Best Rated CDs

Classical
1992

A Selection Guide to

Orchestral Music
Chamber Music
Instrumental Music
Early Music
Choral Music
Opera
Solo Vocal Music

The Peri Press

Hemlock Ridge, P.O. Box 348
Voorheesville, NY 12186

ISBN 1-879796-07-4

Photo Credits:

Front Cover

Alexander Markov	Jacques Sarrat/Elektra International Classics

Back Cover

Center:

Zubin Mehta/Israel Philharmonic Orchestra	Sony Classical

Clockwise from upper left:

Yuri Bashmet	Laurie Lewis/RCA Victor Red Seal
Michala Petri	Suzie Maeder/Rca Victor Red Seal
Lorin Maazel	Ben Spiegel/Sony Classical
Murray Perahia	Susesch Bayat/Sony Classical

Cover design: Mike Moreno, The Graphics Shop, Albany, NY

Table of Contents

CD Review Digest
Classical

Introduction

This inaugural edition of the *Classical* volume of *Best Rated CDs* lists the most highly rated classical musical performances issued on compact disc from 1983-1992 . Like its companion, *Best Rated CDs—Jazz, Popular etc.*, it will appear annually, with the 1993 editions of each scheduled for late fall of this year.

As the title indicates, the objective for the *Best Rated* volumes is to provide a selection guide to CD recordings. These guides are unique in the ways they provide music lovers of all temperaments and tastes the information needed to determine the specific recordings most compatible with particular musical tastes. They offer readers listings of CD performances for which there has been general agreement among music reviewers and critics that they are outstanding, exceptional—among the best.

Three bases of selection were used for this volume: (1) **awards** a recording has received from major English-language music-review magazines (see Directory of Periodicals), (2) **reviews** carried by those magazines reflecting a predominant opinion of excellence, and (3) **recommendations** by Richard Halsey, author of the generally acclaimed selection guide, *Classical Music Recordings for Home and Library*, ALA, 1976 (o.p.). While receiving at least one award was an initial basis of selection, strength of reviews was one of the most determinative factors. Some recordings were included on this basis even if they had not received an award, and others because they were among Halsey's recommendations. For some works where competition is very strong several outstanding performances have been listed; in a few instances where there was no particularly strong performance of a work one might expect to find in this guide, an acceptable performance was listed.

The symbol "HC"—for Halsey's Choice—signifies (in his words) "works of integrity, elegance, power and beauty that have passed through the filters of professional musical judgement and personal taste and will yield lasting pleasure in performances unlikely to be surpassed in the near future." Widely acknowledged masterpieces lacking HC notations in this issue will be assigned HCs in subsequent issues whenever qualifying performances with acceptable sonics become available.

Entries are arranged in musical categories, with miscellaneous collective works at the end of each section. For each recording included there is a listing of the awards it has received with a rating of 1-5 stars depending on the number, diversity and significance of the awards. These ratings are followed by review excerpts describing distinctive features of a performance and recording and often providing helpful comparisons with other performances (as well as dissenting opinions).

An artist/composer index and a label-number index are included to facilitate finding individual works and artists. Short works in collections listed in *Schwann-Opus* can be located in this guide by using the label-number index. Most of the recordings included are listed in *Opus*; those that aren't should be available from export or used CD sources.

We believe all of these features will be helpful both for pursuing already developed musical interests and for choosing new directions to explore. We believe that the range of opinions expressed in the review excerpts make fascinating reading, and we have sought to arrange them in sequences that would most facilitate comprehension. From more to less positive was one of several ordering ideas used. The excerpts can provide a basis for determining which reviewers reflect a musical sensibility most akin to that of one's own and thus worth reading in full in the review magazines.

It should be noted here that while brief excerpts such as those supplied in the *Best Rated* volumes will generally be helpful in determining one's interest in a particular performance, they are not an adequate substitute for the full reviews themselves. We urge readers to take the excerpts as guides to reviewers the reader is likely to find rewarding to read on a regular basis.

We are aware that there will be occasions where a reader will be convinced that a recording of a particular piece of music or a particular performance not included is superior to one that is. Differences of musical taste arising from differences of cultural backgrounds and individual temperaments and experiences result in similarly divergent appraisals of particular compositions and performances. The sets of review excerpts for listed performances provide numerous examples of this kind of plurality of opinion. We believe, and have continuing reader response supporting this, that the serious collector will find it well worth while to consult the comprehensive listings of *CD Review Digest* (the CDRD annuals) which are also published in twin editions of *Classical* and *Jazz, Popular etc.* and which are also published by The Peri Press. These include all CD recordings released since 1983 which have had one or more reviews in the magazines used as review sources. They include multiple indexes and are available in many libraries, some record stores and from The Peri Press.

In this first edition of *Best Rated CDs—Classical* it is particularly appropriate to remind our readers that we want to minimize errors and omissions in our CD guides. We are grateful for all the assistance we have received from you in the past and urge your continuing critiques and suggestions. It will contribute to bettering future editions of both the *Best Rated CDs* and their parent volumes of *CD Review Digest*.

Janet Grimes
Bill Grimes
Richard Halsey
Editors

Directory of Periodicals Used As Sources

American Music. University of Illinois Press, 54 E. Gregory Drive, Champaign, IL 61820 (quarterly)

The Abso!ute Sound. Pearson Publishing Empire, P.O. Box L, Sea Cliff, NY 11579. Eight issues: U.S. $40, Canada $45, outside North America $70 (bimonthly).

American Record Guide. Record Guide Productions, 4412 Braddock Street, Cincinnati, OH 45204. Individuals $24.50, outside U.S. $30, institutions $36 (bimonthly).

Audio. Hachette Magazines, Inc., 1633 Broadway, New York, NY 10019. Subscriptions: P.O. Box 52548, Boulder, CO 80321-2548. U.S. $21.94, all others add $6 (monthly).

Australian Hi-Fi Magazine and Music Review. Australian HI-FI Publication Services, P.O. Box 341, Mona Vale, NSW, 2103, Australia. $A50. (12 times a year).

Canadian Composer. SOCAN, 41 Valleybrook Drive, Don Mills, Ontario M3B 2S6, Canada (quarterly).

Continuo: The Magazine of Old Music. P.O. Box 327, Hammondsport, NY 14840. U.S. $30, Canada $35 (6 issues a year).

Digital Audio's CD Review (formerly **Digital Audio & Compact Disc Review**). WGE Publishing Inc., Forest Road, Hancock, NH 03449. Subscriptions: P.O. Box 58835, Boulder, CO 80322-8835. U.S. $29.94, Canada add $7 plus 7% EST, all others add $19 (monthly).

Fanfare. Joel Flegler, 273 Woodland Street, P.O. Box 720, Tenafly, NJ 07670. U.S. $27; others $37 (bimonthly).

Gramophone. General Gramophone Publications Ltd., 177-179 Kenton Road, Harrow, Middlesex HA3 0HA, England. U.K. £22.00, U.S. $61 (monthly).

Hi-Fi News & Record Review. Link House Magazines Ltd., 120/126 Lavender Avenue, Mitcham, Surrey CR4 3HP, England. U.K. £23.40, overseas £34.00 or $58 U.S. funds (overseas airmail £54.00 or $92 U.S. funds) (monthly).

High Fidelity. Haymarket Trade and Leisure Publications Ltd., 38-42 Hampton Road, Teddington, Middlesex TW11 OJE. U.K. (ceased publication)

High Fidelity. ABC Consumer Magazines, P.O. Box 10759, Des Moines, IO 50340. (ceased publication)

High Performance Review. High Performance Review Publishing Inc., P.O. Box 346, Woodbury, CT 06798. Individuals $20.97 (quarterly).

The Horn Call. International Horn Society, Department of Music, SE Oklahoma State University, Durant, OK 74701. $15 (annual membership) (semi-annual).

Kurt Weill Newsletter. Kurt Weill Foundation for Music, 7 East 20th Street, New York, NY 10003-1106.

Music and Musicians International. Orpheus Publications, 4th Floor, Centro House, Mandela Street, London, NW1 0DU. Subscriptions to: Competition House, Farndon Road, Market Harborough, Leicestershire, England LEI6 9NR. (ceased publication)

Music Journal. Hampton International Communications, 60 East 42nd Street, New York, NY 10017. (ceased publication)

Musical America: The Journal of Classical Music. ABC Consumer Magazines, Inc.,

825 Seventh Avenue, New York, NY 10019. (ceased publication)

The Musical Times. Novello & Co., Ltd., Borough Green, Sevenoaks, Kent (0732 883261), England. (ceased publication)

The NATS Journal. National Association of Teachers of Singing, Inc., 2800 University Boulevard N., JU Station, Jacksonville, FL 32211. Members $16, non-members $23 (bi-monthly except July and August).

The New York Times (Sunday edition). 229 West 43rd Street, New York, NY 10036-3959

Opera. 1a Mountgrove Road, London N5 2LU. Subscritpions to: DSB, 14/16 The Broadway, Wickford, Essex, SS11 7AA.

Opera Canada. Foundation for Coast to Coast Opera Publication, 366 Adelaide Street East, Suite 433, Toronto, Ontario M5A 3X9. Canada $16, all others $21 (quarterly).

Opera News. Metropolitan Opera Guild, Circulation Department, 70 Lincoln Center Plaza, New York, NY 10023-6593. U.S. $30, all others $39.50 (monthly May-November, bi-weekly December-April).

The Opera Quarterly. The University of North Carolina Press, P.O. Box 2288, Chapel Hill, NC 27515.

Organists' Review. Incorporated Association of Organists, Borough Green, Kent. Subscriptions: Philip Brereton, 18 Duffins Close, Shawclough, Rochdale, Lancs. OL 12 6XA 0706 43575 (quarterly).

Opus: The Classical Music Magazine. Historical Times Inc., 2245 Kohn Road, P.O. Box 8200, Harrisburg, PA 17105-8200. (ceased publication),

Ovation. Classical Music Publications, Ltd., 33 West 60th Street, New York, NY 10023. (ceased publication)

Pan Pipes. Sigma Alpha Iota, Inc., 4119 Rollins Avenue, Des Moines, IA 50312. $15 (quarterly).

The $ensible Sound. John A. Horan, 403 Darwin Drive, Snyder, NY 14226. U.S. $20, outside North America $30 (quarterly).

Stereo Review. Hachette Magazines, 1633 Broadway, New York, NY 10019. Subscriptions to: Stereo Review, P.O. Box 55627, Boulder, CO 80322-5627. U.S. $13.94, Canada $18.94, all others $21.94. (monthly).

Stereo Review Presents: Compact Disc Buyers' Guide

Stereophile. Stereophile, 208 Delgado Street, Santa Fe, NM 87501. U.S. $35 (monthly).

Videoworld. Australian HI-FI Publications Services Pty. Ltd. P.O. Box 341 Mona Vale, NSW, 2103, Australia. (monthly, bound with Australian Hi-Fi and Music Review).

The Wire. Richard Cook, Units G & H, 115 Cleveland Street, London W1P 5PN, England. UK £20, U.S. $50, European £25, other overseas: surface £25. airmail £40 (monthly).

Abbreviations

INSTRUMENTS

acdn	accordion
ac	acoustic
a fl	alto flute
a sax	alto sax
arr	arranger
bar	baritone
bar sax	baritone sax
b clar	bass clarinet
bsn	bassoon
bgos	bongos
c	conductor
clar	clarinet
clvcd	clavicord
contr	contralto
crnt	cornet
ctr-ten	counter-tenor
cymb	cymbals
dir	director
dbl bass	double bass
dbl trb	double trombone
el	electric
Eng horn	English horn
fdl	fiddle
fl	flute
flgl	flugelhorn
ftpno	fortepiano
Fr horn	French horn
glknspl	glockenspiel
gtr	guitar
hca	harmonica
hpscd	harpsichord
kbd	keyboard
mndln	mandolin
mrba	marimba
mez-sop	mezzo-soprano
nar	narrator
orgn	organ
perc	percussion
pno	piano
pclo	piccolo
psthn	posthorn
rec	recorder
rds	reeds
sax	saxophone
sop	soprano
s sax	soprano sax
spkr	speaker
synth	synthesizer
Sync	Synclavier
ten	tenor
tn sax	tenor sax
trb	trombone
tpt	trumpet
tymp	tympani
vphn	vibraphone
vla	viola
vla d'amore	viola d'amore
vla da gamba	viola da gamba
vln	violin
voc	vocals
vcdr	vocorder
wndhp	wind harp
wdwnd	woodwind

DATES

Ja	January
F	February
Mr	March
Ap	April
My	May
Je	June
Jl	July
Ag	August
S	September
O	October
N	November
D	December
Spr	Spring
Summ	Summer
Fall	Fall
Wtr	Winter

RATINGS

P65-100: Performance rated 65-100%
S65-100: Sound rated 65-100%

Orchestral Music

ABEL, CARL FRIEDRICH

1001. Symphonies (6), Opus 7.
Adrian Shepherd (c). Cantilena.
CHANDOS 8648 DDD 59:27

★*Awards:* The Want List 1989, *Fanfare* N/D '89 (Nils Anderson).

"Anyone interested in this period and its lesser figures will find this disc pure pleasure. The sound, as always with this ensemble, is excellent. Highly recommended."
Fanfare 12:66 Jl/Ag '89. Nils Anderson (250w)

"The small-scale, Scottish-based Cantilena ensemble...is distinguished by clear, clean tone, good attacks and accurate playing. The conductor...has become a specialist in 18th Century music without having succumbed to the current craze for 'authenticity.' What they produce, together, is a full-bodied, rich sound, with just enough restraint to mirror the simplicity of the music—all very pleasing to the ear."
American Record Guide 52:9 Jl/Ag '89. Michael Mark (200w)

"Occasionally I felt Andantes to be a little slack, and horns are recorded with less than ideal focus....As far as No. 6 goes, this is its first recording with Abel's oboes rather than Mozart's clarinets. This makes a surprising difference in the outer movements' second subjects, where woodwind trio disports itself joyously. Joyously played, too, which applies equally to the rest of the band."
Music and Musicians International 37:38 My '89. Bob Dearling (600w)

"I am no longer greatly enamoured of performances of music of this period which use conventional modern instruments but recordings of Abel's music are rare and these performances are enthusiastic and stylistically appropriate-....The recording quality is excellent." *P95 S95*
Australian Hi-Fi 21(2):51:16 '90. Chris Green (210w)

Gramophone 67:23 Je '89. Stanley Sadie (350w)

ADAMS, JOHN

1002. The Chairman Dances (Foxtrot for Orchestra); Christian Zeal and Activity; Common Tones in Simple Time; Short Ride in a Fast Machine; Tromba Iontana.
Edo De Waart (c). San Francisco Symphony Orchestra.
ELEKTRA 79144 DDD 51:00

✔**HC** ★*Awards:* Critics' Choice 1988, *Gramophone* D '88 (John Milsom).

"Everything about this release comes as close to perfection as one might imagine: the marvelously persuasive performances, the unobtrusively vivid recording, and, by no means least, Steinberg's invaluable explications."
Stereo Review 52:190 N '87. Richard Freed (425w)

"Scores of this composer's works are hard to come by in London, but de Waart's performances seem faithful and idiomatic. Certainly the recording is excellent."
Hi-Fi News & Record Review 33:93 F '88. Max Harrison (305w) (rev. of LP)

"This recording illuminates just how for the minimalist movement has developed over the past decade, and it can be recommended to anyone with even a cursory interest in modern music."
Audio 72:120-1 F '88. Michael Aldred (495w)

"A well-spring of music minutiae and eccentric tendencies, tempered by a minimalist's sensibility."
down beat 54:28 S '87. John Diliberto (200w)

"In truth John Adams is the richest and most evocative composer to ever come out of American minimalism."
Music and Musicians International 36:28 Ag '88. Mark J. Prendergast (805w)

"I reviewed the SD in *Fanfare* 10:6....Sound on the CD is more brilliant than on the LP, and more present especially in the bass....I still highly recommend the disc for two of its five works, the shimmering *Common Tones in Simple Time*, and the hauntingly ironic *Christian Zeal and Activity*."
Fanfare 11:78 N/D '87. Kyle Gann (200w)

Ovation 8:38-9 O '87. David Patrick Stearns (780w)

Gramophone 66:276 Ag '88. John Milsom (340w)

American Record Guide 50:9-10 N/D '87. Arved Ashby (565w)

Fearful Symmetries, for Orchestra. See No. 8001

ARNOLD, MALCOLM

1003. Dances: Four Cornish Dances, Opus 91 (1966); Four Irish Dances, Opus 126 (1986); Four Scottish Dances, Opus 59 (1957); English Dances (8 dances in two sets), Opus 27 (1950) and Opus 33 (1951); Solitaire: Sarabande and Polka.
Malcolm Arnold (c). London Philharmonic Orchestra. 1990; 1979 reissue.
LYRITA 201 ADD/DDD 61:00

★*Awards:* Best of the Month, *Hi-Fi News & Record Review*, Ja '91.

"To the original threesome Lyrita have added new versions of the 'Solitaire' items and *Irish Dances*, making a programme identical to that of Thomson's Chandos CD reviewed in December. Much as I enjoyed that recent compilation, this is the one I would return to every time with even greater glee. It's not merely that the recordings (digital or otherwise) are nothing short of demonstration-worthy throughout, more that the composer's readings add an extra dimension to his own inspiration." *P100 S100*
Hi-Fi News & Record Review 36:95 Ja '91. Andrew Achenbach (140w)

"Arnold recorded the Irish Dances and the two *Solitaire* pieces digitally last year, while all the other material on this disc goes back to 1979 analog sessions and was issued on LP. There is a little more brightness in the 1990 material, but the sound is really first-rate throughout the disc. A splendid introduction to this composer's music."
Stereo Review 56:79 Jl '91. Richard Freed (230w)
Gramophone 68:1197 D '90. Edward Greenfield (470w)
Digital Audio's CD Review 7:68 Ap '91. Sebastian Russ (210w)

1004. Sinfoniettas: No. 1, Opus 48; No. 2, Opus 65; No. 3, Opus 81. Concerto No. 1 for Flute and Orchestra, Opus 45; Concerto for Oboe and Orchestra, Opus 39.
Ross Pople (c). Edward Beckett (fl); Malcolm Messiter (oboe). London Festival Orchestra.
HYPERION 66332 DDD 60:00

✔**HC** ★*Awards:* The Want List 1990, *Fanfare* N/D '90 (Robert McColley).

"I judge this disc worth having for the First Sinfonietta alone, but the other four works are equally engaging....As expected, the performances are superb and the sound is fine."
Fanfare 13:68-9 Jl/Ag '90. Ron McDonald (300w)

"This program makes for an hour of the kind of breezy delight that Arnold brings to lighter forms....Both soloists...are excellent. The recorded sound has a slight edge in the treble but is otherwise superb."
Musical America 110:68 N '90. Robert R. Reilly (230w)
Gramophone 67:1595 Mr '90. Malcolm MacDonald (280w)

1005. Symphony No. 7, Opus 113; Symphony No. 8, Opus 124.
Vernon Handley (c). Royal Philharmonic Orchestra.
CONIFER 177 DDD 64:00

★★*Awards:* Best of the Month, *Hi-Fi News & Record Review*, Ap '91. Disc of the Month, *Digital Audio's CD Review*, N '91.

"Magnificent accounts of both works from Vernon Handley and a thoroughly committed, superbly incisive RPO. As ever from a Keener/Tryggvason enterprise, production values are unimpeachable." *P100 S100*
Hi-Fi News & Record Review 36:81 Ap '91. Andrew Achenbach (240w)
Gramophone 68:1657 Mr '91. Ivan March (655w)
Digital Audio's CD Review 8:40 N '91. Sebastian Russ (med)

BACH, CARL PHILIPP EMANUEL

1006. Orchestral Symphonies, "Hamburg Symphonies": in C, H.659 (W.182, no. 3); in A, H.660 (W.182, no. 4); in B minor, H.661 (W.182, no. 5). **Concerti:** in C minor for Harpsichord and Orchestra, H.474 (W.43, no. 4); in E flat for Oboe and Orchestra, H.468 (W.165).
Thomas Hengelbrock (c). Peter Westermann (oboe); Andreas Staier (hpscd). Freiburg Baroque Orchestra.
DEUTSCHE HARMONIA MUNDI 77187 DDD 71:00

★*Awards:* Critics' Choice 1991, *Gramophone*, Ja '92 (Nicholas Anderson).

"It has taken the Freiburg Baroque Orchestra to renew my faith that authentic groups can still deliver the shock of the old. Strings have a keen edge and chording is accurate in ensemble and intonation, virtues more than ever necessary in the unforgiving sound-world of CPE Bach, whose open textures rely upon absolute accuracy, and whose iconoclasm needs the proper observance of dynamic contrasts....All three symphonies, supported by a strong bassline with harpsichord, receive energetic, powerful readings which tellingly realize their importance." *P95 S95*
Hi-Fi News & Record Review 36:88 Mr '91. Robert Dearling (200w)

"This is in all ways an excellent disc. First off, it offers a sampling of some of C.P.E. Bach's best work in three genres. Thus it can be highly recommended as a 'sampler' for those who want to see what he was like....Moreover, all the performances are excellent....Sound is excellent, very full and warm."
Fanfare 14:103 My/Je '91. William Youngren (200w)

"Certainly these are competitive performances, expertly played by soloists and ensemble alike. My only reservation is Hengelbrock's propensity for pounding out rhythms a little more emphatically than seems necessary."

American Record Guide 54:36 S/O '91. John W. Barker (med)

Gramophone 68:1822 Ap '91. Nicholas Anderson (320w)

1007. Orchestral Symphonies (6), "Hamburg Symphonies" (H.657-662), W.182, No.'s 1-6.
Trevor Pinnock (c). English Concert.
DEUTSCHE GRAMMOPHON 415 300

✔**HC** ★***Awards:*** *Gramophone* Critics' Choice 1986 (John Duarte).

Gramophone 63:1396 My '86. John Duarte (175w)

BACH, JOHANN SEBASTIAN

1008. Brandenburg Concerti (6), BWV.1046/51.
Age of Enlightenment Orchestra.
VIRGIN 90747 DDD 93:00 2 discs

★★***Awards:*** Critics' Choice 1989, *Gramophone* D '89 (Julie Anne Sadie). *American Record Guide* Overview: Bach: Brandenburg Concertos and Orchestral Suites.

"The playing is of an exceptionally high standard throughout with some peerless concertino performances. Especially dazzling is the viola combination of Monica Huggett and Pavlo Beznosiuk in Concerto no. 6 in B flat and the trumpeter, Mark Bennett, who achieves just the right balance in Concerto no. 2 in F with a bright sound and light articulation as well as some mesmerising ornaments."

The Musical Times 130:550 S '89. Jonathan Freeman-Attwood (435w)

"Ensemble lacks precision at a number of points, brass especially having problems, and there is very much the sense that a stronger hand is wanted at the helm....In a way, this is all a great shame, because this is probably the best-*sounding* set of authentic Brandenburgs."

Stereophile 13:191+ Ap '90. Les Berkley (300w)

"I'll state flat out that I prefer to hear the Brandenburgs on period instruments....My current recommendations are Pinnock or Hogwood."

American Record Guide 53:17 Ja/F '90. Carl Bauman (125w)

"The biggest surprise...is the sixth concerto, with its uncommonly fast tempos....The one disappointment was No. 2, in which Mark Bennett's trumpeting hasn't the zip that distinguishes some of the better versions. One the whole, however, this is a commendable effort, well worth hearing....The recording is first-rate."

Fanfare 13:105-6 N/D '89. George Chien (220w)

"The performances...sound curiously uncohesive and inconsistent, both between and within the actual works....Warts and all, the recording generally maintains the high standards we are coming to expect of Virgin Classics." *P75/85 S95*

Hi-Fi News & Record Review 34:97 N '89. Stephen Daw (320w)

Gramophone 67:165-66 Jl '89. Nicholas Anderson (875w)

1009. Brandenburg Concerti (6), BWV.1046/51; Concerto in A minor for Flute, Violin, Harpsichord and Orchestra, BWV.1044.
Reinhard Goebel (c). Wilbert Hazelzet (fl); Andreas Staier (hpscd). Cologne Musica Antiqua.
DEUTSCHE GRAMMOPHON 423 116 DDD 106:00 2 discs

✔**HC** ★***Awards:*** The Want List 1988, *Fanfare* N/D '88 (Edward Strickland).

"If there were any question as to who has taken over at the cutting edge of the early music movement, this recording leaves no doubt...The ensemble exhibits here the two traits which have marked almost every one of its previous releases: flawless, supremely virtuosic playing which can be breathtakingly innovative or mischievously provocative, but which is always compelling....The recorded sound is a match for the performances, bright, hard and somewhat baffling....for those ready to meet their challenge, they are the Brandenburgs of the decade."

Continuo 12:23-4 Je '88. Scott Paterson (500w)

"MAK's set of the Brandenburgs will excite all but those for whom period instruments are an auditory bowl of hemlock."

American Record Guide 52:15 Ja/F '89. Teri Noel Towe (460w)

"This recording of the *Brandenburg* Concertos is characterized by the brilliance of its sound and the energy and drive of the performances. The exciting thing about the sound is the exceptional instrumental balance."

Stereo Review 53:99-100 Jl '88. Stoddard Lincoln (210w)

"On first hearing I thought these were the worst *Brandenburgs* I had ever heard...A few days later I returned to find myself almost mesmerized by much of the recording....After four or five close hearings I'll give it the silver or bronze, but I warn you that this is not a *Brandenburgs* for everyone, and that Pinnock remains the prime recommendation."

Fanfare 11:101-3 Jl/Ag '88. Edward Strickland (1200w)

Gramophone 65:1305 Mr '88. Nicholas Anderson (760w)

1010. Brandenburg Concerti (6), BWV.1046/51; "Concerto" (trans. Duncan Druce) from Sonata BWV.1029; "Concerto" (Sinfonia) from Cantata, BWV.194.
Andrew Parrott (c). Taverner Players.
EMI 49806 DDD 110:00 2 discs

★*Awards: American Record Guide* Overview: Bach: Brandenburg Concertos and Orchestral Suites, My/Je '90.

"Interesting as their fillers may be, the Taverner's *Brandenburgs* are still the main attraction. Violinist John Holloway—who, as far as I can tell, has *not* recorded this music before—is excellent in the solo parts of all the concertos...Among the highlights of the set are the robust horn playing in No. 1, a splendid No. 4, and a sparkling No. 2, featuring Marion Verbruggen, recorder, Paul Goodwin, oboe, and David Staff, trumpet, as well as Holloway-....Overall, another worthy entry in the *Brandenberg* sweepstakes."

Fanfare 13:92-3 Ja/F '90. George Chien (725w)

"If you're not already glutted with a surfeit of *Brandenburgs*, this new set is well worth your attention."

Stereo Review 55:95 Ap '90. Stoddard Lincoln (250w)

Gramophone 67:1319-20 Ja '90. John Duarte (430w)

1011. Brandenburg Concerti (6), BWV.1046/51 (No.'s 1-3).
Trevor Pinnock (c). English Concert.
DEUTSCHE GRAMMOPHON 410 500

✔HC ★★*Awards: Fanfare* Want List 1984 (George Chien). *American Record Guide* Overview: Bach: Brandenburg Concertos and Orchestral Suites.

"Pinnock's new version quickly and easily moves to the head of the class, eclipsing the Marriner in nearly every meaningful respect. Quite apart from The English Concert's authentic instrumentation and attention to musicological detail are the brightness, the vitality, the security and subtlety of the instrumental playing, and the exemplary teamwork of the ensemble. Any of the concertos could be cited for its excellence, and the overall impression is overwhelmingly positive."

Fanfare 7:113 Jl/Ag '84. George Chien (380w)

Gramophone 61:865 Ja '84. Lionel Salter (245w)

Hi-Fi News & Record Review 29:79 Mr '84. John Atkinson (90w)

Hi-Fi News & Record Review 29:73 Je '84. John Atkinson (165w)

1012. Brandenburg Concerti (6), BWV.1046/51 (No.'s 4-6).
Trevor Pinnock (c). English Concert.
DEUTSCHE GRAMMOPHON 410 501

✔HC ★★*Awards: Fanfare* Want List 1984 (George Chien). *American Record Guide* Overview: Bach: Brandenburg Concertos and Orchestral Suites.

See No.'s 1-3 for review excerpt.

Fanfare 7:113 Jl/Ag '84. George Chien (380w)

Gramophone 61:865 Ja '84. Lionel Salter (245w)

Hi-Fi News & Record Review 29:79 Mr '84 (90w) (rev. of LP); 29:73 Je '84 (165w) (rev. of CD). John Atkinson

Fantasia in G for Organ, BWV.572 (Gravement section only). See No. 1162.

1013. Suites (4) for Orchestra, BWV.1066/9; Suite in G Minor for Orchestra, BWV.1070 (attrib. W.F. Bach).
Reinhard Goebel (director). Cologne Musica Antiqua.
DEUTSCHE GRAMMOPHON 415 671 110:36 2 discs

★★*Awards: American Record Guide* Overview: Bach: Brandenburg Concertos and Orchestral SuitesRecord of the Month, *Hi-Fi News & Record Review*, O '86.

"Both Goebbel and Gardiner...have revealed the music in an entirely new light....Never before have I heard the astonishing variety of Bach's Terpsichorean rhythms so tightly, lightly sprung...The Musica Antiqua players, in particular, leap into your living room as if offering an invitation to the dance which is hard to resist....The players have the technique and imagination to astonish and delight and the recording sound exemplary to me, so full-bodied, indeed, that I wondered whether the instruments were, in fact, 'authentic'!...I cannot imagine a more thrilling account of this music."

Hi-Fi News & Record Review 31:97 O '86. Hugh Canning (650w)

"There are so many fine recordings of the suites it's hard to get excited about these. I'd first investigate Gardiner's subtlety, La Petite Bande's vigor, and Pinnock's crackling energy."

Fanfare 10:59-60 Ja/F '87 Edward Strickland (900w)

"These are not the most exciting or virtuosic versions of the suites available...but the quiet urgency that characterizes them is highly appealing....Excellent recording."

Ovation 8:32 Jl '87 Paul Turok (360w)

Gramophone 64:561-2 O '86. Nicholas Anderson (735w)

Stereo Review 52:141 Ja '87 Stoddard Lincoln (115w)

1014. Suites (4) for Orchestra, BWV.1066/9.
Ton Koopman (c). Wilbert Hazelzet (fl). Amsterdam Baroque Orchestra.
DEUTSCHE HARMONIA MUNDI 77864 DDD 79:00 2 discs

★★*Awards:* Baroque (Non-vocal) Record Award 1990, *Gramophone* D '90. *American Record Guide* Overview: Bach: Brandenburg Concertos and Orchestral Suites.

"Koopman's players use period instruments-...The sound of the orchestra is generous and warm, not at all scrawny or abrasive....if you've a hole in your repertoire or plenty of space on your shelves, Koopman's overtures wouldn't be a bad way to fill either or both."

Fanfare 13:121-22 Mr/Ap '90. George Chien (350w)

"In the larger-scaled Suites 3 and 4 my feeling is that the various excellent parts of the ensembles somehow just fail to add up to a convincing and coherent whole; such things as tuning, timing and engineering balance—as well as distribution—are variable. Nevertheless one of the best sets of these works to have, others being AAM/Hogwood (good in the large Suites) and, in its own odd way, the diversely-treated MAK." *P100/85 S85*

Hi-Fi News & Record Review 35:87 My '90. Stephen Daw (285w)

"Koopman's are the most inspiriting period-instrument performances recorded so far—perhaps the most stimulating of all available versions at present, using either modern *or* 'original' instruments."

Stereo Review Presents: Compact Disc Buyers' Guide Summer 1990 p.55 Richard Freed (100w)

Gramophone 67:1319 Ja '90. Nicholas Anderson (600w)

Gramophone 68:725 O '90. Nicholas Anderson (140w)

BACH, P.D.Q. See SCHICKELE, PETER. See No. 1321.

BALAKIREV, MILY

1015. Symphony No. 1 in C; Tamara (symphonic poem).
Thomas Beecham (c). Royal Philharmonic Orchestra. 1962, 1955 reissue.
EMI 63375 ADD (m) 61:00

✔**HC** ★*Awards:* The Want List 1990, *Fanfare* N/D '90 (John Bauman).

"Beecham's recording of the symphony remains the best (Karajan tried) and the best-sounding....*Tamara* may not sound as good as Ansermet's (when available), but no apologies are needed."

American Record Guide 53:28+ S/O '90. Donald R. Vroon (210w)

"*Tamara*...makes the perfect coupling for Sir Thomas's unequaled reading of the Balakirev Symphony in C. I am mildly disappointed in the sonic results...Ownership of this CD is imperative."

Fanfare 14:155-56 N/D '90. John Bauman (560w)

Gramophone 68:207 Jl '90. Alan Sanders (395w)

Stereo Review Presents: Compact Disc Buyers' Guide 1991 p.39 Richard Freed (150w)

The Absolute Sound 16:172 S/O '91. Thomas Hathaway (brief)

BANTOCK, GRANVILLE

1016. Celtic Symphony (1940); Tone Poem No. 5, The Witch of Atlas (1902); The Sea Reivers (1917); Hebridean Symphony (1915).
Vernon Handley (c). Royal Philharmonic Orchestra.
HYPERION 66450 DDD 73:00

★★★*Awards:* Best of the Month, *Hi-Fi News & Record Review*, Je '91. Critic's Choice: 1991, *American Record Guide*, Ja/F '92 (Michael Carter). Editors' Choice—Best CDs of the Year, *Digital Audio's CD Review*, Je '92.

"There's obviously a keenly imaginative, fastidious musical mind at work here. Despite an overriding impression of heady sensuality, scoring is always lucid, with countless examples readily revealing the composer's textural mastery....And yet...What bothers me most about Bantock's music (even after repeated hearings) is a dearth of real distinction and personality, as well as a worrying tendency towards rhapsodic aimlessness....this is stunningly natural sound, state-of-the-art." *P95 S100*

Hi-Fi News & Record Review 36:67 Je '91. Andrew Achenbach (390w)

"His contemporaries included Bax, Ireland, Vaughan-Williams, Holst, and Delius—not a bad lineup. Unfortunately fickle fame has thus far consigned Bantock to a place not with them but with Joseph Holbrooke and Rutland Boughton, ambitious composers who made a stir in their day but are rarely heard from in ours....this first serious attempt to establish Bantock discographically should awaken some listeners to this virtues."

Fanfare 14:105-6 Jl/Ag '91. David Johnson (750w)

"Vernon Handley's [*Hebridean Symphony* follows another recent issue on Marco Polo (8.223274) by the Philharmonic of Kosice under the baton of another English conductor, Adrian Leaper. Both men seem equipped with the necessary tools and talent, but Handley's orchestra is more polished....The real gem in this release is the *Celtic Symphony*...it is vital, full-blooded, even youthful....[*Witch of Atlas* and *The Sea Rivers*] are glorious tone poems-...It is an attractive, fascinating colorful disc."

American Record Guide 54:39-40 S/O '91. Michael Carter (med)

Digital Audio's CD Review 7:56 S '91. Sebastian Russ (350w)

BARBER, SAMUEL

Die Natali: Chorale Preludes for Christmans, Opus 37. See No. 6026

1017. Essay No. 1 for Orchestra; Essay No. 2 for Orchestra, Opus 17; Medea's Meditation and Dance of Vengeance, Opus 23a; Overture to The School for Scandal, Opus 5; Adagio for Strings (arr. from the String Quartet, Opus 1).
Leonard Slatkin (c). Saint Louis Symphony Orchestra. 1988.
EMI 49463 DDD 61:11

✔**HC** ★★*Awards:* Critics' Choice 1989, *Gramophone* D '89 (Edward Seckerson); Top Disks of the Year, *The New York Times* D 24, '89 (John Rockwell).

"Without stooping to exaggeration, Slatkin flavors nearly every measure, adding caressing, subtle inflections of dynamics and tempos-....One might wish that Saint Louis's strings were lusher in tone, but their lean sound may be Slatkin's personal antidote to a potential overdose of lyricism."

High Fidelity 39:62+ Je '89. K. Robert Schwarz (250w)

"The performances are superbly disciplined yet fiery in pursuit of Barber's melancholy vision."

The New York Times Je 11 '89, p. 30. Andrew L. Pincus (75w)

"Slatkin's must be considered the finest all-Barber orchestral recording to date, better played (and recorded, of course) than the once-definitive Schippers issue."

Fanfare 12:54-8 Jl/Ag '89. Walter Simmons (1250w)

"All of these works have been recorded before-....The strongest competition comes from Schippers, who...had a wonderful feel for the music....Slatkin brings a different perspective to the music. His interpretations are more conservative and restrained but, in their own way, excellent."

American Record Guide 52:16 Jl/Ag '89. Karl Miller (300w)

"It gives us a good cross-section of his music in excellent performances." *P95/100 S95*

Hi-Fi News & Record Review 34:97-8 N '89. Kenneth Dommett (265w)

"Leonard Slatkin's readings of these works are generally less than definitive....Angel has provided wonderfully full-bodied sonics." *P80 S95*

Stereo Review 54:140 O '89. David Hall (260w)

Gramophone 67:645 O '89. Edward Seckerson (550w)

Digital Audio's CD Review 5:64+ Ag '89. Lawrence Johnson (260w)

1018. Fadograph of a Yestern Scene, for Orchestra; Medea (complete ballet suite), Opus 23; Essay No. 3 for Orchestra, Opus 47.

Andrew Schenk (c). New Zealand Symphony Orchestra.

KOCH 7010 DDD 47:00

★★*Awards:* Pick of the Month, North American Perspective (Christopher Pollard) *Gramophone* Ja '91; The Highs, 1990, *The New York Times* D 30 '90 (John Rockwell).

"The New Zealand band, surprisingly, can compete easily with Leonard Slatkin's overrated St. Louis Orchestra. Schenck does all the right things....Most importantly, he does not underplay Barber's almost irrepressible emotionalism and melodic gift....These recordings can be highly recommended for their music, performances, and surprisingly excellent sound."

The Absolute Sound 16:186+ S/O '91. Arthur B. Lintgen (med)

"I particularly like the program chosen for...[this] disc even though, in terms of value for money, it should have been extended."

Stereophile 15:173+ Mr '92. Barbara Jahn (med)

"Regardless of version, *Medea* is a most impressive achievement, but I find the orchestral suite richer and more satisfying than the one-movement version, and Schenck and the New Zealand Symphony give it an intense, exciting performance...*Fadograph of a Yestern Scene*-...is a dark, haunting meditation for orchestra and, according to *New Grove*, two sopranos. No singers are heard on this otherwise excellent recording, and the liner notes contain no information about whether their presence is optional....excellent sound."

Musical America 111:67-8 My '91. Terry Teachout (245w)

"The New Zealand Symphony, while offering a solid, committed performance [of Medea], lacks the desirable urgency and tautness....I have discussed *Essay No. 3* several times before in these pages. In *Fanfare* 12:6 (pp.54ff), I noted that Leonard Slatkin's performance with the St. Louis Symphony revealed a Straussian sweep and opulence that lent more character to the work than I had previously sensed. While lacking the polish and precision of that reading, Schenck's New Zealand performance convincingly highlights the works' virtues."

Fanfare 14:142-3 Mr/Ap '91. Walter Simmons (460w)

Stereo Review 56:98 Ja '91. Eric Salzman (115w)

American Record Guide 54:24+ Jl/Ag '91. Kyle Rothweiler (med)

Gramophone 68:1369 Ja '91. Peter Dickinson (300w)

Medea. See No. 1153.

1019. Symphony No. 1, Opus 9; Concerto for Piano and Orchestra, Opus 38; Souvenirs, Opus 28.

Leonard Slatkin (c). John Browning (pno). Saint Louis Symphony Orchestra.

RCA 0732 DDD 70:00

✔**HC** ★*Awards:* Top Twelve Albums of the Year, 1991, *Stereo Review*, F '92.

"Blazing virtuosity."

Stereo Review 57:43 F '92. (brief)

"Although the First Symphony has never suffered from a paucity of recordings, only recently have performances begun to reflect an overall understanding of the deeper and subtler aspects of Barber's compositional rhetoric. From this perspective, both Slatkin's and Jarvi's renditions are noteworthy....Slatkin's reading of the Symphony No. 1...[is] a successful effort to articulate this fundamentally lyrico-dynamic work from the perspective of a thorough understanding of the composer's expressive syntax....In summary, therefore, I would recommend Slatkin's interpretation to those just discovering this richly appealing work, and Jarvi's to those already familiar enough with it to enjoy an 'alternative' approach."

Fanfare 15:353-6 N/D '91. Walter Simmons (long)

"As far as the symphony is concerned, this too is a performance to treasure....Browning and Slatkin together on one piano sound to be having great fun with *Souvenirs*...Slatkin seems to be inside this music in a very special way and it's his recording I'd put at the top of my list at present." *PS 95*

Hi-Fi News & Record Review 37:81+ Ap '92. Mark Lowther (long)

"The last recording of the Barber First by a top-ranked conductor and orchestra was made in 1942 by...Bruno Walter and the New York Philharmonic....Two recordings of his First Symphony have recently appeared. The first one is part of an all-Barber CD...Slatkin and his orchestra are in exceptional form, and one comes away from this outstanding recording convinced that the Barber First is one of the two or three greatest symphonies ever composed by an American. The coupling is a fire-breathing performance of Barber's 1962 Piano Concerto...Browning recorded the concerto with George Szell and the Cleveland Orchestra, but this new version is no less musically impressive and benefits from fine digital sound."

Musical America 111:37-8 N/D '91. Terry Teachout (med)

"Leonard Slatkin's well-knit new reading is better than the two other recordings currently available...Browning and Slatkin make a wonderful keyboard team, and their joy in musicmaking shines through every measure. The sound is top of the line."

Stereo Review 56:91 S '91. David Hall (med)

John Browning's "playing is as brilliant as ever [in the Barber Piano Concerto]. Yet I can't feel that it replaces the earlier one [with George Szell and the Cleveland Orchestra]-...Slatkin's First Symphony is far superior to the Schermerhorn/Milwaukee or Strickland/Japan Philharmonic versions on all counts."

American Record Guide 54:26+ N/D '91. Carl Bauman (long)

Gramophone 69:82 N '91. Edward Greenfield (long)

BARTOK, BELA

1020. Concerto for Orchestra. JANACEK, LEOS. Sinfonietta (1926).

Karel Ancerl (c). Czech Philharmonic Orchestra. reissue.

DENON/SUPRAPHON 8038 ADD 60:13

✔HC ★*Awards:* Top Choices—1989, *American Record Guide* Ja/F '90 (Stephen Chakwin).

"The Bartok stands with the best recordings of this popular work...As for the Janacek, I defy anyone to find me a better recorded performance. These musicians have this music in their blood and it shows. The CD transfer is exemplary."

American Record Guide 52:23 S/O '89. Allen Linkowski (100w)

Fanfare 12:75+ My/Je '89. John Wiser (b.n.)

1021. Concerto for Orchestra; Music for Strings, Percussion and Celesta.

Fritz Reiner (c). Chicago Symphony Orchestra. 1955; 1958.

RCA 5604 ADD 65:00

✔HC ★*Awards:* Records to Die for: 1 of 5 Recommended Recordings, *Stereophile* Ja '91 (Mortimer H. Frank).

"If you are already familiar with these performances you know that they are as definitive as we are likely to get."

American Record Guide 50:12-3 N/D '87. Kurt Moses (435w)

"This remake [of the Concerto] is a phonographic classic....MSPC is, if anything, even better. Despite some tape hiss (more noticeable in the Concerto), the sound retains a natural ambience and impact remarkable for 30-year-old recordings."

Stereophile 14:135 Ja '91. Mortimer H. Frank (b.n.)

High Fidelity 37:60 Ap '87 Terry Teachout (125w)

Fanfare 10:204-5 My/Je '87 Mortimer H. Frank (210w)

1022. Divertimento for String Orchestra. STRAVINSKY, IGOR. Apollo (Apollon Mussagete). BERG, ALBAN. Lyric Suite for String Quartet.

Sandor Vegh (c). Salzburg Mozarteum Camerata Academica. Salzburg, Alte Aula. May 1988; November 1988; March 1989.

CAPRICCIO 10300 DDD 73:58

✔HC ★*Awards:* The Want List 1990, *Fanfare* N/D '90 (John Wiser).

"Throughout this production, the strings of the Camerata Academica are as precise and reactive as any string ensemble I've ever encountered on record...This disc doesn't entirely put in the shade the work of Orpheus Chamber Orchestra in the Divertimento (DG 415 668-2), but it does set down quite resoundingly all past essays upon *Apollo*. Recommended with the greatest urgency."

Fanfare 13:123-24 Mr/Ap '90. John Wiser (550w)

1023. Miraculous Mandarin—Suite; Music for Strings, Percussion, and Celesta.

Antal Dorati (c). Detroit Symphony Orchestra. United Artists Auditorium in Detroit.

LONDON/DECCA 411 894 60:31

✔HC ★*Awards: Stereo Review* Best of the Month, N '85.

"*The Miraculous Mandarin* has long been a Dorati specialty...To be sure, the chase scene was faster and more exciting in the old Chicago version, but...this account has a feeling of rightness and inevitability that keeps one thoroughly engrossed....The Detroit Symphony...really outdoes itself in playing of tremendous vitality and virtuosity. The many solo clarinet passages are especially impressive....As heard on CD, Decca's recording proves remarkably lifelike, the organ in the *Mandarin* registering with enormous impact, every timpani stroke in the *Music* captured with extreme clarity. Warmly recommended."
Opus 2:35 Ap '86. John Canarina (375w)

"In view of the exceptional sound quality of this extraordinary CD...Dorati and the orchestra should perhaps share honors with London/Decca's engineers."
Stereo Review 50:96 N '85. Richard Freed (650w)

"But I've never encountered a reading—either live or recorded, of the full ballet or of the suite—that caught the elusive mix of honey and cyanide. Dorati's is no different: it's powerful but not sufficiently perverse....Still, while it's not the recording I've been hoping for, it's as effective as any I know; and...Dorati's *Music for Strings, Percussion, and Celesta* is-...vigorous, if a bit heavy of tread in the even-numbered movements; somewhat unsubtle elsewhere...The recording of the *Mandarin* is exceptionally vivid, providing both crushing weight and brilliant clarity of detail—only the very low bass seems puffy at times...That flaw has more serious impact on *MSPC*, which-...ends up sounding a trace muddy."
Fanfare 9:116 N/D '85. Peter J. Rabinowitz (525w)

"For some, the dissonance of this music may be off-putting. For everyone else, this CD is an absolute must."
Audio 71:124 Ja '87 Bert Whyte (190w)

Gramophone 63:25 Je '85. Arnold Whittall (365w); John Borwick (85w)

Hi-Fi News & Record Review 30:86 S '85. Edward Seckerson (175w)

BAX, ARNOLD

1024. Symphony No. 5 (1932); Russian Suite (1919).
Bryden Thomson (c). London Philharmonic Orchestra.
CHANDOS 8669 DDD 62:00

✔HC ★*Awards:* Critics' Choice 1989, *Gramophone* D '89 (Robert Layton).

"The performance by the LPO and Bryden Thomson is, as usual, excellent. They bring out the magical and brooding qualities superbly, and Thomson's overall grasp of the symphony's form and direction is uncanny-....The remainder of the disc is devoted to the Russian Suite."
Music and Musicians International 37:57 Ag '89. Michael Stewart (700w)

"This final release in Bryden Thomson's now-definitive Bax symphonic cycle is a triumphant copestone to the series....The Chandos sound-spectrum remains unsurpassed anywhere in today's recording industry."
Fanfare 13:128-29 S/O '89. Paul A. Snook (500w)

"A further highly coloured yet sensitive performance." *P95 S95*
Hi-Fi News & Record Review 34:98 N '89. Max Harrison (315w)

"Fine though the Lyrita/MHS performances by Del Mar, Fredman, and Leppard were, they are equalled or exceeded by Bryden Thomson and the LPO....warmly endorsed."
American Record Guide 52:33-4 N/D '89. Carl Bauman (200w)

Gramophone 67:294 Ag '89. Michael Kennedy (820w)

The New York Times Ag 13 '89, p. H 26. Scott Cantrell (175w)

1025. The Tale the Pine-trees Knew; Into the Twilight; In the Faery Hills; Rose-Catha.
(Tone Poems, Volume 2).
Bryden Thomson (c). Ulster Orchestra.
CHANDOS 8367 56:46

✔HC ★*Awards: Gramophone* Critics' Choice 1985 (Michael Oliver).

"This is a treasurable CD, offering the first recordings of three symphonic poems of Arnold Bax—*Into the Twilight, Rosc-Catha,* and *In the Faery Hills*—as well as the better-known *Tale the Pine-trees Knew*....wonderfully evocative scores, well presented by Bryden Thomas and the Ulster Orchestra, and Chandos's engineering gets top marks for clarity and richness."
High Fidelity 36:61 Ag '86. Robert E. Benson (160w)

"Committed performances by conductor Bryden Thomson and his orchestra....Highly recommended.'
Fanfare 9:117 N/D '85. John Ditsky (250w)

"A very welcome disc."
Hi-Fi News & Record Review 30:103 O '85. Doug Hammond (120w)

"The music deserves, though it discourages, an attentive ear, especially when played with the love Bryden Thomson and the Ulster Orchestra evince here."
Opus 3:26 D '86 Matthew Gurewitsch (255w)

Gramophone 63:333-4 S '85. Michael Oliver (525w)

BEETHOVEN, LUDWIG VAN

Egmont: incidental Music, Opus 84. See No. 1068.

1026. Symphonies (9) (complete).
Nikolaus Harnoncourt (c). Chamber Orchestra of Europe. The Stefaniensaal, Graz. June 29, 1990 live; July 3 and 5, 1990 live; June 21, 1991 live.
TELDEC 46452 DDD 358:00 5 discs

★★*Awards:* Critics' Choice 1991, *Gramophone*, Ja '92 (Stephen Johnson); Disc of the Month, *Digital Audio's CD Review*, D '91 (David Vernier). Editors' Choice—Best CDs of the Year, *Digital Audio's CD Review*, Je '92.

"This is the finest set of Beethoven symphonies to appear since Gunter Wand's...A magnificent achievement."
Fanfare 15:164-5 Ja/F '92. David Hurwitz (long)

"In his new Teldec set of the Beethoven symphonies there is as much that is comfortable and reassuring as there is that is startling-...Teldec has come through with exemplary recordings whose clarity splendidly points up the clarity of the performances themselves as well as their warmth and color. Those who feel there is no compelling reason to buy an "integral" set of the Beethoven symphonies owe it to themselves to hear this one."
Stereo Review 57:142 F '92. Richard Freed (long)

"Taken from concerts given at Graz—June-July 1990 and June '91 (the Ninth)—these recordings sound more 'live' than Abbado's with the Vienna Philharmonic [DG], and more rugged than in the sleek, smaller-scaled Tilson Thomas cycle [Sony], divided between the ECO and St. Luke's Orchestra...The symphonies are paired so that each CD makes a 'programme'" 1/3, 6/8, 2/5, 4/7, 9...For [Harnoncourt] the COE produces a very different quality from that in their Abbado recordings. Throughout, the brass are encouraged in a relentless coarseness which becomes wearing. Ultimately, I think the many expressive twists and turns Harnoncourt insinuates into these readings diminish the stature of the music. The Teldec sound is very consistent—except marginally in transfer levels." P95/75 S95
Hi-Fi News & Record Review 37:88 Ja '92. Christopher Breunig (long)

"Whatever one may think about Harnoncourt's previous recordings, there can be no question that this is one of the most arresting cycles of 'The Nine' to have appeared in some time-....these performances present Beethoven in a remarkably illuminating light....this five-CD set is a release that anyone who cares about Beethoven cannot afford to overlook."
Stereophile 15:262+ Ap '92. Mortimer H. Frank (long)

"All of these performances are of a very high quality with no interpretive tricks to make artificial points....The presence of the audience is rarely felt—only in some shuffling between movements....The sound is very good; though a bit too distant, details are usually clear....The playing of the Chamber Orchestra of Europe is beyond reproach, nothing short of remarkable. All repeats are observed. A truly distinguished cycle then, enhanced by Hartmut Krones's detailed notes. It takes its place among the best committed to posterity: Toscanini (1939—currently available in a Nuova Era box), Mengelberg (Philips—recently deleted), Karajan (1961 and 1977 cycles on DG), Klemperer (Angel), Walter (now in a budget box—Sony), Norrington (thought-provoking, but not aesthetically complete—Angel), to name a few."
American Record Guide 55:31-2 Mr/Ap '92. Allen Linkowski (long)

Digital Audio's CD Review 8:74 D '91. David Vernier (long)

Gramophone 69:83 N '91. Stephen Johnson (long)

1027. Symphonies (9) (complete). Overtures: Coriolan; Egmont.
Herbert Von Karajan (c). Gundula Janowitz (sop); Hilde Rossel-Majdan (alto); Waldemar Kmentt (ten); Walter Berry (bar). Berlin Philharmonic Orchestra. 1963.
DEUTSCHE GRAMMOPHON 429 036 ADD 332:00 5 discs

✔HC ★★★★*Awards:* The Want List 1990, *Fanfare* N/D '90 (David Claris); Records to Die for: 1 of 5 Recommended Recordings, *Stereophile* Ja '91 (Richard Schneider); Critic's Choice: 1990, *American Record Guide* Ja/F '91 (Arved Ashby); Critic's Choice: 1990, *American Record Guide* Ja/F '91 (Stephen Chakwin).

"Karajan's first (1961-62) traversal of the Nine-...is probably the most widely disseminated Beethoven cycle in phonographic history, and it is certainly one of the great ones. For one thing, it is superbly recorded, and in this laser transfer sounds better than ever."
Fanfare 13:120-21 My/Je '90. Mortimer H. Frank (235w)

"The recorded sound and remastering—a few traces of analog hiss aside—are exemplary. At this price, this should be most people's first choice for an integral Beethoven set, or for an antidote to many of the others."
American Record Guide 53:17-8 S/O '90. Stephen D. Chakwin, Jr. (190w)

"I hope the CDphobes have the vinyl original of this 1963 cycle in good shape. For the rest of us, DG has done an excellent transfer of naturally produced analog recordings before DG and Karajan went mad at the mixing consoles-....This set remains *the* post-WWII Beethoven Symphony statement on recording."
Stereophile 14:165 Ja '91. Richard Schneider (b.n.)

Gramophone 67:1320-21 Ja '90. Michael Kennedy (370w)

The New York Times Mr 18 '90, p. H 27+. Richard Freed (225w)

1028. Symphonies (9) (complete). Overtures: Fidelio; The Consecration of the House; Leonore No. 3.
Riccardo Muti (c). Cheryl Studer (sop); Delores Ziegler (mez); Peter Seiffert (ten); James Morris (bass). Philadelphia Orchestra; Westminster Choir. 1985, 1987, 1988.
EMI 49487 DDD 392:00 6 discs

★★*Awards:* The Want List 1989, *Fanfare* N/D '89 (James Camner); Top Choices—1989, *American Record Guide* Ja/F '90 (Lawrence Hansen).

"Muti's Beethoven has a beautiful fetch. It breathes. It has what the Italians call *slancio*—impulse, impetuosity. His sentences are big lines and phrases, and he builds them up into elegant and dramatic musical stories. It works very well."

Stereo Review 54:128 Ja '89. Eric Salzman (400w)

"Among recently recorded integral cycles, this is certainly a good one, perhaps one of the best—overall as good as Haitink's recent edition on Philips. Its strengths and weaknesses complement rather than duplicate Haitink's."

American Record Guide 52:23-6 Ja/F '89. John P. McKelvey (2100w)

"Haitnik's Concertgebouw Orchestra is his set's principal attraction. Muti, by contrast, unites his strong interpretive profile to the Philadelphia's superlative playing, and produces one of the finest Beethoven cycles in years."

Ovation 9:46-7 D '88. David Hurwitz (785w)

"If Riccardo Muti's recordings of all nine Beethoven symphonies equaled his superb performances of the First, Fifth, Seventh, the slow movement of the Ninth, and the *Leonore* Overture No. 3—and if they were as well recorded—then this set would be a landmark-....For what it's worth, the soloists in the Ninth Symphony are excellent, the voice of soprano Cheryl Studer being particularly outstanding."

Musical America 110:56+ Ja '90. Thomas Hathaway (720w)

"Sonically, this set is hardly any better than it is musically. A claustrophobic closeness flattens perspective and exposes a number of extramusical details that one does not want to hear-....Ultimately, such defects in engineering bespeak a lack of musical sensibility evident also in Muti's dogged observation of every last one of Beethoven's repeats, regardless of what context, structure, or simple common sense dictate. Except for those with some special interest in Muti or his orchestra, I cannot see who might be interested in this set."

Fanfare 12:98-100 Mr/Ap '89. Mortimer H. Frank (1000w)

Digital Audio's CD Review 5:24-5 Jl '89. Lawrence Johnson (635w)

Gramophone 66:1141 Ja '89. Stephen Johnson (1405w)

1029. Symphonies (9) (complete). Overtures: Prometheus; Coriolan; Egmont.
Roger Norrington (c). Yvonne Kenny (sop); Sarah Walker (mez); Patrick Power (ten); Petteri Salomaa (bass). Schutz Choir; London Classical Players.
EMI 49852 DDD 353:00 6 discs

★★★*Awards:* The Want List 1990, *Fanfare* N/D '90 (Peter J. Rabinowitz). Top Disks of the Year, *The New York Times* D 24, '89 (John Rockwell); Top Choices—1989, *American Record Guide* Ja/F '90 (Allen Linkowski).

"If I had to live with only one stereo Nine, this would be it."

Fanfare 13:134-37 Mr/Ap '90. Peter J. Rabinowitz (1075w)

Gramophone 67:881-82 N '89. Richard Osborne (445w)

1030. Symphonies (9) (complete). Leonore Overture No. 3, Opus 72A.
Arturo Toscanini (c). Eileen Farrell (sop); Nan Merriman (alto); Jan Peerce (ten); Norman Scott (bass). Robert Shaw Chorale; NBC Symphony Orchestra. February 3, 1951; March 22, 1952; November 10, 1951; November 4, 1939 live.
RCA 0324 ADD 337:00 5 discs

✔HC ★★*Awards:* Critic's Choice: 1990, *American Record Guide* Ja/F '91 (Lee Milazzo); Critics Choice, *Hi Fi News & Record Review*, Ap '91 Supplement (Simon Cargill).

"It is my impression that the sound in every case is superior to any previous issue."

American Record Guide 53:33-6 S/O '90. Gerald S. Fox (1395w)

"These, to me, are an absolute household necessity....these are the urtext."

HighPerformanceReview 7:81 Winter '90-91. Bert Wechsler (120w)

"The natural sound of most of the originals turns out, amazingly, to have been spacious, resonant, lustrous, and sweet—in short, everything a Toscanini recording has been perceived *not* to have been—and excellent for its period-....To hear these CDs, then, is to hear Toscanini's recordings as if for the first time, and to discover what audiences and musicians of his day found so impressive about his performance."

Musical America 110:42-6 Jl '90. Thomas Hathaway (1065w)

"This release presents volumes one through five of a projected eighty-two compact disc and nine video cassette (and video disc) series that will ultimately comprise Arturo Toscanini's offical RCA recorded legacy-....Comparing Toscanini's performances of the Beethoven Nine with most modern versions is rather like comparing Raphael to Andy

Warhol. These performances are truly *sui generis*....My carpings about the technical quality aside, this is a monumental and monumentally worthy endeavor."

Fanfare 13:91-2 Jl/Ag '90. William Zagorski (1200w)

"Why invest in digitally remastered analog recordings from the early '50s when DDD recordings of these works abound? First, because tape noise notwithstanding, the sound is sumptuous. More importantly, because Toscanini's interpretations simply swing more; are more lyrical, in the sense of singer and song; are more organic from first note to last; and present a vigorous, unified conception of this as living, breathing music."

Musician 142:85-6 Ag '90. Chip Stern (490w)

Digital Audio's CD Review 7:42 Mr '91. Octavio Roca (b.n.)

Gramophone 67:1969 My '90. Alan Sanders (720w)

1031. Symphonies (9) (complete).
Gunter Wand (c). North German Radio Chorus; Hamburg State Opera Chorus; North German Radio Symphony Orchestra.
RCA 0090 68:04, 68:56, 58:25, 50:03, 44:09, 66:21 6 discs

★***Awards:*** The Want List 1989, *Fanfare* N/D '89 (William Zagorski).

"Those who want all the Beethoven symphonies in one box should find this the all-round most satisfying set on CD so far—not because of homogeneity, but because each of the nine works shines with its own distinctive character."

Stereo Review Presents: Compact Disc Buyers' Guide 1990 p.66 Richard Freed (125w)

"In spite of some soft spots, this is really a very good edition. Wand creates the proper sound world each of these works inhabits—perhaps the most fundamental thing a conductor must accomplish...I consider this set about equal, overall, to Weller's edition. I would choose Weller in 3, 5, and 6 and Wand in 4, 7, and 9, with the others more or less a toss-up. The Wand edition is very satisfactorily recorded."

American Record Guide 53:25-6 Ja/F '90. John P. McKelvey (465w)

"Were the reissue of Karajan's 1977 set complete on DG's Galleria label, it might well be my first choice...only those of Bernstein (DG) and Kegel (Capriccio) are competitive with Wand's....The shortcomings in Wand's cycle rest with an orchestra that is not quite the equal of the world's best and with tempos in the opening movement of the 'Pastorale' and the finale of the Second that might benefit from just a shade more elan. But just about everything else boasts a persuasive rightness and communicative impact that convey the quintessential Beethoven."

Fanfare 13:137-38 N/D '89. Mortimer H. Frank (500w)

"Like other commanding traversals—Karajan's from 1977, Bernstein's from 1978 (both DG), and Kegel's more recent effort (Capriccio)—Wand's is not without failings. His orchestra lacks the virtuosity and sumptuous tone of Karajan's Berlin ensemble and Bernstein's VPO, the Hamburg brass at times being a bit anemic, horns, in particular, wanting the color and bite that Beethoven demands. Then, too, the engineering, though generally admirable, occasionally veils detail in a bit too much resonance. But the sound has great presence and impact, and benefits from accurate timbres (especially string tone) and a wide dynamic range. Most of all, though, it is Wand's probing vision of these warhorses that carries the day, typified by a number of subtleties absent from many of today's faceless readings."

Stereophile 13:223+ Ja '90. Mortimer H. Frank (680w)

"The interpretations are solid and unexceptional."

The New York Times O 29 '89, p. H 27. John Rockwell (240w)

1032. Symphonies: No. 1 in C, Opus 21; No. 6 in F, Opus 68, "Pastorale".
Roger Norrington (c). London Classical Players. 1987.
EMI 49746 DDD 66:00

✔**HC** ★★***Awards:*** Critics' Choice 1988, *Gramophone* D '88 (Richard Osborne). Cream of the Crop IV, *Digital Audio's CD Review*, 6:41 Je '90.

"Norrington...understands that Beethoven's First is a musical eighteenth-century comedy of manners....His performance is heady, headlong, and delightful....Next to Norrington, Weller, Dohnanyi, and Abbado seem dour and tight-lipped."

Fanfare 13:137-44 S/O '89. William Zagorski (680w)

"Of my two initial quibbles about this coupling only one still remains: I find the rallentando over the opening four bars of the *Pastoral*...in both exposition and repeat, effete in manner. And I thought the First rather lacked any sense of the young lion roaring."

Hi-Fi News & Record Review 33:103 D '88. Christopher Breunig (320w)

"He lays his philosophy on the line: 'The point about playing Beethoven on old instruments-...is to make him sound new; to recapture much of the exhilaration and sheer disturbance that his music certainly generated in his day.' There is no question that Norrington does this."

Stereophile 12:207 Ja '89. Barbara Jahn (135)

"I urge the skeptical listener to try this disc along with the rest of this continuing series-

....You will never hear Beethoven with the same ears again."
American Record Guide 52:26 Ja/F '89. Allen Linkowski (250w)

"Norrington's readings here of the First and Sixth Symphonies are startlingly different from what we are accustomed to hearing....once you get used to Norrington's brisk tempos, these two readings offer an exhilarating listening experience. EMI's recorded sound is also absolutely first-rate throughout."
Stereo Review 54:163-64 F '89. Stoddard Lincoln (225w)

"What then most sets these Norrington efforts apart form traditional ones? Most conspicuously, their sound: thin vibratoless strings, colorful winds, biting brass, explosive timpani (especially impressive in the Storm of the 'Pastorale'), and a leanness and transparency of texture often missing in other performances-....However one ultimately feels about these performances, they should be heard by all those interested in Beethoven or in performance-practice. Both mark big improvements over what still strikes me as Norrington's faceless reading of the Ninth Symphony. As one might expect, the conductor observes all repeats and injects da capos in the reprise of the First Symphony's third movement. EMI's recording is close, very clear, and a trifle strident, with a tremendous dynamic range that in the two closing movements of the 'Pastorale' may shake many walls."
Fanfare 12:100-2 Mr/Ap '89. Mortimer H. Frank (750w)

"He uses twenty violins, eight violas, and six each of cellos and basses in both the First and Sixth symphonies....The numbers translate into a heftier sonority and a more dramatic impact."
High Fidelity 39:61+ Ap '89. Scott Cantrell (185w)

Digital Audio's CD Review 6:70 N '89. Lawrence Johnson (b.n.)

Gramophone 66:407-8 S '88. Richard Osborne (474w)

Symphony No. 1 in C, Opus 21. See No. 1266.

1033. Symphonies: No. 2 in D, Opus 36; No. 4 in B flat, Opus 60.
Leonard Bernstein (c). Vienna Philharmonic Orchestra. reissue.
DEUTSCHE GRAMMOPHON 423 049 ADD 70:09

★*Awards: American Record Guide* Overview: Beethoven Symphonies, Ja/F '89.

"Personally I'm captivated by that warm, glistening *molto vibrato* which puts paid to the ghost of Haydn in No 2's Larghetto, by the lurking tension banishing the 'morning mists' image of the introduction to 4(i)—and making thorough sense of the high-powered hymn to life which follows."
Hi-Fi News & Record Review 33:94 Ap '88. David Nice (150w)

"Both performances easily surpass Bernstein's earlier efforts with the New York Philharmonic...a most welcome addition to the CD catalog."
Fanfare 11:82-3 My/Je '88. Mortimer H. Frank (175w)

Gramophone 66:278 Ag '88. Stephen Johnson (250w)

1034. Symphony No. 2 in D, Opus 36. MOZART, WOLFGANG AMADEUS. Symphony No. 39 in E flat, K.543.
Frans Bruggen (c). Eighteenth Century Orchestra. The Netherlands. 1988.
PHILIPS 422 389 DDD 63:00

✔**HC** ★*Awards:* Top Disks of the Year, *The New York Times* D 24, '89 (John Rockwell).

"This disc can be enthusiastically recommended. The main point for the buyer is that the 'period' instruments, very well played, and the approach of the conductor to performance practice do not produce significantly different audible results, at least in these two symphonies, from Karajan and two outstanding 'modern' orchestras."
American Record Guide 53:92 N/D '90. David G. Mulbury (275w)

"The success of [this K.543]...consists of being quite a bit more than merely punctilious in translating score into sound....If this had come to me on vinyl or whatever they now use for a cassette tape base, it would have been well on its way to wearing out by now....a good reading [of Opus 36], but [it] partakes not of the marvel of its discmate. A distinguished CD, nonetheless, strongly recommended."
Fanfare 13:248-50 Mr/Ap '90. John Wiser (140w)

"In this account of 2, he has given us what is easily the finest period-instrument recording of the score and one of the very best in any style available on CD....The Mozart 39...is almost as good, spoiled only by slightly affected phrasing in the slow movement and a finale that moves just a shade too slowly to suggest its bubbly *moto-perpetuo* humor. Never, however, have I encountered a more commanding account of the first movement."
Stereophile 13:178-79 My '90. Mortimer H. Frank (150w)

"Delectable performances to two of the symphonic masterworks that nowadays we have every chance to take too much for granted-....The slight disappointment concerns the recorded balance, which cushions the rather backward winds from the vibrant exposure they require and indeed deserve." *P95 S85*
Hi-Fi News & Record Review 34:98 N '89. Peter Branscombe (145w)

Gramophone 67:24 Je '89. Stephen Johnson (420w)

Digital Audio's CD Review 6:57 Ja '90. David Vernier (260w)

1035. Symphonies: No. 2 in D, Opus 36; No. 8 in F, Opus 93.
Roger Norrington (c). London Classical Players. 1986.
EMI 47698 DDD 58:40

> ★★*Awards:* *Opus* Record Award, 1987; *Opus* Christmas List, 1987 (John Alan Conrad); *Gramophone* Period Performance Award, 1987.

"This release delighted me with its message that even in this day and age, a new recording of a Beethoven symphony can be a major revelation."
Opus 4:53-4 D '87. Jon Alan Conrad (80w)

"Highly recommended to all who are receptive to a new Beethoven listening experience."
American Record Guide 50:18-9 N/D '87. Kurt Moses (390w)

"Controversy aside, these are still excellent performances....Recorded sound is realistic and warm, but without much depth. "
HighPerformanceReview 5:83 Ap '88. D. C. Culbertson (175w) (rev. of LP)

"There is, however, more to Norrington's approach than tempo...Norrington is a dramatist at heart, and his infallible theatrical sense results in the most vivid and personal historical performances I have heard."
High Fidelity 38:63-4 Je '88. K. Robert Schwarz (505w)

Opus 3:31 O '87. Richard Taruskin (900w)

Hi-Fi News & Record Review 32:91-92 Ap '87 Christopher Breunig (345w) (rev. of LP)

Gramophone 64:1248+ Mr '87 Richard Osborne (925w)

Digital Audio's CD Review 6:70 N '89. Lawrence Johnson (b.n.)

1036. Symphony No. 3 in E flat, Opus 55, "Eroica"; Overtures: Leonora 2 and 3.
Otto Klemperer (c). Philharmonia Orchestra. 1955, 1954.
EMI 63855 ADD (m) 76:04

> ✔**HC** ★*Awards:* Classical Hall of Fame, *Fanfare*, Mr/Ap '92 (James H. North).

"I confess to astonishment at the technical quality of EMI's transfer here...It is, of course, one of the greatest of interpretations, and now its resoluteness, its sense of the whole structure held in tonal intellectual command, shine brighter than ever....Add to this two excellent-...items from Otto Klemperer's 1955 LP of all four overtures to *Fidelio* and you have a Beethoven bargain without parallel....Reissue of the month." *P100(historic) S85/75(100) P95 S75*
Hi-Fi News & Record Review 36:125 O '91. Christopher Breunig (brief)

Klemperer's 1955 monaural recording with the Philharmonia of the "Eroica" "hit the record world like a bombshell: an 'Eroica' with all the excitement of Mengelberg, the tension of Toscanini, the sweep of Furtwangler, and the balance and wisdom of Weingartner; even devotees of those great conductors celebrated this recording....Soon came stereo, and Klemperer's remake was eagerly awaited. It was a terrible disappointment...That infamous stereo remake is still around, so make sure your copy says '1954-55 Mono Recordings' on the cover. This is the definitive performance of the greatest music ever written."
Fanfare 15:474 Mr/Ap '92. James H. North (long)

Gramophone 69:44 Ap '92. Richard Osborne (long)

1037. Symphony No. 3 in E flat, Opus 55, "Eroica"; Marche funebre: Second movement (rehearsal sequence).
Pierre Monteux (c). Concertgebouw Orchestra. 1963 reissue.
PHILIPS 420 853 ADD 62:00

> ★*Awards:* Critics' Choice 1988, *Gramophone* D '88 (Richard Osborne).

"Enormously compelling, a strongly etched performance...clean, dynamic recording that responds to the *NoNoise* treatment."
Hi-Fi News & Record Review 33:96 Jl '88. Robert Cowan (100w)

"This *Eroica*...is one of the most distinguished accounts of the score now available."
American Record Guide 52:27-8 Ja/F '89. Allen Linkowski (150w)

Gramophone 66:22 Je '88. Richard Osborne (525w)

1038. Symphony No. 3 in E flat, Opus 55, "Eroica"; Overture: Prometheus.
Roger Norrington (c). London Classical Players. October 1987.
EMI 49101 DDD 49:00

> ★★★*Awards:* Critics' Choice 1989, *Gramophone* D '89 (Stephen Johnson); Top Choices—1989, *American Record Guide* Ja/F '90 (Kurt Moses). Editors' Choice, *Digital Audio's CD Review*, 6:34 Je '90; Cream of the Crop IV, *Digital Audio's CD Review*, 6:41 Je '90.

"Of specific interest here are the tempos, which are faster than all Eroica tempos, live or recorded, that I've ever heard except for Hermann Scherchen's 1950 Vienna recording-...The effect of the faster tempo is to make the work sound lighter, more Haydnesque, and not as grand or monumental....Angel's sound is clear, spacious, and generally first-rate. I recommend this disc as a fascinating and compelling recreation of one of music's greatest masterpieces....Controversial it may be; boring it is not."
American Record Guide 52:23-4 Jl/Ag '89. Kurt Moses (490w)

"I must admit that there are occasional moments when I think that Norrington could have let up a bit, and by the end of the work I wished that there could have been more sensuous beauty to the sound, but on the whole I felt that I was truly hearing this piece for the first time and couldn't help but wonder that if Beethoven had had our modern instruments, whether his music would have been the same. I think not."

HighPerformanceReview 7:1:68-9 '90. Lauren Jakey (785w)

"If the Overture to *The Creatures of Prometheus* comes near to an ideal tempo, parts of the *Eroica* fall rather short of the mark....Many felicities of orchestration emerge with startling clarity...The various soloists excel in their various tasks, and in combination their ensemble bids fair to outdo the best in the profession."

Musical America 109:52-4 S '89. Denis Stevens (740w)

"I don't find Norrington's treatment of the second theme particularly convincing. I do, however, like the dramatic point and the whiplash precision of Norrington's performance in general....Norrington, incidentally, opens this recording with a fleet and brilliant performance of the *Creatures of Prometheus Overture*."

Fanfare 13:137-44 S/O '89. William Zagorski (680w)

"Although Roger Norrington and Roy Goodman are both committed to replicating what early audiences would have heard, they deviate in the matter of tempi....This first movement is not for me....The LCP's crisply disciplined playing is a joy to hear....But the Hanover Band *Eroica* has a superb feeling of devoted enthusiasm, and despite a few slips I find it irresistible."

Hi-Fi News & Record Review 34:85-6 My '89. John Crabbe (280w)

Gramophone 66:1574 Ap '89. Richard Osborne (455w)

Digital Audio's CD Review 6:70 N '89. Lawrence Johnson (b.n.)

1039. Symphonies: No. 4 in B flat, Opus 60; No. 5 in C minor, Opus 67.

Georg Solti (c). Chicago Symphony Orchestra. 1986, 1987.
LONDON/DECCA 421 580 DDD 71:51

✔**HC** ★*Awards:* Best Recordings of the Month, *Stereo Review* Ja '89.

"Sir Georg has never made a happier Beethoven coupling."

Hi-Fi News & Record Review 33:103 D '88. Christopher Breunig (280w)

"This is a thinking man's Beethoven Fifth....a Beethoven Fifth that searches out and delivers the musical essence of the work rather than mere theatrics. Solti's approach to the lyrically expansive Fourth Symphony is warmly straightforward."

Stereo Review 54:104 Ja '89. David Hall (425w)

"The Fourth is dramatically intense....This is a Fifth in the grand manner."

American Record Guide 52:28 Ja/F '89. Allen Linkowski (150w)

"There're no big revelations here; just solid, traditional, big-orchestra interpretations....the recorded sound is really quite splendid."

HighPerformanceReview 6:70 Mr '89. James Primosch (180w)

"If this new Fourth remains firmly rooted in the Toscanini tradition, Solti's reappraisal of the Fifth shows a decided conversion to Furtwanglerian views. The performance is far more sensual and gradual than it was on either of the older recordings....My own tastes in this music incline more toward performances with sharper definition and greater militancy...but even so, I find Sir Georg's rethinking both intriguing and persuasive in its introspective way."

Musical America 109:54-5 My '89. Harris Goldsmith (730w)

"I know of few recordings that capture a virtuoso orchestra with such realism and detail. There is no false resonance here, just an accurate reproduction of a full-sounding orchestra playing straightahead versions of major works. Solti is solid throughout....Occasionally, there is an exaggerated change in dynamics....Elsewhere the only faults I hear involve Solti's rhythmic drive."

Fanfare 12:124 Ja/F '89. Michael Ullman (300w)

"I cannot see the need for the dismissive sting in the tail of the November '88 *Gramophone* review....these are careful, accurate, 'formal,' Beethoven readings that will withstand a good deal of repetition."

Stereophile 12:209 J '89. Christopher Breunig (400w)

Digital Audio's CD Review 5:50 Mr '89. Tom Vernier (160w)

Gramophone 66:772 N '88. Richard Osborne (210w)

1040. Symphonies: No. 5 in C minor, Opus 67; No. 8 in F, Opus 93; **Overtures:** Fidelio.

Leonard Bernstein (c). Vienna Philharmonic Orchestra. 1980, 1978.
DEUTSCHE GRAMMOPHON 419 435 ADD 69:05

★*Awards: American Record Guide* Overview: Beethoven Symphonies, Ja/F '89 (No. 5).

"When this VPO cycle is complete on CD, it will surely rank as one of the very best available."

Fanfare 11:152 S/O '87. Mortimer H. Frank (200w)

"It's hard to forget the violins' transformation of the fate rhythm in the Fifth's first-movement development, the singing freedom of the Andante that follows...or the vivacity of the classical spirit—when allowed the briefest of manifestations—in the Eighth." *P100 S100*

Hi-Fi News & Record Review 32:90-91 Ag '87 David Nice (120w)

Gramophone 65:35 Je '87 Edward Greenfield (255w)

1041. Symphonies: No. 5 in C minor, Opus 67; No. 6 in F, Opus 68, "Pastorale".
Erich Kleiber (c). Concertgebouw Orchestra. reissues 1954.
LONDON/DECCA 417 637 ADD (m) 73:00

✔HC ★★*Awards:* Critics Choice, *Hi Fi News & Record Review*, Ap '91 Supplement (Antony Hodgson). *American Record Guide* Overview: Beethoven Symphonies, Ja/F '89.

This transfer is "an essential component for a classical collection."

Hi-Fi News & Record Review 32:110 O '87. Doug Hammond (180w)

"This new CD transfer is amazingly successful. Tape hiss is virtually inaudible....I could spend pages in this magazine attempting to describe this shattering performance—it is superior to that given by Kleiber's son, Carlos, which is clearly based on his father's account—but I can only urge you, with all the passion at my command, to get hold of this CD somehow."

Music and Musicians International 36:45 N '87. Robert Matthew-Walker (280w)

"I used to think that Kleiber's 'Fifth' was the performance of a lifetime....I still find the performance fascinating but too tense and angry-....a curiosity, while acknowledging that it has achieved the status of recorded classic....The 'Pastorale' gets whipped up from time to time also, but it's a far more genial reading-...although....This CD *is* mono...but the sound quality as such is virtually contemporary."

Fanfare 12:124 Ja/F '89. Leslie Gerber (275w)

Gramophone 65:400 S '87 Robert Layton (365w)

1042. Symphony No. 6 in F, Opus 68, "Pastorale".
Bruno Walter (c). Columbia Symphony Orchestra. reissue.
CBS 36720 ADD 40:53

✔HC ★★★★★*Awards:* Pick of the Crop Reissues, *The New York Times* S 16, '90 (Sedgwick Clark). Records to Die for: 1 of 5 Recommended Recordings, *Stereophile* Ja '91 (J. Gordon Holt). The Super Compact Disk List, *The Absolute Sound*, Ap '92 (Harry Pearson). *American Record Guide* Overview: Beethoven Symphonies, Ja/F '89.

"Perhaps no other conductor has so conveyed the composer's springtime joy at arriving in the countryside as did Walter in the autumn of his years. The transfer to CD—one is almost tempted to say the transformation—is a great success....one of the all-time greats."

Stereophile 10:153 O '87. Tom Gillett (140w)

"There is less of a feeling of 'interpretation' in this reading than in any other recorded 'Pastorale'; the music speaks for itself. If you think you're fed up with hearing this symphony, give this recording a try."

Stereophile 14:143 Ja '91. J. Gordon Holt (105w)

1043. Symphony No. 7 in A, Opus 92.
Carlos Kleiber (c). Vienna Philharmonic Orchestra.
DEUTSCHE GRAMMOPHON 415 862

✔HC ★★★*Awards:* *Gramophone* Critics' Choice 1986 (Trevor Harvey). *American Record Guide* Overview: Beethoven Symphonies, Ja/F '89.

Gramophone 63:1025 F '86. Trevor Harvey (280w)

1044. Symphony No. 8 in F, Opus 93. MENDELSSOHN, FELIX. Symphony No. 4 in A, Opus 90, "Italian". SCHUBERT, FRANZ. Symphony No. 8 in B minor, "Unfinished," D.759.
Thomas Beecham (c). Royal Philharmonic Orchestra. 1953, 1952 reissue.
EMI 63398 ADD (m) 79:00

★★★*Awards:* The Want List 1990, *Fanfare* N/D '90 (John Bauman); Critics' Choice 1990, *Gramophone* D '90 (Richard Osborne); Critic's Choice: 1990, *American Record Guide* Ja/F '91 (Allen Linkowski).

"Can anyone find anywhere a more lovingly phrased Andante in the Schubert 8th? Bruno Walter comes close....The Beethoven 8th is graceful and spirited, tempos just right, sound just beautiful....In Mendelssohn's 4th Beecham decided, as Karajan later would, to slow down the third movement...The 1952 monaural sound on this disc is consistently good, with minor, easily-ignored hiss and plenty of brightness and presence."

American Record Guide 53:28+ S/O '90. Donald R. Vroon (210w)

Fanfare 14:474-76 N/D '90. William Zagorski (160w)

Gramophone 68:284 Jl '90. Richard Osborne (760w)

The Absolute Sound 16:71 S/O '91. Thomas Hathaway (brief)

1045. Symphony No. 9 in D minor, Opus 125, "Choral".
Roger Norrington (c). Yvonne Kenny (sop); Sarah Walker (mez); Patrick Power (ten); Petteri Salomaa (bass). Schutz Choir; London Classical Players. 1987.
EMI 49221 DDD 62:23

✔HC ★★★★*Awards:* *Gramophone* Critics' Choice (Richard Osborne), 1987; *Stereo Review* Best of the Month Mr '88. Record of the Year, Third Place and Orchestral, First Place, Mumm Champagne Classical Music Award 1988—Presented by *Ovation*, *Ovation* N '88; The Want List 1988, *Fanfare* N/D '88 (Robert Levine).

"Now that we have it on records...I would say the Norrington Beethoven Ninth was not so much 'revelatory' as controversial at certain key points."

Hi-Fi News & Record Review 33:99+ Ja '88. Christopher Breunig (425w) (rev. of LP)

"Taken on their own terms, everyone should know that Mr. Norrington and his players are splendid, as are his soloists for this recording."

The New York Times F 7 '88, p. H29-30. Bernard Holland (1200w)

"The point of Norrington's cycle...is not merely to record all the Beethoven symphonies using period instruments, but also to follow Beethoven's metronome markings, which in many instances call for brisker tempos than those we've been accustomed to in 'traditional' interpretations....All the participants, instrumental and vocal, are splendidly responsive on a very high level, and the documentation is splendid, too."

Stereo Review 53:87-8 Mr '88. Richard Freed (600w)

"What is immediately striking is the wonderful clarity of texture created here, lucid enough for one to hear the work afresh....The horn's interjections in the third movement are particularly awkward, but on the whole I welcome the new vistas that Norrington's concept brings into view....the recorded sound is slightly raw-edged, but it is crisp and immediate."

Stereophile 11:163+ Ap '88. Barbara Jahn (585w)

"It's startling at times, but to my ears it rings true as does no other performance-....Norrington's Beethoven performances...are probably the most important since Toscanini's."

Ovation 9:41-3 My '88. Scott Cantrell (285w)

"This record is indispensable because the evidence strongly suggests that it comes closer to what Beethoven actually *wrote* than any other performance within memory, and it is significantly different from any other Beethoven Ninth (I feel safe in saying) that you've ever heard."

American Record Guide 51:15-6 My/Je '88. Kurt Moses (750w)

"I can pay Norrington no greater compliment than to say that, midway through the Ninth Symphony, I forgot I was listening to a historical performance."

High Fidelity 38:63-4 Je '88. K. Robert Schwarz (500w)

"This is a remarkable performance. After a century of both ponderous and overdriven tempi, there is an initial shock reaction, but with familiarity comes a truly new, refreshing, and convincing understanding of this great work."

Musick 10:9-10 Fall '88. John Sawyer (490w)

Gramophone 65:572+ O '87 Richard Osborne (1260w)

Digital Audio's CD Review 6:70 N '89. Lawrence Johnson (b.n.)

1046. Symphony No. 9 in D minor, Opus 125, "Choral".

Arturo Toscanini (c). Eileen Farrell; Nan Merriman; Jan Peerce; Norman Scott. Robert Shaw Chorale; NBC Symphony Orchestra. March-April 1952.
RCA 5936 ADD (m) 64:54

★*Awards:* *American Record Guide* Overview: Beethoven Symphonies, Ja/F '89.

"So what we have here is even better than any issue of this great performance that we have had before."

Fanfare 11:154-5 S/O '87. William Youngren (510w)

"Arturo Toscanini's interpretation of the Ninth Symphony changed over the years....the first movement of the 1952 performance is diminished....the deliberation and clarity with which it unfolds in the 1938 performance is gone. With this one reservation, Toscanini's 1952 performance of the Ninth Symphony is among the most beautiful and sensitive on record."

High Fidelity 37:84 N '87. Thomas Hathaway (735w)

"Though the performance is not immune from criticism...the blazing conviction of this Carnegie Hall Ninth...is scarcely dimmed here....The importance of this classic recording is that it not only gives us a measure by which to relate present-day interpreters of Beethoven, as disparate as Norrington or Tate, but stands as one of the great testaments."

Hi-Fi News & Record Review 33:99 Ja '88. Christopher Breunig (185w)

"As reprocessed here—with especially impressive bass—it sounds better than ever."

American Record Guide 51:118-9 Mr/Ap '88. Peter J. Rabinowitz (300w)

Gramophone 65:1305-6 Mr '88. Stephen Johnson (125w)

Music and Musicians International 36:45 N '87. Robert Matthew-Walker (40w)

Opus 3:30+ O '87. Harris Goldsmith (815w)

BENJAMIN, GEORGE

1047. Antara. BOULEZ, PIERRE. Derive, for Flute, Clarinet, Violin, Cello, Vibraphone and Piano; Memoriale, for Solo Flute and 8 Instruments. HARVEY, JONATHAN. Song Offerings.

George Benjamin (c). Penelope Walmsley-Clark (sop). London Sinfonietta.
NIMBUS 5167 DDD 50:00

★★★★*Awards:* Contemporary Record Award 1990, *Gramophone* D '90; Records to Die for: 1 of 5 Recommended Recordings, *Stereophile* Ja '91 (Barbara Jahn). Critics' Choice 1989, *Gramophone* D '89 (Arnold Whittall). Best of the Month, *Hi-Fi News & Record Review*, My '90.

"Acoustics vary with venue, but results are equally superb."
Stereophile 14:147 Ja '91. Barbara Jahn (b.n.)

"All three composers on this stimulating disc have been associated with IRCAM, the music-cum-technology center headed by Boulez in Paris. However, only the Benjamin work makes use of IRCAM's computer facilities-...Good performances, excellent sonics; a recommended release."
HighPerformanceReview 8(1):63 '91. James Primosch (270w)

"I'd offer to buy this CD from anyone who gets it on my recommendation and finds it disappointing (if I could afford such gestures)."
Fanfare 13:125-26 Ja/F '90. Mike Silverton (625w)

"The appeal of this record is strictly to the ardent devotee of contemporary music."
American Record Guide 53:29 Ja/F '90. Timothy D. Taylor (250w)

"There's nothing really noisy or frightening here for any collector with a mind that's open enough to enjoy a little pop, jazz, or plainsong with his or her Beethoven and Tchaikovsky, and there is some lovely playing and singing." *P100 S100*
Hi-Fi News & Record Review 35:88 My '90. Stephen Daw (315w)

"The sonic simplicity of *Antara* is reflected in its design, a basic sonata-allegro pattern of thematic ideas stated, developed, and resolved. It is arguably not so deep a piece as Jonathan Harvey's 1985 settings of rapturous, mystical love poetry by Rabindranath Tagore, and it is certainly not so packed with musical information as the two brief Boulez works. But it is a solid composition, and—like the 19th-century concertos that are its models—a viscerally exciting one; its easy accessibility is just one of its many assets."
Musical America 110:72 Jl '90. James Wierzbicki (375w)

Gramophone 67:646 O '89. Arnold Whittall (420w) (rev. of LP); 68:726 O '90. Arnold Whittall (140w) (rev. of CD)

BERG, ALBAN

Lyric Suite, for String Quartet (1926) or Orchestra (1929) (3 movts.). See No. 1022, 8008

1048. Three Pieces for Orchestra, Opus 6. SCHOENBERG, ARNOLD. Five Pieces for Orchestra, Opus 16. WEBERN, ANTON. Six Pieces for Orchestra, Opus 6.
James Levine (c). Berlin Philharmonic Orchestra.
DEUTSCHE GRAMMOPHON 419 781 DDD 52:21

✔HC ★★*Awards: Awards: Stereo Review* Best Recordings of the Month Mr '88; International Record Critics Award (IRCA) Winner 1988, *High Fidelity* N '88 and *Musical America* N '88; The Want List 1988, *Fanfare* N/D '88 (Kyle Gann).

"So crammed are these scores [Berg] - and these performances - with beautiful, exotic, surreal, scarifying sounds, that I hardly know where to begin....And I've not even touched upon the neurotic, always questing, Schoenberg pieces - again, brilliantly realized. One of my year's best. Definitely."
Hi-Fi News & Record Review 32:107 N '87 Edward Seckerson (390w)

"The playing is out of this world, and the recording is stunning."
Music and Musicians International 36:48-9 N '87. Robert Hartford (40w)

"All is excellently vivid in this DG recording-....If these performances do not convince you of the innumerable virtues of this music, nothing will."
Stereophile 10:161+ D '87. Barbara Jahn (470w)

"Interpretively and especially sonically, this is one of the most spectacular recordings of the Second Viennese School ever produced....I'd venture to guess that these three works...have never before sounded so close to the way they were heard by their composers' inner ears."
Fanfare 11:91-2 Ja/F '88. Kyle Gann (610w)

"James Levine's new recording...of what might well be termed basic works of the so-called Second Viennese School...makes this music more accessible than it has been in almost any of its previous recordings."
Stereo Review 53:89 Mr '88. Richard Freed (550w)

"In spite of its reputation as one of the world's premier orchestras, the Philharmonic, like the Chicago Symphony Orchestra, has passed its prime....It doesn't take long to realize that the many audible edits—the most noticeable one among them coming at bar 23 in the *Funeral March* of Webern's *Six Pieces*—point not just to DG's technical sloppiness, but to an ensemble whose virtuosity isn't what it once was....I cannot recommend this disc."
Musical America 108:54+ S '88. David Hurwitz (760w)

Gramophone 65:287 Ag '87 Arnold Whittall (350w)

BERLIOZ, HECTOR

Beatrice et Benedict: Overture. See No. 1148.

1049. Symphonie Fantastique, Opus 14. La Damnation de Faust: Hungarian March; Ballets des Sylphes; Menuet des Follets. **Overture:** Le Carnaval Romain.
John Barbirolli (c). Halle Orchestra. 1966 reissues.
EMI 63762 ADD 75:00

★*Awards:* Critic's Choice: 1991, *American Record Guide*, Ja/F '92 (John McKelvey).

"The Vanguard LPs were excellent musically, but sonically left a lot to be desired, dim and fuzzy, lacking brilliance but not surface noise. The Angel CDs are a vast improvement....the *Fantastique*...allows one to see clearly just how fine a Berlioz conductor Barbirolli was."

American Record Guide 54:31 My/Je '91. John P. McKelvey (490w)

Gramophone 68:1659 Mr '91. John Warrack (200w)

"Sir John Barbirolli's 1966 Halle Orchestra reading has quite a lot against it—an orchestra which doesn't reach the technical standards of either the Baltimore or Milwaukee ensembles, let alone the Cleveland Orchestra, and a closely miked, screechy, and comparatively compressed recording that is prone to overload distortion during some of the louder moments in the score....I prefer this kind of recording to our more modern fondness for recreating a realistic concert hall experience....Barbirolli's presents a highly personalized, romantic view of this most Romantic of scores....Dohnanyi, Marcal, and Zinman are trying to reach the heart of this score analytically. Barbirolli succeeds in doing so intuitively."

Fanfare 15:164-67 S/O '91. William Zagorski (long)

1050. Symphonie Fantastique, Opus 14; Les Troyens—Royal Hunt and Storm; Le Corsaire Overture, Opus 21.
Thomas Beecham (c). Beecham Choral Society; French National Radio Orchestra; Royal Philharmonic Orchestra. reissues 1961; 1961; 1959.
EMI 47863 ADD 70:12

✔HC ★*Awards:* Records to Die for: 1 of 5 Recommended Recordings, *Stereophile* Ja '91 (J. Gordon Holt).

"One of the symphonic 'blockbusters' of our time, this is usually played as loudly as possible and much too fast. Beecham's way with it is much slower than we are accustomed to, but it creates an atmosphere of dreamlike fantasy and nightmarish dread that none of the other recorded performances has ever matched."

Stereophile 14:145 Ja '91. J. Gordon Holt (b.n.)

"This is simply the most imaginative, most creative piece of orchestral interpretation on record."

The $ensible Sound 10:65 Fall '88. John J. Puccio (40w)

"In sum, pre-Eminent, classic, and *de rigeur*."

Fanfare 11:159 S/O '87. Adrian Corleonis (150w)

"With 72:12 of music and sound that has hardly dated at all, this disc is a must."

High Fidelity 37:68+ O '87. David Hurwitz (200w)

Musical America 110:53-5 S '90. Denis Stevens (180w)

Gramophone 65:1072+ Ja '88. Edward Greenfield (125w)

1051. Symphonie Fantastique, Opus 14.
Leonard Bernstein (c). French National Orchestra.
EMI 69002 52:12

★*Awards:* *American Record Guide* Overview: Berlioz, Mr/Ap '91.

"Reviewing this superb collaboration...came as a breath of fresh air after Batiz's dismal affair with a tired sounding Royal Philharmonic ....This performance vies with Colin Davis' more classical yet equally hair-raising Concertgebouw recording for top honors among CD versions, along with the incomparable Beecham."

Fanfare 11:84-5 My/Je '88. Michael Fine (185w)

Hi-Fi News & Record Review 32:110 O '87 John Crabbe (150w)

Gramophone 65:393-4 S '87 Stephen Johnson (75w)

American Record Guide 50:81 N/D '87. John J. Puccio (75w)

1052. Symphonie Fantastique, Opus 14.
Charles Munch (c). Boston Symphony Orchestra. 1962 reissue.
RCA 7735 ADD 48:58

✔HC

"At last, the finest and best-sounding of Munch's four *Fantastiques* on compact disc...RCA's 1962 sound, despite general boominess and tape hiss, puts to shame any number of latter-day state-of-the-art productions for sheer detailed intimacy....This is cornerstone material and not to be missed."

Fanfare 12:112-3 S/O '88. Adrian Corleonis (125w)

1053. Symphonie Fantastique, Opus 14.
Roger Norrington (c). London Classical Players. 1988.
EMI 49541 DDD 53:00

★★★★★*Awards:* Best Recordings of the Month, *Stereo Review* Jl '89. Critics Pick Some Favorites of the Year, *The New York Times* N 26, '89 (John Rockwell); Critics' Choice 1989, *Gramophone* D '89 (John Warrack); Top Disks of the Year, *The New York Times* D 24, '89 (John Rockwell); Top Choices—1989, *American Record Guide* Ja/F '90 (Steven Haller). The Year's Best, *Hi Fi News & Record Review*, May '90 Supplement.

"What we have in this CD is outstanding. It is new in color, balance, and thought; it has immense assurance and panache, and the overall impression is one of immense energy."

Musical America 109:55-7 S '89. Denis Stevens (1520w)

"Norrington's *Symphonie Fantastique* should be hailed as an important milestone in the history of classical music on record. His performance goes beyond the mere documentation of a work as performed on period instruments. It is an interpretation which possesses artistic importance....the scaled down orchestra, controlled tempos and, above all, the virtuoso performances help us to hear moments in the score that have never previously been so clearly presented."

Continuo 13:24 O '89. David Cavlovic (535w)

"The performance reveals endless subtleties of phrasing, tone-colour and instrumental repartee, and while I'm not sure that Norrington allows quite enough Romantic fervour into the picture, there's no gainsaying this issue's great qualities." *P95/100 S100*

Hi-Fi News & Record Review 34:87 My '89; p.18 My '90 Supplement. John Crabbe (420w)

"EMI has come through with the only sort of sonics that would do in this case—a recording of outstanding excellence in its own right that allows all the performance's wonderful points to be made most clearly and directly....Before I got to the end I knew that *this* was the *Fantastique* that will be the 'basic' recording from now on, and the others will be the alternates."

Stereo Review 54:68 Jl '89. Richard Freed (725w)

"Sonically it is quite splendid, and insofar as one wishes to hear everything that is going on-...one need look no further. However, I would have liked a few more signs of romantic ardor glinting through the elegant skin of Norrington's performance. He argues that an exact rendition should reveal all, and almost proves his point in a recording that must be heard; but I would not wish this to be the *only* version in my collection."

Stereophile 12:163+ Jl '89. John Crabbe (475w)

"Taken as a performance of a very familiar work, it must be admitted that there is a whiff of pedantry about Norrington's interpretation-....This is not the first time I have felt an unresolved tension between Norrington's research findings and his expressive instincts....Yet, for all the positive reasons outlined above, lovers of Berlioz can not afford to miss this revelatory recording."

Ovation 10:64 Je '89. Paul Turok (335w)

"The unprompted listener...may be forgiven for finding this, on first hearing, a coarse and diminished *Fantastique* in which the Berliozian gamut—from the macabre to the sublime—has dwindled to varieties of the quaint. In fact, a number of attentive hearings may be required for the ear to relinquish its expectation that this curious dryness will blossom and, at last, begin to relish it....while Norrington is a capable and often fine conductor...he touches the surface where such as Beecham, Monteux, Munch, Davis, Bernstein, and Previn, for starters, have mined essential veins of Berliozian power and poetry. Still, one is grateful for this excursion-...a noble experiment and eminently self-commending."

Fanfare 12:99-101 Jl/Ag '89. Adrian Corleonis (1300w)

"This is a recording that will surely be studied avidly by generations to come, most likely punctuated by frequent exclamations of awe at myriad daring orchestral touches. Gratefully ensconced in sonics of the utmost clarity and integrity, this is one recording of the *Fantastique* which no one with any claim to interest in Berlioz's music can afford to be without."

American Record Guide 52:27-8 Jl/Ag '89. Steven J. Haller (550w)

Gramophone 66:1574 Ap '89. John Warrack (735w)

Digital Audio's CD Review 6:70 N '89. Lawrence Johnson (b.n.)

Symphonie Fantastique, Opus 14. See No. 6031

Symphonie Funebre et Triomphale, Opus 15. See No. 6030

BERWALD, FRANZ

1054. Symphonies (4) (complete).
Neeme Jarvi (c). Gothenburg Symphony Orchestra. DEUTSCHE GRAMMOPHON 415 502 2 discs

✔HC ★*Awards:* *Gramophone* Critics' Choice 1986 (Robert Layton).

"There have been distinguished recordings of Berwald's orchestral repertoire...but Neeme Jarvi and the Gothenburg Symphony sweep the field with the dynamism and beauty of their performances, and the sonics are superb as well."

Stereo Review 51:162 N '86 David Hall (400w)

"Until and maybe even beyond the point where EMI de-quads the Bjorlin performances...Jarvi and his now-familiar band have produced the preeminent survey of Franz Berwald's symphonic canon. It is strongly recommended."

Fanfare 9:101-2 Jl/Ag '86. John D. Wiser (550w)

"The Gothenburg Symphony's playing is first-rate...The only quality lacking is the sense of exaltation one gets from Jarvi's work at its very best."

Ovation 8:36 F '87 Paul Turok (360w)

"Written within a short period of hardly four years....Berwald's four essays stand quite apart from any other music of the period....their unique mixture of healthy vigor, fiery passion, exquisite humor, and gossamer, quicksilver lightness brings Haydn to mind....In general, these are exceedingly beautiful performances, by and large the best ever recorded of these marvelous works....An album that by any standard is one of the most successful of the year and the definite recommendation as far as Berwald's symphonies are concerned.

High Fidelity 36:76 N '86 Harry Halbreich (780w)

The Musical Times 128:145 Mr '87 Paul Banks (125w) (rev. of LP)

Gramophone 63:780 D '85. Robert Layton (875w)

BIRTWISTLE, HARRISON

1055. Silbury Air; Carmen Arcadiae Mechanicae Perpetuum; Secret Theatre.
Elgar Howarth (c). London Sinfonietta.
ETCETERA 1052 DDD 58:00

★★★★*Awards: Hi-Fi News & Record Review* Record of the Month, Je '88; The Want List 1988, *Fanfare* N/D '88 (Stephen Ellis); Contemporary Record Award 1988, *Gramophone* O '88.

"These performances are exemplary. Recorded sound is excellent...I highly recommend this 'fiery entertainment'."
HighPerformanceReview 5:77 S '88. James Primosch (225w)

"Recommended to everyone who is interested in the music of our own time."
American Record Guide 51:22 Mr/Ap '88. Timothy D. Taylor (375w)

"Howarth and his London Sinfonietta bring about this music most elegantly and convincingly....Etcetera's sound is dimensional and crystal clear. True devotees of modern music won't want to be without this release."
Fanfare 11:85-6 My/Je '88. Stephen W. Ellis (600w)

"If you are the slightest bit interested in what music of substance and import is being written today, then this disc is simply indispensable—and that is no hyperbole."
Hi-Fi News & Record Review 33:81 Je '88. Stephen Pettitt (270w)

"The orchestra is unendingly colorful and full of fantasy, but the line of musical thought is difficult to grasp and to follow."
Stereo Review 53:136 Je '88. Eric Salzman (160w)

Gramophone 65:1448 Ap '88. Arnold Whittall (350w) (rev. of LP); 66:549 O '88. Arnold Whittall (200w) (rev. of CD)

BIZET, GEORGES

1056. L'Arlesienne: Suites 1 and 2; Carmen Suites 1 and 2.
Charles Dutoit (c). Montreal Symphony Orchestra.
LONDON/DECCA 417 839 DDD 73:00

✔HC ★*Awards:* Critics' Choice 1988, *Gramophone* D '88 (Christopher Headington).

"An outstanding and immensely enjoyable record."
Hi-Fi News & Record Review 33:103+ O '88. Jeremy Siepmann (245w)

"Dutoit's disc should become the version of choice for anyone interested in this combination, though Beecham's recording of the *L'Arlesienne* suites (on the same disc with the Symphony in C) still tops the list."
Fanfare 12:146-7 N/D '88. George Chien (275w)

"Although as crisp and beautifully played as one has come to expect from Montreal, these new performances of music for the stage are something of a disappointment....other versions are much more dramatic, if less transparent in texture."
American Record Guide 51:18-9 N/D '88. Arved Ashby (375w)

"Thoroughly pedestrian....There's no shame in being unable to do everything equally well; at the same time, there's also little doubt that London has seriously miscast this orchestra and conductor."
Musical America 109:63-4 Ja '89. David Hurwitz (350w)

Gramophone 66:27 Je '88. Christopher Headington (435w)

1057. Symphony No. 1 in C. BRITTEN, BENJAMIN. Simple Symphony, Opus 4. PROKOFIEV, SERGEI. Symphony No. 1 in D, Opus 25, "Classical".
Orpheus Chamber Orchestra.
DEUTSCHE GRAMMOPHON 423 624 DDD 64:00

★★★*Awards:* Best Recordings of the Month, *Stereo Review* My '89. The Want List 1989, *Fanfare* N/D '89 (Ron McDonald); Critics' Choice 1989, *Gramophone* D '89 (Ivan March).

"The recording locale, the concert hall at the State University of New York at Purchase, is ideal for the Orpheus ensemble, enhancing the astonishingly powerful sonorities they generate. Unhesitatingly recommended."
Stereo Review 54:104 My '89. David Hall (300w)

"There's no lack of fine performances of any of these pieces...But the present versions are as delectable as any and more exhilarating than many. Strongly recommended."
Fanfare 12:274 My/Je '89. George Chien (290w)

"Superb performances, recorded with skill and taste, this is an outstanding release."
Fanfare 12:274 My/Je '89. Ron McDonald (265w)

"Best on the Orpheus release is the Britten symphony, delivered with just the right wit and charm. The Prokofiev performance is stodgy and leaden except for the Gavotte, which manages a bracing elegance."
The New York Times N 26 '89, p. 32 H. Martin Bookspan (b.n.)

"Orpheus' reading of the slow movement is nobly sustained, but the other movements are all a hair or more too fast—even for the fleet-footed NYCB *corps*....Still, the Orpheus players turn in an exhilarating performance, and the other works on the disc, Prokofiev's *Classical* Symphony and Britten's *Simple Symphony*, are done to perfection. Between these two superb performances and the gorgeous slow movement of the Bizet, this CD is definitely worth having."

Musical America 110:61-2 Ja '90. Terry Teachout (135w)

Gramophone 66:1145-46 Ja '89. Ivan March (150w)

Hi-Fi News & Record Review 34:109 F '89. Christopher Breunig (210w)

Fanfare 14:74+ S/O '90. John Wiser (b.n.)

BLISS, ARTHUR. Checkmate (excerpts). See No. 1202.

BLOCH, ERNEST

1058. Concerti Grosso: No.'s 1 and 2; Schelomo, Hebrew Rhapsody for Cello and Orchestra.
Howard Hanson (c). Georges Miquelle (cello). Eastman-Rochester Orchestra. 1960 reissue.
MERCURY 432 718 ADD 63:05

"This is some of the most accessible and passionate music composed in this, or any other, century. The highest praise I can give this version of Concerto 1 is that it is the equal of Rafael Kubelik's (monophonic) performance with the Chicago Symphony on one of the earliest Mercury Living Presence recordings. That is to say, it is dynamic, impulsive, and lyrical, as appropriate...Concerto 2 is equally vital, with moments reminiscent of Elgar's most noble passages (high praise)...highly recommended."

Stereophile 15:243+ Ja '92. Wallace Chinitz (long)

"Hanson's Bloch is right there in the room with you, its opulently saturated string masses as palpable as anything I've ever experienced in a recording...The Miquelle/Hanson *Schelomo*...is a gripping one, recorded in the same massively intimate sonics...Miquelle's cello is sweet in tone and impassioned in style...with the solo image in front but still surrounded by the orchestra."

The Absolute Sound 16:181-2 Ja '92. Arthur S. Pfeffer (long)

In *Schelomo* "Miquelle...hasn't the opulent tone of [Leonard Rose or Mstislav Rostropovich]...but he makes up for that in eloquence. Hanson's accompaniment is second only to Bernstein's for Rostropovich...and the recording really enables the listener to hear details in the orchestration usually obscured...Hanson's [performance of the First Concerto Grosso] is second only to Kubelik [not yet on CD] and is in stereo...This disc makes a great introduction to Bloch's music and the remastering is good."

American Record Guide 55:34 Ja/F '92. John Landis (long)

"These are *extraordinary* recordings for their time, given new life through the marvels of the CD medium....The weak link in these performances—and it is not all that weak—is the level of orchestral execution. The Eastman-Rochester Orchestra, mainly comprising conservatory students, lacked the solidity, richness of tonal blend, and confidence displayed by a major professional orchestra....it is the *Concerti Grossi* that make this reissue so valuable....In summary, this is a most worthwhile reissue and can be safely recommended to anyone who would like to have both *Concerti Grossi* on a single disc."

Fanfare 15:274-5 N/D '91. Walter Simmons (long)

BOCCHERINI, LUIGI

1059. Symphonies: in C for Guitar, 2 Violins, Cello, 2 Oboes, and Orchestra, Opus 21, No. 3, G.523; 4 in D minor for Orchestra, Opus 12, No.4; in A for Orchestra, Opus 37, No. 4, G.518.
Claudio Scimone (c). Dagoberto Linhares (gtr); Sonig Tchakerian (vln); Bettina Mussemeli (vln); Glauco Bertagnin (vln); Gianantonio Viero (cello); Paolo Pollastri (oboe); Helene Devilleneuve (oboe). I Solisti Veneti.
ERATO 45486 63:00

★*Awards:* The Want List 1991, *Fanfare* N/D '91 (Nils Anderson).

"This is a delightful disc, and it can be recommended to anyone interested in the composer as well as the casual listener. The sound is fine."

Fanfare 14:158 Mr/Ap '91. Nils Anderson (250w)

"Scimone approaches the works with his usual vigor and emotional expressiveness. Slow movements tend to be too deliberate, but Scimone never allows the musical interest to flag. The strings play with admirable ensemble, and the wind playing is superb."

American Record Guide 54:33 Ja/F '91. Paul Laird (220w)

"Over the years I have lived quite happily with Adrian Shepherd's Chandos version of seven Boccherini symphonies (on Chandos BDRD-3005) containing op. 34, no. 4, and op. 12, no. 4 ["La casa del diavolo"] in common with this release. Next to Scimone, Shepherd is four-square and tendentious. Scimone's little orchestra outplays Shepherd's group handily, and both the luscious tone of his winds and his own vital flexibility of beat and elegance of phrasing make these unsung little symphonies really sing."

Fanfare 14:158-9 Mr/Ap '91. William Zagorski (500w)

BORODIN, ALEXANDER

1060. Prince Igor: Polovtsian Dances. RIMSKY-KORSAKOV, NIKOLAI. Scheherazade, Opus 35.

Thomas Beecham (c). Beecham Choral Society; Royal Philharmonic Orchestra. reissues 1974; 1958.
EMI 47717 58:03

✔HC ★★★*Awards:* *Fanfare* Want List 1987 (John Bauman); Records to Die for: 1 of 5 Recommended Recordings, *Stereophile* Ja '91 (J. Gordon Holt). *American Record Guide* Overview: Russian Orchestral Favorites, N/D '89 (Scheherazade).

"Beecham's classic *Scheherazade* is simply twice as beautiful, twice as seductive, as any other recording I know."
Hi-Fi News & Record Review 32:119 O '87 Edward Seckerson (210w)

"Although these recordings are three decades old, the sound is more natural than many recent digital recordings. The balances are ideal, there is clarity and impact in percussion, and the overall effect of an orchestra playing in a first-class auditorium....This is an essential item for any orchestral CD collection."
High Fidelity 37:72 O '87. Robert E. Benson (185w)

"The Borodin makes a spicy fill-up to a disc nobody should be without."
Music and Musicians International 36:54 N '87. Robert Hartford (40w)

"Although no one has ever equaled the sensuousness and atmosphere of Stokowsky's mono performances of this, Beecham's only stereo recording comes the closest. The sound is hardly demo calibre, but it is good enough that it never gets between the listener and the music."
Stereophile 14:145 Ja '91. J. Gordon Holt (b.n.)

Musical America 110:53-5 S '90. Denis Stevens (180w)

Gramophone 65:403 S '87 Edward Greenfield (400w)

1061. Symphonies: No. 1 in E flat; No. 2 in B minor.
Valery Gergiev (c). Rotterdam Philharmonic Orchestra.
PHILIPS 422 996 DDD 66:00

★*Awards:* Critic's Choice: 1991, *American Record Guide*, Ja/F '92 (Steven J. Haller).

"Valery Gergiev is...well attuned to this kind of music, as his well-balanced, highly dynamic, and propulsive reading attests. The recording, especially of the Second Symphony, is a knockout....One of Philips' best recent CD recordings."
Audio 75:106 O '91. Bert Whyte (brief)

"The Borodin First Symphony is a charmer, especially in this alertly played and beautifully recorded performance...the disc is definitely a winner in terms of sonics and orchestral execution."
Stereo Review 57:93 Ja '92. David Hall (med)

BOULEZ, PIERRE. Derive, for Flute, Clarinet, Violin, Cello, Vibraphone and Piano; Memoriale, for Solo Flute and 8 Instruments. See No. 1047. **Figures, Doubles, Prismes, for Orchestra.** See No. 8014

BOYCE, WILLIAM

1062. Symphonies (8) (complete).
Trevor Pinnock (c). English Concert. 1986.
DEUTSCHE GRAMMOPHON 419 631 DDD 60:00

✔HC ★*Awards:* *Gramophone* Critics' Choice (Stanley Sadie), 1987.

"The focus, along with deliciously accurate orchestral playing, is a specialty of the English Concert, and it is lavished in abundance here upon minor music that blooms under such considerate treatment....This recording is warmly recommended."
Fanfare 11:109-10 N/D '87. John D. Wiser (390w)

"The performances...are just as bubbly and energetic as the music."
Stereo Review 53:152 Ja '88. Stoddard Lincoln (75w)

"If you're one of those who still thinks that the use of 'original instruments' spells expressive blandness (and God knows that, in some hands, it does), you're in for a treat....Orchestral balances and timbres have been captured by Archiv's engineers with appealing naturalness, and instruments are securely placed spatially."
Stereophile 11:134-5 F '88. Gordon Emerson (525w)

Ovation 8:21 Ja '88. Karen Monson (240w)

Digital Audio 4:60+ N '87. David C. Vernier (375w)

Gramophone 65:403 S '87 Stanley Sadie (400w)

BRAHMS, JOHANNES

Simple Symphony, Opus 4. See No. 1057.

1063. Symphonies (4) (complete). Music of Brahms: Concerto in A minor for Violin, Cello and Orchestra, Opus 102 (Mischa Mischakoff (vln) and Frank Miller (cello)); **Variations on a Theme by Haydn for Orchestra, Opus 56a; Tragic Overture, Opus 81; Academic Festival Overture, Opus 80; Hungarian Dances (No.'s 1, 17, 20, 21) for Orchestra; Gesang der Parzen, Chorus and Orchestra** (Robert Shaw Chorale), **Opus 89; Liebeslieder Waltz for Piano 4 Hands, Opus 52** (Artur Balsam, Joseph Kahn (pno)).
Arturo Toscanini (c). Mischa Mischakoff (vln); Frank Miller (cello); Artur Balsam (pno); Joseph Kahn (pno). Robert Shaw Chorale; NBC Symphony Orchestra. reissues.
RCA 0325 ADD (m) 267:00 4 discs

✔HC ★*Awards:* Critic's Choice: 1990, *American Record Guide* Ja/F '91 (Lee Milazzo).

"It is my impression that the sound in every case is superior to any previous issue."
American Record Guide 53:33-6 S/O '90. Gerald S. Fox (1395w)

"The natural sound of most of the originals turns out, amazingly, to have been spacious, resonant, lustrous, and sweet—in short, everything a Toscanini recording has been perceived *not* to have been—and excellent for its period-....To hear these CDs, then is to hear Toscanini's recordings as if for the first time, and to discover what audiences and musicians of his day found so impressive."
Musical America 110:42-6 Jl '90. Thomas Hathaway (1065w)

"Anyone knowing his Beethoven but coming upon his Brahms readings for the first time can't help but be impressed by their expansiveness, lyricism, and warmth...I found the transfer generally glaring and harsh, and often lacking in weight and impact....As to the performances I don't like, it's nice to know that a great musical genius occasionally can exhibit feet of clay. And as to the performances I do like, it's wonderful to reacquaint myself with a myth that years later still proves to be true."
Fanfare 13:107-9 Jl/Ag '90. William Zagorski (985w)

"Why invest in digitally remastered analog recordings from the early '50s when DDD recordings of these works abound? First, because tape noise notwithstanding, the sound is sumptuous. More importantly, because Toscanini's interpretations simply swing more; are more lyrical, in the sense of singer and song; are more organic from first note to last; and present a vigorous, unified conception of this as living, breathing music."
Musician 142:85-6 Ag '90. Chip Stern (490w)

Digital Audio's CD Review 7:42 Mr '91. Octavio Roca (b.n.)

Gramophone 67:1970 My '90. Alan Sanders (770w)

1064. Symphony No. 1 in C minor, Opus 68; Variations on a Theme by Haydn, Opus 56a.
Wilhelm Furtwangler (c). Berlin Philharmonic Orchestra. 1952, 1950.
DEUTSCHE GRAMMOPHON 415 662;
DEUTSCHE GRAMMOPHON 427 402 68:23

✔**HC** ★*Awards:* Classical Hall of Fame, *Fanfare*, S/O '91. *Fanfare* Want List 1986 (Henry Fogel).

"This account [of Brahm's First Symphony] by the Berlin Philharmonic...is the greatest performance of this majestic human drama I have ever heard."
High Fidelity 36:73 D '86 Thomas L. Dixon (160w)

"For those unfamiliar with Furtwangler's conducting, this [Brahms] is the place to start....This is a Brahms First for *every* collection, large or small, serious or casual....The performance is such that anyone who cares about this symphony would be foolish not to acquire it."
Fanfare 15:472-73 S/O '91. Henry Fogel (med)

Reviewed in a survey of works conducted by Furtwangler.
Opus 3:24-29 Ag '87 David Hamilton (325w)

Opus 3:48 D '86 Paul L. Althouse (105w)

1065. Symphony No. 1 in C minor, Opus 68. WAGNER, RICHARD. Tannhauser: Bacchanale.
Jascha Horenstein (c). Beecham Choral Society; London Symphony Orchestra; Royal Philharmonic Orchestra. London. January 29-30, 1962; September 29-30, 1962.
CHESKY 019 58:00

★★★*Awards:* Records to Die for: 1 of 5 Recommended Recordings, *Stereophile* Ja '91 (Richard Lehnert). *American Record Guide* Overview: Brahms: Symphonies and Piano Concertos, My/Je '89.

"One of the Cheskys' (and Wilkinson/Gerhardt's) greatest sonic achievements."
Stereophile 14:151+ Ja '91. Richard Lehnert (b.n.)

The Symphony is "an admirable job, well recorded....It's a beautifully played, middle-of-the-road effort that captures both the grandeur and the many detailed felicities of this work-....What may be lacking for some is that hair-raising intensity that the greatest conductors could bring to this familiar music."
American Record Guide 52:31 My/Je '89. Kurt Moses (250w)

"It is a performance [of the Brahms] worthy of comparison with the finest Romantic interpreters...a performance to treasure....The recording is good for the early '60s, hardly showing its age."
HighPerformanceReview 6:90 Je '89. Kenneth Krehbiel (140w)

"Chesky has shown the industry, yet again, how to present a vintage recording on CD with honesty, clarity, and without hamfisted noise reduction. Is it *the* best Brahms 1? If not, it is certainly within the highest category as a recording and as a performance."
Stereophile 12:165+ Jl '89. Richard Schneider (600w)

Brahms' *Symphony No. 1 in C minor* and Dvorak's *Symphony No. 9 in E minor* are "two of the finest standard-repertory recordings ever made, very stirring in Chesky's excellent digitalizations....These discs, with their Wilkinsonian immediacy and spaciousness, are greatly preferable to today's eviscerated DDDs."
The Absolute Sound 17:126+ Ap '92. Arthur S. Pfeffer (med)

1066. Symphony No. 2 in D, Opus 73; Variations on a Theme by Haydn, Opus 56a.

Christoph von Dohnanyi (c). Cleveland Orchestra.
TELDEC 44005 DDD 60:49

✔HC ★*Awards:* The Want List 1988, *Fanfare* N/D '88 (Justin R. Herman).

"Among CD Brahms Seconds, the slightly overemphatic Solti on London 414 487 is probably the safest recommendation, though the new Karajan (coupled with the remake of the Variations) may change the picture....In the Variations, Furtwangler's hypnotic performance (DG 415 6622, CD—with the First Symphony) is well worth hearing."
American Record Guide 51:23-4 N/D '88. Stephen D. Chakwin, Jr. (325w)

"This performance of the Symphony No. 2 cleaves to the pastoral spirit of the score with more powerful results than anything to come along since Kertesz's LSO reading, and in the long run, has such a sense of elevation and lyrical grandeur that it effaces all but a few of the very many recordings made of this music, *ever*....Strongly recommended."
Fanfare 11:136 Jl/Ag '88. John D. Wiser (300w)

"This new 2 is especially distinguished: transparent, unmannered, aptly lyrical, yet surgingly assertive, it features spectacular orchestral playing, the Cleveland horns, in particular, boasting an astonishing richness and virtuosity....the *Haydn Variations*, marked by dramatic contrasts, virtuosic execution, and textural clarity, recall the glories of the 1936 Toscanini recording. Where...[this CD] disappoints is in the excessively close miking of the orchestra."
Stereophile 13:193+ S '90. Mortimer H. Frank (110w)

Gramophone 66:156+ Jl '88. Alan Sanders (245w)

1067. Symphony No. 4 in E minor, Opus 98.
Christoph von Dohnanyi (c). Cleveland Orchestra.
TELDEC 43678 DDD 42:00

✔HC ★*Awards:* The Want List 1988, *Fanfare* N/D '88 (Justin R. Herman).

"Dohnanyi's performance...is forthright, with a rock-steady pulse and ample drive if not the passion of, say, Leonard Bernstein....If you want classic Brahms set forth in a truly state-of-the-art recording, this one, particularly on CD, will fill the bill very nicely."
Stereo Review 53:152 Ja '88. David Hall (175w)

"This is one of the finest discs Christoph von Dohnanyi has made with the Cleveland Orchestra, surpassing in every way the two-decade-old Brahms 4 recorded by Dohnanyi's most famous predecessor in Cleveland, George Szell. As one might expect, this new recording is vastly superior sonically....But of greater significance, Dohnanyi's reading goes more directly to the musical point....A warmly recommended release."
Stereophile 11:161 Ja '88. Mortimer H. Frank (410w)

"On balance...this is one of the preferred CDs of this warhorse."
Fanfare 11:99-100 Ja/F '88. Mortimer H. Frank (145w)

Gramophone 65:1074 Ja '88. Alan Sanders (475w)

1068. Symphony No. 4 in E minor, Opus 98. BEETHOVEN, LUDWIG VAN. Egmont: incidental Music, Opus 84.
Fritz Reiner; Rene Leibowitz (c). Royal Philharmonic Orchestra. reissue.
CHESKY 006 ADD 47:30

★★★*Awards:* Classical Hall of Fame, *Fanfare*, N/D '91; Top Choices—1989, *American Record Guide* Ja/F '90 (Robert Connelly). *American Record Guide* Overview: Brahms: Symphonies and Piano Concertos, My/Je '89.

"The opening movement is the most difficult to characterize....Clearly an iron hand directed by a probing mind is in charge, yet somehow the movement seems cold and detached. This is, I admit, a highly subjective view that others might not share....Rene Leibowitz's account of Beethoven's *Egmont* Overture is fleet, superficially exciting, but a bit short on subtlety."
Fanfare 11:100-1 Ja/F '88. Mortimer H. Frank (290w)

"The sound characteristics of the RCA LP and the Chesky CD are pretty much identical, indicating that the Cheskys decided not to monkey around with Charles Gerhardt's original recording, despite the fact that it's a below-par effort for him."
Fanfare 11:100-1 Ja/F '88. James Miller (250w)

"It is a *great* CD....The Chesky transfer into the digital format is one of the finest of its type I have ever heard."
Stereophile 11:136-7 F '88. Richard Schneider (750w)

"This disc belongs in every music-lover's collection where future generations can hear for themselves what made the diminutive Fritz Reiner a giant among his peers."
American Record Guide 51:26 Mr/Ap '88. Steven J. Haller (300w)

"While the sound of the Brahms is excellent, even by today's standards, the accompanying recording of the *Egmont* Overture is even more remarkable sonically....Highly recommended."
Musical America 108:59 My '88. Robert E. Benson (150w)

"I've singled out this Brahms performance (and I'm not the first to do it) as an example of how good a simple recording technique can sound if it's properly done....There's a density and weight to the orchestral sound, a sweetness to the strings, and a large and seamless soundfield that combine to convey a feeling of naturalness—of 'liveness,' if you will—that later, more complicated recording procedures quite simply lost sight of."

Fanfare 15:603-4 N/D '91. Mike Silverton (med)

Hi-Fi News & Record Review 33:87 Jl '88. Christopher Breunig (125w)

Digital Audio 4:54 Ap '88. Tom Vernier (180w)

BRIAN, HAVERGAL

1069. Comedy Overture: The Tinker's Wedding. Symphonies: No. 31; No. 7.
Charles Mackerras (c). Royal Liverpool Philharmonic Orchestra.
EMI 49558 DDD 64:00

✔HC ★*Awards:* The Want List 1988, *Fanfare* N/D '88 (Paul Rapoport).

"No assessment of contemporary British music will ever be possible until we come to grips with the achievements of Havergal Brian, England's greatest and most prolific symphonist....Sir Charles Mackerras and the Royal Liverpool Philharmonic Orchestra do themselves and the music proud on this outing. I have no question about this being the most important recording of British music issued in years....EMI has decided not to release this disc in the United States...Buy it while you can."

Musical America 109:52-4 N '89. David Hurwitz (545w)

"Get this disc...and listen for yourself to one of the strongest and most original musical minds of the century."

Fanfare 11:137-8 Jl/Ag '88. Paul Rapoport (1175w)

"Sir Charles Mackerras gives us a really glorious performance, somewhat broader in pace than Newstone, but more expressively varied in tempo and phrasing, and this evident feeling for Brian's music carries over into 31....the superb playing of the Royal Liverpool Philharmonic is backed by worthy engineering."

American Record Guide 52:38-41 Ja/F '89. Richard E. Tiedman (1535w)

"The Liverpool Philharmonic have already done sterling work for Brian's music, and here, again, their skill and dedication bear fruit in performances of splendid vigour and conviction."

Hi-Fi News & Record Review 34:94-5 F '89. Doug Hammond (315w)

Gramophone 65:1448+ Ap '88. Michael Kennedy (480w)

1070. Symphony No. 1, "Gothic".
Ondrej Lenard (c). Slovak Philharmonic Chorus; Slovak National Theatre Opera Chorus; Slovak Folk Ensemble Chorus; Lucnica Chorus; Bratislava Chamber Choir; Bratislava Children's Choir; Youth Echo Choir; Czech-Slovak Radio Symphony Orchestra, Bratislava; Slovak Philharmonic Orchestra.
MARCO POLO 8.223280/1 DDD 111:00 2 discs

★★★*Awards:* The Want List 1990, *Fanfare* N/D '90 (Henry Fogel); The Want List 1990, *Fanfare* N/D '90 (Paul Rapoport). The Want List 1991, *Fanfare* N/D '91 (Benjamin Pernick).

"To me, this is the greatest choral/orchestral work since Beethoven's Ninth, and one of the greatest achievements in Western music altogether. It follows that this recording is one of the most important in the entire history of recorded sound. I'm sorry if this isn't more 'objective.' It can't be."

Fanfare 14:186-89 N/D '90. Paul Rapoport (1920w)

"As a musical experience, the symphony ranges from the near indigestible to episodes of sublime and fascinating beauty....the singing here approaches the superlative. The orchestral forces do give their all in playing of the utmost conviction, and the recording engineers have done a remarkable job with music whose demands in terms of balance must be almost impossible to meet."

Stereo Review 56:97-8 Ja '91. David Hall (705w)

"Based on the evidence here, Bratislava, Czechoslovakia, must be a tremendously musical city—which is lucky for us because a majority of the population seems to have participated in the making of this recording. Unfortunately, that doesn't mean that everything goes smoothly....On the other hand, it's obvious that everyone is doing their best. The musicians play with great conviction. Ondrej Lenard's pacing is sure and supple, and the singers really do themselves proud snatching notes for some hair-raising tone clusters that come seemingly out of nowhere. This is not easy music, nor would one expect it to be: Brian was one of the least cosmetic composers imaginable."

Musical America 111:73-4 Ja '91. David Hurwitz (405w)

"Ondrej Lenard has not been content to make his way in workman-like fashion through the gigantic score but has attempted to impose his own vision on the music. If I do not always agree with his choice of tempo and manner of phrasing, nevertheless he has brought a resounding dramatic tension to the orchestral sections and an empowering sonority to the choral music of Part 2....While I would have liked more tonal body, Marco Polo's sonics are marvelously clear....In sum, a release of surpassing fascination of a landmark in the music of this century."

American Record Guide 54:47-9 Mr/Ap '91. Richard E. Tiedman (1180w)

"This performance by Czech forces (fairness would emphasize the strong Slovak contributions here) could not be considered an ideal representation of (Englishman) Brian's ideas, yet it has commitment and singleness of purpose to recommend it....The richness of the overall sound and the excellence of the long-term pacing by the conductor, Ondrej Lenard, more than compensate for the occasional intonation problem and some ineffectual climax-building....In total, then, this issue is far from perfect but more than adequate, and should not be dismissed by those interested in this work."

Stereophile 14:172-73 My '91. Barbara Jahn (270w)

"I fear that, on disc at any rate, Havergal Brian's massive 'Gothic' Symphony still awaits a decent trial [execution?]....both performance and recording here do scant justice to Brian's extraordinary vision." *P85/75(100) S75*

Hi-Fi News & Record Review 35:90 Ag '90. Andrew Achenbach (295w)

The intensity of the music "is reinforced by Ondrej Lenard, the conductor of this vastly ambitious Czechoslovak recording, and the skill of the myriad forces under his command."

The New York Times My 12 '91, p. 32 H. John Rockwell (med)

The New York Times O 7 '90, p. 34. Mark Swed (150w)

Gramophone 68:208 Jl '90. Michael Oliver (840w)

1071. Symphony No. 8; Symphony No. 9.
Charles Groves (c). Royal Liverpool Philharmonic Orchestra. 1978 reissue.
EMI 69890 52:28

✔HC ★*Awards:* The Chosen Few: The Best Sounding Discs of 1989. *New Hi-Fi Sound Supplement* D '89.

"For comments on the LP, see *Fanfare* 2:2, pp. 38-39....Havergal Brian (1876-1972) was a self-taught genius whose throwaway ideas dwarf in importance much of what we hear now extended to inordinate length....The digital remastering makes a lot of difference....There are still problems in the performances...But I wouldn't pass up the opportunity to hear this music, especially No. 8 and the slow movement of No. 9."

Fanfare 13:158 N/D '89. Paul Rapoport (320w)

"Groves's excellent readings of 8 and 9 continue to sound most impressive on CD, and the playing of the RLPO, whilst not the last word in refinement, positively oozes commitment." *P95 S95/100*

Hi-Fi News & Record Review 35:90 Ag '90. Andrew Achenbach (295w)

BRITTEN, BENJAMIN

1072. Young Person's Guide to the Orchestra, Opus 34; Variations on a Theme of Frank Bridge, Opus 10; Simple Symphony for Strings, Opus 4.
Benjamin Britten (c). September, 1964; November 1967; June, 1969.
LONDON/DECCA 417 509 60:52

"Not all older recordings emerge particularly well from digital transfer but luckily for CD addicts, this present coupling of definitive versions of three of Britten's most popular works presents them newly polished and with barely an extra blemish."

Hi-Fi News & Record Review 31:111 D '86 Doug Hammond (105w)

Gramophone 64:1010 Ja '87 Edward Greenfield (235w)

High Fidelity 37:60 Ag '87 Terry Teachout (100w)

BRUCKNER, ANTON

1073. Symphony No. 3 in D minor (1877 version).
Bernard Haitink (c). Vienna Philharmonic Orchestra.
PHILIPS 422 411 DDD 62:00

✔HC ★★★*Awards:* Pick of the Month, North American Perspective (Christie Barter), *Gramophone* Mr '91; Record of the Month, *Hi-Fi News & Record Review*, Mr '91. *American Record Guide* Overview: Bruckner, My/Je '91.

"The Third has the most complex history of revisions of all the symphonies, but most Brucknerians would probably rate the revision of 1876-7 (*edited by Fritz Oeser for the Brucknerverlag) as the finest. We are unlikely to get a more exciting, moving and satisfying account of it than this splendid new CD." *P100/95 S100*

Hi-Fi News & Record Review 36:87 Mr '91. Peter Branscombe (250w)

"This is not quite the same Bruckner Third we are used to hearing. This is the Oeser version-....Philips gives us their usual sound: no warmth or depth...The Vienna Philharmonic is a considerable asset if you want to record Bruckner—but not if the sound turns out this cold."

American Record Guide 54:40-1 My/Je '91. Donald R. Vroon (500w)

"His Vienna Bruckner Third is rather good. Haitink holds together the architecture of the sprawling first movement—no small task with this straggliest stretch of Bruckner's very imperfect masterwork. At the same time he never loses sight of its lyrical, Schubertian heritage-...Two things prevent Haitink's Third from being completely recommendable. The first is fairly serious: his performance of the Andante-...Here it's too slow, becomes soggy, loses cogency...The other failing is more serious yet. Philips's sound is awful: the aural equivalent of what baseball players call dead air. All sounds flat, bass is rolled off, dynamics are homogenized...Haitink conducts the 1877 version of the score edited by Oeser...It's longer, looser, less densely orchestrated than the 1889 Nowak edition most conductors favor...My favorite [Bruckner 3] Jochum's Dresden performance on Angel, comes only as part of a set of the nine symphonies."

Stereophile 15:261 Ja '92. Kevin Conklin (long)

Gramophone 68:1662 Mr '91. Richard Osborne (750w)

1074. Symphony No. 4 in E flat, "Romantic".
Karl Bohm (c). Vienna Philharmonic Orchestra.
LONDON/DECCA 411 581 67:56

✔HC ★★*Awards:* Critics Choice, *Hi Fi News & Record Review*, Ap '91 Supplement (Antony Hodgson). *American Record Guide* Overview: Bruckner, My/Je '91.

"If the performance is not quite flawless it has great majesty and beauty, and the combined effect of broad dynamic range, sonic precision, and all the atmosphere one could hope for, is memorable."

Hi-Fi News & Record Review 30:78 Jl '85. Peter Branscombe (130w)

Gramophone 62:1327 My '85. Edward Greenfield (175w)

1075. Symphony No. 4 in E flat, "Romantic"; Overture in G minor.
Marek Janowski (c). French Radio Philharmonic Orchestra.
VIRGIN 91206 DDD 73:00

★★*Awards:* *American Record Guide* Overview: Bruckner, My/Je '91.

"Janowski and the French Philharmonic orchestra are on fine form, especially the horns and heavy brass in the Symphony's blazing finale. The sound is warm and the dynamic range impressive."

High Fidelity 3:95 My '91. Andrew Stuart (b.n.)

"One of the greatest Bruckner recordings and one of the very best 4ths. (If you count sound, it's one of the two best....the Overture...meanders like the early versions of some of his symphonies. But it is rare on records, and now you can hear for yourself why it's never played."

American Record Guide 54:42 My/Je '91. Donald R. Vroon (365w)

"Performances are respectable, if not superlative."

Fanfare 14:130-1 Jl/Ag '91. Ron McDonald (200w)

P95/85 S85

Hi-Fi News & Record Review 36:83 Ap '91. Antony Hodgson (180w)

Gramophone 68:1824 Ap '91. Richard Osborne (455w)

1076. Symphony No. 5 in B flat.
Michael Gielen (c). Southwest German Radio Symphony Orchestra.
INTERCORD/SAPHIR 830 872 DDD 70:30

★★*Awards:* *American Record Guide* Overview: Bruckner, My/Je '91.

"Mr. Gielen makes more sense out of this symphony than any of the big name living conductors....Everything about this recordings is clean and clear, direct and powerful....but I'm hooked on the Klemperer and all that romantic warmth....it's still first choice for the Bruckner 5th."

American Record Guide 53:42 N/D '90. Donald R. Vroon (230w)

"He instills overwhelming drive and energy into the music, and when the final chorale arrives, the trumpets announce the occasion by taking a few notes up an octave. The movement has a visceral impact and seemingly improvisatory freedom that one imagines characterized Bruckner's organ playing—we seem to be eavesdropping on the creative process itself. Heightened by the best brass playing this symphony has ever been given, and great sound courtesy of German Radio, this performance may be the sleeper of the year."

Musical America 111:74-5 Mr '91. David Hurwitz (105w)

1077. Symphony No. 5 in B flat.
Jascha Horenstein (c). BBC Symphony Orchestra. September 15, 1971.
DESCANT 003 73:18

✔HC ★*Awards:* Top Choices—1989, *American Record Guide* Ja/F '90 (Gerald Fox).

"Overall, Horenstein's is the only Bruckner Fifth to equal Karajan's decade-old benchmark. It also has the economic and operational benefit of being on one disc....Highest recommendation."

Fanfare 13:104-6 S/O '89. Ben Pernick (485w)

This release is "magnificent in all important respects: performance, sonics, even album notes-....Horenstein's Bruckner Fifth is not only the greatest performance in my experience, but the recording also has the finest sound of any I have ever heard of this work."

American Record Guide 52:73+ S/O '89. Gerald S. Fox (380w)

"This live Horenstein recording...is one of the best architectural interpretations. The effect is of high tragedy, of thrilling climaxes and contemplative but never completely relaxed interludes....Sound is hissy and a bit unfocused, but quite vivid in timbres and dimensions."

Stereophile 13:195+ Ap '90. Kevin Conklin (205w)

1078. Symphony No. 5 in B flat.
Otto Klemperer (c). Philharmonia Orchestra. 1967 reissue.
EMI 63612 ADD 80:00

★★*Awards:* *American Record Guide* Overview: Bruckner, My/Je '91.

"Mr. Gielen makes more sense out of this symphony than any of the big name living conductors....but I'm hooked on the Klemperer and all that romantic warmth....it's still first choice for the Bruckner 5th."

American Record Guide 53:42 N/D '90. Donald R. Vroon (230w)

"There are a few minor problems in this release. The New Philharmonia plays well, but there are some untidy moments in the final movement. The recording is spacious and generally satisfactory, but at times the brass sounds unrefined and strident."

Fanfare 14:171-72 Ja/F '91. Ron McDonald (480w)

"Where Gielen finds propulsive energy, Klemperer projects a polyphonic clarity so intense that it becomes almost expressionistic-....The New Philharmonia Orchestra executes Klemperer's vision with complete security, and at midprice this issue represents a terrific bargain."

Musical America 111:74-5 Mr '91. David Hurwitz (105w)

Gramophone 68:1662+ Mr '91. Richard Osborne (350w)

1079. Symphony No. 6 in A.
Otto Klemperer (c). New Philharmonia Orchestra. 1965.
EMI 63351 ADD 55:00

★★★*Awards:* Critics' Choice 1990, *Gramophone* D '90 (Richard Osborne); Critics' Choice 1990, *Gramophone* D '90 (Michael Stewart). *American Record Guide* Overview: Bruckner, My/Je '91.

Gramophone 67:1598+ Mr '90. Richard Osborne (385w)

"Except in the scherzo, Klemperer is consistently faster than Muti (July/Aug 1989) but *sounds* slower. Muti is highly accented, crisp, and refined. Klemperer is hardly accented at all, simply presented, straightforward, deliberate, even plodding....may I suggest you acquire them both? It's good to hear such opposite but equally valid approaches."

American Record Guide 53:37-8 My/Je '90. Donald R. Vroon (150w)

"The performance of the Symphony No. 6 is one of his best, and the New Philharmonia Orchestra produces a rich, glorious sound. Unfortunately the recording...lacks clarity in this CD transfer and there is some annoying harshness in it."

Fanfare 13:116 Jl/Ag '90. Ron McDonald (235w)

1080. Symphony No. 6 in A.
Riccardo Muti (c). Berlin Philharmonic Orchestra.
EMI 49408 DDD 57:00

★★*Awards:* Top Choices—1989, *American Record Guide* Ja/F '90 (Donald Vroon). *American Record Guide* Overview: Bruckner, My/Je '91.

"This new recording is well played and well recorded, and there is much to admire in Muti's performance....If you can only have one recording, seek out the Keilberth CD."

Fanfare 12:153 My/Je '89. Ron McDonald (500w)

"Muti's Sixth is a far more successful performance than his earlier account of the Fourth, and it is given a vastly superior recording-....There is something of the wildness of the unrevised Fourth Symphony in this movement [the finale], and Muti responds by emphasizing its raw, almost primal power. Overall, his account can be easily recommended."

High Fidelity 39:56-7 Jl '89. David Hurwitz (350w)

"It is impossible to imagine a greater orchestra than the one we hear on this recording. In the true sense of the word, they are simply *awesome*."

American Record Guide 52:33 Jl/Ag '89. Donald R. Vroon (475w)

Gramophone 66:994 D '88. Richard Osborne (320w)

1081. Symphony No. 7 in E (Nowak).
Kurt Eichhorn (c). Bruckner Orchestra Linz.
CAMERATA 165 DDD

"This is an excellent performance of the Seventh Symphony...Eichhorn lets the orchestra unfold the musical argument with great naturalness, and the slightly rough edge to the brass playing, like that of other great orchestras such as the Czech Philharmonic, only serves to enhance the feeling of something primal being communicated. Certainly, the musicians have this music in their blood...but beyond that, they have the confidence to let it speak simply and eloquently. And that was one of Bruckner's special gifts."

Fanfare 15:135-6 My/Je '92. David Hurwitz (long)

"No other orchestra in the world has as much experience playing Bruckner, as much sensitivity to his style and message. No other orchestra is made up of people who share (as much as possible over time) his culture and milieu-....The Japanese engineers have captured the warm but airy (never muddy) sound of the Brucknerhaus. This sounds much better than Karajan's last recording in Vienna (DG) and it's more idiomatic, too. It's also cleaner and airier than the Angel Karajan, though that remains one of the all-time great performances. The interpretation, as expected, is Exactly Right....this is one of the great Bruckner recordings."

American Record Guide 55:39-40 Mr/Ap '92. Donald R. Vroon (long)

1082. Symphony No. 7 in E.
Herbert Von Karajan (c). Vienna Philharmonic Orchestra.
DEUTSCHE GRAMMOPHON 429 226 DDD 66:00

✔HC ★★★★Awards: The Highs, 1990, *The New York Times* D 30 '90 (John Rockwell). Editors' Choice, *Digital Audio's CD Review*, Je '92. Critic's Choice: 1991, *American Record Guide*, Ja/F '92 (Stephen Chakwin). Record of the Month, *Hi-Fi News & Record Review*, Je '90; *American Record Guide* Overview: Bruckner, My/Je '91.

"If you are tired of the exaggerations of egotistical conductors, turn to Karajan here and be refreshed. I would not have recommended previous Karajan recordings of this....But the more I listen to it the more I am inclined to call it one of the greatest statements...of one of the greatest conductors of the century."

American Record Guide 54:39-40 Ja/F '91. Ralph V. Lucano (350w)

"It is magisterial, quite beautifully played, in a recording of warmth, clarity and spaciousness that moves easily between the most delicate *ppp* and the awe-inspiring clangour of the climaxes." *P100/95 S100*

Hi-Fi News & Record Review 35:93 Je '90. Peter Branscombe (300w)

"All in all, this recording is a fine souvenir of Karajan's interpretive mastery in Bruckner, which he retained to the very end. I confess, however, my continued partiality to Riccardo Chailly's Berlin Radio Symphony CD on London, a luminous reading in superb sound."

Stereo Review 56:92 Mr '91. David Hall (250w)

"Both conceptually and sonically, this account of the Seventh lacks the impact of the 1977 recording (now on CD; 419 195)."

Musical America 111:70 Jl '91. Steven Lowe (400w)

"There are countless other conductors who make more of the work than he does. To name only two, I would recommend the reissued performance in a complete set of Bruckner symphonies with Eugen Jochum conducting the Staatskapelle Dresden (EMI CZS 7 62935 2), which should eventually be available on a single disc, or the outstanding performance with Libor Pesek conducting the Czech Philharmonic Orchestra (Supraphon CO-72647)."

Fanfare 14:171 Mr/Ap '91. Ron McDonald (400w)

Gramophone 67:1971 My '90. Richard Osborne (490w)

Digital Audio's CD Review 8:39-40 Ap '92. Lawrence B. Johnson (med)

1083. Symphony No. 8 in C minor.
Herbert Von Karajan (c). Vienna Philharmonic Orchestra.
DEUTSCHE GRAMMOPHON 427 611 DDD
83:00 2 discs

✔HC ★★★★★Awards: The Want List 1990, *Fanfare* N/D '90 (Ron McDonald); Critic's Choice: 1990, *American Record Guide* Ja/F '91 (Stephen Chakwin). Top Disks of the Year, *The New York Times* D 24, '89 (John Rockwell); Critics' Choice 1989, *Gramophone* D '89 (Robert Layton); Critics' Choice 1989, *Gramophone* D '89 (Richard Osborne); Best Recordings of the Month, *Stereo Review* Ja '90. *American Record Guide* Overview: Bruckner, My/Je '91.

"When maestro von Karajan brought the Vienna Philharmonic to New York in what clearly was a farewell concert, he chose Bruckner's magnificent *Eighth Symphony* for his valediction. And for those fortunate enough to have been present, the performance was a sublime, a religious experience. The current recording reflects something of what obviously was its grandeur, but it is also frustratingly flawed."

HighPerformanceReview 7:64 Winter '90-91. Thomas Wendel (360w)

"In all, an interesting and impressive Eight: more so than the Giulini, or Wand live recordings." *P95 S75/95*

Hi-Fi News & Record Review 34:105 O '89. Christopher Breunig (665w)

"His reading differs little from the craggy and awesome 1976 version. There is more intensity in the climactic episodes than before, but this may be a factor of the recording itself, which makes an even more powerful impact than the earlier one at the bass end of the spectrum-....Karajan's interpretation of the symphony has unsurpassed drama and scope, essential requirements in this work."

Stereo Review 55:103-04 Ja '90. David Hall (395w)

"This performance goes to the top of the list of the finest Bruckner Eighths currently available. Karajan, the VPO, and Deutsche Grammophon are all at their level best."

Fanfare 13:149 Ja/F '90. William Zagorski (400w)

"Except for the old Furtwangler EMI recording-...nobody has approached Karajan in this symphony. If you already have the Berlin version, there probably isn't enough of a difference to make the new one an essential purchase....The Vienna recording is currently the first choice."

American Record Guide 53:36-7 Mr/Ap '90. Stephen D. Chakwin, Jr. (380w)

Musical America 110:32-4 Jl '90. Thor Eckert Jr. (200w)

Gramophone 67:647 O '89. Richard Osborne (560w)

Digital Audio's CD Review 7:66 O '90. Lawrence Johnson (230w)

1084. Symphony No. 8 in C minor.
Gunter Wand (c). North German Radio Symphony Orchestra. Schleswig-Holstein Festival. August 22-23, 1987 live.
EMI 49718 DDD 86:00 2 discs

★★*Awards:* Critics' Choice 1988, *Gramophone* D '88 (Richard Osborne). *American Record Guide* Overview: Bruckner, My/Je '91.

"This is one of the major releases of the decade. Not only does it rank among the finest recordings ever of Bruckner's Eighth Symphony, but as a performance it stands virtually unparalleled as a testimony to the conductorial art of Gunter Wand....the sound is superb, barring an edit or two."

High Fidelity 39:65-8 Ja '89. David Hurwitz (365w)

Gramophone 66:283 Ag '88. Richard Osborne (490w)

1085. Symphony No. 9 in D minor.
Daniel Barenboim (c). Berlin Philharmonic Orchestra. The Philharmonie, Berlin. October 1990 live. TELDEC 72140 DDD 63:00

★*Awards:* Best Recordings of the Month, *Stereo Review*, Ja '92 (David Hall).

"Barenboim's new Bruckner 9 is splendid in every way—the best performance of his I've ever heard, the best available version of the symphony I've heard, and possibly one of the greatest Bruckner performances on records...Teldec's sound is warm, spacious, detailed, and excellent in balance and perspective."

American Record Guide 55:40 Ja/F '92. John P. McKelvey (long)

"Those who find the readings of Christoph von Dohnanyi on London, Herbert von Karajan on Deutsche Grammophon, and Georg Solti, also on London, too cyclopean and tough-fibered for their taste will respond very positively to this one by Barenboim, who makes the most of Bruckner's long-spanned melodic lines...here is a recorded realization of the Bruckner Ninth that does credit to all concerned—conductor, orchestra, and production staff."

Stereo Review 57:72 Ja '92. David Hall (long)

"It is a powerful performance, and a more affirmative and brighter view of this rather dark and somber music than usually is encountered...There is much to enjoy in this performance, but it simply is not in the same league as those recorded by the Berlin Philharmonic Orchestra with Furtwangler, Karajan, and Jochum."

Fanfare 15:190 Ja/F '92. Ron McDonald (long)

Gramophone 69:76 O '91. Richard Osborne (long)

1086. Symphony No. 9 in D minor.
Christoph von Dohnanyi (c). Cleveland Orchestra. LONDON/DECCA 425 405 DDD 58:00

✔HC ★★★*Awards:* Critic's Choice: 1990, *American Record Guide* Ja/F '91 (Stephen Chakwin). Critics' Choice 1989, *Gramophone* D '89 (Richard Osborne). The Year's Best, *Hi Fi News & Record Review*, May '90 Supplement. *American Record Guide* Overview: Bruckner, My/Je '91.

"A performance of vivid intensity and flowing beauty....Of CD versions I would rate this alongside the Haitink and Karajan performances." *P95 S95*

Hi-Fi News & Record Review 34:86 S '89. Peter Branscombe (150w)

"From the mysteriously superb opening pages, Dohnanyi imparts a kind of electric energy that is absolutely riveting....I cannot give a too-strong recommendation for this disc. Quite simply, it is a treasure."

HighPerformanceReview 7:64-5 Winter '90-91. Thomas Wendel (290w)

"Dohnanyi's Bruckner 9 moves apace, practically motoring across the first two of its three movements of cosmic expanse. The effect of the conductor's efficiency is to drain the music of much depth and anguish, aspects vital to Bruckner's devotional meaning....The CD also sounds clear and precise rather than warm, and reveals few of the secrets of Cleveland's Masonic auditorium. In the last movement, Dohnanyi takes the symphony to a level of meaning one might not anticipate from his aloofness in the first two movements."

Stereophile 14:249+ Ja '91. Kevin Conklin (425w)

"It is superbly played by the Cleveland Orchestra and magnificently recorded, but more important Dohnanyi provides a convincing interpretation. The performance is an energetic, propulsive one, faster than some but not to the point of being rushed....This release does not supplant the earlier ones mentioned above, but it is on a par with many of them. If you want a thoughtful performance of this work, well played and beautifully recorded, this release is an excellent choice."

Fanfare 13:149-50 Ja/F '90. Ron McDonald (425w)

"Though there are a few places in the first movement where the tempo is a bit rushed, this is a thoughtful, well-planned, and beautifully conceived performance....I have not given up my admiration for earlier versions by Walter (CBS) and Haitink (Philips), but musically this is in the same class and sonically it is even finer. I guess that has to add up to an extremely positive recommendation."

American Record Guide 53:38 Ja/F '90. John P. McKelvey (250w)

"He conjures an abundance of lovely sounds, but his faith in Bruckner is tempered with a cheerful calculation not to bore his transatlantic colleagues. He left me good-tempered but unsatisfied."

The Musical Times 130:690 N '89. Robert Anderson (185w)

Musical America 110:32-4 Jl '90. Thor Eckert Jr. (200w)

P95 S95

Hi-Fi News & Record Review p.19 My '90 Supplement. Peter Branscombe (175w)

Gramophone 67:26+ Je '89. Richard Osborne (875w)

1087. Symphony No. 9 in D minor.
Carlo Maria Giulini (c). Vienna Philharmonic Orchestra. Grosser Saal of the Musikverein, Vienna. June 1988 live.
DEUTSCHE GRAMMOPHON 427 345 DDD 68:00

★★*Awards:* The Want List 1990, *Fanfare* N/D '90 (William Zagorski); Critic's Choice: 1990, *American Record Guide* Ja/F '91 (Stephen Chakwin). *American Record Guide* Overview: Bruckner, My/Je '91.

"This is a very beautiful performance of Bruckner's score...It does seem to me, however, to be a reading of remarkable self-indulgence, with tempos in the first and last movements not only even slower than those of his Chicago reading for EMI in 1977, but absolutely the longest-playing of the 25-odd known to me." *P85 S95*

Hi-Fi News & Record Review 34:86 S '89. Peter Branscombe (125w)

"There are so many felicitous moments in this performance that listing them would truly inflate the size of this magazine to that of the Manhattan White Pages....No Brucknerian should deny himself this recording."

Fanfare 13:162 Mr/Ap '90. William Zagorski (470w)

"Giulini's previous Bruckner recordings have been mixed blessings, but this new Ninth, if you can live with the slow tempos of the outer movements, is a total success....Karajan (DG 419 083) is still the safest all-around recommendation in this work."

American Record Guide 53:37 Mr/Ap '90. Stephen D. Chakwin, Jr. (275w)

"The overall effectiveness of the performance is enhanced not only by the magnificent response of the Vienna Philharmonic players but also by the contribution of the Deutsche Grammophon production team, which has here achieved one of the finest live concert recordings yet made in Vienna's Musikverein."

Stereo Review 55:95-6 Ap '90. David Hall (225w)

"Giulini's deliberate tempos, the abysslike depth of his sonorities, the heart-easing richness of the Vienna strings, the magisterial impact of the brass, make this a very memorable version, the more remarkable in that it is also a live performance."

The Musical Times 130:690 N '89. Robert Anderson (185w)

Gramophone 67:296 Ag '89 Richard Osborne (470w); 68:132 Je '90 Ivan March (b.n.)

Musical America 110:32-4 Jl '90. Thor Eckert Jr. (200w)

CHABRIER, EMMANUEL

1088. Espana; Suite Pastorale; Fete Polonaise; Danse Slave; Gwendoline Overture; Joyeuse Marche; Bouree Fantasque. ROUSSEL, ALBERT. Suite in F for Orchestra (Prelude, Sarabande and Gigue), Opus 33.
Paul Paray (c). Detroit Symphony Orchestra.
MERCURY 434 303 67:00

✔HC ★*Awards:* The Super Compact Disk List, *The Absolute Sound*, Ap '92 (Harry Pearson).

"The thrice familiar *Espana* may be taken as a microcosm of Paul Paray's way with this music. So many mediocre performances of this warhorse have careened past in recent times—both the Tortelier ([*ARG*] Mar/Apr 1991) and the Clark ([*ARG*] Jan/Feb 1992) readily fall into this category—that we tend to forget what an innovative, even seminal work this is....If it is *Espana* that sets the stage, the other works on this disc are of no less interest....In short, while there are worthy collections of Chabrier, most recently the two CDs by Plasson for EMI, I know of none so infectious and uninhibited as this. Few other releases in the Mercury catalog are so likely to bring pleasure. Recommended with the warmest enthusiasm."

American Record Guide 55:44 Mr/Ap '92. Steven J. Haller (long)

"Some of the more recent Mercury releases strike me as being, overall, a more accurate representation of the master tape (or rather what's on the master tape) than what we have on the analogue discs....Some of the newer are much superior to the earlier releases....Give the latest generation Mercurys a listen. Some of them are among the jewels of analogue-to-digital technology."

The Absolute Sound 17:118+ Ap '92. Harry Pearson (med)

Espana; Suite Pastorale. See No. 1113.

CHAUSSON, ERNEST. Symphony in B flat, Opus 20. See No. 1146.

CHERUBINI, LUIGI

1089. Symphony in D; Overtures: Medee; Iphigenia in Aulide; Le Crescendo.
Donato Renzetti (c). Toscanini Orchestra.
FREQUENZ 011 042 DDD 53:00

✔HC ★*Awards:* Top Choices—1989, *American Record Guide* Ja/F '90 (Steven Haller).

"In short, for anyone seeking the stereo successor to Toscanini for Cherubini's wonderful symphony, Renzetti is your man."

American Record Guide 52:51 N/D '89. Steven J. Haller (350w)

"This impresses me as the finest-ever recording of Cherubini's symphony....this winning disc...is enthusiastically urged upon you all."

Fanfare 13:178 N/D '89. James H. North (300w)

COPLAND, AARON

1090. Appalachian Spring (complete); Grohg—Cortege macabre; Letter from Home; John Henry.
Leonard Slatkin (c). Saint Louis Symphony Orchestra.
EMI 49766 DDD 61:00

★*Awards:* Best of the Month, *Hi-Fi News & Record Review*, N '89.

"It's a beautiful performance, sensitively paced and very expressive. Since EMI's engineer William Hoekstra has done a superb job of capturing the sound of the full orchestra, this becomes a highly recommendable disc."
Fanfare 12:134-5 S/O '88. Leslie Gerber (280w)

"A most attractive and well-recorded release."
Music and Musicians International 38:63-4 O '89. Peter Dickinson (620w)

"The sound quality throughout is brilliant and exciting. Altogether this is one of the best of the new crop of Copland collections." *P100 S95*
Hi-Fi News & Record Review 34:100 N '89. Kenneth Dommett (320w)

"So there are bits of Copland here that we seldom hear...But none of it adds much to our knowledge or love of Copland. Nor does Mr Slatkin's *Appalachian Spring* challenge such fine recordings as the Bernstein...Ormandy-...Mehta...or, indeed, the composer's own."
American Record Guide 51:19 Jl/Ag '88. Donald R. Vroon (230w)

Gramophone 67:893-94 N '89. Edward Seckerson (575w)

1091. Appalachian Spring (complete); Lincoln Portrait; Billy the Kid: Suite.
Aaron Copland (c). Henry Fonda (narrator). Columbia Chamber Ensemble; London Symphony Orchestra.
1968, 1969, 1973 reissues.
CBS 42431 ADD 68:53

✔HC ★*Awards:* Records to Die for: 1 of 5 Recommended Recordings, *Stereophile* Ja '91 (Robert Hesson).

"I wouldn't want to be without these CDs, and I recommend them to anyone interested in Copland's music."
Fanfare 11:147-8 Jl/Ag '88. Leslie Gerber (300w)

"These soft-edged performances are distinctly unidiomatic....A firmer hand on the podium would have helped matters considerably. So would have extra rehearsals....Faults and all, though, these recordings are important."
Musical America 109:59-60 Mr '89. Terry Teachout (85w)

Digital Audio 5:64+ N '88. Brian J. Murphy (515w)

"This is one of the most powerfully moving musical performances I have ever heard....The remixed CD version is duller and less involving all around than the LP."
Stereophile 14:141-2 Ja '91. Robert Hesson (b.n.)

1092. Appalachian Spring (original version); Music for the Theater; Quiet City, for Trumpet, English Horn and Orchestra; Three Latin American Sketches.
Hugh Wolff (c). Saint Paul Chamber Orchestra.
TELDEC 46314 DDD 76:00

★★*Awards:* Critics' Choice 1991, *Gramophone*, Ja '92 (Edward Seckerson).

"This is Copland's original chamber version of *Appalachian Spring*, the complete score as played in the theatre for Martha Graham's ballet....This performance has plenty of brio and a good feeling for the music's Mexican origins, but not as much polish as Orpheus." *P95 S95*
Hi-Fi News & Record Review 36:73 S '91. Kenneth Dommett (med)

"I would characterize all the performances as elegant rather than energetic or gutsy. It is beauty of motion rather than high energy and drive, thoughtfulness and intensity rather than playfulness and humor, that take center stage here."
Stereo Review 56:72 O '91. Eric Salzman (brief)

"Fine performances in faultless sound....heartily recommended to collectors attracted by the combination of works offered."
Fanfare 15:304-5 N/D '91. Robert McColley (med)

"Wolff and his players give an attractive performance...Teldec's sonics are clear and robust."
American Record Guide 54:54-5 N/D '91. Arved Ashby (long)

"This disc offers a generous selection of Copland's more accessible works, well-played and smartly directed...Teldec's sonic perspective is close-up, full of detail but cool, dry, and a little short on warmth and resonance."
American Record Guide 55:45 Ja/F '92. John P. McKelvey (med)

"There is St. Paul's playing, which is not only unfailingly energetic, but also virtuosic in its precision. St. Paul is on a par with the world's finest chamber orchestra....Wolff's...ascetic, electrifying performances perfectly capture Copland's pulsating urgency and Stravinskyan timbres, but they do less well at conveying the composer's nostalgic, hushed lyricism....On the basis of these two recordings [Copland and Haydn's Symphonies No's. 85, 86], I'd say that Wolff knows well how to communicate excitement, sustain momentum and clarify shape and form. He still, however, has something to learn when it comes to conveying evocative mystery or tender poetry."

Musical America 111:50 N/D '91. K. Robert Schwarz (med)

1093. Appalachian Spring: Suite; Quiet City, for Trumpet, English Horn and Orchestra; Short Symphony; Three Latin American Sketches.
Raymond Mase (tpt); Stephen Taylor (cor ang). Orpheus Chamber Orchestra. 1989.
DEUTSCHE GRAMMOPHON 427 335 DDD 61:00

★*Awards:* Critic's Choice: 1990, *American Record Guide* Ja/F '91 (Stephen Chakwin).

"As Anthony Burton's excellent liner notes explain so clearly, this is not the usually encountered *Appalachian Spring*....It would be hard to imagine a more graceful, singing approach to this evergreen score....*Quiet City* has almost uncannily well-tuned playing from the trumpet and English Horn soloists...This performance echoes in the mind long after the playing has stopped. The rhythmically tricky Mexican postcards are handled with flair. The Symphony, on the other hand, doesn't really come off with forces this small....the engineering is a model of its kind."
American Record Guide 53:39-40 Mr/Ap '90. Stephen D. Chakwin, Jr. (325w)

"Despite plenty of competition in this repertoire, the Orpheus Chamber Orchestra's Copland CD stands out, not least for its topnotch sonics." *P90 S95*
Stereo Review 54:142 O '89. David Hall (275w)

"An admirably played and recorded programme."
Hi-Fi News & Record Review 34:96 Ag '89. Kenneth Dommett (240w)

"Enough has been said about producer/engineer Wolf Erichson's good work in the studio with this chamber orchestra. One can hear *everything*. Here is a collective opinion about Aaron Copland's music that is urgently worthy of your attention."
Fanfare 13:180-81 N/D '89. John Wiser (750w)
Fanfare 14:74+ S/O '90. John Wiser (b.n.)
Gramophone 67:301 Ag '89. Edward Greenfield (420w)
Digital Audio's CD Review 6:58-9 My '90. Lawrence Johnson (200w)

1094. Applachian Spring: Suite; El Salon Mexico; Danzon Cubano; Fanfare for the Common Man.
Leonard Bernstein (c). New York Philharmonic Orchestra.
CBS 37257 ADD 45:00

"There may be individual performances of some of these pieces that equal Bernstein's, but I haven't heard any better ones."
Fanfare 12:148-49 Ja/F '89. Leslie Gerber (150w)

"This is close to definitive on Copland...Final Score: Bernstein 6, everwyone else 0."
American Record Guide 51:18-9 Jl/Ag '88. Donald R. Vroon (90w)

1095. Billy the Kid: suite; Rodeo: suite.
Leonard Bernstein (c). New York Philharmonic Orchestra.
CBS 36727 ADD 39:00

"There may be individual performances of some of these pieces that equal Bernstein's, but I haven't heard any better ones."
Fanfare 12:148-49 Ja/F '89. Leslie Gerber (150w)

"This is close to definitive on Copland...Final Score: Bernstein 6, everyone else 0."
American Record Guide 51:18-9 Jl/Ag '88. Donald R. Vroon (90w)

1096. Connotations, for Orchestra; El Salon Mexico, for Orchestra; Music for the Theatre (orchestral suite); Concerto for Clarinet and String Orchestra.
Leonard Bernstein (c). Stanley Drucker (clar). New York Philharmonic Orchestra. Avery Fisher Hall, New York. October 1989 live.
DEUTSCHE GRAMMOPHON 431 672 DDD 74:00

✔HC ★★*Awards:* Critics' Choice 1991, *Gramophone*, Ja '92 (Peter Dickinson). Editors' Choice—Best CDs of the Year, *Digital Audio's CD Review*, Je '92.

"There is a coherence and an excitement in these performances that is most appealing....the wonderful *Music for the Theatre*, has its finest hour. Avery Fisher Hall never sounded better, either."
Stereo Review 57:84 My '92. Eric Salzman (med)

"This, despite Copland's own performance of it, is electrifying and comes across as fresh as if it were again being premiered....As a cross-section of Copland's varied career this could scarcely be bettered; it certainly could not be played with greater conviction." *P100 S95*
Hi-Fi News & Record Review 36:115 O '91. Kenneth Dommett (med)

"Bernstein and the orchestra are in top form and [the] sound is quite stunning."
Fanfare 15:198 Ja/F '92. David Hurwitz (brief)

"Bernstein's reading [of *Connotations*] is strident but grandiose, searching for the anguished emotional undercurrent, and finding it...Rarely-...have I heard such an expansive, flexible Clarinet Concerto, graced by Stanley Drucker's languid, long breathed solo line. Bernstein takes the time to really interpret Copland."
Musical America 112:42-3 Ja/F '92. K. Robert Schwarz (long)

"The only interpretation I did not like is *El Salon Mexico*...This new version [of the Clarinet Concerto] is even better [than soloists from the NYP (July/Aug 1988)]...This new [*Music for the Theatre*] is...an improvement, but only slight [over Bernstein's CBS recording]...The CBS recording [of *Connotations*] was splendid but this new issue is better...The sonics are outstanding."

American Record Guide 55:45-6 Ja/F '92. Gerald S. Fox (long)

"The Clarinet Concerto...has been recorded by an increasing number of artists, but William Blount, who has recorded it with the St. Lukes Orchestra under Dennis Russell Davies on Music Masters, is the only currently active one to give one pause if a *single* preferred recording of the Concerto is the primary consideration....the sound of the clarinet, loud in the high register, gets annoyingly shrill on the DG....it does detract from the otherwise excellent DG production. Bernstein recorded *El Salon Mexico* on two prior occasions, but this is by far the most successful in doing justice to its range, from tenderness to rowdy vulgarity, with an almost Szell-like polish. The same applies to an even greater degree in the cabaret-style *Music for the Theatre*....Despite the duplication in repertoire, a real Copland collector has to acquire each volume of the *Copland Collection* as they are issued. But the audiophile collector with an interest in Copland must have Bernstein's last public thoughts on the subject of the American composer he most admired, in sound that will put any system through strenuous paces."

Stereophile 15:265-6 Ap '92. Richard Schneider (long)

Gramophone 69:38 Ja '92. Peter Dickinson (brief)

Digital Audio's CD Review 8:52+ Mr '92. Richard Perry (long)

1097. Orchestral Works: El salon Mexico. Danzon cubano. An Outdoor Overture. Quiet City. Our Town. Las agachadas. Fanfare for the Common Man. Lincoln Portrait. Appalachian Spring Suite. Rodeo: Four Dance Episodes. Billy the Kid Orchestral Suite. Music for Movies. Letter from Home. John Henry. Symphony No. 3. Clarinet Concerto.
("The Copland Collection, Volume 1: Copland Conducts Copland, Orchestral and Ballet Works, 1936-1948").
Aaron Copland (c). Benny Goodman (clar); Henry Fonda (nar). New England Conservatory Chorus; New Philharmonic Orchestra; London Symphony Orchestra; Columbia Symphony Orchestra. 1963-1976.
SONY 46559 ADD 226:00 3 discs

★***Awards:*** Classical Hall of Fame, *Fanfare*, My/Je '92 (Scott Wheeler).

"This compilation of Copland performing Copland was made for CBS, mostly in London with his favourite orchestra the LSO...It is by no means an exhaustive gleaning of the archive, since it excludes recordings from his later, less populist phase...nor does it include the two early symphonies or the Piano Concerto which he played under Bernstein's direction....It need hardly be emphasised that he was a more than adequate interpreter of his own music...The sound throughout is very good." *P95/100 S95*

Hi-Fi News & Record Review 36:81 Ag '91. Kenneth Dommett (140w)

"All told...this reissue...is a real treat, and Sony deserves laurels and palms for unearthing so many rarities."

American Record Guide 54:48-9 Jl/Ag '91. Arved Ashby (685w)

"This could be called the essential Copland, at least before he dabbled in serialism, and all conducted by the composer which makes the performances sort of definitive."

HighPerformanceReview 8(3):76 '91. Bert Wechsler (brief)

"Like a fine landscape, Copland's orchestral output rewards continued close listening. Yes, it feels satisfyingly familiar, but its spirit of adventure remains strong....It's great to have them all in this format."

Fanfare 15:379-80 My/Je '92. Scott Wheeler (med)

"Fortunately, the analog masters were excellent, with a broad dynamic range, fine spatial separation and little extraneous noise. Sony's transfers only enhance those qualities. The performances are idiosyncratic but mostly first-rate."

The New York Times My 12 '91, p. 34 H. K. Robert Schwarz (med)

Gramophone 69:42 Jl '91. Peter Dickinson (420w)

1098. Orchestral Works: Dance Symphony; Two Pieces for String Orchestra; Symphony for Organ and Orchestra; Music for the Theatre; Concerto for Piano and Orchestra; Symphonic Ode; Short Symphony; Statements.
("The Copland Collection, Volume 2: Early Orchestral Works, 1922-1935").
Aaron Copland; Leonard Bernstein (c). Aaron Copland (pno). London Symphony Orchestra; New York Philharmonic. reissues.
SONY 47232 ADD 74:35; 69:31 2 discs

★***Awards:*** Classical Hall of Fame, *Fanfare*, My/Je '92 (Scott Wheeler).

"For the devotee of American music, all volumes will be necessary acquisitions."

Fanfare 15:197-8 Ja/F '92. John Wiser (long)

"Just as these are, almost without exception, important and immensely enjoyable works, these performances remain as honest, vivacious, and sincere as old friends, and outshine the few often slicker renditions that have appeared. The Bernstein performances in this set are particularly fine...Skillfully remastered, the sound has come up remarkably fresh and free of distortion...a classic set."

American Record Guide 55:46 Ja/F '92. Arved Ashby (long)

See Volume 1 for review excerpt.

Fanfare 15:379-80 My/Je '92. Scott Wheeler (med)

1099. Orchestral Works: The Red Pony; Preamble for a Solemn Occasion; Orchestral Variations; Dance Panels; Connotations; Down a Country Lane; Music for a Great City; Inscape; Three Latin-American Sketches.
("The Copland Collection, Volume 3: Late Orchestral Works, 1948-1971").
Aaron Copland; Leonard Bernstein (c). New Philharmonic Orchestra; London Symphony Orchestra; New York Philharmonic. 1962-72 live.
SONY 47236 AAD/ADD 70:22; 71:31 2 discs

★*Awards:* Classical Hall of Fame, *Fanfare*, My/Je '92 (Scott Wheeler).

See Volume 2 for review excerpt.
Fanfare 15:197-8 Ja/F '92. John Wiser (long)

"This set represents historic re-recordings of the American composer himself conducting most of these works. The two exceptions are *Connotations* and *Inscape*, both conducted by Bernstein....The remixing for CD format is generally pleasing if perhaps a little hard-toned, a little bright....In all, this is an interesting and valuable set of CDs. It gives us a record not only of Copland's own interpretations of his works, but also of the antipodal nature of his output."
High Performance Review 9:69-70 Spr '92. Thomas Wendel (long)

"The broad, predominantly tonal vernacular (exemplified by *The Red Pony* and *The Tender Land*) seems to have little in common with the ascetic, unmelodious Copland of *Connotations* or *Inscape*. The Sony collection offers a generous sampling of both Coplands...Copland is not always the best conductor of his own music, but his *Pony* is...[lively and] idiomatic. (Sony should have used Andre Previn's Columbia taping, the best recorded performance to date)....Leonard Slatkin recently made the second-ever recording [of *Music for a Great City*] ([*ARG*] M/J 1991) and the work benefits from a seasoned conductorial hand; sonically, there is again no contest—even though RCA's recording is recessed, its natural qualities are greatly preferable to the hyped-up Sony sound. The *Dance Panels* are available from Schwarz ([*ARG*] J/A 1989) and the choice there is pretty much analogous to the Slatkin situation. For the rest of the Sony set, there are few other convincing options—but then these are, for many, works of lesser interest."
American Record Guide 55:48 Mr/Ap '92. Mark Koldys (med)

See Volume 1 for review excerpt.
Fanfare 15:379-80 My/Je '92. Scott Wheeler (med)

1100. Symphony No. 3; Quiet City, for Trumpet, English Horn and Orchestra.
Leonard Bernstein (c). New York Philharmonic Orchestra. Avery Fisher Hall, New York. December 1985.
DEUTSCHE GRAMMOPHON 419 170

✔**HC** ★*Awards: Opus* Record Award, 1987; *Opus* Christmas List, 1987 (John Canarina).

"This totally committed version [of the symphony], recorded at 1985 concert performances, surpasses even his previous, excellent New York Philharmonic account."
Opus 4:53 D '87. John Canarina (150w)

"All in all it is a superb performance, the best this work is likely to have for a long time."
Fanfare 10:101-2 Mr/Ap '87 Walter Simmons (650w) (rev. of LP)

"One hears incredible refinement of detail, uncanny ensemble, immaculate balancing of choirs, and of course, spontaneity—or a compelling illusion of spontaneity....The chording within sections is also perfectly balanced, by conductor and engineers....I know that this recording is some sort of pseudodocumentary, art, not life itself—that what I'm hearing is a kind of sounding score (the retakes, the idealized mixing). Still, somehow I respond to it wholeheartedly, as if it were a real event. It is so musical; it seems to have the breath of life, a disarming mix of calculation and spontaneity-....(Bernstein's filler, *Quiet City*, though predictably drawn out and over-affectionate, is effective.)"
Opus 4:22-5 F '88. William Malloch (1475w)

"The orchestra plays brilliantly here, but the conductor's no-holds-barred version overemphasizes the score's bombastic moments."
Ovation 8:33-34 Mr '87 Paul Turok (135w)

Stereo Review 52:102+ Mr '87 Richard Freed (115w)

Gramophone 64:706 N '86 Michael Oliver (330w) (rev. of LP); 64:1104 F '87 Robert Layton (240w) (rev. of CD)

Hi-Fi News & Record Review 31:113 D '86 Kenneth Dommett (200w)

1101. Symphony No. 3; Music for the Theatre (orchestral suite).
Yoel Levi (c). Atlanta Symphony Orchestra. 1989.
TELARC 80201 DDD 65:00

★*Awards:* Records to Die for: 1 of 5 Recommended Recordings, *Stereophile* Ja '91 (Richard Lehnert).

"This is a definitive performance [of the Symphony]. As is Telarc's recording."
Stereophile 14:153 Ja '91. Richard Lehnert (b.n.)

"The Atlanta Symphony plays authoritatively—an impeccable performance in every way. The Levi approach is relatively relaxed; he emphasizes the long line. His is a lyrical approach. Bernstein (Deutsche Grammophon G-419-170-2) is more visceral, while Mata (Angel CDC-7 47606 2) falls someplace in between. The *The-*

ater Music makes for a highly contrasted companion to the Alpinic *Third*....Maestro Levi and the Atlanta players nicely capture the jazz/classic atmosphere of the piece."
HighPerformanceReview 8(2):62 Summer '91. Thomas Wendel (200w)

"The Atlanta Symphony Orchestra...has never sounded better than on this recording, which captures the whole range of Copland's genius—his tender lyricism, his potent rhythmic force, his translucent textures. And Telarc provides stunning sonics, possessed of a hair-raising dynamic range and a natural, lifelike presence."
The New York Times D 10 '89, p. 33+ H. K. Robert Schwarz (278w)

"Good notes, Telarc sound. Recommended-...this is solid—but not stolid."
Fanfare 13:156 Ja/F '90. John Ditsky (245w)

"The Telarc sound...is of near-breakthrough quality....I don't hold Levy's inability to phrase the third movement with Bernstein's Mahler-like agogics against him, but I'm embarrassed for him at the ponderous tempo of the scherzo coda....Otherwise, he's got the piece down. Levy/ASO and Telarc are far less successful with *Music for the Theatre*."
Stereophile 13:187+ Mr '90. Richard Schneider (275w)

"Yoel Levi's [reading of the symphony] is as good or better than most, and the Atlanta Symphony acquits itself in a manner not unlike our best orchestras....Still, I like the performance better than Bernstein's latest effort...The engineering is good...Yet, the recording is deficient in concert hall atmosphere...*Music for the Theatre* is not merely a generous coupling, it is also as good a performance and recording as you will find."
American Record Guide 53:40 Mr/Ap '90. Gerald S. Fox (420w)

Digital Audio's CD Review 6:58-9 My '90. Lawrence Johnson (200w)

Gramophone 67:1322 Ja '90. Edward Seckerson (430w)

1102. Symphony No. 3; Music for a Great City.
Leonard Slatkin (c). Saint Louis Symphony Orchestra. RCA 0149 DDD 67:00

★*Awards:* Critics' Choice 1991, *Gramophone*, Ja '92 (Edward Seckerson).

"Of all the CD recordings of Symphony 3 (I have heard all but the Mata), Slatkin's is the best performance. It is similar to Dorati's superb 11953 Mercury recording in its power, 'American' ebullience, and apposite tempos and phrasing...Slatkin is a far better conductor than Copland was, but *MFAGC* was one of the composer's finest recordings...All in all, both performances are good; but then there is the engineering....the sonic faults are not gross and the recording is still good, but it should have been better."
American Record Guide 54:47-8 My/Je '91. Gerald S. Fox (480w)

"Of all his works, Copland's Third Symphony contains the most complete portrait of its composer...Heretofore, my favorite performance has been Eduardo Mata's, with the Dallas Symphony (Angel/EMI 47606, LP only; OP), despite some odd balances in the recording. Leonard Slatkin, however, sets a new standard in this music....the sound is warm and true. With the jazz suite *Music for a Great City* as the substantial filler, equally well done, this release becomes the performance of choice in both works."
Musical America 111:72-3 My '91. David Hurwitz (280w)

"In many respects, Slatkin/St. Louis have given us a viable alternative to Bernstein/NYPO on DG. St. Louis lacks the brawny power which the NYPO brings to the piece, and Slatkin, to his credit, does not attempt to ape the overstated epic grandeur which Bernstein, as only he could have, drew from his aggregate of 'hunky brutes.'...Fans of the more cerebral Copland should be able to enjoy this performance without embarrassment. *Music for a Great City* is a recycled film score...This new recording by Slatkin/St. Louis speaks very well for the work."
Stereophile 14:241+ Je '91. Richard Schneider (550w)

"Because Bernstein was so closely associated with Copland, and because we have been so forcefully reminded of the fact by their deaths in 1990, it is hard to review the new RCA recording objectively. Certainly Slatkin and the St. Louis Symphony have a lot of experience with Copland's music, and producer Joanna Nickrenz, along with engineer William Hoekstra, have done a magnificent job of capturing the orchestra's sound."
Fanfare 14:191-2 Mr/Ap '91. Robert McColley (400w)

"Sony Classical has just released a number of Copland's own recordings...His 1960s recording with the London Symphony of *Music for a Great City* is not part of the current reissue, however, and too bad, because it's far more effective than Slatkin's account, which at the moment, is the only recording available...Slatkin's reading is admirable in terms of technical execution but plodding rhythmically and mundane poetically...Slatkin is solid but leaden...Add Bernstein's more dramatic (to put it mildly) approach in general, and Deutsche Grammophon's superior sonics, and Slatkin's recording becomes negligible in the balance."
High Performance Review 8:73 Wtr '91/92. Timothy Mangan (long)

P95 S95

Hi-Fi News & Record Review 36:02 Mr '91. Kenneth Dommett (200w)

High Fidelity 3:97 Ap '91. Andrew Stuart (b.n.)

Digital Audio's CD Review 7:58+ Ap '91. Tom Vernier (310w)

Gramophone 68:1500+ F '91. Edward Seckerson (630w)

CORELLI, ARCANGELO

1103. Concerti Grossi (12), Opus 6.
Trevor Pinnock (c). Simon Standage (vln); Micaela Comberti (vln); Jaap Ter Linden (cello); Trevor Pinnock (hpscd). English Concert.
DEUTSCHE GRAMMOPHON 423 626 DDD
130:00 2 discs

✔HC ★★★*Awards:* The Want List 1989, *Fanfare* N/D '89 (Nils Anderson); The Want List 1989, *Fanfare* N/D '89 (Edward Strickland); Early Music (Baroque) Record Award 1989, *Gramophone*, D '89.

"The CD catalogue does not want for available complete recordings of this set, yet this new one presents performances of unflagging vivacity and virtuosity, shot through with a keen sense of Baroque style and Corelli's personal idiom. Authentic instruments and performance practices are used, and the strong contrasts inherent in the music boldly drawn without violating the essential elegance that underlies even the most folk-based aspects of this music."
Hi-Fi News & Record Review 34:103-5 Ap '89. Doug Hammond (350w)

"In all, I would have to say that Pinnock runs a very close second choice [to Kuijken] in the realm of original instruments, offering slightly faster performances with more 'body'-....Archiv's sound is excellent."
Fanfare 12:166-67 My/Je '89. Nils Anderson (350w)

"Corelli's concertos receive a polished and energetic reading typical of The English Concert."
Continuo 13:23 Je '89. Scott Paterson (120w)

Gramophone 66:1149 Ja '89. Julie Ann Sadie (805w)

1104. Concerti Grossi, Opus 6: No's. 1-6.
Nicholas McGegan (c). Philharmonia Baroque Orchestra. 1989.
HARMONIA MUNDI 907014 DDD 60:00

★★★*Awards:* Editors' Choice, *Digital Audio's CD Review*, 6:34 Je '90; Cream of the Crop IV, *Digital Audio's CD Review*, 6:41 Je '90; Records to Die for: 1 of 5 Recommended Recordings, *Stereophile* Ja '91 (Arnis Balgalvis). Hall of Fame, *Digital Audio's CD Review*, Ja '92.

"The Philharmonia Baroque Orchestra...give us very nearly an hour of splendid playing in the best middle-Baroque style. These *concerti grossi*...represent the epitome of the Italian style. The Philharmonia Baroque plays them with stylish grace...I hear real violin sound on the LP and not on the CD. The later is dry and harmonically poor; there is all string and no soundboard."
Stereophile 13:195+ Je '90. Les Berkley (585w)

"The sounds reaching your ears are sure to please. The instruments have been captured having a most vivid time with the music....It's smooth and sumptuous, yet poignant and commanding."
Stereophile 14:127 Ja '91. Arnis Balgalvis (b.n.)

"The instrumental sounds produced by this estimable group are lovely. Ensemble work seems impeccable. Dynamics and shading are fine. But the performances are dull, with little excitement. I prefer less authentic, but more enthusiastic, recordings."
American Record Guide 53:41-2 Ja/F '90. Stephen R. Max (125w)

"McGegan...tends toward a certain abruptness and occasionally uses faster tempos than I would prefer (e.g., his opening largo in no. 1), but these performances hold together well-....The sound is forward, open, and clear."
Fanfare 13:181-82 N/D '89. Nils Anderson (200w)

"McGegan's musical revelations are fairly modest ones. Corelli still doesn't have the emotional depth of Bach or Handel, but he does emerge here as more than a mere charmer."
P80 S95

Stereo Review 54:155 N '89. David Patrick Stearns (125w)

Gramophone 67:1458+ F '90. Julie Ann Sadie (450w)

Digital Audio's CD Review 6:70+ O '89. David Vernier (300w)

CORIGLIANO, JOHN

1105. Symphony No. 1.
Daniel Barenboim (c). Chicago Symphony Orchestra. Orchestra Hall, Chicago. March 15-17, 1990 live.
ERATO 45601 DDD 41:00

★★★★★*Awards:* Choice Pick, *Musical America* N '91; The Want List 1991, *Fanfare* N/D '91 (Marc Mandel); The Want List 1991, *Fanfare* N/D '91 (James H. North). Critics' Choice 1991, *Gramophone*, Ja '92 (Edward Greenfield); Top Twelve Albums of the Year, 1991, *Stereo Review*, F '92.

"This is truly a smashing recording...The piece is modern, and in some senses challenging, but by no means does it sound hostile to the audience....This is a remarkable CD, and I recommend it highly." *P95 S95*
The $ensible Sound 12:59 Summ '91. Karl W. Nehring (med)

"It is potent music, beyond its moving program; several hearings suggest that it grows deeper as one gets to know it. The Chicago Symphony plays with the enormous conviction necessary for such a piece; that they are technically superb goes without saying....This disc is a must for anyone interested in music after

Mahler, with whom the symphony shares many moods."

Fanfare 15:193-94 S/O '91. James H. North (med)

"A triumph."

Stereo Review 56:91-2 S '91. David Patrick Stearns (med)

"With John Corigliano's Symphony No. 1, American contemporary composition finally enters the age of AIDS....Corigliano has created one of the finest American symphonies since World War II....Not surprisingly, much of this symphony is brutal, violent, one long halluncinatory scream. What is surprising is its exquisite delicacy of timbre and its willingness to engage in expressive (but never sentimental) lyricism....The Chicago Symphony Orchestra-...plays it with dazzling virtuosity and harrowing power, and Barenboim's masterful shaping of an exceptionally difficult score is a paragon of clarity and design. No one who cares about contemporary music can afford to ignore this disc."

Musical America 111:43 S/O '91. K. Robert Schwarz (long)

"In composing his first symphony, John Corigliano has sought to express in music his deepest personal feelings regarding the AIDS crisis....Symphony 1 is socially relevant art, and highly effective...I recommend this recording to anyone willing to tackle a piece of honestcontemporary music, which takes on what may come to be regarded as the most compelling moral crisis of our time. The music is perfectly accessible, but its emotional demands are not for the faint-hearted."

Stereophile 14:233+ D '91. Richard Schneider (long)

"John Corigliano's 40-minute No. 1, which won the $150,000 University of Louisville Grawemeyer Award, is a searing, vividly emotional response to the AIDS crisis...the symphony presents its ideas in a rich chromatic language that is not shy of expressive dissonance but adheres to an essentially Romantic syntax-....The symphony, Mr. Corigliano's valedictory as resident composer of the Chicago, was recorded during its first performances, in March 1990...the recorded sound is remarkably clean."

The New York Times Ag 25 '91, sec H p. 24. Allan Kozinn (long)

"This is disturbing music, often dissonant, full of anguish, conveying timely feelings and expressing a universal message of human suffering....Perhaps the fact that the symphony was recorded 'live' has something to do with the less than satisfactory sonics? But there is no audience noise!"

American Record Guide 54:63 S/O '91. Diederik C. D. De Jong (long)

The New York Times Jl 21 '91, p. 23 H. Gerald Gold (brief)

CRESTON, PAUL. Corinthians XIII, for Orchestra, Opus 82. See No. 6026.

DE FALLA, MANUEL

1106. Three Cornered Hat; El Amor Brujo.

Charles Dutoit (c). Colette Boky; Huguette Tourangeau. Montreal Symphony Chorus and Orchestra.

LONDON/DECCA 410 008 DDD 62:11

> ✔HC ★★*Awards:* Perfect 10/10, *Digital Audio*, Mr '88. *Gramophone* Critics' Choice 1983 (Edward Greenfield). Critics Choice, *Hi Fi News & Record Review*, Ap '91 Supplement (Kenneth Dommett).

This "is brilliant, joyful music-making abetted by the clarity and transparency of London's recording."

High Performance Review 3(1):94 Ag '84. (170w)

Ovation 4:48 Ja '84. Paul Turok (180w)

Digital Audio 2:20 Ja '86. David Vernier (200w)

Gramophone 61:144 Jl '83. Edward Greenfield (420w)

DEBUSSY, CLAUDE

1107. Images (Gigues; Iberia; Rondes de Printemps) pour Orchestre; Le Martyre de St. Sebastien (incidental music).

Pierre Monteux (c). London Symphony Orchestra. 1963 reissue.

PHILIPS 420 392 ADD 57:38

> ✔HC ★*Awards:* Pick of the Crop Reissues, *The New York Times* S 16, '90 (Sedgwick Clark).

"This is Debussy exquisitely scored, and marvellously unified thematically - features which Monteux points up with customary finesse. Excuse me while I go off to listen to it again."

Hi-Fi News & Record Review 32:97 S '87 Roger Bowen (140w)

Gramophone 65:489 S '87 Alan Sanders (120w)

Fanfare 11:110-11 Ja/F '88. James Miller (200w)

1108. La Mer; Prelude a l'apres-midi d'un Faune; Jeux—Poeme Danse.

Serge Baudo (c). London Philharmonic Orchestra. reissue 1986.

EMI 9502 DDD 51:33

> ✔HC ★*Awards:* *Gramophone* Critics' Choice (Stephen Johnson), 1987.

"CD transforms the qualities of this All Saints' Tooting production as presented by the LP (September '86 p87)....Though I still have reservations over the leader's few solos...Jonathan Snowden (flute) is outstandingly lovely in *L'apres-midi* - climaxes flower erotically!....A definite upgrade."

Hi-Fi News & Record Review 32:113 O '87 Christopher Breunig (110w)

"Baudo's expertise in French music needs no touting from me, and his Debussy collection is

about as good as I expected it to be, if somewhat marred by an overresonant recording."
Fanfare 11:110-1 Ja/F '88. James Miller (200w)

Gramophone 65:571-2 O '87 Stephen Johnson (105w)

DELIUS, FREDERICK

1109. Music of Delius: Over the Hills and Far Away (fantasy overture) (1895-7); 2 Pieces (Sleigh Ride; Marche caprice) (188708); Brigg Fainan English Rhapsody (1907); Florida Suite (1887) (rev. & ed. Beecham); Dance Rhapsody No. 2 (1916); Summer Evening (1890) (ed. & arr. Beecham); 2 Pieces for Small Orchestra (On Hearing the First Cuckoo in Spring, 1912; Summer Night on the River, 1911); A Song Before Sunrise (1918); Fennimore and Gerda (1909-10)—Intermezzo; Irmelin (1890-92)—Prelude; Songs of Sunset (1906-7).
Thomas Beecham (c). Maureen Forrester (contr); John Cameron (bar). Royal Philharmonic Orchestra; Beecham Choral Society. 1956-7 reissues.
EMI 47509 ADD 146:00 2 discs

✔HC ★★★*Awards:* Pick of the Crop Reissues, *The New York Times* S 16, '90 (Sedgwick Clark); *Gramophone* Remastered CDs Award, 1987; *Opus* Christmas List, 1987 (David Hamilton).

"Sir Thomas knew these would be valedictory recordings and he bestowed a lifetime's care and affection on the music; now they are preserved for posterity, can future generations do other than marvel at the sounds this great conductor conjured from his orchestra?"
Music and Musicians International 36:49 N '87. Robert Hartford (65w)

"Admirers of Delius, like myself, who have always been frustrated by black discs that seem to have a little pop or scratch to distract from the delicate textures, can revel in the pristine silence of these CDs, which permit the performances to be heard in all of their exquisite beauty."
Musical America 107:59 Ja '88. Robert E. Benson (250w)

"These stereo recordings of most of the important Delius works...have never, ever, been done better...the late fifties sound holds up remarkably well, give or take a little tape hiss."
The $ensible Sound 10:65 Fall '88. John J. Puccio (60w)

"Sir Thomas Beecham, one of the century's great conductors, made few stereo recordings, none better-sounding than these."
High Fidelity 37:59 Jl '87 David Hurwitz (100w)

"PH [Peter Herring] (Sept '85, p94)...found the LP pressings troublesome. That limitation is eliminated on CD."
Hi-Fi News & Record Review 32:93 Jl '87 Doug Hammond (70w)

"Needless to say, this collection is a landmark, classic and indispensable....the present collection is fine as far as it goes but it needs to be supplemented by compact disc editions of the World Records volumes—especially of the magical, breathtaking 1948 recording of *A Village Romeo and Juliet.*"
Fanfare 11:133-4 N/D '87. Adrian Corleonis (480w)

Musical America 110:53-5 S '90. Denis Stevens (180w)

Opus 4:56 D '87. David Hamilton (90w)

Gramophone 65:38+ Je '87 Ivan March (630w)

Digital Audio 4:48+ Ag '88. Wayne Green (350w)

1110. Music of Delius: Paris, the Song of a Great City; Eventyr; *Fennimore and Gerda:* Intermezzo; Over the Hills and Far Away; Irmelin Prelude.
Thomas Beecham (c). London Philharmonic Orchestra. 1935, 1937, 1939.
BEECHAM 002 ADD 61:00

✔HC ★*Awards:* Historical (Non-vocal) Record Award 1990, *Gramophone* D '90.

"The orchestral playing is inconsistent, but the conduction is unique in its charm and panache."
Musical America 111:88 Ja '91. Terry Teachout (b.n.)

Gramophone 67:98 Je '89 (210w); 68:728 O '90 (140w). Alan Sanders

DIAMOND, DAVID

1111. Concerto for Small Orchestra; Symphony No. 2 (1944); Symphony No. 4 (1948).
Gerard Schwarz (c). New York Chamber Symphony Orchestra; Seattle Symphony Orchestra.
DELOS 3093 DDD 73:17

★★★★★*Awards:* The Want List 1990, *Fanfare* N/D '90 (Benjamin Pernick); Records to Die for: 1 of 5 Recommended Recordings, *Stereophile* Ja '91 (Gordon Emerson); Critic's Choice: 1990, *American Record Guide* Ja/F '91 (James Ginsburg). Pick of the Month, North American Perspective (Christie Barter), *Gramophone* Ap '91; The Want List 1991, *Fanfare* N/D '91 (Paul Snook); The Want List 1991, *Fanfare* N/D '91 (Jon Tuska).

"The Second is given a performance of great conviction and persuasiveness by Schwarz and his Seattle Symphony, and so is the far more succinct Fourth, the only one of Diamond's symphonies, I believe, to have been recorded before....The sound is first-rate throughout the disc."
Stereo Review 55:159 N '90. Richard Freed (515w)

Musical America 110:20+ N '90. K. Robert Schwarz (535w)

"The works on Delos's disc demonstrate Diamond's mastery of the ardent, American orchestral sound cultivated by Roy Harris and Aaron Copland....The performances are, in a word, marvelous. The Seattle Symphony proves it must be counted (with SF and LA)

among the three left coast orchestras today on a par with the East-of-the-Mississippi 'big 5'. The NY Chamber Symphony, no stranger to 20th Century American music, acquits itself admirably too."

American Record Guide 53:47-8 N/D '90. James S. Ginsburg (480w)

"This is very likely the most important release of American music of the season and a required purchase for all serious collectors who are not victims of the 'warhorse' syndrome. A fine start to an exceptional cycle showcasing an exceptional composer."

Fanfare 14:214-15 N/D '90. Paul A. Snook (750w)

"On the evidence of this recording, the Seattle Symphony continues to grow and develop impressively under its imaginative and courageous young conductor, Gerard Schwarz. If I had to choose one single epithet for Diamond's music, I think I would call it mellifluous; Webster defines it as 'flowing sweetly and smoothly.' That quality comes naturally from the composer of some of the finest songs ever composed to English language texts."

Audio 75:124+ Ja '91. Paul Moor (405w)

"Each [piece] overflows with soaring melody, brilliant orchestral colors, and imaginative thematic development. There is also plenty of rhythmic fire, potently realized by Schwarz and his colleagues in performances that radiate stylistic understanding."

Stereophile 14:133 Ja '91. Gordon Emerson (b.n.)

"Although everything on this CD is interesting, my particular favorite is Diamond's Symphony #4, which is simply delightful....Highly recommended!" *P95 S90*

The $ensible Sound 12:59-60 Summ '91. Karl W. Nehring (brief)

Gramophone 68:1827 Ap '91. Peter Dickinson (315w)

Digital Audio's CD Review 7:62 Ap '91. Linda Kohanov (325w)

Stereophile 14:251+ Ja '91. Gordon Emerson (475w)

The Absolute Sound 16:182+ S/O '91. Arthur B. Lintgen (med)

1112. Symphony No. 3; Music for Shakespeare's Romeo and Juliet; Kaddish, for Cello and Orchestra; Psalm, for Orchestra.

Gerard Schwarz (c). Janos Starker (cello). Seattle Symphony Orchestra; New York Chamber Orchestra. DELOS 3103 DDD 74:15

★*Awards:* The Want List 1991, *Fanfare* N/D '91 (James Miller).

"The performances by the Seattle Symphony and the New York Chamber Symphony are all resplendent, and Delos has provided sonics to match."

Stereo Review 56:72-3 O '91. David Hall (med)

"The half-hour Symphony No. 3 is the highlight of this disc....The Diamond symphonies are proving to be the equal of those by Harris, Schuman, and Mennin. Schwarz's performances and Delos's recordings of them are everything we could ask; they are appearing about once a year. I concur with Paul Snook's opinion (*Fanfare* 14:2) of their importance."

Fanfare 15:311-2 N/D '91. James H. North (long)

"Delos's care and devotion to this repertoire makes this CD not a Diamond in the rough, but one among many native gems."

American Record Guide 54:58 N/D '91. James Ginsburg (long)

"The poignant, expansive lyricism, the bittersweet modality, the percussive rhythms and the lean, open textures are all as evident now as they were during the 1940's....As for the Third (1945), it is far less compelling than either the harrowing Second or the compact Fourth (both released last year on Delos DE 3093). Still, there is much to recommend here: the mellow, understated intensity of Mr. Starker's performance of the 'Kaddish,' the irresistible 'Romeo and Juliet' music and the fine, committed playing of both orchestras."

The New York Times Ag 25 '91, sec H p. 24. K. Robert Schwarz (med)

Diamond's music "is notoriously inconsistent in quality. The 1936 *Psalm*...is an attractive but rather faceless piece of post-Copland great-American-symphony-type music...*Music for Shakespeare's 'Romeo and Juliet'* (1947) is a delightfully fresh five-movement suite that would make an elegant ballet score. Best of all is a gorgeous *Kaddish*...superlatively performed on this CD by Janos Starker."

Musical America 111:44-5 N/D '91. Terry Teachout (med)

D'INDY, VINCENT. Symphony on a French Mountain Air, Opus 25. See No. 1148.

DUKAS, PAUL

1113. La Peri (fanfare and poeme danse); L'Apprenti Sorcier (The Sorcerer's Apprentice). CHABRIER, EMMANUEL. Espana; Suite Pastorale.

Yan Pascal Tortelier (c). Ulster Orchestra. CHANDOS 8852 DDD 56:51

★*Awards:* Critics' Choice 1991, *Gramophone*, Ja '92 (Christopher Headington).

"In an earlier review of the Ulster Orchestra's work under Vernon Handley (*Fanfare* 13:4) I found the orchestra in fine fettle, but its guidance from the podium lacking. In this release, the orchestra is still excellent, but here it is being led by an energetic, occasionally impetuous, but, on balance, very persuasive, conductor, who in his flamboyant brilliance recalls

Munch—and the results are superb....This is the kind of persuasive, committed music-making that I thought had disappeared for good a generation ago."

Fanfare 14:203 Mr/Ap '91. William Zagorski (350w)

"In short, a mixed bag, difficult to recommend wholeheartedly and yet not entirely unworthy. The warm, cushiony sonics make perhaps the best case for *La Peri* since Ansermet's London recording."

American Record Guide 54:61-2 Mr/Ap '91. Steven J. Haller (250w)

P100/95/85 S95

Hi-Fi News & Record Review 35:95 N '90. Christopher Breunig (390w)

Gramophone 68:1522 F '91. Christopher Headington (305w)

The Sorcerer's Apprentice. See No. 1317.

DVORAK, ANTONIN

1114. Slavonic Dances, Opus 46 and 72 (complete).
Vaclav Talich (c). Czech Philharmonic Orchestra. 1950 reissue.
SUPRAPHON 110 647 ADD (m) 75:00

✓HC ★★*Awards:* The Want List 1990, *Fanfare* N/D '90 (John Bauman); The Want List 1990, *Fanfare* N/D '90 (Mortimer H. Frank).

"Here is one of the prime examples of the Talich legacy. The performances are absolutely seductive."

American Record Guide 53:51 N/D '90. Carl Bauman (155w)

1115. Symphony No. 1 in C minor, B.9, "The Bells of Zlonice"; Heroic Song (symphonic poem), Opus 111.
Neeme Jarvi (c). Scottish National Orchestra.
CHANDOS 8597 DDD 74:00

★★★*Awards:* The Year's Best, *Hi Fi News & Record Review*, May '90 Supplement. *American Record Guide* Overview: Dvorak Symphonies, Ja/F '90.

"This conductor has amply certified his understanding of and sympathy with an idiom which has defeated many comers, including some of the composer's fellow countrymen. Strongly recommended."

Fanfare 12:137-38 Jl/Ag '89. John Wiser (475w)

"Stirring, vibrant performances."

The New York Times Ap 9 '89, p. 25. Barrymore L. Scherer (125w)

"There is a sense of emotional kinship and involvement in 1 that seldom wanes, from the carefully nurtured buildup in the introduction of the first movement to the brash, spellbinding coda of movement four. Phrasings are fresh throughout, and have a sure-handed vitality....Two older recordings of Symphony 1 by the LSO, one under Istvan Kertesz on London and one under Witold Rowicki on Philips, give much more rewarding views of the work."

Stereophile 13:195 F '90. Robert Hesson (180w)

"Neither Kertesz nor Rowicki has yet made the transition from black disc. This is particularly regrettable in the case of Kertesz, still the definitive set...Still, heard over a wide-ranging stereo system there is a comfortable ambience to the Chandos, which combined with Jarvi's energetic and sympathetic direction makes this one of the best of the set. Add to this the splendid *Heldenlied*...and the new disc becomes well-nigh irresistible."

American Record Guide 52:42-3 Jl/Ag '89. Steven J. Haller (425w)

"Where this new version [of The Hero's Song] scores is in the quality of the sound, which has wide range and is bell-like in its clarity compared with the Czech product [by Gregor for Supraphon]. The symphony also receives a splendid performance, though, since Jarvi's version is uncut and observes all repeats, its length becomes more than 'heavenly'. The sense of commitment everyone brings to the performance alleviates some though not all of the *longeurs* native to the work." *P95 S95/100*

Hi-Fi News & Record Review 34:79 Jl '89; p.19 My '90 Supplement. Kenneth Dommett (245w)

Gramophone 66:1577-78 Ap '89. Edward Greenfield (455w)

1116. Symphony No. 3 in E flat, Opus 10; Carnival Overture, Opus 92; Symphonic Variations, Opus 78.
Neeme Jarvi (c). Scottish National Orchestra.
CHANDOS 8575 DDD 63:00

★*Awards:* *American Record Guide* Overview: Dvorak Symphonies, Ja/F '90.

"Jarvi's tempos are judiciously chosen and momentum never flags. He emphasizes the strongly rhythmic, brilliant and dynamic aspects of the score, qualities that make for a truly exciting *Carnival* Overture as well."

Music Magazine 11:42 S/O '88. Robert Markow (220w)

"The symphony is the reason to buy this: it belongs with the best. The sound does too."

American Record Guide 51:41 S/O '88. Donald R. Vroon (250w)

"This Symphony No. 3...contains much more self-conscious music than its predecessors-...Jarvi's distinctly frenzied *Carnival Overture* is neither cheerful nor in any other way celebratory in sense; better aimed, altogether more satisfactory is the control of detail and variety of character the conductor finds in the equally familiar *Symphonic Variations*."

Fanfare 12:145-6 S/O '88. John Wiser (390w)

"It is...not a particularly memorable symphony and it takes a conductor of unusually sympathetic gifts to make it seem as if it were. Kertesz was one. Jarvi is another....Balance here tends to favour the winds, but no-one is likely to quibble too much about that in the face of such exhilarating performances."

Hi-Fi News & Record Review 33:85 Je '88. Kenneth Dommett (260w)

"The fabulous *Symphonic Variations* is perhaps the best performed work on the disc-....Jarvi plays it in a stunningly virtuosic manner....Once more, Chandos has apparently sunk conductor and orchestra into a deep well whose thick walls bounce the music reverberatingly into the microphones....None of this flatters any of this music, but it is particularly cruel to the turgidly scored *Third Symphony*."

HighPerformanceReview 7:66-7 Winter '90-91. Thomas Wendel (390w)

Gramophone 65:1590 My '88. Edward Greenfield (350w)

1117. Symphony No. 4 in D minor, Opus 13; The Golden Spinning Wheel (symphonic poem), Opus 109.
Istvan Kertesz (c). London Symphony Orchestra. reissue 1967; 1971.
LONDON/DECCA 417 596 ADD 66:45

★*Awards:* *American Record Guide* Overview: Dvorak Symphonies, Ja/F '90.

"These reissues from Kertesz's integral LSO set of the Dvorak symphonies from the 1960s-...remain among the finest recorded performances of this extraordinary conductor."

Music and Musicians International 36:49 N '87. Robert Matthew-Walker (30w)

"The LSO throughout the series was in top condition; one can make a case for these ADRM-processed reissues as absolutely viable alternatives to the all-digital work of Jarvi and the Scottish National Orchestra....If any performance in the series has a fault, it is the air of mischievous innocence with which Kertesz bears down upon the last two movements of the Symphony No. 4 in D Minor, which are operatically vulgar nearly beyond redemption."

Fanfare 14:235-8 S/O '90. John Wiser (190w)

Hi-Fi News & Record Review 32:97 S '87 Kenneth Dommett (90w)

Gramophone 65:290 Ag '87 Ivan March (105w)

1118. Symphony No. 5 in F, Opus 76; The Water Goblin (symphonic poem), Opus 107.
Neeme Jarvi (c). Scottish National Orchestra.
CHANDOS 8552 DDD 61:00

★★★*Awards:* Critics' Choice 1988, *Gramophone* D '88 (Edward Greenfield). *American Record Guide* Overview: Dvorak Symphonies, Ja/F '90.

"This latest installment of Jarvi's Dvorak cycle is quite the best so far."

Hi-Fi News & Record Review 33:95 F '88. Kenneth Dommett (240w)

"Chandos has given its performers a typically vivid and atmospheric sound documentation, entirely comparable to earlier issues in the series (*Fanfare* 10:6, pp. 101-02; 11:2, pp. 135-36). The latest installment also earns warm recommendation."

Fanfare 11:103-4 Mr/Ap '88. John D. Wiser (425w)

"On balance, while both Kertesz and Jarvi have different, if equally valid, approaches to the symphony, the performance of the tone poem inclines me toward this new release as a first choice."

Ovation 9:38 Ap '88. Jon Tuska (250w)

"Jarvi's direction is softer than that of his most famous rival's, Kertesz's performance from the late-sixties (now available on London CD)...I have a special fondness for Kertesz's emphatically vital interpretation, but Jarvi provides a reasonable alternative."

The $ensible Sound 10:63 Fall '88. John J. Puccio (220w)

Gramophone 65:942 D '87. Edward Greenfield (385w)

"Once again Jarvi and his sturdy ensemble play their hearts out, and once again the Chandos engineers come along and smother them in reverberation....Jarvi's F Major is fully on a par with the finest Dvorak he's given us so far...under normal circumstances it could provide some healthy competition for the newly reissued Kertesz...Jarvi's filler...is colorfully done and for some reason relatively free of excess reverb."

American Record Guide 51:41 S/O '88. Steven J. Haller (250w)

1119. Symphony No. 5 in F, Opus 76; Overture, "My Home," Opus 62; Hustiska, dramatic overture, Opus 87.
Istvan Kertesz (c). London Symphony Orchestra. 1965-66.
LONDON/DECCA 417 597 ADD 64:11

✔HC ★*Awards:* *Opus* Christmas List, 1987 (James R. Oestreich). *American Record Guide* Overview: Dvorak Symphonies, Ja/F '90.

"The LSO throughout the series was in top condition; one can make a case for these ADRM-processed reissues as absolutely viable alternatives to the all-digital work of Jarvi and the Scottish National Orchestra."

Fanfare 14:235-8 S/O '90. John Wiser (190w)

"CD has opened out the sound afresh to reveal to a new generation the treasures contained within these performances."

Hi-Fi News & Record Review 32:97 S '87 Kenneth Dommett (100w)

"Digitally remastered, the recordings sound fresh as new, and 'fresh' well describes Kertesz's approach to this composer, always inspiriting."

Opus 4:59 D '87. James R. Oestreich (120w)

"These reissues from Kertesz's integral LSO set of the Dvorak symphonies from the 1960s-...remain among the finest recorded performances of this extraordinary conductor."

Music and Musicians International 36:49 N '87. Robert Matthew-Walker (30w)

Gramophone 65:290 Ag '87 Ivan March (105w)

1120. Symphony No. 6 in D, Opus 60. JANACEK, LEOS. Taras Bulba.
Christoph von Dohnanyi (c). Cleveland Orchestra.
LONDON/DECCA 430 204 DDD 66:00

★*Awards:* Best Recordings of The Month, *Stereo Review*, D '91 (David Hall).

A "sensitive performance by Dohnanyi and the Cleveland Orchestra...with a superb recording to back it up, this has to be one of the best versions of the symphony I've heard....This is not-...a performance that portrays the death of *Taras Bulba* and his two sons with terrifying intensity. Nevertheless, it is aesthetically pleasing and a worthwhile addition to a very desirable disc."

Stereophile 15:266-7 Ap '92. Barbara Jahn (med)

"The Sixth Symphony, one of Dvorak's most unaffectedly joyous, has had the benefit of several memorable recordings...Any new version, therefore, has strong competition to meet-...Dohnanyi...contrives to pick out the essential elements of rhythm (a splendidly conceived Scherzo/Furiant) and colour that put him in the highest class....compared with Mackerras-...Dohnanyi does not give the impression of deep personal involvement with the tragic destiny of Taras Bulba and his sons. The sound, in common with all these Cleveland issues, is superb." *P100/85 S95/100*

Hi-Fi News & Record Review 36:70 Ag '91. Kenneth Dommett (200w)

"Christoph von Dohnanyi's way with the music in his new London recording is along the same lines as in his other Dvorak symphony recordings—lean and rhythmically vital but by no means lacking in sentiment where it's called for...Rafael Kubelik with the Bavarian Radio Symphony Orchestra and, more recently, Charles Mackerras with the Vienna Philharmonic have given us stirring recordings of [*Taras Bulba*] and both are available on CD. Dohnanyi's new one is leaner in texture but remarkable in its care for detail...The very good recorded sound is not as rich as Mackerras's but more than matches the other competing versions."

Stereo Review 56:100 D '91. David Hall (long)

"Taras Bulba...[is] expertly managed by the Cleveland Orchestra. In the Dvorak my preference would be the mellower Kertesz, despite the first-movement repeat."

American Record Guide 54:62-3 N/D '91. Paul L. Althouse (med)

"This is a particularly likable account [of the symphony] in several respects: orchestral excellence, *en masse* and in detail, prevails throughout, and that major asset is lovingly captured in London's recording process....*Taras Bulba* also has a great deal of orchestral prettiness and textural clarity going for it, bUt Janacek's music should be wilder than Dohnanyi's topiary treatment permits....This one is tame, so that one feels it's not quite the conductor's meat, but something prettified into cinema score unobtrusiveness. But for the Dvorak, which is the main matter the CD is strongly recommended."

Fanfare 15:316-7 N/D '91. John Wiser (med)

Gramophone 69:45 Jl '91. Edward Greenfield (335w)

1121. Symphony No. 6 in D, Opus 60; The Noon Witch (symphonic poem), Opus 108.
Neeme Jarvi (c). Scottish National Orchestra. 1986.
CHANDOS 8530 DDD 56:00

★*Awards:* *Gramophone* Critics' Choice (Edward Greenfield), 1987.

"This is by far the best of Jarvi's Dvorak series to date....Comparisons are bound to be made between this new version and Kertesz's classic twenty-year old one. Both are magnificent."

Hi-Fi News & Record Review 32:97 S '87 Kenneth Dommett (200w) (rev. of LP)

"These performances are more than merely adequate; combined with the secondary consideration of a well-filled CD of dependably solid and detailed sound quality, this production proves easy to endorse with enthusiasm."

Fanfare 11:135-6 N/D '87. John D. Wiser (410w)

"Whereas Jarvi is propulsive and forward-driving in an altogether captivating manner, Kertesz's performance is more reflective, responsive to the multiplicity of musical ideas and aware of a depth of emotion that tends to escape Jarvi's more extroverted treatment; and yet Jarvi's rhythmic grasp is more sure and satisfying."

Ovation 9:38 Ap '88. Jon Tuska (250w)

"The Kertesz Sixth, newly reissued on CD-...though drier in sound, still gives a better idea of what the composer had in mind than the Chandos."

American Record Guide 51:22 Ja/F '88. Stephen J. Haller (150w)

Gramophone 65:733 N '87 Edward Greenfield (610w)

Digital Audio 4:62 F '88. Tom Vernier (240w)

1122. Symphony No. 6 in D, Opus 60; Symphonic Variations, Opus 78.
Istvan Kertesz (c). London Symphony Orchestra. reissue 1966; 1971.
LONDON/DECCA 417 598 ADD 69:05

★*Awards:* *American Record Guide* Overview: Dvorak Symphonies, Ja/F '90.

See Symphony No. 5, London/Decca 417 597 for review excerpt.
Fanfare 14:236-8 S/O '90. John Wiser (190w)

1123. Symphony No. 6 in D, Opus 60; In Nature's Realm (concert overture), Opus 91.
Libor Pesek (c). Czech Philharmonic Orchestra.
VIRGIN 90791 DDD 58:00

★*Awards:* The Year's Best, *Hi Fi News & Record Review*, May '90 Supplement.

"I think it is fair to say that Pesek really does have an instinctive empathy for the idiom, even though he reflects that in a rather more relaxed, laid-back approach than we are used to-....The *In Nature's Realm* overture...is joyous but simple and unaffected—a charming coupling to such a worthy disc."
Stereophile 13:217+ D '90. Barbara Jahn (155w)

"If not perhaps the crispest performance of the symphony on record—though the Furiant is sharp enough—this is certainly one of the most affectionate. The playing throughout is almost fulsome in its exuberance, and there is a lovely warmth about the strings and an exciting vibrancy in the brass....The recording...emphasizes the brass slightly, but is spacious and appropriately atmospheric." *P95 S95*
Hi-Fi News & Record Review 34:105+ O '89; p.19 My '90 Supplement. Kenneth Dommett (250w)

"In general, these are not heavy-weight, high-tension performances of the variety we became accustomed to in Maestro Szell's lifetime, but lighter, quicker-moving accounts with formal fine-bred bones more than hinted at....[they] earn positive endorsement in a strong field."
Fanfare 13:174-75 Mr/Ap '90. John Wiser (550w)

"When one listens to this by itself one hears an incredibly good orchestra, interesting conducting, with some nice phrasing and detail, and very beautiful sound. When one compares to Kertesz and Kubelik the orchestra becomes merely good, the sound seems less real, less tangible, and the conductor falls into third place."
American Record Guide 53:47 Ja/F '90. Donald R. Vroon (190w)

Gramophone 67:449-50 S '89. Edward Greenfield (230w)

1124. Symphony No. 7 in D minor, Opus 70.
Christoph von Dohnanyi (c). Cleveland Orchestra.
LONDON/DECCA 417 564 DDD 36:28

✔HC ★*Awards:* Editors' Choice, *Digital Audio*, 1988.

"A bracing and exhilarating performance. The almost startling clarity of orchestral detail is a tribute not only to the Decca/London recording engineers—who here have produced yet another demonstration-class disc—but to the virtuosity of the Clevelanders."
High Fidelity 38:80 O '88. Robert R. Reilly (165w)

"Christoph von Dohnanyi's performance of the Seventh is another success in his traversal of the Dvorak symphonies. He conducts the Cleveland with a Beethovian vigor without becoming manic, and brings out a wealth of orchestral details without dawdling over them."
Musical America 107:60 N '87. Robert R. Reilly (180w)

"Rarely since George Szell died 17 years ago has the Cleveland Orchestra played as well as it does here....The recording is crisp, detailed, but with an ample sense of space. The performance is...humane, lovable, and has more of a Czech feel than many other recordings of this work currently available....The only drawback-...is the amount of music provided....Other than that...highly recommended."
Fanfare 10:101 Jl/Ag '87 John Bauman (275w)

"I found the performance too dispassionate compared with the other versions on compact disc."
Stereo Review 52:88 Ag '87 David Hall (140w)

Hi-Fi News & Record Review 32:97 Ap '87 (rev. of LP) (210w); 32:94 My '87 (rev. of CD) (60w). Kenneth Dommett

Gramophone 64:1260 Mr '87 Ivan March (245w)

Ovation 8:39-40 O '87. Paul Turok (280w)

Digital Audio 4:78+ O '87. Tom Vernier (215w)

1125. Symphony No. 7 in D minor, Opus 70; Symphony No. 8 in G, Opus 88; Symphony No. 9 in E minor, Opus 95, "New World".
Vaclav Neumann (c). Czech Philharmonic Orchestra. reissue.
SUPRAPHON 110 559 DDD 56:28, 57:29 2 discs

"These are substantial, lively, exactingly stylish readings in which the most serious shortcomings are a too-slow introduction to the opening movement of the Ninth, and elision of the exposition repeat thereof...For all the good work done in various quarters since, Neumann's is still the benchmark set in this music. It continues to justify an urgent recommendation."
Fanfare 14:192-95 Ja/F '91. John Wiser (385w)

Gramophone 69:65-6 D '91. Ivan March (long)

1126. Symphony No. 7 in D minor, Opus 70; Symphony No. 8 in G, Opus 88.
Libor Pesek (c). Royal Liverpool Philharmonic Orchestra.
VIRGIN 90756 DDD 75:00

★★★*Awards:* The Year's Best, *Hi Fi News & Record Review*, May '90 Supplement. *American Record Guide* Overview: Dvorak Symphonies, Ja/F '90.

"The recording is excellent....for those building a library or extending an existing collection,

this disc can be warmly recommended. If your requirements are for a rather more gutsy display, try Dohnanyi on London (421 082-2)."
Stereophile 13:217+ D '90. Barbara Jahn (155w)

"In general, these are not heavy-weight, high-tension performances of the variety we became accustomed to in Maestro Szell's lifetime, but lighter, quicker-moving accounts with formal fine-bred bones more than hinted at....[they] earn positive endorsement in a strong field."
Fanfare 13:174-75 Mr/Ap '90. John Wiser (550w)

"Paita's performance [of 7] has become an accepted standard for this symphony, but his version on his own label, Lodia, is very hard to come by. More readily available and in line with it is Dohnanyi's (Decca), and it is into this company that Pesek slips quite comfortably. His version of No. 8, however, is rather more hard-driven than might have been expected after his ebullient Sixth." *P95 S95*
Hi-Fi News & Record Review 34:107 O '89; p.19 My '90 Supplement. Kenneth Dommett (260w)

Gramophone 67:449-50 S '89. Edward Greenfield (230w)

1127. Symphony No. 7 in D minor, Opus 70; Overture: My Home.
Andre Previn (c). Los Angeles Philharmonic Orchestra. Royce Hall, UCLA, Los Angeles, CA. May 4, 1988.
TELARC 80173 DDD 48:00

★★*Awards:* Top Choices—1989, *American Record Guide* Ja/F '90 (Donald Vroon). *American Record Guide* Overview: Dvorak Symphonies, Ja/F '90.

"Never has there been a more beautiful recording of this music. Never has the Los Angeles orchestra sounded so good."
American Record Guide 52:32-3 Mr/Ap '89. Donald R. Vroon (315w)

"Dvorak's Seventh is glorious, flowing and bold thrust and long-arc shaping throughout; the climactic *tuttis*, with their brass needles poking through the thickly padded string cushions, have a burnished gleam."
Ovation 10:51-2 S '89. Tom Di Nardo (250w)

"Performance style...for the D Minor has tended to polarize between a stressed, taut approach and a warmly lyrical one....Andre Previn definitely hews to the latter course in this recording....Throughout, he makes a good case for his interpretation, and he is aided by fine orchestral execution and Telarc's gorgeous recorded sound."
Stereo Review 54:116-17 Je '89. David Hall (250w)

"Previn's account certainly merits consideration. Predictably, the recording is full and transparent."
Fanfare 12:184-85 My/Je '89. George Chien (150w)

"I would recommend the Dohnanyi version [of the 7th] over any other, especially the comparatively passionless effort by Neeme Jarvi with the Scottish National Orchestra. But Previn illuminates the score in many ways....*My Home*, is very much in the character of the symphony, but seems more diffuse in conception."
Stereophile 12:179-80 S '89. Robert Hesson (245w)

"In all, a disappointing disc."
HighPerformanceReview 6:75-6 Je '89. Thomas Wendel (160w)

Gramophone 66:1578 Ap '89. Edward Greenfield (245w)

1128. Symphony No. 8 in G, Opus 88; Scherzo Capriccioso, Opus 66.
Christoph von Dohnanyi (c). Cleveland Orchestra.
LONDON/DECCA 414 422 49:04

★*Awards:* *Stereo Review* Best of the Month, Ag '86.

"It is hard to imagine a more straightforward, rousing, rollicking rendition of this non-neurotic, extroverted music....The playing and sound are a pure joy."
High Fidelity 36:71 S '86. Robert R. Reilly (150w)

"The CD confirms the high expectations raised by the LP."
Hi-Fi News & Record Review 31:117 My '86. Kenneth Dommett (50w)

"Strongly recommended."
Stereo Review 51:103 Ag '86. David Hall (300w)

"Except that Christoph von Dohnanyi appends an admirably spirited, spit-'n'-polish performance of the *Scherzo capriccioso*, his performance of the G-major Symphony conspicuously fails to dump Vaclav Neumann from first place on the CD list."
Fanfare 9:131 Jl/Ag '86. Roger Dettmer (270w)

Ovation 7:42 S '86. Paul Turok (185w)

Gramophone 63:1027 F '86 (rev. of LP) (385w); 63:1402 My '86 (rev. of CD) (75w). Edward Greenfield

Hi-Fi News & Record Review 31:101 Mr '86. Kenneth Dommett (200w) (rev. of LP)

1129. Symphony No. 8 in G, Opus 88; Slavonic Dances, Opus 46 and Opus 72.
George Szell (c). Cleveland Orchestra.
EMI 47618 48:34

★*Awards:* *American Record Guide* Overview: Dvorak Symphonies, Ja/F '90.

"There are many excellent performances of the Eighth on the market, but Szell and his Clevelanders in top form outshine them all."
High Fidelity 37:75 D '87. David Hurwitz (90w)

1130. Symphony No. 8 in G, Opus 88. SMETANA, BEDRICH. The Moldau (Vltava); From Bohemian Fields and Groves (symphonic poem), from Ma Vlast.

Vaclav Talich (c). Czech Philharmonic Orchestra. 1954 reissue.
SUPRAPHON 110 627 ADD (m) 59:00

✔HC ★★*Awards:* The Want List 1990, *Fanfare* N/D '90 (John Bauman); The Want List 1990, *Fanfare* N/D '90 (Mortimer H. Frank).

"At last, on CD...we have a prime example of the work of 'legendary' conductor Vaclav Talich, leading the Czech Philharmonic Orchestra...Strongly recommended, particularly to people who wonder what all the fuss is about."

Fanfare 13:135 Jl/Ag '90. John Wiser (360w)

"I have long maintained that the Talich recording of the Dvorak Eighth is the standard against which all others must be judged....The sound is not modern stereo, and yet the mono has transferred better than I had feared....You should own this disc if you love Dvorak."

American Record Guide 53:49-50 My/Je '90. Carl Bauman (280w)

1131. Symphony No. 9 in E minor, Opus 95, "New World". WAGNER, RICHARD. Siegfried Idyll; Overture: Fliegende Hollander.
Jascha Horenstein (c). Royal Philharmonic Orchestra. 1962 reissue.
CHESKY 031 ADD 68:00

★★*Awards:* Records to Die for: 1 of 5 Recommended Recordings, *Stereophile* Ja '91 (Gary A. Galo); Records to Die for: 1 of 5 Recommended Recordings, *Stereophile* Ja '91 (Robert Hesson).

'Horenstein's 'New World' is one of the finest in stereo, holding its own with Kubelik and Kertesz....The Royal Philharmonic's playing is first-rate....The recording has excellent clarity complemented by a warm acoustic."

Stereophile 14:137 Ja '91. Gary A. Galo (b.n.)

"You will hear few performances of any work that are as passionate as this one....This is also the best modern-instrument orchestral recording I have heard, and I don't know of many that really come close."

Stereophile 14:142 Ja '91. Robert Hesson (b.n.)

"There are over 50 'New Worlds' in the catalog. Whether you have every one of them or none of them, buy this one. It is fat with passion....Pure, ripened, bone-true passion....At the core of the nearly unprecedented sound quality of this CD is its timbre....Wagner's *Siegfried-Idyll* and *Flying Dutchman Overture* are added in renditions nearly as gratifying."

Stereophile 13:199 Ap '90. Robert Hesson (400w)

Brahms' *Symphony No. 1 in C minor* and Dvorak's *Symphony No. 9 in E minor* are "two of the finest standard-repertory recordings ever made, very stirring in Chesky's excellent digitalizations....These discs, with their Wilkinsonian immediacy and spaciousness, are greatly preferable to today's eviscerated DDDs....The Wagner couplings...are uniformly excellent, with a combination of clean recording and whirlwind performances."

The Absolute Sound 17:126+ Ap '92. Arthur S. Pfeffer (med)

"The *Flying Dutchman* Overture really takes off. This is by far the most powerful and impressive recording of it....Apart from that piece, Horenstein's conducting is not particularly striking....The sound is absolutely outstanding."

American Record Guide 53:47-8 Ja/F '90. Donald R. Vroon (175w)

"*Siegfried Idyll* fares best in a delicate, carefully wrought account...But the overture gets a distinctly low-voltage performance. The atmosphere of *Parsifal*, of all things, hangs over this 'New World' like a humid day in August; nothing much happens until the third movement, while the finale begins with real energy and power but levels off just as the music begins to soar. The CD sound is quite splendid."

Fanfare 13:176-77 Mr/Ap '90. Paul Sargent Clark (175w)

1132. Symphony No. 9 in E minor, Opus 95, "New World"; Scherzo Capriccioso, Opus 66.
Rafael Kubelik (c). Berlin Philharmonic Orchestra; Bavarian Radio Symphony Orchestra. 1973.
dg 427 202 55:27

✔HC

"Fresh, unaffected, and poetic Ninth—my own first choice, unless I wanted Toscanini, or Ancerl's."

Hi-Fi News & Record Review 34:97 My '89. (40w)

1133. Symphony No. 9 in E minor, Opus 95, "New World".
Zdenek Macal (c). London Philharmonic Orchestra.
MUSICAL HERITAGE 512 245 42:00

★*Awards:* *American Record Guide* Overview: Dvorak Symphonies, Ja/F '90.

"What a wonderful performance this is!—fiery, spirited, and passionate; brilliantly played and conducted....Of its kind this beats all the others—even George Szell. And the quality of the sound is definitely part of the excitement."

American Record Guide 52:49 Ja/F '89. Donald R. Vroon (200w)

1134. Symphony No. 9 in E minor, Opus 95, "New World"; Serenade in E for String Orchestra, Opus 22.
Vaclav Talich (c). Czech Philharmonic Orchestra; Prague Soloists. 1949, 1950, 1951.
SUPRAPHON 110 290 ADD 68:56

✔HC ★*Awards:* The Want List 1990, *Fanfare* N/D '90 (John Bauman).

"Here is a truly great performance [of the New World Symphony] that transcends its historical status in every respect."

Musical America 110:73-5 N '90. David Hurwitz (560w)

"This CD earns an urgent recommendation, and I hope the people in charge at Supraphon have duty bumps to compel them to keep the Talich reissues coming."

Fanfare 14:192-95 Ja/F '91. John Wiser (385w)

"While this disc cannot be considered a primary version in this day of stereo/digital sound, it certainly remains my favorite performance of the *New World* Symphony from a purely musical standpoint....The recorded sound is exceptional for the period....The Serenade for Strings was recorded (on tape) in 1951. It is also a definitive reading."

American Record Guide 53:53 N/D '90. Carl Bauman (250w)

1135. Symphony No. 9 in E minor, Opus 95, "New World".

Klaus Tennstedt (c). Berlin Philharmonic Orchestra.
EMI 47071

★*Awards:* *Stereo Review* Best of the Month, My '85.

"The Tennstedt performance reminds me of Klemperer in its slow, monumental grandeur and of Walter in its affability....The sound is among the best from Berlin."

The $ensible Sound 9:53 Fall '87. John J. Puccio (45w)

"The most formidable interpretive rival to Tennstedt's *New World*...is James Levine's RCA recording...Levine is more generous with the repeats, and his highly charged reading is, overall, perhaps more taut and ferociously dramatic. Tennstedt's, on the other hand, is both brillliant and passionate....*Chacun a son gout!*"

Stereo Review 50:90 My '85. David Hall (450w)

Hi-Fi News & Record Review 30:103 Mr '85. John Crabbe (175w)

Gramophone 62:1327-8 My '85. Edward Greenfield (490w)

Fanfare 8:137 My/Je '85. Roger Dettmer (350w)

1136. Symphony No. 9 in E minor, Opus 95, "New World".

Bruno Walter (c). Columbia Symphony Orchestra.
CBS 42039

★★★*Awards:* *American Record Guide* Overview: Dvorak Symphonies, Ja/F '90. *Gramophone* Critics' Choice 1986 (Trevor Harvey).

"As always in his later recordings, Walter is relaxed and dignified, and if it weren't for the sound, this disc would probably be rated above Solti or Dohnanyi."

The $ensible Sound 9:53 Fall '87. John J. Puccio (50w)

Gramophone 64:711 N '86 Trevor Harvey (30w)

ELGAR, EDWARD

1137. Enigma Variations, Opus 36; Pomp and Circumstance Marches (5), Opus 39.

Adrian Boult (c). London Symphony Orchestra; London Philharmonic Orchestra. reissues in part.
EMI 64015 ADD 55:00

✔HC

Gramophone 69:46-8 Ap '92. Michael Kennedy (med)

1138. Enigma Variations, Opus 36; Cockaigne Overture, Opus 40; Froissart Overture, Opus 19.

Leonard Slatkin (c). London Philharmonic Orchestra.
RCA 0073 DDD 64:00

★*Awards:* The Year's Best, *Hi Fi News & Record Review*, May '90 Supplement.

"Slatkin's *Enigma* is dark but never heavy, its serious point made with the most delicate of brushstrokes....The London Philharmonic has never sounded healthier." *P100 S100*

Hi-Fi News & Record Review 34:123 D '89; p.21 My '90 Supplement. David Nice (490w)

"Slatkin lays bare the pages of Elgar's personal photograph album where many another conductor has been content merely to point the objective baton at a selection of stylized portraits."

Stereophile 13:173 Ag '90. Barbara Jahn (145w)

"This is a patient, brooding, even anguished reading [of the Variations]. It's not quite as deliberately provoking as Bernstein's (the only slower recording I can think of), but it is still a challenge to received opinion regarding this score....The shorter works get high-quality readings as well."

Fanfare 13:203-04 N/D '89. Peter J. Rabinowitz (310w)

"The overtures are spirited and they shimmer in turn-of-the-century joie de vivre."

HighPerformanceReview 8(1):66 '91. John Mueter (190w)

"The drawbacks to Slatkin's reading of the Second Symphony are as nothing...compared with his misrepresentations of the *Enigma Variations*....The playing of the London Philharmonic in the *Variations* is curiously generalized and lackluster. But, filling out the release, the orchestra turns in quite respectable accounts of the *Froissart* and *Cockaigne* overtures."

Musical America 110:72-4 Mr '90. Scott Cantrell (355w)

"The theme gets an overly studied and hesitant statement...and variations are characterized in almost a perverse fashion....If Elgar had heard a performance like this, he'd likely have had apoplexy."

American Record Guide 53:49 Mr/Ap '90. Stephen D. Chakwin, Jr. (210w)

Gramophone 67:301-2 Ag '89. Michael Kennedy (430w)

1139. Enigma Variations, Opus 36; Cockaigne Overture, Opus 40; Serenade in E minor for Strings, Opus 20; Salut d'Amour, Opus 12.
David Zinman (c). Baltimore Symphony Orchestra. 1989.
TELARC 80192 DDD 61:55

★★*Awards:* Best of the Month, *Hi-Fi News & Record Review*, Mr '91. Editors' Choice, *Digital Audio's CD Review*, 6:34 Je '90; Cream of the Crop IV, *Digital Audio's CD Review*, 6:41 Je '90.

"Nowadays, it seems, it takes an American or two to probe the introspective core of Elgar's *Enigma*. First there was Andrew Litton, winning some of the most refined playing from the LPO on Virgin Classics (if only the lines had moved forward a little more); Leonard Slatkin followed suit, dark and controversially slow but all of a piece; and now comes David Zinman, with a keen, bright American orchestra to complement in perhaps the most meticulously detailed performance of them all." *P100 S100*
Hi-Fi News & Record Review 36:92-3 Mr '91. David Nice (180w)

"The clean, beautifully balanced recording is a mirror image of his performance. He finds some delightful color in painting his portraits, and if his palette seems more sharply focused than Slatkin's impressionistic reservoir, his interpretation is as deeply searching."
Stereophile 13:173 Ag '90. Barbara Jahn (145w)

"Compare this release with Leonard Slatkin's recent RCA accounts of the 'Enigma Variations,' 'Cockaigne' and the serenade, and Zinman easily emerges as the more sympathetic Elgarian....Apart from an ill-tuned flute in the 'W.N.' variation of the 'Enigma,' the Baltimore orchestra plays splendidly, and Telarc supports it with sonics both forward and spacious."
The New York Times D 10 '89, p. 38 H. Scott Cantrell (125w)

"Zinman's is a refined, reserved, restrained, deftly paced account that veers a little too much toward the finicky and pallid for me to take it completely to heart....Telarc's sound is resplendent...The album is nicely filled out with an exciting account of the sprawling, brawling, bustling *Cockaigne* Overture and a rather-too-diffuse rendering of the perennially popular Serenade...all topped off by a perfectly adequate *Salut d'amour* chestnut trifle."
American Record Guide 53:50 My/Je '90. Lawrence Hansen (250w)

"Zinman's colors tend toward the pastel, his emotions toward the muted...In the end, I find it too slack, sentimental, even timid; but those who prefer their Elgar on the refined side will be pleased to find that Baltimore's redolent strings and soft-edged woodwinds...amply meet the demands of Zinman's interpretation. Telarc's engineering...offers plenty of atmosphere."
Fanfare 13:177-79 Mr/Ap '90. Peter J. Rabinowitz (200w)

Digital Audio's CD Review 6:64-5 F '90. Lawrence Johnson (200w)

Gramophone 68:739 O '90. Michael Kennedy (315w)

1140. Orchestral Music: Symphony No. 1 in A flat, Opus 55; Serenade in E minor for Strings, Opus 20; Chanson de Nuit, Opus 15, No. 1; Chanson de Matin, Opus 15, No. 2; Overture: Cockaigne, Opus 40; Symphony No. 2 in E flat, Opus 63; Enigma Variations, Opus 36; Pomp and Circumstance Marches (5), Opus 39.
Adrian Boult (c). London Philharmonic Orchestra; London Symphony Orchestra. reissue.
EMI 63099 AAD/ADD 69:08, 68:12, 55:32 3 discs

★*Awards:* Critics Choice, *Hi Fi News & Record Review*, Ap '91 Supplement (David Nice).

"With these timeless interpretations, Boult created a model for generations to come."
New Hi-Fi Sound 6:115 Jl '89. Jonathan Kettle (240w)

"As I believe the cited reviews make clear, Miller finds most of these Boult performances—and so do I—to be benchmark quality: thoughtful, deeply expressive, compellingly authoritative....Newcomers well supplied with pelf will do well to become owners of a splendidly consistent lot."
Fanfare 13:197-98 S/O '89. John Wiser (180w)

1141. Serenade in E minor for String Orchestra, Opus 20. WARLOCK, PETER (PHILIP HESELTINE). Capriol Suite. HOLST, GUSTAV. Saint Paul's Suite. Oriental Suite (Beni Mora).
Malcolm Sargent (c). Philharmonia Orchestra; Royal Philharmonic Orchestra; BBC Symphony Orchestra. 1971, 1966 reissue.
EMI 2141 AAD 51:00

★*Awards:* Top Choices—1989, *American Record Guide* Ja/F '90 (Robert Connelly).

"Here we have four prime examples of [Sargent's]...work...all recorded near the end of his life in 1966 and 1971 If you love Elgar as I do and want to hear a modern recording of the *Serenade* virtually as the composer himself did it, no one else in my experience comes close. Add to it superb 1971 sound with near-perfect stereo balance....it is the excessive reverberation that keeps it from absolute perfection-....Here we have what I consider the finest St. Paul's Suite since the previous standard by Boyd Neel and his group c. 1948 on London. The *Beni Mora* is entirely new music to me and a true delight."
American Record Guide 52:47 My/Je '89. Robert M. Connelly (250w)

"This is a significant reissue providing valuable documentation of a worthy musician. To me, the Holst 'Beni Mora' Suite alone is worth the price of admission. Recommended for Sargent devotees, or for Holst fans who really must have the 'Beni Mora' Suite at all costs."
Fanfare 12:191 My/Je '89. William Zagorski (525w)

1142. Symphony No. 1 in A flat, Opus 55.
Andre Previn (c). Royal Philharmonic Orchestra.
PHILIPS 416 612 51:43

> ★*Awards: Gramophone* Critics' Choice 1986 (Alan Blyth).

"From the very first bars of Andre Previn's performance, you can breathe a sigh of rich satisfaction along with the thought, 'Ah! He's really got it right!'...Highly recommended."
Stereo Review 51:132 D '86 David Hall (210w)

"The combination of conviction, performance, and superlative recording makes the CD indispensable, if not definitive."
High Fidelity 37:65 My '87 Robert R. Reilly (200w)

"Once past his prosaic account of the Introduction...Previn rises to the occasion, dusting off the score with a refreshingly lean and sassy perspective on the music, marked by splashy colors and bracing—even jazzy—rhythms (parts of the first movement, in fact, summon up the spirit of Gershwin)."
Fanfare 10:140-2 N/D '86 Peter J. Rabinowitz (375w)

"Like Boult and Barbirolli, Previn has a highly personal way with Elgar, but with perhaps sharper pin-pointing of what makes this symphony tick. Personally, I lean more to the two B's."
American Record Guide 51:27 My/Je '88. Michael Mark (225w)

Previn's "overindulgent pullings and tuggings rob the music of essential urgency; ardor is replaced by a dreamy, sentimental aimlessness."
Ovation 8:35-36 Mr '87 Scott Cantrell (170w)

"Andre Previn and the Royal Philharmonic-...may strike those accustomed to Boult's deftness as straightforward to the point of lacking subtlety. Tempos are standard and inflections wholly predictable."
Fanfare 10:142 N/D '86 J.F. Weber (150w)

Hi-Fi News & Record Review 31:80 Ag '86. Christopher Breunig (325w)

1143. Symphony No. 1 in A flat, Opus 55; In the South, Opus 50, "Alessio".
Leonard Slatkin (c). London Philharmonic Orchestra.
RCA 0380 DDD 74:00

> ★*Awards:* The Gramophone Awards, Nominations, Orchestral, *Gramophone*, N '91.

"When Slatkin chooses to be slow in Elgar, he is—as usual—very slow indeed, but (also as usual) I remain convinced....I shall treasure this Elgar First as a persuasive alternative to Barbirolli and Boult; if anything, Slatkin has even more to say about the expressive possibilities and refinements of Elgarian introspection."
P100/95 S95/(85)
Hi-Fi News & Record Review 36:70 Je '91. David Nice (380w)

"As it progresses, Slatkin's Elgar series increasingly confirms his stature as one of the more penetrating Elgarians around....Slatkin's First stands out for its refusal to mediate the symphony's conflicting stylistic demands....an exceptionally high-contrast performance...*In the South* gets a similarly complex reading that plays up both its ethereal tracery and its Straussian extravagance....In sum, Slatkin's First stands with Previn's and Thomson's very different accounts (see 10:2) at the top of the list of modern performances, and as a worthy heir to the classic recordings by Boult, Barbirolli, and Elgar himself. Highly recommended."
Fanfare 14:155-6 Jl/Ag '91. Peter J. Rabinowitz (525w)

Gramophone 69:38 Je '91. Michael Kennedy (350w)

1144. Symphony No. 2 in E flat, Opus 63; Serenade in E minor for Strings, Opus 20.
Leonard Slatkin (c). London Philharmonic Orchestra.
RCA 0072 DDD 67:00

> ★*Awards:* Critics' Choice 1989, *Gramophone* D '89 (Michael Kennedy).

"Although Elgar's two symphonies may be an acquired taste, one need not necessarily have cultivated that taste in order to relish this recording. It is enthusiastically recommendable on all counts to Elgar neophytes and devotees alike....The *Serenade for Strings*....receives a sensitive performance....Still, this is merely a bonus; the symphony is the true prize."
HighPerformanceReview 7:67-8 Winter '90-91. Kenneth Krehbiel (330w)

"On the whole, this is a low-tension performance [of the 2nd] more notable for its shimmering textures than its rhythmic detail, more notable for its luminous warmth...than its searing pain. By any standards, it's an important recording; and for those who find Sinopoli too wrenching and Thomson too ethereal, it may well belong at the top of the post-Boultian list-....In the *Serenade*, Slatkin extracts the poignance while filtering out the sap."
Fanfare 13:203-04 N/D '89. Peter J. Rabinowitz (310w)

"A formidable controlling perception is at work here, leading us steadily to the inchoate terror buried deep beneath the confident surface of Elgar's Second Symphony, and back

again....The *Serenade* catches the essence of this conductor's Elgar." *P100 S85/95*
Hi-Fi News & Record Review 34:121+ D '89. David Nice (425w)

"Leonard Slatkin brings ideas of his own to the music without altering its essential character; his performance of the Second Symphony is possibly the most convincing yet recorded, and the serenade, too, has never been more enticing."
Stereo Review Presents: Compact Disc Buyers' Guide 1990 p.66-7 Richard Freed (105w)

"Leonard Slatkin now comes forward with an Elgar Second (55:10, for the record) to make one sit up and take notice; it's not without misjudgments, but its finest moments are fine indeed....The coupling on this recording, the String Serenade in E minor, receives a respectable reading of its finale, but the second movement...is maudlin, and the first movement lacks spontaneity."
Musical America 110:72-4 Mr '90. Scott Cantrell (355w)

"Slatkin's Elgar 2 is the best conducting I've heard from him to date....There is room for a quibble here and there about an instrumental voicing or the way a climax is built, but this is as good a performance as any in the catalog."
American Record Guide 53:49 Mr/Ap '90. Stephen D. Chakwin, Jr. (210w)

"The performance [of the Symphony] ends on a note of majestic triumph, proving itself, for me, the most exciting and moving modern reading in the catalog. The *Serenade* confirms that the dynamism of Slatkin's Elgar runs deep; an easy fluidity frames his subtly graded rubato, but the intensity of his vision is never lost, even within these pastoral shades."
Stereophile 13:183+ My '90. Barbara Jahn (260w)

Gramophone 67:301-2 Ag '89. Michael Kennedy (430w)

FASCH, JOHANN FRIEDRICH

1145. Music of Fasch: Suites: in D minor for 3 Flutes, 3 Oboes, Bassoon, Strings and Continuo; in B flat for Double Orchestra. Concertos: in B flat for Chalumeau, Orchestra and Continuo; in D for Trumpet, 2 Oboes, Strings, and Continuo; in D for Triple Ensemble. Sonata in C minor for Oboe, Violin and Continuo. Cantata, Bestandigkeit bleibt mein Vergnugen, for Tenor and Continuo. Missa (brevis) in D, for 4 Solo Voices, Choir, Orchestra, and Continuo.
Ludwig Guttler (c). Peter Schreier (ten); Andrea Ihle (sop); Elisbeth Wilke (contr); Reinhart Ginzel (ten); Olaf Bar (bass). Halle Madrigalists; Virtuosi Saxoniae. Lukaskirche, Dresden. November 1986, May 1987. CAPRICCIO 10218/9 DDD 60:35, 56:37 2 discs

✔HC ★*Awards:* The Want List 1988, *Fanfare* N/D '88 (Nils Anderson).

"I find this a remarkable set, performed in rare style by soloists...and ensembles alike, and highly recommend it to any and all, especially those interested in exploring a 'new' personality."
Fanfare 12:181 N/D '88. Nils Anderson (500w)

"These recordings can hold their own even with the celebrated Archiv series put out in West Germany by Deutsche Grammophon."
High Fidelity 39:68-9 Ja '89. Paul Moor (700w)

"Right now, I can think of several much-recorded period instrument ensembles who would give their eye teeth for the kind of blend, intonation and open-handed joy in the music that prevail here."
HighPerformanceReview 6:76 Je '89. Rodney Shewan (460w)

"The Virtuosi Saxoniae are simply not very stylistically informed—their emotional palette ranges from staid to lukewarm, and Guttler seems unable to find the lightness of touch and shapely turning of phrase that we have come to expect from a number of period-instrument ensembles."
Musical America 109:58 Ja '89. Christopher Rothko (440w)

FAURE, GABRIEL

1146. Pelleas et Melisande (orchestral suite), Opus 80; Masques et Bargamasques (suite for orchestra), Opus 112; Penelope (drama lyrique in 3 acts): Prelude. CHAUSSON, ERNEST. Symphony in B flat, Opus 20. ("The Ansermet Edition", Volume 5).
Ernest Ansermet (c). Suisse Romande Orchestra. LONDON/DECCA 433 715

✔HC

FINZI, GERALD

1147. The Fall of the Leaf, Opus 20; New Year Music, Opus 7. MOERAN, ERNEST JOHN. Sinfonietta; Serenade in G.
Richard Hickox (c). Northern Sinfonia. EMI 49912 DDD 62:00

★*Awards:* The Year's Best, *Hi Fi News & Record Review*, May '90 Supplement.

"If you are fond of the choral and vocal works of Elgar, Vaughan Williams, and, perhaps, Walton, but you don't know the music of Gerald Finzi (1901-56), don't hesitate for another minute. Combining Elgar's nobility of utterance and Vaughan Williams's spacious grandeur, with a touch of Walton's exuberance, Finzi may lack their breadth and depth, but the extraordinarily poignant sensitivity with which he could reflect poetic meaning through simple diatonic melody is second to no one.,..If you already know *Intimations of Immortality* through the 1975 Lyrita recording...be assured that, on the basis of vastly superior choral and orchestral execution, this new release represents a distinct and significant improvement. Need I say more?"

Fanfare 14:196-97 Ja/F '91. Walter Simmons (350w)

"Both [Finzi] pieces are played with the utmost sympathy. At long last Moeran's delectable *Serenade* is available in a decent modern recording, and in a dashing performance-....Hickox's invigorating new performance [of the Sinfonietta] resembles Del Mar's in many respects, but he is more sensitive to the lyrical elements in (i) and (ii) and, at the same time, does not miss out on the irrepressible high spirits in the last movement. Like everything...a resonant, wide-ranging recording." *P95/100 S95/100*

Hi-Fi News & Record Review 35:107 Mr '90; p.24 My '90 Supplement. Andrew Achenbach (420w)

"The performances by Hickox and his players are deft, lively, and well-proportioned. Angel has provided clear, translucent, and spacious recorded sound."

American Record Guide 53:72 Jl/Ag '90. John P. McKelvey (265w)

Gramophone 67:1461 F '90. Michael Kennedy (245w)

FRANCK, CESAR

1148. Symphony in D minor. D'INDY, VINCENT. Symphony on a French Mountain Air, Opus 25. BERLIOZ, HECTOR. Beatrice et Benedict: Overture.

Pierre Monteux; Charles Munch (c). Nicole Henriot-Schweitzer (pno). Chicago Symphony Orchestra; Boston Symphony Orchestra. 1961 reissue.
RCA 6805 ADD 71:48

✔**HC** ★*Awards:* Pick of the Crop Reissues, *The New York Times* S 16, '90 (Sedgwick Clark).

"Though Beecham, Munch, and Cantelli also left estimable performances of the [Franck] symphony, Monteux's remains preeminent for having taken the work...at face value with rock-solid dignity and virtuoso attention to detail-....With Henriot-Schweitzer raptly *en rapport*, Munch's ecstatically lambent way with d'Indy's most winning work complements the brisk elan of that other classic performance by Casadesus and Ormandy....Need you be told that this is cornerstone material?"

Fanfare 12:152-3 S/O '88. Adrian Corleonis (240w)

"Monteux...leads the orchestra through an honest, heartfelt, yet utterly unexaggerated performance of a work [Symphony in D minor] which many of us have come to disdain, and the result becomes an archive treasure....Produced from the session master, the CD unveils the tuttis with awesome power and a degree of clarity which should not send you running to your volume control. Admittedly, the possibility of high-level saturation remains, but the CD provides such an improvement over the LP as to constitute the difference between night and day....The performance [of Symphony on a French Mountain Air] by Nicole Henriot-Schweitzer, with the BSO under Charles Munch, transcends the musical substance of the work, as only Munch and his eccentric and characterful BSO could do. Delightful."

Stereophile 12:169-71 My '89. Richard Schneider (675w)

"On CD [The Chicago Franck Symphony]...re-emerges as a recording of majestic weight and marvellous transparency. The fillers...have come up well too, although there is a hint of coarseness in the Berlioz climaxes. Exemplary conducting."

Hi-Fi News & Record Review 34:105 Ag '89. (110w)

Gramophone 66:1414 Mr '89. Michael Oliver (175w)

Variations Symphoniques. See No. 4090

FUCIK, JULIUS

1149. Einzug der Gladiatoren, 68; Wintersturme, Opus 184; Mississippi River, Opus 160; Donausagen, Opus 233; Attila, Opus 211; Traumideale, Opus 69; Triglav, Opus 72; Marinarella Overture, Opus 215.

Vaclav Neumann (c). Czech Philharmonic Orchestra.
ORFEO 147 861 58:00

★*Awards: Gramophone* Critics' Choice (Andrew Lamb), 1987.

"Splendid stuff, beautifully recorded with plenty of body and brilliance."

Hi-Fi News & Record Review 32:93 Jl '87 Kenneth Dommett (210w)

"Many of the marches and waltzes by relatively obscure composer...recorded in the early seventies by this very same orchestra and conductor are now available as an alternate CD recommendation (Teldec 8.42337)....Choice between the two CDs is about even."

The $ensible Sound 10:64 Fall '88. John J. Puccio (120w)

"In *Fanfare* 10:4 I sang the praises of this recording on LP....I am even more strongly impressed by the CD."

Fanfare 10:108-9 Jl/Ag '87 John Bauman (145w)

Gramophone 65:406 S '87 Andrew Lamb (265w)

GERSHWIN, GEORGE. An American in Paris. See No. 2064

GLIERE, REINHOLD

1150. Symphony No. 3 in B minor, Opus 42, "Ilya Murometz".

Harold Farberman (c). Royal Philharmonic Orchestra. 1979.

UNICORN-KANCHANA 2014/5 DDD 93:00 2 discs

✔HC ★*Awards:* Top Choices—1989, *American Record Guide* Ja/F '90 (Gerald Fox).

"When Jack Diether reviewed the LP in February 1980 he called it the only complete stereo recording. That is still so. He also called it 'musically and sonically stupendous'. It still is-....this is the orchestral equivalent of *Gurrelieder*—romanticism at its most sinfully sumptuous. Mid-price and worth every cent."

American Record Guide 52:52-3 My/Je '89. Donald R. Vroon (100w)

"Sonically it is a good, though not outstanding, issue....I would suggest buying this 1911 work in this version if you don't have Scherchen, the only other uncut version, for it is well worth knowing."

Fanfare 12:203 My/Je '89. John Bauman (350w)

Digital Audio's CD Review 6:62+ My '90. Wayne Green (240w)

GLINKA, MIKHAIL. Overture: Ruslan and Ludmilla. See No. 6117.

GOULD, MORTON

1151. Fall River Legend.
Milton Rosenstock (c). Morton Gould (conversation); Agnes De Mille (conversation); Brock Peters (voc). National Philharmonic Orchestra.
ALBANY 035 DDD 73:35

"Although the composer's well-known concert suite emphasizes the more immediately appealing sections, this recording—made in England for the Dance Theatre of Harlem in a stirring interpretation under the veteran Broadway maestro Milton Rosenstock—provides a first opportunity to experience, outside the theater, the full, uncut original preserved in all its varied dramatic chiaroscuro and with all of its seamless narrative fluency intact. Nearly half of its forty-seven-minute length contains music never before recorded...[other than Brock Peter's 100-second indictment] this release...is a major and irreplaceable addition to our native discography."

Fanfare 14:165-6 Jl/Ag '91. Paul A. Snook (315w)

"This disc is recommended."

HighPerformanceReview 8(3):74 '91. Bert Wechsler (long)

"What we have here is the first recording of the complete ballet...the National Philharmonic sounds good, but I suspect could have sounded even better with a little more rehearsal time....Despite the reservations noted, I would not want to be without this recording."

American Record Guide 54:59 Jl/Ag '91. Mark Koldys (200w)

Gramophone 69:48 Ap '92. Peter Dickinson (long)

1152. Music of Gould: Housewarming; American Symphonette No. 2; Symphony of Spirituals; Flourishes and Galop; Concerto for Viola and Orchestra; Columbia; Soundings.
Lawrence Leighton Smith; Jorge Mester; Morton Gould (c). Robert Glazer (vla); Leon Rapier (tpt). Louisville Orchestra. reissues.
ALBANY 013/4 AAD/DDD 49:40, 57:58 2 discs

★★*Awards:* The Want List 1989, *Fanfare* N/D '89 (Stephen Ellis); Top Choices—1989, *American Record Guide* Ja/F '90 (Mark Koldys).

"Every decade of Gould's prolific composing career except the 1950s is represented in this choice and generous survey....one remains aware of the same fundamental and immediately recognizable and approachable temperament in all this music: urbane, inventive, mostly positive and ingratiating, craftsmanlike, thoughtful, and eclectically receptive to the full gamut of our native musical experience."

Fanfare 12:153-54 Jl/Ag '89. Paul A. Snook (800w)

"The playing of the Louisville Orchestra is excellent....While some of the performances sound rather tame, don't miss this set. It is a rare opportunity to hear some of the best music by one of our most gifted musicians."

American Record Guide 52:46-7 Jl/Ag '89. Karl Miller (625w)

"At its best, Morton Gould's music is spirited, spontaneous, good-humored and it wears well. At its worst, it just sounds like warmed-over Copland....The remastering is first-rate, the accompanying booklet informative, and the packaging quite shiny."

Ovation 10:55-6 Ag '89. Philip Kennicott (380w)

Gramophone 67:657-58 O '89. David J. Fanning (625w)

1153. Spirituals for Orchestra; Fall River Legend (ballet suite). BARBER, SAMUEL. Medea.
Howard Hanson (c). Eastman-Rochester Orchestra. reissues.
MERCURY 432 016

✔HC ★*Awards:* The Super Compact Disk List, *The Absolute Sound*, Ap '92 (Harry Pearson).

"The Hanson-conducted disc of Gould and Barber is a special favorite of mine....We are talking about some of the best LPs ever made versus some the best CDs, and I have no reservations in crediting both versions with doing as much justice to the music as the states of their arts permit."

The Absolute Sound 16:136+ N/D '91. Arthur S. Pfeffer (brief)

"Some of the more recent Mercury releases strike me as being, overall, a more accurate representation of the master tape (or rather what's on the master tape) than what we have on the analogue discs....Some of the newer are much superior to the earlier releases....Give the latest generation Mercurys a listen. Some of them are among the jewels of analogue-to-digital technology."

The Absolute Sound 17:118+ Ap '92. Harry Pearson (med)

GRIEG, EDVARD

1154. Peer Gynt (complete incidental music), Opus 23; Sigurd Jorsalfar (incidental music), Opus 22.

Neeme Jarvi (c). Barbara Bonney; Marianne Eklof; Kjell Magnus Sandve; Urban Malmberg; Carl Gustaf Holmgren. Gosta Ohlin's Vocal Ensemble; Pro Musica Chamber Choir; Gothenburg Symphony Orchestra. 1987.
DEUTSCHE GRAMMOPHON 423 079 DDD
124:00 2 discs

✔HC ★★★★★*Awards:* Editors' Choice, *Digital Audio*, 1988; Record of the Month, *Hi-Fi News & Record Review*, Mr '88; The Want List 1988, *Fanfare* N/D '88 (George Chien). Critics' Choice 1988, *Gramophone* D '88 (Robin Golding); Critics' Choice 1988, *Gramophone* D '88 (Alan Sanders).

"It isn't merely Neeme Jarvi's determined adherence to the sparser score of 1875 which makes this new issue so special, nor his willingness to give his three fine actors their head with long stretches of crucial drama when the music's role becomes vitally supportive-....Grieg's detailed advice to the conductor of the 1886 production has been followed to the letter and beyond."

Hi-Fi News & Record Review 33:95 Mr '88. David Nice (400w)

"While Dreier's recording of *Peer Gynt* was useful, Jarvi's is truly indispensable."

Musical America 108:76-7 Jl '88. Bill Zakariasen (800w)

"The recording quality is crisply transparent and a music landscape is opened before you with splendid natural ambience and sparkling vivid imagery."

Australian Hi-Fi 19(11):97 '88. (200w)

"The performances are excellent....and the engineering is excellent as well."

Ovation 10:46 F '89. Paul Turok (325w)

"This album is highly recommended. Perhaps the only way I could think of to improve on DG's album (apart from engaging Ameling to sing Solveig's music) would have been to have had Sir Thomas Beecham at the controls."

Fanfare 11:133-5 My/Je '88. George Chien (650w)

Digital Audio 4:55 My '88. David C. Vernier (500w)

Gramophone 65:1219 F '88. Alan Sanders (595w)

1155. Peer Gynt (incidental music), Opus 23; Symphonic Dances, Opus 64 (No. 2); In Autumn (concert overture), Opus 11.

Thomas Beecham (c). Ilse Hollweg (sop). Beecham Choral Society; Royal Philharmonic Orchestra. 1957.
EMI 69039 ADD 58:15

✔HC

This "recording has been for three decades the benchmark for Grieg's *Peer Gynt*. And here it is, digitally remastered...sounding better than ever....this disc is indispensable."

Fanfare 11:134-5 My/Je '88. George Chien (650w)

"Sometimes the Beecham magic works here...Recording is worthy of its vintage, though CD hasn't sharpened up the definition as I thought it might."

Hi-Fi News & Record Review 33:90 Jl '88. David Nice (200w)

Musical America 110:53-5 S '90. Denis Stevens (180w)

Gramophone 66:1153 Ja '89. Ivan March (225w)

1156. Peer Gynt (incidental music), Opus 23 (excerpts).

Herbert Blomstedt (c). Mari-Anne Haeggander (sop); Urban Malmberg (bar). San Francisco Symphony Chorus; San Francisco Symphony Orchestra.
LONDON/DECCA 425 448 DDD 73:00

★*Awards:* Best of the Month, *Hi-Fi News & Record Review*, Jl '90.

"Overall...London and Blomstedt have given us an excellent single-disc view of *Peer Gynt*. The recording is first-rate. Warmly recommended."

Fanfare 13:160-61 Jl/Ag '90. George Chien (675w)

"Probably the best selection of music is Mr. Blomstedt's...and in the London booklet Michael Steinberg offers the most useful background information and plot synopsis. But the San Francisco Symphony's playing, although satisfactory, is tonally less distinguished than the Dresden State Orchestra's in Mr. Blomstedt's earlier, more abbreviated recording (EMI/Angel 4AM 34701; cassette)....However one chooses among them, the new-breed 'Peer Gynt' recordings demonstrate that Grieg's contribution has been persistently undervalued."

The New York Times Ag 25 '91, sec H p. 19+. Kenneth Furie (long)

"For those who want every note of Grieg's original, there is a splendid Neeme Jarvi recording on two Deutsche Grammophon CD's, combined with the composer's less interesting incidental music to *Sigurd Jorsalfer*. But if you just want the essential *Peer Gynt* music, you can't do better than with this superbly recorded Blomstedt performance."

Stereo Review 55:89 Ag '90. David Hall (225w)

"Whichever way we greet this, it is unlikely that we will like Solveig. She is scratchy and unsmooth—anything but soothing."

American Record Guide 53:56 My/Je '90. Donald R. Vroon (130w)

"This is the third 'complete' *Peer Gynt*...Unless one desperately wants Dreier's extra little bit of music there cannot be much doubt as to which of the two to choose, but DN, reviewing Jarvi in March 88, was enthusiastic about that, and it has for bonus the complete music for *Sigurd Jorsalfar*." *P95/100 S100*

Hi-Fi News & Record Review 35:81 Jl '90. Kenneth Dommett (315w)

Digital Audio's CD Review 6:46+ Je '90. David Vernier (520w)

Gramophone 67:1658+ Mr '90. Alan Sanders (360w)

1157. Symphonic Dances, Opus 64; Norwegian Dances (4), Opus 35.
Neeme Jarvi (c). Gothenburg Symphony Orchestra.
DEUTSCHE GRAMMOPHON 419 431 DDD 68:03

✔HC ★*Awards:* *Gramophone* Critics' Choice (Alan Sanders), 1987.

"Altogether, this is an admirable issue and is well worth savouring."

Hi-Fi News & Record Review 32:97 Mr '87 Doug Hammond (325w)

"The present album is thoroughly enjoyable and is highly recommended."

Fanfare 10:117-8 Jl/Ag '87 George Chien (300w)

"Jarvi secures fine playing from the Gothenburg Symphony Orchestra, and his readings are vigorous and exciting, if a bit undershaped in the slow movements."

High Fidelity 37:76 D '87. Christopher Rothko (205w)

Gramophone 64:1013-14 Ja '87 Alan Sanders (310w)

GRIFFES, CHARLES TOMLINSON

1158. The Pleasure-Dome of Kubla Khan, for Piano (orch. 1917); The White Peacock; Poem for Flute and Orchestra; Three Tone-Pictures; Bacchanale. TAYLOR, DEEMS. Through the Looking Glass.
Gerard Schwarz (c). Scott Goff (fl). Seattle Symphony Orchestra.
DELOS 3099 DDD 71:50

"This performance of the great *Kubla Khan* rivals one by the Boston Symphony Orchestra on a New World compact disc....The Seattle strings become a bit congested in the Taylor but are pure and radiant in Griffes's more subtle instrumentations, and his many woodwind solos are superbly played. The Delos recording is lush and sumptuous, far finer than the New World disc; both are essential Griffes."

Fanfare 14:227-8 Mr/Ap '91. James H. North (390w)

"The real prize here is the suite *Through the looking Glass*...This is one of the finest orchestral recordings I have heard recently—everything well-balanced and details miraculously clear without artificial spotlighting."

American Record Guide 54:115-6 My/Je '91. Carl Bauman (350w)

HANDEL, GEORGE FRIDERIC

1159. Concerti Grossi (6), Opus 3.
Trevor Pinnock (c). English Concert.
DEUTSCHE GRAMMOPHON 413 727 54:54

✔HC ★*Awards:* *Gramophone* Critics' Choice 1985 (Nicholas Anderson).

"Musical dynamics, commitment and consistency of style and approach, and a recorded balance which is never less than musical, if a little 'cold', make this a 'hot' CD."

Hi-Fi News & Record Review 30:99 Mr '85. John Atkinson (105w)

"None of the recordings I have heard can challenge the sonic excellence of the present issue...Trevor Pinnock...infuses his performance with a *joie de vivre* that is infectious."

American Record Guide 48:65 S/O '85. Carl Bauman (300w)

Gramophone 62:1063 Mr '85. Nicholas Anderson (385w)

1160. Concerti Grossi, Opus 6 (No.'s 1-4).
Robert Salter (vln). Guildhall String Ensemble. 1988.
RCA 7895 DDD 44:00

✔HC ★*Awards:* Critics' Choice 1990, *Gramophone* D '90 (John Duarte).

"Light and airy is the order of the day, yet not lacking in substance, and with fine cohesion and articulation....The sound is clear and open, and the disc warmly recommended."

Fanfare 13:195 Ja/F '90. Nils Anderson (100w)

"This recording...is refreshing to hear. The tone is clear and bright, and the ensemble plays with a vitality that brings joy to the music. Their excellent reading...certainly attests to the validity of this wonderful music on modern instruments."

Stereo Review 55:98 Mr '90. Stoddard Lincoln (b.n.)

"These are lively, alert accounts, with at times almost spiky solo violin work—crisp, pointed and distinctive. There are occasional touches of untidiness in the tuttis, the occasional sign of enthusiasm not completely held in check—but the exuberant music-making, the response to Handel's quicksilver changes of mood and texture, are very attractive." *P95/85 S95/85*

Hi-Fi News & Record Review 35:90 My '90. Peter Branscombe (270w)

"For those who wish *only* to hear stylish, balanced, well-tuned, nicely articulated, finely paced, and literate if literal renderings of these great masterpieces I would recommend this set unreservedly."

American Record Guide 53:56-7 My/Je '90. Alan Heatherington (b.n.)

Digital Audio's CD Review 6:84 D '89. David Vernier (325w)

Gramophone 67:1461-62 F '90. John Duarte (320w)

1161. Overtures (Alceste; Agrippina; Pastor Fido; Saul, Acts 1 & 2; Teseo; Samson).
Trevor Pinnock (c). English Concert.
DEUTSCHE GRAMMOPHON 419 219

★*Awards: Fanfare* Want List 1987 (George Chien).

"Pinnock invests all with wonderful zest and vitality, which are captured with lively realism by Archiv's engineers...the present album—easily among the best of this superb series—is joyfully recommended."
Fanfare 10:127 My/Je '87 George Chien (400w)

"Here, in a collection of sinfonie and preludes-...is an unexpected pendant which confirms Pinnock's orchestra's supremacy in this music. I treasure the astringent string timbres, the athletic wind playing, the rhythmic buoyancy and vivid attack of their music-making."
Hi-Fi News & Record Review 31:118-9 D '86 Hugh Canning (215w)

Gramophone 64:867-8 D '86 Nicholas Anderson (405w)

1162. Royal Fireworks Music. HOLST, GUSTAV. Suites (2) for Band (1909, 1911). BACH, JOHANNES SEBASTIAN. Fantasia in G for Organ, BWV.572 (Gravement section only).
Frederick Fennell (c). Cleveland Winds.
TELARC 80038 DDD

✔HC

1163. Water Music (complete).
Nicholas McGegan (c). Philharmonia Baroque Orchestra. Lone Mountain College Chapel, San Francisco CA. October 1987 & March 1988 reissue.
HARMONIA MUNDI 907010 AAD 56:38

★★*Awards:* Records to Die for: 1 of 5 Recommended Recordings, *Stereophile* Ja '91 (Robert Harley); Records to Die for: 1 of 5 Recommended Recordings, *Stereophile* Ja '91 (Robert Hesson).

"This is a *Water Music* to conjure with. It is witty, vital, vivacious, and thoroughly delightful....This one goes near the top of a long list. Highly recommended."
Fanfare 12:174-75 Ja/F '89. George Chien (230w)

"There may be far too many recordings of the *Water Music*, but this new one, which includes a couple of tracks devoted to rarely heard variations, is well worth adding to your collection."
Stereo Review 54:164 F '89. Stoddard Lincoln (190w)

"The recording is of analog origins but wonderfully clear and handsomely processed....Everything about McGegan's performance is musical and vital: this is not just a reading but a genuine rendition. For those who want a period-instruments version of this wonderful music, I would recommend the Gardiner recording and this new one by McGegan; pressed to narrow the choice to one, I guess I would even opt for McGegan alone, as offering about the freshest and least distractingly freighted version to be had just now."
American Record Guide 52:54 My/Je '89. John W. Barker (490w)

"This release is a luminous, revelatory expression of the grandeur of intensely felt and lovingly crafted music, preserved in a recording that can stand as a landmark in the art and science of high fidelity."
Stereophile 12:168 Jl '89. Robert Hesson (400w)

"This performance and recording convey the essence of Handel's *Water Music*....What really makes this particular version stand out (apart from the wonderful performance) is the gorgeous recording."
Stereophile 14:141 Ja '91. Robert Harley (b.n.)

"McGegan's *Water Music* is alive with spirit. Totally absent is the often dull, scholarly cast of the original-instrument movement. The players here are superb—and obviously thrilled to be playing the music....It is perhaps the most natural-sounding recording I have heard and is absolutely stunning in every respect."
Stereophile 14:142 Ja '91. Robert Hesson (b.n.)

"An oft-played, hackneyed favorite, the *Water Music* glistens anew in this brisk, spiky performance....The San Francisco-based Philharmonia Baroque Orchestra plays with great panache. The fine recording was made in 1987 and 1988, but is analog."
HighPerformanceReview 6:77 Je '89. Kenneth Krehbiel (110w)

Gramophone 66:1282 F '89. Nicholas Anderson (360w)

1164. Water Music (complete).
Trevor Pinnock (c). English Concert.
DEUTSCHE GRAMMOPHON 410 525 DDD 54:15

✔HC ★★*Awards:* Records to Die for: 1 of 5 Recommended Recordings, *Stereophile* Ja '91 (Peter W. Mitchell). Perfect 10/10, *Digital Audio*, Mr '88.

"What's so satisfying about Pinnock's early-instruments group is this: they play with such freshness, variety, and toe-tapping rhythmic swing that every time I put on this disc I feel I am hearing this wonderful music for the first time. The sound is crisp, clear, full-bodied, spacious, and (happily) does not suffer from the hardness that afflicts many other Archiv digitals."
Stereophile 14:159 Ja '91. Peter W. Mitchell (b.n.)

"If the original performance of Handel's *Water Music* was comparable to this recording by the

English Concert, it is no small wonder that on that summer evening in 1717 'his Majesty-...caused it to be played over three times in going and returning.'"
Musick 6:36 Mr '85. Gregory Johnston (400w)

"If you do not already have a complete *Water Music* on early instruments, get this one. If you do, get this one anyway."
Stereo Review 49:102-3 S '84. Stoddard Lincoln (75w)

Ovation 5:50-1 Ag '84. Allan Kozinn (480w) (rev. of LP); 6:29-30 Jl '85. Scott Cantrell (100w) (rev. of CD)

Digital Audio 1:69-70 Je '85. Roland Graeme (120w)

Gramophone 61:971 F '84. Lionel Salter (105w)

Hi-Fi News & Record Review 29:73 Je '84. John Atkinson (90w)

HANSON, HOWARD

1165. Symphonies: No. 1 in E minor, "Nordic", Opus 22; No. 2, "Romantic", Opus 30; **Song of Democracy, for Chorus and Orchestra.** (Mercury Living Presence).
Howard Hanson (c). Eastman School of Music Chorus; Eastman-Rochester Orchestra. 1960, 1958, 1957 reissues.
MERCURY 432 008 ADD 66:40

★★★*Awards:* The Want List 1991, *Fanfare* N/D '91 (Peter Burwasser). Pick of the Month, North American Perspective (Christopher Pollard) *Gramophone* F '91. The Super Compact Disk List, *The Absolute Sound*, Ap '92 (Harry Pearson).

"Enjoyable of their kind, these symphonies are not great music but they are genuine—authoritatively played, of course, and nice to come back to now and again....*The Song of Democracy*...celebrates an education association centenary [and is the]...sort of thing Americans seem to love—Whitman and his 'fair auroral skies'—it is, like the occasion, eminently forgettable." *P95 S95/85*
Hi-Fi News & Record Review 36:77 Je '91. Kenneth Dommett (245w)

"Not so easy to recommend this one without reservations....the *Song of Democracy*...[is] the best performance and recording on the disc—stunning beyond belief."
American Record Guide 54:132+ My/Je '91. John Landis (150w)

The Absolute Sound 15:146+ N/D '90. Arthur S. Pfeffer (120w)

Fanfare 14:112-17 Ja/F '91. Ron McDonald (260w)

Gramophone 68:1506 F '91. Edward Seckerson (290w)

Musical America 111:65-8 Mr '91. Terry Teachout (120w)

The New York Times S 30 '90, p. 28+ H. Richard Freed (b.n.)

1166. Symphonies: No. 1 in E minor, "Nordic", Opus 22; No. 2, "Romantic", Opus 30; **Elegy in Memory of Serge Koussevitzky, Opus 44.**
Gerard Schwarz (c). Seattle Symphony Orchestra. 1989.
DELOS 3073 DDD 71:00

✔HC ★★★★*Awards:* Best Recordings of the Month, *Stereo Review* S '89. The Want List 1989, *Fanfare* N/D '89 (James Miller); The Want List 1989, *Fanfare* N/D '89 (Walter Simmons); Top Choices—1989, *American Record Guide* Ja/F '90 (Karl Miller). Editors' Choice, *Digital Audio's CD Review*, 6:34 Je '90.

"A brilliant, impassioned reading."
The New York Times Mr 4 '90, p. H 34. K. Robert Schwarz (100w)

"The performances of both works...stand up to the very best, including the composer's own, and are recorded in most resplendent fashion."
Stereo Review 54:126 S '89. David Hall (450w)

"Delos engineering means fantastic sound: clear and open, never congested, and completely natural. Mr. Schwarz is also a natural, emphasizing what the music itself seems to call attention to and understating surrounding material."
American Record Guide 52:61 S/O '89. Donald R. Vroon (335w)

"Schwarz's subdued approach to Hanson works best in the *Elegy in Memory of Serge Koussevitsky*. It is plainly stated: moving, but never maudlin. Overall, these are fine performances, very well played and recorded. As for the judgement that true passion is lacking—that is, admittedly, highly subjective—no doubt some listeners would find anything more than is offered here excessive, false or banal."
HighPerformanceReview 8(1):68 '91. Kenneth Krehbiel (380w)

"In common with most 20th-century music, the works...require rhythmic security as well as subtlety—qualities Schwarz and his colleagues possess in abundance....In addition to finely wrought performances brimming with passion and stylistic understanding, the sonics are also splendid—detailed but with enough air to please those (including present company) who cherish clarity of line and timbre as long as it sounds natural."
Stereophile 13:233+ O '90. Gordon Emerson (305w)

"Gerard Schwarz and his excellent orchestra deserve our gratitude for this revival recording. Schwarz revels unapologetically in these three works' unabashed Romanticism without ever descending to wallow in it. The high strings occasionally sound incongruously thin, but otherwise the technical niveau of the recording measures up to the exceptional standards of that spunky little California firm, Delos."
Audio 73:142+ D '89. Paul Moor (825w)

Gramophone 67:1604 Mr '90. Edward Seckerson (595w)

Digital Audio's CD Review 6:74 My '90. Lawrence Johnson (215w)

"Over the years, I have reiterated my contention *ad nauseam* that Hanson's 'Romantic' Symphony is a decidedly inferior composition-...By contrast, I have argued, the 'Nordic' Symphony...is a far superior work in every respect—perhaps the most distinctive, fully realized American symphony of the first quarter of this century. Now, this fine new recording...offers an excellent opportunity for the reader to arrive at his own conclusion."

Fanfare 13:228-31 N/D '89. Walter Simmons (1160w)

Musical America 110:20+ N '90. K. Robert Schwarz (535w)

Symphony No. 2, Opus 30, "Romantic". See No. 2008.

Symphony No. 3, Opus 33; Symphony No. 6. See No. 2066

HARRIS, ROY

1167. Symphony No. 3. SCHUMANN, ROBERT. Symphony No. 3 in E flat, Opus 97, "Rhenish".

Leonard Bernstein (c). New York Philharmonic Orchestra. Avery Fisher Hall, New York. December 1985 live.

DEUTSCHE GRAMMOPHON 419 780 DDD 51:00

> ✔HC ★*Awards:* Second Place Orchestral Mumm Champagne Classical Music Award 1988—Presented by *Ovation, Ovation* N '88.

"Bernstein says all that there is to say about these marvellous pieces."

Hi-Fi News & Record Review 32:127 D '87. Edward Seckerson (280w)

This new recording "is more expansive than the conductor's previous ones...both symphonies are enhanced by the auditorium's strident ambience and by the New York Philharmonic's austere textures."

The New York Times F 7 '88, p. H32. K. Robert Schwarz (150w)

"There has never been a conductor who could project the spirit and vitality of this music with as much conviction as Bernstein can....for many reasons this new release represents an important historical document in the recorded history of American symphonic music."

Fanfare 11:195-6 Mr/Ap '88. Walter Simmons (900w)

"Harris's famous Third has been recorded six times now...This new one...is a truly definitive statement of this music...I was convinced that the wise, mature Lenny and the largely cleaned-up 1985 NYPO would be unable to surpass the youthfully exuberant Lenny with the often funky and sometimes out-of-kilter 1959 NYPO-...the new one is remarkable for the improvement in Bernstein's control of the enormous energy of the music and its complex figurations. The final coda is like a big band on a construction site. It's not funky anymore, but it still kicks ass."

Stereophile 11:167+ Je '88. Richard Schneider (780w)

"The mischief begins in the lyrical and pastoral sections of the Harris, where totally exposed solo woodwinds repeatedly play ragged attacks and inexact rhythms."

High Fidelity 38:57 My '88. Paul Moor (275w)

"It is a lack of bite in attack, the sense that the players are not being made to dig in, that lends this performance [of Harris] its slightly tired air....[in the Schuman] Bernstein is slower than before, yet he comes far closer to duplicating the thrust and drive of his earlier version than he does in the Harris. But here he is let down by the recording engineers with sound that does less than justice to the details and dynamics of Schuman's complex scoring."

American Record Guide 51:34-5 My/Je '88. Richard E. Tiedman (825w)

Stereo Review 53:99 Mr '88. David Hall (285w)

Gramophone 65:737 N '87 Michael Oliver (515w)

HARVEY, JONATHAN. Song Offerings. See No. 1047.

HAYDN, FRANZ JOSEPH

1168. Symphonies (complete).

Antal Dorati (c). Philharmonia Hungarica. Also available as eight four-disc sets.

LONDON/DECCA 430 100 ADD 2191:00 32 discs

> ★*Awards:* Critics' Choice 1991, *Gramophone*, Ja '92 (Richard Wigmore). Pick of the Month, North American Perspective (Christie Barter) *Gramophone* Je '91.

"There is as yet no other...recording with the Philharmonia Hungarica of the complete symphonies from the early 70's."

The New York Times S 22 '91, sec H p. 25+. Matthew Gurewitsch (long)

Gramophone 69:40+ Je '91. Richard Wigmore (2910w)

1169. Symphonies: No. 6 in D, "Le Matin;" No. 7 in C, "Le Midi;" No. 8 in G, "Le Soir".

Trevor Pinnock (c). Trevor Pinnock (hpscd). The English Concert.

DEUTSCHE GRAMMOPHON 423 098 DDD 65:00

> ✔HC ★*Awards: American Record Guide* Overview: Haydn, Mr/Ap '92.

"The sound is crystal clear, and the genius of Haydn's inventive writing is heard to fullest advantage."

Music and Musicians International 36:46-7 Ap '88. Robert Hartford (125w)

"In a recording that maintains the balance Pinnock has striven for and which presents the earthy qualities of these instruments without undue coloration or added warmth, these unprettified but very enjoyable performances must come closest to the sound Haydn would have heard."
Stereophile 11:165 N '88. Barbara Jahn (330w)

"There are moments in these performances where I wish Pinnock and his band would pick up a bit on the underlying tempo...Otherwise, the playing and the quality of direction combine delectability with scholarly punctiliousness in familiar English Concert fashion. The competition is slight....Strongly recommended."
Fanfare 11:142-3 My/Je '88. John D. Wiser (240w)

Gramophone 65:1076 Ja '88. Stanley Sadie (470w)

1170. Symphonies: No. 22 in E flat, "Der Philosoph"; No. 63 in C, "La Roxelane" (second version); No. 80 in D minor.
Orpheus Chamber Orchestra. State University of New York, Purchase. March 1988.
DEUTSCHE GRAMMOPHON 427 337 DDD 63:00

✔**HC** ★*Awards: American Record Guide* Overview: Haydn, Mr/Ap '92 (No. 22).

"The performances, granted, are on modern instruments, but...they play with finesse and sensitivity." *P90 S90*
Stereo Review 54:144 O '89. David Hall (220w)

"A delightful issue...Throughout, the players convey full appreciation of Haydn's achievements, revealing an equally happy hand in tiny points of detail and balance, and in the broad sweep of each movement and work. The acoustic has keen presence...one feels one is sitting in a very good seat at an uncommonly rewarding concert." *P95 S100*
Hi-Fi News & Record Review 34:101 N '89. Peter Branscombe (175w)

"This bouquet of Haydn symphonies, I undertake to warrant, will not wilt or fade with time or under the most intense critical scrutiny. Wolf Erichson continues to provide this splendid conductorless chamber orchestra with recording quality of transparency and vital corporeality. Urgently recommended."
Fanfare 13:238-39 N/D '89. John Wiser (260w)

"The Philosopher of 22 is more pompous than usual....The *Roxelane* variations in 63 are subdued. Mackerras brought more light and shade to 80 on Conifer 165, though his orchestra wasn't as assured as the one here. The playing is very good, especially the intonation, which approaches the uncanny. Consider the disc as an alternative or supplement to Fischer's 22 (Nimbus 5179) and as a stopgap for 63 until Marriner's is reissued."
American Record Guide 55:73 Mr/Ap '92. Stephen D. Chakwin, Jr. (brief)

Fanfare 14:68+ S/O '90. John Wiser (b.n.)

1171. Symphonies: No. 22 in E flat, "Der Philosoph"; No. 24 in D; No. 45 in F# minor, "Farewell".
Adam Fischer (c). Austro-Hungarian Haydn Orchestra.
NIMBUS 5179 DDD 62:24

★*Awards: American Record Guide* Overview: Haydn, Mr/Ap '92 (No. 45).

"All these symphonies are performed well, bringing out all their drama and wit, yet somehow the 'farewell' section of *No. 45* does not really give a good feel of the musicians gradually leaving, as do some other recordings-....Nimbus is to be commended for their superb recording job."
HighPerformanceReview 8(2):67 Summer '91. D. C. Culbertson (320w)

"If these performances aren't always the last word in *brio* (indeed, the term 'stately' comes too easily to mind), it is clear that Fischer and his orchestra are comfortably at home in the middle range of Haydn symphonies, a mine as rich as any in the symphonic literature."
Fanfare 13:238 N/D '89. Paul Sargent Clark (190w)

Gramophone 67:1130 D '89. Edward Greenfield (225w)

Stereophile 13:207+ N '90. Mortimer H. Frank (b.n.)

1172. Symphonies: No. 22 in E flat, "Der Philosoph"; No. 78 in C minor; No. 82 in C, "The Bear".
Esa-Pekka Salonen (c). Stockholm Chamber Orchestra.
SONY 45972 DDD 57:52

★*Awards:* Best Recordings of the Month, *Stereo Review* S '91.

"The performances are...a startling personal distillation of the lessons of the authentic-instruments movement within the context of a chamber orchestra of modern instruments....Stockholm Chamber Orchestra...achieves a transparency and lightness of texture that one associates with original-instruments ensembles, while also giving a rhetorical weightiness to the music that is possible only with conventional modern instruments."
Stereo Review 56:68 S '91. David Patrick Stearns (med)

With Mr. Salonen's "touch Haydn springs to the empyrean possessed of all the ingenuity, humor and depth...Mr. Salonen begins with Symphony No. 82 ('The Bear'), another from the Paris set, combining the fanfares, winged melody and theatrical sighs of the opening Vivace assai in a swirl of irresistible festivity. In less than 30 seconds with its dashing maestro, the Stockholm Chamber Orchestra has opened to view an enchanting array of colors, contours and densities. As the movement unfolds, the ideas keep streaming forth in cascading abundance, speeding by yet never hasty, never breathless."

The New York Times S 22 '91, sec H p. 25+. Matthew Gurewitsch (long)

"Salonen takes most of the movements here at breathtaking tempos, sometimes shockingly fast, as in the Adagio opening of 'The Philosopher,' but his menuets are slow, elegant, and forceful....This is all wonderful Haydn playing: imaginative, daring, intelligent, and refreshing-....There are advantages to collecting Haydn by sets—Kuijken's 'Paris' Symphonies, for example, or Bernstien's—but don't miss this stunning disc."

Fanfare 15:232-33 S/O '91. James H. North (med)

"There is a nice contrast and variety on this disc that should make it attractive to those who do not want to fill their shelves with *all* the Haydn symphonies but rather want some of the best ones. Add to that superb playing by the Stockholmers and Mr. Salonen, in which crisp articulation, plenty of electricity and energy, and an ability to relax when necessary to bring out the individual character of each movement and each work, go hand-in-hand with Sony's pleasantly clear but resonant 'high definition sound'."

American Record Guide 54:83 S/O '91. Lawrence Hansen (med)

"Mr Salonen tries too hard. When he looks at a Haydn score he sees a coiffeur salon of hairpins....It is as if the conductor is saying 'Watch me cleverly shape this bit', and 'Listen to the inner parts, damn you!' Haydn does not need this treatment. Neither does he survive it." *P65(95) S95*

Hi-Fi News & Record Review 36:84 Ap '91. Robert Dearling (140w)

"There are too many conductors who have devoted their lives to Haydn and Mozart to add this disc to one's shelf simply because it's new."

High Performance Review 8:87 Wtr '91/92. Bert Wechsler (brief)

Gramophone 69:62 S '91. Richard Wigmore (long)

1173. Symphonies: No. 26 in D minor, "Lamentatione"; No. 52 in C minor; No. 53 in D, "Imperial".
Sigiswald Kuijken (c). Petite Bande.
VIRGIN 90743 DDD 62:00

★*Awards:* *American Record Guide* Overview: Haydn, Mr/Ap '92.

"Neat, clean, and sonorous performances of three of Haydn's lesser-known symphonies—and all well worth a closer acquaintance. The orchestral balance is excellent, featuring clarity within cohesion, and the recorded sound transports the listener effortlessly to Esterhaz."

Musical America 109:61-2 S '89. Denis Stevens (340w)

"The recorded sound is spectacular....Performances are alert and judiciously paced. The result is a thoroughly engaging issue."

American Record Guide 52:66-7 N/D '89. Carl Bauman (115w)

1174. Symphonies: No. 31 in D, "Hornsignal"; No. 45 in F# minor, "Farewell".
Charles Mackerras (c). Saint Luke's Orchestra. 1988.
TELARC 80156 DDD 68:26

✔**HC** ★*Awards:* *American Record Guide* Overview: Haydn, Mr/Ap '92 (No. 31).

"Mackerras conducts absolutely ideal performances."

Fanfare 13:217-18 S/O '89. James H. North (165w)

"The performances, granted, are on modern instruments, but...they play with finesse and sensitivity." *P80 S95*

Stereo Review 54:144 O '89. David Hall (220w)

"The playing is very accomplished, with fine detail as well as a bold sweep in the fast movements, and warm lyricism in the slow movements....The recording is warm, sonorous, easy on the ear." *P95 S95*

Hi-Fi News & Record Review 34:101 N '89. Peter Branscombe (170w)

"A wonderful release which I recommend most enthusiastically."

American Record Guide 52:67 N/D '89. Allen Linkowski (230w)

Gramophone 67:1604+ Mr '90. Edward Greenfield (455w)

Digital Audio's CD Review 6:78 S '89. David Vernier (200w)

1175. Symphonies: No. 41 in C; Symphony No. 48 in C, "Maria Theresia"; No. 65 in A. ("Sturm and Drang" Symphonies, Volume 3).
Trevor Pinnock (c). English Concert.
DEUTSCHE GRAMMOPHON 429 399 DDD 58:00

✔**HC** ★*Awards:* Best of the Month, *Hi-Fi News & Record Review*, Ag '90.

"Fantastic period-instrument playing, clearly recorded in the spacious acoustic of the Henry Wood Hall....Not to be missed!"

High Fidelity 1:109 Ag '90. Andrew Stuart (b.n.)

"Here is festive music, imaginatively scored, and projected vibrantly with virtuosic playing....A disc well worth acquiring."

Stereophile 14:255+ O '91. Mortimer H. Frank (brief)"

"Strongly recommended."

Fanfare 15:347-9 N/D '91. John Wiser (brief)

The playing, as playing, is still outstanding, and the care that has gone into every aspect of these performances pays off over and

over...There's an extra dimension to this furious music...that Pinnock's forces downplay."
American Record Guide 54:79-80 N/D '91. Stephen D. Chakwin, Jr. (long)

"True to form, Pinnock leads performances which are technically accomplished and carefully considered, making the most of the music's technical innovations and highly-strung nervous energy."
Continuo 14:29 O '90. Scott Paterson (b.n.)

"No number of words could do justice to these richly contrasting symphonies or the performances...the recording quality [is] up to Archiv's very best." *P100 S95*
Hi-Fi News & Record Review 35:91 Ag '90. Peter Branscombe (120w)

Gramophone 68:210+ Jl '90. Richard Wigmore (440w)

1176. Symphonies: No. 42 in D; No. 44 in E minor, "Trauer"; No. 46 in B.
("Sturm and Drang" Symphonies, Volume 5).
Trevor Pinnock (c). The English Concert.
DEUTSCHE GRAMMOPHON 429 756 DDD 63:00

✔HC ★★★*Awards:* Critics' Choice 1990, *Gramophone* D '90 (Richard Wigmore). *American Record Guide* Overview: Haydn, Mr/Ap '92 (No. 44).

"The technical quality of the production is excellent, with good, natural balance, plenty of presence and a warm glow to the timbres that never threatens to inhibit clarity." *P100 S100*
Hi-Fi News & Record Review 35:93 D '90. Peter Branscombe (215w)

"Strongly recommended."
Fanfare 15:347-9 N/D '91. John Wiser (brief)

See Volume 4 for review excerpt.
American Record Guide 54:79-80 N/D '91. Stephen D. Chakwin, Jr. (long)

Gramophone 68:513-4 S '90. Richard Wigmore (550w)

1177. Symphonies: No. 43 in E flat, "Mercury"; No. 51 in B flat; No. 52 in C minor.
("Sturm and Drang" Symphonies, Volume 4).
Trevor Pinnock (c). English Concert.
DEUTSCHE GRAMMOPHON 429 400 DDD 65:00

✔HC ★*Awards:* Best of the Month, *Hi-Fi News & Record Review*, Ag '90.

"No number of words could do justice to these richly contrasting symphonies or the performances...the recording quality [is] up to Archiv's very best." *P100 S95*
Hi-Fi News & Record Review 35:91 Ag '90. Peter Branscombe (120w)

"Strongly recommended."
Fanfare 15:347-9 N/D '91. John Wiser (brief)

"Fantastic period-instrument playing, clearly recorded in the spacious acoustic of the Henry Wood Hall....Not to be missed!"
High Fidelity 1:109 Ag '90. Andrew Stuart (b.n.)

See Volume 3 for review excerpt.
—*Continuo* 14:29 O '90. Scott Paterson (b.n.)

—*American Record Guide* 54:79-80 N/D '91. Stephen D. Chakwin, Jr. (long)

Gramophone 68:210+ Jl '90. Richard Wigmore (440w)

1178. Symphonies: No. 82 in C, "The Bear"; No. 83 in G minor, "The Hen"; No. 84 in E flat.
Sigiswald Kuijken (c). Age of Enlightenment Orchestra.
VIRGIN 90793 DDD 78:00

★*Awards:* *American Record Guide* Overview: Haydn, Mr/Ap '92.

"Virgin provides beautifully realistic sound. It is rich, vibrant, and smooth, with no hint of harshness. Kuijken and the period instrument orchestra are at their best....I know no other version of these three works that is so satisfying."
American Record Guide 53:59 My/Je '90. Carl Bauman (b.n.)

"Although the Orchestra of the Age of Enlightenment uses only five more strings than Glover's forces, they make a much greater impact; not so much because they use original instruments, but because of the way they play. These are big, rough performances—very different from the polish of the Concertgebouw, but certainly appropriate for these symphonies."
Fanfare 13:187-89 My/Je '90. James H. North (225w)

"The Orchestra of the Age of Enlightenment-...shares members with the English Concert-...Although their band of 36 is far smaller than that of the commissioning society, they compensate by means of a lively, unfettered wit, capitalizing on the music's folk-inflected content and cultivatedly outrageous pranks."
Musical America 110:78-9 S '90. K. Robert Schwarz (270w)

Musick 12:18 Fall '90. Peter Slemon (150w)

Gramophone 67:1462 F '90. Stanley Sadie (355w)

Stereophile 14:255+ O '91. Mortimer H. Frank (brief)

1179. Symphonies: No. 83 in G minor, "The Hen"; No. 84 in E flat, "In Nomine Domine"; No. 88 in G.
Jane Glover (c). London Mozart Players.
ASV 677 DDD 67:00

★*Awards:* *American Record Guide* Overview: Haydn, Mr/Ap '92 (No.'s 83, 84).

"A delightful programme with three masterpieces from the mid-1780s. The playing is unfailingly alert, the recording atmospheric without artificial highlighting, the musical direction full of good sense, humour, style." *P95 S85/95*
Hi-Fi News & Record Review 34:123 D '89. Peter Branscombe (150w)

"Her disc is well-filled, well-recorded and well-annotated. All in all, it's a solid release."
American Record Guide 53:74-5 S/O '90. Stephen D. Chakwin, Jr. (205w)

"Like Kuijken's 83, Glover's [performance] lacks a bit of needed tension, but it is far more pointedly nuanced, especially in its subtle dynamic shading in the slow movement....In 84 and 88, however, Glover holds her own with anybody....Given the fine-grained engineering, this stands as one of today's finest Haydn CDs."
Stereophile 14:255+ O '91. Mortimer H. Frank (brief)

1180. Symphonies: No. 85 in B flat, "La Reine"; No. 86 in D; No. 87 in A.
Sigiswald Kuijken (c). Age of Enlightenment Orchestra.
VIRGIN 90844 DDD 79:00

✔**HC** ★*Awards:* Critic's Choice: 1991, *American Record Guide*, Ja/F '92 (Stephen Chakwin). *American Record Guide* Overview: Haydn, Mr/Ap '92.

"This is the finest set of the *Paris* Symphonies, on any kind of instruments, that I've heard."
American Record Guide 54:79-80 N/D '91. Stephen D. Chakwin, Jr. (long)

"Using a fairly large orchestra...Kuijken...elicits some fine performances, which emphasize Haydn's formal mastery without sacrificing any of the verve and wit which are such crucial components of the composer's style."
Continuo 14:29 O '90. Scott Paterson (b.n.)

"The first volume of Kuijken's 'Paris' Symphonies was reviewed in *Fanfare* 13:5; everything said there still applies...This is probably the best set of these six symphonies on compact discs...The Virgin Classics disc are near-ideal performances; their recorded sound is excellent."
Fanfare 14:216-17 Ja/F '91. James H. North (500w)

"Superb sound and performances."
High Fidelity 1:103 Je '90. Andrew Stuart (b.n.)

"Apart from a few moments when the harpsichord could have been more present, this bright recording charms the ear. No.85 is the star performance, but all three are admirable." *P100/95 S95*
Hi-Fi News & Record Review 35:90 My '90. Antony Hodgson (380w)

Stereophile 14:255+ O '91. Mortimer H. Frank (brief)

Gramophone 67:1976 My '90. Edward Greenfield (350w)

1181. Symphonies: No. 86 in D; No. 88 in G.
Frans Bruggen (c). Eighteenth Century Orchestra. The Netherlands. November 1988 live.
PHILIPS 426 169 DDD 49:00

✔**HC** ★★★★*Awards:* Top Disks of the Year, *The New York Times* D 24, '89 (John Rockwell). The Year's Best, *Hi Fi News & Record Review*, May '90 Supplement. *American Record Guide* Overview: Haydn, Mr/Ap '92 (No. 86).

"As period-instrument readings, these are preferred editions, Bruggen being particularly successful in conveying the dramatic transformations that lie at the core of sonata style and the humor that pervades these works."
Stereophile 14:255+ O '91. Mortimer H. Frank (brief)

"A vivid pairing of symphonies...Frans Bruggen directs both with great immediacy and flair, and the live recording deserves the adjective for two reasons (though you are hard put to it to find evidence of the audience). Period instruments help greatly in creating the lean, lively textures, though there is plenty of impact to the big tutti with blazing trumpets, horns and timpani." *P95 S95*
Hi-Fi News & Record Review 35:104 Mr '90; p.22 My '90 Supplement. Peter Branscombe (175w)

"The new account [of 86] has all the assets to be found in earlier CD issues on the same subject (*Fanfare* 12:3, 13:2)....In the finale [of 88], Bruggen's refinement gets slightly out of hand, taking the edge off general jollity and treating all the slyly delayed thematic returns with a poker face. But this is a small debit in the course of a record, and a series, which has established a firmly positive balance."
Fanfare 13:189-90 My/Je '90. John Wiser (280w)

Gramophone 67:1129-30 D '89. Nicholas Anderson (395w)

1182. Symphonies: No. 88 in G; No. 89 in F; No. 92 in G, "Oxford".
Karl Bohm (c). Vienna Philharmonic Orchestra.
DEUTSCHE GRAMMOPHON 429 523 76:00

★★*Awards:* Critic's Choice: 1991, *American Record Guide*, Ja/F '92 (John McKelvey); Critic's Choice: 1991, *American Record Guide*, Ja/F '92 (Stephen Chakwin).

"This is Austrian music-making *par excellence*; the smooth, bright, resinous strings and clearly projected brass and woodwind sound is so *Viennese* you can almost cut it with a knife, like pastry....you will search the catalog in vain for comparable performances of these works at any price, and at the low figure asked, they're a steal."
American Record Guide 54:66 My/Je '91. John P. McKelvey (230w)

1183. Symphonies (12) "The Salomon Symphonies": No. 93 in D; No. 94 in G, "Surprise"; No. 95 in C minor; No. 96 in D, "Miracle"; No. 97 in C; No. 98 in B flat; No. 99 in E flat; No. 100 in G, "Military"; No. 101 in D, "Clock"; No. 102 in B flat; No. 103 in E flat, "Drumroll"; No. 104 in D, "London".

Adam Fischer (c). Austro-Hungarian Haydn Orchestra.
NIMBUS 5200/04 DDD 69:42, 79:03, 51:24, 56:27, 58:27 5 discs

"There is little to quarrel with and much to enjoy in this set....I don't expect a better set of these works to come along soon and would be hard pressed to assemble one from the current catalog."
American Record Guide 53:74-5 S/O '90. Stephen D. Chakwin, Jr. (205w)

"The instruments are modern, but the concert-hall is ultra-authentic and the warm-toned Austro-Hungarian Haydn Orchestra is extremely responsive to its founder-conductor Adam Fischer....It is unfortunate that so many of Haydn's dramatically sudden changes of orchestral colour go for so very little in these readings, but the engineers cannot take the entire blame since many forte passages are played without their essential ruggedness. I loved the gorgeous acoustic, but it always seemed difficult to get close to the music." *P85 S75/85*
Hi-Fi News & Record Review 35:97 F '90. Antony Hodgson (775w)

"The Haydnsaal...tends to blur ensemble passages or make them seem bloated...This conductor lavishes as much attention on the development sections of first movements (and some finales) as on the more obviously melodic expositions, which tends to give him access to the core of the composer's genius....Why...do I so often return to Beecham, Szell, Monteux, Casals, Bernstein, Jochum, Dorati, and Toscanini? Perhaps it's because these conductors were able to make more sound like less—they got a lighter, learner sound with orchestras twice the size of Fischer's forty-five-piece group."
Fanfare 13:239-40 N/D '89. Paul Sargent Clark (1190w)

The New York Times Mr 4 '90, p. H 31. Martin Bookspan (930w)

Gramophone 67:1130 D '89. Edward Greenfield (225w)

1184. Symphonies: No. 93 in D; No. 94 in G, "Surprise;" No. 96 in D, "Miracle".
Colin Davis (c). Concertgebouw Orchestra.
PHILIPS 412 871 DDD 67:23

✔**HC** ★*Awards:* Record of the Eighties, *Gramophone*, D '89 (Robin Golding).

"In his July 1982 review of the LP set of all the Salomon symphonies, PB extolled the sound quality of these three, the only digitally recorded items in the album, and he was full of praise for Colin Davis' outstanding performances. The CD enhances all these qualities."
Hi-Fi News & Record Review 31:107 Ja '86. Kenneth Dommett (100w)

"I received these performances with warm enthusiasm when they first appeared on LP (see *Fanfare* 6:3 & 5)....A release not to be missed."
Fanfare 11:219-20 S/O '87. Mortimer H. Frank (300w)

Gramophone 63:916 Ja '86. Robin Golding (210w)

1185. Symphonies: No. 93 in D; No. 95 in C minor; March for the Royal Society of Musicians.
Adam Fischer (c). Austro-Hungarian Haydn Orchestra.
NIMBUS 5216 DDD 49:49

"This is the best Haydn series in 20 years....The best 93 ever was George Szell's, the best 95 Fritz Reiner's. Bernstein's 95 must also place ahead of this one. But Adam Fischer belongs in the exalted company of the best Haydn interpreters."
American Record Guide 53:75-6 S/O '90. Donald R. Vroon (280w)

Stereophile 13:207+ N '90. Mortimer H. Frank (b.n.)

"The music on this single disc is also available on the five-disc set containing all of Haydn's London symphonies....[which was reviewed in *Fanfare* 13:2]. I agree with Clark's judgments about these recordings made in the overly resonant Esterhazy Palace....That same resonance makes the big Finales rather exciting, but, listening elsewhere to Fischer, I miss something of Haydn's verve."
Fanfare 13:169-70 Jl/Ag '90. Michael Ullman (100w)

1186. Symphonies: No. 101 in D, "Clock"; No.103 in E flat, "Drum Roll".
Frans Bruggen (c). Eighteenth Century Orchestra. Netherlands. March, November 1987 live.
PHILIPS 422 240 DDD 60:00

✔**HC** ★★★*Awards:* Top Disks of the Year, *The New York Times* D 24, '89 (John Rockwell). *American Record Guide* Overview: Haydn, Mr/Ap '92.

"Easy motion, microscopically fine melodic articulation and beautifully graded rhythmic swing are Bruggen's keys to effective Haydn interpretation. Nor does all the polish detract from vitality...urgently recommended."
Fanfare 13:238-39 N/D '89. John Wiser (260w)

"This release has major shortcomings, but comprises one of the most communicative period-instrument presentations that I have heard and the most commanding performances that Frans Bruggen has recorded to date....Philips' sound is close, clear, and richly detailed."
Stereophile 12:209-10 N '89. Mortimer H. Frank (320w)

Digital Audio's CD Review 6:74 Mr '90. Lawrence Johnson (175w)

Gramophone 66:1153 Ja '89. Nicholas Anderson (445w)

HINDEMITH, PAUL

1187. Mathis der Maler (symphony); Concert Music for Strings and Brass, Opus 50; Der Schwanendreher, for Viola and Orchestra.
William Steinberg; Daniel Barenboim (c). Daniel Benyamini (vla). Boston Symphony Orchestra; Paris Orchestra. 1972, 1980 reissues.
DEUTSCHE GRAMMOPHON 423 241 ADD 70:00

"Both Steinberg performances with the BSO contrive to impose great tonal weight and considerable expansiveness upon their subjects, while nicely avoiding any sense of sluggishness."

Fanfare 12:93 My/Je '89. John Wiser (170w)

Gramophone 66:600+ O '88. Lionel Salter (305w)

1188. Nobilissima Visione (ballet suite) (1938); Concerto for Horn and Orchestra (1949); Konzertmusik, Opus 50; Symphony in B flat (1951).
Paul Hindemith (c). Dennis Brain (horn). Philharmonia Orchestra. 1956.
EMI 63373 ADD 73:00

✔HC

"All one can say of this lot is that Paul Hindemith knew what he wanted, and knew how to get the players of the Philharmonia Orchestra to give it to him. It could be documented in sound of greater body and impact, but hardly with greater clarity than EMI has restored to it. As documentation, this reissue is essential listening for anyone who takes an interest in twentieth-century music."

Fanfare 14:177-8 Jl/Ag '91. John Wiser (275w)

"Dennis Brain's classic 1956 account of the Horn Concerto, made just a few months before his untimely death in a car smash, is especially vivid even though the sound is slightly thinner than for the other works (recorded in 1959)."

High Fidelity 2:115 N '90. Andrew Stewart (110w)

P historic S historic

Hi-Fi News & Record Review 36:101 F '91. Christopher Breunig (b.n.)

Gramophone 68:1506 F '91. John Steane (460w)

HODKINSON, SYDNEY. Sinfonia Concertante (1980). See No. 1201.

HOLST, GUSTAV

1189. The Planets, Opus 32.
Adrian Boult (c). Geoffrey Mitchell Choir; London Philharmonic Orchestra. 1979 reissue.
EMI 69045 AAD 47:57

"This is *The Planets* to buy. Though a classic performance of an overworked warhorse, it shows that in the hands of a master like the late Sir Adrian Boult, even a warhorse can have something fresh to say."

Stereophile 11:161+ Mr '88. George Graves (600w)

"Boult is outstanding with *Mars, Mercury,* and *Jupiter*, less effective, but certainly competent on the other movements."

Fanfare 11:144-5 My/Je '88. James Miller (525w)

Gramophone 65:1959 My '88. Ivan March (185w)

1190. The Planets, Opus 32.
Charles Dutoit (c). Montreal Symphony Orchestra.
LONDON/DECCA 417 553 DDD 52:52

✔HC ★★★*Awards:* *Gramophone* Engineering and Production Award, 1987; *Fanfare* Want List 1987 (Michael Ullman); First Place Production and Engineering, and Third Place Orchestral Mumm Champagne Classical Music Award 1988—Presented by *Ovation, Ovation* N '88.

This work "has rarely sounded more entrancing than in this new version from Montreal. The color and vitality of all sections of this fine orchestra, as deployed by Dutoit and the London engineers, produce fascinating and valid new balances at many points."

Opus 4:35-6 D '87. Jon Alan Conrad (450w)

One of 20 classical CDs reviewed and recommended as "outstanding for their musical interest and their performance as well as for their technical quality."

Stereo Review Presents: Compact Disc Buyer's Guide 1988 p.40. William Livingstone and Christie Barter (125w)

"There are of course many recordings of Holst's great and popular piece of program music....Still I have heard none, including the Karajan on DG, that have the impact of this ravishing interpretation by Charles Dutoit. Stunningly recorded by London, its broad, smooth, spacious sound serves Dutoit well."

Fanfare 11:157 N/D '87. Michael Ullman (180w)

"Those who have been waiting need wait no longer: This stunningly recorded account is the *Planets* of choice."

High Fidelity 37:77 D '87. David Hurwitz (375w)

"This stunning recording ranks right up there with the Previn/Royal Philharmonic version on Telarc and the Davis/Toronto Symphony version on Angel."

Audio 71:146 D '87. John Eargle (310w)

"Another disappointing 'Planets', I'm afraid."

Hi-Fi News & Record Review 32:96 Je '87 Edward Seckerson (210w)

Gramophone 64:1412 Ap '87 Michael Kennedy (320w)

1191. The Planets, Opus 32.
Andre Previn (c). Royal Philharmonic Orchestra. Watford Town Hall, London. April 14-15, 1986.
TELARC 80133 DDD 50:57

★*Awards:* Editors' Choice, *Digital Audio*, 1988.

"This is as fine a recording of Holst' pleasant work as likely to be found....Astrologers, this is your disk!"

HighPerformanceReview 4:89 S '87. Thomas H. Wendel (60w)

"There are other CD versions of *The Planets*, but none to date as satisfying as this new Previn version....[In comparison with Haitink on Philips (LP and out of print)] Previn captures the Majesty—'Jupiter' is by far the most successful of the sections—but misses the Mysticism and Mystery."

Stereophile 10:179 Je '87 Tom Gillett (250w)

"I'd have to consider...[this] one the very best available—possibly the most desirable of all on CD, though I haven't heard every one in that medium. Of those I do know, Previn surpasses Davis in poetry in the more intimate moments, Karajan in rightness of color and balance, and Solti in almost every respect."

Opus 3:37-38 Ap '87 Jon Alan Conrad (525w)

"Before explaining why Previn falls short of himself in his new recording of *The Planets*, let me say that Telarc's sound for the most recent version of Holst's galactical glitz-fest is among the most sensational that has ever poured through my speakers."

Fanfare 10:125-6 Ja/F '87 Vincent Alfano (225w)

"If...you're content with an uneccentric and impeccably executed account of a score that is too often reduced to a garish spectacular, this new issue is vastly superior to the limp Andrew Davis recording recently released on Angel (DS-37362), especially given the exceptional quality of the engineering."

Ovation 8:35 Ap '87 Peter J. Rabinowitz (360w)

"If it comes to selecting one top choice, it's still [Previn] on EMI."

The $ensible Sound 9:60-1 Spring '88. John J. Puccio (250w)

Stereo Review Presents: Compact Disc Buyers' Guide p. 50 Spr '87 William Livingstone and Christie Barter (100w)

Music Journal p.73 Fall/Wint '86 Bert Wechsler (50w)

Stereo Review 52:146+ Ja '87 David Hall (225w)

Gramophone 64:868 D '86 Michael Kennedy (230w)

Digital Audio 4:76 N '87. Octavio Roca (280w)

Saint Paul's Suite. Oriental Suite (Beni Mora). See No. 1141.

Suites (2) for Band (1909, 1911). See No. 1162.

HONEGGER, ARTHUR

1192. Orchestral Music: Pacific 231 (Mouvement symphonique No. 1); Pastorale d'Ete; Rugby (Mouvement symphonique No. 2); Mouvement symphonique No. 3; Symphony No. 1.

Charles Dutoit (c). Bavarian Radio Symphony Orchestra.
ERATO 88171

✔HC ★★*Awards:* *Gramophone* Critics' Choice 1986 (Robert Layton). *Gramophone* Critics' Choice (Geoffrey Horn), 1987.

"These new performances have some strong assets in their favor, not least some of the most elegant playing that the Bavarian Radio Symphony Orchestra has ever been heard to produce. Dutoit is fastidious in achieving clarity and depth in the strings, very much the foundation of every symphony, but he does so at the expense of body....Tempos are good, pacing flexible and balance invariably superb. Not a bad exchange if one must make trade-offs, particularly in these very high-impact recordings."

Ovation 8:34 Mr '87 John D. Wiser (315w)

"This final installment in Dutoit's impressive and rewarding Honegger symphony cycle is characteristically distinguished."

Hi-Fi News & Record Review 31:119+ D '86 Andrew Keener (195w)

"The best modern versions of these three shorter works remain those by Jean Martinon for In Sync, but the Dutoit program is a must for every Honeggerian."

High Fidelity 37:82-83 Ja '87 R.D. Darrell (310w) (rev. of cassette)

"Perhaps the CD will reveal depths not apparent on this LP."

Fanfare 10:168-9 S/O '86 Royal S. Brown (335w) (rev. of LP)

"I had thought that the CD would perhaps alter my opinion somewhat, but this has not been the case. What the CD does, however is to considerably clarify Honegger's scoring, and this can only be considered a plus."

Fanfare 10:136 Mr/Ap '87 Royal S. Brown (210w)

Gramophone 64:868 D '86 Geoffrey Horn (90w)

Opus 3:40 F '87 John Canarina (690w)

1193. Symphony No. 2 for String Orchestra (with trumpet ad lib.); Symphony No. 3, "Liturgique".

Herbert Von Karajan (c). Berlin Philharmonic Orchestra. 1973 reissue.
dg 423 242 ADD 59:00

✔HC

"In many respects, these accounts stand alone: they tend to avoid the almost hysterical tone of Baudo's performances and are much more opulently recorded; yet they are tauter, better played, and more sensibly paced than their counterparts in Dutoit's recent and well-recorded cycle."

American Record Guide 51:40-1 N/D '88. Arved Ashby (325w)

"The power, perspectives and textural clarity set this recording apart as an object lesson in the art."

Hi-Fi News & Record Review 33:123 N '88. David Prakel (105w)

"Thoroughly recommendable."

High Fidelity 38:70-1 D '88. David Hurwitz (110w)

"These gripping performances from 1973 are my first choice for both works, although I will not cease to approve of the rawer-toned expositions once offered by Baudo and the Czech Philharmonic, which are not in the sonic running with DG's entry."

Fanfare 12:70+ N/D '88. John Wiser (115w)

"Although the Berlin Philharmonic under Karajan...makes these symphonies seem as lurid and emotional as film scores, they remain uneven works, their anguished lyricism and rhythmic urgency are marred by patches of banality and (in No. 2) a victorious affirmation that rings false."

The New York Times Ag 7 '88, p. H23+. K. Robert Schwarz (150w)

Gramophone 66:28 Je '88. Robert Layton (245w)

IBERT, JACQUES

1194. Escales (Ports of Call). RAVEL, MAURICE. Rapsodie Espagnole; Alborado del Gracioso; Pavane pour une Infante Defunte; La Valse; Le Tombeau de Couperin. (Mercury Living Presence).
Paul Paray (c). Detroit Symphony Orchestra. reissues.
MERCURY 432 003 ADD 67:38

★★*Awards:* The Want List 1991, *Fanfare* N/D '91 (George Chien). Critic's Choice: 1991, *American Record Guide*, Ja/F '92 (Mark Koldys).

"I cannot think of any Mercury Living Presence recordings more deserving of release on compact disc than these masterworks of French music, in performances that are not just definitive, but historic....And then, there's the sound-....the new format eliminates the distortion, noise,and inconvenience of the LP without losing one bit (no pun intended!) of the music. When a compact disc can reproduce these 30-year-old recordings with such impact and realism, one cannot deny that the LP vs CD debate is over."

American Record Guide 54:106 Mr/Ap '91. Mark Koldys (220w)

"Cool, disciplined playing....Nowadays there are warmer, more freely imaginative interpretations of greater appeal." *P85/75 S85/75*

Hi-Fi News & Record Review 36:107 Ja '91. Christopher Breunig (105w)

"Should you get this disc? Unless *Escales* is your favorite work here I would recommend against—you can do much better on the Ravel pieces even with reissues from the same period by munch, Ormandy, and Reiner."

American Record Guide 54:132 My/Je '91. John Landis (200w)

The Absolute Sound 15:146+ N/D '90. Arthur S. Pfeffer (120w)

Fanfare 14:112-17 Ja/F '91. Ron McDonald (260w)

Musical America 111:65-8 Mr '91. Terry Teachout (120w)

Digital Audio's CD Review 7:66 Ja '91. Lawrence B. Johnson

Gramophone 68:1830 Ap '91. John Steane (255w)

The New York Times S 30 '90, p. 28+ H. Richard Freed (b.n.)

IVES, CHARLES

1195. Orchestral Music: Country Band March; Set of Four Ragtime Dances; Postlude in F; Calcium Light Night; Yale-Princeton Football Game; Set for Theatre Orchestra; Largo Cantabile (hymn); Three Places in New England (First Orchestral Set).
James Sinclar; Kenneth Singleton (c). Christopher Oldfather (pno); Steven Thomas (cello). Orchestra New England.
KOCH 7025 DDD 55:00

★*Awards:* Honorable Mention, Records of the Year, 1991, *Stereo Review*, F '92.

"What comes through from the beginning to the end of this program is the zest, the passion, and the consummate musicianship that animate each and every performance. The Sprague Hall acoustics provide just the kind of bright yet intimate sound needed for this music. No matter how much recorded Ives has come your way before, do not on any account pass up this album."

Stereo Review 56:97 Ap '91. David Hall (475w)

"In new critical editions, we have several smaller works, the longest being *Three Places in New England* in the small orchestra arrangement. Only a few minutes each, the others are gems and very typical of Ives. He certainly could write Ragtime, for instance, as well as marches and hymns in his unique manner. The performances are all fun."

HighPerformanceReview 8(2):79 Summer '91. Bert Wechsler (b.n.)

"There is a whiff of the original-instruments movement about this disc: new interpretations of revised scores based on the latest scholarship, using a reduced orchestra....All goes well here: the reduced body of strings does allow everything to be heard clearly; winds and brass also play with plenty of gumption....Congratulations to all on a sparkling production."

Fanfare 14:245 Mr/Ap '91. James H. North (425w)

"Their Ives cannot be faulted....James Sinclair, who founded this orchestra in 1974 and still directs it, is one of the leading Ives scholars and executive director of the Charles Ives Society."

American Record Guide 54:58 Ja/F '91. Donald R. Vroon (180w)

"The playing of the chamber-sized Orchestra New England is sprightly and a little rough-and-ready—from what is known about Ives, it is the type of playing he preferred....The sound is perfectly adequate."

Musical America 111:77 Mr '91. Josiah Fisk (350w)

Gramophone 68:1506+ F '91. Peter Dickinson (635w)

Digital Audio's CD Review 7:72+ My '91. David Vernier (290w)

1196. Orchestral Music: Symphony No. 2; The Gong on the Hook and Ladder; Tone Roads—No. 1; A Set of Three Short Pieces: Largo Cantabile, Hymn, Hallowe'en; Central Park in the Dark; The Unanswered Question.

Leonard Bernstein (c). New York Philharmonic Orchestra. Avery Fisher Hall, New York. April 1987, November 1988 live.

DEUTSCHE GRAMMOPHON 429 220 DDD 68:00

✔HC ★★★*Awards:* Best Recordings of the Month, *Stereo Review* N '90; Critics' Choice 1990, *Gramophone* D '90 (Edward Seckerson); Critic's Choice: 1990, *American Record Guide* Ja/F '91 (Lee Milazzo); The Gramophone Awards, Nominations, Orchestral, *Gramophone,* N '91.

"This is a glorious disc."

Fanfare 14:219 Ja/F '91. James H. North (400w)

"Bernstein at his best."

High Fidelity 1:105 S '90. Andrew Stuart (105w)

"This wonderful amalgam of European symphonic tradition with olde Americana is the very subject of this amazingly successful symphony, a creative hodgepodge that never sounds like anything but a perfectly natural and ingratiating work of art....The CD comes with a classic and very perceptive Bernstein essay on the symphony. Even more important, it contains a classic and very perceptive, contemporary performance of this great 'old' symphony."

Stereo Review 55:131-2 N '90. Eric Salzman (615w)

"The Symphony, *Central Park* and *The Unanswered Question* are the quintessential Ives and have seldom been heard to greater advantage than here, where Bernstein is at his most persuasive, most devotional and most disciplined." *P95/100 S95*

Hi-Fi News & Record Review 35:95-6 N '90. Kenneth Dommett (350w)

"Bernstein's new Ives Second (recorded in concert, as usual for him these days) is a considerable improvement sonically and orchestrally over his previous effort...The interpretation has deepened a little as well....The shorter pieces are all well done."

American Record Guide 53:70 N/D '90. Stephen D. Chakwin, Jr. (265w)

"A great interpretation [of the Symphony]-....DG...delivers somewhat close-up (Bernstein grunts, groans, and wheezes throughout) but very believable, very vivid sound, if a bit cold-....it's one of the more easy, pleasurable jobs I've had as a reviewer to strongly recommend this generous CD as fitting closure and a return to roots for a quintessentially American conductor and composer and an unjustly neglected American masterpiece."

Stereophile 14:256-7 Ja '91. Richard Lehnert (870w)

"The new Deutsche Grammophon recording is quite nice in many ways. It features hearty sound, the expected directorial flamboyance, and firm playing, particularly in many of the individual wind and brass lines, which are especially prominent in the smaller-scaled works included on the disc. Yet, in spite of its many strengths, this release is not an improvement over the 1958 recording...it's still worth buying, if only for the secondary pieces, which are well played indeed."

Musical America 111:74-5 Ja '91. Josiah Fisk (410w)

Gramophone 68:366 Ag '90. Edward Seckerson (790w)

Wire 81:68 N '90. Graham Lock (175w)

1197. Symphony, "Holidays" (complete); The Unanswered Question; Central Park in the Dark.

Michael Tilson Thomas (c). Chicago Symphony Chorus; Chicago Symphony Orchestra.

CBS 42381 DDD 63:20

★*Awards:* Best Recordings of the Month, *Stereo Review* N '88.

"The music of Charles Ives is one of the things Michael Tilson Thomas does best....it is one of the best-sounding orchestral recordings yet to appear on this label."

Stereo Review 53:107-8 N '88. Richard Freed (400w)

"This is music to clean out your ears and run up your heart rate....stunningly recorded."

Stereo Review Presents: Compact Disc Buyer's Guide 1989 p.61 Richard Freed (105w)

"Thomas...dwells lovingly on the sentimental, and throws himself ecstatically into the melee, pulling his orchestra unresistingly along with him....Tilson Thomas manages to be more revealing than Bernstein, whose classic versions are obscured by opaque sound. Whether any

but the aficionado really wants the *Question* asked twice is another unanswered question."
Hi-Fi News & Record Review 34:106 Ja '89. Kenneth Dommett (340w)

"Thomas, employing newly published critical editions as the bases of his performances, is contributing yeoman service in the drive to appreciate Ives....The Chicago Symphony plays superbly....The recording is excellent....Kudos to CBS for this important and essential release."
Musical America 109:62-3 Mr '89. David Hurwitz (310w)

"Highly recommend for Ives fans or those seeking an introduction to this truly unique composer."
HighPerformanceReview 6:78-9 Mr '89. James Primosch (220w)

"The accuracy and tone of the Chicago Symphony are beyond praise, except, perhaps in *Central Park in the Dark*....On the other hand, Bernstein pulled an overwhelming amount of joy and brilliance out of the piece, some of which Thomas and the Chicagoans fail to recreate."
American Record Guide 52:59-60 Ja/F '89. Arved Ashby (570w)

"As Tilson Thomas matures as a conductor, his Ives grows progressively more civilized—to the point where these holidays exhibit more caution than celebration....*Central Park* gets the gutsiest reading on the disc—but even here, he corks the climax....Not recommended."
Fanfare 12:207 N/D '88. Peter J. Rabinowitz (300w)

"Rarely have I heard such a murky recording per se....Especially in this hellishly intricate music, the lack of crystalline transparency becomes a serious impediment."
High Fidelity 38:65 D '88. Paul Moor (350w)

Gramophone 66:605 O '88. Edward Seckerson (280w)

1198. Symphonies: No.'s 1 and 4 (including original hymn settings).
Michael Tilson Thomas (c). Chicago Symphony Orchestra. Medinah Temple.
SONY 44939 DDD 77:00

★*Awards:* Pick of the Month, North American Perspective (Christopher Pollard) *Gramophone* F '91. Best of the Month, *Hi-Fi News & Record Review*, Jl '91.

"I recommend this disc very strongly."
American Record Guide 54:69-70 Jl/Ag '91. David W. Moore (1050w)

"This 'critical edition' is the second large-scale attempt to piece together fragments left lying about unassorted...The performances one must take as definitive...Sound in both recordings is superior...With the Fourth especially, the acoustic is only limited by your reproducing equipment."
High Performance Review 8:75 Wtr '91/92. Bert Wechsler (long)

"It was once assumed that no conductor could handle such complexity [as is contained in the 4th] single-handed...Michael Tilson-Thomas, however, armed with the new edition, an excellent orchestra and chorus, and aided by recording of improbably clarity—it is nearly possible to pick one's way through the brawling climaxes—has succeeded beyond expectation in imposing some sort of order on the music and extracting from it a whiff of the transcendentalism the composer sought to distil." *P100 S95/100*
Hi-Fi News & Record Review 36:64 Jl '91. Kenneth Dommett (375w)

"Morton Gould conducted this same orchestra in the premiere recording of the First, which has remained the standard for twenty-five years. Thomas's Chicago Symphony is sweeter, more delicate, as if cleaning up the score has led to a cleaner performance....Both recordings are fine; the 1966 RCA LP from the post-shaded-dog era was virtually up to their best, but the new Sony disc is cleaner, sweeter, and better balanced....Now that Thomas's views of all four symphonies have been heard, a consistency of approach becomes apparent. He brings beauty and gentleness to the fore where we were used to more raucous excitement from Bernstein, Gould, and Stokowski. The more interpretations we hear, the more this music has to offer, which is a sign of its strength. Certainly Thomas will not be the last word on Ives's symphonies."
Fanfare 15:242-43 S/O '91. James H. North (long)

"If Medinah Temple does not provide the sharp aural focus needed for the Ives First Symphony, it is just about ideal for the separated groupings of the Fourth and for its massive climaxes."
Stereo Review 56:92+ Je '91. David Hall (320w)

Gramophone 68:1509 F '91. Peter Dickinson (840w)

Digital Audio's CD Review 7:72+ My '91. David Vernier (290w)

JANACEK, LEOS

1199. Sinfonietta. MARTINU, BOHUSLAV. Symphony No. 6, "Fantaisies Symphoniques". SUK, JOSEF. Fantasticke Scherzo, Opus 25.
Jiri Belohlavek (c). Czech Philharmonic Orchestra.
CHANDOS 8897 DDD 65:00

✔**HC** ★★★*Awards:* The Highs, 1990, *The New York Times* D 30 '90 (John Rockwell). The Want List 1991, *Fanfare* N/D '91 (John Bauman); Critics' Choice 1991, *Gramophone*, Ja '92 (Edward Seckerson).

"Czechs stand fast against the invader in the two most substantial works here, which offset each other to glorious effect....this is a reading to make more human sense than any other of Martinu's sad and lonely references, throughout the symphony, to the Dvorak *Requiem*; and in a Martinu centenary year which has seen not a single performance of a Martinu symphony in London, passionate pleadings like this (and Jarvi's on BIS) ought to put promoters to shame. Suk's *Fantastic Scherzo* makes a real charmer of a bonus." *P100 S100/85*

Hi-Fi News & Record Review 36:98 Ja '91. David Nice (480w)

"How much of the sound to be heard in this CD is the responsibility of the conductor, and how much is owed to the engineering, is difficult to estimate on short acquaintance, but one thing is certain: the Czech Philharmonic has never before sounded quite so elegant on record....If this is the quality of work we shall be getting from the Czech Philharmonic under its new director, and the quality also of recording under Chandos's exclusive arrangement, we're in for some gems. This one is strongly recommended."

Fanfare 14:269-70 Mr/Ap '91. John Wiser (510w)

"Readers of this journal may have noted previously my enthusiasm for the playing of the Czech Philharmonic, and this disc fully lives up to expectations, with the possible exception of one very vulgar trombone solo in the *Sinfonietta*. The recorded sound is superb in every respect...The only possible misgiving is in the choice of repertory."

American Record Guide 54:70 My/Je '91. John Landis (225w)

Gramophone 68:1375 Ja '91. Edward Seckerson (610w)

Sinfonietta (1926). See No. 1020.

Taras Bulba. See No. 1120.

JOSEPHS, WILFRED. Variations on a Theme of Beethoven. See No. 1201.

KODALY, ZOLTAN

1200. Concerto for Orchestra; Summer Night; Harry Janos: Suite.

Zoltan Kodaly; Ferenc Fricsay (c). Budapest Philharmonic Orchestra; Berlin Radio Symphony Orchestra. 1962, 1963 reissue.
DEUTSCHE GRAMMOPHON 427 408 ADD 67:00

✔HC ★*Awards:* Records to Die for: 1 of 5 Recommended Recordings, *Stereophile* Ja '91 (Bill Sommerwerck).

"The Kodaly performance of his own works (which has to be considered definitive) is almost startling in the focus and 'roundness' of its images....how often does one hear a recording with such a lifelike image?"

Stereophile 14:169 Ja '91. Bill Sommerwerck (b.n.)

"There are no outright bloopers here, but the orchestra sometimes sounds tentative, and the conductor's direction is more knowledgeable than inspiring....The considerable bonus, Fricsay's *Hary Janos*, shows up the other material. The sound (from only a year later) is much superior, as is the playing of the orchestra."

Fanfare 13:229-30 S/O '89. Leslie Gerber (275w)

Gramophone 66:1730 My '89. John Warrack (150w)

KORTE, KARL

1201. Symphony No. 3. HODKINSON, SYDNEY. Sinfonia Concertante (1980). JOSEPHS, WILFRED. Variations on a Theme of Beethoven.

Lawrence Leighton Smith; Gerhardt Zimmermann (c). Louisville Orchestra. 1985, 1986.
LOUISVILLE 001 AAD 65:20

★*Awards:* The Want List 1990, *Fanfare* N/D '90 (Stephen Ellis).

"What makes this CD indispensable: the Symphony No. 3 of Karl Korte (b. 1928)....If you know the recordings of Korte's fine Concerto for Piano and Winds or his piano trio, then you should suspect that the Third Symphony is a strong work constructed out of seemingly disparate influences: serial procedures, jazz, and some pop elements....There is plenty in Korte's Third Symphony to reward rehearings. Under Lawrence Leighton Smith, the mid- to late-1980s Louisville Orchestra has become a *major* U.S. orchestra. Their response and sensitivity to different modern styles is remarkable. The disc's sound is warm and full, balanced and honest."

Fanfare 13:174-75 Jl/Ag '90. Stephen Ellis (800w)

American Record Guide 53:125 Jl/Ag '90. Kyle Rothweiler (250w)

Digital Audio's CD Review 6:52 Jl '90. Peter Golub (295w)

LAMBERT, CONSTANT

1202. Horoscope: Suite. WALTON, WILLIAM. Facade: Suite. BLISS, ARTHUR. Checkmate (excerpts).

David Lloyd-Jones (c). English Northern Philharmonia Orchestra.
HYPERION 66436 DDD 74:14

✔HC ★★*Awards:* Best of the Month, *Hi-Fi News & Record Review*, F '91. The Gramophone Awards, Nominations, Orchestral, *Gramophone*, N '91; Critics' Choice 1991, *Gramophone*, Ja '92 (Ivan March).

"Devotees of British music...have been given a CD release which solidly advances the repertoire. Strongly recommended."

Fanfare 14:203-4 My/Je '91. John Wiser (550w)

"All three composers are magnificently served."
American Record Guide 54:135-6 My/Je '91. Richard E. Tiedman (585w)

High Fidelity 3:99 Mr '91. Andrew Stuart (b.n.)

Gramophone 68:1659 Mr '91. Ivan March (420w)

Lambert *P95 S95/100*, Walton *P95/100 S95* and Bliss *P95 (85) S95/85*
Hi-Fi News & Record Review 36:91 F '91. Andrew Achenbach (355w)

LANDOWSKI, MARCEL

1203. Symphonies: No. 1, "Jean de la Peur" (1949); No. 3, "Des Espaces" (1964); Symphony No. 4 (1988).
Georges Pretre (c). French National Orchestra.
ERATO 45018 DDD 66:36

★*Awards:* The Want List 1990, *Fanfare* N/D '90 (Stephen Ellis).

"In short—a super CD of challenging, rewarding listening....Pretre's [performance] shows a special control and insight that owners of the other versions will be glad to have, even if they acquire this CD primarily for the previously unrecorded Fourth Symphony."
Fanfare 13:182-83 Jl/Ag '90. Stephen Ellis (750w)

"At the conclusion of his Symphony 1 (1949), the full orchestra engages in several minutes of densely polyphonic ranting while the piccolo screams helplessly overhead; it is a stupendously horrifying finish. The problem is that this symphony is hopping mad all the way through, and so are the other two....Still, his strange, bitter music is far from negligible; structurally it is quite unorthodox, motivic and with a powerful rhythmic thrust....and it is superbly performed and recorded here."
American Record Guide 53:73 N/D '90. Kyle Rothweiler (230w)

Audio 75:108 Ap '91. Robert Long (255w)

Gramophone 68:50 Je '90. Arnold Whittall (355w)

LLOYD, GEORGE

1204. Symphony No. 4, "Arctic".
George Lloyd (c). Albany Symphony Orchestra.
ALBANY 002 DDD 65:00

★*Awards:* The Want List 1988, *Fanfare* N/D '88 (John Bauman).

"The musicians turn in an impassioned and beautifully played performance here, helped by the superb acoustics of the Troy Music Hall in which the warm, natural-sounding recording was made....In the main, this is brilliant playing, and a deeply convincing reading, vividly directed by the composer."
Fanfare 12:187-8 S/O '88. Henry Fogel (755w)

"As in the case of [Lloyd's Symphony] 11 on Conifer, the Albany Symphony acquits itself with a very high level of proficiency. Lloyd is evidently a persuasive interpreter of his own work...The recording is clear and realistic, made in the much praised Troy Savings Bank Music Hall."
American Record Guide 51:51 N/D '88. Carl Bauman (330w)

"The Albany Symphony plays beautifully in this composer-conducted account of the score, and the sound is splendid. There aren't many new avenues that conservative listeners can explore with greater confidence than this one."
Musical America 109:63 Mr '89. David Hurwitz (350w)

"Certain moments test the Albany SO under the veteran composer, but the performance has atmosphere and spirit."
The Musical Times 130:94 F '89. Robert Anderson (190w)

Gramophone 66:1153 Ja '89 (285w) (rev. of LP); 67:1332 Ja '90 (220w) (rev. of CD). Malcolm MacDonald

1205. Symphony No. 6; Symphony No. 10, "November Journeys; John Socman: Overture.
George Lloyd (c). BBC Philharmonic Brass; BBC Philharmonic Orchestra.
ALBANY 015 DDD 57:00

★*Awards:* Critics' Choice 1989, *Gramophone* D '89 (Malcolm MacDonald).

"Definitive...highly recommended."
American Record Guide 53:63-4 My/Je '90. Carl Bauman (200w)

"The three pieces on this disc range widely across Lloyd's repertoire....Conducted by the composer and played vigorously by the BBC Philharmonic Brass—the band for whom the piece was written—the *Tenth* could have no stronger execution than this....Overall...the sound is clean and spacious."
New Hi-Fi Sound 6:105 Ag '89. David Prakel (260w)

"Lloyd's [overture to the] opera *John Socman*-...is, as the composer describes it, short (just over five minutes) and light—attractive but, in the context of Lloyd's music that has become available, lightweight and conventional. The Sixth Symphony, a product of the locust years and undated, is also, rather surprisingly perhaps, light and romantic in tone...The tenth, on the other hand, is both impressive and grand." *P95 S95*
Hi-Fi News & Record Review 35:99 O '90. Kenneth Dommett (325w)

"All three performances are winningly conducted by the composer who is an extremely effective interpreter of his own work. The BBC Philharmonic clearly has a deep devotion for this man and his music, and they dig in to a degree quite uncommon in performances of new scores. The occasional thin string sound or slightly tentative brass entrance are minor blemishes on excellent achievements. Albany's sound quality is rich and warm, at no sacrifice of clarity."

Fanfare 13:267-68 N/D '89. Henry Fogel (650w)

1206. Symphony No. 7.
George Lloyd (c). BBC Philharmonic Orchestra.
CONIFER 143 50:13

★★*Awards:* The Want List 1988, *Fanfare* N/D '88 (John Bauman). The Want List 1987, *Fanfare* N/D '88 (Henry Fogel).

"Over 30 years after its conception, George Lloyd's 7th Symphony has eventually found its way onto disc and, thankfully, has been blessed with a superb performance and recording."

Hi-Fi News & Record Review 32:117 N '87 Doug Hammond (280w)

"The BBC Symphony, as expected, plays very well."

American Record Guide 51:52-3 Mr/Ap '88. Carl Bauman (300w)

Fanfare 10:152-3 My/Je '87 James Miller (350w)

Gramophone 64:1126 F '87 Malcolm MacDonald (375w) (rev. of LP)

1207. Symphony No. 11.
George Lloyd (c). Albany Symphony Orchestra. 1986.
CONIFER 144 DDD 59:00

★★*Awards:* The Want List 1988, *Fanfare* N/D '88 (John Bauman). *Gramophone* Critics' Choice (Malcolm Macdonald), 1987.

"The Albany Symphony plays beautifully, we need make no allowances for them at all; and the deep but detailed recording was made at the Troy Music Hall, a place you've probably never heard of, but many musicians who've played there smile with pleasure at the memory—I've heard people not given to hyperbole call it one of the great concert halls in the United States."

Fanfare 11:230-1 S/O '87. James Miller (600w)

Digital Audio 4:66 N '87; 5:106 Je '89. Wayne Green (200w)

American Record Guide 51:52-3 Mr/Ap '88. Carl Bauman (300w)

LUTOSLAWSKI, WITOLD

1208. Concerto for Orchestra. RESPIGHI, OTTORINO. Feste Romane. STRAUSS, RICHARD. Don Juan, Opus 20.
(Bravura).
James De Priest (c). Oregon Symphony Orchestra. May 1987.
DELOS 3070 DDD 70:24

★★*Awards:* The Super Compact Disk List, *The Absolute Sound*, Ap '92 (Harry Pearson). Cream of the Crop IV, *Digital Audio's CD Review*, 6:42 Je '90.

"Although conductor James De Priest provides a fine idiomatic performance of 'Don Juan', whose famous French horn theme soars resonantly in the hall, it is the musical and sonic values of the Respighi and Lutoslawski pieces that merit special accolades....De Priest must be reckoned as a formidable conductor....His incandescent leadership and John Eargle's spectacular engineering blaze new trails in the musical and sonic firmament."

Audio 72:96 Ap '88. Bert Whyte (575w)

"James DePriest and his Oregonians have made an auspicious beginning with this release."

HighPerformanceReview 5:87 Ap '88. John Mueter (380w)

"This is a very well-planned, well-played, well-conducted, and especially well-recorded debut by the Oregon Symphony."

High Fidelity 38:64 F '88. David Hurwitz (250w)

"The Oregon Symphony's first commercial recording is a triumph for all involved."

Ovation 8:19 Ja '88. Paul Turok (450w)

Digital Audio's CD Review 6:78+ D '89. Tom Vernier (320w)

"DePriest...conducts the work to the manor born, and not a little unlike the old maestro himself. It's a first-rate interpretation, though without some of the moonlight and mystery of the Maazel/Cleveland collaboration...Nevertheless, DePriest and his men have fun with this, and the recording is eye-popping, especially at the bottom end of the frequency range....if you want to know what a gifted engineer can do with an intransigent digital technology—even several seasons ago—here is proof that the mind of the engineer is more potent than the sword of his technology."

The Absolute Sound 17:120 Ap '92. Harry Pearson (long)

"This is a recording which is perfectly decent in its modest way....De Priest doesn't seem to have much to say about these pieces."

American Record Guide 51:56-7 My/Je '88. Stephen D. Chakwin, Jr. (380w)

"The musicians have been stabbed in the back by producers from Flatland, who seem to have decided that orchestral sounds exist only in the plane of the proscenium."

Opus 4:53 Ap '88. Andrew Stiller (190w)

1209. Symphony No. 3; Les Espaces du Sommeil, for Baritone and Orchestra. MESSIAEN, OLIVIER. Turangalila-symphonie.
Esa-Pekka Salonen (c). John Shirley-Quirk (bar). Philharmonia Orchestra; Los Angeles Philharmonic Orchestra. August, 19.
CBS 42271 DDD 124:38 2 discs

★★★★★*Awards: Opus* Contemporary Music Award, 1987; *Gramophone* Critics' Choice (Arnold Whittall), 1987; Perfect 10/10, *Digital Audio*, Mr '88. Classical Hall of Fame, *Fanfare*, S/O '91. *Fanfare* Want List 1986 (Paul Snook).

"All told, this is a highly recommended disc, especially for contemporary-music enthusiasts."
Stereo Review 51:119 Ag '86. David Hall (350w)

"Everyone connected with this recording seems to have done a superlative job....Much of the credit must go to the newly fledged Finnish conductor Esa-Pekka Salonen, who has taken the trouble to really get under the skin of these new works, and has the talent to fully communicate both sweep and detail to his orchestra....If you care at all about contemporary music, this record belongs in your collection."
Opus 2:42-43 O '86 Andrew Stiller (1110w) (rev. of LP)

"Every so often, an ambitious recording project comes out completely and utterly right-....Somebody up there really loves Messiaen and Lutoslawski, and I expect the much-talked-about young conductor Esa-Pekka Salonen is it. It is unlikely that these performances will be superseded anytime soon....The Lutoslawski pieces make wonderful companions to (and, on CD, disc-mates with) the Messiaen."
Ovation 8:38 F '87 David Patrick Stearns (1170w)

"Salonen has taken *Turangalila*'s measure *most* convincingly, and the Philharmonic plays it as well, it seems to me, as an orchestra can. Bud Graham's engineering wants special mention for its detail and clout...The two Lutoslawski works are very good and appropriate fillers."
Fanfare 15:473 S/O '91. Mike Silverton (med)

"In short, no one approaching this exciting composition through Salonen's record should be disappointed."
American Record Guide 50:40-1 My/Je '87 Ashby (1000w)

High Fidelity 37:64 Je '87 K. Robert Schwarz (350w)

Gramophone 65:45 Je '87 Arnold Whittall (140w)

Digital Audio & Compact Disc Review 107:87-88 Je '87 Roland Graeme (850w)

Audio 70:92+ Ag '86. Edward Tatnall Canby (630w)

Gramophone 64:550 O '86 Arnold Whittall (235w) (rev. of CD)

MAHLER, GUSTAV

1210. Symphonies (complete): No's. 1-9 and Symphony No. 10—Adagio; Das Lied von der Erde.
Eliahu Inbal (c). Helen Donath (sop); Faye Robinson (sop); Teresa Cahill (sop); Hildegard Heichele (sop); Jard Van Nes (alto); Doris Soffel (alto); Livia Budai (alto); Jane Henschel (alto); Peter Schreier (ten); Kenneth Riegel (ten); Hermann Prey (bar); Harald Stamm (bass); North German Radio Chorus; Dale Warland Singers; Limburger Domsingknaben; Frankfurt Kantorei Women's Chorus; Bavarian Radio Chorus; Sudfunkchor; West German Radio Chorus; Berlin RIAS Chamber Choir; Hessian Radio Children's Chorus. Frankfurt Radio Symphony Orchestra.
DENON/SUPRAPHON 2589/604 DDD 771:00 16 discs

★*Awards:* Top Choices—1989, *American Record Guide* Ja/F '90 (Gerald Fox).

"Inbal certainly was a dark horse among Mahler conductors until these records were issued. They prove him to be an outstanding interpreter. On the whole, his set is better than most other integral versions and as good as the best-....Our editor has directed me to include only summaries of those recordings already reviewed in *ARG*, an exquisite torture for me because I have much to say about each one."
American Record Guide 52:55-8 Jl/Ag '89. Gerald S. Fox (900w)

"Summing up briefly: this is the best, as well as the most important, set of the Mahler symphonies since Bernstein/CBS. If you intend to collect multiple performances, this set makes a good starting point or cornerstone, especially if it comes at a reduced price. My choices for single performances: 1—Inbal or Litton. 2—Bernstein/CBS, Kaplan or Bernstein/DG. 3—Bernstein, Horenstein or Haitink. 4—Szell, Inball or Bernstein/DG. 5—Inbal, Levine or Solti. 6—Bernstein or Inbal. 7—Bernstein/CBS, Inbal or Bernstein/DG. 8—Bernstein, Solti or Tennstedt. *Das Lied*—King/Fischer-Dieskau, Bernstein; van Nes/Schreier/Inbal; or Fassbaender/Araiza/Giulini. 9—Bernstein/DG or Horenstein. 10 (Cooke version)—Chailly, Levine or Rattle."
Fanfare 12:174-78 Jl/Ag '89. Ben Pernick (2500w)

1211. Symphony No. 1 in D.
Leonard Bernstein (c). Concertgebouw Orchestra. Concertgebouw, Amsterdam. October 1987 live.
DEUTSCHE GRAMMOPHON 427 303 DDD 56:00

✔HC ★★*Awards:* Critics' Choice 1989, *Gramophone* D '89 (Edward Seckerson). Critics Choice, *Hi Fi News & Record Review*, Ap '91 Supplement (Antony Hodgson).

"The great orchestra is in top form, the sound rich and well focused. In sum, a distinguished addition to the discographies of both Bernstein and Mahler."
Stereo Review 54:145 S '89. Richard Freed (280w)

"A great First. One of the best. Highly recommended."
Fanfare 13:240-41 S/O '89. Ben Pernick (285w)

"Whereas Bernstein's earlier version of the First, for CBS, featured agogics that distorted the musical line, here everything breathes naturally....Surely this is what Mahler had in mind when he spoke of a continuously flexible pulse. The Concertgebouw Orchestra plays magnificently; especially fine are the incomparable winds in the first movement."

Musical America 110:77-8 Mr '90. David Hurwitz (250w)

"This is a performance that grows in stature as it progresses. Even if you have a version of the symphony already, this is one to consider."

Music and Musicians International 37:22 Je '89. Simon Cargill (600w)

"This is Bernstein's second account of the work on CD, and...This time he is more expansive than ever, yet he maintains a power and authority that seem absolutely right in all but the very opening sequence." *P85 S80*

The $ensible Sound 12:67 Summ '91. John J. Puccio (brief)

"Bernstein frequently shifts tempos or momentarily holds back without the least justification in the score....Others have also indulged in this manufactured shift in tempo markings, but to less positive effect. For Bernstein does turn in a very exciting and heroic performance notwithstanding....bass response is fuzzy and balances (particularly in brass) are uneven."

American Record Guide 52:58-9 Jl/Ag '89. Lewis M. Smoley (950w)

"Not by any means...the clear recommendation one had hoped for. Haitink for more immaculate playing; Horenstein for his idiomatic but severe reading (mid-price); Bernstein for possessiveness, insights, and the unacceptably gross."

Hi-Fi News & Record Review 34:109 Ap '89. Christopher Breunig (540w)

"One wonders if the virtuosity is misplaced: whether this youthful music is probed too deeply....My first recommendation for a Mahler 1 is the Litton."

Stereophile 12:210-11 N '89. Kevin Conklin (315w)

Gramophone 66:1428 Mr '89. Edward Seckerson (665w)

Digital Audio's CD Review 6:66 D '89. Lawrence Johnson (175w)

1212. Symphony No. 1 in D.

Christoph von Dohnanyi (c). Cleveland Orchestra. LONDON/DECCA 425 718 DDD 55:00

★*Awards:* Best Recordings of the Month, *Stereo Review* N '90.

"Those who have tired of the usual blockbuster approach to Mahler's First Symphony may find the antidote in the fascinating new recording by Christoph von Dohnanyi and the Cleveland Orchestra. Clarity of line, dynamic refinement, and elicitation of the work's poetic element get top priority in this performance, and for me the whole listening experience was remarkably refreshing....The recording itself is so clean and so beautifully shaded dynamically that you could almost copy out the score from hearing it."

Stereo Review 55:136 N '90. David Hall (320w)

"This performance of Mahler's First Symphony must be somewhat unique in having stripped the score of every vulgarity, the orchestration of every wild hyperbole, and the music of every unsettling, contradictory emotion....Mahler's symphonies can be so much a visceral experience that I am left perplexed when, as here, I find this dimension absent, when the only warmth is electronic and not spiritual, when even the ugly and awkward are fine tuned and smoothed away, and when all sense of a child's wonder amid menacing shadows has been replaced with stylish elegance."

Fanfare 14:261 N/D '90. Jon Tuska (310w)

"Dohnanyi elicits a superb orchestral performance of this most frequently recorded of Mahler's symphonies, highlighting the Cleveland Orchestra's renown for highly-polished technique and warm, legato string sound. But-....this performance lacks in enthusiasm, spirit, and dramatic effect whatever it offers in proficiency."

American Record Guide 54:62-3 Ja/F '91. Lewis M. Smoley (340w)

"In his search for 'correct' dynamics and 'correct' tempi, he seems to have lost the wood for the trees. The first movement development proceeds in fits, starts and uneasy warmings to life; the strings' hysteria in the finale is too self-conscious to be believed." *P75 S85/75*

Hi-Fi News & Record Review 35:85 S '90. David Nice (210w)

Gramophone 68:212+ Jl '90. Edward Seckerson (365w)

1213. Symphony No. 2 in C minor for Soprano, Mezzo and Orchestra, "Resurrection".

Leonard Bernstein (c). Barbara Hendricks (sop); Christa Ludwig (mez). Westminster Choir; New York Philharmonic Orchestra. Avery Fisher Hall, New York. April 1987 live.
DEUTSCHE GRAMMOPHON 423 395 DDD 94:00 2 discs

★★*Awards:* Best of the Year, *Opera News* D 24 '88; Best Recordings of the Month, *Stereo Review* D '88.

"I am so deeply moved by this performance and so favorably impressed by the production which DG has given it, that I have no conpunction in declaring it to be definitive in a way which is unlikely to bear substantial competition at any time in the foreseeable future."

Stereophile 11:165+ N '88. Richard Schneider (1290w)

"Bernstein's new recordings are classics, moments frozen in time that surely would require a lifetime of listening to savor completely."

Ovation 9:52 D '88. Lawrence B. Johnson (230w)

"This may be the lengthiest *Resurrection* ever preserved for posterity, but such is Bernstein's control of tension and momentum that it never sounds slow. Moreover, the Westminster Choir, Barbara Hendricks, Christa Ludwig, and above all the New York Philharmonic give Bernstein the all-out support his interpretation requires....Here at last is a recording of the Second Symphony that deserves the term 'definitive'."

High Fidelity 39:62-3 Ja '89. David Hurwitz (310w)

"The basic shape of Bernstein's dramatic conception remains more intact than it does in his new Fifth and Ninth. Where this Second excels over its predecessors is in the sheer quality of the orchestral playing....an easy first choice for anyone seeking an up-to-date 'Resurrection'."

Fanfare 12:198-99 Ja/F '89. Peter J. Rabinowitz (470w)

"Bernstein's new recording...is in much the same idiosyncratically expansive vein as his fabled second recording of the work....The major advantages of the remake...are first-rate sound and good balances throughout."

Stereo Review 53:114 D '88. David Hall (425w)

"This is Bernstein's third complete recording-...though the engineering is not outstanding, the sound is far superior to both earlier efforts. I wish I could say the same for the performance....my less-than-enthusiastic remarks are in relation only to the highest standards, which are also Bernstein's own. Conducted by anyone else, this would be considered an outstanding interpretation."

American Record Guide 51:52-4 N/D '88. Gerald S. Fox (530w)

1214. Symphony No. 2 in C minor for Soprano, Mezzo and Orchestra, "Resurrection".

Simon Rattle (c). Arleen Auger (sop); Janet Baker (sop). City of Birmingham Symphony Orchestra Chorus; City of Birmingham Symphony Orchestra.
EMI 47962 DDD 86:00 2 discs

✔HC ★★★★*Awards:* *Gramophone* Critics' Choice (Michael Kennedy), 1987; *Stereo Review* Best Recordings of the Month Je '88; Orchestral Record Award 1988, *Gramophone* O '88; Engineering and Production Record Award 1988, *Gramophone* O '88.

"I'm not going to pretend that you get from Rattle the burning emotional statement of a Tennstedt or Bernstein. Nor do you get the lifetime's experience of a Bruno Walter. What you do get, however, is something scrupulously prepared, unfailingly musical, and just now and again, pretty startling."

Hi-Fi News & Record Review 32:117 N '87 Edward Seckerson (650w) (rev. of LP)

"It needs a conductor who recognizes (and revels in) its lack of discretion....Rattle offers any number of gorgeous illuminations...But I don't think it's unfair to say that the music's histrionic side is often held in check....In the end, then, this recording inspires deep respect—which, for me, simply isn't enough."

Fanfare 11:158-9 My/Je '88. Peter J. Rabinowitz (650w)

"This CD suggests that EMI is slowly getting its digital act together....the CBSO and Chorus-...play with delicacy and balance...this CBSO recording convinces me that he [Rattle] is the first conductor since Bernstein to *earn* the right to conduct a full Mahler cycle."

Stereophile 11:169+ Je '88. Kevin Conklin (1060w)

Rattle "opts for a predominantly lyrical treatment...Janet Baker makes a major contribution with her rapt rendering of the *Urlicht* solo in the fourth movement...The choral forces acquit themselves superbly."

Stereo Review 53:114 Je '88. David Hall (350w)

"Simon Rattle's recording succeeds because, as he has proved in earlier recordings, he resonates to Mahler's emotional vibrations and is not inhibited about conveying them. However, he ignores many of Mahler's details and instructions and misinterprets others...which compromises the performance enough to keep it from the first rank. It is a tribute to Rattle that, despite these shortcomings, it is quite compelling!"

American Record Guide 51:52-4 N/D '88. Gerald S. Fox (530w)

"Rattle's account of the Second is so bad that it's practically a joke."

High Fidelity 38:63-4 Jl '88. David Hurwitz (600w)

Gramophone 65:583 O '87 (585w) (rev. of LP); 65:944 D '87 (275w); 66:550 O '88 (rev. of CD) (200w) Michael Kennedy; 66:553 O '88 John Borwick (200w) (rev. of CD)

1215. Symphony No. 3 in D minor for Mezzo-Soprano and Orchestra; Songs from Ruckert (5).

Leonard Bernstein (c). Martha Lipton (sop). New York Philharmonic Orchestra; Schola Cantorum Boys' Chorus.
CBS 42196

★★*Awards:* *Fanfare* Want List 1987 (Peter J. Rabinowitz). *American Record Guide* Overview: Mahler, Jl/Ag '88.

"For those who want the whole set by a single conductor, then, this [cycle] remains the clear first choice; and for those who want to pick and choose, a no-compromise, all-CD cycle can at least be put together. Obviously with Sinopoli's cycle and Bernstein's second both getting started on DG, any recommendations are subject to revision; still, my current choices

would be as follows: No. 1: Abbado; No. 2: Slatkin; No. 3: Bernstein; No. 4: Mengelberg (or Bernstein if you insist on stereo); No. 5: sinopoli; No. 8: Bernstein; Das Lied: Giulini; No. 9: Bernstein; No. 10 (complete): Levine."
Fanfare 10:169-71 N/D '86 Peter J. Rabinowitz (1600w)

Reviews of Bernstein's Mahler cycle.
—*Gramophone* 64:868+ D '86 Richard Osborne (1270w)
—*Ovation* 7:29-30 Ja '87 Lawrence B. Johnson (570w)

1216. Symphony No. 4 in G.
Leonard Bernstein (c). Helmut Wittek (boy sop). Concertgebouw Orchestra. Concertgebouw, Amsterdam. June 1987 live.
DEUTSCHE GRAMMOPHON 423 607 DDD
57:00 2 discs

★*Awards:* Critics' Choice 1988, *Gramophone* D '88 (Richard Osborne).

"His new Concertgebouw Fourth is among the best in a crowded catalog, positive and ebullient where the NYPO was straightjacketed. It compares favorably with Mengelberg's recently reissued 1939 reading with the same orchestra....On sound, there's good news."
Stereophile 12:157-61 F '89. Kevin Conklin (500w)

"He has added some retrograde ideas, but, for the most part, his conducting represents a more reasoned and mature approach with less extrovert eccentricities....The playing he elicits from the Concertgebouw is simply magical....This is probably one of the best DG recordings in years."
Audio 73:163-64 Ja '89. Bert Whyte (315w)

"For me, the tone of the boy soprano brings Mahler's delicate orchestral imagery even more vividly to life."
High Fidelity 39:62-3 Ja '89. David Hurwitz (310w)

"The most salient feature of Bernstein's new Fourth is his decision to use a boy soprano-....this choice of soloist makes most other readings seem arch and artificial....But not even the exceptionally well-characterized playing by the Concertgebouw...can turn this into one of Bernstein's more revelatory performances."
Fanfare 12:198-99 Ja/F '89. Peter J. Rabinowitz (470w)

"The finale has a childlike charm, but it doesn't have the beauty of Kathleen Battle, who alone would make Maazel's recording worth hearing. Bernstein's soloist, Helmut Wittek, is truly refreshing, however....A triumph...and a high point thus far of a cycle that has had several."
HighPerformanceReview 6:81 Mr '89. Kenneth Krehbiel (220w)

"Except for the miscalculation, in my view, of using a boy soprano instead of a female singer in the finale...the most successful in his Mahler cycle for Deutsche Grammophon." *P90 S90*
Stereo Review 54:144 O '89. David Hall (145w)

"It is most unfortunate that Maestro Bernstein did not provide us with details of his interpretive vision here. For this reading is both extremely different from his earlier approach (reissued on CD - CBS 42197) and quite often at odds with its competition....But for a very different and most provocative reading, Bernstein's latest effort is well worth the price."
American Record Guide 51:56-8 N/D '88. Lewis M. Smoley (1080w)

"It may be only in the immediate comparison with the Second and Fifth that Bernstein's achievement seems a fraction less compelling."
Ovation 9:52 D '88. Lawrence B. Johnson (230w)

Gramophone 66:286 Ag '88. Richard Osborne (820w)

1217. Symphony No. 4 in G for Soprano and Orchestra.
Bernard Haitink (c). Roberta Alexander (sop). Concertgebouw Orchestra. Concertgebouw, Amsterdam.
PHILIPS 412 119 55:19

✔HC ★*Awards:* *Stereo Review* Best of the Month, Je '85.

"Warmth and a fine sense of flow characterize Haitink's new reading, and the sonics...are rich and transparent almost to a fault....Of special interest...is the contribution of the gifted American soprano Roberta Alexander."
Stereo Review 50:75 Je '85. David Hall (350w)

"The most introspective and dreamlike landscape of all" the Fourths now on CD.
The $ensible Sound 8:56 Fall '86 John J. Puccio (65w)

"A superbly idiomatic reading....Alexander sings without mannerism."
HighPerformanceReview 4(1):165-6 '86 Thomas H. Wendel (480w)

"Lovely."
Hi-Fi News & Record Review 30:82 Jl '85. Andrew Keener (100w)

"Haitink seems not only to be brisker in fettle but temperamentally perkier than one found in his digital remake of Symphony No.7 some 10 months earlier. There's a *lot* of character in his interpretation...The orchestra plays with an authority born of long advocacy...When all's been heard and weighed, though, I find myself drawn all over again to Abbado's CD version."
Fanfare 8:159-60 My/Je '85. Roger Dettmer (700w)

Audio 70:109 Jl '86. Bert Whyte (210w)

Gramophone 62:1069 Mr '85. Richard Osborne (245w)

1218. Symphony No. 4 in G, for Soprano and Orchestra; Songs of a Wayfarer.
George Szell (c). Judith Raskin (sop). Cleveland Orchestra.
SONY 46535 ADD

✔HC

1219. Symphony No. 5 in C# minor.
Leonard Bernstein (c). Vienna Philharmonic Orchestra. Alte Oper, Frankfurt. September 1987.
DEUTSCHE GRAMMOPHON 423 608 DDD 75:00

★★*Awards:* The Want List 1989, *Fanfare* N/D '89 (Henry Fogel); The Want List 1989, *Fanfare* N/D '89 (Peter J. Rabinowitz).

"Very impressive it sounds, the handsome mahogany-clad surfaces of the hall doing wonderful things for an orchestra that—let's face it—doesn't need too much flattery....Listening has been a privilege."
Hi-Fi News & Record Review 33:111 N '88. Edward Seckerson (340w)

"Bernstein's new recordings are classics, moments frozen in time that surely would require a lifetime of listening to savor completely."
Ovation 9:52 D '88. Lawrence B. Johnson (230w)

"Having his latest thoughts on the Fifth so eloquently committed to disc is like finding a chapter that has long been missing from a great novel."
High Fidelity 39:61-3 Ja '89. David Hurwitz (310w)

"Once again Bernstein proves himself to be Mahler's greatest living interpreter....This is a great performance. No matter how many versions you have, it is worth acquiring."
American Record Guide 52:63-4 Ja/F '89. Lewis M. Smoley (750w)

"Bernstein's Fifth establishes itself immediately as a statement of significance....On sound, there's good news....I would certainly place this new Fifth as the best of Bernstein's new cycle, with the Fourth not far behind."
Stereophile 12:157-61 F '89. Kevin Conklin (250w)

"In sum, this is probably not a good introduction to the score; but if you've lived long with the music, it will reveal a mean streak that you probably haven't heard before. The sound is a bit thick and congested, but that's hardly enough to obscure the quality of the performance."
Fanfare 12:198-99 Ja/F '89. Peter J. Rabinowitz (470w)

Gramophone 66:286 Ag '88. Michael Kennedy (335w)

1220. Symphony No. 5 in C# minor.
Eliahu Inbal (c). Frankfurt Radio Symphony Orchestra.
DENON/SUPRAPHON 1088 DDD 72:42

★*Awards:* Records to Die for: 1 of 5 Recommended Recordings, *Stereophile* Ja '91 (Gary A. Galo).

"There is - and I say this with confidence - no more illuminating or satisfying account of this score on record or Compact Disc."
Hi-Fi News and Record Review 32:95-6 Jl '87 Edward Seckerson (310w)

"Make no mistake about it; both as a performance and as a recording, this Denon release can stand with any in the catalog....This is definitely off-limits for those who like their Mahler logical and detached: from the agonizingly slow and uncompromisingly brutal account of the first movement to the crushing chorale statement near the end of the finale, this reading makes the most of Mahler's emotional intensifiers....Highest recommendation."
Fanfare 10:155-6 Mr/Ap '87 Peter J. Rabinowitz (515w)

"Of currently available performances on CD, the Inbal is my first recommendation by a comfortable margin."
American Record Guide 50:43-44 Ja/F '87 Stephen D. Chakwin, Jr. (750w)

"Inbal makes structural sense out of these difficult works, a refreshing contrast to Bernstein's 'climax every five minutes' approach....the sound is spacious and natural, with excellent accuracy of individual instrumental timbres. Probably the best recorded Mahler Fifth."
Stereophile 14:137 Ja '91. Gary A. Galo (b.n.)

"In sum, it is the *angst*, the demonic qualities, and the ecstatic elements of Mahler's vision that are missing from Inbal's sane and prettified reading. Without those elements, the essence of Mahler is gone. The advice here is to turn elsewhere for satisfaction in Mahler's Fifth."
Fanfare 10:155-6 Mr/Ap '87 Henry Fogel (515w)

"Inbal's reading seems distracted, his attention unfocused, the symphony undigested. Problematic and eccentric as were his readings of the first four symphonies, they at least all had unified visions; not so here. Not recommended."
Stereophile 10:153+ N '87. Richard Lehnert (720w)

Gramophone 64:1017 Ja '87 Michael Kennedy (210w)

1221. Symphony No. 5 in C# minor; Symphony No. 10 (Adagio).
James Levine (c). Philadelphia Orchestra.
RCA 2905 2 discs

★★*Awards: American Record Guide* Overview: Mahler, Jl/Ag '88. *Gramophone* Critics' Choice 1985 (Michael Kennedy).

Gramophone 63:236 Ag '85. Michael Kennedy (420w) (rev. of LP)

1222. Symphony No. 5 in C# minor.

James Levine (c). Philadelphia Orchestra.
RCA 5453

★*Awards: American Record Guide* Overview: Mahler Symphonies, Jl/Ag '88.

"Not only does it surpass his Seventh Symphony with the Chicago Symphony, it betters all of the Mahler Fifths since Karajan's Berlin surprise for DG, and that one too in the last two movements. RCA's transfer level is subdued, however; I can't even guess why but it is."

Fanfare 9:199-200 N/D '85. Roger Dettmer (300w)

1223. Symphony No. 5 in C# minor.
Giuseppe Sinopoli (c). Philharmonia Orchestra.
DEUTSCHE GRAMMOPHON 415 476

★★*Awards: Fanfare* Want List 1986 (Peter J. Rabinowitz); *Gramophone* Critics' Choice 1986 (Geoffrey Horn).

"While four of its predecessors are formidable realizations by Karajan, Levine, Solti, and Tennstedt, to my ears Sinopoli and the remarkable Philadelphia Orchestra go right to the top of the heap....My only criticism of this marvelous performance, in fact, is of the conductor's vocal embellishments (which again recall Toscanini). The recorded sound is spectacular."

Stereo Review 51:70+ Ap '86. David Hall (450w)

"If the rest of Sinopoli's series can maintain the standards of this first installment, it may well stand as the first Mahler cycle to pose a real challenge to Bernstein's."

Fanfare 9:179-80 My/Je '86. Peter J. Rabinowitz (560w)

"At thirty-nine, he is the strongest personality among the younger generation of conductors (next to him, I would place only Simon Rattle),and if his performances at times unleash strong controversy, it is because they do not hesitate to overthrow obsolete traditions in order to take a fresh view of scores on which routine performances have allowed the dust to settle....as a whole, this stands out as the most recommendable Mahler Fifth available at the moment, superior to those by Herbert von Karajan, Georg Solti, and Klaus Tennstedt (to name the leading contenders on Compact Disc). I only hope CBS Masterworks will release the Bruno Walter performance on CD."

High Fidelity 36:68-9 Je '86. Harry Halbreich (450w)

Gramophone 63:916+ Ja '86. Geoffrey Horn (400w)

1224. Symphony No. 5 in C# minor.
Klaus Tennstedt (c). London Philharmonic Orchestra. Royal Festival Hall, London. December 13, 1988 live.
EMI 49888 DDD 73:00

★*Awards:* The Want List 1990, *Fanfare* N/D '90 (Benjamin Pernick).

"The febrile excitement and emotional atmosphere of his reading are such that I found myself unable to break from the recording, even to pause momentarily to take notes for this review...The playing of the London Philharmonic is brilliant, especially since this is a concert performance and the recording evidently was not corrected by splicing in passages or notes from a later studio session...The recording, though very good, and even better than Tennstedt's earlier effort, *is* a little dry—a characteristic of its venue, London's Royal Festival Hall....this gripping new Tennstedt goes to the top of my list."

American Record Guide 53:68-70 My/Je '90. Gerald S. Fox (390w)

"Tennstedt gives us Mahler in italics, in bold, and underlined. With its emotional extremes, wayward or unorthodox tempos, near-losses of control, and other exaggerations, it is the most manic-depressive Fifth I've ever encountered-....Considering the...location...EMI's sound is good....For those who like their Mahler on (and occasionally over) the brink and can take Tennstedt's extremes, strongly recommended."

Fanfare 13:211 My/Je '90. Ben Pernick (510w)

"In many ways, this recording is superior to Tennstedt's studio recording of the same work."

High Fidelity 1:119 Mr '90. Andrew Stuart (b.n.)

"This live recording...may not boast quite the sonic richness of the 1979 Angel recording of the work by the same forces, but it displays greater sureness and spontaneity of execution."

Stereo Review 55:108 My '90. David Hall (190w)

"Some may complain about a weak backbone to Tennstedt's conducting, but his flexibility is exactly what makes the interpretation work, bringing excitement to the contrasts between the symphony's ripeness and its violence. The failings that drop Tennstedt's performance a notch below Bernstein/VPO are the few places where the chance is *not* taken...Despite these small interpretive faults, and the usual flubs in execution one would expect from a live performance, Tennstedt's must be considered among the best available CDs of Mahler 5. Unfortunately, the live sound deserves no such lofty ranking."

Stereophile 13:201+ Je '90. Kevin Conklin (320w)

"The London Philharmonic plays well, aside from a little raggedness here and there and a truly unforgivable timpani entrance one bar early in the middle of the scherzo. Tennstedt's interpretation is tremendously exciting and full of almost schizoid contrasts of emotion....The recorded sound is respectable."

Musical America 111:76-7 Ja '91. David Hurwitz (175w)

"This is the second recording of Mahler's *Fifth* on EMI for Tennstedt and the London....there are certainly no noise artifacts on it, but the previous recording is gorgeous, perhaps even a bit more feeling."

HighPerformanceReview 7:60 Fall '90. Bert Wechsler (200w)

Gramophone 67:1132 D '89. Edward Seckerson (630w)

The New York Times Ja 21 '90, p. 26 H. Andrew L. Pincus (145w)

Digital Audio's CD Review 6:56 My '90. Lawrence Johnson (190w)

1225. Symphonies: No. 6 in A minor; No. 8 in E flat, "Symphony of a Thousand".
Leonard Bernstein (c). Erna Spoorenberg; Gwenyth Jones; Gwyneth Annear; Anna Reynolds; Norma Procter; John Mitchinson; Vladimir Ruzdjak. Leeds Festival Chorus; Orpington Junior Singers; Highgate School Boys' Choir; Finchley Children's Music Group; London Symphony Chorus; New York Philharmonic Orchestra; London Symphony Orchestra. February, 1968; December, 1966.
CBS 42199 159:00 3 discs

★★*Awards:* Pick of the Crop Reissues, *The New York Times* S 16, '90 (Sedgwick Clark). *American Record Guide* Overview: Mahler, Jl/Ag '88.

Reviews of Bernstein's Mahler cycle:

—*Gramophone* 64:868+ D '86 Richard Osborne (1270w)

—*Ovation* 7:29-30 Ja '87 Lawrence B. Johnson (570w)

Fanfare 10:169-71 N/D '86 Peter J. Rabinowitz (1600w)

American Record Guide 50:66-71 Mr/Ap '87 Gerald S. Fox (420w)

1226. Symphony No. 6 in A minor; Kindertotenlieder.
Leonard Bernstein (c). Thomas Hampson (bar). Vienna Philharmonic Orchestra.
DEUTSCHE GRAMMOPHON 427 697 DDD
115:00 2 discs

★*Awards:* Critics' Choice 1990, *Gramophone* D '90 (Edward Seckerson).

"Standing a quarter-century later before a European ensemble, Bernstein records another Sixth. The accomplishment is no less great than in New York; the creative sense is very different....By comparison, the New York reading is a bit callow....no performance before Hampson's has evoked in me such feeling for Ruckert's cathartic poetry, nor such understanding of Alma's rage at her husband for tempting fate by setting these songs [*Kindertotenlieder*]. The DG recording team captures a full and powerful sound."

Stereophile 13:235+ O '90. Kevin Conklin (750w)

"Bernstein's conception still calls, from time to time, upon his undiminished capacity for theatrical flair. But on the whole, this is a more deliberate account—slower, more detailed, and more deeply considered....The Vienna Philharmonic plays superbly. Not that there's much conventional beauty of tone: the trumpets, in particular, often scream coarsely and unyieldingly. But the players offer just what the performance demands, both in detail...and in mass-...Like so many DG recordings, the sound has an odd perspective...but the problems are rarely serious enough to undermine the performance. As for the coupling...it hardly has the same interpretive depth as the Sixth....A major release nonetheless."

Fanfare 13:190-91 Jl/Ag '90. Peter J. Rabinowitz (650w)

"Although this performance [of the Symphony] is certainly more effective than its predecessor, certain lingering concerns remain. Several sonic effects are jumbled or too overladen with ragged brass to be thoroughly effective....Such personal music which touches the depths of one's soul almost defies full realization....For now, Bernstein's version, along with Horenstein, Karajan, and perhaps Tennstedt, is the best we have. Thomas Hampson makes every effort to convey the tragedy in his passionate reading of *Kindertotenlieder*, a perfect coupling for the Sixth....Orchestral playing is excellent and the sonics are marvelous."

American Record Guide 53:68-9 Jl/Ag '90. Lewis M. Smoley (805w)

Gramophone 67:1333 Ja '90. Edward Seckerson (385w)

1227. Symphony No. 6 in A minor.
James Levine (c). London Symphony Orchestra.
RCA 3213 2 discs

★*Awards:* *American Record Guide* Overview: Mahler Symphonies, Jl/Ag '88.

"James Levine's eloquent performance...strikes me as the finest single segment of his still uncompleted survey of the symphonies....and the fine analog recording sounds better than new in this especially successful transfer to CD."

Stereo Review 51:136 D '86 Richard Freed (136w)

1228. Symphony No. 6 in A minor; Symphony No. 10 (unfinished)—Adagio.
Giuseppe Sinopoli (c). Philharmonia Orchestra.
DEUTSCHE GRAMMOPHON 423 082 DDD
126:00 2 discs

★*Awards:* The Record of the Month, *Music and Musicians International* Ap '88; The Want List 1988, *Fanfare* N/D '88 (Peter J. Rabinowitz).

"Giuseppe Sinopoli and the Philharmonia Orchestra deliver a performance of Mahler's Sixth Symphony that is transparent, finely detailed, and often mesmerizing....Deutsche Grammophon provides a recording of great clarity and impact for the gorgeous playing of the Philharmonia Orchestra."

High Fidelity 38:80 N '88. Robert R. Reilly (225w)

"It is a measure of Sinopoli's insight into the creative process that he catches Mahler's meanings as few others: the result, with superbly committed playing from the Philharmonia, is a triumph of identification and sympathetic interpretation."

Music and Musicians International 36:46 Ap '88. Robert Hartford (165w)

"Forced to choose one version—I'd still stick with Bernstein's more overtly theatrical recording. But Sinopoli's is so radically different, and so compelling on its own terms, that it certainly deserves a place on the shelf right beside it....A major release."

Fanfare 11:159-60 My/Je '88. Peter J. Rabinowitz (600w)

"The problem with his general approach becomes evident as soon as the main theme appears. From here on, the sense of dramatic intensity is weakened and dynamic levels restrained."

American Record Guide 51:58-9 S/O '88. Lewis M. Smoley (1025w)

"How can an artist do so many things right, and still come out mediocre?...The result is just more unremarkable output from the relentless Mahler production line operating this last decade at the major record labels."

Stereophile 11:153+ Ag '88. Kevin Conklin (930w)

"The pity is that the Philharmonia play so marvellously throughout these performances-....But...spiritually and emotionally this is not the Mahler I know and love. I don't think I have ever felt so far removed from the 6th, so unaffected by it."

Hi-Fi News & Record Review 33:103 Mr '88. Edward Seckerson (650w)

Gramophone 65:1076+ Ja '88. Richard Osborne (365w)

1229. Symphony No. 7 in E minor.
Leonard Bernstein (c). New York Philharmonic Orchestra.
DEUTSCHE GRAMMOPHON 419 211

★★★*Awards: Opus* Record Award Nominee, 1987; *Fanfare* Want List 1987 (Henry Fogel). *American Record Guide* Overview: Mahler, Jl/Ag '88.

"Comparisons with Abbado tell the full story-....This isn't in the same class....So, if I've left you in no doubt as to the safer all-round recommendation, let me also leave you in no doubt that Bernstein's Mahler 7—the danger, the immediacy, the unashamed emotionalism of it—is somehow closer in spirit to the composer."

Hi-Fi News & Record Review 32:103 Ja '87 Edward Seckerson (365w)

"The New York concert hall is notoriously unfavorable—the new DG recording of Copland's Symphony confirms this—but it is indicative that where the technical approach is too dissective, the end product can fail to communicate."

Stereophile 10:185-7 Ja '87 Christopher Breunig (275w)

Gramophone 64:871 D '86 Michael Kennedy (265w); 64:1104 F '87 Robert Layton (50w)

Ovation 9:46 S '88. Paul Turok (240w)

Audio 72:156+ Ja '88. Edward Tatnall Canby (350w) (Rev. of LP)

Fanfare 10:156-7 Mr/Ap '87 Peter J. Rabinowitz (525w)

1230. Symphonies: No. 7 in E minor; No. 9 in D; No. 10 (unfinished by the composer): Adagio.
Leonard Bernstein (c). New York Philharmonic Orchestra. June, 1966; September, 1968; April, 1976.
CBS 42200 186:00 3 discs

★★★*Awards: Fanfare* Want List 1987 (Peter J. Rabinowitz); *Fanfare* Want List 1987 (Mortimer H. Frank). *American Record Guide* Overview: Mahler, Jl/Ag '88.

Reviews of Bernstein's Mahler cycle:

—*Gramophone* 64:871 D '86 Michael Kennedy (780w)

—*Ovation* 7:29-30 Ja '87 Lawrence B. Johnson (570w)

Gramophone 64:1104 F '87 Robert Layton (140w)

Fanfare 10:169-71 N/D '86 Peter J. Rabinowitz (1600w)

American Record Guide 50:66-71 Mr/Ap '87 Gerald S. Fox (420w)

1231. Symphony No. 7 in E minor.
Claudio Abbado (c). Chicago Symphony Orchestra.
DEUTSCHE GRAMMOPHON 413 773 76:00 2 discs

✔HC ★★★*Awards: American Record Guide* Overview: Mahler, Jl/Ag '88. *Fanfare* Want List 1985 (Roger Dettmar).

"So if you insist on Mahler performances that accentuate all of the music's startling and unsettling disjunctions, then this one is not for you. But if your interest, like Abbado's and like mine, is in what sense can be made of the whole rather than on how to milk every local effect, then you must give this performance a hearing."

Fanfare 8:210-1 Jl/Ag '85. William Youngren (650w)

"Abbado is, as always, an intensely lyrical conductor, and Deutsche Grammophon has provided a recording of tremendous refinement and a dynamic range almost too wide for home listening....Perhaps this performance would have been slightly different if Abbado had read the essay [in the liner notes] before he studied the symphony. If you want this work on CD, the field appears to be made up of this new release, with the considerable virtues and equally considerable drawbacks I have outlined."

American Record Guide 49:75-77 S/O '86 Stephen D. Chakwin, Jr. (1735w)

Gramophone 62:1069 Mr '85 (420w) (rev. of LP); 62:1218 Ap '85 (210w) (rev. of CD). Richard Osborne

Hi-Fi News & Record Review 30:79 Jl '85. Ivor Humphreys (180w)

Stereo Review 50:65-6 Ag '85. David Hall (250w)

Audio 70:90 F '86. Bert Whyte (525w)

Opus 2:20-2 Ap '86. Nancy Miller (2850w)

1232. Symphony No. 7 in E minor.
Jascha Horenstein (c). New Philharmonia Orchestra. Royal Festival Hall, London. August 29, 1969 reissue. DESCANT 002 74:53

★***Awards:*** Top Choices—1989, *American Record Guide* Ja/F '90 (Gerald Fox).

"A superlative Seventh; equal to Bernstein/CBS and Inbal. And, on a single disc, a bargain. Highly recommended."
Fanfare 13:104-6 S/O '89. Ben Pernick (485w)

This release is "magnificent in all important respects: performance, sonics, even album notes-....If Horenstein's interpretation does not replace Bernstein's as Number One, it certainly nudges it a bit....Bernstein emphasizes the symphony's phantasmagoria...and, in the last movement, its wild madness. Horenstein, while certainly not ignoring the symphony's quirkiness, brings a more conventional orderliness to the work....For those who do not react favorably to Bernstein's emphasis of that facet of the music, Horenstein's performance may be just the ticket....superb, open sound."
American Record Guide 52:73+ S/O '89. Gerald S. Fox (380w)

"The tense and analytical precision of his fourth-movement *Andante amoroso* robs it of its sex. And while the string counterpoint and *portamento* of the finale are dispatched with verve and exactitude, it is also evident that something is missing: what is called for is more the spirit of Mozart's 'Jupiter' Symphony than of Bach....Inner voices lack transparency: clarinets and middle strings are hard to hear, detracting from the luminosity of the score."
Stereophile 13:191+ Mr '90. Kevin Conklin (300w)

1233. Symphony No. 7 in E minor.
Eliahu Inbal (c). Frankfurt Radio Symphony Orchestra.
DENON/SUPRAPHON 1553/4 DDD 77:49 2 discs

★***Awards:*** *Gramophone* Critics' Choice (Michael Kennedy), 1987.

"This is quite possibly the best-*played* Seventh ever—the performance has much of the electricity of a live performance, *sans* audience noises and orchestral fluffs....If this be multimiking, patch on! The recording is superb, the ambience, so far as I can tell, unimpaired-....Highly recommended."
Stereophile 10:157+ D '87. Richard Lehnert (1040w)

"Those who have always found the Seventh intractable may well find that Inbal makes sense of it in a convincing new way; and even those who think they know and love it are apt to find his perspective refreshing....Highly recommended."
Fanfare 11:238-9 S/O '87. Peter J. Rabinowitz (475w)

Inbal "plays it all for its considerable worth and, perhaps because it is comparatively unfamiliar music, brings off a performance remarkable for its freshness and cohesion. The recorded sound is first rate."
Music and Musicians International 36:51 N '87. Robert Hartford (85w)

"These are the only recorded performances fit to stand beside Leonard Bernstein's in their total comprehension of, and identification with, Mahler's sound world. The interpretations are exciting, lucid, and, above all, idiomatic."
High Fidelity 38:57+ Ja '88. David Hurwitz (365w)

"Only one thing is lacking in this realization of Mahler's Seventh, and that is the ultimate measure of orchestral virtuosity the Chicago Symphony displays under both Levine and Abbado. But for spirit and conviction, Inbal need bow to no one."
Stereo Review 52:188+ N '87. David Hall (390w)

"[Inbal's] 7th may yield a point or two to Bernstein and Maazel, or even Tennstedt, for theatricality, to Abbado for sheer beauty, but it's a strong, assertive, texturally audacious account all the same: honestly, passionately, Mahlerian."
Hi-Fi News & Record Review 32:99 S '87 Edward Seckerson (305w)

Gramophone 65:296 Ag '87 Michael Kennedy (120w)

1234. Symphony No. 7 in E minor.
James Levine (c). Chicago Symphony Orchestra. RCA 4581 DDD 2 discs

★★***Awards:*** Perfect 10/10, *Digital Audio*, Mr '88. *American Record Guide* Overview: Mahler, Jl/Ag '88.

"The first thing to mention about this CD set is the startlingly rich quality of the bass response...In fact, this is the best-sounding CD I have yet heard—clear from top to bottom of the frequency and dynamic spectrum, with sound both natural and realistic throughout....Levine's reading...neither overplays nor underplays this most complex of Mahler symphonies. In his middle-of-the-road view, Levine sees to it that everything is played cleanly, clearly, with sweep and power. The CD reveals just how careful Levine has been in these matters."

Ovation 5:58 Jl '84. Thor Eckert, Jr. (260w)

"Of all of James Levine's Mahler performances that I've heard to date—whether live, on broadcasts, or on discs—this one, albeit only this one, impresses me."

Fanfare 8:210 Jl/Ag '85. Roger Dettmer (275w)

Digital Audio 1:78-9 N '84. Norman Eisenberg (275w)

1235. Symphony No. 8 in E flat, "Symphony of a Thousand".

Klaus Tennstedt (c). Elizabeth Connell (mez); Edith Wiens (sop); Felicity Lott (sop); Trudeliese Schmidt (sop). Tiffin Boys School Choir; London Philharmonic Chorus; London Philharmonic Orchestra. March 1987.

EMI 47625 DDD 82:39 2 discs

✔HC ★★★★*Awards:* *Gramophone* Orchestral Award, 1987; *Opus* Record Award, 1987; *Stereo Review* Best of Month, O '87. Records to Die for: 1 of 5 Recommended Recordings, *Stereophile* Ja '91 (Robert Levine).

"The recorded sound [is]...a knockout....Tennstedt has made a strong bid for top honors. Anyone who loves this work will have to hear what he has done with it."

Opus 3:45-46 Ag '87 Jon Alan Conrad (1275w)

"With the release of this new Compact Disc, Klaus Tennstedt's well-earned reputation as a visionary Mahler conductor has finally been sustained by a recording and performance worthy of him."

High Fidelity 37:68 Ag '87 David Hurwitz (500w)

"Buy this, and relish a true Mahlerian in full cry. Few have communicated so great a love for the piece, few have made it work so convincingly."

Hi-Fi News & Record Review 32:99 Ap '87 Edward Seckerson (480w) (rev. of LP)

"Tennstedt leads the best all-around reading of this mammoth work available, bringing out every nuance, from the hushed, otherworldly opening of the second part to the gorgeous hymn which closes the work....The choirs have to be heard to be believed—they'll knock your socks off."

Stereophile 14:155 Ja '91. Robert Levine (b.n.)

"Tennstedt here is in a relaxed but majestic mood, with enough in reserve for when the BIG climaxes come. There is an air of rightness about this performance that is compelling."

Musical America 107:62 N '87. Robert E. Benson (300w)

"All in all, Tennstedt's is one of the best of the many cycles that have proliferated since Bernstein's pioneering effort. In fact, I would rate it second only to Bernstein's."

American Record Guide 50:29-30 Fall '87. Gerald S. Fox (950w)

"Among those [current recordings of Mahler's Eighth that] I have heard, the new Tennstedt recording is one of the most outstanding, the other being Georg Solti's very different 1971 recording with the Chicago Symphony. The distinctive features of Tennstedt's recording stem from his conception of the Mahler Eighth as an inner-directed, poetic work."

Stereo Review 52:89-90 O '87. David Hall (450w)

"One of the most fascinating features of Klaus Tennstedt's approach to Mahler's Eighth Symphony...is the way he encourages his performers to capture the often neglected intimacy of this most public of works. The London Philharmonic Orchestra and Chorus...respond to this interpretation with a flexibility and virtuosity which is refreshing....other features diminish its impact, most notably the soloists' contribution....The recording is also less than ideal, failing to offer either the organ or the off-stage brass group adequate weight within the sound spectrum of the climaxes."

The Musical Times 129:26 Ja '88. Paul Banks (270w) (rev. of LP)

"His hell-bent-for-leather attack leaves little room for the opportunities for introspection offered by even this most overt of Mahler's symphonies....The singing is a problem....The London Philharmonic Choir's tenor section, however, is a force to be reckoned with, both in volume and grace....Listening to this flat, bright recording directly after the Denon's deeper, darker, transparent, effortless sound was hardly flattering to the EMI, and proved once again that there is digital sound, and then there is digital sound....Recommendation? Not as good as Solti or Inbal, though considerably better than Ozawa, Haitink, or Kubelik. Recommended, but not highly."

Stereophile 11:163+ Ja '88. Richard Lehnert (1090w)

"Very little to add to my LP review, of April p99."

Hi-Fi News & Record Review 32:97 Je '87 Edward Seckerson (140w)

Gramophone 64:1265 Mr '87 (665w) (rev. of LP); 64:1554 My '87 (230w) (rev. of CD) Michael Kennedy

1236. Symphony No. 9 in D.

Herbert Von Karajan (c). Berlin Philharmonic Orchestra. 1982.

DEUTSCHE GRAMMOPHON 410 726 DDD

✔HC ★★★★*Awards:* *Gramophone* Record Award Winner 1984—Orchestral Award and Record of the Year. Record of the Eighties, *Gramophone*, D '89 (Richard Osborne). *American Record Guide* Overview: Mahler, Jl/Ag '88.

Gramophone 62:123 Jl '84. Richard Osborne (700w)

Ovation 5:61 S '84. Paul Turok (715w)

"Herbert von Karajan has recorded Mahler's Ninth Symphony once before...Apparently feeling that he had still more to say, and being the perfectionist he is, Karajan steered a second, live recording through DG's A&R division in 1982, and this double-CD package is the spectacular result."

Stereo Review 49:100+ N '84. Christie Barter (350w)

"In sum, this is a distinguished release, far outclassing the CD competition; but it certainly doesn't match interpretively the the Walter/Vienna (Turnabout THS 65008-9) or the Giulini/Chicago (DG 2707 097), to mention but two of the best currently available on record."

Fanfare 8:243-4 Mr/Ap '85. Peter J. Rabinowitz (650w)

"The most remarkable aspect of this recording is that it is *indexed*!!! For once the manufacturer is living up to the promise of CD technology....That indeed may be the major reason to own this recording....There are, in short, greater recordings of this immense work."

HighPerformanceReview 4(1):166 '86 Thomas H. Wendel (320w)

1237. Symphony No. 9 in D.

Bruno Walter (c). Vienna Philharmonic Orchestra. Musikvereinsaal, Vienna. January 16, 1938.
EMI 63029 ADD 70:00

> ★★*Awards:* Historical (Non-vocal) Record Award 1989, *Gramophone*, D '8. The Want List 1990, *Fanfare* N/D '90 (William Youngren).

"This performance is quite clearly the model on which so many modern recordings have been based; justifiably too. It is the definitive *Mahler Nine*."

New Hi-Fi Sound 6:109 S '89. Jonathan Kettle (200w)

Gramophone 67:373 Ag '89. Robert Layton (315w)

1238. Symphony No. 10 (Deryck Cooke performing version). SCHOENBERG, ARNOLD. Verklarte Nacht, Opus 4.

Riccardo Chailly (c). Berlin Radio Symphony Orchestra.
LONDON/DECCA 421 182 DDD 110:00 2 discs

> ★*Awards:* Critics' Choice 1988, *Gramophone* D '88 (Michael Kennedy).

"To sum up: Chailly's 10th is excellent and his *Verklarte Nacht* is the finest I've heard—in concert or on disc. Levine may cover a greater emotional spectrum, but RCA's sound is cramped, unfocused, and poorly balanced. Rattle's performance is more neutral. Angel's sound, while better than RCA's, is not as good as London's....Recommended."

Fanfare 12:219-20 N/D '88. Benjamin Pernick (625w)

"This is unquestionably the most accomplished, and the most thoroughly prepared account of the Cooke 'performing version' yet to have made it to disc. Why then my nagging doubts?...The closer I get to Cooke's masterful 'restoration,' the more I start to consider where Mahler might have taken us."

Hi-Fi News & Record Review 33:97 My '88. Edward Seckerson (560w)

"While it is interesting to hear this Tenth, and Chailly's account has rich rewards in its own right, I am struck by the way it alters perception of the Ninth, now a lamentation but not a final gasp of despair....together with a miraculous version of Schoenberg's romantic hit, these are a couple of very fine discs indeed."

Music and Musicians International 36:53 Jl '88. Robert Hartford (150w)

"Its many merits deserve high praise, particularly for a conductor coming to Mahler for the first time....my current choice for the Cooke revised version must be the superb rendition by the Berlin Symphony under Kurt Sanderling."

American Record Guide 51:59-60 S/O '88. Lewis M. Smoley (830w)

Gramophone 65:1313 Mr '88. Michael Kennedy (525w)

Digital Audio 5:62+ O '88. Octavio Roca (440w)

1239. Symphony No. 10. BRAHMS, JOHANNES. Quartet No. 1 in G minor for Piano and Strings, Opus 25.

Simon Rattle (c). Bournemouth Sinfonietta; City of Birmingham Symphony Orchestra.
EMI 47300 2 discs

> ★*Awards:* *American Record Guide* Overview: Mahler Symphonies, Jl/Ag '88.

"This new version is my recommendation for the piece [the 10th] and I urge all those who enjoy Mahler's music to buy it....The recorded sound is lovely in both works, the two orchestras play up to international standards."

American Record Guide 50:31-2 Fall '87. Stephen D. Chakwin, Jr. (1245w)

MARTIN, FRANK

1240. Concerto for 7 Wind Instruments, Timpani, Percussion and String Orchestra (1949); Etudes for String Orchestra (1955-6); Petite Symphonie Concertante (1945).

Ernest Ansermet (c). Suisse Romande Orchestra. 1962, 1951 reissues.
LONDON/DECCA 430 003 ADD (m) 58:00

> ✔HC ★*Awards:* Critics' Choice 1990, *Gramophone* D '90 (Robert Layton).

"Ansermet's flair for effective performance of Frank Martin's music is borne out by the stereo recordings of the Concerto for Seven Winds and the *Etudes*...The *Petite Symphonie Concertante* is still the best work of the three, and it is unfortunate that Ansermet did not make a stereo recording....Still, for Ansermet and the OSR's vivid work in the balance of the program, strongly recommended."

Fanfare 14:211-12 My/Je '91. John Wiser (275w)

Gramophone 68:1208+ D '90. Robert Layton (460w)

MARTINU, BOHUSLAV

1241. Double Concerto for 2 String Orchestras, Piano and Timpani; Concerto for String Quartet and Orchestra; Sinfonia Concertante.

Richard Hickox (c). Nicholas Daniel (oboe); Stephen Reay (bsn); Stephen Orton (cello); John Alley (pno); Charles Fullbrook (tymp). Endellion String Quartet; City of London Sinfonia.
VIRGIN 91099 DDD 61:27

★***Awards:*** The Highs, 1990, *The New York Times* D 30 '90 (John Rockwell).

"All told, Virgin Classics appears to have come up with one of the most attractive of all Martinu bouquets. Strongly recommended!"

Fanfare 14:212-14 My/Je '91. John Wiser (390w)

"Richard Hickox is a conscientious but not always penetrating interpreter of Martinu....Despite the caveats do not be deterred from sampling the music if you come fresh to Martinu. There is plenty to enjoy." *P95/85 S85*

Hi-Fi News & Record Review 35:97+ N '90. Kenneth Dommett (315w)

"The *Double Concerto* is an old standby...I have six recordings...The Virgin performance is a polished one in superb sound, but it lacks the vigor of the other versions. Yet this issue gives us the only modern recording of the *Quartet With Orchestra*...The performance here is completely satisfying....The Virgin players are magnificent [in the Sinfonia Concertante]."

American Record Guide 54:79-80 My/Je '91. Carl Bauman (240w)

Gramophone 69:44 Je '91. Stephen Johnson (280w)

1242. Double Concerto for 2 String Orchestras, Piano and Timpani; Les Fresques de Piero della Francesca, for Orchestra.

Charles Mackerras (c). Prague Radio Symphony Orchestra.
SUPRAPHON 103 393; DENON/SUPRAPHON 1056 DDD 39:25

★***Awards:*** *Fanfare* Want List 1987 (Elliott Kaback).

"The recording is wholly satisfying on all counts. Highly recommended!"

Stereo Review 52:178 F '87 David Hall (275w)

"It is good to have this outstanding recording on CD...There have been seven recordings, but this is the best."

American Record Guide 53:71 My/Je '90. Donald R. Vroon (130w)

"Charles Mackerras leads the Prague Radio Symphony Orchestra in dedicated, thoughtful performances of both works, but much of the impact of the Double Concerto and the iridescent beauty of the *Frescos* is only suggested, to some extent because of the rather dry sound."

High Fidelity 37:68 Mr '87 Robert E. Benson (260w)

"Of the two performances of the double concerto, Mackerras's (welcomed by John Ditsky in *Fanfare* 10:3) is the more volatile...And Mackerras's transparent performance of the *Frescoes*...makes a good alternative to the Ancerl recording reviewed last issue (Urania 5166). But the Supraphon timings *are* unusually short—and those on a budget should know that Sejna's double concerto...is equally committed, and that what it lacks in nuance is compensated for by demonic energy—enough so that one hardly notices the harsh sonics."

Fanfare 13:213-14 My/Je '90. Peter J. Rabinowitz (185w)

Music Journal p. 25 Spr '87 Bert Wechsler (70w)

Fanfare 10:141 Ja/F '87 John Ditsky (200w)

1243. Symphonies: No. 1; No. 2.

Neeme Jarvi (c). Bamberg Symphony Orchestra. reissues 1942-45.
BIS 362 DDD 61:00

★★***Awards:*** The Want List 1988, *Fanfare* N/D '88 (John Bauman). *Gramophone* Critics' Choice (Lionel Salter), 1987.

"Jarvi's conducting is impressive [in the First]-....He imbues the music with as great a sense of power and forward motion as does Neumann, but in decidedly better sonics....If I prefer Jarvi to Neumann [in the Second]..., it is mainly on the basis of the recorded sound-....The BIS recordings are at a slightly higher level and produce a weightier, more opulent sound."

Fanfare 11:171-3 N/D '87. John Bauman (590w)

"Jarvi has immersed himself in Martinu's highly individual sound world, and his performances have power....BIS's sound...is bell-like in its clarity and dramatic in its impact, the Domanikanbau acoustic giving the performance a genuine concert-hall feel."

Hi-Fi News & Record Review 32:131 D '87. Kenneth Dommett (250w)

"The Bambergers sound like a major orchestra here, far more polished than I have heard them sound in other recordings. BIS has provided sound that complements the performances—spectacularly good and utterly natural."

American Record Guide 51:42-3 My/Je '88. Stephen D. Chakwin, Jr. (425w)

Gramophone 65:409-10 S '87 Lionel Salter (290w)

1244. Symphonies: No. 3; No. 4.

Neeme Jarvi (c). Bamberg Symphony Orchestra. May 1987.
BIS 363 DDD 63:00

✔HC ★★Awards: The Want List 1988, *Fanfare* N/D '88 (John Bauman). *Gramophone* Critics' Choice (Lionel Salter), 1987.

"In the Third Symphony I prefer Jarvi to Neumann....He provides a hard-edged brilliance, while Neumann is more introspective-....The BIS recordings are at a slightly higher level and produce a weightier, more opulent sound....(I do prefer Neumann outright in the Fourth)."

Fanfare 11:171-3 N/D '87. John Bauman (590w)

Jarvi's "ability to get inside the spirit of the composers he espouses is perhaps his greatest strength, and his success with Martinu is, apart from an occasional divergence from the text, surprising, and a source of delight."

Hi-Fi News & Record Review 32:131 D '87. Kenneth Dommett (240w)

"These are excellent performances worthy of being heard."

HighPerformanceReview 5:83 Ap '88. George S. T. Chu (180w)

Gramophone 65:409-10 S '87 Lionel Salter (290w)

1245. Symphonies: No. 5; No. 6, "Fantaisies symphoniques".
Neeme Jarvi (c). Bamberg Symphony Orchestra.
BIS 402 DDD 59:16

✔HC ★Awards: The Want List 1988, *Fanfare* N/D '88 (John Bauman).

"Jarvi imposes rhythmic point and projection that is nearly the equal of Munch's, and far beyond the accomplishments to date of Neumann-....highly recommended."

Fanfare 12:177-9 N/D '88. John Wiser (525w)

"Jarvi treats both works as big Romantic symphonies, with often exciting but ultimately unsatisfying results."

Ovation 9:43 Ja '89. David Hurwitz (145w)

"The completion of Jarvi's Martinu symphony cycle maintains the excellence of its two predecessors....it has to be admitted that BIS, usually so good at shining light into dark corners, have not been wholly successful in illuminating these complex tapestries. Not that the recordings are unsuccessful....Where they do succeed, and magnificently, is in their interpretive quality."

Hi-Fi News & Record Review 34:109 Ap '89. Kenneth Dommett (245w)

Gramophone 66:1003 D '88. Lionel Salter (290w)

Symphony No. 6, "Fantaisies Symphoniques". See No. 1199.

MENDELSSOHN, FELIX

1246. Symphony No. 2 in B flat, Opus 52, "Lobgesang", for 2 Sopranos, Tenor, Orchestra and Chorus.
Riccardo Chailly (c). Margaret Price (sop); Sally Burgess (sop); Siegfried Jerusalem (ten). London Philharmonic Choir and Orchestra. 1980.
PHILIPS 416 470 70:37

★Awards: *American Record Guide* Overview: Mendelssohn, Mr/Ap '88.

"It is most gratifying to hear this sprawling work without a break. There is certainly no finer edition of it currently available, including those by Karajan, Abbado, Sawallisch, and Masur."

Fanfare 10:158-9 My/Je '87 John Bauman (150w)

Gramophone 64:1128 F '87 Trevor Harvey (315w)

Hi-Fi News & Record Review 32:99 Ap '87 Peter Branscombe (120w)

1247. Symphonies: No. 3 in A minor, Opus 56, "Scottish;" No. 4 in A, Opus 90, "Italian".
Semyon Bychkov (c). London Philharmonic Orchestra.
PHILIPS 420 211 DDD 69:00

★Awards: *Stereo Review* Best Recordings of the Month Jl '88.

"A first-rate recording in every way."

HighPerformanceReview 6:81-2 Mr '89. John Mueter (140w)

"I've enjoyed both these performances on several hearings and can recommend them for their great vitality, warmth of feeling and breadth of conception....It must be added that these are highly personal interpretations, stressing the romantic rather more than the classical side of the composer and allowing a freedom of declamation which some may find excessive."

Hi-Fi News & Record Review 33:99 S '88. Jeremy Siepmann (380w)

"From the very outset...it is clear that this conductor knows exactly what he wants—and he gets it from the London Philharmonic Orchestra....The sonics in both symphonies are spacious and crystalline."

Stereo Review 53:82 Jl '88. David Hall (300w)

"Some may object to the fairly fast *coda* that ends the performance, but an accumulation of delights makes this 'Scottish' one of the best-...and better, on the whole that competing CDs by Abbado and Ivan Fischer, and the duplicate 'Italian' couplings by Marriner and Solti."

Fanfare 11:200-1 Jl/Ag '88. James Miller (215w)

"This is easily the best album from this conductor so far, although it is not without aspects which cause an occasional shiver. Among these are a tendency to overdo matters in the 'Italian'...overall, this is a good performance without being ideal. The 'Scotch', however, re-

ceives a very fine performance throughout-...this album is an impressive achievement."
Music and Musicians International 36:46 Je '88. Robert Matthew-Walker (170w)

"Tempo-wise Bychkov is all over the map-...Perhaps now that Bychkov has gotten this sort of thing out of his system, some kind A&R man could gently but firmly steer him back to more congenial fare."
American Record Guide 51:42 Jl/Ag '88. Steven J. Haller (150w)

Gramophone 65:944+ D '87. Edward Greenfield (160w)

1248. Symphony No. 4 in A, Opus 90, "Italian". SCHUBERT, FRANZ. Symphony No. 8 in B Minor, "Unfinished", D.759.
Giuseppe Sinopoli (c). Philharmonia Orchestra.
DEUTSCHE GRAMMOPHON 410 862 DDD 61:09

✔HC ★*Awards:* *Gramophone* Critics' Choice 1984 (Edward Greenfield).

"One thing is sure, after you hear this performance you will never hear the *Unfinished* with quite the same ears again."
Stereo Review 49:79 Jl '84. David Hall (140w)

"True concert-hall ambience....highly poetic vision of [the *Unfinished*]....Sinopoli is one of those rare maestros (like his compatriot Chailly) who has something new to say about works of the traditional repertoire....Highly recommended."
HighPerformanceReview 4(1):4 '86 Thomas H. Wendel (260w)

Gramophone 61:1177 Ap '84. Edward Greenfield (350w)

Hi-Fi News & Record Review 29:75 Je '84. David Prakel (130w)

Digital Audio 1:74-5 Jl '85. John Marks (520w)

Symphony No. 4 in A, Opus 90, "Italian". See No. 1044.

MESSIAEN, OLIVIER

1249. Des Canyons aux Etoiles; Oiseaux Exotiques; Couleurs de la Cite Celeste.
Esa-Pekka Salonen (c). Paul Crossley (pno); Michael Thompson (horn); James Holland (xylorimba); David Johnson (glknspl). London Sinfonietta.
CBS 44762 DDD 66:51, 54:31 2 discs

★★*Awards:* Top Disks of the Year, *The New York Times* D 24, '89 (John Rockwell); Top Choices—1989, *American Record Guide* Ja/F '90 (Arved Ashby).

"When Salonen is combined with virtuosos like the pianist Paul Crossley and the London Sinfonietta, the result is a performance of etched linearity, sonic brilliance and searing intensity."
The New York Times F 19 '89, p. 32. K. Robert Schwarz (125w)

"Salonen's *Des canyons aux etoiles*...brilliantly performed and accompanied by two of the master's most popular orchestral works, is an absolute must-have for those who love *Turangalila* and are looking for more of the same."
Fanfare 12:211-14 Mr/Ap '89. Kyle Gann (385w)

"Crossley is attempting a personal interpretation of Messiaen's highly individual piano writing....Technically he emerges triumphant from this sternest of tests....[a] thoroughly recommendable disc."
The Musical Times 130:220 Ap '89. Roger Nichols (550w)

"The London Sinfonietta is a coming-together of experienced soloists; and as usual, their ensemble performances are brilliant, technically faultless, and full of life....the CBS recording is remarkably clear and realistically balanced, if slightly lacking in depth. No person taking an interest in 20th Century music will want to miss this collection of rarely-heard Messiaen."
American Record Guide 52:65-6 My/Je '89. Arved Ashby (630w)

"The performance [of From the Canyons to the Stars] is basically excellent. Individual players are amazingly strong....*Oiseaux Exotiques*, dating from 1956, is a delightful score....The performance is lovely, capturing the work's exuberance with virtuosity....*Couleurs*...is well-performed, but without the degree of conviction Boulez brought to it years ago for CBS. All three works are excellently recorded, with the difficult instrumental balances superbly resolved."
Ovation 10:52-3 Jl '89. Paul Turok (825w)

"This is a wonderful compilation...What I feel is lacking [in Canyons], despite wonderful and dedicated playing, is a warmth and generosity of spirit. Pacing is to blame too: By waiting to build only to the exultant climaxes of the large-scale movements, Salonen misses out on other momentous landmarks along the way....This is all wonderful music and, for completeness, the Messiaen enthusiast should have this set until other recordings present themselves as more satisfying possibilities."
Stereophile 12:183 Ag '89. Barbara Jahn (340w)

"The portion highlighting the Horn is titled *Appel Interstellaire*; it is a virtuoso solo display piece, exploiting avant garde effects to represent bird calls of species indigenous to Bryce Canyon, Utah....The Gramophone comments (February, 1989), 'A most distinguished issue and an essential constituent of any library of twentieth-century music'."
The Horn Call 20:81 O '89. Julian Christopher Leuba (120w)

Gramophone 66:1284-86 F '89. Michael Oliver (805w)

Turangalila-symphonie. See No. 1209.

MOERAN, ERNEST JOHN. Sinfonietta; Serenade in G. See No. 1147. **Whythorne's Shadow, for Orchestra.** See No. 2083

MOZART, WOLFGANG AMADEUS

1250. Contradances: in C, K.587, "Der Sieg vom Helden Koburg"; in D, K.534, "Das Donnerwetter"; in C, K.535, "La Bataille"; in G, K.610, "Les Filles Malicieuses"; in E flat, K.607, "Il Trionfo Delle Donne. **Gallimathias Musicum, K.32. German Dances:** K.567; K.605; K.611, "Die Leyerer". **March in D, K.335, No. 1. Musical Joke, K.522.**
Orpheus Chamber Orchestra.
DEUTSCHE GRAMMOPHON 429 783 DDD 69:00

✔HC ★*Awards:* Pick of the Month, North American Perspective (Christie Barter), *Gramophone* Ap '91.

"A generous selection warmly performed....- The recording is warm, rounded and beautiful—balance is exemplary and it is not the engineers' fault that the timpani have rather to much bass content." *P95/85 S95*
Hi-Fi News & Record Review 36:72 Je '91. Antony Hodgson (315w)

"Unfortunately, the Orpheus Chamber Orchestra mistakenly assumes that Mozart's humor, of which there is plenty here, comes off best with a deadpan delivery. The approach may be refined, but it also falls flat."
Stereo Review 56:86+ Ag '91. David Patrick Stearns (160w)

Gramophone 68:1835 Ap '91. Ivan March (525w)

1251. Divertimenti: in D, K.131; in E flat, K.113. **Menuett in E flat, K.122; Musical Joke, K.522.**
Sandor Vegh (c). Salzburg Mozarteum Camerata Academica.
CAPRICCIO 10333 DDD 61:06

✔HC ★*Awards:* Classical Hall of Fame, *Fanfare*, Mr/Ap '92 (Jon Tuska).

"Vegh's rhythms are well inflected and sprightly throughout. He secures superb intonation from his orchestra, and his sense of instrumental balance allows for a full realization of Mozart's harmonic structure."
Fanfare 15:284-85 S/O '91. William Zagorski (med)

"Sandor Vegh and the Camerata Academica des Mozarteums Salzburg in their ten-disc series devoted to Mozart's so-called *Erhaltungsmusik* have consistently brought freshness and vitality. This volume—No. 7—is no exception. What makes it especially notable, however, is that these works have been less frequently recorded than many of the others in this series-....What we have here is one of those proverbial desert island discs which is totally satisfying and sufficient unto itself so that it is not likely to be soon or readily surpassed."
Fanfare 15:474-5 Mr/Ap '92. Jon Tuska (med)

"I heartily recommend the entire program, lesser works and all, for its profound insight into the inner workings of the most mysterious of music's geniuses."
Fanfare 14:290 Mr/Ap '91. Elliott Kaback (260w)

American Record Guide 54:89-90 My/Je '91. Thomas F. Marshall (120w)

1252. Serenade (No. 10) in B flat for 13 Wind Instruments, K.361.
Frans Bruggen (c). Eighteenth Century Orchestra.
PHILIPS 422 338 DDD 51:00

★*Awards:* Best of the Month, *Hi-Fi News & Record Review*, S '89. The Year's Best, *Hi Fi News & Record Review*, May '90 Supplement.

"Another period version of this most opulent of wind serenades...this latest version is at once the most disciplined, most gracious on the ear, and most aptly paced of all. It also happens to be superbly well recorded." *P100 S100*
Hi-Fi News & Record Review 34:91 S '89; p.25 My '90 Supplement. Kenneth Dommett (150w)

"No fancier of the sweet-and-sour sonorities of 'original' instruments will want to miss this version."
The New York Times S 17 '89, p. H 34. James R. Oestreich (125w)

"Never a particularly high-profile interpreter, Bruggen lets the music unfold as if on its own. Though his relaxed tempos sometimes allow the momentum to sag momentarily, the music blooms naturally, in rich colors." *P90 S90*
Stereo Review 54:156 N '89. David Patrick Stearns (120w)

"Bruggen and his band here commit the third period-instrument account on record, not far behind Octophoros (Accent Acc 68642, *Fanfare* 11:4, p. 163), and the Amadeus Winds under Hogwood (L'Oiseau-Lyre 421 437-2, *Fanfare* 13:1)....In the long run, I find Octophoros under Kuijken the most enlivening and engaging period-instrument performance, with Bruggen trailing, not by a vast interval."
Fanfare 13:295-96 N/D '89. John Wiser (425w)

"Generally...the playing is of a very high order."
The Musical Times 130:618 O '89. Niall O'Loughlin (220w)

Gramophone 66:1587 Ap '89. Stanley Sadie (315w)

1253. Serenade (No. 13) in G, K.525, "Eine Kleine Nachtmusik;" Divertimento in D, K.136; Musical Joke, K.522.
Academy of St. Martin-in-the-Fields Chamber Ensemble.
PHILIPS 412 269 DDD 50:51

"A silent background, beautifully focused sound, and one player per part contribute to the exceptional clarity of these readings, all of which are aptly spirited, stylish, and polished....The accompanying notes for this release, incidentally, although brief, feature some of the most intelligent comments I have ever encountered about Mozart's *Joke*, citing all of the compositional 'errors' consciously committed."

Fanfare 9:189 S/O '85. Mortimer H. Frank (150w)

"This genial group of Mozart works in chamber music guise has the benefit of equally genial sound on silver disc....Only deadness of ambience between some movements is contrary to the general *finesse* of the production."

Hi-Fi News & Record Review 30:87 Je '85. Doug Hammond (115w)

Gramophone 62:1353 My '85. Robin Golding (315w)

Digital Audio 2:45+ D '85. David H. Blombach (365w)

Serenade (No. 13) in G, K.525, "Eine Kleine Nachtmusik". See No. 1281.

1253a. Symphonies (complete).
Karl Bohm (c). Berlin Philharmonic Orchestra.
DEUTSCHE GRAMMOPHON 427 241 ADD 767:00 12 discs

★*Awards:* *American Record Guide* Overview: Mozart Symphonies, N/D '87.

"As a whole this edition outclasses existing ones by Hogwood (Oiseau Lyre), Marriner (Philips), and Leinsdorf (MCA), and can really only be compared in incomplete editions by Walter, Klemperer, and Beecham. The CD transfer is clear and highly detailed, though a little overbright, about 3db of bass boost being necessary to display its inherent warmth and spaciousness....at mid-price this superb edition is easy to recommend."

American Record Guide 53:84 My/Je '90. John P. McKelvey (320w)

Gramophone 67:900 N '89. Stephen Johnson (420w)

1254. Symphonies (complete): Early Symphonies, 1764-1771.
(Volume 1).
Christopher Hogwood (c). Academy of Ancient Music. June 1982.
OISEAU-LYRE 417 140 140:00 2 discs

✔HC ★*Awards:* Record of the Eighties, *Gramophone*, D '89 (Stanley Sadie).

Hi-Fi News & Record Review 32:105 Ja '87 Kenneth Dommett (205w)

Gramophone 64:1130 F '87 John Duarte (230w)

1255. Symphonies (complete): Salzburg: 1766-1772.
(Volume 2).
Christopher Hogwood (c). Academy of Ancient Music. August 1981.
OISEAU-LYRE 417 518 139:05 2 discs

✔HC ★*Awards:* Record of the Eighties, *Gramophone*, D '89 (Stanley Sadie).

Hi-Fi News & Record Review 32:99 Mr '87 Kenneth Dommett (75w)

Gramophone 64:1266 Mr '87 John Duarte (210w)

1256. Symphonies (complete): Salzburg: 1772-1773.
(Volume 3).
Christopher Hogwood (c). Academy of Ancient Music. 1979.
OISEAU-LYRE 417 592 176:00 3 discs

✔HC ★*Awards:* Record of the Eighties, *Gramophone*, D '89 (Stanley Sadie).

Gramophone 65:584 O '87 John Duarte (350w)

1257. Symphonies (complete): Salzburg, 1773-1775.
(Volume 4).
Christopher Hogwood (c). Academy of Ancient Music. reissue 1980.
OISEAU-LYRE 417 841 171:00 3 discs

✔HC ★*Awards:* Record of the Eighties, *Gramophone*, D '89 (Stanley Sadie).

"Some lack of sharpness and clarity of detail in the analog originals have been put right in the process, and one may now more fully appreciate the qualities of these epoch-making performances."

Hi-Fi News & Record Review 33:109 Ja '88. Kenneth Dommett (130w)

Gramophone 65:948 D '87. John Duarte (325w)

1258. Symphonies (complete).
(Volume 5: Salzburg, 1775-1783).
Christopher Hogwood (c). Academy of Ancient Music. 1981 reissue.
OISEAU-LYRE 421 104 185:30 3 discs

✔HC ★*Awards:* Record of the Eighties, *Gramophone*, D '89 (Stanley Sadie).

"Mercifully there is no such thing as a definitive Mozart performance, but we can hardly hope for more vital and commanding 'authentic' interpretations than these of the symphonies of 1775-83."

Hi-Fi News & Record Review 33:109+ Ja '88. Peter Branscombe (175w)

Gramophone 65:1454 Ap '88. John Duarte (300w)

1259. Symphonies (complete): No. 31 in D, K.297, "Paris"; No. 35 in D, K.385, "Haffner"; No. 38 in D, K.504, "Prague"; No. 39 in E flat, K.543; No. 40 in G minor, K.550; No. 41 in C, K.551, "Jupiter".
(Volume 6).
Christopher Hogwood (c). Academy of Ancient Music. 1983 reissue.
OISEAU-LYRE 421 085 DDD 191:00 3 discs

✔HC ★*Awards:* Record of the Eighties, *Gramophone*, D '89 (Stanley Sadie).

Gramophone 66:418 S '88. John Duarte (175w)

1260. Symphonies (complete): No. 6 in F, K.43; No. 7 in D, K.45; No. 7a in G, K.45a, "Alte Lambacher;" No. 8 in D, K.48; (No. 37) in G, K.425a; No. 40 in G minor, K.550 (2nd version); (No. 43) in F, K.42a (K.76); in A minor, K.16a; in G, K.45a; in D, K.46a (K.51), "La Finta Semplice"; in B flat, K.74g, (K.Anh216/C11.03).
(Volume 7).
Christopher Hogwood (c). Academy of Ancient Music. 1980, 1987 reissues.
OISEAU-LYRE 417 135 DDD 196:00 3 discs

✔HC ★*Awards:* Record of the Eighties, *Gramophone*, D '89 (Stanley Sadie).

"The dozen scores as here performed are not uniformly successful....There is however, plenty of vigour and style; we are unlikely to be taken closer to the letter or the spirit of Mozart's intentions overall. The recorded sound is fresh and sparkling."
Hi-Fi News & Record Review 34:109 Ja '89. Peter Branscombe (430w)

Gramophone 66:418 S '88. John Duarte (175w)

1261. Symphonies: No. 25 in G minor, K.183; No. 29 in A, K.201; No. 33 in B flat, K.319.
Ton Koopman (c). Amsterdam Baroque Orchestra.
ERATO 75498 DDD 60:14

★*Awards:* Top Disks of the Year, *The New York Times* D 24, '89 (John Rockwell).

"Koopman...mediates readings of strong pulse and easy flexibility....strongly recommended."
Fanfare 13:248-50 Mr/Ap '90. John Wiser (140w)

"Rarely have I heard a more caring and beguiling reading [of the A major symphony]; it just glows from beginning to end. Koopman's imaginative continuo playing adds in no small measure to its overall success. The B-flat symphony, too, is wonderfully rendered. My only reservations concern the so-called 'little' G-minor symphony...Otherwise this disc can be recommended especially to those interested in period-instrument performance."
American Record Guide 53:84-5 My/Je '90. Allen Linkowski (160w)

1262. Symphonies: No. 29 in A, K.201; No. 31 in D, K.297, "Paris"; No. 34 in C, K.338; No. 35 in D, K.385, "Haffner"; No. 36 in C, K.425, "Linz"; No. 38 in D, K.504, "Prague"; No. 39 in E flat, K.543; No. 40 in G minor, K.550; No. 41 in C, K.551, "Jupiter".
Thomas Beecham (c). London Philharmonic Orchestra. reissues.
EMI 63698 ADD (m) 211:00 3 discs

✔HC ★*Awards:* Classical Hall of Fame, *Fanfare*, Mr/Ap '92 (Jon Tuska). *American Record Guide* Overview: Mozart Symphonies, N/D '87.

"There is a suppleness and beauty in these symphonic performances that [Sir Thomas Beecham]...would never achieve again....Decades have passed, but in these symphonies, and the last three especially, are the fire and delicacy which is the quintessential Mozart....Having first heard these performances in their Columbia Masterworks long-playing transfers and then, later, in the World Record Club edition, I am pleased also to report that Keith Hardwick's digital transfers provide the finest sound they have yet had. This set will always constitute a cornerstone in any comprehensive Mozart disc library."
Fanfare 15:470-2 Mr/Ap '92. Jon Tuska (long)

"These are wonderful performances that won critical raves in their time and have hardly been surpassed since. If you want a real treat and wish to avoid the claptrap of the 'original instrument' craze now flooding the market, I urge you to purchase this."
American Record Guide 54:98 Mr/Ap '91. Robert M. Connelly (b.n.)

"Interpretive defects notwithstanding, this is a valuable reissue, documenting not only an historically significant approach to Mozart, but also the way in which our tastes and our view of the composer have changed during the half century that has elapsed since these performances were recorded."
Fanfare 14:239-40 My/Je '91. Mortimer H. Frank (690w)

Gramophone 68:1574 F '91. Alan Sanders (530w)

1263. Symphonies: No. 29 in A, K.201; No. 32 in G, K.318; No. 33 in B flat, K.319; No. 35 in D, K.385, "Haffner"; No. 36 in C, K.425, "Linz"; No. 38 in D, K.504, "Prague"; No. 39 in E flat, K.543; No. 40 in G minor, K.550; No. 41 in C, K.551, "Jupiter".
("The Symphony Edition" (also available as a set, Deutsche Grammophon 429 677)).
Herbert Von Karajan (c). Berlin Philharmonic Orchestra.
DEUTSCHE GRAMMOPHON 429 668 3 discs

✔HC ★*Awards:* Critic's Choice: 1990, *American Record Guide* Ja/F '91 (Arved Ashby).

"Karajan was a Mozart proponent to be ranked with Bruno Walter and George Szell, as anyone who has heard his dramatic second recording of the *Requiem* (DG 429 821) or his famous *Figaro* with Schwarzkopf and Seefried (Angel 69639) will attest. Among the eight sets included in this edition, the Mozart performances gave me the most unalloyed joy and kept me enthralled from first note to last. Tempos, always a difficult matter in this music, are perfect."
American Record Guide 53:12+ S/O '90. Arved Ashby (315w)

1264. Symphonies: No. 31 in D, K.297, "Paris;"No. 36 in C, K.425, "Linz".
Frans Bruggen (c). Eighteenth Century Orchestra.
PHILIPS 416 490 40:16

★★*Awards:* *Opus* Record Award Nominee, 1987; *Opus* Christmas List, 1987 (Matthew Gurewitsch). *Gramophone* Critics' Choice (Stanley Sadie), 1987.

"Here are two 'authentic' performances strikingly different from the 'authentic' accounts of both works by the Academy of Ancient Music under Christopher Hogwood....On balance, I find Bruggen's reading more imaginative, more probing, and (at times) a bit more musical than Hogwood's."

Fanfare 10:166-7 My/Je '87 Mortimer H. Frank (550w)

This group's "latest Mozart speaks with a full-voiced grandeur, ablaze with energy, purpose, and passion."

"These are wonderful performances of their kind. But if you buy them, you should be aware of what their kind is: namely, nineteenth century performances on eighteenth-century instruments."

Opus 4:45-6 D '87. Richard Taruskin (1000w)

"Apart from the obligatory whine of the violins, these performances triumphantly survive their 'periodicity'."

Hi-Fi News & Record Review 32:109 F '87 Jeremy Siepmann (165w)

Opus 4:56 D '87. Matthew Gurewitsch (75w)

Continuo 12:24 Je '88. Michael Berton (480w)

Gramophone 64:875 D '86 (rev. of LP) Stanley Sadie (390w); 64:1266 Mr '87 (rev. of CD) Richard Osborne (320w)

Ovation 8:41-42 Je '87 Robert Levine (215w)

1265. Symphonies: No. 38 in D, K.504, "Prague"; No. 39 in E flat, K.543.
John Eliot Gardiner (c). English Baroque Soloists.
PHILIPS 426 283 DDD 66:00

★★*Awards:* The Want List 1991, *Fanfare* N/D '91 (Mortimer H. Frank). Record of the Month, *Hi-Fi News & Record Review*, D '90; Critics Choice, *Hi Fi News & Record Review*, Ap '91 Supplement (Antony Hodgson).

"Here are exceptionally musical, dramatic, and stylish readings, virtues that have their root in clarity of texture and voicing, stark contrasts in dynamics and timbre, and an apt suggestion of grandeur and power all too rare in Mozart recordings...as period-instrument readings, these performances may well be unchallenged."

Stereophile 15:195 F '92. Mortimer H. Frank (long)

"From the moment that the gripping adagio introduction of the *Prague* Symphony leads to an Allegro in which the 'Don Giovanni' fanfares are played with all the dramatic power of late Beethoven, it is obvious that John Eliot Gardiner is to bring revelatory interpretive skills to Mozart. Under his inspired direction, the English Baroque Soloists provide direct, forthright Mozart, beautifully balanced and superbly played....the following grading is given only because the *HFN/RR* system has nothing higher available." *P100 S100*

Hi-Fi News & Record Review 35:91 D '90. Antony Hodgson (385w)

"This recording...belongs to a group of landmark achievements. If Hogwood's decade-old Mozart symphony survey was something of a pioneering venture, Gardiner's work is a consolidation, comparable in enterprise and vastly superior in sheer musicality and strength....This recording is urgently recommended."

Fanfare 14:239-40 Jl/Ag '91. John Wiser (275w)

"Gardiner's performances use period instruments (of course) and with all kinds of repeats seem to go on forever. Given that approach, however, the English conductor delivers well-balanced if somewhat rigid readings, and his cause is much assisted by excellent sound."

American Record Guide 54:97 Jl/Ag '91. Kurt Moses (190w)

"The detailed writing for strings and wind in both symphonies, often obscured in performances using conventional instruments, comes across superbly, aided by a carefully recorded musical balance."

High Fidelity 2:107 D '90. Andrew Stewart (120w)

Gramophone 68:1510 F '91. Stanley Sadie (505w)

"The ideal authentic-instrument coupling of these works is yet to come, but Gardiner's is certainly the best so far."

Stereo Review 56:94+ Mr '91. David Patrick Stearns (250w)

Symphony No. 39 in E flat, K.543. See No. 1034.

1266. Symphony No. 40 in G minor, K.550. BEETHOVEN, LUDWIG VAN. Symphony No. 1 in C, Opus 21.
Frans Bruggen (c). Eighteenth Century Orchestra.
1985 live.
PHILIPS 416 329

★★*Awards:* *Gramophone* Critics' Choice 1986 (Stephen Johnson); Perfect 10/10, *Digital Audio*, Mr '88.

"Frans Brueggen offers a luminous version of these two symphonies, both recorded in concert. Under Brueggen's direction, the Mozart unfolds naturally, flowing according to its own inexorable logic....Positive remarks are also called for concerning the Beethoven....On the down side is the fact that the microphone captures too well, the kind of sound heard by audience members. The blend, due in large part to the halls, is warm and flattering, but the woodwinds are on the soft side. The horns lack bite."

Continuo 12:16-7 Summ '88. Philip Gottling (340w)

"These are wonderful performances of their kind. But if you buy them, you should be aware of what their kind is: namely, nineteenth-

century performances on eighteenth-century instruments."
Opus 4:45-6 D '87. Richard Taruskin (1000w)

"In sum, not a complete triumph, but a release well worth investigating for Bruggen's persuasive view of the Mozart."
Fanfare 9:194-5 Jl/Ag '86. Mortimer H. Frank (500w)

"In short, a fine disc."
Stereo Review 51:122+ S '86. David Hall (200w)

"Uncluttered and unaffected, these are nonetheless, powerful readings."
High Fidelity 36:68 N '86 James Wierzbicki (145w)

"To hear this well-known music played by a correctly-sized orchestra on authentic instruments is a revelation."
HighPerformanceReview 4:112 Wint '86/'87 D.C. Culbertson (195w) (rev. of LP)

Audio 71:126+ Ja '87 Edward Tatnall Canby (545w)

Hi-Fi News & Record Review 31:115 Ap '86 (215w) (rev. of LP); 31:115 Je '86 (60w) (rev. of CD). Kenneth Dommett

The Musical Times 128:274 My '87 William Drabkin (125w) (rev. of LP)

Ovation 7:38 D '86 Scott Cantrell (310w)

Digital Audio & Compact Disc Review 107:95 Je '87 Tom Vernier (390w)

Opus 3:31 O '87. Richard Taruskin (900w)

1267. Symphonies: No. 40 in G minor, K.550; No. 41 in C, K.551, "Jupiter".
Charles Mackerras (c). Prague Chamber Orchestra.
TELARC 80139

★*Awards:* *Opus* Record Award Nominee, 1987; *Opus* Christmas List, 1987 (William Malloch).

"These are exciting, impressive performances of the kind that will open the ears and the mind of the listener who is lulled by conventional readings....The recording is fresh, spacious and clear....A challenging issue, which I have greatly enjoyed."
Hi-Fi News & Record Review 32:97 Je '87 Peter Branscombe (240w)

"It's just conceivable that Mozart knew what he was talking about when he praised Prague for understanding him best of all."
Opus 4:57 D '87. William Malloch (110w)

"This is probably the closest one can come to the 'original instrument' approach to Mozart without actually using original instruments, with brisk tempos, an orchestra of twenty to twenty five players (though it often sounds larger), and a minimum of string vibrato. And what exhilarating and powerful performances these are (albeit often disappointing expressively)."
Opus 4:44+ D '87. John Canarina (725w)

"These are the most refreshing modern-instruments recordings of these two symphonies that I have heard in a long time. They compelled me to listen extra closely."
American Record Guide 50:41-2 Fall '87. John W. Barker (590w)

"What bothers me...is a remarkable rigidity of tempo, straight through like a machine, with never the slightest 'give' for moments of special import and expressiveness—even for beginnings and endings of major sections....On the other hand, it is simply impossible to force these Prague players into any sort of hard performance. They play warmly and beautifully as well as with remarkable accuracy. No single phrase is just *played*; all are shaped, melodious, and fluent. That redeems the recordings, decidedly."
Audio 72:170 D '88. Edward Tatnall Canby (125w)

"A hands-down loser!"
Stereophile 10:179 Je '87 J.Gordon Holt (100w)

"What might be termed the adverse effects of the 'authenticity' movement are concentrated in these superficial readings....In short, a disappointing disc."
Fanfare 10:167 My/Je '87 Mortimer H. Frank (250w)

Music Journal p. 25 Spr '87 Bert Wechsler (65w)

Ovation 8:41-42 Je '87 Robert Levine (215w)

Stereo Review 52:114 My '87 David Hall (175w)

The $ensible Sound 33:59-60 Spr '87 John J. Puccio (190w)

Gramophone 64:1557 My '87 Edward Greenfield (455w)

1268. Symphonies: No. 40 in G minor, K.550; No. 41 in C, K.551, "Jupiter".
Yehudi Menuhin (c). Sinfonia Varsovia. 1989.
VIRGIN 91082 DDD 58:00

✔HC ★*Awards:* The Want List 1990, *Fanfare* N/D '90 (Elliott Kaback).

"Put as simply as possible, this is one of the very finest items to be sent my way in my twelve years of reporting for this journal. It goes to the top of the list of modern recordings of these immortal works."
Fanfare 14:317-8 S/O '90. Elliott Kaback (540w)

"Sir Yehudi Menuhin...a lithe and delicately poised account of the G minor at speeds that, though very much on the fast side, are within canonical specifications....The *Jupiter* is a little less impressive."
American Record Guide 53:91-2 N/D '90. John P. McKelvey (165w)

Gramophone 67:1614 Mr '90. Edward Greenfield (290w)

"Even those who know these works well are likely to discover something new from what

Menuhin reveals of them. With a small ensemble of what I would guess to number 40 or 50, he captures the 'authentic' spirit of the music while (with modern instruments) avoiding the fundamentalist's attempt to recreate how it may have sounded two centuries ago....very close, clean sound free of harshness and relatively flat in perspective."

Stereophile 14:260-1 Ja '91. Mortimer H. Frank (175w)

Digital Audio's CD Review 7:54 S '90. Tom Vernier (400w)

MUSSORGSKY, MODEST

1269. Pictures at an Exhibition (orch. Ravel). RAVEL, MAURICE. Bolero; Rapsodie Espagnole.

Herbert Von Karajan (c). Berlin Philharmonic Orchestra.
DEUTSCHE GRAMMOPHON 413 588 DDD 64:25

★*Awards:* *American Record Guide* Overview: Russian Orchestral Works, N/D '89 (Pictures).

"Those tired of a brash *Pictures* may find much to admire in Karajan's dispassionate but strangely engaging account. The conductor's new *Bolero* recalls Ravel's own 1928 recording...it comprises a reading free of the raucousness favored by some conductors...On the other hand, his reserve in the *Rapsodie Espagnole* borders on excess. Sonically, these Karajan recordings are sumptuous"

Stereophile 11:173+ Je '88. Mortimer H. Frank (645w)

"For sheer polish, these performances have no superiors but I find them overproduced."

Fanfare 11:184 Ja/F '88. James Miller (155w)

"The textures may be gorgeous, but the ensemble is far from immaculate in the outer movements of *Rapsodie.* And *Pictures* is sometimes downright flaccid....*Bolero* is singularly unseductive alongside the recent Chailly/Concertgebouw account."

Hi-Fi News & Record Review 32:117 O '87 Edward Seckerson (280w)

Ovation 9:21 Ag '88. Jon Tuska (280w)

Gramophone 65:298 Ag '87 Edward Greenfield (500w)

1270. Pictures at an Exhibition (orch. Ravel). STRAVINSKY, IGOR. Firebird: Suite (1919 version).

Riccardo Muti (c). Philadelphia Orchestra.
EMI 47099 ADD 51:07

✔HC ★*Awards:* Records to Die for: 1 of 5 Recommended Recordings, *Stereophile* Ja '91 (Bill Sommerwerck).

"Those who prefer the composer's drier approach to the *Firebird* may be put off by Muti's technicolor brilliance—I think it's quite appropriate and makes the performance a worthy companion to Muti's *Petrouchka* and *Sacre.*"

Fanfare 8:179 My/Je '85. James Miller (220w)

"Until the Muti performance, I had heard no stereo recording that so clearly conveyed the structure and movement of the work [Pictures]. Muti's *Firebird Suite* is equally entertaining."

Stereophile 14:167+ Ja '91. Bill Sommerwerck (b.n.)

Gramophone 62:1220+ Ap '85. Robert Layton (210w)

Hi-Fi News & Record Review 30:92 My '85. Christopher Breunig (180w)

Ovation 7:30 F '86. Thor Eckert, Jr. (245w)

NIELSEN, CARL

1271. Aladdin, Opus 34—Suite; Springtime in Funen for Soprano, Tenor, Baritone, Orchestra and Chorus.

Tamas Veto (c). Inga Nielsen (sop); Kim von Binzer (ten); Jergen Klint (bar). Odense Symphony Orchestra.
UNICORN-KANCHANA 9054

★★*Awards:* *Gramophone* Critics' Choice 1986 (Stephen Johnson; David Fanning).

"These are pleasant, well-made pieces performed with sympathy and considerable competence by the slightly limited resources of the Odense Symphony."

Ovation 8:41+ F '87 John D. Wiser (200w)

Hi-Fi News & Record Review 31:106 Jl '86. Edward Seckerson (210w) (rev. of LP)

1272. Symphony No. 2, Opus 16, "Four Temperaments"; Symphony No. 3, Opus 27, "Sinfonia Espansiva".

Herbert Blomstedt (c). Nancy Wait Fromm (sop); Kevin McMillan (bar). San Francisco Symphony Orchestra.
LONDON/DECCA 430 280 DDD 67:00

★★★*Awards:* The Gramophone Awards, Nominations, Orchestral, *Gramophone,* N '91; Best Orchestral Recording 1991, *Gramophone,* D '91. Critics' Choice 1990, *Gramophone* D '90 (Stephen Johnson); Critics' Choice 1990, *Gramophone* D '90 (Robert Layton).

"This completes Blomstedt's second cycle of the Nielsen symphonies and, one may say with some confidence, the best of any so far....As with the previous releases from this source, Decca's engineers have secured brilliant sound quality and a spacious setting for these memorable performances." *P100 S95*

Hi-Fi News & Record Review 35:95+ D '90. Kenneth Dommett (280w)

"For the last few years, four conductors have been in a kind of race to finish the first complete cycle of the six Nielsen works for CD-....Happily for the Nielsen enthusiast, choices and recommendations are difficult, since current levels are mostly very high....In the final reckoning, though, I think my choice here [in the 2nd] goes to Myung-Whun Chung, the Korean conductor leading the Gothenburg Symphony for Bis...As for the Third...It is again to Chung...that I turn for a performance (Bis 321) of wonderful lilt and spirit. Blomstedt is only slightly behind him, however, and has the advantage of the most sharply focussed and revealing sound yet applied to this score, furthered by the crisp playing of the San Francisco musicians."

American Record Guide 54:99 Mr/Ap '91. John W. Barker (355w)

"All in all, this project has been a beautifully played but I think fundamentally misconceived enterprise, with the wrong man at the helm."

Fanfare 14:240-42 My/Je '91. John Wiser (330w)

Gramophone 68:376 Ag '90. Robert Layton (550w)

1273. Symphony No. 3, Opus 27, "Sinfonia Espansiva"; Concerto for Clarinet and Orchestra, Opus 57; Maskarade—Overture.
Kyung-Wha Chung (c). Olle Schill (clar). Gothenburg Symphony Orchestra.
BIS 321 66:44

★*Awards:* *Gramophone* Critics' Choice 1986 (David Fanning).

"Once again, the young Korean conductor shows a splendidly firm grasp of the tricky Nielsen idiom, and in the case of the *Espansiva*, he gives a reading of immense heroic breadth and power that recalls Leonard Bernstein's superb performance of it with the Royal Danish Orchestra some 25 years ago."

High Fidelity 36:72 D '86 Bill Zakariasen (175w)

"This disc is essential to Nielsen collectors."

American Record Guide 50:42 Mr/Ap '87 Carl Bauman (350w) (rev. of LP)

"In the *Espansiva*, Chung may not offer quite the visceral excitement of Leonard Bernstein's 1965 Danish recording for CBS or the uninhibited romanticism of Yuri Ahronovitch's 1981 Danish Radio Symphony performance on Unicorn-Kanchana, but we do get a magnificently controlled reading that lays bare both the architecture and the brilliantly linear writing that suffuses the first and third movements....Olle Schill...makes this recording [of the Clarinet Concerto] yet another of the several distinguished versions that have gone in and out of the catalog since the middle Fifties....This release combines an outstanding program, first-rate performances, and exemplary sonics."

Stereo Review 51:171 N '86 David Hall (435w)

"[This] is a good performance, well played by a remarkably improving orchestra....If you want the finest contemporary version of this work...it is Audiofon's release of a 1984 Kennedy Center concert performance by Sixten Ehrling and the Danish Radio Orchestra. The *Maskarade* Overture is likewise coupled, in a dazzlingly animated performance by the Danes of their national heritage."

Fanfare 10:202-3 S/O '86 Roger Dettmer (600w) (rev. of LP)

Hi-Fi News & Record Review 31:85 Ag '86. Edward Seckerson (300w)

Gramophone 64:1104 F '87 Robert Layton (75w)

1274. Symphony No. 4, Opus 29, "The Inextinguishable"; Symphony No. 5, Opus 50.
Herbert Blomstedt (c). San Francisco Symphony Orchestra.
LONDON/DECCA 421 524 DDD 71:59

✔HC ★*Awards:* Perfect 10s, *Digital Audio's CD Review*, Mr '89; Editors' Choice, *Digital Audio's CD Review*, Je '89.

"Here is a recording that represents peak value in musicality, program content, and playing time."

Stereo Review 53:144+ N '88. David Hall (490w)

"Not since Monteux's recordings have I heard the orchestra play so splendidly...Engineering, too, is exceptional...The notes...are superior as well...On all accounts, an auspicious release."

Fanfare 12:241-2 N/D '88. Peter J. Rabinowitz (500w)

"Blomstedt brings Nielsen's quirky, surprising, endearing music to life perhaps better than anyone on the musical scene today."

Musical America 108:56-7 N '88. Paul Moor (225w)

"These are commanding performances, rich in nuance (beautiful pianissimos) with eloquent melodic lines and powerfully affirmative."

Hi-Fi News & Record Review 34:115 Ja '89. Kenneth Dommett (310w)

"Blomstedt makes the traditional Grand Statement out of the Fourth's motto theme, but he manages it with great warmth and imparts an almost autumnal quality to his interpretation that precludes bombast....Nonetheless, and in spite of Blomstedt's undoubted inspiration, I prefer Berglund's Fourth and Esa-Pekka Salonen's new Fifth."

High Fidelity 38:68 D '88. David Hurwitz (245w)

"What is pleasing about this new London release is to find how far Blomstedt has come with the Fifth....By far the most impressive recording of the Fifth just now, and one of the best ever made, is Myung-Whun Chung's-....The sound BIS accords him seems much more honest than the rather slick sonics in London's release."

American Record Guide 52:66-7 Mr/Ap '89. John W. Barker (500w)

Blomstedt's "release, pairing the two greatest symphonies, leaves absolutely nothing to be desired interpretively, and his orchestra sounds world-class in London's surpassingly vivid, well-balanced sonic frame. One of the outstanding orchestral releases of the decade."

Stereo Review Presents: Compact Disc Buyers' Guide Summ 1989 p.59 Richard Freed (100w)

"If you already own Blomstedt's multiple-LP EMI box of the complete orchestral works of Nielsen, you will find few surprises....The improvements are twofold: The San Francisco Symphony is a more opulent and disciplined instrument than the Danish Radio Symphony, and the new London digital recording is superb....It is difficult to imagine better sound engineering."

Ovation 10:51-2 Ag '89. Octavio Roca (200w)

The New York Times F 19 '89, p. 32. Allan Kozinn (125w)

Stereophile 12:205-7 Ap '89. Richard Schneider (525w)

Digital Audio 5:62 O '88. Nigel Reid (370w)

Gramophone 66:611 O '88. Robert Layton (735w)

PADEREWSKI, IGNACE JAN. Symphony in B minor, Opus 24, "Polonia". See No. 2117

PANUFNIK, ANDRZEJ

1275. Sinfonia Sacra (1963); Arbor Cosmica (1983).

Andrzej Panufnik (c). Concertgebouw Orchestra; New York Chamber Orchestra.
ELEKTRA 79228 DDD 59:00

★★★★*Awards:* Critics' Choice 1991, *Gramophone*, Ja '92 (Peter Dickinson); Critics' Choice 1991, *Gramophone*, Ja '92 (Jonathan Swain). The Want List 1990, *Fanfare* N/D '90 (Walter Simmons); The Highs, 1990, *The New York Times* D 30 '90 (John Rockwell).

"Although Mr. Panufnik's tonal, accessible work has always shunned the avant-garde, its darkly colored dissonance and fascination with intricate structure mark it as a product of our era....in light of the changed face of Poland, the thrilling Sinfonia Sacra—with its militant fanfare, violent percussion and triumphant, climactic hymn—seems positively prescient in its faith in the invincibility of the human spirit."

The New York Times Ag 5 '90, p. 26 H. K. Robert Schwarz (b.n.)

"The *Sinfonia Sacra*...is the most appealing of Panufnik's symphonies....The playing and sound are ideal. The Concertgebouw strings are naturally a lot juicier than Chicago's. I think this is Panufnik's best work."

American Record Guide 53:81-2 Jl/Ag '90. Donald R. Vroon (260w)

"Excellent recording." *P95 S95*

Hi-Fi News & Record Review 36:82-3 My '91. Simon Cargill (350w)

Fanfare 14:306-9 N/D '90. Walter Simmons (350w)

Gramophone 68:2017-8 My '91. Michael Stewart (465w)

PART, ARVO

1276. Fratres (2 versions); Cantus in Memory of Benjamin Britten, for String Orchestra and Bell; Tabula Rasa.

Saulus Sondeckis; Dennis Russell Davies (c). Gidon Kremer (vln); Tatjana Grindenko (vln); Keith Jarrett (pno); Alfred Schnittke (prepared piano). Berlin Philharmonic Cellists; Lithuanian Chamber Orchestra; Stuttgart State Orchestra.
ECM 817 764 AAD 55:04

★★*Awards: Fanfare* Want List 1985 (Edward Strickland); *Gramophone* Critics' Choice (John Milsom), 1987.

"As shown by the impressive roster of artists on this record, Part has won friends and admirers in high places. They serve his unique music well, making this release one of the most valuable and interesting of recent years."

American Record Guide 50:46-47 My/Je '87 Ashby (850w)

"Part's *Tabula Rasa*...shines as a spectacular piece of work: this decade, this half of the century....ECM's notes are as informative as could be imagined."

Fanfare 11:351-2 Jl/Ag '88. Jurgen Gothe (275w)

"Quite audible tape hiss mars the many silences of the 12-celli version of 'Fratres,' and the live recording (a 1977 Cologne radio broadcast) of the title piece is *very* live, with lots of page rustling, chair squeaking, coughs, door closings, footsteps up the aisles, and that inevitable hiss....Even so, the dynamic range of the 12-celli 'Fratres' is overwhelming, AAD and all."

Stereophile 10:157+ N '87. Richard Lehnert (1060w)

The New York Times Mr 26 '89, p. 25. Allan Kozinn (375w)

Digital Audio 2:59-60 Ag '86. Laurel E. Fay (600w)

PERGOLESI, GIOVANNI BATTISTA. Sinfonia in F for Cello and Continuo (attrib.). See No. 1419.

PISTON, WALTER

1277. Sinfonietta (1941); Symphony No. 2 (1944); Symphony No. 6 (1955).

Gerard Schwarz (c). Seattle Symphony Orchestra; New York Chamber Symphony Orchestra.
DELOS 3074 DDD 67:00

★★*Awards:* Pick of the Month, North American Perspective (Christopher Pollard), *Gramophone* S '90. The Want List 1990, *Fanfare* N/D '90 (James Miller).

"The earliest of the works...is the Sinfonietta of 1941...The somewhat dry acoustic of the 92nd Street YMHA...is ideally suited to the nature of the music...Schwarz and the Seattle

Symphony give Munch and the Bostonians a real run for their money [in the 6th], even if they don't quite match the senior orchestra's preternatural nimbleness in the scherzo. The new recording's state-of-the-art sound, however, as well as the vigor and warmth of the performance, makes it the one to have."

Stereo Review 55:87 Ag '90. David Hall (400w)

"Both orchestras are absolutely first-rate. The Seattle Symphony, playing at home in the opera house, sounds rich and balanced in all sections. The moderately dry acoustic assures that the lushness does not become florid. In the *Sinfonietta*, the New York ensemble enjoys equal rapport with Schwarz."

HighPerformanceReview 8(1):74 '91. Robert J. Sullivan, Jr. (380w)

"The Sixth Symphony, both for its music and its realization, merits the price of this CD many times over. And my lack of total involvement in the Second Symphony and Sinfonietta should not be construed as a lack of support for an admirable project such as this."

Fanfare 14:333-4 S/O '90. Royal S. Brown (570w)

"In common with most 20th-century music, the works...require rhythmic security as well as subtlety—qualities Schwarz and his colleagues possess in abundance....In addition to finely wrought performances brimming with passion and stylistic understanding, the sonics are also splendid-detailed but with enough air to please those (including present company) who cherish clarity of line and timbre as long as it sounds natural."

Stereophile 13:233+ O '90. Gordon Emerson (305w)

"Although Piston is hardly unknown in American music, his appearances on record have been spotty....For the current recording, Schwarz has chosen early pieces: the *Sinfonietta* from 1941 for fairly light forces, and Symphony 2 from 1943-44, for which Piston won the Music Critics' Circle Award. Sinfonietta, which was recorded at the 92nd Street Y with the New York Chamber Symphony, turns out to be a work of considerable substance for its title and Haydn-scaled orchestra....Although long out of print on vinyl and not yet reissued, the Munch/BSO [performance of Symphony 6] remains one of the treasures of its period and provides a genuine challenge to newcomers....[This] performance displays its own degree...of excellence, and...suffers ever so slightly when compared to Munch/BSO....Eargle's sound seems just a bit closed-in, but I'm drawn to his deep...bass. Schwarz's seating plan for the strings, almost unique today (violins left and right, violas right, cellos left, basses left rear) gives his recording a special interest. As I said, it's a very close call."

Stereophile 15:179+ Mr '92. Richard Schneider (long)

"Schwarz finds a lofty eloquence in the slow movement of the Second Symphony—perhaps the most moving music Piston ever wrote—while the finale has the requisite jaunty vigor. I find Schwarz a mite careful in the Sixth-....The sound is rich but overly blended....Still, the coupling of two of the finest American symphonies on one disc, with the substantial Stravinsky-induced Sinfonietta thrown in, is just about irresistible."

American Record Guide 54:74-5 Ja/F '91. Richard E. Tiedman (520w)

Musical America 110:20+ N '90. K. Robert Schwarz (535w)

Gramophone 68:532+ S '90. Edward Seckerson (560w)

PROKOFIEV, SERGEI

1278. Cinderella, Opus 87 (complete ballet).
Vladimir Ashkenazy (c). Cleveland Orchestra.
LONDON/DECCA 410 162 2 discs

★★*Awards:* *Gramophone* Critics' Choice 1986 (Trevor Harvey). *American Record Guide* Overview: Prokofieff/Shostakovich, S/O '91.

"The Cleveland Orchestra and the sound are simply gorgeous."

The American Record Guide 54:16 S/O '91. Donald R. Vroon (b.n.)

Gramophone 64:272 Ag '86. Trevor Harvey (175w)

1279. Cinderella, Opus 87 (excerpts): No's. 1-9, 20-28, 46-50.
Gennady Rozhdestvensky (c). USSR Radio Symphony Orchestra. reissue.
EURODISC 7937 ADD 54:03

★*Awards:* *American Record Guide* Overview: Prokofieff and Shostakovich, S/O '91.

"Rozhdestvensky's acidic baton cuts through most objections to the editorial decisions—this disc is, therefore, still a viable alternative to the more up-to-date, and more intelligently selected, excerpts recorded by Slatkin (...*Fanfare* 8:5 and 6). Eurodisc provides a wider soundstage than MHS does, but the sonic properties are otherwise nearly identical: not up to the highest current standards, but more than adequate."

Fanfare 12:239-40 Mr/Ap '89. Peter J. Rabinowitz (300w)

1280. Cinderella (excerpts).
Leonard Slatkin (c). Saint Louis Symphony Orchestra.
RCA 5321

★*Awards:* *American Record Guide* Overview: Prokofieff and Shostakovich, S/O '91.

"With an especially vivid recording, this release is another triumph for all concerned."

Opus 2:34 D '85. John Canarina (250w)

"This has to be RCA engineer Paul Goodman's masterpiece; it's even better than his Grammy Award-winning recording of Prokofiev's Fifth Symphony with these same forces. Paul has caught the perfect balance between fine orchestral detail and the warm ambience of Powell Hall in Saint Louis. The sound is very clean, tonally rich and sumptuous, with splendid depth and instrumental localization."

Audio 70:86+ Ap '86. Bert Whyte (300w)

Ovation 6:18 My '85. David Hall (200w)

Fanfare 8:243 Jl/Ag '85. Peter J. Rabinowitz (100w)

The $ensible Sound 8:50 Wint '86/'87 John J. Puccio (210w)

Lieutenant Kije Suite, Opus 60. See No. 6116, 6117

1281. Peter and the Wolf, Opus 67. SAINT-SAENS, CAMILLE. Carnival of the Animals, Opus 67. MOZART, WOLFGANG AMADEUS. Serenade in G, K.525, "Eine Kleine Nachtmusik".
Richard Stamp (c). John Gielgud (nar); Anton Nel (pno); Keith Snell (pno). Academy of London.
VIRGIN 90786 DDD 66:55

★★*Awards:* Critics' Choice 1989, *Gramophone* D '89 (Ivan March)The Year's Best, *Hi Fi News & Record Review*, May '90 Supplement.

"The American-born Richard Stamp conducts an elegant, witty, charming performance [of Peter and the Wolf], with razor-sharp playing. Mr. Gielgud's storytelling has a fine sense of the dramatic."

The New York Times N 26 '89, p. 32 H. Martin Bookspan (b.n.)

"The Academy of London's recording is designed for children in a way that the Menuhin, with its recordings of the Prokofiev violin concerto and of the 'Classical' Symphony, was not....I recommend this clearly recorded disc, especially to those readers with children."

Fanfare 13:262 Mr/Ap '90. Michael Ullman (340w)

"The new Virgin Classics release is an outstanding one in all respects."

Fanfare 13:288-89 Jl/Ag '90. Ron McDonald (200w)

"Richard Stamp...directs three winning performances in a row, the Prokofiev making you realize anew just what a little masterpiece it is-....There is no speech with the Saint-Saens...the most striking feature of this disc is that there's a complete absence of that routine, or rushed, feeling of a record being completed to a deadline. Everyone seems to have time and feeling for the pieces. And the sound-quality...is exceptionally good." *P100 S100*

Hi-Fi News & Record Review 34:100 Ag '89; p.25-6 My '90 Supplement. Christopher Breunig (455w)

"Best of all is still the Previn on Telarc, both for musical virtues and for the avuncular narration....Stamp's recording comes with a sprightly reading of the Mozart and the added virtue that artist royalties are being donated to a center for physically handicapped children."

American Record Guide 53:98 N/D '90. Stephen D. Chakwin, Jr. (b.n.)

Gramophone 67:474 S '89. Ivan March (735w) (rev. of LP); 66:302 Ag '88. Edward Greenfield (380w) (rev. of CD)

1282. Romeo and Juliet (complete ballet).
Lorin Maazel (c). Cleveland Orchestra. 1973.
LONDON/DECCA 417 510 ADD 71:48; 68:53 2 discs

★*Awards: American Record Guide* Overview: Prokofieff and Shostakovich, S/O '91.

"The Cleveland Orchestra is in smashing form for this sensitive, powerful performance."

High Fidelity 37:68 O '87. Robert E. Benson (100w)

"For this listener, Mr. Maazel's taut, charged rendition, sounding even better on CD, remains the quintessential symphonic *Romeo*, with Mr. Ozawa's a close second."

The New York Times My 15 '88, p. H40. James R. Oestreich (150w)

"Stunning playing and a recording of great brilliance, heightened and sharpened in its digital remastering."

Hi-Fi News & Record Review 32:109+ F '87 Edward Seckerson (105w)

Gramophone 64:1132 F '87 Alan Sanders (230w)

1283. Romeo and Juliet (excerpts). TCHAIKOVSKY, PIOTR ILYICH. The Nutcracker, Opus 71 (excerpts).
Evgeny Mravinsky (c). Leningrad Philharmonic Orchestra. December 30-31, 1981 live.
PHILIPS 420 483 ADD 59:00

✔HC ★★*Awards:* The Want List 1989, *Fanfare* N/D '89 (Henry Fogel); The Want List 1989, *Fanfare* N/D '89 (Peter J. Rabinowitz).

"From the very beginning...Mravinsky's often individual way with articulation and balance brings out the acid beneath Prokofiev's deceptive lushness....As for the Tchaikovsky: those who know Mravinsky's white-hot performances of the last three symphonies may wonder how he fares in the more delicate world of *The Nutcracker*. The answer is that his *Nutcracker* has nothing delicate or child-like about it....Ardently recommended."

Fanfare 12:233-34 Ja/F '89. Peter J. Rabinowitz (575w)

Gramophone 66:293 Ag '88. David J. Fanning (130w)

1284. Symphony No. 1 in D, Opus 25, "Classical"; Symphony No. 5, Opus 100.
Charles Dutoit (c). Montreal Symphony Orchestra.
LONDON/DECCA 421 813 DDD 59:00

✔HC ★*Awards:* Top Disks of the Year, *The New York Times* D 24, '89 (John Rockwell).

"Charles Dutoit's performance of the *Classical* is careful and precise in the first three movements and like a well-oiled machine in the finale. His reading of the Fifth is notable for its wealth of textural detail and poise in the first movement and for a fine sostenuto quality throughout the intensely tragic slow movement." *P85 S90*

Stereo Review 54:150 S '89. David Hall (150w)

"This is not, then, an especially individual reading: not as neurotic as the Bernstein/Israel, not as balletic as the Slatkin, not as creamy as the Previn/LA, not as bardic as the Jarvi. But for those seeking a modern and uncontroversial Fifth, it stands near the top of the list."

Fanfare 13:321-22 N/D '89. Peter J. Rabinowitz (345w)

"While the silky sound of the Montreal ensemble never fails to please, its blandness, particularly in the Fifth, fails to convey Prokofiev's striking sense of orchestral color...Even worse, Dutoit insists on slow and draggy tempos in both symphonies...Both performances on this disc sound too heavy, deficient in both fancy and vividness."

Musical America 110:79-80 My '90. Harlow Robinson (795w)

Gramophone 67:183 Jl '89. Edward Seckerson (490w)

1285. Symphony No. 1 in D, Opus 25, "Classical"; Symphony No. 5, Opus 100.
Herbert Von Karajan (c). Berlin Philharmonic Orchestra. 1982, 1969 reissues.
DEUTSCHE GRAMMOPHON 423 216 58:00

★*Awards: American Record Guide* Overview: Prokofieff and Shostakovich, S/O '91.

"The recording remains a little bass-shy in this CD reissue, but the sonorous playing amply compensates. As the coupling, Karajan's more recent traversal of Prokofiev's First, the *Classical* Symphony, lacks something in lightness and charm but is acceptable, and his Fifth is indispensable."

High Fidelity 38:72 O '88. David Hurwitz (150w)

"This performance of the Fifth has been around since 1969...Karajan and the orchestra were at their peak. It's thrilling. The 1968 sound stands up nicely 20 years later."

American Record Guide 51:48 Jl/Ag '88. Donald R. Vroon (200w)

Gramophone 65:1434 Ap '88. Richard Osborne (275w)

1286. Symphony No. 1 in D, Opus 25, "Classical"; Romeo and Juliet (excerpts).
Georg Solti (c). Chicago Symphony Orchestra.
LONDON/DECCA 410 200 59:57

★★*Awards: Stereo Review* Best of the Month, Ap '84; *Fanfare* Want List 1984 (Roger Dettmar).

High Fidelity 34:58-9 Jl '84. Thomas W. Russell III (230w); 35:73 O '85. Robert E. Benson (35w)

"Solti's performance of the symphony has a level of finesse that I can only compare with Koussevitzky's performances with the Boston Symphony in the Thirties....[In the *Romeo and Juliet* excerpts] Solti and the Chicago Symphony play the music to the hilt, achieving a passionate intensity that I have rarely heard equaled."

Stereo Review 49:77-8 Ap '84. David Hall (450w)

Gramophone 61:624 N '83. Robert Layton (405w) (rev. of LP)

Ovation 5:61 Ag '84. Paul Turok (75w)

Hi-Fi News & Record Review 29:73-4 Je '84. Ivor Humphreys (120w)

Fanfare 8:285-6 S/O '84. Peter J. Rabinowitz (255w)

Symphony No. 1 in D, Opus 25, "Classical". See No. 1057.

RACHMANINOFF, SERGEI

1287. Isle of the Dead, Opus 29; Symphonic Dances, Opus 45.
Vladimir Ashkenazy (c). Royal Concertgebouw Orchestra.
LONDON/DECCA 410 124 DDD 54:46

★★★*Awards: Gramophone* Critics' Choice 1984 (Edward Greenfield). Records to Die for: 1 of 5 Recommended Recordings, *Stereophile* Ja '91 (Martin Colloms). *American Record Guide* Overview: Rachmaninoff, S/O '90.

"Ashkenazy does wonderful things with Rachmaninoff, and this performance of the *Symphonic Dances* has astonishing impact. Somehow the full potential dynamic range of the CD medium is exploited with electrifying climaxes."

Stereophile 14:131 Ja '91. Martin Colloms (b.n.)

Gramophone 62:976 F '85. Edward Greenfield(140w)

Digital Audio 2:61 Ag '86. Tom Vernier (250w)

1288. Symphonic Dances, Opus 45; Isle of the Dead; Vocalise, Opus 34, No. 14; Aleko—Intermezzo, Women's Dance.
Andre Previn (c). London Symphony Orchestra. reissue 1976-7.
EMI 69025 71:00

✔HC ★*Awards: American Record Guide* Overview: Rachmaninoff, S/O '90 (Symphonic Dances and Isle of the Dead).

"I particularly like Previn's *Symphonic Dances*-....EMI's punchy, highly-colored recording sounds well in its CD remastering."

Hi-Fi News & Record Review 32:135 D '87. Edward Seckerson (100w)

"Andre Previn's exceptional sympathy for Rachmaninoff's music has never been better documented than in these excellent perfor-

mances of *The Isle of the Dead* and *Symphonic Dances*."
High Fidelity 38:56 Ja '88. David Hurwitz (120w)

"Previn's interpretations are shapely and thoughtful but a bit cool."
Musical America 108:61 My '88. Terry Teachout (185w)

"Not only are the performances sympathetic (and, for Previn, kind of snappy), the digital remastering minimizes the great weakness of the original LPs, a certain tubbiness typical of Abbey Road products of the 70s."
Fanfare 13:326 N/D '89. James Miller (100w)

Gramophone 65:393-4 S '87 Stephen Johnson (75w)

American Record Guide 50:82 N/D '87. John J. Puccio (80w)

1289. Symphony No. 1 in D minor, Opus 13. Isle of the Dead, Opus 29.
Andrew Litton (c). Royal Philharmonic Orchestra.
VIRGIN 90830 DDD 67:00

★★★*Awards:* Critics' Choice 1990, *Gramophone* D '90 (Edward Seckerson); Best Recordings of the Month, *Stereo Review* D '90; Records to Die for: 1 of 5 Recommended Recordings, *Stereophile* Ja '91 (Lewis Lipnick).

"If Litton's speeds are (without exception, I believe) a little more expansive than Rachmaninov suggested, the Royal Philharmonic...fleshes out every detail with playing that is at once rich and focused." *P100/95 S100/95*
Hi-Fi News & Record Review 35:97-8 Je '90. David Nice (395w)

"The beautifully proportioned account of the First is preceded by a noble and impassioned realization of *The Isle of the Dead*; both are gloriously recorded."
Stereo Review 55:100 D '90. Richard Freed (240w)

"With these performances, Andrew Litton has established himself as 'the' interpreter of Sergei Rachmaninoff's orchestral music."
Stereophile 14:157+ Ja '91. Lewis Lipnick (b.n.)

"If you already have satisfactory recordings of these pieces [on Virgin 90830,1,2], Litton's will make a fine supplement...If you don't have some or any of these pieces, there is no collection of them that I would recommend more urgently."
Fanfare 14:281-82 Ja/F '91. James Miller (b.n.)

"The weaknesses of Symphony 1 are not as well disguised here as in Ashkenazy's hands, but then Litton searches out the score's finer points, allowing the structure to reveal its seams."
Stereophile 14:241+ D '91. Barbara Jahn (med)

"Rachmaninoff's orchestral music...could benefit from the architectural control exerted by a great Bruckner conductor...The gifted Andrew Litton does not yet possess such veteran patience and dynamic control...The best news...is Virgin's thrilling sound, with its impeccable clarity and balance, and enormous dynamic range."
American Record Guide 54:104-5 Mr/Ap '91. Arved Ashby (150w)

Gramophone 67:1982 My '90. Edward Seckerson (340w)

1290. Symphony No. 2 in E minor, Opus 27. Vocalise, Opus 34, No. 14.
Andrew Litton (c). Royal Philharmonic Orchestra.
VIRGIN 90831 DDD 70:05

★★*Awards:* Best Recordings of the Month, *Stereo Review* D '90; Records to Die for: 1 of 5 Recommended Recordings, *Stereophile* Ja '91 (Lewis Lipnick).

"Kaspszyk also offers the *Vocalise* on his admirable Collins disc, but Litton's greater sense of momentum is apparent everywhere. The precision and richness he draws from the Royal Philharmonic are wondrous."
Stereo Review 55:100 D '90. Richard Freed (240w)

"Symphony 2 I found altogether less attractive [than Symphony 1], for here the recording definitely stands in the way of the music's emotional force...I much prefer the confidence with which Ashkenazy and Previn quite unashamedly let their hair down. With a rather limp *Vocalise* as companion, this is not a disc I could recommend."
Stereophile 14:241+ D '91. Barbara Jahn (med)

See Symphony No. 1 for review excerpts.
—*Hi-Fi News & Record Review* 35:97-8 Je '90. David Nice (395w)

—*Stereophile* 14:157+ Ja '91. Lewis Lipnick (b.n.)

—*Fanfare* 14:281-82 Ja/F '91. James Miller (b.n.)

—*American Record Guide* 54:104-5 Mr/Ap '91. Arved Ashby (150w)

Gramophone 67:1982 My '90. Edward Seckerson (340w)

1291. Symphony No. 2 in E minor, Opus 27.
Gennady Rozhdestvensky (c). London Symphony Orchestra.
MCA 6272 DDD 66:13

✔HC ★★*Awards:* Best Recordings of the Month, *Stereo Review* Je '89. Top Choices—1989, *American Record Guide* Ja/F '90 (John McKelvey).

"Rozhdestvensky's version may not be...what Rachmaninoff had in mind. But...this conductor puts it all together better than anyone else I know of. It is not only deeply felt, but brilliantly realized. If this doesn't raise your goose bumps, nothing will. Guaranteed, or your money back!"
American Record Guide 52:102 N/D '89. John P. McKelvey (185w)

Rozhdestvensky's "own successful efforts are enhanced here by outstanding sonics, with a balance of warmth and brilliance ideally suited to this performance. Neither the LSO nor the Rachmaninoff Second has ever sounded better in a recording."
Stereo Review 54:94 Je '89. Richard Freed (460w)

"I find this recording a great disappointment-....what we have is one of the slowest, heaviest, most ponderous interpretations I have ever heard of this work....The sound is outstanding."
Fanfare 12:217 Jl/Ag '89. Ron McDonald (150w)

1292. Symphony No. 3 in A Minor, Opus 44; Symphony in D Minor (one movement).
Vladimir Ashkenazy (c). Concertgebouw Orchestra. 1983.
LONDON/DECCA 410 231

★*Awards: American Record Guide* Overview: Rachmaninoff, S/O '90.

"Vladimir Ashkenazy and the Concertgebouw players give us a passion-filled account of these two lesser-known symphonies by Rachmaninov....Coupled with a high quality digital recording, the warmth and dynamics come through cleanly."
High Performance Review 3 (3):116-7 '85. (125w)

Gramophone 61:972 F '84. Edward Greenfield (125w)

Hi-Fi News & Record Review 29:79 Mr '84. John Atkinson (80w)

1293. Symphony No. 3 in A minor, Opus 44. Symphonic Dances, Opus 45.
Andrew Litton (c). Royal Philharmonic Orchestra.
VIRGIN 90832 DDD 78:00

★★*Awards:* Best Recordings of the Month, *Stereo Review* D '90; Records to Die for: 1 of 5 Recommended Recordings, *Stereophile* Ja '91 (Lewis Lipnick).

"This disc is the one I would recommend, although Ashkenazy still holds all the trump cards for the three symphonies as far as I'm concerned (London/Decca 421 065-2)."
Stereophile 14:241+ D '91. Barbara Jahn (med)

"Here, I feel, Litton's pacing is just a little too broad. Momentum doesn't slacken, but the tension does somewhat. There's no slackening in the Dances, though."
Stereo Review 55:100 D '90. Richard Freed (240w)

See Symphony No. 1 for review excerpt.
—*Stereophile* 14:157+ Ja '91. Lewis Lipnick (b.n.)

—*Fanfare* 14:281-82 Ja/F '91. James Miller (b.n.)

—*Hi-Fi News & Record Review* 35:97-8 Je '90. David Nice (395w)

See Symphony No. 1 for review excerpts.
American Record Guide 54:104-5 Mr/Ap '91. Arved Ashby (150w)

Gramophone 67:1982 My '90. Edward Seckerson (340w)

RAMEAU, JEAN PHILIPPE

1294. Les Boreades (suite); Dardanus (suite).
Frans Bruggen (c). Eighteenth Century Orchestra. 1986.
PHILIPS 420 240 DDD 57:49

✔HC ★★*Awards: Gramophone* Critics' Choice 1987 (Nicholas Anderson; David Fanning).

"Controversial they may be in Mozart and Beethoven, but here...I find Bruggen's Orchestra of the 18th-Century magnificent....Period instruments have liberated this music from the library vaults."
Hi-Fi News & Record Review 33:92 Jl '88. Hugh Canning (335w)

"This is relaxed, stylish playing...Superb fare."
Ovation 9:43-4 O '88. Christopher Greenleaf (210w)

"Bruggen is most successful here in the more raucous and primitive-exotic sections, such as the Bruit de guerre and Tambourins in *Dardanus*, yet the more quiet movements are nicely calibrated and effectively juxtaposed to their more aggressive brethren."
Fanfare 11:197 Ja/F '88. Edward Strickland (200w)

"Frans Bruggen's Orchestra of the Eighteenth Century...rise magnificently to the technical challenge of the score. Precision of rhythm and articulation, even in the most virtuoso passages, is simply staggering, while intonation is almost always flawless....Compared to Gardiner's recording...tempi can be a bit on the slow side....there are enough delightful moments...[here] to sweep away such slight reservation as I may have, earning it a well-deserved recommendation."
Continuo 12:18-9 O '88. Pierre Savaria (400w)

Gramophone 64:1557-58 My '87 (rev. of LP); 65:915 D '87 (85w) (rev. of CD). Nicholas Anderson (455w)

RAVEL, MAURICE

1295. Bolero; Ma Mere l'Oye (ballet); Pavane pour une Infante Defunte; Rapsodie Espagnole.
Claudio Abbado (c). London Symphony Orchestra.
DEUTSCHE GRAMMOPHON 415 972

✔HC ★*Awards: Stereo Review* Best of the Month, F '87.

"While many collectors will already have one or more satisfactory recordings of [some of these works]...Abbado's wonderfully refined performances and the very good recorded sound, especially on CD, make the package extremely appealing."
Stereo Review 52:172 F '87 David Hall (850w)

Hi-Fi News & Record Review 31:117 N '86. Sue Hudson (275w)

Ovation 8:42 D '87. Lawrence B. Johnson (220w)

Fanfare 10:160 Ja/F '87 James Miller (100w)

High Fidelity 37:59 Je '87 Robert E. Benson (100w)

Opus 3:45-46 Je '87 John Canarina (430w)

Stereo Review Presents: Compact Disc Buyers' Guide p. 51 Spr '87 William Livingstone and Christie Barter (90w)

Gramophone 64:883 D '86 Ivan March (235w)

1296. Bolero; Alborada del Gracioso; Rapsodie Espagnole; Valses Nobles et Sentimentales; La Valse.
Jesus Lopez-Cobos (c). Cincinnati Symphony Orchestra. Music Hall, Cincinnati, OH. 1988.
TELARC 80171 DDD 66:45

★★*Awards:* The Want List 1988, *Fanfare* N/D '88 (Justin R. Herman); Best CD of the Month, *Digital Audio* N '88; Perfect 10s, *Digital Audio's CD Review*, Mr '89.

"*Bolero*...is by far the best interpretation in this hour-plus of Spanish music....the tempo is both slow and relentless, allowing the wonderful combination of solo instruments, each time around, to make a maximum impact. The relentlessness brings out precisely what Ravel meant—a horrible, fascinating, hideous, glassy sweet, almost poisonous buildup, to the final hair-raising change of key as the music suddenly collapses."
Audio 73:130-2 Ap '89. Edward Tatnall Canby (325w)

"The combination of technical and musical excellence in this release attains a standard that few can equal."
HighPerformanceReview 6:84 Je '89. John Mueter (100w)

"Most *HFN/RR* readers need have no qualms about this CD, whose sonics are excellent in all respects. The performances are mostly very good too....a fine issue overall."
Hi-Fi News & Record Review 34:111 Ap '89. John Crabbe (280w)

"To sum up, wonderful atmospheric performances from the musicians coupled with a recording of exceptional clarity without the excessive close-up glare that is often meted out to these orchestral showpieces." *P95 S95*
Australian Hi-Fi 21(3):51:13 '90. John Aranetta (345w)

"This is a very good Ravel collection, but anyone who already owns most or all of the 'complete' Ravels of, say, Dutoit, Mata, or Skrowaczewski, can do without it."
Fanfare 12:255 N/D '88. James Miller (200w)

"The Telarc release...is not quite as highly recommendable as the [Dutoit] London release. Lopez-Cobos draws refined, energized, sensitive playing from the Cincinnati Orchestra, and is decidedly more attuned to Ravel than Inbal and his French band."
Stereophile 12:165-67 F '89. Bernard Soll (200w)

"The skillful playing by what is becoming one of this country's finest orchestras is not without value. But the problem with these readings is that, way down deep, they are shallow."
American Record Guide 51:72-3 N/D '88. Mark Koldys (175w)

Digital Audio 5:66 N '88. Wayne Green (200w)

Gramophone 66:1008-12 D '88. Lionel Salter (265w)

Bolero; Rapsodie Espagnole. See No. 1269.

1297. Daphnis et Chloe (complete ballet).
Bernard Haitink (c). Tanglewood Festival Chorus; Boston Symphony Orchestra. 1989.
PHILIPS 426 260 DDD 58:00

★*Awards:* Best of the Month, *Hi-Fi News & Record Review*, S '90.

"Haitink's new *Daphnis* is sensational, comparable to Monteux's classic stereo performance as an interpretation and equal to Dutoit's in terms of sound....Throughout, the Boston orchestra is flawless...Breathtaking stuff."
High Fidelity 1:105 S '90. Andrew Stuart (100w)

"Haitink's first recorded encounter with the Bostonians is a triumph....For a start, there's that wonderful Boston acoustic...Then there's the contribution of the Boston Symphony itself: super-refined, hugely eloquent, obviously basking in the security of Haitink's direction-...And lastly, of course, we have Haitink's intensely flexible, characterful interpretation." *P100 S100*
Hi-Fi News & Record Review 35:91 S '90. Andrew Achenbach (585w)

"I must say that I regard this issue as representative of Haitink's finest work, and quite as satisfying in the end as Dutoit's."
American Record Guide 53:101-2 N/D '90. John P. McKelvey (250w)

"If I have any complaint at all about this recording, it's that I don't especially like what is nearly a conductor's ear perspective...The orchestra, especially its wind section, plays beautifully for Haitink, and Philips's close perspective yields a wealth of detail....If this sounds like your kind of *Daphnis*, I don't think you'll regret purchasing it."
Fanfare 14:325 N/D '90. James Miller (145w)

"Classical purity has a place in this music, but Haitink conducts a performance chaste unto death, featuring lumbering tempos and a coloristic sense more suited to Whistler than Matisse."
Musical America 110:78-9 N '90. David Hurwitz (170w)

Gramophone 68:376+ Ag '90. Edward Greenfield (385w)

Digital Audio's CD Review 7:74-5 O '90. David Vernier (405w)

1298. Daphnis et Chloe (complete ballet); Rapsodie Espagnole; Pavane pour une Infante Defunte.
Pierre Monteux (c). Royal Opera House Chorus, Covent Garden; London Symphony Orchestra. 1959, 1962 reissues.
LONDON/DECCA 425 956 ADD (m) 74:00

★★*Awards:* Critics' Choice 1990, *Gramophone* D '90 (Alan Sanders; Jonathan Swain).

"Even without the suave and sultry *Rapsodie espagnole* and the perfectly gauged *Pavane* as fillers, this disc would be right up there with Munch's as the clear first choice in this repertoire."
Fanfare 14:78+ S/O '90. Peter J. Rabinowitz (195w)

"One of the most valuable of all CD reissues and a fine buy at midprice."
Stereo Review Presents: Compact Disc Buyers' Guide 1991 p.40 Richard Freed (b.n.)

"Monteux's account has been a classic since its first issue in 1959, and it sounds just terrific in this new transfer, a bit of background hiss aside."
Musical America 110:78-9 N '90. David Hurwitz (170w)

"The *Rapsodie Espagnole/Pavane* are fillers. These sound astonishingly convincing. Ravel's *Daphnis* is hardly less impressive." *P95 S95/100*
Hi-Fi News & Record Review 35:88 Jl '90. Christopher Breunig (150w)

"The original LP of *Daphnis* (CS 6147) featured lovely sound of the sweet, warm, feathery variety, rather distantly but spaciously staged. The CD, I am happy to report, wreaks little damage; in fact, the big climaxes are bigger—and much cleaner—on the CD, and the fine digital transfer also manages to polish up the surfaces of the instrumental and vocal sound as well....I'm quite impressed by the CD's ability to equal or exceed the old LP in differentiating the instrumental colors....I love Monteux's Ravel...Monteux actually accomplished what Pierre Boulez, an inferior conductor with a superior press agent, was later spuriously credited with. This *Daphnis* presents a clear-eyed classicism whose bright Aegean surfaces eclipse the dark Freudian recesses of modernism."
The Absolute Sound 16:135-6 My/Je '91. Arthur S. Pfeffer (735w)

"Pierre Monteux's way with these French Impressionist masterpieces has always had many admirers, and they will be pleased with these re-releases of stereo recordings...The overall sound, quite good for its time, is now no longer competitive....[in the *Rapsodie* and the *Pavane*] the remastered sound is better."
American Record Guide 53:101 N/D '90. Kurt Moses (225w)

The New York Times My 13 '90, p. 29 H. Will Crutchfield (110w); S 16 '90, p. 48 H. Sedgwick Clark (210w)

Gramophone 67:1985 My '90. Alan Sanders (385w)

1299. Daphnis et Chloe (complete ballet). ROUSSEL, ALBERT. Bacchus et Ariane Suite No. 2.
Charles Munch (c). Boston Symphony Orchestra. 1955; 1952.
RCA 0469 ADD 70:40

✔HC ★*Awards:* Classical Hall of Fame, *Fanfare*, Ja/F '92 (Jon Tuska).

"Although it's less colorful [than the Chesky LP], the CD embodies a healthy vitality of its own. It neither shrieks nor shrills, nor does it bore you into inattentiveness. In short, the CD sounds like the LP, only a little less....As a filler, BMG offers Munch/BSO's highly characterful 1952 mono recording of Roussel's second Suite from *Baccus et Ariane*...here's your chance to hear this recording as it was never intended to be heard, yet surely somehow meant to be heard."
Stereophile 15:268+ Ja '92. Richard Schneider (long)

"The brilliant accentuation and articulate phrasing of a Munch performance at its best are evident in abundance on this disc."
Fanfare 15:474 Ja/F '92. Jon Tuska (long)

"The RCA CD of the Munch/Boston *Daphnis et Chloe* is a terrific transfer of a 1955 recording that is one of the greatest recordings ever made in Symphony Hall....The CD's sparkling colors, dynamic honesty, and spatial amplitude easily compensate for its reduced warmth. This is one RCA CD reissue I would not want to be without....The CD takes top honors for sheer focus, the LP for all around musical balance. How nice to have both, especially when the RCA CD throws in the BSO's inimitable 1952 recording of Roussel's *Bacchus et Ariane* suite-....The recording...seems to accent the superb focus and color of the mono tape. I was lucky to hear the BSO at Tanglewood under Munch and Monteux, and—with the exception of stage width—this is just what they sounded like: rich, glorious, fulfilling, perfect."
The Absolute Sound 17:124+ Ap '92. Arthur S. Pfeffer (long)

"There are times when Munch's tendency to get carried away by the excitement of the moment results in some roughness and trampling of the orchestral balance. This was part of his conducting personality, and one simply accepts it or goes on to the next good version [of the ballet], of which there are several....There have been quite a few good recordings of the second *Bacchus and Ariadne* Suite."
Fanfare 14:260-1 Jl/Ag '91. James Miller (650w)

Gramophone 69:158 D '91. Robert Layton (long)

1300. Fanfare (for the ballet L'Eventail de Jeanne); Sheherazade, for Mezzo-soprano and Orchestra; Alborada del Gracioso; Miroirs: La Valle des Cloches (arr. Grainger); **Ma Mere l'Oye; La Valse.**
Simon Rattle (c). Maria Ewing (mez). City of Birmingham Symphony Orchestra.
EMI 54204 DDD 75:00

★★★*Awards:* Pick of the Month, North American Perspective (Christie Barter) *Gramophone* Ag '91. Critics' Choice 1991, *Gramophone*, Ja '92 (Jonathan Swain). Best Recordings of the Month, *Stereo Review*, D '91 (Richard Freed).

"There are at least two items on Simon Rattle's generously filled new EMI disc that give it a unique appeal. The first, and more substantial one, is the downright irresistible performance of *Sheherazade* by the soprano Maria Ewing....No other recorded performance of this stunning song cycle has so fully realized its intoxicating impact....this version is a must, and it surely justifies duplicating the other works on the disc. One of them, however, is not to be found anywhere else: Rattle's appears to be the very first recording of *La Vallee des Cloches* as orchestrated in 1944 by Percy Grainger....his version of *La Vallee* is a fascinating piece....EMI's fine sound emphasizes richness without neglecting clarity."
Stereo Review 56:102 D '91. Richard Freed (long)

"We get a sense that the orchestra isn't crowding us and that decisions about balance have been left strictly in the hands of the conductor....Its advantages include a coherent sonority (we hear the orchestral colors pretty much as the composer must have intended) and vast dynamic range (the climaxes are really loud without being strident); the disadvantage is that a certain amount of detail gets lost."
Fanfare 15:453-55 N/D '91. James Miller (med)

Fanfare for "L'Eventail de Jeanne"; Menuet Antique; Le Tombeau de Couperin. See No. 2133

1301. Ma Mere l'Oye (ballet); Pavane pour une Infante Defunte; Le Tombeau de Couperin; Valses Nobles et Sentimentales.
Charles Dutoit (c). Montreal Symphony Orchestra.
LONDON/DECCA 410 254 DDD 66:15

✓HC ★*Awards: Gramophone* Record Award Winner 1985—Engineering and Production Award.

"Charles Dutoit and his Montreal orchestra take to the music of Ravel like ducks to water, and they have the good fortune to have a fine recording locale."
Stereo Review 50:70 F '85. David Hall (200w)

"This is one disc where Dutoit's performances are easily worthy of their superior sonics, and I recommend this CD...very highly."
Fanfare 8:278 Mr/Ap '85. James Miller (150w)

Ovation 6:42 Ap '85. Paul Turok (440w)

Audio 69:94+ S '85. Bert Whyte (265w)

Digital Audio 2:48 Ja '86. Wayne Green (210w)

Gramophone 62:611 N '84. Lionel Salter (135w)

Ma Mere l'Oye (ballet). See No. 1316.

Rapsodie Espagnole; Alborado del Gracioso; Pavane pour une Infante Defunte; La Valse; Le Tombeau de Couperin. See No. 1194.

REGER, MAX

1302. Bocklin Suite, Opus 128; Hiller Variations, Opus 100.
Neeme Jarvi (c). Royal Concertgebouw Orchestra.
CHANDOS 8794 DDD 67:00

★★*Awards:* Best of the Month, *Hi-Fi News & Record Review*, Mr '90; The Year's Best, *Hi Fi News & Record Review*, May '90 Supplement. Critics' Choice 1990, *Gramophone* D '90 (Robert Layton).

"This disc, the first Concertgebouw Reger since the days of 78s, is a major breakthrough. Both pieces are played marvelously here....the Chandos is now my prime recommendation among all discs of Reger's orchestral music."
Fanfare 13:263-64 My/Je '90. James H. North (235w)

"If one single record can once and for all dispel the many myths surrounding Reger's music-...then this is it. The two works featured here are amongst his very finest...these are superlative performances and the Royal Concertgebouw play like angels for Jarvi throughout....Glorious recording." *P100 S100*
Hi-Fi News & Record Review 35:108-09 Mr '90. Andrew Achenbach (420w)

P100 S100

"All-in-all, this is fine issue and easily recommended just on the strength of the Hiller Variations."
American Record Guide 53:94-5 My/Je '90. Carl Bauman (400w)

"The special character of the CGB strings, warm and rich yet lean and clear, comes through beautifully, as does the somewhat astringent quality of the CGB woodwind and brass....Jarvi/CGB play each of these pieces as though it were their last day on earth."
Stereophile 13:213+ N '90. Richard Schneider (425w)

"All of the music...has been recorded before, but it's safe to say that these versions surpass the competition in most respects."
Musical America 110:83 Jl '90. David Hurwitz (235w)

Gramophone 67:1616+ Mr '90. Michael Oliver (490w)

1303. Eine Romantische Suite, after Eichendorff, Opus 125; Tondichtungen (4) nach Arnold Bocklin, Opus 128.

Gerd Albrecht (c). Berlin Radio Symphony Orchestra. 1988.
KOCH-SCHWANN 311 011 DDD 57:00

★★*Awards:* The Want List 1988, *Fanfare* N/D '88 (David K. Nelson); Critics' Choice 1988, *Gramophone* D '88 (Robin Golding). Record of the Month, *Hi-Fi News & Record Review*, My '90.

"Yet another outstanding Reger release, well on a par with Jarvi's recent Chandos issue (which is certainly saying something!); and if anything the coupling here makes more sense too." *P100 S95/100*

Hi-Fi News & Record Review 35:87 My '90. Andrew Achenbach (390w)

"These two works are Reger's only forays into program music...Schmidt-Isserstedt [Acanta 43077] is more old-fashioned, putting beauty before truth; Albrecht is stylistically modern, concentrating on detail and structure. This consistency of differences provides a means of choice: if you like lush sounds, go for Schmidt-Isserstedt; if you prefer clarity and drama, choose Albrecht."

Fanfare 12:246-47 Mr/Ap '89. James H. North (300w)

"If you like Reger you'll want this well-produced disc. If you don't know, I wouldn't start here."

American Record Guide 51:73-4 N/D '88. Donald R. Vroon (240w)

Gramophone 67:308 Ag '89. Robin Golding (190w)

REICH, STEVE

1304. Drumming (1970-71).
Steve Reich; others.
ELEKTRA 79170 DDD 56:46

★*Awards:* Critics' Choice 1988, *Gramophone* D '88 (John Milsom).

"For the first time, Reich is willing to compromise the audibility of process in favor of a luxuriant timbral blend, and when the work culminates in a final burst of drums, marimbas, glockenspiels, and voices, the effect is as sensuous as it is exhilarating."

High Fidelity 38:64-5 F '88. K. Robert Schwarz (250w)

"In place of the languid pace of the DG recording is a new tautness, a directionalized thrust, that is partly the result of crystal-clear sonics and partly of a driving, savagely energetic interpretation."

The New York Times F 7 '88, p. H32. K. Robert Schwarz (200w)

"*Drumming* has no pauses or changes in key but graduated alterations in rhythm and timbre. These uncanny transitions are achieved by a 'build-up and reduction' technique where rests are substituted for notes and vice-versa. All in all *Drumming* is and was a vitally necessary recording. (It predated Mike Oldfield's '73 *Tubular Bells* and its terrain can be clearly observed in the work of say Jon Hassell)."

Music and Musicians International 36:54-5 Jl '88. Mark J. Prendergast (500w)

"The recording is excellent, superior not only to the DG but to the two Reich CDs issued earlier by Nonesuch....The work is a Minimalist landmark, unfolding slowly but interestingly from a bongo duet to a marimba/women's voices dialog to one for glockenspiel, whistling, and piccolo to the compelling combination of all forces in the final section."

Fanfare 11:199-200 Ja/F '88. Edward Strickland (240w)

"You may find that once you get into *Drumming*, it may well get into you. It represents minimalism to the max."

Audio 72:120-1 F '88. Michael Aldred (495w)

"The 1974 recording lasts 85:11, the new version a mere 56:46....In the original recording the musicians help the listener get a grasp on the patterns by holding steady for considerable lengths of time; in the new version, right from the outset they seem to be rushing through the piece, altering the patterns almost as soon as they are established."

Musical America 108:61-2 My '88. James Wierzbicki (270w)

Gramophone 66:312 Ag '88. John Milsom (220w)

RESPIGHI, OTTORINO

Ancient Airs and Dances Suite No. 3. See No. 1482.

Feste Romane. See No. 1208.

1305. The Fountains of Rome; The Pines of Rome; Feste Romane.
Charles Dutoit (c). Montreal Symphony Orchestra.
LONDON/DECCA 410 145 DDD 60:24

✔**HC** ★★*Awards:* Perfect 10/10, *Digital Audio*, Mr '88. Records to Die for: 1 of 5 Recommended Recordings, *Stereophile* Ja '91 (Gary A. Galo).

"Dutoit and his orchestra strike a lovely balance between showmanship and expressiveness....Highly recommended."

High Performance Review 3 (2):117 '84. (120w)

"The Montreal Symphony's playing is world-class, captured in a reference-quality recording. The tremendous high-frequency energy of Respighi's orchestrations, realistically recorded, will tax many CD players and systems. The soundstage is large and three-dimensional, with pinpoint localization of instruments and incredible inner detail complemented by natural hall ambience."

Stereophile 14:137 Ja '91. Gary A. Galo (b.n.)

"Much of what sounded spectacularly brilliant and beautiful at first hearing of this disc did not quite stand up under repetition, especially in comparison to some other performances I have heard both on and off records....For sonic exhibitionists, however, this and the Catacombs movement of *Pines* and the outer movements of *Feste Romane* will more than justify investment in this disc."

Stereo Review 49:100-1 F '84. David Hall (250w)

Audio 68:78 Ag '84. Bert Whyte (180w)

Digital Audio 1:83-4 N '84. Steve Birchall (1000w); 2:22 Ja '86. David Vernier (200w)

Gramophone 61:349 S '83 (315w) (rev. of LP); 61:626 N '83 (210w) (rev. of CD). Edward Greenfield

RIMSKY-KORSAKOV, NIKOLAI

1306. Capriccio Espagnol, Opus 34; Russian Easter Overture, Opus 36. TCHAIKOVSKY, PIOTR ILYICH. Capriccio Italien, Opus 45; Marche Slave, Opus 3.

Eugene Ormandy (c). Philadelphia Orchestra.
CBS 42248 ADD 57:55

★*Awards:* *American Record Guide* Overview: Russian Orchestral Favorites, N/D '89.

"The two *Capriccios* ravish the ear, the *Marche slave* is one of the more potent on records, and the *Russian Easter Overture*, if not quite on their level and showing its age more readily for that reason, is still more than merely reputable."

Fanfare 13:335 N/D '89. James Miller (100w)

1307. Scheherazade, Opus 35; Capriccio Espagnol, Opus 34.

Charles Mackerras (c). London Symphony Orchestra. 1990.
TELARC 80208 DDD 60:00

✔**HC** ★*Awards:* Critics' Choice 1990, *Gramophone* D '90 (Ivan March).

"This is one of the best *Scheherazades* to surface in more than recent history....Telarc's sound is of demonstration quality—for once a demonstration-quality recording with a content worth demonstrating. The *Capriccio espagnol* filler merely offers a sumptuous dessert to an already fine and satisfying musical feast."

Fanfare 14:289-90 Ja/F '91. William Zagorski (775w)

"Mackerras's *Capriccio* is serviceable but does not displace Stokowski, Ancerl..., Ormandy, and Jarvi as my favorites. For *Scheherazade* Stokie's London version remains my first choice. Its vibrant, vivid, colorful three-dimensional analog sound surpasses Telarc's in every way."

American Record Guide 54:82 Ja/F '91. Lawrence Hansen (180w)

"The sound is a little dry and anonymous. In the event it matters little: the performance is just as lacklustre." *P85/75 S85*

Hi-Fi News & Record Review 35:101 N '90. Simon Cargill (285w)

"For sheer exhilaration, his account does not match the zeal of Fritz Reiner (RCA) or Kiril Kondrashin (Philips); and for lyricism, the Beecham performance (EMI) is still the one to beat...But for listeners interested in a sturdy, straightforward performance done up in the latest digital sound, with maybe the biggest bass drum of all, Mackerras and Telarc will not disappoint."

The $ensible Sound 13:66-7 Fall/Wtr '91. John J. Puccio (long)

Gramophone 68:744+ O '90. Ivan March (700w)

Digital Audio's CD Review 7:56 N '90. Lawrence Johnson (305w)

Scheherazade, Opus 35. See No. 1060.

1308. Symphony (No. 1) in B minor; Antar (symphonic suite), Opus 9 ("Symphony No. 2"); Symphony No. 3 in C; Capriccio Espagnol, Opus 34; Russian Easter Overture, Opus 36.

Neeme Jarvi (c). Gothenburg Symphony Orchestra.
DEUTSCHE GRAMMOPHON 423 604 DDD 60:19, 66:01 2 discs

★*Awards:* *American Record Guide* Overview: Russian Orchestral Favorites, N/D '89 (Capriccio Espagnol and Russian Easter Overture).

"Jarvi here gives us the 1897 score [of Antar] in a definitive performance full of passion and urgency....a fascinating package of Russian music and history."

Stereo Review 54:94+ Jl '89. David Hall (325w)

"Jarvi draws the richest of oriental colours from his Gothenburg players [in Rimsky's First]....Their role in the Third Symphony, too, does the imaginative orchestration credit....The *Capriccio*, in any case, ignites as Jarvi's account of the overture (cadenzas apart) somehow doesn't: every *con forza* bites deep, and a wild, devil-may-care abandon sweeps us at ever-increasing speeds from the fandango to the end."

Hi-Fi News & Record Review 33:115-17 D '88. David Nice (385w)

"Neeme Jarvi and his orchestra are in splendid form throughout this attractive program, their stunning performances enhanced by first-rate sound."

Stereo Review Presents: Compact Disc Buyers' Guide Summ 1989 p.59 Richard Freed (100w)

"This set is a treat and I heartily recommend it."

American Record Guide 52:80-1 Jl/Ag '89. Allen Linkowski (375w)

"The orchestra plays superbly, Jarvi rises to moments of passion, and the engineers are competent. But there seems to be no coherent ideas behind any of this. There are some pleasing, passing immediate effects, but no apparent design other than to make fine-sounding compact discs that provide another cycle of symphonies and toss in a couple of popular works as fillers. No one is cheated. The music is interesting and in ample amounts, but the results are just not very exciting. Jarvi's Rimsky-Korsakov would not be my first choice for the proverbial desert island."

Fanfare 12:249-50 Mr/Ap '89. Ron McDonald (550w)

Gramophone 66:1929 F '89. John Warrack (570w)

ROREM, NED

1309. String Symphony; Sunday Morning (after Wallace Stevens' poem), for Orchestra; Eagles (after Whitman's The Dalliance of Eagles).

Robert Shaw; Louis Lane (c). Atlanta Symphony Orchestra. Symphony Hall, Atlanta, GA. May 6, 1986; November 7, 1987.
NEW WORLD 353 DDD 51:18

★*Awards:* Classical Hall of Fame, *Fanfare*, Jl/Ag '91.

"Rorem has emerged at the age of 65 as quite possibly the best composer we have."

High Fidelity 39:70-1 Ja '89. Terry Teachout (425w)

"*Eagles*...has dramatic force but *Sunday Morning* has the most original and inspired music on the record. Its brief, poetic movements are brilliantly orchestrated, with an impressive subtlety of coloration and expression....Good performances here."

Stereo Review 53:152-60 D '88. Eric Salzman (225w)

"If you are unfamiliar with Rorem, I can think of no better introduction than this recording, particularly if you enjoy orchestral music of the spectacular persuasion. The fact that Rorem has the capacity to challenge our minds without alienating, and to touch our hearts without embarrassing, sets him nearly in a class by himself among today's composers."

Stereophile 12:170-71 Mr '89. Richard Schneider (435w)

"This most significant release of 1988 was savaged by an ex-*Fanfare* reviewer whose sympathies lay clearly elsewhere. But this reviewer feels strongly that not only does it demonstrate conclusively that Rorem has always been capable of moving beyond the small-master art-song ghetto he has so often been confined to, but also that his idiom and his goals underwent a radical expansion and enrichment during the past very productive fifteen years....In short, a disc that should be an outstanding part of every collection of American music."

Fanfare 14:421-2 Jl/Ag '91. Paul A. Snook (500w)

"The performances are very good...Recommended."

HighPerformanceReview 7:67 Fall '90. Allan Blank (235w)

"Rorem's *String Symphony* is one of the best of his recent efforts....This disc is one of the high points in the series from New World."

American Record Guide 51:75-6 N/D '88. Karl Miller (275w)

"The Atlanta Symphony Orchestra's strings sound strained and occasionally ragged in the virtuosic *String Symphony*, but their vitality and commitment offer adequate compensation-....All three works are recorded with a sonic brilliance that is a welcome departure from the usually sedate New World productions. Those who fear new music will find this recording utterly user-friendly."

Musical America 109:79-80 Mr '89. K. Robert Schwarz (420w)

"'Sunday Moring' and 'Eagles' are both tone poems, the former based on Wallace Stevens' work of the same name, the latter on Walt Whitman's 'The Dalliance of the Eagles.' But it is the 'String Symphony' that is of primary interest—partly because its abstract nature is a departure for Rorem, but mostly because of its swirling colors and melodic beauty....Performances throughout are solidly prepared and committed, though one might have wished for a bit more bite to those acerbic edges."

Audio 73:167-68 Ja '89. Susan Elliott (500w)

"All three are brilliantly performed, resplendently recorded. *Eagles* has historic interest for the Americana buff. The others are devoid of soul or backbone."

Fanfare 12:261 N/D '88. Kyle Gann (340w)

"None of this music is particularly profound or monumental. Rather, it is pleasantly evocative and atmospheric. One almost might describe such music as being like whiffs of perfume were it not as rugged and bracing—perhaps whiffs of cologne is a more apt metaphor-....This is an expert and heartfelt performance by the Atlanta Symphony and Robert Shaw, to whom the work is dedicated. A disturbing lack of clarity, however, is evident in some of the busier passages, especially in the double basses. This may be unavoidable, considering the rapid, virtuosic fireworks given to the bass section from time to time."

American Music 7:355-57 Fall '89. Howard Pollack (840w)

The New York Times Je 18 '89, p. 23. Andrew L. Pincus (100w)

ROSNER, ARNOLD

1310. Concerto Grosso No. 1, Opus 60; The Chronicle of Nine, Opus 81: Prelude to Act 2; Five Meditations, for English Horn, Harp and

Strings, Opus 36; A Gentle Musicke, for Flute and Strings, Opus 44; Magnificat, Opus 72.
David Amos (c). Saint Paul's Cathedral Choir; San Diego Clarion Brass; Jerusalem Symphony Orchestra.
LAUREL 849 ADD/DDD 66:20

★*Awards:* The Want List 1990, *Fanfare* N/D '90 (Walter Simmons).

"This is an important release, sure to appeal to the not insignificant number of listeners who have already discovered Rosner's music through the Opus One recordings of his French horn sonata and cello sonata, released during the past few years (see *Fanfare* 8:1, p. 299 and 9:5, p. 226)....Of the pieces presented here, the most stunning is the six-minute Prelude to act II of the opera, *The Chronicle of Nine*...David Amos, who is developing quite a reputation as a champion of unjustly neglected twentieth-century music, provides some of his most persuasive performances on this disc....Sound quality is extremely good."
Fanfare 13:279-81 Ja/F '90. Walter Simmons (1000w)

"Rosner...has turned out some very finely crafted, deliberately anachronistic pieces that, for the most part, escape the blight of bloat but are not entirely free themselves from what Rosner asserts is the principal failing of most Baroque music: its predictability....The performances throughout are very good, as is the sound."
Musical America 110:84 Jl '90. Robert R. Reilly (215w)

"Performances and recordings are good."
American Record Guide 53:91 Jl/Ag '90. David W. Moore (175w)

ROSSINI, GIOACCHINO

1311. Overtures: Tancredi; L'Italiana in Algeri; L'Inganno Felice; Il Barbiere di Siviglia; Il Signor Bruschino; La Cambiale di Matrimonio; Il Turco in Italia.
Orpheus Chamber Orchestra. State University of New York, Purchase. 1985.
DEUTSCHE GRAMMOPHON 415 363 53:23

✔HC ★*Awards:* *Gramophone* Critics' Choice 1985 (Ivan March).

"The precision and sparkle achieved in these conductorless performances is altogether remarkable....The CD can be recommended without reservation."
Stereo Review 51:86-7 Ap '86. David Hall (175w)

"This is as much fun as any Rossini recording I know, registered with clear, airy sound on CD."
Opus 2:47+ Je '86. David Hamilton (785w)

"The sonics here have real bass, warmth, and, of all things, depth. In fact, this is the best, most natural, recording I have ever heard from DG."
The $ensible Sound 8:55 Wint '86/'87 (175w); 33:58 Spr '87 (50w) John J. Puccio

"No application of grim precisionism a la Toscanini or Reiner can deal with the amiability and vivid atmosphere potential to Rossini's best overtures. These knowing and affectionate readings are a joy."
Fanfare 14:72+ S/O '90. John Wiser (b.n.)

"The players may not be, each and every one, Philadelphia Orchestra or Chicago Symphony virtuosi...but they play *con brio* as well as *con amore*, and make you glad that a lot of big-band barnacles have been scraped off the hull of Rossini's variously droll, effervescent, abundantly tuneful, charmingly wistful, inventively wealthy music."
Fanfare 9:217-8 Mr/Ap '86. Roger Dettmer (550w)

"While other hands (notably Arturo Toscanini's and Sir Thomas Beecham's) have given us more characterful recordings of Rossini, the youthful high spirits of these outstanding players, combined with the delights of hearing the composer's original instrumentation, lend this album a very special charm of its own." Review of Cassette.
High Fidelity 36:68-9 Ap '86. Terry Teachout (225w)

Ovation 7:34 My '86. Paul Turok (160w)

Hi-Fi News & Record Review 31:111 Mr '86. Doug Hammond (230w)

Gramophone 63:510 O '85. Ivan March (245w)

1312. Overtures: La Scala di Seta; Il Signor Bruschino; L'Italiana in Algeri; Il Barbiere di Siviglia; La Gazza Ladra; Semiramide; Guillaume Tell.
Roger Norrington (c). London Classical Players.
EMI 54091 DDD 60:00

★★*Awards:* The Gramophone Awards, Nominations, Orchestral, *Gramophone*, N '91. Critic's Choice: 1991, *American Record Guide*, Ja/F '92 (Steven J. Haller); Critics' Choice 1991, *Gramophone*, Ja '92 (Richard Osborne).

"There are more than two dozen other discs of Rossini overtures currently available, but none rival this one....Unleashing the music on period instruments makes the colors and contrasts as vivid as they were to Rossini and his audiences....you can't afford to do without this disc."
Musical America 111:50 S/O '91. Robert Levine (med)

"The...clarity and sparkle are astonishing even to those of us used to the Toscanini tradition of Rossinian high spirits....Actually, quite bearable. In fact, adorable."
Stereo Review 56:76 O '91. Eric Salzman (brief)

"Norrington leads these occasionally episodic pieces with a sure hand and the players obviously relish their chances to shine in the many challenging solo passages."

Continuo 15:23-5 Ag '91. Scott Paterson (140w)

"A set of performances that present this presumably familiar music in a new and decidedly flattering light."

American Record Guide 54:115-16 S/O '91. Steven J. Haller (brief)

"If trombones disappoint in *Tell*, most of these performances enthrall." *P95 S95*

Hi-Fi News & Record Review 36:67 Jl '91. Robert Dearling (350w)

"In place of the customary homogeneous blend of big-band Rossinian ensembles, Norrington offers an aural kaleidoscope in which dazzling orchestral colors collide and vie with each other for the listener's attention....Norrington's performance also enjoys a superb recording that is warm and atmospheric without being overresonant....However, if listeners insist upon performances by a chamber ensemble, then the recording of the early overtures by the conductorless Orpheus Chamber Orchestra is hard to resist. Their playing has even more flair and imagination than that of Norrington's London Classical Players, as well as an intimacy born of a natural interplay between genuine chamber musicians that seems second nature."

Fanfare 15:324-25 S/O '91. Ronnie Yip (long)

"Mr. Norrington and his unmerry marauders can't take all the fun out of Rossini....For *spiritually* authentic Rossini, among current listings consider Carlo Maria Giulini (Angel CDM 69042; also Seraphim cassettes), Neville Marriner (Philips 412 893-2; CD) and the Orpheus Chamber Ensemble (Deutsche Grammophon 415 363-2; CD)."

The New York Times My 12 '91, p. 32 H. Kenneth Furie (brief)

Gramophone 68:1842+ Ap '91. Richard Osborne (980w)

Digital Audio's CD Review 8:88 D '91. Tom Vernier (long)

ROUSE, CHRISTOPHER

1313. Symphony No. 1; Phantasmata.
David Zinman (c). Baltimore Symphony Orchestra.
ELEKTRA 79230 DDD 46:30

★★★*Awards:* The Want List 1990, *Fanfare* N/D '90 (Marc Mandel; James H. North). Classical Hall of Fame, *Fanfare*, Ja/F '92 (Mike Silverton).

"Rarely does a recording bring the listener through the canned musical experience to something like the live as convincingly as this. It's certainly among the better orchestral recordings I've heard—thunderous where required and handsomely detailed within a well-dimensioned soundstage...Particular thanks to Paul Zinman and Judith Sherman, who engineered these rewarding goings-on."

Fanfare 15:464-5 Ja/F '92. Mike Silverton (long)

"This 1986 composition stems from a commission by the Baltimore Symphony Orchestra, and Rouse has been their composer-in-residence since that date. He is fortunate to have David Zinman (my candidate for most under-appreciated conductor) at the helm, and to have Joseph Meyerhoff Symphony Hall as the 1988 recording venue: this is a staggering performance and recording....Bravo!..urgently recommend[ed]"

Fanfare 13:209-11 Ja/F '90. James H. North (400w)

"On the basis of the superb performance by the Baltimore Symphony Orchestra under David Zinman, this is a symphony that deserves to be heard more frequently."

The New York Times D 10 '89, p. 33 H. K. Robert Schwarz (278w)

ROUSSEL, ALBERT. Suite in F for Orchestra (Prelude, Sarabande and Gigue), Opus 33. See No. 1088. **Bacchus et Ariane Suite No. 2.** See No. 1299.

RUBBRA, EDMUND

1314. Symphonies: No. 3, Opus 49; No. 4, Opus 53; **A Tribute, Opus 56. Resurgam (overture), Opus 149.**
Norman Del Mar (c). Philharmonia Orchestra.
LYRITA 202 DDD 73:00

✔**HC** ★★*Awards:* Critics' Choice 1990, *Gramophone* D '90 (Robert Layton); Best of the Month, *Hi-Fi News & Record Review*, Ja '91.

"What impresses me most about these marvellous symphonies is their irresistible sense of purpose....Norman Del Mar and the Philharmonia have collaborated once before on an excellent Lyrita/Rubbra disc (coupling Symphonies 6 & 8) and I can assure everyone that the performances on this new compilation are just as superb. Technically, too, Lyrita's Abbey Road recording is absolutely outstanding....Heartily recommended." *P100 S100*

Hi-Fi News & Record Review 36:103 Ja '91. Andrew Achenbach (420w)

"These performances...are always polished and professional, but, to these ears, they lack that final edge of passionate intensity and exultation which Rubbra's music calls for to take flight into the worshipful empyrean that is both its ground and its ultimate goal....In any case, and needless to say, no one interested in British music or the symphonic summits of our time can afford to pass up this magisterial disc."

Fanfare 14:270-71 My/Je '91. Paul A. Snook (750w)

Gramophone 68:986 N '90. Robert Layton (525w)

SAARIAHO, KAIJA

1315. Music of Saariaho: Verblendungen, for Orchestra and Tape (1982-84); Lichtbogen, for 9 Musicians and Live Electronics (1985-86); Io, for Chamber Orchestra, Tape and Live Electronics (1986-87); Stilleben ("A Radiophonic Composition"), for Tape (1987-88).
Jukka-Pekka Saraste; Eric-Olof Soderstrom (c). Francoise Girard (voc); Jurgen Schlelke (voc); Tuula-Marja Tuomela (sop); Eva Tigerstedt (fl). Avanti Chamber Orchestra; Finnish Chamber Choir. Helsinki. August 1987—March 1989.
FINLANDIA 374 ADD 67:30

★*Awards:* The Critics' Choice 1990—Composition Award: No. 12 of 15 *Wire* 82/3 '91.

"The striking thing about her electronic sounds is not their singularity of timbre or effect but, rather, their easy compatibility with more or less normal instrumental sounds. The high-tech music seems but an expansion of familiar human sonorities....For the listener, and presumably for the composer as well, the aesthetic ends here are vastly more important than the technological means. And those ends are both noble and well-met....Her music is almost never 'pretty,' but often it is profoundly beautiful."

Musical America 110:79 N '90. James Wierzbicki (300w)

"*Verblendungen* opens with a bang, and so did my ears. The composer's command is simply stunning. She's equally and abundantly at ease within both electronic and acoustic spheres. The woman's music makes sparks fly-....Strongly recommended to adventuresome types, or those who would like to get that way in short, painless steps. First-rate recorded sound."

Fanfare 13:273 My/Je '90. Mike Silverton (320w)

"Saariaho...writes in an idiom which seems to emphasise texture and timbre over structure, but which is nonetheless disciplined by a painstaking consciousness of instrumental resources and a fine poetic awareness....She has an extravagant talent, which, so far, she has refused to overindulge."

Wire 77:54 Jl '90. Brian Morton (170w)

"No, modern instruments simply do not do this music justice. For Morton Subotnick, O.K. For dozens of talented film composers, definitely. But not for works that aspire to be classics of the original electronic muse."

Fanfare 15:464 N/D '91. David Hurwitz (brief)

SAINT-SAENS, CAMILLE

1316. Carnival of the Animals. RAVEL, MAURICE. Ma Mere l'Oye (ballet).
Andre Previn (c). Joseph Villa (pno); Patricia Prattis Jennings (pno). Pittsburgh Symphony Orchestra.
PHILIPS 400 016

"I have never heard the 'Carnival' performed with as much attention to musical detail, and Previn's play on dynamics is a good part of this....Sonically, everything is glorious, and this CD is highly recommended."

Audio 68:50 Ja '84. John M. Eargle (150w)

"Since I like the performances of Boulez, Martinon, Ozawa, and Skrowaczewski as much as I like Previn's and *prefer* their sound...I'd suggest that you pass this one up."

Fanfare 7:121 S/O '83. James Miller (220w)

Gramophone 60:1152 Ap '83. Edward Greenfield (350w)

Ovation 4:38 S '83. Paul Turok (180w)

Carnival of the Animals, Opus 67. See No. 1281.

1317. Symphony No. 3 in C minor, Opus 78, "Organ". DUKAS, PAUL. The Sorcerer's Apprentice.
James Levine (c). Simon Preston (orgn). Berlin Philharmonic Orchestra.
DEUTSCHE GRAMMOPHON 419 617 DDD 47:04

✔HC ★★*Awards:* *Gramophone* Critics' Choice (Ivan March), 1987; The Want List 1988, *Fanfare* N/D '88 (Haig Mardirosian).

"The majestic grandeur of this symphony is made the most of by Levine and the tension is well-built to cataclismic finale which leaves you emotionally drained....The recording quality is fabulous."

Australian Hi-Fi 19(11):97 '88. (200w)

"This is a winner—a Saint-Saens Third in the grand manner, big of gesture, sumptuous of sonority....[Both performances are] representative of the ripest and most exciting sounds I've heard from DG in ages. The Dukas is particularly successful, uncommonly vivid."

Hi-Fi News & Record Review 32:123 N '87 Edward Seckerson (350w)

"The interpretation is flowing, and dignified, but not as freely joyous as the Munch. There the finale is as powerful, but carefree, a romp as ever played. Here, balance and restraint still hem in unbridled happiness if not massive, brassy, musculature. In all other ways, however, the Levine comes as a splendid addition to the library."

Fanfare 11:204 Ja/F '88. Haig Mardirosian (425)

"Dukas's delightful *The Sorcerer's Apprentice* is superbly played here, but the recording is marred by Levine's offensive grunts and exhortations to the orchestra."

High Fidelity 38:60 Jl '88. Robert E. Benson (240w)

"This orchestra records so often—and its recorded repertoire is so wide—that people may actually think that weightless brass, small-toned horns, sloppy percussion, and Lothar Koch's air-raid siren oboe constitute the way this ensemble, and orchestras in general, ought to sound....Credit must go then to James Levine for forcing DG to give him a reasonably clean, attractive sonority and for encouraging this often overrefined orchestra to play at full tilt. Unfortunately, problems remain."

Musical America 108:79 Jl '88. David Hurwitz (350w)

"Levine's is in general one of the better 3rds on CD....Barenboim...is easily the most exciting interpreter on silver discs, if one can take the hoked-up acoustics...Ormandy's is at least as good a performance as Levine's, and Telarc's recording...is staggering. And then there's Munch, a long-time favorite of many collectors, sabotaged by RCA's careless CD processing...that allows distortion to ruin the exciting climax."

American Record Guide 51:59-60 Ja/F '88. Mark Koldys (375w)

Gramophone 65:300 Ag '87 Ivan March (350w)

SAMMARTINI, GIOVANNI BATTISTA

Concerti Grossi in E minor and in G minor; Concerto in F for Recorder and Orchestra. See No. 1318.

1318. Sinfonias in D and G; Quintet in G. SAMMARTINI, GIUSEPPE. Concerti Grossi in E minor and in G minor; Concerto in F for Recorder and Orchestra.

Chiara Banchini (c). Conrad Steinmann (recorder). Ensemble 415.
HARMONIA MUNDI 901245 DDD

★*Awards:* *Gramophone* Critics' Choice (Julie Anne Sadie), 1987.

"Recommended."

Fanfare 10:184-5 My/Je '87 Nils Anderson (550w)

"At a time when pathetically little of the music of either of the Sammartini brothers is available on disc it is especially good to be able to welcome a pleasing recital containing three characteristic pieces by each."

Hi-Fi News & Record Review 32:101 Ap '87 Peter Branscombe (180w) (rev. of LP)

"One cannot say enough about the fine playing of Ensemble 415....The performances also benefit from excellent, full-bodied, yet thoroughly crisp sound."

Musical America 107:62-3 Ja '88. Christopher Rothko (530w)

"I greatly enjoyed the LP (April, p101)....The clarity and atmosphere of the recording are enhanced on the silver disc."

Hi-Fi News & Record Review 32:99 Jl '87 Peter Branscombe (70w)

Gramophone 64:1416 Ap '87 Julie Anne Sadie (300w)

SAXTON, ROBERT

1319. Concerto for Orchestra; The Ring of Eternity; The Sentinel of the Rainbow; The Circles of Light.

Oliver Knussen (c). BBC Symphony Orchestra; London Sinfonietta.
EMI 49915 DDD 65:00

★*Awards:* The Critics' Choice 1990—Composition Award: No. 14 of 15 *Wire* 82/3 '91.

"This is wonderfully evocative contemporary music—probing, surprising, virtuosic, entertaining. It's orchestration is thrilling....The CD sound is gorgeous....In short, I can see no reason for every collection of late-twentieth-century music not having this CD of Robert Saxton's music."

Fanfare 14:365-6 S/O '90. Stephen Ellis (700w)

Gramophone 67:1788 Ap '90. Arnold Whittall (350w)

SCELSI, GIACINTO

1320. Quattro Pezzi per Orchestra; Anahit, for Violin and Chamber Orchestra; Uaxuctum, for Chorus and Orchestra.

Jurg Wyttenbach (c). Jadwiga Jakubiak (sop); Irena Urbanska (sop); Josef Dwojak (ten); Krzysztof Szafran (ten); Tristan Murail (Ondes Martenot). Polish Radio and Television Chorus and Symphony Orchestra.
ACCORD 20061 DDD 49:40

★★*Awards:* The Want List 1990, *Fanfare* N/D '90 (Mike Silverton). The Critics' Choice 1990—Composition Award: No. 3 of 15 *Wire* 82/3 '91.

"This is perhaps *the* necessary Scelsi recording."

Wire 76:63 Je '90. Richard Barrett (150w)

"One rarely senses so unequivocally that he listens to performances in total harmony with the composer's intent....The recorded sound is airy and smooth, with a splendid dynamic and low end....Recommended to the skies!"

Fanfare 13:246 Jl/Ag '90. Mike Silverton (590w)

Gramophone 68:381 Ag '90. Arnold Whittall (260w)

Music and Musicians International 38:48 Mr '90. P. Grahame Woolf (135w)

SCHICKELE, PETER

1321. 1712 Overture and Other Musical Assaults.

Walter Bruno; Peter Schickele (c). Peter Schickele (nar/pno/devious instrumentalist/intellectual guide).

The Greater Hoople Area Off-Season Philharmonic Orchestra. 1989.
TELARC 80210 DDD 63:12

★★*Awards:* The Want List 1989, *Fanfare* N/D '89 (John Bauman). Editors' Choice, *Digital Audio's CD Review*, 6:34 Je '90; The Editors Pick 6, *Digital Audio's CD Review*, 6:31 Je '90; Cream of the Crop IV, *Digital Audio's CD Review*, 6:41 Je '90.

"We can only be grateful that Prof. Schickele, who has devoted his life to the study of the music of P.D.Q. Bach, has shown such herculean restraint in releasing only the best of those fragments of a life ill-spent....this disc sports the best sound any of P.D.Q.'s music has received...Don't miss this one, if you can."
Stereophile 12:193+ O '89. Richard Lehnert (700w)

"Unfortunately, Peter Schickele is back with more of the disgusting creations of P. D. Q. Bach, the last and least son of old J. S. Worse yet, Telarch has lavished their vaunted superior recording quality on his musical drivel....Lest anyone be deceived by the seemingly negative comments above, I would like to urge all admirers of P. D. Q. Bach and Professor Schickele to immediately invest in this issue. It is certainly one of the best (that is to say worst) in the series."
Fanfare 13:119-20 N/D '89. John Bauman (550w)

"The *Bach Portrait* is the best thing here. It deserves a place beside Schickele's classic play-by-play sportscast of Beethoven's Fifth Symphony....The sonics lavished on this enterprise are certainly sparkling and wide-range. All Schickele-sharers will want to have this one, and perhaps the audiophile presentation package will find new fans for his mad musical adventures."
American Record Guide 53:19-20 Ja/F '90. John Sunier (350w)

Digital Audio's CD Review 6:68+ N '89. Wayne Green (125w)

SCHMIDT, FRANZ

1322. Symphony No. 1 in E.
L'udovit Rajter (c). Bratislava Radio Symphony Orchestra. Also available as a boxed set, Opus 9530 1852/4.
OPUS 9350 1851 DDD 47:00

★*Awards:* The Want List 1988, *Fanfare* N/D '88 (Henry Fogel). Critics' Choice 1988, *Gramophone* D '88 (John Warrack).

"It is an intoxicating work, and Schmidt manages to sustain it despite the length. Rajter captures this soaring quality wonderfully."
American Record Guide 51:77-9 N/D '88. John W. Barker (335w)

"Strongly recommended to collectors with even a mild sense of adventure."
Fanfare 11:183-5 Mr/Ap '88. Henry Fogel (250w)

Originally reviewed in *Fanfare* 11:4, pp.183-85. "Scrub performances of music which deserves far better treatment...My disappointment is quite intense."
Fanfare 12:245-6 S/O '88. John Wiser (850w)

Gramophone 65:1199-200 F '88. John Warrack (180w)

The New York Times S 4 '88, p. H21. Mark Swed (120w)

1323. Symphony No. 2 in E flat.
Neeme Jarvi (c). Chicago Symphony Orchestra. April 20-22, 25, 1989 live.
CHANDOS 8779 DDD 46:55 Orchestra Hall, Chicago discs

★★★*Awards:* The Want List 1991, *Fanfare* N/D '91 (John Wiser); Best of the Month, *Hi-Fi News & Record Review*, F '90; The Year's Best, *Hi Fi News & Record Review*, May '90 Supplement. Critic's Choice: 1990, *American Record Guide* Ja/F '91 (Lee Milazzo).

"Jarvi/CSO has given us a revelation. Symphony 2 is crafted by a sure professional hand possessed of an excellent application of traditional form, a full palette of harmonic and melodic colors, and it's brilliantly orchestrated-....However, for me, this is a case where the performance transcends the music."
Stereophile 13:213+ N '90. Richard Schneider (425w)

"All of the music...has been recorded before, but it's safe to say that these versions surpass the competition in most respects."
Musical America 110:83 Jl '90. David Hurwitz (235w)

"It is difficult to imagine a more thoroughly enjoyable performance than this one. The orchestra is absolutely superb, the sonics simply magnificent—these merits alone overshadow the competition."
American Record Guide 53:99-100 My/Je '90. Lewis M. Smoley (600w)

"Schmidt deserves such enthusiastic and distinguished advocacy as is displayed here and I now impatiently await the remaining three symphonies: above all the magnificent Fourth."
P95/100 S95/100
Hi-Fi News & Record Review 35:100 F '90; p.26 My '90 Supplement. Andrew Achenbach (525w)

"Make no mistake about it, this recording comprises a real performance, and a wholly effective one. I'm inclined to regard it as the first occasion in which a Schmidt symphony has been recorded by major artists with complete understanding of the composer's idiosyncratic manner."
Fanfare 14:302-3 Ja/F '91. John Wiser (525w)

"This recording, with Jarvi doing his best and the Chicago Symphony lending their patented sound, matched by the recording engineer, gives Schmidt his due: it's just that his due is not overdue."

HighPerformanceReview 8(1):76 '91. Bert Wechsler (160w)

Gramophone 67:1618 Mr '90. John Warrack (245w)

Digital Audio's CD Review 7:50 S '90. Daniel Wakin (330w)

1324. Symphony No. 2 in E flat.
L'udovit Rajter (c). Bratislava Radio Symphony Orchestra. Also available as a boxed set with Opus 9530 1851,3,4.
OPUS 9350 1852 DDD 50:00

★*Awards:* The Want List 1988, *Fanfare* N/D '88 (Henry Fogel).

"The only previous recording of this rich and fascinating work was...led by Milan Horvat-....Rajter is more exuberant, and is able to shape and direct the flow of the score with considerably greater expressiveness, earning clear preference."

American Record Guide 51:77-9 N/D '88. John W. Barker (335w)

See Symphony No. 1 for review excerpts from:
Fanfare 11:183-5 Mr/Ap '88, Henry Fogel (250w), and *Fanfare* 12:245-6 S/O '88, John Wiser (850w)

Gramophone 65:1199-200 F '88. John Warrack (180w)

The New York Times S 4 '88, p. H21. Mark Swed (120w)

1325. Symphony No. 3 in A.
L'udovit Rajter (c). Bratislava Radio Symphony Orchestra. Also available as a boxed set with Opus 9530 1851,2,4.
OPUS 9350 1853 DDD 55:00

★*Awards:* The Want List 1988, *Fanfare* N/D '88 (Henry Fogel).

"Each Slovak conductor has something to say about this work, but I suspect Rajter's more mellow reading will be the one to live with."

American Record Guide 51:77-9 N/D '88. John W. Barker (335w)

See Symphony No. 1 for review excerpts from:
Fanfare 11:183-5 Mr/Ap '88, Henry Fogel (250w), and *Fanfare* 12:245-6 S/O '88, John Wiser (850w)

Gramophone 65:1199-200 F '88. John Warrack (180w)

The New York Times S 4 '88, p. H21. Mark Swed (120w)

1326. Symphony No. 4 in C.
L'udovit Rajter (c). Bratislava Radio Symphony Orchestra. Also available as a boxed set with Opus 9530 1851/3.
OPUS 9350 1854 DDD 49:00

★*Awards:* The Want List 1988, *Fanfare* N/D '88 (Henry Fogel).

"I think it can be said that only in Rajter's performance does Schmidt's Fourth finally stand out as one of the genuine symphonic masterpieces of the century. Even allowing some competition from its CD rivals, then, Rajter's performances are clearly desirable individually, while unmatchable as a group."

American Record Guide 51:77-9 N/D '88. John W. Barker (335w)

See Symphony No. 1 for review excerpts from:
Fanfare 11:183-5 Mr/Ap '88, Henry Fogel (250w), and *Fanfare* 12:245-6 S/O '88, John Wiser (850w)

Gramophone 65:1199-200 F '88. John Warrack (180w)

The New York Times S 4 '88, p. H21. Mark Swed (120w)

SCHNITTKE, ALFRED

1327. Symphony No. 1.
Gennady Rozhdestvensky (c). USSR Ministry of Culture State Symphony Orchestra.
MELODIYA 00062 DDD 64:27

★*Awards:* The Want List 1991, *Fanfare* N/D '91 (Paul Rapoport).

"This is all strong stuff but Schnittke brings it off with elan and great skill and the work is expertly performed. This is not easy-listening music nor is it for the faint-hearted or for those who like their music soothing and melodious....The demands on the musicians' skills are heavy and kudos should especially go to the brass....The CD sounds excellent considering the complexity of much of the orchestral fabric."

American Record Guide 54:118-9 Jl/Ag '91. Diederik C. D. De Jong (515w)

"Performances are excellent. The recordings are sub-standard...worth hearing."

American Record Guide 55:102-3 Ja/F '92. Timothy D. Taylor (med)

"The performance [of Symphony No. 1] seems splendidly prepared, with a great deal of striking solo work from jazz violinist Paul Magi and trumpeter Viktor Guseinov, as improvisors, and from a half-dozen others with written-out important solo parts."

Fanfare 15:306-7 Mr/Ap '92. John Wiser (med)

SCHOECK, OTHMAR

1328. Serenade for Orchestra, Opus 1; Concerto in B flat for Violin and Orchestra, Opus 21; Suite in A flat, Opus 59.
Howard Griffiths (c). Ulf Hoelscher (vln). English Chamber Orchestra.
NOVALIS 150 070 DDD 70:16

★*Awards:* Critic's Choice: 1991, *American Record Guide*, Ja/F '92 (Donald Vroon).

"Attractive minor masterworks, loving performances in buxomly immediate, nearly transparent sound, and a handsome production graced

with informed annotations compel one to acknowledge this as a classic and take it to heart."
Fanfare 14:274-75 My/Je '91. Adrian Corleonis (320w)

"Othmar Schoeck wrote very lyrical music....The violin concerto is played with great beauty and vitality by Ulf Hoelscher...The Suite for Strings is warmly conveyed by the ever-dependable orchestra....A delightful discovery—a delectable disc."
American Record Guide 54:101-2 My/Je '91. Donald R. Vroon (250w)

Gramophone 69:62 Jl '91. Robert Layton (525w)

SCHOENBERG, ARNOLD

1329. Chamber Symphony in E, Opus 9; Chamber Symphony, Opus 38; Verklarte Nacht, Opus 4 (arr. string orchestra).
Orpheus Chamber Orchestra. State University of New York, Purchase. April 1989.
DEUTSCHE GRAMMOPHON 429 233 DDD 69:00

✔HC ★★★★*Awards:* Record of the Month, *Hi-Fi News & Record Review*, S '90. The Want List 1990, *Fanfare* N/D '90 (John Wiser); Critics' Choice 1990, *Gramophone* D '90 (James Jolly; Arnold Whittall).

"Here is a record in a thousand—a record that seems to defy the laws of musical performance-....In an astonishing display of large-scale ensemble playing that seems to fly in the face of what has hitherto been considered possible, the conductorless Orpheus Chamber Orchestra have contrived to commit to disc performances of three of Schoenberg's most complex works—and they are performances which, in their beauty and coherence, manage to overshadow virtually every other version in the catalogue....Part of the credit must go to the beautifully judged recording which makes it all seem child's play." *P100 S100*
Hi-Fi News & Record Review 35:81 S '90. Simon Cargill (420w)

"Orpheus and COE, recorded within two months of each other in 1989, bring superb performances, encompassing the work's many moods with coherence and, above all, elan-....Choosing between the two recordings is impossible."
American Record Guide 54:111-12 Mr/Ap '91. Stephen D. Chakwin, Jr. (170w)

"These are rambunctious and arrestingly accomplished performances, thrilling for technique and full, rich tone alone. Ultimately, however, the lack of a conductor is missed on music as personal as the darkly sexual *Verklarte Nacht* or the First Chamber Symphony—although this is less noticeable in the neoclassical second Chamber symphony, which is less emotionally demanding. As for Berg's Chamber Concerto, Holliger's hothouse approach is, again, highly engrossing—and soloists Thomas Zehetmair and Oleg Maisenberg are both dynamite—but here...the young players don't have quite the sonic sweep to bring out the old-fashioned romanticism of the composer."
Musical America 111:83 My '91. Mark Swed (170w)

"For my taste, *VN* gets pushed along just a bit too emphatically, although it is beautifully managed in proportion from section to section-....This is the first account of Chamber Symphony No. 2 to come my way which doesn't ever go slack for a moment, anywhere."
Fanfare 14:74+ S/O '90. John Wiser (b.n.)

Gramophone 68:226 Jl '90. Arnold Whittall (560w)

1330. Chamber Symphony in E, Opus 9; Three Pieces for Chamber Orchestra (1910); Lied der Waltaube (arr. cpsr. for mezzo-soprano and chamber orchestra); Five Pieces for Orchestra, Opus 16.
Reinbert De Leeuw (c). Jard Van Nes (mez). Schoenberg Ensemble.
KOCH-SCHWANN 311 009 DDD 53:00

★*Awards:* Critics' Choice 1989, *Gramophone* D '89 (Arnold Whittall).

"If this magazine were to designate best recordings of the year, this would be one of my nominees."
American Record Guide 52:110-11 N/D '89. Stephen D. Chakwin, Jr. (270w)

"A record of rarities....The playing is excellent, and Reinbert de Leeuw has a real feel for the schizophrenic changes of mood that are such a feature of the idiom....If there were only just a little more air around the sound, everything would be ideal." *P95 S85*
Hi-Fi News & Record Review 35:101 F '90. Simon Cargill (410w)

Gramophone 67:308+ Ag '89. Arnold Whittall (385w)

Chamber Symphony in E, Opus 9. See No. 2029, 3117.

Five Pieces for Orchestra, Opus 16. See No. 1048.

Verklarte Nacht, Opus 4. See No. 1238.

SCHUBERT, FRANZ

1331. Rosamunde (incidental music), D.797 (complete).
Claudio Abbado (c). Anne-Sofie von Otter (mez). Ernst Senff Chamber Chorus; Chamber Orchestra of Europe.
DEUTSCHE GRAMMOPHON 431 655 DDD 59:38

✔HC ★*Awards:* Best Recordings of the Month, *Stereo Review* N '91.

"Abbado, Schubert, and the young performers are in sync; the performances are lively, colorful, and fresh."
Stereo Review 56:74 N '91. Eric Salzman (med)

"The music sounds so good. It sounds particularly good with Claudio Abbado conducting. His expansive tempos, and the warm, sensuous playing he seems to evoke from whatever orchestra he is conducting, are ideally suited to Schubert's lyrical, evocative writing here-....One can also hear well-played excerpts from *Rosamunde* by James Levine (Deutsche Grammophon), Gunter Wand (Angel), and, inexpensively, Adam Fischer (White Label). I was unable to find the Philips recording by Kurt Masur, but I imagine it is worth hearing as well."

Fanfare 15:473-74 N/D '91. Michael Ullman (med)

"Abbado brings his unusual impeccable pacing, relaxed phrasing, and level-headedness to this complete recording of Schubert's incidental music. The Chamber Orchestra of Europe-...delivers extremely clean rhythms and tonal sophistication...Apart from placing the singer too close to the microphones...[this is] a very warm and well-balanced recording. A good recommendation, certainly preferable to the Masur on Philips."

American Record Guide 55:106 Ja/F '92. Arved Ashby (long)

1332. Symphonies (8) (complete); Grand Duo in C, D.812 (orch. J. Joachim); Rosamunde, D.644: Overture, "Die Zauberharfe".
Claudio Abbado (c). Chamber Orchestra of Europe.
DEUTSCHE GRAMMOPHON 423 651 DDD
320:00 5 discs

★★*Awards:* Orchestral Record Award 1989, *Gramophone*, D '89; Top Choices—1989, *American Record Guide* Ja/F '90 (Paul Althouse).

"The Chamber Orchestra of Europe, an international group founded by former members of the European Community Youth Orchestra, is a wonderful group, about as far from the stereo typical 'student orchestra' as you can get. Their ensemble and distinguished wind playing are on a level with the best....while their numbers are modest...the orchestra seems well nourished and closer in sound to a large orchestra than a 'chamber' one....The first six symphonies under Abbado are as satisfying as in any collected set I have encountered. I enjoyed all six except perhaps for No. 6, which seems tepid. The *Unfinished* and Ninth occupy a more exalted rank among the symphonies and have more to offer probing interpreters. Much as I admire Abbado, then, I cannot forget wonderful Eighths by Casals, Furtwangler and (in different veins) Cantelli and Sinopoli; nor will the Ninths of Krips, Furtwangler or Bohm go away."

American Record Guide 52:87-8 Jl/Ag '89. Paul L. Althouse (470w)

"Abbado's style is all-encompassing. He understands what Schubertian lyricism is all about and coaxes succulent sounds from his wood-wind soloists....As befits an operatic conductor, his sense of dramatic timing is impeccable, and he has a better ear for balance than all the digital didgerydoos in the Common Market. Moreover, he insists that every one of his musicians use an original instrument."

Musical America 109:58-60 N '89. Denis Stevens (1010w)

"Here is a very rewarding set, one that challenges preconceptions and offers rich insights....Overall this is probably the most desirable basic set of Schubert's symphonies, though I would myself opt for Marriner's 6-CD box both for the bonus of the realizations of the sketched works and the unfailingly stylish performances."

Hi-Fi News & Record Review 34:93 Mr '89. Peter Branscombe (455w)

"Most listeners will want to decide between this collection and the six discs of Schubert Symphonies by Neville Marriner on Philips....I find Abbado's a better choice of music, and its five discs make his collection a better buy, but—and I realize this evaluation may not be helpful—overall I prefer Neville Marriner's renditions."

Fanfare 12:241-42 Jl/Ag '89. Michael Ullman (650w)

Gramophone 66:1297 F '89. Edward Greenfield (420w)

1333. Symphony No. 3 in D, D.200; Symphony No. 5 in B flat, D.485; Symphony No. 6 in C, "Little Symphony," D.589.
Thomas Beecham (c). Royal Philharmonic Orchestra.
1960, 1956 reissue.
EMI 63750 ADD 78:18

✔HC ★★*Awards:* The Want List 1990, *Fanfare* N/D '90 (John Bauman). *American Record Guide* Overview: Schubert Symphonies, Ja/F '88.

1334. Symphony No. 5 in B flat, D.485; Symphony No. 8 in B minor, D.759, "Unfinished".
Leonard Bernstein (c). Royal Concertgebouw Orchestra. Concertgebouw, Amsterdam. June 1987, October 1987 live.
DEUTSCHE GRAMMOPHON 427 645 DDD 57:00

★*Awards:* The Highs, 1990, *The New York Times* D 30 '90 (John Rockwell).

"These performances serve Schubert well....Despite the considerable resonance of the Concertgebouw, the recording retains clarity and, with its distant perspective, an aura of concert-hall realism still all too infrequent in today's productions."

Fanfare 14:278-79 My/Je '91. Mortimer H. Frank (155w)

"Two things distinguish this pair of live recordings...first, the conductor's success in conveying that the two works emanate from entirely different expressive worlds; and second, the aura of the live performance, which captures the intensity of both pieces in a way that is far more difficult to obtain in a studio recording....The sound throughout is spacious and resonant."

Musical America 111:87-8 Jl '91. Nancy Raabe (280w)

"With Norrington I had no sense that he admired or even cared for what he was doing-....With Bernstein we find no shortage of either admiration or caring....A welcome release, then, from a conductor little associated with Schubert. The orchestra's beautiful playing is admirably captured by DG."

American Record Guide 54:105 My/Je '91. Paul L. Althouse (175w)

Gramophone 67:1336+ Ja '90. Edward Greenfield (230w)

Stereo Review 56:102 Ap '91. Eric Salzman (115w)

1335. Symphonies: No. 5 in B flat, D.485; No. 8 in B Minor, D.759 "Unfinished".
Georg Solti (c). Vienna Philharmonic Orchestra.
LONDON/DECCA 414 371 58:55

✔HC ★*Awards:* *Gramophone* Critics' Choice 1985 (Trevor Harvey).

"These recordings compare favorably with any now available. Solti's version of the Fifth is surely the best in the current domestic LP catalog."

American Record Guide 49:39 My/Je '86. John P. McKelvey (450w) (rev. of LP)

Ovation 7:34-5 Jl '86. Paul Turok (205w); 7:44 N '86 Lawrence B. Johnson (140w)

Gramophone 63:353 S '85. Trevor Harvey (350w)

Hi-Fi News & Record Review 30:115 D '85. Christopher Breunig (105w)

Symphony No. 8 in B minor, "Unfinished," D.759. See No. 1044, 1248.

1336. Symphony No. 9 in C, D.944, "The Great".
Leonard Bernstein (c). Royal Concertgebouw Orchestra. Concertgebouw, Amsterdam. October 1987 live.
DEUTSCHE GRAMMOPHON 427 646 DDD 50:00

★★*Awards:* The Highs, 1990, *The New York Times* D 30 '90 (John Rockwell). Critic's Choice: 1991, *American Record Guide*, Ja/F '92 (Kurt Moses).

"This superb reading of the Great C Major comes to us from a Concertgebouw concert in October 1987, and it shoots immediately to the top of my list....A top recommendation."

American Record Guide 54:106 My/Je '91. Kurt Moses (250w)

"This glorious account of the Schubert Ninth is Bernstein at the very peak of his powers....It is unquestionably a major addition to the catalog, one of the great recorded Ninths, and now a very special reminder of a conductor who gave all music-lovers so much."

Musical America 111:85+ Mr '91. Thor Eckert, Jr. (340w)

"Along with the versions of Karajan (both his DG and EMI accounts), Tennstedt (EMI), Wand (RCA), and Dohnanyi (Telarc), and Szell (CBS), this release must be counted among the preferred editions of this 'Great' score."

Fanfare 14:311 Ja/F '91. Mortimer H. Frank (255w)

"Bernstein....hews pretty close to the pacing we're accustomed to in standard big-orchestra readings, except for some uncomfortable gear shifting at the close of the first movement-....The Royal Concertgebouw is in top form, and the recorded sound is lovely in its bloom, body, and sense of space."

Stereo Review 56:90 My '91. David Hall (150w)

Gramophone 67:1336+ Ja '90. Edward Greenfield (230w)

1337. Symphony No. 9 in C, D.944, "The Great".
Christoph von Dohnanyi (c). Cleveland Orchestra. Masonic Auditorium, Cleveland OH. 1985.
TELARC 80110 49:38

✔HC ★*Awards:* *American Record Guide* Overview: Schubert Symphonies, Ja/F '88.

"There are so many 'high spots' in this performance, that one can only advise the reader to go out and purchase the CD in order to judge it for himself....This is a very great recording of a very great work....a superb engineering job...just enough reverberation to give the illusion of concert-hall ambience."

HighPerformanceReview 4(1):184-5 '86 Thomas H. Wendel (200w)

"The new recording of the Schubert Ninth Symphony is, by all odds, the most satisfactory in terms of sound and performance to be issued on CD. Christoph von Dohnanyi...provides a classically structured 'middle-European' performance of great power and elegance."

Audio 70:88 Ap '86. Bert Whyte (180w)

"Dohnanyi's view of the Great C Major flowers its heavenly breadth with quite earthly delights. Affectionate, minutely and yet warmly detailed, devoid of pomposity from first to last, this performance turns the music's sublime spirit to ecstatic affirmation. It is a hymn of intellectual beauty imbued with the directness of folk song....Telarc has delivered this magnificent affair with a naturalism and immediacy that are to be prized in themselves."

Ovation 7:44 N '86 Lawrence B. Johnson (245w)

"There are probably only two recordings I would recommend above this new one: Krips on a bargain-label Decca/London and Tennstedt on EMI. Both have greater spring to their rhythms and more song-like bite."

The $ensible Sound 8:56-57 Wint '86/'87 John J. Puccio (195w)

"Among current recordings of this score, Dohnanyi's can take its place beside Tennstedt's (Angel) as one of the best."

Fanfare 9:211-2 Ja/F '86. Mortimer H. Frank (500w)

"This is indeed a 'Great' C major—an account that can be mentioned in the same breath as the sublime 1941 Toscanini/Philadelphia Orchestra miracle (RCA, OP). Greater praise could hardly be tendered from this quarter!"

Opus 2:47 F '86. Harris Goldsmith (440w)

Gramophone 63:632+ N '85. Trevor Harvey (420w)

Hi-Fi News & Record Review 30:119 D '85. Peter Branscombe (150w)

1338. Symphony No. 9 in C, D.944, "The Great".

Charles Mackerras (c). Age of Enlightenment Orchestra. 1987.
VIRGIN 90708 DDD 59:30

★★*Awards:* Best Recordings of the Month, *Stereo Review* F '89. Cream of the Crop IV, *Digital Audio's CD Review*, 6:43 Je '90.

"Mackerras's Schubert 9 may not only be the first recording of this work on authentic instruments, but also the first performance as Schubert would have heard it....While the difference in sound is not as startling as that on Norrington's Beethoven 9 (Vol.11 No.4), it does reveal some beautiful scoring that glows with a warmth and clarity rarely heard in modern performance."

Stereophile 11:159-162 Ag '88. Barbara Jahn (390w)

"A mild revelation....the textures of the Ninth make much more sense when correct brass and wind timbres are heard."

Hi-Fi News & Record Review 33:75+ Je '88. Christopher Breunig (175w)

"This may not be the only way to do the 'Great' C Major, but it is an especially bracing refreshing account of it, and it makes great musical sense. It is also superbly recorded, with a fine open-air quality that makes the most of those crisp 'period' brasses and woodwinds and allows the strings to charm without becoming soupy."

Stereo Review 54:114 F '89. Richard Freed (490w)

"My first choice for this symphony remains the wondrous Furtwangler....This version will also attain a special fondness in my affections for the gorgeous instrumental sounds it contains as well as for Sir Charles's idiomatic reading."

American Record Guide 52:87 Ja/F '89. Carl Bauman (250w)

"Though Sir Charles Mackerras leads performances which are intriguing in their scholarship, they are also...lacking in romantic passion."

Continuo 13:15 Ag '89. David Cavlovic (130w)

"Mackerras' reading is somewhat unorthodox and at times refreshing. For my taste, however, it is too bland, too lacking in drama and in sufficient number of plateaus of tension....this is a release that at least deserves a hearing."

Fanfare 12:253-4 S/O '88. Mortimer H. Frank (680w)

Gramophone 66:35 Je '88. Richard Osborne (525w)

Ovation 10:64-5 Ap '89. Scott Cantrell (385w)

Digital Audio's CD Review 5:92+ Je '89. Lawrence Johnson (325w)

SCHUMANN, ROBERT

1339. Symphonies (4) (complete).

("The Symphony Edition" (also available as a set, Deutsche Grammophon 429 677)).
Herbert Von Karajan (c). Berlin Philharmonic Orchestra. 1972 reissue.
DEUTSCHE GRAMMOPHON 429 672 ADD (m) 132:00 2 discs

✔HC ★★*Awards:* Records to Die for: 1 of 5 Recommended Recordings, *Stereophile* Ja '91 (Mortimer H. Frank); Critic's Choice: 1990, *American Record Guide* Ja/F '91 (Arved Ashby).

"Anyone who doubts Karajan's greatness should hear these performances."

Stereophile 14:137 Ja '91. Mortimer H. Frank (b.n.)

Gramophone 68:227-28 Jl '90. John Steane (330w)

American Record Guide 53:12+ S/O '90. Arved Ashby (315w)

1340. Symphonies: No: 1 in B flat, Opus 38, "Spring"; No. 4 in D Minor, Opus 120.

Leonard Bernstein (c). Vienna Philharmonic Orchestra.
DEUTSCHE GRAMMOPHON 415 274

★★*Awards:* *Fanfare* Want List 1986 (James Miller). *American Record Guide* Overview: Schumann, My/Je '88.

Bernstein "does take Schumann seriously and he allows the orchestration, so often regarded as bungling and inept, to speak plainly and strongly for itself."

The Musical Times 128:90 F '87 Hugh Macdonald (175w) (rev. of LP)

"My favorite in the Schumann symphony cycle that Leonard Bernstein recorded for Columbia in the early Sixties has remained the *Spring* symphony...Bernstein' performance of the D Minor Symphony, however, seems lacking in drive through most of the first movement, and the pacing is generally on the heavy side....The sound throughout is rich and detailed, though, making for an extraordinarily transparent orchestral texture."

Stereo Review 51:126-7 Je '86. David Hall (300w)

High Fidelity 36:63 Jl '86. Thomas L. Dixon (175w)

Ovation 7:42-43 D '86 Peter J. Rabinowitz (705w)

1341. Symphony No. 1 in B flat, Opus 38, "Spring"; Symphony No. 2 in C, Opus 61.
Christoph von Dohnanyi (c). Cleveland Orchestra. 1987/88.
LONDON/DECCA 421 439 DDD 71:00

★*Awards:* Best Recordings of the Month, *Stereo Review* Ap '89.

"Highly recommended."
Stereo Review 54:32 Ap '89. David Hall (290w)

"These are deeply considered readings, remarkable for their clarity of texture...a powerfully organic sense of developing structure, and a spacious lyricism which deftly avoids sentimentality and self-indulgent 'sensitivity'. The composer emerges as thoroughly healthy and virile, and the stature of the works seems so self-evident that their well-aired defects pale into insignificance....These performances may lack the febrile intensity of a Toscanini, the galvanic energy of a Solti or the epic nobility of a Furtwangler, but they should find an honoured place on many a music-lover's shelf, and rightly so."
Hi-Fi News & Record Review 34:111-13 Ap '89. Jeremy Siepmann (190w)

"To me, the performances don't add up to much except that: (1) Dohnanyi is a proficient, 'sensitive' maestro; (2) the Cleveland Orchestra can still play beautifully; (3) London Records can capture them in vivid, powerful sound....I could even recommend them to somebody who's looking for 'safe' performances of the Schumann symphonies, but I don't *love* them."

Fanfare 12:316-18 My/Je '89. James Miller (250w)

Gramophone 66:1161 Ja '89. Edward Seckerson (330w)

Digital Audio's CD Review 6:76-7 S '89. Lawrence Johnson (200w)

1342. Symphony No. 2 in C, Opus 61; Concerto in A minor for Cello and Orchestra, Opus 129.
Leonard Bernstein (c). Mischa Maisky (cello). Vienna Philharmonic Orchestra.
DEUTSCHE GRAMMOPHON 419 190 67:15

★*Awards:* *American Record Guide* Overview: Schumann, My/Je '88.

"At last, Leonard Bernstein's Schumann cycle comes to an end, with performances...that are as great a pleasure to recommend as were the two previous discs in this splendid series-....From all parties concerned, then, a truly magnificent accomplishment. Schumann has rarely been so well served."

High Fidelity 37:68 O '87. Thomas L. Dixon (250w)

"There's something to be said for a conductor who leads a piece as if every bar were a matter of life and death to him, and I'll gladly live with Bernstein's eccentricities (some of which I like) in preference to the solid routine of Haitink or the hard-boiled intensity of Sinopoli, the present CD competition."
Fanfare 10:202-3 Mr/Ap '87 James Miller (575w)

Hi-Fi News & Record Review 32:103 Ap '87 Christopher Breunig (210w)

Ovation 7:42-43 D '86 Peter J. Rabinowitz (705w)

Gramophone 64:718 N '86 Robert Levine (485w)

Symphony No. 3 in E flat, Opus 97, "Rhenish". See No. 1167.

SCRIABIN, ALEXANDER

1343. Symphony No. 3 ("Divine Poem"), Opus 43; Symphony No. 4 ("The Poem of Ecstasy"), Opus 54.
Giuseppe Sinopoli (c). New York Philharmonic Orchestra.
DEUTSCHE GRAMMOPHON 427 324 DDD 70:00

✔HC ★*Awards:* The Want List 1989, *Fanfare* N/D '89 (Walter Simmons).

"Sinopoli makes a surprisingly strong argument for the symphonic structure—each climax in the outer movements is more brilliant than the last, so any momentary sense of 'back to the beginning' with the ever-insistent motto is immediately banished by fresh energy. It may be the tighter invention of the *Poem of Ecstasy* which finds him more lavish with rubato and expressive exuberance (first trumpet Philip Smith, so good in the *Divine Poem*, is even more dazzling here)." *P95/100 S95/100*
Hi-Fi News & Record Review 34:92-3 S '89. David Nice (320w)

"An antidote to even the finest of the conventional approaches [to the 3rd], which never fully succeed in mitigating the impression of an unwieldy, elephantine work, Sinopoli's reading creates a buoyant transparency that expands its range of textures, reducing its tendency toward monotony and enabling it to stand without embarrassment or apology among other monumental works of its time-....Confirming the stature of this new DG release as the most important Scriabin orchestral recording of recent years, Sinopoli and the NYP bring a comparable level of artistry to 'Le Poeme de l'Extase."
Fanfare 13:324-26 S/O '89. Walter Simmons (250w)

"Listening to these soaring, surging performances, it's easy to understand why Soviet radio chose Scriabin's *Poem of Ecstasy* to accompany the first manned spaceflight...Such music—especially in Giuseppe Sinopoli's sensational interpretation—is not of this earth-....the Third Symphony makes much ado about a very small amount of musical material—one brassy, insistent motif ever so reminiscent of the lovesick Wagner of *Tristan und Isolde*. Just when you think the composer couldn't possibly reach any higher level of supersensual abandon, he does. Sinopoli stays with Scriabin all the way, right through the coital acceleration to the sublime final tranquility, bringing to marvelous muscularity to this divine decadence."

Musical America 110:83-4 Mr '90. Harlow Robinson (440w)

"Sinopoli's conducting sheds the most revealing of lights on the composer's orchestral textures, but his commitment seems more to the niceties of this music than to its underlying spirit. His punctiliousness works better in *Le Poeme de l'Extase*, where tight control gives the climax a real sense of authority. DG's recording is spatially cramped and dynamically restricted in the *Third Symphony*, and only marginally more open and communicative in *Le Poeme de l'Extase*."

New Hi-Fi Sound 6:105 Ag '89. George Entwistle (240w)

"Conductor Giuseppe Sinopoli has the New York Philharmonic playing at the top of their form in a lush, effusively romantic performance of 'Le Divin Poeme,' but the gem on this CD is the searing emotional intensity and passion of 'Le Poeme de l'Extase'....The sound is very clean and well detailed, with great weight."

Audio 74:146 Ja '90. Bert Whyte (430w)

"Having inconclusively debated the relative merits of Muti and Pritchard in the July/August issue, I now find myself greatly appreciating the ripe Philadelphia sound as well as Muti's control and subtlety of rubato. These are all characteristics sorely missing from Sinopoli's account...I also find the sound of the New York Philharmonic as recorded in Manhattan Center coarse and difficult to enjoy."

American Record Guide 52:117 N/D '89. Arved Ashby (205w)

"Sinopoli's recording disappoints on a number of counts, but most obviously in the recorded sound."

The Musical Times 130:420-21 Jl '89. Matthew Rye (340w)

Gramophone 67:44 Je '89. Michael Oliver (420w)

SESSIONS, ROGER

1344. Symphonies: No.'s 1-3.

Akeo Watanabe; Dimitri Mitropoulos; Igor Buketoff (c). Japan Philharmonic Orchestra; New York Philharmonic Orchestra; Royal Philharmonic Orchestra. reissues.
CRI 573 ADD (stereo/mono) 74:22

★*Awards:* The Want List 1991, *Fanfare* N/D '91 (Royal S. Brown).

"This is one of the most important and most enjoyable of all CD reissues of American music."

Fanfare 14:289 Jl/Ag '91. James H. North (350w)

"It's wonderful to see these fine performances of Roger Sessions's first three symphonies, which I've known and loved for so many years, together in the convenient (and, in the case of the First Symphony, sonically improved) CD format."

American Record Guide 54:124-5 Jl/Ag '91. Mark L. Lehman (560w)

1345. Symphony No. 4; Symphony No. 5; Rhapsody for Orchestra.

Christian Badea (c). Columbus Symphony Orchestra.
NEW WORLD 345 DDD 54:00

✔HC ★★★★*Awards:* *Opus* Repertoire Enhancement Award, 1987; *Fanfare* Want List 1987 (Paul Snook); *Fanfare* Want List 1987 (Paul Rapoport); *Fanfare* Want List 1987 (Stephen W. Ellis).

"A CD I'll return to again and again with pleasure."

HighPerformanceReview 5:90 S '88. James Primosch (180w)

"Those Ohioans do a whale of a job on this tough music....New World's sound is top-notch."

Fanfare 11:294-5 S/O '87. Stephen W. Ellis (850w)

"The *Rhapsody*, incidentally, was recorded years ago on Argo ZRG 702, in a performance which is noticeably faster and in some places technically more secure. That performance is not as clear, however, as this one,; the intricacies of Sessions' counterpoint and the iridescence of his orchestration seem made for compact discs (or very well produced LPs). That said, it must also be admitted that the earlier performance has more drive in places....But I don't want to take away from the extraordinary achievement which this disc represents."

Fanfare 11:295-6 S/O '87. Paul Rapoport (740w)

"That an American regional orchestra, not one of the majors, and in its recording debut at that, should be able to perform these complex and intricate scores with such assurance and aplomb is cause for rejoicing and reflects much credit on orchestra and conductor Christian Badea alike."

Opus 4:39+ D '87. John Canarina (900w)

"The Columbus Symphony is a fine orchestra, well-balanced in sound and technically competent in this demanding music. The only aspect one might question is a certain lack of brilliance in the sound which one suspects is due to a rather dry recorded ambience."

American Record Guide 50:71-2 N/D '87. David W. Moore (275w)

"These pieces are extremely difficult to play, and Christian Badea has rehearsed his orchestra to the point of great accuracy."
Ovation 9:42 F '88. Paul Turok (405w)

"Christian Badea and the Columbus Symphony turn in performances that are astonishing. The orchestra sounds absolutely world-class. Special praise must go to the violins for managing the perilously high writing so cleanly."
High Fidelity 38:77 Ap '88. David Hurwitz (250w)

Gramophone 65:584+ O '87 Michael Oliver (560w)

SHAPERO, HAROLD

1346. Symphony for Classical Orchestra; Nine-Minute Overture.
Andre Previn (c). Los Angeles Philharmonic Orchestra. 1988 live.
NEW WORLD 373 DDD 54:48

★*Awards:* Top Choices—1989, *American Record Guide* Ja/F '90 (Gerald Fox).

"The clean, taut textures and tonal harmonic language are a delight...Shapero's intellectual vantage doesn't grip the emotions as much as compel an immense regard for his craft, but let's hope we don't have to wait as long for more treasure from this creator."
Ovation 10:51-2 S '89. Tom Di Nardo (250w)

"This is an absolutely stunning performance—recorded 'live' with all the attendant crackle of immediacy—that completely revises one's view of the work: where before one heard stiffness and overfastidiousness, Previn shows us how gracefully supple, songful, and ingratiating Shapero can be. He is also very successful in clarifying the work's incisive tissue of polyphonic textures and its architectonic mastery of formal development without ever sacrificing the momentum of forward motion."
Fanfare 12:274-75 Mr/Ap '89. Paul A. Snook (700w)

"Harold Shapero's symphony inspires more admiration than affection....Nor is such an attachment encouraged by the composer; on the contrary, he clearly and deliberately avoids the potential for it....This recording...supersedes Bernstein's excellent one in mono on Columbia....Previn is a degree or two colder, but equally committed to the work, and includes the overture, a Pistonesque, toccata-like exercise in going nowhere fast."
American Record Guide 52:82 Mr/Ap '89. Kyle Rothweiler (280w)

"Previn...responds enthusiastically to both works, extracting from them their colour and vitality and essential Americanism. The sound...is rather fierce but clear and sparkling."
Hi-Fi News & Record Review 34:84 Jl '89. Kenneth Dommett (280w)

The New York Times Ag 20 '89, p. H 29. Andrew L. Pincus (110w)

SHOSTAKOVICH, DMITRI

1347. Symphony No. 1 in F, Opus 10; Symphony No. 6 in B minor, Opus 54.
Vladimir Ashkenazy (c). Royal Philharmonic Orchestra. 1988.
LONDON/DECCA 425 609 DDD 64:00

★★*Awards:* Critic's Choice: 1990, *American Record Guide* Ja/F '91 (James Ginsburg). *American Record Guide* Overview: Prokofieff/Shostakovich, S/O '91.

"Having recently tabbed Rozhdestvensky's First (Melodiya 161) as 'the most compelling version so far on silver disc' (July/Aug 1990), I am pleased to report that Ashkenazy's better played and recorded account rivals the Russian in interpretation....the lack of emotion at the start of the Sixth signals trouble ahead."
American Record Guide 53:116-17 N/D '90. James S. Ginsburg (480w)

"This Shostakovich First may not quite have the character one finds in every measure of Leonard Bernstein's recent recording, but it certainly comes in a close—very close—second among the CD performances, and there are those who may prefer the excitement it generates to Bernstein's slightly more controlled emotivity....An above-average Shostakovich Sixth, but not at the top of the heap."
Fanfare 14:355-56 N/D '90. Royal S. Brown (275w)

"If these were live performances they would doubtless be cheered to the rafters. It is the ability to withstand repetition, however, that must be the chief criterion for a recording-....Good versions then, in good sound; but lacking that little something." *P95/85 S95*
Hi-Fi News & Record Review 35:103 N '90. Simon Cargill (330w)

Digital Audio's CD Review 7:52 F '91. Tom Vernier (400w)

Gramophone 68:61-2 Je '90. Michael Oliver (430w)

1348. Symphony No. 1 in F, Opus 10; Symphony No. 7 in C, Opus 60, "Leningrad".
Leonard Bernstein (c). Chicago Symphony Orchestra. Orchestra Hall, Chicago. June 1988 live.
DEUTSCHE GRAMMOPHON 427 632 DDD 120:00 2 discs

★★★★*Awards:* Best Recordings of the Month, *Stereo Review* Ap '90. Records to Die for: 1 of 5 Recommended Recordings, *Stereophile* Ja '91 (Richard Schneider); Critic's Choice: 1990, *American Record Guide* Ja/F '91 (James Ginsburg). *American Record Guide* Overview: Prokofieff/Shostakovich, S/O '91.

"I...was just going to listen to part of the first movement. But I sat in my chair and couldn't move until the whole symphony was over....That's how terrific the performance was."

Musical America 111:48 N/D '91. Cho-Liang Lin (brief)

"I hate to use the adjective, but I can find no other to describe the...performance of the...First Symphony...than 'perfect'....all other versions of the symphony might just as well be thrown away....Adding to all this excellence is recorded sound that is...perfect...Bernstein's interpretation [of the 7th] throughout is noticeably more careful and measured than the New York Philharmonic version and therefore lacks some of that performance's electricity....he gets much better, much fuller, much more committed playing from the Chicago Symphony than from the overrated New York Philharmonic."

Fanfare 13:295-99 Mr/Ap '90. Royal S. Brown (245w)

"The DG [recording] shows up most of the better recordings of the past several years as being no more than adequate....he draws from [the CSO]...two of their finest recorded performances since the Reiner era, performances of great subtlety and refinement, as well as the extreme emotional range embodied in works of Shostakovich."

Stereophile 13:203+ Ap '90. Richard Schneider (185w)

"Bernstein's new reading [of the Seventh] is invested with a somewhat different sort of intensity than his first one...The orchestra's playing reflects the same level of conviction and is simply beyond praise....The accompanying First Symphony sounds a little larger than life here-...Rozhdestvensky is incomparably convincing in this work, on Melodiya, but Bernstein's intensity and the Chicago Symphony Orchestra's beautiful playing may persuade you that you need a second version."

Stereo Review 55:77 Ap '90. Richard Freed (700w)

"Here Bernstein is in his element! He presents the symphony as the story of the complete corruption and destruction of a world that could be peaceful and beautiful....The performance offers 84 minutes of the finest music-making on disc....DG offers closely miked yet effectively though not perfectly balanced sound—the trombones are a little too forward, for example—not without ambiance."

American Record Guide 53:108-09 My/Je '90. James S. Ginsburg (400w)

"A recording that sounds more like the real Chicago Symphony really sounds than almost any recording since the Martinon/CSO Varese *Arcana*/Martin Concerto for 7 Winds of 1966 in pre-renovation Orchestra Hall for RCA."

Stereophile 14:167 Ja '91. Richard Schneider (b.n.)

Gramophone 67:1338 Ja '90. Michael Oliver (350w)

1349. Symphony No. 4 in C minor, Opus 43.

Bernard Haitink (c). London Philharmonic Orchestra. 1979 reissue.
LONDON/DECCA 421 348 ADD 68:00

⇑ ★*Awards: American Record Guide* Overview: Prokofiev/Shostakovich, S/O '91.

"London's transfer of this 1979 analogue recording proves quite successful, a little warmer than average, with tremendous dynamics, natural string sound, and an enormous stage. The CD presents an orchestral image closer than in some recent DDDs and with not a lot less atmosphere and depth than an LP....cymbals and gong are not among the most realistic I've heard on a CD—huge blasts without compression of the initial stroke or generalizing of shimmery fragments. Haitink has an affinity for Shostakovitch....The LPO doesn't make an authentically Russian or spiky sound, but I guarantee it will wake you up and keep you up—this disc is the musical equivalent of 12 cups of espresso."

The Absolute Sound 15:162+ S/O '90. Arthur S. Pfeffer (460w)

"Unless you want to wait to hear how Ashkenazy's new RPO recording comes out, this Kingsway Hall production is recommended—not just for its shattering weight in Shostakovich's big tutti scoring, but for the certain sense of logic conveyed by Haitink. Whereas on LP it seemed rather cool (see *Penguin's* dismissal), remastering brings enhanced presence."

Hi-Fi News & Record Review 34:113 Ap '89. Christopher Breunig (245w)

Gramophone 66:1437 Mr '89. Michael Oliver (190w)

1350. Symphony No. 4 in C minor, Opus 43.

Neeme Jarvi (c). Scottish National Orchestra.
CHANDOS 8640 DDD 61:00

★★*Awards:* Record of the Month, *Hi-Fi News & Record Review*, F '90; The Year's Best, *Hi Fi News & Record Review*, May '90 Supplement. *American Record Guide* Overview: Prokofieff/Shostakovich, S/O '91.

"This massive, commanding masterpiece has a troubled history, including not years but decades of neglect and oblivion. The blazing performance it gets here, brilliantly recorded, provides us a welcome opportunity for discovery-....as a whole, the work requires courageous, adventurous listening."

Audio 74:112+ Je '90. Paul Moor (950w)

"Both Neeme Jarvi's conducting of the *Fourth* and the Chandos recording of it are superlative achievements. This is one of those rare recordings that will elicit continual amazement and satisfaction with each new hearing. It is a marvel of technical skill to have brought this performance to CD."

HighPerformanceReview 8(1):79 '91. John Mueter (280w)

"Yet another Shostakovich work affected by the cruel politics of his day....The recording is simply another gem in Jarvi's superb Shostakovich cycle....The Fourth has enjoyed fine recordings in the past (Previn and Ormandy immediately spring to mind) but never with sound like this!"

American Record Guide 53:107-08 Mr/Ap '90. James S. Ginsburg (225w)

"This team has been giving us a major Shostakovich series, of which this recording may be the most important entry to date."

Stereo Review 55:112 My '90. Eric Salzman (110w)

"No question of a single choice for a symphony like this, so Ashkenazy *P100 S100*, Jarvi*P100 S95/100*

Hi-Fi News & Record Review 35:94 F '90; p.11 My '90 Supplement. David Nice (365w)

"The Scottish National Orchestra executes the music with its usual expertise...But, for all the music's 'alienation' effects, it calls for a tad more involvement than comes across in this rendition."

Fanfare 13:295-99 Mr/Ap '90. Royal S. Brown (245w)

Gramophone 67:1143 D '89. Michael Oliver (285w)

1351. Symphony No. 5 in D minor, Opus 47; Five Fragments, Opus 42.

Vladimir Ashkenazy (c). Royal Philharmonic Orchestra. Walthamstow Assembly Hall, London. March 1987.
LONDON/DECCA 421 120 DDD 56:00

✔HC ★*Awards:* The Want List 1988, *Fanfare* N/D '88 (Royal S. Brown).

"Sonically speaking, Decca, of course, spoiled us for good with their spectacular Concertgebouw/Haitink recording....But Ashkenazy's reading has a temperament and emotional force that quite eluded Haitink, and what the RPO lack here in finish and subtlety they more than compensate for in spirit and commitment."

Hi-Fi News & Record Review 33:103 S '88. Edward Seckerson (515w)

"Ashkenazy, the Royal Philharmonic, and London make *this* Shostakovich Fifth the most attractive—by far—on CD....Throughout, Ashkenazy finds the perfect pace for allowing the music to reveal its innermost workings....he exploits the full emotional potential of the symphony's dynamic shadings better than any conductor I've heard."

Fanfare 12:278-82 N/D '88. Royal S. Brown (350w)

"Vladimir Ashkenzay's account of the Shostakovich Fifth is tantalizingly close to a fine performance. Unfailingly lyrical in his approach, the conductor probes those aspects of the work that relate to Mussorgsky, rather than to Mahler....The result is a rhapsodic performance that at best is suggestively brooding but at worst sounds as if Ashkenzay is waving his arms at the melody instruments and letting the rest of the band take care of itself....Jansons' is still the best of the recent recordings of the symphony."

Musical America 109:80-1 Mr '89. Paul Turok (380w)

"From beginning to end, in every aspect, this is a terrific recording."

HighPerformanceReview 6:86-7 Je '89. Timothy Mangan (200w)

Gramophone 66:36 Je '88. David J. Fanning (540w)

1352. Symphony No. 5 in D minor, Opus 47.

Bernard Haitink (c). Concertgebouw Orchestra.
LONDON/DECCA 410 017 DDDPerfect 10/10, *Digital Audio*, Mr '88.

"Bernard Haitink's disc...combines a powerfully tense interpretation, electrifying sonics, and impeccable playing to produce the most awe-inspiring account of the work ever recorded."

American Record Guide 52:88 Ja/F '89. James Ginsberg (50w)

"Haitink's Fifth...is now the third performance to make it to CD, and I will say immediately that this is the version I will pull off the shelves and listen to the most often."

Fanfare 9:248 My/Je '86. Royal S. Brown (500w)

"If forced to choose...[between this disc and the Rostoprovich with the National Symphony Orchestra of Washington, DC] I would have to take the Haitink recording....simply on the basis that the Concertgebouw is a finer orchestra...neither Rostropovich...nor his orchestra have the technique or the quality of Haitink and his band."

High Performance Review 3 (2):122-3 '84. Thomas H. Wendel (150w)

"A superb performance gains in stature and impact on CD. Haitink's reading may not be as visceral as, say, Bernstein's latest with the New York Philharmonic on CBS (IM 35854), or the very recent Rostropovich account on Deutsche Grammophon (2532 076), but the Dutch maestro is nevertheless unexpectedly energetic, committed and passionate in this score. The climaxes are not shirked, but it is in the moments of deep introspection and morose brooding that Haitink and the Concertgebouw make this reading so special. Here, the orchestra's unique string tone takes on a haunting plagency, and all work together to make the undercurrent of despair really suffuse the piece. The CD, with its quiet background, adds to that sense of desolation, of aridity."

Ovation 5:50 F '84. Thor Eckert, Jr. (165w)

An "unexpectedly earthbound performance—conscientious and artful but not [a compelling interpretation]...I favor Lorin Maazel's reading, as deeply felt as Haitink's but smoother, less self consciously 'interpretive'."

Fanfare 7:256-7 Mr/Ap '84. Roger Dettmer (200w)

Gramophone 61:349 S '83. Robert Layton (140w)

Digital Audio 1:76-7 O '84. Norman Eisenberg (600w)

1353. Symphony No. 5 in D minor, Opus 47; The Bolt—Ballet Suite No. 5, Opus 27a.
Neeme Jarvi (c). Scottish National Orchestra.
CHANDOS 8650 DDD 76:12

> ★***Awards:*** *American Record Guide* Overview: Prokofiev/Shostakovich, S/O '91.

"*The Bolt*...is unremitting in its almost manic high spirits....Jarvi and the SNO attack it (the word is used advisedly) as if they believe in every note. Combined with a characteristically spectacular recording, it all adds up to an exciting if occasionally numbing musical experience....this is a version [of the Fifth] that should prove very easy to live with. If, however, you are looking for the maximum sensitivity at the beginning of the slow movement, you may be better off elsewhere." *P95 S95/85*

Hi-Fi News & Record Review 34:93 S '89. Simon Cargill (275w)

"Not only is there nothing wrong with this Shostakovich Fifth, it is right—superb—in so many ways that I can only begin to note them here....Chandos deserves much credit for taking advantage of the CD format by including Shostakovich rarities along with the symphonies."

Fanfare 13:326-29 S/O '89. Royal S. Brown (280w)

"Chandos's sound is superb as always...Jarvi's distinctive interpretation joins Haitink's more massive reading (London 410 017 -praised in Jan/Feb 1989), in the first line of Shostakovich Fifths on CD."

American Record Guide 52:119 N/D '89. James S. Ginsburg (350w)

Gramophone 67:1801 Ap '90. Michael Oliver (315w)

1354. Symphonies: No. 6 in B minor, Opus 54; No. 11 ("Year 1905"), Opus 103; **Concerto No. 1 for Piano, Trumpet and Orchestra; Concerto No. 2 in F for Piano and Orchestra; Fantastic Dances (3) for Piano, Opus 5.**
Paavo Berglund (c). Cristina Ortiz (pno).
Bournemouth Symphony Orchestra. 1980, 1975 reissues.
EMI 47790 ADD 143:00 2 discs

> ★***Awards:*** *American Record Guide* Overview: Prokofiev/Shostakovich, S/O '91 (Concerto).

"I reviewed the LP recording of the two symphonies all the way back in *Fanfare* 4:3 (January/February 1981). Then, as now, Berglund's Sixth remained and remains one of the most persuasive interpretations ever of this magnificent symphony."

Fanfare 12:278-82 N/D '88. Royal S. Brown (350w)

Gramophone 65:1608 My '88. Michael Oliver (420w)

1355. Symphony No. 8 in C minor, Opus 65.
Bernard Haitink (c). Concertgebouw Orchestra.
LONDON/DECCA 411 616 DDD 61:24

> ★★★***Awards:*** *Fanfare* Want List 1985 (Royal S. Brown); *Fanfare* Want List 1984 (Elliott Kaback). *American Record Guide* Overview: Prokofieff/Shostakovich, S/O '91.

"Haitink, as in the best of his previous Shostakovich recordings, here offers...fresh insights, and he is aided by the superb playing of his orchestra and topflight digital recording."

Stereo Review 49:109-10 Ap '84. David Hall (360w)

Gramophone 61:1182 Ap '84. Geoffrey Horn (245w)

Hi-Fi News & Record Review 29:74 Je '84. Andrew Keener (210w)

Ovation 5:56-7 Ag '84. Paul Turok (390w)

Digital Audio 1:58 My '85. Bill Storrer (660w)

1356. Symphony No. 8 in C minor, Opus 65.
Evgeny Mravinsky (c). Leningrad Philharmonic Orchestra. Leningrad. February 1982 live.
PHILIPS 422 442 ADD 60:00

> ✔**HC** ★★***Awards:*** Critics' Choice 1989, *Gramophone* D '89 (Stephen Johnson). *American Record Guide* Overview: Prokofieff/Shostakovich, S/O '91.

"Playing is everywhere utterly beyond reproach...it is a pity I cannot recommend this CD....since Philips did not check speeds when they transferred to digital tape the performance sounds about 3% fast (half a semitone sharp). This alters the whole character of the sound and performance."

Hi-Fi News & Record Review 34:101 Ag '89. Richard Black (410w)

"The not-always-secure playing of the Leningrad Philharmonic cannot compare with an inspired Concertgebouw under Haitink (London 411 616)....the disc at hand offers an intriguing interpretive alternative, but Haitink remains king of the hill."

American Record Guide 52:120 N/D '89. James S. Ginsburg (230w)

"Mravinsky's Eighth maintains every bit of what Robert Layton, in his excellent notes, calls the music's 'bitter suffering'—indeed, it is this quality that strongly marked an earlier version done years ago by the same forces."

Fanfare 13:359-62 N/D '89. Royal S. Brown (300w)

"The performance is magnificent. The recording...is technically excellent....However, if you can have only one I recommend the Haitink (London 411 616). Interpretation and playing are equal to Mravinsky, but London's engineering is spectacular."

American Record Guide 53:109 My/Je '90. Gerald S. Fox (425w)

"This recording leaves many messages, makes many impressions. In the hands of Mravinsky the multifaceted and potent Shostakovich *Eighth* emerges as a historical testament as well as a worthy memorial to a great conductor."

HighPerformanceReview 8(1):79-80 '91. Kenneth Krehbiel (320w)

"Aside from some thrilling as well as haunting moments, this 1981 performance lacks the energy or tension to suggest its origins. The drab, colorless, bass-shy production offers scant evidence of stereo, and there's little to draw us into Shostakovich's world."

Stereophile 13:203+ Ap '90. Richard Schneider (185w)

Digital Audio's CD Review 6:57-8 Ap '90. Lawrence Johnson (220w)

The New York Times Ja 7 '90, p. 27 H. Barrymore L. Scherer (100w)

Gramophone 67:44 Je '89. Michael Oliver (245w)

1357. Symphony No. 9 in E flat, Opus 70; Festival Overture, Opus 96; Katerina Izmaylova: Suite; Tahiti Trot, Opus 16 (tr. of Youman's Tea for Two).

Neeme Jarvi (c). Scottish National Orchestra. Henry Wood Hall, Glasgow, Scotland UK. April 14-17, 1987.
CHANDOS 8587 DDD 52:00

✔HC ★★★*Awards:* The Record of the Month, *Music and Musicians International* Ag '88; Best Recordings of the Month, *Stereo Review* N '88. *Gramophone* 66:170 Jl '88. Michael Oliver (590w).

"Most of us agree that there's something nasty in the woodpile of Shostakovich's Ninth Symphony; it just takes time to come out. Jarvi, however, spares not a moment on the work's seemingly innocuous surface...The spectacular open-hall acoustic is from Chandos's most successful, least reverberant Scottish venue, the Henry Wood Hall."

Music and Muscians International 36:27 Ag '88. David Nice (310w)

"The very resonant sound somewhat gobbles up some of the Ninth Symphony's chamber-like subtleties. But that reservation aside, I find this to be a most satisfying Ninth...Shostakovich's incredibly witty, almost cubistic arrangement of 'Tea for Two' is great icing on a nearly perfect cake."

Fanfare 12:263 S/O '88. Royal S. Brown (250w)

"First-rate performances and interpretations in superb sound."

Stereo Review 53:110 N '88. David Hall (275w)

"These are all invigorating renditions of infrequently-heard music that are very welcome to the catalog."

American Record Guide 51:86-7 N/D '88. Arved Ashby (515w)

"What a showcase for the SNO brass....Jarvi's Ninth is in deadly earnest...In Jarvi's hands, the melancholic *Moderato* and those long mournful bassoon laments in the *Largo* are weighty utterances indeed...I like Jarvi's tough, hard-hitting vein of satire...Very impressive recording."

Hi-Fi News & Record Review 33:85 Ag '88. Edward Seckerson (285w)

"The performances...are basically good, with emphasis on brilliance rather than great refinement. Chandos' recorded sound is bright and clear, and a bit edgy."

HighPerformanceReview 5:84 D '88. James Primosch (180w)

1358. Symphony No. 10 in E minor, Opus 43; Ballet Suite No. 4.

Neeme Jarvi (c). Scottish National Orchestra. Caird Hall, Dundee. 1988.
CHANDOS 8630 DDD 66:00

✔HC ★★★*Awards:* Editors' Choice, *Digital Audio's CD Review*, Je '89. Top Choices—1989, *American Record Guide* Ja/F '90 (James Ginsburg); Top Choices—1989, *American Record Guide* Ja/F '90 (Mark Koldys). *American Record Guide* Overview: Prokofieff/Shostakovich, S/O '91.

"Neeme Jarvi...conducts...one of the best performances I have heard of one of Shostakovich's best symphonies, the Tenth-....Chandos's very rich sound, within which only a slight feeling of digital void bothered me from time to time, contributes greatly to the overall excellence here."

Fanfare 12:321-24 My/Je '89. Royal S. Brown (300w)

"The label's customary, wide-ranging, reverberant acoustic fits Shostakovich's monumental symphony to a tee....No recording recreates the Tenth's intense dramatic atmosphere better than this. The plaintive dialog between clarinet and strings at the work's outset has never sounded more poignant. The myriad of tone colors called for by Shostakovich's ingenious orchestration is stunningly reproduced. In addition to his sublime attention to detail, Jarvi demonstrates an uncanny sense of pacing as each crescendo positively pulsates toward its apex."

American Record Guide 52:91 Jl/Ag '89. James S. Ginsburg (325w)

"This symphony makes heavy demands on performances....The Scottish National Orchestra rise to the challenge. The strain tells on the violas at figures 63 and 64 of this opening movement....Yet this Chandos account can be safely recommended, for it offers impassioned power, tension and virtuosity, with smooth sound in the believable but not overstated acoustic of the Caird Hall, Dundee."

Music and Musicians International 37:63 Ap '89. David Heaton (810w)

"The *Ballet Suite No. 4* that serves as filler is of decidedly less interest than the symphony; here Shostakovich really is being banal, particularly in the second and third movements. It is the symphony that commands our attention on this CD: one of Shostakovich's most impressive efforts in a god performance."

HighPerformanceReview 7:77 Winter '90-91. James Primosch (295w)

"The contemporary *Ballet Suite, ie* 1953, compensates with its delicious grand (and silly!) Waltz for slight disappointments in the symphony (judged by the standards of expectation established so often by this team on disc—Shostakovich 7, for instance)."

Hi-Fi News & Record Review 34:95 Mr '89. Christopher Breunig (240w)

Gramophone 66:1437-38 Mr '89. Michael Oliver (280w)

Digital Audio's CD Review 5:104 Je '89. David Vernier (360w)

1359. Symphony No. 11 ("Year 1905"), Opus 103.

James De Priest (c). Helsinki Philharmonic Orchestra. May 1988.
DELOS 3080 DDD 68:00

★★★★*Awards:* The Want List 1989, *Fanfare* N/D '89 (Jon Tuska); Critics' Choice 1989, *Gramophone* D '89 (Michael Oliver); Top Choices—1989, *American Record Guide* Ja/F '90 (James Ginsburg). *American Record Guide* Overview: Prokofieff/Shostakovich, S/O '91.

"For listeners in this country, James De Priest's Shostakovich will be something of a bolt from the blue. Everything you need to bring the problematic, public-statement Eleventh to life is here....The recording is a model of natural perspective—atmospheric to match the playing whenever the camera pans across the static scene, but sensitive to each new stroke of instrumental colour that Shostakovich introduces against the chilly backcloth; no spectacular boosting of the bloodbath climaxes, either." *P100 S100*

Hi-Fi News & Record Review 35:95 My '90. David Nice (385w)

"Overall, the performance is one of total conviction, once again eloquently making the case for the value of the work itself. The recording is a model of clean sound and wide dynamic range."

Stereo Review 54:115 Je '89. David Hall (350w)

"While I would never be without Stokowski's electrifying performance, the Helsinki Philharmonics's superlative playing, DePreist's masterly direction, and Delos's breathtaking sound make the new disc a clear first choice. Highest recommendation."

American Record Guide 52:88-9 My/Je '89. James S. Ginsburg (375w)

"As Shostakovich Elevenths go, James DePriest's ranks near the top, although I would still go for the Berglund version on EMI as my first choice."

Fanfare 13:326-29 S/O '89. Royal S. Brown (280w)

"While the ensemble is quite conscientious, their sound is not especially rich or refined. The recorded sound is basically good, although the strings occasionally are a bit distant."

HighPerformanceReview 6:91 Mr '89. James Primosch (200w)

Gramophone 66:1735-36 My '89. Michael Oliver (500w)

1360. Symphony No. 13, "Babi Yar," for Bass, Orchestra and Chorus, Opus 113.

Bernard Haitink (c). Marius Rintzler (bass). Concertgebouw Chorus and Orchestra.
LONDON/DECCA 417 261 64:30 2 discs

★★*Awards:* *Gramophone* Critics' Choice 1986 (Michael Oliver). *American Record Guide* Overview: Prokofieff/Shostakovich, S/O '91.

"Bernard Haitink's new account...is in certain ways the best recorded performance of the symphony yet."

High Fidelity 37:59 Je '87 Terry Teachout (125w)

"Symphony No. 13 is not music for the faint-hearted. Music and text both deal with major human and moral issues....Haitink and his choral-orchestra forces turn in an excellent job, and London has provided powerful and wide-ranging sonics. The weak link in this recording is the soloist, Marius Rintzler, whose essentially lyrical style seems inappropriate much of the time."

Stereo Review 51:174+ N '86 David Hall (400w)

Haitink and the Concertgebouw Orchestra excel in communicating the full impact of the symphony's often shifting dramatic patterns...I maintain quite a fondness for the warmth of the version recorded some years ago by Eugene Ormandy for RCA (a version no longer available). But in Haitink's hands the symphony continues to reach into the emotions at a depth one would almost not suspect possible, and this premiere CD is most welcome."

Fanfare 10:217-8 N/D '86 Royal S. Brown (620w).

"This is the best of the disappointing installments I've heard in Haitink's Shostakovich cycle."

Opus 3:49 F '87 Kenneth Furie (960w)

Hi-Fi News & Record Review 31:117-8 Je '86 (320w) (rev. of LP); 31:109 Jl '86 (75w) (rev. of CD). Edward Seckerson

1361. Symphony No. 15 in A, Opus 141; From Jewish Folk Poetry (song cycle), for Soprano, Contralto, Tenor and Piano, Opus 79.
Bernard Haitink (c). Elisabeth Soderstrom (sop); Ortrun Wenkel (mez); Ryszard Karczykowski (ten). London Philharmonic Orchestra.
LONDON/DECCA 417 581 73:27

★*Awards: American Record Guide* Overview: Prokofiev/Shostakovich, S/O '91 (Symphony No. 15).

"Highly recommended."
High Fidelity 37:71 O '87. David Hurwitz (165w)
Hi-Fi News & Record Review 32:101 My '87 Edward Seckerson (120w)
Gramophone 64:1418 Ap '87 Michael Oliver (320w)

1362. Symphony No. 15 in A, Opus 141; October (symphonic poem), Opus 131; Overture on Russian and Khirgiz Folk Themes, Opus 115.
Neeme Jarvi (c). Gothenburg Symphony Orchestra.
DEUTSCHE GRAMMOPHON 427 616 DDD 65:57

★★*Awards:* The Year's Best, *Hi Fi News & Record Review*, May '90 Supplement. *American Record Guide* Overview: Prokofieff/Shostakovich, S/O '91.

"This is a refreshing performance [of 15]—without doubt the finest among the three now available....Jarvi gives exceptionally fine performances of two brief works...with the turbulent, snare-drum dominated *October* often suggesting the Tenth Symphony and transcending its occasional basis."
American Record Guide 53:109 Mr/Ap '90. Arved Ashby (400w)

"Maxim Shostakovich (the composer's son), Eugene Ormandy, and Bernard Haitink all made memorable early recordings of this score. Now Neeme Jarvi, with the Gothenburg Symphony, has give us the first digital recording, and it is on an equally high interpretive level....The dynamics range from deathly stillness punctuated by eerie woodwind chords to floor-shaking tuttis. In short, one could hardly ask for a more ideal demonstration vehicle for the CD medium."
Stereo Review 55:158 F '90. David Hall (360w)

"This CD is a triumphant success."
New Hi-Fi Sound 7:109 D '89. Jonathan Kettle (260w)

"Balances can be uncomfortably close, though no-one would deny that the feeling of a live performance has been carried over with admirable presence." *P95/100 S85/100*
Hi-Fi News & Record Review 34:109 N '89; p.27 My '90 Supplement. David Nice (525w)

"Even though I was mildly turned off by Deutsche Grammophon's somewhat cold digital sonics (Chandos's are much warmer and less harsh, but DG definitely also hints a kind of concert-hall realism in parts) and by an occasional slip within the orchestral forces, Jarvi's is absolutely the best Shostakovich Fifteenth I have hard. And he accomplishes this excellence not by tinkering around with the symphony's sometimes mystifying amalgam of the minimal and the epic but by actually making deep sense of it, both musically and emotionally....Something less than a masterpiece, the rarely recorded *October* gets a crisp, refreshingly un-heavy-handed performance from Jarvi and his forces."
Fanfare 13:304-06 Ja/F '90. Royal S. Brown (285w)
Gramophone 68:2021-2 My '91. Stephen Johnson (260w)

SIBELIUS, JEAN

1363. Finlandia, Opus 26; The Swan of Tuonela (from 4 Legends, Opus 22); Valse Triste (from Kuolema, Opus 44); Tapiola, Opus 112.
Herbert Von Karajan (c). Berlin Philharmonic Orchestra.
DEUTSCHE GRAMMOPHON 413 755

✔HC ★*Awards: Gramophone* Critics' Choice 1984 (Robert Layton).

"The unusually deliberate pace here...may raise a few eyebrows, but the enormous dynamic range Karajan elicits from the orchestra gives the reading great power."
Stereo Review 50:185 S '85. David Hall (150w)
Gramophone 62:480 O '84. Robert Layton (385w) (rev. of LP); 62:884 Ja '85. John Borwick (140w) (rev. of CD)
Fanfare 8:264 Jl/Ag '85. Roger Dettmer (600w)

1364. Pelleas et Melisande (incidental music), Opus 46; The Oceantides, Opus 73; Symphony No. 7 in C, Opus 105; Tapiola, Opus 112.
Thomas Beecham (c). Royal Philharmonic Orchestra. reissue.
EMI 63400 ADD (m) 76:00

★★*Awards:* The Want List 1990, *Fanfare* N/D '90 (John Bauman); Critic's Choice: 1990, *American Record Guide* Ja/F '91 (Arved Ashby).

"The sweetest, most lovable *Pelleas and Melisande* ever recorded....Both [*Tapiola* and the 7th] are definitive recordings, approached by only one competitor: Karajan. The entire disc is in gorgeous, peak-of-the-art sound....Indispensable if you like Sibelius."
American Record Guide 53:28+ S/O '90. Donald R. Vroon (210w)
Gramophone 68:228 Jl '90. Robert Layton (280w)
Fanfare 14:474-76 N/D '90. William Zagorski (160w)
The Absolute Sound 16:71 S/O '91. Thomas Hathaway (brief)

1365. Symphony No. 1 in E minor, Opus 39; Karelia Suite, Opus 11.

Vladimir Ashkenazy (c). Philharmonia Orchestra.
LONDON/DECCA 414 534

✓HC ★★*Awards: Fanfare* Want List 1986 (James Miller). *American Record Guide* Overview: Sibelius Symphonies, Mr/Ap '89.

"Ashkenazy responds to the First Symphony with all the requisite sweep and ardor...The three movements of the *Karelia* Suite come off with just the right spirit, color, and tenderness."
Stereo Review 51:98 O '86. David Hall (300w)

"I venture to say that this, the last installment in Ashkenazy's Sibelius cycle, is also the best."
High Fidelity 37:59 Je '87 Robert R. Reilly (150w)

"Ashkenazy's pride of place is not merely alphabetical—he combines most of the virtues of his predecessors (including the thundering timpani of Collins!) into one splendid performance that has both epic sweep and virtuoso brilliance....He certainly does the *Karelia Suite* better than Karajan....London's sound...is clear and impactful, worthy of the special performance it perpetuates."
Fanfare 10:218-20 N/D '86 James Miller (220w)

"For both works, these are hardly the only interpretations one would want to live with; still, I would not want to be without the chance to hear such stimulatingly unconventional rethinkings of them. London's sound is clean, vivid, and powerful, in a handsomely engineered pressing."
American Record Guide 49:36-37 S/O '86 John W. Barker (300w) (rev. of LP)

"Here I will come as close as possible to recommending Ashkenazy in the complete Sibelius. And in any event, his First Symphony is sure to please because nothing else on CD comes close."
The $ensible Sound 9:60 Spring '88. John J. Puccio (275w)

"All in all, despite excellent playing, this performance never quite jells."
Opus 3:49-50 F '87 John Canarina (375w)

Hi-Fi News & Record Review 31:87 Ag '86. Edward Seckerson (300w)

Opus 3:51 D '86 Harris Goldsmith (105w)

Musical America 107:63 Mr '87 R.D. Darrell (175w) (rev. of cassette)

1366. Symphony No. 1 in E minor, Opus 39; Karelia Overture, Opus 10; Karelia Suite, Opus 11; Finlandia, Opus 26.
Jukka-Pekka Saraste (c). Finnish Radio Symphony Orchestra.
RCA 7765 DDD 69:24

★★★*Awards:* Top Choices—1989, *American Record Guide* Ja/F '90 (Kurt Moses); Top Choices—1989, *American Record Guide* Ja/F '90 (Donald Vroon). *American Record Guide* Overview: Sibelius Symphonies, Mr/Ap '89.

"Conductor Saraste seems to have a knack for eliciting transcendent playing from uncompromising ensembles....Altogether a successful and promising issue, strongly recommended."
Fanfare 12:263-5 S/O '88. John Wiser (300w)

"Although I find the sound of this CD quite thrilling, I'll not call is as *beautiful* as the Colin Davis/Boston on Philips....Still, Mr. Saraste makes a far more coherent piece of music out of this than Davis does—or Maazel, for that matter....The *Karelia Suite* is as attractive as the symphony....The performance here may be described as *jaunty*....This is an exciting record."
American Record Guide 52:87 Mr/Ap '89. Donald R. Vroon (300w)

Gramophone 66:786 N '88. Robert Layton (350w)

1367. Symphony No. 2 in D, Opus 43.
John Barbirolli (c). Royal Philharmonic Orchestra. 1966.
CHESKY 003 43:55

★*Awards: American Record Guide* Overview: Sibelius Symphonies, Mr/Ap '89.

"The music has never been better served, even if Sir John is a bit on the emotionally conservative side—which does no harm at all to this flamboyant music! I'd call it close to a definitive recording on all counts."
Audio 72:170-1 N '88. Edward Tatnall Canby (350w)

"The performance and sonic quality of this CD are of the highest standard."
High Fidelity 37:75 D '87. Robert E. Benson (225w)

"It seems to me that this Sibelius Second has an extra charge of energy along with a richness of orchestral sonority not heard on the Angel discs (it's a shade faster). I still prefer a tauter, leaner type of performance...but those whose tastes incline toward a blowzier, more sensuous approach should find Barbirolli's way with the score quite pleasing."
Fanfare 11:299 S/O '87. James Miller (240w)

American Record Guide 50:67-8 n/D '87. Stephen J. Haller (225w)

1368. Symphony No. 2 in D, Opus 43; Valse Triste (from Kuolema, Opus 44); The Swan of Tuonela (from 4 Legends, Opus 22); Pohjola's Daughter, Opus 49.
Eugene Ormandy (c). Philadelphia Orchestra. reissue 1973.
RCA 6528 72:00

★*Awards: American Record Guide* Overview: Sibelius Symphonies, Mr/Ap '89.

"This performance of *Pohjola's Daughter* probably is the best one currently in the catalog. The Second Symphony...fares splendidly as well."
High Fidelity 38:58 F '88. David Hurwitz (100w)

"I think this Ormandy is the most attractive Sibelius 2 on CD. Nor will you find a better

Pohjola or *Swan*....Ormandy understood Sibelius as few conductors have."

American Record Guide 51:65 My/Je '88. Donald R. Vroon (250w)

Gramophone 65:716+ N '87 Ivan March (125w)

1369. Symphony No. 3 in C, Opus 52; King Christian II (orchestral suite), Opus 27.
Neeme Jarvi (c). Gothenburg Symphony Orchestra.
BIS 228 DDD 54:50

★★*Awards:* Perfect 10/10, *Digital Audio*, Mr '88. *American Record Guide* Overview: Sibelius Symphonies, Mr/Ap '89.

"Jarvi's version of the Third Symphony...[is] an unqualified success, particularly in the last movement, though his treatment of the extensive filler—the *King Christian II* Suite—is oddly ponderous."

High Fidelity 36:62 F '86. Bill Zakariasen (100w)

"While I am eagerly awaiting Sir Alexander's new Chandos CD, I can safely say that Jarvi has successfully plumbed the mysteries of this work, which for reasons beyond my comprehension, has remained relatively obscure among this composer's symphonies. The gentle music from Adolf Paul's play *King Christian II* is given a sympathetic reading."

American Record Guide 48:73-5 Ja '85. Carl Bauman (165w)

"The Gothenburg Symphony Orchestra is powerful, almost to the point of overpowering this relatively slender work, and the total effect is curiously lumpy...."*King Kristian II* is one of the many lovely scores Sibelius contributed to the theater; here the performance seems perfectly tailored to the music. Bis' CD reproduction is superbly clear."

Ovation 5:71 O '84. Paul Turok (160w)

"A vital and coherent performance of a difficult work right up to the big tune in the finale, akin to Brahms' in the last movement of the C-minor Symphony. Both need what the Germans call *Schwung* ('swing' or 'swagger' in English don't suggest the feeling: A gait, pace, and implicit rwhythmic spring that Jarvi withholds. He gets yeasty instead...The incidental music for *King Kristian II*, however, is markedly richer-sounding and more sonorous on CD; the tonal excellence of this performance is underscored, while the music is revealed as genuinely and consistently beautiful minor Sibelius."

Fanfare 8:260-2 N/D '84. Roger Dettmer (330w)

Gramophone 62:480+ O '84. Robert Layton (175w)

Digital Audio 2:54+ N '85. David C. Vernier (150w)

1370. Symphony No. 4 in A minor, Opus 63; Luonnotar, Opus 70; Finlandia, Ous 26.
Vladimir Ashkenazy (c). Elisabeth Soderstrom (sop). Philharmonia Orchestra.
LONDON/DECCA 400 056 DDD

★★*Awards:* Perfect 10/10, *Digital Audio*, Mr '88. *American Record Guide* Overview: Sibelius Symphonies, Mr/Ap '89.

1371. Symphony No. 4 in A minor, Opus 63; Symphony No. 5 in E flat, Opus 82.
Herbert Blomstedt (c). San Francisco Symphony Orchestra.
LONDON/DECCA 425 858 DDD 68:00

✓HC ★★★*Awards:* Editors' Choice, *Digital Audio and CD Review*, Je '92. Pick of the Month, North American Perspective (Christie Barter) *Gramophone* Jl '91; Record of the Month, *Hi-Fi News & Record Review*, Ag '91.

"A superb presentation: depth, spaciousness and realism combine to make this a glowing, exciting recording. The San Francisco Orchestra has qualities I had not previously comprehended, enhanced by the superb balancing: for example the many important woodwind passages are strongly imposing, yet the instruments are always set in correct perspective." *P100 S100*

Hi-Fi News & Record Review 36:69 Ag '91. Antony Hodgson (210w)

"Both performances have a take-it-or-leave-it quality, with more advocacy felt from the work of individual players than anything emanating from the podium. In the long run, then, these are beautifully played and long-wearing accounts, in London's best present-day sound....This is a good second recording to explore after Gibson and Colin Davis (Chandos and Philips respectively)."

Fanfare 15:327-9 Mr/Ap '92. John Wiser (long)

"The readings are well conceived, well played, and handsomely recorded, but there is no tensile strength in the phrasing or dynamics to match that of the Nielsen recordings....[In the Fourth Symphony] Vladimir Ashkenazy, Simon Rattle, and Herbert von Karajan all meet the work's demands with notably more success in their recordings....The shortcomings...[in the] performance [of the Fifth Symphony] are evident in comparisons with those by Jukka-Pekka Saraste, Rattle, and Leonard Bernstein."

Stereo Review 56:77 O '91. David Hall (med)

These performances "of Symphonies 4 and 5 on London are well-recorded, impeccably paced, conventionally well played, and competently directed, but that's really about all; and despite their undeniable professionalism, they strike me as something of a flop."

American Record Guide 55:115-6 Ja/F '92. John P. McKelvey (long)

Gramophone 69:62 Jl '91. Robert Layton (370w)

Digital Audio's CD Review 8:74+ D '91. Lawrence B. Johnson (long)

1372. Symphony No. 4 in A Minor, Opus 63; Symphony No. 6 in D Minor, Opus 104.
Herbert Von Karajan (c). Berlin Philharmonic Orchestra. 1966.
DEUTSCHE GRAMMOPHON 415 107 65:21

★*Awards:* *American Record Guide* Overview: Sibelius Symphonies, Mr/Ap '89.

Gramophone 63:44 Je '85. Robert Layton (245w)

High Fidelity 36:66 Ap '86. Robert E. Benson (50w)

1373. Symphony No. 4 in A minor, Opus 63; Symphony No. 6 in D minor, Opus 104.
Simon Rattle (c). City of Birmingham Symphony Orchestra.
EMI 47711 DDD 67:00

★★★*Awards:* *Hi-Fi News & Record Review* Record of the Month, Ag '88. Critics' Choice 1988, *Gramophone* D '88 (Robert Layton). *American Record Guide* Overview: Sibelius Symphonies, Mr/Ap '89.

"These performances...are as good as any now available in any recorded format, and moreover reveal insights into Sibelius's austere and withdrawn and inner world not to be found elsewhere....These recordings furnish evidence that Rattle has molded the CBSO into a major British orchestra."
American Record Guide 51:84 S/O '88. John P. McKelvey (200w)

"Superb orchestral playing, sharp attacks, first-rate ensemble all go for naught in a reading that is metrically literal, enervated...A similar terminal case of the blahs infects No. 6."
Fanfare 12:264-5 S/O '88. John Wiser (300w)

"We have here two of the most illuminating Sibelius performances ever committed to disc-....The recording *has* to be the finest yet from this source: in balance, depth of field, tonal range. Exemplary."
Hi-Fi News & Record Review 33:77 Ag '88. Edward Seckerson (380w)

"While it does not replace previous issues by Sixten Ehrling...and Sir John Barbirolli...it is to be preferred among all those currently available, including Jarvi's recent account."
Ovation 9:53 D '88. Jon Tuska (260w)

"A must for everyone who cares about the Sibelius symphonies and a good bet for anyone who has yet to be drawn to them."
Stereo Review 53:160-62 D '88. Richard Freed (325w)

Gramophone 65:1314+ Mr '88. Robert Layton (590w)

1374. Symphony No. 5 in E flat, Opus 82; Pohjola's Daughter, Opus 49.
Leonard Bernstein (c). New York Philharmonic Orchestra. 1983.
CBS 38474 ADD 44:35

★*Awards:* *American Record Guide* Overview: Sibelius Symphonies, update, Jl/Ag '89.

Originally reviewed in *Fanfare* 7:1.
"Bernstein's plush phrasing mutes the icy colors, and his stress of grand gestures and outward drama obscures the music's special tone of voice, rugged and often cryptic. But the sense of culmination—especially in the superbly sculpted arc of the first movement—is so powerful that, as you're listening, you're almost compelled to submit to Bernstein's vision. *Pohjola's Daughter* is similarly conceived and almost as persuasive."
Fanfare 13:331 S/O '89. Peter J. Rabinowitz (90w)

1375. Symphony No. 5 in E flat, Opus 82; Symphony No. 7 in C, Opus 105.
Herbert Von Karajan (c). Berlin Philharmonic Orchestra. 1966.
DEUTSCHE GRAMMOPHON 415 108 55:09

★*Awards:* *American Record Guide* Overview: Sibelius Symphonies, Mr/Ap '89.

"The warmth, depth and concert-hall perspective found here are missing in many of his [von Karajan's] newer recordings. These performances with the Berlin Philharmonic Orchestra are models of power and expressiveness."
High Fidelity 36:66 Ap '86. Robert E. Benson (50w)

Gramophone 63:44 Je '85. Robert Layton (245w)

1376. Symphony No. 5 in E flat, Opus 82; Concerto in D minor for Violin and Orchestra, Opus 47.
Simon Rattle (c). Nigel Kennedy (vln). City of Birmingham Symphony Orchestra.
EMI 49717 DDD 62:27

★*Awards:* Best Recordings of the Month, *Stereo Review* O '88.

"The CD-only release is especially attractive because the symphony is coupled with a uniquely lovely performance of the Sibelius Violin Concerto in which soloist Nigel Kennedy displays the same intense musicality and prowess as in his now-famous recording of the Elgar concerto."
Stereo Review 53:90 O '88. David Hall (330w)

"I would rate this performance of the Sibelius Fifth as just about the best I've ever heard-....Shlomo Mintz plays this concerto much better on a recent DG release...but James Levine and the Berlin Philharmonic let the side down with an accompaniment that has all the clarity and sparkle of a glass of prune juice. On CD, that leaves Gidon Kremer or Itzhak Perlman."
American Record Guide 51:84 S/O '88. John P. McKelvey (200w)

"As ever with Kennedy's work, the impression here is of an extended improvisation from a fertile imagination....As for Rattle's account of the 5th Symphony...a great performance, vividly recorded: high impact, no tricks."

Hi-Fi News & Record Review 33:103-4 S '88. Edward Seckerson (390w)

"The performance of the Fifth coupled with the violin concerto is new...I find it less firm of outline than its predecessor...There is likewise very little that is compelling about Nigel Kennedy's solo playing in the concerto...There hasn't been a recording of such sheer brute dullness since Belkin and Ashkenazy had at it in the mid-'70s."

Fanfare 12:263-5 S/O '88. John Wiser (300w)

"The choice of young Nigel Kennedy as soloist is not an altogether happy one....What is truly remarkable about Rattle's effort is the outstanding fluidity and transparency he brings to the rather opaque orchestration."

Ovation 9:53 D '88. Jon Tuska (260w)

"While nothing atrocious happens in either of these performances, enough goes wrong to preclude a recommendation."

Musical America 108:84-5 Jl '88. David Hurwitz (980w)

Gramophone 65:1461 Ap '88 (450w) (rev. of LP). Robert Layton; 66:423-4 S '88 (295w) (rev. of CD)

The New York Times My 29 '88, p. H23. John Rockwell (400w)

1377. Symphony No. 5 in E flat, Opus 82; Pohjola's Daughter, Opus 49.
Esa-Pekka Salonen (c). Philharmonia Orchestra.
CBS 42366 DDD 47:31

★★*Awards:* *Stereo Review* Best Recordings of the Month, Ja '88. The Record of the Month, *Music and Musicians International* Ja '88.

"This coupling is competitive with the best currently available recordings, highly recommended."

Fanfare 11:190-1 N/D '87. John D. Wiser (475w)

Salonen "starts off with a splendidly expansive performance of the symphony....*Pohjola's Daughter* receives a less imaginative, rather heavy-handed, grim performance, both in terms of tempos and dynamics."

American Record Guide 51:62 Ja/F '88. Kurt Moses (425)

"The first and last movements of this masterpiece receive the most completely realised recorded performances I have ever heard-....'Pohjola' is also given a masterly performance."

Music and Musicians International 36:44 Ja '88. Robert Matthew-Walker (150w)

"To be frank, I like Salonen's Sibelius where it is most unconventional....I am less happy with the braking of the natural momentum in (i), though. The perspective/dynamics relationships here strike me as wholly false, in David Mottley's production, and that is a disappointment."

Stereophile 11:169 Mr '88. Christopher Breunig (425w)

"This is probably the worst account of Sibelius' Fifth Symphony before the public."

Musical America 108:61-2 Mr '88. David Hurwitz (460w)

Hi-Fi News & Record Review 33:101 F '88. Edward Seckerson (455w)

Gramophone 65:956 D '87. Robert Layton (585w)

Stereo Review 53:126+ Ja '88. Steve Simels (400w)

1378. Symphony No. 7 in C, Opus 82; Tapiola, Opus 112.
Vladimir Ashkenazy (c). Philharmonia Orchestra. Kingsway Hall, London. March 1982.
LONDON/DECCA 411 935 40:37

✔**HC** ★*Awards:* *American Record Guide* Overview: Sibelius Symphonies, Mr/Ap '89.

"A beautifully integrated performance that features powerful climaxes with measured intensity and balance....Compared with existing records and, perhaps, recordings to come, Ashkenazy will have the advantage of the outstanding sound quality realized by engineer Stan Goodall in the superb acoustics of Kingsway Hall."

High Performance Review 3 (4):145 '85. (95w)

Gramophone 62:480 O '84. Robert Layton (210w)

Hi-Fi News & Record Review 29:133 D '84. John Atkinson (75w)

SIMPSON, ROBERT

1379. Symphony No. 6; Symphony No. 7.
Vernon Handley (c). Royal Liverpool Philharmonic Orchestra. Philharmonic Hall, Liverpool UK. September 3-4, 1987.
HYPERION 66280 DDD 60:00

★★★*Awards:* Critics' Choice 1988, *Gramophone* D '88 (David Fanning; Stephen Johnson; Robert Layton).

"The recording...is excellent...and so are the performances under Vernon Handley, as vigorous and committed as the notes and the ideas themselves."

Hi-Fi News & Record Review 33:115 O '88. Stephen Pettitt (245w)

"The idea behind the Symphony No. 6...may be unique: the processes of life from conception through birth to maturity....The Seventh Symphony is a different matter emotionally, altogether tougher and grimmer...Anyone knowing the other Simpson symphonies on records (Nos. 1 and 3) will not need persuading to get this disc."

Fanfare 12:265-6 S/O '88. Paul Rapoport (525w)

"Fine performances, well recorded...Simpson can and does trace back to Beethoven many of his guiding principles: organic unity...construction from intervallic cells, and an uncompromising dialectic that presupposes (wrongly, I believe) a phenomenological continuum between melodic intervals, harmonic intervals, form and tonality."

The Musical Times 130:480-81 Ag '89. Stephen Banfield (410w)

"Simpson's music is worth getting to know, especially for contemporary-music aficionados who subscribe to the idea that the 'validity' of a new piece is dependent on its form and content being somehow on the cutting edge. It's worth getting to know because Simpson—who produces well-wrought and compelling music that is valid in every way—represents the very antithesis of the avant-garde."

Musical America 108:64 N '88. James Wierzbicki (290w)

"Vernon Handley's performances seem authoritative, the Royal Liverpool Philharmonic plays well, and the sound is excellent."

High Fidelity 39:70 Je '89. David Hurwitz (425w)

"All the elements of a proper symphony parade by, and sometimes they make for moments that aren't unattractive. But the gestures lack a real freshness and vitality....Both performances and recording quality seem good."

HighPerformanceReview 5:84 D '88. James Primosch (180w)

"The overall impression is one of determined stolidity. Simpson can compose, all right, but his conception of the composer's calling is severely restricted by his programmatic, extramusical intentions."

Ovation 10:60-1 Je '89. George Gelles (230w)

Gramophone 66:36 Je '88. David J. Fanning (455w)

1380. Symphony No. 9 (1987).
Vernon Handley (c). Bournemouth Symphony Orchestra.
HYPERION 66299 DDD 68:00

★*Awards:* Contemporary Record Award 1989, *Gramophone*, D '89.

"Simpson sounds very European to this listener...I think of older styles, Beethoven at times, Bach in this symphony particularly....for those who wish to explore the work with the composer personally, there is an 18-minute commentary afterwards in which we meet the pleasant and witty man himself, who takes us through the symphony with musical examples-....The orchestra plays smoothly and with rich sonority, and the recording is excellent."

American Record Guide 52:92 Jl/Ag '89. David W. Moore (225w)

"One can imagine a lighter approach to parts of this symphony...More obvious is the need for certain moving lines to be more prominent, for parts of the climaxes to be less monolithic. The problem here could lie anywhere (orchestration, conducting, orchestra). The recorded sound could improve some, too. The distinct strands of sound, the 'analytical' separation which digital recording is famous for, needs to be evident in a number of places where it is lacking."

Fanfare 12:280-81 Mr/Ap '89. Paul Rapoport (800w)

Gramophone 66:1012-14 D '88. David J. Fanning (385w)

SMETANA, BEDRICH

The Moldau (Vltava); From Bohemian Fields and Groves (symphonic poem), from Ma Vlast. See No. 1130.

1381. My Fatherland ("Ma Vlast"). The Bartered Bride: Overture; Dances.
Eliahu Inbal (c). Frankfurt Radio Symphony Orchestra. 1989.
TELDEC 35838; TELDEC 44183 DDD 51:40, 39:35 2 discs

★*Awards:* Cream of the Crop IV, *Digital Audio's CD Review*, 6:43 Je '90.

"Inbal gives one of the most sweeping, epic performances the cycle has ever had on recordings with fine playing and a decent recording."

American Record Guide 53:91 Ja/F '90. Stephen D. Chakwin, Jr. (585w)

"Eliahu Inbal responds strongly to the lyrical-poetic aspects of the first three of Smetana's six tone poems gathered under the title *Ma vlast* and celebrating the beauties and past glories of Bohemia....The sonics are pleasing throughout, if not quite on the level of Inbal's Mahler cycle with the same orchestra." *P90 S80*

Stereo Review 54:156 S '89. David Hall (250w)

"This exactly replicates the programme on Levine's DG set with the VPO, and runs it neck and neck on quality of performance and engineering." *P100 S100*

Hi-Fi News & Record Review 34:93 S '89. Kenneth Dommett (150w)

"Inbal seems to have absolutely no feeling for the special character and color of this music. Textures are mushy and brass-heavy, like Bruckner. Attacks lack unanimity, ensemble is slack and routine....Dismal."

Fanfare 13:331-32 S/O '89. Elliott Kaback (160w)

"I find this a depressing set: the orchestral playing is competent but Inbal seems determined to treat this heroic cycle as little more than a series of orchestral showpieces and the results are uninspiring."

The Musical Times 130:752 D '89. Nigel Simeone (120w)

Digital Audio's CD Review 6:55-6 F '90. Lawrence Johnson (230w)

Gramophone 67:672 O '89. John Warrack (460w)

1382. My Fatherland ("Ma Vlast").

Rafael Kubelik (c). Czech Philharmonic Orchestra. Smetana Hall, Council House, Prague. May 12, 1990 live.
SUPRAPHON 111 208 DDD 77:46

★★★★★*Awards:* The Want List 1991, *Fanfare* N/D '91 (John Bauman); The Want List 1991, *Fanfare* N/D '91 (Ron McDonald). Critics' Choice 1991, *Gramophone*, Ja '92 (James Jolly); Top Twelve Albums of the Year, 1991, *Stereo Review*, F '92; Critics' Choice 1991, *Gramophone*, Ja '92 (Alan Sanders).

"I can imagine a hypothetical sonic ideal for Smetana's masterpiece that may not have been quite achieved here, but I doubt that a more gripping musical realization will be captured on disc anytime soon."
Stereo Review 56:92 Je '91. David Hall (525w)

"All the great past performances of *Ma Vlast* have been done by the Czech Philharmonic under Czech conductors. Karel Ancerl produced a compelling and satisfying reading in the early stereo era...far earlier, Vaclav Talich produced, for my ears, the finest, and most fully realized performance of this symphonic cycle...Kubelik delivers his finest *Ma Vlast*—a performance worthy of comparison with the best podium masters of the past."
Fanfare 14:293-4 Jl/Ag '91. William Zagorski (900w)

"Gripping."
Stereo Review 57:43 F '92. (brief)

"This is the fourth *Ma Vlast* by Kubelik on records, so there are no surprises; but his interpretation has become a bit broader, more searching, and more deliberate; and this concert performance continues that trend....The most questionable aspect of this recording is the variable quality of the sound....Until Kubelik's old Chicago performance is re-mastered, the choice is between this disc and his Boston Symphony recording released last year by DG. I'd favor the latter...primarily because of the better sound."
American Record Guide 54:110-11 My/Je '91. Kurt Moses (300w)

Gramophone 69:73 S '91. Alan Sanders (med)

1383. My Fatherland ("Ma Vlast").
Libor Pesek (c). Royal Liverpool Philharmonic Orchestra.
VIRGIN 91100 DDD 76:00

✔HC ★*Awards:* Critics' Choice 1990, *Gramophone* D '90 (Ivan March).

"Levine, coming to the music as a foreigner [DG] brought spectacular colour and pace to it, aided by remarkable recording, but Pesek's comparatively subdued response is ultimately more persuasive, and his orchestra echoes with remarkable fidelity his fervent espousal of what is in effect Czechoslovakia's national hymn. The recording is spacious and natural. What more could one ask?" *P95/100 S95*
Hi-Fi News & Record Review 35:94 Ag '90. Kenneth Dommett (155w)

Gramophone 68:228+ Jl '90. Ivan March (590w)

STENHAMMAR, WILHELM

1384. Orchestral Music: Serenade in F, Opus 34; Chitra (concert suite in three movements, adapted in 1959 by Hilding Rosenberg from Stenhammar's incidental music for the play by Rabindranath Tagore), Opus 43; **Mid-Winter (Swedish Rhapsody for Orchestra and Chorus), Opus 24.**
Esa-Pekka Salonen (c). Swedish Radio Symphony Choir and Orchestra. Berwald Hall, Stockholm.
CAPRICE/MUSICA SVECIAE 626 DDD 64:35

★*Awards:* Record of the Month, *Hi-Fi News & Record Review*, Ja '91.

"All three works show great originality and a most individual sensibility within a conventional language....Strongly recommended, not least for well-balanced, highly detailed orchestral recording."
Fanfare 14:363 N/D '90. John Wiser (450w)

"Recommended."
Musical America 111:81-2 Ja '91. Thomas L. Dixon (120w)

"A marvellous disc. If there are any *HFN/RR* readers who have yet to discover the delights of Stenhammer's Serenade (his finest orchestral work), then I can only passionately urge that they try to hear this latest instalment in the ambitious 'Musica Sveciae' series from Conifer....Superbly played...and stunningly well recorded...as sheer sound this is fabulous: rich, transparent, glare-free, with a sumptuously well-defined bass—this goes straight into the 'unmissable' category as far as I'm concerned." *P100 S100*
Hi-Fi News & Record Review 36:95 Ja '91. Andrew Achenbach (455w)

"Salonen's performances are every bit as fine [as Jarvi's] and Musica Sveciae's digital recording very nearly equals the BIS ones. The problems come in matters of completeness."
American Record Guide 54:101-2 Ja/F '91. Carl Bauman (235w)

Gramophone 68:1038 N '90. Robert Layton (390w)

STRAUSS FAMILY

1385. Strauss Program: New Year's Day Concert in Vienna. J. Strauss II: *Die Fledermaus:* Overture. Annen Polka, Opus 117. Vergnungszug, Opus 281. Unter Donner und Blitz, Opus 324. Fruhlingsstimmen, Opus 410. An der schonen, blauen Donau, Opus 314. **Josef Strauss:** Spharenklange, Opus 235. Delirien, Opus 212. Ohne Sorgen, Opus 271. **J. Strauss II/Josef Strauss:** Pizzicato Polka. **J. Strauss I:** Beliebte Annen Polka, Opus 137. Radetzky-Marsch, Opus 228.

Herbert Von Karajan (c). Kathleen Battle. Vienna Philharmonic Orchestra. Grosser Musikvereinsaal, Vienna. January 1, 1987.
DEUTSCHE GRAMMOPHON 419 616 DDD 69:00

★★*Awards:* *Gramophone* Critics' Choice (Ivan March), 1987. Record of the Eighties, *Gramophone*, D '89 (Ivan March).

"The subtle rhythmic lilt, the unique inflections, the seductive warmth of sound from the Vienna Philharmonic are in evidence throughout this well-recorded disc."

Fanfare 11:236-7 N/D '87. Howard Kornblum (155w)

"This time DG have the right orchestra, and Karajan collectors will give this issue a place next to the marvellous 1960 RCA 'Soria' LP with the VPO."

Hi-Fi News & Record Review 33:119 Ja '88. Christopher Breunig (300w)

Gramophone 65:754 N '87 Ivan March (585w)

STRAUSS, JOHANN (II)

1386. Music of Johann Strauss: Gunstwerber—Waltz, Op. 4 Herzenslust—Polka, Op. 3. Phonix-Schwingen—Waltz, Op. 125. Debut-Quadrille, Op. 2. Zehner-Polka, Op. 121. Klangfiguren—Waltz, Op. 251. Maskenzug—Polka francaise, Op. 240. Nocturne-Quadrille, Op. 120. Freut euch des Lebens—Waltz, Op. 340. Fledermaus-Polka, Op. 362. Bein uns z'Haus—Waltz, Op. 361. Veilchen—Mazurka, Op. 256.
(J. Strauss, Jr. Edition, **Volume 1).**
Alfred Walter (c). CSSR Philharmonic Orchestra.
MARCO POLO 8.223201 DDD 65:00

"Anyone who enjoys Strauss will enjoy any of the records in this series. To the dedicated collector, they are essential."

American Record Guide 53:119-20 N/D '90. David Mason Greene (195w)

"Overall, the performances...are fluent and idiomatic....All manner of treasure is unearthed in these recordings, and, by association, a good deal of social and political history as well-....one wishes that the scholarly apparatus in so ambitious a project were more enlightening."

The New York Times My 6 '90, p. 25 H. Barrymore L. Scherer (165w)

"Glitterlingly performed and recorded." *P95 S95*

Australian Hi-Fi 21(8):51:12 '90. John Aranetta (200w)

"The recorded sound, aside from a slightly lightweight bass, is good...Alfred Walter...conducts Strauss with a deft and knowing hand (though not equal to Krauss). He draws playing of considerable finesse from the Kosice players....Considering the generous playing time and the unusual interest of much of the contents, these are three highly desirable CDs."

Fanfare 13:312-15 Ja/F '90. John Bauman (170w)

Gramophone 67:1380 Ja '90. Andrew M. Lamb (190w)

1387. Music of Johann Strauss: Czechen-Polka, Opus 13. Die jungen Wiener—Waltz, Opus 7. Satanella-Polka, Opus 124. Cytheren-Quadrille, Opus 6. Solonspruche—Waltz, Opus 128. Fantasieblumchen—Polka-mazurka, Opus 241. Wo die Zitronen bluhn—Waltz, Opus 364. Indra-Quadrille, Opus 122. Tik-Tak—Polka schnell, Opus 365. Vermahlungs-Toaste—Waltz, Opus 136. Neue Pizzicato-Polka, Opus 449. Kaiser Franz Joseph I Rettungs-Jubel-Marsch, Opus 126.
(J. Strauss, Jr. Edition, **Volume 2).**
Alfred Walter (c). CSSR Philharmonic Orchestra.
MARCO POLO 8.223202 DDD 68:00

"There are close to 500 opus numbers to his name plus a number of unpublished pieces. That's a lot of waltzes, fast polkas, French polkas, quadrilles, marches, etc. By my calculations that will mean more than 40 volumes in the series. As a totally committed fanatic where this wonderful music is concerned, I'm in 3/4 time heaven! The CSSR Philharmonic of Kosice...is a very good orchestra and its members play with enthusiasm and affection and without any real glitches."

American Record Guide 53:114-15 My/Je '90. Michael Mark (120w)

See Volume 1 for review excerpts.

—*Fanfare* 13:312-15 Ja/F '90. John Bauman (170w)

—*The New York Times* My 6 '90, p. 25 H. Barrymore L. Scherer (165w)

Gramophone 67:1380 Ja '90. Andrew M. Lamb (190w)

1388. Music of Johann Strauss: Berglieder—Waltz, Opus 18. Jux-Polka, Opus 17. Wiener Punsch-Lieder—Waltz, Opus 131. Damonen-Quadrille, Opus 19. Freudengruss-Polka, Opus 127. Liebeslieder—Waltz, Opus 114. Vergnugungszug—Polka schnell, Opus 281. Satanella-Quadrille, Opus 123. Die Oesterreicher—Waltz, Opus 22. Aeskulap-Polka, Opus 130. Lind-Gesange-Waltz, Opus 21. Amazonen-Polka, Opus 9.
(J. Strauss, Jr. Edition, **Volume 3).**
Alfred Walter (c). CSSR Philharmonic Orchestra.
MARCO POLO 8.223203 DDD 68:00

See Volume 1 for review excerpts.

—*Fanfare* 13:312-15 Ja/F '90. John Bauman (170w)

—*The New York Times* My 6 '90, p. 25 H. Barrymore L. Scherer (165w)

See Volume 2 for review excerpt.

American Record Guide 53:114-15 My/Je '90. Michael Mark (120w)

Gramophone 67:1380 Ja '90. Andrew M. Lamb (190w)

1389. Music of Johann Strauss: Hopser Polka, Opus 28; Serailtanze, Opus 5; Austria Marsch, Opus 20; Veilchen Polka, Opus 132.
(J. Strauss, Jr. Edition, **Volume 4**).
Richard Edlinger; Oliver Dohnanyi (c). CSSR Philharmonic Orchestra.
MARCO POLO 8.223204 DDD 62:00

"There are near masterpieces among even his earliest compositions and only the occasional is somewhat less than first quality....Any collector who is seriously interested in Johann Junior's music will want the whole series."
Fanfare 13:302-3 My/Je '90. John Bauman (b.n.)

See Volume 1 for review excerpt.
The New York Times My 6 '90, p. 25 H. Barrymore L. Scherer (165w)

See Volume 2 for review excerpt.
American Record Guide 53:114-15 My/Je '90. Michael Mark (120w)

Gramophone 67:1871 Ap '90. Andrew M. Lamb (105w)

1390. Music of Johann Strauss: Heiligenstadter Rendezvous Polka, Opus 78; Nachtfalter, Opus 157; Quadrille sur des Airs Francaises, Opus 290; Musen Polka, Opus 147.
(J. Strauss, Jr. Edition, **Volume 5**).
Richard Edlinger; Oliver Dohnanyi (c). CSSR Philharmonic Orchestra.
MARCO POLO 8.223205 DDD 55:00

See Volume 1 for review excerpt.
The New York Times My 6 '90, p. 25 H. Barrymore L. Scherer (165w)

See Volume 2 for review excerpt.
American Record Guide 53:114-15 My/Je '90. Michael Mark (120w)

See Volume 4 for review excerpt.
Fanfare 13:302-3 My/Je '90. John Bauman (b.n.)

Gramophone 67:1871 Ap '90. Andrew M. Lamb (105w)

1391. Music of Johann Strauss: Warschauer Polka, Opus 84; Wellen und Wogen, Opus 141; Caroussel March, Opus 133; Camelien Polka, Opus 248.
(J. Strauss, Jr. Edition, **Volume 6**).
Richard Edlinger; Oliver Dohnanyi (c). CSSR Philharmonic Orchestra.
MARCO POLO 8.223206 DDD 60:00

See Volume 1 for review excerpt.
The New York Times My 6 '90, p. 25 H. Barrymore L. Scherer (165w)

See Volume 2 for review excerpt.
American Record Guide 53:114-15 My/Je '90. Michael Mark (120w)

See Volume 4 for review excerpt.
Fanfare 13:302-3 My/Je '90. John Bauman (b.n.)

Gramophone 67:1871 Ap '90. Andrew M. Lamb (105w)

1392. Music of Johann Strauss: Zeitgeister, Opus 25; Bachus-Polka, Opus 38; Odeon-Quadrille, Opus 29; Schnee-Glockchen Walzer, Opus 143; Neuhauser-Polka, Opus 137; Kron-Marsch, Opus 139; Ballg'schichten, Opus 150; Furioso-Polka, Opus 250; Deutscher Kriegermarsch, Opus 284; Colonnen Walzer, Opus 262; Kriegers Liebchen, Opus 379; Nordseebilder, Opus 390.
(Johann Strauss Jr. Edition, **Volume 7**).
Oliver Dohnanyi (c). Polish State Philharmonic Orchestra.
MARCO POLO 8.223207 DDD 68:00

"These performances do capture the Strauss style. Considering the wealth of pieces available here, it is almost impossible to select one or two for special mention. The recorded sound is good, though not demonstration quality....Considering the interest of the material, the majority of which is not available elsewhere, I have no hesitation in recommending all three discs—as well as their six predecessors—to all ardent Straussians."
Fanfare 14:393-4 S/O '90. John Bauman (105w)

"In the May/June ARG I wrote most enthusiastically about vols. 2-6 of this series...and I'm delighted to no end to give volumes 7, 8, and 9 an equally rapturous endorsement."
American Record Guide 53:116-17 S/O '90. Michael Mark (155w)

Gramophone 68:279-80 Jl '90. Andrew M. Lamb (215w)

1393. Music of Johann Strauss: Die Sanguiniker, Opus 27; Pepita Polka, Opus 138; Erzherzog Wilhelm Genesungs, Marsch, Opus 149; Schallwellen, Opus 148; Wiedersehen, Polka, Opus 142; "Un Ballo in Maschera", Opus 272; Carnevals, Botschafter, Opus 270; Leichtes Blut, Opus 319; Saison, Quadrille, Opus 283; Cagliostro, Walzer, Opus 370; Banditen Galopp, Opus 378; Lagunen, Walzer, Opus 411.
(Johann Strauss Jr. Edition, **Volume 8**).
Oliver Dohnanyi (c). Polish State Philharmonic Orchestra.
MARCO POLO 8.223208 DDD 75:00

See Volume 7 for review excerpts.
—*Fanfare* 14:394 S/O '90. John Bauman (105w)

—*American Record Guide* 53:116-17 S/O '90. Michael Mark (155w)

Gramophone 68:279-80 Jl '90. Andrew M. Lamb (215w)

1394. Music of Johann Strauss: Carnevalsbilder (Waltz), Opus 357; Annen-Polka, Opus 117; Indigo-Marsch, Opus 349; Albion-Polka, Opus 102; Gedanken auf den Alpen, Opus 172; Festival-Quadrille, Opus 341; Hapsburg Hoch! (March), Opus 408; Nachtveilchen (Polka Mazur), Opus 170; Luzifer Polka, Opus 266; Kaiserwalzer, Opus 437.
(Johann Strauss Jr. Edition, **Volume 9**).

Johannes Wildner (c). Polish State Philharmonic Orchestra.
MARCO POLO 8.223209 DDD 62:00

See volume 7 for review excerpts from
—*American Record Guide* 53:116-17 S/O '90. Michael Mark (155w)

—*Fanfare* 14:394 S/O '90. John Bauman (105w)

Gramophone 68:279-80 Jl '90. Andrew M. Lamb (215w)

1395. Music of Johann Strauss: Morgenblatter, Walzer, Opus 279. Bauern, Polka, Opus 276. Juristenball, Polka, Opus 280. Myrthenbluthen, Walzer, Opus 395. Blumenfest, Polka, Opus 111. Panacea-Klange, Walzer, Opus 161. Diabolin, Polka, Opus 244. Lieder, Quadrille, Opus 275. Pesther Csardas, Opus 23. Feuilleton, Walzer, Opus 293.
(Johann Strauss Jr. Edition, **Volume 10**).
Johannes Wildner (c). Polish State Philharmonic Orchestra.
MARCO POLO 8.223210 DDD 68:00

"As in the previous issues, we have a mix of unknown and better-known pieces....To those who have the other nine volumes, the mere existence of these will be recommendation enough. All others are advised to investigate the series."
Fanfare 14:364-65 N/D '90. John Bauman (225w)

See Volume 1 for review excerpt.
American Record Guide 53:119-20 N/D '90. David Mason Greene (195w)

Gramophone 68:615-6 S '90. Andrew M. Lamb (175w)

1396. Music of Johann Strauss: Herrmann, Polka, Opus 91. Klange aus der Walachei, Walzer, Opus 50. Revolutions, Marsch, Opus 54. Haute, volee Polka, Opus 155. Glossen, Walzer, Opus 163. Handels, Elite, Quadrille, Opus 166. Patrioten, Polka, Opus 274. Aus den Bergen, Walzer, Opus 292. L'africaine, on Themes from Meyerbeer's Opera, Quadrille, Opus 299. Waldine, Polka Mazurka, Opus 385. Donauweibchen, Walzer, Opus 427. Frisch heran, Polka scnell, Opus 386.
(Johann Strauss Jr. Edition, **Volume 11**).
Alfred Walter (c). Polish State Philharmonic Orchestra.
MARCO POLO 8.223211 DDD 64:00

★***Awards:*** Critics' Choice 1990, *Gramophone* D '90 (Andrew Lamb).

See Volume 10 for review excerpt.
American Record Guide 53:119-20 N/D '90. David Mason Greene (195w)

Gramophone 68:615-6 S '90. Andrew M. Lamb (175w)

1397. Music of Johann Strauss: Harmonie, Polka, Opus 106. Die Gemuthlichen,, Walzer, Opus 70. Aurora, Polka, Opus 165. Fest, Quadrille, Opus 44. Ella, Polka, Opus 160. Man lebt nur einmal,, Walzer, Opus 167. Kronungs, Marsch, Opus 183. Neues Leben,, Polka francaise, Opus 278. Hafball, Tanze,, Walzer, Opus 298. Sturmisch in Lieb und Tanz,, Polka schnell, Opus 393. Wiener Frauen,, Walzer, Opus 423. Souvenir, Polka, Opus 162.
(Johann Strauss Jr. Edition, **Volume 12**).
Alfred Walter (c). Polish State Philharmonic Orchestra.
MARCO POLO 8.223212 DDD 57:00

See Volume 10 for review excerpt.
American Record Guide 53:119-20 N/D '90. David Mason Greene (195w)

Gramophone 68:615-6 S '90. Andrew M. Lamb (175w)

1398. Music of Johann Strauss: Jolly Folk, Polka, Opus 26. Zillerthal Folk, Waltz in Landler-style, Opus 30. Dancing Bear, Polka, Opus 134. Sirens, Waltz, Opus 164. Patriots' March, Opus 8. Demolition Men, Polka, Opus 269. Thermal Springs, Waltz, Opus 245. Quadrille on Themes from the opera "The Siege of Rochelle," Opus 31. Let's Away!, Quick Polka, Opus 383. New melodies Quadrille, Opus 254. Lovers Are Fond of Teasing, French Polka, Opus 399. Egyptian March, Opus 335.
(Johann Strauss, Jr. Edition, **Volume 13**).
Alfred Walter; Johannes Wildner (c). Czech-Slovak State Philharmonic Orchestra; Czech-Slovak Radio Symphony Orchestra, Bratislava.
MARCO POLO 8.223213 DDD 57:56

"It is perhaps unfair to Marco Polo to not write a detailed review of each disc, but it hardly seems necessary. The performances seem all to be absolutely first-rate....The recorded sound is even better in these volumes than in previous ones in the series with special praise reserved for those produced by Teije van Geest."
Fanfare 14:323 Ja/F '91. John Bauman (b.n.)

"The more discs Marco Polo issues in its Strauss Edition, the more flabbergasted I become over just how sophisticated and cosmopolitan Strauss could be....Wonderful music, fine performances. Such adventurous programming; the label is well named."
American Record Guide 54:102 Ja/F '91. Michael Mark (95w)

Gramophone 68:1563 F '91. Andrew M. Lamb (170w)

1399. Music of Johann Strauss: Whiplashes, Polka, Opus 60. Harvest Dances Waltz, Opus 45. Champagne Polka, Opus 211. Phenomena, Waltz, Opus 193. Romance No. 1 in D minor, Opus 243. Children's Games, French Polka, Opus 304. Gifts of Cheerfulness, Waltz, Opus 73. St. Petersburg, Quadrille on Russian Themes, Opus 255. Voslau Polka, Opus 100. Banisher of Gloom, Waltz, Opus 247. Country Ball, Quadrille on French Airs, Opus 303. Yoand You, Waltz, Opus 367.
(Johann Strauss, Jr. Edition, **Volume 14**).
Alfred Walter; Johannes Wildner (c). Czech-Slovak State Philharmonic Orchestra; Czech-Slovak Radio

Symphony Orchestra, Bratislava.
MARCO POLO 8.223214 DDD 67:19

See Volume 13 for review excerpts from
—*American Record Guide* 54:102 Ja/F '91. Michael Mark (95w)

—*Fanfare* 14:323 Ja/F '91. John Bauman (b.n.)

Gramophone 68:1563 F '91. Andrew M. Lamb (170w)

1400. Music of Johann Strauss: Alexander Quadrille, Opus 33. The Jovial Ones, Waltz, Opus 34. Joke Polka, Opus 72. The Viennese Lady, Polka-Mazurka, Opus 144. Trinkets Quadrille, Opus 169. Spirit Levels, Waltz, Opus 180. Jewels, French Polka, Opus 242. Votes, Waltz, Opus 250. In Praise of Women, Polka-Mazurka, Opus 315. Joyous Festival March, Opus 396. Imperial Jubilee, Waltz of Rejoicing, Opus 434. (Johann Strauss, Jr. Edition, **Volume 15**).
Alfred Walter; Johannes Wildner (c). Czech-Slovak State Philharmonic Orchestra; Czech-Slovak Radio Symphony Orchestra, Bratislava.
MARCO POLO 8.223215 DDD 72:16

See Volume 13 for review excerpts from
—*American Record Guide* 54:102 Ja/F '91. Michael Mark (95w)

—*Fanfare* 14:323 Ja/F '91. John Bauman (b.n.)

Gramophone 68:1563 F '91. Andrew M. Lamb (170w)

1401. Music of Johann Strauss: Ligourian Sighs, Joke Polka, Opus 57. Singers' Journeys, Waltz, Opus 41. The Bohemian Girl Quadrille, Opus 24. Express Mail Polka, Opus 159. Salvos of Joy, Waltz, Opus 171. Prince Bariatinsky March, Opus 212. Students Polka, Opus 263. Motors, Waltz, Opus 265. Long Live the Hungarian!, Quick Polka, Opus 332. The Lullaby Quadrille, Opus 194. Civic Airs, Waltz, Opus 306. Looking for a Bride, Polka, Opus 417.
(Johann Strauss Jr. Edition, Volume 16).
Alfred Walter (c). Czech-Slovak State Philharmonic Orchestra.
MARCO POLO 8.223216 DDD 59:23

"I could go on about individual pieces, but, by now, serious collectors need no urging to purchase every disc in this series."
Fanfare 14:300 Jl/Ag '91. John Bauman (500w)

1402. Music of Johann Strauss: Songs of Freedom, Waltz, Opus 52. Poor People's Ball-Polka, Opus 176. Melodies Quadrille, Opus 112. Windsor Echoes, Waltz, Opus 104. There's only One Imperial City! There's Only One Vienna!, Polka, Opus 291. Public Spirit, Waltz, Opus 295. Sweetheart, Sway!, Polka-Mazurka, Opus 394. Fairy-Tales, Waltz, Opus 312. Festival Polonaise for Full Orchestra, Opus 352. Adele Waltz, Opus 424. Violetta, French Polka, Opus 104. Kaiser Franz Joseph March, Opus 67.
(Johann Strauss Jr. Edition, **Volume 17**).
Alfred Eschwe (c). Czech-Slovak Radio Symphony Orchestra, Bratislava.
MARCO POLO 8.223217 DDD 73:34

See Volume 16 for review excerpt.
Fanfare 14:300 Jl/Ag '91. John Bauman (500w)

1403. Music of Johann Strauss: Students March, Opus 56. Streams of Lava, Waltz, Opus 74. Invitation to the Polka, Mazurka, Opus 277. Cagliostro Quadrille, Opus 369. Grand Duchess Alexandra, Waltz, Opus 181. Either-or!, Quick Polka, Opus 403. Alliance March, Opus 158. Patronesses, Waltz, Opus 264. People of Leopoldstadt, Polka, Opus 168. The Publicists, Waltz, Opus 321. Town and Country, Polka-Mazurka, Opus 322. City Hall Ball Dances, Waltz, Opus 438.
(Johann Strauss Jr. Edition, **Volume 18**).
Alfred Walter (c). Czech-Slovak State Philharmonic Orchestra.
MARCO POLO 8.223218 DDD 58:50

See Volume 1 for review excerpt.
Fanfare 14:300 Jl/Ag '91. John Bauman (500w)

Gramophone 69:120 My '92. Andrew M. Lamb (long)

STRAUSS, RICHARD

1404. Eine Alpensinfonie, Opus 64; Till Eulenspiegels Lustige Streiche, Opus 28.
Vladimir Ashkenazy (c). Cleveland Orchestra.
LONDON/DECCA 425 112 DDD 65:00

> ★*Awards:* The Year's Best, *Hi Fi News & Record Review*, May '90 Supplement.

"*Till Eulenspiegel* [is]...deft, beautifully played, and not without some humor...[the *Alpine Symphony* is] majestic in sound and playing, fully competitive with anyone's, whether you happen to prefer it to those of Karajan, Previn, Haitink, Mehta, or some other 'consensus' ones is largely a matter of whim."
Fanfare 13:306-08 Mr/Ap '90. James Miller (505w)

P100/95 S95

Hi-Fi News & Record Review p.28 My '90 Supplement. David Nice (395w)

Gramophone 67:1144 D '89. Michael Kennedy (330w)

1405. Eine Alpensinfonie, Opus 64; Don Juan, Opus 20.
Herbert Blomstedt (c). San Francisco Symphony Orchestra. 1988.
LONDON/DECCA 421 815 DDD 70:00

> ★★*Awards:* Critics' Choice 1990, *Gramophone* D '90 (Michael Kennedy). Editors' Choice, *Digital Audio's CD Review*, Je '91.

"Blomstedt and his orchestra offer a splendidly played *Don Juan*...that strikes me as a bit cool-...and lean....This is an outstanding recording of the piece [an Alpine Symphony], but I couldn't say that it's better than Previn's second one, Ashkenazy's, Haitink's, or Mehta's first one."

Fanfare 14:395-7 S/O '90. James Miller (315w)

"Blomstedt...[recorded *Don Juan*] only a few years ago in his Strauss cycle for Denon with the Dresden State Orchestra...But no allowances need be made for the San Franciscans; their *Don Juan* is superior orchestrally as well as sonically to the Dresden recording, and the big work is sheer glory. Blomstedt shows ample warmth of heart without ever hinting at overindulgence, and he makes the strongest case imaginable for the structural integrity of the supposedly sprawling score."

Stereo Review 55:118 O '90. Richard Freed (170w)

"Still, the *Alpine Symphony*'s the thing, and sound in the Davies Symphony Hall takes us one step beyond the rest in decent taming of the massive orchestration. I was prepared to say that Decca couldn't afford a fourth recording of the work, but now I might happily say farewell to the other three (even, on reflection, Ashkenazy's)." *P100/95/85 S100/95*

Hi-Fi News & Record Review 35:99 Je '90. David Nice (490w)

Gramophone 68:62 Je '90. Michael Kennedy (420w)

The New York Times O 21 '90, p. 36. Martin Bookspan (b.n.)

Digital Audio's CD Review 7:94+ D '90. Lawrence B. Johnson (135w)

Audio 75:109-10 Ap '91. Paul Moor (530w)

1406. Eine Alpensinfonie, Opus 64.
Bernard Haitink (c). Concertgebouw Orchestra.
PHILIPS 416 156 49:30

★★*Awards:* *Opus* Christmas List, 1987 (John Alan Conrad). *American Record Guide* Overview: Strauss Tone Poems, Mr/Ap '90.

"Haitink and his orchestra have finally made me see what the *Alpine Symphony* is about, and I recommend their magnificent rendition to anyone else who may previously have found this chunk of musical sightseeing an indigestible experience."

Opus 4:54 D '87. Jon Alan Conrad (80w)

"Bernard Haitink and the Concertgebouw Orchestra are expert guides on this journey, delivering a flawless performance. If one comes away without the sense of vision and spirituality imparted by Karajan...or the exhilaration of Solti...it's because Haitink's great integrity and seriousness of purpose do not normally lend themselves to music requiring a certain bit of flair to put across."

Opus 3:50 Ag '87 John Canarina (425w)

"Haitink's performance is well calculated, giving us, perhaps, the best of both worlds—logic and romance....If Mehta's impassioned response to the music makes him my favorite LP, Haitink's common sense and command of his resources make his my favorite CD."

Fanfare 10:187-8 Ja/F '87 James Miller (650w)

High Fidelity 37:63 Mr '87 Robert E. Benson (150w)

Hi-Fi News & Record Review 31:88 Ag '86. Edward Seckerson (280w)

Ovation 8:43-44 Je '87 Peter J. Rabinowitz (375w)

1407. Eine Alpensinfonie, Opus 64.
Zubin Mehta (c). Los Angeles Philharmonic Orchestra. Royce Hall, UCLA. 1975.
LONDON/DECCA 417 717 ADD 48:09

★*Awards:* *American Record Guide* Overview: Strauss Tone Poems, Mr/Ap '90.

"To complement the lush but still clearly articulated low end of Mehta's *Alpine Symphony*, Decca has provided liquid, silky sweet violins with no trace of hardness, even on CD. In fact, the mid-priced CD yields little to the British Decca LP; it is the richest, warmest sounding CD I have ever heard. The organ has a palpable warmth and depth rarely encountered in any recording—let alone a CD....Mehta's performance of the *Alpine Symphony* is in that same ultra-romantic tradition....He gets closer to the music than the insipid boredom of the critically adored Haitink."

The Absolute Sound 15:156+ Jl/Ag '90. Arthur B. Lintgen (335w)

"In the face of formidable competition, Strauss's musical travelogue of the Alps receives its finest CD representation on this London Jubilee disc....this is an example of London's finest sonics."

High Fidelity 38:55 Ja '88. Robert E. Benson (210w)

1408. Also Sprach Zarathustra, Opus 30; Don Juan, Opus 20.
Herbert Blomstedt (c). Dresden State Orchestra.
DENON/SUPRAPHON 2259 DDD 51:00

✔HC ★*Awards:* Best Recordings of the Month, *Stereo Review* Mr '89.

"While there is plenty of brilliance and power in both performance and sonics, the blockbuster aspect is incidental to a presentation that is intensely lyrical and poetic....*Also sprach Zarathustra* is coupled with a *Don Juan* that is on the same high level....two Strauss interpretations that are colorful and highly dramatic, yet impressively controlled."

Stereo Review 54:103-4 Mr '89. David Hall (340w)

"Given the orchestra's cultivated ease and the natural-sounding recording (even the dubbed-in organ seems to fit in), it's a safe recommendation for those who want their Zarathustra up-to-date and uncontroversial."

Fanfare 12:273-74 Ja/F '89. Peter J. Rabinowitz (300w)

"Unreservedly recommended."
American Record Guide 52:91 Ja/F '89. Allen Linkowski (275w)

"Both [the Telarc and Denon discs] convey to perfection the full weight of Strauss's opulent orchestration for *Zarathustra* without the slightest hint of distortion, despite the huge dynamic range both employ....Choice might well be determined by the fillers on each disc."
Stereophile 12:220 Je '89. Barbara Jahn (125w)

"Perhaps the palm just goes to Telarc, for their new VPO/Previn *Zarathustra/Tod und Verklarung* coupling...but this Lukaskirche production is one of the most natural-sounding, large orchestra, digital releases I have heard."
Hi-Fi News & Record Review 33:117 D '88. Christopher Breunig (245w)

Gramophone 66:424 S '88. Michael Kennedy (185w)

1409. Also Sprach Zarathustra, Opus 30; Till Eulenspiegels Lustige Streiche, Opus 28; Salome: Dance of the Seven Veils.
Herbert Von Karajan (c). Michel Schwalbe (vln). Berlin Philharmonic Orchestra. 1974 reissues.
DEUTSCHE GRAMMOPHON 415 853 61:00

★*Awards:* *American Record Guide* Overview: Strauss Tone Poems, Mr/Ap '90 (Zarathustra).

"This performance...will doubtless some day have historical value as one of the conductor's greatest. It is also one of the finest accounts of a Strauss work ever put on record, and demands to be heard by everyone who values his music."
American Record Guide 51:89-90 N/D '88. Arved Ashby (170w)

Gramophone 65:1439 Ap '88. Ivan March (250w)

1410. Also Sprach Zarathustra, Opus 30; Death and Transfiguration, Opus 24.
Giuseppe Sinopoli (c). New York Philharmonic Orchestra.
DEUTSCHE GRAMMOPHON 423 576 DDD 66:00

★*Awards:* *American Record Guide* Overview: Strauss Tone Poems, Mr/Ap '90 (Death and Transfiguration).

"Highest recommendation."
Fanfare 12:273-74 Ja/F '89. Peter J. Rabinowitz (300w)

"Heaviness abounds where there should be light, air and movement."
Hi-Fi News & Record Review 33:117 O '88. David Nice (315w)

Gramophone 66:424 S '88. Michael Kennedy (185w)

1411. Death and Transfiguration, Opus 24; Metamorphosen, for 23 Solo Strings; Drei Hymnen, Opus 71.
Neeme Jarvi (c). Felicity Lott (sop). Scottish National Orchestra. 1988/89.
CHANDOS 8734 DDD 72:00

★*Awards:* Critics' Choice 1990, *Gramophone* D '90 (Michael Kennedy).

"Transfiguration in Jarvi's skillful hands *is* the resolution of death and the gentle release from its terrors. Only Karajan himself has grappled as powerfully with this tension (unless one can identify with the remarkable soul of Celibidache). But Jarvi's pacing is even better, showing a wholly convincing restraint at the very points where Karajan stumbles forward-....The rash of recent recordings of *Metamorphosen* may make it one of the most over-represented works in the catalog, but very few of these fully reveal what lies beyond the many notes and heaves and sighs. Jarvi's belongs among those few, happily convincing us that there *is* life after Karajan."
American Record Guide 53:115-16 My/Je '90. Alan Heatherington (300w)

"Though not as technically tight [as Blomstedt's performance], his performance is emotionally much bigger, and surely its warmth and ardor secure just the right degree of emotion that Strauss must have felt....Jarvi's *Tod und Verklarung* is driven by the same urgency, but its spontaneity is never allowed to dilute the rich sensuousness of its themes and sounds-....Jarvi's trump card is played by the inclusion of the little-known *Hymnen.*"
Stereophile 13:227 D '90. Barbara Jahn (150w)

P95/85 S95
Hi-Fi News & Record Review 35:92-3 Ap '90. David Nice (250w)

Fanfare 13:303-4 My/Je '90. Peter J. Rabinowitz (320w)

Digital Audio's CD Review 6:30 Ag '90. Tom Vernier (310w)

Gramophone 67:1620 Mr '90. Michael Kennedy (460w)

1412. Death and Transfiguration, Opus 24; Don Quixote, for Cello and Orchestra Opus 35.
Arturo Toscanini (c). Frank Miller (cello); Carlton Cooley (vla). NBC Symphony Orchestra. reissue.
RCA 0295 ADD 64:35

✔HC ★*Awards:* Critic's Choice: 1990, *American Record Guide* Ja/F '91 (Lee Milazzo).

"All the qualities I liked in the 50s are still there, and the CD *is* superior to the LP...-Toscanini's splendid *Don Quixote* hasn't changed...but I have and it is now one of many valid performances, not *numero uno*....the performance [of *Death and Transfiguration*] is so intense, it's almost hair-raising....RCA Victor's mono sound has held up very well; in a performance that carries so potent a charge, sonic considerations seem almost irrelevant."
Fanfare 14:365-66 N/D '90. James Miller (1250w)

Gramophone 68:1416 Ja '91. Richard Osborne (240w)

Stereophile 14:205 Mr '91. Igor Kipnis (b.n.)

Death and Transfiguration, Opus 24. See No. 3141

1413. Don Juan, Opus 20; Don Quixote, for Cello and Orchestra, Opus 35; Salome: Dance of the Seven Veils.
Rudolf Kempe (c). Paul Tortelier (cello); Max Rostal (va). Dresden State Orchestra. 1973, 1974, 1975 reissues.
EMI 47865 ADD 65:27

✔HC ★*Awards:* Critics' Choice 1988, *Gramophone* D '88 (Michael Kennedy).

These performances "represent some of the finest Strauss conducting and playing ever committed to disc."
High Fidelity 37:71 O '87. David Hurwitz (120w)

"The competition pales alongside these *Dons.* Not a phoney, calculated bar in ear shot....I had forgotten, too, how exciting these recordings sounded....incomparable."
Hi-Fi News & Record Review 33:93 Jl '88. Edward Seckerson (105w)

Gramophone 66:297 Ag '88. Michael Kennedy (150w)

Fanfare 10:187-8 Jl/Ag '87 William Youngren (185w)

Don Juan, Opus 20. See No. 1208.

1414. Ein Heldenleben, Opus 40; Four Last Songs.
Neeme Jarvi (c). Felicity Lott. Scottish National Orchestra.
CHANDOS 8518 DDD 67:00

★★*Awards: Hi-Fi News & Record Review* Record of the Month, D '87; *Gramophone* Critics' Choice (Michael Kennedy), 1987.

"Felicity Lott's *Four Last Songs* is so magical that that alone seems to qualify this issue for 'Record of the Month'....But Jarvi's *Heldenleben* is equally worth having."
Hi-Fi News & Record Review 32:119 D '87. Christopher Breunig (875w)

"Felicity Lott, I think, gives more pleasure in these songs than anyone who has recorded them since Lisa della Casa's exquisite version with Karl Bohm....As for the grandiose tone of the poem itself, it seems to suit Jarvi's temperament, and the Scottish orchestra responds on a level of virtuosity that surpasses anything it has done on records before."
Stereo Review 53:196 F '88. Richard Freed (275w)

"Highly recommended."
Stereophile 11:147+ F '88. Barbara Jahn (415w)

"Felicity Lott's voice seemed, on first hearing, less distinctive than that of Dame Kiri Te Kanawa (CBS) or Jessye Norman (Philips), but repeated hearings convinced me hers is a voice meant to sing these songs."
American Record Guide 51:83 Mr/Ap '88. Robert Follet (300w)

"My advice would be to buy Jarvi for *Heldenleben*—and buy all of the others mentioned [Norman, Flagstad, Janowitz, Stich-Randall, Schwarzkopf, Tomowa-Sintow, Popp] for the *Songs.*"
Fanfare 11:207-8 Mr/Ap '88. Michael Fine (750w)

"Jarvi knows his Strauss."
High Fidelity 38:61 My '88. David Hurwitz (250w)

"Lott's performance of this cycle—which occupies only one third of the CD—makes this a disc worth owning. And its combination with such a fine *Heldenleben* makes the recording unusually worthwhile."
Musical America 108:69 Jl '88. Paul Moor (315w)

Gramophone 65:589 O '87 (410w) (rev. of LP); 65:956+ D '87 (265w) (rev. of CD). Michael Kennedy

1415. Metamorphosen, for 23 Solo Strings; Sonatina No. 1 in F for 16 Winds.
Andre Previn (c). Vienna Philharmonic Orchestra.
PHILIPS 420 160 DDD 62:00

✔HC ★*Awards: American Record Guide* Overview: Strauss Tone Poems, Mr/Ap '90 (Metamorphosen).

"Previn delivers a finely-conceived and dignified reading of 'Metamorphosen' with a superbly-controlled seamless flow which is very impressive. The Vienna Philharmonic strings play with fine character and in general this is an impressive achievement."
Music and Musicians International 36:49 Je '88. Robert Matthew-Walker (150w)

"The poignantly elegiac *Metamorphosen*-...emerges with great warmth and eloquence under Previn's direction, if not with the searing intensity of Karajan's realization with the Berlin Philharmonic on Deutsche Grammophon-....The delightful surprise in this release, however, is the F Major Sonatina...The performance here is of the very best, with sound to match."
Stereo Review 53:94 Ag '88. David Hall (255w)

"*Metamorphosen* receives a darkly passionate performance, the Sonatina a limpid and elegant one, and one suspects that Andre Previn's natural restraint and the lushness of the Vienna Philharmonic served each other very well."
High Fidelity 38:73 O '88. Terry Teachout (120w)

"For *Metamorphosis*, this disc can be highly recommended."
Fanfare 12:272-3 S/O '88. Peter J. Rabinowitz (215w)

"The entire recording is a winner from beginning to end."
American Record Guide 51:90 N/D '88. John P. McKelvey (270w)

Gramophone 65:1462 Ap '88. Michael Kennedy (350w)

1416. Der Rosenkavalier Suite. Salome: Dance of the Seven Veils; Capriccio: Prelude; Intermezzo; Morgen mittag um elf!
Neeme Jarvi (c). Felicity Lott (sop). Scottish National Orchestra.
CHANDOS 8758 DDD 65:00

★*Awards:* Critic's Choice: 1990, *American Record Guide* Ja/F '91 (Donald Vroon).

"Everything wonderful that can be lifted out of the context of the opera is here [in this concert suite]....Conducting, playing, and sound are simply *ideal*."
American Record Guide 53:112-13 Mr/Ap '90. Donald R. Vroon (325w)

"Jarvi and the SNO's collaboration with Chandos certainly reached a high point with their disc of the three operatic excerpts from *Rosenkavalier*, *Salome*, and *Capriccio*. This is surely one of the most satisfying of the lot (if you'll excuse the pun)."
Stereophile 14:201+ Ag '91. Barbara Jahn (150w)

"Salome's Dance is the stunner of the disc: teasingly slow speeds stretched even beyond Karajan's means, and matched to sharply focused sensuousness in the playing, make the flesh creep and thrill like no other unveiling I can recall. And there is more to disorientate the sense immediately afterwards, in quick succession, as the six solo strings sprucely embark on the cool neoclassical argument that begins *Capriccio*." *P95/100 S95/100*
Hi-Fi News & Record Review 35:111 Mr '90. David Nice (490w)

"For once I have no gripes about the blowzy Chandos sound, which complements Jarvi's juicy performance [of the Rosenkavalier Suite], and I guess you can imagine that he stirs up the pot quite enthusiastically in the dance from *Salome*....Recommended."
Fanfare 13:306-08 Mr/Ap '90. James Miller (505w)

Gramophone 67:1471 F '90. Michael Kennedy (330w)

Till Eulenspiegels Lustige Streiche, Opus 28. See No. 3142

STRAVINSKY, IGOR

Apollo (Apollon Mussagete). See No. 1022.

1418. Le Baiser de la Fee (Divertimento); Suites No's. 1 and 2 for Small Orchestra; Chamber Music: Octet for Wind Instruments; Fanfare for a New Theatre, for 2 Trumpets; Three Pieces for Clarinet.
Riccardo Chailly (c). Paul Archibald; Antony Pay (clar); James Watson. London Sinfonietta. 1980.
LONDON/DECCA 417 114 52:38

★*Awards:* *Gramophone* Critics' Choice 1986 (Robin Golding).

"You'll enjoy these alert, quick-witted performances. Elegance walks hand in hand with precision, charm with vulgarity."
Hi-Fi News & Record Review 31:129 My '86. Edward Seckerson (60w)

"These performances crackle with verve and virtuosity, giving the distinct impression that the musicians really relish the music....The result is a CD which would grace anyone's burgeoning collection."
Fanfare 9:236-7 Jl/Ag '86. Don C. Seibert (300w)

"This is Stravinsky at his most mellifluous-....Two short bonuses on this CD are *Three Pieces* for solo clarinet (1919) and the very short *Fanfare for a New Theatre*....Those who know these masterful miniatures will be entranced by Chailly's deft touch and the very beautiful playing of the London Sinfonietta"
High Fidelity 36:68 N '86 Robert R. Reilly (300w)

"In all of this material, there have been, and remain, more forceful, sharply profiled recordings....But if you like your Stravinsky on the more delicate—not to say bland—side, then you will enjoy this record."
American Record Guide 49:37-38 N/D '86 John W. Barker (600w)

Audio 71:82-83 Jl '87 Edward Tatnall Canby (275w)

High Fidelity 36:60 Ag '86. Terry Teachout (90w) (rev. of cassette)

Ovation 7:43-44 O '86 Paul Turok (370w)

1419. "Dumbarton Oaks" Concerto in E flat; Pulcinella (ballet, after Pergolesi), for Soprano, Tenor, Bass and Orchestra. GALLO, DOMENICO. Trio Sonatas: No. 1 in G: Moderato; No. 2 in B flat: Presto, Presto; No. 7 in G minor: Allegro. **PERGOLESI, GIOVANNI BATTISTA. Sinfonia in F for Cello and Continuo (attrib.).**
Christopher Hogwood (c). Bernadette Manca di Nissa (mez); David Gordon (ten); John Ostendorf (bass); Christopher Hogwood (hpscd); Romuald Tecco (vln); Thomas Kornacker (vln); Peter Howard (cello). Saint Paul Chamber Orchestra.
LONDON/DECCA 425 614 DDD 66:00

★*Awards:* Best of the Month, *Hi-Fi News & Record Review*, Ag '90.

"The musical content and technical quality of recording make this one of the most attractive Stravinsky selections to come along in years-....Strongly recommended."
Fanfare 14:402 S/O '90. John Wiser (405w)

"With stylish, light-toned singing from the soloists, and a fascinating appendix which presents some of Stravinsky's borrowed material in its original form, this disc is surely a must for any Stravinskyan." *P100 S95*

Hi-Fi News & Record Review 35:94 Ag '90. Simon Cargill (325w)

Gramophone 68:62-3 Je '90. Michael Oliver (460w)

1420. Firebird (complete ballet); Scherzo Fantastique, Opus 3; Fireworks, Opus 4.
Charles Dutoit (c). Montreal Symphony Orchestra. October, 1986.
LONDON/DECCA 414 409 62:32

✔HC ★★*Awards:* *Stereo Review* Best of the Month, Mr '87; *Gramophone* Critics' Choice 1986 (Edward Greenfield).

"All that one would expect of Dutoit/Montreal: sensual, rarified textures, those cultured woodwinds to coax, beguile and luxuriate."
Hi-Fi News & Record Review 32:113 Ja '87 Edward Seckerson (270w)

This performance "is, to my ear, the finest issue yet from this team, a gorgeous complete *Firebird* that surpasses the most distinguished previous recordings of this glittering but very substantial score." Record of the Month.
Stereo Review 52:72+ Mr '87 Richard Freed (810w)

"This recording will probably be a best-seller, and deservedly so."
Fanfare 10:214-5 Mr/Ap '87 Peter J. Rabinowitz (275w)

Ovation 8:44 My '87 Paul Turok (200w)

Stereo Review Presents: Compact Disc Buyers' Guide p. 52 Spr '87 William Livingstone and Christie Barter (110w)

Gramophone 64:585-6 O '86 (470w) (rev. of LP); 64:883 D '86 (120w) (rev. of CD) Edward Greenfield

1421. Firebird (complete ballet); Scherzo a la Russe (versions for jazz ensemble and orchestra); Etudes (4) for Orchestra.
Simon Rattle (c). City of Birmingham Symphony Orchestra. The Arts Centre, Warwick, England.
EMI 49178 DDD 65:00

★★★*Awards:* *Hi-Fi News & Record Review* Record of the Month, My '89; Best Recordings of the Month, *Stereo Review* Ag '89. Critics' Choice 1989, *Gramophone* D '89 (Edward Seckerson). The Year's Best, *Hi Fi News & Record Review*, May '90 Supplement.

"Rattle's *Firebird*...is splendid....He is helped by fine engineering which gives a wide, but not grotesquely wide, dynamic range and catches the power of the tuttis well....The orchestral work is fine, some slightly prosaic woodwind solos aside."
American Record Guide 52:125-26 N/D '89. Stephen D. Chakwin, Jr. (130w)

"Certainly, this is the most memorable account [of the Firebird] since the famous LSO/Dorati Mercury LP...an obvious choice for 'Record of the Month'." *P100 S100*
Hi-Fi News & Record Review 34:85 My '89; p.12 My '90 Supplement. Christopher Breunig (700w)

"The performances are brilliant, the sound stunningly vivid."
Stereo Review 54:73 Ag '89. David Hall (320w)

"Granted, there's a good deal of sheer visceral impact to the performance here...But if Rattle can make early Mahler sound too much like late Elgar, here he blurs early Stravinsky into late Glazunov...Add to this some rather ill-defined orchestral playing, and not even the civilized naughtiness of *Scherzo a la Russe*...and the urbanity of the *Etudes*...can make this a major discographic event."
Fanfare 13:335-36 S/O '89. Peter J. Rabinowitz (240w)

"The City of Birmingham Symphony has real weaknesses in its wind section (particularly in the flutes), and the principal horn sounds very precarious at its crucial entry in the final section....Rattle's performances of the two versions of the *Scherzo a la russe* are interesting, but the piece hardly deserves the attention. The same is true of the *Four Studies for Orchestra*."
Musical America 110:86 Mr '90. David Hurwitz (180w)

Gramophone 66:1591-92 Ap '89. Edward Seckerson (520w)

Firebird: Suite (1919 version). See No. 1270.

1422. Fireworks for Orchestra, Opus 4; The Firebird; Tango; Scherzo a la Russe; The Song of the Nightingale.
Antal Dorati (c). London Symphony Orchestra. 1959; 1964.
MERCURY 432 012 ADD 74:07

★★*Awards:* Pick of the Month, North American Perspective (Christie Barter), *Gramophone* N '91. Critics' Choice 1991, *Gramophone*, Ja '92 (Ivan March).

"The *Scherzo a la russe*...feature a congested blare of braying brasses that couldn't sound attractive in the finest hall in the world...in *Firebird*...The CD warms and focuses the LP sound, abandoning little of its liquid quality....I know of *no* DDD that sounds as real as the *Tango*, music for lounge lizards."
The Absolute Sound 16:136+ N/D '91. Arthur S. Pfeffer (med)

"The sound is wonderfully bright and clear. The performances are exceptional as well....I still prefer the Stravinsky I've heard by Boulez, but this is an unusually generous, unusually valuable release."
Fanfare 14:303-4 Jl/Ag '91. Michael Ullman (225w)

"This 1959 recording of the *Firebird* was only the second one ever made...There are some orchestral errors that should have been remade."
American Record Guide 54:129 Jl/Ag '91. John Landis (175w)

Gramophone 69:102 N '91. Ivan March (long)

1423. L'Histoire du Soldat (complete).

Igor Markevitch (c). Jean Cocteau; Peter Ustinov; instrumental ensemble. 1963 reissue.
PHILIPS 420 773 ADD 54:00

✔HC

A "witty, robust account...with hugely characterful contributions from Jean Cocteau (Le lecteur), Peter Ustinov (Le diable), Jean Marie Fertey (Le soldat), Anne Tonietti (La princesse) and a supporting group of instrumentalists that includes the likes of Maurice Andre and the late Manoug Parikian."

Hi-Fi News & Record Review 33:96 Jl '88. Robert Cowan (140w)

Gramophone 65:1634 My '88. Arnold Whittall (210w)

1424. L'Histoire du Soldat (complete).
Kent Nagano (c). Ian McKellen (nar); Sting; Vanessa Redgrave; members of the London Sinfonietta. London Sinfonietta.
PANGAEA 6233; PANGAEA 461 048 DDD 60:00

"Stravinsky's music is performed brilliantly by violinist Nona Liddell and the six other instrumentalists under Kent Nagano's direction, and it has never been more vividly recorded. The spoken parts are mostly excellent, too...but I found Redgrave too arch by at least half...But that is a personal reaction...if you want the work spoken in English, this new Pangaea recording is definitely the one to go for."

Stereo Review 53:123-4 O '88. Richard Freed (325w)

"This is surely ahead of competing versions in the sound department as well as in overall performance values."

American Record Guide 52:92-3 Ja/F '89. John Sunier (405w)

"It seems safe to say that until you have heard this performance you have not heard *L'Historie du soldat*....The always admirable London Sinfonietta consists in this instance of only seven of its finest instrumentalists, virtuosos all. To the role of the Soldier the rock star Sting brings an authentic, thoroughly becoming proletarian (in his case, Cockney) accent, a certain guttersnipe toughness, and, under the theatrical guidance of James Mallinson and Christine Reed, surprising histrionic ability....Vanessa Redgrave, flourishing a vast array of accents and personalities, pulls off a characterization of bravura dimensions."

Musical America 109:81-2 Mr '89. Paul Moor (230w)

"In sum, most of this is hugely enjoyable, well paced by Redgrave, McKellen, and by Nagano's team."

Hi-Fi News & Record Review 34:105 F '89. Christopher Breunig (480w)

Gramophone 66:1605 Ap '89. Edward Seckerson (350w)

1425. Music of Stravinsky: "The Igor Stravinsky Edition" (complete).
Volume 1: Ballets, volume 1: The Firebird (Columbia Symphony Orchestra); Scherzo a la russe (Columbia SO); Scherzo Fantastique (CBC Symphony Orchestra); Fireworks (Columbia SO); Petrushka (Columbia SO); The Rite of Spring (Columbia SO); Les Noces (Mildred Allen, sop; Regina Sarfaty, mez; Loren Driscoll, ten; Richard Oliver, bass; Samuel Barber, Lucas Foss, Aaron Copland, Roger Sessions (pno); American Concert Choir; Columbia Percussion Ensemble); Renard (George Shirley, Driscoll, tens; William Murphy, bar; Donald Gramm, bass; Toni Koves, cimbalom; Columbia Chamber Ensemble); L'Histoire du Soldat Suite (Columbia Chbr Ens).

Volume 2, Ballets, volume 2: Apollo (Columbia SO). Agon (Los Angeles Festival Symphony Orchestra); Jeu de cartes (Cleveland Orchestra); Scenes de ballet (CBC SO); Bluebird—Pas de deux (Columbia SO); Le baisir de la fee (Columbia SO); Pulcinella (Irene Jordan, sop; Shirley, ten; Gramm, bass; Columbia SO); Orpheus (Chicago Symphony Orchestra).

Volume 3, Ballet Suites: Petrushka. Pulcinella. The Firebird (Columbia SO).

Volume 4, Symphonies: Symphony No. 1 in E flat major (Columbia SO); Stravinsky in Rehearsal; Stravinsky in His Own Words; Symphony in Three Movements (Columbia SO). Symphony in C (CBC SO); Symphony of Psalms (Toronto Festival Singers; CBC SO).

Volume 5, Concertos: Piano Concerto (Philippe Entremont, pno; Columbia SO); Capriccio (Entremont; Columbia SO); Movements (Charles Rosen, pno; Columbia SO); Violin Concerto (Isaac Stern, vln; Columbia SO).

Volume 6, Miniature Masterpieces: Greeting Prelude (Columbia SO); Concerto in E flat major "Dumbarton Oaks" (Columbia SO); Circus Polka (CBC SO); Eight Instrumental Miniatures (mbrs of CBC SO); Four Etudes for Orchestra (CBC SO); Four Norwegian Moods (CBC SO); Concerto in D major.

Volume 7, Chamber Music and Historical Recordings: Preludium (Columbia Jazz Ens); Concertino for 12 Instruments (Columbia Chbr Ens); Octet (Columbia Chbr Ens); Rag-Time (Columbia Chbr Ens); Tango (Columbia Jazz Ens); Septet (Columbia Chbr Ens); Ebony Concerto (Benny Goodman, clar; (Columbia Jazz Ens); Symphonies of Wind Instruments (Northwest German Radio Symphony Orchestra); Duo concertante (Joseph Szigeti, vln; Igor Stravinsky, pno); Serenade in A major (I. Stravinsky, pno); Concerto for Two Pianos (I. and Soulima Stravinsky, pnos); Piano-Rag-Music (I. Stravinsky, pno); Sonata for Two Pianos (Arthur

Gold, Robert Fizdale, pnos); Sonata (Rosen).

Volume 8, Operas and Songs: Le Rossignol (Reri Grist, sop; Driscoll; Marina Picassi, sop; Kenneth Smith, bass; Gramm; Herbert Beattie, bass; Elaine Bonazzi, contr; Chorus and Orchestra of the Opera Society of Washington); Mavra (Susan Belinck, sop; Mary Simmons, mez; Patricia Rideout, contr; Stanley Kolk, ten; CBC SO); Faun and Shepherdess, Opus 2 (Simmons; CBC SO); Two Poems of Paul Verlaine (Gramm; Columbia SO); Two Poems of Konstantin Bal'mont; Three Japanese Lyrics (Evelyn Lear, sop; Columbia SO); Three Little Songs. Pribaoutki (Cathy Berberian, mez; Columbia SO); Cat's Cradle Songs (Berberian; Columbia Chbr Ens); Four Russian Peasant Songs (Gregg Smith Singers/Gregg Smith); Four Russian Songs (Adrienne Albert, mez; Louise Di Tullio, fl; Dorothy Remsen, harp; Laurindo Almeida, gtr); Three Songs from Willim Shakespeare (Berberian; Columbia Chbr Ens); In memoriam Dylan Thomas (Alexander Young, ten; Columbia Chbr Ens); Elegy for JFK (Berberian; Paul E. Howland, Jack Kreiselmann, Charles Russo, clars); The Owl and the Pussycat (Albert, mez; Craft, pno); Tilimbom (Lear; Columbia SO).

Volume 9, The Rake's Progress (Young; Judith Raskin, sop; Reardon; Sarfaty, mez; Kevin Miller, ten; Jean Manning, mez; Don Garrard, bass; Peter Tracey, bar; Sadler's Wells Opera Chorus; Royal Philharmonic Orchestra).

Volume 10, Oratorio and Melodrama: Oedipus Rex (John Westbrook, nar; Shirley, ten; Shirley Verrett, mez; Gramm; Chester Watson, bass; Reardon; Driscoll; Chor and Orch of the Opera Soc of Washington); The Flood (Laurence Harvey, Sebsatian Cabot, Elsa Lanchester, nars; Paul Tripp, nar/ten; Richard Robinson, ten; Reardon; Oliver; chorus; Columbia SO); Persephone (Vera Zorina, nar; Michele Molese, ten; Ithaca College Concert Choir; Texas Boys' Choir of Fort Worth; G. Smith Sngrs; Columbia SO); Ode (Cleveland Orch); Monumentum pro Gesualdo di Venosa ad CD annum (Columbia SO).

Volume 11, Sacred Works: Chorale Variations on Von Himmel hoch. Zvezdoliki (Toronto Fest Sngrs); Credo (G. Smith Sngrs); Pater noster (Toronto Fest Sngrs); Cantata (Albert; Young; G. Smith Sngrs; Columbia Chbr Ens); Mass (Annette Baxter, sop; Albert; G. Smith Sngrs; Columbia Symphony Wind and Brass); Babel (John Calicos, nar; Toronto Fest Sngrs; CBC SO); Canticum sacrum ad honorem Sancti Marci nominis (Robinson; Howard Chitjian, bar; Los Angeles Fest Chor and SO0; Introitus—T. S. Eliot in memoriam (G. Smith Sngrs; Columbia Chbr Ens); A Sermon, a Narrative and a Prayer (John Horton, nar; Verrett; Driscoll; CBC SO); Anthem—The Dove Descending (Toronto Fest Sngrs); Threni (Bethany Beardslee, sop; Beatrice Krebs, contr; William Lewis, James Wainner, tens; Mac Morgan, bar; Oliver; Schola Cantorum; Columbia SO).

Volume 12, Robert Craft Conducts: Le chant du rossignol (Columbia SO); Danses concertantes (Columbia SO); Epitaphium (Arthur Gleghorn, fl; Kalman Bloch, clar; Remsen); Double Canon (Israel Baker, Otis Igleman, vlns; Sanford Schonbach, vla; George Neikrug, cello); Abraham and Isaac (Richard Frisch, bar; Columbia SO); Requiem Canticles (Linda Anderson, sop; Bonazzi; Charles Bressler, ten; Gramm; Ithaca Coll Con Ch; Columbia SO).
Each volume also available separately, Sony 46291-46302. 1982.
SONY 46290 ADD 1507:00 22 discs

★★★***Awards:*** Critics' Choice 1991, *Gramophone*, Ja '92 (Alan Sanders). Critical Choice, *Musical America*, N/D '91 (Terry Teachout). Editors' Choice—Best CDs of the Year, *Digital Audio's CD Review*, Je '92.

"The sound quality is generally free of distortion and enjoys natural balances...Taken as a whole, this handsomely packaged and generally well-recorded edition is a most valuable addition to the catalog."
American Record Guide 54:152-5 N/D '91. Arved Ashby (long)

"This set contains nearly all of Stravinsky's music, the bulk of it in performances conducted, played or accompanied by the composer....[The Recorded Legacy's] a more or less complete survey of Stravinsky's compositional output...The results, despite various flaws, are highly impressive....Unfortunately, several of Stravinsky's stereo remakes were artistically inferior to the mono 'originals'...Anyone who cares about Stravinsky's music must hear them and should own them...To my mind, the complete package is an unrivaled bargain and should be snapped up at once, warts and all, but collectors who insist on picking and choosing should be sure to acquire 'Chamber Music and Historical Recordings' (SM 2K 46297). This two-CD set contains a...rare recording of the Concerto for Two Solo Pianos which Stravinsky made with his son Soulima in 1938, reissued here for the first time."
Musical America 111:42-3 N/D '91. Terry Teachout (long)

1426. Petrouchka (complete ballet); Le Sacre du Printemps.
Igor Stravinsky (c). Columbia Symphony Orchestra. reissue.
CBS 42433 ADD 64:26

✔HC ★***Awards:*** The Want List 1988, *Fanfare* N/D '88 (Mortimer H. Frank). Critics' Choice 1988, *Gramophone* D '88 (Michael Oliver).

"Had he lived to record still further versions of these...works, Stravinsky might well have left us very different readings. But for a man of his years...the control, exhilaration, and raw power of his direction, some lapses in ensemble not withstanding, remain astonishing. In every way these CD transfers are magnificent."

Stereophile 11:175-6 N '88. Mortimer H. Frank (320w)

"Though flashier conductors and more glamorous orchestras have taken advantage of the latest technical advances to overwhelm us with ever-more-perfect *Sacres* and *Petrouchkas*, the composer's own blunt and slightly shaggy recordings have retained their pungency....The older LPs are more aggressively brilliant and synthetic than the mellower, more natural CDs. Only *Petrouchka* fails to gain from this adjustment, possibly because the original masters are a bit on the thin and opaque side."

Fanfare 11:261-2 Jl/Ag '88. Elliott Kaback (210w)

"The digital remixing of *Le Sacre* improves on the old LP transfers ."

Hi-Fi News & Record Review 33:85-6 Ag '88. Frances Handford (245w)

"CBS has chosen to reissue Stravinsky's stereo remakes rather than the earlier mono recordings, which are frequently far superior both as interpretations and as performances....Faults and all, though, these recordings are important."

Musical America 109:59-60 Mr '89. Terry Teachout (85w)

1427. Le Sacre du Printemps.
Lorin Maazel (c). Cleveland Orchestra.
TELARC 80054

★*Awards:* *Fanfare* Want List 1983 (Paul Turok).

"This is a clean, polished, brilliant reading of Stravinsky's remarkable score....Everything is tightly controlled—as if Stravinsky himself were conducting....the sonics of this compact disc are superb."

High Performance Review 3 (1):127 Ag '84. Thomas H. Wendel (200w)

Audio 67:88 N '83. John M. Eargle (185w)

Originally reviewed in *Fanfare* IV:4, p. 181.

Fanfare 7:109-10 S/O '83. William Youngren (235w)

Ovation 4:34 O '83. Paul Turok (120w)

American Record Guide 47:80 Mr '84. Carl Bauman (190w)

Gramophone 61:978+ F '84. Robert Layton (150w)

Symphony in C; Symphony in Three Movements. See No. 6132

SUK, JOSEF. Fantasticke Scherzo, Opus 25. See No. 1199. **Serenade in E flat for String Orchestra, Opus 6.** See No. 2081.

SUPPE, FRANZ VON

1428. Overtures: Leichte Kavallerie; Tantalusqualen; Die Irrfahrt um's Gluck; Die Frau Meisterin; Ein Morgen, ein Mittag, ein Abend in Wien; Pique-Dame; Wiener Jubel; Dichter und Bauer.
Neville Marriner (c). Academy of St. Martin-in-the-Fields.
EMI 54056 DDD 61:00

★*Awards:* Critics' Choice 1990, *Gramophone* D '90 (Andrew Lamb).

"Anyone wanting every available overture of Suppe will want the new Marriner as well. Those trying to decide between the two Marriner recordings might be best advised to buy the EMI now and wait for Philips to reissue the Paray, which includes far more winning versions of *Beautiful Galatea* and *Boccaccio* than Marriner's Silver Line disc."

American Record Guide 54:127-28 Mr/Ap '91. Steven J. Haller (210w)

"Mehta's recent VPO recording for CBS re-alerted us (as Kuhn's Eurodisc collection failed, relatively, to do) to Suppe's lively if limited imagination. Marriner extends the sense of worth by adding some solidity to the colour—the opening of *Pique Dame* is very powerful—without sacrificing any of the essential Viennese brilliance." *P95 S95*

Hi-Fi News & Record Review 35:107 O '90. Kenneth Dommett (235w)

"What of the current competition? Dutoit (London) is predictably slick, handsomely played and richly recorded, but faceless. Mehta (CBS) received my endorsement (*Fanfare* 13:5), and it retains it strongly....With a respectful bow to Marriner's high gloss, I'll stick with Mehta and the Viennese."

Fanfare 14:399-400 Mr/Ap '91. Elliott Kaback (150w)

The New York Times O 21 '90, p. 36. Barrymore L. Scherer (b.n.)

Gramophone 68:827 O '90. Andrew M. Lamb (280w)

TAYLOR, DEEMS. Through the Looking Glass. See No. 1158.

TCHAIKOVSKY, PIOTR ILYICH

1429. Capriccio Italien, Opus 45; Symphony No. 3 in D, Opus 29, "Polish".
Herbert Von Karajan (c). Berlin Philharmonic Orchestra.
DEUTSCHE GRAMMOPHON 419 178 63:33

★*Awards:* *American Record Guide* Overview: Russian Orchestral Favorites, N/D '89 (Capriccio).

High Fidelity 37:66 Je '87 Robert E. Benson (65w)

Capriccio Italien, Opus 45; Marche Slave, Opus 3. See No. 1306.

1430. Francesca da Rimini, Opus 32; Hamlet, Fantasy Overture, Opus 67.

Leopold Stokowski (c). New York Stadium Symphony Orchestra. 1958.
DELL'ARTE 9006 42:35

✔HC ★*Awards:* Critics' Choice 1988, *Gramophone* D '88 (Ivan March).

"These performances...are without question the finest these works have ever received....The remastered sound has a relatively high level of hiss but it is otherwise fine."

High Fidelity 38:57 Ag '88. David Hurwitz (170w)

Fanfare 11:215-6 Mr/Ap '88. James Miller (200w)

Gramophone 65:1462 Ap '88. Ivan March (575w)

1431. Manfred (symphony), Opus 58.
Mariss Jansons (c). Oslo Philharmonic Orchestra. Oslo Philharmonic Concert Hall. November 26-29 and December 5, 1986.
CHANDOS 8535 DDD 53:00

★*Awards:* Critics' Choice 1988, *Gramophone* D '88 (Edward Greenfield).

"Triumphant conclusion to a magnificent series....The work...is played with all the insight it merits, the recording is quite superb in its rich sonorities...here is a winner, no mistake."

Music and Musicians International 36:55 Jl '88. Robert Hartford (70w)

"Here at last is a *Manfred* worthy of its subject matter, a fitting climax to Jansons's series of the Tchaikovsky symphonies....a stunning disc."

American Record Guide 51:88 S/O '88. Steven J. Haller (300w)

"Highly recommended, but not necessarily the best version! Muti's (EMICDC 7 47412 2, recorded in 1982 with the Philharmonia Orchestra) is even more highly charged, with equally fine shaping, somewhat slower at critical points, and with perhaps an even finer orchestra."

Fanfare 12:276-7 S/O '88. Howard Kornblum (150w)

"Jansons is a skillful operator. He 'hears' the music well: balances are generally exemplary, rhythms precisely articulated, climaxes well placed. But characterization? The music beyond the notes?...A rather low-key finish to a cycle."

Hi-Fi News & Record Review 33:94 Jl '88. Edward Seckerson (350w)

"In the present recording, Jansons continues his no-nonsense approach to the Russian master's music. Of the many versions available, this one may be the most livable. It is a consistently exciting, straightforward reading-....A word as to the sonics: they are adequate but a little on the dry side, lacking just a bit in depth and color."

HighPerformanceReview 6:88 Je '89. Thomas Wendel (210w)

"Mariss Jansons and Chandos have foundered on the rocks of the *Manfred* Symphony."

High Fidelity 38:69 D '88. David Hurwitz (365w)

Ovation 10:59-60 Je '89. Peter J. Rabinowitz (130w)

Gramophone 65:1611 My '88. Edward Greenfield (425w)

1432. Manfred (symphony), Opus 58.
Riccardo Muti (c). Edith Gabry (sop). Philharmonia Orchestra. July 1982.
EMI 47412 DDD 58:13

★★*Awards:* Perfect 10/10, *Digital Audio*, Mr '88. Perfect 10s, *Digital Audio's CD Review*, Mr '89. *American Record Guide* Overview: Tchaikovsky, Ja/F '92.

"Subsequent releases will have a mark to shoot at, for Muti and his virtuosic orchestra turn in a splendid reading."

Ovation 8:44-45 My '87 Paul Turok (90w)

"Muti's is clearly the best of...[the recent *Manfreds*], so it is good that his is the first *Manfred* to be issued on CD....it must be added that none of them is especially moving or really penetrates to the heart of this rather special score."

Fanfare 10:194-5 Ja/F '87 Don C. Seibert (450w)

"CB [Christopher Breunig] wasn't happy back in '82. Neither am I."

Hi-Fi News & Record Review 32:113+ Ja '87 Edward Seckerson (180w)

Gramophone 64:1138 F '87 Ivan March (140w)

Digital Audio 4:59-60 Ja '88. Joe Roberts (130w)

1433. The Nutcracker, Opus 71 (complete ballet); **Eugen Onegin:** Entr'acte; Waltz; Polonaise.
Semyon Bychkov (c). Berlin State Boys' Choir; Berlin Cathedral Boys' Choir; Berlin Philharmonic Orchestra.
PHILIPS 420 237 102:00 2 discs

✔HC ★*Awards:* Editors' Choice, *Digital Audio*, 1988.

"Young master Bychkov...can stand alongside Dorati without embarrassment while viewing the score in an entirely different light."

American Record Guide 51:86-7 Mr/Ap '88. Steven J. Haller (400w)

Gramophone 65:419 S '87 Ivan March (525w)

Ovation 8:43 D '87. Dan F. Cameron (650w)

1434. The Nutcracker, Opus 71 (excerpts); **Swan Lake, Opus 20** (excerpts).
Neeme Jarvi (c). Scottish National Orchestra.
CHANDOS 8556 DDD 75:00

★*Awards:* Top Choices—1989, *American Record Guide* Ja/F '90 (Lawrence Hansen).

"The playing and conducting here are so full of life, so pointed and charming that I felt cheated by not having the complete work-....Much the same is true of the eight excerpts from *Swan Lake*."

Fanfare 12:263 Jl/Ag '89. Howard Kornblum (100w)

"The SNO acquits itself like a world-class ensemble of great refinement and responsiveness—step aside Chicago and Berlin, there's a new kid on the block—and it is captured in better-than-average sonics....The performance is outstanding, the sound fine, and the disc well-filled."

American Record Guide 52:101 Jl/Ag '89. Lawrence Hansen (525w)

"An interesting release, perhaps suggesting a certain element of coldness in this conductor's makeup?"

Hi-Fi News & Record Review 34:96 Mr '89. Christopher Breunig (225w)

Gramophone 66:1438 Mr '89. Ivan March (210w)

The Nutcracker, Opus 71 (excerpts). See No. 1283.

1435. Orchestral Music: Hamlet, Fantasy Overture, Opus 67; Romeo and Juliet (fantasy overture); Festival Overture in D (on the Danish national hymn); Serenade for Nikolai Rubinstein's Name-Day; Mazeppa (incidental music).
Geoffrey Simon (c). London Symphony Orchestra.
CHANDOS 8310 2 discs

★*Awards:* *Fanfare* Want List 1984 (John Bauman).

"One of my strongest recommendations yet."

Hi-Fi News & Record Review 29:81 Ag '84. Angus McKenzie (175w)

"This two-disc set is, in fact, a winner in every respect."

American Record Guide 48:68-9 My/Je '85. John P. McKelvey (400w)

Ovation 5:72 D '84. Paul Turok (140w)

"D.C.S. and P.T. were glowing in their comments (*Fanfare* V:6) while I was equally enthusiastic about the MHS reissue (*Fanfare* VII:2)-....Buy this one by all means if you don't have the other disc versions already."

Fanfare 8:275 N/D '84. John Bauman (140w)

Gramophone 62:127 Jl '84. Ivan March (210w)

1436. Overture 1812, Opus 49; Marche Slave, Opus 31; Romeo and Juliet.
Leonard Bernstein (c). New York Philharmonic Orchestra.
CBS 36723 44:29

★*Awards:* *American Record Guide* Overview: Russian Orchestral Works, N/D '89.

"In the *1812 Overture* the cannons are hefty enough, though a little more reverb would not have been amiss; Bernstein's Slavs march a bit more briskly than some, and the coda is even more up-tempo....But the *piece de resistance* is still Bernstein's youthful thoughts on Tchaikovsky's equally youthful depiction of Shakespeare's timeless tragedy, in which the passion of the 'star-crossed lovers' and the hammer blows of sword on sword, taken at a hell-for-leather tempo with a few extra cymbal crashes thrown in for good measure, make this wonderful music sound as fresh and virile as when the composer first set pen to paper."

American Record Guide 50:63-64 Ja/F '87 Steven J. Haller (325w)

1437. Suites for Orchestra: No. 3 in G, Opus 55; No. 4 in G, Opus 61 ("Mozartiana").
Neville Marriner (c). Stuttgart Radio Symphony Orchestra. March 1987.
CAPRICCIO 10200 DDD 64:00

★*Awards:* The Want List 1988, *Fanfare* N/D '88 (Don C. Seibert).

"For lovers of the music of Tchaikovsky, this disk is a must....Sir Neville and the Stuttgart players are entirely up to these works' enormous technical demands."

HighPerformanceReview 6:91-2 Mr '89. Thomas Wendel (220w)

"Marriner's 'Mozartiana' proves to be a triumph for him and his German radio orchestra-....The total effect is delectable....Regrettably, Marriner's Third Suite is not so commendable. It is expertly played, but the effect is a bit cool and matter-of-fact."

Fanfare 11:224 My/Je '88. Don C. Seibert (340w)

"Glowing accounts...Performances, recording, and presentation are first-rate."

Music and Musicians International 36:55 Jl '88. Robert Hartford (80w)

"These works are not easy for performers to get just right....With his extensive experience in—and empathy for—18th Century repertory, Marriner's accounts are splendid, passionate readings of this soaringly lyrical music."

American Record Guide 51:62-3 Jl/Ag '88. Lawrence Hansen (550w)

"It wouldn't be fair to suggest that Sir Neville entirely ignores the composer's markings...but too much is dully generalized."

Hi-Fi News & Record Review 33:93 Jl '88. David Nice (250w)

Digital Audio 4:82 Je '88. John Holdren (125w)

Gramophone 65:1611 My '88. Ivan March (200w)

1438. Symphony No. 1 in G minor, Opus 13, "Winter Dreams"; Symphony No. 2 in C minor, Opus 17, "Little Russian".
Andrew Litton (c). Bournemouth Symphony Orchestra.
VIRGIN 91119 DDD 80:00

★★*Awards:* Critic's Choice: 1991, *American Record Guide*, Ja/F '92 (Donald Vroon). Critics' Choice 1990, *Gramophone* D '90 (Edward Greenfield). *American Record Guide* Overview: Tchaikovsky, Ja/F '92.

"The orchestra is incredibly good—more than 'provincial', something like the Cincinnati Symphony. I hear no weaknesses....[Litton] has

Tchaikovsky figured out! So few do. This is the real thing, and I am thrilled!"
American Record Guide 54:130-31 Mr/Ap '91. Donald R. Vroon (375w)

"Vigorous, clean performances, with Litton offering effectively paced shapings of both pieces, clearly recorded. Although I still prefer the Jansons/Oslo performances on Chandos (you'd have to buy two discs to get them), and the Abbado/Chicago performance of No. 2 on CBS, it's convenient to have these two symphonies on one disc."
Fanfare 14:301 My/Je '91. Howard Kornblum (120w)

"Yes, Litton's neat yet flexible manner is endearing in its way (nowhere more so than in the Trio of 'Winter Dreams'—gloriously shaped here) but this vernally fresh music ends up sounding just a little too episodic and ramshackle in design for its own good. Enjoyable music-making, certainly, but not the kind to linger long in the memory." *P995/85 S95*
Hi-Fi News & Record Review 36:105 Ja '91. Andrew Achenbach (245w)

Gramophone 68:1219 D '90. Edward Greenfield (480w)

1439. Symphony No. 2 in C minor, Opus 17, "Little Russian;" Capriccio Italien, Opus 45.
Mariss Jansons (c). Oslo Philharmonic Orchestra. CHANDOS 8460 DDD 48:00

★*Awards:* *American Record Guide* Overview: Tchaikovsky, Ja/F '92 (Symphony No. 2).

"As was true with the other five Tchaikovsky symphonies on Chandos, Jansons and his alert, rich-sounding orchestra give us a fresh and enchanting version of the No. 2."
Fanfare 11:220 Ja/F '88. Howard Kornblum (175w)

"The superlatives ran dry some issues ago. So let me just say that Jansons's *Little Russian* is typical of his cycle as a whole....If I have any reservation at all, it is this. I do sometimes wish that Jansons's Tchaikovsky were cut of a slightly coarser cloth."
Hi-Fi News & Record Review 32:141 D '87. Edward Seckerson (280w)

"That I have actually enjoyed this disc must say a lot for Jansons's advocacy, his fresh enthusiastic players, and the splendid sound of Chandos's top-notch recording."
Music and Musicians International 36:49 Ja '88. Robert Hartford (75w)

"I've heard more impetuous and virtuosic readings [of Capriccio Italien], but the Oslo performance retains much of this show piece's charm and fire."
HighPerformanceReview 5:89-90 Ap '88. James Primosch (130w)

"The orchestra has no tone; I don't think any orchestra can sound as dry and dull as the Oslo Philharmonic does here."
American Record Guide 51:65-6 Ja/F '88. Donald R. Vroon (370w)

Gramophone 65:750 N '87 Edward Greenfield (370w)

Ovation 10:59-60 Je '89. Peter J. Rabinowitz (130w)

1440. Symphony No. 2 in C Minor, Opus 17, "Little Russian".
Geoffrey Simon (c). London Symphony Orchestra. CHANDOS 8304

★*Awards:* *Fanfare* Want List 1984 (Peter J. Rabinowitz).

"The sound is very spacious, the ambience absolutely right and the clarity quite amazingly good, giving an overall open sound which allows me to recommend this disc very highly-....it is one of my personal favourites."
Hi-Fi News & Record Review 29:91 Ja '84. Angus McKenzie (160w)

"A major release."
American Record Guide 47:73-4 S'84. Peter J. Rabinowitz (400w)

"The original 1872 version recorded here for the first time shows marked differences from the later 1880 score....with imposing Chandos sonics and a performance of civilized stature from Geoffrey Simon, this is a disc to be reckoned with."
The Sensible Sound 7:53 Fall '85. John J. Puccio (170w)

"Our resident Tchaikovskian, D.C.S., reviewed the conventional disc of this performance at length in *Fanfare* VII:4 and...concludes with the estimate that Simon's performance is 'thoroughly satisfying.'"
Fanfare 7:264-5 Jl/Ag '84. James Miller (220w)

Audio 68:317 O '84. Bert Whyte (200w)

Gramophone 61:877 Ja '84. John Warrack (210w)

Ovation 5:52 My '84. Paul Turok (330w)

1441. Symphony No. 3 in D, Opus 29, "Polish".
Mariss Jansons (c). Oslo Philharmonic Orchestra. CHANDOS 8463 44:52

★★*Awards:* *American Record Guide* Overview: Tchaikovsky, Ja/F '92; *Gramophone* Critics' Choice 1986 (Edward Greenfield).

"Once again, Jansons and his spirited Norwegians give us a vivid, forthright Tchaikovsky."
Fanfare 10:227-8 N/D '86 Howard Kornblum (110w)

"Brilliance and maximal contrast in both dynamics and differentiation of episodic elements are the hallmarks of this interpretation of Tchaikovsky's youthful not-quite-masterwork-....The sound throughout is resplendent."

Stereo Review 51:176+ N '86 David Hall (215w)

"For those willing to put up with a certain amount of smudged ensemble...young Maestro Jansons's rendition is a joy to hear, brisk, to the point, and satisfying."

American Record Guide 50:58-59 Mr/Ap '87 Steven J. Haller (350w)

The $ensible Sound 33:60 Spr '87 John J. Puccio (150w)

Hi-Fi News & Record Review 31:88 Ag '86. Edward Seckerson (215w)

1442. Symphony No. 4 in F minor, Opus 36; Nutcracker Suite, Opus 71A.
Thomas Beecham (c). Royal Philharmonic Orchestra. 1959 and 1956 reissues.
EMI 63380 mono 65:00

★★*Awards:* The Want List 1990, *Fanfare* N/D '90 (John Bauman); Critic's Choice: 1990, *American Record Guide* Ja/F '91 (Allen Linkowski).

"This is one of the great Tchaikovsky Fourths, no question about it....One doesn't much miss the stereo....The 1954 *Nutcracker Suite*...is the perfect CD companion....this is a truly magical, worth-going-out-of-your-way-for recording."

American Record Guide 53:28+ S/O '90. Donald R. Vroon (210w)

Gramophone 68:546 S '90. Alan Sanders (385w)

Fanfare 14:474-76 N/D '90. William Zagorski (160w)

The Absolute Sound 16:172 S/O '91. Thomas Hathaway (brief)

1443. Symphonies: No. 4 in F minor, Opus 36; No. 5 in E minor, Opus 64; No. 6 in B minor, Opus 74, "Pathetique".
Guido Cantelli (c). NBC Symphony Orchestra. 1952-1954.
MUSIC & ARTS 602 AAD (m) 128:00 2 discs

★*Awards:* The Want List 1990, *Fanfare* N/D '90 (Peter J. Rabinowitz).

"These are tough-minded readings, tightly wound...even bordering in spots on cruelty-...Cantelli has little patience for Tchaikovsky's self-indulgent side...In all, a major addition to the catalog."

American Record Guide 53:138-42 Ja/F '90. Peter J. Rabinowitz (125w)

"In many respects, this NBC 'Pathetique' scores over Cantelli's studio effort with the Philharmonia Orchestra....Here is a performance suggesting the Toscanini sonority and purity, but one infused with greater breadth and consequently purged of the nervous intensity the older conductor brought to the music-....The same might be said of Cantelli's account of the Fourth Symphony, probably...the most valuable item in this set....A warmly recommended set."

Fanfare 13:311-12 My/Je '90. Mortimer H. Frank (480w)

"A CD SoundRing helps in taming the shrill-sounding brass of 4, some tape hiss is noticeable in 5, and, throughout, NBC's typically close and unatmospheric miking of the winds throws the conductor's carefully balanced orchestral panorama askew. For historical reasons, however, this issue is a most valuable document."

Stereophile 13:205 Je '90. Igor Kipnis (205w)

"These performances are remarkable for the clarity of thought and sure control that Cantelli brings to them....The production captures the unmistakably dry, somewhat harsh Studio 8H acoustic, a little wearing after a while, but at least it's uncluttered."

HighPerformanceReview 8(1):83-4 '91. Timothy Mangan (400w)

1444. Symphony No. 4 in F minor, Opus 36.
Mariss Jansons (c). Oslo Philharmonic Orchestra.
CHANDOS 8361 41:29

✔**HC** ★*Awards:* *Gramophone* Critics' Choice 1985 (Edward Greenfield).

"One of the freshest and most exciting Fourths in recent memory (see LP review p. 93 August)."

Hi-Fi News & Record Review 30:86 S '85. Edward Seckerson (75w)

"Both as a performance and as a sonic treat, the Chandos release is a welcome change from other recent digitals—from the undernourished Previn (Philips) and Maazel (Telarc) discs to the frenzied new Solti (London) effort-....Jansons has the field to himself."

The Sensible Sound 7:52-3 Fall '85. John J. Puccio (270w)

"In reviewing Tchaikovsky's Fifth by these performers (Chandos ABRD 1111, *Fanfare* VIII:5), I wrote that Jansons and the orchestra 'combine talents and offer as affecting and as powerful a performance of Tchaikovsky's Fifth as I know....' Change one word (Fifth to Fourth) and you have the same impression from me for this new disc."

Fanfare 9:268-9 N/D '85. Howard Komblum (375w)

"How well one receives this recording of the Symphony No. 4 hinges on the approach one prefers toward this vividly dramatic work. Jansons clearly favors a cooler, 'Norwegian' approach to this music. Tempos are straightforward and nowhere extreme; phrasings are understated. While there is no lack of drama, neither is there any attempt to pump additional blood into the veins."

American Record Guide 49:39-40 S/O '86 Mark Koldys (480w) (rev. of LP)

Gramophone 63:128 Jl '85 (rev. of LP). Edward Greenfield (450w); 63:359 S '85 (rev. of CD). Ivan March (350w)

1445. Symphony No. 5 in E minor, Opus 64; Romeo and Juliet (fantasy overture).
Leonard Bernstein (c). New York Philharmonic Orchestra. Avery Fisher Hall, New York. November 1988, October 1989 live.
DEUTSCHE GRAMMOPHON 429 234 DDD 76:00

★★*Awards:* The Want List 1991, *Fanfare* N/D '91 (William Zagorski); Critic's Choice: 1991, *American Record Guide*, Ja/F '92 (James Ginsburg). *American Record Guide* Overview: Tchaikovsky, Ja/F '92 (Symphony No. 5).

"A viable, gripping performance of the symphony, so different from the generalized 'heroics' that grace so many of our record labels. *Romeo and Juliet* fares less well....Still, for those who like their music caught on the wing, there is little one could really criticize." *P95/85 S95/85*
Hi-Fi News & Record Review 36:95 Mr '91. Simon Cargill (180w)

"These live recordings...represent the late Leonard Bernstein in his more willful aspect. Exaggerated tempo contrasts and heavy underlining of emotional high points are found throughout."
Stereo Review 56:102 Ap '91. David Hall (125w)

"True to the tendencies of his later years. Bernstein's...performance is broad and romantically oversized in almost every detail except in the third-movement Valse, where his tempo is very close to Koussevitzky's in this 1944 recording."
Musical America 111:87 My '91. Gary Lemco (160w)

"Here, as with his unparalleled *Pathetique* ...Bernstein reveals Tchaikovsky as a troubled Mahlerian (never mind chronology)....The New Yorkers play so idiomatically it is hard to believe this is not a Russian orchestra! The recording from subscription concerts is spectacularly direct and natural, far superior to most studio productions. Bernstein's third recording of *Romeo and Juliet* was an unnecessary exercise since the maestro got it right on the second try-....get that *Romeo and Juliet*, and the Fifth at hand, and you will own the most captivating versions of both pieces!"
American Record Guide 54:117-8 My/Je '91. James S. Ginsburg (475w)

"This is not only a significant performance of a tired old warhorse, but an inspirational one as well. As to the even *more* tired overture, it goes in like fashion."
Fanfare 14:308-9 Jl/Ag '91. William Zagorski (1050w)

Bernstein's performance is "exciting and, most of all, enthralling. The NYPO string sound is quite sumptuous too; in fact, the entire orchestra is outstanding."
Stereophile 14:225 N '91. Barbara Jahn (brief)

Gramophone 68:1219-20 D '90. Edward Greenfield (260w)

1446. Symphony No. 6 in B minor, Opus 74, "Pathetique".
Mariss Jansons (c). Oslo Philharmonic Orchestra.
CHANDOS 8446 43:35

✔**HC** ★*Awards: Gramophone* Critics' Choice (Edward Greenfield), 1987.

"A pristine Pathetique....Yet...something inside tells me that clear-headed Jansons has not entirely surrendered to the *Pathetique*, to the uncompromising weight and force of its *angst*."
Hi-Fi News & Record Review 32:111 F '87 Edward Seckerson (320w) (rev. of LP)

Gramophone 64:1026 Ja '87 (210w) (rev. of LP); 64:1563 My '87 (225w) (rev. of CD). Edward Greenfield

Hi-Fi News & Record Review 32:104-5 Mr '87 Edward Seckerson (105w)

1447. Symphony No. 6 in B minor, Opus 74, "Pathetique".
Eugene Ormandy (c). Philadelphia Orchestra. 1960.
CBS 37768

★*Awards: American Record Guide* Overview: Tchaikovsky, Ja/F '92.

"It is *the* Ormandy version to have. However, competition these days is greater than it has ever been."
Ovation 10:50-1 F '89. Jon Tuska (450w)

"I think his most impressive issue was the early LP...But it's supremely well played, with the strings of the orchestra astonishing in their richness and precision. The recording still sounds decent."
Fanfare 12:312-13 Mr/Ap '89. Howard Kornblum (65w)

"The *Pathetique* was an Ormandy specialty; he recorded it many times. This, the first stereo version was made in 1960 and remains the finest moderate version available....the Ozawa (Erato) is the only one that sounds better, and Ormandy knows and feels the music better than Ozawa does."
American Record Guide 52:100 Mr/Ap '89. Donald R. Vroon (220w)

TELEMANN, GEORG PHILIPP

1448. Musique de Table (Tafelmusik) (complete).
Reinhard Goebel (c). Musica Antiqua Koln.
DEUTSCHE GRAMMOPHON 427 619 DDD 254:00 4 discs

★*Awards:* The Want List 1990, *Fanfare* N/D '90 (George Chien).

"I came to the version by Musica Antiqua Koln with high expectations, as a longtime admirer of their work. Their *Tafelmusik* met my expectations. The sound is warm, resonant, and balanced, with the finest details of even the continuo harpsichord audible....The collection is a true embarrassment of riches, but make sure that these are the riches that you seek. The uninitiated might prefer excerpts."

American Record Guide 53:123-24 S/O '90. Paul Laird (415w)

"Here's an album that's about as close to self-recommending as I can imagine....The performances are done with all the breathtaking virtuosity that we have come to expect from the group....Archiv's recording is superb....Listeners who still consider Goebel and MAK to be extremist may wish to hold out for the possibility of a complete transfer of the Bruggen set-....Highly recommended."

Fanfare 13:314-15 My/Je '90. George Chien (550w)

"I have not heard Harnoncourt's recent recording for Teldec...but I have no reservation in giving the Musica Antiqua Koln's version the highest recommendation. The quality of the recorded sound is excellent."

Continuo 14:16 Ag '90. Pierre Savaria (520w)

"Both Musica Antiqua Koln and Concentus Musicus Wien, groups long familiar to early-music enthusiasts, have recently released recordings of the complete *Musique de table*. The recordings have an almost equal number of virtues, but they offer surprisingly different advantages as well as unique ensemble approaches....Concentus Musicus is consistently musical, combining verve and vigor with a greater sense of weight. Ultimately, that tips the scales slightly in its favor."

Musical America 110:80 N '90. Christopher Rothko (225w)

Gramophone 67:679-80 O '89. Nicholas Anderson (735w)

1449. Musique de Table (Tafelmusik) (complete).

Nikolaus Harnoncourt (c). Vienna Concentus Musicus. 1986-88.
TELDEC 35670; TELDEC 44688 DDD 261:00 4 discs

✔HC ★*Awards:* Critics' Choice 1989, *Gramophone* D '89 (Nicholas Anderson).

"Both Music Antiqua Koln and Concentus Musicus Wien, groups long familiar to early-music enthusiasts, have recently released recordings of the complete *Musique de table*. The recordings have an almost equal number of virtues, but they offer surprisingly different advantages as well as unique ensemble approaches....Concentus Musicus is consistently musical, combining verve and vigor with a greater sense of weight. Ultimately, that tips the scales slightly in its favor."

Musical America 110:80 N '90. Christopher Rothko (225w)

Gramophone 67:679+ O '89. Nicholas Anderson (735w)

Digital Audio's CD Review 6:76-7 N '89. Octavio Roca (200w)

TIPPETT, MICHAEL

1450. Concerto for Double String Orchestra; Fantasia Concertante on a Theme of Corelli, for String Orchestra; Songs for Dov, for Tenor and Small Orchestra.

Michael Tippett (c). Nigel Robson (ten). Scottish Chamber Orchestra.
VIRGIN 90701 DDD 70:55

★*Awards:* Critics' Choice 1988, *Gramophone* D '88 (Michael Oliver).

"Both string works receive sinewy readings that dig deep into the music, as if Tippett was searching for the original motivations...Indeed, the toughness almost suggests that Tippett might be wrestling with another composer's thinking."

Hi-Fi News & Record Review 33:75 Je '88. Christopher Breunig (350w)

"I was quite moved by his autumnal reading of the Concerto...The complexities of his Corelli Fantasia unravel themselves without any force of hand here...Songs for Dov is something of a revelation too...All three works are recorded with a clarity and balance that does them full justice."

Stereophile 11:159-62 Ag '88. Barbara Jahn (390w)

"This is an excellent disc in every respect."

Fanfare 12:283-4 S/O '88. John Ditsky (200w)

Gramophone 66:39 Je '88. Michael Oliver (430w)

TOCH, ERNST. Jephta, Rhapsodic Poem (Symphony No. 5). See No. 6026.

TORKE, MICHAEL

1451. The Yellow Pages; Slate; Adjustable Wrench; Vanada; Rust.

Kent Nagano; David Miller (c). Michael Torke (pno); Edmund Niemann (pno); Nurit Tilles (pno); James Pugliese (xylophone); Gary Schall (mrba). London Sinfonietta. 1989.
ARGO 430 209 DDD 55:00

★★★*Awards:* Critics' Choice 1990, *Gramophone* D '90 (Michael Stewart); Pick of the Month, North American Perspective (Christopher Pollard), *Gramophone* D '90; Disc of the Month, *Digital Audio's CD Review*, Mr '91. Editors' Choice, *Digital Audio's CD Review*, Je '91.

"As several of his titles imply, Torke is synesthetic: he sees colors in chords....The music does not suggest the term crossover, nor does it recall the self-conscious collages of Gunther Schuller's Third Stream; rather it seems a natural outcome for a young composer who has grown up awash in modern media. Minimalism has always been around during Torke's life, as has pop culture, so Madonna is as much of an icon as Glass or even Stravinsky."

Fanfare 14:303-4 My/Je '91. James H. North (600w)

"Whether Torke's technical finesse is enough to make his music endure I have no idea; it seems quite enough that it has loads of appeal for the classical music audience of the fast-paced 1990s....The recordings are clean, the performances appropriately spiffy and lively."
Musical America 111:91 Jl '91. James Wierzbicki (390w)

"Five works by Torke without a break are simply too much. At this stage, at least, his music does not offer sufficient diversity to sustain anything more than about 15 minutes. The details are charming, and in *Adjustable Wrench* [*Torke wrench* one assumes?] Torke has created a modern equivalent of a Mozart Divertimento, with all the skill and craftsmanship which that implies." *P95/85 S85/75*
Hi-Fi News & Record Review 36:95-6 Mr '91. Simon Cargill (210w)

Digital Audio's CD Review 7:40 Mr '91. David Vernier (325w)

Gramophone 68:1228+ D '90. Michael Stewart (630w)

TUBIN, EDUARD

1452. Symphonies: No. 2 "Legendaire"; No. 6.
Neeme Jarvi (c). Swedish Radio Symphony Orchestra.
BIS 304 63:31

★*Awards:* Record of the Eighties, *Gramophone*, D '89 (Robert Layton).

"This disc is the best place to make first acquaintance with one of the truly outstanding symphonists of the postwar period."
Fanfare 9:241-2 Mr/Ap '86. Paul Snook (750w)

"Both of these issues are important additions to the library of one who is serious about the music of our own time. Don't let lack of familiarity dissuade you from purchase. Both the Bamberg Symphony and Swedish Radio Symphony perform very well for Jarvi. I cannot imagine finer performances becoming available at any time in the near future. BIS has provided its usual superb recording quality."
American Record Guide 49:88-89 S/O '86 Carl Bauman (930w)

"The Swedish Radio Symphony Orchestra premiered the Sixth Symphony in 1955, and its reprise here is extremely potent in execution and stunning in sound. Ditto for the Second."
High Fidelity 37:78-79 Ja '87 Robert R. Reilly (525w)

Ovation 8:48 F '87 Paul Turok (525w)

Hi-Fi News & Record Review 31:131 My '86. Kenneth Dommett (210w)

The New York Times My 20 '90, p. H 27. Andrew L. Pincus (140w)

1453. Symphony No. 3; Symphony No. 8.
Neeme Jarvi (c). Swedish Radio Symphony Orchestra. Berwald Hall, Stockholm. June 16-19, 1986.
BIS 342 DDD 62:46

★★★*Awards:* *Fanfare* Want List 1987 (Henry Fogel); *Fanfare* Want List 1987 (John Ditsky); Critics' Choice 1988, *Gramophone* D '88 (Robert Layton). Record of the Eighties, *Gramophone*, D '89 (Robert Layton); Engineering and Production Record Award 1989, *Gramophone*, D '89.

"The performances are quite good...The recording is good."
HighPerformanceReview 5:90 Ap '88. James Primosch (240w)

"No need to comment on the performances which are uniquely authoritative."
Hi-Fi News & Record Review 32:106 S '87 Kenneth Dommett (240w)

"BIS has done well, again, by these symphonies. The background is quiet, the orchestra up to the mark, and the overall sound excellent."
Fanfare 11:329-30 S/O '87. John Ditsky (660w)

Gramophone 66:430 S '88. Robert Layton (585w)

Digital Audio's CD Review 6:58 F '90. David Vernier (290w)

Musical America 110:86-8 My '90. Robert R. Reilly (230w)

The New York Times My 20 '90, p. H 27. Andrew L. Pincus (140w)

1454. Symphony No. 4, "Sinfonia Ilirica"; Symphony No. 9; Toccata.
Neeme Jarvi (c). Bergen Symphony Orchestra; Gothenburg Symphony Orchestra. December, 1983; March, 1985.
BIS 227 65:24

✔**HC** ★*Awards:* Record of the Eighties, *Gramophone*, D '89 (Robert Layton). *Gramophone* Critics' Choice 1986 (Robert Layton).

"These unique recordings and performances make an ideal introduction to the composer."
Hi-Fi News & Record Review 31:117 O '86. Kenneth Dommett (140w)

"A Terribly Important Recording among CDs issued to date."
Fanfare 10:229-30 N/D '86 John Ditsky (165w)

"Any Tubin collection should include this excellent CD."
High Fidelity 37:70 Ag '87 Robert R. Reilly (350w)

The New York Times My 20 '90, p. H 27. Andrew L. Pincus (140w)

American Record Guide 50:59 Mr/Ap '87 Carl Bauman (385w)

Gramophone 64:586-7 O '86 Robert Levine (210w)

1455. Symphony No. 5 in B minor; Kratt Suite.
Neeme Jarvi (c). Bamberg Symphony Orchestra.
BIS 306 DDD 54:40

★*Awards:* Record of the Eighties, *Gramophone*, D '89 (Robert Layton). *Fanfare* Want List 1986 (John Bauman).

"The recording is very fine, and the performances by the German orchestra of both the symphony and the suite are first-rate."
High Fidelity 37:78-79 Ja '87 Robert R. Reilly (525w)

"Jarvi—thanks to whom Tubin's stature has been steadily growing for a couple of years now—is able to get superb performances out of this German orchestra. The SD is good, but the CD is even better; the music is overpowering in the latter medium....A highly recommended release, probably one of the year's best."
Fanfare 10:241 S/O '86 John Ditsky (670w)

"Both of these issues are important additions to the library of one who is serious about the music of our own time. Don't let lack of familiarity dissuade you from purchase. Both the Bamberg Symphony and Swedish Radio Symphony perform very well for Jarvi. I cannot imagine finer performances becoming available at any time in the near future. BIS has provided its usual superb recording quality."
American Record Guide 49:88-89 S/O '86 Carl Bauman (930w)

The New York Times My 20 '90, p. H 27. Andrew L. Pincus (140w)

Hi-Fi News & Record Review 32:115 Ja '87 Kenneth Dommett (165w)

VAN DE VATE, NANCY

1456. Distant Worlds; Dark Nebulae; Journeys; Concertpiece for Cello and Small Orchestra.
Szymon Kawalla (c). Janusz Mirynsky (vln); Zdislaw Lapinski (cello). Polish National Radio Symphony Orchestra.
CONIFER 147 AAD 52:00

"The veneer of wide-ranging eclecticism conceals music of real substance."
Hi-Fi News & Record Review 33:110-11 Mr '88. Stephen Pettitt (275w)

"The exotic sonorities will delight those who listen sensuously, yet the music stays close enough to melody to suit those who consider that aspect essential. The performances exhibit a high (if inconsistent) level of virtuosity...Recorded sound is marvelously transparent."
Fanfare 11:224 Ja/F '88. Kyle Gann (350w)

"Her music has grandeur and an emotional sweep that fills out the titles of her works and makes them good descriptions of the content....The performances are convincing and the recording, though slightly cavernous in sound, is realistic and will provide an effective test of your equipment's capacity for large and colorful noises."
American Record Guide 51:64 Jl/Ag '88. David W. Moore (120w)

"Van de Vate's interest in orchestra colors is evident, as is her skill and imagination in selecting and using them....The Polish orchestra and soloists demonstrate a remarkable affinity for this music; this recording is recommended with great enthusiasm."
Sigma Alpha Iota Pan Pipes 80:15 Wint '88. Jocelyn Mackey (400w)

"*Distant Worlds* is a marvelous work. I'm not prone to selecting favorites; nevertheless, of the works represented, 'Distant Worlds' would get my vote....All of the performances appear well-executed, and exhibit sensitive understanding of the music....This is in every way an excellent release offering the listener powerful music that commands attention and merit—musically and sonically, a very satisfying experience."
International League of Women Composers Newsletter Wint '88/'89 p.10. Elizabeth Hayden Pizer (735w)

"These performances...are remarkably forceful and vivid. The recording is as clean and vibrant as any analog transcription."
High Fidelity 38:77-8 Ap '88. James Wierzbicki (425w)

"The orchestra...does a fine job."
HighPerformanceReview 5:90 Ap '88. Allan Blank (215w)

Gramophone 65:590 O '87. Arnold Whittall (285w)

VARESE, EDGAR

1457. Music of Varese: Ionisation, for 13 Percussionists (1929-31); **Ameriques** (1921); **Arcana** (1925-7); **Density 21.5, for Solo Flute** (1936); **Offrandes, for Soprano and Chamber Orchestra** (1921); **Octandre, for Flute, Winds and Brass** (1923); **Integrales, for 11 Winds and 4 Percussionists** (1924-5).
Pierre Boulez (c). Rachel Yakar (sop); Lawrence Beauregard (fl). New York Philharmonic Orchestra; Ensemble Intercontemporain. 1985 reissues.
SONY 45844 ADD/DDD 77:00

✔HC ★★*Awards:* Critics' Choice 1990, *Gramophone* D '90 (Michael Stewart). The Want List 1991, *Fanfare* N/D '91 (William Youngren).

"Comprising recordings made with the New York Philharmonic in the mid-'70s and more recent digital offerings courtesy of the Ensemble InterContemporain, this disc is a must for anyone fascinated by the origins of 20th-century Modernism." *P100/95 S95/85*
Hi-Fi News & Record Review 35:97 S '90. Simon Cargill (325w)

"Since these are generally the best recordings of these Varese works, it's a welcome arrival."
American Record Guide 54:132 Jl/Ag '91. Timothy D. Taylor (b.n.)

Gramophone 68:748+ O '90. Michael Stewart (590w)

VAUGHAN WILLIAMS, RALPH

1458. Job, A Masque for Dancing.
Vernon Handley (c). David Nolan (vln). London Philharmonic Orchestra. 1984 reissue.
EMI 9506 DDD 48:00

✔HC ★*Awards: Gramophone* Critics' Choice (Stephen Johnson), 1987. Records to Die for: 1 of 5 Recommended Recordings, *Stereophile* Ja '91 (Lewis Lipnick).

"The engineering by Mr. Baer...is remarkable, with natural soundstaging and awesome dynamic range, without any unnatural spotlighting of instruments. This piece requires the transparency of an English orchestra, and the London Philharmonic doesn't disappoint."
Stereophile 14:159 Ja '91. Lewis Lipnick (165w)

"This is a winner."
Music and Musicians International 36:44 O '87. Robert Hartford (50w)

"Handley's poetical account of this work...was welcomed three years ago as a very acceptable alternative to Boult's 1971 classic."
Hi-Fi News & Record Review 32:141-2 D '87. Barbara Jahn (95w)

"The sound is representative of EMI's mid-'80s art in body and definition....Handley's account has sufficient understanding, and the orchestral playing enough refinement and strength, for this CD to stand very well on its own. I recommend it urgently."
Fanfare 11:229-30 My/Je '88. John D. Wiser (350w)

Gramophone 65:571-2 O '87 Stephen Johnson (105w)

1459. Music of Vaughan Williams: A Sea Symphony; Fantasia on a Theme of Thomas Tallis; A London Symphony; A Pastoral Symphony; Symphony No. 4 in F minor; Symphony No. 5 in D; Symphony No. 6 in E minor; Sinfonia Antartica; Aristophanic Suite, "The Wasps"; Symphony No. 8 in D minor; Symphony No. 9 in E minor; Serenade to Music; In the Fen Country; The Lark Ascending; Norfolk Rhapsody No. 1; English Folk Song Suite; Fantasia on "Greensleeves".
(Boult Conducts Vaughan Williams).
Adrian Boult (c). Sheila Armstrong (sop); John Carol Case (bar); Norma Burrowes (sop); Margaret Price (sop); Hugh Bean (vln). London Philharmonic Choir; Sixteen Vocal Soloists; London Philharmonic Orchestra; New Philharmonia Orchestra; London Symphony Orchestra. reissue.
EMI 63098 ADD/AAD 65:28, 59:51, 71:20, 68:46, 68:10, 63:37, 65:43 7 discs

"For those of us of the pre-Previn generation who learnt our Vaughan Williams from Boult's old Decca set, this new Compact Disc box set is a rare treasure."
New Hi-Fi Sound 6:105 Jl '89. Christopher Palmer (660w)

"As I believe the cited [*Fanfare*] reviews make clear, Miller finds most of these Boult performances—and so do I—to be benchmark quality: thoughtful, deeply expressive, compellingly authoritative....Newcomers well supplied with pelf will do well to become owners of a splendidly consistent lot."
Fanfare 13:197-98 S/O '89. John Wiser (180w)

Overture: The Wasps. See No. 1479.

1460. Symphony No. 1, "A Sea Symphony", for Soprano, Baritone, Chorus and Orchestra.
Adrian Boult (c). Sheila Armstrong (sop); John Carol Case (bar). London Philharmonic Choir; London Philharmonic Orchestra. 1968.
EMI 47212

✔HC ★*Awards: Opus* Christmas List, 1987 (Paul L. Althouse).

"The work is not uniformly strong, but the opening and closing movements contain music as wonderful as any."
Opus 4:52 D '87. Paul L. Althouse (100w)

"HMV's recording and performance may not quite fulfill one's ideals, but the only competition, with the LSO conducted by Andre Previn for RCA, is blown out of the water."
Fanfare 10:223-4 Mr/Ap '87 John D. Wiser (125w)

Music Journal p. 26 Spr '87 Bert Wechsler (70w)

Hi-Fi News & Record Review 32:113 F '87 Doug Hammond (40w)

Gramophone 64:1138 F '87 Alan Sanders (125w)

Ovation 9:17 Ag '88. Scott Cantrell (70w)

1461. Symphony No. 1, "A Sea Symphony", for Soprano, Baritone, Chorus and Orchestra.
Bernard Haitink (c). Felicity Lott (sop); Jonathan Summers (bar). London Philharmonic Chorus; Cantilena; London Philharmonic Orchestra.
EMI 49911 DDD 71:00

★★*Awards:* Orchestral Record Award 1990, *Gramophone* D '90. *American Record Guide* Overview: 20th Century British Symphonies, My/Je '92.

"Orchestral and choral forces are splendid, and his soloists (Felicity Lott most notably) outperform most others on record. Angel's recording is of exceptional clarity and presence, with chorus in perfect focus...Above all, Haitink has assembled a performance of great strength and passionate conviction, which casts light on many previously unexplored passages, and delivers its diverse messages with surprising eloquence, albeit without a British accent."
American Record Guide 53:130 N/D '90. John P. McKelvey (475w)

"Anyone should be delighted with this new EMI disc."
Fanfare 14:296-7 S/O '90. Robert McColley (360w)

"Bernard Haitink leads the London Philharmonic and Choir in a lovely performance of this work, capturing the lyric and free qualities which Vaughan Williams drew from the majestic poetry: 'Away O Soul! hoist instantly the anchor...O farther, farther sail!' Soprano Felicity Lott and baritone Jonathan Summers perform the extensive solo roles with wondrous ease. The miking of the performance is a bit distant and it is difficult to detect the words of the chorus, but this does not detract significantly from this fine production of an important but little-known work."

HighPerformanceReview 8(1):84 '91. George S. T. Chu (240w)

Gramophone 68:729 O '90. Michael Kennedy (140w)

1462. Symphony No. 1, "A Sea Symphony", for Soprano, Baritone, Chorus and Orchestra.

Vernon Handley (c). Joan Rodgers (sop); William Shimell (bar); Ian Tracey (chorus master). Liverpool Philharmonic Choir; Royal Liverpool Philharmonic Orchestra. Philharmonic Hall, Liverpool. July 1988.
EMI 2142; EMI 69867 DDD 69:39

★*Awards:* Records to Die for: 1 of 5 Recommended Recordings, *Stereophile* Ja '91 (Richard Schneider).

"The quality of the performance and the recording is very high indeed and the *Scherzo* 'The Waves' is exciting listening." *P95 S95*

Hi-Fi News & Record Review 34:93-4 S '89. William McVicker (275w)

"Hearing a recording such as this reveals more options than I had believed possible in this work....of the few great conductors alive today, I would bet only on Bernstein or Kleiber to obtain a *Sea Symphony* as definitive as this one-....Shimell has an unfortunate wobble in the high tessituras, and in other places tends to search for pitch. These caveats aside, each soloist's identification with the meaning of the text and the musical flow far outweigh invidious comparisons with their competition. The production...is one of the best recordings of a choral orchestral work I have ever heard."

Stereophile 13:we9+ Ja '90. Richard Schneider (560w)

"An incredible mid-price sleeper, practically an after-thought in the EMI catalog, this is one of the finest audio productions of a large-scale work to come out of digital technology....For me...the EMI wins [over Virgin] for Handley's incredible architectonic mastery of the score, and, by the closest call, a more convincing illusion of overall reality in the production."

Stereophile 14:167 Ja '91. Richard Schneider (b.n.)

Gramophone 66:1300 F '89. Ivan March (480w)

1463. Symphony No. 2, "London"; Fantasia on a Theme by Thomas Tallis.

Bernard Haitink (c). London Philharmonic Orchestra.
EMI 49394 DDD 65:51

★★*Awards:* *Stereo Review* Best Recordings of the Month Ap '88. Critics Choice, *Hi Fi News & Record Review*, Ap '91 Supplement (John Crabbe).

"Both the music and the recorded sound here evoke the majesty of English cathedral architecture. Bernard Haitink and this excellent orchestra, in both works, rise handsomely to the occasion."

High Fidelity 38:84 O '88. Paul Moor (285w)

"It is state-of-the-art realization of the work that I have been waiting for since the advent of compact disc."

Stereo Review 53:82 Ap '88. David Hall (300w)

"The clouds of war really do seem to gather over Haitink's daybreak. This is a darker, more 'serious' reading of the score than any in my experience...Fine too, is the Tallis Fantasia-...The recording (Abbey Road) is broad, deep and handsome, reminding me of EMI's palmiest days gone by."

Hi-Fi News & Record Review 33:99-100 My '88. Edward Seckerson (350w)

"Haitink give an outstanding reading....The recording itself is somewhat distant in perspective...Of the available performances the Boult/Angel remains my choice."

American Record Guide 51:71-2 My/Je '88. Carl Bauman (300w)

"Though there are various times when I prefer Boult's or either of Previn's performances, this one is quite competitive and boasts clear, powerful sound that makes it my narrow favorite."

Fanfare 11:230 My/Je '88. James Miller (125w)

Gramophone 65:959 D '87 (370w) (rev. of LP); 66:172 Jl '88 (130w) (rev. of CD). Michael Kennedy

1464. Symphony No. 2, "London;" Concerto Academico, for Violin and Orchestra; The Wasps: Overture.

Andre Previn (c). James Buswell (vln). London Symphony Orchestra. 1970s reissue.
RCA 0581 ADD 71:00

★★*Awards:* *American Record Guide* Overview: 20th Century British Symphonies, My/Je '92.

"The bright, brilliant, primary-colored Previn recordings catch the essence of the music better for me than the Boult ones—yet we would be much poorer without Sir Adrian's never less than excellent accounts."

Fanfare 14:338-40 Ja/F '91. Robert McColley (170w)

"I have always disliked the recordings [of RVW's music] by English conductors—especially Sir Adrian Boult, who seems to underline the composer's alien Englishness, making him more staid and boring than he need be....Previn does these best."

American Record Guide 54:134 Mr/Ap '91. Donald R. Vroon (130w)

P85/95 S95/75

Hi-Fi News & Record Review 35:113 O '90. Christopher Breunig (b.n.)

Gramophone 68:1678+ Mr '91. Michael Stewart (190w)

Digital Audio's CD Review 7:42-3 Mr '91. Octavio Roca (b.n.)

1465. Symphony No. 3, "Pastoral"; Symphony No. 4 in F minor.
Andre Previn (c). Heather Harper (sop). London Symphony Orchestra. 1972.
RCA 0583 ADD 72:00

★★★*Awards: American Record Guide* Overview: 20th Century British Symphonies, My/Je '92.

See Symphony No. 2 (Previn, LSO, RCA 0581) for review excerpt.

American Record Guide 54:134 Mr/Ap '91. Donald R. Vroon (130w)

See Symphony No. 2 (Previn, LSO, RCA 0581) for excerpt of review of the cycle.

Fanfare 14:338-40 Ja/F '91. Robert McColley (170w)

P85/95 S95/75

Hi-Fi News & Record Review 35:113 O '90. Christopher Breunig (b.n.)

Digital Audio's CD Review 7:42-3 Mr '91. Octavio Roca (b.n.)

Gramophone 68:1678+ Mr '91. Michael Stewart (190w)

1466. Symphony No. 5 in D; Concerto for 2 Pianos and Orchestra.
Yehudi Menuhin (c). Ralph Markham (pno); Kenneth Broadway (pno). Royal Philharmonic Orchestra.
VIRGIN 90733 DDD 69:00

★★*Awards:* The Want List 1989, *Fanfare* N/D '89 (Howard Kornblum); Critics' Choice 1989, *Gramophone* D '89 (Michael Kennedy).

"It's gratifying to report that his readings of the Fifth Symphony and the Concerto for Two Pianos leave little to be desired."

Musical America 109:77-8 S '89. David Hurwitz (270w)

"This is an unjustly neglected work, and you could do far worse than investigate it, especially in such a fine performance and such excellent recorded sound."

Stereophile 12:197 D '89. Barbara Jahn (215w)

"Menuhin obviously loves this music and I chose the word 'loves' deliberately because there is, in his performance of the Fifth Symphony in particular, a strong stress on the affective qualities of the work. His engineers also seem to be emphasising this by highlighting the higher registers so that the soaring strings make their presence unmistakably felt from the very opening of the symphony—though this is also at the expense of other things in the music which seem to recede by comparison....This recording of the *Double Concerto* certainly supersedes any of its predecessors and is well worth the price of this record, whatever reservations one might entertain about Menuhin's account of the symphony." *P95 S95*

Australian Hi-Fi 20(11):51:15-6 '89. John Aranetta (360w)

"Strongly recommended."

Fanfare 12:340-41 My/Je '89. John Wiser (500w)

"The orchestra plays well for Menuhin...but his interpretation is straightforward to the point of plainness, and there is a squareness about his phrasing that makes the bar lines intrude when they're least wanted....The best thing about this release is the *Concerto for Two Pianos*, an excellent work not heretofore available on CD. Fortunately, it is better performed than the symphony."

American Record Guide 52:102 Jl/Ag '89. John P. McKelvey (350w)

"Menuhin makes the Symphony's first-movement curiously static, especially the central Allegro section; and this emerges very clearly from comparison with another recent recording—by Bryden Thomson with the LSO-...where every note tingles with life, even when the music is at its slowest and most quiet-....The performance [of the concerto] is a vigorous one, though not always shaped firmly enough."

Hi-Fi News & Record Review 34:97 Mr '89. Max Harrison (280w)

Gramophone 66:1166 Ja '89. Michael Kennedy (455w)

1467. Symphony No. 5 in D; Three Portraits (from "The England of Elizabeth," 1955 film score); Concerto in F minor for Bass Tuba and Orchestra.
Andre Previn (c). John Fletcher (tuba). London Symphony Orchestra. reissue.
RCA 0586 ADD 72:16

★★*Awards: American Record Guide* Overview: 20th Century British Symphonies, My/Je '92.

See Symphony No. 2 (Previn, LSO, RCA 0581) for review excerpt.

American Record Guide 54:134 Mr/Ap '91. Donald R. Vroon (130w)

See Symphony No. 1 (Previn, LSO, RCA 0580) for excerpt of review of the cycle.

Fanfare 14:338-40 Ja/F '91. Robert McColley (170w)

P85/95 S95/75

Hi-Fi News & Record Review 35:113 O '90. Christopher Breunig (b.n.)

Digital Audio's CD Review 7:42-3 Mr '91. Octavio Roca (b.n.)

Gramophone 68:1678+ Mr '91. Michael Stewart (190w)

1468. Symphony No. 6 in E minor; Symphony No. 9 in E minor.

Andre Previn (c). London Symphony Orchestra. reissue.
RCA 0588 ADD 73:10

★*Awards: American Record Guide* Overview: 20th Century British Symphonies, My/Je '92.

See Symphony No. 1 (Previn, LSO, RCA 0580) for excerpt of review of the cycle.
Fanfare 14:338-40 Ja/F '91. Robert McColley (170w)

P85/95 S95/75
Hi-Fi News & Record Review 35:113 O '90. Christopher Breunig (b.n.)

Digital Audio's CD Review 7:42-3 Mr '91. Octavio Roca (b.n.)

Gramophone 68:1678+ Mr '91. Michael Stewart (190w)

1469. Symphony No. 6 in E minor; Fantasia on a Theme by Thomas Tallis; The Lark Ascending (Romance for Violin and Orchestra).
Andrew Davis (c). Tasmin Little (vln). BBC Symphony Orchestra.
TELDEC 73127 DDD 62:00

✔HC ★★*Awards:* Best of the Month, *Hi-Fi News & Record Review*, O '91. Critics' Choice 1991, *Gramophone*, Ja '92 (Michael Stewart).

"Tasmin Little's account of the solo part [*Lake Ascending*] makes it difficult to prefer either Hugh Bean's (with Boult) or Iona Brown's, on the earlier ASM recording for Argo. Andrew Davis's tempi here, and throughout the CD, I find more than persuasive...and his is a reading with an unusual depth of feeling and quotient of pathos....Davis conducts an impressive performance of the Sixth too...here the BBC strings are glowing and rich (Tony Faulkner's magic again), and give a fluent and varied performance." *P95/100 S100*
Hi-Fi News & Record Review 36:121+ O '91. Christopher Breunig (med)

"If only the first movement had just a touch more violence, this would have been the VW6 for the ages. As it is, it's very fine, and the recording itself is simply stunning—one of the finest-sounding discs I have ever heard...The two fillers are exquisitely done, the recording flattering the BBC strings to a remarkable degree."
Fanfare 15:359 Ja/F '92. David Hurwitz (long)

"I had never thought of the BBC Symphony as a particularly good orchestra, but the playing in all departments is at every moment first-rate-...RVW would have thought well of this effort [in the Sixth Symphony]; it joins Thomson's and Boult's third recording as a desirable and illuminating performance of a powerful and original score, and outstrips both of them in sheer impact as a recording. If there were nothing else on the record, it would still get my urgent recommendation...[In the *Tallis Fantasia* and *Lark*, Tasmin Little's] playing is fine-grained and warm. Lightness and transparency reign here in the sound as well; worthy additions to the main work."
Fanfare 15:359-61 Ja/F '92. John Wiser (long)

"The Davis must reluctantly be discarded in favor of [Boult on EMI (currently on CD: 63308) and Stokowski with the New York Philharmonic (last available on an English CBS LP)]...The recording sabotages Davis's work here—muddy and indistinct with recessed winds in an over-reverberant church, an unnatural acoustic for an orchestra."
American Record Guide 55:132-3 Ja/F '92. John Landis (long)

1470. Symphony No. 7 (Sinfonia Antartica).
Bernard Haitink (c). Sheila Armstrong (sop). London Philharmonic Choir; London Philharmonic Orchestra. October, 1985.
EMI 47516 41:35

★★★*Awards: Gramophone* Record Award Winner 1986—Orchestral Award. *American Record Guide* Overview: 20th Century British Symphonies, My/Je '92.

"What a thoroughly absorbing and fascinating piece this is!...Much credit must go to Haitink's magnificent realization of the score, with superb playing by the London Philharmonic—which, of course, learned the work from Adrian Boult (Angel LP, 36763). This is not to slight Haitink's achievement, for his pacing is tauter and more forward-moving than Boult's....On the basis of this disc I can only say to Haitink and Angel: More Vaughan Williams, please!"
Opus 2:53 O '86 John Canarina (510w)

"Although this won *The Gramophone's* award for orchestral recording of 1986 it might just as well have been for engineering."
Hi-Fi News & Record Review 32:113 F '87 Christopher Breunig (135w)

"Somehow, for all this precision and energy, Haitink fails to approximate the intensity achieved by Boult when the score was brand-new....A notice of the LP issue may be found in *Fanfare* 9:4, p. 243."
Fanfare 10:198-9 Ja/F '87 John D. Wiser (380w)

Gramophone 64:554 O '86 (250w) (rev. of LP); 64:1031 Ja '87 (170w) (rev. of CD) Alan Sanders

1471. Symphony No. 7, "Sinfonia Antartica"; Symphony No. 8 in D minor.
Andre Previn (c). Heather Harper (sop); Ralph Richardson (spkr). Ambrosian Singers; London Symphony Orchestra. reissue.
RCA 0590 ADD 73:05

★*Awards: American Record Guide* Overview: 20th Century British Symphonies, My/Je '92.

Fanfare 14:338-40 Ja/F '91. Robert McColley (170w)

P85/95 S95/75
Hi-Fi News & Record Review 35:113 O '90. Christopher Breunig (b.n.)

Digital Audio's CD Review 7:42-3 Mr '91. Octavio Roca (b.n.)

Gramophone 68:1678+ Mr '91. Michael Stewart (190w)

VILLA-LOBOS, HEITOR

1472. Bachianas Brasileiras (9) (complete); Concerto for Guitar and Orchestra.
Enrique Batiz (c). Alfonso Moreno (gtr). Royal Philharmonic Orchestra.
EMI 47901 DDD 185:00 3 discs

★*Awards:* The Want List 1988, *Fanfare* N/D '88 (Henry Fogel, James Miller).

"If I had only a few competing recordings and especially if I had none at all, I'd suggest buying this set, packed as it is with good performances of exotic, colorful, energetic music that will not be easily surpassed in the future."
Fanfare 12:306-7 N/D '88. James Miller (225w)

"Batiz has the heart and head for this music: where it works best, as in Nos. 2, 4, and 7, his drive and sense of style make the music bubble with life....The smaller-scale works are recorded with clarity, but where the forces are larger the sound easily becomes saturated above the *forte*, and although Batiz and the orchestra retain a firm control over the balance of Villa-Lobos's typically loaded, multi-layered textures, the recording smudges rather than elucidates these."
Hi-Fi News & Record Review 33:115 Ja '88. Doug Hammond (455w)

Gramophone 65:753 N '87 Michael Oliver (770w)

1473. Bachianas Brasileiras (9) (complete).
Isaac Karabtchevsky (c). Leila Guimaraes (sop). Brazil Symphony Orchestra.
SIGLA 600 208 ADD 70:35, 42:40, 61:15 3 discs

✔HC ★*Awards:* The Want List 1989, *Fanfare* N/D '89 (Jon Tuska).

"In every phrase of every movement of every one of the *Bachianas* there is an effortless and irresistible evocation of the fantasy world Villa-Lobos created by comingling native sources and Bachian forms....In No. 5...Leila Guimaraes is so deep inside the piece that there is no point in making comparisons with other performances. It's not just a matter of her singing in her native language and a familiar idiom; it's as if that delicious voice—rich and creamy and incredibly luminous—had been created just for this music, or the music written in anticipation of it."
Stereo Review 54:87 Ap '89. Richard Freed (400w)

"How fitting that this version should be 100% Brasilian—from artists to record label. Even the note writer and translator are Brasilian. Apart from the last, they are all more than adequate to the task."
American Record Guide 52:103-4 Mr/Ap '89. Donald R. Vroon (550w)

"The performances in this extraordinary set are all-surpassing, not only collectively but in each of the individual works—even the famous No. 5, for soprano and cellos, in which the wonderful Leila Guimaraes eclipses all previous performers with her unfeigned warmth and enthusiasm."
Stereo Review Presents: Compact Disc Buyers' Guide Summ 1989 p.60 Richard Freed (125w)

"Idiomatic performances....Although recorded a bit closer to the orchestra, the sound is less detailed than that vouchsafed Batiz, whose performances are generally more spirited than Karabtchevsky's."
Fanfare 12:330 Mr/Ap '89. James Miller (200w)

1474. Choro No. 6; Bachiana Brasileira No. 7.
Heitor Villa-Lobos (c). Berlin Radio Symphony Orchestra. 1954.
VARESE SARABANDE 47257 54:30

★*Awards:* *Fanfare* Want List 1987 (James Miller).

"The composer-conducted Varese Sarabande CD is a very important reissue....Varese Sarabande has found a richness and tonal body that I never would have believed existed on the originals, and that renders useless the earlier issues even if you do own them."
Fanfare 10:231-3 Mr/Ap '87 Henry Fogel (285w)

"Regardless of future CD releases of new recordings of the works, the composer's eye-opening interpretations will remain of permanent value."
Ovation 8:38 Ap '87 Paul Turok (180w)

"These performances are excellent and are presented here in their best light."
American Record Guide 50:80 N/D '87. David W. Moore (235w)

Choro No. 9 for Orchestra. See No. 2152

WAGNER, RICHARD. Siegfried Idyll; Overture: Fliegende Hollander. See No. 1131. **Tannhauser: Bacchanale.** See No. 1065.

WALTON, WILLIAM

Facade: Suite. See No. 1202.

1475. Film Music: As You Like It (a five-secton "poem for orchestra" arranged by Christopher Palmer from Walton's music for the 1936 Olivier film); **Hamlet** (a nine-section "scenario for orchestra" arr. Christopher Palmer). (Walton: Film Music, Volume 1).
Neville Marriner (c). Catherine Bott (sop). Academy of St. Martin-in-the-Fields.
CHANDOS 8842 DDD

★*Awards:* Critic's Choice: 1991, *American Record Guide*, Ja/F '92 (Steven J. Haller).

"These recordings sweep the field for many reasons, chief among them being the completeness of the music and the performances by Marriner and the greatly expanded Academy of St. Martin in the Fields Orchestra...All of the film music except the *Christopher Columbus* Suite was recorded in St. Jude's Church, and sounds much alike. It is generally top-drawer."
The Absolute Sound 16:184+ Ja '92. Arthur B. Lintgen (long)

1476. Film Music: Spitfire Prelude and Fugue; A Wartime Sketchbook; Escape Me Never; The Three Sisters; Battle of Britain Suite. (Volume 2).
Neville Marriner (c). Academy of St. Martin-in-the-Fields.
CHANDOS 8870 65:00

★*Awards:* The Want List 1991, *Fanfare* N/D '91 (James Miller); The Want List 1991, *Fanfare* N/D '91 (Benjamin Pernick).

"I can only echo colleague Haller's comments about the performances: they are excellent. Long may the series continue."
American Record Guide 54:139 Mr/Ap '91. Charles Parsons (b.n.)

See Volume 1 for review excerpt.
The Absolute Sound 16:184+ Ja '92. Arthur B. Lintgen (long)

"Sir Neville is too much the professional to let the resonance of the St. Jude's NW11 acoustic interfere with the brio of his orchestra's performances; even so, a drier ambience would have been better matched." *P95/100 S95(85)*
Hi-Fi News & Record Review 36:96 Mr '91. Christopher Breunig (170w)

1477. Film Music Collection. Walton: Henry V. **Farnaby:** Rosa Solis. **Anon.:** Watkin's Ale. **Canteloube:** Obal, dinlou Limouzi.
(Walton: Film Music, Volume 3).
Neville Marriner (c). Christopher Plummer (nar). Westminster Abbey Choir; Academy of St. Martin-in-the-Fields Chorus; Academy of St. Martin-in-the-Fields.
CHANDOS 8892 DDD 67:00

★★★★*Awards:* The Want List 1991, *Fanfare* N/D '91 (Benjamin Pernick). Critics' Choice 1991, *Gramophone*, Ja '92 (Edward Greenfield). Pick of the Month, North American Perspective (Christie Barter), *Gramophone* Ap '91; Best CD of the Month, *Digital Audio's CD Review*, Ap '91; Best of the Month, *Hi-Fi News & Record Review*, My '91.

"'A Shakespeare Scenario' occupies sixty-one minutes of this disc. The stirring music that Sir William Walton wrote for Sir Laurence Olivier's film is the principal attraction, but in addition to the music we have Christopher Plummer declaiming over 300 lines from the play....On the Chandos disc speech and music sometimes alternate, and sometimes go on simultaneously....The playing does full justice to Walton's music...Chandos deserves high praise for the thoughtfully designed thirty-six-page booklet that accompanies the disc."
Fanfare 14:320-21 My/Je '91. Robert McColley (400w)

"Walton's score for the film was the match of Olivier's approach: lavish, exciting, strikingly dramatic, innovative but respectful of the past (in its skillful borrowing of theme from the *Fitzwilliam Virginal Book*, a couple of Canteloube's *Chants d'Auvergne*, and the old French tune, the 'Agincourt Song', that gloriously caps off the score and the movie itself)-....Chandos's disc is subtitled 'A Shakespeare Scenario' and was arranged by Christopher Palmer from the complete film score-....Chandos's characteristic, rather echoey 'house' acoustic is well suited to this music, and the recorded sound is demonstration, watch-your-speakers quality."
American Record Guide 54:125-6 My/Je '91. Lawrence Hansen (475w)

"In all, another winner of a CD in what's turning out to be a msot distinguished series."
P95/100 S100
Hi-Fi News & Record Review 36:85 My '91. Andrew Achenbach (210w)

See Volume 1 for review excerpt.
The Absolute Sound 16:184+ Ja '92. Arthur B. Lintgen (long)

Gramophone 68:1848 Ap '91. Edward Greenfield (560w)

Digital Audio's CD Review 7:56 Ap '91. Sebastian Russ (300w)

Musical America 111:62-3 Jl '91. Terry Teachout (165w)

1478. Symphony No. 1 in B flat minor (1932-5); Variations on a Theme by Hindemith.
Vernon Handley (c). Bournemouth Symphony Orchestra.
EMI 49671 DDD 66:00

★*Awards:* Best Recordings of the Month, *Stereo Review* F '90.

"In his new EMI recording of William Walton's richly Neoromantic First Symphony of 1935, Handley not only far surpasses his own previous recording of the work (issued here by Nonesuch in 1981), but he fully measures up to the wonderful recording made in 1967 by Andre Previn....Fine as the symphony is, my greatest pleasure in this disc came from the coupler piece...the whole recording is a splendid musical, interpretive, and sonic achievement."
Stereo Review 55:141 F '90. David Hall (600w)

"Vernon Handley's new recording [of the *Hindemith Variations*]...is ideal in every way. Handley even provides an ideal coupling: a superb performance of Walton's First Symphony that is not quite so violent as Andre Previn's justly celebrated 1966 recording...but that is no less effective in its elegant lucidity. *Very highly recommended.*"

Musical America 110:88-9 My '90. Terry Teachout (205w)

"To those who own a recording of neither piece, the CD has my enthusiastic recommendation. Those who already own a satisfactory recording of the symphony but can't wait for Szell's *Variations* to hit CDs might also give Handley some consideration."

Fanfare 13:342-43 My/Je '90. James Miller (425w)

"The third movement...receives as moving an account as I've ever heard. But pride of place goes to the scherzo, which, in the revelation of all its constructional details, beats 'em all. If you have any recording of Walton 1 other than Previn/RCA, too bad. If you have the Previn/RCA, you may duplicate it with this one as a more than worthy alternative, and receive Variations on a Theme by Hindemith."

Stereophile 13:215+ Ap '90. Richard Schneider (550w)

"EMI's new Handley version [of the Symphony], this time with the Bournemouth Orchestra, is altogether finer if still not a completely effective tour of this tremendously exciting score....Despite the caveats, this is a recommendable release."

American Record Guide 53:123-24 Mr/Ap '90. Richard E. Tiedman (450w)

Gramophone 67:319 Ag '89. Edward Greenfield (635w)

The Musical Times 130:551 S '89. Robert Anderson (155w)

1479. Symphony No. 1 in B flat minor. VAUGHAN WILLIAMS, RALPH. Overture: The Wasps.

Andre Previn (c). London Symphony Orchestra. 1966 reissue.
RCA 7830 ADD 52:15

✔HC ★★*Awards:* *American Record Guide* Overview: 20th Century British Symphonies, My/Je '92.

"Previn made later versions of the symphonies, neither surpassing these mid-priced reissues [RCA 6801 and RCA 7830]....Indeed, the Walton and Shostakovich might well be cited as Previn's finest recorded work with the LSO."

Hi-Fi News & Record Review 34:99 Mr '89. Christopher Breunig (280w)

"If anything, it's clearer in its digital remastering...I'd still call it the best all-around Walton First and I don't expect anyone to beat it very soon....Recommended."

Fanfare 12:341 Mr/Ap '89. James Miller (300w)

"A fast, taut, no-nonsense interpretation played with dazzling virtuosity, this performance has been correctly regarded as definitive ever since its initial release. It puts every other recording of the Walton First in the shade."

High Fidelity 39:76 Je '89. Terry Teachout (125w)

"Though Previn left a few stones unturned, and was just slightly less tidy, his landmark recording still gets the nod for its overall, start-to-finish visceral involvement. Moreover, the analog sound of Previn's recording is far more listenable than the Virgin digital."

Stereophile 12:167-68 My '89. Richard Schneider (375w)

Digital Audio's CD Review 6:84 O '89. Octavio Roca (125w)

Gramophone 66:1300 F '89. Edward Greenfield (125w)

1480. Symphony No. 1 in B flat minor; Portsmouth Point Overture.

Leonard Slatkin (c). London Philharmonic Orchestra.
VIRGIN 90715 DDD 50:00

★*Awards:* Record of the Month, *Hi-Fi News & Record Review* Ag '88.

"Once again, an American conductor shows the establishment a thing or two about this score...Andrew Keener's Virgin production proves quite outstanding; even its slight abrasive edge is entirely apt to this coupling, and the impact of the brass is stunning....An unqualified A*:1*."

Hi-Fi News & Record Review 33:89 S '88. Christopher Breunig (645w)

"Slatkin and the London Philharmonic are in brilliant form throughout the sprawling sweep of the epic finale....I would have liked just a little more weight in the opening movement and more passion in the slow movement, but compared with other recordings available at the moment this one has a slight edge, not least for the inclusion of *Portsmouth Point*."

Stereo Review 53:164 D '88. David Hall (175w)

"There has been much debate as to whether this recording is a 'real challenge to Previn's 1966 RCA performance,' as Virgin stated it would be. I would say that Previn's is still the classic performance....But I must admit to finding Slatkin's *Finale* convincing, with its last devastating chords ringing on menacingly in the resonant acoustic of St. Augustine's—and all so deftly handled by Andrew Keener."

Stereophile 11:197 D '88. Barbara Jahn (190w)

"This is the first opportunity that an American-born conductor has had to deal with this challenging symphony on discs, though with an English orchestra. Leonard Slatkin's taut and energetic performance is perhaps closest to the composer's own, with its emphasis on an incessant forward thrust even at the expense of a greater range of expressions....The sound on this new Virgin Classics disc is somewhat lacking in tonal body—certainly so compared with Gibson on Chandos—and rather lacks natural presence."

American Record Guide 52:105-6 Mr/Ap '89. Richard E. Tiedman (1200w)

"The recording...is brassy and aggressive; one appreciates all that detail, but I found the sonority tiresome...rapid string passages tend to emerge blurred the way Slatkin rips into them. On the whole, I'd rather hear the piece done this way than the more paunchy, dignified rendition Previn leads on Telarc."

Fanfare 12:310 N/D '88. James Miller (225w)

WARLOCK, PETER (PHILIP HESELTINE). Capriol Suite. See No. 1141.

WEBERN, ANTON

1481. Complete Works: Passacaglia, Opus 1. Entflieht auf leichten Kahnen, Opus 2. Five Songs from "Der siebente Ring", Opus 3. Five Songs, Opus 4. Five Movements, Opus 5. Six Pieces, Opus 6. Four Pieces, Opus 7. Two Songs, Opus 8. Six Bagatelles, Opus 9. Five Pieces, Opus 10. Three Little Pieces, Opus 11. Four Songs, Opus 12. Four Songs, Opus 13. Six Songs, Opus 14. Five Sacred Songs, Opus 15. Five Canons on Latin Texts, Opus 16. Three Songs, Opus 18. Two Songs, Opus 19. String Trio, Opus 20. Symphony, Opus 21. Quartet, Opus 22. Three Songs from "Viae inviae", Opus 23. Concerto, Opus 24. Three Songs, Opus 25. Das Augenlicht, Opus 26. Piano Variations, Opus 27. String Quartet, Opus 28. Cantata No. 1, Opus 29. Variations, Opus 30. Cantata No. 2, Opus 31. Five Movements, Opus 5—orchestral version. **Bach (orch. Webern):** Musikalischen Opfer, BWV.1079—Fuga (Ricercata) No. 2. **Schubert (orch. Webern):** Deutsche Tanze, D.820.

Pierre Boulez (c). Various others. London Symphony Orchestra; Julliard Quartet. 1967-72.
SONY 45845 ADD 223:00 3 discs

★***Awards:*** The Want List 1991, *Fanfare* N/D '91 (William Youngren).

"The tonal beauty and relative leisureliness of all the performances make one sharply aware not only of the continuity between Webern and the Austro-German musical tradition he prized so highly but also between the earlier Webern of the lush songs and pieces for large orchestra-...So despite the fact that these performances (aside from Webern's own of the Schubert dances) were recorded between 1967 and 1972, and that a few of them have been bettered in the years since their original release, this is the set to get if you want to become acquainted with the music of this twentieth-century master."

Fanfare 15:394-95 S/O '91. William Youngren (long)

"Wow! If anything is an important document, this is it....I do not suggest listening to this whole set in one hearing, although I did, and it's not difficult: but this collection is more for study. One work at a time, perhaps....The booklet accompanying this recording, with notes by Humphrey Searle and musical analyses by Susan Bradshaw is a reading must."

High Performance Review 9:91 Spr '92. Bert Wechsler (long)

"Generally speaking, the performances here could very well have been electronically produced, so precisely are the pitches centered, the rhythmic values meted out, the tones absolved of any variety of color...Boulez's renditions of the orchestral works generally form the highlights of the set...his Opus 30 Variations and orchestral Opus 5 are very impressive and still sound good."

American Record Guide 54:169-70 N/D '91. Arved Ashby (long)

Gramophone 69:55 Je '91. Arnold Whittall (455w)

Six Pieces for Orchestra, Opus 6. See No. 1048.

WOLF, HUGO

1482. Italian Serenade in G for Orchestra (1892). RESPIGHI, OTTORINO. Ancient Airs and Dances Suite No. 3. MALIPIERO, GIAN FRANCESCO. Quartet No. 1 for Strings, "Rispetti e Strambotti".

I Solisti Italiani.
DENON 9150 DDD 46:15

"If this program sounds appealing, this disc is well worth hearing."

Fanfare 15:460 N/D '91. George Chien (med)

"This recording [of the Respighi] doesn't entirely erase memories of Marriner or I Musici, but it holds its own...The Wolf and Malipiero pieces are originally for string quartet and are here performed by 11 string players. They lose nothing in intimacy and gain a lot in sonority...Recommended."

American Record Guide 55:98-9 Ja/F '92. John Landis (long)

WORDSWORTH, WILLIAM (BROCKLESBY)

1483. Symphonies: No. 2 in D, Opus 34; No. 3 in C, Opus 48.

Nicholas Braithwaite (c). London Philharmonic Orchestra.
LYRITA 207 DDD 71:00

★***Awards:*** The Gramophone Awards, Nominations, Engineering, *Gramophone*, N '91. Best Engineered Recording 1991, *Gramophone*, D '91.

"If you like the music of George Lloyd or Daniel Jones and enjoy expert string writing and dramatic contrasts, then I recommend this disc. The LPO is in fine fettle, Nicholas Braithwaite conducts with finesse, and the sound is what we can expect from the Lyrita engineers."

American Record Guide 54:128-9 My/Je '91. Diederik C. D. De Jong (420w)

"Excellent playing; stunning, razor-sharp quality of sound in the best Lyrita tradition." *P95 S100*

Hi-Fi News & Record Review 36:105 Ja '91. Andrew Achenbach (315w)

"More conspicuous for its *gravitas* than its *humanitas*, Wordsworth's stuff is for the most part unrelievedly grim—or at least gray—in tone and almost completely humorless. But his music still has very important things to say, however imperfect some of its specific formulations may be....For some reason that this reviewer cannot exactly pinpoint, Braithwaite does not always seem to be giving us forceful enough readings here to make the best possible case for Wordsworth....Nonetheless, caviling at the quality of the fare on such a heretofore bare table may be presumptuous, if not downright churlish."

Fanfare 14:323-24 My/Je '91. Paul A. Snook (650w)

Gramophone 68:995 N '90. Michael Kennedy (455w)

XENAKIS, IANNIS

1484. Kraanerg.

Roger Woodward (c). Alpha Centauri Ensemble. 1988.
ETCETERA 1075 DDD 71:00

★***Awards:*** Cream of the Crop IV, *Digital Audio's CD Review*, 6:43 Je '90.

"Strongly recommended."

Fanfare 13:353 Ja/F '90. Ben Pernick (400w)

"This is a terrifying work. Not only is it long, but violent, with great, daring pauses which are only pauses; the violence returns undiminished for almost 71 minutes....I was not aware of a *composer* in this work, much less performers—which is probably the best thing I could say about Roger Woodward's and Alpha Centauri's performance. Recommended, but not for the fainthearted."

American Record Guide 53:108 Ja/F '90. Timothy D. Taylor (205w)

Gramophone 67:1148 D '89. Arnold Whittall (315w)

Digital Audio's CD Review 6:51 Ap '90. Octavio Roca (150w)

ZEMLINSKY, ALEXANDER VON

1485. Die Seejungfrau (fantasy after Andersen); Psalm XIII for Chorus and Orchestra, Opus 24.

Riccardo Chailly (c). Berlin Radio Symphony Chorus Orchestra.
LONDON/DECCA 417 450

★***Awards:*** *Fanfare* Want List 1987 (David Johnson); *Fanfare* Want List 1987 (Kyle Gann).

"This is one of those rare recordings of music I have not previously heard where one listening convinces me that I am in the presence of a masterwork—in this case, two masterworks-....Riccardo Chailly conducts both compositions with great eloquence, everything firmly under control but with latitude for expressivity and passion when called for....The digital sound is London/Decca at its best."

Fanfare 11:259-60 N/D '87. David Johnson (950w)

"An excellent performance."

The New York Times Ja 10 '88, p. H27. Paul Turok (75w)

"A belated review for a disc which must rank as one of the finest CD issues of 1987....The recording and performance make for exhilarating listening."

Hi-Fi News & Record Review 33:107 Ap '88. David Prakel (320w)

The New York Times S 4 '88, p. H21. Mark Swed (120w)

ZWILICH, ELLEN TAAFFE

1486. Concerto Grosso 1985 (after Handel); Symbolon (1988); Concerto for Trumpet and Five Players (1984); Double Quartet for Strings (1984).

Zubin Mehta; Ellen Taaffe Zwilich (c). Philip Smith (tpt). New York Philharmonic Orchestra; New York Philharmonic Ensemble. 1988.
NEW WORLD 372 DDD 63:53

✔**HC** ★***Awards:*** The Want List 1989, *Fanfare* N/D '89 (Benjamin Pernick).

"Zwilich is fortunate to have superb interpreters...All are enhanced by the hair-raisingly lifelike recorded sound, perhaps the finest I have heard from New World."

Musical America 109:65 N '89. K. Robert Schwarz (400w)

"Good performances, solid and intelligent annotations, fine sound. Another major issue from New World."

Fanfare 13:419 N/D '89. Peter J. Rabinowitz (710w)

"To me at least, Zwilich's music becomes more, not less, significant with each hearing."

American Record Guide 53:109 Ja/F '90. Kyle Rothweiler (355w)

"All the performances are consistently excellent and serve the composer very well. Informative liner notes by Alan Rich will add to the listener's enjoyment of this disc."

HighPerformanceReview 7:83-4 Winter '90-91. Allan Blank (360w)

The New York Times Ag 20 '89, p. H 29. Andrew L. Pincus (110w)

Digital Audio's CD Review 6:51 Ap '90. Linda Kohanov (155w)

Orchestral Music—Collections

Berlin Philharmonic Orchestra

1487. Furtwangler: The Rediscovered Berlin Recordings. For contents, see Deutsche Grammophon 427 774/783.
Wilhelm Furtwangler (c). Berlin Philharmonic Orchestra. reissue.
DEUTSCHE GRAMMOPHON 427 773 ADD (m) 573:00 10 discs

★★*Awards:* The Want List 1990, *Fanfare* N/D '90 (Henry Fogel). Critics' Choice 1989, *Gramophone* D '89 (Alan Sanders).

"These 10 discs enshrine Furtwangler's ideals (even in the indulgent Strauss *Sinfonia*, brought to vivid life). Those unable to afford the complete set should start with the Brahms concerto, the Beethoven Fourth; the Fifth/Seventh pairing, then the Ravel/Strauss/Sibelius." *P-historic S-historic*

Hi-Fi News & Record Review 34:101 O '89. Christopher Breunig (b.n.)

The New York Times N 19 '89, p. H29. David Hamilton (100w)

Gramophone 67:557-58 S '89. Alan Sanders (100w)

London Symphony Orchestra

1488. Skyscrapers and Other Music of the American East Coast School. Carpenter: Skyscrapers. **Paine:** Oedipus Tyrannus—Prelude, Opus 35. **MacDowell:** Lamia, Symphonic Poem, Opus 29. **Foote:** Suite in E for Strings, Opus 29. **Buck:** Festival Overture on *The Star Spangled Banner*.
Kenneth Klein (c). London Symphony Orchestra.
EMI 49263 DDD 67:42

★*Awards:* The Want List 1988, *Fanfare* N/D '88 (Benjamin Pemick, George Chien).

"Kenneth Klein...has done a more than competent job on all of this diversity and, coupled with spacious sound and good engineering, has made an excellent case for reviving these essences of East Coast America."

Hi-Fi News & Record Review 33:119+ O '88. Kenneth Dommett (340w)

"Good performances from this busy English orchestra under its American conductor. Recommended!"

Fanfare 11:276-7 Ja/F '88. John Ditsky (215w)

"The performances are very good. Klein is obviously a versatile conductor, making the most of the giddiness of the Carpenter and the high drama of the MacDowell."

American Record Guide 51:105-6 Mr/Ap '88. Kyle Rothweiler (425w)

"Kenneth Klein...makes his debut on EMI/Angel apparently trying to turn the London Symphony into a chamber orchestra. While he does very well with the amusement-park sounds of the Carpenter and the grandiosity of the Buck, he has made much of the rest of the music sound inappropriately bloodless."

Ovation 9:46 My '88. Karen Monson (375w)

"Kenneth Klein...obviously feels completely at ease in this thoroughly American music, and the ever reliable London Symphony responds to him with professional finesse."

Musical America 108:83-4 S '88. Paul Moor (360w)

"Rehearsal time must have been limited to the Carpenter, because the strings sound ragged indeed in the other works. By itself, however, *Skyscrapers* is worth the price of purchase."

Gramophone 66:795 N '88. John Milsom (420w)

High Fidelity 38:65 Mr '88. K. Robert Schwarz (365w)

Montreal Symphony Orchestra

1489. Fete a la Francaise. Chabrier: Joyeuse marche; Espana. **Dukas:** L'Apprenti Sorcier. **Satie (orch. Debussy):** Gymnopedies—No's. 1 and 3. **Saint-Saens:** *Samson et Dalila:* Bacchanale. **Bizet:** Jeux d'Enfants. **Thomas:** *Raymond:* Overture. **Ibert:** Divertissement.
Charles Dutoit (c). Montreal Symphony Orchestra. 1987.
LONDON/DECCA 421 527 DDD 70:00

★★★*Awards:* Critics' Choice 1989, *Gramophone* D '89 (Christopher Headington); Best of the Month, *Hi-Fi News & Record Review*, D '89; Editors' Choice, *Digital Audio's CD Review*, Je '89. Cream of the Crop IV, *Digital Audio's CD Review*, 6:41 Je '90.

"An immensely enjoyable disc....one is treated to a cavalcade of Gallic wit, precision and elegance which happily makes no reference to the recent bicentennial mania....it seems inconceivable to me that anyone could emerge from listening to this disc in anything but the highest good humour." *P100 S100*

Hi-Fi News & Record Review 34:135 D '89. Jeremy Siepmann (145w)

"This particular collection of French lollipops is so suave and stylish that it's miles above similar collections....these clean, beautifully engineered performances offer much to enjoy."

Stereo Review 54:96 Jl '89. David Patrick Stearns (180w)

"Overall, a pleasant experience which should serve well enough as a stopgap until such time as Philips makes good on its promise to reissue the Paray recordings on CD."

American Record Guide 53:109-10 Ja/F '90. Steven J. Haller (160w)

"Apart from one rather premature double-bass entry in the *Divertissement*, the playing is excellent and though the recording does tend to make the *Danse Bacchanale* into a castanet concerto it is in Decca's top bracket and I most strongly recommend it to you."

Music and Musicians International 37:19 Je '89. David Denton (240w)

Digital Audio's CD Review 5:62+ Ag '89. David Vernier (300w)

Fanfare 13:440 S/O '89. Leslie Gerber (250w)

Gramophone 67:48 Je '89. Christopher Headington (245w)

New York Philharmonic Orchestra

1490. Arturo Toscanini and the Philharmonic-Symphony Orchestra of New York: The Great Recordings 1926-1936. **Mendelssohn:** Midsummer Night's Dream Suite. **Verdi:** La Traviata, Preludes to Acts I and III. **Haydn:** Symphony 101, Clock. **Mozart:** Symphony 35, Haffner. **Dukas:** Sorcerer's Apprentice. **Gluck:** Dance of the Blessed Spirits. **Beethoven:** Symphonies 5 + 7. **Wagner:** Dawn and Siegfried's Rhine Journey; Lohengrin: Preludes to Acts I and III; Siegfried Idyll. **Brahms:** Haydn Variations. **Rossini:** Overtures: Semiramide; Italiana in Algeri; Barber of Seville.
Arturo Toscanini (c). New York Philharmonic Orchestra.
PEARL 9373 ADD 230:00 3 discs

★★★*Awards:* The Want List 1990, *Fanfare* N/D '90 (Marc Mandel; Michael Ullman; William Youngren).

"Put simply, the 1933 effort is the finest Toscanini account of the work [the 5th] I have ever heard...in Marc Obert-Thorn's transfer the sound is exceptionally fine for its vintage-....Those who know Toscanini only from his later NBC years should find this set an ear-opener."

Stereophile 13:219 Ap '90. Mortimer H. Frank (130w)

Musical America 109:69 N '89. Terry Teachout (b.n.)

Gramophone 67:1700+ Mr '90. Alan Sanders (390w)

American Record Guide 53:159-61 Mr/Ap '90. David Radcliffe (360w)

1491. Willem Mengelberg and the Philharmonic-Symphony Orchestra of New York. **Handel (arr. Gohler):** Alcina: Suite. **Bach (arr. Mahler):** Suite No. 3 in D, BWV.1068: Air. **J. C. Bach (arr. Stein:** Sinfonia in B flat, Opus 18, No. 2. **Mozart:** *Die Zauberflote:* Overture. **Beethoven:** *Egmont, Opus 84:* Overture. **Mendelssohn:** *Athalie:* War March. **Meyerbeer:** *Le Prophete: Coronation March.* **Wagner:** *Siegfried:* Forest Murmurs. **Humperdinck:** *Hansel und Gretel: Overture.* **Saint-Saens.** Le Rouet d'Omphale, Opus 31.
Willem Mengelberg (c). New York Philharmonic Orchestra. 1928-30.
PEARL 9474 AAD (m) 72:38

★*Awards:* Classical Hall of Fame, *Fanfare*, Mr/Ap '92 (Jon Tuska).

"Mengelberg's considerable legacy with the Philharmonic-Symphony ought not to be overlooked and his achievements with that orchestra are well documented by these transfers made by Mark Obert-Thorn....the sound throughout on this disc is actually superior to that on the Teldec Mengelberg reissues from a few years ago mastered from more recent performances but using pressings inferior to those employed here....The transfers of his recordings of Mozart, Beethoven, Mendelssohn, and Meyerbeer here stand as a brilliant testament to his unique talent, and they only whet the appetite for other notable recordings he made in New York, among the the First and 'Eroica' Symphonies of Beethoven."

Fanfare 15:470 Mr/Ap '92. Jon Tuska (long)

"I have been bitterly disappointed by the sound quality of every previous reissue of Mengelberg's commercial recordings; here at last is a superb one."

Fanfare 14:384-85 My/Je '91. James H. North (250w)

"A brilliantly played assortment of overtures and other shorter works by Bach, Handel, Mozart, Beethoven, Wagner and other composers."

Musical America 111:46 N/D '91. Terry Teachout (brief)

"Previous releases of Mengelberg on CD have been disappointing, so I am happy to report that in this case sonic justice has been done."

American Record Guide 54:215-9 N/D '91. David Radcliffe (long)

Vienna Philharmonic Orchestra

1492. Legendary Conductors. Haydn: Symphony 88 in G. **Mozart:** Symphony 39 in E flat, K.543. **Gluck:** Alceste: Overture. **Beethoven:** Leonora Overture No. 3, Opus 72a.
Clemens Krauss; Erich Kleiber; Willem Mengelberg; Bruno Walter (c). Vienna Philharmonic Orchestra; Berlin State Opera Orchestra; Concertgebouw Orchestra.
KOCH 7011 (m) 67:00

★*Awards:* *American Record Guide* Overview: Haydn, Mr/Ap '92.

"Be assured that these fine performances bear out the good fame attached to these famous conductors."
American Record Guide 53:184-88 N/D '90. David Radcliffe (390w)

"Given the exceptional high quality of this release and its great documentary value, it is disappointing that the notes do not include more discographic information, particularly about the pressings Obert-Thorn used for these transfers. But this is the only blemish on a release that augurs well for a most distinguished series."
Fanfare 14:471-72 N/D '90. Mortimer H. Frank (450w)

Orchestral Music with Soloists

ARNOLD, MALCOLM

Concerto No. 1 for Flute and Orchestra, Opus 45. See No. 1004.

Concerto for Oboe and Orchestra, Opus 39. See No. 1004.

2001. Concerto for 2 Violins and Orchestra, Opus 77; Concerto No. 1 for Clarinet and Strings, Opus 20; Concerto No. 1 for Flute and Strings, Opus 45; Concerto No. 2 for Horn and Strings, Opus 58.
Karen Jones (fl); Michael Collins (clar); Richard Watkins (horn); Kenneth Sillito (vln); Lyn Fletcher (vln). Mark Stephenson (c). London Musici.
CONIFER 172 DDD 56:00

★*Awards:* Record of the Month, *Hi-Fi News & Record Review*, S '89; The Year's Best, *Hi Fi News & Record Review*, May '90 Supplement.

"These concertos are often witty, even jolly, but they are never comic and, indeed, have sustained serious episodes. That is especially true of the concerto for two violins and strings from 1962, the most recent work on the disc. The London Musici, making their debut on this disc, play brilliantly, and each soloist plays with admirable skill and expressiveness."
Fanfare 13:86-7 Ja/F '90. Ron McDonald (300w)

"The recordings are expansively staged—an image both deep and wide...In short, pithy, approachable modern works, inventive, essentially non-derivative in expression." *P95 S95*
Hi-Fi News & Record Review 34:85 S '89; p.9 My '90 Supplement. Christopher Breunig (250w)

"The overall performances are first class; the composer was consulted extensively in preparing the recording. The sound: near perfect."
American Record Guide 54:20+ Ja/F '91. Carl Bauman (260w)

The Musical Times 130:690-91 N '89. Stephen Banfield (360w)

Gramophone 67:293 Ag '89. Edward Greenfield (535w)

BACH, CARL PHILIPP EMANUEL

2002. Concerto in A minor for Cello and Orchestra, H.432 (W.170); Concerto in B flat for Cello and Strings, H.436 (W.171); Concerto in A for Cello and Orchestra, H.439 (W.172).
Anner Bylsma (cello). Gustav Leonhardt (c). Age of Enlightenment Orchestra.
VIRGIN 90800 DDD 70:00

✔HC ★*Awards:* Critics' Choice 1990, *Gramophone* D '90 (Nicholas Anderson).

"The orchestra of the Age of Enlightenment plays with little vibrato and much security-....Anner Bylsma, by contrast, allows a touch of Romantic sentiment to creep in from time to time. The disparity is not disturbing....The band is near but surrounded by plenty of reverberant space. The space is so live, in fact, that the engineers evidently had a problem with the pauses between movements."
Audio 74:132 N '90. Robert Long (575w)

"Fine performances well recorded."
High Fidelity 1:119 Mr '90. Andrew Stuart (b.n.)

"All Saints' Church Petersham seems to have been ignored by record companies in recent years [Decca excepted] but here Virgin takes advantage of its warm, even acoustic to present three fine concerti with clarity and colour-....The sound is always beautiful but with the solo cello a little closer than ideal...and nowhere is the phrasing other than stylishly authentic." *P95 S95*
Hi-Fi News & Record Review 35:101 Mr '90. Antony Hodgson (385w)

"The peerless Bylsma has now given us versions that are effortless, expressive, and elegant, lithe in rhythm and very eloquent in the slow movements. Leonhardt and his band are perfect in accompaniment. The sound too is splendid...I must add that this is not by any means the best of C.P.E. Bach."
Fanfare 14:141-42 N/D '90. William Youngren (225w)

"Although certainly not CPE Bach's finest music, the performances will make this disc worthwhile to some."
American Record Guide 53:40 S/O '90. Paul Laird (340w)

Gramophone 67:1455 F '90. Nicholas Anderson (410w)

Concerti: in C minor for Harpsichord and Orchestra, H.474 (W.43, no. 4); in E flat for Oboe and Orchestra, H.468 (W.165). See No. 1006.

BACH, JOHANN SEBASTIAN

Concerto in A minor for Flute, Violin, Harpsichord and Orchestra, BWV.1044. See No. 1009.

2003. Concerti (7) for Harpsichord and Strings, BWV.1052-1058; Concerto No. 8 in D minor for Harpsichord, BWV.1059; Concerti (3) for 2 Harpsichords and Orchestra, BWV.1060/62; Concerti (2) for 3 Harpsichords and Strings, BWV.1063/4; Concerto in A minor for 4 Harpsichords and Strings, BWV.1065.
Gustav Leonhardt (hpscd); Anneke Uittenbosch (hpscd); Alan Curtis (hpscd); Eduard Muller (hpscd); Herbert Tachezi (hpscd). Nikolaus Harnoncourt (c). Leonhardt Consort; Concentus Musicus. 1968 reissue.
TELDEC 35778 ADD 212:39 3 discs

✔HC ★*Awards:* The Want List 1990, *Fanfare* N/D '90 (David Claris).

"This all sounds much better than the Teldec Vivaldi set." *P95 S85*

Hi-Fi News & Record Review 34:96 S '89. Christopher Breunig (b.n.)

Gramophone 67:1214 D '89. Nicholas Anderson (265w)

2004. Concerto No. 1 in D minor for Harpsichord & Strings, BWV.1052; Concerto No. 5 in F minor, BWV.1056; Concerto No. 7 in G minor, BWV.1058.
Jean Louis Steuerman (pno). James Judd (c). Chamber Orchestra of Europe.
PHILIPS 420 200 DDD 45:00

✔HC ★*Awards:* The Record of the Month, *Music and Musicians International* Je '88.

"A great issue: Steuermann is clearly a Bach interpreter of the very front rank, and he plays these Concertos, on a modern piano, with such style and artistry, such profound insight and musicianship that all arguments surrounding 'authenticity' are swept aside as pedantic irrelevancies....Very strongly recommended indeed."

Music and Musicians International 36:37 Je '88. Robert Matthew-Walker (170w)

"This is a pianist...who conveys the sheer privilege and joy of making music with an infectious vitality."

Hi-Fi News & Record Review 33:83 Je '88. Jeremy Siepmann (280w)

"This is a generally quite stylish account of the three concertos which will please mainstream fans more than the Pinnock accounts which George Chien and I both prefer among available performances."

Fanfare 12:88 S/O '88. Edward Strickland (75w)

"These performances will provide those who prefer their classical music gritlessly baroque many happy hearings."

Ovation 10:51 Jl '89. Joseph Fennimore (245w)

"These are, if you will, new-age performances: respectful of the texts, not disrespectful of older traditions, but emotionally somewhat disinvolved—unquestionable proof that our planet is cooling down."

Musical America 109:51-2 Mr '89. Harris Goldsmith (160w)

Gramophone 65:1577-8 My '88. John Duarte (160w)

2005. Concerti (2) for Violin and Orchestra, BWV.1041/2; Concerto in D minor for 2 Violins and Orchestra, BWV.1043; Concerto in C minor for Violin, Oboe and Orchestra, BWV.1060.
Catherine Mackintosh (vln); Elizabeth Wallfisch (vln); Paul Goodwin (oboe). Robert King (c). King's Consort. 1989.
HYPERION 66380 DDD 59:00

✔HC ★★*Awards:* Critic's Choice: 1990, *American Record Guide* Ja/F '91 (Paul Laird). The Year's Best, *Hi Fi News & Record Review*, May '90 Supplement.

"These are inspired performances combining a satisfying historical approach with interpretations that explore the music's emotional depths-....The King's Consort compares favorably with the English Concert on DG."

American Record Guide 53:16 N/D '90. Paul Laird (130w)

"Performances of exceptional authenticity: period instruments, pitch at A=415, and the minimum of vibrato is used—in many ways this is daring, inasmuch as the solo writing is so exposed that the slightest departure from precise intonation could become immediately noticeable....The Hyperion recordings reveal the thoughtful interpretations in gorgeous detail and all the works have a spacious atmosphere." *P100 S100*

Hi-Fi News & Record Review 35:101 Mr '90; p.15 My '90 Supplement. Antony Hodgson (315w)

"The violin and oboe concerto...receives a particularly energetic, even romping performance from Elizabeth Wallfisch, and Goodwin has his instrument under full control. The end result is one of the better renditions of this popular arrangement that I've heard. The violin concertos share similar virtues but in truth don't differ materially in style or sound from the recordings of Jaap Schroder and Simon Standage."

Fanfare 13:72-3 Jl/Ag '90. David K. Nelson (360w)

Gramophone 67:1769-70 Ap '90. John Duarte (385w)

Digital Audio's CD Review 6:56-8 Je '90. David Vernier (360w)

2006. Concerti (2) for Violin and Orchestra, BWV.1041/2; Concerto in D Minor for 2 Violins, BWV.1043; Concerti (7) for Harpsichord and Strings, BWV.1052/58 (No's. 1, 5);

Concerti (3) for 2 Harpsichords and Orchestra, BWV.1060/2 (No's 1, 2); Concerti (2) for 3 Harpsichords, BWV.1063/4; Cocerto in A minor for 4 Harpsichords, BWV.1065.
Simon Standage (vln); Elizabeth Wilcock (vln); Trevor Pinnock (hpscd); Kenneth Gilbert (hpscd); Lars Ulrik Mortensen (hpscd); Nicholas Kraemer (hpscd). Trevor Pinnock (c). English Concert.
DEUTSCHE GRAMMOPHON 413 634 3 discs

✔HC ★*Awards:* *Gramophone* Critics' Choice 1985 (Lionel Salter).

Simon Standage is "as lively a Baroque fiddler as we have....Sonics...are vibrant, performances full of panache, notes by Werner Breig as orginally (minus the handy table thoroughly explaining the musical provenance of the keyboard concertos)."

Fanfare 8:83-8 My/Je '85. Edward Strickland (460w)

Gramophone 62:1199 Ap '85. Lionel Salter (280w)

BARBER, SAMUEL

2007. Concerto for Cello and Orchestra, Opus 22. BRITTEN, BENJAMIN. Symphony for Cello and Orchestra, Opus 68.
Yo-Yo Ma (cello). David Zinman (c). Baltimore Symphony Orchestra. 1988.
CBS 44900 DDD 62:02

✔HC ★*Awards:* Critics Pick Some Favorites of the Year, *The New York Times* N 26, '89 (Allan Kozinn).

"It is not one of Barber's more distinctive scores. You couldn't tell that from this superlative performance, though, for Yo-Yo Ma and David Zinman and the Baltimore Symphony play the concerto as if it had come straight out of Barber's top drawer....[In the Britten Concerto] The recorded balance between Ma and the orchestra is a good deal more natural than that heard on Raphael Wallfisch's cello-heavy 1984 recording...On the debit side, Wallfisch's playing is significantly more incisive than Ma's, Bedford's conducting more intense than Zinman's. Still, Ma and Zinman give a fine performance."

Musical America 109:52 S '89. Terry Teachout (260w)

"At present the only alternative version [of the Barber concerto]...is by Raphael Wallfisch-...Though both soloists are in full control of their material, Simon's more positive direction and Chandos's incisive recording tip the balance. With the Britten Ma again comes into competition with Wallfisch in another excellent performance. More significantly perhaps, he comes into competition with the Rostropovich/Britten original. He and Zinman fail to match the tautness of Wallfisch/Bedford, nor can they equal the inspired improvisatory character of the original version." *P95/85 S95*

Hi-Fi News & Record Review 34:85 S '89. Kenneth Dommett (250w)

"Ma's performances have his usual effortless accuracy and febrile intensity; though the somewhat dry, analytic sound of the recording robs both works of some of their potential grandeur. On the other hand this is the first technically adequate performance of the Barber on discs-....A slight cavil—certainly the trumpet solo in the Passacaglia shouldn't sound so jauntily Coplandesque."

American Record Guide 52:37 S/O '89. David W. Moore (255w)

"Ma emphasizes restraint rather than excess. Although he never hesitates to mine Barber's vein of tender, yearning lyricism, he maintains a certain reserve that is entirely appropriate in this rhythmic, often percussive concert. That same spirit of Romantic expression tempered by classical propriety informs the performance of Britten's *Cello Symphony*."

High Fidelity 39:62+ Je '89. K. Robert Schwarz (250w)

"In both works, the orchestral support offered by the Baltimoreans is exemplary. Add Yo-Yo Ma's masterful playing, and this release of two important but not often heard 20th-century works is irresistible."

The New York Times Je 11 '89, p. 30. Paul Turok (100w)

"Given his impeccable technique and rock-solid intonation, Ma's straightforward approach invigorates the music...Wallfisch and Simon, on Chandos, stressed its beauty, and the work slipped down the drain. Ma and Zinman stand up and play it straight; it works wonders for the concerto....here the Baltimore Symphony plays beautifully....Definitive Barber."

Fanfare 12:81-2 Jl/Ag '89. James H. North (550w)

Gramophone 67:23-4 Je '89. Michael Kennedy (420w)

Digital Audio's CD Review 6:60-1 Ja '90. Lawrence Johnson (255w)

2008. Concerto for Violin and Orchestra, Opus 14. HANSON, HOWARD. Symphony No. 2, Opus 30, "Romantic".
Elmar Oliveira (violin). Leonard Slatkin (c). Saint Louis Symphony Orchestra.
EMI 47850 DDD 54:48

✔HC ★*Awards:* *Gramophone* Critics' Choice (Ivan March), 1987.

"I don't expect to hear a finer performance of Hanson's most durable, and lovable, work-....No doubt about it: Gerhardt's National Philharmonic account (RCA) was outstanding, but this is better....The Barber is hardly less impressive."

Hi-Fi News & Record Review 32:115 N '87. Edward Seckerson (310w)

"The best review one can imagine for this release is to extend the warmest possible welcome for the entry into the CD catalog of such well-planned and wonderfully executed performances of two established American classics."
Musical America 107:61 N '87. Thomas L. Dixon (350w)

"The approach here is fresh, with the emphasis on subtle inner orchestral textures....In direct comparison to Hanson, Slatkin plays the *Allegro con brio* somewhat more majestically, Hanson featuring a certain 'swagger.'...Soundwise, the recording is first-rate."
Stereophile 10:177+ Je '87 George Graves (600w)

"The LP version...was reviewed at some length in *Fanfare* 10:6 (pp. 56-58). In summary, this recording of the justifiably popular Barber concerto far surpasses all previous efforts-....Though equally rich and luxuriant, the Hanson performance is less successful."
Fanfare 11:111-2 Jl/Ag '88. Walter Simmons (175w)

Opus 3:46 O '87. Andrew Siller (625w)

Gramophone 65:572 O '87 Ivan March (470w)

BARTOK, BELA

2009. Concerti (3) for Piano and Orchestra; Sonata for 2 Pianos and Percussion.
Vladimir Ashkenazy (pno); Vovka Ashkenazy (pno); David Corkhill (perc); Andrew Smith (perc). Georg Solti (c). London Symphony Orchestra. 1978-1981 reissues.
LONDON/DECCA 425 573 ADD/DDD 103:00 2 discs

"If Vladimir Ashkenazy lacks Andra's whimsicality and Sandor's relaxed wisdom, he nevertheless has the music at his fingertips and in his mind....Ashkenazy projects a winning balance of darting and cushioned playing, and Solti...is a commanding, complementing presence, leading an LPO—with fabulous brass!—in peak athletic form."
Musical America 111:64-5 Jl '91. Herbert Glass (150w)

Gramophone 68:2004 My '91. David J. Fanning (205w)

2010. Concerti (3) for Piano and Orchestra; Music for Strings, Percussion and Celeste; Rhapsody for Piano and Orchestra, Opus 1; Scherzo for Piano and Orchestra.
Zoltan Kocsis (pno). Ivan Fischer (c). Budapest Festival Orchestra.
PHILIPS 416 831 DDD 157:00 3 discs

★★★***Awards:*** *Stereo Review* Best Recordings of the Month Je '88; First Place Concerto Mumm Champagne Classical Music Award 1988—Presented by *Ovation, Ovation* N '88; The Want List 1988, *Fanfare* N/D '88 (John Wiser).

"All things considered, this is a very fine modern set of these works...although the orchestral playing is not invariably first-class...and the acoustic is fractionally too resonant."
Music and Musicians International 36:51 Ap '88. Robert Matthew-Walker (400w)

"Although the Kocsis/Fischer collaboration produces plenty of excitement, it is the sheer intelligibility of their performances that makes this release so special....The recordings are excellent, although it is too bad that the particularly brilliant recorded sound of the 'Scherzo' is not present in the First and Second Concertos."
The New York Times My 22 '88, p. H25. Paul Turok (850w)

"These are buoyant performances that should have wide appeal, especially for those who find Pollini's classic accounts of the first two concertos too severe....Unfortunately, Philips' packaging is so inconvenient that it's hard to recommend this release...the sound is variable."
Fanfare 11:76-7 My/Je '88. Peter J. Rabinowitz (615w)

"Kocsis perhaps finds a little more poetry here and there than the other fine pianists who have recorded the concertos, without diminishing any of the music's other qualities, and the outstanding sound makes the most of every detail."
Stereo Review 53:111-2 Je '88. Richard Freed (660w)

"While there is plenty of bite and character to his pianism, I would not automatically choose Kocsis over Maurizio Pollini (DG 415 371-2), who is marginally more incisive."
Ovation 9:16 Ag '88. John Von Rhein (775w)

Gramophone 65:1072 Ja '88. David J. Fanning (460w)

2011. Concerti (2) for Violin and Orchestra.
Midori (vln). Zubin Mehta (c). Berlin Philharmonic Orchestra.
SONY 45941 DDD 63:00

★★★★***Awards:*** Record of the Month, *Hi-Fi News & Record Review*, F '91. Critics' Choice 1991, Modern Composition, *The Wire*, D/Ja '91/92; Editors' Choice, *Digital Audio's CD Review*, Je '91. *American Record Guide* Overview: Popular Violin Concertos, S/O '89.

"These are exemplary performances, quite the most lyrical and integrated as between soloist and conductor of any that have come my way for quite a while." *P100 S95*
Hi-Fi News & Record Review 36:87 F '91. Kenneth Dommett (315w)

In Midori's playing of the First Violin Concerto there "is barely a trace of harshness in her approach; every edge is softened, lyricism dominates, attacks are quite subtle, and lower dynamics are meticulously observed....Mehta's collaborative effort is not to be dismissed, as he draws from the Berlin Philharmonic the most extraordinary orchestral playing ever lavished on this demanding accompaniment....Midori gives a classic, pure, restrained, quietly intense reading [in the Second]."

American Record Guide 54:40-1 S/O '91. Alan Heatherington (med)

"Whenever the two Bartok concertos call for a long, lyrical statement, Midori meets the challenge handily....But whenever the concertos demand sheer force, Midori seems unwilling to revel in the gritty, cutting articulations of the Hungarian folk rhythms, to convey these works' rhapsodic fire. Although she possesses plenty of physical strength, she is simply too controlled, too well-behaved. From a technical point of view, these are impeccable performances."

Musical America 111:68 My '91. K. Robert Schwarz (240w)

"There is little trace of Bartok's Hungarian flavor in this performance [of the 2nd Concerto], which spoils it for me despite the many excellences of Midori's playing....The First Concerto is a total success here."

Fanfare 14:144 Mr/Ap '91. James H. North (600w)

Gramophone 68:1498 F '91. Edward Seckerson (295w)

Digital Audio's CD Review 7:69 Ap '91. Tom Vernier (375w)

BEETHOVEN, LUDWIG VAN

2012. Concerti (5) for Piano and Orchestra (complete); Fantasia in C minor for Piano, Chorus and Orchestra, Opus 80.
Vladimir Ashkenazy (pno); Teresa Cash (sop); D'Anna Fortunato (alto); Jon Garrison (ten); Terry Cooke (bar); Martin Horning (2nd bar). Vladimir Ashkenazy (c). Cleveland Chorus; Cleveland Orchestra.
LONDON/DECCA 421 718 DDD 199:00 3 discs

★★★*Awards:* Critics' Choice 1989, *Gramophone* D '89 (Richard Osborne); Critics' Choice 1989, *Gramophone* D '89 (Robin Golding); Top Disks of the Year, *The New York Times* D 24, '89 (John Rockwell).

"Here the myth of soloist *vs* orchestra is exploded: Ashkenazy, now in dual responsibility, is spiritually of one mind with his colleagues, and the balance of piano with orchestra, of necessity a more integral feature, heightens that impression....Yet I feel a lack of refinement in Concerto 2...As for the piano, it doesn't sound in the best of condition. In fact, the way it resonates is often reminiscent of the fortepiano-....Whether or not to recommend the set is difficult."

Stereophile 12:203 N '89. Barbara Jahn (390w)

"While he is a thoughtful and intelligent musician as well as an excellent technician, Ashkenazy is not the most poetic of pianists; for that reason, some movements of some of the concertos are more convincing than others-....The most successful performance is of the 'Choral' Fantasy, with a perfect balance between piano and orchestra and, later, solo voices and chorus. Ashkenazy plays the cadenzas with requisite authority, and elicits beautiful solo playing from the orchestra, and the singing is first-rate."

Fanfare 12:83-4 Jl/Ag '89. Susan Kagan (525w)

Music and Musicians International 38:59-60 O '89. David Denton (250w)

Gramophone 66:1408-13 Mr '89. Richard Osborne (1295w)

2013. Concerti (5) for Piano and Orchestra (complete).
Alfred Brendel (pno). James Levine (c). Chicago Symphony Orchestra. Orchestra Hall, Chicago. June 14-20, 1983.
PHILIPS 411 189 3 discs

✔HC ★*Awards:* *Gramophone* Critics' Choice 1984 (Stephen Plaistow).

"Everything about these performances is utterly right—so majestic and yet so compassionate, so profound and yet so charged with wit, so filled with Beethovenian spontaneity yet so meticulous in detail, balance, and proportion."

Stereo Review 49:75 Jl '84. Richard Freed (250w)

"Technically...Brendel's 1977 analogue LP cycle with the LPO and Haitink, recorded in Walthamstow Town Hall, has the edge, but this almost unique audio 'snapshot' has an honesty about it which is most appealing."

Hi-Fi News & Record Review 29:83 Ag '84. John Atkinson (160w)

High Fidelity 36:59 My '86. Thomas L. Dixon (35w) (rev. of LP)

Gramophone 62:214 Ag '84. Geoffrey Horn (280w)

2014. Concerti (5) for Piano and Orchestra (complete). MOZART, WOLFGANG AMADEUS. Concerto No. 25 in C for Piano and Orchestra, K.503.
Leon Fleisher (pno). George Szell (c). Cleveland Orchestra. 1959-61 reissue.
CBS 42445 AAD 186:00 3 discs

✔HC ★★★★*Awards:* Second Place Non-Vocal Reissues Mumm Champagne Classical Music Award 1988—Presented by *Ovation*, *Ovation* N '88. *Fanfare* Want List 1987 (Elliott Kaback); *Fanfare* Want List 1987 (Mortimer H. Frank); *Fanfare* Want List 1987 (John Bauman).

"There are those, myself among them, who consider this one of the finest such cycles ever produced...Tape-hiss has been markedly reduced to a point where it is masked in all but the softest of passages; timbres are now truer-...What is more, the remixing...has taken some brittleness away from the piano's upper registers and placed the soloist in a better-focused, more well-defined stereo ambience."

Fanfare 11:145 S/O '87. Mortimer H. Frank (570w)

"This is, quite simply, one of the year's outstanding reissues, offering a substantial sonic improvement on what was already a truly legendary release."

Opus 4:32 D '87. Harris Goldsmith (550w)

Digital Audio 4:50 Ja '88. Joe Roberts (165w)

2015. Concerti (5) for Piano and Orchestra (complete).
Steven Lubin (ftpno). Christopher Hogwood (c). Academy of Ancient Music. 1987.
OISEAU-LYRE 421 408 DDD 164:00 3 discs

★★★★*Awards:* The Want List 1988, *Fanfare* N/D '88 (Mike Silverton); Critics' Choice 1988, *Gramophone* D '88 (Stanley Sadie). The Want List 1989, *Fanfare* N/D '89 (Leslie Gerber); The Want List 1989, *Fanfare* N/D '89 (David Claris).

"Lubin uses, in effect, five different instruments, each of them a reproduction of a fortepiano roughly contemporary with the work at hand....Based though they are on substantial research and experience, these performances are presented only as conjectures....For the listener who has heard the Beethoven concertos played only on modern pianos, any one of Lubin's realizations is startling enough—in terms of sonority alone—to make it seem as though the concerto is being heard for the first time."

Musical America 108:76-7 S '88. James Wierzbicki (265w)

"Lubin...argues that Beethoven's piano music was conceived for instruments he owned and played and receives its best articulation on such pianos....Lubin carries this argument to such a fine point that each of the pianos he uses corresponds to the kind that Beethoven played at the time....Beethoven is here represented, correctly and realistically, as an idealist with perfectly human and earthly roots."

Stereo Review 53:108 S '88. Eric Salzman (935w)

"The recording's greatest asset is that it captures beautifully the subtlety of each of the four fortepianos, their penetrating bass ranges and exquisite, silvery trebles...A valuable set-...for all its faults."

Hi-Fi News & Record Review 33:91 S '88. Stephen Pettitt (420w)

"These less sonorous instruments (particularly the piano!) give us a far different sound picture of Beethoven's music than do performances on modern instruments....We simply can hear the music better....Hogwood and the orchestra are beautifully coordinated with Lubin's conceptions of the music....Lubin's performance is better executed than Badura-Skoda's and more poetic as well."

Fanfare 12:131-3 N/D '88. Leslie Gerber (1250w)

"Let me say straight away that I feel this set belongs in the collection of anyone who has a serious interest in Beethoven's music and how it probably sounded when it was first performed-....Though I find all of the performances entrancing, the passion which Lubin brings to the Third is especially attractive. In the *Emperor* we find the whole emerging with a new-minted splendor."

American Record Guide 52:19-20 Mr/Ap '89. Carl Bauman (575w)

"These are brisk, alert, and, for the most part, thoroughly enjoyable readings, and even though the orchestra sounds at times a bit asthmatic, its playing is in a different class altogether from what one encounters in Hogwood's progressing series of the Beethoven symphonies."

Musical America 109:70-5 My '89. Harris Goldsmith (265w)

Gramophone 65:1578+ My '88. Stanley Sadie (1500w)

The New York Times Jl 3 '88, p. H23. Will Crutchfield (500w)

Digital Audio 5:62+ D '88. Tom Vernier (725w)

Music and Musicians International 38:59 O '89. David Denton (860w)

Concerto No. 1 in C for Piano and Orchestra, Opus 15. See No. 4049.

2016. Concerti for Piano and Orchestra: No. 3 in C minor, Opus 37; No. 4 in G, Opus 58.
Murray Perahia (pno). Bernard Haitink (c). Concertgebouw Orchestra.
CBS 39814 69:21

★★★★★*Awards:* *Gramophone* Critics' Choice 1986 (Stephen Plaistow; Richard Osborne); *Gramophone* Record Award Winner 1986—Concerto Award; Best of the Month, *Stereo Review* Je '86.

"The Third and Fourth Concertos, where Beethoven moved further away from Mozartean precedents, are heard in extremely finished, classically balanced interpretations."

Musical America 109:70-5 My '89. Harris Goldsmith (265w)

"Interpretively, this first installment must be classed with the most select handful of earlier recordings of each of these works, and, not surprisingly, it surpasses them all in quality."

Stereo Review 51:108+ Je '86. Richard Freed (500w)

"Its LP counterpart...[was] very favorably reviewed in *Fanfare* 9:3."

Fanfare 9:90 Jl/Ag '86. Mortimer H. Frank (90w)

Gramophone 64:550 O '86. Robert Layton (200w); 64:562 O '86 Richard Osborne (320w); 64:157-8 Jl '86. Stephen Plaistow (1050w) (rev. of LP)

Ovation 8:39 Je '87 Lawrence B. Johnson (165w)

2017. Concerti for Piano and Orchestra: No. 4 in G, Opus 58; Variations (32) in C minor for Piano, G.191.
Claudio Arrau (pno). Colin Davis (c). Dresden State Orchestra. 1984-85.
PHILIPS 416 144 DDD 49:51

✔**HC** ★***Awards:*** *Stereo Review* Best Recordings of the Month, D '87.

One of 20 classical CDs reviewed and recommended as "outstanding for their musical interest and their performance as well as for their technical quality."

Stereo Review Presents: Compact Disc Buyer's Guide 1988 p.39. William Livingstone and Christie Barter (125w)

"Arrau has never struck me as an ideal interpreter of this score, but his earlier recordings of it with Alceo Galliera (Quintessence) and Bernard Haitink (Philips) come far closer to the spirit of the music. The C-minor Variations suffer from a similar ponderous heaviness."

Fanfare 11:95 N/D '87. Mortimer H. Frank (220w)

Digital Audio 4:59 F '88. Tom Vernier (380w)

"It is a performance that must rank, musically and sonically, with the very greatest ever committed to discs....Not even the legendary Artur Schnabel, in his three recordings of the Fourth Concerto, surpassed the architectural strength and passion of this reading....Arrau's execution is of the utmost brilliance and passion, and the support given him by Sir Colin Davis and the Dresden State Orchestra is entirely on the same level."

Stereo Review 52:136+ D '87. David Hall (425w)

"Arrau has always had a special way of unlocking the broad lyricism inherent in Beethoven's Fourth Piano Concerto, and in this latest version with Sir Colin Davis and the Dresden Staatskapelle he finds willing collaborators."

Ovation 9:36-7 Ap '88. Dan F. Cameron (110w)

"So gorgeous are the sounds Arrau produces that it is easy to forget that he places himself entirely in the service of the music....The 32 Variations in C minor makes an appealing encore to a probing and profound musical journey."

High Fidelity 38:70 Ap '88. David Hurwitz (350w)

"Sir Colin Davis and the Dresden orchestra provide an ideal orchestral framework for this fine performance, and the Philips recording is rich and warmly reverberant to match. The LP is good, but the CD has that extra bit of clarity, transparency, and definition...that makes for near-total realism."

American Record Guide 51:12-14 My/Je '88. John P. McKelvey (325w)

2018. Concerti for Piano and Orchestra: No. 4 in G, Opus 58; No. 5 in E flat, Opus 73 ("Emperor").
Walter Gieseking (pno). Alceo Galliera (c). Philharmonia Orchestra. 1955 reissue.
EMI 62607 68:00

★***Awards:*** *American Record Guide* Overview: Beethoven Piano Concertos, Jl/Ag '89 (No. 5).

"All the hallmarks of the Gieseking style are very much in evidence: the magnificent technique placed solely at the service of the music; the limpid tonal purity, and the essentially no-frills classical approach. The *Emperor* may lack some of the fire of the pianist's legendary 1934 Vienna recording with Bruno Walter, but the interpretative viewpoint remains remarkably similar and Galliera's accompaniment is rhythmically tighter than Walter's....There is background hiss, hardly objectionable given the quality of the music making."

American Record Guide 52:19 Jl/Ag '89. Allen Linkowski (210w)

"These restrained readings are not technically immaculate, but in quiet authority they exemplify this German artist's classical manner...the sound quality is truly amazing for its age-....Galliera emerges as a most under-rated conductor. Of major musical and documentary value."

Hi-Fi News & Record Review 34:78 Jl '89. Christopher Breunig (185w)

"I find the sound on this CD reissue nothing short of astonishing....To put it plainly, Gieseking has never *sounded* so good....My hindsight view of these performances shows them to be animated, expressive, and architecturally sound. This is fine 'old-fashioned' big-orchestra Beethoven—performances that effectively capture the grandeur of the 'Emperor' and the ruminative, lyrical quality of the Fourth Concerto."

Fanfare 13:125-26 N/D '89. William Zagorski (400w)

2019. Concerto No. 5 in E flat for Piano and Orchestra, Opus 73, "Emperor".
Claudio Arrau (pno). Colin Davis (c). Dresden State Orchestra.
PHILIPS 416 215 40:40

✔**HC** ★★***Awards:*** *Stereo Review* Best of the Month, O '86; *Gramophone* Critics' Choice 1986 (Richard Osborne).

"It may seem unrealistic or foolhardy to suggest that any *one* recording of such a work could be recommended as clearly superior to all the others, but this is simply the most glorious recorded *Emperor* I know, and the superb sound does Arrau, Davis, and Beethoven full justice."

Stereo Review 51:83 O '86. Richard Freed (700w)

"Among currently available CD's, this one is preferable to those of Rudolf Serkin and Vladimir Ashkenazy, and can stand beside the different conceptions of Maurizio Pollini and Alfred Brendel as one of the better editions. Of course if sound is not a prime concern, there is the Artur Schnabel traversal (available only as a three-CD set), which remains a *ne plus ultra* in this repertory."

Fanfare 10:100 S/O '86 Mortimer H. Frank (105w)

"So much of...[Davis'] conducting here (and in my experience everywhere) is so deadly serious: no wit, no sparkle, no lightness of touch. Another quality lacking is majesty; Davis is too interested in rhythm to allow for majesty-....From Arrau we get a satisfying performance, with nobility, if not grandeur. Satisfying, but not stunning."

American Record Guide 49:6 S/O '86 Donald R. Vroon (750w) (rev. of LP)

Ovation 8:39 Je '87 Lawrence B. Johnson (165w)

Hi-Fi News & Record Review 31:77 Ag '86. Andrew Keener (300w)

2020. Concerto No. 5 in E flat for Piano and Orchestra, Opus 73 ("Emperor"); Sonata No. 32 in C minor for Piano, Opus 111.
Wilhelm Kempff (pno). Ferdinand Leitner (c). Berlin Philharmonic Orchestra. 1962 reissue.
DEUTSCHE GRAMMOPHON 419 468 ADD 63:00

> ★*Awards:* *American Record Guide* Overview: Beethoven Piano Concertos, Jl/Ag '89.

This is "one of the great recordings of the score: imperious, tonally rich yet never lush, and marked by an exceptional rhythmic sense-...The one disappointing aspect of this most welcome mid-priced CD reissue is a slight yet nonetheless noticeable brightening of the sound."

Fanfare 11:84-5 Ja/F '88. Mortimer H. Frank (185w)

Gramophone 65:896 D '87. Richard Osborne (245w)

2021. Concerto No. 5 in E flat for Piano and Orchestra, Opus 73 ("Emperor").
Murray Perahia (pno). Bernard Haitink (c). Concertgebouw Orchestra.
CBS 42330 DDD 39:00

> ★*Awards:* Record of the Year, Second Place, and Concerto, Third Place, Mumm Champagne Classical Music Awards 1988—Presented by *Ovation*, *Ovation* N '88.

"A performance, in my view, to rank with the very best."

Hi-Fi News & Record Review 32:91 Ag '87 Jeremy Siepmann (240w) (rev. of LP)

"In Perahia's hands, the first movement is taut and chastely phrased, with bracing rhythm and plenty of forward motion....The rondo, however, is playful and darting rather than, as is usual, pounding and weighty. Some will doubtless miss the pomp, but I suspect Perahia is intentionally avoiding the idea of Opus 73 as Great Music."

Musical America 109:70-5 My '89. Harris Goldsmith (265w)

Gramophone 64:1546 My '87 Stephen Plaistow (735w) (rev. of LP)

2022. Concerto No. 5 in E flat for Piano and Orchestra, Opus 73 ("Emperor"); Fantasia in C minor for Piano, Chorus and Orchestra, Opus 80.
Melvyn Tan (ftpno); Nancy Argenta (sop); Evelyn Tubb (sop); Mary Nichols (alto); Caroline Trevor (alto); Rufus Muller (ten); Howard Milner (ten); Richard Wistreich (bass). Roger Norrington (c). London Classical Players; Schutz Choir.
EMI 49965 DDD 52:00

> ★*Awards:* Critic's Choice: 1990, *American Record Guide* Ja/F '91 (Allen Linkowski).

"I have no hesitation in recommending this [5], especially to listeners who lean toward period-instrument performance. What really tips the scale in favor of this release is an absolutely revelatory reading of the *Choral Fantasy*....superb sonics."

American Record Guide 53:46-7 S/O '90. Allen Linkowski (230w)

"To Norrington's feeling for historic colour and structure, Melvyn Tan brings a matching sense of poetry and fun—and an impressive technique....Norrington's seven soloists and choir...make a fine case for the *Fantasia*, but it remains a *piece d'occasion*."

Continuo 14:27-8 O '90. Colin Tilney (495w)

"This last installment of the Tan/Norrington traversal of the Beethoven five piano concertos is a most unrhetorical yet vivacious performance of what is traditionally regarded as Beethoven's most rhetorical and extroverted of piano concertos....This performance is sprightly, alert, and alive both in piano and orchestra, and deeply satisfying in its musical insights and in its exuberant offhandedness....The Chorale Fantasia is a fitting close...The performance is loose, flows admirably, and makes most traditional versions seem stodgy and tendentious by comparison."

Fanfare 13:85-6 Jl/Ag '90. William Zagorski (500w)

Gramophone 67:1770-71 Ap '90. Stanley Sadie (760w)

2023. Concerto in D for Violin and Orchestra, Opus 61. BRAHMS, JOHANNES. Concerto in D for Violin and Orchestra, Opus 77.
Jascha Heifetz (vln). Charles Munch; Fritz Reiner (c). Boston Symphony Orchestra; Chicago Symphony Orchestra.
RCA 5402 72:12

> ★★★*Awards:* *Gramophone* Critics' Choice 1985 (Trevor Harvey). *American Record Guide* Overview: Popular Violin Concertos, S/O '89.

"The Boston Symphony's Beethoven has a thicker, better-balanced sonic quality although reverb takes its toll in tutti passages. The placement is more forward than we hear in Brahms, which Pfeiffer produced 30 years ago in Chicago, with the illusion on CD of perhaps more 'presence.'"

Fanfare 9:124-6 N/D '85. Roger Dettmer (725w)

Opus 2:32+ F '86. Richard Freed (425w)

Gramophone 63:336 S '85 (160w) (rev. of LP); 63:503 O '85 (265w) (rev. of CD). Trevor Harvey

High Fidelity 35:73 D '85. Robert E. Benson (50w)

2024. Concerto in D for Violin and Orchestra, Opus 61. MENDELSSOHN, FELIX. Concerto in E minor for Violin and Orchestra, Opus 64.
Yehudi Menuhin (vln). Wilhelm Furtwangler (c). Philharmonia Orchestra; Berlin Philharmonic Orchestra.
EMI 47119

✔HC ★*Awards:* *Fanfare* Want List 1985 (Harry Townsend).

"For the spiritual qualities in evidence here, realized with a sonic fullness quite beyond any previous release of these readings, this CD is recommended with enthusiasm."

Fanfare 8:146 Jl/Ag '85. Henry Fogel (275w)

Gramophone 63:26 Je '85. Michael Oliver (280w)

Ovation 6:42 D '85. Paul Turok (95w)

2025. Concerto in D for Violin and Orchestra, Opus 61.
Itzhak Perlman (vln). Carlo Maria Giulini (c). Philharmonia Orchestra. 1982.
EMI 47002

★*Awards:* *American Record Guide* Overview: Popular Violin Concertos, S/O '89.

"This is a broad and masterful performance, a true partnership between soloist and conductor."

American Record Guide 47:74 Jl '84. Matthew B. Tepper (125w)

"In *Fanfare* V:4 I wrote, 'This is one of the great recordings of the Beethoven concerto, worthy of rank beside those of Isaac Stern, Arthur Grumiaux, David Oistrakh, and, to go back further into the past, Joseph Szigeti and Bronislaw Huberman.' In the two years since I wrote that, rehearing this performance has not changed that impression, but has, if anything, strengthened it."

Fanfare 7:142 My/Je '84. Philip Hart (350w)

Gramophone 61:964 F '84. Trevor Harvey (350w)

Hi-Fi News & Record Review 29:84 Mr '84. David Prakel (130w)

Ovation 5:54 Ap '84. Paul Turok (135w)

Audio 68:102+ Je '84. Bert Whyte (285w)

2026. Concerto in D for Violin and Orchestra, Opus 61. MENDELSSOHN, FELIX. Concerto in E minor for Violin and Orchestra, Opus 64. PAGANINI, NICCOLO. Caprice for Solo Violin, "La Chasse".
Joseph Szigeti (vln). Bruno Walter; Thomas Beecham (c). British Symphony Orchestra; London Philharmonic Orchestra. 1932, 1933.
MUSIC MEMORIA 30272 AAD (m) 72:11

★*Awards:* Classical Hall of Fame, *Fanfare*, Jl/Ag '91.

"In terms of color, warmth, and vital expressiveness this has long been for me *the* recording of Beethoven's violin concerto....the surfaces are much quieter [than the Pearl 9345 reissue] and the transfer to compact disc far more effective, the sound having been given a bloom and presence it has not had on any of the vinyl incarnations since its original 78-rpm issue. This is a performance that will reward repeated hearings well into the next century. The Mendelssohn E Minor has had many fine recordings down through the years...but, once more, if I could only choose one: Szigeti/Beecham would be it....'*la chasse*' provides a fitting encore for such an exceptionally masterful release in transfers that capture more of the original sound than can be heard at any time in the past nearly six decades."

Fanfare 14:422-23 Jl/Ag '91. Jon Tuska (long)

Gramophone 69:198 O '91. Alan Sanders (brief)

2027. Concerto in C for Violin, Cello, Piano and Orchestra ("Triple Concerto"), Opus 56. BRAHMS, JOHANNES. Concerto in A minor for Violin, Cello and Orchestra, Opus 102.
David Oistrakh (vln); Sviatoslav Knushevitzky (cello); Lev Oborin (pno); Pierre Fournier (cello). Malcolm Sargent; Alceo Galliera (c). Philharmonia Orchestra. 1958, 1956.
EMI 62854 ADD 69:51

✔HC

"Not even Karajan and his soloists, although together they constitute my first choice [in the triple concerto], can surpass Sargent and his for the beauty of phrasing and flowing majesty of the Largo. Equally, while Karajan brings greater panache to the final movement, there is no denying the gracefulness Sargent achieves....If I were compelled to choose but one low-priced version [of the double concerto], I would be hard pressed since Walter's has only the *Tragic Overture* whereas to have these two performances together at a budget price is a bargain indeed."

Fanfare 13:86 Jl/Ag '90. Jon Tuska (355w)

2028. Concerto in C for Violin, Cello, Piano and Orchestra, Opus 56; Sonata No. 17 in D minor for Piano, Opus 31, No. 2, "Tempest".
David Oistrakh (vln); Sviatoslav Richter (pno); Mstislav Rostropovich (cello). Herbert Von Karajan (c). Berlin Philharmonic Orchestra. 1970, 1961 reissues.
EMI 69032 ADD 60:00

★*Awards:* *American Record Guide* Overview: Beethoven Piano Sonatas, Jl/Ag '91.

Gramophone 65:1426 Ap '88. Christopher Headington (250w)

"One of the best Beethoven 'Triples' of its time, this performance is here given an excellent transfer."

Fanfare 11:79-80 My/Je '88. Mortimer H. Frank (115w)

BERG, ALBAN

2029. Chamber Concerto for Piano, Violin and 13 Wind Instruments. SCHOENBERG, ARNOLD. Chamber Symphony in E, Opus 9.
Oleg Maisenberg (pno); Thomas Zehetmair (vln). Heinz Holliger (c). Chamber Orchestra of Europe. TELDEC 46019 DDD 63:00

★★★*Awards:* Critic's Choice: 1991, *American Record Guide*, Ja/F '92 (Stephen Chakwin). Critics' Choice 1991, Modern Composition, *The Wire*, D/Ja '91/92. Best Recordings of the Month, *Stereo Review* Ap '91.

"Both of these performances are distinguished by unusual sensitivity to style....Teldec's latest entry is strongly recommended."

Fanfare 14:155 Mr/Ap '91. John Wiser (150w)

"Orpheus and COE, recorded within two months of each other in 1989, bring superb performances, encompassing the work's many moods with coherence and, above all, elan-....Choosing between the two recordings is impossible."

American Record Guide 54:111-12 Mr/Ap '91. Stephen D. Chakwin, Jr. (170w)

"There are finally musicians...to whom this music [the Chamber Symphony] speaks a comprehensible and expressive language and to whom its formidable technical challenges are a means to an end and not just obstacles to be (grudgingly) overcome. Still not easy listening, but immensely worthwhile....Berg's Chamber Concerto...is the most opaque work of a composer usually considered to be the most accessible of the twelve-toners, but Heinz Holliger, in his role as conductor, and the Chamber Orchestra of Europe have a skillful and valiant go at it."

Stereo Review 56:85 Ap '91. Eric Salzman (375w)

"Heinz Holliger's performance of the 1906 Chamber Symphony No. 1...focuses extraordinarily detailed attention on Schoenberg's plethora of expressive markings. The result seems both very nineteenth-century (the influence of Mahler is everywhere) and, because there is so much simultaneous expression occurring, almost Cage-like. Indeed, never have I heard a performance of Schoenberg that captures both extremes of the composer so effectively at once."

Musical America 111:82-3 My '91. Mark Swed (170w)

"Harmonically, neither of the composers here is particularly abstruse in their writing when compared with the dissonances we are exposed to in much film and TV incidental music. No, the problem is that there is more going on at once than most ears (or for that matter microphones) can take in....the coupling is a useful one if one desires the Berg. Most Second Viennese buffs will still prefer the extraordinary account of the *Chamber Symphony* by the Orpheus CO on DG, though." *P95 S95*

Hi-Fi News & Record Review 36:80 My '91. Simon Cargill (350w)

Gramophone 68:1498 F '91. Arnold Whittall (365w)

2030. Concerto for Violin and Orchestra (1935); **Lyric Suite, for String Quartet** (1926) **or Orchestra** (1929).
Louis Krasner (vln). Anton Webern (c). BBC Symphony Orchestra; Galimir Quartet. reissues. TESTAMENT 1004 ADD (mono) 57:00

★★*Awards:* The Gramophone Awards, Nominations, Historical—non-vocal, *Gramophone*, N '91. Best Historical Recording Non Vocal 1991, *Gramophone*, D '91.

Gramophone 69:94 Je '91. Robert Layton (630w)

2031. Concerto for Violin and Orchestra (1935); **Three Pieces for Orchestra, Opus 6.**
Gidon Kremer (vln). Colin Davis (c). Bavarian Radio Symphony Orchestra.
PHILIPS 412 523 DDD 47:00

✔HC ★*Awards:* *American Record Guide* Overview: Popular Violin Concertos, S/O '89.

"His tone is sweet throughout, with hardly a hint of the grit that characterized, say, Krasner's pioneering performance. As a result, such passages as the achingly beautiful second chorale variation fairly glow in his hands. Yet his performance is more varied than Perlman's, and for that reason I find it ultimately preferable....Kremer also has the advantage of far better orchestral support....The sound in both works is moderately good, although the tuttis are slightly congested...and there's little sense of space...But with playing of this caliber, you barely notice the deficiencies."

Fanfare 9:129 N/D '85. Peter J. Rabinowitz (500w)

Opus 2:24-5 F '86. David Hamilton (160w); 3:50 D '86 Jon Alan Conrad (85w)

Gramophone 63:116 Jl '85. Michael Oliver (490w)

Hi-Fi News & Record Review 30:83 Ag '85. David Prakel (105w)

Digital Audio 2:36-7 My '86. Laurel E. Fay (350w)

BERLIOZ, HECTOR

2032. Harold in Italy, for Viola and Orchestra, Opus 16; Reverie et Caprice for Violin and Orchestra, Opus 8.
Yehudi Menuhin (vla/vln). Colin Davis; John Pritchard (c). Philharmonia Orchestra. 1963, 1965 reissue. EMI 63530 53:11

✔HC ★*Awards:* Critics Choice, *Hi Fi News & Record Review*, Ap '91 Supplement (John Crabbe).

"Colin Davis's superb command of the old Philharmonia Orchestra, with Yehudi Menuhin in the unusual role of solo violist, produced a uniquely satisfying amalgam of rhythmic fire and reflective melancholy, while the sound is of EMI's best Kingsway Hall vintage....A great reissue." *P100 S100/95*

Hi-Fi News & Record Review 35:113 O '90. John Crabbe (205w)

2033. Harold in Italy, for Viola and Orchestra, Opus 16; Overtures: Rob Roy; Le Corsaire.

Pinchas Zukerman (vln). Charles Dutoit (c). Montreal Symphony Orchestra.
LONDON/DECCA 421 193 DDD 66:00

★*Awards:* *American Record Guide* Overview: Berlioz, Mr/Ap '91.

"This [Harold in Italy] would quite definitely be my first choice among available recordings."

Ovation 10:58-9 Ap '89. Jon Tuska (300w)

"The best thing about this sixth CD *Harold* is Zukerman's contribution....Dutoit's somewhat laid-back manner fails to provide an adequate range of rhythmic and dynamic inflections to offset the violist's introspective musings."

Hi-Fi News & Record Review 33:91-2 S '88. John Crabbe (315w)

"Dutoit is certainly not above fireworks, and he delivers them fully in the fourth movement, the 'Brigands' Orgy.' Pinchas Zukerman gives a well-studied interpretation of the solo-viola part."

Stereo Review 53:132-3 N '88. David Patrick Stearns (275w)

"Dutoit is outclassed in *Le Corsaire* by Beecham, Munch, and Davis, all recently reissued on CD, while Sir Alexander Gibson and the Scottish National Orchestra evince an edge in finesse in *Rob Roy*. For *Harold*, one is advised to turn to classic performances by Scherchen-...and Toscanini, or—if up-to-date sound is a requirement—Maazel's with the Berlin Philharmonic, to cite only those available on silver discs. The present issue is not recommended."

Fanfare 12:145-6 N/D '88. Adrian Corleonis (165w)

"Recommended with reservations, but still recommended."

American Record Guide 52:32 Ja/F '89. Steven J. Haller (275w)

Gramophone 66:280 Ag '88. Edward Greenfield (480w)

BERNSTEIN, LEONARD

2034. Prelude, Fugue and Riffs (1950). **COPLAND, AARON. Concerto for Clarinet and String Orchestra. CORIGLIANO, JOHN. Concerto for Clarinet and Orchestra.**

Richard Stoltzman (clar). Lawrence Leighton Smith (c). London Symphony Orchestra.
RCA 7762 DDD 56:00

✔HC ★★*Awards:* The Want List 1989, *Fanfare* N/D '89 (Jon Tuska); Top Disks of the Year, *The New York Times* D 24, '89 (John Rockwell).

"This is an outstanding release."

Ovation 10:47 My '89. Jon Tuska (405w)

"Stoltzman's playing throughout is little short of miraculous....Balances between soloist and orchestra are excellent and the recording has terrific presence and range."

Hi-Fi News & Record Review 34:95 My '89. Kenneth Dommett (315w)

"Richard Stoltzman plays with dazzling agility, articulation, and coloration, Lawrence Leighton Smith and the London Symphony provide superb backing, and the digital sonics are truly state of the art."

Stereo Review 54:89+ Jl '89. David Hall (375w)

"This disc belongs in the absolutely-must-have category. As a sound recording it's among the dozen or so best I've heard....I shouldn't be surprised if the Corigliano soon establishes itself as a front-rank American masterpiece....I urge you to get it."

Fanfare 13:152 My/Je '90. Mike Silverton (250w)

"The early Bernstein [is] ...a showcase for the supreme artistry of Richard Stoltzman. No technical obstacle stands in his way, enabling him to project the difficult Corigliano work using the full resources of his instrument. His highly individual reading of the Copland is absolutely rivetting...An essential release."

American Record Guide 53:40-1 Jl/Ag '90. Allen Linkowski (290w)

Gramophone 66:1574-77 Ap '89. David J. Fanning (350w)

The New York Times Ag 20 '89, p. H 29. Andrew L. Pincus (110w)

BIRTWISTLE, HARRISON

2035. Endless Parade, for Trumpet and Orchestra. BLAKE WATKINS, MICHAEL. Concerto for Trumpet and Orchestra. MAXWELL DAVIES, PETER. Concerto for Trumpet and Orchestra.

Hakan Hardenberger (tpt); Paul Patrick (vphn). Elgar Howarth (c). BBC Philharmonic Orchestra.
PHILIPS 432 075 DDD 79:00

★★*Awards:* The Gramophone Awards, Nominations, Contemporary, *Gramophone*, N '91. Critics' Choice 1991, Modern Composition, *The Wire*, D/Ja '91/92.

"Birtwistle's trumpet concerto is a modern classic. It's also the most approachable score of his I've yet heard. Maxwell Davies's concerto reaffirms his return to relative tonal orthodoxy-

...There is too much to write on these remarkable works...this is a recording to play and savour many times."

The Wire 90:50 Ag '91. Andy Hamilton (long)

"Maxwell Davies's mature command of rhetoric and dramatic gesture—firmly grounded in the past, but very much of the present—is everywhere in evidence, and there's not a dull or mechanical moment in all of the piece's half-hour length. (He also gives the soloist plenty of virtuoso writing.) A rewarding and moving work....Both [the Watkins]...and the Birtwistle were commissioned for Hakan Hardenberger, and he plays all three works with extraordinary technical ease and expressive assurance. Elgar Howarth and the BBC Philharmonic turn in really first-rate work as well....Strongly recommended. Potential buyers, and especially Maxwell Davies fans, should however know that another recording of that composer's trumpet concerto has been issued in England (Collins Classics 1181-2) paired with his Symphony No. 4. That performance, with John Wallace the soloist and the composer conducting the Royal Scottish National Orchestra, was judged marginally preferable in the June 1991 *Gramophone*. Take your pick; but it would be a shame to miss the Birtwistle."

Fanfare 15:411-2 Mr/Ap '92. Nicholas Deutsch (long)

Gramophone 69:46 Je '91. Arnold Whittall (235w)

Digital Audio's CD Review 8:57-8 F '92. Tom Vernier (long)

BLAKE WATKINS, MICHAEL. Concerto for Trumpet and Orchestra. See No. 2035.

BLISS, ARTHUR

2036. Concerto for Cello and Orchestra; The Enchantress (Scene for Contralto and Orchestra); Hymn to Apollo for Orchestra.
Raphael Wallfisch (cello); Linda Finnie (mez). Vernon Handley (c). Ulster Orchestra.
CHANDOS 8818 DDD 56:00

★★*Awards:* Best of the Month, *Hi-Fi News & Record Review*, S '91. Critics' Choice 1991, Modern Composition, *The Wire*, D/Ja '91/92.

"Taken as a whole, the excellent Ulster CD offers a most satisfying stylistic overview of Bliss's compositional career....Passionate, urgently disciplined performances under Vernon Handley...with vividly natural recording a bonus." *P95/100 S95/100*

Hi-Fi News & Record Review 36:72 S '91. Andrew Achenbach (brief)

"This disc...is strongly recommended to all who love 20th Century British music."

American Record Guide 55:33 Ja/F '92. John Landis (long)

"All in all, except for the viola sonata [Chandos 8770], Chandos has not done Bliss as great a service as we would have wished or expected, particularly in view of their earlier work on behalf of British music."

Fanfare 15:168-69 S/O '91. Paul A. Snook (med)

Gramophone 69:41-2 Jl '91. Michael Kennedy (265w)

BLOCH, ERNEST. Schelomo, Hebrew Rhapsody for Cello and Orchestra. See No. 1058, 2062.

BOCCHERINI, LUIGI

2037. Concerti for Cello and Orchestra: No. 7, G.480, No. 10, G.483. **Symphonies:** G.497; G.506.
Anner Bylsma (cello). Jean Lamon (c). Tafelmusik Baroque Orchestra.
DEUTSCHE HARMONIA MUNDI 78670 DDD 67:00

✔**HC** ★*Awards:* Critics Pick Some Favorites of the Year, *The New York Times* N 26, '89 (John Rockwell).

"Here is a particularly well-chosen mixture of Boccherini symphonies and concertos that are exquisitely performed on authentic period instruments by a group of musicians who know how to render the delicate little details so essential to a full realization of this composer's fragile, Rococo sensibility."

Stereo Review 55:153-54 F '90. David Patrick Stearns (125w)

"Easily recommended."

Fanfare 13:151 Mr/Ap '90. John Wiser (300w)

"As a baroque cellist, I find any release that includes the playing of Anner Bylsma irresistible-....Bylsma has proved his affinity for the works of Luigi Boccherini in recordings of the cello sonatas (Pro Arte 117) with cellist Wieland Kuijken and guitarist Hopkinson Smith. This latest release has the same verve and polish and includes the fine accompaniement of Tafelmusik."

American Record Guide 53:32-3 My/Je '90. Paul Laird (300w)

Gramophone 67:1456 F '90. Stanley Sadie (345w)

BRAHMS, JOHANNES

2038. Concerti for Piano and Orchestra: No. 1 in D Minor, Opus 15; No. 2 in B flat, Opus 83; **Fantasies (7) for Piano, Opus 116.**
Emil Gilels (pno). Eugen Jochum (c). Berlin Philharmonic Orchestra.
DEUTSCHE GRAMMOPHON 419 158 2 discs

★*Awards:* *American Record Guide* Overview: Brahms: Symphonies and Piano Concertos, My/Je '89.

"This B flat Concerto is far less fiery and volatile than the magnificent Gilels-Reiner version of 1958 (now available on an RCA CD), but this version with Jochum offers its own rewards and is far more tasteful, musical, and coherent than the recent Zimerman-Bernstein DG edition. And this D-minor Concerto can stand beside the best expansive versions, notably Serkin-Szell, Curzon-Szell, and (in mono) Solomon-Kubelik."

Fanfare 10:121 N/D '86 Mortimer H. Frank (220w)

2039. Concerto No. 1 in D minor for Piano, Opus 15.
("The Rubinstein Collection").
Artur Rubinstein (piano). Fritz Reiner (c). Chicago Symphony Orchestra. reissue 1955.
RCA 5668 46:00

★*Awards:* *American Record Guide* Overview: Brahms: Symphonies and Piano Concertos, My/Je '89.

"On this collaboration with Reiner, Rubinstein made what may well be his greatest concerto recording. It remains one of the two or three finest Brahms Firsts on discs...sonically speaking, Rubinstein's achievement is fresher than ever."

High Fidelity 37:67 O '87. Thomas L. Dixon (125w)

"Beyond the exceptional sonic quality of the collection lies its value as documentation for posterity of one of the great pianistic personalities of the century."

American Record Guide 52:118-21 Jl/Ag '89. Donald Manildi (55w)

Gramophone 65:404 S '87 Trevor Harvey (175w)

2040. Concerto No. 1 in D minor for Piano and Orchestra, Opus 15. STRAUSS, RICHARD. Burleske in D minor for Piano and Orchestra.
Rudolf Serkin (pno). George Szell; Eugene Ormandy (c). Cleveland Orchestra; Philadelphia Orchestra. 1969, 1970 reissues.
CBS 42261 ADD 67:00

✔HC ★★*Awards:* Pick of the Month, North American Perspective (Christie Barter) *Gramophone* Jl '91. *American Record Guide* Overview: Brahms: Symphonies and Piano Concertos, My/Je '89.

"This Op. 15, Serkin's last recording of the work, may lack some of the fire and thrust of his two earliest versions, but it is nonetheless a strong, stylish reading....[The filler is] less distinguished."

Fanfare 10:72-73 Jl/Ag '87 Mortimer H. Frank (125w)

Gramophone 69:40-1 Jl '91. Richard Osborne (210w)

2041. Concerto No. 2 in B flat for Piano and Orchestra, Opus 83. BEETHOVEN, LUDWIG VAN. Sonata No. 23 in F minor, Opus 57, "Appasionata".
Sviatoslav Richter (piano). Erich Leinsdorf (c). Chicago Symphony Orchestra. 1961 reissues.
RCA 6518 ADD 71:21

✔HC ★★*Awards:* Critics' Choice 1988, *Gramophone* D '88 (Ivan March). *American Record Guide* Overview: Brahms: Symphonies and Piano Concertos, My/Je '89; *American Record Guide* Overview: Beethoven Piano Sonatas, Jl/Ag '91.

"Richter's inspired account of the B-flat Concerto...was, is, one of the great piano recordings; and as a piece of engineering it still sounds good. A MUST."

Hi-Fi News & Record Review 32:107 N '87 Frances Handford (190w)

"If you want the Brahms Second Concerto, this is the one to have. And you even get along with it the best Beethoven *Appassionata* I've ever heard, and a sensible 15 seconds of silence between them."

American Record Guide 51:19-20 My/Je '88. Donald R. Vroon (225w)

"The magical snap that defines a transcendental Richter performance is absent [from the Brahms concerto]...Richter described this recording [of Beethoven's Sonata] as 'not particularly good,' preferring a searing live version recorded in Moscow in June 1960....this version is not particularly bad either."

Music Magazine 11:42 N/D '88. Robert McAlear (420w)

Gramophone 65:1580 My '88. Ivan March (360w)

2042. Concerto No. 2 in B flat for Piano and Orchestra, Opus 83; 4 Pieces for Piano, Opus 119.
Rudolf Serkin (pno). George Szell (c). Cleveland Orchestra. Severance Hall, Clevland OH; Guilford VT. January 1966, May 1979.
CBS 42262 64:40

★*Awards:* *American Record Guide* Overview: Brahms: Symphonies and Piano Concertos, My/Je '89.

"One gets the feeling one is listening to Brahms rather than listening to Serkin play Brahms....Recorded sound is really quite fine; you wouldn't guess that this recording is 23 years old. The album is rounded out with the four piano pieces of Op. 119...Piano sound is slightly less vivid here, and when listening with headphones, I was bothered by the sound of what seems to be Serkin's labored breathing. But these performances are also very fine."

HighPerformanceReview 6:72 Je '89. James Primosch (150w)

Fanfare 10:72-73 Jl/Ag '87 Mortimer H. Frank (125w)

2043. Concerto No. 2 in B flat for Piano, Opus 83.
Krystian Zimerman (pno). Leonard Bernstein (c). Vienna Philharmonic Orchestra.
DEUTSCHE GRAMMOPHON 415 359

★*Awards:* *American Record Guide* Overview: Brahms: Symphonies and Piano Concertos, My/Je '89.

"Zimerman's energy and urgency combine with Bernstein's ecstatic intensity to produce a heady, wildly exciting, yes, *joyful*, performance....So if you want a stunning, live-with-it-for-a-lifetime Brahms Second on LP or CD, Zimerman/Bernstein is it."

American Record Guide 50:13 Mr/Ap '87 Donald R. Vroon (150w) (rev. of LP)

"The opening moments of this performance—with the horn call sounding so spacious, expansive and utterly lofty—promise greatness. And, for the most part, the rest of the recording delivers just that....The finest recordings currently available of this work include the Gilels/Jochum (Deutsche Grammophon 413 229), which remains unsurpassed for its authority and heroism: the Richter/Leinsdorf (RCA Gold Seal ALK1-9350, cassette), the ultimate in imagination and individuality; and the Fischer/Furtwangler (recently rereleased on French Emi 2909701; dist. by International Book and Record), which cannot be touched for an intensity bordering on madness. Zimerman/Bernstein offer generous helpings of all these qualities, but the hallmark of the performance is its sense of balance."

Ovation 8:32 Ap '87 David Patrick Stearns (570w)

"For all his superb gifts, Bernstein has a maddening tendency to love romantic music almost to death—death by suffocation—as he does here repeatedly, with sudden, musically unmotivated ritards bordering on the apocalyptic. Zimerman displays similar irresponsibility."

High Fidelity 37:61 F '87 Paul Moor (260w)

Gramophone 63:914 Ja '86. Ivan March (300w)

2044. Concerto in D for Violin and Orchestra, Opus 77.
Gidon Kremer (vln). Leonard Bernstein (c). Vienna Philharmonic Orchestra. 1983.
DEUTSCHE GRAMMOPHON 410 029

★*Awards:* *American Record Guide* Overview: Popular Violin Concertos, S/O '89.

"Overall, this is an enjoyable, inspiriting performance, with much beautiful playing from both soloist and orchestra."

Stereo Review 49:103-4 Ap '84. Richard Freed (175w)

Gramophone 61:140+ Jl '83 (315w) (rev. of LP); 61:234 Ag '83 (140w) (rev. of CD). Edward Greenfield

2045. Concerto in D for Violin and Orchestra, Opus 77. SIBELIUS, JEAN. Concerto in D minor for Violin and Orchestra, Opus 47.
Ginette Neveu (vln). Issay Dobrowen; Walter Susskind (c). Philharmonia Orchestra. 1948; 1946.
EMI 61011 70:12

★*Awards:* Historical (Non-vocal) Record Award 1988, *Gramophone* O '88.

"The searingly intense Sibelius performance is simply one of the most illuminating readings of the work ever recorded, getting close to the heart and soul of this music as have few in phonographic history....This along with Heifetz-...and Camilla Wicks...stands as one of the great recordings of this music. So too, the Brahms, recorded almost a year later....Most enthusiastically recommended."

American Record Guide 52:85-6 Mr/Ap '89. Allen Linkowski (225w)

"This is strong, forceful fiddling: masculine in profile, yet frequently sensitive. I have to say that many subsequent recordings of the Brahms strike me as having a wider expressive range...Neveu's hardy resilience seems more appropriate in the Sibelius, but I'd unhesitatingly choose Heifetz as my 'reference' in this particular work."

Hi-Fi News & Record Review 33:104-5 My '88. Robert Cowan (250w)

Gramophone 65:1306 Mr '88 (315w); 66:553 O '88 (200w). Robert Layton

Concerto in D for Violin and Orchestra, Opus 77. See No. 2023.

Concerto in A minor for Violin, Cello and Orchestra, Opus 102. See No. 1063, 2027.

BRIDGE, FRANK. Phantasm for Piano and Orchestra. See No. 2073.

BRITTEN, BENJAMIN. Symphony for Cello and Orchestra, Opus 68. See No. 2007.

BROUWER, LEO

2046. Concerto No. 3, "Concerto Elegiaco," for Guitar and Orchestra. RODRIGO, JOAQUIN. Fantasia para un gentilhombre for Guitar and Orchestra.
Julian Bream (gtr). Leo Brouwer (c). RCA Victor Chamber Orchestra.
RCA 7718 DDD 45:32

"To put matters simply, this is among the best recordings of this work [*Fantasia para un Gentilhombre*] I have heard, and on that score alone the disc can be recommended to the needful....The sound is excellent in both vehicles, and Brouwer's reading of his own tightly constructed concerto...must be considered definitive."

Fanfare 11:139 Jl/Ag '88. John Ditsky (250w)

"This long-awaited recording features exquisite playing from Bream and the most sympathetic support from the composer/conductor with the RCA Victor Chamber Orchestra."

Music and Musicians International 36:32 S '88. Graham Wade (350w)

"Although competition for the Rodrigo rages fiercely, the inclusion of the Brouwer Concerto here makes this a very desirable version."

Hi-Fi News & Record Review 33:117 D '88. Doug Hammond (245w)

"This is an aristocratic performance made more so by the unusually sensitive direction of Brouwer and the refined playing of the orchestra. The sound of the disc matches the remarkable playing from all concerned: a silken, almost lush quality that I find quite attractive." *P100 S100*

Australian Hi-Fi 20(7):51:3 '89. John Aranetta (320w)

Gramophone 66:280 Ag '88. John Duarte (350w)

BRUCH, MAX

2047. Concerto No. 1 in G minor for Violin and Orchestra, Opus 26; Scottish Fantasy for Violin and Orchestra, Opus 46.
Cho-Liang Lin (vln). Leonard Slatkin (c). Chicago Symphony Orchestra.
CBS 42315 53:01

★★***Awards:*** *Gramophone* Critics' Choice (Edward Greenfield), 1987. *American Record Guide* Overview: Popular Violin Concertos, S/O '89 (Scottish Fantasy).

"If you are a bit jaded by the staples of the violin repertoire, try these well-performed, excellently recorded Bruch pieces."

Audio 71:124 S '87. Bert Whyte (210w)

"What Lin lacks is a certain rhapsodic, romantic fervor that would turn these technically superlative performances into a truly arresting musical experience."

High Fidelity 37:78 N '87. K. Robert Schwarz (200w)

"Highly recommended."

Ovation 8:37 D '87. Paul Turok (315w)

"Recommendable."

Hi-Fi News & Record Review 32:93 Ap '87 Christopher Breunig (250w) (rev. of LP)

Gramophone 64:1256+ Mr '87 (490w) (rev. of LP); 65:178 Jl '87 (rev. of CD). Edward Greenfield

Stereo Review 52:85 Ag '87 David Hall (160w)

Fanfare 10:79-80 Jl/Ag '87. James Miller (350w)

2048. Concerto No. 1 in G minor for Violin and Orchestra, Opus 26. MENDELSSOHN, FELIX. Concerto in E minor for Violin and Orchestra, Opus 64.
Gil Shaham (vln). Giuseppe Sinopoli (c). Philharmonia Orchestra.
DEUTSCHE GRAMMOPHON 427 656 DDD 55:00

✔**HC** ★***Awards:*** Best Recordings of the Month, *Stereo Review* Ag '90.

"I hear a welcome degree of freshness and exploration to the Bruch, which is given a high-contrast, powerful interpretation, distinguished by the imaginative work of Sinopoli, who leads into the tender Adagio magnificently....In the third movement, and in portions of the Mendelssohn, Shaham overforces the instrument, and I hear strain when he plays high on the G string....Shaham's musical comprehension seems very promising, indeed, certainly more than mere boyish enthusiasm, and this is an impressive outing."

Fanfare 14:155-6 S/O '90. David K. Nelson (390w)

"The concertos of Bruch and Mendelssohn are the special province of the young, where freshness and spontaneity have not yet given way to standardization. One need only listen to Perlman's recordings to see how much can be lost in later, more 'mature' remarks. Shaham is the ideal interpreter of both concertos, and his readings so outshine those of other violinists (there are more than a dozen couplings readily available) as to make this the recording of choice."

American Record Guide 53:40-1 N/D '90. Alan Heatherington (425w)

"Considering Shaham's choice of repertory—the overplayed Mendelssohn and Bruch concertos—it's hard to say whether he has the range and maturity of his 19-year-old colleague, Midori. But time, and a broader repertory, will tell. In the meantime, this is a most auspicious debut, one enhanced by the thoughtful (if overly expansive) accompaniments of Giuseppe Sinopoli."

Musical America 111:74 Ja '91. K. Robert Schwarz (300w)

"These concertos have been played in almost as many different ways as there are different violinists who have played them...Not everyone will warm to Shaham's expansive interpretations, but surely everyone whose ears are in working order must admire and enjoy such musicianship in its own right."

Stereo Review 55:72 Ag '90. Richard Freed (450w)

"Shaham is by no means a callow youth; but his version of the Bruch never really recovers from its low-key opening, and the feeling that he is tied to note-lengths and bar-lines....It is much the same story in the Mendelssohn." *P85 S95/85*

Hi-Fi News & Record Review 35:88-9 Ap '90. Simon Cargill (280w)

Gramophone 67:1598 Mr '90. Edward Greenfield (295w)

BUSONI, FERRUCCIO

2049. Concerto in C for Piano and Orchestra (with male chorus), Opus 39.
John Ogdon (pno). Daniell Revenaugh (c). John Alldis Choir; Royal Philharmonic Orchestra. 1967.
EMI 69850 ADD 69:00

✔**HC** ★***Awards:*** Best of the Month, *Hi-Fi News & Record Review*, Ag '90.

"This 1967 recording of Busoni's piano concerto catches him at the zenith of his career and in the blush of one of his most resplendent triumphs....The recent Ohlsson/Dohnanyi recording (Telarc CD-80207, *Fanfare* 13:4) rivals this in a more sumptuously relaxed account...though this crisper, muscularly brisker, and more dramatically charged performance remains preeminent....Recommendation is superfluous."

Fanfare 13:119-20 Jl/Ag '90. Adrian Corleonis (505w)

"For all Ohlsson's superior technique and glossy finish, I still find Ogdon's pioneering version that bit more involving and, ultimately, more moving....EMIs 1967 Abbey Road recording is now beginning to show its age, inclining to shrillness in tuttis." *P95/100 S95/85*

Hi-Fi News & Record Review 35:91 Ag '90. Andrew Achenbach (190w)

Gramophone 67:1772 Ap '90. Michael Oliver (455w)

Stereophile 13:215+ D '90. Igor Kipnis (150w)

2050. Concerto in C for Piano and Orchestra (with male chorus), Opus 39.

Garrick Ohlsson (pno). Christoph von Dohnanyi (c). Cleveland Orchestra Men's Chorus; Cleveland Orchestra. 1989.
TELARC 80207 DDD 72:00

★★*Awards:* The Want List 1990, *Fanfare* N/D '90 (Adrian Corleonis). Best of the Month, *Hi-Fi News & Record Review*, Ag '90.

"Busoni's concerto is a work of great mastery and vision. And it has, as this performance clearly demonstrates, the power to speak to our time."

Stereo Review 55:153 F '90. Eric Salzman (330w)

"A landmark recording, awesome and indispensable."

Fanfare 13:162-63 Mr/Ap '90. Adrian Corleonis (400w)

"Telarc's superb recorded sound captures in spectacular fashion both the brilliance of Ohlsson's technique and some top-notch playing by the Cleveland Orchestra....This is a sententious, deeply felt interpretation, but one that is at times more ponderous than profound-....there is no compelling reason (except the sound) to buy it if you have the Ogdon LP. When the latter appears on compact disc, it will prevail."

American Record Guide 53:37 Mr/Ap '90. Mark Koldys (175w)

"I must admit I never thought anyone could surpass John Ogdon's hair-raising virtuosity in this piece but if anything Garrick Ohlsson is an even more dauntingly accurate advocate-...[However] for all Ohlsson's superior technique and glossy finish, I still find Ogdon's pioneering version that bit more involving and, ultimately, more moving....the crystalline clarity of Ohlsson's Bosendorfer has been excitingly captured by sound engineer Jack Renner-...Get one or the other—Busoni fans will surely want both." *P95 S95/100*

Hi-Fi News & Record Review 35:91 Ag '90. Andrew Achenbach (190w)

Stereophile 13:215+ D '90. Igor Kipnis (150w)

Gramophone 67:1772 Ap '90. Michael Oliver (455w)

Digital Audio's CD Review 6:72 Mr '90. Tom Vernier (360w)

CARTER, ELLIOTT

2051. Concerto for Oboe and Orchestra; Esprit Rude/Esprit Doux, for Flute and Clarinet; Penthode, for 5 Groups of 4 Instruments; A Mirror on Which to Dwell (6 poems of Elizabeth Bishop), for Soprano and Chamber Ensemble.

Heinz Holliger (oboe); Phyllis Bryn-Julson (sop); Sophie Cherrier (fl); Andre Trouttet (clar). Pierre Boulez (c). Ensemble Intercontemporain.
ERATO 45364 DDD 63:00

✔HC ★★*Awards:* Critics' Choice 1990, *Gramophone* D '90 (Arnold Whittall).

"Everything about this musical tribute derives from the very best of contemporary thought and art: the stunning performance of the soloists, the wonderful poetry of Elizabeth Bishop, the superb artistic direction of Pierre Boulez, the first-rate performances of the Ensemble Inter-Contemporain, Paris's eminent new music ensemble, and not the least the very sophisticated and profound writing of Elliott Carter....[The Oboe Concerto] was exciting and stimulating, personal and melancholic, comfortably familiar and then at times new to the ears....Both the composition *Esprit Rude/Esprit Doux* and this performance of it are remarkable....Cherrier and Trouttet give an incredible performance. I loved hearing *A Mirror on Which to Dwell* and Bryn-Julson shows herself a true virtuoso in this performance....This recording is a fascinating and historic event and having participated in and even thrown artistic bashes myself, I felt privileged to be invited to the party by hearing this record."

American Record Guide 55:41-2 Mr/Ap '92. Sara Lambert Bloom (long)

"Boulez leads the recent works with a kind of transcendental confidence that tempts a listener with every detail, and Heinz Holliger's performance of the concerto contains some of the greatest solo oboe playing found anywhere on disc."

Musical America 111:71-2 Jl '91. Mark Swed (160w)

"I can't see anyone remotely interested in the music of Elliott Carter passing up this disc."

Fanfare 14:134-6 Jl/Ag '91. Art Lange (625w)

Gramophone 67:1500+ F '90. Arnold Whittall (300w)

2052. Concerto for Piano and Orchestra.
Ursula Oppens (pno). Michael Gielen (c). Cincinnati Symphony Orchestra. Music Hall, Cincinnati, Ohio. October, 1984; October, 1985.
NEW WORLD 347 45:02

> ✔**HC** ★★***Awards:*** *Fanfare* Want List 1987 (William Youngren); *Gramophone* Critics' Choice (Arnold Whittall), 1987.

"New World Records' first Compact disc release brings together two of Carter's loftiest creations—the 1955 *Variations for Orchestra* and the 1965 Piano Concerto—in performances led by a conductor who apparently responds as much to the music's emotive content as to its technical workings...these performances are, quite simply, superb."
High Fidelity 37:64-65 My '87 James Wierzbicki (775w)

"The performances here, recorded live, are both excellent. Michael Gielen is the master of this kind of modernism, and his collaboration with Ursula Oppens is particularly notable."
Stereo Review 52:100 Mr '87 Eric Salzman (310w)

"Ms. Oppens plays the intricate solo part of Elliott Carter's Piano Concerto magnificently-...Otherwise the orchestration gives a messy, monochrome effect."
Ovation 8:32-33 Mr '87 Paul Turok (215w)

Gramophone 64:1410 Ap '87 Arnold Whittall (410w)

CHOPIN, FREDERIC

2053. Concerto No. 1 in E minor for Piano and Orchestra, Opus 11. LISZT, FRANZ. Concerto No. 1 in E flat for Piano and Orchestra.
Emil Gilels (pno); Charles Rosen (pno). Eugene Ormandy; John Pritchard (c). Philadelphia Orchestra; New Philharmonia Orchestra. 1964, 1966.
CBS 37804 ADD 58:07

> ★***Awards:*** *American Record Guide* Overview: Romantic Piano Concertos, Jl/Ag '90 (Chopin).

"The reason for getting this release is Gilels, in one of his finest records."
Fanfare 12:135 Mr/Ap '89. Howard Kornblum (175w)

"This is the most beautiful recording of the Chopin you'll ever hear. The soloist is sensitive and poetic, and the conductor follows him all the way. The Phildelphia winds and strings make a major contribution to the excellence of the performance....The 1964 sound is everything I want from a recording."
American Record Guide 52:38-9 My/Je '89. Donald R. Vroon (160w)

COPLAND, AARON

Concerto for Clarinet and String Orchestra. See No. 1096, 2027.

Quiet City, for Trumpet, English Horn and Orchestra. See No. 1092, 1093, 1100.

CORIGLIANO, JOHN

Concerto for Clarinet and Orchestra. See No. 2034.

2054. The Pied Piper Fantasy (concerto for flute and orchestra); Voyage, for Flute and String Orchestra.
James Galway (fl). David Effron (c). Eastman Philharmonia Chamber Orchestra.
RCA 6602 DDD 45:45

> ★***Awards:*** Third Place Contemporary Composer Mumm Champagne Classical Music Award 1988—Presented by *Ovation, Ovation* N '88.

"This interpretation by the score's commissioner and dedicatee—the astonishing James Galway—must be considered perforce definitive....RCA has done a superb job of capturing the visceral excitement and the variegated dynamics and color of Corigliano's remarkable conception."
Fanfare 11:98 Mr/Ap '88. Paul Snook (600w)

"Corigliano's musical style is as effective as it is conservative—even the cacophony is easy to take. Galway, with his outstanding low register, plays the music as if it belonged to him, which it essentially does."
Ovation 9:34 Jl '88. Karen Monson (350w)

"Children will love The Rats: sneaky, twitching long-nosed creatures, squealing and writhing around, serried in ranks of age. Older listeners may switch to War Cadenza for the sheer sophistication of Galway's playing....I am underlining the negative qualities of this issue, but it is one I have enjoyed: the 'Galway sound' in itself is magically individual, and the wonderful transparency of the scoring is finely served by Jay David Saks's production."
Hi-Fi News & Record Review 34:105 Ja '89. Christopher Breunig (535w)

"Despite (or, maybe, in part because of) the album photo cover of James Galway in Pied Piper garb playing while a pack of chubby-faced brats listen enthralled...this strikes me as an extremely cynical release. Much of the music sounds like a film score...like one by John Corigliano—stylistically diffuse, gimmicky, and fuzzy-minded in its dramatic intent."
American Record Guide 51:29 N/D '88. Kyle Rothweiler (400w)

Gramophone 66:595 O '88. Michael Oliver (270w)

Digital Audio 4:43-4 My '88. Tom Vernier (325w)

DELIUS, FREDERICK

2055. Concerto for Violin and Orchestra; Suite for Violin and Orchestra; Legende for Violin and Orchestra.

Ralph Holmes (vln). Vernon Handley (c). Royal Philharmonic Orchestra.
UNICORN-KANCHANA 9040 53:57

★★*Awards: Gramophone* Critics' Choice 1985 (Ivan March); *Gramophone* Critics' Choice 1985 (Max Harrison).

"Although the works of Frederick Delius aim at native English ears, Delians of any nationality won't want to pass this rare collection by."
High Fidelity 37:59 Je '87 Paul Moor (175w)

"Warmly recommended for all but severe classicists."
American Record Guide 48:63-4 S/O '85. John P. McKelvey (500w)

"There could be no finer performances of this music than you'll find here."
Stereo Review 50:121-2 N '85. Richard Freed (275w)

"Unicorn's close, clear sound is marginally brighter and fuller on CD....Recommended."
Fanfare 9:151 N/D '85. Adrian Corleonis (190w)

"All three works are played to perfection by Holmes."
Opus 2:40-1 F '86. John Canarina (440w)

"A superb CD, with splendid performances and natural, wide-range sonics."
High Fidelity 36:56 Mr '86. Robert E. Benson (85w)

Gramophone 63:122+ Jl '85 (385w) (rev. of LP); Max Harrison; 63:339 S '85 (140w) (rev. of CD) Ivan March

DIAMOND, DAVID. Kaddish, for Cello and Orchestra. See No. 1112.

D'INDY, VINCENT. Symphony on a French Mountain Air, for Piano and Orchestra, Opus 25. See No. 1148.

DITTERSDORF, KARL DITTERS VON

2056. Concerto in D minor for Oboe and Orchestra. LEBRUN, LUDWIG AUGUST. Concerto No. 1 in D minor for Oboe and Orchestra. SALIERI, ANTONIO. Concerto in D for Violin, Oboe, Cello and Orchestra.
Heinz Holliger (oboe); Thomas Demenga (cello). Thomas Furi (c). Berne Camerata. 1980, 1983.
DEUTSCHE GRAMMOPHON 427 125 DDD 60:00

✔HC ★*Awards:* The Want List 1989, *Fanfare* N/D '89 (George Chien).

"If you don't like this, there's something wrong with you." *PS 95*
Fanfare 13:89-90 S/O '89. Eric Van Tassel (200w)

Gramophone 66:1722 My '89. John Warrack (80w)

DOHNANYI, ERNST VON

2057. Variations on a Nursery Song for Piano and Orchestra, Opus 25; Capriccio in F minor for Piano (from Opus 28). TCHAIKOVSKY, PIOTR ILYICH. Concerto No. 1 in B flat minor for Piano and Orchestra, Opus 23.
Earl Wild (pno). Christoph von Dohnanyi; Anatole Fistoulari (c). New Philharmonia Orchestra; Royal Philharmonic Orchestra. 1962.
CHESKY 013 AAD 60:00

✔HC ★*Awards: American Record Guide* Overview: Romantic Piano Concertos, Jl/Ag '90.

"This is simply the best recording of the Tchaikovsky ever made. The pianist is outstanding-....The coupling is imaginative."
American Record Guide 51:87 S/O '88. Donald R. Vroon (175w)

"The sound is nearly state-of-the-art....This CD far outclasses the Quintessence pressings of these Reader's Digest originals. Good annotations accompany this outstanding issue."
Fanfare 12:140 S/O '88. John Bauman (300w)

"The only competition for this coupling is the dreadful Andras Schiff/Georg Solti version on London...Even Chesky's recorded sound is superior to London's."
High Fidelity 38:72 O '88. David Hurwitz (175w)

"Of considerably lesser artistic value are the orchestral fillers....Not having heard this in its original vinyl incarnation, the intensity of his impassioned playing—very capably supported by Fistoulari and the Royal Philharmonic—almost took my breath away....In the Dohnanyi Variations...Wild again exhibits a similar blend of digital wizardry and sensitive artistry."
Stereophile 12:227-29 Ja '89. Bernard Soll (315w)

Wild's "clean fingering, his power and his ability to project mood are demonstrated fully in these recordings, and remind us that his talent was never regarded in this country for what it was....The piano comes through cleanly, but the orchestral sound shows definite signs of age on the inner grooves, particularly in the Liszt. Despite this, it is a worthwhile rescue operation for a gifted artist."
American Record Guide 52:41 My/Je '89. Michael Mark (225w)

"This release can only be termed a qualified success....On the plus side, there is the ever-impressive artistry of Earl Wild....On the other hand, the sonic qualities of these resurrected recordings...while satisfactory, fall short of the highest standards."
HighPerformanceReview 7:80 Winter '90-91. John A. Mueter (250w)

Digital Audio 5:50-2 Ja '89. Tom Vernier (180w)

Variations on a Nursery Song for Piano and Orchestra, Opus 25. See No. 2126.

DUTILLEUX, HENRI

2058. Concerto for Cello and Orchestra ("Tout un monde lointain"). LUTOSLAWSKI, WITOLD. Concerto for Cello and Orchestra.
Mstislav Rostropovich (cello). Serge Baudo; Witold Lutoslawski (c). Paris Orchestra. 1976 reissue.
EMI 49304 ADD 53:00

★★*Awards:* The Want List 1988, *Fanfare* N/D '88 (Royal S. Brown). Critics' Choice 1988, *Gramophone* D '88 (Arnold Whittall).

"These are definitive performances."
Musical America 108:55 N '88. Paul Moor (275w)

"One of the most important releases ever of contemporary music has now appeared on a magnificently recorded compact disc that reproduces both the solo instrument and the various orchestral components with stunning clarity and fullness."
Fanfare 11:157-8 Jl/Ag '88. Royal S. Brown (425w)

Gramophone 65:1590 My '88. Arnold Whittall (200w)

2059. L'Arbre de Songes, for Violin and Orchestra. MAXWELL DAVIES, PETER. Concerto for Violin and Orchestra.
Isaac Stern (vln). Lorin Maazel; Andre Previn (c). French National Orchestra; Royal Philharmonic Orchestra. Salle Wagram, Paris, Walthamstow Town Hall, Loudon. 1985, 1986.
CBS 42449 DDD 56:00

✔HC ★★★*Awards:* The Want List 1988, *Fanfare* N/D '88 (Royal S. Brown, Paul A. Snook). Critics' Choice 1988, *Gramophone* D '88 (Arnold Whittall).

"The recording brings the listener right up close and personal....Stern demonstrates clearly the formal and aesthetic differences between the two works."
Music Magazine 11:41-2 S/O '88. Alan Gasser (710w)

"*L'Arbre des Songes* receives an incredibly intense, committed performance...supported by brilliant playing from France's Orchestre National...and by some of the warmest, richest, and fullest sound I have yet heard on CD."
Fanfare 11:100-101 Mr/Ap '88. Royal S. Brown (560w)

"Isaac Stern is at the top of his form in both performances, as are the two orchestras and conductors and the CBS production team."
Stereo Review 53:99 Ap '88. Richard Freed (450w)

"Stern and Maazel's performance is exemplary, more committed and passionate, I feel, than the excellent live performances given by the soloist with Rattle/CBSO last December, and the recording, though not of the highest standards to which CBS now aspire..is very clear and atmospheric."
Hi-Fi News & Record Review 33:95 My '88. Hugh Canning (550w)

"In both concertos, Stern sounds better that I have heard him in years."
High Fidelity 38:55+ My '88. K. Robert Schwarz (475w)

"It is impossible to imagine more imaginative performances or finer recorded sound than on this CBS release...Recommended with all possible enthusiasm."
American Record Guide 51:25-6 My/Je '88. Arved Ashby (275w)

"Though very different in style and form, these lyrical, accessible pieces become eloquent vehicles for both composers in the hands of Stern, who brings a high degree of commitment to his usual impassioned, intuitive playing....Recording quality is good, though not distinguished....Recommended with enthusiasm."
Stereophile 11:151 Ag '88. L. Hunter Kevil (380w)

"Neither work has lived up to expectations."
HighPerformanceReview 5:76-7 D '88. John Mueter (260w)

Gramophone 65:1181 F '88. Arnold Whittall (490w)

Fanfare 11:100-102 Mr/Ap '88. Paul Snook (850w)

DVORAK, ANTONIN

2060. Concerto in A minor for Violin and Orchestra, Opus 53; Romance in F minor for Violin and Orchestra, Opus 11; Carnival Overture, Opus 92.
Midori (vln). Zubin Mehta (c). New York Philharmonic Orchestra.
CBS 44923 DDD 53:00

✔HC ★*Awards:* Top Disks of the Year, *New York Times* D 24 '89 (John Rockwell).

"Compared with Kyung-Wha Chung's recent Angel recording of the Dvorak concerto and romance, Midori takes a decidedly more extroverted view of both works. Her playing of the concerto's first movement is volatile and brilliant....The familiar *Carnival* Overture, which gets no more than a smart run-through at the end of the program, seems tacked on simply to give the buyer more music for the money."
Stereo Review 55:130 Ja '90. David Hall (200w)

"She conjures up a surging, fiery emotive force, swelling and receding in a blaze of passion. Her ability to convey a variety of moods is due to an unusual timbral range—one that extends from hushed, breathy restraint to throbbing, focused intensity. And she revels in the joy of the long Romantic line, spinning out phrases in beautifully shaped arches."

Musical America 110:72 Mr '90. K. Robert Schwarz (305w)

"Her sound is exquisitely beautiful, never edgy or forced but brilliant when appropriate....All the Allegro giocoso finale [of the concerto] requires is consummate technique that allows the violinist and the listener to smile rather than wince, which is why both Midori and Chung succeed (as does Perlman) where most others have failed hopelessly. CBS has done better than usual with sound quality on this disc, giving Midori a natural presence and the New York Philharmonic an unaccustomed roundness to its sonority."

American Record Guide 53:45 Mr/Ap '90. Alan Heatherington (525w)

"Midori, one of the most technically polished of the younger crop of violin virtuosos, displays more personality in this recording than in her Paganini concerto for Philips....In a field of CD performances ranging from the overstuffed (Stern and Mintz) to the astringent (Ricci), I can't say Midori outranks Suk/Ancerl on Fidelio or Milstein on EMI, but I do think she equals Perlman and surpasses Luca. In other words, this is one of the better versions available, and is in up-to-date sound to boot. The *Romance*, reworked from a quartet movement, receives a gentle interpretation marred by some slightly sour wind playing."

Fanfare 13:170 Ja/F '90. David K. Nelson (400w)

"CBS have their soloist rather far back, giving the impression (especially in the chordal passages) that though she has a sweet and pure tone Midori is not a strong player." *P95 S85*

Hi-Fi News & Record Review 35:103 Mr '90. Kenneth Dommett (250w)

Gramophone 67:894 N '89. Edward Greenfield (245w)

ELGAR, EDWARD

2061. Concerto in E minor for Cello and Orchestra, Opus 85; Sea Pictures, Opus 38.

Jacqueline du Pre (cello); Janet Baker. John Barbirolli (c). London Symphony Orchestra. 1965 reissue. EMI 47329 AAD 54:04

✔**HC** ★*Awards:* Records to Die for: 1 of 5 Recommended Recordings, *Stereophile* Ja '91 (Peter W. Mitchell).

"Elgar wrote the greatest of all cello concertos, and this performance is one of the most life-affirming musical events ever committed to disc, thanks to a pairing of the old master Barbirolli with the sparkling young du Pre in her prime. Even the LSO seems energized by the occasion."

Stereophile 14:159 Ja '91. Peter W. Mitchell (b.n.)

2062. Concerto in E minor for Cello and Orchestra, Opus 85. BLOCH, ERNEST. Schelomo—Hebrew Rhapsody for Cello and Orchestra.

Steven Isserlis (cello). Richard Hickox (c). London Symphony Orchestra. VIRGIN 90735 DDD 51:00

★★*Awards:* Critics' Choice 1989, *Gramophone* D '89 (Edward Seckerson); The Year's Best, *Hi Fi News & Record Review*, May '90 Supplement. *Hi-Fi News & Record Review* Record of the Month, Jl '89.

"I am impressed by his musicianship and straightforward, economical, though eloquent, rhetorical style....Artistically and sonically...it's hard to avoid giving this recording top marks."

American Record Guide 53:47 Mr/Ap '90. John P. McKelvey (225w)

"Isserlis and Hickox take a grave, perhaps too grave view of the Elgar....The Bloch *Schelomo*...fiendishly difficult from a technical point of view...is a thoroughly rewarding work."

New Hi-Fi Sound 6:101 Ag '89. Jonathan Kettle (280w)

"Isserlis may, at times, be slightly more self-conscious than Du Pre; but no other post-Du Pre performance of this increasingly popular work has so thoroughly captured the music's evasive shimmers, its subtle oscillations between the resigned and the defiant (in the finale especially), between the full-bodied and the rarefied, between the assured and the self-obliterating."

Fanfare 13:177-79 Mr/Ap '90. Peter J. Rabinowitz (200w)

"Steven Isserlis is an exceptional cellist, and his account of Elgar's autumnal masterpiece may be the finest on disc....*Schelomo*, however, is another matter—not because of Isserlis, who plays beautifully, but because Hickox and the orchestra are simply too restrained for this florid piece of musical slush."

Musical America 110:72 My '90. David Hurwitz (180w)

"Under Hickox, there is some magnificent and committed playing, a nice transparency of texture...Yet this is clearly Isserlis's record: it's another performance which shows his rare sensitivity and musicianship....I think some readers will find Steven Isserlis's Elgar very understated—but not undercharacterised....What is readily apparent is the admirable differentiation between the sound-worlds of the two composers."

Hi-Fi News & Record Review 34:77 Jl '89. Christopher Breunig (1000w)

P100 S100

Hi-Fi News & Record Review p.9 My '90 Supplement. Christopher Breunig (1020w)

Gramophone 67:172+ Jl '89. Edward Seckerson (700w)

2063. Concerto in B minor for Violin and Orchestra, Opus 61.

Nigel Kennedy (vln). Vernon Handley (c). London Philharmonic Orchestra.
EMI 47210

★★★**Awards:** *Stereo Review* Best of the Month, Ja '86; *Gramophone* Record Award Winner 1985—Concerto Award and Record of the Year. Record of the Eighties, *Gramophone*, D '89 (Edward Seckerson).

"More than any other I have heard, this recording probes to the core of the work's poetic essence....The recorded sound is surpassingly rich in both body and detail."

Stereo Review 51:71-2 Ja '86. David Hall (400w)

"Despite gorgeous passages, it can turn long-winded and saccharine....The abundance of emotion requires a soloist who will throw himself into Elgar's world with unrepentant Romanticism yet always beware of overwhelming the music with too much feeling. Violinist Nigel Kennedy...is just such a performer-....Kennedy's Elgar is not likely to be surpassed for years to come."

High Fidelity 36:61 Jl '86. K. Robert Schwarz (430w)

"I'm not about to give up my copy of the Menuhin/Elgar performance—nor, for that matter, the Perlman...But if I had to choose a single modern performance to live with, it would be this new one by Kennedy. Highest recommendations."

Fanfare 9:136 Ja/F '86. Peter J. Rabinowitz (500w)

"More than the Cello Concerto, the one for violin forces the soloist to cover a wide emotional range, and this Kennedy cannot manage....The London Philharmonic Orchestra...plays smoothly but with no particular subtlety, and the recorded sound is shallow and boxy."

Ovation 9:38 Ap '88. Michael Fleming (150w)

Gramophone 63:784 D '85. Edward Greenfield (175w)

Digital Audio 2:25 Ja '86. David Vernier (300w)

The New York Times My 29 '88, p. H23. John Rockwell (400w)

Hi-Fi News & Record Review 31:109 Ap '86. Edward Seckerson (55w)

EYBLER, JOSEPH LEOPOLD EDLER VON. Concerto in B flat for Clarinet and Orchestra. See No. 2084.

FASCH, JOHANN FRIEDRICH. Concertos: in B flat for Chalumeau, Orchestra and Continuo; in D for Trumpet, 2 Oboes, Strings, and Continuo; in D for Triple Ensemble. See No. 1145.

GERSHWIN, GEORGE

2064. Rhapsody in Blue, for Piano and Orchestra; Concerto for Piano and Orchestra in F; An American in Paris.
Andre Previn (pno). Andre Previn (c). Pittsburgh Symphony Orchestra.
PHILIPS 412 611

✔**HC** ★**Awards:** Perfect 10/10, *Digital Audio*, Mr '88; Record of the Eighties, *Gramophone*, D '89 (Edward Greenfield).

"The *Rhapsody* sounds oddly unfamiliar after the plethora of 'authentic' versions, but the Piano Concerto, with its joyously bluesy adagio...must take pride of place on CD. The transplanted *American* also sparkles, with an even more idiomatic reading than the Cincinnati Orchestra under Kunzel."

Hi-Fi News & Record Review 31:107 Ja '86. John Atkinson (175w)

Ovation 6:26 Ja '86. John Von Rhein (425w)

Gramophone 63:620 N '86. (560w)

GLAZUNOV, ALEXANDER. Concerto in A minor for Violin and Orchestra, Opus 82. See No. 2141.

GOULD, MORTON. Concerto for Viola and Orchestra. See No. 1152.

GRIEG, EDVARD. Concerto in A minor for Piano and Orchestra, Opus 16. See No. 2136, 2146, 4108.

GRIFFES, CHARLES TOMLINSON. Poem for Flute and Orchestra. See No. 1158.

GUBAIDULINA, SOFIA

2065. Offertorium (Concerto for Violin and Orchestra); Hommage a T. S. Eliot, for Octet and Soprano.
Gidon Kremer (vln); Christine Whittlesey (sop); Isabelle Van Keulen (vln); Tabea Zimmermann (vla); David Geringas (cello); Alois Posch (dbl bass); Eduard Brunner (clar); Klaus Thunemann (bsn); Radovan Vlatkovic (horn). Charles Dutoit (c). Boston Symphony Orchestra.
DEUTSCHE GRAMMOPHON 427 336 DDD 69:00

★★★**Awards:** The Want List 1990, *Fanfare* N/D '90 (William Wians). Top Disks of the Year, *The New York Times* D 24, '89 (John Rockwell); Best CD of the Month, *Digital Audio's CD Review*, F '90. Editors' Choice, *Digital Audio's CD Review*, 6:34 Je '90; Cream of the Crop IV, *Digital Audio's CD Review*, 6:41 Je '90.

"Although there are many hints of tonality in Gubaidulina's *Offertorium* the most pervasive influence at its opening is that of Lutoslawski-....the music is never less than inventive....it all adds up to a performance that grows more impressive with each hearing....The *Hommage a TS Eliot* is altogether more testing—an impression exaggerated by the slightly drier recording." *P95 S95/85*

Hi-Fi News & Record Review 34:87 S '89. Simon Cargill (300w)

"Sofia Gubaidulina (born 1931) was one of the most interesting Soviet composers discovered by the audiences at the 'Making Music Together' festival put together by Sarah Caldwell in Boston two years ago. This is the first

recording of any of her music to come my way, and it presents her in the very strongest light....Both works receive the most committed, eloquent, altogether impressive performances a composer could wish, and they have been superbly recorded."
Stereo Review 55:130+ Ja '90. Richard Freed (465w)

"This release commands attention for two reasons: Sofia Gubaidulina, in recent years, has established herself as probably the most important female composer in history, and this impressive recording recently won the International Record Critics' Association's Koussevitzky prize annually awarded the best first recording of a contemporary work....You will find her full of surprises. She ranges from rock-solid tonality to the latest western compositional wrinkles and instrumental innovations-....Both works get the sort of performances composers dream about but all too rarely enjoy."
Fanfare 13:191 Ja/F '90. Paul Moor (375w)

"Strongly recommended."
Fanfare 13:191-92 Ja/F '90. John Wiser (650w)

"Both her orchestral and chamber music seem to emanate from a single source, a well-spring of uncompromising spirituality, both personal and universal....Kremer brings to *Offertorium* the same blistering intensity and intellectual rigor that infuse his interpretations of even the most hackneyed repertory items....Kremer's friends from the Lockenhaus festival—especially Christine Whittlesey, with her soaring soprano—contribute a similarly impassioned, focused performance of *Hommage a T.S. Eliot.*"
Musical America 110:76-7 My '90. K. Robert Schwarz (330w)

"Many seem to hear great significance in these two works. They educed in me the wish that Sofia Gubaidulina would doff the emperor's new academicisms and put her obvious gifts to more personal, musically significant use. It must be said that these performances radiate supreme dedication to the cause, and DG's sound is impeccable."
American Record Guide 54:53 Ja/F '91. Arved Ashby (280w)

Digital Audio's CD Review 6:50 F '90. David Vernier (500w)

Gramophone 67:454 S '89. Michael Oliver (545w)

HANSON, HOWARD

2066. Fantasy Variations on a Theme of Youth, for Piano and String Orchestra; Symphony No. 3, Opus 33; Symphony No. 6.
Carol Rosenberger (pno); Michael Crusoe (tymp); Randolph Baunton (snare drums); Howard Gilbert (snare drums). Gerard Schwarz (c). New York Chamber Symphony Orchestra; Seattle Symphony Orchestra.
DELOS 3092 DDD 68:00

★★*Awards:* The Want List 1991, *Fanfare* N/D '91 (Walter Simmons). The Highs, 1990, *The New York Times* D 30 '90 (John Rockwell).

"The performances of both the Third and the Sixth by the Seattle Symphony are superbly executed, with passionate conviction, and the recorded sound is excellent."
Stereo Review 56:85+ My '91. David Hall (325w)

"If you're one of those who has been turned off by the modern music you've heard but would still like to find some you can both understand and enjoy, Delos's Great American Composers series may well fill the bill....As usual, Schwarz and his musicians acquit themselves admirably and the recorded sound is airy and transparent, marred only by an occasional stridency, particularly during full-tilt tuttis."
Stereophile 14:175 My '91. Gordon Emerson (410w)

"Philips has begun to reissue the composer's own Eastman performances on mid-priced CDs...those composer-conducted performances, most of which originally appeared during the 1950s, are excellent renditions, as well as landmarks of recording technology. Listeners who are new to Hanson and are interested in saving a few dollars or are inclined toward 'composer-authenticated' performances are assured that there is no reason to avoid those reissues. On the other hand, older listeners who know the Hanson symphonies primarily through the Eastman performances will welcome the perspective offered by Schwarz's fresh new interpretations, as well as the increased richness and depth of the sonic aspect....All three works are sympathetically interpreted, stunningly performed, and beautifully recorded. I found this to be an even more satisfying release than its predecessor."
Fanfare 14:211-12 Ja/F '91. Walter Simmons (875w)

"The playing of the Seattle Symphony is superb on the new disc, so my few criticisms are directed at the conductor."
American Record Guide 54:54-5 Ja/F '91. John Landis (480w)

"This set "is pleasant, rather than otherwise, and has a few moments of genuine drama but adds little to our general knowledge of Hanson's work or its stature." *P95 S95*
Hi-Fi News & Record Review 36:73 S '91. Kenneth Dommett (brief)

Gramophone 68:1504+ F '91. Edward Seckerson (455w)

Musical America 110:20+ N '90. K. Robert Schwarz (535w)

HAYDN, FRANZ JOSEPH

2067. Concerti (2) in C and D for Cello and Orchestra.
Heinrich Schiff (cello). Neville Marriner (c). Academy of St. Martin-in-the-Fields.
PHILIPS 420 923 DDD 47:13

"With Sir Neville and the Academy providing limpid, fresh-toned accompaniments with much felicitous detail, and the Philips production team offering a bright, forward recording that enhances the performances, this is a clear winner."
Hi-Fi News & Record Review 34:98 F '89. Peter Branscombe (220w)

"Heinrich Schiff's playing in both the standard-repertoire D major and recently discovered C major...concertos is restrained and refined, with light, deft bowing—he's practically skimming over the strings....he uses almost no ornamentation, which is decidedly 'out of period.' Also, in the the C major concerto, his cadenza does not work as well as the one Haydn provided....The Academy of St. Martin, under the ever-reliable baton of Maestro Marriner, provides its usual rock-solid accompaniment to the soloist, with a light, clear sound."
HighPerformanceReview 6:77 Mr '89. D. C. Culbertson (160w)

"The warm but crisply clear sonics with which Philips endows their Academy recordings lends an immediacy to these performances that sets off Schiff's virile attacks and pointed phrases to great advantage....These are some of the most highly polished and exciting readings this reviewer has heard lately."
American Record Guide 52:54 My/Je '89. David W. Moore (75w)

"These are self-assured, no-nonsense, and somewhat impersonal readings, aided considerably by Marriner's skilled voicing of wind chords. The digital sound is a bit harsh....I think Schiff will wear better than Maisky, however, and this recording is recommended."
Fanfare 12:175-76 Ja/F '89. David K. Nelson (175w)

Gramophone 66:776 N '88. Hilary Finch (265w)

2068. Concerto No. 1 in D for Horn and Orchestra; Symphony No. 31 in D, "Horncall". HAYDN, MICHAEL. Concerto in D for Horn and Orchestra.
Anthony Halstead (natural horn). Roy Goodman (c). Hanover Band.
NIMBUS 5190 DDD 61:00

✔HC ★*Awards:* Critic's Choice: 1990, *American Record Guide* Ja/F '91 (Barry Kilpatrick).

"Scintillating horn playing, mostly from Anthony Halstead and his natural horn...Each concerto is enjoyable, but the two together make it eminently clear why it is Franz Joseph we have come to revere rather than Joseph Michael."
Fanfare 13:198-99 Ja/F '90. James H. North (240w)

"Halstead has a distinguished performance record...His performances here are so good that the concerto by Michael Haydn is just as fascinating as the one by his more skillful brother. It's not slick and elegant playing. Halstead plays with flair, verve, grit and determination—every note and phrase has character."
American Record Guide 53:52-3 Ja/F '90. Barry Kilpatrick (360w)

"Anthony Halstead's handling of the valveless horn in Joseph Haydn's Concerto is remarkably accomplished....Michael Haydn's 'Concerto' (probably three movements from an unidentified serenade) is less spectacular but just as demanding. The Hanover Band is excellent in its accompanying role, and the driving force of the first movement of the Symphony is admirably conveyed."
Music and Musicians International 39:44 S '90. Robert Dearling (240w)

"Anthony Halstead plays the concertos with considerable panache and deft control on a natural horn, equally at home when scaling the heights and plumbing the depths....The recording though clean and well balanced is quite close, and for my taste over-resonant—it suggests too large a scale for music of the 1760s and '70s." *P95 S85*
Hi-Fi News & Record Review 34:101+ N '89. Peter Branscombe (175w)

The Musical Times 130:751 D '89. Lindsay Kemp (295w)

Gramophone 67:897 N '89. Nicholas Anderson (420w)

2069. Concerto in E flat for Trumpet and Orchestra; Concerto in C for Clavier and Orchestra, H.XVIII, No. 2; Concerto No. 1 in D for Horn and Orchestra.
Friedemann Immer (tpt); Christopher Hogwood (chamber orgn); Timothy Brown (horn). Christopher Hogwood (c). Academy of Ancient Music. 1986-87.
OISEAU-LYRE 417 610 DDD 53:00

★*Awards:* Critics' Choice 1988, *Gramophone* D '88 (Stanley Sadie).

"Here is a fascinating and convincing demonstration of the efficacy of performing early classical concertos on authentic instruments....The AAM is in top form, the recording...has plenty of presence and natural warmth, textures beautifully clear and precisely weighted."
Hi-Fi News & Record Review 33:101 Mr '88. Peter Branscombe (250w)

"An engagingly adventurous disc and a nice retrospective on Haydn."
Fanfare 11:174-5 Jl/Ag '88. Edward Strickland (220w)

"The sound is first-rate, and these are, in the end, acceptable performances. But this is repertory in which I would opt for modern instruments, at least for the present."

High Fidelity 38:64 Ag '88. Christopher Rothko (320w)

Gramophone 65:1076 Ja '88. Stanley Sadie (445w)

Digital Audio 5:78+ N '88. Tom Vernier (230w)

HAYDN, MICHAEL. Concerto in D for Horn and Orchestra. See No. 2068.

HEADINGTON, CHRISTOPHER

2070. Concerto for Violin and Orchestra. STRAUSS, RICHARD. Concerto for Violin and Orchestra.

Xue Wei (vln). Jane Glover (c). London Philharmonic Orchestra.
ASV 780 DDD 63:00

★★*Awards:* Critics' Choice 1991, *Gramophone*, Ja '92 (Richard Osborne). Pick of the Month, *Gramophone*, D '91 (Christie Barter).

"This first recording of Christopher Headington's glorious Violin Concerto will give great pleasure to many music lovers...Xue-Wei's playing in both works is ravishing, the London Philharmonic sounds wonderful, and the recorded sound is splendid. Congratulations to all—and let's have more Headington soon!."

American Record Guide 55:75 Mr/Ap '92. Mark L. Lehman (long)

"This is the Strauss concerto's first outing in a long time; performance and recording are superior to a decades-old one by Caroll Glenn, the only other I know....Once again Xue-Wei plays gorgeously [in the Headington concerto], never losing his lustrous tone. This disc should please both fiddle fanciers and repertoire-oriented collectors; I welcome it on both counts."

Fanfare 15:213-4 Mr/Ap '92. James H. North (long)

Gramophone 69:71 D '91.Michael Jameson (med)

HINDEMITH, PAUL

2071. Concerto for Horn and Orchestra. STRAUSS, RICHARD. Concerto No. 1 in E flat for Horn and Orchestra, Opus 11; Concerto No. 2 in E flat for Horn and Orchestra.

Dennis Brain (horn). Paul Hindemith; Wolfgang Sawallisch (c). Philharmonia Orchestra. reissue 1957, 1959.
EMI 47834 ADD (m) 53:21

✔HC ★*Awards:* *Fanfare* Want List 1987 (John D. Wiser).

"The legendary reputation Dennis Brain left behind...is splendidly confirmed on this disc."

Ovation 8:37-38 Je '87 Paul Turok (120w)

"I can't imagine anyone wanting a different recording of these concertos: Dennis Brain is the acknowledged master of his instrument, and these remastered performances sound, not up-to-date, but remarkably solid and forthright."

Fanfare 10:188 Jl/Ag '87 Michael Ullman (125w)

"I believe the Strauss works were once reissued in electronic stereo—I'm glad to say that this remastering is more wholesomely faithful to my well-worn second-hand copy of them."

Hi-Fi News & Record Review 32:141 D '87. David Nice (270w)

Digital Audio 4:68 N '87. Andrew Taylor (450w)

Gramophone 65:580 O '87 Alan Sanders (315w)

Concerto for Horn and Orchestra (1949). See No. 1188.

Der Schwanendreher, for Viola and Orchestra. See No. 1187.

HUMMEL, JOHANN NEPOMUK

2072. Concerto in A minor for Piano and Orchestra, Opus 85; Concerto in B minor for Piano and Orchestra, Opus 89.

Stephen Hough (pno). Bryden Thomson (c). English Chamber Orchestra.
CHANDOS 8507; MUSICAL HERITAGE 512071 DDD 66:18

✔HC ★*Awards:* *Gramophone* Concerto Award, 1987.

"If the English go on producing pianists of this quality to play the neglected masterworks of Hummel throughout this anniversary year and beyond, I will go on shouting their praises....It is a splendid performance of two of the greatest piano concertos ever written....Bryden Thomson does his best conducting to date on this recording. Everything about it is auspicious."

Fanfare 11:221-4 S/O '87. David Johnson (1950w)

"Both concertos are expertly played...with superlative accompaniments...The reproduction is extraordinarily fine."

High Fidelity 37:72 O '87. Robert E. Benson (190w)

"Stephen Hough is at least as good as Martin Galling, but has a heavier touch....The A minor, with its tricky, jazzy rhythms, is especially well done."

American Record Guide 51:47 Mr/Ap '88. Donald R. Vroon (315w)

"Sparkling performance."

Hi-Fi News & Record Review 32:96 Je '87 (55w); 32:97 My '87 (225w) (rev. of LP). Peter Branscombe

Gramophone 64:1412 Ap '87 Lionel Salter (320w)

IRELAND, JOHN

2073. Concerto in E flat for Piano and Orchestra. BRIDGE, FRANK. Phantasm for Piano and Orchestra. WALTON, WILLIAM. Sinfo-

nia Concertante for Piano and Orchestra (original version).
Kathryn Stott (pno). Vernon Handley (c). Royal Philharmonic Orchestra.
CONIFER 175 DDD 70:00

★***Awards:*** Best of the Month, *Hi-Fi News & Record Review*, Mr '90; The Year's Best, *Hi Fi News & Record Review*, May '90 Supplement.

"This is one of the most stimulating and, at the same time, emotionally compelling piano concertante discs issued in years....Do NOT miss it!"

American Record Guide 53:77-8 S/O '90. Thomas L. Dixon (185w)

"*Phantasm*...A forgotten masterpiece if ever I heard one. It receives a performance here which can only be described as magnificent, a term which applies to the whole of this disc." *P100 S100*

Hi-Fi News & Record Review 35:105+ Mr '90 (490w); p.23 My '90 Supplement (525w). Andrew Achenbach (490w)

Gramophone 67:1321 Ja '90. Michael Kennedy (350w)

"One expects fine performances from Vernon Handley and the Royal Philharmonic, and both are right on form this time....all these performances are excellent, and the sound is as clear, natural, and wide-range as any audiophile could wish. Strongly recommended."

Fanfare 13:341-42 My/Je '90. Robert McColley (480w)

JONGEN, JOSEPH

2074. Symphonie Concertante for Organ and Orchestra. FRANCK, CESAR. Fantaisie in A for Organ.
Michael Murray (orgn). Edo De Waart (c). San Francisco Symphony Orchestra.
TELARC 80096

★***Awards:*** *Fanfare* Want List 1985 (Haig Mardirosian).

"Murray, de Waart, and the San Francisco Symphony obviously enjoy what they are doing and they do it superbly. Telarc's engineer, Jack Renner, has given us a superlative disc of demonstration quality."

American Record Guide 48:66 Ja '85. Carl Bauman (300w)

Fanfare 8:183 Ja/F '85. Haig Mardirosian (405w)

Ovation 6:34-5 N '85. Scott Cantrell (470w)

Gramophone 62:1064 Mr '85. Ivan March (335w)

Audio 69:126 Je '85. Bert Whyte (460w)

LEBRUN, LUDWIG AUGUST. Concerto No. 1 in D minor for Oboe and Orchestra. See No. 2056.

LISZT, FRANZ

2075. Concerti (2) for Piano and Orchestra; Fantasy on Hungarian Folk Tunes for Piano and Orchestra.
Barry Douglas (pno). Jun'ichi Hirokami (c). London Symphony Orchestra.
RCA 7916 DDD 54:00

★***Awards:*** Best Recordings of the Month, *Stereo Review* S '90.

"What it brings to my mind is the all-too-short career of the British pianist Solomon, who was equally master of the intellectual peaks of the repertory and of its bravura showpieces. That Douglas, an Irishman, has a similar potential is well demonstrated in this program....The excellence of the musicianship is enhanced by the recording, in which piano and orchestra are captured in a single acoustic perspective, with no sense of the piano's being in your lap."

Stereo Review 55:100 S '90. David Hall (400w)

"I haven't heard all the versions of these concertos in the listings, but this offering is at the top of my list, and is in fact one of the finest concerto recordings I've ever heard."

American Record Guide 54:73 My/Je '91. John P. McKelvey (400w)

"Both Concertos are given clear-sighted and vigorous performances though they lack the scintillating bravura and poetic fancy that made Krystian Zimerman's recent DG versions so memorable....there is too little personal involvement or poetic commitment....although the *Hungarian Fantasy* is more urgently propelled and realized, it is difficult to see these performances as competitive....the recordings are generally smooth and refined." *P75 S95/85*

Hi-Fi News & Record Review 35:92 Ag '90. Bryce Morrison (325w)

"Only briefly, in the *Hungarian* Fantasy, does his power translate into pounding, perhaps in response to Hirokami's square conducting. But generally, these are excitingly fluent interpretations, with the pianist moving easily between thundering octaves and gracefully articulated elegance."

Jazziz 8:82 Ja '91. Susan Elliott (695w)

"Douglas's muscular swagger, stiffening in overbearing steeliness, is met by Hirokami with noisy overkill so that these pieces literally come apart at the seams—the rattled off episodes, rounded with orchestral flourishes, stubbornly resisting integration. The overall effect is machine-like and wearying."

Fanfare 14:275 S/O '90. Adrian Corleonis (150w)

Gramophone 68:367 Ag '90. David J. Fanning (445w)

Digital Audio's CD Review 7:66+ Ap '91. Tom Vernier (205w)

2076. Concerti (2) for Piano and Orchestra.

Sviatoslav Richter (pno). Kirill Kondrashin (c). London Symphony Orchestra. 1961.
PHILIPS 412 006 41:12

★★*Awards: American Record Guide* Overview: Romantic Piano Concertos, Jl/Ag '90. *Gramophone* Critics' Choice 1984 (Stephen Plaistow).

"It is a debatable point as to whether Philips could have got more from the master tapes than has been presented here."
Hi-Fi News & Record Review 29:137 D '84. David Prakel (105w)

Gramophone 62:747 D '84. Max Harrison (140w)

2077. Concerti (2) for Piano and Orchestra; Totentanz for Piano and Orchestra.
Krystian Zimerman (pno). Seiji Ozawa (c). Boston Symphony Orchestra.
DEUTSCHE GRAMMOPHON 423 571 DDD 56:00

✔HC ★★★★*Awards:* Critics' Choice 1988, *Gramophone* D '88 (Christopher Headington); Best Recordings of the Month, *Stereo Review* Mr '89. Top Choices—1989, *American Record Guide* Ja/F '90 (David Mulbury). *American Record Guide* Overview: Romantic Piano Concertos, Jl/Ag '90.

"Music-making on the highest level....Worthy of any collection."
Ovation 10:54 Mr '89. Stuart Isacoff (210w)

"The intensity and flexibility of his playing, in both its hair-raising and seductive facets, made me think of Zimerman as a sort of Mengelberg of pianists, but the Mengelberg role is actually filled by Ozawa, in perhaps the most sympathetic partnering any conductor has provided in recordings of these works, and the Boston Symphony is in absolutely glorious form. The recording itself represents a high mark for DG-....A triumphant and irresistible record."
Stereo Review 54:105 Mr '89. Richard Freed (575w)

"One's response is less visceral than 'appreciative'...Nice try."
Fanfare 12:201 Mr/Ap '89. Adrian Corleonis (100w)

"This is the finest of all CD versions of the two Liszt Concertos, with the added bonus of the *Totentanz*....Pianistically only Richter in his legendary Philips recording...commands such intrepid virtuosity though Zimerman is more characterful, more vividly and teasingly alive to every facet of Liszt's poetry and barnstorming theatricality."
Music and Musicians International 37:58 Ap '89. Bryce Morrison (210w)

"Zimerman's...Liszt is technically astonishing-....Ozawa and the Boston Symphony provide ideal accompaniments...Deutsche Grammophon's sound...is excellent. Despite the fact that most collectors will already own various versions of most, if not all, of this music, these performances deserve the highest recommendation."
High Fidelity 39:64 Je '89. David Hurwitz (275w)

"Krystian Zimerman...turns out to be a phenomenally persuasive Lisztian, going all out in the grand manner and obviously relishing every sweeping phrase. Seiji Ozawa, with his orchestra in brilliant form, doesn't just 'accompnay' but takes part in a real give-and-take...exceptionally vivid, well-balanced sound."
Stereo Review Presents: Compact Disc Buyers' Guide Summ 1989 p.58 Richard Freed (120w)

Gramophone 66:776 N '88. Christopher Headington (350w)

"This is an explosively brilliant recording on every count....Zimerman is one of the premier pianists of our time. A highly recommended CD and surely one of the year's outstanding releases."
American Record Guide 52:70 S/O '89. David G. Mulbury (320w)

"The two Concerto performances lie at the opposite pole from Arrau's, with LSO/Davis. They have a nervous energy, with a mix of ravishing refinement and near-mannerism, where Arrau's readings are I think too dignified and reposeful. What makes the DG less than comfortable is the excessive 'help' given by the production team."
Hi-Fi News & Record Review 34:107 Ja '89. Christopher Breunig (280w)

Concerto No. 1 in E flat for Piano and Orchestra. See No. 2053.

LITOLFF, HENRY CHARLES. Concerto Symphonique No. 4 in D minor for Piano and Orchestra, Opus 102: Scherzo. See No. 2126.

LOCATELLI, PIETRO ANTONIO

2078. Concerti (12) for Violin, Strings and Continuo with 24 Caprices Ad Libitum, Opus 3, "L'Arte del Violino": No. 1 in D; No. 2 in C minor; No. 3 in F.
(Volume 1).
Diego Conti (vln). I Virtuosi Dell'Accademia.
RODOLPHE 32513 DDD 56:35

✔HC ★*Awards:* Critics' Choice 1990, *Gramophone* D '90 (John Duarte).

"An auspicious start for a welcome project-...The sound is good....Recommended to aficionados of the fiddle and those who sport a musical peruke."
Fanfare 13:238 S/O '89. Nils Anderson (300w)

"No period instruments here, but music that sings....Crisp, clean recording. Everyone who buys this is keeping the true authenticity alive."
American Record Guide 52:75 N/D '89. Donald R. Vroon (125w)

Gramophone 67:1610 Mr '90. John Duarte (420w)

LUTOSLAWSKI, WITOLD

2079. Concerto for Cello and Orchestra; Dance Preludes (5) for Clarinet, Harp, Piano, Percussion and Strings; Concerto for Oboe, Harp and Chamber Orchestra.
Heinrich Schiff (cello); Eduard Brunner (clar); Heinz Holliger (oboe); Ursula Holliger (harp). Witold Lutoslawski (c). Bavarian Radio Symphony Orchestra. Herkulessaal, Munich. January 1986.
PHILIPS 416 817 DDD 52:00

★*Awards:* First Place Contemporary Composer Mumm Champagne Classical Music Award 1988—Presented by *Ovation, Ovation* N '88.

"All three works, however you may respond to them personally, are given performances of unique authority and vitality."
Stereo Review 52:188 N '87. Richard Freed (230w)

"The performances here are brilliant, the recording noiseless and exquisitely transparent-...The Holligers play flawlessly, Brunner's clarinet tone is rich and jubilant."
Fanfare 11:169-70 N/D '87. Kyle Gann (325w)

"Personally, I prefer the original EMI recording of the Cello Concerto, with Rostropovich and the composer, but this new version is at least currently on sale and is a very impressive piece of work from all concerned."
Music and Musicians International 36:50-1 N '87. Robert Matthew-Walker (135w)

"Competing versions of all three can be had, but the excellent performances, ideal sonics, and career-spanning, all-Lutoslawski program make this the clear winner in each case."
Opus 4:44-5 F '88. Andrew Stiller (390w)

Gramophone 65:296 Ag '87 Arnold Whittall (315w)

Concerto for Cello and Orchestra. See No. 2058.

2080. Partita for Violin, Orchestra and Obbligato Piano. STRAVINSKY, IGOR. Concerto in D for Violin and Orchestra.
Anne-Sophie Mutter (vln); Phillip Moll (pno). Witold Lutoslawski; Paul Sacher (c). BBC Symphony Orchestra; Philharmonia Orchestra. 1988.
DEUTSCHE GRAMMOPHON 423 696 DDD 56:00

✔HC ★★★*Awards:* Editors' Choice, *Digital Audio's CD Review*, Je '89; Best CD of the Month *Digital Audio's CD Review*, Ag '89. The Want List 1989, *Fanfare* N/D '89 (William Zagorski); Critics' Choice 1989, *Gramophone* D '89 (Arnold Whittall). Cream of the Crop IV, *Digital Audio's CD Review*, 6:43 Je '90.

"So flexible and fiery are Mutter's performances that one feels she lives and breathes this music, much as a gypsy fiddler lives and breathes his demonic improvisations."
High Fidelity 39:61-2 Jl '89. K. Robert Schwarz (315w)

"A highly recommended disc."
Fanfare 12:261-63 Jl/Ag '89. David K. Nelson (370w)

Digital Audio's CD Review 5:58+ Ag '89. David Vernier (380w)

Gramophone 66:1282-84 F '89. Arnold Whittall (450w)

MARTINU, BOHUSLAV

2081. Sinfonietta Giocosa, for Piano and Small Orchestra. SUK, JOSEF. Serenade in E flat for String Orchestra, Opus 6.
Dennis Hennig (pno). Charles Mackerras (c). Australian Chamber Orchestra.
CONIFER 170 DDD 59:00

★*Awards:* Critics' Choice 1989, *Gramophone* D '89 (Edward Seckerson).

"This is a truly delightful performance...Altogether a treasurable disc."
The Musical Times 130:752 D '89. Nigel Simeone (120w)

"Mackerras's antipodean dealings with Josef Suk the elder and Bohuslav Martinu makes an elegant, uncommonly illuminating coupling-....Conifer's recording is transparent, generous in ambience. Mackerras demonstrates here, not for the first time, that it isn't absolutely essential to be any kind of Czech to get the music right. Strongly recommended!"
Fanfare 13:319 Ja/F '90. John Wiser (325w)

"Conifer's remasterings strike a sensible compromise between the pure transcriptions of sizzly 78s favored by Pearl and the excessive noise-reduction of other labels. The voice emerges clearly and vividly."
American Record Guide 54:177-78 Mr/Ap '91. Ralph V. Lucano (210w)

"The Serenade...receives a rapt performance full of subtlety and light....This lively and idiomatic performance...admirably played by Dennis Hennig, admirably fills a gap in the Martinu CD catalogue with a recording that is well balanced and fresh-sounding." *P95 S95*
Hi-Fi News & Record Review 34:115 O '89. Kenneth Dommett (210w)

"These are good performances. They just don't efface the memories of others."
American Record Guide 53:94-5 Ja/F '90. Carl Bauman (230w)

Gramophone 67:304 Ag '89. Edward Seckerson (525w)

The New York Times O 15 '89, p. H 29+. Richard Freed (195w)

MAXWELL DAVIES, PETER

Concerto for Trumpet and Orchestra. See No. 2035.

Concerto for Violin and Orchestra. See No. 2059.

MENDELSSOHN, FELIX. Concerto in E minor for Violin and Orchestra, Opus 64. See No. 2024, 2026, 2048, 2115, 2148, 2149.

MERCADANTE, GIUSEPPE SAVERIO

2082. Concerti for Flute and Orchestra: in D; in E minor; in E.
James Galway (fl). Claudio Scimone (c). I Solisti Veneti. 1987.
RCA 7703 DDD 62:23

✔**HC** ★★★*Awards:* Perfect 10s, *Digital Audio's CD Review*, Mr '89; Editors' Choice, *Digital Audio's CD Review*, Je '89; Best of the Month, *Hi-Fi News & Record Review*, O '89. The Year's Best, *Hi Fi News & Record Review*, May '90 Supplement. Cream of the Crop IV, *Digital Audio's CD Review*, 6:42 Je '90.

"This is a record of some very ingratiating music that is so well achieved that it should win new friends for all of the performers involved—and possibly win back friends for James Galway, since it's the best I've heard from him for some time." *P100 S100*

Hi-Fi News & Record Review 34:109 O '89; p.24 My '90 Supplement. Stephen Daw (215w)

"Galway...plays everything in sight with wonderful fluency, splendid bravura, flawless intonation and warmly clear tone. I Solisti...do all that one might ask...in a brightly clear recording that, whilst it makes charming and civilised listening, may be of interest mainly to lovers of the flute—or those who prefer opera to instrumental music."

Music and Musicians International 36:35 Ag '88. John Duarte (570w)

"If the Italian music of the early 19th century (all three were written no later than 1819) is one of your interests, by all means pick this CD up."

Fanfare 12:223 N/D '88. John Ditsky (200w)

"All three of these works appeared on RCA about 1980 with Jean-Pierre Rampal as soloist and Scimone as conductor....I find both performances superb....Good though Rampal is, Galway's runs and trills are even more breathtaking."

American Record Guide 52:66-7 Ja/F '89. Carl Bauman (175w)

Digital Audio 5:36-40 Ja '89. Tom Vernier (150w)

MOERAN, ERNEST JOHN

2083. Concerto for Violin and Orchestra; Lonely Waters, for Orchestra; Whythorne's Shadow, for Orchestra.
Lydia Mordkovitch (vln). Vernon Handley (c). Ulster Orchestra.
CHANDOS 8807 DDD 49:00

★*Awards:* Best of the Month, *Hi-Fi News & Record Review*, S '90.

"A gorgeous performance of a gorgeous concerto....The playing here has just the right degree of intensity (her vibrato is never really a problem) allied to an admirable technical discipline throughout...Both orchestral miniatures here, too, have never sounded more magical than in the hands of these performers, and the Ulster Hall recording is absolutely outstanding." *P100 S100*

Hi-Fi News & Record Review 35:85+ S '90. Andrew Achenbach (280w)

"This appears to be the first recording ever of Ernest John Moeran's violin concerto...One reaches for new superlatives with which to praise it: Lydia Mordkovitch plays with technical security, idiomatic expression, and singing tone...Such dazzling playing and recording all but conceal the weakness of the piece: it sprawls....But having dutifully noted its weakness, one must add that the work nevertheless rewards repeated listenings."

Fanfare 14:284-85 N/D '90. Robert McColley (425w)

"The performances are brilliant. The Ulster Orchestra is wonderfully assured and Mordkovitch digs into her solos and plays with technical brilliance and a sense of conviction. The Chandos sound is brilliant."

American Record Guide 54:84-5 My/Je '91. Carl Bauman (300w)

"For those who would like to venture beyond the standard repertoire for violin concertos, this tuneful, folk music-inspired piece by underappreciated British composer E. J. Moeran is quite rewarding."

Audio 75:141 D '91. Bert Whyte (brief)

Gramophone 68:523 S '90. Michael Kennedy (350w)

MOZART, WOLFGANG AMADEUS

2084. Concerto in A for Clarinet and Orchestra, K.622. SUSSMAYR, FRANZ XAVER. Concerto in D for Clarinet and Orchestra. EYBLER, JOSEPH LEOPOLD EDLER VON. Concerto in B flat for Clarinet and Orchestra.
Dieter Klocker (clar). English Chamber Orchestra.
NOVALIS 150 061 DDD 62:41

★★*Awards:* The Want List 1991, *Fanfare* N/D '91 (George Chien). Critic's Choice: 1991, *American Record Guide*, Ja/F '92 (Michael Carter).

"Klocker has a history of breathing new life into obscure works, and his notes for the present disc tell us more about two nearly forgotten composers than we'll find in most reference books. The sound from Novalis is excellent. Strongly recommended."

Fanfare 14:285-7 Mr/Ap '91. George Chien (1025w)

"Dieter Klocker is a man with a mission and there seems to be no end to the rare orchestral and chamber literature unearthed by this musical archaeologist (N/D 1990, pp. 146-148). I am quite amazed at the quality of much of this esoteric repertoire. As a performer, he is above reproach....The sound is spacious, clear and natural, and has a nice focus."

American Record Guide 54:154 Jl/Ag '91. Michael Carter (310w)

2085. Concerto in A for Clarinet and Orchestra, K.622; Concerto in C for Oboe and Orchestra, K.314.

Antony Pay (clar); Michel Piguet (oboe). Christopher Hogwood (c). Academy of Ancient Music.
OISEAU-LYRE 414 339 46:48

★*Awards: Gramophone* Critics' Choice 1986 (Stephen Plaistow).

"It's no exaggeration to say that Pay's vivacious, graceful, and deeply expressive performance is as much a revelation as is the work's original version itself. One could hardly imagine the music's being more happily served."

Opus 3:40-41 Ap '87 Nancy Miller (1110w)

"With this account, Christopher Hogwood and Anthony Pay...restore the full emotional range of the music."

High Fidelity 37:59 F '87 Charles McCardell (200w)

The basset clarinet "gives the concerto a darker, more voluptuous sound...and this is without doubt the way in which the Mozart Clarinet Concerto should now be performed."

Musical America 107:62 Mr '87 Terry Teachout (210w) (rev. of LP)

In the LP review...I was a trifle hard on performance aspects and now up-rate slightly....apart from the absence of noise the CD is not a revelatory improvement."

Hi-Fi News & Record Review 31:123 My '86. Kenneth Dommett (50w)

The Musical Times 128:273-4 My '87 William Drabkin (125w) (rev. of LP)

Opus 3:49 D '86 John W. Barker (150w)

Hi-Fi News & Record Review 31:107 Mr '86. Kenneth Dommett (205w) (rev. of LP)

2086. Concerto in A for Clarinet and Orchestra, K.622; Quintet in A for Clarinet and Strings, K.581.

David Shifrin (clar). Gerard Schwarz (c). Mostly Mozart Orchestra; Chamber Music Northwest. Masonic Temple Auditorium; Rutgers Prebyterian Church, New York, New York. July, 1984; December, 1984.
DELOS 3020 63:00

"What truly distinguishes the disc is the glowing performances it contains."

Stereo Review 52:148 Ja '87 Stoddard Lincoln (110w)

"The entire disc is a gem. Not to be missed."

Ovation 8:42 Je '87 Robert Levine (400w)

"Anyone not convinced about the new scholarship will be surprised to hear in this recording (and a couple of others recently released) that the passages using the extended range of the altered clarinet sound more correct than the versions which have been performed for so many years....I never thought that I would hear anything to rival Leopold Wlach's playing of Mozart's clarinet work, but David Shifrin's performance does just that."

HighPerformanceReview 4:83 Spr '87 Ann Viles (320w)

"This release is 62 minutes and 19 seconds of sheer delight and, if it were an LP, would already be wearing out from my repeated playings....I can only recommend this disc as strongly as possible."

American Record Guide 50:47 Ja/F '87 Stephen D. Chakwin, Jr. (675w)

"These works are so beautifully played that there is a sort of dreaminess about them. Some may prefer a heartier approach...Delos's superb sound makes this CD irresistible."

High Fidelity 38:66 Ap '88. Robert R. Reilly (125w)

Gramophone 64:1265-66 Mr '87 John Warrack (210w)

2087. Concerto No. 1 in G for Flute and Orchestra, K.313; Andante in C for Flute and Orchestra, K.315; Concerto in C for Flute, Harp and Orchestra, K.299.

Susan Palma (fl); Nancy Allen (harp). Orpheus Chamber Orchestra. State University of New York, Purchase. December 1988.
DEUTSCHE GRAMMOPHON 427 677 DDD 58:00

★*Awards:* Critics' Choice 1990, *Gramophone* D '90 (Christopher Headington).

"The whole disc offers lovely playing from everyone involved...Warm, lively, well-defined sonics, too...It's a winner on all counts."

Stereo Review 55:93-4 Jl '90. Richard Freed (140w)

"How does the Orpheus Chamber Orchestra do it, anyway? Not only do they manage to perform superbly without a conductor, regardless of the repertoire, but every recording they turn out is as excellent as the one that preceded it. This all-Mozart disc is no exception...The recorded sound is good though a little dry. If you don't already have recordings of these pieces, you can't go wrong with this disc."

High Performance Review 8:79 Wtr '91/92. D. C. Culbertson (long)

"I like my Mozart played with a lot of guts and liberal helpings of vim, vigor, and vitality. Whether it is period instruments or modern, a large string section or small matters not to the writer. What does matter is that the participants be aware of the communicative factors involved in performance and endeavor to make the listener aware of them as well....[this recording gets] high marks here....Excellent recordings on all counts."

American Record Guide 53:84-5 N/D '90. Michael Carter (255w)

Gramophone 67:1610+ Mr '90. Christopher Headington (285w)

"Susan Palma's performance is lilting, bright, lissome, readily preferable to Grafenauer's more academic approach, but for all that my first choice remains Jean-Louis Beaumadier's with Jean Leber leading the Ensemble Orchestral de Marseille (Calliope CAL-9216)....However, the real triumph here is the flute and harp concerto, in large measure because of the sumptuous tone and brilliant articulation of Nancy Allen...If I continue to prefer as a first choice Francette Bartholomee's collaboration with Jean-Louis Beaumadier on the Calliope release, it is only because their interchanges are a bit more intimate, vulnerable, and ultimately involving while being no less accomplished."

Fanfare 13:204 Jl/Ag '90. Jon Tuska (320w)

Fanfare 14:70+ S/O '90. John Wiser (b.n.)

Digital Audio's CD Review 7:58 Ap '91. Tom Vernier (100w)

2088. Concerto in C for Flute, Harp and Orchestra, K.299; Concerto No. 1 in G for Flute and Orchestra, K.313; Concerto No. 2 in D for Flute and Orchestra, K.314.

Jean-Louis Beaumadier (fl); Francette Bartholomee (harp). Jean Leber (c). Marseille Ensemble Orchestra. July 1989.
CALLIOPE 9216 DDD 74:12

"I am inclined to place this Calliope disc...in the very first rank....Do not be put off by the relative unfamiliarity of these artists...They have all the magic of Marriner's early Argo recordings with the Academy, and you are certain to find this disc especially rewarding."

Fanfare 13:237-38 Mr/Ap '90. Jon Tuska (300w)

"There may not be a crying need for new versions of these works; but this release, conveniently coupling all three on one generously filled disc, is certainly as good as a dozen or so others."

American Record Guide 53:77-9 My/Je '90. Lawrence Hansen (235w)

2089. Concerti (4) for Horn and Orchestra, K.412, 417, 447, 495.

Dennis Brain (horn). Herbert Von Karajan (c). Philharmonia Orchestra. reissue 1954.
EMI 61013 ADD (m) 55:00

"This recording, more than most, qualifies as a Great Recording of the Century. Enough said?"

American Record Guide 51:65 S/O '88. Carl Bauman (110w)

"Later orchestras have held up their end in these works with better technical command, and later hornists have in the same respect come near the mark set by Dennis Brain. But for sheer insouciance, and for sending a long line flying, nobody has ever matched him. Essential listening."

Fanfare 12:216-17 Mr/Ap '89. John Wiser (200w)

Dennis Brain's horn "is so unfailingly tasteful and well played that comment from me is superfluous....it only remains for me to report on the CD transfer, which has cleaned up the original tape at the expense of vinyl's cushioning warmth."

Hi-Fi News & Record Review 33:105 My '88. Robert Cowan (90w)

Gramophone 65:1193-4 F '88. Ivan March (455w)

2090. Concerti (4) for Horn, K.412, 417, 447, 495.

Barry Tuckwell (horn). Barry Tuckwell (c). English Chamber Orchestra.
LONDON/DECCA 410 284

✔**HC** ★***Awards:*** *Stereo Review* Best of the Month, Ap '85.

"One can strongly recommend the CD to anyone who wants to hear the horn concertos under the best possible present conditions."

Fanfare 8:255-6 Mr/Ap '85. John D. Wiser (650w)

"All told, this is a splendid set, splendidly recorded. Bravo Mozart! And bravo Barry Tuckwell!"

Stereo Review 50:60 Ap '85. Stoddard Lincoln (375w)

"This volume represents a milestone in the distinguished career of Barry Tuckwell....Try as I might, however, I simply can't ignore a nagging perfunctoriness in his approach that deprives the music of much of its inner life."

Opus 2:42-3 Ap '86. Nancy Miller (1120w)

Gramophone 62:224 Ag '84. Robin Golding (800w) (rev. of LP); 62:606 N '84. Geoffrey Horn (90w) (rev. of CD)

Audio 69:127 Je '85. Bert Whyte (175w)

2091. Concerti (25) for Piano and Orchestra (complete); Concerto for 2 Pianos, No. 10 in E Flat, K.365; Concerto for 3 Pianos, No. 7 in F, K.242.

Alfred Brendel (pno); Imogen Cooper (pno). Neville Marriner (c). Academy of St. Martin-in-the-Fields.
PHILIPS 412 856 635:42 10 discs

★★***Awards:*** *Gramophone* Critics' Choice 1986 (Richard Osborne). *American Record Guide* Overview: Mozart Piano Concertos, N/D '88.

"As with all integral cycles of any significant body of music, this one is not without flaws. But taken as a whole, it sustains a high level-....Perhaps the biggest limitation in Alfred Brendel's musical, sensitive readings is his restricted, sometimes brittle tone....And sometimes one senses that Brendel does not really *feel* the music....More often than not, however, Brendel goes right to the heart of the Mozartean matter....Perhaps a general distinction that can be drawn between this set and its major CD competitor, the Perahia edition, is that Brendel began *his* traversal on a very high level and sustained it throughout. Perahia, in contrast, is more variable: Sometimes (as in K. 466) he is no match for Brendel; but at his best (as in K. 456) he scales heights that Brendel does not attain."

Fanfare 10:190-91 S/O '86 Mortimer H. Frank (800w)

Hi-Fi News & Record Review 31:105 Mr '86. Kenneth Dommett (340w)

2092. Concerti for Piano and Orchestra: No. 6 in B flat, K.238; No. 7 in F for 3 Pianos, K.242; No. 10 in E flat for 2 Pianos, K.365.
Malcolm Bilson (ftpno); Robert Levin (ftpno); Melvyn Tan (ftpno). John Eliot Gardiner (c). English Baroque Soloists.
DEUTSCHE GRAMMOPHON 427 317 DDD 68:00

> ✔HC ★*Awards:* Top Disks of the Year, *The New York Times* D 24, '89 (John Rockwell).

"A strong recommendation is given; mostly for an intensely poetic K. 365."

Fanfare 13:236-37 Ja/F '90. John Wiser (335w)

"Playing is crisp, alert, and beautifully balanced. The recordings allow all of the wondrous detail of Mozart's scoring to be heard. The interplay between soloist(s) and orchestra is superb....Strongly recommended."

American Record Guide 53:67-8 Ja/F '90. Carl Bauman (215w)

"The playing is very polished...and the whole an exemplary demonstration of how scholarship and engineering may combine to teach us a valuable lesson on how such music ought to be heard. I acknowledge the lesson humbly, but am left wondering quite what all the fuss is about." *P95 S95*

Hi-Fi News & Record Review 34:89+ S '89. Kenneth Dommett (225w)

Gramophone 67:304+ Ag '89. Stanley Sadie (490w)

2093. Concerti for Piano and Orchestra: No. 6 in B flat, K.238; No. 13 in C, K.387b (415).
Murray Perahia (pno). Murray Perahia (c). English Chamber Orchestra.
CBS 39223

> ★★*Awards:* *American Record Guide* Overview: Mozart Piano Concertos, N/D '88 (No. 6); *Gramophone* Critics' Choice 1985 (Stephen Plaistow).

"In the final installment in the single-issues series, Perahia's dealings with the relatively undistinguished Concerto No. 6 are as conscientiously graceful as anything he has done."

Fanfare 9:186 Ja/F '86. John D. Wiser (300w)

Gramophone 63:508 O '85. Stephen Plaistow (245w)

2094. Concerti for Piano and Orchestra: No. 8 in C, K.246; No. 27 in B flat, K.595.
Rudolf Serkin (pno). Claudio Abbado (c). London Symphony Orchestra.
DEUTSCHE GRAMMOPHON 410 035

> ★★*Awards:* *Stereo Review* Best of the Month, Je '85; *Gramophone* Critics' Choice 1984 (Trevor Harvey).

"The quality of the recording itself, in both works, ensures that all the vividness of their music making, as well as its affectionate character, comes through with the fullest impact, especially on CD."

Stereo Review 50:73-4 Je '85. Richard Freed (425w)

"In sum, then, this release is not so disappointing as some others in the Serkin-Mozart series, but it still falls short of capturing this great pianist at his best."

Fanfare 8:167-8 My/Je '85. Mortimer H. Frank (400w)

Gramophone 62:747-8 D '84. Trevor Harvey (315w)

2095. Concerti for Piano and Orchestra: No. 9 in E flat, K.271; No. 11 in F, K.413.
Malcolm Bilson (ftpno). John Eliot Gardiner (c). English Baroque Soloists.
DEUTSCHE GRAMMOPHON 410 905

> ✔HC ★★*Awards:* *Stereo Review* Best of the Month, Ag '84; *Gramophone* Critics' Choice 1984 (Robin Golding).

"Both [concertos] are brought off beautifully, and the recorded sound of the fortepiano as integrated with Gardiner's English Baroque Soloists is first-rate."

Stereo Review 49:73 Ag '84. Stoddard Lincoln (350w)

"All too frequently early string instruments can sound somewhat shrieky, but this time they seem sweeter and natural....The disc shows a welcome improvement in Archiv's balancing and tonal quality...I find the soloist's finger work a little irregular sometimes."

Hi-Fi News & Record Review 29:89 S '84. Angus McKenzie (120w)

Ovation 5:52-3 S '84. Harris Goldsmith (560w) (rev. of LP)

Gramophone 61:1177 Ap '84. Robin Golding (490w); Geoffrey Horn (85w)

2096. Concerti for Piano and Orchestra: No. 9 in E flat, K.271; No. 13 in C, K.387b (415).
Andras Schiff (pno). Sandor Vegh (c). Salzburg Mozarteum Camerata Academica.
LONDON/DECCA 425 466 DDD 59:00

> ★*Awards:* The Gramophone Awards, Nominations, Concerto, *Gramophone*, N '91.

"At this point, it hardly seems necessary to indicate in so many words the excellences of this performing team, which achieves readings of such definite character that all but a few predecessors seem bland and routine by comparison....Only in the Bilson-Gardiner out-and-out period instrument readings does one find orchestral details considered with comparable acuity, and even in their K.415, the sense of speed and loft in the outer movements is not so strong....Strongly recommended!"

Fanfare 14:287-88 N/D '90. John Wiser (225w)

"Schiff's performance is marked by his refined touch and elegant use of pedal. Although these readings may at times feel a trifle lacking in personality, they are consistently lovely....For both concertos Alfred Brendel presents superlative competition...but you'll have to buy the complete set...to sample those wonderfully joyous performances (an investment I would readily urge upon all Mozart lovers)."

American Record Guide 53:85 N/D '90. James S. Ginsburg (110w)

Gramophone 68:217-18 Jl '90. Stephen Plaistow (390w)

2097. Concerti for Piano and Orchestra: No. 11 in F, K.413; No. 12 in A, K.414; No. 14 in E flat, K.449.
Murray Perahia (pno). Murray Perahia (c). English Chamber Orchestra. reissue 1976.
CBS 42243 70:23

✔HC ★*Awards: American Record Guide* Overview: Mozart Piano Concertos, N/D '88 (No. 11).

"The only competition for Perahia's traversal, and it is pretty much an even bet in every respect, is Alfred Brendel's work for Philips-...But I think that for sheer intensity where it is most needed...Perahia's performances have a distinct edge."

Fanfare 11:247 S/O '87. John D. Wiser (55w)

Gramophone 65:410 S '87 Christopher Headington (150w)

2098. Concerti for Piano and Orchestra: No. 13 in C, K.387b (415); No. 15 in B flat, K.450.
Malcolm Bilson (pno). John Eliot Gardiner (c). English Baroque Soloists.
DEUTSCHE GRAMMOPHON 413 464 51:54

✔HC ★★*Awards: Fanfare* Want List 1985 (Edward Strickland); *Gramophone* Critics' Choice 1985 (Robin Golding).

"Lithe, stylish and often revealing performances make for another very satisfying issue."

Hi-Fi News & Record Review 30:83 Je '85. Peter Herring (190w)

"Bilson's playing is a delight. He has the brightness of spirit and the even technique to keep the music sparkling, as most of it in these pieces should sound....In short, this is not only a recommendable production but almost an essential one for Mozart lovers."

Fanfare 8:224-5 Jl/Ag '85. Leslie Gerber (550w)

"A few critics have charged that in Bilson's concerto performances the piano is 'drowned out' by the orchestra; and so it is, if you expected it to sail out over a deferential accompaniment like Ethel Merman over a pit band-....Paradoxically, the instrument that 'almost avoids resonance' can sing more lyrically than the Romantic giant, for its lyricism is of the most serious, adult kind. What Bilson has to teach us is that Mozart doesn't ask for the expressive generalization or approximation of the big legato line: When he speaks of grief or resignation or exaltation, he understands that these emotions unfold amid ambiguities and complexities, that in a mature heart there is no steady state of feeling, but rather a continuing dialectic of hesitation and growth—a dialectic that finds its best expression in the infinitely subtle and constantly changing articulations of the fortepiano."

Opus 2:26-27+ O '86 Eric Van Tassel (2445w)

Gramophone 62:1332 My '85. Robin Golding (420w)

2099. Concerti for Piano and Orchestra: No. 18 in B flat, K.456; No. 19 in F, K.459.
Peter Serkin (pno). Alexander Schneider (c). English Chamber Orchestra.
RCA 2244

★*Awards: American Record Guide* Overview: Mozart Piano Concertos, N/D '88 (No. 18).

"The recordings of the six Mozart concertos made by Peter Serkin in the early '70s were among the extraordinary releases of the decade-...[this] CD transfer simply reinforces the astonishing impression they made when released."

Fanfare 10:145 Ja/F '87 Mortimer H. Frank (200w)

2100. Concerti for Piano and Orchestra: No. 18 in B flat, K.456; No. 19 in F, K.459.
Mitsuko Uchida (pno). Jeffrey Tate (c). English Chamber Orchestra.
PHILIPS 422 348 DDD 56:30

★*Awards:* Best of the Month, *Hi-Fi News & Record Review*, Mr '90.

"Even those who find Uchida's playing too restrained in some Mozart are probably going to love the disc containing K.456 and 459. These pieces are perfectly suited to her style, and the inherent joyousness of the music comes out clearly....Highly recommended."

Fanfare 14:301-2 S/O '90. Leslie Gerber (125w)

"The Uchida/Tate cycle is coming on very nicely, with a fascinating creative tension between the innately delicate, even reticent approach of the pianist, and the vigour and strength of the conductor. The ECO plays quite beautifully, and the firm, natural piano tone and excellent recording balance—just the right degree of resonance, every detail in place—are further pleasing features of this issue." *P100 S100*

Hi-Fi News & Record Review 35:108 Mr '90. Peter Branscombe (240w)

"Exquisitely crafted performances...Tate's collaboration is absolutely top-drawer. Rhythmically vital and with every voice clearly heard, this is Mozart conducting at its very finest-....Philips has put the icing on the cake with glowing sonics."

American Record Guide 53:74 Jl/Ag '90. Allen Linkowski (125w)

Stereophile 15:265+ Ja '92. Mortimer H. Frank (long)

Gramophone 68:217-18 Jl '90. Stephen Plaistow (390w)

Digital Audio's CD Review 7:57 S '90. Tom Vernier (260w)

2101. Concerti for Piano and Orchestra: No. 19 in F, K.459; No. 20 in D minor, K.466.
Rudolf Serkin (pno). George Szell (c). Cleveland Orchestra. 1964 reissue.
CBS 37236 AAD 63:25

★***Awards:*** *American Record Guide* Overview: Mozart Piano Concertos, N/D '88.

"Musically, these performances are generally more winning than Serkin's remakes for DG, in good measure because of Szell's more idiomatic accompaniment."

Fanfare 11:170 Ja/F '88. Mortimer H. Frank (155w)

"The performances on this CD are Mozart's music realized to perfection. Brilliant, witty, lively, subtle, magnificent, are among a few of the adjectives that come to mind....On the black disc his [Serkin's] vocal contributions were almost inaudible. The clarity of the silver disc brings these intrusions much more to our attention."

American Record Guide 51:59 Mr/Ap '88. Carl Bauman (275w)

2102. Concerti for Piano and Orchestra: No. 20 in D minor, K.466; No. 21 in C, K.467.
Malcolm Bilson (ftpno). John Eliot Gardiner (c). English Baroque Soloists.
DEUTSCHE GRAMMOPHON 419 609 DDD 58:00

✔**HC** ★★★***Awards:*** The Want List 1988, *Fanfare* N/D '88 (Mortimer H. Frank, Nick Rossi, Edward Strickland).

"This latest installment in Malcolm Bilson's cycle of the Mozart concertos proves as distinguished as its predecessors....from the opening of K.466, with its sharply defined syncopations, growling bases, and explosive tuttis (made all the more pungent by tight, well-focused timpani), it is clear that this will be a D minor of demonic *Sturm und Drang* punch."

Fanfare 11:170-1 My/Je '88. Mortimer H. Frank (400w)

"Bilson, playing on his 1977 Philip Belt reproduction of an early 1780's Anton Walter fortepiano, performs with greater technical finish and flair; he adds some very stylish cadenzas and lead-ins, and even effectively and tastefully fills out several of the barer passages. There is a nice sense of space around his instrument...Perhaps my only genuine complaint about the reproduction has to do with the harshness of the loudest orchestral passages."

Stereophile 11:175 O '88. Igor Kipnis (325w)

"The pairing of K466/467 seems to me the most exciting product of the series yet....the partnership of Malcolm Bilson, John Eliot Gardiner and the English Baroque Soloists has continued to grow in authority and skill."

Hi-Fi News & Record Review 33:105 Mr '88. Peter Branscombe (400w)

"An outstanding recording of well known repertoire."

Continuo 12:16 D '88. David Cavlovic (550w)

"On interpretive points, this recording rightfully goes near the top of the list, but its sonics keep it out of the No. 1 slot."

High Fidelity 38:64 Jl '88. Christopher Rothko (315w)

Gramophone 65:1082 Ja '88. Stanley Sadie (910w)

The New York Times Jl 3 '88, p. H23. Will Crutchfield (500w)

2103. Concerti for Piano and Orchestra: No.'s 20-27.
Malcolm Bilson (pf). John Eliot Gardiner (c). English Baroque Soloists.
DEUTSCHE GRAMMOPHON 427 846 DDD
57:38; 59:47; 61"15; 61:03 4 discs

✔**HC** ★★***Awards:*** Best CD of the Month, *Digital Audio's CD Review*, S '90. The Want List 1990, *Fanfare* N/D '90 (Elliott Kaback).

"This set, among all the recent Mozart recordings, commands special attention because it is so satisfying. These performances seem to realize with special immediacy Mozart's operatic way of balancing disturbing violence and utter grace, which is what makes the concertos such dramatically fulfilling works."

The New York Times N 4 '90, p. 27+. Mark Swed (1125w)

"As Mortimer Frank has noted in reviewing most of the series, the ultimate test is not of 'authenticity' but of musical taste and technique. Both soloist and conductor pour out these essences unstintingly, convincing us (again) that no greater body of concertos than these has yet been written....The set is being sold at full price."

Fanfare 14:302 S/O '90. Elliott Kaback (450w)

"Overall, it's as if Bilson has filtered all of his playing through the elegiac, reflective side of Mozart's genius and left out too much of the high spirits and immediacy of the music. It's an approach that leads to some rewards....So far Mozart—a few happy exceptions aside—seems to be better played on the less well-suited modern instruments than on those he would have recognized."

American Record Guide 53:85-6 N/D '90. Stephen D. Chakwin, Jr. (225w)

Digital Audio's CD Review 7:44 S '90. Lawrence Johnson (605w)

2104. Concerti for Piano and Orchestra: No. 20 in D minor, K.466; No. 21 in C, K.467; Sonata No. 12 in F for Piano, K.332.
Artur Schnabel (pno). Walter Susskind; Malcolm Sargent (c). Philharmonia Orchestra; London Symphony Orchestra. reissues.
ARABESQUE 6591 AAD 73:12

★*Awards:* The Want List 1989, *Fanfare* N/D '89 (Michael Ullman).

"Schnabel's interpretation...has a needed dramatic tension that, all too often, one misses, even today, in Mozart playing....Those who own everything here need not rush, then, to acquire CD replacements. But those who may be coming to these glorious performances for the first time should seek them in the new format."

Fanfare 12:218-20 Mr/Ap '89. Mortimer H. Frank (300w)

"These particular CD transfers have been cleaned and tidied to the point that the modern reproduction has taken on more value than the original antique—something to make the antiquarian throw up his hands in despair. We hear Schnabel much better now than did record buyers in 1937."

The New York Times My 21 '89, p. 25. Bernard Holland (260w)

Gramophone 67:1536+ F '90. Richard Osborne (275w)

2105. Concerti for Piano and Orchestra: No. 20 in D minor, K.466; No. 21 in C, K.467.
Mitsuko Uchida (piano). Jeffrey Tate (c). English Chamber Orchestra.
PHILIPS 416 381 DDD 62:08

★★*Awards:* *Gramophone* Critics' Choice 1986 (Stephen Plaistow); Record of the Month, *Hi-Fi News & Record Review* S '86.

The D-minor "seems to me to fulfil all that one might have expected of Tate and Uchida....Together, Uchida and Tate convey the *surprises* in Mozart's writing...It is that kind of insightful playing which gives this record rare distinctiveness."

Hi-Fi News & Record Review 31:83 S '86. Christopher Breunig (820w)

"The texture of Mozart's music shines anew, quite uncorrupted by cleverness."

The Musical Times 128:90 F '87 Alec Hyatt King (320w) (rev. of LP)

"The real glory of Uchida's disc...is No. 21-....The playing of the slow movement...is gorgeous on all counts."

Ovation 8:33 Je '87 Paul Turok (125w)

"Despite a long association in the concert hall, the pianist seems constrained by the orchestra, and her playing, in the D minor at least, is uncharacteristically self-conscious and low key-....The sound is generally disappointing."

Hi-Fi News & Record Review 31:83 S '86. Kenneth Dommett (280w)

Fanfare 10:161 My/Je '87 Elliott Kaback (400w)

Digital Audio & Compact Disc Review 107:61 Jl '87 Tom Vernier (200w)

2106. Concerti for Piano and Orchestra: No. 21 in C, K.467; No. 23 in A, K.488.
Rudolf Serkin (pno). Claudio Abbado (c). London Symphony Orchestra.
DEUTSCHE GRAMMOPHON 410 068

★*Awards:* *American Record Guide* Overview: Mozart Piano Concertos, N/D '88 (No. 21).

"Although one might supplement this disc with another performance closer to today's interpretive style, this recording is a must. Serkin's Mozart is a unique and profoundly moving account."

High Performance Review 3 (1):102-3 Ag '84. Thomas H. Wendel (330w)

"M.H.F.'s review of the conventional disc of these concertos (*Fanfare* VII:3)...finds nothing good to say beyond a nod to the engineers-....Given the total divergence of our reactions, one can only advise careful audition. For myself, this CD is near the top of a short list of best buys for this format."

Fanfare 8:266-7 S/O '84. Elliott Kaback (270w)

Gramophone 61:341 S '83. Ivan March (245w)

2107. Concerti for Piano and Orchestra: No. 22 in E flat, K.482; No. 24 in C minor, K.491.
Murray Perahia (pno). Murray Perahia (c). English Chamber Orchestra.
CBS 42242 66:43

★*Awards:* *American Record Guide* Overview: Mozart Piano Concertos, N/D '88 (No. 24).

"The only competition for Perahia's traversal, and it is pretty much an even bet in every respect, is Alfred Brendel's work for Philips-...But I think that for sheer intensity where it is most needed...Perahia's performances have a distinct edge."

Fanfare 11:247 S/O '87. John D. Wiser (55w)

Gramophone 65:296+ Ag '87 Stephen Plaistow (490w)

2108. Concerti for Piano and Orchestra: No. 22 in E flat, K.482; No. 23 in A, K.488.
Andras Schiff (pno). Sandor Vegh (c). Salzburg Mozarteum Camerata Academica.
LONDON/DECCA 425 855 DDD 63:00

✔HC ★*Awards:* Critical Choice, *Musical America*, N/D '91 (Harris Goldsmith).

"As always, Schiff's unselfconsciously beautiful tone production is a joy in itself, as is the almost otherworldly level of the wind playing, but the overall satisfaction goes far beyond the sum of the component parts—among which must be counted the exemplary recording quality."

Stereo Review 56:74 O '91. Richard Freed (brief)

"Intelligent recorded balance and great immediacy of sound complete an attractive picture; for K.482, urgently recommended; for K.488, judgment must be reserved."

Fanfare 15:396-97 N/D '91. John Wiser (med)

"The latest in the Andras Schiff-Sandor Vegh Mozart Concerto series presents two more typically stylish interpretations that blend modern and period performance practices in an uncommonly satisfactory ratio....Very highly recommended."

Musical America 111:49 N/D '91. Harris Goldsmith (med)

Gramophone 69:51-2 Jl '91. Christopher Headington (325w)

2109. Concerti for Piano and Orchestra: No. 22 in E flat, K.482; No. 23 in A, K.488.
Mitsuko Uchida (pno). Jeffrey Tate (c). English Chamber Orchestra.
PHILIPS 420 187 DDD 61:12

★★*Awards:* *Gramophone* Critics' Choice (Stephen Plaistow), 1987. Perfect 10s, *Digital Audio's CD Review*, Mr '89.

"The performances of both concertos are a delight. Uchida, always a thoughtful interpreter of Mozart though occasionally a flaccid one-...seems to have acquired new strength....The recording, apart from a tendency to emphasize the lower notes of the piano, is beautifully detailed and balanced."

Hi-Fi News & Record Review 32:119 N '87 Kenneth Dommett (315w)

Ovation 8:40 D '87. Dan F. Cameron (360w)

Digital Audio 4:42 My '88. Octavio Roca (215w)

Gramophone 65:296+ Ag '87 Stephen Plaistow (490w)

2110. Concerti for Piano and Orchestra: No. 23 in A, K.488; No. 27 in B flat, K.595.
Vladimir Ashkenazy (pno). Vladimir Ashkenazy (c). Philharmonia Orchestra.
LONDON/DECCA 400 087

★*Awards:* *American Record Guide* Overview: Mozart Piano Concertos, N/D '88 (No. 23).

"Ashkenazy offers stylish, but characteristically un-self-conscious readings: the first movement of the A-major Concerto and the finale of K. 595 strike me as occasionally tentative interpretively, but the rest of these concertos are as beautiful as I have ever heard this music played."

Fanfare 7:115-6 S/O '83. Philip Hart (200w)

Ovation 4:37 D '83. Allan Kozinn (105w)

Gramophone 60:1011-2 Mr '83. Lionel Salter (175w)

Audio 68:97 Mr '84. John M. Eargle (95w)

2111. Concerti for Piano and Orchestra: No. 23 in A, K.488; Sonatas for Piano: No. 13 in B flat, K.333.
Vladimir Horowitz (pno). Carlo Maria Giulini (c). Milan La Scala Orchestra. 1987.
DEUTSCHE GRAMMOPHON 423 287 DDD 50:00

★*Awards:* *Stereo Review* Best Recordings of the Month, F '88.

"Horowitz moves through both concerto and sonata with the vigor and irrepressible humor of a man one-fourth his age...In addition to humor, this performance of the sonata displays the utmost care over phrasing, color, and articulation of compound voices....This is a performance to make one forget all others, and the recorded sound is admirably clear and faithful."

American Record Guide 51:47-8 My/Je '88. Arved Ashby (325w)

"Regardless of all the other fine recordings of these Mozart works, and especially of the concerto, this one is well worth owning. The fine sonics are wholly appropriate to the music and to the intimate scale of the performances."

Stereo Review 53:178 F '88. David Hall (525w)

"As a document of a dying 19th-century view of Mozart, Horowitz's account of the sonata is valuable. But his concerto performance transcends an era, breathing life into Mozart in the timeless manner that only a genius can achieve."

Musical America 108:78-9 Jl '88. K. Robert Schwarz (375w)

"Mr. Horowitz plays the A major with many inflections that will be considered 'Romantic.' Dirty word, that. He strives for color, for rhythmic flexibility and expressivity, all within the bounds of good taste....In the program notes Mr. Horowitz puts in a good case for his approach, based on Mozart's letters....Would it be heretical to suggest that Mr. Horowitz is closer to the true Mozart style than today's more 'learned' but antiseptic Mozartean specialists?"

The New York Times O 23 '88, p. H26. Harold C. Schonberg (245w)

"Everything [in K.488] seems geared to show not the composer's genius but the performer's digital dexterity....K. 333 is, if anything, even less stylish...one thing is certain: Mozart performances like these will not be heard from any other living artist."

Fanfare 11:157-8 Mr/Ap '88. Mortimer H. Frank (500w)

"Beyond question, a formidable keyboard technician is at work here. Every note can be heard, with details often veiled in other performances laid bare in bold relief. It is the kind of detail, however, that one encounters when looking through a fluoroscope: clinical, one-dimensional, and soulless....DG's recording boasts ideal sound."

Stereophile 11:173 Ap '88. Mortimer H. Frank (400w)

"Edward Greenfield's exemplary notes here quote Vladimir Horowitz...brandishing intimidating material from Mozart's own letters to justify everything audacious he does in this recording—and God knows he does quite a lot-....Giulini himself deviates a bit."

High Fidelity 38:60 My '88. Paul Moor (325w)

"From the use of the Busoni cadenza to the occasional exaggeration of the bass line, the Horowitz point of view permeates this performance [of the Concerto]. The result is vintage Horowitz, but not the most moving Mozart-....Horowitz's performance of the *Sonata* No. 13 is much more enjoyable."

HighPerformanceReview 6:82 Mr '89. Ann Viles (120w)

Stereo Review Presents: Compact Disc Buyer's Guide Summer 1988 p.51. William Livingstone (75w)

Digital Audio 4:46 My '88. David C. Vernier (350w)

Gramophone 65:740 N '87 Edward Greenfield (610w)

2112. Concerti for Piano and Orchestra: No. 24 in C minor, K.491; No. 27 in B flat, K.595.
Malcolm Bilson (ftpno). John Eliot Gardiner (c). English Baroque Soloists.
DEUTSCHE GRAMMOPHON 427 652 DDD 63:00

★★*Awards:* Best of the Month, *Hi-Fi News & Record Review*, F '90; The Year's Best, *Hi Fi News & Record Review*, May '90 Supplement. Critics' Choice 1990, *Gramophone* D '90 (Stanley Sadie).

"The C-minor and final B-flat Concerts are a glorious pairing: the one passionate and dramatic, the other tinged with the melancholy that, whatever Mozart may have thought, comes from our knowing it to be the last-....Bilson...is strong, supple and sensitive...John Eliot Gardiner obtains vivid and sensitive playing from his English Baroque Soloists, with excellent balance, and fresh clarity from the winds. The recorded quality is again admirable: clean, spacious, precise." *P100 S100*

Hi-Fi News & Record Review 35:99 F '90; p.24-5 My '90 Supplement. Peter Branscombe (290w)

"The Bilson-Gardiner performances complete their distinguished period-instrument traversal of the concertos...orchestral color is bracing; piquant winds, bright brass, and slightly nasal, vibrato-free strings. As always, Gardiner is a superb accompanist...Bilson's tone is somewhat less colorful than in some of his earlier efforts, but his playing retains the taste and musicality he has always exhibited...Among many distinguished recordings of these two concertos, Bilson's most recall the arresting understatement favored by Curzon...A warmly recommended release."

Stereophile 15:265+ Ja '92. Mortimer H. Frank (long)

"Overall, it's as if Bilson has filtered all of his playing through the elegiac, reflective side of Mozart's genius and left out too much of the high spirits and immediacy of the music. It's an approach that leads to some rewards....So far Mozart—a few happy exceptions aside—seems to be better played on the less well-suited modern instruments than on those he would have recognized."

American Record Guide 53:86 N/D '90. Stephen D. Chakwin, Jr. (225w)

Gramophone 67:1467 F '90. Stanley Sadie (735w)

Concerto No. 25 in C for Piano and Orchestra, K.503. See No. 2014.

2113. Concerti No. 26 in D for Piano and Orchestra, K.537, "Coronation;" Rondo in D for Piano and Orchestra, K.382; Rondo in A for Piano and Orchestra, K.386.
Murray Perahia (pno). Murray Perahia (c). English Chamber Orchestra.
CBS 39224

✔**HC** ★*Awards: Gramophone* Critics' Choice 1985 (David Fanning).

"Perahia's is probably the best currently available performance of this concerto."

American Record Guide 49:30 My/Je '86. John P. McKelvey (290w)

"*Distinguished* is the only word for these recordings and for Perahia's series as a whole."

Fanfare 8:168-9 My/Je '85. John D. Wiser (230w)

"The *Coronation* Concerto may be he weakest of Mozart's mature concertos, but Perahia reminds us that to be least in such a group is hardly an embarrassment....Perahia plays his own tasteful ccadenzas in all three works, and CBS has come through with rich, warm, altogether lifelike sonics."

Stereo Review 49:102+ N '84. Richard Freed (200w)

Ovation 5:69 N '84. Dean Elder (425w) (rev. of LP)

Gramophone 63:626 N '85. David J. Fanning (105w)

2114. Concerti for Violin and Orchestra: No. 3 in G, K.216; No. 5 in A, K.219.
Cho-Liang Lin (vln). Raymond Leppard (c). English Chamber Orchestra.
CBS 42364 DDD 62:01

✔**HC** ★★*Awards: Stereo Review* Best Recordings of the Month, D '87. Critics' Choice 1988, *Gramophone* D '88 (Edward Greenfield).

"Lin has a shiningly lovely tone and plays these pieces with natural elegance. Even Grumiaux seems a little calculating by

comparison....The recorded sound is fine. This is a wonderful disc and I recommend it to all."
American Record Guide 51:48 My/Je '88. Stephen D. Chakwin, Jr. (130w)

"The performances of these two works...can stand beside the very best, and they come with an appropriate additional piece, the Adagio in E major, K. 261."
Stereo Review 52:135 D '87. Richard Freed (430w)

"This is one of the better recent versions of these works. Lin plays with delicacy and athletic grace....all is close to the Mozartean ideal-....sound is quite natural, though in no way spectacular."
Fanfare 11:179 N/D '87. John Bauman (260w)

Lin "plays these two concertos sympathetically enough, but as yet without the emotional rapport needed to turn good performances into great ones....The sound quality is good, clear and spacious."
Hi-Fi News & Record Review 33:102 Ap '88. Kenneth Dommett (200w)

Ovation 8:21 Ja '88. Lawrence B. Johnson (510w)

Gramophone 65:948 D '87. Edward Greenfield (390w)

2115. Concerto No. 4 in D for Violin and Orchestra, K.218. PROKOFIEV, SERGEI. Concerto No. 1 in D for Violin and Orchestra, Opus 19. MENDELSSOHN, FELIX. Concerto in E minor for Violin and Orchestra, Opus 64.
Joseph Szigeti (vln). Thomas Beecham (c). London Philharmonic Orchestra.
PEARL 9377

★*Awards:* The Want List 1990, *Fanfare* N/D '90 (William Youngren).

"Put simply, the 1933 effort is the finest Toscanini account of the work [the 5th] I have ever heard...in Marc Obert-Thorn's transfer the sound is exceptionally fine for its vintage-....Those who know Toscanini only from his later NBC years should find this set an ear-opener."
Stereophile 13:219 Ap '90. Mortimer H. Frank (130w)

"Recommendable."
The New York Times Ag 12 '90, p. 30 H. Will Crutchfield (b.n.)

Musical America 111:88 Ja '91. Terry Teachout (b.n.)

Musical America 109:69 N '89. Terry Teachout (b.n.)

Gramophone 67:1700+ Mr '90. Alan Sanders (390w)

American Record Guide 53:159-61 Mr/Ap '90. David Radcliffe (360w)

NIELSEN, CARL

Concerto for Clarinet and Orchestra, Opus 57. See No. 1273.

2116. Concerto for Violin and Orchestra, Opus 33; Concerto for Flute and Orchestra; Concerto for Clarinet and Orchestra, Opus 57.
Kim Sjogren (vln); Toke Lund Christiansen (fl); Niels Thomsen (clar). Michael Schonwandt (c). Danish Radio Symphony Orchestra.
CHANDOS 8894 DDD 80:00

★★*Awards:* The Gramophone Awards, Nominations, Concerto, *Gramophone*, N '91. Best of the Month, *Hi-Fi News & Record Review*, Je '91.

"To get all Nielsen's concertos onto one record is something of a triumph. And to have them all so well played is an added cause for celebration....Add fine, well-balanced sound and we have here a Nielsen record to bring unequivocal pleasure and praise." *P100 S95*
Hi-Fi News & Record Review 36:74 Je '91. Kenneth Dommett (210w)

"Possibly the best all-round Violin Concerto, with a slightly under-par Flute Concerto and one of the finest Clarinet Concertos' adding up to a package of high merit."
American Record Guide 54:102-3 S/O '91. John W. Barker (long)

"In respect to the violin concerto, Tellefsen holds the lead, and is unlikely to be bettered soon, if ever. The new Chandos issue, however, is a mightily attractive conflation, in which the flute and clarinet concertos are supreme, and the violin concerto account a much more than merely respectable contribution. Typical roomy sound aids in establishing atmosphere and in no way impedes character and abundant detail. Strongly recommended."
Fanfare 14:240-42 My/Je '91. John Wiser (330w)

Gramophone 68:1838+ Ap '91. Robert Layton (515w)

Concerto for Violin and Orchestra, Opus 33. See No. 2143.

PADEREWSKI, IGNACE JAN

2117. Polish Fantasy for Piano and Orchestra, Opus 19; Symphony in B minor, Opus 24, "Polonia".
Regina Smendzianka (pno). Stanislaw Wislocki; Bohdan Wodiczko (c). Warsaw National Philharmonic Orchestra; Pomeranian Philharmonic Symphony Orchestra, Bydgoszcz. 1964, 1973.
OLYMPIA 305 AAD 75:12

★*Awards:* Top Choices—1989, *American Record Guide* Ja/F '90 (Steven Haller).

"The sound in both instances is clear and spacious....In the *Fantasy* the orchestra is as active and cogent as the piano....Hearing Smendzianka and the Warsaw Philharmonic play it, after knowing only the Blumenthal recording, is like hearing a new and infinitely finer work....Paderewski remains his own man in this symphony, creating a work of strong profile and powerful drama. I shall come back to it from time to time; it is worth regular, if not frequent, rehearings."

Fanfare 12:233-34 Mr/Ap '89. David Johnson (550w)

"Miss Smendzianka is perhaps closer in style to Felicia Blumenthal's recording for Turnabout, tempering Paderewski's daunting passagework with a lyricism largely absent from Wild's reading. Coupled with the Symphony, the total package is both generous and compelling, making this CD essential to any music library but especially those to whom the name of Ignacy Jan Paderewski may conjure up no more than faded memories of the recital hall....a record to cherish."

American Record Guide 52:72-3 Jl/Ag '89. Steven J. Haller (750w)

PAGANINI, NICCOLO

2118. Concerto No. 1 in D for Violin and Orchestra, Opus 6. TCHAIKOVSKY, PIOTR ILYICH Serenade melancolique for Violin and Orchestra, Opus 26; Valse-Scherzo for Violin and Orchestra, Opus 34.

Midori (vln). Leonard Slatkin (c). London Symphony Orchestra. London. 1987.

PHILIPS 420 943 DDD 52:00

★*Awards:* *American Record Guide* Overview: Popular Violin Concertos, S/O '89.

"The young virtuosa is not playing it safe [in the Paganini concerto]: all the technical fireworks are securely in place, and relaxed tempos actually make the demands even more fiendish. The playing may lack the effortless perfection of Kogan or the Italian temperament of Accardo or the pervasive warmth of Perlman; but it makes its own statement convincingly and brilliantly and in the process documents the continued growth of Midori's artistry."

American Record Guide 52:67 Mr/Ap '89. Alan Heatherington (325w)

Midori's "playing is not only technically dazzling, with flawless intonation, brilliant passage work, and sumptuous tone, but she is innately musical as well....Leonard Slatkin and the London Symphony Orchestra deliver solid support throughout, and Philips provides expert sonics."

HighPerformanceReview 6:83 Je '89. John Mueter (160w)

"As good, even wonderful, as it is, this recording does not enter my personal pantheon of Paganini First Concertos....The Tchaikovsky fillers are pleasant, the sound is fine....Don't misconstrue what I'm saying—this is a very enthusiastic reception for Midori's Paganini, and if, like me, you like to keep track of the new crop of fiddle players, the recording is virtually self-recommending."

Fanfare 12:227 Ja/F '89. David K. Nelson (450w)

Gramophone 66:290 Ag '88. Ivan March (350w)

Digital Audio 5:38 Ja '89. David Vernier (250w)

2119. Concerto No. 1 in D for Violin and Orchestra, Opus 6. VIEUXTEMPS, HENRI. Concerto No. 5 in A minor for Violin and Orchestra, Opus 37.

Viktoria Mullova (vln). Neville Marriner (c). Academy of St. Martin-in-the-Fields.

PHILIPS 422 332 DDD 55:00

★*Awards:* Critics' Choice 1989, *Gramophone* D '89 (Lionel Salter).

"Mullova has all that it takes to play these works better than anyone else. Greater attention to musical subtleties can be found in the Midori Paganini, but Mullova has more panache and a few moments of hysterical intensity. The Vieuxtemps...has never fared better in recorded performance and is the clear choice over Perlman/Barenboim and Heifetz/Sargent."

American Record Guide 53:87 My/Je '90. Alan Heatherington (225w)

"She has a nobler notion than most of what virtuosity is all about, and the seriousness with which she takes these works is exactly what makes these performances so exciting....Neville Marriner, a former violinist himself, is a perfect partner in both works, and Philips provides an ideal sonic focus."

Stereo Review Presents: Compact Disc Buyers' Guide Summer 1990 p.57 Richard Freed (125w)

"There isn't a technical demand made by these two virtuoso concertos that Viktoria Mullova does not meet with ease. While we expect big techniques nowadays, what makes this recording a success is Mullova's ability to convey the drama and temperament in this operatic music....A recommended recording."

Fanfare 13:240-41 My/Je '90. David K. Nelson (380w)

Gramophone 67:671 O '89. Lionel Salter (425w)

PENDERECKI, KRZYSZTOF

2120. Concerto No. 2 for Cello and Orchestra; Partita for Harpsichord, Electric Guitar, Bass Guitar, Harp, Contrabass and Orchestra.

Mstislav Rostropovich (cello); Elzbieta Stefanska-Lukowicz (hpscd); Annemarie Schmeisser (harp); Helga Bohnstedt (gtr); Wolfgang Bargel (gtr); Norbert Brenner (d-bass). Krysztof Penderecki (c). Philharmonia Orchestra; Southwest German Radio Orchestra.

ERATO 75321 DDD (Concerto)/AAD (Partita) 51:00

★★*Awards:* Second Place Contemporary Composer Mumm Champagne Classical Music Award 1988—Presented by *Ovation*, *Ovation* N '88; The Want List 1988, *Fanfare* N/D '88 (David K. Nelson).

"Rostropovich revels in this rich, Slavic material, and the digital recording is equal to the performance."
Stereo Review 53:193 F '88. Eric Salzman (275w)

"That Rostropovich accomplishes incredible feats here is undeniable, and if finding out how fast the master can play random-sounding tremolos is your bag, have at it. Recorded sound is excellently present, though with a little background hiss in the AAD Partita recording."
Fanfare 11:188 Ja/F '88. Kyle Gann (300w)

"Rostropovich's performance alone would be worth the price of the disc. This ever youthful cellist of unquenchable energy tears into the concerto with savage intensity."
Musical America 108:80-1 Jl '88. K. Robert Schwarz (480w)

Gramophone 66:290 Ag '88. Arnold Whittall (315w)

Ovation 9:39-40 F '88. Peter J. Rabinowitz (265w)

POULENC, FRANCIS

2121. Concerto in G minor for Organ, Strings, Timpani and Orchestra; Gloria in G; Motets (4) pour un Temps de Penitence.
Maurice Durufle (organ); Rosanna Carteri (sop). Georges Pretre (c). Rene Duclos Choir; French National Radio Chorus; French National Radio Orchestra. 1961, 1963 reissues.
EMI 47723 64:00

"In essence, a classic transferred with bonus to Compact Disc."
Hi-Fi News & Record Review 33:105+ Mr '88. Frances Handford (240w)

Gramophone 65:801 N '87 Christopher Headington (245w)

PROKOFIEV, SERGEI

2122. Concerti for Piano and Orchestra (5) (complete).
Vladimir Ashkenazy (pno). Andre Previn (c). London Symphony Orchestra. 1975.
LONDON/DECCA 425 570 ADD (m) 126:00 2 discs

★*Awards:* *American Record Guide* Overview: Prokofieff/Shostakovich, S/O '91.

"Aside from Prokofiev's own recording of the Third, the benchmark among his recorded piano concertos is, I suppose, the London/Decca complete set of 1975, with Vladimir Ashkenazy backed by Andre Previn and the London Symphony....There are marked differences [in these performances and Berman/Jarvi on Chandos 8791] . The sound, for one thing: Close-up, as you might hear it if you were an assistant of Jarvi's, as opposed to the old 'ideal' of a 13th-row orchestra seat approximated in the London set."
Audio 75:90+ F '91. Robert Long (430w)

Gramophone 67:1616 Mr '90. Edward Seckerson (170w)

2123. Concerto No. 3 in C for Piano and Orchestra, Opus 26. TCHAIKOVSKY, PIOTR ILYICH. Concerto No. 1 in B flat minor for Piano and Orchestra, Opus 23.
Martha Argerich (pno). Charles Dutoit; Claudio Abbado (c). Royal Philharmonic Orchestra; Berlin Philharmonic Orchestra.
DEUTSCHE GRAMMOPHON 415 062 62:39

"A definitive version of the Tchaikovsky Piano Concerto...coupled...with an equally good version of the Prokofiev."
The $ensible Sound 10:56 Fall, '86 John J. Puccio (45w)

Gramophone 62:1338 My '85. Edward Greenfield (280w)

High Fidelity 35:73 O '85. Robert E. Benson (50w)

Concerto No. 3 in C for Piano and Orchestra, Opus 26. See No. 2132.

2124. Concerti (2) for Violin and Orchestra.
Isaac Stern (vln). Eugene Ormandy (c). Philadelphia Orchestra. 1963.
CBS 38525 ADD 47:11

★*Awards:* *American Record Guide* Overview: Prokofiev update, N/D '91.

"At mid price this is self-recommending."
American Record Guide 52:95-6 N/D '89. Allen Linkowski (145w)

"Other than boomy bass, I have no complaints to make about the sound, and can strongly recommend the Prokofiev CD."
Fanfare 12:192-93 Jl/Ag '89. David K. Nelson (200w)

Concerto No. 1 in D for Violin and Orchestra, Opus 19. See No. 2115.

Concerto No. 2 in G minor for Violin and Orchestra, Opus 63. See No. 2139, 2141.

RACHMANINOFF, SERGEI

2125. Concerti for Piano and Orchestra: No. 1 in F# minor, Opus 1; No. 3 in D minor, Opus 30.
Jean-Philippe Collard (pno). Michel Plasson (c). Toulouse Capitole Orchestra.
EMI 69115

★*Awards:* *American Record Guide* Overview: Rachmaninoff, S/O '90 (No. 1).

"Collard's recognisably Gallic verve and brilliance are a tonic and life-affirming dismissal of the old French snobbery and hostility regarding Rachmaninov....The pace of No 1 is white hot, the reflexes bold and inflammatory, and if the recording now seems unduly shallow, the

Toulouse Orchestra hardly the acme of refinement, there are many scintillating compensations....In the Third Concerto Collard again competes at the highest level, Occasionally less fervent than in No 1...it is still given with an often supreme sense of romantic ebb of flow."

Music and Musicians International 37:44 D '88. Bryce Morrison (425w)

2126. Concerto No. 1 in F# minor for Piano and Orchestra, Opus 1. DOHNANYI, ERNST VON: Variations on a Nursery Song for Piano and Orchestra, Opus 25. LITOLFF, HENRY CHARLES. Concerto Symphonique No. 4 in D minor for Piano and Orchestra, Opus 102: Scherzo.
Arthur Ozolins (pno). Mario Bernardi (c). Toronto Symphony Orchestra.
CBC ENTERPRISES 5052 58:32

★*Awards: American Record Guide* Overview: Rachmaninoff, S/O '90.

"While it has been rumored for some time that Ozolins is the greatest virtuoso pianist in Canada, this release...should help promote a higher claim: that he is currently one of the greatest young virtuoso artists in the world."

High Fidelity 37:66 My '87 Thomas L. Dixon (275w)

2127. Concerto No. 1 in F# minor for Piano and Orchestra, Opus 1; Rhapsody on a Theme of Paganini, Opus 43.
Mikhail Pletnev (pno). Libor Pesek (c). Philharmonia Orchestra. 1987.
VIRGIN 90724 DDD 51:00

✔**HC** ★*Awards:* Critics' Choice 1989, *Gramophone* D '89 (Robert Layton).

"This is very powerful playing, even if the tone is not especially warm. I was definitely impressed by Pletnev's rendition of the concerto...The Rhapsody, so often recorded and available in so many excellent versions, is, if anything, even more stunning. Here, again, excitement mingles with poetic sensibility, a really sensational performance that I will play with pleasure for any music-minded visitor to my home as an example of a really top-rate performance."

Stereophile 12:199+ O '89. Igor Kipnis (220w)

"Pletnev...sweeps through the intricacies of Rachmaninoff's scores with exuberance, poetry and effortless technique—not to mention his piano sound, which is of uncommon quality and richness....either the Philharmonia players or the Virgin engineers (possibly both) fail to bring us the sumptuous orchestral sonority that this music demands."

American Record Guide 52:98-9 N/D '89. Donald Manildi (165w)

"What we have here is brilliant pianism, especially where repeated notes and brisk octave work are concerned....I was impressed with Pesek's responsive conducting: he and Pletnev leap in, out, and around each other without as much as a moment's breathing space! The sound is excellent, too."

Hi-Fi News & Record Review 33:115 D '88. Robert Cowan (345w)

"The First Concerto...is given with a towering strength, a weight and musical authority inacessible to all but a mere handful of pianists; even those of world class. The continuity is superb and if others are more darting and fanciful (the composer) or more volatile, few could compete with Pletnev's overall command-....Pesek and the Philharmonia are admirable partners and the recordings are of a fine bloom and resonance."

Music and Musicians International 37:43-4 D '88. Bryce Morrison (350w)

"This whole CD sounds terrific."

Fanfare 12:282-83 My/Je '89. James Miller (700w)

Gramophone 66:1008 D '88. David J. Fanning (330w)

Digital Audio's CD Review 6:94+ O '89. Tom Vernier (190w)

2128. Concerti for Piano and Orchestra: No. 1 in F# minor, Opus 1; No. 2 in C minor, Opus 18.
Peter Rosel (pno). Kurt Sanderling (c). Berlin Symphony Orchestra.
ARS VIVENDI 049 66:54

★*Awards: American Record Guide* Overview: Rachmaninoff, S/O '90 (No. 1).

"These full-blooded performances will not suite everyone, for in playing the brooding lyricism to the hilt, Rosel slights the neoclassical side of Rachmaninov's muse...and snubs some of his more genial splashes of color...But if you can take your Rachmaninov without wit, you'll find Rosel's arch-romantic performances gripping in their fervor....Highly recommended."

Fanfare 13:230-31 Jl/Ag '90. Peter J. Rabinowitz (350w)

"Most hearing these performances [would declare]...both performances entirely too heavy, even perhaps flat-footed. I did at first—until around the fifth hearing, when I realized what stunning artistry is at work....a first choice? No. A choice version? Indeed, yes....Strongest recommendation."

American Record Guide 53:100 S/O '90. Thomas L. Dixon (275w)

2129. Concerti for Piano and Orchestra: No. 1 in F minor, Opus 1; No. 4 in G minor, Opus 40. **Rhapsody on a Theme of Paganini, Opus 43.**
Earl Wild (pno). Jascha Horenstein (c). Royal Philharmonic Orchestra. reissue.
CHESKY 041 ADD 69:07

★*Awards:* *American Record Guide* Overview: Rachmaninoff, S/O '90.

"These fleet and often angular performances have generated heated controversy on these pages...I still find them a constant source of fascination....In the end, where Shelley engages us, Wild seizes us; and while I don't think that the rather high-minded Horenstein is quite a match for Thomson in this repertoire, the accompaniments are undoubtedly well conceived-....Chesky's expert remastering (with 128 times oversampling) certainly inspires renewed appreciation of how much producer Charles Gerhardt captured in his original master tapes. Highest recommendation."
Fanfare 14:255-57 My/Je '91. Peter J. Rabinowitz (280w)

2130. Concerto No. 2 in C minor for Piano and Orchestra, Opus 18. TCHAIKOVSKY, PIOTR ILYICH. Concerto No. 1 in B flat minor for Piano and Orchestra, Opus 23.
Van Cliburn (pno). Kiril Kondrashin; Fritz Reiner (c). RCA Symphony Orchestra; Chicago Symphony Orchestra. reissue 1958; 1963.
RCA 5912 AAD 67:30

★*Awards:* *American Record Guide* Overview: Rachmaninoff, S/O '90.

"Few other pianists have ever played a Tchaikovsky more inherently musical, more tonally sumptuous or controlled. Most remarkable of all RCA have re-mastered this famous record with much of the vividness and sheen of a modern recording; the pianist's glorious sound can be heard in all its richness and fullness-....The shimmer and sweep of the Chicago strings and Fritz Reiner's full-blooded direction are a perfect complement."
Music and Musicians International 37:63-4 Ap '89. Bryce Morrison (600w)

"The Chicago Symphony musicians could probably play Rachmaninoff Two in their sleep. It was not the kind of music to spark Reiner's deepest sympathies. Cliburn valiantly tries to budge Reiner's impassivity. the maestro should have heeded Cliburn more closely. In this music, youth can be wiser than experience."
Ovation 10:58-9 S '89. Joseph Fennimore (330w)

2131. Concerto No. 2 in C minor for Piano and Orchestra, Opus 18; Etudes-Tableaux for Piano, Opus 39.
Evgeny Kissin (pno). Valery Gergiev (c). London Symphony Orchestra. 1988.
RCA 7982 DDD 60:00

★*Awards:* Best Recordings of the Month, *Stereo Review* Ap '89.

"During the three years that separate his Prokofiev from his Rachmaninoff, Mr. Kissin's musical range broadened and deepened. His immense technical facility and uninhibited emotional sweep remain unchanged, but they are balanced by a newly thoughtful, poetic sensibility."
The New York Times S 24 '89, p. H 27. K. Robert Schwarz (160w)

"Judging from this recording debut, Kissin has formidable digital equipment, and the kind of decisive personality one encounters too rarely these pianistic days. The prize here is the sampling of the Op. 39 *Etudes Tableaux*, fairly bristling with spontaneity and yet never far from the music's sinister undercurrents."
Ovation 10:51 Mr '89. Scott Cantrell (380w)

"Kissin, who was all of sixteen when he recorded these performances last May, is not only the most exciting teenage virtuoso to appear since Anne-Sophie Mutter started recording violin concertos with Karajan, but one of the most impressive pianists of any age to come along in decades. If this recording is truly representative, he is a master musician of astounding maturity and depth."
Stereo Review 54:84 Ap '89. Richard Freed (650w)

"But if the Concerto hardly compares with the finest available recordings, the Etudes *are* truly astonishing. With volcanic temperament and technique to burn, Kissin already suggests one of the most dazzling and unsettling talents to have emerged since the young Horowitz."
Hi-Fi News & Record Review 34:110-11 Ap '89. Bryce Morrison (245w)

"Though this might be a minority report, I must admit to being disappointed interpretively by much of what emerges here. Overall, the most impressive moments occur in the finale of the concerto, where real excitement finally fires up the performance....The smooth-sounding reproduction of the piano and well-detailed orchestra, nicely imaged, is impressively rich and full-bodied."
Stereophile 12:165-67 My '89. Igor Kipnis (200w)

"I wouldn't recommend this type of reading [of the concerto] to those who prefer the more brilliant, mercurial style represented by the composer's own recording, but those with more conventional tastes ought to find it very satisfying, even exciting at times, as I do."
Fanfare 12:283-84 My/Je '89. James Miller (485w)

"The orchestral contribution might have been more inspired and delivered more firmly within the sonic frame, but it's quite adequate. The solo pieces are downright mesmerizing."
Stereo Review Presents: Compact Disc Buyers' Guide Summ 1989 p.59 Richard Freed (100w)

"The major talent is certainly in evidence; but, for all but the most avidly curious (this critic among them!), this performance can safely be ignored. There is nothing new or truly arresting, rest assured."

American Record Guide 53:75 Ja/F '90. Thomas L. Dixon (115w)

Gramophone 66:1434-37 Mr '89. David J. Fanning (630w)

The New York Times Ja 7 '90, p. 27 H. Barrymore L. Scherer (100w)

Digital Audio's CD Review 6:75 O '89. Tom Vernier (250w)

2132. Concerto No. 3 in D minor for Piano and Orchestra, Opus 30. PROKOFIEV, SERGEI. Concerto No. 3 in C for Piano and Orchestra, Opus 26.
Santiago Rodriguez (pno). Emil Tabakov (c). Sofia Philharmonic Orchestra.
ELAN 2220 DDD 69:00

★***Awards:*** *American Record Guide* Overview: Rachmaninoff, S/O '90.

"As if a world-class Rachmaninoff Three were not enough for one release, pianist and conductor also throw in a stupendously virile Prokofieff Third...Everything said earlier about the Rachmaninoff performance applies equally here, if not more so. Get this one!"
American Record Guide 53:90-1 Mr/Ap '90. Donald Manildi (565w)

"Based on what I knew of their recordings of other music, I expected that Rodriguez and Tabakov would give a good account of themselves on this Rachmaninov/Prokofiev CD and I found my expectations confirmed by the comparatively fast tempo they adopt at the beginning of the Rachmaninov....I wish I could tell you more clearly (and more succinctly) why I think this is one of the better versions of the piece, but aren't most reviews, ultimately, attempts to objectify the subjective?"
Fanfare 13:257-59 My/Je '90. James Miller (1550w)

"Santiago Rodriguez and Bulgarian conductor Emil Tabakov convey the most positively macho, dramatic, and emotionally riveting performance [of the Rachmaninoff Concerto] within long memory....Similarly, Prokofiev's Third Concerto, which graces the remainder of this sensational disc, is presented in an interpretation so witty, impudent, and blatantly imaginative as to surpass even the versions by Martha Argerich, Weissenberg, and Kapell-....The sound, while not of demonstration quality, is of such lovely immediacy as to make the listening quite compulsive."
Musical America 110:18 Jl '90. Thomas L. Dixon (455w)

"Rodriguez...is sadly let down in both works by the orchestra, which is simply not competitive in works that demand the same level of virtuosity from that quarter as from the soloist."
Stereo Review 55:94 Jl '90. Richard Freed (185w)

"He plays too obviously for effect, willfully ignoring Rachmaniov's directions...in favour of an often flashy alternative. The musical personality is too inconsistent and lacking in cogency to make such an elaborate show of 'difference', or individuality, truly convincing-....Elan's recording is of limited range and quality." *P75 S75*
Hi-Fi News & Record Review 35:93 Ag '90. Bryce Morrison (390w)

"Rodriguez, in sum, comes on a little too much like a matinee idol to be altogether convincing, attractive as his sensibilities and technique are in themselves."
Audio 75:90+ F '91. Robert Long (430w)

Gramophone 67:1982+ My '90. Stephen Johnson (260w)

RAVEL, MAURICE

2133. Concerto in G for Piano and Orchestra; Concerto in D for Piano (left hand) and Orchestra; Orchestral Music: Fanfare for "L'Eventail de Jeanne"; Menuet Antique; Le Tombeau de Couperin.
Martha Argerich (pno); Michel Beroff (pno). Claudio Abbado (c). London Symphony Orchestra. 1984, 1987.
DEUTSCHE GRAMMOPHON 423 665 DDD 65:00

★★***Awards:*** Best Recordings of the Month, *Stereo Review* O '89. Cream of the Crop IV, *Digital Audio's CD Review*, 6:42 Je '90.

"The new performance [of the G Major Concerto] may not quite match the intensity and drive of the earlier one, but it is not wanting in vivacity or wit, and it surpasses all current rivals, I think, in terms of finesse and the level of integration between soloist and orchestra."
Stereo Review 54:108 O '89. Richard Freed (390w)

"The standard of quality here is a high one-....Highly recommended."
Fanfare 13:329-30 N/D '89. James Miller (210w)

Gramophone 66:1291-92 F '89. Christopher Headington (390w)

Hi-Fi News & Record Review 34:93 Mr '89. Christopher Breunig (420w)

Digital Audio's CD Review 6:82 D '89 Lawrence Johnson (250w); 6:62 Je '90 Tom Vernier (160w)

RODRIGO, JOAQUIN. = Fantasia para un gentilhombre for Guitar and Orchestra. See No. 2046.

ROSNER, ARNOLD. Five Meditations, for English Horn, Harp and Strings, Opus 36; A Gentle Musicke, for Flute and Strings, Opus 44. See No. 1310.

SAINT-SAENS, CAMILLE

2134. Concerti for Piano and Orchestra: No. 2 in G minor, Opus 22; No. 4 in C minor, Opus 44.

Jean-Philippe Collard (pno). Andre Previn (c). Royal Philharmonic Orchestra. July, 1985.
EMI 47816 DDD 50:00

★*Awards:* *Gramophone* Critics' Choice (Robert Layton), 1987.

"The playing is gorgeous, the sound stunning."
High Fidelity 38:65 Mr '88. Robert R. Reilly (300w)

"From the incisive, dramatically pregnant toccata that opens Jean-Philippe Collard's account of the Saint-Saens Second Piano Concerto to the headlong surge that carries the problematic Fourth to a heady finish, this collaboration with Andre Previn proves a thoroughgoing triumph. It may be the most satisfying coupling of these oft-mated concertos ever committed to discs."
Ovation 9:21-2 Ag '88. Lawrence B. Johnson (215w)

"Multimiking of a sort not ordinarily encountered from EMI puts soloist and orchestra mostly on the same plane, with ambiguous imaging and an unnatural level of detail. The sound is brighter than Erato's, and decidedly aggressive....Collard and Previn are among the most deadly-serious interpreters the piece [the G minor] has ever fallen afoul of on record, in a hard-pressed, hard-toned, and consistently unsmiling account of otherwise exemplary clarity."
Fanfare 11:211-2 N/D '87. John D. Wiser (370w)

Gramophone 65:186-7 Jl '87 Robert Layton (310w) (rev. of LP); 65:639 O '87 Alan Sanders (95w) (rev. of CD)

Digital Audio 4:58-9 Ja '88. Tom Vernier (295w)

SALIERI, ANTONIO. Concerto in D for Violin, Oboe, Cello and Orchestra. See No. 2056.

SAMMARTINI, GIUSEPPE. Concerti Grossi in E minor and in G minor; Concerto in F for Recorder and Orchestra. See No. 1318.

SCELSI, GIACINTO. @REFTITLE = Anahit, for Violin and Chamber Orchestra. See No. 1320.

SCHNITTKE, ALFRED

2135. Concerti for Violin and Orchestra: No. 1 (1957, rev. 1962); No. 2 (1966).
Mark Lubotsky (vln). Eri Klas (c). Malmo Symphony Orchestra. Malmo Concert Hall.
BIS 487 DDD 61:00

★*Awards:* The Want List 1991, *Fanfare* N/D '91 (Mike Silverton).

"Prokofiev, Bartok, Bloch among others are elicited by Schnittke's imaginative harmonic resources [in No. 1], and by his way of using coloristic devices....[Concerto No. 2] is far more firmly shaped in respect to the solo playing than Lubotsky's earlier recording, which originated with Melodiya but so far as I know appeared only on the Eurodisc label. The orchestra, too, seems to have under Eri Klas a more secure sense of what the music is about than the Leningrad players under Rozhdestvensky of the older recording (ca. 1976)....a strong recommendation."
Fanfare 15:339-41 S/O '91. John Wiser (med)

"Lubotsky's clean bowing is throughout this CD a pleasure in itself, and the orchestral playing under Eri Klas is crisp and rhythmically alert. Both works are finely balanced, in the classic manner of the best BBC transmissions: excellent perspectives, and well judged ambience." *P95 S95*
Hi-Fi News & Record Review 36:87 Ap '91. Christopher Breunig (240w)

"Alfred Schnittke (b 1934) is probably one of the most overrated and over-performed of currently practicing composers. But his First Violin Concerto...is a pleasant surprise...I think it is the best piece of his I've heard. More typical is the Second Concerto for violin and chamber orchestra."
American Record Guide 54:101 My/Je '91. Kyle Rothweiler (110w)

Gramophone 68:1845 Ap '91. David J. Fanning (385w)

SCHOECK, OTHMAR. Concerto in B flat for Violin and Orchestra, Opus 21. See No. 1328.

SCHUMANN, ROBERT

Concerto in A minor for Cello and Orchestra, Opus 129. See No. 1341.

2136. Concerto in A minor for Piano and Orchestra, Opus 54. GRIEG, EDVARD. Concerto in A minor for Piano and Orchestra, Opus 16.
Geza Anda (pno). Rafael Kubelik (c). Berlin Philharmonic Orchestra.
DEUTSCHE GRAMMOPHON 415 850 63:00

★*Awards:* *American Record Guide* Overview: Schumann, My/Je '88.

Gramophone 65:281-2 Ag '87 Ivan March (160w)

2137. Concerto in D minor for Violin and Orchestra; Fantasy in C for Violin and Orchestra, Opus 131.
Thomas Zehetmair (vln). Christoph Eschenbach (c). Philharmonia Orchestra.
TELDEC 44190 DDD 45:00

✔**HC** ★*Awards:* Critics' Choice 1990, *Gramophone* D '90 (Joan Chissell).

Gramophone 67:1792 Ap '90. Joan Chissell (455w)

SHCHEDRIN, RODION. Concerto No. 1 in D for Piano and Orchestra. See No. 4179.

SHOSTAKOVICH, DMITRI

2138. Concerti for Cello and Orchestra: (No. 1) in E flat, Opus 107; No. 2, Opus 126.
Heinrich Schiff (cello). Maxim Shostakovich (c). Bavarian Radio Symphony Orchestra.
PHILIPS 412 526 DDD 62:54

✔HC ★★*Awards: Fanfare* Want List 1986 (Royal S. Brown); *Gramophone* Critics' Choice 1985 (Robert Layton).

"Although I never thought I'd hear myself relegating Mstislav Rostropovich to second place in anything, I certainly prefer the Schiff/Maxim Shostakovich version of the Second Cello Concerto to the Rostropovich/Ozawa one on DG 2530 653-....Adding to the attractiveness of the Philips package (a perfect coupling, by the way) is the clarity, richness, and range of the CD sound."
Fanfare 9:251-2 N/D '85. Royal S. Brown (775w)

"Elegant, imbued playing from Schiff."
Hi-Fi News & Record Review 30:109 O '85. Ivor Humphreys (90w)

"Shostakovich's two Cello Concertos receive knowledgeable if not entirely successful presentations."
High Fidelity 36:57 Mr '86. Bill Zakariasen (150w)

"The Austrian cellist Heinrich Schiff offers probing readings that well hold their own alongside Rostropovich's....As heard on CD, the sound is astonishingly realistic."
Gramophone 63:242 Ag '85 (475w) (rev. of LP); 63:510+ O '85 (195w) (rev. of CD). Robert Layton

Stereo Review 51:98 Ja '86. Richard Freed (300w)

Opus 2:52-3 Ap '86. John Canarina (360w)

Digital Audio 2:52 Ap '86. Laurel E. Fay (600w)

Concerto No. 2 in F for Piano and Orchestra. See No. 1354.

Concerto No. 1 for Piano, Trumpet and Orchestra. See No. 1354

2139. Concerto No. 1 in A minor for Violin and Orchestra. PROKOFIEV, SERGEI. Concerto No. 2 in G minor for Violin and Orchestra, Opus 63.
Viktoria Mullova (vln). Andre Previn (c). Royal Philharmonic Orchestra. 1988.
PHILIPS 422 364 DDD 60:00

★★*Awards:* Best Recordings of the Month, *Stereo Review* N '89. Editors' Choice, *Digital Audio's CD Review*, 6:34+ Je '90.

"Shostakovich's First Violin Concerto is by all odds one of the most remarkable such works composed in our century, trembling, it would seem, on the edge of the so-called 'standard repertoire.' The new Philips recording by Viktoria Mullova, with the Royal Philharmonic under Andre Previn, might well push the work over that edge, to a permanent place beside the concertos of Beethoven, Brahms, and Tchaikovsky....Magnificent is the word for this recording."
Stereo Review 54:123-24 N '89. Richard Freed (650w)

"She captures the emotional and timbral extremes, juxtaposing grim, haunted desperation with shrill, lean, mocking humor."
The New York Times S 24 '89, p. H 27. K. Robert Schwarz (160w)

"Philips' recording has quite exceptional depth-...The Prokofiev G-minor fares best where the mood is delicate and inward-looking...This disc is more or less indispensable for Shostakovich 1: a riveting performance that can stand comparison with CBS's classic Oistrakh/NYPO/Mitropoulos version from 1955."
Hi-Fi News & Record Review 34:82 Jl '89. Robert Cowan (525w)

"Mullova...offers technically expert, straightforward interpretations in which the greatest attribute, perhaps, is the utter fluidity of her playing....I also particularly like the quality of Mullova's vibrato....Mullova is just a tad underrecorded in the Shostakovich."
Fanfare 13:359-62 N/D '89. Royal S. Brown (300w)

"Here is unmistakably great music making and violin playing on a level of consistency achieved by few artists of any age or specialization. The conducting and the orchestral playing are fairly pedantic, which is definitely disappointing but not so damaging as to detract from Mullova's accomplishments. Philips engineer Roger de Schot has reached a level of sonic success too seldom encountered on this label."
American Record Guide 53:75-6 Ja/F '90. Alan Heatherington (225w)

"She slashes into the second movement of Shostakovich's Concerto No. 1 with electrifying elan and vigor, turning austere and stoic in the Passacaglia that follows. Her performance of the showy finale led me to conclude that here she has made a recording musically superior to those done in Moscow and New York by David Oistrakh, for whom Shostakovich wrote the piece. The Prokofiev's first movement presents Mullova at her warmest, and its Mozartean middle movement unfolds under her incandescent, vaulting lyricism."
Musical America 110:76 My '90. Paul Moor (125w)

Digital Audio's CD Review 6:64 N '89. David Vernier (620w)

Gramophone 67:43 Je '89. Edward Seckerson (455w)

2140. Concerto No. 1 in A minor for Violin and Orchestra, Opus 77 (1947-8 version); Concerto No. 2 in C# minor for Violin and Orchestra, Opus 129.
David Oistrakh (vln). Maxim Shostakovich; Yevgeny Svetlanov (c). New Philharmonia Orchestra USSR State Symphony Orchestra. Royal Festival Hall, London. November 20, 1972 live; August 1968 live.
INTAGLIO 7241 ADD 60:48

✔HC

SIBELIUS, JEAN

2141. Concerto in D minor for Violin and Orchestra, Opus 47. PROKOFIEV, SERGEI. Concerto No. 2 in G minor for Violin and Orchestra, Opus 63. GLAZUNOV, ALEXANDER. Concerto in A minor for Violin and Orchestra, Opus 82.
Jascha Heifetz (vln). Walter Hendl; Charles Munch (c). Chicago Symphony Orchestra; Boston Symphony Orchestra; RCA Symphony Orchestra. reissue.
RCA 7019 68:55

★*Awards:* *Gramophone* Critics' Choice 1986 (Alan Sanders).

"One of the most heartening aspects of the current CD boom lies in the concern of the major companies for the restoration of historic and classic performances. This disc is a prime example....Except for the Glazunov (a 1963 studio production), these performances hardly show their age, thanks to the expert RCA restoration....Greater playing and a finer value are simply not to be had."

High Fidelity 36:62 Ag '86. Thomas L. Dixon (225w)

"This is major-league violin playing of the kind that made him [Heifetz] as awesome to most of his colleagues as he was to the general public, and RCA has done a good job with the digitalization."

Fanfare 11:252 Jl/Ag '88. James Miller (70w)

Gramophone 64:575 O '86 Alan Sanders (315w)

2142. Concerto in D minor for Violin and Orchestra, Opus 47 (original 1903-04 version and final 1905 version).
Leonidas Kavakos (vln). Osmo Vanska (c). Lahti Symphony Orchestra.
BIS 500 DDD 75:00

★★★*Awards:* The Gramophone Awards, Nominations, Concerto, *Gramophone*, N '91; The Want List 1991, *Fanfare* N/D '91 (David K. Nelson). Best Concerto Recording 1991, *Gramophone*, D '91.

"For those who are interested only in the final, definitive thoughts of a composer, half of this disc will hold no interest. For those who are fascinated by the creative process, this is a gold mine....Both versions are superbly conducted by Vanska; and the orchestra, while clearly not among the world's top ten, is certainly better than most that we hear regularly-....This is one of the best of BIS technically, as is so often the case when Robert von Bahr himself produces the recording. Overall, I would place this almost on a plane with Heifetz/Beecham and Oistrakh/Rozhdestvensky as a performance. It clearly surpasses them in sound."

American Record Guide 54:109-10 My/Je '91. Carl Bauman (720w)

"This original score is recorded only with the express permission of the composer's family (it will be 2007 before they allow another hearing, apparently); young Greek virtuoso Leonidas Kavakos certainly makes out a persuasive case for it...Likewise, his performance of the final version we all know and love is neat, thoughtful and profoundly musical. Osmo Vanska and the excellent Lahti SO provide most idiomatic support throughout, and, as ever, BIS have given us a natural, concert-hall balance, though some will find the soloist a bit too backwardly placed if anything." *P95 (100)/historic S95*

Hi-Fi News & Record Review 36:75 Je '91. Andrew Achenbach (450w)

"Kavakos's big technique and warm sound are recorded realistically (do heed BIS's warnings about dynamic range), meaning that when Sibelius presents a balance problem, it sounds like a balance problem. Kavakos softens the acute angles of some phrases, so I was reminded of Miriam Fried's warm and passionate recording on Finlandia; Kavakos's smoldering temperament also called Bustabo to mind. I prefer fire-and-ice artists like Heifetz or Ricci, but this is far, far more than merely an adequate performance or a token gesture....The revision is greater music but the original has considerable merits above and beyond pure novelty....a near-mandatory purchase for the Sibelian."

Fanfare 14:290-1 Jl/Ag '91. David K. Nelson (750w)

"This is a recording of considerable interest to violinists for it presents the premiere of the original 1903 version of the well-known Sibelius *Violin Concerto*...The violinist, Leonidas Kavakos, is clearly a major talent...he performs both versions with superb technique and musicality."

HighPerformanceReview 8(2):76 Summer '91. George S. T. Chu (200w)

Digital Audio's CD Review 7:64+ S '91. David Vernier (485w)

Gramophone 68:1845 Ap '91. Robert Layton (630w)

2143. Concerto in D minor for Violin and Orchestra, Opus 47. NIELSEN, CARL. Concerto for Violin and Orchestra, Opus 33.
Cho-Liang Lin (vln). Esa-Pekka Salonen (c). Philharmonia Orchestra; Swedish Radio Symphony Orchestra. Watford Town Hall, London; Berwald Hall,

Stockholm. 1987, 1988.
CBS 44548 DDD 69:17

✔HC ★★*Awards:* Concerto Record Award 1989, *Gramophone*, D '89. Editors' Choice, *Digital Audio's CD Review*, 6:36 Je '90; Cream of the Crop IV, *Digital Audio's CD Review*, 6:43 Je '90.

"In contrast with the recent highly poetic Nigel Kennedy-Simon Rattle performance [of the Sibelius] on Angel, this one by Cho-Liang Lin and Esa-Pekka Salonen is fiery and impetuous—brilliantly virtuosic in the old Heifetz manner. But what really distinguishes this release is the pairing of the Sibelius with an outstanding performance of the Violin Concerto of Denmark's Carl Nielsen...The sound in both works is absolutely superb—clean, powerful, and well balanced."
Stereo Review 54:124+ Je '89. David Hall (275w)

"So far as Sibelius is concerned, I'm inclined to favor this performance over all current competition. [In] The Nielsen concerto....Lin and *his* competition, violinist Dong-Suk Kang (BIS CD-370, *Fanfare* 11:2, pp. 190-91; 11:3, pp.184-85), are more or less on a par in organization, but Lin has a range of shading, and an inclination to use it well, that puts him out in front."
Fanfare 12:268-69 Ja/F '89. John Wiser (310w)

"The present recording is a sensible pairing-...Lin...proves highly responsive to their differing demands, giving excellent accounts of both."
Hi-Fi News & Record Review 34:113 Ap '89. Kenneth Dommett (200w)

"Some listeners will choose this performance as totally satisfying. For my taste, however, Lin is given to *attacking* this beautiful music, leaving rough edges everywhere and too frequently losing any sense of melodic line except in the middle movement. Too much protesting. Salonen exacerbates matters with his self-indulgent dynamic splashes and unidiomatic balances....The filler work...suffers from the same defects."
American Record Guide 52:84-5 Mr/Ap '89. Alan Heatherington (235w)

"This release is an injustice to Sibelius and Nielsen. Do them—and yourself—a favor. Choose any recording but this one."
Stereophile 12:167 My '89. Robert Hesson (350w)

Gramophone 66:1158 Ja '89. Robert Layton (235w)

Digital Audio's CD Review 5:68 Ap '89 Philip Hald (340w); 5:54+ Jl '89 Lawrence Johnson (205w)

2144. Concerto in D minor for Violin and Orchestra, Opus 47; Overture in A minor; Menuetto; In Memoriam, Opus 59.
Silvia Marcovici (vln). Neeme Jarvi (c). Gothenburg Symphony Orchestra. 1986-87.
BIS 372 DDD 54:00

★*Awards:* *American Record Guide* Overview: Popular Violin Concertos, S/O '89.

"Marcovici and Jarvi have achieved a recorded miracle that serves Sibelius spectacularly well-....Somehow Marcovici, who has played this work for many years, allows the listener to move beyond technique-consciousness to a realm where only the stunningly beautiful music is heard. Jarvi effortlessly allows this to happen....I have not run out of superlatives, nor will I run out of pleasure in hearing this disc despite countless recent repetitions in futile quest of some fault."
American Record Guide 52:84-5 Mr/Ap '89. Alan Heatherington (235w)

"The smaller orchestral works coupled with the concerto are not very distinguished music-....Quite sufficient back is put by conductor and orchestra into the task of making this sorry lot presentable....But there is tough competition for the concerto."
Fanfare 12:278-29 Mr/Ap '89. John Wiser (450w)

Gramophone 66:1158 Ja '89. Robert Layton (235w)

Digital Audio's CD Review 5:53 Mr '89. David Vernier (325w)

The New York Times N 12 '89, p. H 29. George Jellinek (b.n.)

Concerto in D minor for Violin and Orchestra, Opus 47. See No. 2045.

STENHAMMAR, WILHELM. Two Sentimental Romances for Violin and Orchestra, Opus 28. See No. 6131.

STONE, CARL

2145. Four Pieces: Wall Me Do; Hop Ken; Shing Kee; Sonali.
Carl Stone (synth).
ELECTRO-ACOUSTIC MUSIC 201 DDD 55:15

★★*Awards:* The Want List 1990, *Fanfare* N/D '90 (Kyle Gann); The Want List 1990, *Fanfare* N/D '90 (Mike Silverton).

"This is the best contemporary electronic music I know."
American Record Guide 53:113 Jl/Ag '90. Timothy D. Taylor (410w)

"*Wall Me Do* and *Sonali* entertain on several levels, and can therefore be enjoyed entirely at their richly delighting surfaces: both are essentially pop-inspired, with substance enough for distancing from the congenital simple-mindedness in which their models dwell (a form of musical irony I especially enjoy)....*Shing Kee* [is], the earliest and for me most purely magical work on the disc."
Fanfare 13:279-80 Jl/Ag '90. Mike Silverton (400w)

STRAUSS, RICHARD

Burleske in D minor for Piano and Orchestra. See No. 2040.

Concerto No. 1 in E flat for Horn, Opus 11; Concerto No. 2 in E flat for Horn. See No. 2071.

Concerto for Violin and Orchestra. See No. 2070.

2145a. Don Quixote, for Cello and Orchestra, Opus 35; Death and Transfiguration, Opus 24.
Pierre Fournier (cello); Giusto Cappone (vla). Herbert Von Karajan (c). Berlin Philharmonic Orchestra. 1967; 1974.
DEUTSCHE GRAMMOPHON 429 184 ADD 71:00

★*Awards:* *American Record Guide* Overview: Strauss Tone Poems, Mr/Ap '90.

Gramophone 67:1802+ Ap '90. Michael Kennedy (315w)

2145b. Don Quixote, for Cello and Orchestra, Opus 35; Till Eulenspiegels Lustige Streiche, Opus 28.
Antonio Meneses (cello); Wolfram Christ (viola). Herbert Von Karajan (c). Berlin Philharmonic Orchestra.
DEUTSCHE GRAMMOPHON 419 599 DDD 58:32

★★*Awards:* *Hi-Fi News & Record Review Record of the Month, S '87. Gramophone* Critics' Choice (David Fanning), 1987.

"Whatever else the Maestro may have in store, these loving fresh tributes to scores he cares about will surely remain among the glories of his later years."
Hi-Fi News & Record Review 32:93 S '87 David Nice (410w)

"Karajan and Meneses have given us a solid *Don Quixote*, but, ultimately, a disappointing one....Karajan's finely crafted reading [of *Till Eulenspiegel* is superlatively played but perhaps a shade too refined for his raffish subject."
Fanfare 11:216-7 Ja/F '88. George Chien (450w)

"The Berlin Philharmonic produces some predictably ravishing sounds here [*Don Quixote*], but Karajan's marginal lessening of tempo and DG's papery recording (this is another Telemondial soundtrack) are fatal to the cohesiveness of this protracted score....Karajan conducts *Till Eulenspiegel* with all the energy and command evinced in his 1973 recording, and even the sound quality has the ingratiating warmth DG provided fifteen years ago."
American Record Guide 51:84 Mr/Ap '88. Arved Ashby (365w)

"*Don Quixote*, the most humane of the tone poems, gets a rather detached treatment in this new recording...*Till Eulenspiegel* gets an efficient run-through, with all dramatic and coloristic points duly made but with less of the style and savagery this music needs to become a memorable listening experience."
Stereo Review 53:107-8 Ap '88. David Hall (175w)

Gramophone 65:302+ Ag '87 Michael Kennedy (420w)

Don Quixote, for Cello and Orchestra Opus 35. See No. 1412, 1413.

STRAVINSKY, IGOR

Concerto in D for Violin and Orchestra. See No. 2080.

Music of Stravinsky: Concertos: Piano Concerto (Philippe Entremont, pno; Columbia SO); Capriccio (Entremont; Columbia SO); Movements (Charles Rosen, pno; Columbia SO); Violin Concerto (Isaac Stern, vln; Columbia SO). Concerto in D major. Concerto for Two Pianos (I. and Soulima Stravinsky, pnos). See No. 1425.

SUSSMAYR, FRANZ XAVER. Concerto in D for Clarinet and Orchestra. See No. 2084.

TCHAIKOVSKY, PIOTR ILYICH

2146. Concerto No. 1 in B flat minor for Piano and Orchestra, Opus 23. GRIEG, EDVARD. Concerto in A minor for Piano and Orchestra, Opus 16.
(The Rubinstein Collection).
Artur Rubinstein (pno). Erich Leinsdorf (c). Boston Symphony Orchestra. reissue.
RCA 6259 ADD 63:14

★*Awards:* *American Record Guide* Overview: Romantic Piano Concertos, Jl/Ag '90.

"Beyond the exceptional sonic quality of the collection lies its value as documentation for posterity of one of the great pianistic personalities of the century....these 35 CDs ["The Rubinstein Collection"] must be regarded as the cornerstone of any collection of piano recordings."
American Record Guide 52:118-21 Jl/Ag '89. Donald Manildi (55w) (rev. of the collection)

Fanfare 11:215 Mr/Ap '88. Howard Kornblum (150w)

Concerto No. 1 in B flat minor for Piano and Orchestra, Opus 23. See No. 2057, 2123, 2130.

2147. Concerto in D for Violin and Orchestra, Opus 35. WIENIAWSKI, HENRYK. Concerto No. 2 in D minor for Violin and Orchestra, Opus 22.
Joshua Bell (vln). Vladimir Ashkenazy (c). Cleveland Orchestra. 1988, 1989.
LONDON/DECCA 421 716 DDD 59:00

★*Awards:* The Want List 1989, *Fanfare* N/D '89 (Jon Tuska).

"Bell's performance is scintillating. He dances above the surface with a lightness and felicity that is at times little short of astonishing. The engineers have elected to place Bell on something of a sonic promontory. Here we may examine his perfection of tone with almost clinical precision. Some listeners may find the effect slightly unbalanced and 'unrealistic' but given that the Concerto is a showpiece, the decision to 'feature' Bell is not unreasonable."

Australian Hi-Fi 20(1):Music Review 16 '89. (400w)

"This is still how an adolescent might feel the extremes of Tchaikovsky's emotional barometer, given the technique which one can now take for granted with Bell. Listen to the wonderfully improvisatory quality of the opening flourishes in the outer movements—teasing our expectations of the main event, slyly nudging up to the B-flat before careering off into the finale proper."

Hi-Fi News & Record Review 34:96-7 Mr '89. David Nice (315w)

"There may be other recordings of the Tchaikovsky with more flair and excitement, but none of either work, I think, that is more musically sound."

Stereo Review 54:92 Ap '89. Richard Freed (100w)

"This release proves that Bell has got the chops. It also reaffirms that he is an uncommonly interesting musician...Bell is recorded in a flattering acoustic, fortunately."

Fanfare 12:334 My/Je '89. David K. Nelson (525w)

"Bell virtually lurches into Tchaikovsky's more romantic statements, and rushes through the rest....In this beautifully recorded disc, Ashkenazy follows every vagary of his soloist, whose obvious talents as a fiddler do not produce a continuous performance. I should say that Bell does an altogether better job on the lesser work recorded here."

Fanfare 12:334-35 My/Je '89. Michael Ullman (160w)

Bell's "account of the Tchaikovsky is infinitely more conventional than, say, Nigel Kennedy's eccentric reading (Angel EMI)...in fact, many of his mannerisms seem drawn from long-honored conventions....there is much to praise in this recording—not the least of which is the Cleveland Orchestra's flexible, perfectly balanced, genuinely enthusiastic accompaniment."

High Fidelity 39:71 Je '89. K. Robert Schwarz (300w)

Music and Musicians International 38:51 N '89. David Denton (140w)

Digital Audio's CD Review 6:95 D '89. Lawrence Johnson (190w)

Gramophone 66:1014 D '88. Edward Greenfield (215w)

2148. Concerto in D for Violin and Orchestra, Opus 35. MENDELSSOHN, FELIX. Concerto in E minor for Violin & Orchestra, Opus 64.

Kyung-Wha Chung (vln). Charles Dutoit (c). Montreal Symphony Orchestra.
LONDON/DECCA 410 011

★*Awards: Gramophone* Critics' Choice 1983 (Edward Greenfield).

"Chung's rich tone rings out in full beauty on CD....This is one of the best available recordings of the popular pairing."

High Performance Review 3 (1):128-9 Ag '84. (150w)

"Kyung Wha Chung recorded these same two violin concertos for London/Decca early in her career....In this splendid new digital recording, her performances clearly reflect growth and maturity as a violin virtuoso of international renown....Dutoit's Montrealers get better and better, and his accompaniment for the violinist is nicely balanced, displaying a good rapport between these artists."

Audio 70:354 O '86 Bert Whyte (295w)

Gramophone 61:241 Ag '83. Edward Greenfield (245w)

Ovation 5:44 Mr '84. Paul Turok (175w)

2149. Concerto in D for Violin and Orchestra, Opus 35; Serenade Melancolique for Violin and Orchestra. Opus 26; Serenade in C for Strings, Opus 48: Waltz. MENDELSSOHN, FELIX. Concerto in E minor for Violin and Orchestra, Opus 64.

Jascha Heifetz (vln). Fritz Reiner (c). Chicago Symphony Orchestra. reissue.
RCA 5933 64:24

✔**HC** ★★*Awards:* First Place Non-Vocal Reissues Mumm Champagne Classical Music Award 1988—Presented by *Ovation, Ovation* N '88. *American Record Guide* Overview: Popular Violin Concertos, S/O '89.

"This fabulous reissue is certainly not recommend to those with high blood pressure or to anyone with prim or conventional tastes....Only those who think the standard classics should be exciting and provide unsuspected thrills should investigate the Heifetz."

High Fidelity 37:78 N '87. Thomas L. Dixon (200w)

"A fine reissue."

Fanfare 11:239 N/D '87. Howard Kornblum (200w)

"For their legions of fans, these classic, late-fifties Heifetz recordings of the Tchaikovsky and Mendelssohn Violin Concertos need little comment. Suffice it to say that they have made the transfer to CD exceptionally well—perhaps they're a little brighter now, but clearer, cleaner, and more detailed than they have ever sounded on LP."

American Record Guide 51:87-8 Mr/Ap '88. John J. Puccio (525w)

Serenade melancolique for Violin and Orchestra, Opus 26; Valse-Scherzo for Violin and Orchestra, Opus 34. See No. 2118.

TELEMANN, GEORG PHILIPP

2150. Concerto in F for Recorder, Bassoon, and Strings, Concerto in C for Recorder and Strings. VIVALDI, ANTONIO. Concerto in F for Bassoon and Orchestra; Concerto in G minor for Flute, Bassoon and Strings, R.104, "La Notte".
Clas Pehrsson (recorder); Michael McGraw (bassoon). Drottningholm Baroque Ensemble.
BIS 271 DDD 51:31

✓HC ★*Awards:* Perfect 10/10, *Digital Audio*, Mr '88.

"These readings offer spirit and personality, and I am particularly pleased with their performance of the Vivaldi bassoon concerto...heartily recommended."
Fanfare 9:233 Ja/F '86. Nils Anderson (400w)

"I enjoyed this collection very much."
Hi-Fi News & Record Review 31:129+ My '86. John Atkinson (210w)

"In summary, a fine recording of some unfamiliar though interesting and enjoyable music. Warmly recommended."
American Record Guide 49:88 S/O '86 John P. McKelvey (210w)

Digital Audio 2:54 Ja '86. David Vernier (355w)

TISHCHENKO, BORIS IVANOVICH

2151. Concerto No. 2 for Violin and Orchestra, Opus 84.
Sergei Stadler (vln). Vasili Sinaisky (c). Leningrad Philharmonic Orchestra.
MELODIYA 123; OLYMPIA 123 AAD 52:00

★★★*Awards:* The Want List 1989, *Fanfare* N/D '89 (Royal S. Brown); The Want List 1989, *Fanfare* N/D '89 (Benjamin Pernick); Critics' Choice 1989, *Gramophone* D '89 (David Fanning).

"From the outset, Stadler captures the acidic humor of the opening violin motif; he then goes on to meet every emotional and technical challenge with amazing sensitivity to the composer's style and with stunning expertise....by and large, the ensemble plays off well against Stadler....A major release."
Fanfare 12:266-67 Jl/Ag '89. Royal S. Brown (450w)

"In *Fanfare* 12:6, I raved about the Olympia release of this work: I also included it in my 1989 Want List as 'simply the best new work of 'classical' music I have heard over the past twelve months.' Get it."
Fanfare 13:317 My/Je '90. Royal S. Brown (b.n.)

Gramophone 66:1014 D '88. David J. Fanning (320w)

VAN DE VATE, NANCY. Concertpiece for Cello and Small Orchestra. See No. 1456.

VAUGHAN WILLIAMS, RALPH

Concerto Academico, for Violin and Orchestra. See No. 1464.

Concerto for 2 Pianos and Orchestra. See No. 1466.

The Lark Ascending (Romance for Violin and Orchestra). See No. 1469.

VIEUXTEMPS, HENRI. Concerto No. 5 in A minor, Opus 37. See No. 2119.

VILLA-LOBOS, HEITOR

2152. Choros: No. 8, for 2 Pianos and Orchestra; No. 9 for Orchestra.
Kenneth Schermerhorn (c). Hong Kong Philharmonic Orchestra.
RECORDS INTERNATIONAL 7002

★*Awards:* *Fanfare* Want List 1986 (Paul Snook).

"This outstanding release fills one of the most conspicuous gaps in the Villa-Lobos discography and is an indispensable acquisition for all admirers of the irrepressible creative dynamo that Oliver Messiaen once likened to a natural force and described as 'ce grand musicien bresilien.'...One of the essential records of the year."
Fanfare 9:269-70 My/Je '86. Paul Snook (600w)

"Hong Kong is surely an unexpected source for this music...but the performances by that city's philharmonic under Kenneth Schermerhorn sound thoroughly idiomatic, some thin violin sound notwithstanding....The reproduction is extremely vivid; anything less would not do for this music."
Opus 2:54 Je '86. John Canarina (610w)

"*Choro* No. 8 is one of Villa-Lobos's masterpieces...Villa-Lobos's complex and rich fabric cries out for the most sophisticated sound quality, which is exactly what it gets here."
High Fidelity 36:63 Jl '86. Harry Halbreich (250w) (rev. of LP)

Concerto for Guitar and Orchestra. See No. 1472.

VIVALDI, ANTONIO

Concerto in F for Bassoon and Orchestra; Concerto in G minor for Flute, Bassoon and Strings, R.104, "La Notte". See No. 2150.

2153. Concerti for Cello and Orchestra: R.424; R.416; R.418; R.412; R.401; R.413.

Christophe Coin (cello). Christopher Hogwood (c). Academy of Ancient Music.
OISEAU-LYRE 421 732 DDD 58:00

★*Awards:* Critics' Choice 1989, *Gramophone* D '89 (Nicholas Anderson).

"Coin and Hogwood have refreshingly chosen to accent Vivaldi's subtle use of tonal colour and melodic shape rather than the overtly virtuosic element of these concertos, although Coin is more than equal to the challenges Vivaldi poses."
Continuo 14:30 O '90. Scott Paterson (120w)

"Hogwood's performances are among his most committed in years. In addition to his usual feeling for the style of the music, he is unusually attuned to its minute emotional twists, eliciting its volatility. As for Coin, sometimes the cello lines can be downright craggy, but he never tries to smooth them out into something suave and bland. On the other hand, his articulation on the authentic instruments (a cello and a cello piccolo) is so much more fluid than what we're used to hearing on a modern cello that the virtuosic aspects of the music don't call attention to themselves but seem like an integrated part of the total expression."
Stereo Review 55:134 Ja '90. David Patrick Stearns (215w)

"In sum, a delightful disc that can be highly recommended to both the Vivaldian and the casual listener. The sound is excellent."
Fanfare 13:336 Ja/F '90. Nils Anderson (275w)

"The once-rigid, austere conductor seems to have loosened up considerably—and since he was always at his best in early 18th century repertory, what was good before has become excellent indeed."
Musical America 110:87+ Mr '90. K. Robert Schwarz (380w)

"The recording is proportioned and spaced so as to give a lyrically warm, chamber-music impression. Perhaps there is a very slight danger that Coin may sound too casual in the longer slow solos...however, even this 'laid back' impression is, in its own way, extremely beguiling." *P100/95 S95*
Hi-Fi News & Record Review 35:99 My '90. Stephen Daw (215w)

2154. Concerti for Flute and Orchestra: R.427, 438, 440, 533, 428, 436, 429.
Janet See (flute). Nicholas McGegan (c). Philharmonia Baroque Orchestra.
HARMONIA MUNDI 905193 DDD 60:00

★*Awards:* Best CD of the Month, *Digital Audio* D '88. Perfect 10s, *Digital Audio's CD Review*, Mr '89; Editors' Choice, *Digital Audio's CD Review*, Je '89.

"See...has a clean and fluent technique and can call upon a variety of tone colors in accord with the music. She plays a copy (made by Rod Cameron in 1982) of a Rottenburgh instrument from about 1745; its wood lends her tone a dulcet warmth no metal flute could match—or even produce."
Musical America 109:83-4 Ja '89. Paul Moor (250w)

"Such slight, Baroque works as these almost always reveal their modest riches more readily with authentic instruments."
Ovation 9:42 Je '88. David Patrick Stearns (240w)

"After picking my nits, I must say this is an enjoyable disc with first-rate sound. Recommended."
Fanfare 12:293 S/O '88. Nils Anderson (150w)

"A fairly pleasing but hardly revelatory collection."
Hi-Fi News & Record Review 33:104 S '88. Christopher Breunig (240w)

Gramophone 66:300 Ag '88. Nicholas Anderson (420w)

2155. Concerto in G for 2 Mandolins and Orchestra, R.532; Concerto in C for Mandolin and Orchestra, R.425; Concerti for Diverse Instruments (R.558); Concerto in D for Guitar and Orchestra, R.93.
Ugo Orlandi (mndln); Dorina Frati (mndln). Claudio Scimone (c). I Solisti Veneti.
ERATO 88042 DDD 43:12

★*Awards:* *Fanfare* Want List 1985 (Nils Anderson).

"The performances are infectiously alive and imaginative....Recommended."
American Record Guide 48:75-6 Ja '85. Carl Bauman (75w)

Digital Audio 3:40 S '86. Pierre Beauregard (500w)

2156. Concerti for Recorder and Orchestra: R.108; R.441; R.444; R.445; R.442; R.443.
Peter Holtslag (rec). Peter Holman (c). Parley of Instruments.
HYPERION 66328 DDD 60:00

★*Awards:* The Year's Best, *Hi Fi News & Record Review*, May '90 Supplement.

"In sum, this is a release which, whilst conforming to authenticist requirements, must appeal equally to the general collector with its crisp but warmly expressive playing and attractive programme-content." *P100 S100*
Hi-Fi News & Record Review 34:102 Ag '89; p.29 My '90 Supplement. Christopher Breunig (245w)

"Three of the works are for sopranino recorder, an astonishing tiny instrument....Remember the piccolo in Sousa marches? It's that kind of music but nonstop, the most astonishing virtuoso stuff you'll ever hear....The other concertos feature a larger recorder, the treble, which is better known in the U.S. as the soprano in C. Lovely stuff, this too."
Audio 74:80 Jl '90. Edward Tatnall Canby (425w)

"My only complaint is that the second movement, a Siciliano, of RV. 442 might have had a bit more soul. Otherwise, a beautiful collection and warmly recommended. The sound is first-rate."

Fanfare 13:399-400 N/D '89. Nils Anderson (120w)

Digital Audio's CD Review 6:54 Je '90. Tom Vernier (190w)

Gramophone 67:319 Ag '89. John Duarte (295w)

2157. Concerti for Violins and Orchestra (Collections): La Cetra, Opus 9.
Monica Huggett (vln). Nicholas Kraemer (c). Raglan Baroque Players.
EMI 47829 DDD 116:44 2 discs

✔HC ★★★★*Awards:* *Fanfare* Want List 1987 (Nils Anderson); *Gramophone* Critics' Choice (Nicholas Anderson; John Duarte; Stanley Sadie), 1987.

"Huggett...is up to her best form here. In all, this is a marvelous set and a must for any Vivaldian, or for anyone interested in the music. The sound is clean and clear with good acoustics. Excellent program."

Fanfare 11:253 N/D '87. Nils Anderson (350w)

"Special praise goes to Nigel North, whose fine theorbo continuo provides the perfect complement for the solo passages. High marks also go to Angel EMI for sound."

High Fidelity 38:65 F '88. Christopher Rothko (175w)

Gramophone 64:1420 Ap '87 Nicholas Anderson (665w) (rev. of LP)

2158. Concerti for Violins and Orchestra (Collections): Il Cimento dell'Armonia e dell'Inventione, Opus 8 (excerpts), No's. 1-6. Concerto in G for 2 Violins, R.516; Concerto in A for Violin and Cello, R.546.
Monica Huggett (vln); Elizabeth Wallfisch (vln); Tim Mason (cello). Nicholas Kraemer (c). Raglan Baroque Players.
VIRGIN 90803 DDD 123:00 2 discs

★*Awards:* The Want List 1990, *Fanfare* N/D '90 (Nils Anderson).

"Rarely on record have I experienced period performance infused with such warmth and commitment. Virgin's luminous sonics have something to do with this; but surely the quality of the playing cannot be overlooked."

American Record Guide 54:137 Mr/Ap '91. Allen Linkowski (215w)

"In a world of violinists afraid or unable to ornament a line, Monica Huggett is a treasure-....Excellent sound adds to the clarity of these performances. Highly recommended."

Fanfare 14:391 N/D '90. Nils Anderson (275w)

Huggett "ornaments like an 18th-century speed-demon, and she renders Vivaldi's onomatopoeic passages with the sheer verve they require. The Raglans charge along behind her like the Light Brigade...the sound on this release is pretty good. It sounds more or less like what I hear at a live concert on original instruments...You want this set."

Stereophile 14:245-6 D '91. Les Berkley (long)

"The Abbey Road recording is clear, forward, natural and well-rounded. The soloist is present but never over-forward. Accept her occasionally willful tempi and this set offers rich rewards." *P95 S100*

Hi-Fi News & Record Review 35:99 My '90. Antony Hodgson (560w)

Stereo Review 55:165 N '90. Eric Salzman (130w)

Gramophone 67:1806 Ap '90. John Duarte (250w)

2159. Concerti for Violins and Orchestra (Collections): The Four Seasons, Opus 8, No's. 1-4; Concerto for Violin and Orchestra, R.577.
Viktoria Mullova (vln). Claudio Abbado (c). Chamber Orchestra of Europe.
PHILIPS 420 216 DDD 49:00

★*Awards:* Critics' Choice 1988, *Gramophone* D '88 (John Duarte).

"The playing is a fiddler's delight throughout. The instrumentally luxurious Dresden Concerto is also very well played and recorded—the best I have heard on record."

Hi-Fi News & Record Review 33:94 Jl '88. Stephen Daw (160w)

"This new Abbado performance with Viktoria Mullova...far surpasses his earlier one....At last, after an overlong period of O.K. 'Seasons,' this one is worth recommending without reservation. RV. 577...makes its CD debut in an excellent performance. The sound is Philips' best, and this disc can be heartily recommended."

Fanfare 11:275-6 Jl/Ag '88. Nils Anderson (175w)

Gramophone 65:1095 Ja '88. John Duarte (340w)

2160. Concerti for Violins and Orchestra (Collections): The Four Seasons, Opus 8, No's. 1-4.
Nils-Erik Sparf (vln). Drottningholm Baroque Ensemble.
BIS 275 DDD 39:53

✔HC ★★*Awards:* *Fanfare* Want List 1986 (Nils Anderson); *Gramophone* Critics' Choice 1986 (Nicholas Anderson).

"Much though I love a number of ther recordings of these extremely fashionable Concertos, I have to confess to being completely bowled over by this magnificent version....Not only is Sparf one of the best baroque musicians to emkerge since the early 1970s, but he persuades me consistently as he plays that this is exactly how Vivaldi himself would have played the concertos. To me, he simply *is* Vivaldi. *P100 S100*

Hi-Fi News & Record Review 31:125 Ap '86. Stephen Daw (190w)

"Highly recommended."
Fanfare 9:251-2 Mr/Ap '86. Nils Anderson (260w)

"No, I'm delighted to say, it's not just another version of 'The Four Seasons.'...I don't believe in 'best' or 'definitive' recordings, but this is as good a performance as I've heard of the music."
Fanfare 10:213-4 My/Je '87 Leslie Gerber (450w)

Digital Audio 2:42+ Mr '86. David Vernier (285w)

2161. Concerti for Violins and Orchestra (Collections): The Four Seasons, Opus 8, No's. 1-4.
Simon Standage (vln). Trevor Pinnock (c). English Concert.
DEUTSCHE GRAMMOPHON 400 045 38:00

✔**HC** ★***Awards:*** *Fanfare* Want List 1983 (George Chien).

"Unquestionably one of the finest of the current wave of 'original instrument' recordings, this is also a superbly reproduced one."
Fanfare 7:376 S/O '83. Philip Hart (100w)

"N.A. was disappointed in Standage and Pinnock on the Archiv LP version (VI:3), which he compared unfavorably with their earlier effort for Vanguard (from CRD). Not being acquainted with the latter (or, as a matter of fact, with the Archiv LP), I have nothing but praise for the English Concert's CD."
Fanfare 7:126+ S/O '83. George Chien (200w)

"Given the range of LP *Seasons* to choose from, though, Pinnock's is the one I'd take to a desert island."
High Fidelity 34:60 My '84. Allan Kozinn (930w)

Gramophone 60:1015 Mr '83. Lionel Salter (245w)

Audio 67:30 Ag '83. John M. Eargle (175w)

Ovation 4:35 O '83. Paul Turok (90w)

Digital Audio 1:75-6 O '84. John Marks (225w)

2162. Concerti for Violins and Orchestra (Collections): La Stravaganza, Opus 4.
Monica Huggett (vln); Christopher Hogwood (hpscd/orgn). Christopher Hogwood (c). Academy of Ancient Music.
OISEAU-LYRE 417 502 DDD 101:15 2 discs

★★***Awards:*** *Fanfare* Want List 1987 (Nils Anderson); Second Place Concerto Mumm Champagne Classical Music Award 1988—Presented by *Ovation, Ovation* N '88.

"The high quality of both recording and playing which I noted when I heard the LP version-...is most effectively reinforced in the quality of the CDs."
Hi-Fi News & Record Review 32:105 Ap '87 (180w) (rev. of LP); 32:102 Jl '87 (70w) (rev. of CD) Stephen Daw

"Hogwood allows Vivaldi's *stravaganza* (i.e., 'eccentricity') to come through rather than applying his own...His direction is crisp and precise...Monica Huggett fiddles up a storm here in what must be one of her best recorded performances to date."
Fanfare 11:344 S/O '87. Nils Anderson (225w)

"The Academy of Ancient Music gives stylish, committed performances...although the playing occasionally lacks buoyancy, and the phrasing, in particular, is a touch more legato than I'd like."
High Fidelity 38:65 F '88. Christopher Rothko (175w)

Gramophone 64:1274 Mr '87 Nicholas Anderson (700w)

2163. Concerti for Violins and Orchestra (Collections): La Stravaganza, Opus 4.
Simon Standage (vln); Micaela Comberti (vln); Jane Coe (cello). Trevor Pinnock (c). English Concert.
DEUTSCHE GRAMMOPHON 429 753 DDD 99:00 2 discs

★★***Awards:*** The Want List 1991, *Fanfare* N/D '91 (Nils Anderson).

"The solo performances are excellent throughout, and the occasional minor deviation in pitch can be easily overlooked in view of the level of virtuosity required of and met by the players. The supporting orchestra performs to its usual high standards under Trevor Pinnock's direction."
Musick 13:23-4 Wtr '91. Gregory S. Johnston (long)

WALTON, WILLIAM. Sinfonia Concertante for Piano and Orchestra (original version). See No. 2073.

WEBER, CARL MARIA VON

2164. Concerti for Clarinet and Orchestra: No. 1 in F minor, Opus 73; No. 2 in E flat, Opus 74.
Antony Pay (clar). Antony Pay (c). Age of Enlightenment Orchestra.
VIRGIN 90720 DDD 53:00

★***Awards:*** The Want List 1989, *Fanfare* N/D '89 (John Bauman).

"A recording of these pieces is a must for clarinet fans....this one is among the best....The recorded sound is excellent, too. This is a terrific recording."
American Record Guide 52:116-17 S/O '89. Stephen R. Max (155w)

"If you need these concertos in your collection or want still another view of them, this brilliantly engineered recording can be heartily recommended, not because it is authentically period but because it is authentically Weber."
Fanfare 13:374-75 S/O '89. David Johnson (575w)

"The naturally unwieldy instrument lacks a bit of the fluidity that is necessary for this music, and the articulation, especially in the upper register, can be fuzzy. Nevertheless, Pay gives superb performances. He is one of those accomplished professional musicians who shows evidence of having used his brain for something else...His playing is tasteful and suave, and he avoids Romantic excesses of rubato and vibrato, although at moments one wishes for a bit more soul."

Musical America 110:73 Ja '90. Dan Wakin (310w)

WIENIAWSKI, HENRYK. Concerto No. 2 in D minor for Violin and Orchestra, Opus 22. See No. 2147.

WUORINEN, CHARLES

2165. Concerto No. 3 for Piano and Orchestra; The Golden Dance.
Garrick Ohlsson (pno). Herbert Blomstedt (c). San Francisco Symphony Orchestra.
ELEKTRA 79185 DDD 53:02

★*Awards:* Critics Pick Some Favorites of the Year, *The New York Times* N 26, '89 (Allan Kozinn).

"As both the expansive works under review make plain, [Wuorinen]...shuns the minimalist vogue in favor of the grand, sweeping gesture-....[A] brilliant recording."

High Fidelity 39:62-3 Jl '89. Paul Moor (550w)

"These may not be deep, serious masterpieces, but they are flashy, exciting music, with plenty of structure and intellectual glue to hold them together through many hearings. One might wistfully regret that never—well, hardly ever—during these fifty-three minutes is a bow drawn its full length across a string....The digital engineering is bright and clear; if it sacrifices warmth for a glossy sheen, that is completely in accord with the music....Recommended to all; especially to those who want to like new music but have been frightened or disappointed in the past."

Fanfare 12:362-63 My/Je '89. James H. North (625w)

The New York Times Je 18 '89, p. 23. Andrew L. Pincus (100w)

Orchestral Music with Soloists—Collections

Belov, Rudolf

2166. Balalaika Favorites.
(Mercury Presence).
Rudolf Belov (domra). Vitaly Gnutov (c). Osipov State Russian Folk Orchestra. reissue.
MERCURY 432 000 ADD 49:30

✔HC ★★*Awards:* The Super Compact Disk List, *The Absolute Sound,* Ap '92 (Harry Pearson); Editors' Choice, *Digital Audio's CD Review,* Je '91.

"Stylish performances by artists well-versed in the music, and recorded in the best technology then available...of all ten [Mercury] reissues this [*Balalaika Favorites*] is the most essential, the one that everyone should buy."

American Record Guide 54:131-2 My/Je '91. John Landis (120w)

"At last the first ten releases of the distinguished and legendary Mercury Living Presence series (see *Fanfare* 12:2) have appeared from Philips....These reissues represent some of the best of what was achieved by analog recording technology, and they make a strong case for what can be achieved through digital duplication."

Fanfare 14:112-17 Ja/F '91. Ron McDonald (260w)

"One should regard these [Mercury CDs] not so much as an audiophile or collector/nostalgia series, but a teasury of performances."

Hi-Fi News & Record Review 36:107 Ja '91. Christopher Breunig (875w)

"Sonically speaking, the series is an unqualified triumph. Heard on CD, 'Living Presence' sound proves to be fully as good as remembered: warm, clean, crisp, beautifully balanced, unfailingly natural. Musically speaking, Philips's initial 'Living Presence' release is slightly uneven."

Musical America 111:65-8 Mr '91. Terry Teachout (120w)

"Wilma Cozart Fine's efforts (aided by Robert Eberenz, Dennis Drake, and others) have delivered ten marvels of digital transfer that recapture the essential Living Presence sound: its palpable liveness, three-dimensional focus, spaciousness, midrange realism, bass power and definition, dynamic impact, and intense tonal color. These disks momentously challenge but cannot overcome the inherent limitations of the CDs present sampling rate and high-frequency response....Nevertheless, the Mercury CDs push the digital envelope to its very edges. They audibly constitute the 1990 state of the CD art. They offer probably ninety-five percent of the virtues of the LPs while simultaneously curing some LP deficiencies, thereby running up an impressive total score....A listener who wishes to dip a toe into the Mercury CD waters should probably start with the

Kodaly-Bartok, which offers a spectacular introduction to the world of Mercury sound."

The Absolute Sound 15:146+ N/D '90. Arthur S. Pfeffer (120w)

The New York Times S 30 '90, p. 28+ H. Richard Freed (b.n.)

Digital Audio's CD Review 7:66 Ja '91. Lawrence B. Johnson (85w)

Golani, Rivka

2167. Chaconne: Music for Viola and Orchestra. Colgrass: Chaconne. **Bloch:** Suite Hebraique. **Hindemith:** Trauermusik. **Britten:** Lachrymae, Opus 48a.
Rivka Golani (vla). Andrew Davis (c). Toronto Symphony Orchestra.
CBC ENTERPRISES 5087 DDD 61:48

★***Awards:*** The Want List 1990, *Fanfare* N/D '90 (James H. North).

"I have never heard finer performances of the Bloch, Hindemith, or Britten works, and that of the Colgrass is breathtaking....Great music, superlative performances, and gorgeous recordings: as I said at the top, this is a magnificent disc."

Fanfare 14:449 N/D '90. James H. North (500w)

"All in all, this recording possesses matter of interest for even the most casual fanciers of fine viola playing. I recommend it strongly."

Fanfare 13:163-65 My/Je '90. John Wiser (315w)

Hardenberger, Hakan

2168. Trumpet Concertos. Hummel: Trumpet Concerto in E. **Hertel:** Trumpet Concerto in D; **J. Stamitz (realized Boustead):** Trumpet Concerto in D. **Haydn:** Trumpet Concerto in E flat, H.VIIe/1.
Hakan Hardenberger (tpt). Neville Marriner (c). Academy of St. Martin-in-the-Fields. 1986.
PHILIPS 420 203 DDD 59:00

★***Awards:*** Critics' Choice 1988, *Gramophone* D '88 (Ivan March).

"Hakan Hardenberger is that rare trumpeter who is both a fabulous technician and a sensitive musician....He plays with the subtlety of a fine oboist, bringing each phrase to its climactic point and turning it perfectly. Add to this the wonderful playing of the Academy...and you are assured of nearly an hour of delightful listening. The music itself is also well worth hearing."

Stereo Review 53:109 S '88. Stoddard Lincoln (150w)

"These are real enrichments to the repertoire, challenging and attractive. Hakan Hardenberger's agility and expressivity never lead him astray...Emphatically not just another virtuosic trumpet record."

Hi-Fi News & Record Review 33:105 F '88. Peter Branscombe (175w)

"Neville Marriner and his modern-instruments orchestra are poised and effortlessly dancelike-...The young Swede...is an exceptionally gifted performer."

Fanfare 11:175 Jl/Ag '88. Edward Strickland (220w)

"Playing slightly above the pitch only thins his sound to a buzzing whirr which undermines his honestly amazing technique."

American Record Guide 51:113 S/O '88. Gwendolyn Haverstock (125w)

Gramophone 65:960+ D '87. Ivan March (460w)

Digital Audio 5:78+ N '88. Tom Vernier (230w)

Hermansson, Soren

2169. Horn Concertos. Jacob: Concerto for Horn and Orchestra. **Larsson:** Concertino for Horn and Orchestra. **Seiber:** Notturno for Horn and Strings. **Reger:** Scherzino for Horn and Strings. **Atterberg:** Concerto for Horn and Orchestra.
Soren Hermansson (horn). Edvard Tjivzjel (c). Umea Sinfonietta.
BIS 376 DDD 68:23

★***Awards:*** The Want List 1988, *Fanfare* N/D '88 (Stephen Ellis).

"No equivocating. This is a dream horn collection—undeniably the finest gathering of 20th-century horn-and-orchestra works ever put on one disc."

Fanfare 11:263-4 My/Je '88. Stephen W. Ellis (550w)

"Never mind that all of the performers are likely to be unfamiliar. They perform outstandingly well. A most attractive disc."

American Record Guide 51:76-7 Jl/Ag '88. Carl Bauman (425w)

"Hermansson is a strong performer who gives one a feeling of certainty, both technically and musically, at all times; the orchestra is well prepared and recorded. This is an important recording."

The Horn Call 19:93 O '88. Julian Christopher Leuba (205w)

"This, I believe, marks his recording debut here. It shows him—at 32—to be a player of considerable technical skill and the possessor of a full, rounded tone....If there is room for criticism here it is perhaps that, Reger apart, the general tone of the music is introverted and reflective and, since all but Atterberg use only a string orchestra, tends to lack colour contrasts. The Umea orchestra under its conductor, Edvard Tjivzjel, however, respond very positively to the challenges set down by such varied idioms."

Hi-Fi News & Record Review 34:114 Ap '89. Kenneth Dommett (315w)

Isserlis, Steven

2170. Concertante Cello Works. Tchaikovsky: Variations on a Rococo Theme, Opus 33; Pezzo capriccioso, Opus 62; Nocturne, Opus 19 No. 4; Andante Cantabile, Opus 11. **Glazunov:** Two Pieces, Opus 20; Chant du menestrel, Opus 71. **Rimsky-Korsakov:** Serenade, Opus 37. **Cui:** Deux morceaux; Opus 36: Scherzando; Cantabile.
Steven Isserlis (cello). John Eliot Gardiner (c). Chamber Orchestra of Europe.
VIRGIN 91134 DDD 64:00

> ★*Awards:* Best of the Month, *Hi-Fi News & Record Review*, D '90.

"Isserlis has an appealing, dusky tone, with which he shapes impressive phrases, giving the charming variations a brilliant and convincing performance, as good as any I know....The other pieces here are attractively and superbly played. The Glazunov op. 71 is a delight. The accompaniment is handled sensitively, and the reproduction is O.K., making this a fine release."

Fanfare 14:489-90 Mr/Ap '91. Howard Kornblum (150w)

"Collaboration is the keynote here, and it could hardly be otherwise given the concertante flair of the COE. Flutes and oboes weave magic with Tchaikovsky's ritornello each and every time." *P100/95 S100*

Hi-Fi News & Record Review 35:100 D '90. David Nice (390w)

"I don't like his tonal quality. It lacks the heft I expect from a cello and reminds me of a viola. In addition, the Chamber Orchestra of Europe sounds too small for much of this music, particularly the *Rococo Variations*-....Whatever problems I have with this disc are greatly overshadowed by the selections and the generally sympathetic interpretations."

American Record Guide 54:142 My/Je '91. Justin Herman (100w)

Gramophone 68:751-2 O '90. Ivan March (280w)

Digital Audio's CD Review 7:77-8 My '91. Tom Vernier (185w)

Johnson, Emma

2171. Works for Clarinet and Orchestra. Weber: Concerto No. 1 in F minor for Clarient and Orchestra. **Crusell:** Introduction, Theme and Variations on a Swedish Air. **Tartini (arr. Jacob):** Concertino for Clarinet and Strings. **Debussy:** Premiere Rapsodie.
Emma Johnson (clar). Yan Pascal Tortelier (c). English Chamber Orchestra.
ASV 585 DDD 53:45

> ★*Awards:* *Gramophone* Critics' Choice (Edward Greenfield), 1987.

"Forced to make choices, and leaving aside Emma Johnson's unquestioned talents, first choice for Weber would be De Peyer, with King for Crusell. There is no serious rival for the Jacob though, and the Debussy will withstand the competition easily enough."

Hi-Fi News & Record Review 32:110 S '87 Kenneth Dommett (190w)

"Emma Johnson...continues to amaze and delight in her third release on the ASV label-....The 1987 digital sound dazzles."

Fanfare 11:284-5 N/D '87. David Johnson (640w)

"The mellowness of tone, the richly varied phrasing and the subtle dynamic gradations are amazing."

American Record Guide 51:73 Ja/F '88. Carl Bauman (320w)

Gramophone 65:420+ S '87 Edward Greenfield (530w)

Mutter, Anne-Sophie

2172. The Great Violin Concertos. Mozart: Concerto No. 3 in G, K.216; No. 5 in A, K.219. **Beethoven:** Concerto in D, Opus 61. **Mendelssohn:** Concerto in E minor, Opus 64. **Bruch:** Concerto No. 1 in G minor, Opus 26. **Brahms:** Concerto in D, Opus 77.
Anne-Sophie Mutter (vln). Herbert Von Karajan (c). Berlin Philharmonic Orchestra. reissues.
DEUTSCHE GRAMMOPHON 415 565 ADD; AAD; DDD; DDD 57:58; 48:11; 56:30; 40:04 4 discs

"A remarkable consistency of approach marks Mutter's playing of these standards of the violin literature. The Mozart concertos, made when she was only fourteen, already showed her to be a major talent....As for the Brahms, it is the best thing in the set."

Ovation 9:45 Ap '88. John Von Rhein (300w)

"The overall impression is of an astonishingly talented and musical violinist still seeking an interpretive view of these warhorses....All the same, as an anthology of a developing and uncommonly precocious talent, this package comprises a remarkable and fascinating document. DG's transfers are admirable."

Fanfare 11:259-60 My/Je '88. Mortimer H. Frank (250w)

Paillard Chamber Orchestra

2173. Recital. Pachelbel: Kanon (and Gigue in D). **Albinoni:** Adagio in G minor for Organ and Strings. **Bach:** Wachet auf (from Cantata 140); Jesu, Joy of Man's Desiring (from Cantata 147), Air on the G String (arr. from Orchestral Suite 3), Minuet (from Suite 2). **Clarke:** Trumpet Voluntary. Plus excerpts by **Handel, Vivaldi, Zipoli, Marcello, Rameau, and Molter.**
Jean-Francois Paillard (c). Paillard Chamber Orchestra.
RCA 5468 DDD 73:00

"These are new, all-digital recordings by the team that made the Pachelbel Canon famous [5 years on *Billboard*'s Hit Parade]....Here it's a minute faster....the whole disc is a nice gift to introduce someone to the baroque. Despite the faster tempo here, Paillard does own the Pachelbel Canon, and you really should own one of his recordings if you like the piece."

American Record Guide 54:145 Mr/Ap '91. Donald R. Vroon (120w)

Petri, Michala

2174. Recorder Concertos. Vivaldi: C for Soprano Recorder, R.443; **G. Sammartini:** F for Descant Recorder; **Telemann:** C for Treble Recorder; **Handel:** F for Treble Recorder.
Michala Petri (rec). Iona Brown (c). Academy of St. Martin-in-the-Fields.
PHILIPS 400 075

"In short, these are very recommendable performances, expertly backed up by the Academy of St. Martin's strings under Iona Brown's direction. The recording is superb, as well."

Fanfare 7:125-6 S/O '83. George Chien (220w)

"Recommended."

Fanfare 8:250-1 My/Je '85. Nils Anderson (150w)

"The delights of the performance aside, this disc also offers plenty of fragile, upper-range passage-work for the CD system to grapple with. The sound...is ravishing; but then, the high recorder sound hasn't posed any problem on Petri's LPs either."

High Fidelity 33:66 N '83. Allan Kozinn (325w)

Ovation 5:46 Mr '84. Allan Kozinn (220w); 6:30 Jl '85. Paul Turok (100w)

Gramophone 61:155 Jl '83. Nicholas Anderson (210w)

Zabaleta, Nicanor

2174. Harp Collection. Mozart: Concerto in C for Flute, Harp and Orchestra, K.299. **Spohr:** Variations sur l'air "Je Suis encore dans mon printemps." for Solo Harp, Opus 36. **Handel:** Concerto in B flat for Harp and Orchestra, Opus 4, No. 6. **Wagenseil:** Concerto in G for Harp and Orchestra.
Karlheinz Zoeller (fl); Nicanor Zabaleta (harp). Ernst Marzendorfer; Paul Kuentz (c). Berlin Philharmonic Orchestra; Kuentz Chamber Orchestra. reissue.
DEUTSCHE GRAMMOPHON 427 206 AAD

✔HC

Chamber Music

ARNOLD, MALCOLM

3001. Chamber Music: Violin Sonatas 1 and 2; Viola Sonata; Piano Trio; Duo for 2 Cellos; Pieces (5) for Violin and Piano. (Volume 1).
Nash Ensemble.
HYPERION 66171 65:45

✔HC ★*Awards:* Record of the Eighties, *Gramophone*, D '89 (Malcolm MacDonald).

"The recordings are very realistic, the performances first class....emphatically endorsed."
American Record Guide 52:11 Mr/Ap '89. Carl Bauman (30w)

"While the pranks, as well as the range of expression, that he can pull off with a full orchestra are missing, one can only marvel at the level of invention and wit manifest in many of these miniatures—including a goodly number for solo instruments....These three engaging and entertaining CDs are a triumph for the composer, the brilliant Nash Ensemble, the Hyperion engineers—indeed, for all concerned."
Musical America 110:55-6 Ja '90. Robert R. Reilly (130w)

"I'd collect these valuable CDs in reverse order [vol.3-2-1]."
Hi-Fi News & Record Review 33:99 O '88. Christopher Breunig (350w)

Gramophone 66:1169 Ja '89. Michael Kennedy (240w)

BACH, JOHANN CHRISTIAN

3002. Quartet in B flat for Oboe and Strings. HAYDN, MICHAEL. Divertimenti in C for Oboe, Viola and Double Bass, P.98 and P.115. MOZART, WOLFGANG AMADEUS. Adagio in C for English Horn and Strings, K.580a.
Heinz Holliger (crnt ang/oboe); Antonio Salvatore (vln); Massimo Paris (vla); Vito Paternoster (cello); Lucio Buccarella (d-bass).
DENON/SUPRAPHON 7119

✔HC ★*Awards:* *Gramophone* Critics' Choice 1984 (Lionel Salter).

Gramophone 62:491 O '84. Lionel Salter (225w)

3003. Quintet in D for Flute, Oboe, Violin, Cello and Harpsichord, Opus 22/1; Sextet in C for Oboe, 2 Horns, Violin, Cello and Keyboard; Quintets for Flute, Oboe, Violin, Viola and Continuo, Opus 11: No's. 1 and 6.
The English Concert.
DEUTSCHE GRAMMOPHON 423 385 DDD 69:00

✔HC ★*Awards:* Critics' Choice 1988, *Gramophone* D '88 (Stanley Sadie).

"Heartily recommend[ed]...the sound...is excellent."
Fanfare 12:115-7 N/D '88. William Youngren (315w)

"After listening to this disc, I cannot imagine wanting to hear this music on modern instruments. The sound is excellent."
American Record Guide 51:10 N/D '88. Stephen R. Max (120w)

"A delight. Galant music at its best, beautifully performed and excellently recorded."
Hi-Fi News & Record Review 33:83 Je '88. Jeremy Siepmann (220w)

"Bach's music is aided by some exemplary musicianship here...The sound is quite clear in the three quintets, but a little woolly in the sextet. A winner."
High Fidelity 39:64 Ja '89. Christopher Rothko (200w)

"These are delightful selections, delightfully played by the core members of the English Concert."
Musical America 109:50-2 My '89. Benjamin S. Dunham (250w)

Gramophone 65:1612 My '88. Nicholas Anderson (425w)

BACH, JOHANN SEBASTIAN

3004. A Musical Offering, BWV.1079; Art of the Fugue, BWV.1080; Canons (14) for 2 Harpsichords, BWV.1087.
Reinhard Goebel (c). Musica Antiqua Koln.
DEUTSCHE GRAMMOPHON 413 642 ADD; DDD; DDD 2:19:53 3 discs

"Though some critics find the playing coarse rather than gutsy, the rather raw-toned strings and lively tempos of the account have worn well for me and it [*Musical Offering*] remains my version of preference....Perhaps the Koln *Offering* is *de trop* for the M-O-R listener, but just listen to the contrast of moods between the augmentation canon and its neighbors on either side."

Fanfare 8:83-8 My/Je '85. Edward Strickland (460w)

Gramophone 62:1199 Ap '85. Lionel Salter (385w)

Digital Audio 1:58-9 Ag '85. Jerry Schwartz (475w)

3005. Sonatas (7) for Flute and Harpsichord, BWV.1030/35, BWV.1020 (omits BWV.1020); Partita in A minor for Flute, BWV.1013.
Stephen Preston (fl); Trevor Pinnock (hpscd); Jordi Savall (vla da gamba). 1975.
CRD 33145 ADD 43:00, 54:46 2 discs

✔HC ★*Awards:* Critics' Choice 1990, *Gramophone* D '90 (John Duarte).

"Preston plays with admirable sensitivity and grace, as do his collaborators, Pinnock and Savall....In comparison with Rampal, Preston sounds restrained, even reticent, in the first movement of the great B-Minor Sonata, which opens his disc. But there is no lack of vitality on Preston's part elsewhere in his album, where the joy of Bach's music is fully evident."
Fanfare 13:123 S/O '89. George Chien (300w)

Gramophone 67:1342 Ja '90. John Duarte (225w)

3006. Sonatas (6) for Violin and Harpsichord, BWV.1014-19.
Arthur Grumiaux (vln); Christiane Jaccottet (hpscd).
PHILIPS 426 452

✔HC

BARTOK, BELA

3007. Quartets (6) for Strings (complete).
Emerson Quartet.
DEUTSCHE GRAMMOPHON 423 657 DDD
149:00 2 discs

✔HC ★★★★★*Awards:* *Hi-Fi News & Record Review* Record of the Month, Ja '89. Critics Pick Some Favorites of the Year, *The New York Times* N 26, '89 (Allan Kozinn); Critics Pick Some Favorites of the Year, *The New York Times* N 26, '89 (K. Robert Schwarz); The Want List 1989, *Fanfare* /D '89 (John Wiser); Record of the Year 1989, *Gramophone*, D '89; Top Choices—1989, *American Record Guide* Ja/F '90 (Allen Linkowski); Top Choices—1989, *American Record Guide* Ja/F '90 (Kurt Moses); Top Choices—1989, *American Record Guide* Ja/F '90 (James Ginsburg). Editors' Choice, *Digital Audio's CD Review*, 6:34 Je '90.

"Any faults are trivial....These are truly excellent performances, committed and constantly engaging and eminently recommendable in the face of all current competition."
The New York Times N 13 '88, p. H27. James R. Oestreich (875w)

"Throughout the six quartets, example after example can be cited of what might be termed clarification, through technical means, of passages that remain surprisingly murky on other recordings. What is not present in these performances is a sense of fantasy."
Ovation 9:43 Ja '89. Paul Turok (380w)

"All six Quartets—but particularly the two middle ones—emerge as incisive, dramatic, yet perfectly comprehensive and at times almost romantic works....For once it is possible to see the six Quartets as an evolving sequence, not just a series of unconnected leaps from experiment to experiment...the Emersons have drawn attention to something often missed, namely that Bartok's melodic lines run across all four voices and the ear must be able to follow them."
Hi-Fi News & Record Review 34:101 Ja '89. Kenneth Dommett (525w)

"The recording is certainly the most impressive the Emerson has made so far, and it is one of the most satisfying in the by now long list of integral recordings of Bartok's quartets. The Emerson makes these quartets as appealing as any in the literature, taking an almost—or perhaps a little more than 'almost'—Romantically expressive approach without, however, rounding off any of the Bartokian corners or smoothing over passages meant to sting."
Stereo Review 54:163 F '89. Richard Freed (425w)

"Though their performances on disc are not without mannerism, their virtuosity and stamina are never in question. Like the Tokyo and Lindsay Quartets, their main rivals, they are completely on top of the music technically-....These are essentially big-boned performances. They are marginally less convincing in the more fragile or elusive stretches of the first two quartets, than in the uninhibited middle-period pieces, nos. 3, 4 and 5."
The Musical Times 130:162 Mr '89. Stephen Walsh (600w)

"The main yardstick by which every Bartok quartet performance must be measured is in specificity of character, in how strongly and directly the players get to the central point of each movement and each complex of movements. This is so consistently well achieved [by both the Berg and the Emerson quartets]-...that it is virtually impossible to express preference for one over the other."
Fanfare 12:88-90 Mr/Ap '89. John Wiser (500w)

"The Emerson players revel in breadth of gesture and tonal suavity, whereas the Juilliard never attempted such sensuousness....But can the Emerson match the unbridled ferocity of the Juilliard? To a great extent, yes. And if the four seem unwilling to turn quite as scrappy in tone, they are every bit as forceful and pointed in articulation....Although I remain devoted to the Juilliard's Bartok, I think that the Emerson Quartet, by demonstrating the interpretive range possible among these six works, has performed a valuable service....this traversal not only sets a new standard, but offers a model for countless youthful quartet players."

High Fidelity 39:61-2 Je '89. K. Robert Schwarz (685w)

"Every performance has much to offer, and if you don't already have a recording of these works, this excellent-value set, with over 70 minutes of music on each CD, should not fail to satisfy."

Stereophile 12:162 Jl '89. Barbara Jahn (235w)

"For an ensemble to bring off all of the composer's indications is in itself a challenge of Olympian proportion. For a quartet to scale beyond those heights and imbue these pieces with imagination and spirit of their own is a truly phenomenal accomplishment. The musicians of the Emerson Quartet manage both brilliantly...*American Record Guide* does not indulge in bubbly 'Record of the Year' contests; but if we did, the Emerson discs would be my choice for the chamber music award!"

American Record Guide 52:17-18 Jl/Ag '89. James S. Ginsburg (250w)

Gramophone 66:1016-17 D '88. David J. Fanning (595w)

3008. Rhapsody No. 1 for Violin and Piano; Sonata No. 2 for Violin and Piano. BEETHOVEN, LUDWIG VAN. Sonata No. 9 in A for Violin and Piano, Opus 47, "Kreutzer". DEBUSSY, CLAUDE. Sonata No. 3 in G minor for Violin and Piano.

Joseph Szigeti (vln); Bela Bartok (pno). Library of Congress. April 13, 1940.
VANGUARD 72025 ADD (m) 70:03

✔HC ★*Awards:* Third Place Non-Vocal Reissues Mumm Champagne Classical Music Award 1988—Presented by *Ovation*, *Ovation* N '88. Classical Hall of Fame, *Fanfare*, Jl/Ag '91.

"A disc which every lover of classical music should have and listen to at regular intervals as a reminder of how great music-making can be."

American Record Guide 52:21-2 Ja/F '89. Stephen D. Chakwin, Jr. (530w)

"Everything about this CD is remarkable...This is not merely a great, but a genuinely *important* recording."

Fanfare 14:423 Jl/Ag '91. David K. Nelson (300w)

"Even in the context of the mammoth recorded documentation issued by Hungaroton at his centenary, this recital is of paramount interest in Bartok's discography. What is more, the sound is miraculously clean and detailed. The Rhapsody and Sonata No. 2 offer authoritative guidance for tempos, voicing, and a swarm of nuances that never could make their way into the printed music....Required listening!"

Fanfare 12:130-1 N/D '88. John Wiser (200w)

"This Washington Library of Congress recital-...preserves Bartok's first, important, American concert. The inclusion of two of his own pieces adds to the historical significance of this reissue (a quite good transfer, but losing some of the sweetness of Szigeti's tone and exaggerating the cramping of climaxes, which were freer in analogue)." *PS-historical*

Hi-Fi News & Record Review 35:99 S '90. Christopher Breunig (185w)

Gramophone 68:1419 Ja '91. Lionel Salter (330w)

3009. Sonata for 2 Pianos and Percussion. BRAHMS, JOHANNES. Variations on a Theme by Joseph Haydn, Opus 56b.

Murray Perahia (pno); Georg Solti (pno); David Corkhill (perc); Evelyn Glennie (perc). Snape Maltings Concert Hall, Snape. 1987.
CBS 42625 DDD 45:48

✔HC ★★*Awards:* Second Place ChamberMumm Champagne Classical Music Award 1988—Presented by *Ovation*, *Ovation* N '88. Editors' Choice, *Digital Audio's CD Review*, Je '89.

"Ensemble work with the percussion, which serves mostly for accompaniment, is flawless-....in this lively, first-rate recording."

Ovation 9:38 O '88. Lee Lourdeaux (325w)

"It is Perahia who takes the first piano part, though Solti naturally directs the performance [Bartok]; and a superlatively fine one it is, quite the best I have heard on record...[the Brahms] receives a full-blooded performance, rich in colour yet not at all lacking either subtlety or grace."

Hi-Fi News & Record Review 33:93 My '88. Kenneth Dommett (315w)

"Superbly recorded...The results here are for the most part highly felicitous, particularly in the well-integrated Bartok Sonata...I have somewhat mixed feelings about the very warm but decidedly expansive view of the Brahms/Haydn Variations."

Stereophile 11:149 Ag '88. Igor Kipnis (280w)

"Part of the Bartok performing 'tradition' dictates a percussive approach to the piano. Musicians familiar with Bartok's own playing will therefore appreciate this performance of the Sonata for Two Pianos and Percussion as part of the true and, sorrowfully, lost tradition....A splendid and loving rendition of the Brahms Haydn Variations caps off the disc."

Music Magazine 11:41 N/D '88. Robert McAlear (355w)

"It is a tense, graceful, cleanly set out reading, musically competitive with anything currently to be found on CD....the lack of atmosphere is lethally distracting from an otherwise very presentable performance."

Fanfare 11:75-6 My/Je '88. John D. Wiser (300w)

"The recent Hungaroton recording of the Bartok with Zoltan Kocsis and Dezso Ranki (reviewed in *HPR*, Vol.5 No.3) stands up to Perahia/Solti in every way. In fact, one might give it a light edge for the sheer immediacy and excitement."

HighPerformanceReview 5:73 D '88. John Mueter (185w)

"This disc is highly recommended."
Audio 72:170-72 D '88. Bert Whyte (410w)

Digital Audio 5:50-1 F '89. Tom Vernier (200w)

Gramophone 65:1321 Mr '88. David J. Fanning (340w)

Sonata for 2 Pianos and Percussion. See No. 2009.

BAX, ARNOLD

3010. Quintet in G minor for Piano and Strings; Quartet No. 2 in E minor for Strings.
David Owen Norris (pno). Mistry Quartet.
CHANDOS 8795 DDD 77:00

★*Awards:* Critic's Choice: 1991, *American Record Guide*, Ja/F '92 (Michael Carter).

David Owen Norris brings poignant sensitivity to the quintet and his technical agility is perfectly suited to the virtuosic and demanding piano part. The Mistry Quartet's contributions are elegant, producing a full, mellow sonority that nicely complements Norris in the quintet. As usual for Chandos, the production is topnotch."
American Record Guide 54:28+ Jl/Ag '91. Michael Carter (430w)

"There's absolutely no denying the passionate sweep and huge eloquence of the present performance—this is music-making of great technical assurance, enormous imaginative scope and truly spellbinding commitment....the Mistry plays superbly, and Chandos's recording both here and in the Quintet possesses striking lustre and clarity." *P100 S95*
Hi-Fi News & Record Review 36:82 Ap '91. Andrew Achenbach (200w)

"The recording is roomy but well balanced. One could hardly ask for a better outing on CD for each of these considerable if flawed chamber-music pieces. It is recommended."
Fanfare 14:109-10 Jl/Ag '91. John Wiser (550w)"Pianist

Australian Hi-Fi 22(5):92 '91. Cyrus Meher-Homji (brief)

Gramophone 68:1850 Ap '91. Michael Kennedy (245w)

BEETHOVEN, LUDWIG VAN

3011. Quartets for Strings: No. 4 in C minor, Opus 18, No. 4; No. 15 in A minor, Opus 132.
Borodin Quartet. 1989.
VIRGIN 90746 DDD 70:00

✔**HC** ★*Awards:* The Chosen Few: The Best Music of 1989. *New Hi-Fi Sound Supplement* D '89.

"For a long time I've sworn by the beautifully sparse, wan account of this late quartet, by the Quartetto Italiano on Philips. But the vigour, integrity and astonishing expressive intensity displayed by the Borodin Quartet is more than a match for it. The coupling of the Op 132 quartet, with the early Op 18 No 4, is very effective."
New Hi-Fi Sound 6:117 Jl '89. Jonathan Kettle (230w)

"The Borodin Quartet play like men possessed, and their unity of purpose is such that their music could have been played by a single person."
New Hi-Fi Sound Supplement 7:32 D '89. Jonathan Kettle (325w)

"The disc is a memorable achievement."
The Musical Times 130:752 D '89. Robert Anderson (175w)

"Their playing always has great intensity and conviction as well as absolute tonal security. They never make an ugly sound. Their romantic interpretations may not be to everyone's taste, and theirs is certainly not the only way to play this great music, but I enjoyed their work very much and I suspect most listeners would too....the sound is excellent...Highly recommended."
American Record Guide 53:22-3 Ja/F '90. Kurt Moses (275w)

Digital Audio's CD Review 6:59-60 F '90. Lawrence Johnson (180w)

Gramophone 67:55 Je '89. David J. Fanning (350w)

3012. Quartets for Strings: No. 4 in C minor, Opus 18, No. 4; No. 5 in A, Opus 18, No. 5; No. 6 in B flat, Opus 18, No. 6.
Medici Quartet.
NIMBUS 5186 DDD 75:32

★*Awards:* Critic's Choice: 1990, *American Record Guide* Ja/F '91 (Allen Linkowski).

"In many ways, the *Op. 18* quartets are the most difficult to play of all the Beethoven quartets. The classical texture is so clear, the precision demanded of the four players so intense that the pristine clarity and instrumental lightness is difficult to realize. The Medici String Quartet is certainly up to the task, performing the quartets with unstinting enthusiasm, control and expression. The sound is excellent as is the balance and separation between the four instruments."
HighPerformanceReview 8(1):63 '91. Walter Gray (180w)

"These are 'modern' strings....often they sound like a single instrument in the hands of one flawless musician....and emotion is an equal part of their achievement. While I remain partial to the Three Bs of performing quartets (Busch, Budapest, and Alban Berg)...if DDD is what you demand, you can't do better than the

Medici series, which was very honestly recorded at The Maltings, Snape."

Fanfare 13:130 N/D '89. Paul Sargent Clark (400w)

"A completely unqualified recommendation-....The playing is honest and totally lacking the slick superficiality that often passes for profundity in today's jet-setting musical environment."

American Record Guide 53:22 Jl/Ag '90. Allen Linkowski (135w)

3013. Quartets for Strings: No.'s 7-10, Opus 59 and 74.
Quartetto Italiano.
PHILIPS 420 797 ADD 165:00 3 discs

✔HC ★*Awards:* Critics Choice, *Hi Fi News & Record Review*, Ap '91 Supplement (John Crabbe).

Gramophone 67:1479 F '90. Robert Layton (240w)

3014. Quartets for Strings: No.'s 7-11, Opus 59, 74, 95.
Tokyo Quartet. Princeton University's Richardson Hall.
RCA 0462 DDD 161:00 3 discs

✔HC ★*Awards:* Record of the Month, *Hi-Fi News & Record Review*, O '91.

"One expects good work form the Tokyo String Quartet, which was clearly a major quartet ensemble well before it reached its current level of excellence, but this set of Beethoven's middle quartets is extraordinary beyond expectations....Urgently recommended!"

Fanfare 15:153-54 S/O '91. John Wiser (med)

"The Tokyo performances have a degree of expressive flow and spontaneity that, for me, even surpasses the superbly caring and authoritative, but sometimes slightly stolid, Vermeer interpretations [Op. 59: Teldec 46016; Opp. 74, 95: 44929]....The Teldec sound for the Vermeer is much cleaner....an enthusiastic recommendation for the Tokyo's truly eloquent interpretations."

Musical America 111:42-3 S/O '91. Harris Goldsmith (long)

"To the 'middle period' works...the Tokyo restore some of the cultivation and softer outlined elegance of the disbanded Quartetto Italiano...The Tokyo create marvellous atmospheres of mystery in slow introductions; take the *ppp* before the final page *Allegro* in Op.95—how faithfully they adhere to the markings, *sempre p, leggieramente*; and always what they are doing is interesting....A stimulating and enduring group of performances: I would not have anticipated the height of achievement from their earlier Schubert CDs." *P100 S95*

Hi-Fi News & Record Review 36:109 O '91. Christopher Breunig (long)

"This is the best overall presentation of these quartets since the Budapest Quartet dominated the market in the 1950s."

American Record Guide 55:27-8 Ja/F '92. Stratton Rawson (long)

Gramophone 69:63 Mr '92. Robert Layton (long)

3015. Quartets for Strings: No. 10 in E flat, Opus 74, "Harp"; No. 14 in C# minor, Opus 131.
Guarneri Quartet.
PHILIPS 422 341 DDD 71:00

✔HC ★*Awards:* The Want List 1990, *Fanfare* N/D '90 (Michael Ullman).

"The performances convey heroic struggles and ultimate triumphs, and even the 'slighter' Op. 74 emerges as a rugged and profound creation. In the intricate interweaving lines of Op. 131's Presto, the playing is quite spectacular."

The New York Times Jl 8 '90, p. 22 H. Martin Bookspan (175w)

"These new Guarneri performances are among the best that have been recorded."

Fanfare 13:116 My/Je '90. Michael Ullman (320w)

"The sound here is full, rich, and warm; the approach boldly extroverted....The earlier work is given the more satisfying performance. While lacking that exciting feeling of discovery brought to it by such ensembles as the Talich (Calliope), the Italiano (Philips) and the Alban Berg (Angel), the Guarneris offer a committed reading: big and bold and technically flawless-....Very good, then, but not first choice. The C-sharp minor quartet presents a much different landscape....Listen to the Talich players or to the Vegh (Valois) and you enter a vastly different sphere: intimate, probing, even disturbing."

American Record Guide 54:28+ Ja/F '91. Allen Linkowski (220w)

"They lack, perhaps, a sense of reverence in the presence of one of history's greatest spiritual autobiographers. That said, there *is* something touching about the Beethoven the Guarneri present us with. He might lack Olympian calm, but he appears all the more human for it....On a more practical level, however, the Guarneri's enthusiasm for wide vibrato and consistently rich tone (beautifully revealed on the gorgeous recording) means they seldom achieve a true *pp*." *P85/95 S95*

Hi-Fi News & Record Review 35:97 Ja '90. Simon Cargill (300w)

Gramophone 67:1342 Ja '90. Stephen Johnson (305w)

Quartet No. 11 in F minor for Strings, Opus 95, "Quartetto Serioso". See No. 3122.

3016. Quartets for Strings: No. 12 in E flat, Opus 127; No. 16 in F, Opus 135.
Alban Berg Quartet.
EMI 47135 ADD/DDD 62:00

✔HC ★Awards: *Gramophone* Record Award Winner 1985—Chamber Award.

Ovation 6:29-30 O '85. David Hall (800w)

Gramophone 62:1234 Ap '85 (140w) (rev. of LP) Roger Fiske; 63:250 Ag '85 (490w); 66:1170 Ja '89 Robert Layton

Hi-Fi News & Record Review 30:107 O '85. Christopher Breunig (85w)

Digital Audio 2:43-4 S '85. David Vernier (355w)

Gramophone 66:1170 Ja '89. Robert Layton (235w)

3017. Septet in E flat for Strings and Winds, Opus 20; Trio No. 7 in B flat for Clarinet (or Violin), Cello and Piano, Opus 11.
Nash Ensemble.
VIRGIN 91137 DDD 60:30

"An exceptionally beautiful recording of the Septet, made in a Berkshire church with the instruments set back in a spacious but not over-resonant acoustic....The Clarinet Trio is a trifle by comparison, but it is beautifully played and the different acoustic (Abbey Road) is no disadvantage....Altogether a fine presentation, although some may find the impetuousness of the faster movements of the Septet unsettling." *P95/85 S95*

Hi-Fi News & Record Review 36:95-6 Ja '91. Antony Hodgson (350w)

"The horn playing by Frank Lloyd stands out among the numerous special joys, as do the contributions of Van Kampen, and the recording itself is a model for future endeavors in the realm of chamber music."

Stereo Review 56:85 My '91. Richard Freed (160w)

"If the lighter side of Beethoven takes your fancy, this CD should prove to be a real treasure. Strongly recommended."

Fanfare 14:128-29 My/Je '91. John Wiser (275w)

"Although this new recording is not the fine one of the Beethoven Trio with Antony Pay on clarinet of several years ago it ranks with the best....These are as good as any available of these youthful and entertaining works....Add excellent sound and readable notes, and we have a highly recommended record."

American Record Guide 54:34 Jl/Ag '91. Stephen R. Max (140w)

Gramophone 68:1684 Mr '91. Joan Chissell (440w)

3018. Sonatas for Cello and Piano (complete).
Mstislav Rostropovich (cello); Sviatoslav Richter (pno). 1963 reissue.
PHILIPS 412 256 2 discs

✔HC ★Awards: *Gramophone* Critics' Choice 1985 (Roger Fiske).

"Ever since this set of recordings was first issued in 1963, it has been the touchstone for all subsequent issues. A few have come close but none have excelled so consistently in all categories, including that of recording quality, as has this one....Warmly endorsed to all, not just to collectors of historic performances."

Fanfare 9:122 S/O '85. John Bauman (190w)

Ovation 6:46 O '85. Paul Turok (125w)

Gramophone 62:889 Ja '85. Roger Fiske (245w)

3019. Sonatas (5) for Cello and Piano (complete); Piano Music: Variations in G minor on "See the Conquering Hero Comes" from Judas Maccabeus, WoO.45; Variations (7) in E flat on "Bei Mannern, welche Liebe fuhlen" from "Die Zauberflote", WoO.46; Variations (12) in F on "Ein Madchen oder Weibchen" from "Die Zauberflote", Opus 66.
Jacqueline Du Pre (cello); Daniel Barenboim (pno). Edinburgh Festival. 1970 live.
EMI 63015 ADD 142:00 2 discs

✔HC ★★★Awards: Critics' Choice 1989, *Gramophone* D '89 (Joan Chissell).

Gramophone 67:324 Ag '89. Joan Chissell (270w)

3020. Sonata No. 4 in A minor for Violin and Piano, Opus 23; Sonata No. 5 in F for Violin and Piano, Opus 24, "Spring".
Gidon Kremer (vln); Martha Argerich (pno).
DEUTSCHE GRAMMOPHON 419 787 DDD 43:00

✔HC ★Awards: The Want List 1988, *Fanfare* N/D '88 (John Wiser).

"Criticism falls silent in the face of this sort of achievement."

Music and Musicians International 36:50 Ap '88. Bryce Morrison (240w)

"On top of all this virtue, if one can use such a term for the play of these rampant temperaments, DG has provided high-impact sound of absolute transparency and even balance."

Fanfare 11:82 My/Je '88. John D. Wiser (225w)

Gramophone 65:1321 Mr '88. Edward Greenfield (315w)

Sonata No. 9 in A for Violin and Piano, Opus 47, "Kreutzer". See No. 3008.

3021. Trios for Piano, Violin and Cello: No. 6 in B flat, Opus 97 ("Archduke"); No. 9 in G, "Kakadu," Opus 121a.
(Volume 2).
Kalichstein, Laredo, Robinson Trio.
MCA 25193 DDD 61:00

★Awards: *American Record Guide* Overview: Getting to Know Chamber Music: Piano Trios, N/D '90 (No. 6).

"Kalichstein, Laredo, and Robinson constitute one of the finest trios before the public today. The sound is fine."

American Record Guide 51:17 N/D '88. Stephen R. Max (200w)

"Laredo doesn't always play spot on pitch, and Sharon Robinson is sometimes excessively utilitarian in tone, but neither string player offends as often in these regards as Cohen and Greenhouse of the Beaux Arts, and they are never as bland—particularly in this piece [the 'Archduke' Trio]—as Angel's Perlman and Harrell (with Ashkenazy)."

Fanfare 11:123-4 Jl/Ag '88. John D. Wiser (190w)

3022. Trios for Strings (5), Opus 3, 8 ("Serenade"), 9 (complete).
Anne-Sophie Mutter (vln); Bruno Giuranna (vla); Mstislav Rostropovich (cello). 1989.
DEUTSCHE GRAMMOPHON 427 687 DDD
139:00 2 discs

✔HC ★★*Awards:* The Chosen Few: The Best Sounding Discs of 1989. *New Hi-Fi Sound Supplement* D '89; Best of the Month, *Hi-Fi News & Record Review*, D '89. The Year's Best, *Hi Fi News & Record Review*, May '90 Supplement.

"In a life ostensibly too busy for such luxuries, I've already returned several times to these performances for the sheer pleasure of it....the performances are all one might expect—technically superb, highly characterized, keenly alert and responsive in conversation, and so naturally 'plotted' in large-scale structure that the whole has a sense of enchanting inevitability, ruling out, for the moment, the notion that the music could or should go in any other way. Add to these virtues a brilliantly lifelike recorded sound." *P100 S100*

Hi-Fi News & Record Review 34:119 D '89; p.17 My '90 Supplement. Jeremy Siepmann (300w)

"These are genial performances—tonally well cultured, vibrant and dynamic. I hankered after a little more by way of introspection in the *E flat major Trio*, but the sunny mood of the players suited the *D major Serenade*, included as a filler on the first of these CDs, admirably-....The recording is internally consistent and stable."

New Hi-Fi Sound 6:101 Ag '89. George Entwistle (225w)

"The recording is close-up and decidedly dry, lacking ambience to the extent of cooling off string tone....We've all become rather spoiled by commonly adopted refinements of the recording art designed to divert attention to the fact that what we're listening to is indeed a recording. This production calls one's attention to it. No matter. The art embodied in these performance is all on an extremely high level of technical and interpretive accomplishment. It is entirely traditional in approach, untouched by period-instrument developments...these heavy hitters are as adept at illuminating Beethoven's string trios as anyone in their generation(s)-....Easily recommended."

Fanfare 13:143-44 N/D '89. John Wiser (550w)

Digital Audio's CD Review 6:60-1 F '90. Tom Vernier (325w)

Gramophone 67:191+ Jl '89. Joan Chissell (595w)

BERG, ALBAN. Lyric Suite for String Quartet; Quartet, Opus 3. See No. 2030, 3116.

BIBER, HEINRICH VON

3023. Mensa Sonora; Sonata Violino Solo Representativa.
Reinhard Goebel (vln). Reinhard Goebel (c). Cologne Musica Antiqua.
DEUTSCHE GRAMMOPHON 423 701 DDD 61:49

★★*Awards:* The Want List 1989, *Fanfare* N/D '89 (George Chien); Critics' Choice 1989, *Gramophone* D '89 (Nicholas Anderson).

"The group's impeccable sense of ensemble and their feeling for instrumental colour make something special of these vivacious occasional pieces."

Continuo 13:23 Je '89. Scott Paterson (120w)

"Musica Antiqua Koln's *Mensa Sonora*...not only marks the work's recorded premiere but it is Baroque music of exceptional quality, barely known and executed with the usual aplomb of the foremost interpreters of 'German' chamber music."

The Musical Times 130:420 Jl '89. Jonathan Freeman-Attwood (400w)

"The *Mensa Sonora* comprises six parts...it is certainly easy on the ear, especially as played here by Reinhard Goebel and the other members of Musica Antiqua Koln....The *Sonata representativa* is a most amusing, programmatic diversion....you can hear it here, along with Biber's table music, all superbly played and recorded. Most highly recommended."

Fanfare 12:102-3 Jl/Ag '89. George Chien (450w)

"This issue is as delightful for the music it contains as it is for the performances, and the recording quality does not lag far behind."

Hi-Fi News & Record Review 34:103 Ap '89. Peter Branscombe (280w)

Gramophone 67:915 N '89. Nicholas Anderson (405w)

3024. The Mystery (or Rosary) Sonatas (15) for Violin and Continuo Instruments.
John Holloway (vln); Davitt Moroney (hpscd/orgn). Tragicomedia Instrumental Ensemble.
VIRGIN 90838 DDD 131:00 2 discs

★★★★*Awards:* The Gramophone Awards, Nominations, Baroque—non-vocal, *Gramophone*, N '91; The Want List 1991, *Fanfare* N/D '91 (Tom Moore). Critic's Choice: 1991, *American Record Guide*, Ja/F '92 (Stephen Chakwin); Best Baroque Recording Non Vocal 1991, *Gramophone*, D '91.

"The sheer color and vibrancy of these pieces, as played here, is overwhelming; and the power and beauty of the passacaglia...beggars description. The recording, made in a church, has exactly the right blend of immediacy and atmosphere. This is an outstanding issue of one of the glories of baroque music."

American Record Guide 54:48-9 S/O '91. Stephen D. Chakwin, Jr. (long)

"It would be difficult to imagine a performance more effective and liberating than Holloway's. His crystalline, non-vibrato, luminous tone is at the service of a note-perfect technique that encompasses all the vagaries of Biber's intense musical vision. The extra dimension given by the varying colors of the continuo adds greatly to the music's drama. The accompanying booklet is a model of its kind."

Musical America 111:67 Jl '91. Shirley Fleming (380w)

"My review of Franzjosef Maier's traversal of these works...concluded that his readings, though the best to date, were not entirely satisfying. John Holloway's superb recording leaves no such reservations....Virgin's sound is just right....Highly recommended."

Fanfare 14:121 Jl/Ag '91. Tom Moore (155w)

"To bring off Biber's stimulating effects a period violin and a study of Baroque technique are vital. Holoway's performances are wholly admirable....The sound is churchy, with warm ambience but admirable clarity and a pleasant sense of space." *P95 S95*

Hi-Fi News & Record Review 36:88 F '91. Robert Dearling (430w)

"This set does full justice to Biber's important and affecting music."

Continuo 15:30 Ap '91. Scott Paterson (220w)

"The scordatura is intriguing in the way it creates a different tone color, a different set of double-stop possibilities for each sonata. Other than that, despite many imaginative, even striking moments, the pieces sounded mostly just pleasant and quaint and often tedious."

HighPerformanceReview 8(3):69 '91. Timothy Mangan (long)

Gramophone 68:2024+ My '91. Nicholas Anderson (325w)

BLOCH, ERNEST

3025. Quartet No. 2 for Strings; Prelude for Quartet; Night; Two Pieces for String Quartet.
Pro Arte Quartet. 1984 reissue.
LAUREL 826 ADD 53:41

"In view of the peerless performance offered here, the release must be considered an indispensable document of 20th-century chamber music at its best."

Fanfare 12:114-5 S/O '88. Walter Simmons (525w)

The New York Times S 18 '88, p. H29. George Jellinek (350w)

"The quality of the recorded sound greatly enhances what is one of the most thrilling listening experiences I have had in a long time....The fill-ups...are most welcome recording premieres."

High Fidelity 34:60-1 Ag '84. Harry Halbreich (300w)

"Nothing less than virtuosic technique and elevated musicianship will do. The members of the Pro Arte possess such qualities in abundance; as an ensemble they offer consistently absorbing and stylistically faithful realizations that burst into searing intensity when called for and are filled with a sense of joy and discovery....the LP is warmer, the CD a bit cleaner and more immediate."

Stereophile 12:211+ Je '89. Gordon Emerson (395w)

"The Pro Arte Quartet's magnificent reading of the Second Quartet sounds even better on CD than it does on the original LP....The shorter works are less significant than the quartet, but they are small only in terms of duration. This is essential listening for anyone interested in great chamber music, and Laurel's analog sound is excellent."

Musical America 109:53-4 Ja '89. David Hurwitz (185w)

"The Pro Arte Quartet's hard-driven, surly performances are no doubt appropriate versions of this music....Still, their playing is sharp and vivid, and so is the recording."

American Record Guide 52:25-6 Ja/F '89. Kyle Rothweiler (135w)

3026. Violin and Piano Music: Sonata No. 1 for Violin and Piano; Suite No. 1 for Solo Violin; Suite hebraique, for Viola (or Violin) and Piano (or Orchestra); Abodah, for Violin and Piano. (Complete Music for Violin and Piano, Volume 1).
Weilerstein Duo.
ARABESQUE 6605 55:23

★*Awards:* The Want List 1989, *Fanfare* N/D '89 (Walter Simmons).

"The Weilersteins play with impeccable ensemble and balance, the violin often dominating according to the dictates of the writing but the piano always displaying technical assurance and artistic sensitivity."

American Record Guide 52:41-2 N/D '89. Alan Heatherington (470w)

"Violinist Donald Weilerstein proves a sensitive and dynamic interpreter in every respect. Bloch's piano writing is every bit as demanding, but Vivian Hornik Weilerstein turns in a set of performances that sound as if she was weaned on this music. The Weilerstein's efforts are enhanced by recorded sound that effectively captures the feel of a live recital in an intimate but warmly reverberant space, though the piano often figures too prominently."

Stereophile 13:225+ Ja '90. Gordon Emerson (325w)

"Barely a year after the appearance of the brilliant ADDA CD (581044) featuring the two sonatas in excellent performances by violinist Alexis Galperine and pianist Frederic Aguessy (see *Fanfare* 12:3, pp. 131-32), the admirable new set arrives...I must confess to a slight preference for the Galperine performance [in Sonata No. 1]...Weilersteins have the edge [in No. 2]...due to a most egregious wrong note that mars the other version. A noteworthy feature of the Arabesque set is what I believe to be the first recording ever of *Nuit Exotique*."

Fanfare 13:150-51 N/D '89. Walter Simmons (1190w)

3027. Violin and Piano Music: Sonata No. 2 for Violin and Piano, "Poeme Mystique"; Suites (2) for Solo Violin; Abodah, for Violin and Piano; Nuit Exotique, for Violin and Piano. (Complete Music for Violin and Piano, Volume 2).
Weilerstein Duo.
ARABESQUE 6606 51:39

★*Awards:* The Want List 1989, *Fanfare* N/D '89 (Walter Simmons).

See Volume 1 for review excerpts.

—*Fanfare* 13:150-51 N/D '89. Walter Simmons (1190w)

—*Stereophile* 13:225+ Ja '90. Gordon Emerson (325w)

—*American Record Guide* 52:41-2 N/D '89. Alan Heatherington (470w)

BOULEZ, PIERRE. Derive, for Flute, Clarinet, Violin, Cello, Vibraphone and Piano; Memoriale, for Solo Flute and 8 Instruments. See No. 1047.

BRAHMS, JOHANNES

3028. Quartets for Strings: No. 1 in C Minor, Opus 51, No. 1; No. 3 in B flat, Opus 67.
Tokyo Quartet.
MOSS MUSIC GROUP/VOX 10039 64:31

✔HC ★*Awards:* *Stereo Review* Best of the Month, My '87.

"Enthusiastically recommended."

Opus 3:33 Ap '87. Harris Goldsmith (510w)

"If you think you've grown tired of Brahms, this surpassingly beautiful issue is, at the moment, the very strongest corrective I can think of."

Stereo Review 52:80 My '87. Richard Freed (290w)

Here is the first Brahms string quartet recording to be taken seriously since the late-'70s complete set by the Alban Berg Quartet-....Strongly recommended...Those who file their *Fanfares* will find a precis of my feelings about the Brahms Quartet competition in 6:4, pp. 136-37."

Fanfare 10:91 Mr/Ap '87 John D. Wiser (225w)

Ovation 8:40 Mr '87 Paul Turok (15w)

3029. Quartets (3) for Piano and Strings (complete), Opus 25, 26 and 60.
Emanuel Ax (pno); Isaac Stern (vln); Jaime Laredo (vla); Yo-Yo Ma (cello).
SONY 45846 DDD 127:32 2 discs

★★*Awards:* The Gramophone Awards, Nominations, Chamber, *Gramophone*, N '91. Best Chamber Recording 1991, *Gramophone*, D '91; Critics' Choice 1991, *Gramophone*, Ja '92 (Edward Seckerson). Pick of the Month, North American Perspective (Christie Barter), *Gramophone* Mr '91.

"In sum, while these performances are commendable (especially if you want the entire set), they are individually not the best available."

American Record Guide 54:45 Mr/Ap '91. Kurt Moses (325w)

"In sum, not bad but not up to the potential, let alone the past achievement, of all concerned. I'm still fond of the Cantilena recordings for Arabesque, opaque as they are, and also admire the sharp-edged and direct playing of Domus in a pair of separately available Virgin Classics CDs."

Fanfare 14:135-37 My/Je '91. John Wiser (180w)

"The rapport between these artists is always superb and represents a worthy survey of these fine works, if with not quite the technical support one might have hoped for. The background roar—especially the New York variety—should surely have been checked out before approving the venues." *P95 S85/75*

Hi-Fi News & Record Review 36:88-9 F '91. Antony Hodgson (455w)

Gramophone 68:1682 Mr '91. Edward Seckerson (490w)

3030. Quintet in B minor for Clarinet and Strings, Opus 115. MOZART, WOLFGANG AMADEUS. Quintet in A for Clarinet and Strings, K.581.
Melos Ensemble of London. 1964, 1965.
EMI 63116

✔HC

3031. Sextet in B flat for Strings, Opus 18; Sextet in G for Strings, Opus 36.
Raphael Ensemble.
HYPERION 66276 DDD 74:00

✔HC ★★★*Awards:* The Want List 1989, *Fanfare* N/D '89 (Mortimer H. Frank); Critics' Choice 1989, *Gramophone* D '89 (Alan Sanders). The Year's Best, *Hi Fi News & Record Review*, May '90 Supplement.

"These performances go to the very top of the not-very-long list of CDs coupling the two sextets."

Fanfare 14:135-57 My/Je '91. John Wiser (180w)

"A treasure trove. Glorious music, gloriously played....If I have criticisms worth voicing, they are few (perhaps only two) and relatively negligible." *P95 S100*

Hi-Fi News & Record Review 34:88 My '89; p.18 My '90 Supplement. Jeremy Siepmann (390w)

"Here are two of Brahms's most beautiful chamber works beautifully performed and recorded. Sonically, this release is a model of how a small ensemble should be reproduced-...Musically these are extraordinarily tasteful, youthfully vital, yet mature readings....A warmly recommended release."

Stereophile 13:227 Ja '90. Mortimer H. Frank (230w)

Gramophone 66:1175 Ja '89. Alan Sanders (380w)

3032. Trio No. 1 in B for Piano, Violin and Cello, Opus 8; Trio No. 3 in C minor for Piano, Violin and Cello, Opus 101.
Joseph Kalichstein (pno); Jaime Laredo (vln); Sharon Robinson (cello). 1984.
MOSS MUSIC/VOX 10042 DDD 54:09

✔HC ★★★*Awards:* Perfect 10/10, *Digital Audio*, Mr '88; Editors' Choice, *Digital Audio*, 1988. Perfect 10s, *Digital Audio's CD Review*, Mr '89. *American Record Guide* Overview: Getting to Know Chamber Music: Piano Trios.

"Good as the Borodin Trio is in their Chandos survey on two CDs of all Brahms' piano trios (CHAN 8334/5, *Fanfare* 9:2, pp. 127-28), the KLR combination makes a measurably more vivid impression. Strongly recommended."

Fanfare 11:170-1 S/O '87. John D. Wiser (310w)

Digital Audio 4:59-60 F '88. Tom Vernier (265w)

3033. Trio No. 1 in B for Piano, Violin and Cello, Opus 8. IVES, CHARLES. Trio for Piano, Violin and Cello (1911).
Fontenay Trio.
TELDEC 44924 DDD 57:00

★★*Awards:* Critic's Choice: 1990, *American Record Guide* Ja/F '91 (Donald Vroon). *American Record Guide* Overview: Getting to Know Chamber Music: Piano Trios.

"You hear right away the boldness and mastery of real pros. The music is smooth and suave but infused with ardor and feeling. It is also shaped: everything fits into a plan....The sound is utterly natural."

American Record Guide 53:52 S/O '90. Donald R. Vroon (175w)

"The three noticeably young Europeans who form the Trio Fontenay (pianist Wolf Harden, violinist Michael Mucke, and cellist Niklas Schmidt) do well indeed by their *Landsmanner* Mendelssohn [Teldec 44947] and Brahms, but they absolutely knock the spots off the trio by that crusty old Connecticut Yankee, Charles Ives."

Musical America 111:72-3 Ja '91. Paul Moor (285w)

"Whatever the mood, Trio Fontenay shows they're up to it. Each member is obviously an excellent player in his own right, and they play with a wonderful sense of ensemble....The recorded sound is equally excellent. Recommended."

HighPerformanceReview 8(3):70 '91. D. C. Culbertson (med)

"Trio Fontenay's Brahms makes little impression, good or bad; they lack a consistent interpretive viewpoint."

Fanfare 14:200-1 S/O '90. James H. North (225w)

Gramophone 67:1813-14 Ap '90. Alan Sanders (245w)

BRIDGE, FRANK

3034. Quartet No. 3 for Strings. WALTON, WILLIAM. Quartet in A minor for Strings.
Endellion String Quartet. 1962.
VIRGIN 91196 DDD 62:00

★*Awards:* Best of the Month, *Hi-Fi News & Record Review*, O '91.

Gramophone 69:84 S '91. Arnold Whittall (med)

The Third Quartet "is a work of real anguish and pain, yet suffused with a tender introspection in many of its quieter havens, above all in the half-lit coda to the ambitious Finale...The exhilarating Walton Quartet...makes an ideal foil. Drawing as it does upon huge reserves of rhythmic vitality and melodic fecundity, this has always struck me as an enormously appealing creation...A wonderful coupling." *P100/95 S100/95*

Hi-Fi News & Record Review 36:113 O '91. Andrew Achenbach (long)

"At last! Someone has finally had the sense to record the single most important chamber composition by a British composer. Period. I refer of course to Frank Bridge's Third Quartet...The Endellion String Quartet is one of Britain's finest, and they play all of this music with superb attack, beautiful tone, and accurate intonation....Needless to say, urgently recommended."

Fanfare 15:288-9 N/D '91. David Hurwitz (med)

"The interpretive style of the Endellion Quartet...[is well] suited to the intensely lyrical and moving Third Quartet by Bridge...Sonics are excellent."

American Record Guide 55:38 Ja/F '92. Karl Miller (long)

BROUWER, LEO

3035. Guitar Music: Danza Caracteristica; Cantium; Cancion de Cuna, "Berceuse"; Elogio de la Danza; Ojos Brujos; Guajira Criolla. **ORBON, JULIAN. Preludio y Danza for Guitar. VILLA-LOBOS, HEITOR. Preludes (5) for Guitar.**
Manuel Barrueco (gtr).
EMI 49710 DDD 49:00

★★*Awards:* Critic's Choice: 1990, *American Record Guide* Ja/F '91 (William Ellis). Top Disks of the Year, *The New York Times* D 24, '89 (John Rockwell).

"Manuel Barrueco's approach to this music is one of the utmost simplicity. His tempos tend to be slightly deliberate; he keeps his rubatos to a minimum, employing them only when the harmonic structure warrants, and he is exceptionally attuned to the coloristic possibilities of the music....The recording is excellent...All in all a fine performance by an exciting artist."
Fanfare 13:465 N/D '89. William Zagorski (425w)

"I can't recall having heard a more furious reading of *Danza caracteristica.* The performance is truly arresting. *Elogio de la danza* is another brilliant interpretation from Barrueco-...In Villa-Lobos's *Preludes,* Barrueco gives a bare-bones reading, siesta-laden and quite different from any other artist's."
American Record Guide 53:37 Ja/F '90. William Ellis (350w)

Gramophone 67:504 S '89. John Duarte (315w)

CARTER, ELLIOTT

Esprit Rude/Esprit Doux, for Flute and Clarinet. See No. 2051.

3036. Quartets for Strings: No. 1 (1951); **No. 4** (1986).
Arditti Quartet.
ETCETERA 1065 DDD 59:00 2 discs

✔HC ★★*Awards:* Critics' Choice 1989, *Gramophone* D '89 (Arnold Whittall); Top Disks of the Year, *The New York Times* D 24, '89 (John Rockwell).

"These are rich works that deserve to be heard and which may prove to be of enduring value and prominence....[The] complete set...is a must for quartet lovers of adventuresome spirit who are committed to music as an ongoing art form, not merely an archival one."
American Record Guide 52:34 Jl/Ag '89. Stephen R. Max (100w)

"I found the two groups [the Arditti and the Composers] quite evenly matched, with the Arditti perhaps having a slight edge—more subtle differentiation of voices, greater rhythmic freedom, wider textural variety....But of course what really makes the Arditti release newsworthy is the presence of Quartet No. 4, in its first recorded performance ever....What is one to say about this new work? I found it immediately engrossing, enjoyable to follow through its various changes of texture and mood, and extremely difficult to describe."
Fanfare 12:155-58 My/Je '89. William Youngren (580w)

Gramophone 66:1742 My '89. Arnold Whittall (220w)

3037. Quartets for Strings: No. 2 (1959); **No. 3** (1971).
Arditti Quartet.
ETCETERA 1066 DDD 45:00 2 discs

✔HC ★★*Awards:* Critics' Choice 1989, *Gramophone* D '89 (Arnold Whittall); Top Disks of the Year, *The New York Times* D 24, '89 (John Rockwell).

See above for review excerpt.
—*Fanfare* 12:155-58 My/Je '89. William Youngren (580w)

—*American Record Guide* 52:34 Jl/Ag '89. Stephen R. Max (100w)

Gramophone 66:1742 My '89. Arnold Whittall (220w)

CHAUSSON, ERNEST

3038. Quartet in A for Piano, Viola, Violin and Cello, Opus 30; Trio for Piano, Violin and Cello in G minor, Opus 3.
Les Musiciens. reissue 1984.
HARMONIA MUNDI 901115 ADD 72:00

"The performances of both works by Les Musiciens, an ensemble associated with Radio France, are superb....The rendition of the piano quartet exhibits exquisite tonal refinement, underlining the work's impressionistic hints....Sound quality is extraordinarily fine—both rich and transparent. This is an essential release for all Chausson admirers."
Fanfare 13:152-53 Ja/F '90. Walter Simmons (375w)

Gramophone 65:430 S '87 Robert Layton (360w)

CORELLI, ARCANGELO

3039. Sonatas (12) for Violin and Continuo Instruments, Opus 5 (complete).
Nigel North (lute). Trio Sonnerie.
VIRGIN 90840

✔HC ★★*Awards:* The Want List 1990, *Fanfare* N/D '90 (Nils Anderson); Critics' Choice 1990, *Gramophone* D '90 (Tess Knighton).

"Quite simply, this is the finest integral recording of Corelli's Op. 5 yet made."
American Record Guide 53:59 S/O '90. John W. Barker (550w)

"This performance by Trio Sonnerie with lutenist Nigel North does most eloquent justice to this marvellous music. Throughout the recording the playing is impeccable, infused with warmth and joy."
Continuo 14:17 Ag '90. Alison Melville (300w)

"The Trio Sonnerie is made up of three very talented ladies: Monica Huggett (violin), Mitzi Meyerson (harpsichord and organ), and Sarah Cunningham (cello)....The sound is excellent, and the set highly recommended."
Fanfare 14:205 N/D '90. Nils Anderson (290w)

"There is a consistent intimacy, urbanity, and graciousness about her [Huggett's] playing seldom found elsewhere. Energy abounds in most fast movements but never unbridled, always caringly put in the service of musical intelligibility. So frequently there is a sweet, smiling countenance bestowed upon the major mode movements—a countenance lacking in the more aggressive approaches of Banchini and Melkus—while a darker, *misterioso* side comes out in the minor keys....It is the wonderful ensemble, the unfailing unity of purpose, and the sheer musicality between all participants which makes this such a truly memorable disc....Virgin Classics has combined a rich, resonant ambience with a remarkable intimacy and clarity."

Musick 12(3):9-12 Winter-D '90.John E. Sawyer (635w)

Gramophone 68:556 S '90. Tess Knighton (330w)

3040. Sonatas (12) for Violin and Continuo Instruments, Opus 5; Sonata in A for Violin and Continuo, Opus 5, No. 9 (elaborated by Geminiani).
Locatelli Trio.
HYPERION 66381/2 DDD 63:25; 63:52 2 discs

★★★***Awards:*** The Want List 1991, *Fanfare* N/D '91 (Nils Anderson). Critic's Choice: 1991, *American Record Guide*, Ja/F '92 (Paul Laird); Critics' Choice 1991, *Gramophone*, Ja '92 (Julie Anne Sadie).

"Wallfisch is now the best choice on baroque violin...The continuo team is splendid."

American Record Guide 54:48 My/Je '91. Paul Laird (200w)

"Hot on the heels of the performances by the Trio Sonnerie with Monica Huggett on Virgin Classics (*Fanfare* 41:2), which I lauded and even included in the 1990 Want List, comes another complete recording of Corelli's opus 5 with original instruments by the Locatelli Trio-....Either set is a delight in its own terms and can be recommended, for it really comes down to a matter of taste. The connoisseur will want to have both sets."

Fanfare 14:192 Mr/Ap '91. Nils Anderson (290w)

Gramophone 68:1684 Mr '91. Julie Ann Sadie (420w)

3041. Trio Sonatas: Opus 1: No's. 1, 3, 7, 9, 12; Opus 2: No.'s 4, 6, 9, 12.
Simon Standage (violin); Micaela Comberti (violin); Anthony Pleeth (cello); Nigel North (archlute); Trevor Pinnock (organ/hpscd).
DEUTSCHE GRAMMOPHON 419 614 DDD 63:23

★***Awards:*** *Gramophone* Critics' Choice (Julie Anne Sadie), 1987.

"I don't want to overdo this, but there are many moments of breath-taking and occasionally heart-rending beauty in this program, aided by the clear and natural Archiv sonics at the Abbey Road Studios. I think if I had one Corelli disc for the desert island, this would be it."

Fanfare 11:129 N/D '87. Edward Strickland (240w)

"This is a most satisfying album."

Ovation 9:50 D '88. Christopher Greenleaf (155w)

"Apart from questions of instrumentation, the playing...is first-rate in all respects."

Musick 10:7-9 Fall '88. John Sawyer (905w)

"The ensemble is excellent...comparisons with the La Petite Bande concerto recordings made me yearn for something less classical and more athletically evocative. But this is very good, anyway."

Hi-Fi News & Record Review 32:97 S '87 Stephen Daw (230w)

Gramophone 65:66 Je '87 Julie Anne Sadie (420w)

DEBUSSY, CLAUDE

3042. Quartet in G minor for Strings, Opus 10. RAVEL, MAURICE. Quartet in F for Strings.
Quartetto Italiano. 1986 reissue.
PHILIPS 420 894 ADD 57:00

"The high-level CD transfer brings the music a bit more vividly to life than did the LP. Musically, the Quartetto Italiano performances are as fine as any."

High Fidelity 39:74 Ap '89. David Hurwitz (100w)

Gramophone 66:628 O '88. Christopher Headington (200w)

3043. Sonata No. 1 in D minor for Cello and Piano. SCHUBERT, FRANZ. Sonata for Arpeggione and Piano, D.821. SCHUMANN, ROBERT. Funt Stucke im Volkston, Opus 102.
Mstislav Rostropovich (cello); Benjamin Britten (piano). reissue 1970; 1962.
LONDON/DECCA 417 833 59:24

✔**HC** ★***Awards:*** *Gramophone* Critics' Choice (Joan Chissell), 1987.

"If you cannot lay your hands on the LP originals...then this CD is a must for you collection."

Hi-Fi News & Record Review 32:125 N '87 Doug Hammond (70w)

Gramophone 65:430 S '87 Joan Chissell (350w)

3044. Sonata No. 3 in G Minor for Violin and Piano. FRANCK, CESAR. Sonata in A for Violin and Piano. RAVEL, MAURICE. Sonata in G for Violin and Piano.
Yefim Bronfman (piano) Shlomo Mintz (violin).
DEUTSCHE GRAMMOPHON 415 683 58:55

✔**HC** ★★***Awards:*** *Gramophone* Critics' Choice 1986 (J. Methuen-Campbell); *Gramophone* Critics' Choice 1986 (Christopher Headington).

"I can think of no preferable version [of the Franck sonata] that I have heard....In the Debussy sonata, other than the Szigetti/Bartok version, I haven't heard another edition that I have liked as well as this one since the Thibaud/Cortot. In the case of the Ravel, the

playing is absolutely spectacular....Reason enough to purchase this superb issue."
Fanfare 10:144 N/D '86 John Bauman (300w)

"Like his mentor, Isaac Stern, Mintz occasionally shows a tendency to coarsen his tone during forte passages...Elsewhere, however, both performers are flawless technicians operating on a high plateau of musical inspiration."
High Fidelity 37:79+ Ja '87 K. Robert Schwarz (315w)

Stereo Review 52:176+ F '87 Richard Freed (145w)

Hi-Fi News & Record Review 31:107 N '86. Andrew Keener (330w)

3045. Sonata No. 3 in G minor for Violin and Piano; Sonata No. 2 for Flute, Viola and Harp. FRANCK, CESAR. Sonata in A for Violin and Piano. RAVEL, MAURICE. Introduction and Allegro for Harp, Flute, Clarinet and String Orchestra.
Kyung-Wha Chung (vln); Radu Lupu (hpscd). Melos Ensemble of London.
LONDON/DECCA 421 154 ADD 67:00

✔HC

Gramophone 66:1175 Ja '89. James Methuen-Campbell (45w)

Sonata No. 3 in G minor for Violin and Piano. See No. 3008.

DOHNANYI, ERNST VON

3046. Quintet in C minor for Piano and Strings, Opus 1; Sextet in C for Piano, Clarinet, Horn and String Trio.
Andras Schiff (pno); Kalman Berkes (clar); Radovan Vlatkovic (horn). Takacs Quartet.
LONDON/DECCA 421 423 DDD 59:00

✔HC ★★*Awards:* Top Disks of the Year, *The New York Times* D 24, '89 (John Rockwell); Top Choices—1989, *American Record Guide* Ja/F '90 (Donald Vroon).

"An astonishing performance: urgent, passionate and wholly persuasive....This is a glorious disc which should generate a great deal of enthusiasm for the piece."
The Musical Times 130:690 N '89. Nigel Simeone (275w)

"I doubt that you will hear better quartet playing anywhere in the world today....Both works exude high spirits, and all participants make them a melodious joy to hear."
Musical America 109:60-1 My '89. Paul Moor (200w)

"Anyone who likes romantic chamber music will respond to [the piano quintet]....There's no other performance in current catalogs, but I've heard a couple others and find this one superior in its passion and sweep as well as in sound....The Sextet is from 40 years later-....And again the performance is the best you can get."
American Record Guide 52:40-1 My/Je '89. Donald R. Vroon (225w)

"Schiff and the Takacs foursome make a particularly eventful performance of Erno Dohnnyi's mild-mannered youthful piano quintet....The London recording has a savor about its playing, particularly pianist Schiff's, which indicates a degree of affectionate involvement and understanding not to be found in *any* previous recording, not even in the prewar Eduard Kilenyi/Roth Quartet 78s once available on the Columbia label....I recommend this CD strongly."
Fanfare 12:130-31 Jl/Ag '89. John Wiser (350w)

"Schiff and his partners, aware of the Lisztian connection—Liszt is as strong an influence as Brahms—throw themselves into the music with enthusiasm, and produce performances calculated to win over the growing band of admirers of the late Romantics whose work has suffered the vagaries of fashion."
Hi-Fi News & Record Review 34:105 Ap '89. Kenneth Dommett (280w)

The New York Times My 27 '90, p. 19 H. John Rockwell (175w)

Gramophone 66:1020 D '88. Lionel Salter (350w)

DOWLAND, JOHN

3047. Lachrimae, or Seven Teares.
Jakob Lindberg (lute). Dowland Consort. October 1986.
BIS 315 DDD 66:00

✔HC ★*Awards:* *Gramophone* Critics' Choice (Geoffrey Horn), 1987.

"Important repertoire, expert realizations, full and vivid digital sound, liner notes by the world's leading authority on Dowland and a full sixty-five minutes of music—there is not much more one can ask from a recording. I am happy to give it my highest recommendation."
American Record Guide 49:61-62 N/D '86 Thomas W. Skladony (840w)

"The Dowland Consort's traversal joins two earlier issues...Each takes an approach that was deemed suitably "authentic" in its time, and hearing the three successively yields an interesting overview of how drastically our notions of authenticity have changed during the last twenty-five years....In many respects, the new version is the most attractive of the three, combining some of the better qualities of each predecessor."

"The Consort's ensemble playing is excellent, especially in the Pavans, some of which are taken very slowly indeed."
Continuo 11:12-13 Ja '87 Scott Paterson (560w) (rev. of LP)

"All the music...is expertly performed on original instruments."

The New York Times F 28 '88, p. H27. Paul Turok (75w)

Hi-Fi News & Record Review 31:80 Ag '86. Stephen Daw (200w)

Fanfare 10:138-9 S/O '86 Mortimer H. Frank (275w)

Gramophone 64:591 O '86 (rev. of LP) David Fallows (540w); 64:896 D '86 (rev. of CD) Geoffrey Horn (95w)

Opus 3:30-31 D '86 Allan Kozinn (1140w)

Digital Audio 3:36-7 S '86. David Vernier (280w)

DVORAK, ANTONIN

3048. Quartet in D for Piano and Strings, Opus 23; Quartet in E flat for Piano and Strings, Opus 87.
Ames Piano Quartet.
DORIAN 90125 DDD 69:51

> ✔**HC** ★★★***Awards:*** The Want List 1990, *Fanfare* N/D '90 (Al Fasoldt).

"A recording this good defeats one's critical faculties. It's just so right. If you like Dvorak but don't have this music, its time has now come. Treat yourself."

American Record Guide 53:62 S/O '90. Donald R. Vroon (125w)

"This is one of the most enjoyable chamber music albums I've encountered in some time. Fine performances are served by outstanding recorded sound to make for a most satisfying listening experience....The sound is completely natural, with a pleasing resonance which can probably be traced to the fine acoustic properties of the Troy Savings Bank in upstate New York where the recording was made."

HighPerformanceReview 8(2):63 Summer '91. James Primosch (300w)

"Dorian brought this group to Troy, New York, to record the two piano quartets of Dvorak in that small city's greatest cultural asset, the Troy Savings Bank Music Hall....Of the four CDs coupling these two very different and challenging works, Dorian's is by far the best recorded, the performances also in every sense competitive with their forerunners from Prague, London, and Munich. The disc is strongly recommended."

Fanfare 13:136-39 Jl/Ag '90. John Wiser (350w)

"If I finally recommend other interpretations over those of the Ames Quartet, it is with the admonition that you'll be missing some fine music If you pass these up."

Stereophile 13:217 D '90. Robert Hesson (350w)

"In considering these performances one must take into account their only current competition, by Domus on Hyperion....All things considered, the Domus is the more satisfying version." *P95/85 S85*

Hi-Fi News & Record Review 36:70-1 Ag '91. Kenneth Dommett (100w)

Digital Audio's CD Review 7:70 Ja '91. Lawrence B. Johnson (140w)

Gramophone 68:756+ O '90. Stephen Johnson (245w)

3049. Quartet in D for Piano and Strings, Opus 23; Quartet in E flat for Piano and Strings, Opus 87.
Domus.
HYPERION 66287 DDD 70:00

> ★***Awards:*** Critics' Choice 1989, *Gramophone* D '89 (Stephen Johnson).

"Accounts of considerable strength and intelligence."

Fanfare 12:152-53 Mr/Ap '89. John Wiser (325w)

"Highly recommended."

American Record Guide 52:44 My/Je '89. Stephen R. Max (100w)

"The four young players....are impressively secure technically and convey all the give and take and spontaneity of their live chamber music playing in this exemplary recording, which is certain to give lasting pleasure in performances that are unlikely to be superseded in the near future."

Music and Musicians International 37:34-5 My '89. P. Grahame Woolf (240w)

"This young group's approach is unexpectedly restrained and in marked contrast to the Beaux Arts' performances...the earlier D major...actually responds rather better to Domus's caressingly low-key performance....The later E-flat Quartet, however, could do with a little more drama than Domus find in it....It is an enjoyable performance all the same."

Hi-Fi News & Record Review 34:97 F '89. Kenneth Dommett (210w)

Gramophone 66:1447 Mr '89. Stephen Johnson (320w)

3050. Quartet No. 12 in F for Strings, Opus 96, "American". SMETANA, BEDRICH. Quartet No. 1 in E minor for Strings, "From My Life".
Guarneri Quartet.
PHILIPS 420 803 DDD 52:00

"These are powerful performances which, despite the familiarity of the music, find something new to say about both quartets."

Hi-Fi News & Record Review 33:98 Ap '88. Kenneth Dommett (200w)

"Unreservedly recommended!"

Stereo Review 53:135 Je '88. David Hall (245w)

"Fourteen years and eight months later, their second recording of the 'American' Quartet of Dvorak preserves assets of luxuriant individual tone and good ensemble, and by some minor miracle, no trace of any sense of the routine or workaday."

Fanfare 11:158-60 Jl/Ag '88. John D. Wiser (315w)

"This new issue is not entirely recommendable. The problem lies in the ensemble's approach to tempi...a greater cohesive sense would have made this an outstanding issue."

Music and Musicians International 36:41 Je '88. Robert Matthew-Walker (150w)

Gramophone 65:1209 F '88. Edward Greenfield (210w)

3051. Quintet in E flat for Strings, Opus 97; Sextet in A for Strings, Opus 48.
Raphael Ensemble.
HYPERION 66308 DDD 65:00

✔**HC** ★*Awards:* The Year's Best, *Hi Fi News & Record Review*, May '90 Supplement.

"Throughout the playing is rhythmically alert, sensitively phrased and cleanly fingered. A pleasing touch of asperity to the violins tempers the warm, natural sound." *P95 S95*

Hi-Fi News & Record Review 34:79 Jl '89; p.21 My '90 Supplement. Kenneth Dommett (115w)

"The Raphael players identify completely with both scores. This is warmly effusive playing, captured in exquisite sound....highly recommended."

American Record Guide 54:48 Ja/F '91. Allen Linkowski (120w)

"Ensemble precision and tonal body are conspicuously good, and so is pitch-accuracy. Beyond these more or less mechanical considerations, the picture gets even better."

Fanfare 13:196-200 N/D '89. John Wiser (400w)

"Their performances of these two wonderful Dvorak works are among the happiest chamber-music experiences to come from any source in years....The recording itself is absolutely first-rate."

Stereo Review Presents: Compact Disc Buyers' Guide Summer 1990 p.56 Richard Freed (125w)

Gramophone 67:326 Ag '89. John Warrack (265w)

3052. Trios for Piano, Violin and Cello: No. 3 in F minor, Opus 65; No. 4 in E minor, Opus 90, "Dumky".
Emanuel Ax (pno); Young Uck Kim (vln); Yo-Yo Ma (cello).
CBS 44527 DDD 72:27

✔**HC** ★★*Awards:* Best Recordings of the Month, *Stereo Review*, O '88. *American Record Guide* Overview: Getting to Know Chamber Music: Piano Trios, N/D '90.

"It offers surpassingly fine accounts of the two works by musicians who must love performing together as much as they obviouosly adore the music they're playing."

Stereo Review 53:92 O '88. Richard Freed (525w)

"Ax has never shown greater radiance, nor Ma more warm-hearted animation, and the whole really does seem greater than the sum of even these superb parts."

Stereo Review Presents: Compact Disc Buyer's Guide 1989 pg:61 Richard Freed (125w)

"Previous recordings by the Ax/Ma duo have left me rather cold, their note-for-note perfection shielding a spiritual blandness. But with Kim in the 'Dumky,' they dig to the heart of the music. Voluptuous, almost idiosyncratic phrasing gives the work an irresistible mystical cast."

Stereophile 12:rh Ja '89. Robert Hesson (380w)

"This Ax-Kim-Ma Trio recording has much to recommend it, including realistic sound."

Hi-Fi News & Record Review 34:88 Mr '89. Kenneth Dommett (175w)

"If these are neither of them that fabled animal, a wholly idiomatic Dvorak performance, they come close enough in my estimation to decouple any reservations I might have regarding certain small details. Recommended."

Fanfare 12:179-80 N/D '88. John Wiser (215w)

"The CBS disc is marked by particularly fine playing by Ax. This is the finest playing I have heard from him on disc. His partners are fully up to his standard....the Denon remains a clear first choice. Suk and his colleagues bring a special quality to the rhythm—a kind of poise—which the other groups simply do not command."

American Record Guide 52:33 Mr/Ap '89. Stephen D. Chakwin, Jr. (125w)

"It is a pity to have such fine performances ruined by such a poor reading."

High Fidelity 39:65 F '89. Christopher Rothko (275w)

The New York Times Ap 9 '89, p. 25. Barrymore L. Scherer (b.n.)

Gramophone 66:1447 Mr '89. Stephen Johnson (230w)

FASCH, JOHANN FRIEDRICH. Music of Fasch. See No. 1145.

FAURE, GABRIEL

3053. Sonata in A for Violin and Piano, Opus 13; Sonata in E minor for Violin and Piano, Opus 108.
Krysia Osostowicz (vln); Susan Tomes (pno).
HYPERION 66277 DDD 50:00

✔**HC** ★★*Awards:* Top Choices—1989, *American Record Guide* Ja/F '90 (Arved Ashby). The Year's Best, *Hi Fi News & Record Review*, May '90 Supplement.

"The violin soars through a bit of ambient blur in the piano for an effect of opulent impasto, close and immediate. One of the most fascinating and persuasive readings of Faure—ever."

Fanfare 12:194-95 My/Je '89. Adrian Corleonis (150w)

"To hear chamber music played with such obvious involvement, such careful attention to structural detail at every level, and such soaring, refined intensity is nothing but a pleasure and a privilege....Full marks, too, to the recording team." *P100 S95*

Hi-Fi News & Record Review 34:89 Je '89; p.21 My '90 Supplement. Jeremy Siepmann (245w)

"The two founder members of the Domus piano quartet...play both sonatas with affection and understanding and the recording can be warmly recommended."

Music and Musicians International 37:15 Je '89. P. Grahame Woolf (300w)

"Once in a blue moon a record arrives of such fulfilling music performed with such skill, sensitivity and taste that you cannot avoid setting aside all critical intent and simply becoming captured by the proceedings....Perhaps most deserving of mention is Osostowicz's beautiful, sensitive, and rather dark tone, as constantly shaded and varied as that of an intelligent human voice, and perfectly suited to this music-....Strongly recommended."

American Record Guide 52:44 Jl/Ag '89. Arved Ashby (250w)

Gramophone 66:800 N '88. Joan Chissell (400w)

FINE, IRVING

3054. Notturno for Strings and Harp; Partita, for Wind Quartet; String Quartet; The Hour Glass, for Chorus; Serious Song: A Lament for String Orchestra.

Jean Dane (vla); Susan Jolles (harp). Gerard Schwarz; David Hoose (c). Cantata Singers; New York Chamber Symphony Orchestra; New York Woodwind Quintet; Lydian String Quartet; Los Angeles Chamber Orchestra.

ELEKTRA 79175 DDD 70:14

✔**HC** ★*Awards:* Classical Hall of Fame, *Fanfare*, Ja/F '92 (Mike Silverton).

"More than having aged well, Fine's music demands to be cherished. Performances and recordings are excellent."

Fanfare 15:468-9 Ja/F '92. Mike Silverton (med)

"But nothing on this release takes a second place, especially when the factor of sound quality is considered. There are good Nonesuch notes and rich recorded sound. Very highly recommended.

Fanfare 12:163-64 Mr/Ap '89. John Ditsky (225w)

"It is a well-recorded, well-paced collection with some very fine performances."

Audio 73:132 Ap '89. Susan Elliott (575w)

"For the quality of the music, the caliber of the performances, and the imaginative programming, this CD is a clear winner."

High Fidelity 39:62-3 My '89. Robert R. Reilly (525w)

"Irving Fine was not a prolific composer, but on the evidence of the works recorded here and a few others I have had the opportunity to hear in the past, he was certainly a craftsman-....These performances, recorded at different times and places, have been expertly matched in sound and ambience so that this fact is hardly noticeable. First class playing throughout and good sound." *P95 S95*

Australian Hi-Fi 20(11):51:16-7 '89. John Aranetta (205w)

"Irving Fine...was an individual voice...who wrote beautiful original music...He's not as well remembered today as he ought to be, and I hope that this release by the reliable Nonesuch will help."

American Record Guide 53:51 Mr/Ap '90. Timothy D. Taylor (230w)

FRANCAIX, JEAN

3055. Quintets for Winds: No. 1, No. 2. Divertissement for Wind Trio. Quartet for Winds.

Aulos Quintet.

KOCH-SCHWANN 310 022 DDD 57:39

✔**HC** ★*Awards:* Critics' Choice 1989, *Gramophone* D '89 (Lionel Salter).

"The Aulos group is well-nigh perfect for the music, in terms of technique and interpretation. Further, the recorded sound is outstanding, and the little blurb by Francaix that passes for notes reveals him to be the charming gentleman suggested by his music."

American Record Guide 52:59-60 N/D '89. Stephen R. Max (185w)

"Practically every French composer has had to produce an obligatory piece or two for woodwind ensemble....This CD offering Francaix's four major works in this field brings together a definitive survey of some of the most ingenious scores of this type ever written."

Fanfare 12:148-49 Jl/Ag '89. Paul A. Snook (200w)

Gramophone 67:684+ O '89. Lionel Salter (400w)

FRANCK, CESAR

3056. Sonata in A for Violin and Piano. RESPIGHI, OTTORINO. Sonata in B minor for Violin and Piano. POULENC, FRANCIS. Sonata for Violin and Piano.

("Josef Suk Treasury").

Josef Suk (vln); Jan Panenka (pno); Josef Hala (pno). 1967, 1980, 1967.

SUPRAPHON 110 710 ADD 70:00

"I have owned the LP for 15 years as my only version [of these works], and I have never tired of it or longed for another....Mid-priced, perfect sound and artistry: this is essential for my library, and I recommend it for yours."

American Record Guide 53:49 Jl/Ag '90. Donald R. Vroon (200w)

Fanfare 13:146-47 Jl/Ag '90. David K. Nelson (280w)

Gramophone 67:2058 My '90. Alan Sanders (105w)

Sonata in A for Violin and Piano. See No. 3044, 3045.

GIBBONS, ORLANDO

3057. Fantasias: Six Fantasias a 2—No. 5; Nine Fantasias 1 3—No.'s 1-4, 8, 9; Two Fantasias a 4—No. 1; Four Fantasias a 6, No.'s 1-3. **Gailliard a 3. In Nomine a 4. Three In Nomines a 5—No. 2. Go from my window. Prelude. Ground. Fantasia. The Cries of London.**
Paul Nicholson (orgn). Fretwork.
VIRGIN 90849 DDD 68:00

✔HC ★★★*Awards:* The Want List 1990, *Fanfare* N/D '90 (Tom Moore); Critics' Choice 1990, *Gramophone* D '90 (Julie Anne Sadie); Critics Choice, *Hi Fi News & Record Review*, Ap '91 Supplement (Helena Stoward).

"The spontaneity of the music is intact here; viol players will want to play along, and other listeners will be captured by the intimacy. The music is a true sensual pleasure, beginning with the second entrance on the disc, which is a delicious dissonance against the opening line-....The sonic presence of the recording is admirable; particularly impressive is the bass range."
American Record Guide 53:59 N/D '90. Paul Laird (345w)

"Fretwork's performances here are stunning. What ensemble, what expansiveness of phrase. The recording captures the richness of the beautifully tuned deep tones of the viols, yet the details of each line read through the ensemble sound."
Fanfare 14:233 N/D '90. Tom Moore (200w)

"Fretwork...play with warm tone, accurate ensemble, and deep sympathy for their material....Sonically, this is another Virginal success."
Stereophile 14:217 N '91. Les Berkley (med)

"The thorough, balanced programme...embraces a great variety of fantasias for two to six instruments which more than compensates for the inevitable homogeneity of sound in a recording like this; but there are also frequent occasions when the sheer virtuosity of both Gibbons and Fretwork are little short of riveting." *P95 S85*
Hi-Fi News & Record Review 35:101 Je '90. Helena Stoward (245w)

Gramophone 67:1628 Mr '90. Julie Ann Sadie (385w)

GLASS, PHILIP

3058. Music in 12 Parts.
Philip Glass Ensemble.
VIRGIN 91311 DDD 207:00 3 discs

★★*Awards:* Critics' Choice 1990, *Gramophone* D '90 (John Milsom); The Highs, 1990, *The New York Times* D 30 '90 (John Rockwell). Record of the Eighties, *Gramophone*, D '89 (John Milsom).

"Scored for three electronic keyboards, three amplified winds (flutes and/or saxophones), and a soprano (whose part is wordless), *Music in 12 Parts* literally defines the unique sonic realm of the Philip Glass Ensemble. From deliberately limited resources, Glass elicits a maximum of color, mixing the luminous winds, the hovering solo voice, and the reedy, monochromatic keyboards...into a shimmering, constantly shifting timbral blend....Listening to the ensemble negotiate the layered polyrhythms, shifting metric patterns, melodic augmentation and diminution, exposed unisons and parallelisms, whirling arpeggios and scales—and all within cycles of repetition!—is an exhilarating experience. And it is not accomplished by studio trickery, as Glass's recent live performance of *Music in 12 Parts* in New York made clear."
Musical America 110:77-8 S '90. K. Robert Schwarz (820w)

Gramophone 68:68 Je '90. John Milsom (675w)

GODOWSKY, LEOPOLD

3059. Impressions for Violin and Piano: Legende; Poeme; Perpetuum mobile; Elegie; Valse; Oriental; Tyrolean; Larhetto lamentoso; Profile; Saga; Viennese; Valse macabre.
Gottfried Schneider (vln); Cord Garben (pno).
ETCETERA 1067 DDD 42:00

★*Awards:* The Want List 1989, *Fanfare* N/D '89 (Adrian Corleonis).

"A poignantly pleasurable, lastingly treasurable release, highly recommended."
Fanfare 13:208 S/O '89. Adrian Corleonis (270w)

"Anyone attracted to sophisticated late-romantic violin writing in the Kreisler vein need not hesitate to investigate this release. Schneider-...and Garben treat the music sympathetically and stylishly, though occasionally a greater sense of relaxation might be desirable. The recording presents the performers in a vivid, rather close sonic perspective."
American Record Guide 52:56 S/O '89. Donald Manildi (275w)

Gramophone 67:330 Ag '89. Michael Oliver (375w)

GORECKI, HENRYK MIKOLAJ

3060. Quartet No. 1 for Strings, Opus 62, "Already It Is Dusk"; Lerchenmusik, Opus 53.

Michael Collins (clar); Christopher Van Kampen (cello); John Constable (pno). Kronos String Quartet.
ELEKTRA 79257 DDD 54:00

★★★*Awards:* Wire Winner: Music of Extremes, *The Wire* S '91; The Want List 1991, *Fanfare* N/D '91 (Mike Silverton). Critics' Choice 1991, Modern Composition, *The Wire*, D/Ja '91/92; Disc of the Month, *Digital Audio's CD Review*, Ap '92 (Tom Vernier). Editors' Choice—Best CDs of the Year, *Digital Audio's CD Review*, Je '92.

"This CD [is]...a threefold triumph—music, performance, and timeliness...Get this disc."
Fanfare 15:222-3 Ja/F '92. Mike Silverton (long)

"The dramatic Tatra mountains, inspiration for artists and Romantics, line Poland's southern border with Czechoslovakia. There, fiddle bands of the *gorale* (literally 'mountain-men') play a kind of Polish country music—and it's from their wild, delirious dissonances that Henryk Gorecki, unsung hero of modern music, has taken inspiration....Much of the time you're on your own, in a world of sound of pristine beauty and crafted yet elemental simplicity. Yes, this is minimalism, but developed independently, and intrinsically expressive in its impact."
The Wire 91:48 S '91. Andy Hamilton (med)

"Kronos is, as usual, superb."
American Record Guide 54:68 N/D '91. Timothy D. Taylor (long)

"Unlike most avant-gardists, Gorecki showed a lively interest in his country's [(Poland)] rich folk music...Henryk Gorecki brings a breath of fresh air to the contemporary scene. On this CD, both musicians and technicians have done their very best by him."
Musical America 111:46-7 N/D '91. Paul Moor (long)

Digital Audio's CD Review 8:32 Ap '92. Tom Vernier (long)

Gramophone 69:87 S '91. Arnold Whittall (med)

GUBAIDULINA, SOFIA. Hommage a T. S. Eliot, for Octet and Soprano. See No. 2065.
Rejoice! For Violin and Cello. See No. 3135.

HAYDN, FRANZ JOSEPH

3061. Quartets for Strings: Quartet in B flat, Opus 1, No. 1; Quartet in D, Opus 64, No. 5, "Lark"; Quartet in G minor, Opus 74, No. 3, "Rider".
Hagen Quartet.
DEUTSCHE GRAMMOPHON 423 622 DDD 55:00

✔HC ★*Awards:* Critic's Choice: 1990, *American Record Guide* Ja/F '91 (Stephen Chakwin).

"I am impressed and delighted by their [The Hagen Quartet] performances here of three nicely contrasted works....The recording, resonant yet not lacking intimacy, is natural in sound, allowing a wide range of tonal nuances to make their due effect."
Hi-Fi News & Record Review 34:97 Ag '89. Peter Branscombe (180w)

"The Hagens are flashy all right; attacking like the Tatrai but always with a grace and tonal beauty not shared by the Hungarians. Recording is well balanced and distanced; we share a large room with the players, rather than a concert hall. We are offered an ensemble, yet we can hear any separate thread we choose to follow. A marvelous disc from every standpoint."
Fanfare 13:233-35 N/D '89. James H. North (400w)

"If you care enough about Haydn quartets to have read this far, stop reading, take the information in the heading down carefully and go buy this recording....The Hagen Quartet is a wonderful ensemble, well matched in tone, technically secure and, in these pieces, full of the joy and energy so important for good Haydn performances. DG has supplied a recording of demonstration quality."
American Record Guide 53:58 Mr/Ap '90. Stephen D. Chakwin, Jr. (125w)

Gramophone 67:199 Jl '89. Alan Blyth (280w)

3062. Quartets (6) for Strings, Opus 76.
Tatrai Quartet. Budapest, Hungary. 1964.
HUNGAROTON 12812/3 127:52 2 discs

✔HC ★★*Awards:* *Fanfare* Want List 1986 (John D. Wiser). *Gramophone* Critics' Choice (Joan Chissell), 1987.

"Especially on CD this remains a heart-warming issue and, as in 1966, it has the field to itself."
Hi-Fi News & Record Review 32:98 S '87 Peter Branscombe (100w)

"The Tatrai Quartet is a marvelous ensemble with a warm tone, a sure sense of style, and a deep understanding of the many contrasting elements found in Haydn's Op. 76....They bring depth and feeling to all of these wonderful pieces."
Stereo Review 51:134 D '86 Stoddard Lincoln (175w)

"Although a reissue of a 1964 recording that first appeared in the United States about 15 years ago on the Qualiton label, this set is so extraordinary in its digital revitalization that it virtually counts as a new release....These sonic improvements help to italicize the miraculous execution of the Tatrai....I doubt if one will ever hear Haydn playing to surpass what is offered in this Op. 76 set....It provides prime evidence of how the spirit of authentic style may be captured without seeking a literal authenticity....This reissue might well be the finest Haydn-quartet recording ever made. Surely it is one of them and a set not to be missed."

Fanfare 10:162-3 S/O '86 Mortimer H. Frank (550w)

"Sooner or later, everyone with the faintest interest in this repertoire (which should be just about everyone) should feel compelled to acquaint themselves with the Tatrai Quartet accounts of Op. 76."

Fanfare 10:163 S/O '86 John D. Wiser (350w)

"The Tatrai Quartet has recorded all of the mature quartets of Haydn on LP and this appears to be the beginning of their re-release on CD-....Summing up, the Tatrai performances are sometimes on the slow side and play more on the string than most modern groups and with less vibrato, yet they make the music sound right....The recording is good, with the same warm sound Hungaroton has had consistently and you don't have to change discs but once."

American Record Guide 49:74 S/O '86David W. Moore (345w)

"There is very little to fault either in the quality of the performance or the sound of the recording itself."

HighPerformanceReview 5:89 D '87. Ann Viles (230w)

Gramophone 64:1572+ My '87 Joan Chissell (265w)

3063. Trios (43) for Piano, Violin and Cello (complete).
Beaux Arts Trio. 1971-79 reissues.
PHILIPS 432 061 634:20 9 discs

★*Awards:* Wire Winner: Chamber Music, *The Wire*, S '91 (Graham Lock).

"Charles Rosen, in his invaluable study *The Classical Style*, argues convincingly that Haydn's piano trios are "a third great series of works to set beside the symphonies and the quartets"...the Beaux Arts Trio, on modern instruments, make a superb job of this music: their complete collection of the 43 trios, now reissued as a mid-price, nine-CD box set, won the *Gramophone* Record of The Year Award when it first appeared on LP in 1979. Perhaps the ideal would be to hear the trios performed as skillfully on period instruments, but the Beaux play with such persuasive freshness and sparkle that I think they'll more than do until the real thing comes along."

The Wire 91:48-9 S '91. Graham Lock (long)

"The Beaux Arts Trio has one solution to everything: employing a weighty modern piano, they play in such a way that this instrument predominates and the recording ensures that it does. The violin is always beautiful: silvery clear and immaculately played....Features of the playing include amazing accuracy, delightful touch, generosity with repeats and ideal judgement of speeds....I confess to delight at the opportunity to rediscover these works, but the air of sameness was at times depressing and I could never take more than one or two at a sitting." *P95/85 S75*

Hi-Fi News & Record Review 36:109 N '91. Antony Hodgson (long)

Gramophone 70:70 Jl '92. Richard Wigmore (long)

HAYDN, MICHAEL. Divertimenti in C for Oboe, Viola and Double Bass, P.98 and P.115. See No. 3002.

HENZE, HANS WERNER

3064. Chamber Music 1958, for Tenor, Guitar and 8 Solo Instruments.
Neil Jenkins (ten); Timothy Walker (gtr). Brynmor Llewelyn Jones (c). Scharoun Ensemble.
KOCH-SCHWANN 310 004 DDD 47:59

★*Awards:* Critics' Choice 1989, *Gramophone* D '89 (Arnold Whittall).

"It is all pretty irresistible stuff for anyone who likes vocal chamber music....Neill Jenkins imparts a just-right earnestness and full but not heavy tone to the vocal line....A highly recommended release."

Fanfare 12:199-200 N/D '88. Stephen Ellis (325w)

"For anyone with even slight fondness for contemporary music, Henze's prodigal and prolific inventiveness is not to be missed. A valuable addition to an avant-garde repertoire, and with a sound-quality equally beyond reproach."

Hi-Fi News & Record Review 34:98 F '89. Helena Stoward (325w)

Gramophone 66:1196 Ja '89. Arnold Whittall (320w)

HINDEMITH, PAUL. Sonatas (3) for Viola and Piano: (No. 1) Opus 11, No. 4; (No. 2) Opus 25, No. 4; (No. 3). See No. 4113.

IVES, CHARLES. Trio for Piano, Violin and Cello (1911). See No. 3033.

KIRCHNER, LEON

3065. Concerto for Violin, Cello, 10 Winds and Percussion; Five Pieces for Piano; Music for Twelve; Trio for Violin, Cello and Piano.
Malcolm Lowe (vln); Jules Eskin (cello); Gilbert Kalish (pno); Leon Kirchner (pno). Leon Kirchner (c). Boston Symphony Chamber Players.
ELEKTRA 79188 DDD 58:44

✔**HC** ★*Awards:* The Want List 1990, *Fanfare* N/D '90 (Royal S. Brown).

"What has long characterized Mr. Kirchner's music is a rhapsodic, passionate, even violent temperament....All [works] receive precise, intense performances here."

The New York Times F 18 '90, p. 32 H. K. Robert Schwarz (140w)

"Leon Kirchner is one of the major but also most neglected figures in contemporary music.

This superb, beautifully recorded Elektra/Nonesuch sampling of two early and two recent works from Kirchner's *oeuvre* will, I hope, lead to future recorded investigations of this consummate artist's output....Although I would have liked a tad more presence from the piano, the recorded sound is rich, realistic, and perfectly balanced. One would not suspect digital technology, except in its positive aspects, behind the aural warmth one finds here."

Fanfare 13:199-200 My/Je '90. Royal S. Brown (550w)

"One of America's most memorable composers of the post-Copland generation, Kirchner, like George Perle, Seymour Shifrin, etc, has a capacity for blending neo-classic and Schoenbergian gestures with romantic ardor and lyricism that makes this program satisfying."

American Record Guide 53:62 Jl/Ag '90. David W. Moore (140w)

"Kirchner is self-taught and idiosyncratic as a conductor, but he's also unusually effective. His ventures into the standards of the repertory can be revelations; leading his own works, he is persuasive to a degree few other contemporary composers have matched....The recorded sound is generally first-rate."

Musical America 110:81-2 S '90. Josiah Fisk (870w)

KLEIN, GIDEON

3066. Trio for Strings; Fantasia and Fugue; Sonata for Piano; Quartet for Strings, Opus 2. ULLMANN, VICTOR. Quartet for Strings, Opus 46, No. 3.
(Chamber Music from Theresienstadt).
Virginia Eskin (pno). Hawthorne Quartet.
CHANNEL 1691 DDD 68:14

> ★*Awards:* Critics' Choice 1991, *Gramophone*, Ja '92 (David Gutman).

"These are well-made, expressive works by gifted composers, of far more than reverential documentary interest. I found myself enjoying them increasingly after repeated listenings. Performances are committed and idiomatic, and sound is excellent."

American Record Guide 54:148 Jl/Ag '91. Mark L. Lehman (205w)

"The performances of the Hawthrone String Quartet and pianist Virginia Eskin are meticulously prepared, although one feels that the pianist now and then deals somewhat blandly with matter which deserves more forceful statement....Channel Classics' pioneering disc is a well-made and enlightening production, which deserves the widest possible circulation. The music, on its face, is a positive experience. But if it doesn't give you night thoughts, you haven't gotten the message."

Fanfare 15:567-69 N/D '91. John Wiser (long)

Gramophone 69:98 D '91. David Gutman (long)

Digital Audio's CD Review 8:58-59 Ja '92. David Vernier (long)

KODALY, ZOLTAN. Duo for Violin and Cello, Opus 7. See No. 4117.

KOECHLIN, CHARLES

3067. Flute Music: 14 Chants, Opus 157/2. Premier album de Lilian, Opus 139. Second album de Lilian, Opus 149: Serenade a l'etoile errante; Swimming; Les jeux du clown; Le voyage chimerique. Morceau de lecture, Opus 218. Sonata for Piano and Flute, Opus 52. Sonata for Two Flutes, Opus 75.
Fenwick Smith (fl); Leone Buyse (fl); Jayne West (sop); Martin Amlin (pno).
HYPERION 66414 DDD 66:00

> ★*Awards:* Classical Hall of Fame, *Fanfare*, Ja/F '92 (Adrian Corleonis).

"The American instrumentalists performing here, not to mention soprano Jayne West, are excellent, and the recording is warm and intimate—just what Koechlin would have ordered under the circumstances."

Stereophile 15:195 F '92. Barbara Jahn (med)

This set is an exemplary collection of representative works from Koechlin. "Sound...is generally optimum."

Fanfare 15:469-71 Ja/F '92. Adrian Corleonis (long)

"Smith evinces unerring aplomb as he breathes buoyant life into these small, delectable, and often demanding pieces whose immediate appeal belies their substantial and occasionally complex interest in which the world of Faure is heard to lie somewhat closer than hitherto suspected to Ivesian whimsy and the morbid fantasy of *Pierrot lunaire*. Indeed, while even mediocre flute music may beguile the ear, Koechlin's tempts one to take the instrument up—than which I know no more telling a compliment....In sum, a classic."

Fanfare 14:221 Ja/F '91. Adrian Corleonis (430w)

"Flutist Fenwick Smith—a member of the Boston Symphony—and his recital partners deliver the goods with an admirable combination of flair and polish. Hyperion's sound is what we have come to expect from this prestigious British label, and the annotations—by Mr Smith—further add to this entrancing, enthralling, and entertaining disc."

American Record Guide 54:60 Ja/F '91. Michael Carter (300w)

Gramophone 68:759-60 O '90. Michael Oliver (300w)

KRENEK, ERNST

3068. Quartets for Strings: No. 1, Opus 6; No. 2, Opus 8.

Sonare Quartett Frankfurt.
DABRINGHAUS UND GRIMM 3280 68:53

★★*Awards:* The Want List 1988, *Fanfare* N/D '88 (Benjamin Pernick). The Want List 1990, *Fanfare* N/D '90 (Paul A. Snook).

"The Frankfurt-based Sonare Quartet...plays superbly. MD + G has given them a very naturally balanced recording with nice perspective, good ambience, and the intimacy of a smallish concert hall....My highest recommendation."
Fanfare 11:183 Jl/Ag '88. Benjamin Pernick (300w)

3069. Quartets for Strings: No. 3, Opus 20; No. 7, Opus 96.
Sonare Quartett Frankfurt.
DABRINGHAUS UND GRIMM 3281 DDD 49:32

★*Awards:* The Want List 1990, *Fanfare* N/D '90 (Paul A. Snook).

"Highly recommended."
Fanfare 12:185 Ja/F '89. Benjamin Pernick (400w)
Gramophone 66:1776 Ja '89. David J. Fanning (250w)

3070. Quartets for Strings: No. 5, Opus 65; No. 8, Opus 233.
Sonare Quartett Frankfurt.
DABRINGHAUS UND GRIMM 3282 DDD 67:26

★*Awards:* The Want List 1990, *Fanfare* N/D '90 (Paul A. Snook).

"The Sonare Quartet of Frankfurt is a magnificent ensemble playing beautiful instruments, including an Andreas Amati viola and a Goffriller cello, which have been recorded with clarity and warmth....Notes are by the composer. No finer presentation of these important works could be imagined."
Fanfare 14:269-70 S/O '90. James H. North (475w)

"The Sonare Quartet conveys the poetry of this music so well (especially the Fifth) one stops thinking of it as mathematical in design and gets swept away by its lyric allure instead."
American Record Guide 54:75 Jl/Ag '91. William Ellis (325w)

LARSSON, LARS-ERIK

3071. Quartets (3) for Strings, Opus 31, 44, 65; Intima miniatyrer for String Quartet, Opus 20.
Helsingborg String Quartet.
BIG BEN 872 003 DDD 64:27

★*Awards:* The Want List 1988, *Fanfare* N/D '88 (Paul A. Snook).

"The playing of the Helsingborg Quartet is every bit as fine as I remembered from the vinyl issue.The sound also is just as good, but no better. Anyone interested either in Larsson or 20th Century quartets is advised to obtain this."
American Record Guide 54:81-2 Mr/Ap '91. Carl Bauman (200w)

"The Helsingborg String Quartet plays this music effortlessly...Big Ben's sound is quite good, though the Helsingborg group is a bit distantly recorded."
Fanfare 11:227-8 S/O '87. Stephen W. Ellis (300w)

MACONCHY, ELIZABETH

3072. Quartets for Strings (complete): No.'s 1-4.
(Volume 1).
Hanson Quartet.
UNICORN-KANCHANA 9080 DDD 59:00

✔HC ★★*Awards:* The Want List 1990, *Fanfare* N/D '90 (Paul A. Snook). The Critics' Choice 1990—Composition Award: No. 2 of 15 *Wire* 82/3 '91.

"Interpretation and reproduction are unreservedly top-drawer, making this issue (and future ones in the project) indispensable for all lovers and students of the twentieth-century quartet literature. Let us hope this long-overdue recognition from Unicorn-Kanchana helps to put Maconchy's name in the forefront of living composers—whether male or female—where it unquestionably belongs."
Fanfare 13:208-9 My/Je '90. Paul A. Snook (425w)

"Any temptation to claim an influence by the Bartok cycle collides with the fact that Maconchy's early quartets are exactly contemporaneous with it. The first four are short, less than an hour in total. Nevertheless, they are highly compressed, tonally charged in the way that Alan Bush's solitary masterpiece *Dialectic* is, full of the dissonant counterpoint that in Tippett suggests an encounter group in mid-session but in Maconchy a multi-voiced affirmation of variance....The Hanson String Quartet handle the music superbly and with subtlety."
Wire 72:57-8 F '90. Brian Morton (595w)

"Maconchy's stylistic consistency precludes listening to these works in uninterrupted succession...Each demands individual attention for the same reason that Haydn's quartets do: in that within the basic idiom there lies a wealth of technical and expressive possibilities full appreciation of which repays only the attentive and discerning listener."
Music and Musicians International 38:47 Jl '90. Antony Bye (270w)

"I would advise against listening to all four quartets at one sitting for fear of a certain rigid uniformity setting in—but taken individually they do offer a bracing, refreshing experience, particularly when played as well as they are here by the Hanson Quartet. Admirable recording." *P95 S95*
Hi-Fi News & Record Review 35:88 Ap '90. Andrew Achenbach (275w)

Gramophone 67:916 N '89. David J. Fanning (560w)

3073. Quartets for Strings (complete): No.'s 5-8.
(Volume 2).
Bingham String Quartet.
UNICORN-KANCHANA 9081 DDD 69:00

✔**HC** ★★*Awards:* The Want List 1990, *Fanfare* N/D '90 (Paul A. Snook); Critics' Choice 1990, *Gramophone* D '90 (Arnold Whittall).

"'My string quartet music is an impassioned argument,' writes this lucid commentator on her own work, and the passion is almost always evident, never far below the surface. Tough, often violent, never over-cerebral, this gritty uncompromising music compels attention from the listener....For this listener, it is hard to believe that music of such quality could have suffered from such comparative neglect."

Wire 79:64-5 S'90. Andy Hamilton (450w)

"This splendid project—the complete recording of no doubt the greatest string-quartet cycle ever penned by a woman and also one of the major achievements in this genre by any twentieth-century composer—continues brilliantly apace....this Maconchy cycle represents a most important addition to the twentieth-century string-quartet repertoire and as such will remain forever indispensable."

Fanfare 14:283-4 S/O '90. Paul A. Snook (580w)

"The players are never less than accomplished here, and most of the time they bring a feeling of new discoveries, of freshness to these works-....all these quartets are meant for audiences-....Don't be misled by their modesty: you may find yourself, like me, listening to this disc over again to pick out which quartet you like the best—this month."

American Record Guide 53:82 S/O '90. Stratton Rawson (515w)

"Maconchy's stylistic consistency precludes listening to these works in uninterrupted succession...Each demands individual attention for the same reason that Haydn's quartets do: in that within the basic idiom there lies a wealth of technical and expressive possibilities full appreciation of which repays only the attentive and discerning listener."

Music and Musicians International 38:47 Jl '90. Antony Bye (270w)

"For all the superb craftsmanship on offer, there's a relentless quality to much of Maconchy's writing, which I tend to find rather monochrome in expression. No complaints, though, about either the Bingham Quartet's committed performances or the admirably realistic sound-quality." *P95 S95*

Hi-Fi News & Record Review 35:82 Jl '90. Andrew Achenbach (245w)

Gramophone 68:71 Je '90. Arnold Whittall (355w)

MARAIS, MARIN

3074. Viola da gamba Music: Pieces de Viole: Book 3, Suite No. 7 in G; Book 4, Le Labyrinthe; Book 2, Tombeau pour M. de Lully; Couplets de Folies.
Sarah Cunningham (vla da gamba); Mitzi Meyerson (hpscd); Ariane Maurette (vla da gamba).
ASV 112 DDD 50:00

"There may be no new, hitherto unrecorded masterpieces in this collection, but what is here belongs in the first rank of Marais recordings, distinctive and definitive. Very highly recommended."

Fanfare 13:246 S/O '89. Jon Tuska (200w)

Gramophone 66:1742-45 My '89. Julie Ann Sadie (385w)

3075. Viola da gamba Music: La Gamme en forme de petit Opera, for Violin, Bass Viol and Harpsichord; Sonata a la Maresienne, for Violin and Continuo.
Charles Medlam (c). London Baroque. August, 1983.
HARMONIA MUNDI 901105 ADD 47:08

"These are extraordinarily compelling discs, full of an intimacy achieved in good part by refusing to let the microphones get too intimate with the instruments. The sonic ambience is warm and chamber-like rather than meticulous in detail....Perhaps I'm too dour by nature, but to me this is just an appendix to the essential Marais corpus....But let me note that the playing is full of verve, both by the gambists and the practitioner of that Italian *arriviste* the violin."

Fanfare 13:217-18 Ja/F '90. Edward Strickland (130w)

Gramophone 64:1424 Ap '87 Julie Anne Sadie (195w)

Fanfare 10:107-8 My/Je '87 Edward Strickland (125w)

3076. Viola da gamba Music: Pieces de Viole, Book 1: Selections.
Jordi Savall (vla da gamba); Christophe Coin (vla da gamba); Ton Koopman (hpscd); Hopkinson Smith (theorbo). reissue.
AUVIDIS-ASTREE 7769 AAD 62:27

"These are extraordinarily compelling discs, full of an intimacy achieved in good part by refusing to let the microphones get too intimate with the instruments. The sonic ambience is warm and chamber-like rather than meticulous in detail....let me note that the playing is full of verve, both by the gambists and the practitioner of that Italian *arriviste* the violin."

Fanfare 13:217-18 Ja/F '90. Edward Strickland (130w)

3077. Viola da gamba Music: Pieces de Viole, Book 2: Selections.
Jordi Savall (vla da gamba); Anne Gallet (hpscd); Hopkinson Smith (theorbo). reissue.
AUVIDIS-ASTREE 7770 AAD 50:53

See Book 1 for review excerpt.
Fanfare 13:217-18 Ja/F '90. Edward Strickland (130w)

MENDELSSOHN, FELIX

3078. Octet in E flat for Strings, Opus 20; Quintet No. 1 for Strings, Opus 18.
Hausmusik.
EMI 49958 DDD 63:27

✔HC ★*Awards:* Critics' Choice 1990, *Gramophone* D '90 (John Warrack). The Gramophone Awards, Nominations, Chamber, *Gramophone*, N '91.

"This group's name, a German term....means music to be played in the home, usually by amateurs of some accomplishment. It neither describes the nature of these wholly professional string players, nor the extremely demanding music of Mendelssohn to be heard on this CD. But that is the only quibble one can devise in the face of otherwise unexceptionable excellence....Recommended with pleasure."
Fanfare 14:292-3 S/O '90. John Wiser (370w)

"An engaging first recording by the period-instrument group, led by Monica Huggett, Hausmusik. A severe-sounding name, and an impression of severity prevailed as I listened to the beginning of the Octet." *P100/95 S95*
Hi-Fi News & Record Review 35:91+ My '90. Christopher Breunig (280w)

High Fidelity 1:105 S '90. Andrew Stuart (b.n.)

Gramophone 68:558+ S '90. John Warrack (245w)

3079. Sonata in F minor for Violin and Piano, Opus 4; Sonata in F for Violin and Piano (unpublished).
Shlomo Mintz (violin); Paul Ostrovsky (piano).
DEUTSCHE GRAMMOPHON 419 244 DDD 50:53

★★*Awards: Gramophone* Critics' Choice (Alan Sanders), 1987; Chamber Record Award 1988, *Gramophone* O '88.

"It is difficult to imagine more satisfying performances of these two works. Mintz's elegance of phrasing and sweet tone lend just the right mood. Balance and ensemble with the piano are excellent....Highly recommended."
American Record Guide 51:55-6 Mr/Ap '88. Robert Follet (275w)

"Superbly recorded, highly recommended."
Fanfare 11:144 Mr/Ap '88. Howard Kornblum (100w)

"Shlomo Mintz is one of the most refined violinists of his generation, and—ably partnered by Paul Ostrovsky—he keeps all of Mendelssohn's musical elements in balance."
Ovation 9:41 N '88. Peter J. Rabinowitz (215w)

"On CD then (and CD only), this present issue stands alone."
Hi-Fi News & Record Review 32:116 O '87 Doug Hammond (225w)

Gramophone 65:316 Ag '87 (280w) (rev. of LP); 66:546 O '88 (200w) (rev. of CD). Alan Sanders

3080. Trios for Piano, Violin and Cello: No. 1 in D minor, Opus 49; No. 2 in C minor, Opus 66.
Fontenay Trio.
TELDEC 44947 DDD 58:00

★★*Awards:* Critic's Choice: 1990, *American Record Guide* Ja/F '91 (Donald Vroon). *American Record Guide* Overview: Piano Trios, N/D '90.

"In Mendelssohn's two trios, the piano part almost turns into a concerto, but Harden rises admirably to the occasion. He has technique to spare, though he does suffer slightly (who wouldn't) when compared with Arthur Rubinstein in that pianist's nonpareil collaboration with Jascha Heifetz and Gregor Piatigorsky (RCA CD 7768-2, coupled with the Tchaikovsky Trio)....The Fontenay group also gets some respectable competition from the Borodin Trio (Chandos CHAN 8404), which takes a somewhat more settled attitude toward the scores, in contrast with the Fontenay's endearing coltishness....They absolutely revel in Mendelssohn's infinite melodiousness; here they sing as much as play. Their performances take on added excitement in the fast movements, which turn into daredevil, will-they-or-won't-they-make-it feats of bravado virtuosity."
Musical America 111:72-3 Ja '91. Paul Moor (285w)

"It was only Sept/Oct 1988 that Lawrence Hansen reviewed a Denon recording of Trio Fontenay's Mendelssohn No. 1. He called it 'resplendent'....Trio Fontenay has now redone No. 1 and coupled it more sensibly with 2. Teldec's sound is mellower, less insistent, than Denon's...Since the playing is pretty much the same, this now becomes No. 1 of No. 1....[and] No. 2 is just fine."
American Record Guide 53:79-80 N/D '90. Donald R. Vroon (200w)

The Fontenay Trio's playing "is mature and perceptive....If you want both trios, this disc is an excellent choice. The musicianship is first-rate and the studio sound pickup superb."
Audio 75:93+ N '91. Robert Long (med)

"Tempos throughout are conventional, balances unexceptionable, collective ensemble superbly precise, and tone is warmish. But these two accounts on record do not grow upon one when they are repeated; in fact, they seem more mannered and less attractive with every audition. With all that CD competition, why bother?"
Fanfare 14:241-42 Ja/F '91. John Wiser (250w)

Gramophone 68:558 S '90. John Warrack (315w)

MOZART, WOLFGANG AMADEUS

Adagio in C for English Horn and Strings, K.580a. See No. 3002.

3081. Quartets (4) for Flute and Strings, K.285, 285a, 285b, 298.
Philippa Davies (fl). Nash Ensemble. 1988.
VIRGIN 90740 DDD 52:00

★★*Awards:* Critic's Choice: 1990, *American Record Guide* Ja/F '91 (Donald Vroon); Editors' Choice 1992, *Digital Audio's CD Review* Je '92.

"A delightful new version of Mozart's four flute quartets—Philippa Davies is now blithe, now a touch soulful, always precise and musicianly, in these superficially undemanding works, and the trio from The Nash Ensemble provide far more than merely dutiful accompaniment....A real challenge to the long supremacy of Bennett/Grumiaux on Philips, and the period-instrument Kuijkens on Accent." *P95 S95*

Hi-Fi News & Record Review 35:99 F '90. Peter Branscombe (175w)

"There is a sense of joyous music-making here that is not always present in this music....The flute quartets receive a topnotch reading from Grauwels...but I do find myself preferring the Nash Ensemble's readings with their greater flexibility of tempo....The Virgin Classics recording is good to the point of being a demonstration disc to show how a group like this should sound."

Fanfare 13:204-5 Jl/Ag '90. John Bauman (140w)

"Philippa Davies has nothing to fear from anyone who has recorded these works—some very famous artists have, and there has not been a clear first choice until now."

American Record Guide 53:95 S/O '90. Donald R. Vroon (b.n.)

Digital Audio's CD Review 7:42 Ag '91. Tom Vernier (150w)

Gramophone 67:1345 Ja '90. Stanley Sadie (355w)

3082. Quartet in F for Oboe and Strings, K.370; Adagio in C, K.580a; Divertimento No. 11 in D, K.251.
Heinz Holliger (oboe/cor ang); Hermann Baumann (horn); Michel Gasciarrino (horn); Henk Guldemond (d-bass). Orlando Quartet.
PHILIPS 412 618 50:12

✔HC ★*Awards:* *Fanfare* Want List 1986 (George Chien).

"Holliger's mastery has lost none of its cunning...the elegant and purposeful string playing is a major contribution to the success of a record which is further enhanced by fine balancing, natural focusing and a warm acoustic."

Hi-Fi News & Record Review 31:115 Je '86. Kenneth Dommett (160w)

Gramophone 63:648 N '85. John Warrack (295w)

3083. Quartet in F for Oboe and Strings, K.370; Quintet in A for Clarinet and Strings, K.581; Quintet in E flat for Horn and Strings, K.407.
Stephen Hammer (oboe); Antony Pay (b clar); Michael Thompson (horn). Academy of Ancient Music Chamber Ensemble.
OISEAU-LYRE 421 429 DDD 74:00

★*Awards:* Critics' Choice 1989, *Gramophone* D '89 (Stanley Sadie).

"These performances are as good as any one is likely to encounter....The recorded sound is beautiful."

American Record Guide 52:89 N/D '89. Stephen R. Max (110w)

"Strongly recommended."

Fanfare 12:249-50 My/Je '89. John Wiser (310w)

"The outstanding performance...is Stephen Hammer's in the F Major Oboe Quartet....Antony Pay's reading of the A Major Clarinet Quintet, on the other hand, is a disaster." *P70 S75*

Stereo Review 54:144-45 O '89. Stoddard Lincoln (165w)

Gramophone 66:1027 D '88. Stanley Sadie (820w)

3084. Quartets (2) for Piano and Strings: in G Minor, K.478, and in E flat, K.493.
Bruno Giuranna (vla). Beaux Arts Trio.
PHILIPS 410 391 61:07

✔HC ★*Awards:* *Stereo Review* Best of the Month, Mr '85.

"In whatever format you choose, this is an absolutely indispensable issue."

Stereo Review 50:65 Mr '85. Richard Freed (320w)

Gramophone 62:496 O '84. Robin Golding (350w) (rev. of LP). 62:770 D '84. Roger Fiske (70w) (rev. of CD)

Hi-Fi News & Record Review 30:111 Ja '85. Ivor Humphreys (120w)

3085. Quartets (2) for Piano and Strings, in G minor, K.478; in E flat for Piano and Strings, K.493.
Malcolm Bilson (ftpno); Elizabeth Wilcock (vln); Jan Schlapp (vla); Tim Mason (cello).
DEUTSCHE GRAMMOPHON 423 404 DDD 61:00

★★*Awards:* *Hi-Fi News & Record Review* Record of the Month, Ap '89. The Want List 1989, *Fanfare* N/D '89 (John Wiser).

"First-rate sound...Even if you aren't readily drawn to period instruments, I'd strongly recommend that you give this disc a hearing."

American Record Guide 52:87 N/D '89. Allen Linkowski (315w)

"The two Piano Quartets...are a marvellous pair, especially when recreated as lovingly as in these fresh, warm-toned, and stylish performances....If some readers still associate period instruments with scrawny string tone and a jangling keyboard, they should hear this revelatory CD."

Hi-Fi News & Record Review 34:101 Ap '89. Peter Branscombe (220w)

"The assets of this pairing lie primarily in the sensitivity, affection, good judgment, and technical mastery bestowed upon both works....Bilson and the EBS members take a point of view more active in the line than the fine accounts of Richard Burnett with members of the Salomon Quartet (Amon Ra CD-SAR 31, *Fanfare* 11:2, pp. 185-86)....Either of these pairs of performances stands up well in comparison with the best available recordings in current-practice modes...Strongly recommended!"

Fanfare 13:292-94 N/D '89. John Wiser (320w)

Gramophone 66:1448 Mr '89. Stanley Sadie (630w)

3086. Quartets (23) for Strings (complete).
Quartetto Italiano. reissue 1966, 1970-73.
PHILIPS 416 419 466:07 8 discs

✔HC ★*Awards:* *Gramophone* Critics' Choice (Christopher Headington), 1987.

"Luxuriant tone, polished attention to detail, and a sense of execution seem to me the salient properties of this long-lived but no longer extant ensemble. Their manner works well indeed in the early quartets...The others, to my ears, seem often bland and lacking in tension-...Dynamics are distinctly expanded, detail gratifyingly more prominent."

Fanfare 11:251-2 S/O '87. John D. Wiser (260w)

"Listening again to these twenty-three quartets has been like meeting old friends after a long absence and realising just how well they all look."

Hi-Fi News & Record Review 32:99+ S '87 Kenneth Dommett (400w)

Gramophone 65:321 Ag '87 Christopher Headington (560w)

3087. Quartets for Strings: ("The Haydn Quartets"): No. 14 in G, K.387; No. 15 in D minor, K.421.
(Volume 1).
Chilingirian Quartet. 1979-80.
CRD 3362 DDD 54:00

✔HC ★*Awards:* Critics' Choice 1990, *Gramophone* D '90 (Richard Wigmore).

"The playing is worthy of the music: poised, affectionate, of technical excellence...The recording is vivid yet warm, aptly conveying the atmosphere of chamber-music playing of great distinction." *P95 S95*

Hi-Fi News & Record Review 35:96 Je '90. Peter Branscombe (140w)

"The sound does not have the presence or the clarity of today's best recordings...The interpretations and the playing are, by and large, earnest and solid, but not very imaginative or finely nuanced."

American Record Guide 54:88 My/Je '91. Kurt Moses (100w)

Gramophone 68:561 S '90. Richard Wigmore (475w)

3088. Quartets for Strings: ("The Haydn Quartets"): No. 16 in E flat, K.428; No. 17 in B flat, K.458, "Hunting".
(Volume 2).
Chilingirian Quartet.
CRD 3363 DDD 55:30

✔HC ★*Awards:* Critics' Choice 1990, *Gramophone* D '90 (Richard Wigmore).

Gramophone 68:561 S '90. Richard Wigmore (475w)

See Volume 1 for review excerpt.

American Record Guide 54:88 My/Je '91. Kurt Moses (100w)

3089. Quartets for Strings: ("The Haydn Quartets"): No. 18 in A, K.464; No. 19 in C, K.465, "Dissonant".
(Volume 3).
Chilingirian Quartet.
CRD 3364 DDD 67:30

✔HC ★*Awards:* Critics' Choice 1990, *Gramophone* D '90 (Richard Wigmore).

Gramophone 68:561 S '91. Richard Wigmore (475w)

See Volume 1 for review excerpt.

American Record Guide 54:88 My/Je '91. Kurt Moses (100w)

3090. Quartets for Strings: No. 20 in D, K.499; No. 22 in B flat, K.589.
Endellion String Quartet.
VIRGIN 90772 DDD 51:00

✔HC ★*Awards:* Best of the Month, *Hi-Fi News & Record Review*, O '90.

"Previously, the straightforward, no-nonsense approach of Quartetto Italiano on Philips established an admirable standard for these works. Hearing the Endellion approach to K.589, and especially its languorous *Moderato* minuet, performed with admirable firmness and strength (notably so in the cello part), this ensemble seems set to determine the criteria for the 1990s in these works." *P100/95 S100*

Hi-Fi News & Record Review 35:101 O '90. Antony Hodgson (245w)

Gramophone 68:760 O '90. Richard Wigmore (440w)

Quintet in A for Clarinet and Strings, K.581. See No. 3030.

3092. Sonatas for Violin and Piano: K.301, 302, 303, 304.
Itzhak Perlman (vln); Daniel Barenboim (pno).
DEUTSCHE GRAMMOPHON 410 896

✔HC ★*Awards:* *Fanfare* Want List 1984 (Elliott Kaback).

"Wonderful music wonderfully performed. The sound is splendid with the piano taking perhaps just a bit more back seat than is required. Highly recommended."
High Performance Review 3 (3):111 '85. Thomas H. Wendel (140w)

"These two major soloists have been treated with too much individuality, thus affecting the chamber ensemble integration."
Hi-Fi News & Record Review 29:75 Je '84. Felicity Mulgan (105w)

Ovation 6:72 F '85. Paul Turok (60w)

Gramophone 61:1190 Ap '84. Geoffrey Horn (60w); Robin Golding (350w)

Stereo Review 49:92 O '84. Stoddard Lincoln (100w)

3093. Sonatas for Violin and Piano: K.377; K.8; K.379. **Variations in G minor on "Helas, J'ai Perdu Mon Amant," for Violin and Piano, K.360.**
(Volume 1).
Pinchas Zukerman (vln); Marc Neikrug (pno). New York's Manhattan Center.
RCA 0447 DDD 61:44

★★*Awards:* Critical Choice, *Musical America*, N/D '91 (Dennis D. Rooney). Best Recordings of the Month, *Stereo Review* Jl '91.

"Accardo and Messiereur are polar opposites but what they find in the music really is there; I've praised both. This RCA series will be more readily available, and is going to be an attractive option....RCA provides good sound and useful notes to this ambitious project, one to be followed with anticipation."
Fanfare 14:237-8 Jl/Ag '91. David K. Nelson (375w)

"What they give us here is not a demonstration of instruments or technique but honest and especially tasteful musicmaking. As the sound itself could hardly be better with respect to the balance between the two instruments or the overall realism, this is a splendid launching of what promises to be a distinguished cycle. More to the point, it is simply one of the most enjoyable records of its kind, for the Mozart year or any year."
Stereo Review 56:58 Jl '91. Richard Freed (400w)

"This is Zukerman's show, from start to finish. Neikrug, his longtime duo partner, is an estimable musician, but his phrasing is slack when compared to the violinist. Thus, the keyboard part is constantly in the background even when it has the chief musical material...Zukerman's sound has been exceedingly well miked...And what a sound it is! For many listeners, Zukerman's tone is the most sheerly beautiful since Heifetz's....Almost defiantly, Zukerman and Neikrug...seem to be ignoring currently fashionable notions about the performance of 18th-century music. In one crucial respect, however, Zukerman is supremely 'authentic': his fiddling flows like oil, which for Mozart was the alpha and omega of violin playing."
Musical America 111:49-50 N/D '91. Dennis D. Rooney (long)

"In this disc [Zukerman]...sacrifices himself-...to the crisp, brisk, and accurate playing of Neikrug. In keeping with 18th Century convention, the keyboard dominates these sonatas."
American Record Guide 54:121 N/D '91. Thomas F. Marshall (med)

Digital Audio's CD Review 7:49-50 Ag '91. Tom Vernier (250w)

Gramophone 69:98+ Ap '92. Christopher Headington (long)

3094. Sonatas for Violin and Piano: K.454; K.526.
Arthur Grumiaux (vln); Clara Haskil (pno). 1956.
PHILIPS 416 478 43:00

"We have here a sensitivity to Mozart that remains all too rare—poised, elegant, yet vibrant, and attuned to all of the astonishing subtleties and bold strokes in the music....Exceptional artistry."
Fanfare 10:184 N/D '86 Mortimer H. Frank (175w)

"Grumiaux's playing radiates ineffable good taste. It is elegant, patrician Mozart, showing a remarkable control of phrasing and a refined, introspective musicality."
High Fidelity 37:84-85 Ja '87 K. Robert Schwarz (220w)

Ovation 10:69-70 Ap '89. Michael Fleming (205w)

Hi-Fi News & Record Review 31:84 Ag '86. Andrew Keener (70w)

PART, ARVO. Fratres (for 8 celli). See No. 1276.

POULENC, FRANCIS

3095. Chamber Music: Sextet for Flute, Oboe, Clarinet, Bassoon, Horn and Piano. Sonata for Clarinet; Sonata for Flute; Sonata for Oboe; Trio for Oboe, Bassoon and Piano.
Patrick Gallois (fl); Maurice Bourgue (oboe); Michel Portal (clar); Amaury Wallez (bsn); Andre Cazalet (horn); Pascal Roge (pno). 1988.
LONDON/DECCA 421 581 DDD 72:00

✔HC ★★*Awards:* Critics' Choice 1989, *Gramophone* D '89 (Robert Layton). Editors' Choice, *Digital Audio's CD Review*, 6:34 Je '90; Cream of the Crop IV, *Digital Audio's CD Review*, 6:42 Je '90.

"No performance here is less than distinguished. Finely aligned recorded balance, presence, and sharp detail complete the picture. Strongly recommended."
Fanfare 13:262 Ja/F '90. John Wiser (375w)

"Temperamentally, these performances by Roge and his colleagues are hotter, tighter, and more incisive than others on discs. Comparisons suggest that it helps to be French to show these works at their piquant best."

Stereo Review 55:114 Je '90. David Patrick Stearns (200w)

"The overall feeling of blandness is compounded as the disc plods along, with the popular Flute Sonata a particular bore. Distant miking, resulting in sound with little impact, does nothing to help the cause."

American Record Guide 53:74-5 Ja/F '90. James S. Ginsburg (115w)

Digital Audio's CD Review 6:76+ D '89. Lawrence Johnson (350w)

Gramophone 67:330 Ag '89. Lionel Salter (560w)

Sonata for Violin and Piano. See No. 3056.

Sextuor for Piano and Woodwind Quintet; Trio for Oboe, Bassoon and Piano. See No. 8036.

PRAETORIUS, MICHAEL

3096. Terpsichore (instrumental dances).
Philip Pickett (c). New London Consort.
OISEAU-LYRE 414 633

✔HC ★*Awards:* Critics Choice, *Hi Fi News & Record Review*, Ap '91 Supplement (Antony Hodgson).

"Perennial favourites, these dances from the huge collection made by Praetorius are very attractively scored by Philip Pickett and the New London Consort."

Hi-Fi News & Record Review 32:109 Ja '87 Roger Bowen (140w)

Gramophone 64:715-6 N '86 David Fallows (420w)

PROKOFIEV, SERGEI

3097. Sonatas (2) for Violin and Piano, Opus 80, 94a.
Shlomo Mintz (vln); Yefim Bronfman (pno).
DEUTSCHE GRAMMOPHON 423 575 DDD 56:00

✔HC ★★★★*Awards:* The Want List 1989, *Fanfare* N/D '89 (Elliott Kaback); Critics' Choice 1989, *Gramophone* D '89 (David Fanning); Critics' Choice 1989, *Gramophone* D '89 (Stephen Johnson); Top Choices—1989, *American Record Guide* Ja/F '90 (John McKelvey).

"I have delighted in watching this duo blossom and mature...Yet I was unprepared for the stunning impact of their Prokofiev sonatas."

High Fidelity 39:57-8 Jl '89. K. Robert Schwarz (625w)

"These are nothing less than wonderful performances, so searching and so authoritative that the current competition, while perhaps not buried, certainly has to make room for these as coequals with the best....Highly recommended."

Fanfare 12:109-10 Jl/Ag '89. David K. Nelson (350w)

"Some may find the lighter-textured and more swiftly moving Zimmermann/Lonquich performances more to their liking. But for me, this new version of the F minor Sonata in particular has an extra dimension of depth and dark foreboding that is not so strikingly evident in the Angel recording. In the lighter and less serious D major Sonata the choice is more difficult, and it is hard to define a clear superiority for either version."

American Record Guide 52:74 Jl/Ag '89. John P. McKelvey (200w)

"The recording, like the performances, is rich and vibrant, halfway between mellow and melodramatic." *P85 S85*

Stereo Review 54:150 S '89. Eric Salzman (150w)

"Bronfman is a very able partner but does not always quite pull his weight, sounding a touch uninvolved. Nevertheless, the musicians clearly empathise, and the result is most satisfying. What is basically a quite natural recording, albeit a little harsh but with good ambience, is spoiled by a persistent 17-18kHz whistle of varying level, noticeable on loudspeakers and seriously irritating on headphones."

Hi-Fi News & Record Review 34:92 Mr '89. Richard Black (275w)

Gramophone 66:1306-8 F '89. David J. Fanning (270w)

3098. Sonata No. 2 for Violin and Piano, Opus 94a. RAVEL, MAURICE. Sonata for Violin and Piano. STRAVINSKY, IGOR. Divertimento for Violin and Piano.
Viktoria Mullova (vln); Bruno Canino (pno). 1989.
PHILIPS 426 254 DDD 61:00

★★*Awards:* Best of the Month, *Hi-Fi News & Record Review*, S '90. The Highs, 1990, *The New York Times* D 30 '90 (John Rockwell).

"There is, as everyone knows, art; but there is also the art that conceals art. Viktoria Mullova is very much a practitioner of the latter....The playing is not exactly demonstrative; yet neither is it coy or reticent. It is simply exquisitely *apt*. She gives the impression that one is not so much witnessing a public performance as being played to by a good friend. Even at her most showy, she still preserves an essential intimacy. It is a remarkable achievement....Of the recording, one can only say that it is as apt and undemonstrative as the playing...Both instruments are beautifully balanced and set within a believable acoustic." *P100 S95/100*

Hi-Fi News & Record Review 35:93+ S '90. Simon Cargill (255w)

"The playing is so extraordinary that this must finally be regarded as one of the finest violin/piano recitals ever recorded."

American Record Guide 54:155-6 N/D '91. Alan Heatherington (long)

"Philips's clear sound catches Canino's assertive pianism particularly well; indeed, his playing increases in authority and range with each example I encounter. Each work is never less than beautifully played, always sympathetic, and often compelling."

Fanfare 14:367-68 N/D '90. David K. Nelson (350w)

"In the Divertimento, Mullova brings off the spiky accents and *tres sec* flavor splendidly; in this endeavor she is expertly matched by pianist Bruno Canino. It's a performance that communicates some real pleasure, and the disc would be smashing if the players had equalled their traversal of the Stravinsky with comparable readings of the Ravel and Prokofiev sonatas."

Musical America 111:81 My '91. Dennis D. Rooney (180w)

Gramophone 68:388 Ag '90. Michael Oliver (250w)

Digital Audio's CD Review 7:58 N '90. David Vernier (220w)

RACHMANINOFF, SERGEI

3099. Trio in D minor for Piano, Violin and Cello, Opus 9, "Elegiaque". SHOSTAKOVICH, DMITRI. Trio No. 2 in E minor for Piano, Violin and Cello, Opus 67.

Tchaikovsky Trio. February 1986.
DYNAMIC 023 ADD 69:00

★*Awards: American Record Guide* Overview: Getting to Know Chamber Music: Piano Trios, N/D '90.

"What we have here is some of the richest, most full-bodied, present, and realistic sound one is apt to hear on a chamber-music recording. What we also have...are some outstanding performances...the Tchaikovsky Trio's virtuosity serves the music exceedingly well, although slightly more creative solutions to the work's *longeurs* might have been found."

Fanfare 12:279-82 N/D '88. Royal S. Brown (350w)

"If I had to find fault with this excellent performance I would complain that in the last movement they start out a bit too fast. But the music catches up to them! If I had to find fault with the sound, I might note that the violin sounds a bit metallic at times....But it's hard to find fault with something I have enjoyed so much."

American Record Guide 51:74-5 S/O '88. Donald R. Vroon (305w)

"I found the Shostakovich E *minor trio* to be more attractive [than the Rachmaninoff]. There are some telling moments here, all played brilliantly."

HighPerformanceReview 6:86 Mr '89. James Primosch (140w)

Gramophone 66:634 O '88. Stephen Johnson (220w)

RAVEL, MAURICE

Introduction and Allegro for Harp, Flute, Clarinet and String Orchestra. See No. 3045.

Quartet in F for Strings. See No. 3042.

Sonata for Violin and Piano. See No. 3044, 3098.

REICH, STEVE

3100. Different Trains, for String Quartet and Pre-Recorded Tape (1988); Electric Counterpoint, for Guitar and Pre-Recorded Tape (1987).

Pat Metheny (gtr). Kronos String Quartet.
ELEKTRA 79176 DDD 42:00

★★★★★*Awards: Hi-Fi News & Record Review* Record of the Month, Je '89. Critics Pick Some Favorites of the Year, *The New York Times* N 26, '89 (K. Robert Schwarz); The Want List 1989, *Fanfare* N/D '89 (John Ditsky; Leslie Gerber; Don C. Seibert; Frederic Silber); Critics' Choice 1989, *Gramophone* D '89 (John Milsom; Richard Osborne); Top Choices—1989, *American Record Guide* Ja/F '90 (William Ellis). The Year's Best, *Hi Fi News & Record Review*, May '90 Supplement.

"I have no hesitation at all in labeling *Different Trains* a masterpiece....*Electric Counterpoint*, for its part, is pretty nifty, too, though it doesn't aim as high as *Different Trains*....The recorded sound for both works is magnificently clear and real."

Musical America 109:65-6 S '89. Andrew Stiller (760w)

"*Different Trains* is one of Reich's masterpieces....After this shattering experience, *Electric Counterpoint* comes as a distinct letdown....For *Different Trains*, this release is most enthusiastically recommended. I think it will be one of the standout new-music recordings of the year."

Fanfare 13:298-99 S/O '89. Leslie Gerber (450w)

"*Different Trains*...represents the very apex of his creative output so far. Prior to hearing it, I wondered whether anyone could possibly forge a convincing piece of art out of Holocaust imagery: Reich has answered my question in the affirmative with a statement of great power and beauty. *Electric Counterpoint* is lighter, brighter—and slighter! Pat Metheney plays eleventh guitar in harmony with ten...that he prerecorded....I loved it...but *Different Trains* is something else again."*P100 S100*

Hi-Fi News & Record Review 34:85 Je '89; p.10-11 My '90. Robert Cowan (650w)

"Steve Reich has scored a significant breakthrough in *Different Trains*, a work in which he seems to have grasped at a number of various techniques to jump-start his inspiration after years of writing fairly lifeless minimalist pieces....*Electric Counterpoint* exemplifies the creative doldrums from which *Different Trains* arose." *P85 S80*

Stereo Review 54:152 S '89. David Patrick Stearns (325w)

"*Different Trains*....is an ugly, inhuman, mechanized 26 minutes of Reich autobiography-...Why does Kronos record such music...*Electric Counterpoint* is...slightly jazzy, predictable, unchallenging."

American Record Guide 53:93-4 Mr/Ap '90. Timothy D. Taylor (220w)

"*Trains* evinces no real interior development-...Kronos, playing well enough, is reduced to parrotting the words and the various whistles, sirens, and locomotive chug-chuffs...*Electric Counterpoint*, on the other hand, for multiple overdubbed electric guitars played by Pat Metheny, is considerably more successful-....Definitely a mixed bag, recommended for *Electric Counterpoint* alone."

Stereophile 12:175 S '89. Richard Lehnert (460w)

Gramophone 67:61 Je '89. John Milsom (420w)

REICHA, ANTON

3101. Quintets for Wind Instruments (complete): No's. 14, 5, 1.
(Complete Wind Quintets, Volume 1).
Albert-Schweitzer-Quintett.
CPO 999 022 DDD 72:46

★★***Awards:*** The Want List 1988, *Fanfare* N/D '88 (John Wiser). The Want List 1990, *Fanfare* N/D '90 (Leslie Gerber).

"Although the players are technically masterful, one does not get the sense of a convening of five competing virtuosi, but of a splendidly integrated team....CPO's recording is close-up but transparent and cleanly balanced....No wind-quintet fancier can afford not to sample this series."

Fanfare 12:236-7 S/O '88. John Wiser (180w). See also Volume 7 for a 2nd review by John Wiser covering all 10 volumes.

Gramophone 66:1515 Mr '89. Alan Sanders (185w)

3102. Quintets for Wind Instruments (complete): No's. 11, 4, 3.
(Complete Wind Quintets, Volume 2).
Albert-Schweitzer-Quintett.
CPO 999 023 DDD 74:22

★★***Awards:*** The Want List 1988, *Fanfare* N/D '88 (John Wiser). The Want List 1990, *Fanfare* N/D '90 (Leslie Gerber).

See Volume 1 for review excerpt.

Fanfare 12:236-7 S/O '88. John Wiser (180w)

3103. Quintets for Wind Instruments (complete): No's. 19, 10; Adagio in D minor for English Horn and Wind Quartet.
(Complete Wind Quintets, Volume 3).
Albert-Schweitzer-Quintett.
CPO 999 024 DDD 67:00

★★***Awards:*** The Want List 1988, *Fanfare* N/D '88 (John Wiser). The Want List 1990, *Fanfare* N/D '90 (Leslie Gerber).

See Volume 1 for review excerpt.

Fanfare 12:236-7 S/O '88. John Wiser (180w)

3104. Quintets for Wind Instruments (complete): No.'s 16, 17.
(Complete Wind Quintets, Volume 4).
Albert-Schweitzer-Quintett.
CPO 999 025 DDD 57:22

★★***Awards:*** The Want List 1988, *Fanfare* N/D '88 (John Wiser). The Want List 1990, *Fanfare* N/D '90 (Leslie Gerber).

See Volume 1 for review excerpt.

Fanfare 12:236-7 S/O '88. John Wiser (180w)

3105. Quintets for Wind Instruments (complete): No's. 6, 9, 21).
(Complete Wind Quintets, Volume 5).
Albert-Schweitzer-Quintett.
CPO 999 026 DDD 75:54

★★***Awards:*** The Want List 1990, *Fanfare* N/D '90 (Leslie Gerber).

"From an entirely personal viewpoint: I have been so far unable to audition a single one of these CDs without playing the damned thing straight through; that is how seductively entertaining these quintets are in these performances....To the experienced Reicha enthusiast: You have *never* heard these works played on record with such consistent alertness and understanding....Strongly recommended."

Fanfare 13:299 S/O '89. John Wiser (80w)

"The performances are outstanding: as good or better than the best previous issues. The sound is a textbook example of the way this music should be recorded...Outstanding notes."

American Record Guide 52:104 N/D '89. Carl Bauman (115w)

Gramophone 68:1690+ Mr '91. John Warrack (230w)

3106. Quintets for Wind Instruments (complete): No's. 7, 23, 18.
(Complete Wind Quintets, Volume 6).
Albert-Schweitzer-Quintett.
CPO 999 027 DDD 78:09

★★***Awards:*** The Want List 1990, *Fanfare* N/D '90 (Leslie Gerber).

See Volume 5 for review excerpts.

—*Fanfare* 13:299 S/O '89. John Wiser (80w)

—*American Record Guide* 52:104 N/D '89. Carl Bauman (115w)

Gramophone 68:1690+ Mr '91. John Warrack (230w)

3107. Quintets for Wind Instruments (complete): No's. 2, 13, 25.
(Complete Wind Quintets, Volume 7).
Albert-Schweitzer-Quintett.
CPO 999 028 DDD 74:04

★*Awards:* The Want List 1990, *Fanfare* N/D '90 (Leslie Gerber).

"The bare fact of existence of such a recorded survey represents a notable discographic milestone; that the performances happen to be uniformly alert, polished, and sensitive is a blessed endorsement of chance....The entire series is urgently recommended."
Fanfare 13:272-73 Mr/Ap '90. John Wiser (165w)

"In previous reviews of the others in this series, I have raved about the quality of the music, the playing and the extremely vivid recorded sound. The notes, too, are outstanding-....I would urge acquisition of all ten discs."
American Record Guide 53:94 Mr/Ap '90. Carl Bauman (b.n.)

3108. Quintets for Wind Instruments (complete): No's. 12, 24, Andante in E flat for English Horn, Flute, Clarinet, Horn and Bassoon.
(Complete Wind Quintets, Volume 8).
Albert-Schweitzer-Quintett.
CPO 999 029 DDD 69:50

★*Awards:* The Want List 1990, *Fanfare* N/D '90 (Leslie Gerber).

See Volume 5 for review excerpts.
—*Fanfare* 13:299 S/O '89. John Wiser (80w)
—*American Record Guide* 52:104 N/D '89. Carl Bauman (115w)
Gramophone 68:1690+ Mr '91. John Warrack (230w)

3109. Quintets for Wind Instruments (complete): No's. 15, 22.
(Complete Wind Quintets, Volume 9).
Albert-Schweitzer-Quintett.
CPO 999 030 DDD 60:15

★*Awards:* The Want List 1990, *Fanfare* N/D '90 (Leslie Gerber).

See Volume 7 for review excerpts.
—*Fanfare* 13:272-73 Mr/Ap '90. John Wiser (165w)
—*American Record Guide* 53:94 Mr/Ap '90. Carl Bauman (b.n.)

3110. Quintets for Wind Instruments (complete): No's. 8, 20. Andante No. 2 for English horn.
(Complete Wind Quintets, Volume 10).
Albert-Schweitzer-Quintett.
CPO 999 043 DDD 64:45

See Volume 7 for review excerpts.
—*Fanfare* 13:272-73 Mr/Ap '90. John Wiser (165w)
—*American Record Guide* 53:94 Mr/Ap '90. Carl Bauman (b.n.)

RESPIGHI, OTTORINO. Sonata in B minor for Violin and Piano. See No. 3056.

RILEY, TERRY

3111. Salome Dances for Peace, for String Quartet.
Kronos String Quartet. 1988.
ELEKTRA 79217 DDD 121:00 2 discs

★*Awards:* Editors' Choice, *Digital Audio's CD Review*, 6:34 Je '90; Cream of the Crop IV, *Digital Audio's CD Review*, 6:42 Je '90.

"*Salome* firmly establishes Riley as an important, imposing talent who has clearly given a counter-revolutionary new identity to the string quartet with his tonal but completely individual style. *Salome Dances for Peace* may eventually be counted among the great works composed in the Eighties....Riley has created a sound world so full of entrancing effects, so vividly realized by the Kronos Quartet, that it's a highly enjoyable place to spend two hours."
Stereo Review 55:156 F '90. David Patrick Stearns (380w)

"Riley has made a coherent musical statement and a sincere aesthetic statement which could easily have been forced or mishandled...The Kronos Quartet is terrific....Most contemporary music which tries to be spiritual fails...*Salome Dances for Peace* is exceptional—one of the great works of the penultimate decade of our century."
American Record Guide 53:95-6 Mr/Ap '90. Timothy D. Taylor (450w)

"Riley combines Eastern and Western, folk and high-art, serious and popular traditions so deftly that *Salome Dances for Peace* never sounds like a pastiche....Perhaps only a West Coaster like Riley, open to a whole world of musical traditions, could have assimilated so many musics and then reinterpreted them in such a coherent manner....This piece finds the Kronos Quartet at the height of its powers."
Musical America 110:83-4 Jl '90. K. Robert Schwarz (550w)

"As a sustained exhibition of modern string quartet playing, these discs take some beating. Ensemble is well-nigh perfect, while their blend (often using little or no vibrato) verges on the miraculous....Unlike so much minimalism *Salome Dances for Peace* is definitely *music*." *P100 S95*
Hi-Fi News & Record Review 35:83 Jl '90. Simon Cargill (385w)

"The complete work has a curious appeal, though that appeal may not extend to dogged opponents of the California new-music esthetic. The music is simple, innocent, yet within its own terms, intelligent and compelling, reaching beyond European modernism to embrace the Orient and universal mystic rituals."

The New York Times D 10 '89, p. 38 H. John Rockwell (115w)

"I've played this set over several weeks. I'm still not sure somehow what to make of it, assuming anything is to be 'made,' but on an emotional level I suspect it will find a place among the most respected works not only of Riley but of contemporary American music. The superbly nuanced playing of Kronos will do nothing to hurt its chances, nor will the obvious care taken with the project by Nonesuch."

Fanfare 13:275 Mr/Ap '90. Edward Strickland (410w)

Gramophone 68:562 S '90. John Milsom (455w)

Digital Audio's CD Review 6:64-5 Mr '90. Linda Kohanov (445w)

ROSENBERG, HILDING

3112. Quartets for Strings: No's 4, 7; Moments (6) Musicaux.

Fresk Quartet; Berwald Quartet; Gotland Quartet. reissue in part.
CAPRICE 21353 AAD/DDD 69:32

★★***Awards:*** The Want List 1989, *Fanfare* N/D '89 (Stephen Ellis); The Want List 1989, *Fanfare* N/D '89 (Paul A. Snook).

"The Fourth Quartet...is an 'immediate,' attractive score, excitingly rendered by the Fresk Quartet in a transfer from LP....The [7th] quartet was recorded once before, in 1962, by the Kyndel Quartet for Swedish RCA, which the current interpretation easily surpasses in clarity-....*Six Moments musicaux*...is a premiere recording, beautifully done."

Fanfare 13:303-6 S/O '89. Stephen Ellis (775w)

"The notes are most informative and the transfers to CD have been extremely well done."

Hi-Fi News & Record Review 34:100 Ag '89. Kenneth Dommett (140w)

Gramophone 67:2003-04 My '90. Robert Layton (290w)

ROSSINI, GIOACCHINO

3113. Sonatas (6) for Strings.

Camerata Bern.
DEUTSCHE GRAMMOPHON 413 310 DDD 54:39

✔**HC** ★***Awards:*** *Gramophone* Critics' Choice 1985 (Lionel Salter).

"Even were there silver disc competition in *Schwann*, which there's not, this would be a notable value musically and sonically."

Fanfare 9:205-6 Ja/F '86. Roger Dettmer (300w)

"This is delightful music, delectably and brilliantly performed, although I will admit that four sonatas in a row do present a bit of sameness."

Opus 2:50 Ap '86. John Canarina (290w)

"The brilliant string writing is carried off with technical perfection. However, one misses Italian verve and temperament."

HighPerformanceReview 4:113-4 Wint '86/'87 Shirley L. Thomson (150w) (rev. of LP)

Stereo Review Presents: Compact Disc Buyers' Guide p. 51 Spr '87 William Livingstone and Christie Barter (75w)

Gramophone 63:126-7 Jl '85. Lionel Salter (335w)

Hi-Fi News & Record Review 30:109 N '85 Doug Hammond (120w); 31:72 D '86 K. Robert Schwarz (145w)

Digital Audio 2:46 Ja '86. David Vernier (285w)

SAMMARTINI, GIOVANNI BATTISTA. Quintet in G. See No. 1318.

SCELSI, GIACINTO

3114. Quartets (5) for Strings (complete); Trio for Strings; "Khoom", for Female Voice, Horn and Quartet (1962).

Michiko Hirayama (sop); Frank Lloyd (horn); Maurizio Ben Omar (perc). Arditti Quartet.
SALABERT 8904/5 DDD 122:00 2 discs

✔**HC** ★★★★★***Awards:*** The Want List 1991, *Fanfare* N/D '91 (Art Lange); The Want List 1991, *Fanfare* N/D '91 (Benjamin Pernick); The Want List 1991, *Fanfare* N/D '91 (Mike Silverton). Critics' Choice 1990, *Gramophone* D '90 (Arnold Whittall). The Critics' Choice 1990—Composition Award: No. 9 of 15 *Wire* 82/3 '91.

"Quartets two to four, all written in the early 60s, form points along a progression towards the total refinement of Scelsi's string style, resulting (in the fourth) in a single accumulation of expressive tension in which each string of each instrument is eventually notated separately, to accommodate the unprecedented timbral sophistication of the writing....Needless to say, the Arditti Quartet is probably uniquely qualified to clarify such complexities, and, again, comparison with their earlier recording shows a striking increase in interpretative depth."

Wire 76:63 Je '90. Richard Barrett (150w)

"Scelsi's quartets writhe like restrained boa constrictors in these performances, with an intensity only achievable by performers to whom difficulties of intonation, microtones, and extremely long notes have long ago become child's play. The recordings aren't quite as present as I'd like for such subtle works, but they're clear enough, and hiss is minimal. What can I say? Ignore this disc, and there'll be a gap in your twentieth-century European collection big enough to perform *Gruppen* in."

Fanfare 14:299-300 Ja/F '91. Kyle Gann (970w)

"There is no finer string quartet in the world for this kind of thing. You have but to hear their Elliott Carter quartet performances on Etcetera to understand their value to a living art.

The present recordings, produced by Cologne's West-German Radio, couldn't be better....On all counts, this Salabert set is a jewel of inestimable value."

Fanfare 14:299-301 Ja/F '91. Mike Silverton (655w)

"*Khoom*...is a seven-movement chamber aria of almost primal intensity—a study in nonverbal communication ranging from rapt contemplation to a savage frenzy that makes Brunnhilde's '*Hojotoho*' sound like mere petulance. Scelsi's five string quartets and string trios are no less fascinating explorations in sound, and they are magnificently performed here by the Arditti Quartet."

Musical America 111:85 Jl '91. David Hurwitz (160w)

Gramophone 68:562 S '90. Arnold Whittall (270w)

SCHNITTKE, ALFRED

3115. Concerto Grosso No. 1 for 2 Violins, Harpsichord, Piano and Strings; Quasi Una Sonata; Moz-Art a la Haydn.
Gidon Kremer (vln); Tatjana Grindenko (vln); Yuri Smirnov (hpscd/prep pno/ pno). Heinrich Schiff; Gidon Kremer (c). Chamber Orchestra of Europe. Kammermusiksaal, Berlin. September 1988 live.
DEUTSCHE GRAMMOPHON 429 413 DDD 62:00

★★*Awards:* The Critics' Choice 1990—Composition Award: No. 1 of 15 *Wire* 82/3 '91.

"Kremer plays like a man possessed, flailing against the might of the orchestras as sledgehammer chords chase his jagged violin lines and dissonant piano flurries whirl around glimpses of keening lyricism, until, in a fantastic climax, orchestra and piano try to pulverise the violin into submission, only to hear it twist and wriggle, squeal and snarl its independence in a final solo flourish. Monstrously exciting stuff!"

Wire 81:64-5 N'90. Graham Lock (320w)

"Like that of Shostakovich, Schnittke's humour seems to embody irony and terror in equal measure. It is something that violinists Gidon Kremer and Tatiana Grindenko revel in; and given the forceful, realistic recording it is not perhaps a disc to take at one sitting." *P95 S95*

Hi-Fi News & Record Review 35:101 N '90. Simon Cargill (295w)

Gramophone 68:538 S '90. David J. Fanning (455w)

SCHOENBERG, ARNOLD

3116. Quartets (5) for Strings (complete). WEBERN, ANTON. Five Movements for String Quartet, Opus 5; Quartet; Six Bagatelles for String Quartet, Opus 9; Quartet, Opus 28. BERG, ALBAN. Lyric Suite for String Quartet; Quartet, Opus 3.
(Neue Wiener Schule: String Quartets).
Margaret Price (sop). LaSalle Quartet. 1971 reissue.
DEUTSCHE GRAMMOPHON 419 994 ADD 238:10 4 discs

★*Awards:* The Want List 1988, *Fanfare* N/D '88 (Mike Silverton).

"Seven years ago in the pages of *HFN/RR* I referred to the La Salle boxed set of Second Viennese String Quartet music as a 'keystone' recommendation. Today, for a most welcome reissue on CD, that recommendation still stands."

Hi-Fi News & Record Review 33:103-4 My '88. David Prakel (300w)

"The most fitting welcome I can offer you upon this return to currency is to say that we can still learn a great deal about the music from these recordings."

Fanfare 11:265-6 My/Je '88. John D. Wiser (700w)

3117. Serenade for Septet and Baritone, Opus 24; Chamber Symphony in E, Opus 9.
Thomas Paul (bass); Jaime Laredo (vln); Samuel Rhodes (vla); Madeline Foley (cello); Harold Wright (clar); Donald Stewart (b clar); Stanley Silverman (gtr); Jacob Glick (mndln); Felix Galimir (vln); Sarah Kwak (vln); James Dunham (vla); John Sharp (cello); Carolyn Davis (dbl bass); Odile Renault (fl/pclo); Rudolf Vrbsky (oboe); Robbie Lynn Hunsinger (Eng horn); Cheryl Hill (clar); Steven Jackson (clar); Kenneth Radnofsky (b clar); Patricia Rogers (bsn); Donald MacCourt (ctr bsn); Stewart Rose (horn); Victoria Eisen (horn). Leon Kirchner (c). 1966, 1982.
SONY 45894 ADD 55:51

★★*Awards:* The Gramophone Awards, Nominations, Contemporary, *Gramophone*, N '91.

"A performance [of the Chamber Symphony] which suggests long and careful rehearsal, and does not dwell overmuch on the composer's penchant for cloudy self-searching: in fact it is almost jovial. So by intention at any rate, is the Serenade Op. 24 directed by Leon Kirchner." *P95 S95*

Hi-Fi News & Record Review 36:79 S '91. Kenneth Dommett (brief)

"The performances should gain new enthusiasts for these rather thorny scores."

The New York Times Ag 26 '90, p. 23 H. Martin Bookspan (165w)

"A generous dollop of superbly played music by Arnold Schoenberg."

Fanfare 14:96+ S/O '90. John Wiser (360w)

Gramophone 69:107-8 Je '91. David Patmore (b.n.)

SCHUBERT, FRANZ

Fantasiestucke for Clarinet and Piano, Opus 73. See No. 3125.

3118. Music for Violin and Piano (complete): Sonatas for Violin and Piano, Opus 137: No. 1 in D, D.384; No. 2 in A minor, D.385; No. 3 in

G minor, D.408. Sonata (Duo) in A for Violin and Piano, Opus 162, D.574. Rondo brilliant in B minor for Violin and Piano, Opus 70, D.895. Fantasie in C for Violin and Piano, Opus 159, D.934.

Jaime Laredo (vln); Stephanie Brown (pno). Troy Savings Bank Music Hall, Troy, NY.
DORIAN 90137 DDD 53:56, 65:59 2 discs

★*Awards:* The Want List 1991, *Fanfare* N/D '91 (David K. Nelson).

"Some of the very best Schubert I've heard. The playing is heartfelt with beautifully nuanced phrases, a wonderful lilt, wide dynamic ranges, and an expressive yet never sentimentalized palette which runs the gamut from utmost brilliance to intimate tenderness."
Stereophile 15:272 Ap '92. Igor Kipnis (med)

"If you contemplate acquiring this music on CD, the Laredo/Brown set is decidedly one to consider....Dorian's sound is impressively transparent and clear...My mention of some alternative recording shouldn't be seen as equivocation as to the merits of this release. This strongly competitive entry sticks to a point of view that eschews wistful sentimentality."
Fanfare 14:279-80 My/Je '91. David K. Nelson (745w)

"This admirably played, spaciously recorded traversal of Schubert's music for violin and piano follows on the heels of Sony's Stern/Barenboim package (S2K 44504, 2 CDs; reviewed in September 1990, page 17)....I much prefer the songful, unpretentious approach of the newcomers to the former duo's altogether inappropriate grandness and pomposity. In the Sonata in A (*Duo*), the merits of Laredo/Brown's modest lyricism and Stern/Barenboim's more assertive drama become more evenly balanced (although neither quite makes me forget Kreisler/Rachmaninoff, Szigeti/Hess, or Goldberg/Lupu). For the two big pieces, however, Stern and Barenboim prevail."
Musical America 111:83 My '91. Harris Goldsmith (220w)

"Laredo is tempted to attack the music with the force and style of a concert artist accustomed to filling large halls and competing with large orchestras....When he does restrain the vigor of his bow strokes, he plays with great beauty and clarity. At other times, he seems to run roughshod over Schubert's remarkably detailed gradations of emphasis, stress, accent, and bite."
American Record Guide 54:143-4 N/D '91. Alan Heatherington (long)

Gramophone 69:78+ Jl '91. Christopher Headington (335w)

3119. Octet in F for Strings and Winds, D.803.

Academy of St. Martin-in-the-Fields Chamber Ensemble.
CHANDOS 8585 DDD 60:00

✔HC ★*Awards:* Critics' Choice 1988, *Gramophone* D '88 (Alan Sanders).

"Only the most determined critic could fail to find pleasure and enchantment in this altogether welcome release."
Hi-Fi News & Record Review 33:103 S '88. Jeremy Siepmann (270w)

"Highly recommended."
Fanfare 12:270-2 N/D '88. John Wiser (230w)

"The Sept/Oct 1988 issue of *ARG* reported enthusiastically on the new DG recording by violinist Gidon Kremer and his Lockenhaus players....The major difference between the ASMF and Kremer is that the latter gives us a performance of extremes (in the positive sense), of ultimate commitment, while the ASMF seems more reserved....Yet the final *Allegro* has more impetus on the Chandos disc, and that may tip the balance for some."
American Record Guide 52:84-5 Ja/F '89. Allen Linkowski (350w)

Gramophone 66:312 Ag '88. Alan Sanders (350w)

3120. Octet in F for Strings and Winds, D.803 (Opus 166).

Atlantis Ensemble. Cologne. 1989.
VIRGIN 91120 DDD 65:00

★*Awards:* Critic's Choice: 1991, *American Record Guide*, Ja/F '92 (Michael Carter).

"The performance...captures the work's Schubertian essence in both its vigor and its animation, and the interplay among the performers suggests the happiest sort of true chamber-music commitment. In short, it is a joy, and for me the most persuasive account of this wonderful work available now."
Stereo Review 56:94+ Je '91. Richard Freed (200w)

"The reading has enough interpretive give and take to allow the music to breathe freely, but not so much that it becomes distracting. Schroeder allows himself a few occasional portamentos that enhance the music's expressive appeal, and Greer's mastery of the natural horn—stopped tones are all but indistinguishable from open ones—is truly amazing."
Musical America 111:87 Jl '91. Nancy Raabe (340w)

"Yes, it is possible to perform on old instruments with feeling, but it requires a keen balance of academic knowledge and musical soul. When these two seemingly different characteristic meld as they do here, the result is a thoroughly rewarding experience."
American Record Guide 54:120 Jl/Ag '91. Michael Carter (290w)

"While there are some modern-instrument performances I would give higher priority than the Atlantis Ensemble, of the two so far to appear in period-instrument form, this seems the CD of choice. See *Fanfare* 12:4, pp. 263-64 for a potted resume, and 14:1, pp. 370-71 for a colleague's attempt to add dubious recordings to a choice group."

Fanfare 14:281-2 Jl/Ag '91. John Wiser (275w)

"A strong and stylish performance using period instruments. Despite occasional lapses of good intonation, there is much character in the playing of the Atlantis Ensemble, especially the clarinet and horn."

High Fidelity 3:97 Ap '91. Andrew Stewart (60w)

"A recording made with period instruments...This is a spacious, decorous account of the work with much lovely detail, though also the occasional flaw in ensemble....The over-resonant recording seems to me unfriendly to the gentle intimacy at which the artists are aiming, and which is most happily caught in many of the lightly-scored passages." *PS 85*

Hi-Fi News & Record Review 37:89 Mr '92. Peter Branscombe (med)

Gramophone 68:1858+ Ap '91. John Warrack (185w)

3121. Quartets for Strings: No. 10 in E flat, D.87; No. 12 in C minor, D.703, "Quartettstaz"; No. 13 in A minor, D.804, "Rosamunde".
Borodin Quartet.
VIRGIN 59047 DDD

✔HC

3122. Quartet No. 14 in D minor for Strings, "Death and the Maiden," D.810. BEETHOVEN, LUDWIG VAN. Quartet No. 11 in F minor for Strings, Opus 95, "Quartetto Serioso".
Emerson Quartet. Troy Music Hall, Troy, New York.
DEUTSCHE GRAMMOPHON 423 398 DDD 57:47

★*Awards:* The Want List 1989, *Fanfare* N/D '89 (Ralph V. Lucano).

"This is virtuoso quartet playing, and no mistake. The brilliance and drive of these performances are exciting both in their own right and for the quite appropriate sense of drama they bring out in the music....The opening of the Beethoven is superbly judged...and there are unexpected parallels with the Schubert, including the effectiveness of keeping the slow movement moving. But for all the dramatic conviction, there is a sense of something missing, some of the inwardness we quite reasonably associate with Beethoven's middle and late quartets."

Stereo Review 54:169-70 F '89. Richard Freed (275w)

"This is a promising release and a worthy purchase for anyone who wants this combination of works."

American Record Guide 52:85 Ja/F '89. Stephen D. Chakwin, Jr. (250w)

"A volatile debut by the Emerson Quartet-....They are especially impressive in the Beethoven 'Serioso'."

Hi-Fi News & Record Review 33:78 Ag '88. Christopher Breunig (270w)

"Impetuosity is...the keynote of the Emerson Quartet's approach to Schubert's great D minor Quartet....the accuracy and technical virtuosity of the players are impressive, but a less headlong tempo would have served the music with greater effectiveness. Beethoven's Quartet in F minor...brings out the best in the Emerson ensemble."

Musical America 108:62 N '88. George Jellinek (240w)

"If this recording can be said to have a fault, it is engineering of slight oddity....Troy Music Hall is a superb concert venue, but it gets away from recording engineers....But this is a small liability in a recording with the largest musical assets, which remains urgently recommended."

Fanfare 12:250-2 S/O '88. John Wiser (325w)

Gramophone 66:172+ Jl '88. David J. Fanning (450w)

3123. Quartet No. 15 in G for Strings, D.887.
Tokyo Quartet.
RCA 0199 DDD 46:00

✔HC ★*Awards:* Critic's Choice: 1990, *American Record Guide* Ja/F '91 (Arved Ashby).

"This is a wonderfully accomplished performance, with playing of great beauty, strength and sensitivity. The recording too is of the highest class." *P95 S95*

Hi-Fi News & Record Review 35:92 Ap '90. Peter Branscombe (170w)

"The Tokyo Quartet is almost perfect, the playing unfailingly beautiful....You ought to hear this great performance at a single sitting, in one vast sweep."

American Record Guide 53:108-9 N/D '90. Stratton Rawson (225w)

"In some of the music's sustained moments such as the introduction to the first movement, the playing takes on an almost otherworldly eerieness that goes right to the heart of the Schubertian matter....Clearly here is strong competition for the Alban Berg Quartet's EMI edition praised by John Wiser in *Fanfare* 11:4-....An imposing release."

Fanfare 13:284 My/Je '90. Mortimer H. Frank (250w)

"This may not be one of the great recordings of this work, but its combined musical and

technical virtues add up to a safe recommendation among those currently available on CD."
Stereo Review 55:120 O '90. Richard Freed (175w)

Gramophone 67:1826+ Ap '90. Stephen Johnson (350w)

3124. Quintet in C for 2 Violins, Viola and 2 Cellos, D.956; Der Hirt auf dem Felsen, for Soprano, Clarinet and Piano, D.965.
Pamela Frank (vln); Felix Galimir (vln); Steven Tenenbom (vla); Julia Lichten (cello); Peter Wiley (cello); Benita Valente (sop); Harold Wright (clar); Rudolf Serkin (pno). 1986; 1960 reissue.
SONY 45901 DDD/ADD 70:23

✔**HC** ★*Awards:* Critics' Choice 1991, *Gramophone*, Ja '92 (David Patmore).

"Desert Island choice." *P95/85 S95/85*
Hi-Fi News & Record Review 36:79 S '91. Kenneth Dommett (brief)

"The soprano Benita Valente is radiant and angelic. The clarinetist Harold wright matches her every step of the way, and Mr. Serkin's performance of the piano part inspires rapt reverie....[In the quintet the] five players represent precisely the Marlboro performing tradition."
The New York Times Ag 26 '90, p. 23 H. Martin Bookspan (165w)

"This reading [of the quintet] exemplifies the Marlboro custom of gathering a youngish group around a player of greater experience (in this case, much greater—violinist Felix Galimir) and giving the older player a tutorial role, yet not quite that of a leader. In this case, as in many of the Marlboro chamber-music road shows to come my way over the years, the idea is superbly realized in a performance of genuine strength, security, and thoughtfulness. The shorter work...finds soprano Benita Valente at her most unmodulated, blandest and brightest, and the isntrumental support chaste beyond necessity....But for the quintet, which unusually occupies a CD in solitary splendor, this performance becomes one of the two or three of choice."
Fanfare 14:96+ S/O '90. John Wiser (360w)

"The music [in the Quintet] never speaks for itself. The ensemble reminds us of its performance choices. I hear solutions to problems I did not know existed....The performance [of *Shepherd on the Rock*] is inspired and inspiring, but not inspiring enough to provide a reason for purchasing this disc."
American Record Guide 53:109-10 N/D '90. Stratton Rawson (830w)

Gramophone 69:107-8 Je '91. David Patmore (b.n.)

Musical America 111:57-9 Jl '91. Steven Lowe (90w)

Digital Audio's CD Review 7:88 D '90. David Vernier (300w)

3125. Sonata for Arpeggione and Piano, D.821. SCHUMANN, ROBERT. Fantasiestucke for Clarinet and Piano, Opus 73; Romances (3) for Oboe and Piano, Opus 94. WEBER, CARL MARIA VON. 7 Variations for Clarinet and Piano, J.128.
Gervase De Peyer (clar); Gwenneth Pryor (pno). Rosslyn Hill Chapel. 1982-83.
CHANDOS 8506 DDD 48:33

★*Awards:* *Fanfare* Want List 1987 (Michael Ullman).

"Here is a clarinetist apart from the standard breed, whose level of impulse occasionally runs amok, but who has never in my hearing let anything get well away from him....At last someone has taken the G-minor clarinet recasting of the 'Arpeggione' out of the slums where Richard Stoltzman found it...and left it."
Fanfare 11:99 Ja/F '88. John D. Wiser (155w)

"De Peyer's interest in 'coloring' his clarinet sound is wholly compatible with his interest in animating the music and filling it with character."
High Fidelity 38:78+ Ap '88. James Wierzbicki (150w)

Sonata for Arpeggione and Piano, D.821. See No. 3043.

Stucke im Volkston (5 pieces for Cello and Piano), Opus 102. See No. 3043.

3126. Trio No. 1 in B flat for Piano, Violin and Cello, Opus 99, D.898; Trio No. 2 in E flat for Piano, Violin and Cello, Opus 100, D.929; Nocturne in E flat, Opus 148, D.897 (piano trio).
(Works for Piano, Violin and Cello).
David Golub (pno); Mark Kaplan (vln); Colin Carr (cello).
ARABESQUE 6580 DDD 51:24

★★*Awards:* The Want List 1988, *Fanfare* N/D '88 (Susan Kagan). *American Record Guide* Overview: Getting to Know Chamber Music: Piano Trios, N/D '90.

"I have no hesitation in recommending these excellent performances to your attention. They are full of sensitive originality of phrasing, well-chosen tempos and an awareness of Schubert's depth as well as his beauty."
American Record Guide 51:81-2 S/O '88. David W. Moore (225w)

"In this excellent performance...the sound is warm and lyrical, and the ensemble playing superb."
Ovation 9:42 N '88. Lee Lourdeaux (325w)

"Before publication, the Trio No. 2 in E flat had in the development section of its finale two 50-bar passages that never made it into print....These players offer two alternatives: Band 4 of the second CD contains the as-published movement, with cuts. Band 5 contains the movement with both passages restored....I like their ensemble playing very much, and they are cleanly recorded. I do not know where in the scheme of whose priorities these restorations-on-record will fall, but they are worthy of consideration along with the general value of these performances, which is considerable."

Fanfare 11:249-50 Jl/Ag '88. John D. Wiser (265w)

"Arabesque's new release...deserves attention for several reasons. The pianist David Golub, the violinist Mark Kaplan and the cellist Colin Carr play with great finesse. Their carefully thought out and brilliantly executed interpretations are thoroughly convincing (although their failure to repeat the opening section of the Op. 99, as indicated by Schubert, is disappointing)."

The New York Times O 30 '88, p. 27. Paul Turok (210w)

Gramophone 66:634 O '88. Christopher Headington (420w)

SCHUMANN, ROBERT

3127. Quartet in E flat for Piano and Strings, Opus 47; Quintet in E flat for Piano and Strings, Opus 44.

Emanuel Ax (pno). Cleveland Quartet. Rochester, New York. November 1986.
RCA 6498 DDD 57:00

★*Awards:* *Stereo Review* Best Recordings of the Month, Ja '88.

"This one will take some effort to beat."

Stereo Review 53:128 Ja '88. Richard Freed (500w)

"This coupling proves thoroughly recommendable, and I prefer it to the equally well-played, harder edged but less full-bodied accounts by the augmented Beaux Arts Trio (Philips, OP)."

Opus 4:49-50 Ap '88. Harris Goldsmith (300w)

"Emanuel Ax's piano playing—secure, incisive, colorful, and powerfully expressive—is worth having for itself....As recorded here, the Cleveland's tone is more granular and shaky than I recall ever hearing it before."

High Fidelity 38:68 D '88. Thomas Hathaway (175w)

"Schumann's piano quartet works rather well in the new Red Seal issue, in which Emanuel Ax shows a level of sensitivity to its melodic content that I would not have thought probable....I wish that the level of organization were as good in the quintet, for it is not easy to recommend half a CD."

Fanfare 11:159-60 Ja/F '88. John D. Wiser (350w)

American Record Guide 51:78-9 Mr/Ap '88. Kurt Moses (175w)

Romances (3) for Oboe and Piano, Opus 94. See No. 3125.

3128. Trios (No.'s 1-3) for Piano, Violin and Cello, Opus 63, 80, 110. Fantasiestucke (4) for Violin, Cello and Piano, Opus 88.

Borodin Trio.
CHANDOS 8832/3 DDD 110:00 2 discs

★*Awards:* Critics' Choice 1990, *Gramophone* D '90 (Joan Chissell).

"The Bordin Trio approaches all of these scores from the inside-out. Their interpretive philosophy is quite unlike the more classically poised Gobel Trio on Thorofon, and far more akin to the venerable Rubinstein, Szeryng, Fournier Trio on RCA Gold Seal 6262-2, which, alas, offers only op. 63, along with a smashing version of Schubert's trio D.898. As integrales of these trios go, this one, given its fine, detailed, well-balanced, and impactful sound (the strings for once sound richly woody), is, by all accounts, outstanding."

Fanfare 14:378-9 Mr/Ap '91. William Zagorski (725w)

"Their performance of the first trio is magnificent, and the finale, labeled *with fire*, is incandescent, noble, potent, uplifting....This group of players trusts Schumann as much as he trusts them. If the composer chooses to end with a whimper instead of a bang, they produce a luscious, regretful whimper."

American Record Guide 54:106-7 My/Je '91. Stratton Rawson (415w)

Gramophone 68:1002 N '90. Joan Chissell (455w)

SHOSTAKOVICH, DMITRI

3129. Quartets for Strings (complete): No. 1 in C, Opus 49; No. 9 in E flat, Opus 117; No. 12 in D flat, Opus 133.

Borodin Quartet. 1979-1984.
EMI 49266 ADD 69:01

"While a perusal of the entire cycle reveals, to my feelings, a deeper commitment by the ensemble to the later quartets (from the Seventh on) than to the earlier ones, the Borodin Quartet's executions and interpretations speak so eloquently for this music that one feels guilty about any minor quibbles....A set for posterity."

Fanfare 12:260-3 S/O '88. Royal S. Brown (410w)

"Older sets...continue to offer valid alternative readings...But this new cycle is easily the best available and likely to prove definitive for some time to come."

Hi-Fi News & Record Review 33:115 O '88. Robert Cowan (665w)

"In their superb set, the Fitzwilliam emphasized the lyrical qualities of the music...The Borodin Quartet, by contrast, exhibits far less legato playing, accentuating individual parts and stressing the music's brilliantly crafted polyphonic textures. The level of musicianship displayed by both ensembles...is beyond reproach."

American Record Guide 51:85-6 N/D '88. James S. Ginsburg (840w)

3130. Quartets for Strings (complete): No. 2 in A, Opus 68; No. 3 in F, Opus 73.
Borodin Quartet. 1979-1984.
EMI 49267 ADD 72:13

See Quartet No. 1 for review excerpt.
—*Fanfare* 12:260-3 S/O '88. Royal S. Brown (410w)

—*Hi-Fi News & Record Review* 33:115 O '88. Robert Cowan (665w)

—*American Record Guide* 51:85-6 N/D '88. James S. Ginsburg (840w)

3131. Quartets for Strings (complete): No. 4 in D, Opus 83; No. 6 in G, Opus 101, No. 11 in F minor, Opus 122.
Borodin Quartet. 1979-1984.
EMI 49268 ADD 68:00

See Quartet No. 1 for review excerpt.
—*Fanfare* 12:260-3 S/O '88. Royal S. Brown (410w)

—*Hi-Fi News & Record Review* 33:115 O '88. Robert Cowan (665w)

—*American Record Guide* 51:85-6 N/D '88. James S. Ginsburg (840w)

Gramophone 66:440 S '88. Michael Oliver (340w)

3132. Quartets for Strings (complete): No. 5 In B flat, Opus 92, No. 15 in E flat minor, Opus 144.
Borodin Quartet. 1979-1984.
EMI 49270 ADD 68:11

See Quartet No. 1 for review excerpt.
—*Fanfare* 12:260-3 S/O '88. Royal S. Brown (410w)

—*Hi-Fi News & Record Review* 33:115 O '88. Robert Cowan (665w)

—*American Record Guide* 51:85-6 N/D '88. James Ginsburg (840w)

Gramophone 66:440 S '88. Michael Oliver (340w)

3133. Quartets for Strings (complete): No. 7 in F# minor, Opus 108; Quartet No. 8 in C minor, Opus 110; Quintet in G minor for Piano and Strings, Opus 57.
Sviatoslav Richter (pno). Borodin Quartet. November, 1985.
EMI 47507 70:00

★*Awards:* *Fanfare* Want List 1987 (Royal S. Brown).

"Older sets...continue to offer valid alternative readings...But this new cycle is easily the best available and likely to prove definitive for some time to come."
Hi-Fi News & Record Review 33:115 O '88. Robert Cowan (665w)

"In their superb set, the Fitzwilliam emphasized the lyrical qualities of the music...The Borodin Quartet, by contrast, exhibits far less legato playing, accentuating individual parts and stressing the music's brilliantly crafted polyphonic textures. The level of musicianship displayed by both ensembles...is beyond reproach."
American Record Guide 51:85-6 N/D '88. James S. Ginsburg (840w)

"This CD is an outstanding value in every respect."
Stereo Review 52:93 Ap '87 Richard Freed (500w)

"The live analog recording, made in 1983, sounds fine in spite of an occasional tubbiness in the piano, and the audience is undetectable until the concluding applause."
High Fidelity 37:61-62 Jl '87 Robert R. Reilly (335w)

Fanfare 10:204-6 Mr/Ap '87 James Miller (315w)

Gramophone 65:639 O '87 Alan Sanders (110w)

3134. Quartets for Strings (complete): No. 10 in A flat, Opus 118; No. 13 in B flat minor, Opus 138; No. 14 in F flat, Opus 142.
Borodin Quartet. 1979-1984.
EMI 49269 ADD 68:11

See Quartet No. 1 for review excerpt.
—*Fanfare* 12:260-3 S/O '88. Royal S. Brown (410w)

—*Hi-Fi News & Record Review* 33:115 O '88. Robert Cowan (665w)

—*American Record Guide* 51:85-6 N/D '88. James S. Ginsburg (840w)

Gramophone 66:440 S '88. Michael Oliver (340w)

3135. Quartet No. 15 in E flat for Strings, Opus 144. GUBAIDULINA, SOFIA. Rejoice! For Violin and Cello.
Gidon Kremer (vln); Daniel Phillips (vln); Kim Kashkashian (vla); Yo-Yo Ma (cello). 1985, 1988.
CBS 44924 DDD 68:01

★*Awards:* The Year's Best, *Hi Fi News & Record Review*, May '90 Supplement. The Want List 1990, *Fanfare* N/D '90 (Edward Strickland).

"Both the works themselves and the performances are remarkable for their spiritual power-...As compelling as the performance of the Shostakovich is, the duo sonata *Rejoice!* by Gubaidulina, whose music Kremer has so conspicuously championed, is the real discovery of this release."
Stereo Review 55:98 Mr '90. Richard Freed (480w)

"All-star ensembles are not always without problems; but there is nothing to complain at here. They opted to record the Shostakovich live...musically the decision is marvelously vindicated....it is very much to the group's credit that they are never afraid to risk ugliness in their efforts to articulate the anguish....To follow it, CBS offer an inspired piece of programme planning: Gubaidulina's *Rejoice*...is light-years away from Shostakovitch's suffocating terror. And there is an intellectual and emotional excitement about this music which eschews *avant-garde angst*...yet still contrives to avoid neo-romantic nostalgia. Kremer and Ma are at the very top of their form and succeed in demonstrating that modern music can still make emotional statements which combine integrity and intelligibility." *P100 S95*

Hi-Fi News & Record Review 35:110 Mr '90; p.27-8 My '90 Supplement. Simon Cargill (535w)

"To my sensibilities, the mournful loneliness of the Shostakovich quartet often transcends to a level of nihilistic mysticism (one feels Mallarme's swan trapped in the ice of a winter pond) that the four very accomplished musicians on this CD do not quite capture....The extraneous sounds...do not help a great deal-....'Rejoice!'...calls for the utter mastery of their instruments that violinist Kremer and cellist Ma show in their rendition of this work."

Fanfare 13:295-99 Mr/Ap '90. Royal S. Brown (245w)

"Both her [Gubaidulina's] orchestral and chamber music seem to emanate from a single source, a well-spring of uncompromising spirituality, both personal and universal....And Yo-Yo Ma, Kremer's partner in *Rejoice!*, exhibits a confident virtuosity and intellectual comprehension to match the violinist's....Kremer's group...emphasize the quartet's obsessively pessimistic tone and monochromatic coloring-...The result is a performance of hair-raising intensity, so riveting that I can only hope it will not be the last Shostakovich we hear from this foursome."

Musical America 110:76-7 My '90. K. Robert Schwarz (330w)

Gramophone 67:1818 Ap '90. David J. Fanning (490w)

Digital Audio's CD Review 6:62 Ja '90. David Vernier (380w)

3136. Quintet in G minor for Piano and Strings, Opus 57; Seven Songs on Poems of Alexander Blok; Two Pieces for String Octet.
Vladimir Ashkenazy (pno); Elizabeth Soderstrom (sop); Christopher Rowland and Jonathan Sparey (violins); Alan George (viola); Iona Davies (cello). Fitzwilliam Quartet.
LONDON/DECCA 411 940 63:51

✔**HC** ★★*Awards: Hi-Fi News & Record Review* Record of the Month, Mr '87. *Gramophone* Critics' Choice (Michael Oliver), 1987.

"Shame on Decca for sitting so long on such treasures....We've really no right to expect a more beautiful or more searching account of the Piano Quintet."

Hi-Fi News & Record Review 32:93 Mr '87 Edward Seckerson (480w)

Fanfare 10:183-4 Jl/Ag '87 Royal S. Brown (230w)

Gramophone 64:1150 F '87 Michael Oliver (490w)

3137. Quintet in G minor for Piano and Strings, Opus 57; Trio No. 2 in E Minor for Violin, Cello and Piano, Opus 67.
Mimi Zweig; Jerry Horner. Borodin Trio.
CHANDOS 8342 DDD 65:27

★*Awards: American Record Guide* Overview: Getting to Know Chamber Music: Piano Trios, N/D '90.

"The Borodins continue their excellent Chandos CD series with fine performances of these two important chamber works."

Hi-Fi News & Record Review 30:101 Mr '85. John Atkinson (190w)

Gramophone 62:1243 Ap '85. Michael Oliver (150w)

Digital Audio 2:66-7 N '85. Laurel E. Fay (700w)

3138. Trio No. 2 in E minor for Piano and Strings, Opus 67; Sonata in D minor for Cello and Piano, Opus 40.
Emanuel Ax (pno); Isaac Stern (vln); Yo-Yo Ma (cello). 1987.
CBS 44664 DDD 58:31

★*Awards: American Record Guide* Overview: Getting to Know Chamber Music: Piano Trios, N/D '90.

"At every quiet opportunity I have been playing the Largo from the Sonata (1934)—which seems to me to exemplify one of those very rare instances where a studio recording (New England Conservatory) has the immediacy and 'timelessness' of a great live performance without the 'real-life' interference of other persons interposed, *ie* audience members, between you and the platform....Both content and intensity of performance, especially with Stern present, make this an important release. Those who normally shy away from Shostakovich's chamber music must hear it."

Hi-Fi News & Record Review 34:96 Mr '89. Christopher Breunig (460w)

"Producer James Mallinson presents the music in a warm atmosphere with excellent depth and stereo imaging. The CBS disc represents the best tradition of recording: great musicians performing compositions about which they obviously care very deeply."

American Record Guide 52:89-90 My/Je '89. James S. Ginsburg (290w)

Gramophone 67:61 Je '89. Stephen Johnson (455w)

Digital Audio's CD Review 6:60 Je '90. Lawrence Johnson (290w)

Trio No. 2 in E minor for Piano, Violin and Cello, Opus 67. See No. 3099.

SIMPSON, ROBERT

3139. Quartets for Strings No.'s 3 and 6.
Delme Quartet.
HYPERION 66376 DDD 72:13

★*Awards:* Critics' Choice 1990, *Gramophone* D '90 (David Fanning).

"Congratulations are due to recording engineer Antony Howell for one of the best quartet sounds I have yet heard on disc and to the Delme Quartet for its dramatic playing. Superb."

High Fidelity 1:107 Jl '90. Andrew Stuart (100w)

"The three works here are as good an introduction as any to his extraordinary world...Recording, like the playing, is excellent, yet always self-effacing. Everything is put at the service of the music. And what music it is." *P100 S95*

Hi-Fi News & Record Review 35:94 Ag '90. Simon Cargill (310w)

"The performances are well focussed and projected. However, especially in the Third Quartet, often we need more second violin and more emphasis on accents. Soft dynamics do not *seem* as soft as they do on most analog recordings."

Fanfare 14:388-9 S/O '90. Paul Rapoport (600w)

Gramophone 68:242 Jl '90. David J. Fanning (665w)

3140. Quartets for Strings: No. 7 and No. 8. Delme Quartet. 1984 reissue.
HYPERION 66117 AAD 51:03

★Awards: The Year's Best, *Hi Fi News & Record Review*, May '90 Supplement.

"Here is some of the finest music by a composer whose neglect has been almost criminal-....The Delme...play like men committed to the validity of every note....the recording handles it all with an unassuming effectiveness so appropriate to the music." *P100 S100*

Hi-Fi News & Record Review 34:109 N '89; p.28 My '90 Supplement. Simon Cargill (230w)

"The Delme Quartet have recorded many of Simpson's quartets and this disc continues a worthy series."

Music and Musicians International 38:47 Jl '90. Anthony Milner (235w)

"Both works are well-crafted and effective, fairly conservative I suppose, but Simpson's music is more deserving of acclaim than much that is in vogue....The Delme Quartet plays well."

American Record Guide 53:111-12 Jl/Ag '90. Timothy D. Taylor (135w)

"The performances are certainly good. The sound defects I mentioned in 1985 are partly removed by the CD: no surface noise, of course, but the dynamics still aren't conveyed ideally."

Fanfare 13:300 Mr/Ap '90. Paul Rapoport (350w)

Gramophone 67:1482 F '90. David J. Fanning (155w)

SMETANA, BEDRICH. Quartet No. 1 in E minor for Strings, "From My Life". See No. 3050.

STRAVINSKY, IGOR

Divertimento for Violin and Piano. See No. 3098.

Fanfare for a New Theatre, for 2 Trumpets. See No. 1418.

Music of Stravinsky: "The Igor Stravinsky Edition" (complete). See No. 1425.

Octet for Wind Instruments. See No. 1418.

Three Pieces for Clarinet. See No. 1418.

3143. Violin and Piano Music: Suite Italienne, for Cello and Piano; Ballad (1947); Petrouchka: Danse Russe; **Chanson Russe (1937); Pastorale (1933); Divertimento (1932); Duo Concertante (1931-2); Tango (arr. Mustonen); Elegie (1944:** arr. vln solo); Prelude et Ronde des Princesses (1929); The Firebird: Berceuse (1929); Scherzo (1933); La Marseillaise (1919: arr. vln solo); Chants du Rossignol et Marche Chinoise (1932).
(Works for Violin and Piano and Solo Violin).
Isabelle Van Keulen (vln); Olli Mustonen (pno). 1931-1937.
PHILIPS 420 953 DDD 96:00 2 discs

★Awards: Critic's Choice: 1990, *American Record Guide* Ja/F '91 (Stephen Chakwin).

"Isabelle van Keulen...does a distinguished job in this music. If few sparks fly, she does have more than enough technique to stay on top of things at all times....Mustonen handles the tricky piano parts with unfailing finesse, and his deft way of bringing out secondary inner voices attracted my attention to many details I had never really noticed before."

Musical America 110:84-5 My '90. Paul Moor (335w)

"Van Keulen is a superbly poised artist with great technical fluency and a silvery, gleaming tone. It is hard to imagine more stylish or tonally elegant playing in these pieces. Certainly nobody in the current catalog even comes close. Mustonen...is an ideal collaborator, handling an often ungrateful piano part articulately and—here's that word again—elegantly. Both individually and together these players have real charisma."

American Record Guide 53:117-18 My/Je '90. Stephen D. Chakwin, Jr. (440w)

"In short, a wonderful idea marred slightly by some interpretive immaturity on the part of the artists, particularly the violinist, admittedly confined to the less important music. Recommended with some cautions; both the Stravinsky admirer and the violin fan will find real attractions here."

Fanfare 13:376-77 N/D '89. David K. Nelson (700w)

Gramophone 67:332 Ag '89. David J. Fanning (490w)

ULLMANN, VICTOR. Quartet for Strings, Opus 46, No. 3. See No. 3066.

VARESE, EDGAR. Music of Varese. See No. 1457.

VILLA-LOBOS, HEITOR

3144. Bachiana Brasileira No. 1, for 8 Celli; Bachiana Brasileira No. 5, for Soprano and 8 Celli. Bach Transcriptions: The Well-tempered Clavier—Prelude in D minor; Fugue in B flat, BWV.846; Prelude in G minor, BWV.867; Fugue in D, BWV.874.
Jill Gomez; Peter Manning (vln). Pleeth Cello Octet.
HYPERION 66257 DDD 54:00

★*Awards:* Critics' Choice 1988, *Gramophone* D '88 (Lionel Salter).

"The Pleeth Cello Octet show here how it [1] should be done...[an] altogether well thought out, well put together issue. Recommended."
Hi-Fi News & Record Review 33:105 Ap '88. Doug Hammond (275w)

"I have heard a few singers whose voices soared over the cello ensemble of the *Bachiana Brasileira No. 5* more imposingly than that of Jill Gomez, but she's extremely proficient and renders the 'Danza' with spirit, having fun with the words. That same sense of fun seems to dominate the 'Sertaneja' movement of the *Suite for Voice and Violin*."
Fanfare 11:228-9 Mr/Ap '88. James Miller (350w)

"Like Gomez, the Pleeth Cello Octet and violinist Peter Manning make a strong case for the composer's wayward but intriguing music. Be warned that defective copies of this CD are circulating."
High Fidelity 38:72 O '88. Terry Teachout (155w)

Stereo Review 53:116+ My '88. Richard Freed (160w)

Gramophone 65:972 D '87. Lionel Salter (350w)

3145. Quartets for Strings: No's. 4-6.
Bessler-Reis Quartet. 65:30.
CHANT DU MONDE 278 901 DDD

★*Awards:* Classical Hall of Fame, *Fanfare*, Mr/Ap '92 (Jon Tuska).

"The Bessler-Reis Quartet...is the best-sounding string ensemble I have ever heard emanating from Brazil....Strongly recommended to those who know that they like this sort of thing."
Fanfare 12:291-2 S/O '88. John Wiser (175w)

"The Bachianas Brasileiras can be said now to be masterfully represented on compact disc with Karabtchewsky's recent traversal and the reissue of the composer's integral set. This has never been the case with the string quartets until the recordings by the Bessler-Reis Quartet began appearing of which this is the second volume....The sound is warm, detailed, and intimate with fine balance. These performances are articulate, totally idiomatic, and compel repeated hearings."
Fanfare 15:476 Mr/Ap '92. Jon Tuska (long)

Gramophone 66:440+ S '88. Lionel Salter (475w)

VIVALDI, ANTONIO

3146. Chamber Concerti: R.105; R.101; R.107; R.103; R.98. **Sonata in A minor for Recorder, Bassoon and Continuo, R.86.**
Ensemble Il Giardino Armonico. Salone Baronale del Castello di Manta. July 10-14, 1988.
NUOVA ERA 6731 DDD 50:48

★*Awards:* The Want List 1989, *Fanfare* N/D '89 (Nils Anderson).

"These are delightfully immediate, lively performances with a clean acoustic and the sound forward....While some tender souls might find these readings here a bit too vigorous for their sensibilities, I will still recommend this disc very highly to anyone interested in the composer or the genre."
Fanfare 12:348-49 My/Je '89. Nils Anderson (170w)

"The ensemble blend favors soloistic pungency, but in rhythmic matters the members remain essentially of one mind. And the recording, in spite of some cloudiness in the bass, gives a pleasing sense of the natural live acoustic. In sum, the work of these eight harmonic gardeners shows energy, confidence, brio, intelligence, style. Great. Now, how about a little weeding and pruning?"
HighPerformanceReview 6:89 Je '89. Rodney Shewan (285w)

WAGNER, RICHARD

3147. Siegfried Idyll. Piano Transcriptions (trans. Gould): *Die Meistersinger von Nurnberg:* Prelude, Act 1; *Gotterdammerung:* Dawn and Sigfried's Rhine Journey. Sigfried Idyll.
Glenn Gould (pno); chamber ensemble (members of the Toronto Symphony Orchestra). Glenn Gould (c). 1982.
SONY 46279 ADD 71:00

★★*Awards:* The Want List 1991, *Fanfare* N/D '91 (Kevin Bazzana; Edward Strickland).

"Gould...somehow manages to go to the heart of the music and make one hear it anew. He does use overdubbing to give himself four hands and thus convey the essential weight of Wagner's writing."
American Record Guide 54:146 S/O '91. Carl Bauman (med)

"It strikes me that *control* is the name of the game throughout. Whether it all amounts to a valid musical experience is a matter of taste."
Stereo Review 56:77-8 O '91. David Hall (brief)

"This disc is a must-buy for the chamber-orchestra version...[of Gould's] *Siegfried Idyll*—you'll not have heard its like."
Stereophile 14:209+ S '91. Richard Lehnert (long)

"Wagner's 'Siegfried Idyll'...[is] a connoisseur's version, with tonal savoring taking precedent over rhythmic momentum and thematic contrast. It'd be insane to recommend this to someone not familiar with the piece; those who know it should, however, take pleasure in Gould's atomizing of Wagner's soundworld, as well as the not-entirely-unexpected deposits of humor....just attempting to render 'Siegfried's Rhine Journey' in pianistic terms is a little mad—call it audacious."
Musician 159:92-3 Ja '92. Richard C. Walls (med)

"The 13 instrument *Idyll* was both [Gould's]-...conducting debut and final recording, further reminding us of the loss of this most original musician at age 50."
High Performance Review 9:72 Spr '92. Bert Wechsler (brief)

"Gould stretches the *Idyll* over his dissecting table a full 24½m (18-21½m is the norm for full-orchestra readings), clinically—or is it *lovingly*—exposing rarely glimpsed internal workings....These somewhat boxy recordings (reissues) are curious and compelling; the *Idyll* too holds you in anticipation, even after several hearings." *P Historic (85) S95/85 P? S85/75*
Hi-Fi News & Record Review 36:89 Ap '91. Christopher Breunig (140w)

"This is not, properly speaking, a performance of Wagner's piece at all but rather a dreamy meditation on it, more akin to the Liszt fantasias on familiar works than to a mere recreation. And, so heard, it's fabulous....As to the performance itself, it has joy, majesty, sweep—all the qualities appropriate to the piece....So one is glad to have these performances for what they teach us about a great musician whom we lost too soon—yes, in a way glad even to have that execrable chamber-orchestra version of the *Siegfried Idyll*, which you, I trust, will join me in never listening to again."
Fanfare 15:388-90 S/O '91. William Youngren (long)

The New York Times Je 16 '91, p. 21 H. James Hunter (long)

Gramophone 68:1873 Ap '91. Arnold Whittall (350w)

Digital Audio's CD Review 8:40 Ap '92. Richard Perry (long)

WALTON, WILLIAM. Quartet in A minor for Strings. See No. 3034.

WEBER, CARL MARIA VON

3148. Clarinet Music: Quintet in B flat for Clarinet and Strings, Opus 34; Grand Duo Concertante for Clarinet and Piano, Opus 48; Introduction, Theme and Variations for Clarinet and Strings, op. posth.; Seven Variations for Clarient and Piano, Opus 33.
(The Complete Clarinet Music, Volume 1: Chamber Music).
Jon Manasse (clar); Samuel Sanders (pno). Manhattan String Quartet.
XLNT MUSIC 18004 DDD 74:02

★*Awards:* The Want List 1989, *Fanfare* N/D '89 (James H. North).

"This first installment of the complete clarinet music of Carl Maria von Weber is a winner in every regard."
American Record Guide 53:105 Ja/F '90. Stephen R. Max (200w)

"Sterling performances and high-quality sound."
Musical America 110:91 S '90. James Wierzbicki (120w)

"Manasse...plays with great verve and spirit-....This new label provides nice production values all around, starting with a clean, honest recording."
Fanfare 13:377 S/O '89. James H. North (250w)

7 Variations for Clarinet and Piano, J.128. See No. 3125.

WEBERN, ANTON

Complete Works. See No. 1481.

Five Movements for String Quartet, Opus 5; Quartet; Six Bagatelles for String Quartet, Opus 9; Quartet, Opus 28. See No. 3116.

ZWILICH, ELLEN TAAFFE. Double Quartet for Strings (1984). See No. 1486.

Chamber Music—Collections

American Brass Quintet

3149. Recital. Bolcom: Quintet for Brass (1980); **Druckman:** Other Voices, for Brass Quintet (1976); **Shapey:** Quintet for Brass (1963); **Wright:** Quintet for Brass (1986).
American Brass Quintet.
NEW WORLD 377 DDD 59:44

★*Awards:* Critic's Choice: 1990, *American Record Guide* Ja/F '91 (Barry Kilpatrick).

"This is as serious and substantive a brass album as I've come across. All four works are solid, and each is representative of its composer to a deeper extent than is common with the medium."
Fanfare 13:409-10 Ja/F '90. Kyle Gann (420w)

"This one is a masterpiece. The works are complex and intense—none fall into the category of easy listening....They play, collectively and individually, the way a great group should: with character and a sense of conviction."
American Record Guide 53:116 Ja/F '90. Barry Kilpatrick (280w)

"None of this is great music, and none of it is a waste of time, either. The performances, however, are just plain spectacular."
Musical America 110:73 Ja '90. Andrew Stiller (b.n.)

The New York Times Je 18 '89, p. 23. Andrew L. Pincus (100w)

Amsterdam Loeki Stardust Quartet

3150. Virtuoso Recorder Music. (Anonymous: Tre Fontane (excerpts). **Palestrina:** Recercar del secondo tuono. **Frescobaldi:** Canzon prima. **Merula:** Canzon 'La Lusignuola." **Vivaldi:** Concerto R.443. **Locke:** Suite 5. **Gibbons:** In nomine. **Simpson:** Ricercar 'Bonny Sweet Robin.' **Black:** Report upon 'When shall my sorrowful sighing slack.' **R. Johnson:** Temporiser. **Byrd: Sermone blando).**
Amsterdam Loeki Stardust Quartet.
OISEAU-LYRE 414 277 DDD 55:34

✔**HC** ★*Awards: Gramophone* Critics' Choice 1986 (John Duarte).

"Marvellous, an excellent demonstration record of immediate appeal."
Hi-Fi News & Record Review 30:119 D '85. Stephen Daw (90w)

"Lovers of the dulcet pipes will find much to savor on this fine-sounding disc."
Fanfare 9:281-2 Jl/Ag '86. George Chien (300w)

"The Amsterdam Loeki Stardust Quartet know exactly what they're doing when it comes to the scholarly details of the 16th-, 17th-, and 18th- century pieces....Their delivery, though, is spiced with more insouciance than the early-music camp has ever known....the super-fast, super-crisp articulations, like the sonics, are always dazzling."
High Fidelity 36:69 N '86 James Wierzbicki (150w)

Digital Audio 2:60-1 Ag '86. Tom Vernier (225w)

Bashmet, Yuri and Mikhail Muntian

3151. Schubert, Schumann, Bruch, Enesco.
Schubert: Sonata for Arpeggione and Piano, D.821. **Schumann:** Marchenbilder (4) for Viola, Opus 113; Adagio and Allegro for Horn and Orchestra, Opus 70. **Bruch:** Kol Nidrei for Cello and Orchestra, Opus 7. **Enescu:** Konzerstuck.
Yuri Bashmet (vla); Mikhail Muntian (pno). 1990.
RCA 0112 DDD 72:49

★*Awards:* The Gramophone Awards, Nominations, Chamber, *Gramophone*, N '91. Critics' Choice 1991, *Gramophone*, Ja '92 (Joan Chissell).

"The playing of each and every work on this recital is of surpassing beauty, and I cannot imagine anyone fond of the sound of this, the most beautiful of all string instruments (and, therefore, of all instruments of any kind), not enjoying this CD. Which is not the same thing as giving a blanket seal of approval on each and every one of the interpretations....on balance this recital is enthusiastically received."
Fanfare 14:307-8 Ja/F '91. David K. Nelson (320w)

"The sounds he gets the viola to make are much wider-ranging than Imai, and the emotional range is downright astounding. Besides ideal performances, the program is ideal....Yuri Bashmet, given half a chance, could probably make the viola as popular as the violin."
American Record Guide 54:113 Mr/Ap '91. Donald R. Vroon (220w)

"Bashmet responds to the particular demands of each piece—no mere all-purpose virtuosity for him....The curiosity of the disc is the Enesco *Konzertstuck*, a showpiece full of rhapsodic tune-spinning, cascading arpeggios, and cavalry charges up and down the fingerboard. Amidst it all, Bashmet makes the viola sound as fine-spun and light on its feet as any violin. The excellent pianist, Mikhail Muntian, keeps pace with him throughout."

Musical America 111:82-3 Ja '91. Shirley Fleming (225w)

"An unusual disc, demonstrating the potential of the viola in a subtle manner....The recording is warm and glowing, with the instruments ideally balanced as equal partners in the rich acoustic of St. George's Church, Brandon Hill, Bristol." *P95 S100*

Hi-Fi News & Record Review 36:97 Mr '91. Antony Hodgson (220w)

Digital Audio's CD Review 7:67 N '90. David Vernier (190w)

Gramophone 68:1231 D '90. Joan Chissell (390w)

California EAR Unit

3152. The California Ear Unit. Jarvinen: Egyptian Two Step. **Steiger:** Quintessence. **Torke:** The Yellow Pages. **Stockhausen:** Dr. K.—Sextet. **Carter:** Enchanted Preludes. Esprit Rude/Esprit Doux. Canon for Four—Homage to William. **Andreissen:** Hoketus. Erika Duke (cello); Lorna Eder (pno); Arthur Jarvinen (perc); Amy Knoles (perc); Robin Lorentz (vln); Gaylord Mowrey (pno); James Rohig (clar); Dorothy Stone (fl); Toby Holmes (el bass); Theresa Tunnicliff (clar); Rand Steiger (cond).
NEW ALBION 019 DDD 67:00

★*Awards:* Critic's Choice: 1990, *American Record Guide* Ja/F '91 (William Ellis).

"The California EAR Unit, a...group founded in 1981, takes highly esoteric music and instills such zeal and mettle into it that the only word for the spirit of this disc is 'fun'....Disregard the awful ear-on-the-beach cover and purchase what will prove to be the most enjoyable contemporary collection to be had."

American Record Guide 53:143 N/D '90. William Ellis (325w)

"The Ear Unit musicians are an impressively well-drilled and virtuosic bunch (clarinetist James Rohrig stands out especially), and these performances are polished and clean."

Musical America 110:82 N '90. Andrew Stiller (440w)

"The real discovery is Louis Andriessen's *Hoketus*, an unrelenting 24-minute work whose pounding rhythms seem static until they suddenly change and blow you out of your seat. The EAR Unit performs with exuberance and razor-sharp precision."

The New York Times Mr 4 '90, p. H 34. K. Robert Schwarz (100w)

"This recommended compilation clearly calls for more....The recorded sound is good, if a touch boxed-in."

Fanfare 13:386 My/Je '90. Mike Silverton (200w)

Gramophone 69:97 S '91. Arnold Whittall (med)

Campbell, James. Impact. See No. 3155.

Equale Brass

3153. Bacchanales. Warlock: Capriol Suite. **Poulenc:** 'Suite.' **Arnold:** Quintet for Brass. **Couperin:** 'Suite.' **Bartok:** Hungarian Sketches. Equale Brass.
NIMBUS 5004 DDD 50:26

★*Awards:* Records to Die for: 1 of 5 Recommended Recordings, *Stereophile* Ja '91 (Bill Sommerwerck).

"A total delight...."Though ordinary stereo reproduction is excellent, in Ambisonic mode the brass players are *right there* in your listening room."

Stereophile 10:193+ Je '87 John Sunier (125w)

"In short, this is a very enjoyable program-....Suggested for all brass lovers."

American Record Guide 47:78-9 My '84. Carl Bauman (375w)

"How many recordings in your collection sound like you're actually standing in front of a group of real musicians performing in a real hall?...the performances are light, crisp, and engaging. A fun recording."

Stereophile 14:167 Ja '91. Bill Sommerwerck (b.n.)

Gramophone 61:993 F '84. Ivan March (225w)

Guildhall String Ensemble

3154. English Music for Strings. Britten: Simple Symphony, Opus 4. **Tippett:** Little Music. **Walton:** Sonata. **Oldham/Tippett/L. Berkeley/Britten/Searle/Walton:** Variations on an Elizabethan Theme, "Sellinger's Round". Robert Salter (vln). Guildhall String Ensemble.
RCA 7846 DDD 69:00

★*Awards:* Critics' Choice 1989, *Gramophone* D '89 (Alan Sanders).

"All in all, this is a disc that can be strongly recommended."

Fanfare 12:408-9 My/Je '89. John Bauman (425w)

"The Guildhall String Ensemble is the most interesting group of its sort to come along since the Camerata Bern. It is small...young...and lively, specializing in 20th Century repertoire-...the sound and playing style are refreshingly individual while the technical level matches that of their better known English rivals."

American Record Guide 52:146 N/D '89. Alan Heatherington (470w)

"The approach [is] sparing on vibrato and (dare one say it) very British in its reticence, with only a handful of rich climaxes to show what this group can manage when it chooses. Slow movements are subtly done...while their faster counterparts are clean and airy...Recording is appropriately clean and full of presence."

Hi-Fi News & Record Review 34:103 Ag '89. David Nice (315w)

Gramophone 66:1741 My '89. Alan Sanders (245w)

Hakkila, Tuija. Contemporary Music for Cello and Piano. See No. 3156.

Johnston, Beverley and Campbell, James

3155. Impact.
Beverly Johnston (perc); James Campbell (clar).
CENTREDISCS 2786

★*Awards: Fanfare* Want List 1987 (John Ditsky).

"Johnston...is a whiz at what she does, with both the virtuoso's knack for making the difficult sound effortless and the true artist's capacity to transcend the limits of her instrument-....Whether you're an aficionado of percussion music or totally unfamiliar with the genre, a splendid time is guaranteed for all."
Opus 4:42-3 F '88. Andrew Stiller (1050w)

Karttunen, Anssi and Tuija Hakkila

3156. Contemporary Music for Cello and Piano. Carter: Sonata for Cello and Piano. **Kaipainen:** Trois Morceaux de l'Aube. **Denisov:** Sonata for Cello and Piano. **Heininen:** Serenade. **Bergman:** Quo Vadis.
Anssi Karttunen (cello); Tuija Hakkila (pno).
FINLANDIA 362 DDD 70:51

★*Awards:* The Want List 1989, *Fanfare* N/D '89 (Stephen Ellis).

"I've praised the performers and music alike. What's left? Finlandia's sound. Topnotch—almost three-dimensional. Well balanced. No listener will soon forget this music."
Fanfare 12:312 Jl/Ag '89. Stephen Ellis (600w)

"Excellent performances of music that is often overlooked in assessments of 20th-century compositions."
Music and Musicians International 39:39 O '90. Anthony Milner (180w)

Kriikku, Kari

3157. The Virtuoso Clarinet. Lindberg: Ablauf, for Clarinet and Two Bass Drums. Linea d'ombra, for Clarinet, Flute, Guitar, and Percussion. **Salonen:** Meeting, for Clarinet and Harpsichord. **Koskelin:** Exalte, for Solo Clarinet. **Xenakis:** Anaktoria, for Octet. **Donatoni:** Clair, for Solo Clarinet. **Ambrosini:** Capriccio, detto l'Ermafrodita, for Solo Bass Clarinet.
Kari Kriikku (clar); members of the Avanti Chamber Orchestra.
FINLANDIA 366 DDD 66:47

★*Awards:* The Want List 1990, *Fanfare* N/D '90 (Stephen Ellis).

"Kari Kriikku certainly is a virtuoso; he plays this difficult music seemingly without effort. The sound and the notes are excellent. This album is recommended for clarinet fans and other adventuresome types."
American Record Guide 53:133-34 Mr/Ap '90. Stephen R. Max (175w)

"If you want to know every possible sound a clarinet can make, and some a clarinetist can make, this disc is for you. It may not have the broadest appeal, but this recording is, at least, an excellent example of the clarinet's modern capabilities....Ambrosini's *Capriccio*...is the disc's most sonically fascinating work."
Musical America 110:88 Jl '90. Dan Wakin (255w)

"These clarinet works are more advanced than you might be prepared for. But since names like Lindberg and Xenakis in small dark type above haven't scared you off to this point, then you are probably ready for what Finlandia is offering....Kari Kriikku can certainly do it all. As a founding member of the Avanti Chamber Orchestra and the Toimii Ensemble, he lives for this type of music, much to the benefit of modern-music fans. He is surrounded by the most capable of complementary musicians on this CD, and Finlandia's sound lacks for nothing. Come for the virtuoso display, stay for the rewarding hijinks of the whole production."
Fanfare 13:378-79 Mr/Ap '90. Stephen Ellis (950w)

Kronos String Quartet

3158. Contemporary Works for String Quartet. Sculthorpe: String Quartet 8. **Sallinen:** String Quartet 3. **Glass:** Company. **Nancarrow:** String Quartet. **Hendrix:** Purple Haze.
ELEKTRA 79111 DDD

★*Awards: Gramophone* Critics' Choice (David Fanning), 1987.

"Let me tell you, this is the kind of album that renews your faith in the human race. Intelligence! Taste! Dedication! Growth! They actually exist! Wow!"
Opus 3:39-40 Ap '87 Andrew Stiller (1300w) (rev. of LP)

"Recordings of contemporary music aren't supposed to be as much fun as this."
Ovation 8:45 My '87 David Patrick Stearns (600w)

"J.D [John Ditsky] and S.W.E [Stephen W. Ellis] doubly reviewed this album in *Fanfare* 10:1, and its variety is such as to send reviewers scurrying off in an amusing number of opposing directions....I find the sound on the CD much richer, more transparent, and more conducive to detail than on the SD."
Fanfare 10:273 Mr/Ap '87 Kyle Gann (275w)

"What may attract Corner readers most is one of the Quartet's famous showstopping encores: Steve Rifkin's arrangement of 'Purple Haze.'

More than anything they have recorded to date this encapsulates the KSQ approach and attitude. There's a whole album in this idea: great rock solos for string quartet."

Fanfare 11:348 Jl/Ag '88. Jurgen Gothe (425w)

Gramophone 65:198 Jl '87 David J. Fanning (280w) (rev. of LP)

—

3159. White Man Sleeps. K. Volans: White Man Sleeps, No's. 1 and 5. **Ives:** A Set of Three Short Pieces—No. 2, Scherzo, Holding Your Own. **J. Hassell:** Pano da Costa. **Lee:** Morango...Almost a Tango. **O. Coleman (arr. Graves 1984):** Lonely Woman. **B. Johnston:** Amazing Grace. **Bartok:** String Quartet No. 3.
Kronos String Quartet.
ELEKTRA 79163 DDD 66:08

> ★*Awards:* *Gramophone* Critics' Choice (David Fanning), 1987; Third Place Mumm Champagne Classical Music Award 1988—Presented by *Ovation*, *Ovation* N '88.

"Another exciting program from our leading avant-garde quartet....Good if cool sonics make this well worth hearing."

Fanfare 11:290 N/D '87. Edward Strickland (235w)

One of 20 classical CDs reviewed and recommended as "outstanding for their musical interest and their performance as well as for their technical quality."

Stereo Review Presents: Compact Disc Buyer's Guide 1988 p.43. William Livingstone and Christie Barter (125w)

"Its burden of premieres alone would make this an extraordinarily noteworthy recording, but there's a topper: Every piece receives a performance so note-perfect (I have the scores before me), trenchant, and insightful that the composers must want to run up and give the quartet a big kiss. Such emotions will, however, be tempered by the ensemble's highhanded programming practices....At worst, though, all this comes under the heading 'trivial annoyances,'-....You will not find a better new disc or tape anywhere this week, this month, this year, this decade."

Opus 4:43-4 F '88. Andrew Stiller (1480w)

"Generally speaking, most of the music performed here gets an inordinate amount of temporal mileage...out of a remarkably scanty quantity of impoverished musical material-....these four remarkably proficient musicians perform everything with extraordinary musical expressivity and almost superhuman virtuosity."

High Fidelity 38:78 Ap '88. Paul Moor (315w)

"By combining newly commissioned works, arrangements of jazz and rock tunes, and an occasional backward glance at 20th-century classicism, the Kronos builds diversified programs that blur the boundaries between 'vernacular' and 'cultivated' musics....Considering how substantial the repertory is on *White Man Sleeps*-...it is ironic that no program notes are provided."

Musical America 108:63 My '88. K. Robert Schwarz (480w)

American Record Guide 51:77-8 Jl/Ag '88. David W. Moore (350w) (rev. of LP)

Gramophone 65:771-2 N '87 David J. Fanning (425w) (rev. of LP)

Hi-Fi News & Record Review 33:107 F '88. Max Harrison (330w) (rev. of LP)

London Brass

3160. Modern Times with London Brass.
Tippett: Praeludium for Brass, Bells and Percussion. **Takemitsu:** Garden Rain. **Xenakis:** Eonta for Piano and Brass. **Britten:** Fanfare for St. Edmundsbury. **Crosse:** Peace for Brass, Opus 53. **Rouders:** Break Dance for Piano and Brass. **Ruggles:** Angels. **Lutoslawski:** Variations on a Theme of Paganini.
London Brass.
TELDEC 46442 DDD 58:14

> ★*Awards:* Critic's Choice: 1991, *American Record Guide*, Ja/F '92 (Barry Kilpatrick).

"As the successor to the now-defunct Philip Jones Brass Ensemble, London Brass is populated by some of the finest brass players in the world. All of the works are marvellous....The final selection...[is] one of the most stunning brass ensemble performances I have ever heard. It alone is worth the price of the disc."

American Record Guide 54:152-3 Jl/Ag '91. Barry Kilpatrick (385w)

"One of the few collections of brass music that can claim equal rank with any chamber or orchestral collection. For once, we have a brass ensemble that in no way condescends to its audience....The London Brass matches any American group for chops and for sound engineering. At the same time, they have put together a program that is adventurous, varied, and showmanlike....The notes are readable and informative. An important disc."

Fanfare 15:439-40 S/O '91. Scott Wheeler (long)

Los Angeles Guitar Quartet

3161. Guitar Music. De Falla: El amor brujo (arr. Kanengiser, Krouse, Tennant). **Sciammarella:** Interlude for Love. **Copland:** *Rodeo:* Corral Nocturne (arr. Kanengiser); Hoe-Down (arr. Nestor). **Brouwer:** Cuban Landscape with Rain. **Krouse:** Antique Suite after Neusiedler.
Los Angeles Guitar Quartet.
GHA 126 001 DDD 53:26

> ★*Awards:* Records to Die for: 1 of 5 Recommended Recordings, *Stereophile* Ja '91 (Igor Kipnis).

"Such fabulous playing by these four guitarists, passionately intense, often darkly atmospheric, and above all rhythmically vital, as heard here has enabled me to enjoy to the fullest both the music and the splendid ensemble, nowhere more so than in the de Falla. In contrast to most record companies' predilections for tunnel acoustics through distant miking, this showcase standout is quite dry, intimately but not oppressively close-up, and well separated."

Stereophile 14:151 Ja '91. Igor Kipnis (b.n.)

"The recording is quite vivid and realistic, with a minimum of extraneous noise. This new Belgian label, apparently devoted to the guitar, does good work."

Fanfare 12:406-7 My/Je '89. Leslie Gerber (400w)

Muntian, Mikhail. Schubert, Schumann, Bruch, Enesco. See No. 3151.

Parley of Instruments

3162. Purcell's London. Keller: Sonata No. 1. **Matteis:** Divisions on a Ground in D minor. **Baltzar:** Pavan and Galliard in C. **Blow:** Chaconne a 4 in G. **Eccles: Symphony for Mercury from "The Judgement of Paris." Anon.:** Sonata in D "con certino." **Croft:** The Twin Rivals—Suite. **Purcell:** Cibell in C, Z.678.
Roy Goodman (dir); Peter Holman (dir). Parley of Instruments.
HYPERION 66108 DDD 50:56

> ★*Awards:* Critics' Choice 1988, *Gramophone* D '88 (Julie Anne Sadie).

"All of the recorded music is delightful, although the one tiny contribution of Henry himself strikes me as the very best item: his *Cibell in C* for trumpet and strings, beautifully played by Crispian Steele-Perkins, with strings and chamber-organ continuo."

Hi-Fi News & Record Review 33:115 D '88. Stephen Daw (175w)

"A treat, in part because of the convincing presentation of varied timbres by Hyperion....I especially enjoyed the Eccles piece, but found the anthology consistently appealing for its verve and diversity."

Fanfare 12:238 Ja/F '89. Edward Strickland (75w)

"The performances are spirited but elegant, with a tangy quality that will appeal to those fond of period-instrument sound and that might even convert those who are not. The engineering is impeccable, and the annotations are exemplary."

American Record Guide 52:111 Mr/Ap '89. John W. Barker (325w)

Gramophone 66:790 N '88. Julie Ann Sadie (240w)

Sluchin, Benny

3163. The Contemporary Trombone. Dutilleux: Choral, Cadence, et Fugato, for Trombone and Piano. **Leibowitz:** Four Bagatelles for Trombone and Piano, Opus 61. **Scelsi:** Three Pieces for Trombone. **Berio:** Sequenza V, for Trombone. **Denisov:** Choral Varie for Trombone and Piano. **Anderson:** Sound the Tucket Sonance and the Note to Mount, for Trombone and Tape. **Xenakis:** Keren, for Solo Trombone. **Dusapin:** Indeed, for Solo Trombone.
Benny Sluchin (trb); Pierre-Laurent Aimard (pno).
ADDA 581 087 DDD 60:25

> ★*Awards:* Critic's Choice: 1990, *American Record Guide* Ja/F '91 (Barry Kilpatrick).

"Recommended to all trombone partisans."

Fanfare 13:478 N/D '89. John Ditsky (175w)

"I highly recommend this recording to trombonists and listeners interested in contemporary music. It is a major contribution to the genre."

American Record Guide 53:125 Ja/F '90. Barry Kilpatrick (235w)

Starobin, David

3164. New Music with Guitar: Selected Works from Volumes 1, 2 and 3. Carter: Changes. **Sondheim:** Sunday Song Set. **Babbitt:** Composition for Guitar. **Takemitsu:** Toward the Sea. **J. A. Lennon:** Another's Fandango. **Kolb:** Three Lullabies. **Bland:** A Fantasy-Homage to Victoria. **Henze:** Carillon, Recitatif, Masque.
David Starobin (gtr); Susan Jolles (harp); Patrick Mason (bar); Susan Palma (a fl); Peter Press (mndln). 1980-85 reissues.
BRIDGE 9009 AAD 69:27

> ★*Awards:* Top Choices—1989, *American Record Guide* Ja/F '90 (William Ellis).

"The recording is superb, resonant and live enough to clearly hear the whisk of his fingers across the fingerboard. It's a pleasure to have Starobin's playing on CD, and perhaps only guitarists would want to pass this up for the fuller repertoire on the original vinyl."

Fanfare 12:398 My/Je '89. Kyle Gann (400w)

"For anyone interested in where the guitar has been and the directions it will likely take, this record is essential listening....If you own only ten guitar records, make this one of them."

American Record Guide 52:126-27 S/O '89. William Ellis (380w)

"Starobin backs up his dedication to contemporary music with superb technique, careful attention to detail and a catholic sense of esthetics that brings each to vivid life."

Ovation 10:72 Ap '89. Karen Campbell (290w)

Digital Audio's CD Review 5:58+ Jl '89. Tom Vernier (200w)

Instrumental Music

ALBENIZ, ISAAC

4001. Iberia (suite for piano, 4 books); Navarra (completed by Deodat de Severac); Suite Espanola.
Alicia De Larrocha (pno). Cambridge University Music School.
LONDON/DECCA 417 887 DDD 126:00 2 discs

✔**HC** ★*Awards:* Critics' Choice 1988, *Gramophone* D '88 (Joan Chissell).

"If her performance, both in the concert hall and on these records, is so deeply satisfying it is partly because of its naturalness....it is hard to imagine this record being superseded."
Hi-Fi News & Record Review 33:99 O '88. (280w)

"It would be difficult, if not impossible, to imagine any of this music brought to life more compellingly by either the performer or the recording team....The annotation, worthy of the occasion, is by Lionel Salter, who, as always, is not merely informative but illuminating."
Stereo Review 53:133 N '88. Richard Freed (350w)

"I'd suggest that this will remain the best *Iberia* for quite some time—it utterly wipes out the 'competing' CD set by Ricardo Requejo (*Fanfare* 11:1....this new *Suite espanola* is almost as fast as her 1964 Columbia recording and more complete."
Fanfare 12:111 N/D '88. James Miller (425w)
Gramophone 66:47 Je '88. Joan Chissell (330w)

"Whatever the recording, you can't miss with De Larrocha's *Iberia.* Her playing reeks of guitars and castanets and rich red blood. The generous fillers on this two-disc set are equally compelling performances."
High Fidelity 38:61 D '88. Terry Teachout (125w)

"It would be hard to imagine any of this music brought to life more compellingly, by either the performer or the recording team."
Stereo Review Presents: Compact Disc Buyer's Guide 1989 pp:60 Richard Freed (105w)

"It is difficult to imagine this music played with greater authority."
American Record Guide 52:13 Ja/F '89. Donald Manildi (165w)

"It is, simply, a superb album."
Stereophile 12:149-51 F '89. Igor Kipnis (130w)

"Poetry and deep consideration characterize the performance as a whole, whereas the pianist's 1960 set...is notable for its impulsive abandon and greater sweep. In any case, the new set will certainly not disappoint."
Musical America 109:50 Mr '89. Christopher Rothko (230w)

"Musically and sonically, this is one of the most outstanding recordings of piano on CD."
Audio 73:111-12 Jl '89. Bert Whyte (425w)

"It goes without saying that her performances are authoritative. If some tempos are a trifle faster than one is accustomed to in the familiar pieces—'Sevilla', for example—the general effect is entrancing. The colour, vitality and articulateness of this playing project the music for all, or more, than it is worth."
The Musical Times 129:537 O '88. Cyril Ehrlich (375w)

"Miss De Larrocha's recorded history with this music represents less a curve of growth than a process of small refinements made to already fixed ideas....What sets the newest recording apart is its technology....One celebrates her strong voice but at the same time mourns the lack of other strong ones—musicians like Mr. Arrau who might tell the listener, 'How beautifully she plays, but I read Albeniz's intentions much differently'."
The New York Times O 16 '88, p. H31-40. Bernard Holland (1410w)

ALBRIGHT, WILLIAM HUGH

4002. Organbook I; Organbook III.
David Craighead (orgn).
GOTHIC 58627 47:00

★★*Awards:* The Want List 1989, *Fanfare* N/D '89 (Haig Mardirosian); Top Choices—1989, *American Record Guide* Ja/F '90 (David Mulbury).

"In sum, Albright's books are wonderfully inventive, widely accessible, brilliantly played, and celebrate a spirit of eager creativity as merged with substantial technique too often missing in today's newly written music. Here is a celebration of the highest magnitude, and a recording which, if justice prevails, should become a modern classic."
Fanfare 12:111-2 N/D '88. Haig Mardirosian (540w)

"This exceptional new release should occupy a special niche in the collection of every lover of organ music....Albright's own notes and the clear, completely realistic recording are additional bonuses for the purchaser of this CD. Bravo, bravissima!"

American Record Guide 52:11 My/Je '89. David G. Mulbury (320w)

BABBITT, MILTON

4003. Piano Music: Three Compositions; Duet; Semi-Simple Variations; Partitions; Post-Partitions; Tableaux; Reflections, for Piano and Synthesizer; Canonical Form; Lagniappe.
Robert Taub (pno).
HARMONIA MUNDI 905160 55:47

✔**HC** ★*Awards: Gramophone* Critics' Choice 1986 (Arnold Whittal).

"Although a number of pianists have tackled the complex and beautifully ordered music of the American composer and pedagogue Milton Babbitt, few have come away from the thicket of notes with characterizations that suggest much beyond the strain of performing those mathematically complex intervallic manipulations. Thus it comes as a distinct delight to hear Robert Taub careening through Babbitt's mazes with the same ease that one finds in the average young string quartet dispatching its Schoenberg."

Ovation 7:36 D '86 Nancy Malitz (345w)

"I raved about the SD version of this release in *Fanfare* 9:6 and included it on my 1986 Want List, and all I can add is that I've come to enjoy Babbitt's sparkling, unpredictable textures more with each listening."

Fanfare 10:52-53 Ja/F '87 Kyle Gann (200w)

"One cannot improve the original rating, but this [performance on CD] is even *more* enjoyable."

Hi-Fi News & Record Review 32:95 Ja '87 Benedict Sarnaker (45w)

"Though restricted to a single instrument...Robert Taub's program confirms a variety of invention, fantasy, and style that you might not suspect from the 'Northeastern-academic-establishment complexity' label, or even from hearing a single work in isolation. What's more, you quickly realize there is no other music quite like this...There's no point in concealing the fact that Babbitt believes in a highly and densely ordered music, asking of the listener considerable aural agility, precision, and recall-....If you enjoy having your perceptions stretched and challenged, then it will be worth your while to explore this music....Taub's program covers the whole chronological range of Babbitt's mature music."

Opus 2:28-30 O '86 David Hamilton (3480w)

"One imagines that this is the kind of thing that goes on inside a computer: bright electrical movement mostly meaningless to the outside world. One can tell from the generally sensitive, frequently delicate sounds Taub makes that he sees much in this music which, with its rapid-fire activity and dynamic changes, is difficult to perform. It is entertaining in its incessant, jerky movements, like the activity of skippers on the surface of the pond."

American Record Guide 49:4 S/O '86 David W. Moore (405w) (rev. of LP)

"Robert Taub plays all these works with exemplary dedication and proficiency."

High Fidelity 38:65 Je '88. Paul Moor (240w)

"Every aspect of the production is first-rate, and the documentation is quite exceptional."

Stereo Review 51:120 Ag '86. Richard Freed (450w)

BACH, JOHANN SEBASTIAN

4004. Art of the Fugue, BWV.1080.
Davitt Moroney (hpscd). reissue.
HARMONIA MUNDI 901169/70 AAD 50:53; 47:48 2 discs

✔**HC** ★★*Awards: Gramophone* Critics' Choice 1986 (Iain Fenlon); *Gramophone* Record Award Winner 1986—Early Music Award (Baroque).

"Both [Leonhardt and Moroney] are indispensable, period....The unparalleled meditative profundity of the Leonhardt recording is matched by Moroney's highly dramatic reading. I never hope to hear a more cogent account of Contrapunctus 11, the emotional and real-time centerpiece of this recording, while the canons, treated by Moroney as appendices under the influence of Gregory Butler's scholarship (see review in *Fanfare* 9:3), are more highly characterized here than anywhere else."

Fanfare 11:99-100 Jl/Ag '88. Edward Strickland (425w)

Originally reviewed in March '86, p.97. "The CD opens up the range, seems to bring the instrument in closer, and certainly firms up the image."

Hi-Fi News & Record Review 31:111 My '86. Roger Bowen (60w)

Gramophone 64:550 O '86 Nicholas Anderson (200w)

Chaconne (from the Violin Partita No. 2, BWV.1004 (arr. Piano O'Riley). See No. 4062.

4005. English Suites (6) for Harpsichord, BWV.806/11.
Andras Schiff (pno). Cambridge University UK. January 1988.
LONDON/DECCA 421 640 DDD 129:00 2 discs

✔**HC** ★*Awards:* Top Disks of the Year, *The New York Times* D 24, '89 (John Rockwell).

"If you skip this performance because you are an authenticist (or, for that matter, an ultra-Romantic), you have only robbed yourself....This recording is an absolute pianistic joy from be-

ginning to end....sound...is of good quality and does not detract materially from enjoyment."
Stereophile 12:170-71 Ag '89. Les Berkley (400w)

"Perhaps the most beautiful aspect of Schiff's new recording of the six English Suites is his tone, something harpsichordists do not have to worry about."
Stereo Review 54:87 Ag '89. Stoddard Lincoln (225w)

"Schiff plays with strength, sensitivity, and elan....Sound is warm, clear and alive. A first-class CD in every regard. Buy it!"
HighPerformanceReview 7:1:66-7 '90. June C. Ottenberg (340w)

"The music is presented deftly, flexibly and with poised detachment. Most repeats are observed, and Schiff adds ornamentation, discreet mostly, apt and sometimes skittish....it is the good sense of Schiff's approach, the joyous spring and wit he brings to the music, that wins the day and cannot fail to delight."
The Musical Times 130:355 Je '89. Robert Anderson (310w)

"Schiff doesn't poke out subordinate lines, as Gould sometimes did; nor does he take, virtually for argument's sake, unexpected tempos. I don't think Schiff hits the heights that Gould did, either. But his performances are perfectly satisfying piano versions of works Bach wrote for another instrument....I recommend these discs highly."
Fanfare 12:78 Jl/Ag '89. Michael Ullman (175w)

"Schiff's skill is, subsequently, most apparent in the slower Preludes, Allemandes and, particularly, the Sarabandes....Unfortunately, the faster movements, where there is less opportunity to demonstrate these aristocratic gestures, are slightly less interesting."
Ovation 10:59 Je '89. Philip Kennicott (270w)

Gramophone 66:1031 D '88. John Duarte (250w)

Digital Audio's CD Review 5:60+ Ag '89. Tom Vernier (320w)

4006. French Suites (6) for Harpsichord, BWV.812/7; Suites (2) for Keyboard: in A minor, BWV.818a and in E flat, BWV.819a.
Davitt Moroney (hpscd). Chateau de Creullet, Normandy.
VIRGIN 91201 DDD 144:00 2 discs

★*Awards:* The Gramophone Awards, Nominations, Baroque—non-vocal, *Gramophone*, N '91.

"This is one of the finest and most satisfying recordings of the French Suites on harpsichord available....The recording, made at the Chateau de Creullet in Normandy, is resonant but clear."
Stereo Review 56:79 Jl '91. David Patrick Stearns (300w)

"Moroney clearly enjoys unleashing the power of his John Phillips copy of Ruckers and Taskin instruments....The recording presents the harpsichord with great immediacy. These exciting sounds are best represented by playing back at a modest volume level. Not only does the engineer capture this fine instrument faithfully but the birds—presumably living in the caves (or roof) of Chateau de Creuillet in Normandy—are represented with extraordinary fidelity. This is not a distraction, however: indeed, it is almost an enhancement." *P95/85 S100*
Hi-Fi News & Record Review 36:79 My '91. Antony Hodgson (455w)

"His performances...are special, emphasizing the French character of these works with a constant variety of ornamentation and rhythmic detail."
Continuo 15:23-5 Ag '91. Scott Paterson (140w)

"Moroney is truly at home in the French style, and that is evident here in Bach's most inviting and least didactic works for harpsichord....Occasionally Moroney chooses a tempo with which I would disagree...but usually he is right on, sounding particularly comfortable with the more stately dances....The recording is close and clear. Warmly recommended."
Fanfare 14:100 Jl/Ag '91. Tom Moore (150w)

"Moroney focuses attention on the two 'extra' suites by placing them first on the recording and by discussing them in some detail in his notes. Unfortunately, his performance of these works is not totally convincing....In general, the performance of the six traditional French Suites is better....The recorded sound is acceptable."
American Record Guide 54:22 Jl/Ag '91. Randolph Currie (420w)

Digital Audio's CD Review 7:50+ Ag '91. Tom Vernier (265w)

Gramophone 68:1862+ Ap '91. Nicholas Anderson (700w)

4007. Goldberg Variations for Harpsichord, BWV.988; Keyboard Music: Chromatic Fantasy and Fugue in D minor, Harpsichord, BWV.903; Inventions: No. 2 in C minor, BWV.773; No. 6 in E, BWV.777; No. 8 in F, BWV.779; Sinfonias: No. 2 in C minor, BWV.788; No. 6 in E, BWV.792; No. 15 in B minor, BWV.801.
Claudio Arrau (pno). 1942, 1945.
RCA 7841 ADD (m) 99:36 2 discs

✔HC ★*Awards:* The Want List 1989, *Fanfare* N/D '89 (Mortimer H. Frank).

"It is a wonderfully bold and exciting performance—highly recommended listening."
Ovation 10:59 Ap '89. Stuart Isacoff (650w)

"None of Arrau's Bach has hitherto been issued commercially so the above, playing for almost 100 minutes, is a pleasant surprise. His approach to most music is fundamentally polyphonic and that attitude here finds its most acute application, Bach's contrapuntal resource and logic being displayed to the greatest possible effect."

Music and Musicians International 37:60+ Ag '89. Martyn Harry (630w)

"If the Aria is rather deliberate, its possibilities as it were 'examined' *in situ*, then the Variations themselves, played without pedal, convey a wide emotional range. One or two of the slow ones do sound contrived on this instrument, although in general Arrau's is—it almost goes without saying—a much more straightforward, cogent account than either of Glenn Gould's....The *Chromatic Fantasy* demands virtuosity, but Arrau's playing is not showy for its own sake."

Hi-Fi News & Record Review 34:101 Ap '89. Christopher Breunig (245w)

"This is not another digital reissue by RCA of Blasts from the Past but correctly labeled a Premiere Recording—although it dates from 1942 (*Goldbergs*) and 1945 (rest)....The surprising thing is how contemporary these accounts sound—relative to the more legato and pedal-ridden accounts of the era. The sound, however, is distinctly uncontemporary."

Fanfare 12:105-6 My/Je '89. Edward Strickland (200w)

"What one hears here...is remarkably objective playing, even at times just a little brusque, with not the slightest hint of sentimentality-....Perhaps most impressive is the humanity that Arrau brings to the composer in these, his only recorded examples of Bach. And, as they emerge here, it is always Bach who appears to be speaking, rather than the interpreter....The high-level, not very colorful monophonic sound reveals very little surface noise, presumably through steep filtering, but at times there is some underlying rumble, as well as slight flutter."

Stereophile 12:161-62 Jl '89. Igor Kipnis (825w)

"His recording deserves to be regarded with respect, even awe, and to be placed alongside such other towering piano versions as Schiff's-...Peter Serkin's second version, for Pro Arte-...and both by Gould...The Inventions, Sinfonias, and the *Chromatic Fantasia and Fugue* are similarly well played and well preserved."

Musical America 110:90-2 Mr '90. Harris Goldsmith (405w)

"Arrau often sounds cumbersome and inhibited-...He even tends to plod...There are compensations, of course, for a great pianist inevitably brings insights to a masterpiece."

The Musical Times 131:37 Ja '90. Cyril Ehrlich (155w)

The New York Times Je 25 '89, p. 27. John Rockwell (b.n.)

Gramophone 67:244 Jl '89. Lionel Salter (360w)

4008. Goldberg Variations for Harpsichord, BWV.988.

Kenneth Gilbert (hpscd). reissue.
HARMONIA MUNDI 901240 DDD 66:46

★*Awards: Hi-Fi News & Record Review Record of the Month, O '87.*

"In Gilbert's hands each variation sparkles with its own strongly drawn character....All is vividly captured with great presence and immediacy. The bright voice of the instrument, though closely miked, never takes on an unpleasant edge, and its limited dynamic capabilities are handled to the maximum effect....This issue must be recommended not only for a structural integrity rarely experienced in other performances of this work, but also for the quality of its recording."

Stereophile 10:151 D '87. Barbara Jahn (390w)

"Singled out in vinyl as 'Record of the Month' for October, the CD transfer gives the Bedard harpsichord an even more bejeweled sound."

Hi-Fi News & Record Review 33:97 Ja '88. Roger Bowen (165w)

"If Gilbert does not displace his prime competitors, Gustav Leonhardt and Trevor Pinnock, he certainly stands firmly beside them. Gilbert steers something of a middle course between Pinnock's athletic flamboyance and Leonhardt's rather cold but highly intense account....it's Leonhardt for depth, Pinnock for excitement, and Gilbert for a relaxed and natural path between the two."

Musical America 108:58 Mr '88. Christopher Rothko (360w)

"I would rank this almost with Leonhardt among harpsichord (and CD) versions and strongly recommend it as a lively supplement to that account."

Fanfare 11:137-8 S/O '87. Edward Strickland (150w)

"Having been bowled over by Kenneth Gilbert's set of the '48'...I looked forward keenly to his reading of the *Goldberg Variations*...and I was not disappointed."

Hi-Fi News & Record Review 32:109 O '87 Roger Bowen (350w) (rev. of LP)

Stereo Review 52:127 O '87. Stoddard Lincoln (165w)

Gramophone 65:72+ Je '87 Nicholas Anderson (500w)

4009. Goldberg Variations for Harpsichord, BWV.988.

Glenn Gould (pno). 1955.
CBS 38479 ADD (m) 38:25

"This magnetic performance is without question one of the great recordings of this century-....An essential recording."

High Fidelity 38:56 Ja '88. Terry Teachout (75w)

"Whatever his material or medium, Gould can only be compared with Gould, and the contrasts with his 1981 digital remake of the Goldbergs (CBS 37779) are considerable...if forced to decide between the two, I would opt for the irrepressible exuberance of the earlier recording."

American Record Guide 51:9-10 My/Je '88. Arved Ashby (515w)

"The wonderful 1955 record, surely a watershed in our perception of keyboard Bach, is appropriately fit for any insomniac, and has long been selected by desert island maroons."

The Musical Times 131:37 Ja '90. Cyril Ehrlich (155w)

"This is about the 10th incarnation of Gould's debut recording to appear in the United States and its first appearance on CD....the digital remastering has not been able to eliminate tape-hiss, which is audible in the more ruminative variations. Nonetheless, this is how I'll be hearing this classic performance from now on."

Fanfare 11:76-7 Ja/F '88. Edward Strickland (180w)

The New York Times Je 25 '89, p. 27. John Rockwell (b.n.)

4010. Goldberg Variations for Harpsichord, BWV.988; Keyboard Music: Italian Concerto in F for Harpsichord, BWV.971; Chromatic Fantasy and Fugue in D minor, Harpsichord, BWV.903.

Wanda Landowska (hpscd). 1933-36.
EMI 61008 71:52

✔HC ★*Awards:* Critics' Choice 1988, *Gramophone* D '88 (Stephen Plaistow).

"Her recordings are items to beg, borrow or steal for."

Ovation 9:43 N '88. Joseph Fennimore (225w)

"Landowska's first (1933) recording of Bach's *Goldberg Variations* justifies the most extravagant words of praise."

Hi-Fi News & Record Review 33:104-5 My '88. Robert Cowan (215w)

Gramophone 65:1618 My '88. Stephen Plaistow (675w)

The New York Times Je 25 '89, p. 27. John Rockwell (b.n.)

4011. Goldberg Variations for Harpsichord, BWV.988.

Gustav Leonhardt (hpscd).
PRO ARTE 010 ADD 47:06

"Though some prefer Leonhardt's Telefunken account, and others Pinnock on Archiv or Tureck on CBS, this remains my choice as the requisite harpsichord supplement to the two Gould accounts. The instrument sounds even more pristine and bell-like in its upper register than originally."

Fanfare 9:108 N/D '85. Edward Strickland (50w)

Digital Audio 2:62-3 N '85. Tom Vernier (725w)

High Fidelity 36:64 My '86. Irving Kolodin (130w)

4012. Lute Music: Suite in E minor, BWV.996; Partita (Suite) in C minor, BWV.997; **Trio Sonatas for Organ:** BWV.525 and 529.

Bream (lute/gtr) Julian; George Malcolm (hpscd). 1965.
RCA 5841; RCA 9654 63:00+

✔HC ★*Awards:* *Gramophone* Critics' Choice 1986 (John Duarte).

"All of this music has been arranged by Bream for guitar and lute. The results are polished, smooth, entirely ingratiating. In other words, typical Bream."

Fanfare 10:58-59 Ja/F '87 Vincent Alfano (150w)

"Smoldering readings of the Lute Suites."

Stereo Review 51:129 D '86 Stoddard Lincoln (90w)

Gramophone 64:66 Je '86. John Duarte (175w)

4013. Organ Music: Preludes and Fugues: BWV.544, 548; Chorale Settings: BWV.653, 654, 658, 662, 663, 664.

Marie-Claire Alain (orgn). Schnitger Ahrend Organ at St. Martin's, Groningen, Holland.
ERATO 88174 DDD

✔HC ★★*Awards:* *Fanfare* Want List 1987 (Haig Mardirosian).

"The marriage of fine organ, generous acoustic and the noble-spirited performance here recorded, marks a high point in this long series of Bach recordings for Erato by Madame Alain. If you are not yet happy with any recording of these works, you would do well to search this one out and judge my enthusiasm for yourself."

Organists' Review 72:250 Jl '87. Gavin Barrett (270w)

"A very worthwhile CD, and a good example of this international artist at her best."

Hi-Fi News & Record Review 31:105-7 D '86 Stephen Daw (135w)

"This is the finest record of Bach organ works to have come my way in some time."

Ovation 8:38 Je '87 Scott Cantrell (320w)

Gramophone 64:728+ N '86 Gordon Reynolds (180w)0:52 Jl/Ag '87 Haig Mardirosian (55w)

4014. Organ Music: Fugue in B Minor for Organ, S.579; Concerti for Organ: BWV.594, 595, 596.

Daniel Chorzempa (orgn). Arlesheim.
PHILIPS 412 116 DDD 51:25

✔HC ★*Awards:* *Gramophone* Critics' Choice 1984 (Gordon Reynolds).

"The unique sound of this instrument is real music to the ear, and the playing is consistently stylish, if perhaps a shade heavy in terms of registration and accenting."

Hi-Fi News & Record Review 29:137 D '84. Trevor Attwell (140w)

"One fault I do find with this release is in the matter of indexing....That gripe aside, this is an enjoyable disc and easily recommended."

Fanfare 8:167-8 Mr/Ap '85. Nils Anderson (350w)

Gramophone 62:775 D '84. Gordon Reynolds (40w)

Ovation 6:29 O '85. Scott Cantrell (315w)

Digital Audio 1:63-4 Jl '85. Jerry Schwartz (500w)

4015. Organ Music: Passacaglia and Fugue in C minor, BWV.582; Preludes and Fugues, BWV. 532, 543, 552; Toccata and Fugue, BWV.565.
Daniel Chorzempa (orgn).
PHILIPS 422 965

✔HC

4016. Organ Music: Preludes and Fugues: BWV.533; BWV.546. Orgelbuchlein: O Lamm Gottes, unschuldig, BWV.618; Christe, du Lamm Gottes, BWV.619 (both versions); Wir danken dir, Herr Jesu Christ, BWV.623; Hilf, Gott, das mir's gelinge, BWV.624; Christ lag in Todesbanden, BWV.625; Jesu Christus, unser Heiland, BWV.626; Ertsanden ist der heil'ge Christ, BWV.628 (both versions). Liebster Jesu, wir sind hier. **BUXTEHUDE, DIETRICH. Organ Music:** Praeludium in A minor, BuxWV.153; Herr Christ, der einig Gottes Sohn—chorale prelude, BuxWV.192; Wie schon leuchtet der Morgenstern—chorale fantasia, BuxWV.223; Passacaglia in D minor, BuxWV.161.
Piet Kee (orgn). St. Lauren's Church organ, Alkmaar, The Netherlands. November 1988.
CHANDOS 0501 DDD 61:00

✔HC ★*Awards:* Cream of the Crop IV, *Digital Audio's CD Review*, 6:41 Je '90.

"I cannot recommend these programmes [Chandos 0501 and 0506] too highly—they are perfectly recorded and come with specifications and full details of registration. But which to choose? Well, you really need both!"

Organists' Review 75:273 D '89. Paul Hale (225w)

"Older LP collectors remember well the landmark Helmut Walcha Bach series on DG Archiv recorded at the Alkmaar Schnitger organ....Piet Kee's revisit to the Schnitger (that is, Franz Caspar, not Arp) reveals a startling difference in sonority. Walcha's discs were cut in the days after the 1949 rebuild by Dirk Flentrop. The Flentrop firm went back for a far more historic restoration in 1981....The instrumental tone, as judged by this CD, is richer, darker, and far fuller in the pedal line (although one can also assume that the lows are a result of the improved reproduction over thirty years)."

Fanfare 13:167-68 N/D '89. Haig Mardirosian (160w)

"I have always held Mr. Kee in high esteem, but most of his Alkmaar registrations are disappointing. There is an oppressive heaviness in so many of the combinations, caused by the organist's disinclination to leave off the 16' manual Prestant, a stop which comes through on this recording with exasperating thickness and prominence."

American Record Guide 53:42-3 S/O '90. David G. Mulbury (240w)

Gramophone 67:339-40 Ag '89. Marc Rochester (315w)

Digital Audio's CD Review 6:98 O '89. David Vernier (100w)

4017. Organ Music: Toccata and Fugue in D minor, BWV.538 ("Dorian"); Partita on Sei gegrusset, Jesu gutig, BWV 768; Fantasia in G, BWV.572; Trio Sonata No. 6 in G, BWV.530; Vater unser in Himmelreich, BWV.682; Jesus Christus, unser Heiland, BWV.688; Prelude and Fugue in A minor, BWV.543.
Ton Koopman (orgn). 1727 Christian Muller organ, Grote Kerk, Leeuwarden.
NOVALIS 150 036 DDD 70:07

✔HC ★*Awards:* Top Disks of the Year, *The New York Times* D 24, '89 (John Rockwell).

"Another fine sample of this great player's passionate drive and of his passionate search for authenticity. He gives best value in the *Partita*, where many contrasts of tone quality and speed lead him to ways of gentleness."

Organists' Review 75:202 S '89. Gordon Reynolds (110w)

"The whole disc is executed in a vigorous, robust and *detache* style which suits the nature of the music well and aids clarity in this spacious church." *P95 S95*

Hi-Fi News & Record Review 34:112 N '89. William McVicker (420w)

"The performances...are energetic and demanding of the listener....The abstract works carry some degree of recommendation, and the chorales, a warning."

Fanfare 12:79 Jl/Ag '89. Haig Mardirosian (200w)

Gramophone 67:345-46 Ag '89. Marc Rochester (125w)

4018. Partitas: No. 1 in B flat for Harpsichord, BWV.825; No. 2 in C minor for Harpsichord, BWV.826; No. 6 in E minor, BWV.830.
(Bach & Tureck at Home).
Rosalyn Tureck (pno). 1989.
ALBANY 008 ADD 74:15

✔HC ★*Awards:* Critic's Choice: 1990, *American Record Guide* Ja/F '91 (Mark Koldys).

"Put simply, this is as fine a set of piano performances of these three partitas as you are likely to hear....A record reviewer runs out of ways to praise exalted interpretations, so I will not try. This is one."

American Record Guide 53:16+ My/Je '90. Mark Koldys (125w)

"Since Troy intends to release the remaining three partitas, these could well serve as an alternative to Gould's for those who, like myself, object to that pianist's perverse eccentricities and off-key grunting noises. If either option appeals to you, try the harpsichord with Pinnock (Archiv) or Gilbert (Harmonia Mundi)."

Fanfare 13:114-15 Mr/Ap '90. David Claris (500w)

Digital Audio's CD Review 6:60 Jl '90. Tom Vernier (185w)

4019. Partita No. 1 in B minor for Violin Unaccompanied, BWV.1002. BARTOK, BELA. Sonata for Solo Violin. PAGANINI, NICCOLO. Introduction and Variations on Paisiello's "Nel cor piu non mi sento" from Paisiello's *La Molinara*, for Solo Violin.
Viktoria Mullova (vln). 1987.
PHILIPS 420 948 DDD 66:00

★★*Awards:* Editors' Choice, *Digital Audio's CD Review*, Je '89; Critics' Choice 1988, *Gramophone* D '88 (Michael Oliver). Cream of the Crop IV, *Digital Audio's CD Review*, 6:41 Je '90.

"The recording captures what sounds like the full range of Ms Mullova's tone, garnished with just a suggestion of ambience. A marvellous CD."

Hi-Fi News & Record Review 33:121 N '88. Robert Cowan (245w)

"Her Bach, taken on its own terms, is a convincing interpretive document...Even more impressive is Bartok's Solo Sonata, filled with improvisatory abandon, sharply chiseled, searing in its intensity."

The New York Times S 24 '89, p. H 27. K. Robert Schwarz (160w)

"Mullova seems most at home in the Paganini, where she shows a playfulness that's rather engaging. But it's too little, too late."

Stereo Review 54:92 Ap '89. David Patrick Stearns (175w)

Gramophone 66:444 S '88. Michael Oliver (420w)

Digital Audio's CD Review 5:56 Ap '89. David Vernier (375w)

4020. Sonatas (3) and Partitas (3) for Violin Unaccompanied (complete), BWV.1001-6.
Gidon Kremer (vln). October 1981.
PHILIPS 416 651 AAD 2 discs

✔HC ★*Awards:* Records to Die for: 1 of 5 Recommended Recordings, *Stereophile* Ja '91 (Guy Lemcoe).

"Partita No. 2 in a, BWV 1003, is as close as one can get to musical nirvana. I have rarely heard more spirituality in music—it's as if I am bonding to a greater reality....Gidon Kremer brings this music to life. In his hands, the notes sing, dance, reach for the sky."

Stereophile 14:153 Ja '91. Guy Lemcoe (100w)

"Despite occasional moments of beauty...I-...find the interpretation lacking in competitive qualities."

Hi-Fi News & Record Review 32:95 Ja '87 Stephen Daw (135w)

Gramophone 64:901 D '86 John Duarte (175w)

4021. Sonatas (3) and Partitas (3) for Violin Unaccompanied (complete), BWV.1001-6.
Shlomo Mintz (violin).
DEUTSCHE GRAMMOPHON 413 810 142:30 3 discs

★*Awards:* *Gramophone* Critics' Choice 1985 (Roger Fiske).

"Near-flawless playing, flawlessly recorded."

Fanfare 9:116 S/O '85. Harry Townsend (100w)

"It is a daring violinist who essays these ultimate tests of virtuosity and musical understanding....But Mintz plays the part amazingly well, maybe not with quite the savoir faire of the great Nathan Milstein's performance of these same works (DG 2709 047), but with zest, understanding, and a tone if anything richer than that of the older master."

HighPerformanceReview 4(1):136 '86 Thomas H. Wendel (330w) (rev. of LP)

Hi-Fi News & Record Review 30:85 Je '85. Stephen Daw (90w)

Ovation 6:30 D '85. Paul Turok (385w)

Gramophone 63:145 Jl '85. Roger Fiske (350w)

High Fidelity 36:58-9 My '86. Shirley Fleming (300w)

Opus 2:27+ Ag '86. Allan Kozinn (900w)

4022. Sonatas (3) and Partitas (3) for Violin Unaccompanied (complete), BWV.1001-6.
Itzhak Perlman (vln). 1986-87.
EMI 49483 DDD 143:00 2 discs

✔HC ★*Awards:* The Want List 1989, *Fanfare* N/D '89 (David K. Nelson).

"Perlman alternates between a Guarnerius and a Stradivarius, with the warmest sounds coming from the Strad....But the basic, well-recorded sound is Perlman, not a particular instrument....Even those who have grown tired of hearing an unaccompanied violin wend its way across this rugged terrain will listen with renewed awe to Perlamn's rewardingly effortless traversal."

American Record Guide 52:15-16 My/Je '89. Alan Heatherington (975w)

"His pure physical dexterity almost defies belief; his playing here is immaculately clean and precise. It is impossible to avoid *that* word: awesome....The sound quality does Perlman no favors....Not all of the discs' shortcomings lie with the recording job. In a few places, Perlman's speed and facility border on glibness, and changes in dynamics sometimes result only in softer or louder music, without adding expression....Let me add, though, that this

is true only in comparison to the very finest of performances, such as that of Nathan Milstein."
Stereophile 12:191+ O '89. Robert Hesson (550w)

"It is...something of a pity that the engineers and producers responsible for the recording-...have chosen to thrust his playing at us so prominently....However, the sheer effortlessness and musical relish of Perlman's playing rivets our attention on the music itself, and no true enthusiast for this music will want to miss this release."
Hi-Fi News & Record Review 34:93 F '89. Stephen Daw (210w)

"I've listed a few reservations, but Perlman's percentage of success is very high, and the set should satisfy and please any purchaser, even a purchaser who does not foreswear allegiance to other versions. The sound and annotations are quite fine."
Fanfare 12:110-11 My/Je '89. David K. Nelson (780w)

Gramophone 66:1031 D '88. John Duarte (185w)

Digital Audio's CD Review 5:60 Ap '89. Lawrence Johnson (280w)

Sonata in D minor for Solo Violin, BWV.1004: Chaconne (arr. Busoni). See No. 4091.

4023. Suites (6) for Cello Unaccompanied, BWV.1007/12: No.'s 1-3.
Pablo Casals (cello). 1936-8.
EMI 61028

"One can summarize a critical assay of these performances in four words: Casals set the standard. The accounts sound almost incredibly good in these CD rejuvenations."
High Fidelity 39:59 My '89. Paul Moor (140w)

"Anyone with some interest in Baroque performance practice must still be impressed by the level of intuition, practical knowledge, and sheer gutsy conviction that shines through every bar of these performances....Essential listening, I think."
Fanfare 12:124-5 N/D '88. John Wiser (175w)

"How can one review such a disc? Casals, surely, *is* the Bach Suites....Keith Hardwick has done a fine job in transferring these from 78s....This is a wonderful issue."
Stereophile 12:151 F '89. Barbara Jahn (175w)

"These are performances to love....Tape hiss is somewhat higher here than in the 3-LP set of Japanese EMI pressings I had on hand for comparison, but the LP's highs are more seriously clipped and, overall, I prefer the CD sound."
Music Magazine 11:50-2 N/D '88. Rick MacMillan (350w)

"These are compelling performances, but I occasionally find the cut'n'thrust of Casals's attack somewhat overbearing; also, certain phrases are wilfully distended. But in other respects, this playing is very much of our own era...they sound well on CD, albeit with an occasional raw edge."
Hi-Fi News & Record Review 33:89 Ag '88. Robert Cowan (150w)

Gramophone 66:1512 Mr '89. Lionel Salter (320w)

4024. Suites (6) for Cello Unaccompanied, BWV.1007/12: No.'s. 4-6.
Pablo Casals (cello). 1938-9.
EMI 61029 (m)

"One can summarize a critical assay of these performances in four words: Casals set the standard. The accounts sound almost incredibly good in these CD rejuvenations."
High Fidelity 39:59 My '89. Paul Moor (140w)

4025. Toccata and Fugue in D minor for Organ, BWV.565; Prelude and Fugue in F minor, BWV.534; Fantasia and Fugue in G minor for Organ, BWV.542; Toccata, Adagio and Fugue in C for Organ, BWV.564; Trio Sonata No. 1 in E flat, BWV.525.
Helmut Walcha (orgn). 1963-1965 reissue.
DEUTSCHE GRAMMOPHON 419 047 ADD 60:59

"Many listeners, like me, will immediately take ear to the familiar, rectilinear, but virtuoso flash on the wonderful Alkmaar Schnitger. The reward comes with the alive, and brilliant, remastering."
Fanfare 11:77-8 Ja/F '88. Haig Mardirosian (120w)

4026. The Well-tempered Clavier, BWV.846/93.
Davitt Moroney (hpscd). 1988.
HARMONIA MUNDI 901285/8 DDD 272:00 4 discs

✔HC ★*Awards:* Top Choices—1989, *American Record Guide* Ja/F '90 (Stephen Chakwin).

"Moroney's performance is serious and weighty, with deliberate tempos that allow utmost clarity in the parts and shed a radiant light on the astonishing beauties in every nook and cranny of the work....Intellectual control is absolute. Moroney also risks much....Yet the performance remains a *tour de force* of concentration and integrity, and is an altogether worthy commentary on Bach's achievement."
The Musical Times 130:355 Je '89. Robert Anderson (310w)

"Moroney's interpretations occupy a solid middle ground between the austere Bach playing of such artists as Gustav Leonhardt and the strongly characterized readings of Anthony Newman. The result is an uncommonly satisfying WTC....What room there is for disagreement with the playing here (curiously, all in Book 1) comes from an occasional lack of intensity or energy....this newcomer is the most consistently satisfying harpsichord version of these pieces currently available."

American Record Guide 52:13 Jl/Ag '89. Stephen D. Chakwin, Jr. (250w)

"Stick with [your]...current favorite for Book I-...and...turn to [Moroney's]...incomparable Book II as beyond all current competition."

Fanfare 12:116-17 My/Je '89. Richard Taruskin (850w)

"There are a number of competing performances, and there are so many fine harpsichordists playing today that there are certain to be wonderful new recordings. At present, however, I suggest that Davitt Maroney is the one to buy....There is...an annoying level difference between Books 1 and 2. This is sloppy in the extreme, as well as easily avoidable."

Stereophile 13:220+ Ja '90. Les Berkley (225w)

Digital Audio's CD Review 5:52+ Jl '89. David Vernier

Gramophone 66:1606-10 Ap '89. Nicholas Anderson (600w)

4027. The Well-tempered Clavier, BWV.846/93 (Book I).
Andras Schiff (pno).
LONDON/DECCA 414 388 DDD 110:16 2 discs

✔HC ★★★*Awards:* *Stereo Review* Best of the Month, N '86; *Fanfare* Want List 1986 (John D. Wiser). *Gramophone* Critics' Choice (Ivan March), 1987.

"The intelligence and good taste that pervade this recording make it recommendable as a reference piano version of *WtC I* although the more erratic and inspired Gould account is hardly superseded, in fact could never be....But-...[Schiff is an interpreter] of such skill that it is hard to imagine anyone disliking this set."

Fanfare 10:100 N/D '86 Edward Strickland (390w)

"Schiff is at his best in those preludes or fugues requiring elegant, poised phrasing...and graceful melody playing....There is obviously much opportunity for the use of these qualities in the '48' but where Schiff is, to my mind, less happy in his approach is in the dramatic or theatrical numbers."

Hi-Fi News & Record Review 31:105 D '86 Roger Bowen (165w)

"At first, his work is very disappointing...Fortunately, he soon gets matters in hand, and...settles down to extremely distinguished playing."

Ovation 8:32 Mr '87 Paul Turok (305w)

"The preludes are exquisitely played. But the momentum of the fugues is often disrupted by ruminative pauses. In addition, Schiff repeatedly lowers the dynamics of the active voices when a new voice enters."

High Fidelity 37:71-2 O '87. Thomas Hathaway (175w)

Gramophone 64:415 S 86. John Duarte (330w)

4028. The Well-tempered Clavier, BWV.846/93 (Book 2).
Andras Schiff (harpsichord).
LONDON/DECCA 417 236 DDD 144:15

✔HC ★*Awards:* *Opus* Record Award Nominee, 1987.

"This careful, almost reverential, (and it must be said musical) interpretation can easily lead to too comfortable a view of the music."

Hi-Fi News & Record Review 32:91 Je '87 Roger Bowen (210w) (rev. of LP)

Gramophone 64:1295 Mr '87 Lionel Salter (415w)

Fanfare 10:54 Jl/Ag '87 Edward Strickland (275w)

4029. The Well-tempered Clavier, BWV.846/93 (Book 1).
Keith Jarrett (pno).
ECM 835 246; ECM 1362/63 DDD 51:28, 54:11 2 discs

★★*Awards:* The Want List 1988, *Fanfare* N/D '88 (Edward Strickland). Critics' Choice 1988, *Gramophone* D '88 (John Duarte).

"If I were permitted (God forbid) to own only one version of WtC 1, this would be it. I believe it bears repeated listening better than any previous version."

Fanfare 12:94-5 S/O '88. Edward Strickland (775w)

"Das Wohltemperierte Klavier is the musical equivalent of a Cathedral, or Gerard Manley Hopkins' Vision of Nature; a complex, yet diverse unity....in an amazing bravura performance that possibly only a performer of Jarrett's background in jazz could have achieved, that diversity is superbly manifested. Jarrett's familiarity with improvisational freedom allows him an insight into the spirit of Bach's underlying structure rather than its strict notation; a necessary virtuosity which allows him to control seeming spontaneity with a strict fidelity for Bach's expressive intention."

Music and Musicians International 36:48 Jl '88. Colin De Suinn (480w) (rev. of LP)

"I would never give up Gould's interpretations-...This said, I do not think it is too much to argue that Jarrett is much closer to the composer, producing a reading that is far more well-tempered—as the pianist himself says, 'nice and singing.'...I highly recommend this record. If you want more information, I also recommend the *Fanfare* interview [Vol. 12 no.3)."

Stereophile 11:147-8 S '88. Les Berkley (500w)

"The jazz pianist has successfully purged his playing of any jazz mannerisms...Jarrett's recording certainly has its appealing moments-...Unfortunately, there are also many passages that sound rather too plain. Jarrett's basic lack of rhythmic spring makes the G-sharp Minor Fugue impossibly heavy-footed. Soon, you hunger for Sviatoslav Richter, whose *Well-Tem-*

pered Clavier...is probably the most *over*-characterized modern recording, but he at least lets the music have light, shade, joy, and mystery."

Stereo Review 53:132 N '88. David Patrick Stearns (320w)

"Compared to the great keyboard masters who have taken on this towering work, Jarrett inevitably comes off sounding rather bland....Even among jazz musicians, ECM could probably have come up with a more interesting *WTC*."

High Fidelity 39:61 Ja '89. Terry Teachout (250w)

The New York Times F 5 '89, p. 26. John Rockwell (160w)

Fanfare 15:46 S/O '91. Edward Strickland (med)

BARTOK, BELA. Sonata for Solo Violin. See No. 4019.

BAX, ARNOLD

4030. Piano Music: Two Russian Tone Pictures: Nocturne (May Night in the Ukraine); Gopak (National Dance); The Maiden with the Daffodil; The Princess's Rose-Garden; Apple-Blossom-Time; On a May Evening; O Dame Get Up and Bake Your Pies (Variations on a North Country Christmas Carol); Nereid; Sleepy-head; A Romance; Burlesque.
(Volume 3).
Eric Parkin (pno).
CHANDOS 8732 DDD 59:00

✔HC ★*Awards:* Best of the Month, *Hi-Fi News & Record Review*, Jl '90.

"Parkin is fully in command of Bax's rather individual piano writing (he had, by all accounts, an unusual flair for the instrument), and he presents it with admirable skill and affection. His performances supersede the earlier mono Lyrita recordings by Iris Loveridge, and Parkin is of course immeasurably aided by first-rate sound."

American Record Guide 53:25-6 N/D '90. Donald Manildi (175w)

"The finest pieces here...have a scale and often a slumbering power which one would never begin to suspect from their coy titles...Parkin captures their languorous, dreamy mood to limpid perfection, just as, equally, he revels in the 'knockabout' fun of the more robust numbers like *Gopak* and *Burlesque*....A lovely disc." *P100 S95*

Hi-Fi News & Record Review 35:79-80 Jl '90. Andrew Achenbach (250w)

"Even at its most serene, this music is never bland. At the same time...they're nowhere near as deep, challenging, or self-expressive as the sonatas or even such small masterpieces as *Winter Waters* ....As on the first two discs, Parkin plays with a thorough command of the Baxian idiom."

Fanfare 14:166 S/O '90. Peter J. Rabinowitz (400w)

Gramophone 68:245 Jl '90. Michael Kennedy (425w)

BEETHOVEN, LUDWIG VAN

4031. Piano Music: Variations and Fugue in E flat for Piano, Opus 35, "Eroica"; Bagatelles, Opus 126; Bagatelle ("Fur Elise"), K.59; Ecossaises for Piano, K.83.
Alfred Brendel (pno).
PHILIPS 412 227 49:36

"Very highly recommended!"

American Record Guide 49:5 N/D '86 Donald R. Vroon (220w) (rev. of LP)

"*Fur Elise* excepted, this release is highly recommended."

Opus 2:37 Ap '86. Harris Goldsmith (450w)

"I must say Brendel's sensibilities in Beethoven raise some antipathies here."

Hi-Fi News & Record Review 30:90 S '85. Christopher Breunig (110w)

"While disagreeing with much of what he does by way of interpretation, I am aware of a tension and dynamism in his playing, and the forceful projection of his ideas."

Fanfare 9:117 Ja/F '86. Susan Kagan (400w)

Gramophone 63:256 Ag '85. Edward Greenfield (350w)

Piano Music: Variations in G minor on "See the Conquering Hero Comes" from Judas Maccabeus, WoO.45; Variations (7) in E flat on "Bei Mannern, welche Liebe fuhlen" from "Die Zauberflote", WoO.46; Variations (12) in F on "Ein Madchen oder Weibchen" from "Die Zauberflote", Opus 66. See No. 3019.

4032. Sonatas for Piano (complete).
Claude Frank (pno). 1970s reissue.
MUSIC & ARTS 640 ADD 66:16; 57:55; 57:06; 65:47; 56:09; 59:43; 63:04; 73:58; 64:01; 59:12 10 discs

★*Awards: American Record Guide* Overview: Beethoven Piano Sonatas, Jl/Ag '91.

"We all have our favorite versions of certain works...This is why I find it hard to recommend anyone's complete set. But I must say that if you have to choose a complete CD version, I would not hesitate to put this one before what I have heard of those by Ashkenazy, Barenboim, Brendel, or Nat....The remastered sound is excellent, with hardly audible hiss."

Fanfare 14:150-1 Mr/Ap '91. Charles Timbrell (750w)

"Having lived comfortably for 20 years with the LP edition of Frank's Beethoven sonata cycle (RCA Victrola 9000), I am glad to see its return in remastered format and at an attractive price...Franks's set...is one of but two cycles I find myself constantly returning to. The

other is Wilhelm Kempff's early-50s mono survey for DG...The compact but full-bodied recording handily captures the ringing but never ugly piano tone that is one of Frank's trademarks. When this is combined with the high level of musical satisfaction and the value offered, a strong recommendation is automatic."
American Record Guide 54:31 Mr/Ap '91. Donald Manildi (325w)

4033. Sonatas for Piano (complete).
Artur Schnabel (pno). 1930-35.
EMI 63765 ADD (mono) 605:00 8 discs

★*Awards:* The Want List 1991, *Fanfare* N/D '91 (Leslie Gerber; Michael Ullman).

Gramophone 69:125 Jl '91. Richard Osborne (920w)

4034. Sonatas for Piano (complete): No. 1 in F minor, Opus 2, No. 1; No. 22 in F, Opus 54; No. 23 in F minor, Opus 57, "Appassionata". (Also available as a boxed set of 11 CDs, Nimbus 1792.).
Bernard Roberts (pno).
NIMBUS 5050 DDD

★*Awards:* Record of Distinction *Ovation* Jl '89.

"These are performances to satisfy both the exploring novitiate and those who know the literature well."
The New York Times Mr 27 '88, p. H35. Bernard Holland (45w)

"Bernard Roberts turns out to be a provocative and artful pianist whose Beethoven speaks with a voice of refreshing originality-....Roberts' rewarding Beethoven series is made all the more beautiful by Nimbus' extraordinary digital sound."
Ovation 10:54-5 Jl '89. Lawrence B. Johnson (75w)

4035. Sonatas for Piano (complete): No. 2 in A, Opus 2, No. 2; No. 24 in F#, Opus 78; No. 28 in A, Opus 101.
Bernard Roberts (pno).
NIMBUS 5051 DDD 57:52

★*Awards:* Record of Distinction *Ovation* Jl '89.

See Sonatas No.'s 1, 22 and 23 for review excerpts.
—*The New York Times* Mr 27 '88, p. H35. Bernard Holland (45w)
—*Ovation* 10:54-5 Jl '89. Lawrence B. Johnson (75w)
Fanfare 10:64 Jl/Ag '87 Michael Ullman (125w)

4036. Sonatas for Piano (complete): No. 3 in C, Opus 2, No. 3; No. 19 in G minor, Opus 49, No. 1; No. 21 in C, Opus 53, "Waldstein".
Bernard Roberts (pno). 1984.
NIMBUS 5052 DDD 62:28

★*Awards:* Record of Distinction *Ovation* Jl '89.

"Frankly, my liking for this playing goes beyond anything I can explain; Roberts' playing is just plain likable, and I look forward to hearing more of this series."
Fanfare 11:98-9 N/D '87. Leslie Gerber (160w)

See Sonatas No.'s 1, 22 and 23 for review excerpts.
—*Ovation* 10:54-5 Jl '89. Lawrence B. Johnson (75w)
—*The New York Times* Mr 27 '88, p. H35. Bernard Holland (45w)
American Record Guide 51:17-8 Mr/Ap '88. Mark Koldys (115w)
Digital Audio's CD Review 6:82-3 O '89. Tom Vernier (b.n.)

4037. Sonatas for Piano (complete): No. 11 in B flat, Opus 22; No. 20 in G, Opus 49, No. 2; No. 15 in D, Opus 28, "Pastoral".
Bernard Roberts (pno).
NIMBUS 5055 DDD 58:14

★*Awards:* Record of Distinction *Ovation* Jl '89.

"Bernard Roberts turns out to be a provocative and artful pianist whose Beethoven speaks with a voice of refreshing originality-....Roberts' rewarding Beethoven series is made all the more beautiful by Nimbus' extraordinary digital sound."
Ovation 10:54-5 Jl '89. Lawrence B. Johnson (75w)

"If you want more performer's style and personality, look elsewhere. If you want more Beethoven, you are at home here."
Stereophile 11:133+ F '88. William A. C. Furtwangler (335w)

See Sonatas No.'s 1, 22 and 23 for review excerpt.
The New York Times Mr 27 '88, p. H35. Bernard Holland (75w)

See Sonatas No.'s 5, 6 and 7 for review excerpt.
Fanfare 11:99 N/D '87. Susan Kagan (100w)
American Record Guide 51:17-8 Mr/Ap '88. Mark Koldys (115w)

4038. Sonatas for Piano (complete): No. 17 in D minor, Opus 31, No. 2, "Tempest"; No. 18 in E flat, Opus 31, No. 3; No. 25 in G, Opus 79.
Bernard Roberts (pno).
NIMBUS 5056 DDD 59:05

★*Awards:* Record of Distinction *Ovation* Jl '89.

"My little reservations prevent me from recommending Roberts' recordings wholeheartedly. I don't think his playing is on a level with that of Richard Goode, for example. But there is still something very likable, enjoyable and captivating about Roberts' performances, and even if these discs aren't my first choices they are still going to stay in my library as welcome guests."
Fanfare 11:117-8 Jl/Ag '88. Leslie Gerber (550w)

See Sonatas No.'s 1, 22 and 23 for review excerpt.
Ovation 10:54-5 Jl '89. Lawrence B. Johnson (75w)

4039. Sonatas for Piano (complete): No. 13 in E flat, Opus 27, No. 1; No. 29 in B flat, Opus 106, "Hammerklavier".
Bernard Roberts (pno).
NIMBUS 5057 DDD 60:40

★*Awards:* Record of Distinction *Ovation* Jl '89.

"I have been enjoying Roberts' Beethoven sonatas as they have appeared, but I wasn't prepared for the way he outdoes himself in the 'Hammerklavier.'"
Fanfare 12:104-5 S/O '88. Leslie Gerber (300w)

"While the performances could be described as adequate and the recording quality excellent I could find greater listening pleasure elsewhere."
Music and Musicians International 37:39-40 D '88. Jeremy Walbank (390w)

"It sustains the lofty level of musicianship displayed by Bernard Roberts elsewhere in the series."
American Record Guide 52:20 Ja/F '89. Mark, Koldys (150w)

See Sonatas No.'s 1, 22 and 23 for review excerpt.
Ovation 10:54-5 Jl '89. Lawrence B. Johnson (75w)

4040. Sonatas for Piano (complete): No. 9 in E, Opus 14, No. 1; No. 16 in G, Opus 31, No. 1; No. 30 in E, Opus 109.
Bernard Roberts (pno).
NIMBUS 5058 DDD 56:49

★*Awards:* Record of Distinction *Ovation* Jl '89.

"Readings...are convincingly musical at all times."
Fanfare 12:117-18 Ja/F '89. Susan Kagan (250w)

See Sonatas No.'s 1, 22 and 23 for review excerpt.
Ovation 10:54-5 Jl '89. Lawrence B. Johnson (75w)

4041. Sonatas for Piano (complete): No. 12 in A flat, Opus 26, "Funeral March"; No. 14 in C# minor, Opus 27, No. 2, "Moonlight"; No. 31 in A flat, Opus 110.
Bernard Roberts (pno). Wyastone Leys, UK. September 10, 1985.
NIMBUS 5059 DDD 56:40

★*Awards:* Record of Distinction *Ovation* Jl '89.

"Bernard Roberts turns out to be a provocative and artful pianist whose Beethoven speaks with a voice of refreshing originality-....Roberts' rewarding Beethoven series is made all the more beautiful by Nimbus' extraordinary digital sound."
Ovation 10:54-5 Jl '89. Lawrence B. Johnson (75w)

"Roberts...opts for the sonic grandeur of the modern Steinway grand. And grand it is. The piano sound is unusually fine. And the playing is also fine. Roberts displays what might be called a conventional approach to the sonatas-....But a careful comparison of this disc with the justly famed Ashkenazy and Brendel recordings leaves little question as to preeminence. Of these, Roberts would be this listener's first choice."
HighPerformanceReview 6:71 Je '89. Thomas Wendel (220w)

"Nimbus' sound is still more reverberant than I like...were [this disc and Nimbus 5059] recoupled more economically they would be even easier to recommend, but they still constitute my favorite complete cycle of Beethoven's piano sonatas yet issued on CD."
Fanfare 12:118 Ja/F '89. Leslie Gerber (150w)

Digital Audio's CD Review 6:82-3 O '89. Tom Vernier (b.n.)

4042. Sonatas for Piano (complete): No. 8 in C minor, Opus 13, "Pathetique"; No. 27 in E minor, Opus 90; No. 32 in C minor, Opus 111.
Bernard Roberts (pno). 1984/85.
NIMBUS 5060 DDD 58:08

★*Awards:* Record of Distinction *Ovation* Jl '89.

"Nimbus' sound is still more reverberant than I like...were [this disc and Nimbus 5060] recoupled more economically they would be even easier to recommend, but they still constitute my favorite complete cycle of Beethoven's piano sonatas yet issued on CD."
Fanfare 12:118 Ja/F '89. Leslie Gerber (150w)

See Sonatas No.'s 1, 22 and 23 for review excerpt.
Ovation 10:54-5 Jl '89. Lawrence B. Johnson (75w)

Digital Audio's CD Review 6:82-3 O '89. Tom Vernier (b.n.)

4043. Sonatas for Piano: No. 2 in A, Opus 2, No. 2; No. 4 in E flat, Opus 7.
Emil Gilels (pno).
DEUTSCHE GRAMMOPHON 415 481 DDD

✔HC ★★*Awards:* *Stereo Review* Best of the Month, Ag '86; *Gramophone* Critics' Choice 1985 (Richard Osborne).

"In short, music making doesn't get much better than this, in any repertoire, and, fortunately, the recorded sound is also just about ideal on all counts. This is a treasurable release."
Stereo Review 51:107 Ag '86. Richard Freed (400w)

Stereo Review Presents: Compact Disc Buyers' Guide p. 50 Spr '87 William Livingstone and Christie Barter (70w)

Gramophone 63: 814+ D '85. Richard Osborne (560w)

Ovation 8:40 N '87. David Patrick Stearns (260w)

4044. Sonatas for Piano: No. 5 in C minor, Opus 10, No. 1; No. 32 in C minor, Opus 111.
Claudio Arrau (pno). La Chaux-de-Fonds, Switzerland. 1985-86.
PHILIPS 420 154 DDD 48:00

✔HC ★*Awards:* Perfect 10s, *Digital Audio's CD Review*, Mr '89.

"Arrau never treats these as museum pieces, and the freshness of his conceptions, combined with a still formidable command of the keyboard, makes this record a tempting buy."
American Record Guide 52:21-2 Mr/Ap '89. Michael Mark (325w)

"The engineers have provided a reverberant sonic ambience (obviously to Mr. Arrau's liking) which, while it is sufficiently clear, contributes to the effect of a slightly nostalgic, enervated performance."
HighPerformanceReview 6:71 Je '89. John Mueter (180w)

"Arrau's realization of the Sonata No. 32 is an exalting one—not the measurable 'best,' perhaps (that being a quite unrealistic notion), but one whose great beauty and unostentatious intellectual power simply cannot be resisted. The earlier sonata in the same key takes on a certain breadth and depth in Arrau's reading without at any point being inflated beyond its true proportions."
Stereo Review 54:120 Mr '89. Richard Freed (275w)

"Essentially, this is for those who want to sit with the score, watching the printed pages become incontrovertible sound....The piano recordings are entirely complementary to the grandeur of the performances."
Hi-Fi News & Record Review 33:83-4 Je '88. Christopher Breunig (540w)

"This release would not be my first choice for either work...but if you care deeply about Beethoven, and about Beethoven interpretation (especially Arrau's performance of the Arietta), this release simply has to form an indispensable part of your collection."
Music and Musicians International 36:38 Je '88. Robert Matthew-Walker (220w)

"Variable successfulness....Op. 10, No. 1, is done in general with greater rhythmic firmness than has been the player's late habit....If the same kind of metrical control had been bestowed upon Op. 111, I would be tempted to say this was an unusually attractive coupling."
Fanfare 12:117 Ja/F '89. John Wiser (150w)

Gramophone 65:1212 F '88. Richard Osborne (245w)

Digital Audio 5:72 D '88. Anne Valdespino (310w)

4045. Sonatas for Piano: No. 8 in C minor, Opus 13, "Pathetique"; No. 20 in G, Opus 49, No. 2; No. 5 in C minor, Opus 10, No. 1; No. 3 in C, Opus 2, No. 3.
Bruno-Leonardo Gelber (pno).
DENON/SUPRAPHON 2203 DDD 69:00

✔HC ★*Awards:* Critics' Choice 1988, *Gramophone* D '88 (James Methuen-Campbell).

"This is awfully good playing that can stand up to the competition on musical and technical grounds. The miking is very close, and there are some extraneous noises noticeable in the 'Pathetique' especially."
Fanfare 12:116 Ja/F '89. Susan Kagan (310w)

"Gelber's masculine Beethoven is a healthy alternative to understated wimpy interpretations."
American Record Guide 52:19-20 Ja/F '89. Mark, Koldys (175w)

"Bruno-Leonardo Gelber has an epic style in this music, and I like it."
Hi-Fi News & Record Review 34:102 Ap '89. Stephen Pettitt (350w)

"Judging from the first issues, three separately available CDs, this performer is definitely worth hearing for his strong interpretive profile-....One important feature particularly recommendable to music teachers or those wishing to understand aspects of sonata form is the indexing, with anywhere from three to as many as eight internal sections per movement being accessible at the push of a button."
Stereophile 12:205 N '89. Igor Kipnis (275w)

Gramophone 66:44 S '88. James Methuen-Campbell (465w)

4046. Sonatas for Piano: No. 8 in C Minor, Opus 13, "Pathetique;" No. 13 in E flat, Opus 27, No. 1; No. 14 in C# Minor, Opus 27, No. 2, "Moonlight".
Emil Gilels (pno). 1983.
DEUTSCHE GRAMMOPHON 400 036

★*Awards:* *American Record Guide* Overview: Beethoven Piano Sonatas, Jl/Ag '91.

"Having expressed in the last issue my great admiration for the superb musicality of Emil Gilels in two other Beethoven sonatas, I can only applaud the first issue from this series in CD...Gilels gives unhackneyed readings that reveal fresh musical ideas and piano textures one seldom hears in this music."
Fanfare 7:108-9 S/O '83. Philip Hart (270w)

"There are some wonderful moments in all these sonatas. Yet Gilels frequently breaks his own momentum with questionable ritards...Nor is this recording exactly a triumph of the compact disc art."
High Performance Review 2 (4):98-9 N '83. Thomas H. Wendel (300w)

Gramophone 60:1275 My '83. Richard Osborne (85w)

Ovation 5:49 My '84. Paul Turok (100w)

4047. Sonatas for Piano: No. 8 in C Minor, Opus 13, "Pathetique;" No. 14 in C# Minor, Opus 27, No. 2, "Moonlight;" No. 15 in D, Opus 28, "Pastoral".
Wilhelm Kempff (pno). 1966.
DEUTSCHE GRAMMOPHON 415 834 60:00

★*Awards: American Record Guide* Overview: Beethoven Piano Sonatas, Jl/Ag '91.

Gramophone 65:281-2 Ag '87 Ivan March (160w)

4048. Sonatas for Piano: No. 11 in B flat, Opus 22; No. 18 in E flat, Opus 31, No. 3.
Earl Wild (pno).
DELL'ARTE 7004 49:34

★*Awards: American Record Guide* Overview: Beethoven Piano Sonatas, Jl/Ag '91 (No. 18).

"Wild's sensitive, finely nuanced and precise playing in both sonatas is beyond reproach, and the music is allowed to speak directly to the listener, unhindered in any fashion. It would be difficult to imagine finer versions of both works. The superbly balanced tones of the Bosendorfer, splendidly caught by the engineers, and the sensible notes by Bryce Morrison, make this a completely treasurable disc."
American Record Guide 53:22+ Jl/Ag '90. Vivian A. Liff (125w)

4049. Sonatas for Piano: No. 12 in A flat, Opus 26, "Funeral March"; No. 24 in F#, Opus 78; **Concerto No. 1 in C for Piano and Orchestra, Opus 15.**
Sviatoslav Richter (pno). Charles Munch (c). Boston Symphony Orchestra. 1960.
RCA 6804 66:00

★*Awards: American Record Guide* Overview: Beethoven Piano Sonatas, Jl/Ag '91 (No. 12); *American Record Guide* Overview: Beethoven Piano Concertos, Jl/Ag '89.

"Richter gives us a broadly-paced, essentially lyrical account of this music, providing youthful brio in full measure where it is required-....The much-improved sound of the CD allows us to hear the crisp, clean and incisive orchestral support provided by the conductor."
American Record Guide 51:20 S/O '88. Allen Linkowski (310w)

4050. Sonatas for Piano: No. 13 in E flat, Opus 27, No. 1; No. 14 in C# minor, Opus 27, No. 2, "Moonlight"; No. 15 in D, Opus 28, "Pastoral".
Bruno-Leonardo Gelber (pno).
DENON/SUPRAPHON 2539 DDD 50:00

✔HC ★*Awards:* Critics Pick Some Favorites of the Year, *The New York Times* N 26, '89 (John Rockwell).

"The piano, a Steinway, is solidly centered in the acoustic space and sounds simply rapturous-....Gelber's playing is expert and assured, although he lacks some of the fire of his rivals. He makes up in clarity, however, for anything he may lack in zeal."
Fanfare 13:487 S/O '89. Al Fasoldt (270w)

"Judging from the first issues, three separately available CDs, this performer is definitely worth hearing for his strong interpretive profile-...One important feature particularly recommendable to music teachers or those wishing to understand aspects of sonata form is the indexing, with anywhere from three to as many as eight internal sections per movement being accessible at the push of a button."
Stereophile 12:205 N '89. Igor Kipnis (275w)

"His playing here has so many virtues that I cannot dismiss it although I have some problems in appreciating the disc....My main problem is with Gelber's climaxes....I doubt that the raucous sound of his loudest playing is the fault of piano or engineering, although it might be."
Fanfare 12:126-27 My/Je '89. Leslie Gerber (550w)

Gramophone 66:1183 Ja '89. James Methuen-Campbell (280w)

4051. Sonatas for Piano: No. 14 in C# minor, Opus 27, No. 2, "Moonlight"; No. 21 in C, Opus 53, "Waldstein"; No. 23 in F minor, Opus 57, "Appassionata".
Mikhail Pletnev (pno).
VIRGIN 90737 DDD 67:00

★★*Awards:* The Year's Best, *Hi Fi News & Record Review*, May '90 Supplement. *American Record Guide* Overview: Beethoven Piano Sonatas, Jl/Ag '91.

"These are stimulating, satisfying, and utterly splendid performances, as fastidious and tasteful as they are brilliant. All three sonatas are demonstrably dramatic works, and Mikhail Pletnev brings out that quality to its full proportions—but never beyond. This is an aristocratic sort of drama: direct, uncluttered, poetic."
Stereo Review 54:147 D '89. Richard Freed (150w)

"Pletnev's pianism is here characterized by an extraordinary cleanness and clarity of detail—but never in the dry, academic sense....Pletnev gives full measure to Beethoven's sense of drama and development, and he binds everything together tightly and convincingly. The recording has immediacy and impact while still preserving an ample sense of space around the instrument."
American Record Guide 53:23-4 Ja/F '90. Donald Manildi (135w)

"The important thing that must be said first about this young Soviet pianist is that he is an artist of major importance....Pletnev tends toward the broadest of emotional extremes...I suspect this Russian Expressionism is no affectation; but sincere or not, it is not always ideally suited to Beethoven."
Fanfare 13:133 N/D '89. Paul Sargent Clark (200w)

"This is Beethoven played with all that the modern grand has to offer; magnificently recorded, it will surely alternately repel and enthral the listener."*P95(?) S95*

Hi-Fi News & Record Review 34:87 My '89; p.17 My '90 Supplement. Christopher Breunig (420w)

Gramophone 66:1610 Ap '89. James Methuen-Campbell (315w)

4052. Sonatas for Piano: No. 15 in D, Opus 28 "Pastorale"; No. 17 in D Minor, Opus 31, No. 2 "Tempest".
Emil Gilels (pno). 1983.
DEUTSCHE GRAMMOPHON 419 161 DDD 51:33

★***Awards:*** *American Record Guide* Overview: Beethoven Piano Sonatas, Jl/Ag '91.

Fanfare 10:107-8 N/D '86 John D. Wiser (475w)

Gramophone 64:688 N '86 Robert Layton (570w)

4053. Sonatas for Piano: No. 17 in D minor, Opus 31, No. 2, "Tempest"; No. 29 in B flat, Opus 106, "Hammerklavier".
Wilhelm Kempff (pno). 1968 reissues.
DEUTSCHE GRAMMOPHON 419 857 ADD 63:00

★***Awards:*** *American Record Guide* Overview: Beethoven Piano Sonatas, Jl/Ag '91 (No. 29).

Gramophone 66:447 S '88. Richard Osborne (425w)

Sonata No. 17 in D minor for Piano, Opus 31, No. 2, "Tempest". See No. 2028.

4054. Sonatas for Piano: No. 21 in C, Opus 53 "Waldstein"; No. 23 in F Minor, Opus 57 "Appassionata"; No. 26 in E flat, Opus 81a "Les Adieux".
Emil Gilels (pno).
DEUTSCHE GRAMMOPHON 419 162

★***Awards:*** *American Record Guide* Overview: Beethoven Piano Sonatas, Jl/Ag '91.

Fanfare 10:107-8 N/D '86 John D. Wiser (475w)

Sonata No. 23 in F minor for Piano, Opus 57, "Appasionata". See No. 2041.

4055. Sonatas for Piano: No. 28 in A, Opus 101; No. 29 in B flat, Opus 106, "Hammerklavier"; No. 31 in A flat, Opus 110; No. 32 in C minor, Opus 111.
Richard Goode (pno). 1986/88.
ELEKTRA 79211 DDD 63:41, 65:31 2 discs

★★★***Awards:*** Best Recordings of the Month, *Stereo Review* O '89. Top Choices—1989, *American Record Guide* Ja/F '90 (Paul Althouse). *American Record Guide* Overview: Beethoven Piano Sonatas, Jl/Ag '91.

"Goode's performances are utterly unselfconscious, as free of phony reverence as of externalized drama....These superb performances have been handsomely recorded by Max Wilcox."

Stereo Review 54:110 O '89. Richard Freed (365w)

"As a newcomer to Richard Goode's artistry, I must admit to being stunned by the sheer poetry and sensitivity of his musical expression. His textural lucidity and total grasp of formal structure, and, what's more, his ability to make this comprehensible to his audience, immediately bring intimations of Alfred Brendel's skill; there is the same intellectual depth, but a different vision emerges, and the added warmth and fluidity of Goode's playing make him just a little less clinically astringent."

Stereophile 13:186 F '90. Barbara Jahn (325w)

"No more than a few minutes is needed to realize the depth and scope of Goode's Beethoven."

American Record Guide 52:36-7 N/D '89. Paul L. Althouse (400w)

This performance "is idiosyncratic, but in the main logical, and at every moment sensitive and alive to possibilities....My strong positive recommendation for this set is rather a forced move, but one I make trusting that others will find these performances as engaging and thought-provoking as I have."

Fanfare 13:135-36 S/O '89. John Wiser (450w)

Gramophone 67:503-4 S '89. David J. Fanning (665w)

Digital Audio's CD Review 6:82 N '89. Tom Vernier (310w)

4056. Sonata for Piano No. 29 in B flat, Opus 106, "Hammerklavier".
Emil Gilels (pno).
DEUTSCHE GRAMMOPHON 410 527

✔**HC** ★★***Awards:*** *Gramophone* Record Award Winner 1984—Instrumental Award. *American Record Guide* Overview: Beethoven Piano Sonatas, Jl/Ag '91.

"The effect is a Cubist view of Beethoven, surely a valid approach to the craggy final fugue, but perhaps less appropriate to the buoyant energies of the opening. Still, an impressive reading that more than once burns through to the heart of this cranky, magisterial work."

High Fidelity 34:56-7 Ag '84. Thomas W. Russell III (350w)

Gramophone 61:798 D '83 (595w) (rev. of LP); 61:994 F '84 (335w) (rev. of CD). Richard Osborne

Hi-Fi News & Record Review 29:79+ Mr '84. John Atkinson (55w)

4057. Sonatas for Piano: No. 30 in E, Opus 109; No. 31 in A flat, Opus 110.
Emil Gilels (pno).
DEUTSCHE GRAMMOPHON 419 174 DDD

✔**HC** ★★★★***Awards:*** *Gramophone* Critics' Choice 1986 (Richard Osborne); *Gramophone* Critics' Choice 1986 (Robert Layton); *Opus* Christmas List, 1987 (Paul L. Althouse). *American Record Guide* Overview: Beethoven Piano Sonatas, Jl/Ag '91.

Ovation 8:40 N '87. David Patrick Stearns (260w)

Opus 4:52 D '87. Paul L. Althouse (120w)

Gramophone 64:688 N '86 Robert Layton (570w)

The Musical Times 128:275 My '87 Robert Anderson (150w) (rev. of LP)

Fanfare 10:66-67 Ja/F '87 John D. Wiser (150w)

Sonata No. 32 in C minor for Piano, Opus 111. See No. 2020.

4058. Variations (33) on a Waltz by Diabelli, for Piano, Opus 120.
Claudio Arrau (pno). reissue 1985.
PHILIPS 416 295 DDD 35:03

✔**HC** ★*Awards:* *Gramophone* Critics' Choice (Richard Osborne), 1987.

"This music can seem bleak and monochromatic in the hands of other interpreters, but, as early as the very first chords of the first variation, with Arrau the music rises—root and branch—from the depths of his wonderful instrument with the force of a rich and mighty affirmation....This is Arrau at the summit of his art."

Ovation 9:36-7 Ap '88. Dan F. Cameron (110w)

"Despite the spate of recent recordings of the *Diabelli Variations*, and the CD reissue of Michael Oelbaum's perceptive interpretation (Bridge BCD 9010), Arrau's account has not been superseded."

Musical America 110:90-2 Mr '90. Harris Goldsmith (405w)

Digital Audio 4:78+ D '87. Tom Vernier (315w)

4059. Variations (33) on a Waltz by Diabelli, for Piano, Opus 120.
Sviatoslav Richter (pno). Concertgebouw, Amsterdam. June 17, 1986, live.
PHILIPS 422 416 DDD 52:00

★★*Awards:* The Want List 1990, *Fanfare* N/D '90 (Leslie Gerber); Critics' Choice 1989, *Gramophone* D '89 (David Fanning).

"Richter's pianism is stunning, and he offers the best view of the volcanic energy permeating this work."

American Record Guide 52:27-8 S/O '89. Stephen D. Chakwin, Jr. (235w)

"It is difficult to conceive that this Olympian masterpiece has ever been played with a more apt or transcendental mastery....Apart from a few 'noises off' the recordings are highly successful."

Hi-Fi News & Record Review 34:78 Jl '89. Bryce Morrison (290w)

"The sound...is focused as effectively as a studio recording and virtually free of audience noise....Richter's is one performance that seems indispensable, projecting at the same time a sense of individuality and of modesty in the face of the music and its creator, a sense of exploration rather than of manipulation, and the sort of momentum that comes most naturally in the live setting."

Stereo Review 54:89 Jl '89. Richard Freed (325w)

"It is harmonic movement, after all, that produces the unifying backbone of these variations. When obscured, as it sometimes is with Richter, the music's nervous system, so to speak, collapses. And there are other problems with Richter's performances."

Stereophile 12:162-63 Jl '89. Mortimer H. Frank (225w)

"This performance...shows Richter at the height of his powers....In short, this is as close to a mandatory purchase as I can imagine. Any listener with the capacity to appreciate and love this difficult, magnificent music will be richly rewarded by this disc."

Fanfare 13:124-25 My/Je '90. Leslie Gerber (300w)

Gramophone 66:1031-32 D '88. David J. Fanning (495w)

"I am amazed that an artist of Richter's exalted standing would consent to the release of such a flawed document—indeed, that he would agree to continue playing on so foully mistuned an instrument—and that so reputable a firm as Philips was willing to issue it. There are *musical* problems, as well."

Musical America 110:90-2 Mr '90. Harris Goldsmith (405w)

Variations (32) in C minor for Piano, G.191. See No. 2017.

BLOCH, ERNEST. Suite No. 1 for Solo Violin. See No. 3026. **Suites (2) for Solo Violin.** See No. 3027.

BOTTERMUND, HANS. Variations (many) for Unaccompanied Cello, after Paganini's Violin Caprice No. 24 (trans. Starker). See No. 4117.

BRAHMS, JOHANNES

Fantasies (7) for Piano, Opus 116. See No. 2038.

Liebeslieder Waltz for Piano 4 Hands, Opus 52. See No. 1063.

4060. Piano Music: Sonata No. 3 in F minor; Intermezzi (3), Opus 117.
Emanuel Ax (pno).
SONY 45933 DDD 53:09

★★*Awards:* Record of the Month, *Hi-Fi News & Record Review*, N '90. Best Recordings of the Month, *Stereo Review* Ja '91.

"Emanuel Ax...is given an atmospheric halo of resonance that emphasizes the poetry of his lyric, unpressured approach to this music...his gentle, perfectly proportioned reading of the sonata in particular brings to mind that of his ontetime mentor, Arthur Rubinstein. (Yes, it is *that* good!) His version easily takes its place with the second Rubinstein (RCA 5672), Arrau

(Philips; OP), Curzon (London; OP), and Lupu (also London; OP)."

Musical America 111:71 My '91. Harris Goldsmith (170w)

"Emanuel Ax's new Sony Classical CD of No. 3, in F Minor, joins more than a half-dozen other versions in the CD medium alone, but his is the one that must make listeners wonder why so fascinating a work is not among the most popular items in its category....Ax refers to the sonata as 'one of the glories of the pianist's repertoire,' and his performance fully supports that encomium."

Stereo Review 56:92 Ja '91. Richard Freed (545w)

"These...are superlative performances by one of the most intensely musical of all young pianists. The recordings are smooth and natural." *P100 S100*

Hi-Fi News & Record Review 35:93 N '90. Bryce Morrison (585w)

"Among other notable exponents of the sonata, Arrau (Philips, deleted) penetrates more into the work's philosophical depths, Curzon (London, likewise) extracts a bit more massive drama, and Zimerman (DG 423 401) delivers youthful individuality. Ax manages to hold his own rather handily, however, and projects an appropriately introspective aura in the Intermezzos. He also has the advantage of a firmly-centered, highly faithful recording."

American Record Guide 54:37 Ja/F '91. Donald Manildi (100w)

"This is an off-and-on reading, more on than otherwise, but, in the long run, hardly competitive with the aforementioned Curzon (despite Curzon's elision of the exposition repeat), somewhat less whole in its deployment of energy than Lupu's more recent recording. But I do not think these analog tapings from English Decca/London have been CD'd, and the current digital competition is not so grand....the three Intermezzi...are here subdued in expression but lovingly outlined. A clean recording of an entirely natural-sounding piano, in a convincing capture of Ax's lovely tone, secures my strong recommendation."

Fanfare 14:163-64 Ja/F '91. John Wiser (275w)

Gramophone 68:1235 D '90. Christopher Headington (360w)

4061. Piano Music: Sonata No. 3 in F minor, Opus 5; Capriccio in B minor, Opus 76, No. 2; Intermezzo in E flat minor, Opus 118, No. 6; *Rhapsodies:* B minor, Opus 79, No. 1; E flat, Opus 119, No. 4.
Murray Perahia (pno).
SONY 47181 DDD 60:00

✔HC ★*Awards:* Critics' Choice 1991, *Gramophone*, Ja '92 (Christopher Headington).

"As in his new Franck/Liszt recital for Sony-...Perahia is apparently striving for a bigger, more heroic manner than has been evident in his playing until now. He succeeds triumphantly, displaying more individuality than Emanuel Ax ([*ARG*] Jan/Feb 1991) if not quite the grand romantic authority of Rubinstein (RCA 5672). Perahia also equals in distinction the diverse readings of Arrau (Philips) and Katchen (London), though both of these are available only as part of multi-disc Brahms collections....Sonically this new Sony release gives us a realistic, firmly-centered piano image."

American Record Guide 55:37 Mr/Ap '92. Donald Manildi (med)

"To them Mr. Perahia brings one of the piano's individual sounds....the Brahms sonata is no less powerful for the uncharacteristic leanness of its sound. In Mr. Perahia's case, the word 'hard' is not a critical pejorative. No detail is corrupted, none left unheard."

The New York Times O 20 '91, sec H p. 31. Bernard Holland (long)

"Although he has his rivals—though not his superiors—in the more heroic peaks of this early masterpiece, his way with the *Andante espressivo*, to say nothing of so many other deep pools of tranquility and reflection, is surely the finest on record....I shall return to this recording for true enlightenment and, indeed, spiritual refreshment....The recordings, as in the Franck and Liszt recital, are exemplary." *PS 100*

Hi-Fi News & Record Review 37:85 Ap '92. Bryce Morrison (long)

Murray Perahia's "account of the extravagant F-Minor Sonata has all the elevation and restraint one could desire, with great rhythmic vivacity, alertness, and chiseled delineation of melodies in the past far too often subjected to fervent sloppiness and excessive fantasizing-....The appended shorter works, approached with the same intensity, don't entirely strike me as constituting a logical program sequence. They are the climaxing or culminating works in their various contexts, and out of those contexts, not all their variety of texture, pace, and melody can tell against such uniformly high expressive intensity....Vivid, close-up, nicely atmospheric recording. In all, this is likely to wear very well as one of the best piano CDs *ever*."

Fanfare 15:164-5 Mr/Ap '92. John Wiser (long)

Gramophone 69:138 O '91. Christopher Headington (long)

BRITTEN, BENJAMIN. Nocturnal after John Dowland for Guitar, Opus 70. See No. 4184.

BUSONI, FERRUCCIO

4062. Fantasia Contrappuntistica (solo piano version, 1910-12); **Mephisto-Waltz** (after Liszt). **BACH, JOHANN SEBASTIAN. Chaconne** (from the Violin Partita No. 2, BWV.1004 (arr. Piano O'Riley).
Christopher O'Riley (pno).
CENTAUR 2036 DDD 59:00

★*Awards:* The Want List 1989, *Fanfare* N/D '89 (Adrian Corleonis).

"Unless I've missed something, this is Christopher O'Riley's solo recording debut and it's a triumph....Enthusiastically recommended."
Fanfare 13:169-71 S/O '89. Adrian Corleonis (405w)

"By any standards Busoni's *Fantasia contrappuntistica*, based on fragments from Bach's *Art of Fugue* mixed into a structure and harmonic idiom of forbidding complexity, is a tough nut to crack for both performer and listeners. O'Riley's performance, however, will go a long way toward making the work more accessible."
American Record Guide 52:34-5 My/Je '89. Donald Manildi (200w)

"Either this disc from O'Riley or the more comprehensive set from Madge is recommended to the Busoni devotee. Each captures the essential flavor of an important, world-class composer, a man who felt himself to be the repository for all of cultural history up to and beyond his personal existence."
Musical America 110:64 Ja '90. Gary Lemco (850w)

Gramophone 67:699 O '89. Michael Oliver (300w)

BUXTEHUDE, DIETRICH. Organ Music. See No. 4016.

CHOPIN, FREDERIC

4063. Piano Music: Preludes (24), Opus 28; Prelude No. 25 in C#, Opus 45; Prelude in A flat, Op. Posth.; Barcarolle in F#, Opus 60; Poloniase in A flat, Opus 53; Scherzo No. 2 in B flat minor, Opus 31.
Martha Argerich (pno). 1977 reissue.
DEUTSCHE GRAMMOPHON 415 836 ADD 62:21

★*Awards:* *American Record Guide* Overview: Chopin, Jl/Ag '92 (Preludes).

"Argerich's volatile and poetic playing of the Preludes...remains for me the best version of these ever-fresh pieces....An outstanding reissue in which the reproduction still holds up well."
Fanfare 11:107-8 Ja/F '88. Howard Komblum (135w)

Gramophone 65:1478 Ap '88. James Methuen-Campbell (475w)

4064. Piano Music: Etudes, Opus 10 and Opus 25.
Vladimir Ashkenazy (pno).
LONDON/DECCA 414 127

★*Awards:* *American Record Guide* Overview: Chopin, Jl/Ag '92.

Gramophone 62:896 Ja '85. Max Harrison (105w)

4065. Piano Music: Ballades (4) for Piano (Opus 23, 38, 47, 52); Berceuse in D flat, Opus 57; Preludes (24) for Piano, Opus 28.
Alfred Cortot (pno). 1926-29.
MUSIC & ARTS 317 AAD (m) 70:20

✔HC ★*Awards:* The Year's Best, *Hi Fi News & Record Review*, May '90 Supplement.

"It would be difficult to over-estimate the importance of this reissue....It is, incidentally, a curious and sobering thought to realize that today probably neither Cortot nor Schnabel would be invited to record. Their concern for music rather than mechanics would render them misfits in the contemporary record scene."*P100(historical) S-historical*
Hi-Fi News & Record Review 34:88 My '89; p.13 My '90 Supplement. Bryce Morrison (700w)

"If the continuing surface swish of a 78 is really abhorrent to you...go on to the next review. But, if music *and* performance remain paramount, please recall that Alfred Cortot (1877-1962) was one of the great pianists of his time....As an emotionally unbound yet aristocratic poet of the piano...he was unrivaled-....This CD presents a unique opportunity to hear the kind of superb playing that otherwise might be lost because of its vintage—and, perhaps not so surprisingly, I find that it speaks to the heart more effectively than most Chopin of our own time."
Stereophile 11:153+ S '88. Igor Kipnis (375w)

"Recent reissues by both British EMI and Music and Arts of Alfred Cortot performing Chopin provide a listening experience just short of enchanting....I would—if *really* pressed—suggest the EMI disc, but only for its somewhat cleaner sonics; the performances themselves are not vastly different."
High Fidelity 39:68 Jl '89. Thomas L. Dixon (200w)

Gramophone 66:1216 J '89. James Methuen-Campbell (260w)

4066. Piano Music: Etudes, Opus 10 and Opus 25.
Andrei Gavrilov (pno).
EMI 47452 DDD 57:00

✔HC ★*Awards:* Critics' Choice 1988, *Gramophone* D '88 (Joan Chissell).

"This is probably the most brilliant recording of Chopin's *Etudes* since Ashkenazy's, for Decca....Perfect keyboard mastery is shown throughout."

Hi-Fi News & Record Review 33:94 My '88. Max Harrison (275w)

"Overall I prefer this account (superbly recorded) to Pollini's or Ashkenezy's celebrated recordings on DG and Decca respectively. And although it is true that few musicians will want to part with particular favourites from Cortot and Moiseiwitsch (another time, another style) they will look in vain for a more stunningly robust or eloquent modern performance."

Music and Musicians International 37:40-1 D '88. Bryce Morrison (420w)

"For the most part, these are exciting performances, some of the best playing I've heard from Gavrilov....But he let me down in the last three pieces of Op. 25...EMI's reproduction is excellent."

Fanfare 12:128 S/O '88. Howard Kornblum (150w)

"From the very beginning of Gavrilov's traversal of these works, it becomes clear that they hold no terrors from him, at least in the technical sense....Only occasionally does Gavrilov allow the music to bloom under his fingers, but when he does he shows himself capable of considerable sensitivity."

Ovation 10:57 Je '89. Dan F. Cameron (250w)

"A wholly satisfactory recording of these works seems as unattainable as ever. Gavrilov's will certainly give pleasure; but by his own high standards it is a disappointment."

American Record Guide 51:34 S/O '88. Arved Ashby (430w)

Gramophone 65:1047-8 Ap '88. Joan Chissell (560w)

The New York Times Ja 15 '89, p. H 27. Harold C. Schonberg (160w)

4067. Piano Music: Sonata No. 2 in B flat minor for Piano, Opus 35; Sonata No. 3 in B minor for Piano, Opus 58; Mazurkas (selected).
William Kapell (pno). 1951-53.
RCA 5998 ADD 73:11

★★★★*Awards: Opus* Christmas List, 1987 (Tim Page); *Fanfare* Want List 1987 (Howard Kornblum); The Want List 1988, *Fanfare* N/D '88 (Peter J. Rabinowitz). *American Record Guide* Overview: Chopin, Jl/Ag '92 (Sonata No. 1 and Mazurkas).

Kapell's "scintillating playing of the Op. 58 puts the performance on a par with the great ones by Pollini, Lipatti, Rubinstein, and Gilels. The appealing simplicity of his phrasing in the mazurkas is on the level of the great Rubinstein performances....[Sonata No. 2] is indeed a rarely beautiful performance."

Fanfare 11:125-6 N/D '87. Howard Kornblum (225w)

"The studio sound is superb, the acetate only fair—but this performance would be worth owning even on the scratchiest of Maplesons."

Opus 4:57-8 D '87. Tim Page (90w)

"At long last RCA seems ready to acknowledge that these super-great piano recordings deserve to be kept alive; and here they are, sounding fresher than ever."

American Record Guide 51:28-9 Mr/Ap '88. Donald Manildi (350w)

"These accounts of Chopin sonatas and mazurkas document the changes in Kapell's approach—toward greater flexibility, color, and subjectivity—that occurred in the last years of his life. Some will think it perverse, but I prefer his earlier and comparatively more straightforward style."

Musical America 108:60+ Jl '88. Harris Goldsmith (980w)

4068. Piano Music: Waltzes No's. 1-14; Barcarolle in F sharp, Opus 60; Nocturne, Opus 27, No. 2; Mazurka, Opus 50, No. 3.
Dinu Lipatti (piano). 1948.
EMI 47390 65:00

✔HC ★★*Awards: American Record Guide* Overview: Chopin, Jl/Ag '92; *Fanfare* Want List 1986 (Howard Kornblum) (Waltzes).

"The performances of the Nocturne, Barcarolle, and Mazurka remain the finest I know. Lipatti's phrasing was of a kind uniquely his: an unrivaled mixture of eloquence, elegance, and creative genius, always striking deeply to the essence of the composer....No one serious about music on records should be without these performances. I think music lovers ought to express gratitude to EMI for having released these unmatched examples of musical mastery on a CD."

Fanfare 10:129 S/O '86 Howard Kornblum (450w)

Gramophone 64:599-600 O '86 Joan Chissell (420w)

High Fidelity 37:62 Mr '87 Terry Teachout (75w)

4069. Piano Music: Etudes, Opus 10 and Opus 25; Nouvelles Etudes (3) for Piano.
Louis Lortie (pno).
CHANDOS 8482 DDD

★★★*Awards: Fanfare* Want List 1987 (Howard Kornblum); *Gramophone* Critics' Choice (Joan Chissell), 1987. *American Record Guide* Overview: Chopin, Jl/Ag '92.

Louis Lortie's "powerful, vivid playing of the etudes stands up remarkably well against the current best: (Pollini on DG and Ashkenazy on London), although there is still no recent complete set of these imaginative pieces that satisfies me (the closest remains a set done years ago by the very young Ashkenazy, circulated here once on the MK label; Ashkenazy, and no one else for that matter, has ever matched that for freshness and vitality)....Lortie's feeling for etudes is robust, warm, and unaffected. His technique in such pieces as Op. 10, No. 4, Op. 10, No. 8, and Op. 25, No. 6, will take your breath away."

Fanfare 10:90-91 Jl/Ag '87 Howard Kornblum (140w)

Ovation 8:39 O '87. Peter J. Rabinowitz (330w)

Hi-Fi News & Record Review 32:103 F '87 Roger Bowen (210w)

Gramophone 64:1044 Ja '87 Joan Chissell (420w)

4070. Piano Music: Sonata No. 2 in B flat minor for Piano, Opus 35; Sonata No. 3 in B flat minor for Piano, Opus 58.
Maurizio Pollini (pno).
DEUTSCHE GRAMMOPHON 415 346 51:53

✔HC ★★*Awards: Fanfare* Want List 1986 (Howard Kornblum); *Gramophone* Critics' Choice 1986 (Christopher Headington).

"Over the years many impressive recordings of these two inventive masterpieces have been made....I think none of these surpasses what Pollini gives us here....The reproduction is first-rate—an indispensable disc for anyone who lives this music."

Fanfare 10:131 N/D '86 Howard Kornblum (225w)

"Pollini....achieves an elegant balance of poetry and power, and his piano is handsomely recorded."

Stereo Review 51:130 D '86 D Richard Freed (150w)

Ovation 8:38 My '87 Peter J. Rabinowitz (255w)

Hi-Fi News & Record Review 31:85+ S '86. Andrew Keener (285w)

4071. Piano Music: Ballades (4) (Op. 23, 38, 47, 52); Scherzos (4) (Opus 20, 31, 39, 54).
("The Rubinstein Collection").
Artur Rubinstein (pno). reissue.
RCA 7156 71:21

★*Awards: American Record Guide* Overview: Chopin, Jl/Ag '92.

"It was Rubinstein's view that despite his physical frailty, Chopin meant his music to be interpreted from a position of strength. 'With sentiment, yes, but not sentimentality,' was Rubinstein's motto, and he managed to walk that elusive line with great conviction all through his career....At the risk of too sweeping a generalization, I would venture that few other pianists came close to matching Rubinstein's blend of elegance and power, which reveals all the drama and poetry of the Ballades and Scherzos, the sensuousness and passion of the Nocturnes, the proud nationalism of the Polonaises, the sophistication of the Waltzes, and the earthiness and vitality of the Mazurkas. (I would add that the 1963 version of the Waltzes, from an incredibly productive single-evening session in Rome, proves a bit disappointing after repeated exposure."

American Record Guide 52:118-21 Jl/Ag '89. Donald Manildi (55w)

"The Rubinstein reissue on CD is a great success for me: the remastering is superb and Max Wilcox has much reason to be proud of this accomplishment."

Fanfare 11:125-6 N/D '87. Howard Kornblum (225w)

4072. Piano Music: Impromptus (4); Barcarolle in F#, Opus 60; Nouvelles Etudes (3) for Piano; Bolero, Opus 19; Berceuse in D flat, Opus 57; Tarantelle in A flat, Opus 43; Andante Spianato and Grande Polonaise, Opus 22.
("The Rubinstein Collection").
Artur Rubinstein (pno). 1962-65.
RCA 5617 ADD 67:20

★*Awards: American Record Guide* Overview: Chopin, Jl/Ag '92 (Impromptus, Barcarolle, Fantasy, Berceuse).

See Ballades and Scherzos (Rubinstein) for review excerpt.

American Record Guide 52:118-21 Jl/Ag '89. Donald Manildi (55w)

Fanfare 10:89-90 Jl/Ag '87 Howard Kornblum (65w)

Digital Audio 4:70 N '87. Tom Vernier (140w)

4073. Piano Music: Mazurkas (51) for Piano (complete).
("The Rubinstein Collection").
Artur Rubinstein (pno).
RCA 5614 69:12; 70:49 2 discs

✔HC ★★★*Awards: Fanfare* Want List 1987 (Howard Kornblum). *American Record Guide* Overview: Chopin, Jl/Ag '92.

See Ballades and Scherzos (Rubinstein) for review excerpt.

American Record Guide 52:118-21 Jl/Ag '89. Donald Manildi (55w)

Fanfare 10:90 Jl/Ag '87 Howard Kornblum (65w)

High Fidelity 37:60 Ag '87 Terry Teachout (45w)

4074. Piano Music: Nocturnes (21) for Piano (complete).
("The Rubinstein Collection").
Artur Rubinstein (pno). reissue.
RCA 5613 54:58; 52:32 2 discs

✔HC ★★★*Awards: Fanfare* Want List 1987 (Susan Kagan); Pick of the Crop Reissues, *The New York Times* S 16, '90 (Sedgwick Clark). *American Record Guide* Overview: Chopin, Jl/Ag '92.

See Ballades and Scherzos (Rubinstein) for review excerpt.

American Record Guide 52:118-21 Jl/Ag '89. Donald Manildi (55w)

Audio 69:97-8 S '85. John M. Eargle (250w)

Fanfare 10:90 Jl/Ag '87 Howard Kornblum (65w)

High Fidelity 37:60 Ag '87 Terry Teachout (45w)

4075. Piano Music: Polonaises for Piano: Opus 26, 40, 44, 61.
("The Rubinstein Collection").
Artur Rubinstein (pno). 1964.
RCA 5615 ADD 59:18

✔HC ★***Awards:*** Editors' Choice, *Digital Audio*, 1988. *American Record Guide* Overview: Chopin, Jl/Ag '9210:89-90 Jl/Ag '87 Howard Kornblum (65w)

See Ballades and Scherzos (Rubinstein) for review excerpt.

American Record Guide 52:118-21 Jl/Ag '89. Donald Manildi (55w)

Digital Audio 4:68+ N '87. Tom Vernier (140w)

4076. Piano Music: Sonata No. 2 in B flat minor, Opus 35; Sonata No. 3 in B minor, Opus 58.
("The Rubinstein Collection").
Artur Rubinstein (pno). 1961-62.
RCA 5616 ADD 60:48

★***Awards:*** *American Record Guide* Overview: Chopin, Jl/Ag '92 (No. 2).

See Ballades and Scherzos (Rubinstein) for review excerpt.

American Record Guide 52:118-21 Jl/Ag '89. Donald Manildi (55w)

4077. Piano Music: Waltzes, No's. 1-14.
("The Rubinstein Collection").
Artur Rubinstein (pno).
RCA 5492

★***Awards:*** *American Record Guide* Overview: Chopin, Jl/Ag '92.

Originally reviewed in *Fanfare* VII:6. "The reproduction is mellow and lovely and the CD format is marvelous."

Fanfare 9:149 Mr/Ap '86. Howard Kornblum (220w)

American Record Guide 52:118-21 Jl/Ag '89. Donald Manildi (55w)

4078. Piano Music: Ballades (4) (Opus 23, 38, 47, 52); Scherzos (4) (Opus 20, 31, 39, 54).
Earl Wild (pno).
CHESKY 044 DDD 69:19

★***Awards:*** *American Record Guide* Overview: Chopin, Jl/Ag '92.

"Competing couplings of the Ballades and Scherzos are by Ashkenazy (London), Katsaris (Teldec), and Rubinstein (RCA). Wild eclipses all but the last, and his warm, roomy sonics surpass all three. In short, a triumph—not just for Wild but also for producer Michael Davis and engineer Ed Thompson."

American Record Guide 54:56-7 Mr/Ap '91. Donald Manildi (200w)

"What besides his physical mastery assures that these recordings will live on? Artistry. And in the scherzos particularly, Wild has some remarkable conceptions....Chesky has improved on the sound of Wild's Medtner recording (which was already outstanding). The bell-like bass is stupendous."

HighPerformanceReview 8(1):65-6 '91. Robert J. Sullivan, Jr. (410w)

"Whether you're looking for your first recording of this music, or whether you've got so many copies that you're running out of shelf space, this superbly engineered disc deserves the highest priority."

Fanfare 14:186-7 Mr/Ap '91. Peter J. Rabinowitz (500w)

"These are large-scale, dramatic readings, generating excitement from far below the surface, and as free of gimmickry as of cliche....It will upset some listeners who have very set ways of regarding Chopin as all gossamer; they will find Wild's way too muscular, too 'Lisztian' by half. But such a notion is unrealistically confining in respect to both Chopin and Liszt."

Stereo Review 56:92 Mr '91. Richard Freed (275w)

4079. Piano Music: Ballades (4) (Op. 23, 38, 47, 52); Barcarolle in F#, Opus 60; Fantaisie in F minor, Opus 49.
Krystian Zimerman (pno). 1987.
DEUTSCHE GRAMMOPHON 423 090 DDD 60:00

✔HC ★★***Awards:*** Critics' Choice 1988, *Gramophone* D '88 (Joan Chissell). The Want List 1989, *Fanfare* N/D '89 (Howard Kornblum).

"Krystian Zimmerman's way with the Chopin ballades is especially winning....The barcarolle, too, exudes a convincing air of poetic inspiration. It's only in the fantasy, at the end of the recorded program, that disappointment sets in-....The sound is quite good without calling attention to itself."

Stereo Review 54:164 F '89. Richard Freed (200w)

"Chopin playing of this calibre is rarely encountered."

Music and Musicians International 37:49 F '89. Bryce Morrison (285w)

"These two brilliant recordings represent music-making on the highest level. They are worthy of any collection."

Ovation 10:54 Mr '89. Stuart Isacoff (210w)

"This is not Chopin for old-timers, but rather a sort of space-age Chopin....Contrasts are very strongly drawn, with an enormous dynamic range....if I can't love these performances, I certainly can admire and respect them, while remaining aware that this isn't really my favorite style of Chopin playing....DG's recording is-...far too close-up for my taste, leading to some shrill climaxes."

Fanfare 12:134-35 Mr/Ap '89. Leslie Gerber (300w)

"Zimerman's Chopin is simply exquisite-...Deutsche Grammophon's sound...is excellent. Despite the fact that most collectors will already own various versions of most, if not all, of this music, these performances deserve the highest recommendation."

High Fidelity 39:64 Je '89. David Hurwitz (275w)

Digital Audio's CD Review 5:50+ Jl '89. Lawrence Johnson (190w)

"I would single out Zimerman's second Ballade as one of the finest performances on records, and the other pieces are not far behind-....DG provides superb recorded sound."

American Record Guide 52:34-5 Jl/Ag '89. Donald Manildi (200w)

Gramophone 66:642 O '88. Joan Chissell (420w)

CLERAMBAULT, LOUIS NICOLAS. Suite No. 2 for Organ (Second Tone Suite). See No. 4082.

COPLAND, AARON

4080. Piano Music: Three Episodes from *Our Town*; **Four Episodes from** *Rodeo*; Four Piano Blues. Piano Variations; Danzon Cubano.
James Tocco (pno); Lukas Foss (pno).
PRO ARTE 183

✔**HC** ★***Awards:*** *Fanfare* Want List 1985 (John Ditsky).

"This is vintage Copland. From the seminal, extraordinary and grimly serious *Piano Variations* to the rollicking *Rodeo* Hoedown we get an overview of one of America's greatest composers in a performance that has to be as close to definitive as that over-worked expression is imaginably possible."

HighPerformanceReview 4(1):151-2 '86 Robert F. Arenz (415w) (rev. of LP)

COUPERIN, FRANCOIS

4081. Pieces de Clavecin (excerpts): L'art de toucher le clavecin: Preludes: C; D minor; G minor; B flat; F minor; A. Premier livre: Troisieme ordre: Allemande La tenebreuse; Courantes I and II; Sarabande La lugubre; L'espagnolete; Chaconne La favorite. Cinquieme ordre: Sarabande La dangereuse; Les ordes. Dieuxieme livre: Sixieme ordre: Les baricades misterieuses. Huitieme ordre: La Raphaele; Allemande L'Ausoniene; Courantes I and II; Sarabande L'unique; Gavotte; Rondeau; Gigue; Passacaille. Troisieme livre; Quinzieme ordre: Le dodo ou L'amour au berceau. Quatrieme livre: Vingt-troisieme ordre: L'arlequine. Vingtquatrieme ordre: Les vieux seigneurs.
Skip Sempe (hpscd).
DEUTSCHE HARMONIA MUNDI 77219 DDD 72:00

★***Awards:*** The Gramophone Awards, Nominations, Baroque—non-vocal, *Gramophone*, N '91.

"Sempe's study of Couperin's ornaments, and his conviction that by *'Toucher'* the composer really meant 'touch' not 'play', have resulted in a thoughtful recital, perhaps somewhat pedestrian here and there, but convincingly stylish. I think I have never heard a better recording of a harpsichord." *P95 S100*

Hi-Fi News & Record Review 36: 96-7 Ja '91. Robert Dearling (275w)

"His playing is admirably free and flexible rhythmically—the shaping of the preludes from Couperin's method is rhapsodic and convincing. Occasionally he is almost too free—the rondeau from Ordre 8 (a minuet) would be difficult to dance to."

Fanfare 14:194 Mr/Ap '91. Tom Moore (175w)

Gramophone 68:1386 Ja '91. Nicholas Anderson (445w)

4082. Pieces d'Orgue Consistantes en Deux Messes (Messe pour les Paroisses; Messe pour les Couvents). CLERAMBAULT, LOUIS NICOLAS. Suite No. 2 for Organ (Second Tone Suite).
Marie-Claire Alain (orgn). 1736/1981 Albi Cathedral organ. April 1989.
ERATO 45460 DDD 107:30 2 discs

✔**HC** ★***Awards:*** The Highs, 1990, *The New York Times* D 30 '90 (John Rockwell).

"Alain plays a 1736 Moucherel organ...the instantaneous response and supple muscularity of tone in both solo registers and large ensembles make it Alain's very willing dance partner. Quite literally, this is Church music with a beat, and a commanding imperative to leap to one's feet....Alain...imparts that knack of love-hate, secularized church that has been part of the fabric of French life since the Middle Ages, furthermore doing so in such vivid, imaginative sound as to totally amuse and delight the audience."

Fanfare 14:206-7 N/D '90. Haig Mardirosian (275w)

"What a sound this instrument makes! It possesses in voluptuous abundance...all the tonal requirements for Couperin and Clerambault. Marie-Claire Alain makes perfect use of them in her so persuasive performances....A must for anyone with even the slightest interest in this music."

Organists' Review 76:216-17 S '90. Paul Hale (360w)

"In spite of all the French obscurities [noted], this is a terrific, maybe sensational, recording of its type—music for organ. Anyone with a bit of patience (and plenty of time) who has thrilled to *any* sort of organ music should have this two-CD album."

Audio 75:88 Mr '91. Edward Tatnall Canby (590w)

"This is the second set of Couperin masses I have heard in a year. The first was by Andre Isoir on Calliope 9903. The performances are remarkably similar, even down to almost identical ornamentation....However, Alain has more sparkle and vitality....The three instruments

Isoir used are excellent in their own rights but pale compared to the Moucherel. Recording quality: again the Erato seems less muddy and has more vitality."

American Record Guide 54:59-60 Mr/Ap '91. David Bond (110w)

DEBUSSY, CLAUDE

4083. **Piano Music:** Preludes for Piano, Books 1 and 2.
Walter Gieseking (pno). 1954, 1955 reissues.
EMI 61004 70:00

✔**HC** ★*Awards:* Critics Choice, *Hi Fi News & Record Review*, Ap '91 Supplement (Kenneth Dommett).

"In this music, the pianist set a standard that no one since has matched. He recorded the first dozen *Preludes* in London in 1953 and the second group in 1954, but as rejuvenated for CD they sound far more recent."

High Fidelity 39:59 F '89. Paul Moor (275w)

"This CD preserves Gieseking's third and last commercial recording of the *Preludes*...the flame of inspiration may be seen burning less brightly than usual here. There are, to be sure, no glaring weaknesses....But there is a perceptible dropping off of freshness that manifests itself in a variety of ways."

Musical America 109:60-1 Mr '89. Harris Goldsmith (430w)

Gramophone 65:1478 Ap '88. David J. Fanning (360w)

4084. **Piano Music:** Pour le Piano; Children's Corner; Estampes; Le Plus que Lente; L'Isle Joyeuse; Deux Arabesques; Page d'Album.
Jean-Bernard Pommier (pno).
VIRGIN 90847 DDD 61:00

★*Awards:* Best of the Month, *Hi-Fi News & Record Review*, N '90.

"This is one of the most impressive Debussy recitals since Gieseking's legendary sets, and it is incomparably better recorded....music-making for connoiseurs." *P100 S100*

Hi-Fi News & Record Review 35:95 N '90. Bryce Morrison (245w)

"The two *Arabesques* and *Pour le piano* respond well to his strong no-nonsense playing. Yet with *Estampes* and the *Children's Corner*, the mature Debussy nuances emerge, and *L'Isle Joyeuse* is both subtle and brilliant. A fine disc."

Music and Musicians International 39:45 S '90. Gordon Reynolds (200w)

"These pungent and often witty readings are, to be sure, not the last word in languor....But he shapes the music horizontally through his superb control of accentuation and weight...and he shapes it vertically through imaginative voicing, which gives even the less elaborate music a sense of inner activity that saves it from fading....Good sound....Warmly recommended."

Fanfare 14:221 S/O '90. Peter J. Rabinowitz (215w)

"Pommier provides a more traditional, more objective Debussy, rhythmically straighter and less urgent....Although he is not as tonally alluring as the Hungarian pianist, he avoids the latter's few moments of tonal hardness. Virgin Classics' reproduction does extremely well by Pommier, presenting highly satisfactory sonics."

Stereophile 14:195-6 Ag '91. Igor Kipnis (100w)

Gramophone 67:1489-90 F '90. James Methuen-Campbell (365w)

4085. **Piano Music:** Etudes (12) for Piano.
Mitsuko Uchida (pno).
PHILIPS 422 412 DDD 47:00

✔**HC** ★★★*Awards:* Critics' Choice 1990, *Gramophone* D '90 (David Fanning); Critics' Choice 1990, *Gramophone* D '90 (Michael Stewart). The Gramophone Awards, Nominations, Instrumental, *Gramophone*, N '91; Critic's Choice: 1991, *American Record Guide*, Ja/F '92 (Stephen Chakwin).

"Mitsuko Uchida's new recording of the piano studies is anything but cool or academic. She brings out an extraordinary range of colour and dynamic range without loss of control. The recording was made using Bitstream Conversion and the sound is extremely realistic and clear without loss of warmth."

High Fidelity 1:109 Ag '90. Andrew Stuart (b.n.)

"I could go on and on about extraordinary details in her accomplishments here, but suffice it to say that she has made a dazzling recording of these forbidding, truly avant-garde works-....In doing so, she has revealed a new and unexpected facet of her formidable talent.."

Musical America 110:70 N '90. Paul Moor (230w)

"Despite the acrobatic virtuosity...what most resonates in your consciousness are her more poetic interpretive touches...Uchida emphasizes the etudes' untraditional structures—the startling breaks in their musical argument—by lighting on each disruption as a miraculous discovery....even with strong competition from Swann, Jacobs, and Keller, the Philips disc would stand as my recommendation in this repertoire were I limited to a single choice."

Fanfare 14:209-10 N/D '90. Peter J. Rabinowitz (215w)

"Her recording is not good or very good or excellent. It is something even better than that. It is as fine a recording as these pieces have had. In fact, with the possible exception of Jacobs, I can't think of another that even comes close."

American Record Guide 54:44-5 Ja/F '91. Stephen D. Chakwin, Jr. (145w)

"Her secret isn't delicacy, but strength; Uchida's command over the instrument is so absolute that it becomes almost unnoticeable."
Musician 140:111 Je '90 J.D. Considine (b.n.)

"Though I would not want to be without Garrick Ohlsson's lavishly affectionate Arabesque disc of the *Etudes* (He also finds room for the complete *Suite Bergamasque*) this recording is, quite simply, in a class of its own." *P100 S100*
Hi-Fi News & Record Review 35:95 Je '90. Bryce Morrison (375w)

The New York Times My 27 '90, p. 19 H. John Rockwell (175w)

Gramophone 68:245-46 Jl '90. David J. Fanning (385w)

Digital Audio's CD Review 7:71 Ja '91. Tom Vernier (160w)

DURUFLE, MAURICE

4086. Organ Music (complete): Prelude sur l'Introit de l'Epiphanie; Prelude et Fugue sur le nom d'Alain; Suite, Opus 5; Scherzo; Prelude, Adagio et Choral varie sur Veni Creator; Fugue sur le Carillon des Heures de la Cathedrale de Soissons.
John Scott (orgn). St. Paul's Willis/Mander organ, St. Paul's Cathedral. April and June 1989.
HYPERION 66368 69:33

★*Awards:* Critics' Choice 1991, *Gramophone*, Ja '92 (Marc Rochester).

"It would indeed be hard to imagine playing which brought more out of these marvellous pieces....Scott has the measure of this music, technically, intellectually and emotionally. A compelling programme, particularly as it includes the lesser-known works."
Organists' Review 76:215 S '90. Robert Lawrenson (360w)

Gramophone 68:1389 Ja '91. Marc Rochester (300w)

FELDMAN, MORTON

4087. Piano Music: Intermission 5; Piano Piece (to Philip Guston); Vertical Thoughts 4; Piano; Palais de Mari (for Francesco Ciamente).
Marianne Schroder (pno).
HAT ART 6035 DDD 63:20

★★*Awards:* The Want List 1991, *Fanfare* N/D '91 (Kyle Gann). The Critics' Choice 1990—Composition Award: No. 11 of 15 *Wire* 82/3 '91.

"Schroeder is that rarest of creatures, the gifted instrumentalist who devotes her energies (so far as I can generalize from what I hear on two CDs) to this age's finest and least known music....I recommend this wonderfully performed and recorded Hat Art disc...with enthusiasm."
Fanfare 14:241 S/O '90. Mike Silverton (360w)

FIOCCO, JOSEPH-HECTOR

4088. Pieces de Clavecin, Opus 1.
Ton Koopman (hpscd).
AUVIDIS-ASTREE 7731 AAD 86:00 2 discs

★*Awards:* Critics' Choice 1990, *Gramophone* D '90 (Julie Anne Sadie).

"The music...is on a par with that of Couperin-....Koopman's playing is stunning. It takes control and taste to render this music....the ornaments...require a virtuoso touch. The sound of the Elsche harpsichord is delicious, with a nasal yet full timbre....Highly recommended—this deserves a place on your shelf."
Fanfare 13:180 Mr/Ap '90. Tom Moore (210w)

Gramophone 67:1639 Mr '90. Julie Ann Sadie (420w)

FRANCK, CESAR

Fantaisie in A for Organ. See No. 2074.

4089. Organ Music: Piece Heroique; Pastorale; Fantasy in A; Trois Chorals; Final; Fantasy in C; Prelude, Fugue et Variation; Cantabile; Priere; Grande Piece Symphonique.
Jean Guillou (orgn). Van Den Heuvel organ, St. Eustache, Paris. June and July 1989.
DORIAN 90135 DDD 74:16, 72:15 2 discs

★★★*Awards:* The Want List 1990, *Fanfare* N/D '90 (Al Fasoldt); Critic's Choice: 1990, *American Record Guide* Ja/F '91 (Arved Ashby). The Want List 1991, *Fanfare* N/D '91 (Al Fasoldt).

"Guillou's playing has appeal to anyone who enjoys the organ works of Franck and is looking for a different slant or insight into these musical pages....This is a superb collection of imaginative performances, beautifully recorded-....top rating."
American Record Guide 53:63-4 S/O '90. Donald E. Metz (290w)

"In these collections [Guillou and Murray] we have two distinct views on a body of organ works which many consider the only one capable of standing comparison to J.S. Bach's....For the audiophile in search of a 'sonic spectacular,' the choice of the Dorian collection is rather easy....Choosing between these releases on a musical basis is not so easy. Guillou is fresh and vivacious. Murray offers patrician restraint and marvelous taste. The former makes the music alive and immediate, but I think the latter will prove to render it more durable."
Stereophile 14:197-98 Mr '91. Robert Hesson (260w)

"Technical wizardry of every kind permeates this complete set of Franck's organ works-...The wizardry of the organ builder and of the distinguished performer are matched by truly fantastic sound engineering, but watch the level you set, in case your ears drop off or your equipment catches fire."

Organists' Review 76:133-34 Je '90. Gordon Reynolds (780w)

"Guillou...has transcended the lessons of the master [Marcel Dupre] with a prodigality which may not be uniformly successful but is never dull....Murray offers the basic Franck, grandly given."

Fanfare 13:145-46 Jl/Ag '90. Adrian Corleonis (175w)

Musical America 110:37-41 Jl '90. Josiah Fisk (230w)

Gramophone 68:83 Je '90. Marc Rochester (170w)

4090. Prelude, Chorale et Fugue, for Piano; Aria et Final; Variations Symphoniques. Jorge Bolet (pno). Riccardo Chailly (c). Concertgebouw Orchestra. 1987 reissue.
LONDON/DECCA 421 714 DDD 62:00

★***Awards:*** Critic's Choice: 1990, *American Record Guide* Ja/F '91 (Arved Ashby).

"The scale is grand, the pace is unhurried; there is power to burn, but it is always subtly controlled, and the overall impression is one of just the sort of spontaneity and flair one wants in this music, along with the touches of poetry and wit one hopes for. Chailly and the orchestra are fine partners in the *Variations symphoniques*, and the sound quality is demonstration-class throughout." *P90 S95*

Stereo Review 54:156 N '89. Richard Freed (130w)

"Bolet's beautifully shaded piano sonority at all dynamic levels, his rhythmic solidity, and the basic sobriety of his musical approach produce outstanding versions of all three works-....Sonically, London's efforts here are first-class."

American Record Guide 53:50 Ja/F '90. Donald Manildi (155w)

"I found this performance rather perfunctory for my taste....The Concertgebouw are marvellous, and I do like the recorded sound of the piano on this Decca disc." *P85 S95*

Hi-Fi News & Record Review 34:107 O '89. William McVicker (340w)

"Notwithstanding that this is the same recording of the *Symphonic Variations* included with Chailly's reading of the Franck symphony (compact disc London 417 487-2 LH, *Fanfare* 11:2), every new release by Bolet seems to document a dynamic and expressive shrinkage. Sound is adequately close and clear."

Fanfare 13:208 N/D '89. Adrian Corleonis (280w)

Gramophone 67:450 S '89. Michael Oliver (315w)

4091. Prelude, Chorale et Fugue, for Piano. BACH, JOHANN SEBASTIAN. Sonata in D minor for Unaccompanied Violin, BWV.1004: Chaconne (arr. Busoni). LISZT, FRANZ. Sonata in B minor for Piano. ("The Rubinstein Collection").
Artur Rubinstein (pno). 1970 and 1965 reissue.
RCA 5673 ADD 60:00

"The Franck and Bach-Busoni performances are...classic. But the Liszt...is oddly laconic....Sound is fuller and brighter on CD, that is, close and crisply detailed. Cornerstone material."

Fanfare 11:312 Jl/Ag '88. Adrian Corleonis (100w)

Gramophone 66:444 S '88. James Methuen-Campbell (105w)

American Record Guide 52:118-21 Jl/Ag '89. Donald Manildi (55w)

Prelude, Choral et Fugue for Piano. See No. 4122.

FROBERGER, JOHANN JAKOB

4092. Harpsichord Music: Canzon No. 2 Capriccio No. 10. Fantasia No. 4 sopra Sollare. Ricercare No. 5. Suites: No. 2; No. 14: Allemande, Lamentation sur ce que j'ay ete vole; No. 30. Toccatas: No. 9; No. 10; No. 14. Lamentation faite sur la mort tres douloureuse de Sa Majeste Imperiale, Ferdinand le troisieme. Tombeau fait a Paris sur la mort de Monsieur Blancrocher.
Gustav Leonhardt (hpscd).
DEUTSCHE HARMONIA MUNDI 7923 DDD 56:58

Gramophone 68:783-4 O '90. Lindsay Kemp (300w)

"Leonhardt conveys the originality of this music with spontaneity and flair in the freer works and with relaxed sobriety in the stricter ones....Highly recommended."

Fanfare 14:199 Ja/F '91. Charles Timbrell (275w)

GINASTERA, ALBERTO

4093. Piano Music: Sonata No. 1 for Piano, Opus 22 (1952); Danzas Argentinas para Piano, Opus 2; American Preludes (12) for Piano, Opus 12.
Barbara Nissman (pno). 1981.
GLOBE 5006 42:00

★★***Awards:*** Critics' Choice 1989, *Gramophone* D '89 (Alan Sanders); Top Choices—1989, *American Record Guide* Ja/F '90 (Karl Miller).

"This is some of the most remarkable piano playing I have heard in many years-....[Nissmann's] playing has personality. Her performances are filled with the extremes to be found in the music, from intense brilliance to sensuous lyricism to an almost naive simplicity."

American Record Guide 52:51-2 My/Je '89. Karl Miller (165w)

"Like it or not, Barbara Nissman's muscular, hell-bent-for-leather approach is, on its own terms, phenomenal....Nissman's...performance of the sonata is far more effective than the old

Somer performance on Desto...I have reservations as to whether Nissman provides a complete enough realization of what this magnificent music is all about."
Fanfare 12:202 My/Je '89. William Zagorski (270w)

GLASS, PHILIP

4094. Dances: No.'s 2 and 4 for Solo Organ; No.'s 1, 3 and 5 for Voice and Instruments.
Michael Riesman (orgn); Philip Glass (orgn). Philip Glass Ensemble.
CBS 44765 ADD 42:17, 66:31 2 discs

★*Awards:* Critics' Choice 1989, *Gramophone* D '89 (John Milsom).

"This work represents a collaboration between Glass and choreographer Lucinder Childs; apparently known for her 'austere, mathematically exact dances'. This quote from the liner notes is certainly an apt description of the music on this double CD....There certainly is a rather joyous sense in this work and it is attractive in its own way. It does, however, tend to go on and on...with, however, a somewhat hypnotic quality to the pieces."
Australian Hi-Fi 20(5):83:10 '89. Gary Crees (180w)

"There is an inventiveness in these two solo organ pieces that makes one long for even more economy of materials in Glass's work—namely, a reduction of the instrumental forces. Or, in other works, instrumental Minimalism."
Ovation 10:50 Mr '89. Karen Campbell (380w)

"The performances and the recording itself are highly effective, with the exception of the very opening of No. 1, which has a switched-on, cut-in effect that, intentional or not, I find distracting."
Stereo Review 54:120+ Mr '89. Eric Salzman (200w)

"Stylistically, the music of *Dance* holds closely to that of *Einstein on the Beach*-...Riesman's solo performance in *Dance* No. 2 is an extraordinary show of keyboard virtuosity."
Musical America 109:62 My '89. James Wierzbicki (500w)

"*Dance Nos 1 - 5*...is clearly descended from *Music In Twelve Parts*....What differentiates *Dance* from the earlier work is its glistening sound, harmonically bright with Glass utilising Farfisa organ and flutes to great effect."
Music and Musicians International 37:15+ Je '89. Mark J. Prendergast (1035w)

"Although doing little to gainsay early accusations of minimalist 'naivety,' and not commensurate in harmonic variety with some of Glass's other works mentioned above, *Dance* is tremendously enjoyable in its particularly clean textures and rhythmic vitality."
American Record Guide 52:45 Jl/Ag '89. Arved Ashby (290w)

"This is a real dog."
Fanfare 12:167-68 Mr/Ap '89. Edward Strickland (400w)
Gramophone 67:450 S '89. John Milsom (490w)

GRAINGER, PERCY

4095. Piano Music: Handel in the Strand; Walking Tune; The Merry King; Molly on the Shore; Jutish Medley; One More Day, My John; Lullaby; The Sussex Mummers' Christmas Carol; The Hunter in His Career; Knight and Shepherd's Daughter; "In a Nutshell" Suite; Colonial Song; Shepherd's Hey; Irish Tune from County Derry; Country Gardens.
(Dished Up for Piano by the Composer).
Nigel Coxe (pno).
TITANIC 155 DDD 66:00

★*Awards:* *Fanfare* Want List 1987 (John D. Wiser).

"This Jamaican-born, English-trained pianist not only seems to recognize how to cut a folk song melody, but leans into Grainger's understandingly formulated piano writing with something approaching the composer's characteristic frenzy....Played with his energy level and finesse, every one of these little essays blossoms into something of measurable significance."
Fanfare 11:146 N/D '87. John D. Wiser (250w)

"The best anthology of Grainger's piano settings to be made available in the United States since Daniel Adni's 1976 Seraphim release-...The close-up yet reverberant sonics are fairly good, but I would have preferred a piano sound that was a little less clattery at times, as well as less shallow on top and richer in the bass."
Musical America 108:75-6 Jl '88. Igor Kipnis (560w)

"The virtue of this disc [lies]...in the lively, open-hearted performances of Nigel Coxe."
American Record Guide 50:19 Fall '87. David W. Moore (165w)

"Coxe's brisk and unaffected playing suggests considerable familiarity with Grainger's own 78-rpm recordings. Kenneth Forfia's boxy digital sound does less than perfect justice to Coxe's tone, but brings out his humming with unwelcome clarity."
High Fidelity 37:90 N '87. Terry Teachout (260w)

"I welcome this refreshing recording, even with its flaws....Nigel Coxe...handles these charming pieces well enough, but if you listen carefully you can actually hear the labored breathing such exertions cost him."
Musical America 107:60-1 N '87. Paul Moor
Gramophone 65:778 N '87 Malcolm MacDonald (345w)

HighPerformanceReview 5:78 Ap '88. Murray Dineen (275w)

Ovation 10:46-7 My '89. Peter J. Rabinowitz (165w)

GRANADOS, ENRIQUE

4096. Allegro de Concierto; Danza Lenta; Goyescas.
Alicia De Larrocha (pno).
RCA 0408 DDD 70:00

✔HC

Gramophone 68:1533-4 F '91. Lionel Salter (455w)

"The London recording is perfectly fine, and its sound is a bit mellower than the new RCA. However, in the end I prefer the RCA, which is more vivid and, if a bit brilliant for my taste, also more convincingly realistic....I recommend this issue strongly, and it's going to become my basic *Goyescas* for certain."

Fanfare 14:176-77 My/Je '91. Leslie Gerber (200w)

"Alicia de Larrocha presents here a wonderfully sensitive and strong recording of works by Enrique Granados...Her impeccable playing is, as we have come to expect, full of revelations as she etches the musical outlines and lends depth to fluctuating shadows and highlights. She tellingly projects that haunting quality that so pervades the pieces but eludes many a pianist...The recording...is clear and warm. Informative and interesting notes are provided by Harris Goldsmith."

High Performance Review 8:74 Wtr '91/92. June C. Ottenberg (long)

"There is little to be said here. If you like Granados's atmospheric piano writing, you'll do no better than this....Larrocha remains the supreme Spanish pianist of our day."

American Record Guide 54:61 My/Je '91. Carl Bauman (75w)

4097. Goyescas (suite of six pieces for piano).
Alicia De Larrocha (pno). 1977.
LONDON/DECCA 411 958 ADD 57:00

✔HC ★*Awards:* Critics' Choice 1989, *Gramophone* D '89 (Christopher Headington).

"This 1977 analogue recording was highly recommended in its day...The piano sound is a little forward, however, and congested at climaxes."

Hi-Fi News & Record Review 29:131 D '84. John Atkinson (70w)

Gramophone 66:1457 Mr '89. Christopher Headington (140w)

4098. Spanish Dances (12), Opus 37.
Alicia De Larrocha (pno). 1982 reissue.
LONDON/DECCA 414 557 56:21

"The 1982 LP has become one of my firm favourites for the freshness and spontaneity of both the music and Alicia de Larrocha's exquisite playing. The CD will ensure a revival in my household."

Hi-Fi News & Record Review 30:103 O '85. Roger Bowen (65w)

Gramophone 63:524 O '85. Max Harrison (125w)

GRIEG, EDVARD

4099. Piano Music (complete): Lyric Pieces, sets 1-4.
(Volume 1).
Eva Knardahl (pno). reissue.
BIS 104 AAD 65:21

★*Awards:* Record of the Eighties, *Gramophone*, D '89 (James Methuen-Campbell).

"CD versions of a most praiseworthy project, both as to conception and to execution."

Fanfare 11:131-2 Ja/F '88. John Ditsky (150w)

"Digital sound may be good, but these transfers show just how fine good analog sound, without any Dolby, can be."

American Record Guide 51:39-40 Mr/Ap '88. Carl Bauman (80w)

Digital Audio 4:58+ Mr '88. D. R. Martin (110w)

4100. Piano Music (complete): Lyric Pieces, sets 5-7.
(Volume 2).
Eva Knardahl (pno). reissue.
BIS 105 AAD 66:54

★*Awards:* Record of the Eighties, *Gramophone*, D '89 (James Methuen-Campbell).

See Volume 1 for review excerpts.

—*American Record Guide* 51:39-40 Mr/Ap '88. Carl Bauman (80w)

—*Fanfare* 11:131-2 Ja/F '88. John Ditsky (150w)

Digital Audio 4:58+ Mr '88. D. R. Martin (110w)

4101. Piano Music (complete): Lyric Pieces, sets 8-10.
(Volume 3).
Eva Knardahl (pno). reissue.
BIS 106 AAD 62:05

★*Awards:* Record of the Eighties, *Gramophone*, D '89 (James Methuen-Campbell).

See Volume 1 for review excerpts.

—*American Record Guide* 51:39-40 Mr/Ap '88. Carl Bauman (80w)

—*Fanfare* 11:131-2 Ja/F '88. John Ditsky (150w)

Digital Audio 4:58+ Mr '88. D. R. Martin (110w)

4102. Piano Music (complete): Four Piano Pieces, Opus 1; Poetic Tone Pictures, Opus 3; Nordraak's Funeral March; Humoresques, Opus 6; Sonata for Piano, Opus 7.
(Volume 4).
Eva Knardahl (pno). reissue.
BIS 107 AAD 64:41

★*Awards:* Record of the Eighties, *Gramophone*, D '89 (James Methuen-Campbell).

See Volume 1 for review excerpts.
—American Record Guide 51:39-40 Mr/Ap '88. Carl Bauman (80w)

—Fanfare 11:131-2 Ja/F '88. John Ditsky (150w)

Digital Audio 4:58: Mr '88. D. R. Martin (110w)

Gramophone 66:316+ Ag '88. James Methuen-Campbell

4103. Piano Music (complete): Norwegian Folksongs and Dances (25), Opus 17; Scenes from Folk Life, Opus 19; Four Album Leaves, Opus 28; Improvisations on Two Norwegian Folksongs, Opus 29.
(Volume 5).
Eva Knardahl (pno). reissue.
BIS 108 AAD 66:29

★***Awards:*** Record of the Eighties, *Gramophone*, D '89 (James Methuen-Campbell).

See Volume 1 for review excerpts.
—American Record Guide 51:39-40 Mr/Ap '88. Carl Bauman (80w)

—Fanfare 11:131-2 Ja/F '88. John Ditsky (150w)

Digital Audio 4:58+ Mr '88. D. R. Martin (110w)

Gramophone 66:316+ Ag '88. James Methuen-Campbell

4104. Piano Music (complete): Ballade in G minor, Opus 24; Peer Gynt: Suite No. 1, Opus 46; Suite No. 2, Opus 55. Three Orchestral Pieces from "Sigurd Jorsalfar," Opus 56.
(Volume 6).
Eva Knardahl (pno). September 1978.
BIS 109 AAD 70:00

★***Awards:*** Record of the Eighties, *Gramophone*, D '89 (James Methuen-Campbell).

"Eva Knardahl plays the program nicely though she might have been more outgoing, more daring in this unabashedly romantic music."
HighPerformanceReview 5:78-9 Ap '88. John Mueter (215w)

See Volume 1 for review excerpts.
—American Record Guide 51:39-40 Mr/Ap '88. Carl Bauman (80w)

—Fanfare 11:131-2 Ja/F '88. John Ditsky (150w)

Digital Audio 4:58+ Mr '88. D. R. Martin (110w)

Gramophone 66:316+ Ag '88. James Methuen-Campbell (100w)

4105. Piano Music (complete): From Holberg's Time, Opus 40; Two Elegiac Melodies, Opus 34; Waltz-Caprices, Opus 37; From "Olav Trygvason," Opus 50; Two Nordic Melodies, Opus 63.
(Volume 7).
Eva Knardahl (pno). reissue.
BIS 110 AAD 64:52

★***Awards:*** Record of the Eighties, *Gramophone*, D '89 (James Methuen-Campbell).

See Volume 1 for review excerpts.
—American Record Guide 51:39-40 Mr/Ap '88. Carl Bauman (80w)

—Fanfare 11:131-2 Ja/F '88. John Ditsky (150w)

Digital Audio 4:58+ Mr '88. D. R. Martin (110w)

Gramophone 66:316+ Ag '88. James Methuen-Campbell (100w)

4106. Piano Music (complete): Norwegian Folksongs (19), Opus 66; Song Arrangements (6), Opus 41; Song Arrangements (6), Opus 52. (Volume 8).
Eva Knardahl (pno). reissue.
BIS 111 AAD 65:56

★***Awards:*** Record of the Eighties, *Gramophone*, D '89 (James Methuen-Campbell).

See Volume 1 for review excerpts.
—American Record Guide 51:39-40 Mr/Ap '88. Carl Bauman (80w)

—Fanfare 11:131-2 Ja/F '88. John Ditsky (150w)

Digital Audio 4:58+ Mr '88. D. R. Martin (110w)

Gramophone 66:316+ Ag '88. James Methuen-Campbell (100w)

4107. Piano Music (complete): Norwegian Peasant Dances, Opus 72; Moods, Opus 73; Three Piano Pieces, Op. posth.
(Volume 9).
Eva Knardahl (pno). reissue.
BIS 112 AAD 72:24

★***Awards:*** Record of the Eighties, *Gramophone*, D '89 (James Methuen-Campbell).

See Volume 1 for review excerpts.
—American Record Guide 51:39-40 Mr/Ap '88. Carl Bauman (80w)

—Fanfare 11:131-2 Ja/F '88. John Ditsky (150w)

Digital Audio 4:58+ Mr '88. D. R. Martin (110w)

Gramophone 66:316+ Ag '88. James Methuen-Campbell (100w)

4108. Piano Music (complete): Norwegian Dances, for Piano, Four-hands, Opus 35; Two Romances, Opus 53; Six Norwegian Mountain Melodies, Opus 112; Concerto in A minor for Piano and Orchestra, Opus 16.
(Volume 10).
Eva Knardahl (pno); Kjell Ingebretsen (pno). Kjell Ingebretsen (c). Royal Philharmonic Orchestra. reissue.
BIS 113 AAD 65:30

★***Awards:*** Perfect 10s, *Digital Audio's CD Review*, Mr '89.

"This is still not the finest available recording of the concerto, but it is more than competent and, in the context of the 'complete' Grieg pianism (it's not quite that), it will surely serve."
Fanfare 11:132 Ja/F '88. John Ditsky (100w)

See Volume 1 for review excerpt.
American Record Guide 51:39-40 Mr/Ap '88. Carl Bauman (80w)

Digital Audio 4:58+ Mr '88. D. R. Martin (110w)

GUILMANT, ALEXANDRE

4109. Organ Music: Sonata No. 1 in D minor; Sonata No. 5 in C minor; Scherzo Symphonique (from Opus 57); March on a Theme of Handel; Grand Choeur in D (alla Handel).
Catherine Ennis (orgn). Rieger organ, St. Marylebone Parish Church, London. August 1988.
EMI 49674

★*Awards:* Best of the Month, *Hi-Fi News & Record Review*, My '90.

"I'm delighted to be able to welcome most warmly this issue. It is a splendid exposition of the lively playing of Catherine Ennis; it is also (I believe) the debut recording of this large new Rieger; not least it begins to restore Guilmant to a position of respectability....Miss Ennis combines flair and enthusiasm for the music with a fine control of a sensitive mechanical action (a product partly, no doubt, of her studies with Nicholas Danby). She has chosen a splendid programme."
Organists' Review 75:274-75 D '89. Robert Lawrenson (500w)

"Ennis's ability to drive the music forward is, perhaps, the most exciting feature of this recording...This recording is strongly recommended." *100 S95/100*
Hi-Fi News & Record Review 35:89-90 My '90. William McVicker (385w)

HANDEL, GEORGE FRIDERIC. Sonatas for Recorder: H.369, H.365, H.358. See No. 6073.

HAYDN, FRANZ JOSEPH

4110. Piano Music (complete).
Walid Akl (pno).
BOURG 30/43 130:07; 134:25; 124:31; 130:07; 129:54; 124:30; 131:49 14 discs

★*Awards:* *Fanfare* Want List 1987 (David Johnson).

"This set...represents a valuable reference and contains many works unlikely to be duplicated soon in the CD catalog. Haydn scholars will doubtless argue happily for years about various aspects of this release, but the general listener will find it an inexhaustable vault of musical treasures waiting to be discovered and appreciated."
American Record Guide 51:30-3 Ja/F '88. Stephen D. Chakwin, Jr. (980w)

Digital Audio 4:90+ D '87. Joe Roberts (750w)

4111. Piano Music: Sonatas for Piano: No. 33 in C minor; No. 38 in F; No. 58 in C; No. 60 in C.
Emanuel Ax (pno). 1988.
CBS 44918 DDD 63:59

✔**HC** ★★★*Awards:* Best Recordings of the Month, *Stereo Review* S '89. Top Choices—1989, *American Record Guide* Ja/F '90 (Lee Milazzo). Best of the Month, *Hi-Fi News & Record Review*, Mr '90; The Year's Best, *Hi Fi News & Record Review*, May '90 Supplement.

"One word sums up Ax's Haydn: satisfying. CBS has supported Ax with excellent reproduction; his piano comes through with bright singing highs and warm solid bass, smoothly integrated across the spectrum."
Fanfare 13:217 S/O '89. James H. North (200w)

"These are four of the finest [of Haydn's sonatas], and none of them has been—or is likely to be—heard to better advantage."
Stereo Review Presents: Compact Disc Buyers' Guide 1990 p.66-7 Richard Freed (115w)

"Ax's command is immaculate yet the music's inner life, quality and poetry are always placed above pianistic know-how or expertise....All Emanuel Ax's performances—beautifully recorded—are of a rare composure and serenity." *P100 S95*
Hi-Fi News & Record Review 35:104-05 Mr '90; p.22-23 My '90 Supplement. Bryce Morrison (245w)

"Ax's disc is a welcome one. His playing is technically fluent and full of evident affection for Haydn's witty asides....The recorded sound is some of the best CBS has given Ax."
American Record Guide 53:55 Jl/Ag '90. Stephen D. Chakwin, Jr. (100w)

"The listener unfamiliar with this part of the beloved composer's output could hardly ask for a handsomer introduction to it. The recorded sound is exemplary...Quite possibly the piano recording of the year."
Stereo Review 54:123-24 S '89. Richard Freed (480w)

Digital Audio's CD Review 6:60 Ap '90. Tom Vernier (360w)

Gramophone 67:1164 D '89. Stephen Johnson (315w)

4112. Piano Music: Sonatas for Piano: H.XVI:40, 41, 42; H.XVII:6; H.XVI:51; 52. (Keyboard Works. Volume 2).
Lola Odiaga (ftpno).
TITANIC 160 DDD 67:12

★*Awards:* The Want List 1988, *Fanfare* N/D '88 (John Wiser).

"How very much better the music of Haydn sounds when the keyboard instrument is the so-called fortepiano....Especially is this true when that essential element, an understanding artist, is involved! Lola Odiaga fills the bill."
Audio 73:163 Ja '89. Edward Tatnall Canby (300w)

"If Odiaga's second CD is part of a continuing series, then it is showing the sort of organization such a series ought to possess....Aside from Alfred Brendel's various Haydn keyboard sets for Philips, I do not know of other performances available on CD that approach this player's dash, comprehension, and grasp of Haydn's musical phraseology....Urgently recommended."

Fanfare 11:141 My/Je '88. John D. Wiser (350w)

HINDEMITH, PAUL

4113. Sonatas (4) for Viola Solo: (No. 1) Opus 11, No. 5; (No. 2) Opus 25, No. 1; (No. 3) Opus 31, No. 4; (No. 4). **Sonatas (3) for Viola and Piano:** (No. 1) Opus 11, No. 4; (No. 2) Opus 25, No. 4; (No. 3).
Kim Kashkashian (vla); Robert Levin (pno).
ECM 833 309; ECM 1330/32 DDD 72:43; 55:07 2 discs

"There are no perceptible flaws in this whole idealistic production, either of sound or of musicianship. The set is of permanent reference value in addition to its strong sensory assets."

Fanfare 12:168-70 S/O '88. John Wiser (550w)

"This remarkable set is a landmark in the history of viola recordings."

American Record Guide 51:40 N/D '88. Robert Follet (275w)

"I've not heard finer viola playing since the days of William Primrose. Robert Levin gives strong, utterly committed performances of the various piano parts and ECM's recording maintains a vivid instrumental profile throughout."

Hi-Fi News & Record Review 33:109 N '88. Robert Cowan (410w)

"With any luck, this collection of sonatas will reopen the book on Hindemith to give the composer the credit he is due. This is superbly rewarding music, compassionately played by Kim Kashkashian and Robert Levin."

Stereophile 11:187-89 D '88. Robert Hesson (590w)

"Her richly assured playing could hardly be bettered....Levin's playing is highly competent but somewhat monochromatic."

High Fidelity 39:60 F '89. Terry Teachout (300w)

"In violist Kim Kashkashian's recording of the seven sonatas, the works are divided by type: the four unaccompanied sonatas on the first disc and the three duo-sonatas on the second. This separation has a top-heavy effect, if one listens to the entire set straight through."

Musical America 109:77-8 Mr '89. Gary Lemco (1420w)

Gramophone 66:628+ O '88. James Methuen-Campbell (680w)

IVES, CHARLES

4114. Sonata No. 2 for Piano, "Concord, Mass., 1840-1860". WRIGHT, MAURICE. Sonata for Piano.
Marc-Andre Hamelin (pno).
NEW WORLD 378 DDD 59:36

> ✔HC ★★*Awards:* The Want List 1990, *Fanfare* N/D '90 (William Wians). Top Choices—1989, *American Record Guide* Ja/F '90 (Arved Ashby).

"Hamelin provides the most poetic rendition of the *Concord* that I have ever encountered...The textures [of the sonata by Maurice Wright] are perhaps reminiscent of Ives, but the orientation is neoclassical—rather mischievously so, in the manner of early Britten or early Hindemith. The melodic material is eminently forgettable, but Wright's control of dissonance, texture, and register is absolute, and this music is thoroughly entertaining...Everyone involved in this project, including those responsible for the close-up but solid sound of the piano, can take pride in it."

American Record Guide 52:65-6 S/O '89. Arved Ashby (350w)

"Hamelin's approach to the *Concord*, one of the most terrifying knuckle-crunchers in the modern piano repertory, is intensely lyrical and, believe it or not, convincingly pianistic. Whether Ives would have *wanted* the *Concord* Sonata to sound this beautiful is, of course, another question....Wright's sonata is a pleasingly well made piece of moderately dissonant musical carpentry. Excellent piano sound by producer Elizabeth Ostrow."

Musical America 110:70 Ja '90. Terry Teachout (270w)

"Marc-Andre Hamelin...races through the fast sections with total abandon and zest...technical problems simply do not exist. Perhaps he misses some of the dreamy grandeur of Gilbert Kalish on a Nonesuch LP...After hearing Hamelin, however, Kalish does seem to lack variety-....A winner."

Fanfare 13:224 S/O '89. James H. North (400w)

Gramophone 67:509 S '89. David J. Fanning (350w)

JANACEK, LEOS

4115. Piano Music: Sonata, "October 1, 1905" (In the Street); In the Mists; On an Overgrown Path; Reminiscence.
Rudolf Firkusny (pno). 1989.
RCA 0147 DDD 71:00

> ★★*Awards:* The Highs, 1990, *The New York Times* D 30 '90 (John Rockwell). The Gramophone Awards, Nominations, Instrumental, *Gramophone*, N '91.

"We have had convincing recordings made over the years by other pianists: Josef Palenicek, Ivan Klansky, Ivan Moravec, Radoslav Kvapil, and, most recently, Scandinavian pianist Jet Roling (*Fanfare* 12:1, but none among them has quite matched the acute muscular grace and pungency of Firkusny's readings, which accurately reflect what he does with the music in concert....There is a Schubertian element at work here, more in spirit than in any physical sense....whatever it may be, it earns this issue the most urgent of recommendations."

Fanfare 14:248-9 Mr/Ap '91. John Wiser (550w)

"Firkusny is, for me, the ideal interpreter of Janacek's piano music, not the least because Janacek was his teacher from age five onwards-....Firkusny's are the most desirable recordings of these works, which rank among the finest piano music of this century....The RCA recording is solid, clean, and almost palpably realistic—required listening."

American Record Guide 54:69-70 My/Je '91. Carl Bauman (120w)

"He captures the music's astonishing emotional range in all its transcendent beauty and shocking ugliness, its impulse rhythms and bold color."

Stereo Review 56:80 Jl '91. David Patrick Stearns (120w)

"Recently DG reissued on CD his 1972 recording....Perhaps it would be impertinent to refer to such differences as there are between the two recordings as a 'maturing'; they are better dscribed as a reassessment of music with which he has been intimately associated all his life. The sound of the new recording is all one could hope for, a natural piano tone that presents the music clearly and unequivocally." *P100 S95*

Hi-Fi News & Record Review 36:85 Ap '91. Kenneth Dommett (180w)

"Both sonically and musically, I find the RCA set preferable [to the DG reissue], but the earlier recordings do at times have a dash of spontaneity the later ones lack."

Musical America 111:75-6 Jl '91. Paul Moor (140w)

Gramophone 68:1700+ Mr '91. John Warrack (160w)

4116. Piano Music: On an Overgrown Path. In the Mists. Theme and Variations, "Zdenka". Sonata for Piano, 1.X.1905, "From the Street".
Rudolf Firkusny (pno). Munich. May 1971.
DEUTSCHE GRAMMOPHON 429 857 ADD 78:48

"These are performances of classic quality unimpaired by their transfer to the newer medium, and represent outstanding value in terms both of price and the amount of music." *P100 S95*

Hi-Fi News & Record Review 35:107 N '90. Kenneth Dommett (105w)

"Firkusny, who studied most of the composer's works with him, does indeed perform this quirky, powerful music with a finesse that has impelled Deutsche Grammophon to reissue on CD recordings originally taped in 1972."

Musical America 111:75-6 Jl '91. Paul Moor (140w)

"There are differences only in minor details, never in overall shape, between these fine performances and the ones recorded by Firkusny in 1989 for RCA Victor Red Seal (*Fanfare* 14:4), or for that matter, the set made for Columbia LP in the early 50s. The fact appears to be that this pianist is directly transmitting the composer's precepts in playing of absolute clarity and control...and conviction....Piano recording is shallower than RCA's in this desirable second alternative."

Fanfare 14:181-3 Jl/Ag '91. John Wiser (290w)

Gramophone 68:1700+ Mr '91. John Warrack (160w)

KLEIN, GIDEON. Sonata for Piano. See No. 3066.

KODALY, ZOLTAN

4117. Sonata for Unaccompanied Cello, Opus 8; Duo for Violin and Cello, Opus 7. BOTTERMUND, HANS. Variations (many) for Unaccompanied Cello, after Paganini's Violin Caprice No. 24 (trans. Starker).
Janos Starker (cello); Jose Gingold (vln). 1970-78.
DELOS 1015 AAD 62:00

✔**HC** ★***Awards:*** Critics' Choice 1989, *Gramophone* D '89 (Robin Golding).

"Starker is recognized as being one of the great cellists...those who appreciate fine playing have learned not to dismiss lightly anything he does, and in the two Kodaly works he is pre-eminent....Sound quality is variable."

Hi-Fi News & Record Review 33:109 D '88. Kenneth Dommett (235w)

Gramophone 66:1172-75 Ja '89. Robin Golding (315w)

LISZT, FRANZ

4118. Piano Music: Sonetti (3) del Petrarca; Legendes—No. 1, "St. Francis d'Assise (la predication aux oiseaux)"; Sonata in B minor for Piano.
Vladimir Feltsman (pno).
CBS 44925 DDD 62:00

★***Awards:*** Critic's Choice: 1990, *American Record Guide* Ja/F '91 (Allen Linkowski).

"Here the head is very much in evidence in the pianist's complete understanding of the structure of this sprawling masterpiece, but so is the heart. This is a deeply-felt performance that grows in stature with each hearing....The shorter pieces are also affectionately played but without the total commitment Feltsman brings to the Sonata."

American Record Guide 53:74-5 N/D '90. Allen Linkowski (165w)

"I re-listened to twelve recordings of the sonata after encountering Feltsman's...Only Anda (Angel 35127, deleted) and Curzon seem to display a commensurate craftsmanship and sense of proportion. My estimation of the other ten recordings diminished severely, and unexpectedly, a reaction you can only understand by hearing Feltsman's performance....An equivalent level of inspiration eludes Feltsman in the three Petrarch settings....Feltsman provides a more nuanced landscape in the exalted Legende than does Ciccolini in his estimable recording. CBS's sound quality is just a bit unyieldingly hard, but is agreeable in perspective, and outstanding in dynamic range."

Fanfare 13:215-17 Mr/Ap '90. Neil Levenson (525w)

"Vladimir Feltsman's Liszt and the B-Minor Sonata in particular seem to me a 20th-century view, precise, somewhat calculated, and a bit hard-toned and dry in color, as well as...mostly anti-rhetorical. There is, to be sure, considerable excitement within these parameters but not a great deal to capture the emotions...Piano tone, least good in the Sonata, is adequate and most attractive in softer sections but without any great sense of depth."

Stereophile 14:244-5 Je '91. Igor Kipnis (120w)

Gramophone 67:2012+ My '90. David J. Fanning (315w)

4119. Piano Music: Mephisto Waltz 1; Venezia e Napoli; Feux Follets; Chasse-neige; Ricordanza; Petrarch Sonnet 123; after Chopin—The Maiden's Wish; after Schubert—Hark, Hark the Lark!; after Schumann—Widmung.
Janina Fialkowska (pno).
CBC 1035 64:00

✔**HC** ★***Awards:*** Critic's Choice: 1991, *American Record Guide*, Ja/F '92 (David Mulbury).

"It has been a long time since I've heard piano playing as good as this!...The recorded sound on this disc is lustrous, clear, and perfectly centered, with ideal room ambience top enhance it-....Here is one of those rare recordings that will yield so much pleasure over repeated hearing that the purchase price bears little or no relationship to the intrinsic value. Do not fail to acquire it for your record library."

American Record Guide 54:75 My/Je '91. David G. Mulbury (450w)

4120. Piano Music: Album Leaf in Waltz Form; Bagatelle sans Tonalite; Landler in A flat; Valse de Bravoure; Valse Melancolique; Valses Oubliees, No.'s 1-4; Valse-impromptu; Mephisto-Waltz (4 versions for solo piano).
Leslie Howard (pno). reissue 1986.
HYPERION 66201 DDD 74:40

★***Awards:*** *Gramophone* Critics' Choice (J. Methuen-Campbell), 1987.

"*This* presentation is in a class by itself by virtue not only of superlative playing but of its informed and impassioned advocacy of an unrecognized canon—details in my review of the SD (Hyperion A66201, *Fanfare* 10:4). One might have preferred somewhat closer sound, though the recording is clear and immediate-....In short, this is one of the most important Liszt offerings of recent years."

Fanfare 11:168-9 N/D '87. Adrian Corleonis (130w)

"Many of Liszt's piano works require an artist who has a soaring virtuoso spirit. Leslie Howard fails here to give that impression, even though he plays even the most difficult passages supremely well and often with appealing lyricism."

American Record Guide 51:42 Ja/F '88. Michael Mark (215w)

"Liszt wrote some of the most difficult piano music ever, but Howard's staggering technique makes it sound like child's play. This entire recording radiates charm."

High Fidelity 39:68 My '89. Paul Moor (170w)

"Despite sharper definition to the piano sound on CD, my LP rating (Dec. '86, p. 121) still stands, as a result of uneasiness over the heavy resonance on most tracks. These are exciting performances, though."

Hi-Fi News & Record Review 32:131 D '87. Barbara Jahn (50w)

Ovation 8:42-3 N '87. Paul Turok (170w)

Gramophone 64:1044 Ja '87 James Methuen-Campbell (345w) (rev. of LP)

4121. Piano Music: Transcendental Etudes (12).
Vladimir Ovchinikov (pno). 1988.
EMI 49821 DDD 64:00

★***Awards:*** The Want List 1990, *Fanfare* N/D '90 (Adrian Corleonis).

"This is phenomenal playing. Not since Lazar Berman's 1976 recording...have the *etudes* been so comprehensively, persuasively...*transcendentally* realized....Enthusiastically recommended."

Fanfare 13:212-13 Ja/F '90. Adrian Corleonis (350w)

"Ovchinikov gives us extraverted, virtuoso readings in the best of taste that provides a happy foil to the more expansive, less viscerally exciting editions by Arrau (Philips) and Bolet (London). He does not quite match the blinding pianistic display that his compatriot Lazar Berman summons forth on his famous version...Nonetheless, Ovchinikov is mightily impressive...Add to these purely musical attractions recorded sound that is ideal in every respect and you have a definite winner in the Liszt sweepstakes."

American Record Guide 53:59-60 Ja/F '90. Donald Manildi (150w)

"Vladimir Ovchinikov...plays with great vividness and immediacy and he has been impressively recorded. At the same time his poetic and, more particularly, his tonal range will hardly erase memories of Richter's truly classic accounts of 5 and 11 (or Norjima's scarcely less brilliant performances), Bolet's musical regality (seriously ruffled, however, by *Feux Follets*' double-note demands), Dziffra's dazzling idiosyncrasies, or Berman's Russian bearhug." *P85/95 S95*

Hi-Fi News & Record Review 34:105 N '89. Bryce Morrison (315w)

"I can imagine still more satisfying accounts of this cycle...But among those recordings available now Ovchinikov's surely takes top honors, and it gives promise of interesting things to come from him."

Stereo Review 55:132 Ja '90. Richard Freed (300w)

Gramophone 67:509 S '89. David J. Fanning (700w)

Digital Audio's CD Review 6:72 Mr '90. Tom Vernier (120w)

4122. Piano Music: Mephisto Waltz No. 1. Annees de Pelerinage: Premiere Annee, "Suisse": Aubord d'une Source; Deuxieme Annee, "Italie": Sonetto 104 del Petrarca. Two Concert Studies. Rhapsodie Espagnole. **FRANCK, CESAR. Prelude, Choral et Fugue for Piano.**
Murray Perahia (pno).
SONY 47180 DDD 60:00

✔HC ★*Awards:* Pick of the Month, North American Perspective (Christie Barter), *Gramophone* O '91.

"Pure Perahia...Perahia's stylish and modifying hand casts its own special light and distinction....The shorter works, too, are played with matchless precision and style, most notably the two Concert Studies, where Liszt's genius is at its most delicate and picturesque....The recordings are beautifully clear and present this new and, for many, unexpected, Liszt champion in a natural and radiant light." *P100 S95*

Hi-Fi News & Record Review 37:86 Ap '92. Bryce Morrison (long)

"Ever the consummate musician, Perahia delivers fabuolous pianism, *qua* pianism—fleet and powerful by turns, frosted with elegant finger work and refinements of touch, striding through difficulties with an elan almost machine-like in its precision—but, for all that, he emerges in this fare as a sort of cultivated Good Humor man....If these performances are all surface, the surfaces are of extraordinary polish."

Fanfare 15:191 Mr/Ap '92. Adrian Corleonis (med)

"The performance of the Franck *Prelude, Choral et Fugue* that opens this program is downright ravishing...[Perahia's] fleet but by no means breathless reading has wonderful momentum and an unfailing sense of proportion; everything unfolds with disarming spontaneity, building to a climax that is charged with radiance. The Liszt portion...is striking in its way, and gorgeous pianism, but one does want a bit more of a splash; Minoru Nojimi manages to give us both the subtlety *and* the splash in his still incomparable Liszt collection on Reference Recordings. *Mephisto* is the only work duplicated on these two discs, and for the rest Perahia is clearly outstanding....The sound is very good; all but two of the performances were taped at the Maltings, Snape, which, for Perahia especially, seems to be a sure-fire recording venue."

Stereo Review 57:80 Mr '92. Richard Freed (long)

"Murray Perahia...is outstanding-especially in Liszt...I've never heard better Liszt than this—and that means *communicative*...The big Franck at the beginning, a major concert piece, is wonderfully clear and balanced, but not as much an accomplishment as the Liszt."

Audio 76:84 Jl '92. Edward Tatnall Canby (med)

"Perahia's patrician account of the Franck joins a distinguished current list dominated by Rubinstein (RCA), Cherkassky (Nimbus), and Bolet (London). As in his concurrently released Brahms disc (this issue) and his so-called 'Aldeburgh recital' ([*ARG*] July/Aug 1991), Perahia's stylistic outlook has broadened considerably, taking on a somewhat tougher fiber where needed for the big moments in the Franck as well as the *Mephisto* and *Spanish Rhapsody*....a well-deserved round of bravos to Perahia and the Sony engineers for a recording of unusual excellence."

American Record Guide 55:58 Mr/Ap '92. Donald Manildi (med)

"If in the Mozart three-piano concerto, Mr. Perahia has perhaps invented virtues, in the Franck he confirms inherent beauties that most pianists leave buried. His clean musicality is a perfect foil to this music's dark mood and sinuous harmony."

The New York Times O 20 '91, sec H p. 31. Bernard Holland (long)

Gramophone 69:139 O '91. Joan Chissell (long)

4123. Piano Music: Piano Sonata in B minor, S.178; Nuages gris, S.199; Unstern: sinistre, disastro, S.208; La Lugubre Gondola I, S.200; R. W.—Venezia, S.201.
Maurizio Pollini (pno). Grosser Saal, Musikverein, Vienna. May 30, 1988 live.
DEUTSCHE GRAMMOPHON 427 322 DDD 46:00

✔HC ★*Awards:* Critics' Choice 1990, *Gramophone* D '90 (David Fanning).

"Maurizio Pollini's new recording of the Liszt Piano Sonata in B minor is, in a word, phenomenal. As always with Pollini, some listeners will find it insufficiently romantic, even cold.

For me, though, it is ideal. Pollini's playing is so aristocratic, impassioned, and virtuosic that 'transcendent' is the only possible description."

Musical America 111:77 Jl '91. Terry Teachout (160w)

"This stands with the Richter and the first Horowitz among the supreme recordings of this popular, but elusive [sonata], score. Pollini fills out the disc with discerning accounts of four of Liszt's late miniatures....Despite the short timing, this disc deserves a spot in any collection of nineteenth-century piano music."

Fanfare 14:205-6 My/Je '91. Peter J. Rabinowitz (360w)

"Despite some clearly audible (and annoying) vocal intrusions from the pianist during the Sonata, the music remains stubbornly earthbound, reduced to a series of problems to be (brilliantly) solved, a set of instructions to be (completely) obeyed."

American Record Guide 54:74 My/Je '91. Donald Manildi (425w)

"A new severity reigns supreme, and purists in particular will celebrate an absence of all beguiling pianistic glamour, tricksiness or sophistication. For them Pollini's performance will imply a moral integrity unknown to previous generations. Others will sense the limitations of Pollini's iron-will and uncompromising vision...Pollini's integrity in 'late' Liszt is, however, total....The recordings are immaculate." *P95/85 S95*

Hi-Fi News & Record Review 35:92 Ag '90. Bryce Morrison (350w)

Gramophone 68:246+ Jl '90. David J. Fanning (965w)

American Record Guide 54:74-5 My/Je '91. Arved Ashby (285w)

4124. Piano Music: Les Jeux d'Eau a la Villa d'Este; Liebestraume; Valses Oubliees No.'s 1 and 2; Sonetti del Petrarca; Konzertetuden, S.145 (Waldesrauschen and Gnomenreigen); Isolde's Liebestod (Wagner); Die Loreley (Liszt).

Mikhail Rudy (pno).
EMI 49842 DDD 74:00

★*Awards:* Best Recordings of the Month, *Stereo Review* Ap '90.

"The whole wonderful recital advances the thought that the most effective interpreter is the musician who has the intellectual and technical equipment required, a reliable heart, and the good sense to avoid getting in the music's way. The recording itself...is demonstration-class."

Stereo Review 55:75-6 Ap '90. Richard Freed (575w)

"Mikhail Rudy's choice of works tells you much about his playing, which is crystalline, mercurial and sophisticated....Clearly, the bombastic or overtly theatrical Liszt holds little appeal for him." *P95 S95*

Hi-Fi News & Record Review 35:96 N '90. Bryce Morrison (290w)

"Angel's sound is a bit distant, but that does not keep me from recommending this outstanding recital."

American Record Guide 53:74-5 N/D '90. Allen Linkowski (165w)

"A perfect complement to business discussion by candlelight."

Fanfare 13:184-85 Jl/Ag '90. Adrian Corleonis (200w)

Gramophone 67:2012+ My '90. David J. Fanning (315w)

4125. Piano Music: Mephisto-Waltz (4 versions for solo piano): No. 1; La Campanella; Harmonies du soir; Feux follets; Sonata in B minor. ("Nojima Plays Liszt").

Minoru Nojima (pno).
REFERENCE 025 DDD 59:24

✔**HC** ★★*Awards:* *Stereo Review* Best Recordings of the Month My '88. Records to Die for: 1 of 5 Recommended Recordings, *Stereophile* Ja '91 (Peter W. Mitchell).

"Minoru Nojima's reading is the first I have heard to combine a musician's understanding of the Sonata's structure with a poet's eloquence and passion, and a near-perfect technique. Yet he steers no bland middle course-...In summary, I'll go out on a limb: this is the first ostensibly audiophile recording of a great Classical work which demands recommendation alongside history's best recorded performances of that work."

Stereophile 11:171+ Ap '88. Kevin Conklin (700w)

"An absolute knockout, vividly recorded and alive with the sort of pianism *and* the sort of music making we don't encounter every other Tuesday."

Stereo Review 53:98 My '88. Richard Freed (630w)

"These are perhaps the most satisfying and consistently realized accounts of the sonata to appear since Daniel Barenboim's introspective, suavely stylized, almost levitated 1981 recording....Not to be missed."

Fanfare 11:153 My/Je '88. Adrian Corleonis (525w)

"While his flying fingers admirably execute Liszt's pyrotechnics, he also brings out structural logic and emotional content that are often overlooked."

Stereophile 14:159+ Ja '91. Peter W. Mitchell (b.n.)

Sonata in B minor for Piano. See No. 4091.

MARTINU, BOHUSLAV

4126. Piano Music: Etudes and Polkas; Fantaisie et Toccata; Julietta (Act 2, Scene 3); Les Ritournelles; Sonata for Piano.
Rudolf Firkusny (pno).
RCA 7987 DDD 59:00

★★*Awards:* Best Recordings of the Month, *Stereo Review* D '89. The Year's Best, *Hi Fi News & Record Review*, May '90 Supplement.

"No one else could bring what Firkusny brings to this music in terms of understanding, commitment, or execution. Each piece opens up entirely and irresistibly to his touch. RCA has done him and Martinu proud with fine sonics and really thoughtful documentation, which includes a striking photograph of Firkusny and Martinu together in Marseilles in 1940 as well as the notes by the pianist himself and by Brian Large, the distinguished biographer of both Martinu and Smetana."
Stereo Review 54:126 D '89. Richard Freed (580w)

"Mr. Firkusny continues to be uniquely authoritative in this music, his piano has been handsomely recorded, and the documentation, too, is exceptional."
The New York Times O 15 '89, p. H 29+. Richard Freed (195w)

Gramophone 67:1167 D '89. Michael Oliver (385w)

"RCA's new CD...offers a gratifying outing for a senior pianist of great musical integrity and strength of personality. Rudolf Firkusny, whose mono Columbia and stereo DG recordings of Janacek once sold that difficult music to many a newcomer, makes a comparably persuasive case for Martinu....Strongly recommended."
Fanfare 13:221-22 Ja/F '90. John Wiser (475w)

"While several earlier discs of Martinu piano music, such as those by Josef Hala and Radoslav Kvapil, have been more than acceptable, Firkusny adds an extra degree of polish and insight, aided considerably by RCA's smooth yet colorful recorded quality."
American Record Guide 53:62 Ja/F '90. Donald Manildi (200w)

P100 S95
Hi-Fi News & Record Review p.24 My '90 Supplement. Kenneth Dommett (315w)

MAYERL, WILLIAM JOSEPH ("BILLY")

4127. Piano Music and Transcriptions: Bats in the Belfry. The Harp of the Winds. Jazzaristrix. Marigold. Insect Oddities: No. 1, Wedding of an Ant; No. 3, Praying Mantis. All-of-a-Twist. Jill all slone. Look Lively. Autumn Crocus. The Jazz Master. Sweet William. Loose Elbows. Shallow Waters. Railroad Rhythm. **F. Fisher:** Peg o'my heart. **P. Braham:** Limehouse Blues. **J. W. Green:** Body and Soul. **Kern:** Smoke gets in your eyes. **P. French:** Phil the Fluter's Ball.
Susan Tomes (pno).
VIRGIN 90745 DDD 59:00

★*Awards:* The Want List 1990, *Fanfare* N/D '90 (Adrian Corleonis).

"Listeners will pick and mix, enchanted at virtually every point by Susan Tomes's beautifully fresh and idiomatic performances. Cool-headed but warm-hearted, she has been excitingly recorded, even when such music cries out for a mellowness and warmth unknown to a modern Steinway." *P95 S85/95*
Hi-Fi News & Record Review 35:99 F '90. Bryce Morrison (420w)

"For sheer flair—lilt, legerdemain, and graciously effortless swing—her performances yield nothing to Mayerl's own (which is, of course, saying a great deal), while her informed, graceful annotations confect a final elegance. Couched in opulently cool ambience, Virgin's sound is scintillantly immediate."
Fanfare 13:216-17 My/Je '90. Adrian Corleonis (415w)

Gramophone 67:1530 F '90. Andrew M. Lamb (310w)

MEDTNER, NIKOLAI

4128. Piano Music: Second Improvisation (Theme & 16 Variations on "The Mermaid's Song"), Opus 47 (1926); Sonate-Idylle, Opus 56 (1937); Vergessene Weisen (Forgotten Melodies), Opus 39 (1919-20).
Earl Wild (pno).
CHESKY 001 DDD 66:00

★★★*Awards:* The Want List 1989, *Fanfare* N/D '89 (Peter J. Rabinowitz); The Want List 1989, *Fanfare* N/D '89 (John Wiser); Top Choices—1989, *American Record Guide* Ja/F '90 (Donald Manildi).

"This performance exhibits one of the greatest pianists of our age at the height of his technical and interpretive genius. And Chesky lets you hear it all, in one of the most natural, realistic acoustics I have experienced among solo piano recordings."
Stereophile 12:214 Je '89. Robert Hesson (400w)

"This release is a winner on every count!"
American Record Guide 52:65 My/Je '89. Donald Manildi (275w)

"Never in my experience has Medtner's music floated in such broad arcs of sound as it does here. I don't mean to suggest that Wild overplays its voluptuous side....he's perfectly attuned to the transparency of texture that so often sets Medtner's music off from Rachmaninov's...he's alert to Medtner's wit, too; and...he understands Medtner's more cryptic utterances as well. But there's no doubt that this music brings out some of the lushest and most expansive playing we've gotten from

Wild...Given that Wild's fingers are as strong as ever, and that his sensitivity to dynamic and timbral nuance has, if anything, reached new heights, this superbly engineered disc merits the highest possible recommendation."

Fanfare 12:178-80 Jl/Ag '89. Peter J. Rabinowitz (345w)

"No fan of Earl Wild's playing, the 'resident specialist' was caught flatfooted with astonishment at how consistently he identifies all the central concerns of this music: rhythmic character, harmonic strength, wholeness of form-....The present CD is recommended strongly."

Fanfare 12:180-81 Jl/Ag '89. John Wiser (560w)

"In performances like these...which are at once dedicated and virtuosic, one can scarcely be unaware of the full-blooded and Romantic character of these pieces...with his vast technique and sensitive range of colours, he [Wild] is ideally suited to Medtner."

Hi-Fi News & Record Review 34:98-9 Ag '89. Max Harrison (160w)

"Always prepared to take chances with lesser known composers, Wild proves that his affinity for Rachmaninoff caries over to Sergei's friend Medtner...He displays a flawless sense of rhythm, without the rubatos that critics say render his Chopin 'wimpy'....The Baldwin piano Wild uses is superbly captured by the Chesky engineers; the upper registers have a faery lightness to them."

HighPerformanceReview 8(1):71 '91. Robert J. Sullivan, Jr. (320w)

Gramophone 69:102 S '91. Michael Stewart (med)

MENDELSSOHN, FELIX. Concerto in E minor for Violin and Orchestra, Opus 64.
See No. 2026.

MENDELSSOHN-HENSEL, FANNY

4129. Das Jahr (The Year).
(Piano Music, Volume 1).
Liana Serbescu (pno).
CPO 999 013 DDD 50:00

> ★*Awards:* Critics' Choice 1989, *Gramophone* D '89 (Joan Chissell).

"Intensely communicative readings...from Romanian pianist Liana Serbescu, who may well be a reviewer's worst nightmare come true: there is simply *nothing* to fault."

American Record Guide 51:39-40 N/D '88. James C. Parsons (270w)

MESSIAEN, OLIVIER

4130. Catalogue d'Oiseaux (Books 1-3), for Piano.
Peter Hill (pno).
UNICORN-KANCHANA 9062 DDD 59:00

"Nearly eighty species of birds appear in this catalogue, since in portraying each bird in its habitat, other birds enter into the musical fabric....Peter Hill plays this exceedingly difficult music with great skill and conviction. He has a warm, full sound which has been accurately captured by Unicorn's engineers. My only qualm is that his control over dynamics occasionally falters."

American Record Guide 51:44-5 Jl/Ag '88. Timothy D. Taylor (465w)

"The technical facility demanded...is daunting, yet Hill accomplishes all this with spectacular panache and an involvement with the music and the quality of piano sound that are a sheer delight to experience....I cannot imagine this being bettered."

Hi-Fi News & Record Review 33:91 Jl '88. Doug Hammond (300w)

"I cannot imagine these pieces played better. Hill is more scrupulous than Troup, has a weightier, richer sound than Loriod, and even brings a smile to the lips from time to time through his precise judgment of the dynamics called for by a particular gesture."

The Musical Times 130:753-54 D '89. Roger Nichols (165w)

Gramophone 65:1624 My '88. Michael Oliver (510w)

4131. Catalogue d'Oiseaux (Books 4-6), for Piano.
Peter Hill (pno).
UNICORN-KANCHANA 9075 DDD 70:00

> ✔**HC** ★★*Awards:* Critics' Choice 1989, *Gramophone* D '89 (Michael Oliver). The Year's Best, *Hi Fi News & Record Review*, May '90 Supplement.

"Hill has a technique that is little short of miraculous...There is no better tribute to the recording than to say it matches the quality and sensitivity of the playing....What the record leaves you with is a sense of overwhelming, ecstatic lyricism." *P100 S100*

Hi-Fi News & Record Review 34:89 S '89. Simon Cargill (300w)

Gramophone 67:510 S '89. Michael Oliver (330w)

"I cannot imagine these pieces played better. Hill is more scrupulous than Troup, has weightier, richer sound than Loriod, and even brings a smile to the lips from time to time through his precise judgment of the dynamics called for by a particular gesture."

The Musical Times 130:753-54 D '89. Roger Nichols (165w)

"Peter Hill's continuing cycle of the complete Messiaen piano music is a major boon for the Messiaen fan, for this is some of the master's best music, and, overall, Hill is my favorite interpreter of it....Hill's strengths are virtuosic control and consummate rhythmic delineating."

Fanfare 13:229-31 Ja/F '90. Kyle Gann (230w)

American Record Guide 53:65-6 Ja/F '90. Arved Ashby (225w)

P100 S100
Hi-Fi News & Record Review p.24 My '90 Supplement. Simon Cargill (390w)

4132. Catalogue d'Oiseaux: Book 7; La Fauvette des Jardins.
Peter Hill (pno).
UNICORN-KANCHANA 9090 DDD 63:00

★***Awards:*** The Gramophone Awards, Nominations, Contemporary, *Gramophone*, N '91.

"This disc is self-recommending....The sound could hardly be bettered." *P100 S95/100*
Hi-Fi News & Record Review 36:72 Je '91. Simon Cargill (210w)

"These performances are certainly imaginative and technically impressive, but treat these scores more as venerable monuments of the 20th-Century piano literature than as fantastic depictions of menacing glories in a natural landscape....Perhaps I did not state my enthusiasm strongly enough for the single-disc Austbo compendium when it appeared: the Norwegian pianist's impulsiveness and the edge to his tone are often gripping, and the clear Fidelio sound is an improvement over the rather dull, airless Unicorn reproduction."
American Record Guide 54:65 Ja/F '91. Arved Ashby (180w)

"Even before the release of this final volume, Peter Hill's *Catalogue* had achieved nearly classic status on these pages...Still, classic status is an ambivalent attribute, and I can't help wondering whether Hill, in so taming Messiaen's birds, hasn't sacrificed the music's capacity to startle....To my ears, the barbaric playing of Yvonne Loriod is more attuned to the music's iconoclastic spirit. Still, many will be convinced by Hill's interpretive strategies—and even for the doubters, his recording remains an extraordinary accomplishment. Highly recommended."
Fanfare 14:243 Ja/F '91. Peter J. Rabinowitz (345w)

4133. Livre du Saint Sacrement.
Jennifer Bate (orgn). Church of Saint Trinite, Paris. October 1986.
UNICORN-KANCHANA 9067/8 DDD 129:00 2 discs

✔**HC** ★***Awards:*** *Gramophone* Critics' Choice (Gordon Reynolds), 1987.

"This is a definitive recording of one of Messiaen's longest works."
Fanfare 11:161-2 Ja/F '88. Kyle Gann (265w)

"How she rivets our attention for over two hours I do not rightly know, but her empathy with this composer's organ music bids fair to become one of the legends of 20th-century performance."
The Musical Times 129:269-70 My '88. Ann Bond (160w)

"The performance is definitive."
High Fidelity 38:69 Je '88. David Hurwitz (190w)

"'Well, what did you think of it?' was the question on people's lips that night in Westminster Cathedral. The work listened to at one sitting is simply too vast to allow an immediate answer to that question. You'll have to decide for yourselves after the repeated hearings which this, Messiaen's largest organ work, calls out for."
Organists' Review 74:59 Ja '88. Paul Hale (225w)

"Some traffic noise must be expected as the price to be paid for an authentic setting....A must for all interested in Messiaen."
Hi-Fi News & Record Review 33:109 Ja '88. Doug Hammond (350w)

"Bate may not be entirely successful in holding together all of the *Livre*'s 130 minutes, but her performance seems impressively prepared and bears the mark of authenticity. The importance of this issue is enhanced even further through the use of Messiaen's own organ at the Church of Saint Trinite in Paris."
American Record Guide 51:56-7 Mr/Ap '88. Arved Ashby (750w)

Gramophone 65:604 O '87 Gordon Reynolds (400w)

4134. Piano Music: Preludes; Quatre Etudes de Rythme; Canteyodjaya.
Peter Hill (pno). 1985, 1986.
UNICORN-KANCHANA 9078 DDD 78:00

★★***Awards:*** Critic's Choice: 1990, *American Record Guide* Ja/F '91 (Arved Ashby); Best of the Month, *Hi-Fi News & Record Review*, S '89.

"Peter Hill...[plays] as if he believes in every note, and the result is as rich a musical experience as any to have come out of post-war Modernism....The recording is excellent." *P100 S95*
Hi-Fi News & Record Review 34:89 S '89. Simon Cargill (320w)

"Peter Hill's continuing cycle of the complete Messiaen piano music is a major boon for the Messiaen fan, for this is some of the master's best music, and, overall, Hill is my favorite interpreter of it....Hill's strengths are virtuosic control and consummate rhythmic delineating."
Fanfare 13:229-31 Ja/F '90. Kyle Gann (230w)

American Record Guide 53:65-6 Ja/F '90. Arved Ashby (225w)

Gramophone 67:510 S '89. Michael Oliver (330w)

MOZART, WOLFGANG AMADEUS

4135. Piano Music (complete solo piano works).

Walter Gieseking (pno).
EMI 63688 ADD 71:29; 65:47; 69:30; 69:25; 66:32; 69:42; 60:08; 69:18 8 discs

✔HC

"Gieseking's use of expressive accents and touch is unmatched in Mozart: this is a Mozart with contrasts less obvious than one might be accustomed to now but with proportion and refinement eluding most other performers. The project took place over two years: not one selection is weak....Hearing any or all of these works is an experience to relish. This is the essential Mozart set."

Fanfare 14:231-2 Jl/Ag '91. Allan Evans (250w)

"Tempi are beautifully crafted...and the playing is immaculate, but the works are all scaled down, classicized....It is quite a luxury to have all of Mozart's piano works readily accessible, attractively packaged, deftly executed and beautifully remastered."

The Absolute Sound 16:146+ N/D '91. Hyperion Knight (med)

4136. Piano Music: Fantasia in C minor for Piano, K.396; Fantasia in D minor for Piano, K.397; Sonatas for Piano: No. 14 in C minor, K.457; Rondo in A minor for Piano, K.511.
Emile Naoumoff (pno). Salle Wagram. 1986.
EMI 49274 DDD 62:00

★*Awards:* Best Recordings of the Month, *Stereo Review* Mr '90.

"EMI's French production team has come through with one of the finest recordings of a piano I have yet heard, every bit as crystalline and well balanced as Naoumoff's superb playing itself."

Stereo Review 55:81 Mr '90. Richard Freed (525w)

"With a pianistic finish and uncanny sense of proportion that brought the name of Lipatti to my mind, Emile Naoumoff springs each of these minor-key Mozart works to life....The perspective is intimate, but not too close...Very highly recommended."

Fanfare 13:242-43 Mr/Ap '90. Neil Levenson (275w)

"From what I have heard here, let me state that I have been won over as a fan of Naoumoff. His playing is innately musical, demonstrating that rarest and most intangible of qualities—the balance of inner tension and serenity. His Mozart is poised, elegant and refined without being selfconscious....Emile Naoumoff is among a mere handful of pianists who come close to doing Mozart justice."

HighPerformanceReview 8(1):71 '91. John Mueter (230w)

"What is lacking in his [Naoumoff's] temperament is a strong dramatic impulse, and sufficient rhythmic definition to enliven Mozart's high-classic piano style."

Fanfare 12:248 My/Je '89. Elliott Kaback (260w)

Gramophone 66:642 O '88. David J. Fanning (340w)

4137. Sonatas (17) for Piano (complete).
Daniel Barenboim (pno).
EMI 47336 348:19 6 discs

✔HC ★*Awards: Stereo Review* Best of the Month, Jl '86.

"In general, I find Barenboim's sobriety more convincing than the studied simplicity of Mitsuko Uchida's not-yet-completed Mozart cycle on Philips. Perhaps it is Andras Schiff, on London, who strikes the happiest balance between brightness and profundity, elegance and effervescence, but Barenboim has reached very deep inside these sonatas, and the artistic level is consistently high throughout the entire set."

Stereo Review 51:93-4 Jl '86. Richard Freed (550w)

"Throughout all six records the listener is made aware of deft fingerwork divorced from any sense of feeling for the emotional content of the music."

Hi-Fi News & Record Review 31:105-6 Jl '86. Kenneth Dommett (240w)

"Barenboim brings to this music the vast experience of the symphonic conductor, the concerto soloist and the orchestral accompanist; the solo recitalist and the chamber-music player, and it shows....All in all, this is one of the finest sets of piano music...that has come my way for years, and I cannot see how this set can fail to become a classic. It is quite magnificent."

Music and Musicians International 36:43-4 N '87. Robert Matthew-Walker (620w)

"Before recommending an omnibus collection such as the two boxes offered here by Angel, I would have to be persuaded of the absolute superiority of the performances. Such is clearly not the case with Barenboim....During the course of preparing this review, I had access to recordings of 11 pianists, and with the possible exception of Glenn Gould, I do not believe Barenboim's musical perceptions to have anywhere sounded superior."

Fanfare 10:198-9 S/O '86 Elliott Kaback (470w) (rev. of LP)

4138. Sonatas for Piano (complete): No. 2 in F, K.280; No. 3 in B flat, K.281; No. 5 in G, K.283; No. 9 in D, K.311; No. 10 in C, K.330; No. 11 in A, K.331.
(Volume 1).
Malcolm Bilson (ftpno).
HUNGAROTON 31009/10 DDD 116:00 2 discs

★★Awards: The Want List 1991, *Fanfare* N/D '91 (John Wiser). Top Disks of the Year, *The New York Times* D 24, '89 (John Rockwell).

"This first volume certainly deserves the attention of everyone interested in this music...Urgently recommended!"

Fanfare 13:236-37 Ja/F '90. John Wiser (335w)

This "set...is a consummate artistic statement. [The sound is dry, but very natural]."

The Absolute Sound 16:146+ N/D '91. Hyperion Knight (med)

"This is an artistic tour-de-force, recorded superbly, accompanied by extensive scholarly and well-written program notes based upon the most recent research on the sonatas. Highly recommended in every respect."

American Record Guide 53:76 Jl/Ag '90. David G. Mulbury (205w)

Digital Audio's CD Review 6:64 Mr '90. Tom Vernier (450w)

Gramophone 67:1167 D '89. Stanley Sadie (700w)

4139. Sonatas (17) for Piano (complete): No. 6 in D, K.284; No. 8 in A minor, K.310; No. 12 in F, K.332; No. 13 in B flat, K.333; No. 16 in B flat, K.570; No. 17 in D, K.576. (Volume 2).
Malcolm Bilson (ftpno).
HUNGAROTON 31011/2 DDD 64:29; 57:44 2 discs

The Want List 1991, *Fanfare* N/D '91 (John Wiser).

"In the second volume of Bilson's traversal of Mozart's piano sonatas, all musical assets are as firmly presented as they were in Volume One...Bilson uses a different fortepiano, a 1979 Louis Dulcken instrument, made by Thomas and Barbara Wolf....As was Volume One, Volume Two is urgently recommended."

Fanfare 14:301-2 Mr/Ap '91. John Wiser (260w)

"This is some of the finest Mozart playing I have heard in years. The recording warmly captures the sound of his fortepiano, a copy of one Mozart himself used. There is a grand sense of style here that I have rarely encountered. Listen, for example to the final Presto of 9 and you will surely fall in love with the results."

can Record Guide 54:90 My/Je '91. Carl Bauman (95w)

See Volume 1 for review excerpt.

The Absolute Sound 16:146+ N/D '91. Hyperion Knight (med)

Digital Audio's CD Review 7:60-1 Ap '91. Tom Vernier (240w)

4140. Sonatas (17) for Piano (complete).
Mitsuko Uchida (pno).
PHILIPS 422 115 DDD 364:00 6 discs

★★Awards: Instrumental Record Award 1989, *Gramophone*, D '89; The Chosen Few: The Best Sounding Discs of 1989. *New Hi-Fi Sound Supplement* D '89.

Gramophone 66:1311 F '89. Joan Chissell (285w)

4141. Sonatas for Piano: No. 4 in E flat, K.282; No. 8 in A minor, K.310; No. 15 in C, K.545.
Sviatoslav Richter (pno). Barbican Hall, London. March 29, 1989 live.
PHILIPS 422 583 DDD 48:01

★★Awards: Best of the Month, *Hi-Fi News & Record Review*, O '90. Best Recordings of the Month, *Stereo Review* F '91.

"In brilliant contrast to the studied 'simplicity' of those performers who surround the striking of each blanched note with pregnant silences betokening some deep and painful spiritual mystery, Richter's playing is marvelously alive. This is not meditation but the most straightforward, refreshing music-making, alive with the color, animation, wit, charm, drama, and overall variety that Mozart, after all, did nothing to conceal....the sound is excellent, ideally focused for the balance between warmth and brightness in these performances."

Stereo Review 56:117-8 F '91. Richard Freed (490w)

"Richter, as usual, humbly places his transcendental technique entirely in the service of the music, making it almost unnoticeable until the realization later strikes you that you have just heard a trill, for instance, or perhaps an ornamentation, of a level bordering almost on the supernatural. In addition, his inflection of melody, even on a percussive instrument such as the piano, comes close to the expressivity of the human voice."

Musical America 111:84 Mr '91. Paul Moor (140w)

"Richter's Mozart is quite unlike Uchida's, with its expression drawing upon all kinds of Mozartian references outside of the specific piece, or of Arrau's, playing burdened down with considerations of form, dramatic allusion, and emotion. With these recital performances, one feels the text is all there is: the phrase has its motivation from the notes, the motion of the music is harmonically, grammatically determined....I nevertheless do find the playing here oddly unsettled, and unsettling....it is as if on this occasion he did not always summon supreme mastery over time and timing. The sound is close, but good. The atmosphere of the hall gives an undeniable electricity."
P95(100) S95

Hi-Fi News & Record Review 35:101+ O '90. Christopher Breunig (400w)

Gramophone 68:1390 Ja '91. Richard Wigmore (435w)

4142. Sonatas for Piano: No. 8 in A minor, K.310; No. 13 in B flat, K.333; No. 15 in C, K.545.
Maria Joao Pires (pno).
DEUTSCHE GRAMMOPHON 427 768 DDD 61:00

✔HC ★*Awards:* Critic's Choice: 1990, *American Record Guide* Ja/F '91 (Allen Linkowski).

"All these performances show an ideal combination of fastidiousness and the most concentrated musical energy. Few pianists have so successfully captured both the *allegro* and *maestoso* of the A-minor Sonata's opening movement, and although the playing is as clear-sighted and honest as the day, it is also relentlessly probing—nervously alive to the music's undertow of Romantic anxiety....The distinctive brightness of her sound is beautifully captured in DG's crystalline recording." *P100 S95*

Hi-Fi News & Record Review 35:89 Ap '90. Bryce Morrison (285w)

"She plays the sonatas for the life that is in them, crisply and clearly, with due regard for color and line—occasionally less than rock-steady, but realizing the seldom-acknowledged substance of K.545, the endearing wit of K.333, and a good deal more with a refreshing vitality that comes from the heart as well as the fingers. Not the last work, perhaps, but deeply pleasing."

Stereo Review 55:105 My '90. Richard Freed (210w)

"She favors a large-scale approach to a repertoire that has, in some hands, returned to the old-fashioned 'Dresden China' manner of interpretation (Mozart in miniature). The Portugese pianist proves that you can broaden the scale without coarsening the material....DG's sound is superb: beautifully balanced and vividly alive."

American Record Guide 53:76 Jl/Ag '90. Allen Linkowski (125w)

"An effectively conceived performance, strong and unaffected and recorded beautifully....This is the kind of Mozart playing I like to hear."

Fanfare 14:312 S/O '90. Michael Ullman (125w)

"The tone is lean, the articulation crisp, with the sustaining pedal rarely used. As a result, textures are generally well-defined, the music's buoyancy and wit well-conveyed. Equally impressive is Pires's sensitivity to the darker side of these pieces...My major reservation concerns Pires's dogged observation of every last repeat Mozart specified, a practice that adds disproportion (rather than balance) to her readings...splendid sound."

Stereophile 14:261 Ap '91. Mortimer H. Frank (225w)

"The most engaging and immediately appealing aspects of Pires's Mozart playing are her warm lyricism and beautiful piano sound. But as noted in her Schubert playing reviewed elsewhere in this issue, her overexpansiveness ultimately does the music harm. Her view of Mozart is unabashedly romantic, and since she takes every indicated repeat of every movement, the overall effect is cloyingly sentimental."

Fanfare 14:299 N/D '90. Susan Kagan (175w)

Gramophone 67:1640 Mr '90. James Methuen-Campbell (425w)

4143. Sonatas for Piano: No. 15 in C, K.545; No. 16 in B flat, K.570; No. 17 in D, K.576; Allegro and Andante in F, K.533 and Rondo in F, K.494 ("Sonata in F for Piano, K.533"). (Volume 6).
Alexei Lubimov (ftpno).
ERATO 45510 DDD 70:53

★★★*Awards:* The Want List 1991, *Fanfare* N/D '91 (Charles Timbrell). Critics' Choice 1991, *Gramophone*, Ja '92 (Stanley Sadie); Critics' Choice 1991, *Gramophone*, Ja '92 (Richard Wigmore).

"Throughout this disc Lubimov demonstrates a fine technical command of the notes and—more importantly—a real Mozartean's ability to project the music in sentences and paragraphs....Lubimov plays on a fortepiano that is a replica by Christopher Clarke of an Anton Walter instrument now in the Germanisches Nationalmuseum in Nuremberg. Its middle range is wonderfully warm and different in timbre, a perfect showcase for the special sound that Mozart might have had in mind for the F-Minor section of K.494....This recording has my highest recommendation."

Fanfare 14:258-59 Ja/F '91. Charles Timbrell (550w)

"These performances of Mozart's last four sonatas reveal scrupulous attention to matters of style, if also considerable freedom in embellishments, and sensitive command of keyboard technique....The instrument is a forte-piano built by Christopher Clarke in 1986 after an original of around 1795 by Anton Walter, Mozart's favourite maker, clearly and delicate in its upper octaves, abundantly rich and rounded lower down." *P95 S95*

Hi-Fi News & Record Review 35:99 N '90. Peter Branscombe (245w)

In "sound quality...[this set combines] nice hall ambience with a very well tuned instrument-....[a] curiosity item...exploring various musicological questions, but not yet having all the answers."

The Absolute Sound 16:146+ N/D '91. Hyperion Knight (med)

"Disappointingly, he takes extremely slow tempos. And like too many pianists, he makes them sound unflowing, as though the feelings they express are somehow blocked....But Mr. Lubimov's slow movements are distinguished by what is far and away the best ornamentation—the most creative and most faithful to period sources—yet to be heard on Mozart recordings."

The New York Times N 18 '90, p. 27+. Will Crutchfield (505w)

"The tone of the instrument on this disc is less harsh and twangy than Newman's two and marginally more powerful and robust of tone. But it ends up sounding more like a rather thin modern instrument than one with a unique voice of its own. The performances are competent, lively, occasionally sensitive, and overall rather charming but faceless and lacking in character....The recorded sound is somewhat muffled, perhaps purposely, to soften the edge of the fortepiano's tone."

American Record Guide 54:97-8 Mr/Ap '91. Lawrence Hansen (b.n.)

Gramophone 68:1869-70 Ap '91. Richard Wigmore (595w)

Sonata in D for 2 Pianos, K.448. See No. 4159.

MUSSORGSKY, MODEST

4144. Pictures at an Exhibition (trans. Guillou). STRAVINSKY, IGOR. Petrouchka (excerpts) (3 dances arr. Guillou).
Jean Guillou (orgn). Kleuker organ, Tonhalle, Zurich. July 1988.
DORIAN 90117 DDD 53:26

★*Awards:* Best of the Month, *Hi-Fi News & Record Review*, N '89. Records to Die for: 1 of 5 Recommended Recordings, *Stereophile* Ja '91 (Peter W. Mitchell).

"Guillou (a composer himself) is well attuned to what Mussorgsky implies beneath his notes-....Guillou's transcriptions of the Stravinsky are quirky, inventive, full of life, and ultimately satisfying...a performing tour de force. Dorian captures Guillou's performances in stunning sound, the kind that defines the possibilities of digital recording technology, and that provides a full realization of his inventive, insightful, and exciting art."

Fanfare 13:252 Ja/F '90. William Zagorski (625w)

"As a performer, Guillou is the antithesis of the largely lethargic style displayed by the organists in the recordings I reviewed previously. Guillou brings light and life to the music, not just through brisker tempos but also through an adroit touch that may be an outgrowth of his fluid piano technique....[this disc] proves that organ playing remains a lively and fascinating art."

Stereophile 13:193+ Mr '90. Robert Hesson (200w)

"The sustaining gloom in the 'Catacombs' is quite impressive on a beautiful, full organ. In it, Guillou is at his best, conveying a sense of the dank, dark depths....it is difficult to imagine something less suited to the organ than the *Petrouchka* excerpts....Jean Guillou not only made these transcriptions, he designed the organ on which they're played, and wrote notes for the recording. Dorian has served him well with a warm, realistic acoustic that foregoes the churchly fog many organ recordings have to be heard through."

HighPerformanceReview 7:1:82 '90. Kenneth Krehbiel (345w)

"Clear and spacious highs, shuddering infrabass that goes lower than most subwoofers, and spirited performances add up to a recording that is far more than a stunt."

Stereophile 14:161 Ja '91. Peter W. Mitchell (b.n.)

"Guillou is offbeat, eccentric, wildly imaginative....Guillou rather overpowers us. But I really think this music can take every bit of the color Guillou brings to it....He's an instinctive musician with tremendous flair and freedom."

American Record Guide 52:64 Jl/Ag '89. Donald R. Vroon (210w)

"Guillou and his student Keith John go out of their way to avoid counterfeiting Ravel....As for summary judgments, I recommend either disc (but doubtless not both) on the basis of adroit musical legerdemain which recolors these *Pictures* on an exceptional instrument."

Fanfare 13:269-71 S/O '89. Haig Mardirosian (605w)

"The performances by John and Guillou are identifiably from the same mould, and both are tremendously exciting *and* radically different." *P95/100 S100*

Hi-Fi News & Record Review 34:113 N '89. William McVicker (210w)

Digital Audio's CD Review 6:80 D '89. Wayne Green (200w)

NANCARROW, CONLON

4145. Studies for Player Piano, Volume 5: No's. 42, 45a, 45b, 45c, 48a, 48b, 48c, 49a, 49b, 49c.
Conlon Nancarrow (pno). Recorded on the composer's custom-altered 1927 Ampico reproducing piano, Mexico City. January 10 and 12, 1988.
WERGO 60165 DDD 51:00

★★*Awards:* The Want List 1989, *Fanfare* N/D '89 (Kyle Gann); The Want List 1989, *Fanfare* N/D '89 (Paul Rapoport).

"Don't miss this brilliant, unique music."

Fanfare 13:271-72 S/O '89. Paul Rapoport (690w)

Gramophone 67:342 Ag '89. David J. Fanning (390w)

PAGANINI, NICCOLO

4146. Caprices (24) for Unaccompanied Violin, Opus 1.
Midori (vln). 1988.
CBS 44944 DDD 77:10

★*Awards:* Critics' Choice 1990, *Gramophone* D '90 (James Methuen-Campbell).

"So confident is her [Midori's] approach, so forceful her personality, that she is able to go

beyond mere technique to interpret these *Caprices* as *music*—possessed of grace, poise, and, most of all, dramatic flair."
Musical America 110:72 Mr '90. K. Robert Schwarz (305w)

"I expected neat-as-a-pin accuracy, but I am slack-jawed at the sheer intensity with which she tackles fingered octaves, trilled octaves, double and triple stops, tenths, bouncing arpeggios: everything. She invests drama and comedy, where appropriate...Except for the rough noises in Nos. 19 and 21, which are caught and magnified by CBS's close sound, Midori has herself completely under control, yet always highly involved and exciting. I will always remain a partisan of Rabin, but I'm very happy to have this astonishing achievement on my shelves."
Fanfare 13:252-53 Mr/Ap '90. David K. Nelson (400w)

"Anyone interested enough in Paganini to have read this far needs *this* complete set. The fiddling alone is astonishing. But that's not reason enough. The tonal spectrum Midori produces is a veritable collage of the best sounds ever brought to this music....Even all that is not reason enough. The real reason you *need* this disc is to hear the musical level at which Midori plays the Paganini *Caprices.*"
American Record Guide 53:84-5 Mr/Ap '90. Alan Heatherington (325w)

"The Paganini Caprices, recorded when she was 17, confirm that the violin poses no technical terrors for her: everything—double stops, left-hand pizzicato, ricochet bow—is tossed off with complete assurance and security."
The New York Times Ja 21 '90, p. 26 H. Martin Bookspan (110w)

"From every aspect, this is a magical disc."
Stereophile 13:177 Jl '90. James Berwin (150w)

Digital Audio's CD Review 6:58 Ja '90. David Vernier (135w)

Gramophone 67:1640+ Mr '90. James Methuen-Campbell (315w)

Caprice for Unaccompanied Violin, "La Chasse". See No. 2026.

Introduction and Variations on Paisiello's "Nel cor piu non mi sento" from Paisiello's a Molinara, for Solo Violin. See No. 4019.

PERLE, GEORGE

4147. Piano Music: Fantasy-Variations; Pantomime, Interlude and Fugue; Short Sonata; Six New Etudes; Suite in C.
Michael Boriskin (pno). 1985.
NEW WORLD 342 DDD 44:52

> ★★*Awards:* Record of Distinction *Ovation* Jl '89. Critics Pick Some Favorites of the Year, *The New York Times* N 26, '89 (Allan Kozinn).

Boriskin "certainly is comfortable with Perle's demands, which are considerable, and seems sympathetic with Perle's individual aesthetic-....A winning release for almost any taste."
Fanfare 10:158 Jl/Ag '87 Stephen W. Ellis (425w)

"The composer and pianist share an evident joy in exploring the nuances of the piano technique; the integration of dazzling virtuosity and musical content in the *Six New Etudes* (1984) brings Chopin to mind. Regrettably, the distant, low-level recording does little to clarify Boriskin's pristine textures. But his powerful, virtuosic performances display both emotional involvement and intellectual comprehension."
High Fidelity 37:67 O '87. K. Robert Schwarz (250w)

"George Perle is a sensational composer, as these releases demonstrate...Pianist Michael Boriskin seems to be the composer's collaborator in creating these wonderfully vivid performances."
Ovation 10:53-4 Jl '89. George Gelles (205w)

Digital Audio's CD Review 6:60-1 Ap '90. Linda Kohanov (330w)

POULENC, FRANCIS

4148. Piano Music: Les Soirees de Nazelles; 3 Mouvements Perpetuels; 3 Novelettes; 9 Improvisations.
Pascal Roge (pno). 1986.
LONDON/DECCA 417 438 DDD 66:23

> ★★★*Awards: Gramophone* Critics' Choice (Joan Chissell); *Gramophone* Critics' Choice (Michael Oliver), 1987; Instrumental Record Award 1988, *Gramophone* O '88.

"As much fun as some of the other players cited above have provided, Roge finds in this music an element not foreign to it but not often previously revealed, of delicacy and almost shockingly decadent sensuality. Strongly recommended."
Fanfare 11:197 N/D '87. John D. Wiser (220w)

"There is nothing on this disc by Pascal Roge (or elsewhere in Poulenc's piano music) of major importance; but we cannot be too grateful for a series of genre pieces that have both wit and feeling....Pascal Roge has just the delicacy of touch to turn these works to perfection."
The Musical Times 129:91 F '88. Robert Anderson (300w)

"To be sure, there have been several more 'important' piano recordings lately, but we haven't had one as pleasurable as this one in years."
Stereo Review 52:141 D '87. Richard Freed (325w)

"The genial pieces forming this collection may not be considered great music, but Pascal Roge responds so readily to their wit and vitality, and to their moments of warmth and charm, that the depth of their personality is irrelevant."

Hi-Fi News & Record Review 32:102 S '87 Barbara Jahn (175w)

"While I still await the CD release of Gabriel Tacchino's wonderful complete recording of Poulenc's solo piano works and the equally fine, if slightly more brilliant, cycle on Ades by that unsung master, Bernard Ringeissen-...this excursion from Roge...ranks as one of the best solo-piano recordings of the year."

High Fidelity 38:64 Mr '88. Thomas L. Dixon (200w)

Digital Audio 4:36 Ag '88. Linda Kohanov (225w)

Gramophone 65:204 Jl '87 Michael Oliver (420w); 66:549 O '88 Lionel Salter (200w)

4149. Piano Music: Humoresque. Nocturnes. Suite in C. Theme varie. Improvisations: No. 4 in A flat; No. 5 in A minor; No. 9 in D; No. 10 in F, "Eloge des gammes"; No. 11 in G minor; No. 14 in D flat. Two Intermezzos. Intermezzo in A flat. Villageoises. Presto in B flat.
Pascal Roge (pno).
LONDON/DECCA 425 862 DDD 63:00

★★*Awards:* The Gramophone Awards, Nominations, Instrumental, *Gramophone*, N '91. Pick of the Month, North American Perspective (Christie Barter), *Gramophone* Ap '91.

"If one is to have but a single CD of Poulenc's music, this must surely be it—with characteristically clean Decca sound as the perfect bonus." *P95 S95*

Hi-Fi News & Record Review 36:74 Je '91. Simon Cargill (220w)

"Now that Roge has made his selection of the best, we needn't bother with Chandos recordings of the hapless (if nimble-fingered) Eric Parkin, which I feel serve only as a prime example of rigid misunderstanding. Tacchino's recently issued large but incomplete survey is in general more shallowly and distantly recorded, and also narrower in interpretive resource; in his very complete set for CBS, Paul Crossley does well by the more overtly lyrical works, but in other respects is not very effective...In short, Pascal Roge's two-CD survey is supreme in current commerce, and strongly recommended."

Fanfare 14:252-3 Jl/Ag '91. John Wiser (250w)

"Pascal Roge takes a focused, highly specific approach to Poulenc's piano music. He plays down its nostalgia and sentimentality and emphasizes its humor, brilliance, rowdiness, and swift sleights of hand with playing that is colorful and elegant...My first choice remains Paul Crossley's thoughtful, atmospheric performances in his three-CD CBS set of Poulenc's complete piano music."

Stereo Review 57:96+ Ja '92. David Patrick Stearns (med)

"[Roge] fluently conveys the *joie de vivre*, the wit, and the nostalgia that permeate these gems and his tonal and technical abilities are exemplary in every respect."

American Record Guide 54:135-6 N/D '91. Donald Manildi (med)

Digital Audio's CD Review 7:60+ S '91. Peter Golub (210w)

Gramophone 68:1870 Ap '91. Christopher Headington (310w)

RACHMANINOFF, SERGEI

4150. Piano Music: Suite No. 1, Opus 5; Russian Rhapsody; Six Morceaux, Opus 11; Two Pieces for Piano, Six-Hands; Polka Italienne; Suite No. 2, Opus 17; Symphonic Dances, Opus 45; Romance in G; Prelude in C# minor. (Complete Works for Two Pianos and Piano Four- and Six-Hands).
Ingryd Thorson (pno); H. Thurber (pno); David Gardiner (pno).
PAULA 046 AAD 62:40

★*Awards:* Critics' Choice 1988, *Gramophone* D '88 (Christopher Headington).

"For anyone who knows and loves Rachmaninov's music, this fine, complete collection for two pianos etc will be indispensable-....Thorson and Thurber have captured the essence of Rachmaninov's sound perfectly....Although the treble of the two Steinway pianos is rather brittle, it is never tiring on the ear, thanks to the careful positioning of the instruments."

Hi-Fi News & Record Review 34:92-3 Mr '89. Barbara Jahn (390w)

"Thorson and Thurber's performances are quite satisfactory although their pianos have a bell-like top that works fine in the final movement of the Suite No. 1 but is less satisfactory in the melancholy movement ('Tears') that precedes it."

Fanfare 12:232 S/O '88. James Miller (240w)

Gramophone 66:634 O '88. Christopher Headington (455w)

RAVEL, MAURICE

4151. Piano Music (complete works for solo piano): Pavane pour une Infante Defunte; Le Tombeau de Couperin; Serenade Grotesque; Jeux d'Eau; Valses Nobles et Sentimentales; La Valse.
(Volume 1).
Louis Lortie (pno). 1988.
CHANDOS 8620 DDD 66:00

★*Awards:* Critics' Choice 1989, *Gramophone* D '89 (David Fanning). The Year's Best, *Hi Fi News & Record Review*, May '90 Supplement.

"The recordings are full and clear, and Vol. 2 is already eagerly anticipated. These are among the most distinguished Ravel performances on record." *P95/100 S95*

Hi-Fi News & Record Review 34:83 Jl '89; o.26 My '90 Supplement. Bryce Morrison (245w)

Gramophone 66:1751 My '89. Joan Chissell (310w)

Digital Audio's CD Review 6:58-9 Je '90. Octavio Roca (200w)

4152. Piano Music: Gaspard de la Nuit; Miroirs.
Minoru Nojima (pno).
REFERENCE 035 DDD 51:00

✔**HC** ★*Awards:* Record of the Month, *Hi-Fi News & Record Review*, My '91.

"Few players have come close to matching what Nojima achieves here...In fact, the eight pieces contained on this CD glow with such warmth, color and sharply-defined character that even those who think they know this music inside out may be in for a totally fresh experience. Engineer Keith Johnson has again come forth with an ideally balanced piano image that captures the tremendous range of Nojima's playing."

American Record Guide 53:103 S/O '90. Donald Manildi (185w)

"Vladimir Horowitz said that *all* music is really Romantic music, and Nojima is not about to say him nay. This is gorgeous playing-....The sonic focus is very warm, too, with a 'liquid' quality that faithfully conveys the live character of Nojima's playing and the particular sound he cultivates."

Stereo Review 55:170 N '90. Richard Freed (370w)

"His performances owe nothing to generally acknowledged traditions but are freshly thought out and suggest a view from the inside. The documentation is as distinguished as the performances."

Stereo Review Presents: Compact Disc Buyers' Guide 1991 p.39-40 Richard Freed (125w)

"The expectations aroused by *Liszt* are more than fulfilled by *Ravel*. Nojima's virtuosity remains astonishing, and his profound musical sensitivity is directed here at some of the most remarkable of all keyboard music....To say that Nojima triumphs over the difficulties understates the case. It is as if the difficulties have ceased to exist. To my mind, this is one of the most startling piano performances ever recorded. It is also one of the most musically satisfying. In truth, I cannot imagine how these works could be played better....exceptionally beautiful and musically appropriate piano sound....The LP version...offers even finer sound than the CD."

The Absolute Sound 15:168+ S/O '90. Robert E. Greene (2150w)

"Along with *Jeux d'eau*, the *Miroirs* and *Gaspard* test a pianist's technique to the limit. Nojima's is more than a match for them to the point that his colorful performances transcend mere accuracy. I normally don't like to hear a piano recorded this closely because the tones never seem to coalesce, but it seems to happen here; all the more credit to the pianist and/or the producer."

Fanfare 14:285 Ja/F '91. James Miller (125w)

"His readings of both *Miroirs* and *Gaspard* are wholly exceptional. The strength of his personality is such that an initially startling and, indeed, cruelly virtuosic way with the score is resolved in a sense of wonder at such flawless brilliance....The recordings are a little clinical but are nonetheless clear and life-like." *P100 S85*

Hi-Fi News & Record Review 36:79 My '91. Bryce Morrison (630w)

"Perlemuter has, of course, recorded all of Ravel's piano music, the analog recordings now transferred to Nimbus CDs, NIM 5005 and 5011. I still find these performances unmatched for musical insight...These discs are still my first recommendations for Ravel's piano music. But Reference's recording is greatly superior to Nimbus's, and Nojima's performances are really quite superb. I only wish there were more of them here."

Fanfare 14:325 N/D '90. Leslie Gerber (300w)

"Perhaps the only reason I do not enthuse as extravagantly about Nojima's Ravel as I did for his Liszt is that the Ravel is better served by stereo recordings, notably Pogorelich's and also Argerich's of *Gaspard*. The latter, also on DG, is a wayward, mercurial statement that has held up for 15 years. That Nojima's new record deserves mention in this company bespeaks it as excellent....strongly recommended for music lovers, audiophiles, *and* the literary-minded."

Stereophile 13:223+ D '90. Kevin Conklin (565w)

Gramophone 68:790 O '90. David J. Fanning (380w)

REUBKE, JULIUS

4153. Sonata in C minor on the 94th Psalm, for Organ; Sonata in B flat minor for Piano.
Jean Guillou (orgn/pno). Aeolian-Skinner organ, Trinity Church, New York City; Troy Savings Bank Music Hall, Troy, New York. 1987.
DORIAN 90106 DDD 50:00

★*Awards:* Critics' Choice 1990, *Gramophone* D '90 (Marc Rochester).

"For organ aficionados, this CD is a must!"

Audio 74:133 N '90. Bert Whyte (265w)

"The 'nearly nine thousand pipes' of the organ of Trinity Church, New York City, are awesomely present on this disc, seeming to levitate my eighty-five-pound speakers several inches off the floor. Guillou gives us a rip-roaring fire-breathing virtuoso performance...[In the piano sonata] Tanski is more powerful, Guillou more brilliant; both revel the poetry and grandeur of Reubke's unknown masterpiece."

Fanfare 13:333-34 N/D '89. James H. North (410w)

"As a performer, Guillou is the antithesis of the largely lethargic style displayed by the organists in the recordings I reviewed previously. Guillou brings light and life to the music, not just through brisker tempos but also through an adroit touch that may be an outgrowth of his fluid piano technique....[this disc] proves that organ playing remains a lively and fascinating art."

Stereophile 13:193+ Mr '90. Robert Hesson (200w)

"These recordings...are truly breath-taking-....The balance here at the Troy Savings Bank Music Hall, Troy, New York, is bright and virile. A fantastic record."

Organists' Review 76:46 Mr '90. Gordon Reynolds (195w)

"Guillou treats the Sonata on the 94th Psalm in an epic, romantic, quasi-romantic fashion and does some very interesting things in matters of tempo and rhythm which lend a convincing spontaneity to his performance....Reubke's Piano Sonata is given a fine, musical performance, but Guillou, excellent musician that he is, does not come near to the Pianism that Claudius Tanski (Nov/Dec review) brings to this sonata."

American Record Guide 53:94-5 Mr/Ap '90. David G. Mulbury (370w)

Gramophone 67:938 N '89. Marc Rochester (190w)

ROSENBOOM, DAVID

4154. Systems of Judgment (1987). (CDCM Computer Music Series, Volume 4).
David Rosenboom.
CENTAUR 2077 63:52

★*Awards:* The Want List 1990, *Fanfare* N/D '90 (Kyle Gann).

"Anyone in the least taken with the possibilities computer technology brings to art music should find in this disc a good deal to admire-....What one does find in abundance is energy, movement, and wide-ranging invention, as well as the sort of hoop-la audiophiles (like me) scoff up like ice cream."

Fanfare 13:276 Mr/Ap '90. Mike Silverton (200w)

"It is eclectic music that explores many vocabularies of today's compositions...It does so with an intelligence and logic guided by the sure hand of an excellent composer. This is an important piece of computer music which should be a part of any serious collection in that genre."

American Record Guide 53:135 Jl/Ag '90. Herbert A. Deutsch (390w)

SATIE, ERIK

4155. Piano Music: Trois Gymnopedies; Six gnossiennes; Embryons desseches; Croquis et agaceries d'un gros homme en bois; Sonatine bureaucratizue; Avant-dernieres pensees; Veritables preludes flasques (pour un chien); Cinq nocturnes; Trois morceaux en form de poire (2 pianos); La belle excentrique (2 pianos).
Aldo Ciccolini (pno); Gabriel Tacchino (pno).
EMI 47474 DDD 70:57

★★*Awards:* *Stereo Review* Best of the Month, Je '87; The Want List 1988, *Fanfare* N/D '88 (Kyle Gann).

"The performances are cool and witty....An ideal CD for Satie enthusiasts."

High Fidelity 37:72 S '87. Terry Teachout (85w)

Stereo Review 52:101-2 Je '87 Richard Freed (310w)

Gramophone 64:1432 Ap '87 Lionel Salter (225w)

SCARLATTI, DOMENICO

4156. Sonatas (555) for Keyboard (performed on Harpsichord) (complete).
Scott Ross (hpscd); Monica Huggett (vln); Christophe Coin (cello); Michel Henry (oboe); Marc Vallon (bsn).
ERATO 75400 DDD 34 discs

★★★*Awards:* Critics' Choice 1988, *Gramophone* D '88 (Robin Golding); Critics' Choice 1988, *Gramophone* D '88 (Lionel Salter). Record of the Eighties, *Gramophone*, D '89 (John Durate).

Gramophone 66:52 Je '88. Lionel Salter (910w)

4157. Sonatas for Keyboard (performed on Harpsichord): K.52, 211/2, 248/9, 261/2, 263/4, 318/9, 347/8, 416/7, 490/2.
Elaine Thornburgh (hpscd).
KOCH 7014 DDD 72:00

★*Awards:* Critics' Choice 1991, *Gramophone*, Ja '92 (Lionel Salter).

Gramophone 69:144 O '91. Lionel Salter (med)

"This is an excellent recording from many perspectives. The sound is clear, lively and *pleasant*...Highly recommended."

American Record Guide 54:140-1 N/D '91. Catherine Moore (long)

"Thornburgh's performances are full of vigour and enthusiasm and take full advantage of the quickly changing moods and textures in these sonatas."

Continuo 15:26-7 F '91. Scott Paterson (130w)

"The first aspect of this release I noticed was the beautiful luminous sound of the harpsichord in its environment....Thornburgh also does a splendid job of fulfilling most of my requirements for successful Scarlatti....She doesn't seem to these ears to have quite the verve and rhythmic drive of the very best Scarlatti players. But she is a sensitive player with sufficient virtuosity to bring off the music. Her performances certainly deserve a recommendation, and they are enhanced by the beautiful recording and generous timing."

Fanfare 14:299 Ja/F '91. Leslie Gerber (225w)

"Thornburgh has all the technical skill needed for these exacting, difficult works, but she lacks that final degree of interpretive vision...The sound on this disc is only so-so; lines are usually clear, but the harpsichord lacks its characteristic richness in the bass, and high notes are somewhat muffled."

The Absolute Sound 16:193+ Ja '92. Judy Davidson (long)

4158. Sonatas for Keyboard (performed on Piano): (15) K.175, 513, 402, 403, 144, 115, 116, 474, 475, 449, 450, 544, 545, 516, 517.
Andras Schiff (pno).
LONDON/DECCA 421 422 DDD 73:00

✔HC ★*Awards:* The Want List 1989, *Fanfare* N/D '89 (John Wiser).

"The Scarlatti sonatas are new territory for Andras Schiff, and they are eminently well suited to his thoroughly pianistic approach." *P95 S80*

Stereo Review 54:152+ S '89. Richard Freed (275w)

"Schiff is wonderfully alive to the composer's range, his sheer fullness of expression, to the most far-reaching romantic and modern implications."

Hi-Fi News & Record Review 34:100 Ag '89. Bryce Morrison (245w)

"There is none of the thundering, note-crunching vulgarity of Koopman's recent recording (see Nov/Dec) but there is restrained virtuosity aplenty. The delightful lilting pastorale of Sonata K 513 is by itself reason enough to own this recording."

American Record Guide 53:82-3 Ja/F '90. Philip Kennicott (210w)

Gramophone 66:1458 Mr '89. Joan Chissell (350w)

SCHAFER, R. MURRAY. Le Cri de Merlin, for Guitar. See No. 4184.

SCHUBERT, FRANZ

4159. Fantasia in F minor for Piano Four Hands, D.940 (Opus 103). MOZART, WOLFGANG AMADEUS. Sonata in D for 2 Pianos, K.448.
Murray Perahia (pno); Radu Lupu (pno).
CBS 39511 DDD

✔HC

4160. Piano Music: Sonata in D, D.850; Sonata in A minor, D.784.
Alfred Brendel (pno). 1987.
PHILIPS 422 063 DDD 63:00

✔HC ★*Awards:* Critics' Choice 1988, *Gramophone* D '88 (Joan Chissell).

"While there may be no trace of sentimentality in this music-making, there is plenty of feeling and excitement....Philips has improved upon their earlier manner of recording this player-....essential listening for Schubertians-...Strongly recommended."

Fanfare 13:297-99 Ja/F '90. John Wiser (135w)

"The A minor in Brendel's hands is a grim, large scale work of almost Beethovenian grittiness....Brendel (like Schubert) lightens up a bit for the D major, but the carefree charm and bittersweet lyricism that some find in Schubert isn't much in evidence here. This is earnest, powerful playing....Brendel's Schubert is worth hearing. Whether you ultimately like it or not (I do) it will enrich your understanding of a composer whose greatness is still not fully appreciated....fine sound."

American Record Guide 52:102 S/O '89. Stephen D. Chakwin, Jr. (165w)

"D.850...blossoms in Brendel's care, his calculated hurrying and swelling of phrases engendering brilliance, a sense of Apollo at play...It is in the last two movements that slight doubts arise. They're played well...Almost makes you forget to notice a loss of emotional flow-....Brendel maintains exquisite tension in the counterpoint of the closing movement [of D.784]; but is his slow, almost halting climax to the first movement's central section to be interpreted as great insight, or just self-absorbed keyboard banging?"

Stereophile 13:235+ Ja '90. Kevin Conklin (350w)

Gramophone 66:822-30 N '88. Joan Chissell (480w)

4161. Piano Music: Sonata in A minor, D.845; Piano Pieces (3), D.946.
Alfred Brendel (pno).
PHILIPS 422 075 DDD 61:00

✔HC ★*Awards:* Best of the Month, *Hi-Fi News & Record Review*, Ja '90; The Year's Best, *Hi Fi News & Record Review*, May '90 Supplement.

"One can hardly imagine anyone playing *Drei Klavierstucke* more beautifully than Alfred Brendel does here. The piano sounds completely natural throughout."

HighPerformanceReview 7:68 Fall '90. John Mueter (175w)

"Brendel's celebrity in Schubert is so familiar that we are in danger of taking it for granted. And to listen to these performances, of an incomparable stature and lucidity, is to be reminded in the most salutary way that great artistry is constantly self-renewing, that the parameters of what is possible or permissable are in a perpetual state of flux and redefinition....The recordings are of demonstration quality, rich, wide-ranging and deeply satisfying." *P100 S100*

Hi-Fi News & Record Review p.26-7 My '90 Supplement. Bryce Morrison (280w)

"Those who value charm above all in Schubert will likely find this too Beethovenish an approach and will flinch from some of the stinging accents and unlovely tone. Those attracted to the intensity of Schubert's dark vision will find Brendel a kindred spirit and relish his sense of drama and ability to phrase and point Schubert's melodies so that they linger hauntingly in the mind....Philips has given Brendel a medium-to-close recording that approximates well what he sounds like in a good concert hall."

American Record Guide 53:98-9 Jl/Ag '90. Stephen D. Chakwin, Jr. (405w)

"The new recording finds Brendel's feelings for the first and third of these oversized so-called Impromptus little changed in the main line but highly refined. But the largest of the three, No. 2 in E flat, is markedly expanded-...Best of a good lot so far, this vividly recorded CD is urgently recommended."

Fanfare 13:285 Mr/Ap '90. John Wiser (295w)

Gramophone 67:704 O '89. Joan Chissell (500w)

4162. Piano Music: Impromptus, D.899 (Opus 90) and D.935 (Opus 142).
Alfred Brendel (pno). 1989.
PHILIPS 422 237 DDD 61:00

✔HC ★*Awards:* Best of the Month, *Hi-Fi News & Record Review*, Ap '90.

"The pianist [is] at his most winning....the new performances are a bit different, somewhat more expansive than before, with at least marginally slower tempos throughout both works-....exceptionally well recorded."

Stereo Review 55:96+ Ap '90. Richard Freed (150w)

"In short, I have rarely, if ever, heard stronger yet more richly engaging Schubert Impromptus. The recordings, when you stop to notice them, are exemplary." *P100 S100*

Hi-Fi News & Record Review 35:92 Ap '90. Bryce Morrison (370w)

"The two sets of Impromptus are played for all their dramatic and lyrical implications, no warmer in tone than the earlier recording...but more strongly stated and emphasized in detail and in whole....Strongly recommended."

Fanfare 13:253-54 Jl/Ag '90. John Wiser (265w)

"The Impromptus are in the same mold as Brendel's older versions and would not appear to have been rethought."

American Record Guide 53:99 Jl/Ag '90. Paul L. Althouse (125w)

Gramophone 67:704 O '89. Joan Chissell (260w)

Digital Audio's CD Review 6:72 My '90. Tom Vernier (150w)

4163. Piano Music: Sonata in B flat, Opus posth., D.960; Wanderer Fantasie, D.760.
Alfred Brendel (pno). 1988.
PHILIPS 422 062 DDD 58:00

✔HC

"Neither the 1988 performance of the Sonata in B flat nor the *Wanderer Fantasy* differs radically in outline from Brendel's earlier accounts; the most notable change is a certain refinement in tone—still narrowly monochrome—and a tendency to bring out bass lines with greater definition and equality of balance....Recommended."

Fanfare 13:254-55 Jl/Ag '90. John Wiser (325w)

"Both [performances (Brendel/Philips and Leonskaja/Teldec)] are so immediately enjoyable, and take one so deep inside the music, that any sort of comparative evaluation must seem at least a little presumptuous. Nonetheless, in the case of the one work common to both, the *Wanderer-Fantasie*, it comes down to Alfred Brendel....Brendel's coupling here is the same as in his earlier Philips recording of the *Wanderer*....This is a more affecting performance overall than his earlier one, particularly in the two inner movements."

Stereo Review 55:172 N '90. Richard Freed (180w)

"For the Fantasy, Brendel is a clear first choice. He doesn't have the keyboard command and elegant musicianship of Pollini (DG) or the ebullience of Kempff (may we have a reissue, DG?). What he does have is a sense of the almost improvisational nature of the piece....This is at least his third recording...This one is the most refined, but loses some of the zip...The sonata is a different story. First, there's that missing first-movement repeat....Second is Brendel's heavily rhetorical approach to the piece....Brendel's can be an ear-opening supplement to another version, but I don't recommend it as anyone's only Schubert B-flat."

American Record Guide 54:114 Mr/Ap '91. Stephen D. Chakwin, Jr. (450w)

Gramophone 67:1352 Ja '90. Joan Chissell (400w)

4164. Piano Music: Sonata in C minor, Opus posth., D.958; Moments Musicaux (6) for Piano, D.780.
Alfred Brendel (pno). September 1987.
PHILIPS 422 076 DDD 58:00

"The remarkable intensity and concentration that marked Brendel's earlier performance are perhaps even more strongly projected here, but with an even greater regard for the integrity of the structure and for the sort of flow that is part of this music's essential character. The *Moments musicaux* show a similar, if less dramatic, benefit of Brendel's rethinking since his earlier recording....The first-rate sound quality is another reason to be happy Brendel is redoing his Schubert. A very distinguished issue." *P95 S95*

Stereo Review 54:157 N '89. Richard Freed (150w)

"The studied, 'intellectual' sense apparent in many of Brendel's previous recordings is absent....Brendel as an interpreter seems to have much more to say about the music [than Pollini]—and he also dispatches any technical obstacles easily....the highest possible recommendations."

HighPerformanceReview 7:1:87 '90. Kenneth Krehbiel (370w)

"D.958...is given a breathtaking reading, with daring balance between forces of impetuosity and catastrophe....This is a performance to make one rethink this sonata entirely, and to discard once and for all the notion that the finale is an unrelievedly death-obsessed dance....Brendel endows the D.780 *Moments musicaux* with the flesh of interpretation, perhaps more flesh than their skeletons can bear."

Stereophile 13:235+ Ja '90. Kevin Conklin (350w)

"While there may be no trace of sentimentality in this music-making, there is plenty of feeling and excitement....Philips has improved upon their earlier manner of recording this player....essential listening for Schubertians...Strongly recommended."

Fanfare 13:297-99 Ja/F '90. John Wiser (135w)

In the sonata, Brendel "everywhere fights shy of allowing himself a true *pp* or *ff*, and the touch always seems perfunctory, cramped by the turgid and colorless sound quality that has become typical of this label....Anyone coming to Brendel's *Moments musicaux* from Curzon's searching and profound performances (London...) will find them superficial and unmoving."

American Record Guide 52:101-2 S/O '89. Arved Ashby (230w)

Gramophone 66:1610 Ap '89. Joan Chissell (415w)

Digital Audio's CD Review 6:72 My '90. Tom Vernier (150w)

4165. Piano Music: Sonata in A, Opus posth., D.959; Hungarian Melody in B minor, D.817; German Dances (16), D.783; Allegretto in C minor, D.915.
Alfred Brendel (pno). 1987.
PHILIPS 422 229 DDD 56:00

"How easy to say that Brendel's Schubert is self-recommending and, with the odd qualification here and there, leave it at that. But such reduction to cliche fails entirely to suggest the absorbing value of Brendel's quest; of his urgent need to communicate once more his consuming passion and sense of Schubert's greatness."

Music and Musicians International 37:61 Ap '89. Bryce Morrison (450w)

"Philips have done Brendel proud, the piano sounding totally natural from ghostly *ppp* to violent *ff*, with warm resonance never impeding clarity."

Hi-Fi News & Record Review 34:93-5 Mr '89. Peter Branscombe (200w)

"Brendel surprises the ear in the first movement of D.959, treating the often tossed-off second subject with more developmental gravity than usual. But his premeditated shaping of the Andantino leaves no surprise at the arrival of the cry of pain at its core, and the Rondo is so leaden as to spoil its miracle of transformation from baser thematic materials....The Hungarian Melody sounds lightweight and diddly, as it usually does no matter who plays. In the German Dances, however, Brendel finds a gem: full of variety, well-paced, completely idiomatic."

Stereophile 13:235+ Ja '90. Kevin Conklin (350w)

Brendel's "1973 recording of the big A Major Sonata, transferred to CD by Philips some time ago...is effectively superseded by this remake—not because of sonic advantages...but because of certain modifications in his approach to the sonata....Pollini's aristocratic but by no means aloof approach, unencumbered by conspicuous interpretive overlay, may wear a bit better than Brendel's more overtly intense and dramatic one, and Pollini includes the first-movement repeat, which Brendel does not."

Stereo Review 54:124 Je '89. Richard Freed (200w)

"While there may be no trace of sentimentality in this music-making, there is plenty of feeling and excitement....Philips has improved upon their earlier manner of recording this player....essential listening for Schubertians...Strongly recommended."

Fanfare 13:297-99 Ja/F '90. John Wiser (135w)

Gramophone 66:1315 F '89. Joan Chissell (300w)

Digital Audio's CD Review 6:73-4 S '89. Tom Vernier (275w)

4166. Piano Music: Sonata in A minor, D.845; Impromptus, D.935 (Opus 142).
Imogen Cooper (pno).
OTTAVO 88817 DDD 71:00

★★***Awards:*** Best of the Month, *Hi-Fi News & Record Review*, Ja '91; Critic's Choice: 1990, *American Record Guide* Ja/F '91 (Donald Vroon).

"I decided to compare the Impromptus to Perahia's...in every piece I prefer Cooper, who makes Perahia sound cold and businesslike-....This has become first choice for the Impromptus....The Sonata is fine, too, but

some will prefer her teacher's recording (Brendel), which gives it more character."
American Record Guide 53:98 Jl/Ag '90. Donald R. Vroon (125w)

"We are not short of great Schubertians on record, but Imogen Cooper's poetic radiance illuminates some of music's most subtle pages: a different light from Brendel's intense drama (Philips) or Schnabel's famed and robust command (EMI)....The recordings are exemplary, as warm and refined as the performances." *P100 S100*
Hi-Fi News & Record Review 36:103+ Ja '91. Bryce Morrison (420w)

"Overall effect remains more than merely satisfying, with plenty of personality and appropriately aimed feeling. The piano recording is consistent with good work done earlier in the series."
Fanfare 13:253-54 Jl/Ag '90. John Wiser (265w)
Gramophone 67:1495 F '90. Joan Chissell (420w)

4167. Piano Music: Impromptus, D.899 (Opus 90) and D.935 (Opus 142).
Lambert Orkis (ftpno).
VIRGIN 91142 DDD 63:05

★*Awards:* The Want List 1991, *Fanfare* N/D '91 (Susan Kagan).

"His genius is a fantastic ability to discern what the old pianos could do for the composers of their own time—and to bring it to the microphone in dramatic musical fashion. Here he plays solo on an 1826 Graf fortepiano, of Schubert's own time and place, Vienna...NOW we know what Schubert should sound like!"
Audio 76:89 F '92. Edward Tatnall Canby (long)

"Orkis's fleet virtuosity and poetic flexibility are perfect for Schubert, and the result is a wonderful set of performances. The only previous CD I have heard of the complete Schubert Impromptus, that of Melvyn Tan (Angel CDC-49102), is relatively stiff and is completely eclipsed by this new release."
Fanfare 14:279-80 Jl/Ag '91. Leslie Gerber (250w)

"In contrast to Melvyn Tan's somewhat cerebral recording of the pieces for EMI, Orkis makes almost orchestral statements of them, using a very wide dynamic range and the considerable colouristic resources of his 1826 Graf instrument."
Continuo 15:30 Ap '91. Scott Paterson (220w)

"The sound of the Graf 1826 fortepiano is warm and lovely....If any performance can be called existential, this can. All of a piece. Listen to it."
HighPerformanceReview 8(3):83 '91. Bert Wechsler (med)

"Schubert's two delicious sets of impromptus...are neatly and expressively played here by Lambert Orkis on a piano ('fortepiano' if you wish) made by Conrad Graf in Vienna in 1826."
Stereo Review 56:76-7 O '91. Eric Salzman (brief)

"Orkis is a volatile player. He tends to get faster when the music gets louder and to drop his instrument's silvery muted tone when it gets soft. Overall, though, he gives simple unaffected readings of these evergreen works. The first set comes off a little less well than the harder (musically and technically) second....If you can have only one set of Impromptus, I suggest Brendel, but this should be the next one you get."
American Record Guide 54:119-20 Jl/Ag '91. Stephen D. Chakwin, Jr. (225w)

"Where it seems to me these performances fall short is in the emotional range; the poignancy is conveyed, but hardly the profundity. The recording (Vleeshuis, Antwerp) is forward and clear and sounds realistic throughout the dynamic range." *P85 S95/85*
Hi-Fi News & Record Review 36:88 Ap '91. Peter Branscombe (120w)
Digital Audio's CD Review 8:86-7 D '91. Tom Vernier (long)

4168. Piano Music: Sonata in A, Opus posth., D.959. **SCHUMANN, ROBERT. Sonata No. 2 for Piano, Opus 22.**
Murray Perahia (pno). 1986.
CBS 44569 DDD 55:00

✔**HC** ★*Awards:* Best Recordings of the Month, *Stereo Review* S '88.

"The highlights of these two performances for me are the beautifully inward, albeit classically restrained slow movements. Classical, in fact, is an apt description for the pianist's approach to the Schubert....It is a splendid performance in almost all respects....The playing throughout is extremely sensitive, as well, in the Schumann, though here, again, Perahia's leanness of tone and color is rather more Apollonian than Dionysian, as in the more temperamental and mercurial Argerich version of the G-minor Sonata."
Stereophile 12:175 Mr '89. Igor Kipnis (150w)

"Murray Perahia gives us exemplary performances here....Highly recommended."
HighPerformanceReview 6:89 Mr '89. James Primosch (240w)

"These are in many ways surprisingly ordinary performances."
American Record Guide 52:85-6 Ja/F '89. Arved Ashby (350w)

"Perahia, unlike some other very persuasive Schubert players, does not probe for the dark side or try to turn the lyric gestures into stark images. He allows the music its inherent radiance, its innate pulse, and it seems to find its own level."

Stereo Review 53:82 S '88. Richard Freed (400w)

"A superlative recording, marred only by a hint of stridency in the middle register...the playing is Perahia at his best, which is to say incomparable....I've never heard a finer or more compelling performance of either work."

Hi-Fi News & Record Review 33:115 O '88. Jeremy Siepmann (170w)

"The analog sound is respectable, but either a flaw in the master tape or too high a level in mastering the CD has caused plainly audible distortion to ruin the climaxes of the *Wanderer Fantasy*. This, coupled with the misgivings noted, causes one to look elsewhere for these works."

American Record Guide 51:81 S/O '88. Mark Koldys (225w)

Gramophone 66:320 Ag '88. David J. Fanning (475w)

The New York Times My 27 '90, p. H 19 John Rockwell (175w); Ja 15 '89, p. H 27 Harold C. Schonberg (b.n.)

4169. Piano Music: Sonata in C minor, Opus posth., D.958; Sonata in A, Opus posth., D.959; Sonata in B flat, Opus posth., D.960; Allegretto in C minor, D.915; Piano Pieces (3), D.946.
Maurizio Pollini (pno). 1988.
DEUTSCHE GRAMMOPHON 419 229 DDD 2 discs

★★★★*Awards: Stereo Review* Best Recordings of the Month Jl '88; Second Place Instrumental Solo Mumm Champagne Classical Music Award 1988—Presented by *Ovation, Ovation* N '88; The Want List 1988, *Fanfare* N/D '88 (Michael Ullman); Critics' Choice 1988, *Gramophone* D '88 (Stephen Plaistow).

"Pollini plays the sonatas with his characteristic elegance and commitment, and the essential Schubert comes to glowing life....In general, the clarity and vividness of the recordings beautifully convey those qualities in the performances themselves."

Stereo Review 53:80 Jl '88. Richard Freed (575w)

"Pollini's accounts are brilliant and intelligent-...But...there is seldom a moment where the listener can say with certainty that the player is showing any trace of emotional or even sensual involvement in his task....Strongly recommended to those who would best be instructed by the set—pianists."

Fanfare 11:208-9 My/Je '88. John D. Wiser (385w)

"How you react to these performances will depend upon what you think of Pollini's playing. If you find him excessively intellectual, his recordings of Beethoven and Schumann chilly and unfeeling, perhaps you should look elsewhere to explore Schubert's last three sonatas-....On the other hand, I can think of no body of Romantic piano work more appropriate to Pollini's talents that Schubert's last sonatas, so impassioned but free of obviously sensualist or virtuosic elements, so rewarding in the hands of a player whose restraint conceals much art-....Needless to say, this set is strongly recommended."

Stereophile 12:173-75 Mr '89. Kevin Conklin (500w)

The New York Times Ja 15 '89, p. H 27. Harold C. Schonberg (b.n.)

Gramophone 65:1480 Ap '88 Stephen Plaistow (665w); 66:1752 My '89 David J. Fanning (140w)

4170. Piano Music: Allegretto in C minor, D.915; Drei Klavierstucke, D.946; 12 Landler, D.970; Vier Impromptus, D.935.
Andras Schiff (pno).
LONDON/DECCA 425 638 DDD 74:00

★*Awards:* Best of the Month, *Hi-Fi News & Record Review*, Ag '90.

"Every nonessential gesture seems to have been eliminated, and the drama, the pathos, the humor all rise out of the music without being coaxed. In sum, a lovely program of performances that go to the heart with unfailing directness."

Stereo Review 55:170+ N '90. Richard Freed (200w)

"A lovely recital, warmly to be welcomed-....The pianism is alert yet relaxed, with a natural feel for the relationship between detail and structure—in Schiff's hands problems of length and shape simply do not arise." *P100 S95*

Hi-Fi News & Record Review 35:94 Ag '90. Peter Branscombe (280w)

"This recital contains much more that is pleasurable than is not, and as a recorded program, it invites listening through as do few others. Strongly recommended."

Fanfare 14:342 N/D '90. John Wiser (325w)

"Andras Schiff has made his name as a Bach interpreter, but his way with the Schubert is equally memorable....I wish, though, that this artist—who can on occasion be such a colorist—had used a more full-blooded Bechstein or Hamburg Steinway, rather than the Bosendorfer, with its fortepiano-like linearity and muted, unresonant bass. But in every other particular, this is a gem of the Schubert discography."

Musical America 111:83 My '91. Harris Goldsmith (160w)

"This is very fine Schubert, as good as we are likely to hear. Even on a Bosendorfer! not at all the proper piano for Schubert."

Audio 75:124 Je '91. Edward Tatnall Canby (350w)

Gramophone 68:252 Jl '90. Joan Chissell (420w)

4171. Piano Music: Impromptus, D.899 (Opus 90) and D.935 (Opus 142).
Krystian Zimerman (pno). Bielefeld.
DEUTSCHE GRAMMOPHON 423 612 DDD 65:00

★*Awards:* Best of the Month, *Hi-Fi News & Record Review*, Ag '91.

"This rather special Schubert record brought me closer to the composer's music than any since, in 1965, I spent days with the piano parts of *Die Winterreise*, after getting the Pears/Britten Decca set (now on CD). Fine DG sound from a hall in Bielefeld; playing of exquisite subtlety." *P100 S95*

Hi-Fi News & Record Review 36:76 Ag '91. Christopher Breunig (245w)

Gramophone 68:2040+ My '91. Joan Chissell (420w)

4172. Sonatas (18) for Piano (complete): in E, D.157 (fragment); in C, D.279 (fragment); in A minor, op. posth. 122, D.568; in B, op. posth. 147, D.575; in F minor, D.625; in A, op. posth. 120, D.664; in A minor, op. posth. 143, D.784; in C, D.840 ("Reliquie") (fragment); in A minor, Opus 42, D.845; in D, Opus 53, D.850; in G, Opus 78, D.894; in C minor, op. posth., D.958; in A, op. posth., D.959; in B flat, op. posth., D.960. Five Piano Pieces ("Sonata in E"), D.459, 459A.
Wilhelm Kempff (pno). 1965-1969.
DEUTSCHE GRAMMOPHON 423 496 ADD
71:23, 65:49, 69:59, 71:13, 68:10, 57:06, 56:51 7 discs

★*Awards:* The Want List 1989, *Fanfare* N/D '89 (David Claris).

"Kempff is a master of pianistic intimacy and fine gradation. Let who will take pleasure in those many passages of Schubert that respond to this approach. I cannot think of better performances in this mode of many early-to-middle sonatas, and for those, DG's reissue is a valuable addition to the discography. DG's recording doesn't vary much from a central standard of cleanliness and fine detail. Although Kempff's performances illuminate the craftsmanly facet of Schubert's genius best, that facet is often too little appreciated. This set is strongly recommended for it."

Fanfare 12:266-67 Mr/Ap '89. John Wiser (390w)

"It may sound silly to say that Kempff's are performances in which the artist does not seem to interpose himself between the listener and Schubert's music, for we obviously would not be hearing anything if that were the case. But such is the effect of Kempff's utterly selfless playing. It is this quality of selflessness, or lack of any artistic anxiety, that, ironically, allows Kempff to be so individual, so expressive and revealing in his very moving interpretations....Pollini's pianism is superb, but he is only playing notes, rather than re-creating the experience the music expresses....one is left to choose between Pollini the supreme pianist and Kempff the sublime artist."

Musical America 109:66+ S '89. Robert R. Reilly (320w)

SCHUMANN, ROBERT

4173. Piano Music: Carnaval, Opus 9; Faschingsschwank aus Wien, Opus 26. Allegro in B minor, Opus 8.
Alicia De Larrocha (pno).
LONDON/DECCA 421 525 DDD 65:00

★*Awards:* The Year's Best, *Hi Fi News & Record Review*, May '90 Supplement.

"The recordings, when you bother to notice them, faithfully capture an immense range of sonority. Piano records of this calibre are a rare event. Even in her matchless performances of the Spanish repertoire Alicia de Larrocha has seldom confirmed her status more magisterially as one of the world's greatest virtuosi." *P100 S95*

Hi-Fi News & Record Review 34:101 Ag '89; p.27 My '90. Bryce Morrison (350w)

"Schumann's B Minor Allegro...brings out the very best in Alicia de Larrocha, who responds with both passion and grace and seems to revel in its dramatic gestures. If only the two more celebrated and more substantial works here had drawn a similar response." *P85 S85*

Stereo Review 54:154 S '89. Richard Freed (150w)

"I can't recommend this collection to anyone except those collecting de Larrocha or Schumann records. London's sound, which is curiously colorless, doesn't help matters at all, but it's the playing itself which is mostly so drab."

Fanfare 13:352-53 N/D '89. Leslie Gerber (250w)

Gramophone 67:65 Je '89. James Methuen-Campbell (210w)

4174. Piano Music: Carnaval, Opus 9; Faschingsschwank aus Wien, Opus 26; Papillons, Opus 2.
Andrei Gavrilov (pno).
EMI 49235 DDD 65:00

★★*Awards:* Critics' Choice 1989, *Gramophone* D '89 (James Methuen-Campbell); Top Choices—1989, *American Record Guide* Ja/F '90 (Arved Ashby).

"Gavrilov's...*Carnaval* brings each one of Schumann's cameos immediately and vividly to life....Gavrilov's *Papillons* and *Faschingsschwank* find him on his best behavior, and as well-attuned to the chaste and sensitive qualities of the former as he is to the more garish elements of the latter. These works fill out a most invigorating and rewarding recital."

American Record Guide 52:104 S/O '89. Arved Ashby (165w)

"If *Papillons* is your chief concern you need look no further, but Alicia de Larrocha is altogether more thoughtful, serene and exploratory in the two major works. The recordings are of an exceptionally high standard and fully reflect Gavrilov's audacity." *P95/85 S95*

Hi-Fi News & Record Review 34:92 S '89. Bryce Morrison (275w)

"Alicia de Larrocha's recent recordings of Schumann's *Carnaval* and *Faschingsschwank*, both more tidy than stimulating, were coupled with his Allegro in B Minor, Op. 8. Andrei Gavrilov here offers the same two larger works but with *Papillons* in place of the Allegro. His record is an altogether more winning proposition...outstanding performances of all three works, and they're exceptionally well recorded, too."

Stereo Review 54:158 D '89. Richard Freed (200w)

Gramophone 67:65 Je '89. James Methuen-Campbell (210w)

4175. Piano Music: Carnaval, Opus 9; Papillons, Opus 2; Toccata, Opus 7.
Cecile Licad (pno).
SONY 45742 DDD 51:28

★*Awards:* Critics' Choice 1991, *Gramophone*, Ja '92 (Joan Chissell).

"Cecile Licad's third Sony disc is surely her finest, and counts among the most distinguished of Schumann recitals....The recordings are exemplary, and so one can only add that further recordings by a pianist of such impeccable taste and serene technical mastery, are clearly a necessity." *P100 S95*

Hi-Fi News & Record Review 36:76-7 S '91. Bryce Morrison (med)

"From the opening measures of the Preamble, Licad evinces complete identification with the impulsive, fanciful world of Schumann's imagination. The combination of spontaneity and control is perfectly balanced...*Carnaval* has been often recorded, and currently available on CD are such fabled performances as those by Rachmaninov and Rubinstein; but make room on your shelves for this disc too."

Fanfare 14:312-13 Ja/F '91. Susan Kagan (260w)

"Her solo-recital recording debut...demonstrates a most welcome ripening and maturation of her abundant and considerable gifts....Licad observes all repeats but unobtrusively varies her playing of them in terms of dynamics and nuance. Her earnestness is tempered by a decidedly appropriate flirtatiousness...and, without ever losing control...she is never afraid to set some exhilaratingly fast tempos....The piano sound, captured at Princeton's Richardson Auditorium, is superlative in its depth and brilliance."

Musical America 111:87-8 Mr '91. Harris Goldsmith (250w)

"I would not say that Licad surpasses Rubinstein (RCA 5667) or Rosen (Globe 5009) [in Carnaval], but there is much to esteem. Her *Papillons* are noteworthy as well, but Perahia (CBS 42448) will probably remain first choice for most listeners."

American Record Guide 54:94-5 Ja/F '91. Mark Koldys (90w)

Gramophone 68:1390+ Ja '91. Joan Chissell (315w)

4176. Piano Music: Fantasiestucke, Opus 12; Waldscenen, Opus 82 (Vogel als Prophet); Romances (3), Opus 28 (No. 2); Carnaval, Opus 9. ("The Rubinstein Collection").
Artur Rubinstein (pno). Manhattan Center, New York; American Academy of Arts and Letters, New York. 1962 and 1963; 1961.
RCA 5667 ADD 65:00

✔HC ★*Awards:* *Fanfare* Want List 1987 (Susan Kagan).

"There can be few finer examples of CD transfers than these superb collections of Rubinstein's playing....The sound of these recordings is rich, natural, fully alive—like the sound of Rubinstein's playing in person....To my mind, Rubinstein's Schumann readings have always represented an ideal way of playing Romantic music without mannerisms or exaggerated rubato, with sentiment but without sentimentality, with faithfulness to the text."

Fanfare 11:370-1 S/O '87. Susan Kagan (120w)

American Record Guide 52:118-21 Jl/Ag '89. Donald Manildi (55w)

Gramophone 65:453-4 S '87 James Methuen-Campbell (165w)

Sonata No. 2 for Piano, Opus 22. See No. 4168.

4177. Symphonic Etudes, Opus 13; Arabeske for Piano, Opus 18.
Maurizio Pollini (pno).
DEUTSCHE GRAMMOPHON 410 916 38:36

✔HC ★★*Awards:* *Stereo Review* Best of the Month, F '85; *Gramophone* Critics' Choice 1984 (Joan Chissell).

"Quite simply, this is one of Pollini's most cherishable recordings."

Opus 2:52 Ap '86. Harris Goldsmith (400w)

"While in the past Pollini has sometimes excited more admiration for his grasp of structure and the cool perfection of his playing, there is a very welcome warmth of heart as well as Olympian breadth in his performance of the etudes. The brief *Arabeske*, Op. 18...is altogether exceptional as well."

Stereo Review 50:62 F '85. Richard Freed (375w)

"Although not the best performance of the *Symphonic Studies* I have heard from Pollini, this is nonetheless one of the finest on disc. It deserves the best recording DG can muster but...I am afraid that a front-row-of-the-stalls approach detracts from the *finesse* of this great pianist."

Hi-Fi News & Record Review 30:109 Ja '85. Doug Hammond (105w)

Gramophone 62:352+ S '84. Joan Chissell (475w)

SCRIABIN, ALEXANDER

4178. Piano Music: Etudes (Opus 8, No.'s 7 and 12; Opus 42/5); Preludes (Opus 11/1, 3, 9, 10, 13, 14, 16; Opus 13/6, Opus 15/2; Opus 16/1, 4; Opus 27/1; Opus 48/3; Opus 51/2; Opus 59/2; Opus 67/1; Piano Sonatas 3 and 5.

Vladimir Horowitz (pno). 1957, 1976, May 22, 1982.
RCA 6215 ADD 66:00

"The steamy, neurotic, supercharged eroticism of so much of this music seems to have struck a sympathetic chord in Horowitz; his performances, more than anyone else's, deliver the full measure of this disquieting, disturbing, and ultimately marvelous stuff...Those in search of 'authentic' performances will find twenty-one of them on this disc."

Fanfare 13:293 Mr/Ap '90. William Zagorski (250w)

"Much of Scriabin's dark ecstasy sounds as if set down with Horowitz in mind...Best of all are the B-flat-minor and C-sharp-minor Etudes taken from Horowitz's 1953 Carnegie Hall recital, quivering with the sort of life and colour that have caused other pianists to pale and exclaim in wonder down the ages." *P95/100 S85-historic*

Hi-Fi News & Record Review 35:103 F '90. Bryce Morrison (385w)

Gramophone 67:1388 Ja '90. Alan Sanders (105w)

American Record Guide 53:121-22 Ja/F '90. Donald Manildi (155w)

SHCHEDRIN, RODION

4179. Piano Music: Prelude and Fugue in C; Prelude and Fugue in A minor; Troika; 3 Pieces from "The Humpbacked Horse"; 2 Polyphonic Pieces; Sonata in C. **Concerto No. 1 in D for Piano and Orchestra.**

Rodion Shchedrin (pno); Vladimir Krainev (pno). Alexander Dmitriev (c). Leningrad Philharmonic Orchestra. 1983.
MELODIYA 259 AAD 63:00

> ★*Awards:* Critic's Choice: 1990, *American Record Guide* Ja/F '91 (James Ginsburg).

"What a stunning recording! Not only is the music refreshing and inventive, but the performances are spectacular....A winner."

Fanfare 14:386 S/O '90. Henry Fogel (360w)

"When composers perform their own music, one is always concerned with the tradeoff between 'authenticity' and interpretive creativity-....Shchedrin, an accomplished virtuoso, has little difficulty getting 'into' his own works and communicating their inventiveness and humor-....Sound is quite good by Russian Standards."

American Record Guide 53:107-8 Jl/Ag '90. James S. Ginsburg (370w)

Digital Audio's CD Review 7:64+ N '90. Octavio Roca (225w)

SHOSTAKOVICH, DMITRI

4180. Preludes and Fugues (24) for Piano, Opus 87 (complete).

Tatiana Nikolaieva (pno). London. 1990.
HYPERION 66441/3 DDD 166:00 3 discs

> ★★★★★*Awards:* Wire Winner: Classical, *The Wire* Je '91; The Gramophone Awards, Nominations, Instrumental, *Gramophone*, N '91; The Want List 1991, *Fanfare* N/D '91 (Art Lange). Best Instrumental Recording 1991, *Gramophone*, D '91. Editors' Choice—Best CDs of the Year, *Digital Audio's CD Review*, Je '92.

"This 1990 version, spread over a mid-price, three-CD box-set, is certain to stand for many years as the definitive performance-....Nikolayeva['s]...touch, her choice of tempi, are impeccable; she plays with a grace, a fluency, a clarity that reveal both the scope and the coherence of Shostakovich's structural genius....It is, in short, a 'classical' performance of a 'classical' work; it is, too, a *great* performance of a *great* work. Absolutely one of the records of the year."

The Wire 88:51-2 Je '91. Graham Lock (long)

"Musically, the set is both fascinating as a technical exercise and contains passages of great emotional power....Richter has also recorded some of the Preludes and Fugues, and...shows more drama and imagination than the renditions at hand....Hyperion...gives us a soft-focussed, recessed, echoey piano sound....The pianist's strongly concentrated playing manages to transcend these problems."

American Record Guide 54:125-26 S/O '91. James S. Ginsburg (long)

"Everything about the performance is big, including the piano sound, which is very closely miked and suffers from too much reverberation. But the cumulative result is musically powerful, and Nikolayeva is truly masterful."

Musical America 111:53-4 S/O '91. Stuart Isacoff (brief)

"The Russian pianist performs...with utmost sensitivity, warm tone, and superb technical control, and the satisfactory piano reproduction, somewhat reverberant and not especially localized, has considerable color. A valuable recording!"

Stereophile 15:272 Ap '92. Igor Kipnis (med)

"Although in almost every case the pianist has opted for somewhat broader tempos than on her original version, her approach shows the same romantic warmth and attention to sonority one feels in listening to her earlier interpretations....While Nikolayeva shows herself capable of crystalline passage-work as in the will-o'-the-wisp A-Minor Prelude, her technique is sometimes less than sure...On the other hand, there is no question that Nikolayeva gets beneath the surface to plumb the music's affect and drama....All in all, this is an important set."

Fanfare 14:289-90 Jl/Ag '91. Royal S. Brown (375w)

"Tatiana Nikolayeva banishes any notions of this music as aridly intellectual. At its most formal, this music nevertheless touches on emotions, moods dear to the composer which we recognize from the more familiar orchestral works....These CDs have a splendid introduction and detailed commentary by Robert Matthew-Walker....This is a major affirmative Shostakovich release." *P95/100 (historic) S95 (85)*

Hi-Fi News & Record Review 36:88 Ap '91. Christopher Breunig (420w)

"There is an element almost of meditation which runs the course of the Preludes and Fugues, heightened by listening to all 24 in one sitting. Rich piano tone, energetic but never strident."

High Fidelity 3:95 My '91. Andrew Stuart (b.n.)

Digital Audio's CD Review 7:40-1 Jl '91. Lawrence B. Johnson (340w)

Gramophone 68:1703 Mr '91. Stephen Johnson (230w)

SOLER, PADRE ANTONIO

4181. Sonatas for Fortepiano: No.'s 18, 19, 41, 72, 78, 87. **Sonatas for Harpsichord:** No.'s 84, 85, 86, 88, 90. **Fandango, M.1A.**
Maggie Cole (ftpno/hpscd).
VIRGIN 91172 DDD 71:00

★*Awards:* Critics' Choice 1991, *Gramophone*, Ja '92 (Lionel Salter).

"If you're like me, you'll find the Soler sonatas unfamiliar but enormously entertaining works....Maggie Cole has done a superb job of bringing these worthy pieces to light....Her fortepiano, based on a Walter model of ca. 1795, is strong and versatile, though the close miking brings out every glitch in its noisy action....Throughout the program and on both instruments, Cole gives spirited and committed performances, and she has a reliable, athletic technique....In fact, I recommend this recording—both the repertoire and the performances—without reservation."

Fanfare 15:362-63 S/O '91. Kevin Bazzana (long)

"Cole reveals an uncommon energy in her playing and she offers warm and propulsive readings....A first-rate introduction to Soler's music."

HighPerformanceReview 8(3):85 '91. Timothy Mangan (med)

"For the first six of her selections she uses a fortepiano by Derek Adlam (1987) after a model by Anton Walter of Vienna (c.1795); for the famous Fandango and the remaining five Sonatas, she plays a grand three-manual harpsichord, complete with 16' range, built in 1986 by Robert Goble after a 1740 model of HA Hass of Hamburg...Both of her instruments are given dry, close, vivid sonics....If you are looking for an appealing one-disc introduction to his keyboard pieces, I would recommend the Cole; though I would also suggest trying to find Igor Kipnis's Nonesuch program (79010), if you can, as another valuable starting-point."

American Record Guide 54:148-9 N/D '91. John W. Barker (long)

Gramophone 68:2043 My '91. Lionel Salter (375w)

SORABJI, KAIKHOSRU SHAPURJI

4182. Opus Clavicembalisticum.
John Ogdon (pno).
ALTARUS 9075 DDD 284:39 4 discs

★★*Awards:* The Year's Best, *Hi Fi News & Record Review*, May '90 Supplement; *Hi-Fi News & Record Review* Record of the Month, Ag '89; Critics' Choice 1989, *Gramophone* D '89 (David Fanning).

"This is not a creation to come to terms with easily, if at all....readers who own Madge's recording should also want this one, simply because a) it's so different; b) the sound is better; c) there may never be another recording of *O.C.* complete....Even when he is wrong, Ogdon is brilliant in this unique work."

Fanfare 13:301-03 Mr/Ap '90. Paul Rapoport (1250w)

"Whether we are thinking of Ogdon's concert performance in London last year, or the above recording, done in only three sessions, this is one of the great pianistic feats of our time. But it is important to grasp that it is far from being a pianistic triumph only. *Oc* is an exceedingly difficult work not just to play but also to understand as a whole, and if there is something more astonishing here than Ogdon's performance it is his musical insight, sustained over vast stretches of terrain." *P100 S100*

Hi-Fi News & Record Review 34:93 Ag '89; p.11-12 My '90 Supplement. Max Harrison (1150w)

"Overall, Habermann's varied offering on LP is, I believe, the more inviting introduction to Sorabji, but the truly adventurous listener (with an abundance of time at his disposal) will certainly want to own Ogdon's gigantic achievement."

Stereophile 13:241+ O '90. Igor Kipnis (570w)

Gramophone 67:512 S '89. David J. Fanning (980w)

4183. Piano Music: Prelude, Interlude and Fugue; Valse-Fantaisie, "Hommage a Johann

Strauss"; St. Bertrand de Commings, "He Was Laughing in the Tower".
Michael Habermann (pno).
MUSICAL HERITAGE 7530; MUSICMASTERS 60118 50:55

★*Awards:* The Want List 1988, *Fanfare* N/D '88 (Paul Rapoport).

"Habermann has the knack of letting the music breathe so that the ear's bewilderment at hearing and attempting to comprehend the complexities of Sorabji's musical argument is eased and at times even completely dispelled....Without the safety-net of the splicing process he has managed to demonstrate a technical finesse and intellectual rigour that go a long way towards establishing Sorabji's piano music as more than just eccentric and entertaining."
The Musical Times 129:90 F '88. Leslie East (625w)

Michael Habermann "has a big, robust sound and is remarkably sure-fingered, but he is more than a technician: his sympathy for Sorabji's music comes through."
American Record Guide 51:81 Mr/Ap '88. Timothy D. Taylor (200w)

Originally reviewed in *Fanfare* 11:2, pp. 230-32. "This is still a superb release of music-...The transcendental scope and difficulty of his music are present in all these pieces (even though on a scale reduced from his norm) and are handled with complete understanding and conviction by Dr. Habermann."
Fanfare 11:218 My/Je '88. Paul Rapoport (200w)

STRAVINSKY, IGOR

Petrouchka (excerpts) (3 dances arr. Guillou). See No. 4144.

Violin and Piano Music. See No. 3143.

TIPPETT, MICHAEL

4184. The Blue Guitar. BRITTEN, BENJAMIN. Nocturnal after John Dowland for Guitar, Opus 70. SCHAFER, R. MURRAY. Le Cri de Merlin, for Guitar.
Norbert Kraft (gtr). 1989.
CHANDOS 8784 DDD 56:00

✔HC ★★★★*Awards:* Editors' Choice, *Digital Audio's CD Review*, 6:36 Je '90; Cream of the Crop IV, *Digital Audio's CD Review*, 6:43 Je '90. Critics' Choice 1990, *Gramophone* D '90 (John Duarte); Critic's Choice: 1990, *American Record Guide* Ja/F '91 (William Ellis).

"Welcome a new master of the classical guitar. Nobert Kraft is among the most intelligent and sensitive guitarists to appear in quite some time....That he has chosen the contemporary guitar as his point of departure is doubly exciting....one of the year's best releases."
American Record Guide 53:119-20 Jl/Ag '90. William Ellis (485w)

"Norbert Kraft, an astonishingly gifted young guitarist from Toronto, has made the best recording of Benjamin Britten's *Nocturnal* since Julian Bream, the dedicatee, first recorded the piece for RCA a quarter of a century ago....The coupling is an equally impressive performance of Sir Michael Tippett's 1983 *The Blue Guitar.*"
Musical America 110:72-3 Jl '90. Terry Teachout (120w)

"For the Britten and Schafer alone, the recording would be worth the price, especially given the detailed, technically assured and emotionally responsive performances. Expert engineering, too. Recommended."
Fanfare 13:316 My/Je '90. Peter J. Rabinowitz (305w)

"Tippett asks of the guitar the exalted songfulness of his vocal music. Britten does, too, transfiguring an Elizabethan song by Dowland into a haunting dreamlike fantasy. The Canadian composer R. Murray Schafer's transforming is more in the realm of natural soundscaping, enchanting sonically rather than musically, but it is enhanced by the disk's irresistibly gorgeous sound."
The New York Times Ja 7 '90, p. 30 H. Mark Swed (130w)

Gramophone 67:1349 Ja '90. John Duarte (385w)

Digital Audio's CD Review 6:51 Ap '90. Octavio Roca (185w)

VARESE, EDGAR. Music of Varese. See No. 1457.

VILLA-LOBOS, HEITOR

4185. Piano Music: Bachianas brasileiras No. 4 (piano); Guia pratico; Poema singelo; Caixinha de musica quebrada; Saudades das selvas brasileiras No. 2; As tres Marias; Valsa da dor; Cirandas—No. 4; O cravo brigou com a rosa: No. 14, A canoa virou; Ciclo brasileiro.
Cristina Ortiz (pno).
LONDON/DECCA 417 650 DDD 67:00

✔HC ★*Awards:* The Want List 1988, *Fanfare* N/D '88 (James Miller).

"She plays beautifully and the music is a delight and I commend this CD to your attention."

"Miss Ortiz has assembled here a fascinating and worthwhile programme, and plays it to the manner born. The recording is flawless. I strongly recommend this very worthwhile issue."
Music and Musicians International 36:50 Je '88. Robert Matthew-Walker (150w)

"I found this very impressive playing....The recording throughout is bright, clear, a little hard at times, but never stridently so."

Hi-Fi News & Record Review 33:92 Je '88. Jeremy Siepmann (280w)

"Cristina Ortiz plays this music with a rather pinging piano sound....Villa-Lobos's piano writing, with its use of African rhythms and simulations of mechanical musical devices, percussion instruments and guitar, takes this treatment well, and the pianist's passionate and intense temperament marries happily with numerous passages of a heightened dramatic nature or relentless motor motion."

Ovation 10:53 Mr '89. Joseph Fennimore (220w)

Gramophone 65:983 D '87. Lionel Salter (225w)

Stereo Review Presents: Compact Disc Buyer's Guide Summer 1988 p.52. William Livingstone (75w)

Fanfare 12:290 S/O '88. James Miller (240w)

WEBER, CARL MARIA VON

4186. Piano Music: Sonatas (4), J.138, 199, 206, 287; Invitation to the Dance, Opus 65; Rondo brillante (La gaite) in E flat, J.252; Momento Capriccioso in B flat, J.56.
Garrick Ohlsson (pno). April 1987 - February 1988.
ARABESQUE 6584 DDD 74:06, 60:48 2 discs

★★★★*Awards:* The Want List 1989, *Fanfare* N/D '89 (David Johnson; Elliott Kaback; Jon Tuska); Critics' Choice 1989, *Gramophone* D '89 (John Warrack).

"The present recording establishes itself far ahead of its contenders, such as they are. This is the recording of the Weber sonatas that we have been waiting for. If it does not convince the doubting Thomas...that Weber is a supremely gifted composer of instrumental music, nothing will....Arabesque's producer, Ward Botsford, has ensured that Ohlsson's Bosendorfer #808 is preserved in all its rainbow of colors. After hearing these CDs no one shall ever convince me that the digital process cannot capture the sound of a piano with concert hall fidelity. Here is one of the great piano recordings of our era. Do not deprive yourself of it."

Fanfare 12:293-96 Ja/F '89. David Johnson (1675w)

"In the somewhat weightier, more dramatic third and fourth sonatas, Ohlsson does not entirely manage to eclipse the splendid earlier interpretations of Richter...and Fleisher....Nonetheless Ohlsson shows definite flair for the unique style of this music."

American Record Guide 52:105 Ja/F '89. Donald Manildi (215w)

"The recorded sound is not as lush and warm as that provided by Delos for Carol Rosenberger's Bosendorfer on a recent Schubert piano music release, but rather drier, less reverberant and perhaps more apt for music which is by turns both Classical *and* Romantic. These sonatas deserve and repay repeated hearings, and Garric Ohlsson has provided benchmark recordings of all four of them."

Ovation 10:51 Ag '89. Jon Tuska (480w)

Gramophone 66:1462 Mr '89. John Warrack (630w)

WRIGHT, MAURICE. Sonata for Piano. See No. 4114.

Instrumental Music—Collections

Fernandez, Eduardo

4187. Spanish and Italian Guitar Music.
Legnani: Caprices, Opus 20 (excerpts). **Giuliani:** Giulianate, Opus 148 (excerpts). **Sor:** Introduction and Variations, Opus 9. **Diabelli:** Guitar Sonata in F. **Paganini:** Sonata in A.
Eduardo Fernandez (gtr).
LONDON/DECCA 414 160 55:20

★*Awards:* *Gramophone* Critics' Choice 1985 (John Duarte).

"This is not just a promising first album but a spectacular demonstration by an accomplished artist."

Stereo Review 51:72+ Ja '86. William Livingstone (700w)

"Fernandez shows a good deal of variety in tone color, particularly in the Diabelli, and sustains Paganini's lovely slow movement to good effect. Fast movements, however, he generally rips through as rapidly as possible, a technique that marks Fernandez as a young virtuoso but which tends to vitiate his undoubted musical abilities."

American Record Guide 49:92 S/O '86 David W. Moore (450w)

"His delicate phrasing and sure technique ensure that one never tires, even after 18 tracks, as can be the case on *some* solo recital CDs."

Hi-Fi News & Record Review 30:107 N '85. Sue Hudson (140w)

Ovation 7:43 S '86. Paul Turok (185w)

Gramophone 63:378+ S '85 (350w) (rev. of LP); 63:663-4 N '85 (140w) (rev. of CD). John Duarte (350w)

Fox, Virgil

4188. Virgil Fox Plays the John Wanamaker Organ—Philadelphia.
Virgil Fox (orgn). John Wanamaker Organ, Philadelphia. 1964.
BAINBRIDGE 8248

★*Awards:* Top Choices—1989, *American Record Guide* Ja/F '90 (Mark Koldys).

"No organ in the world has a richer 'string' sound, a more orchestral character. Mr. Fox's arrangements were made especially for this instrument. There is much to offend musical Puritans here....But Fox was one of the greatest recitalists ever, and had a way of thrilling an audience even if some of them had come to scoff-....He was the Stokowski of the organ, and this is as good a place as any to find out what that means."
American Record Guide 52:115 Mr/Ap '89. Donald R. Vroon (170w)

"There are Virgil Fox fans all over who will welcome this CD, but what intrigues the most here is a pair of more important factors—first, the most famous of big American organs, second in size only to the Convention Hall monster in Atlantic City (pre-casino), and the 'archiving' of this 1964 recording via Colossus, that recent massing of digital bits into an overall digital processing/recording system put together by Lou Dorren....I am not exactly a Fox worshipper, and I did not find much character in the brief classics....No matter—the end result all sounds very Wanamaker and it's good."
Audio 73:112 Mr '89. Edward Tatnall Canby (750w)

Friedman, Ignaz

4189. Complete Solo Recordings, 1923-36.
Ignaz Friedman (pno). reissues.
PEARL 2000 AAD 297:00 4 discs

★*Awards:* *American Record Guide* Overview: Chopin, Jl/Ag '92 (selected mazurkas).

"The sound is extraordinarily good in Pearl's remastering (by Ward Marston); in only a few selections do dimness or scratchiness detract from the performances. We are indebted to Pearl for making an absolutely invaluable historical anthology of a true 'pianist of the century' and for preparing the set so beautifully, as well as to Allan Evans for his excellent, extensive notes on Friedman's career."
American Record Guide 54:167-8 Jl/Ag '91. David G. Mulbury (850w)

"If for no other reason, the four-CD Pearl set must be obtained for two items in particular: the Op. 55 No. 2 Nocturne in E-flat, which has been described, and I can only concur, as one of the greatest Chopin recordings of all time, and the selection of Mazurkas (some with alternate takes) played by Friedman in a folksy, rhythmic manner unmatched by any other pianist. I cannot sufficiently stress the excellence of these fascinating interpretations, or, for that matter, that of the eight Mendelssohn *Songs Without Words*....Sometimes Friedman is idiosyncratic, but his personality, virility, grandeur, and tonal palette are such as to make this album an essential one for any piano enthusiast—unless, of course, an occasional sonic shattering at an overloaded climax or a poor 78 surface is sufficient excuse to bypass one of the great pianists of the early 20th century."
Stereophile 14:183+ My '91. Igor Kipnis (330w)

Musical America 111:88 Ja '91. Terry Teachout (b.n.)

Gramophone 68:1284 D '90. James Methuen-Campbell (605w)

Grimaud, Helene

4190. Recital. **Chopin:** Ballade No. 1 for Piano, Opus 23. **Liszt:** Annees de Pelerinage: 2nd Year, "Italy"—No. 7, "Dante" Sonata. **Schumann:** Sonata in F# minor for Piano, Opus 11.
Helene Grimaud (pno).
DENON/SUPRAPHON 1786 DDD 53:53

★*Awards:* Critics' Choice 1988, *Gramophone* D '88 (James Methuen-Campbell).

Grimaud "demonstrates a full range of impressive qualities...Technically the playing is at once effortless and impeccable, but it is the ardent Romanticism of this Schumann work which comes across most potently....As matters now stand, Grimaud's Schumann sonata surpasses all current editions except Earl Wild's on Dell'Arte, and her only real competition in the Liszt comes from Arrau, Wild and Bolet. Superb sound."
American Record Guide 51:62-3 My/Je '88. Donald Manildi (210w)

"Though recorded in her 17th year, Grimaud's recital shows considerable mastery and imagination allied to an impressive technique which never seems taxed by these works' often overwhelming technical demands."
Fanfare 11:95-6 Mr/Ap '88. Michael Fine (500w)

"Complete technical mastery is shown throughout the Chopin....Liszt's *Dante Sonata* emerges as an even more brilliant feat of execution, though, again, with no real suggestion of fire and brimstone....Perhaps the Schumann finale is best of all, with some moments of real eloquence."
Hi-Fi News & Record Review 33:105 F '88. Max Harrison (250w)

"If a very French force and logic are Miss Grimaud's present *forte* rather than subtle poetic dalliance, her playing is nonetheless highly musical and of an astonishing mastery. Generous length and a fine recording are added bonuses."

Music and Musicians International 36:49 Jl '88. Bryce Morrison (220w)

Gramophone 65:1328 Mr '88. James Methuen-Campbell (310w)

Guillou, Jean

4191. Organ Encores. Bach (arr. Guillou): Cantata 29—Sinfonia. Orchestra Suite No. 2, BWV.1067—Badinerie. Sarabande, BWV.977. Wauchet auf, BWV.645. Fugue in G minor, BWV.577, "Gigue." **Stanley:** Voluntary in A minor. **Purcell:** Trumpet Tune in D. **Jacinto:** Toccata in D minor. **Seixas:** Toccata in G minor. **Handel (arr. Guillou):** Organ Concerto No. 10 in D, Opus 7—Allegro. Water Music—Hornpipe. **Clerambault:** Basse et Desus de Trompette. **Haydn:** Flotenuhrstucke in C; Flotenuhrstucke in D; Flotenuhrstucke in G. **Schumann:** Canon in A flat. Canon in B minor. **Liszt (arr. Guillou):** Valse oubliee No. 1. **Prokofiev (arr. Guillou):** The Love for Three Oranges—March. **Guillou:** Hautbois d'Amour. Tutti Ostinati. Improvisation on Greensleeves.
Jean Guillou (orgn). Kleuker organ at Notre-Dame des Neiges, Alpe d'Huez, France.
DORIAN 90112 DDD 70:04

★***Awards:*** Cream of the Crop IV, *Digital Audio's CD Review*, 6:41 Je '90.

"This disc is Guillou in a nutshell and consistently entertaining. I recommend it highly for all listeners, even those who normally don't listen to organ music."

American Record Guide 52:117 Jl/Ag '89. David Bond (350w)

"As a performer, Guillou is the antithesis of the largely lethargic style displayed by the organists in the recordings I reviewed previously. Guillou brings light and life to the music, not just through brisker tempos but also through an adroit touch that may be an outgrowth of his fluid piano technique....[this disc] proves that organ playing remains a lively and fascinating art."

Stereophile 13:193+ Mr '90. Robert Hesson (200w)

"The Encores album...shows off Guillou's lively, assured technique and the complete understanding he has of his instrument—a striking organ of his own design."

Continuo 13:23-4 Je '89. Scott Paterson (70w)

"Ultimately, Dorian's Guillou outing must be viewed as appallingly brilliant in nature—consummate and original, but sometimes on the fringes of musical reason. Given the excellent technology behind it, couldn't we wish for a more moderate view of repertoire, a concert organ other than this oversexed, overspiced box, and more conventional virtuosity?"

Fanfare 12:392-93 My/Je '89. Haig Mardirosian (775w)

"Some of the many highlights are Guillou's transcriptions of the Sinfonia to Bach's Cantata BWV 29...some will be appalled by Guillou's audacity, but I find him tremendously exciting." *P100 S100*

Hi-Fi News & Record Review 34:113 N '89. William McVicker (245w)

Digital Audio's CD Review 5:89 My '89. Wayne Green (b.n.)

Herrick, Christopher

4192. Organ Fireworks. (Works by **Bonnet, Guilmant, Whitlock, Brewer, Monnikendam, D. Johnson, Widor, Preston, Hovland**). Played on the Hill organ of Westminster Abbey.
Christopher Herrick (orgn).
HYPERION 66121 52:50

★***Awards:*** *Gramophone* Critics' Choice 1986 (Geoffrey Horn).

"The LP was recommended in Aug '84 (p96) as a good selection of excellently played material—despite the title....Both versions are in the top category."

Hi-Fi News & Record Review 31:101+ S '86. Trevor Attewell (40w)

"The SD review appeared in *Fanfare* 8:1 in which I praised both the glowing talents and native aptitude of Westminster Abbey's Sub Organist, Herrick...Where I earlier suggested that the release lived up to its title, I could now add that it is rather too modest!"

Fanfare 9:278 Jl/Ag '86. Haig Mardirosian (90w)

Gramophone 64:193 Jl '86. Geoffrey Horn (155w)

Horowitz, Vladimir

4193. Collection: Prokofiev: Sonata No. 7 in B flat for Piano, Opus 83; Toccata, Opus 11. **Barber:** Piano Sonata, Opus 26. **Kabalevsky:** Piano Sonata No. 3 in F, Opus 46. **Faure:** Nocturne No. 13 in B minor, Opus 119.
Vladimir Horowitz (pno). reissues.
RCA 0377 ADD 64:44

"A magnificent document of an important swerve in Horowitz's development....ardently recommended."

Fanfare 14:278-79 Ja/F '91. Peter J. Rabinowitz (350w)

"Horowitz is simply magnificent here...this honestly dubbed, midprice reissue is an absolute must for any collection of twentieth-century piano music."

Musical America 111:54-6 Jl '91. Harris Goldsmith (125w)

"This disc is an essential acquisition from RCA's ongoing Horowitz reissue campaign."

American Record Guide 54:169 Jl/Ag '91. Donald Manildi (130w)

Musical America 111:94 My '91. Terry Teachout (b.n.)

4194. The HMV Recordings, 1930-51. Bach (arr. Busoni): Chorale Prelude, "Nun freut euch, lieben Christen, BWV.734. **D. Scarlatti:** Keyboard Sonatas—B minor, Kk.87; G, Kk.125. A minor, Kk.188; A, Kk.322. **Haydn:** Keyboard Sonata in E flat, HobXVI/52. **Chopin:** Etudes, Opus 10—No. 4 in C sharp minor; No. 5 in G flat; No. 8 in F. Opus 25—No. 3 in F. Impromptu No. 1 in A flat, Opus 29. Nocturne No. 19 in E minor, Opus 72 No. 1. Mazurkas—F minor, Opus 7 No. 3; E minor, Opus 41 No. 2. C sharp minor, Opus 50 No. 3. Scherzo No. 4 in E, Opus 54. **Debussy:** Etudes—No. 11, Pour les arpeges composes. **Poulenc:** Pastourelle. Trois pieces pour piano—No. 3, Toccata. **Beethoven:** 32 Variations in C minor, Wo.080. **Schumann:** Arabeske, Opus 18. Toccata in C, Opus 7. Fantasiestucke, Opus 12—No. 7, Traumeswirren. Presto passionato in G minor, Opus 22. **Liszt:** Harmonies poetiques et religieuses, S.173—No. 7, Funerailles. Piano Sonata in B minor, S.178. **Rachmaninov:** Piano concerto No. 3 in D minor, Opus 30. Prelude in G minor, Opus 23 No. 5. **Rimsky-Korsakov** (arr. Rachmaninov): The Tale of Tsar Saltan—The flight of the bumble-bee. **Stravinsky:** Petrushka—Danse russe. **Prokofiev:** Toccata, Opus 11.
Vladimir Horowitz (pno). reissues.
EMI 63538 ADD (m) 180:00 3 discs

★★*Awards:* The Want List 1990, *Fanfare* N/D '90 (Howard Kornblum); Critics' Choice 1990, *Gramophone* D '90 (James Methuen-Campbell).

"Most of these performances...are classics of the piano discography and as such require little comment here....The taut, lean playing of the young Horowitz comes through vividly in these restorations by Keith Hardwick (although a few sides are somewhat noisier and less vivid)."
American Record Guide 53:144-45 S/O '90. Donald Manildi (160w)

"Essential...for the Horowitz enthusiast....Since my library contains almost all of the original Horowitz 78s, I was able to make a comparison with a number of these *vs* EMI's CD 're-constitution,' and, without exception, I was able with the original discs to obtain greater depth and transparency as well as very much more vivid and colorful, less boxy and constricted reproduction. It's really too bad that the CD consumer must face such a misguided effort or do without."
Stereophile 13:251+ O '90. Igor Kipnis (225w)

"There are familiar aspects of Horowitz's playing style heard here—mainly, that nervous intensity, slightly pushed kinetic energy that involves the listener with its sheer dynamism; on the other hand, the playing evinces more control, more straightforwardness, than in some of his later performances...the transfers to CD do not offer an appreciable change for the better-....There are performances here that are absolutely peerless, to be treasured over and over, that reveal a master in all his glory."
Fanfare 13:352-53 Jl/Ag '90. Susan Kagan (575w)
Musical America 110:93 Jl '90. Terry Teachout (155w)
Gramophone 67:1708-09 Mr '90. James Methuen-Campbell (595w)

4195. The Last Recording. Haydn: Keyboard Sonata in E flat, HobXVI/49. **Chopin:** Mazurka in C minor, Opus 56 No. 3. Nocturnes: E flat, Opus 55 No. 2; B, Opus 62 No. 1. Fantaisie-impromptu in C sharp minor, Opus 66. Etudes: A flat, Opus 25 No. 1; E minor, Opus 25 No. 5. **Liszt:** "Weinen, Klagen, Sorgen, Zagen", Praludium S.179. **Wagner/Liszt:** Paraphrase on Isoldens Liebestod from "Tristan und Isolde", S.447.
Vladimir Horowitz (pno). 1989.
SONY 45818 DDD 58:00

✔**HC** ★★★★★*Awards:* Critics' Choice 1990, *Gramophone* D '90 (James Methuen-Campbell); Records to Die for: 1 of 5 Recommended Recordings, *Stereophile* Ja '91 (Igor Kipnis); Critic's Choice: 1990, *American Record Guide* Ja/F '91 (Arved Ashby); Editors' Choice, *Digital Audio's CD Review*, Je '91. Best CD of the Month, *Digital Audio's CD Review*, Jl '90; Best Recordings of the Month, *Stereo Review* Ag '90.

"All nine items are valuable additions to Horowitz's already remarkable discography, and it is not merely awareness of the valedictory connotation that suggests these final performances are among the most beautiful he ever recorded. Not the most dazzling or driven, but absolutely the most radiantly beautiful, filled with a sense of joy and continuing discovery that may be more electrifying than mere pyrotechnics after all. The recording itself, made in the pianist's living room, is exemplary in its realism and perspective."
Stereo Review 55:73 Ag '90. Richard Freed (570w)

"After many years of listening to Horowitz, it is something of a revelation to hear his final recording. One is not prepared for the settled, serene character of his playing here, so far removed from the pushed, nervous intensity of his stage persona for so many decades....Last—but hardly least—is the truly magnificent sound achieved by the engineers in Horowitz's living-room...the bass is richly resonant, the treble sings."
Fanfare 14:176-7 S/O '90. Susan Kagan (265w)

"These warm, natural-sounding final tapings are not only among the absolute best that Horowitz ever received, but the playing itself, autumnal in mood, is remarkably free overall from many of the interpretive mannerisms of his later years."
Stereophile 14:151 Ja '91. Igor Kipnis (b.n.)

"Horowitz had an autumnal last period in which he was constantly looking at new literature and playing it in a relaxed, charming manner. Gone were the neuroticism and outsize dynamics that could surge into his playing. In this kind of performance he gives the feeling that now he is no longer out to prove anything, that he is merely having a good time playing the piano. His patented kind of electricity is still there."

The New York Times Ap 22 '90, p. 25 H. Harold C. Schonberg (835w)

Digital Audio's CD Review 6:40 Jl '90. David Vernier (760w)

"Not surprisingly there is a lack of the fierce glitter and clangour of former years, and yet the facility, idiosyncrasy and musical generosity remain astonishing...The gem of the set is surely the Haydn Sonata, where Horowitz's unashamed delight in the composer's wit and inventiveness is clear in every bar." *P95 S85/75*

Hi-Fi News & Record Review 35:95 Ag '90. Bryce Morrison (220w)

"The Haydn is the highlight of the record, Horowitz's approach being more dramatically effective than classically 'correct'."

Stereophile 13:190-91 S '90. Kevin Conklin (180w)

"Another essential collection for the Horowitz aficionado....all are first-time pieces, and represent Horowitz in remarkable form....So far as reproduction is concerned, I'm tempted to describe the Sony album, with its rich, full-sounding piano, as overall the finest sound Horowitz has received."

Stereophile 13:191 S '90. Igor Kipnis (220w)

"Instead of the neurotic fussiness which has marred some of his interpretations, we have a mellow ambience that is recognizably Horowitzian yet cleansed of mannerisms and exaggerations....This is one of the most sheerly beautiful, and generally convincing, recordings that Horowitz made during his 61 years (off and on) in the studio, an he takes his leave by way of some of his most lyrical, poetic playing."

American Record Guide 53:144-45 S/O '90. Donald Manildi (160w)

Gramophone 68:395 Ag '90. James Methuen-Campbell (565w)

Horszowski, Mieczyslaw

4196. Recital. **Mozart:** Fantasia in D minor, K. 397. **Chopin:** Nocturnes in F#, D flat. **Debussy:** Children's Corner. **Beethoven:** Piano Sonata No. 2 in A, Opus 2, No. 2).
Mieczyslaw Horszowski (pno).
ELEKTRA 79160 DDD 55:32

★★*Awards:* *Opus* Record Award, 1987; *Opus* Christmas List, 1987 (Tim Page); *Stereo Review* Best of Month, S '87.

"There is no other descriptive word for these performances than extraordinary....The Debussy pieces are light-fingered and subtly colored; the Chopin Nocturnes are lyrical and flowing. Only the Mozart Fantasy was a little disappointing, with some distortion in matters of meter and rhythm. The LP disc has some surface noise that is completely absent on the CD; the piano sound is quite wonderful, with a good deal of presence and richness."

Fanfare 11:368-9 S/O '87. Susan Kagan (200w)

"Solo recordings by Horszowski have been all too rare...While the playing is anything but faceless, Horszowski is content in each case to allow the composer's own personality to prevail; he never thrusts his own at the listener."

Stereo Review 52:88+ S '87. Richard Freed (675w)

"It's remarkable how much of the Horszowski personality has been captured here...The few technical untidinesses (as if anyone really cared) are offset by all sorts of revelatory nuances, a richly personal, almost improvisatory style, and a deeply ingrained sensibility and musical cultivation."

Opus 4:36 D '87. Harris Goldsmith (685w)

Opus 4:58 D '87. Tim Page (100w)

4197. Recital. **Mozart:** Sonatas for Piano: No. 17 in D, K.576; No. 12 in F, K.332. **Chopin:** Mazurka in C, Opus 24, No. 2; Nocturne in B flat minor, Opus 9, No. 1; Mazurka in B minor, Opus 33, No. 4. **Schumann:** Arabeske, Opus 18; Kinderszenen, Opus 15.
Mieczyslaw Horszowski (pno). May 1988 live.
ELEKTRA 79202 69:00

★*Awards:* The Want List 1989, *Fanfare* N/D '89 (Leslie Gerber).

"These Mozart performances are near-ideal demonstrations of how to play Mozart on the modern piano....highest recommendation....generous in timing, and...very well recorded. That distinctively beautiful sound...must obviously be the pianist's own."

Fanfare 12:252-53 My/Je '89. Leslie Gerber (540w)

"Elegance, charm, masculinity and interpretative insight are words which come to mind as descriptive of what, to one listener at least, is an extraordinary performance."

American Record Guide 52:117 Mr/Ap '89. Michael Mark (310w)

Mieczyslaw Horszowski's "musicianship...is marked by an elegance and vitality that is a sort of unselfconscious distillation of the music's very essence."

Stereo Review Presents: Compact Disc Buyers' Guide Summ 1989 p.59 Richard Freed (100w)

"Mieczyslaw Horszowski recorded a recital disc for Nonesuch just before his 94th birthday-...This second recital, even more noteworthy than the first, was taped two years later...At 97, this artist...is playing some 30 concerts a year, and is, in fact, in even better form than he was three years ago!..This recording, then, is something that every piano lover will want to own.

The recorded sound—from Philadelphia's Curtis Hall...is ideally pleasant and convincing."
Musical America 110:65-6 Ja '90. Harris Goldsmith (440w)

"Perhaps Horszowski cannot dazzle us with sheer power now, but that was never his long suit. His profound authority and apparently instinctive sense of the music's essence certainly do more than merely dazzle....One has a sense of the music's integrity, of its being communicated in its purest form....A splendid presentation of a recording anyone who cares about the piano and its literature will want."
Stereo Review 54:126 Mr '89. Richard Freed (425w)

Hough, Stephen

4198. My Favorite Things: Virtuoso Encores. MacDowell: Hexentanz, Opus 12. **Chopin/Liszt:** Six chants polonais—The Wish, S.480, No. 1. **Quilter (arr. Hough):** The Crimson Petal; The Fuschia Tree. **Dohnanyi:** Capriccio in F minor, Opus 28, No. 6. **Paderewski:** Minuet in G, Opus 14, No. 1; Nocturne in B flat, Opus 16, No. 4. **Schlozer:** Etude in A flat, Opus 14, No. 1. **Gabrilowitsch:** Melodie in E; Caprice-burlesque. **Rodgers (arr. Hough):** My favourite things. **Woodforde-Finden (arr. Hough):** Kashmiri Song. **Friedman:** Music Box. **Saint-Saens (arr. Godowsky):** The Gardens of Buitenzorg. **Levitzki:** Waltz in A, Opus 2. **Palmgren:** En route, Opus 9. **Moszkowski:** Siciliano, Opus 42, No. 2; Caprice espagnole, Opus 37.
Stephen Hough (pno). Note: In England this recording is available under the title *The Piano Album* on Virgin 90732.
MUSICMASTERS 60135; VIRGIN 90732 DDD 63:07

★★*Awards:* The Year's Best, *Hi Fi News & Record Review*, May '90 Supplement. Top Choices—1989, *American Record Guide* Ja/F '90 (Donald Manildi).

"With this cleverly-chosen recital Hough continues to solidify his reputation as a virtuoso of exceptional taste and skill. What is perhaps most remarkable is the relaxed elegance of his playing, as opposed to the high-pressure, hard-toned treatment many younger pianists apply to repertoire of this kind on the rare occasions when they condescend to play it."
American Record Guide 52:122-23 Jl/Ag '89. Donald Manildi (300w)

"From the scorching to the sentimental, from the decadent to the delightful, Hough catches the fully stylistic range of these miniatures without a trace of condescension. Indeed, his tendency to ruffle the textures and to complicate the rhythmic flow strips coats of varnish from the music so that even the more familiar pieces sound revitalized. This is, in sum, the best playing I've heard from Hough."
Fanfare 13:454-55 N/D '89. Peter J. Rabinowitz (125w)

"There have been several recordings in recent decades that have tried to resuscitate the art of the fabled pianists of the early years of this century, but none, I think, have succeeded so awesomely as this release by Stephen Hough-....The sound is a tad too bright and unshaded."
Fanfare 12:385 My/Je '89. David Johnson (400w)

"Twenty pieces written, or arranged by pianist-composers—including Hough—and with Bryce Morrison's accompanying note itself exemplifying 'charm placed at a premium level'-....A lovely collection."

P100/95 S95
Hi-Fi News & Record Review 34:95 My '89; p.29 My '90 Supplement. Christopher Breunig (350w)

Gramophone 66:1191 Ja '89. Christopher Headington (245w)

The Piano Album. See No. 4198.

Hurford, Peter

4199. Romantic Organ Music. Liszt: Prelude and Fugue on the name B-A-C-H, S.260. **Reger:** Benedictus, Opus 59, No. 9. **Widor:** Symphony No. 6 in C minor, Opus 42, No. 1—Allegro. **Brahms:** Chorale Preludes, Opus 122, No. 3, "O Welt, ich muss dich lassen"; No. 9, "Herzlich tut mich verlangen." **Vierne: Symphony No. 1 in D minor, Opus 14—Finale. Peeters:** Suite modale, Opus 43. **Langlais:** Trois paraphrases gregoriennes—Hymne d'Actions de graces, "Te Deum." **Schumann (ed. C.H. Trevor):** Four Sketches, Opus 58—No. 4, Allegretto. **Boellmann:** Suite gothique, Opus 25.
(Volume 2).
Peter Hurford (orgn). Ratzeburg Cathedral, West Germany.
LONDON/DECCA 421 296 DDD 70:00

★*Awards:* Critics' Choice 1988, *Gramophone* D '88 (Christopher Headington).

"If you want an excellent selection of organ pops rather than a diet of specialist organ music, then choose this recording."
Hi-Fi News & Record Review 34:111 F '89. William McVicker (435w)

Gramophone 66:454 S '88. Christopher Headington (245w)

Kissin, Evgeny

4200. Evgeny Kissin in Tokyo. Rachmaninov: Lilacs, Opus 21 No. 5; Etudes tableaux, Opus 39: No. 1 in C minor; No. 5 in E flat minor. **Prokofiev:** Piano Sonata No. 6 in A, Opus 82. **Liszt:** Concert Studies, S.144: La leggierezza; Un sospiro. **Chopin:** Nocturne in A flat, Opus 32, No. 2; Polonaise in F# minor, Opus 44. **Scriabin:** Mazurka in E minor, Opus 25, No. 3; Etude in C# minor, Opus 42, No. 5. **Anon (arr. Saegusa):** Natu: Wa Kinu; Todai: Mori; Usagi.
Evgeny Kissin (pno). Suntory Hall, Tokyo. May 12, 1987 live.
SONY 45931 DDD 73:00

★*Awards:* The Gramophone Awards, Nominations, Instrumental, *Gramophone*, N '91. Critics' Choice 1990, *Gramophone* D '90 (David Fanning).

"At any age, an artist capable of this playing would stand out; Kissin's exceptional youth makes him phenomenal. His performance of the Sonata No. 6 (in my opinion Prokofiev's best) sets a standard probably unmatched since the prime of Sviatoslav Richter."
Audio 76:118+ Ja '92. Paul Moor (long)

"This recital...demonstrates once again that Evgeny Kissin is a prodigy of prodigies....A selection of Japanese encores, a tribute to his hosts in Tokyo, completes the programme and these are given with a skill and affection they scarcely deserve....The recordings fully capture all the excitement of a memorable and volatile occasion." *P100/95 S95*
Hi-Fi News & Record Review 36:96 Mr '91. Bryce Morrison (200w)

"The Rachmaninoff *Etudes-Tableaux* and Scriabin Etude in C sharp minor exist in studio-recorded Kissin performances, but these are wonderfully spontaneous and brilliantly rendered....Piano buff will doubtless want both albums [this and the Carnegie Hall recital] for comparison; most connoisseurs, however, will find Sony's Tokyo disc an excellent (and, at over seventy-three minutes, generous) representation of an ascending star's career in its first stage."
Musical America 111:89-90 My '91. Harris Goldsmith (240w)

"In short, this is not the most essential Kissin item. But if you are interested in hearing early samples of a pianist who is likely to become a major world figure, you will still find this disc well worth the price."
Fanfare 14:380-81 Ja/F '91. Leslie Gerber (500w)

Gramophone 68:1016 N '90. David J. Fanning (455w)

"Despite all the publicity this young performer has engendered...not to mention the hype and hoopla from the record companies, for some reason I still find myself deaf to the finer qualities alleged to inhere in his playing."
American Record Guide 54:158-59 Mr/Ap '91. Mark Koldys (125w)

"This may be a minority report, but his playing, at least in this earlier stage of his career, gave me little cause for enjoyment. Sony reproduces the sound of the live recital, including the harder edge of Kissin's extreme forte dynamics, accurately, applause has sporadically been left in."
Stereophile 14:263 Ap '91. Igor Kipnis (235w)

Kotzia, Eleftheria

4201. The Blue Guitar. Tippett: The Blue Guitar. **Pujal:** Three Preludes. **Villa-Lobos:** Five Preludes. **Delerue:** Mosaiques. **Giorginakis:** Four Greek Images. **Fampas:** Greek Dances: No. 1 (Karaguna); No. 3 (Susta).
Eleftheria Kotzia (gtr).
PEARL 9609 DAD 67:11

★*Awards:* Critics' Choice 1989, *Gramophone* D '89 (John Durate).

"This young performer handles her Jose Romanillos instrument with a sturdy authority that gives credit to her former teachers Julian Bream and Dimitri Fampas...All in all, this CD makes for a fine introduction to a new presence on the international guitar scene, and contains some music new to discs to boot."
Fanfare 12:308 Jl/Ag '89. John Ditsky (200w)

"Three reasons to buy this record: 1: Greek guitarist Kotzia...is a wiz—a strong, sensuous player with bite and sass. 2: This is the premiere recording of Sir Michael Tippett's *Blue Guitar*...3: The Greek compositions of Kiriakos Giorginakis and Dmitri Fampas...are probably unfamiliar to most American ears, as they were to mine, yet what a treat listening to their peculiar scales, dance rhythms and drones."
American Record Guide 52:115 Jl/Ag '89. William Ellis (175w)

"Kotzia's performance here [of the *Blue Guitar*] is impassioned and poetic, providing an excellent recording debut from a young artist."
The Musical Times 130:691 N '89. Graham Wade (320w)

"In live performance her personality invariably allows an easy communication with her audience, and something of that happy knack has been transferred to disc....The recording is excellently engineered; seldom has the instrument sounded so rich and woody, so capable of limitless *espressione*."
Music and Musicians International 38:47 Je '90. Colin Cooper (450w)

Gramophone 67:69 Je '89. John Duarte (300w)

Kremer, Gidon

4202. A Paganini. Milstein: Paganiniana. **Schnittke:** A Paganini. **Ernst:** Mehrstimmige Studien (excerpts). **Rochberg:** Caprice Variations.
Gidon Kremer (vln).
DEUTSCHE GRAMMOPHON 415 484

★★*Awards:* *Gramophone* Critics' Choice 1986 (J. Methuen-Campbell); *Opus* Record Award Nominee, 1987; *Opus* Christmas List, 1987 (Peter G. Davis).

"What really shines through here is the glowing purity and burning intensity of Kremer's musical spirit, which seems to illuminate everything he plays."
Opus 4:55 D '87. Peter G. Davis (125w)

Gidon Kremer, virtuosically dazzling, recreates the charisma, with only an occasional hint of sluggishness. There is little watering down with romantic slush of Paganini's angularity and fugue-ish wildness. Instead, the jazz-like improvisations admirably retain the eerie, arrogant beauty of his inimitable style."

Hi-Fi News & Record Review 31:135 My '86. Sue Hudson (210w)

Fanfare 9:280 Jl/Ag '86. John Bauman (300w)

"An entire disc of unaccompanied violin music including neither Bach nor Paganini is unusual, held together here by each composer's paying homage to Paganini....Kremer plays with great virtuosity and the material is fascinating in its diversity."

American Record Guide 50:53 My/Je '87 David W. Moore (250w) (rev. of LP)

Ovation 8:49 F '87 Paul Turok (40w)

Labeque, Katia and Marielle

4203. Recital. Bizet: Jeux d'Enfants, Opus 22. **Ravel:** Ma Mere l'Oye (4-hand piano suite). **Faure:** Dolly, Opus 56.
Katia Labeque (piano); Marielle Labeque (piano).
PHILIPS 420 159 DDD 56:00

> ✔**HC** ★*Awards: Gramophone* Critics' Choice (Robin Golding), 1987.

"The Labeques play with their usual enthusiasm, and Philips has captured the sound quite nicely."

Fanfare 11:94 Ja/F '88. James Miller (100w)

Gramophone 65:759-60 N '87 Robin Golding (275w)

The New York Times Jl 24 '88, p. H25. Harold C. Schonberg (250w)

Lawson, Peter

4204. American Piano Sonatas. Copland: Piano Sonata (1939-41). **Ives (ed. Cowell):** Three-page Sonata. **Carter:** Piano Sonata (1945-6 rev. 1982). **Barber:** Piano Sonata, Opus 26.
(Volume 1).
Peter Lawson (pno).
VIRGIN 91163 DDD 76:00

> ★★*Awards:* Critics' Choice 1991, *Gramophone*, Ja '92 (Peter Dickinson). Pick of the Month, North American Perspective (Christie Barter), *Gramophone* My '91.

"This disc—the first in an anthology of American piano sonatas—offers four hard-boiled exemplars of the genre in expertly tough-minded performances. As is evident from the steely account of the end of the Ives or from the merciless charge through the finale of the Barber, Lawson's fingers are unflinching; and he uses his commanding technique to detail both texture and rhythm....Superb notes by Wilfred Mellers and (except for a failure to capture some of the pedal effects in the Carter) excellent sound. In sum, an auspicious launch."

Fanfare 15:547-48 N/D '91. Peter J. Rabinowitz (med)

"The notes (in English, German, French) with this disc tell us this is the first of three CDs by Virgin Classics which aim to survey the American Piano Sonata from 1900-1950....This first disc surveys the musical terrain through Ives' Three Page Sonata of the turn of the century, the Copland pre-war Sonata, Carter's post-war work and finally the Barber piece at mid-century. Peter Lawson plays the works with assurance, navigates their more treacherous currents successfully and manages to draw out the typical features of each. The program becomes stronger as it progresses....Notes by Wilfred Mellers are comprehensive and informative as one would expect from this authoritative writer. The sound is clear with good dynamic range, but a bit dry."

High Performance Review 9:65 Spr '92. June C. Ottenberg (long)

"He has broken the ground, understandably enough, with the most familiar examples by four of the most prestigious composers, Copland, Ives, Carter and Barber, whose music spans a very wide range of expression....That Peter Lawson has triumphed so conclusively, and that his work has been so faithfully recorded, are matters for congratulation and one looks forward with interest and eager anticipation to see what the next two collections will bring." *P100 S95*

Hi-Fi News & Record Review 36:79 S '91. Kenneth Dommett (med)

Lawson's "performances [of the Copland and Carter works]...are wonderfully lucid, the finest renditions I have heard anywhere...On the other hand, he misses some of the rusticity and ecstatic nature of the Ives...But I still recommend this disc strongly."

American Record Guide 54:191 N/D '91. Arved Ashby (long)

Gramophone 68:2043 My '91. Peter Dickinson (385w)

Lipatti, Dinu

4205. Collection. Bach: Partita in B flat; Chorale Preludes (2); "Jesu Joy of Man's Desiring (arr. Hess); Siciliano (arr. Kempff). **Scarlatti:** Sonata in E, L.23; in D minor, L.143. **Mozart:** Sonata in A minor, K.310. **Schubert:** Impromptus in G flat and in E flat.
Dinu Lipatti (pno). Besancon Festival. 1947, 1950.
EMI 69800; also EMI 47517 ADD 59:26

> ★★*Awards:* The Want List 1989, *Fanfare* N/D '89 (Susan Kagan); Critics' Choice 1989, *Gramophone* D '89 (Joan Chissell).

"This appears to be identical with EMI CDC 7 47517-2...Reviewing that release in *Fanfare* 10:3, Howard Kornblum wrote eloquently: 'Every piece here is a glowing example of the performer's art.' I would only add that, despite some of the 'stylistic anachronisms' noted by Kornblum...every piece is equally a glowing example of the composer's art....There is some hissy noise in the Schubert, but the rest of the program, digitally remastered, is excellent. It is no exaggeration to say that this disc is a rare treasure."

Fanfare 12:302 Jl/Ag '89. Susan Kagan (200w)

"Here we have the Geneva studio recordings of Bach and Mozart (not the final, recital versions), together with two Schubert Impromptus taken from Besancon—perhaps unwisely, as they show him at less than best, though only in the context of these other most meticulous realizations....Often, professional musicians used the word 'divine' to describe Lipatti's inspiration. There is something arresting and pure in his authoritative, fluent Bach Partita which typifies that quality. (The sound in all five Bach items is very good.) The claims made in the translated French note here, however 'purple' the prose-style, however extravagant and unlikely, *are* met in the playing."

Hi-Fi News & Record Review 34:115-7 Ap '89. Christopher Breunig (385w)

"For anyone interested in the piano, this disc is as close to essential as they come."

Ovation 8:45 Je '87 Peter J. Rabinowitz (150w) (rev. of EMI 47517)

"Lipatti's playing was far from flashy, but his technique was incredible....he was a transcendent interpreter of every one of these pieces-....The sound on these reissues is variable."

American Record Guide 53:122-23 Ja/F '90. Stephen D. Chakwin, Jr. (175w)

"I suspect that those of you who think of recordings as repository of a great music played by supremely great artists will not even notice the age of this reissue, which to my ears was astonishing as a transfer from 78s and *fully* satisfying. Don't pass this up."

Fanfare 10:58 Ja/F '87 Howard Kornblum (320w) (rev. of EMI 47517)

High Fidelity 37:62 Mr '87 Terry Teachout (150w) (rev. of EMI 47517)

Gramophone 67:98 Je '89. Joan Chissell (280w)

MacGregor, Joanna

4206. American Piano Classics. Nancarrow: Prelude; Blues. **Ives:** Varied Air and Variations; Some Southpaw Pitching; The Anti-abolitionist Riots; Concord Sonata—The Alcotts; Three-page Sonata. **Garner (arr. MacGregor):** Erroll's Blues; Erroll's Bounce. **Copland:** Piano Variations. **T. Monk (arr. MacGregor):** Monk's Point. Round Midnight. **Copland:** Blues No's. 2 and 3. **Gershwin (arr. Finnissy):** A Foggy Day; Fidgety Feet; But Not for Me.
Joanna MacGregor (pno).
LDR 1004 DDD 65:00

★***Awards:*** The Year's Best, *Hi Fi News & Record Review*, May '90 Supplement.

"I have rarely encountered a more thrilling or sheerly enjoyable record debut. Joanna MacGregor's tribute to America in all its teeming and restless variety is made with such sensitivity and poetic vitality that it would be hard to equal."*P100 S95*

Hi-Fi News & Record Review 34:87 Jl '89; p.13 My '90 Supplement. Bryce Morrison (315w)

"It lives dangerously by mixing her own transcriptions of Erroll Garner and Thelonius Monk with tougher pieces like Ives's *Three-Page Sonata* and Copland's Piano Variations-....Overall this is an attractive anthology-...which presents American music as it is—infinitely rich and varied."

The Musical Times 130:689 N '89. Peter Dickinson (155w)

Gramophone 67:345 Ag '89. David J. Fanning (350w)

Oppens, Ursula

4207. Contemporary American Piano Music. Nancarrow: Tango? **Bolcom:** The Dead Moth Tango. **Sahl:** Tango from the Exiles Cafe. **Hemphill:** Parchment. **Adams:** Phrygian Gates (1978). **Carter:** Night Fantasies. **Foss:** The Curriculum Vitae Tango. **Jaggard:** Tango.
Ursula Oppens (pno).
MUSIC & ARTS 604 DDD 69:00

★★★***Awards:*** Top Disks of the Year, *The New York Times* D 24, '89 (John Rockwell). The Want List 1990, *Fanfare* N/D '90 (Mike Silverton). The Critics' Choice 1990—Composition Award: No. 15 of 15 *Wire* 82/3 '91.

"This is a wonderful disc. Ursula Oppens has a fine touch, crisp but sonorous, and even when this repertoire calls for percussive attack, she never produces an ugly sound. She gives a fantastically well-constructed program too."

Stereophile 13:253 O '90. Barbara Jahn (250w)

"Her touch is fluent and precise; the pieces themselves prove enchanting."

Wire 75:61 My '90. Graham Lock (b.n.)

"Oppens is to be congratulated for giving us a valuable perusal of the contemporary scene for piano. Recommended."

Fanfare 13:373-74 My/Je '90. William Wians (600w)

"The recorded sound is first-rate...I can't remember when I've been so turned on by a solo-piano CD."

Fanfare 13:350-51 Jl/Ag '90. Mike Silverton (250w)

"Ursula Oppens is, of course, great....This is one to have, but program your CD player to sneak by *Night Fantasies*."

American Record Guide 53:138-39 Mr/Ap '90. Timothy D. Taylor (350w)

Gramophone 67:2023-24 My '90. John Milsom (490w)

Perahia, Murray

4208. The Aldeburgh Recital. Beethoven: 32 Variations in C minor on an Original Theme, WoO.80. **Schumann:** Faschingsschwank aus Wien, Opus 26. **Liszt:** Hungarian Rhapsody No. 12, S.244; Consolation No. 3 in D flat major, S.172. **Rachmaninov:** Etudes-tableaux, Opus 33—No. 2 in C major. Etudes-tableaux, Opus 39—No. 5 in E flat minor; No. 6 in A minor; No. 9 in D major.
Murray Perahia (pno). Snape Maltings Concert Hall, Aldeburgh, England. May 30-June 1, 1989.
SONY 46437 DDD 59:00

★★★★***Awards:*** Best Recordings of the Month, *Stereo Review* Je '91. Critics' Choice 1991, *Gramophone*, Ja '92 (Joan Chissell); Honorable Mention, Records of the Year, 1991, *Stereo Review*, F '92; Critics' Choice 1991, *Gramophone*, Ja '92 (Robert Layton).

"These performances are enlivening in the very best sense, taking the music absolutely on its own terms, touching all the emotional bases and glorying in the virtually orchestral range of colors. That range, along with every other aspect of Perahia's playing, has been splendidly captured in the recording, one of the finest reproductions of piano sound yet achieved on this label (or its predecessors)."
Stereo Review 56:73-4 Je '91. Richard Freed (625w)

"This compendium...is particularly interesting in that it offers record listeners (home viewers, too, via videodisc) their first glimpse of the 'new' Perahia....The engineering is some of the best ever given this distinctive artist."
Musical America 111:93-4 Jl '91. Harris Goldsmith (570w)

"Despite the implications of the title, this was not recorded in concert before a live audience, but under studio conditions in a concert hall in Aldeburgh, with superb results....a disc for piano lovers to savor."
Fanfare 14:361-2 Jl/Ag '91. Susan Kagan (300w)

"The tightly knit, no-nonsense Beethoven and the imaginatively thought-out Schumann are predictably on the top level that Perahia carved out for himself in his earlier performances of these composers. The sound is superb."
American Record Guide 54:173 Jl/Ag '91. Donald Manildi (205w)

Gramophone 68:1874 Ap '91. Joan Chissell (385w)

Digital Audio's CD Review 7:42+ Jl '91. Tom Vernier (250w)

"In Liszt's D-flat *Consolation* only the late Sir Clifford Curzon excelled Perahia in clarity and elegance...but in the *Hungarian Rhapsody* Perahia's pianism glistens and scintillates with the most liberating subtlety and assurance....In more familiar Perahia territory the playing is just a little less vital and illuminating...The recordings...are too close for comfort...Yet, overall, this is an immensely distinguished recital." *P95 S75*
Hi-Fi News & Record Review 36:76 Je '91. Bryce Morrison (630w)

Preston, Simon

4209. Variations on America. Sousa (arr. anon): Stars and Stripes Forever! **Saint-Saens (arr. Lemare):** Danse Macabre, Opus 40. **Ives:** Variations on "America". **Buck:** Variations on "The Last Rose of Summer", Opus 59. **Bossi:** Etudes Symphonique, Opus 78. **Lemare:** Andantino in D flat. **Guilmant:** Sonata No. 1 in D minor, Opus 42.
Simon Preston (orgn). Organ of the Methuen Memorial Music Hall, Massachusetts, USA. March 1988.
ARGO 421 731 DDD 66:00

★***Awards:*** Pick of the Month, North American Perspective (Christopher Pollard), *Gramophone* N '90.

"This famous instrument is well overdue for such a recording. And what an imaginative programme it is—played by an Englishman!...Preston is a master of colouring the organ, chameleon-like, for every different need; the same tutti is seemingly never heard twice."
Organists' Review 76:42 Mr '91. Robert Lawrenson (290w)

"The marvelous...organ...projects itself with eminence and verve and is, once again, seized in splendidly balanced sound on disc-....Preston's admirers will also recognize the blue-blooded reverence for style and architectural shaping of the substantial works he programs."
Fanfare 14:359-60 My/Je '91. Haig Mardirosian (280w)

Gramophone 68:1016 N '90. Ivan March (350w)

Richter, Sviatoslav

4210. Recital. Scriabin: Sonata No. 5 in F#, Opus 53. **Debussy:** Estampes. Preludes, Book 1—Voiles; Le vent dans la plaine; Les collines d'Anacapri. **Prokofiev:** Sonata No. 7 in B flat, Opus 83; Visions Fugitives, Opus 22, No.'s 3, 6, 9.
Sviatoslav Richter (pno). 1963-1965.
DEUTSCHE GRAMMOPHON 423 573 ADD 67:00

✔**HC** ★★***Awards:*** Critics' Choice 1988, *Gramophone* D '88 (David Fanning). Critics Choice, *Hi Fi News & Record Review*, Ap '91 Supplement (David Nice).

"These are some of Richter's best recordings. The Scriabin is particularly astonishing; its color and white-hot delivery have never been equaled in my experience, not even by the excellent Horowitz live performance issued by RCA. But these are all superb performances-...presented in better sound than they've ever had before."
Fanfare 12:265 Ja/F '89. Leslie Gerber (225w)

"Sonic limitations are quickly forgotten in the face of playing of such mastery and musical insight."
Hi-Fi News & Record Review 33:121 O '88. Max Harrison (175w)

"These capture the tension and electricity of live performances, but some curious noise mars the start of the *Visions* excerpts, and at other points the audience's thoughtless coughing makes you think he must have recorded these pieces in the good old U.S.A.."
High Fidelity 39:63 Mr '89. Paul Moor (210w)

Gramophone 66:453 S '88. David J. Fanning (140w)

Romero, Angel

4211. A Touch of Romance. Anon.: Romance. **Sanz:** Suite Espagnole. **Barrios:** Choro da Saudade. Un Sueno en la Foresta. Aire de Zamba. **Albeniz:** Suite Espanola—No. 5, Asturias, "Leyenda" (all arr. A. Romero). **C. Romero:** Suite Andaluza.
Angel Romero (gtr). 1989.
TELARC 80213 DDD 61:00

★*Awards:* Cream of the Crop IV, *Digital Audio's CD Review*, 6:42 Je '90.

"Make no mistake, this is a superb issue....easily recommend[ed]."
Fanfare 13:215-16 N/D '89. John Bauman (165w)

"Florid embellishment of familiar melodies, sprinkled here and there with adventuresome liberties, one eye cocked toward the popular heart—this is what the title, *A Touch of Romance*, conjures. If such is your expectation, Angel Romero's latest album will not disappoint....look forward, as well, to some very impressive guitar playing."
Audio 74:98+ Mr '90. Michael Wright (375w)

"*A Touch of Romance* consoles us with insignificant trifles in a significant way."
American Record Guide 53:134 Mr/Ap '90. William Ellis (225w)

Gramophone 67:1845 Ap '90. John Duarte (315w)

Digital Audio's CD Review 6:84 O '89. Wayne Green (110w)

Rosenberger, Carol

4212. Night Moods. Chopin: Nocturnes, Opus 27/2; Opus 55/2. **Faure:** Nocturne in D flat. **Debussy:** Clair de Lune; La Soiree dans Grenade; La Terrasse des Audiences au Claire de Lune; Reverie; Nocturne in D flat. **Griffes:** Notturno. **Liszt:** Harmonies du Soir.
Carol Rosenberger (pno). 1988.
DELOS 3030 DDD 76:00

★*Awards:* Cream of the Crop IV, *Digital Audio's CD Review*, 6:42 Je '90.

Rosenberger "plays lyrically, songfully and always musically....the recorded sound is lovely."
American Record Guide 52:129 S/O '89. Stephen D. Chakwin, Jr. (b.n.)

Digital Audio's CD Review 6:54 Ap '90. Wayne Green (100w)

Rubinstein, Artur

4213. The Rubinstein Collection. Ravel: Valses nobles et sentimentales; Forlane; La Vallee des cloches. **Poulenc:** Mouvements perpetuels; Intermezzo in A; Intermezzo No. 2 in D flat. **Faure:** Nocutrne in A flat, Opus 33, No. 3. **Chabrier:** Scherzo-Valse. ("The Rubinstein Collection." Editor's Note: This collection includes 35 CDs; other highly rated issues in the collection may be found under various composers—consult the index for a full listing of Rubinstein CDs.).
Artur Rubinstein (pno). 1961.
RCA 5665 ADD 64:00

★*Awards:* *Fanfare* Want List 1987 (Susan Kagan).

"One of the most distinctive qualities of Rubinstein's pianism is the sheer beauty of his tone—easy to admire in and of itself, without regard for the musical uses to which it is put. The rich, robust, almost 'juicy' singing tone which Rubinstein inevitably drew from the instrument must remain his secret; it has never been approached by any other pianist. Rubinstein's sound retains its immediately recognizable character all through his repertoire, whatever the pianistic demands, whatever the musical style involved. It has been superbly caught in Wilcox's CD editions, and lovers of sumptuous piano sonorities can rejoice at the results....Beyond the exceptional sonic quality of the collection lies its value as documentation for posterity of one of the great pianistic personalities of the century....these 35 CDs must be regarded as the cornerstone of any collection of piano recordings."
American Record Guide 52:118-21 Jl/Ag '89. Donald Manildi (55w)

"There can be few finer examples of CD transfers than these superb collections of Rubinstein's playing....The sound of these recordings is rich, natural, fully alive—like the sound of Rubinstein's playing in person."
Fanfare 11:370-1 S/O '87. Susan Kagan (120w)

"Of all the discs issued thus far in RCA's fabulous Artur Rubinstein celebration, this is my personal favorite."
Musical America 107:64 Ja '88. Thomas L. Dixon (175w)

Gramophone 65:453-4 S '87 James Methuen-Campbell (165w)

4214. The Rubinstein Collection: Carnegie Hall Highlights. Debussy: La Cathedral engloutie; Poissons d'or; Hommage a Rameau; Ondine. Szymanowski: Four Mazurkas. **Prokofiev:** 12 Visions Fugitives. **Villa-Lobos:** Prole du Bebe. **Schumann:** Arabesque. **Albeniz:** Navarra.
("The Rubinstein Collection").
Artur Rubinstein (pno). 1963; 1961.
RCA 5670 ADD 47:00

★*Awards:* *Fanfare* Want List 1987 (Susan Kagan).

"Because he loved playing for the public, the almost palpable sense of occasion conveyed by the 'Carnegie Hall Highlights' CD marks this release as particularly valuable."

American Record Guide 52:118-21 Jl/Ag '89. Donald Manildi (55w)

"For many collectors, this issue in Red Seal's 'Rubinstein Collection,'...may be *the* disc to acquire first. It offers Rubinstein 'live' and in prime form...This is a landmark disc for any piano collection."

High Fidelity 37:72 O '87. Thomas L. Dixon (250w)

"Few pianists—or any musicians, for, that matter—project this natural, spontaneous, inspired joy in communicating music to an audience as did Rubinstein. The Carnegie Hall selections capture the infectious spontaneity of those recitals before enthusiastic audiences."

Fanfare 11:370-1 S/O '87. Susan Kagan (120w)

Gramophone 65:453-4 S '87 James Methuen-Campbell (165w)

Segovia, Andres

4215. The Art of Segovia: The HMV Recordings, 1927-1939. Bach (arr. Segovia): Solo Violin Sonata No. 6 in E, BWV.1006—Gavotte; Solo Cello Suite No. 3 in C, BWV.1009—Courante; Clavier buchlein fur W.F. Bach—Prelude in C minor, BWV.926; Lute Suite in E minor, BWV.996—Allemande; Solo Violin Sonata No. 1 in G, BWV.1001—Fugue in G minor; Solo Cello Suite No. 1 in G, BWV.1007—Prelude. **Ponce:** Suite in A; Sonata No. 3—first and second movements; Postlude; Mazurka; Folies d'espagne—Theme, variations and fugue; Petite Valse (arr. Segovia). **Sor:** Theme varie, Opus 9. **De Visee:** Sarabande; Bourree; Menuet. **Froberger:** Gigue. **Torroba:** Sonatina in A—Allegretto; Suite castellana—Fandanguillo; Preludio; Nocturno. **Mendelssohn (arr. Segovia):** String Quartet No. 1 in E flat, Opus 12—Canzonetta. **Malats:** Serenata. **Tarrega:** Recuerdos de la Alhambra; Study in A. **Castelnuovo-Tedesco:** Sonata, "Homage to Boccherini"—Vivo ed energico. **Albeniz:** Suite espanola: No. 1, Granada; No. 3, Sevilla. **Turina:** Fandanguilla. **Granados:** Danzas espanolas, Opus 37: No. 5 in E minor; No. 10 in G.
Andres Segovia (gtr). 1927-39 reissues.
EMI 61047 AAD 119:48 2 discs

★*Awards:* Top Choices—1989, *American Record Guide* Ja/F '90 (William Ellis).

"Segovia...treats us to much varied nuance and tonal colouring, and in the faster pieces his incisive, rhythmic attack is often exciting....Recordings are tight, dry and clear, and transfers are excellent."

Hi-Fi News & Record Review 33:89 Ag '88. Robert Cowan (105w)

"Nobody who has more than a casual interest in the guitar and its history in our time can afford not to know this repertoire in these performances, if only for the perspective they give to everything that has happened since."

Fanfare 12:333-34 Ja/F '89. John Wiser (325w)

"This recent issue erases unhappy memories of Segovia's later performances and replaces them with the unforgettable sound of a phenomenal virtuoso at work."

High Fidelity 38:62 D '88. Terry Teachout (155w)

"These recordings...are integral performances, recorded 'direct-to disc' without the benefit of tape editing available to all today....There is surface noise, but the guitar sound is detached from it so that a great deal of subtlety comes through clearly."

American Record Guide 52:126 S/O '89. John Sunier (200w)

Gramophone 66:1794-98 My '89. John Duarte (385w)

Serkin, Peter

4216. Recital. Wolpe: Form IV: Broken Sequences (1969); Passacaglia (1936); Pastorale (1939). **Stravinsky:** Serenade in A; Sonata for Piano. **Lieberson:** Bagatelles (3) for Piano.
Peter Serkin (pno).
NEW WORLD 344 53:48

✔HC ★*Awards:* *Stereo Review* Best of the Month, F '87. *Gramophone* Critics' Choice (Arnold Whittall), 1987.

"As a demonstration of pianistic fluency and control, Serkin's Wolpe can be placed alongside Robert Taub's amazing realizations of Babbitt's very different but equally arresting Gestalts....'Spontaneous Songs,' is surely one of the most hauntingly restrained lyrics in the recent literature of the keyboard; finally, Stravinsky's (neo) classics of the '20s are given performances by Serkin that are as cool and smooth as the Wolpe *Passacaglia* is heated and jagged—what a range of style and expression this pianist commands!"

Opus 4:29-30 D '87. Richard Taruskin (1200w)

"It is to Peter Serkin's immense credit that the listener is not likely to be aware of the music's difficulty in these performances but only of its stimulating quality and the surprising level of response it commands—on the part of both performer and listener."

Stereo Review 52:170 F '87 Richard Freed (485w)

High Fidelity 37:70 Jl '87 K. Robert Schwarz (325w)

Gramophone 64:1432 Ap '87 Arnold Whittall (300w)

CD Review Digest
Classical

Early Music

ANONYMOUS. L'Homme Arme. See No. 5025.

BRUMEL, ANTOINE

5001. Missa et Ecce Terrae Motus; Dies Irae.
Paul Van Nevel (c). Huelgas Ensemble.
SONY 46348 DDD 67:00

★★*Awards:* The Want List 1991, *Fanfare* N/D '91 (J.F. Weber). Critics' Choice 1991, *Gramophone*, Ja '92 (Mary Berry).

In the Mass "Van Nevel has organized a persuasive performance indeed....there is no doubt that he has captured the monumantality of this extraordinary work....there's no denying the rich diversity of colors or the high quality of singing and playing [in the *Dies irae*]."
American Record Guide 54:56 S/O '91. John W. Barker (long)

"The Huelgas Ensemble performs with excellent intonation and balance, but I would prefer their sibilants to be a bit less prominent; the recording may exacerbate this to some extent."
Stereophile 14:204+ Ag '91. Les Berkley (160w)

"Brumel isn't much heard or heard of today, a fact that amazes after listening to 'Et ecce terrae motus' for 12 voices....Paul van Nevel and the Huelgas Ensemble offer a voluptuous, perfectly tuned and balanced account. Though some of the music might benefit from a drier sound—separated lines and pointed rhythms—it's a thoroughly convincing performance. The *Sequentia 'Dies irae, Dies illa'* is a more somber affair...The performers bring just the right amount of warmth to the music without compromising its severity."
HighPerformanceReview 8(2):61 Summer '91. Timothy Mangan (410w)

Continuo 15:25 Ap '91. Scott Paterson (275w)

Fanfare 14:92+ Mr/Ap '91. J. F. Weber (275w)

Gramophone 68:2051 My '91. Mary Berry (295w)

BYRD, WILLIAM

5002. Gradualia, Volume 1: The Marian Masses.
Gavin Turner (c). William Byrd Choir. 1990.
HYPERION 66451 DDD 79:39

★*Awards:* Critics' Choice 1991, *Gramophone*, Ja '92 (John Milsom).

"Gavin Turner's mixed choir has made only a few records, but they have been uniformly fine. The singing is exquisite, the balance always right, the intensity of devotion always present. The sound is as fine as we expect from this label....texts are printed in translations."
Fanfare 14:147-48 My/Je '91. J. F. Weber (350w)

"Here is the first of what is projected to be a complete issue of the *Mass Propers* of Byrd's great compilation....This disc is an essential purchase for anyone who takes their church music seriously."
Organists' Review 76:134 Je '91. Timothy Hone (265w)

Gramophone 69:136+ N '91. John Milsom (long)

5003. The Great Service; Anthems (O Lord, make thy servant Elizabeth; O God, the proud are risen; Sing joyfully unto God).
Peter Phillips (c). Tallis Scholars. 1987.
ABBEY-GIMELL 011 DDD 53:00

★*Awards:* **Perfect 10/10, *Digital Audio*, Mr '88; Editors' Choice, *Digital Audio*, 1988.**

"A record-of-the-year this."
Hi-Fi News & Record Review 32:111 O '87 Hugh Canning (280w)

"As an example of Byrd's Anglican music, this disc has long been overdue. Very fine work!"
Fanfare 10:82 Jl/Ag '87 J.F. Weber (260w)

Gramophone 65:88-89 Je '87 David Fallows (330w); 67:1223 D '89. Roger Hughes (160w)

Digital Audio 4:78 O '87. Andrew Taylor (390w)

5004. Keyboard Music (Pavans and Galliards).
Davitt Moroney (hpscd).
HARMONIA MUNDI 901241/2 118:37

✔HC ★*Awards:* *Fanfare* Want List 1987 (Edward Strickland).

"I find Moroney thoroughly convincing as an interpreter here. While reconstruction of the works as performed in their time is impossible, Moroney, even more than Hogwood, conveys a 'You Are There' feeling in the music—aided by the vivid sonics....Some of the tempos are surprising (e.g., the Sixth Pavan), but in general moderation rules."
Fanfare 10:81-82 Ja/F '87 Edward Strickland (725w) (rev. of LP)

"I reviewed the LP set last time with great enthusiasm, which has not faded....The sound is recorded at a higher volume, but when that is appropriately adjusted I find the CDs still tend to be crisper and more forward, the LPs more reserved yet warmer."

Fanfare 10:95 Edward Strickland (150w)

"In his notes, Moroney waxes hot and heavy about the significance of the music....I would have settled without regrets for a single disc of the best pieces; and if Moroney feels differently he should have done his selling in deeds, not words."

Opus 3:35 Ag '87 Richard Taruskin (550w) (rev. of LP)

Hi-Fi News & Record Review 32:101 F '87 (150w); 32:95 Ap '87 (45w) Roger Bowen

Gramophone 64:902 D '86 David Fallows (545w)

5005. Keyboard Music: 13 Pieces from the Fitzwilliam Virginal Book: Fantasia in C; The Carman's Whistle; Pavan and Galliard in F; The Woods so Wild; Fantasia in G; The Queen's Alman; Pavan and Galliard in G; The Bells; Walsingham; All in a Garden Green; Lavolta; Pavan and Galliard in G Minor; Ut re mi fa sol la.
Ursula Duetschler (hpscd). 1989.
CLAVES 9001 DDD 70:00

★★*Awards:* The Gramophone Awards, Nominations, Early Music, *Gramophone,* N '91. Critics' Choice 1990, *Gramophone* D '90 (David Fallows).

"This recording seems to be an ideal introduction to an underappreciated composer."

American Record Guide 53:55 S/O '90. Stephen D. Chakwin, Jr. (135w)

"Duetschler plays a very attractive Italian instrument (1677, from Kenneth Gilbert's collection) with a beautiful sound which is nicely captured here, and she has a good sense of style....Recommended."

Fanfare 14:205-6 S/O '90. Tom Moore (160w)

Gramophone 68:778 O '90. David Fallows (315w)

Digital Audio's CD Review 7:58 S '90. David Vernier (190w)

5006. Mass in 4 Parts; Mass in 5 Parts.
George Guest (c). Saint John's College Choir, Cambridge. reissue 1986.
EMI 62015 DDD 48:29

✔HC ★*Awards:* Near-perfect 10/9, *Digital Audio,* Mr '88.

"In place of restraint, Guest gives forcefulness, not the quality I look for here."

Fanfare 11:104 Ja/F '88. J. F. Weber (250w)

Digital Audio 4:92-3 D '87. David C. Vernier (220w)

Gramophone 65:571-2 O '87 Stephen Johnson (105w)

5007. Mass in 4 Parts; Mass Propers for the Feast of Saints Peter and Paul, Nunc scio vere, Constitues eos, Tu es Petrus. Motets: Quomodo cantabimus?; Tu es pastor ovium; Quodcunque ligaveris; Hodie Simon Petrus. **DE MONTE, PHILIPPE. Motet: Super flumina Babylonis.**
Harry Christophers (c). Sixteen.
VIRGIN 91133 DDD 60:00

★*Awards:* The Want List 1991, *Fanfare* N/D '91 (J.F. Weber).

"The adoption of equal numbers of singers per part imbues everything with a rich earthy quality which distinguishes them from almost any other group working today, and somehow conveys the spirit of the rough-hewn performances surmised of Byrd's time. A chapel-like acoustic provides the perfect environment for such music-making." *P95 S95*

Hi-Fi News & Record Review 36:92 Mr '91. Simon Cargill (200w)

"The singing is superb, worthy to rank with the Tallis Scholars if not quite touching the Hilliard Ensemble. Philip Brett furnishes a sympathetic note, and texts are printed with three translations."

Fanfare 14:148-49 My/Je '91. J. F. Weber (325w)

"The 16 sounds large for these pieces and I don't hear the uncanny unanimity of pitch and blend of tone that the best choral ensembles can produce in this music. Nonetheless, these are very accomplished performances of (mostly) unduplicated repertory. I don't know the group well enough to decide whether this is a murky recording of a clear-sounding ensemble or a faithful one of a slightly muddy group, but either way, the essence of the music comes through handsomely."

American Record Guide 54:51-2 Mr/Ap '91. Stephen D. Chakwin, Jr. (210w)

Gramophone 68:1394+ Ja '91. Lindsay Kemp (390w)

CHANT AND LITURGICAL MUSIC

5008. 12th Century Aquitanian Polyphony.
Marcel Peres (c). Ensemble Organum. 1984 reissue.
HARMONIA MUNDI 901134 ADD 52:42

✔HC ★*Awards:* Critics' Choice 1989, *Gramophone* D '89 (Mary Berry).

"The Ensemble Organum gives wonderfully fluid and atmospheric performances that lend the music a real sense of mysticism without allowing it to become weighty or ominous....The sound is appropriately resonant, with just a few traces of tape hiss. Highly recommended for the slightly adventurous."

High Fidelity 38:72 O '88. Christopher Rothko (250w)

"I hailed this program with enthusiasm in *Fanfare* 8:2, p. 319 and put it on my want list for the year in the same issue....Absolutely splendid."

Fanfare 11:308-9 Jl/Ag '88. J. F. Weber (450w)

Gramophone 67:527 S '89. Mary Berry (210w)

5009. Cant de la Sibilla.
Jordi Savall (c). Montserrat Figueras (sop). Capella Reial.
AUVIDIS-ASTREE 8705 DDD 54:30

✔HC ★*Awards:* The Want List 1989, *Fanfare* N/D '89 (J. F. Weber).

"Each of the prophecies is a solo, the verses embellished with choral refrain and the spare use of instruments. The soprano is incredibly lovely, the pathetic melodies soaring endlessly, bounded by the punctuations of chorus and instruments....This altogether unique collection deserves a special place where it won't be overlooked. It may be best to keep it for a quiet moment when you won't begrudge an hour given up to the profound and the mysterious."
Fanfare 12:300 Jl/Ag '89. J. F. Weber (400w)

"Jordi Savall's recording presents three versions of the chant....With the exceptions noted above, these performances are very fine. The recording is on the whole quite clear...There is, however a sameness in the lengthy repetitions of the tunes which does become rather wearing-....In the end it is the Catalan version with its rich instrumental timbres to which I will return with greatest pleasure."
Continuo 14:19-20 Je '90. David Klausner (400w)

5010. Gregorian Chant: Maundy Thursday.
Dom Jean Claire (c). Solesmes St. Peter Abbey Monastic Choir.
PARACLETE 831 DDD 64:05

✔HC ★*Awards:* The Want List 1990, *Fanfare* N/D '90 (J.F. Weber).

"All of the recent Cardine-type recordings are worth studying, but Dom Claire offers a healthy alternative to all of the others....This disc really can't be overlooked for even modest chant collections, and it's essential for all serious students."
Fanfare 13:344 Jl/Ag '90. J. F. Weber (420w)

5011. Gregorian Chant. Volume 1. (A selection of pieces from the Proper).
Father Hubert Dopf (c). Scola of the Vienna Hofburgkapelle.
PHILIPS 411 140 47:51

✔HC ★*Awards:* *Gramophone* Critics' Choice 1984 (Mary Berry).

Hi-Fi News & Record Review 29:137 D '84. David Prakel (130w)

Gramophone 62:145 Jl '84. John Milsom (155w)

5012. Masterpieces of Mexican Polyphony.
Hernando Franco: Salve Regina. **Juan Gutierrez de Padilla:** Deus in adjutorium. Mirabilia testimonium. Incipit Lamentatio Jeremiae. Salve Regina. **Francisco Lopez Capillas:** Alleluia, Dic nobis Maria. Magnificat. **Antonio de Salazar:** O sacrum convivium.
James O'Donnell (c). Westminster Cathedral Choir. June 1989.
HYPERION 66330 DDD 65:10

★*Awards:* Critics' Choice 1990, *Gramophone* D '90 (Tess Knighton); Pick of the Month, North American Perspective (Christopher Pollard) *Gramophone* D' 90. The Gramophone Awards, Nominations, Early Music, *Gramophone*, N '91.

Gramophone 68:1255-6 D '90. Tess Knighton (395w)

"Despite its unfamiliarity, this music is convincingly presented under O'Donnell's direction....Quite unusual, timely, interesting, and beautiful."
Fanfare 14:379 Ja/F '91. J. F. Weber (350w)

"The music sounds as sumptuous in these performances as it appears to be on the printed page and is done full justice by James O'Donnell and the Westminster Cathedral Choir in furtherance of their policy of introducing us to newly discovered treasures."
Organists' Review 76:53 Mr '91. Alan Spedding (600w)

"Quite unusual, timely, interesting, and beautiful."
Fanfare 14:467-8 Mr/Ap '91. J. F. Weber (350w)

"One should expect nothing particularly exotic. Padilla's work—for double choir—is the most complex and grandiose, the *Lamentation* especially effective....Such repertoire is not commonplace on records....O'Donnell permits, in the style of the era, a continuo of organ, harp, and curtal, but the last two are mostly inaudible.The choir sings well, the trebles strong and clear, but the reverberation of the cathedral makes for mushiness."
American Record Guide 54:164-65 Mr/Ap '91. David Mason Greene (470w)

5013. Messe de Tournai.
Marcel Peres (c). Ensemble Organum. texts and translations included.
HARMONIA MUNDI 901353 53:13

★*Awards:* The Want List 1991, *Fanfare* N/D '91 (J.F. Weber).

"By far the best version [of the Tournai Mass] ever is the new recording by Marcel Peres, the tenth release in his fascinating, aggravating, indispensable series on this label....This is the first genuine Tournai Mass on record."
Fanfare 15:414-15 S/O '91. J. F. Weber (long)

"There have been a number of recordings; by far the best was a Deutsche Harmonia Mundi release (99 870) by the Pro Cantione Antiqua led by Mark Brown (not available, but this one is better anyway)....The presentation is vintage Marcel Peres of the best kind, reflecting his long interest in medieval liturgy as a living and coherent tradition. The chant is sung with vigor and convincing inflection, while the polyphonic Mass segments are delivered with flowing sonority. The only lapse comes in the *Communio*, 'Beata viscera', which is melded into the verses of the Magnificat....that slip aside, this is the best recording yet of the Tournai cycle. Atmospheric sound; good notes."

American Record Guide 55:195-6 Mr/Ap '92. John W. Barker (long)

Continuo 15:27 O '91. Scott Paterson (brief)

5014. Old Roman Liturgical Chants: Grand Vespers for Easter Mass for Second Sunday after Michaelmas.
Laszlo Dobszay; Janka Szendrei (c). Schola Hungarica.
HUNGAROTON 12741

✔**HC** ★*Awards:* *Opus* Christmas List, 1987 (James Parsons).

"Remember those subtly refined, evenly paced, oh so elegantly sung (and let's admit it, rather boring) chant recordings by the monks of Solesmes? This one would make them spin!-...If you've ever wondered how this body of music has endured for nearly 2,000 years, part of the reason will be discovered here."

Opus 4:58 D '87. James Parsons (80w)

"Highly recommended."

Fanfare 10:259 Mr/Ap '87 J.F. Weber (175w)

"Much as I welcomed the first disc last month, this new issue is the better introduction to a neglected but much-discussed aspect of Medieval music."

Fanfare 10:240-1 Ja/F '87 J.F. Weber (830w) (rev. of LP)

Gramophone 65:215 Jl '87 Mary Berry (210w)

Plainsong Prayers for the Feast of the Nativity of Our Lady. See No. 5019.

5015. Sarum Chant: Missa in Gallicantu. **Hymns:** *Christe Redemptor Ominum;* Veni, Redemptor Gentium; Salvator Mundi, Domine; A Solis Ortus Cardine.
Peter Phillips (c). Tallis Scholars. Merton College Chapel, Oxford. 1988.
ABBEY-GIMELL 017 DDD 55:00

★*Awards:* The Want List 1989, *Fanfare* N/D '89 (J. F. Weber).

"This is, to my knowledge, the first really systematic commercial recording devoted to a body of Sarum Rite liturgy, and to that interest is added the high quality of the presentation-....A nicely balanced group of nine singers (three each of tenors, baritones, and basses) sings in a stately, sonorous, and flowing style. The sound captures them in rich beauty and clarity. Full texts are included."

American Record Guide 52:164 N/D '89. John W. Barker (290w)

"Once again...the Tallis Scholars...have opened up another chapter of our musical heritage, and with their characteristic professionalism this recording makes an excellent, well balanced introduction to English plainchant which must also delight even the most pedantic of early music lovers with its scrupulous authenticity."

Hi-Fi News & Record Review 34:119 Ja '89. Helena Stoward (350w)

"As an eye-opener to the Sarum use this disc will prove invaluable....The measured approach adopted leaves one time to savour the chant, and the ensemble is admirable."

Organists' Review 75:47 Mr '89. Robert Lawrenson (300w)

"A recording of this particularly English chant is most welcome among the large number of recordings of so-called Gregorian chant....Unfortunately, there are omissions from the chant recorded: the Collect, Epistle and Gospel are replaced by silent spaces on the disc, and the Eucharistic prayer is also lacking....Although not attempting a full reconstruction of the 16th-century Mass, this disc seems to come so close that its omissions are all the more striking."

The Musical Times 130:221-22 Ap '89. Edward Kershaw (480w)

"This is an interesting disc, not only for the variant Sarum chant but for the presentation of a plenary Mass in an alternative version. The sound is typical of Gimell's good work, and each part is tracked. Informative notes, texts, and translations are provided."

Fanfare 12:510-13 My/Je '89. J. F. Weber (690w)

"Very much worth hearing....the sound...is consistent with...a technique [of a single microphone position]."

Stereophile 12:184-85 Ag '89. Les Berkley (235w)

Gramophone 66:1050 D '88. Mary Berry (255w)

Digital Audio's CD Review 5:49 Mr '89. David Vernier (440w)

CLEMENS NON PAPA, JACOBUS

5016. Missa Pastores Quidnam Vidistis. Motets: Pastores quidnam vidistis; Tribulationes civitatum; Pater peccavi; Ego flos campi.
Peter Phillips (c). The Tallis Scholars. 1987.
ABBEY-GIMELL 013 DDD 54:00

✔**HC** ★★*Awards:* Record of the Month, *Hi-Fi News & Record Review*, Ap '88; The Want List 1988, *Fanfare* N/D '88 (Michael Ullman).

"Highly recommendable."

High Fidelity 38:81-2 N '88. Christopher Rothko (170w)

"'Of such is the kingdom of heaven' is the immediate comment that came to mind as I allowed myself to be transported by the serene delights of Clemens' textures...His expressive devices are all the more effective for being held in check, as are those of the Tallis Scholars who are a perfect body to promote this beautiful and little-known music."

Organists' Review 74:70 Ja '88. Paul Hale (110w)

"This release deserves the highest recommendation to all who love Renaissance polyphony."
Fanfare 11:97 Mr/Ap '88. J. F. Weber (290w)

"This is exquisite music, and the performances—and the recording—match it well."
Hi-Fi News & Record Review 33:93 Ap '88. Stephen Pettitt (275w)

Clemens' "music, full of cascading motivic interplay and carefully balanced sonorities, is very well served here by Phillips and his ensemble."
Continuo 12:19 D '88. Scott Paterson (125w)

"Unfortunately, the 4 sopranos slightly overbalance the other singers with only 2 on each part, and I confess to finding their sound a bit too penetrating. The interpretations are fairly straightforward—more abstract than imaginative. Nevertheless, it is an important contribution to the realm of CDs."
HighPerformanceReview 5:78 S '88. George S. T. Chu (160w)

"There is a note in the mass that, in tonal music, would correspond to the dominant, which tends to hoot in one of the sopranos, and which becomes quite distracting....Other than this, the performances are nicely balanced and musically phrased."
American Record Guide 51:35 S/O '88. David W. Moore (100w)

Digital Audio 4:54 My '88. David C. Vernier (275w)

Gramophone 65:989 D '87. John Milsom (420w)

CORNYSH, WILLIAM

5017. Choral Music: Salve regina; Ave Maria, mater Dei; Gaude virgo mater Christi; Magnificat; Ah, Robin; Adieu, adieu, my heartes lust; Adieu courage; Woefully arrayed Stabat mater.
Peter Phillips (c). Tallis Scholars.
ABBEY-GIMELL 014 DDD 65:00

> ✔**HC** ★★★★*Awards:* Critics' Choice 1989, *Gramophone* D '89 (Mary Berry; David Fallows; John Milsom). The Editors Pick 6, *Digital Audio's CD Review*, 6:31 Je '90.

"Since the recorded quality of this release is as sparkling as its performance, and its programme introduces more fascinating treasures from our sadly underexplored musical past, it is definitely one not to be missed, either by enthusiasts or, indeed, anyone seeking an approachable introduction to the riches of English choral history."
Hi-Fi News & Record Review 34:87 Mr '89. Helena Stoward (385w)

"When singing together The Tallis Scholars make a wonderfully impressive sound—full and well-balanced, with the crystal-clear treble sound of the women laser-like in its precision-....The sound here is rich and expressive, if at times the clarity suffers a little....All in all this is a well-produced recording, accurately sung and thoughtfully prepared."
The Musical Times 130:222 Ap '89. Edward Kershaw (480w)

"Phillips's efforts to develop a new realization of the Tudor sound, using young women as treble and mean voices, reaches a new level of perfection and accomplishment here. Gimell provides consistently good engineering, and the church in Norfolk that they used for Gesualdo serves as well here....texts and three translations are printed."
Fanfare 12:167-68 My/Je '89. J. F. Weber (675w)

"Very much worth hearing....the sound...is consistent with...a technique [of a single microphone position]."
Stereophile 12:184-85 Ag '89. Les Berkley (235w)

Gramophone 66:1618 Ap '89. John Milsom (420w)

DE MACHAUT, GUILLAUME

5018. Messe de Nostre Dame; Je ne Cesse de Prier (lai "de la fonteinne"); Ma Fin Est Mon Commencement.
Paul Hillier (c). Hilliard Ensemble.
HYPERION 66358 DDD 54:00

> ✔**HC** ★*Awards:* The Highs, 1990, *The New York Times* D 30 '90 (John Rockwell).

"The main rival the Hilliard Ensemble's performance of Machaut's *Messe de Notre Dame* has to face is the one that attempts to set the music within the kind of ceremonial for which it must have been composed [Taverner Ch/EMI]-....in this strictly medieval work, whose five movements...are united more by commonness of intent than by any musical link, the context of the ritual within which it was first heard is more vital to an appreciation of its richness. That said, the Hilliard Ensemble deliver their usual finely balanced, intense performance."
P95 S95
Hi-Fi News & Record Review 35:88 Ap '90. Stephen Pettitt (310w)

"The lais are the least familiar of Machaut's works, and the present example is one of the few that has been recorded....I find this version of the Mass splendid; the only other CD (Parrott) is more similar than different, although the latter's liturgical format makes a clear choice between them possible on that basis."
Fanfare 13:207-8 My/Je '90. J. F. Weber (900w)

"It was only a matter of time before the Hilliard Ensemble recorded the mass; an example of their usual high standards, the release also raises some interesting questions. The works which fill out the disc, examples of Machaut's extensive output of French songs, are beautifully presented, but probably intended for those with special interest in this area."

American Record Guide 53:67 Jl/Ag '90. Paul Laird (375w)

Gramophone 67:1504+ F '90. Mary Berry (325w)

5019. Messe de Notre Dame. CHANT AND LITURGICAL MUSIC. Plainsong Prayers for the Feast of the Nativity of Our Lady.
Andrew Parrott (c). Taverner Choir; Taverner Consort. 1984 reissue.
EMI 47949 DDD 51:00

★*Awards:* Critics' Choice 1988, *Gramophone* D '88 (Mary Berry).

"I was quite taken with the Machaut disc which, if nothing else, afforded me an adventure of a nostalgic sort."

Fanfare 13:212-13 S/O '89. Ralph V. Lucano (400w)

Gramophone 66:325 Ag '88. Mary Berry (140w)

DE MONTE, PHILIPPE. Motet: Super flumina Babylonis. See No. 5007.

DE SERMISY, CLAUDIN. Chansons. See No. 5028.

DE VICTORIA, TOMAS LUIS

5020. Officium Defunctorum (includes his second Missa pro defunctis) for 6-part Choir.
David Hill (c). Westminster Cathedral Choir.
HYPERION 66250 DDD 58:00

✔HC ★*Awards:* *Gramophone* Critics' Choice (David Fallows), 1987.

"The choice between this and a rival version on CD [Phillips/Tallis Scholars, Abbey-Gimell 012] which was also reviewed last month comes down to taste, since both are vivid interpretations of this masterpiece in Bruno Turner's new edition....Some may prefer the small ensemble of professional singers over my choice of this superb cathedral choir [which]...goes on a short list of recommended recordings for all lovers of great music."

Fanfare 11:228-9 Ja/F '88. J. F. Weber (150w)

"Heartily endorsed."

American Record Guide 51:91 S/O '88. Paul L. Althouse (140w)

"The Hyperion team take a grand liturgical view of the music....I still can't choose between two such outstanding records, though I prefer—again marginally—the clean bright sound of the Gimell issue to Hyperion's atmospheric, but reverberant acoustic."

Hi-Fi News & Record Review 33:102 F '88. Hugh Canning (210w)

Ovation 9:40-1 Ap '88. Scott Cantrell (225w)

Fanfare 11:247-8 N/D '87. J. F. Weber (310w) (rev. of LP)

Gramophone 65:474 S '87 David Fallows (225w)

5021. Officium Defunctorem, for 6-part Choir. LOBO, DUARTE. Versa Est in Luctum.
Peter Phillips (c). Tallis Scholars. 1987.
ABBEY-GIMELL 012 DDD 47:00

★*Awards:* *Gramophone* Critics' Choice (Stephen Johnson), 1987.

"The Tallis Scholars' singing is extraordinarily accomplished...The sound is up to the high standards of Gimmell's previous recordings of the group."

Musical America 108:82 S '88. Christopher Rothko (200w)

"Heartily endorsed."

American Record Guide 51:91 S/O '88. Paul L. Althouse (140w)

"The traditional choir is splendid....The tempi, the speeds, are a bit rigid and just a trace on the plodding side, but this is a minor problem thanks to the excitement, enthusiasm, and excellent shaping of the musical phrases by these singers."

Audio 72:142 Je '88. Edward Tatnall Canby (360w)

"The Gimell group adopt what might be thought of as a chamber approach....Hill's choir comes nearer, I sense, to the spirit: it sounds less precise, perhaps, but marginally more spontaneous."

Hi-Fi News & Record Review 33:102 F '88. Hugh Canning (210w)

Fanfare 11:247-8 N/D '87. J. F. Weber (310w)

Ovation 9:40-1 Ap '88. Scott Cantrell (225w)

Digital Audio 4:64 N '87. David C. Vernier (320w)

Gramophone 65:474 S '87 David Fallows (225w)

5022. Responsories for Tenebrae (ed. Turner).
David Hill (c). Westminster Cathedral Choir.
HYPERION 66304 DDD 75:00

✔HC ★★★*Awards:* Critics' Choice 1989, *Gramophone* D '89 (Iain Fenlon); Critics' Choice 1989, *Gramophone* D '89 (Tess Knighton). The Year's Best, *Hi Fi News & Record Review*, May '90 Supplement.

"This disc is more than the end of a thrilling era...as Bruno Turner...points out [in his notes]-...'all great music bids farewell to its parent-...and takes on a life of its own.' Indeed it does, nowhere more successfully than on this CD. For some reason this recording, taken in the Byzantine-style cathedral, as Malcolm's [on Argo] was, is much richer than his, the sound warmer, wide in range, and understandably cleaner....texts and translations are printed."

Fanfare 13:354-55 S/O '89. J. F. Weber (670w)

"The quality of the singing is exemplary and the clarity of the recording is most pleasing...I do not object in principle to the utilization of the same tapes for repeated sections, and also appreciate the problems of location recording in a busy part of London like Victoria, but 'Animam meam dilectam' contains a few bumps and a little traffic noise, both of which are served up twice. This remains a minor reservation of this outstanding disc."

Hi-Fi News & Record Review 34:86 Jl '89. William McVicker (315w)

"Hill and his choir have faced the challenge of the highest previous competition—their own, as it were—and have met it beautifully. Not to be missed by choral collectors or lovers of great sacred music."

American Record Guide 53:119 Mr/Ap '90. John W. Barker (500w)

P100 S100/95

Hi-Fi News & Record Review p.29 My '90 Supplement. William McVicker (320w)

Gramophone 67:225 Jl '89. Tess Knighton (320w)

DE WERT, GIACHES

5023. Madrigals: Book 7.
Anthony Rooley (c). Consort of Musicke.
VIRGIN 90763 DDD 58:00

★*Awards:* Critics' Choice 1989, *Gramophone* D '89 (Tess Knighton).

"Splendid performances...deluxe packaging-...Heartily recommended."

American Record Guide 53:132 My/Je '90. Arved Ashby (400w)

"With singers of the stature of Emma Kirkby and Evelyn Tubb as part of this one-on-a-part ensemble, the group produces delightfully clear and engaging performances....The absence of texts and translations is an unfortunate one in this release because of the inevitable close relationship of works and musical treatment."

Continuo 14:22-3 F '90. JoAnne Harrop (440w)

"The engineering...is lovely, the notes are helpful...This is by far the most illuminating treatment we have had on records....a must, not to be overlooked."

Fanfare 13:346 My/Je '90. J. F. Weber (540w)

"To each madrigal the Consort of Musicke respond with their usual intensity, though occasionally that goddess of madrigal singing, perfection, eludes even them in matters of ensemble and intonation. Nevertheless an invaluable issue." *P95 S95*

Hi-Fi News & Record Review 35:97 Ap '90. Stephen Pettitt (230w)

Gramophone 67:1195 D '89. Tess Knighton (490w)

DES PREZ, JOSQUIN

5024. Missa Pange Lingua; Missa, "La sol fa re mi".
Peter Phillips (c). The Tallis Scholars. 1986.
ABBEY-GIMELL 009 DDD 61:29

✔HC ★*Awards:* *Gramophone* Record of the Year, 1987.

"Gimell...has achieved something remarkable here in every way."

High Fidelity 38:63-4 Mr '88. Paul Moor (215w)

"I have no word of criticism to add to the chorus of praise which has met it elsewhere."

Hi-Fi News & Record Review 33:86 Je '88. Jeremy Siepmann (245w)

"Mr. Phillips' inspired ensemble has produced a masterpiece with these two Masses. One hears a wonderful variety of moods, articulations, dynamics, and intensities from this select ensemble of eight singers. The setting at Merton College provided an excellent ambiance for the recording."

Musick 12:7-8 Spr '91. J. Evan Kreider (280w)

Fanfare 10:140 Mr/Ap '87 J.F. Weber (600w)

Gramophone 64:1310+ Mr '87 David Fallows (480w)

5025. Missa l'Homme-arme super Voces Musicales; Missa l'Homme Arme Sexti Toni. ANONYMOUS. L'Homme Arme.
Peter Phillips (c). Tallis Scholars.
ABBEY-GIMELL 019 DDD 74:00

✔HC ★★★*Awards:* International Record Critics Award (IRCA) Winner 1990, *Musical America* N '90. Critics' Choice 1989, *Gramophone* D '89 (Iain Fenlon); Critics' Choice 1989, *Gramophone* D '89 (Tess Knighton).

"This coupling was a superb notion, and it has been superbly accomplished. Give a cheer!"

Fanfare 13:226 S/O '89. J. F. Weber (650w)

"The tonal blend and infallibly ingratiating and rounded tone of the Tallis Scholars are perfectly suited to Josquin's airy, duet-laden counterpoint...I do not hear quite the same level of emotional involvement or rapt variation of dynamics here that graced their marvelous accounts of the *Missa Pange Lingua* and *Missa La sol fa re mi* (Gimell 009), but they still demonstrate extraordinary breath control and the most perfectly judged vibrato, and provide many aural thrills."

American Record Guide 53:56 Ja/F '90. Arved Ashby (300w)

"The Tallis Scholars' previous Josquin recording picked up some prestigious awards—there's no reason why this one should not do the same."

Organists' Review 76:52 Mr '90. Simon Mold (300w)

"This is a characteristic English performance as of this brief moment in the long span of musical time...You will like it."

Audio 75:108+ O '91. Edward Tatnall Canby (long)

"It is pointless to heap more praise upon this accomplished choir...I cannot imagine performances of these works that would give me more musical pleasure. Their balance and precision of ensemble border on the miraculous-...[and the recording is] a treat on pure sonic grounds as well."
Stereophile 13:199+ Je '90. Les Berkley (240w)

"The recording is clear but a bit close. This is glorious music, with minimal recorded competition; I recommend this disc in spite of the reservations cited."
Musical America 110:75-6 Jl '90. Christopher Rothko (365w)

"For some reason I find hard to articulate, I wish that the size of the ensemble for this recording could have been slightly larger, even if augmented by just one more voice per part-....but none of this is serious. Indeed, the overall result is one that recommends this disc highly."
Musick 12:8-9 Spr '91. J. Evan Kreider (825w)

Gramophone 67:216 Jl '89. Tess Knighton (420w)

HILDEGARD OF BINGEN

5026. Symphonia Armonie Celestium: Ave Generosa; Columba Aspexit; O Ecclesia; O Euchari; O Ignis Spiritus; O Jerusalem; O Presul Vere Civitatis; O Viridissima Virga.
Christopher Page (c). Emma Kirkby (sop). Gothic Voices.
HYPERION 66039 DDD 44:03

★★★*Awards:* *Gramophone* Record Award Winner 1983—Early Music Award (Medieval and Renaissance). Record of the Eighties, *Gramophone*, D '89 (Mary Berry).

"'High loveliness like this is not common' wrote Peter Turner in his original review of the LP of this collection of sequences and hymns for a single vocal line with occasional reed organ accompaniment, and the Compact Disc of this all-digital recording has lived up to my expectations."
Hi-Fi News & Record Review 30:81 Jl '85. John Atkinson (95w)

Gramophone 63:157 Jl '85. John Borwick (140w)

"We now have on CD the recording of Hildegard's music which has certainly attracted the most attention of several recent issues (*Fanfare* VIII:6). It's absolutely splendid.'
Fanfare 9:183 N/D '85. J. F. Weber (270w)

"This recording addresses a small, specialized audience, but that audience will find it cause for rejoicing....These performances and their recording come as close to perfection as makes no matter."
High Fidelity 37:68 Ap '87 Paul Moor (325w)

JANEQUIN, CLEMENT

5027. Chansons: Le Caquet des femmes; Va rossignol; D'un seul soleil; Bel aubepin verdissant; J'ay double dueil; Au verd boys je m'en iray; Revenes souvent, m'amye; J'ay d'un coste l'honneur; Ce petit dieu qui vole; La Guerre; L'espoir confus; Petite Nymphe folastre; Pourquoy tournes vous vos yeux; C'est a bon droit; Sur l'aubepin qui est en fleur; Ce moys de may; Las, si tu as plaisir; Ventz hardis et legiers; Plus ne suys ce que j'ay; Frere Thibault; La Chasse. **MORLAYE, GUILLAUME. Fantaisie pour Luth; Gaillarde Dieux pour Luth. LE ROY, ADRIAN. Branle de Bourgogne; Branle Gay.**
Clement Janequin Ensemble. Church of St. Martin du Mejan in Arles.
HARMONIA MUNDI 901271 DDD 63:54

✔**HC** ★*Awards:* Critics' Choice 1988, *Gramophone* D '88 (David Fallows).

Gramophone 66:465 S '88. David Fallows (315w)

"This is a group that has carved out a little niche for itself and performs 16th-century French vocal music to perfection....The onomatopoeic songs sound easy here, but I've heard them done very roughly by less accomplished groups. The sound...is bright and immediate."
Fanfare 12:207-8 N/D '88. J. F. Weber (265w)

"The performances are exemplary, and the recorded sound...is rich but not coated with echo."
Musical America 109:60 Ja '89. James Wierzbicki (340w)

"The programme is as varied and cosmopolitan as the Parisian composer was himself, reflecting the popular tastes of the times....Another superlative recording all round."
Hi-Fi News & Record Review 34:114 Ap '89. Helena Stoward (180w)

"Not since the late David Munrow's brilliant Early Music Consort of London have I heard a similar group I would rank even close to these four (occasionally five or six) superlative, jolly French singers."
High Fidelity 39:67-8 Ap '89. Paul Moor (230w)

5028. Chansons: Voulez ouir les cris de Paris; Ung mari se voulant coucher; Du beau tetin; Or vien ca; La Bataille; La Meusniere de Vernon; L'amour, la mort et la vie; Martin menoit son porceau; Au joly jeu du pousse avant. **DE SERMISY, CLAUDIN. Chansons:** Languir me fais sans t'avoir offensee; Je n'ay point plus d'affection; La, la, Maistre Pierre; Secourez moy; Dont vient cela; Jouyssance vous donneray; Au joly boys; Tu disoys que j'en mourroys.
Clement Janequin Ensemble.
HARMONIA MUNDI 901072 DDD

★*Awards:* Critics Choice, *Hi Fi News & Record Review*, Ap '91 Supplement (Helena Stoward).

"Not since the late David Munrow's brilliant Early Music Consort of London have I heard a similar group I would rank even close to these four (occasionally five or six) superlative, jolly French singers."

High Fidelity 39:67-8 Ap '89. Paul Moor (230w)

LASSUS, ORLANDUS (ROLAND DE)

5029. Choral Music: Missa Osculetur me. **Motets:** Osculetur me; Hodie completi sunt; Timor et tremor; Alma Redemptoris mater a 8; Salve regina mater a 8; Ave regina caelorum II a 6; Regina coeli a 7.
Peter Phillips (c). Tallis Scholars.
ABBEY-GIMELL 018 DDD 49:00

✔**HC** ★★*Awards:* Best of the Month, *Hi-Fi News & Record Review*, Ja '90; The Year's Best, *Hi Fi News & Record Review*, May '90 Supplement. The Want List 1990, *Fanfare* N/D '90 (Robert Levine).

"It is pointless to heap more praise upon this accomplished choir...I cannot imagine performances of these works that would give me more musical pleasure. Their balance and precision of ensemble border on the miraculous-...[and the recording is] a treat on pure sonic grounds as well."

Stereophile 13:199+ Je '90. Les Berkley (240w)

"The performances are at the group's usual standard, with sixteen voices of exquisite purity and accuracy of intonation. The engineering is also dependable on this label. Phillips's notes are informative, texts are printed with translations, and twelve tracks are the rich number....Not to be missed."

Fanfare 14:204 My/Je '91. J. F. Weber (255w)

P100 S100

Hi-Fi News & Record Review p.23-4 My '90 Supplement. Helena Stoward (315w)

Gramophone 67:216 Jl '89. David Fallows (315w)

LAWES, WILLIAM

5030. For Ye Violls: Consort Setts a 5: C minor; F. Consort Setts a 6: C minor; F. Divisions in G minor. Airs for Three Lyra Viols: Ffantasie; Humour.
Paul Nicholson (orgn). Fretwork.
VIRGIN 91187 DDD 70:00

★*Awards:* Critics' Choice 1991, *Gramophone*, Ja '92 (Julie Anne Sadie).

"A recording deserving the highest recommendation. New and old Lawes aficionados may be interested to explore further: the Oberlin Consort of Viols has recorded six of the consort setts (including two of those recorded here) for Classic Masters (CMCD-1015), and the Consort of Musicke, among several LPs of Lawes released a decade ago, devoted one to viol consorts (L'Oiseau-Lyre DSLO 560, presently unavailable)."

Fanfare 15:252 S/O '91. Tom Moore (med)

Fretwork's "exemplary work continues for all of the same reasons: intimacy and spontaneity, wonderful balance in the ensemble, the inherent beauty of the repertory, and remarkable sound....this release...carries my highest recommendation."

American Record Guide 54:86 S/O '91. Paul Laird (med)

LE ROY, ADRIAN. Branle de Bourgogne; Branle Gay. See No. 5027.

LOBO, DUARTE. Versa Est in Luctum. See No. 5021.

MORLAYE, GUILLAUME. Fantaisie pour Luth; Gaillarde Dieux pour Luth. See No. 5027.

PALESTRINA, GIOVANNI

5031. Assumpta Est; Missa Assumpta Est; Sicut Lilium; Missa Sicut Lilium.
Peter Phillips (c). Tallis Scholars. 1989.
ABBEY-GIMELL 020 DDD 71:28

✔**HC** ★★★*Awards:* Best Early Music Recording 1991, *Gramophone*, D '91; The Gramophone Awards, Nominations, Early Music, *Gramophone*, N '91. Critics' Choice 1990, *Gramophone* D '90 (Iain Fenlon).

"Their performances have always been of the highest standards, but in the six-part textures of *Assumpta est*, as in *Sicut Lilium*, a new freshness is evident, perhaps related to the fewer singers employed but even more to the group's and conductor's continually expanding experience and deepening knowledge of Palestrina's works and style."

Music and Musicians International 39:47 S '90. Anthony Milner (120w)

"The performances are sublime."

American Record Guide 53:94-5 N/D '90. Catherine Moore (100w)

"The voices project firmly, blend perfectly, and move effortlessly through the polyphonic weave....The sound is just what Gimell has been achieving for a decade, focused but warm. If you don't automatically pick up each disc on this select label, you should still try this one."

Fanfare 13:220 Jl/Ag '90. J. F. Weber (190w)

"A release of some of the best of Palestrina'a work, performed superlatively, and clearly recorded...literally 'brilliant!'" *P100 S100*

Hi-Fi News & Record Review 36:74 Je '91. Helena Stoward (340w)

Digital Audio's CD Review 6:40 Ag '90. David Vernier (270w)

Gramophone 68:591 S '90. Tess Knighton (400w)

5032. Missa Papae Marcelli; Stabat Mater. Mark Brown (c). Pro Cantione Antiqua. PICKWICK IMP 863 59:00

✔**HC** ★*Awards: Gramophone* Critics' Choice (John Milsom), 1987.

Gramophone 65:801-2 N '87 John Milsom (440w)

PEROTIN

5033. Sacred Choral Works: Viderunt omnes; Alleluia; Posui Adiutorium; Dum sigillum summi Patris; Alleluia, Nativitas; Beata viscera; Sederunt principes. **Anon.** (12th c.): Veni Creator Spiritus; O Maria Virginei; Isaias Cecinit. Paul Hillier (c). Paul Hillier (bar). Hilliard Ensemble. ECM 837 751; ECM 1385 DDD 68:00

✔**HC** ★★★★*Awards:* Best of the Month, *Hi-Fi News & Record Review*, Ja '90; The Year's Best, *Hi Fi News & Record Review*, May '90 Supplement. The Want List 1990, *Fanfare* N/D '90 (J.F. Weber); Critics' Choice 1990, *Gramophone* D '90 (David Fallows); The Highs, 1990, *The New York Times* D 30 '90 (John Rockwell).

"This is the first significant recording of Perotin in some years, and the largest collection of his music ever....Anyone familiar with the Hilliard Ensemble's recording of Leonel Power, Dufay, Ockeghem, and Byrd will not be surprised at the surpassing beauty of these renditions....This is an essential addition to medieval collections, not to be missed....highest recommendation."

Fanfare 13:256-57 Mr/Ap '90. J. F. Weber (700w)

"A recording of 12th-century polyphonic pieces by Perotin and others might be expected to have limited appeal, but the immediacy of these performances is irresistible....The whole programme is performed with a tremendous sense of involvement and delight in the sheer sensuality of Perotin's sound-world. A record not to be missed, especially by those to whom Perotin is little more than a name in the history books."

Music and Musicians International 38:48 Ap '90. Peter Aston (290w)

"This is fascinating music that deserves the description beautiful, but the fascination and beauty of it are nothing like that of later polyphonic music. It is, in a word, challenging, and not everyone who generally enjoys early music will find it to his or her taste....The recording-...is attractively reverberant, but with sufficient resolution to allow the strands of this unfamiliar music to be followed at will."

New Hi-Fi Sound 7:98 Ja '90. Keith Howard (220w)

"The sound is clean, but perhaps a little more reverberation would help raise the cathedral ambience. Paul Hillier may not have a major cross-over here, but those interested in this music should give it a listen."

American Record Guide 53:87-8 My/Je '90. Paul Laird (320w)

"If you've ever heard any Perotin (or the music of his predecessor Leonin), you'll instantly remember the mesmerizing effect of the three- and four-voice works in organum style. And you'll realize that, in retrospect, Perotin seems like a proto-minimalist....For the singers—and, consequently, for us—this is living, breathing music....My only qualm centers around the ambience of this recording, a seemingly cavernous, echo-ridden priory in Sussex."

Musical America 110:82 Jl '90. K. Robert Schwarz (695w)

P100 S100

Hi-Fi News & Record Review p.25 My '90 Supplement. Simon Cargill (390w)

Gramophone 67:1509 F '90. David Fallows (400w)

SHEPPARD, JOHN

5034. Sacred Choral Music: Media Vita; Sacris Solemnis; In Manus Tuas I-III. Peter Phillips (c). Tallis Scholars. 1988. ABBEY-GIMELL 016 DDD 55:08

★*Awards:* Top Disks of the Year, *The New York Times* D 24, '89 (John Rockwell).

"Whether you just want to bathe in glorious Tudor choral sound, or want to study in detail a fascinating and neglected Tudor master, you will find this a most rewarding release."

American Record Guide 53:106 My/Je '90. John W. Barker (425w)

"The Hyperion disc, which duplicates three of these pieces, was recorded in January 1988 using four of the same singers....Using just a few less than Christophers's titular sixteen singers, Phillips gets a lighter sound, but there isn't a lot to choose between them....Even if you have the other record, there is enough here to make this a worthwhile addition, most of all *Media vita.*"

Fanfare 14:353 N/D '90. J. F. Weber (450w)

"As I have said on numerous occasions, no one performs this music better than the Tallis Scholars. Their precision of intonation and precise voicing of each chord are the epitome of what is right in the English style of Renaissance choral singing. As usual, Mike Clements's superb recording is entirely supportive of the performance."

Stereophile 14:264-5 Ja '91. Les Berkley (255w)

"If the music never quite merits the description 'inspired,' it is certainly never less than delightful...Altogether, this recording is securely professional, clear recorded sound and stylistic authenticity certainly compensating for the rather mediocre standard of the programme." *P95 S85*

Hi-Fi News & Record Review 35:101 F '90. Helena Stoward (280w)

Musician 136:127 F '90 James Hunter (b.n.)

Digital Audio's CD Review 6:72+ D '89. David Vernier (450w)

Gramophone 67:1364 Ja '90. Tess Knighton (480w)

TALLIS, THOMAS

5035. The Lamentations of Jeremiah. Church Music: Salvator mundi il; O sacrum convivum; Mass for Four Voices; Absterge Domine.
Paul Hillier (c). The Hilliard Ensemble.
ECM 1341; ECM 833 308 DDD 54:14

✔HC ★*Awards:* Critics' Choice 1988, *Gramophone* D '88 (David Fallows); Critics' Choice 1988, *Gramophone* D '88 (Iain Fenlon).

"The Hilliard is of the same stripe as Pro Cantione, and there isn't much basis for choosing one pair of Lamentations over the other, both done rather better than anything earlier....Recommended."

Fanfare 11:263-4 Jl/Ag '88. J. F. Weber (250w)

"This recording represents as fine and varied a selection of Tallis's work as will be found in the catalog....I hesitate to give blanket recommendations, but if you see any other discs with the names of Hilliard and Howell together, go ahead and buy them."

Stereophile 12:227 Ja '89. Les Berkley (375)

Gramophone 65:1488 Ap '88. David Fallows (280w) (rev. of LP)

5036. Latin Church Music I: Videte miraculum; Homo quidam; Audivi vocem; Candidi facti sunt Nazarei; Dum transisset Sabbatum; Honor, virtus et potestas; Hodie nobis; Loquebantur variis linguis; In pace in idipsum; Spem in alium.
Andrew Parrott (c). Taverner Choir; Taverner Consort and Players. November & December 1986.
EMI 49555 DDD 62:00

✔HC ★★*Awards:* Critics' Choice 1989, *Gramophone* D '89 (John Milsom); Top Disks of the Year, *The New York Times* D 24, '89 (John Rockwell).

"I can imagine no more persuasive advocates for Tallis' glorious music than Andrew Parrott's team."

Organists' Review 75:129 My '89. Robert Lawrenson

"The performances here are impeccable, with superb balance, intonation, and clarity of line."

Continuo 13:19-20 D '89. JoAnne Harrop (225w)

"Andrew Parrott has put the most familiar pieces on his second disc [Latin Church Music II], leaving a group of less familiar works to fill out the great *Spem in alium*....his first disc is a superb complement to anything already in your collection."

Fanfare 14:370-72 N/D '90. J. F. Weber (200w)

"While the choir's tone is impelling, warm in the lower voices and shining in the upper ones, it thins out rather disappointingly in the very top registers which Tallis uses for moments of the utmost intensity....as a whole their performance is impressive and most enjoyable...Although I found some of the gaps between tracks irritatingly long, the recorded sound quality was clear throughout, and overall this is an extremely enjoyable release." *P85 S85/95*

Hi-Fi News & Record Review 35:102 F '90. Helena Stoward (375w)

Gramophone 66:1764 My '89. John Milsom (735w)

5037. Missa Salve Intermerata Virgo. TAVERNER, JOHN. Mass a 4, "Western Wynde". Song, "Western Wynde".
George Guest (c). Saint John's College Choir, Cambridge.
EMI 2155 DDD 58:00

✔HC ★*Awards:* Critics' Choice 1990, *Gramophone* D '90 (Mary Berry).

Gramophone 67:1515-16 F '90. Mary Berry (300w)

TAVERNER, JOHN

Mass a 4, "Western Wynde". Song, "Western Wynde". See No. 5037.

5038. Missa and Motet, "Mater Christi"; Motet, "O Wilhelme, Pastor Bone".
Stephen Darlington (c). Christ Church Cathedral Choir, Oxford.
NIMBUS 5218 DDD 70:00

✔HC ★*Awards:* The Want List 1990, *Fanfare* N/D '90 (J.F. Weber).

"This is beautiful, uplifting music, superbly presented, and warmly recommended."

American Record Guide 53:124-25 N/D '90. John W. Barker (165w)

"The Mass for five voices is rendered with the superior quality that Christ Church has been giving us for years....Highly recommended."

Fanfare 13:287-88 Jl/Ag '90. J. F. Weber (310w)

"These compositions date from about 1530-...and in this performance they are complemented by the appropriate plainchants to complete the sung portions of the liturgy, including a magnificent troped Kyrie 'Rex Splendens'-....Chant is sung by the men alone, and they handle it with a light touch and impeccably clear diction. The polyphony is full and resonant where appropriate and the chorus is able to negotiate Taverner's many 'false relations' with ease surety, and perfect intonation."

Continuo 14:15-6 Ag '90. JoAnne Harrop (400w)

"With secure intonation and precise diction throughout...Acoustically, I find the somewhat distanced resonance of Christ Church Cathedral lacks sparkle, but it does support this serious but appealing music well." *P85 S95*

Hi-Fi News & Record Review 35:97 My '90. Helena Stoward (320w)

Gramophone 67:1854+ Ap '90. Mary Berry (320w)

TYE, CHRISTOPHER

5039. Sacred Choral Music: Kyrie, "Orbis factor"; Mass, "Euge bone"; Quaesumus omnipotens; Misere mei, Deus; Omnes gentes, plaudite; Peccavimus cum patribus.
David Hill (c). Winchester Cathedral Choir. March 1990.
HYPERION 66424 DDD 65:00

★*Awards:* Critics' Choice 1991, *Gramophone*, Ja '92 (Mary Berry).

"The Winchester Cathedral Choir under David Hill is almost ideally suited for this music....It is a sound that is at once reserved yet intensely passionate....Admirers of Tye's music may be pleased to learn that this disc has only a couple of motets in common with the recording by Edward Higginbottom and the choir of New College, Oxford (CRD 3405)."

American Record Guide 54:120 My/Je '91. William J. Gatens (250w)

"This is, for the performers, difficult music which demands strenuous effort on many occasions, yet intersperses these highlights with very subdued passages written with no audience in mind except a heavenly one. Yet I doubt whether anyone could remain untouched by the fervour, the vigour, with which David Hill brings it all to life and unifies what might in other hands be hopelessly disparate sections."

Organists' Review 76:138 Je '91. Gordon Reynolds (345w)

"This new series is superior to anything I've ever heard from Winchester in the past, and I look forward to future relases."

Fanfare 14:408 Mr/Ap '91. J. F. Weber (250w)

Gramophone 68:1401 Ja '91. Mary Berry (450w)

Early Music--Collections

Augsburg Ensemble for Early Music

5040. Schlager um 1500. Music of **M. Franck, Heselloher, Mainerio, Fogliano, Isaak, Da Nola, Janequin, Josquin des Prez, Azzaiolo, Susato, Anon.**
Augsburg Ensemble for Early Music.
CHRISTOPHORUS 74572 DDD 62:53

✔HC ★*Awards:* Critic's Choice: 1990, *American Record Guide* Ja/F '91 (Paul Laird).

"Augsburg's Ensemble for Early Music-...brings a vital freshness and sense of exuberance to a delightful repertory....the release includes polished performances that penetrate straight to the core of each composition's meaning, especially in the humorous pieces-....The sound is admirably clear."

American Record Guide 53:141-42 My/Je '90. Paul Laird (300w)

"Expect upbeat tempos and short selections-...Don't be surprised at familiar titles such as *Fortuna desperata* (Isaak's arrangement) and *Scaramella* (Josquin, of course), but the great majority are so unfamiliar that you'll have no worry about duplicating much in your collection....Only six of the twenty-three selections are instrumental, so three of the five instrumentalists double on the vocals....The sound is close."

Fanfare 13:356-57 Mr/Ap '90. J. F. Weber (200w)

Baltimore Consort

5041. On the Banks of Helicon: Early Music of Scotland. Anon.: Over the Hills. Kathren Oggie. In a Garden So Green. My Heartly Service. Scotch Cap. The Flowres of the Forest. Kilt They Coat, Magge. Canareis. I Will Not Go to Bed Till I Suld Die. Jockey Loves His Moggy Dearly. Come My Children Dere. Prince Edward's Pavan. Like as the Dull Solseequium. The Scots Marche. Support Your Servand. O Lusty May. Doun in Yon Bank. Joy to the Person of My Love. **Blackhall:** On the Banks of Helicon. **Cadeac:** Our Father God Celestial. **Du Tertre:** Branles d'Ecosse. **Lauder:** My Lord of Marche Paven.
Custer LaRue (sop); Edwin George (bagpipe/rec); Alice Kosloski (alto). Baltimore Consort.
DORIAN 90139 DDD 65:40

✔HC ★★*Awards:* Editors' Choice, *Digital Audio's CD Review*, Je '91. The Want List 1991, *Fanfare* N/D '91 (Tom Moore).

"This is music to be enjoyed—not high art, but folk song, melancholy (the beautiful *Joy to the person of my love*) or joyous (*O lustie May*). The Baltimore Consort captures its spirit with immediacy and presence. Warmly recommended."

Fanfare 14:348 My/Je '91. Tom Moore (250w)

"Full texts....Waht makes this Baltimore program so rousing is that the two singers and seven instrumentalists fling themselves into their material with lusty abandon, bringing a more overtly folk style to their work. Sometimes this goes a little too far in some of the instrumental playing; but it works wonders in the vocal pieces, some of which are truly haunting-....A fascinating and satisfying program."

American Record Guide 54:154-5 My/Je '91. John W. Barker (200w)

"Soprano Custer LaRue sings very lightly and straightforwardly, but is well able to put across the characterful nature of these songs. The instrumentalists, especially guest bagpiper Edwin George, are obviously quite comfortable with the folk-like elements and use them to good effect. As always, Dorian's recorded sound and presentation are exemplary."

Continuo 15:27-9 Je '91. Scott Paterson (110w)

"The choice of repertory on this disc is as varied as it is appealing and it's played extremely well, achieving a clean-edged precision or a sensuous, almost hypnotic sound....Highly recommended."

HighPerformanceReview 8(3):66 '91. June C. Ottenberg (med)

"After hearing soprano Custer LaRue's incredibly gorgeous rendition of 'In a garden so green', I stopped the disc and just sat for a while getting my breath back. This track alone is worth the price of admission...*On the Banks of Helicon* contains an eclectic mix of material, well representative of a usually neglected area of early music. Most of the works are from the 16th and 17th centuries, and range from the bawdy ('Jockey loves his Moggy') to the spiritual ('Our Father God Celestial')...this disc is yet another splendid-sounding effort from Dorian."

Stereophile 15:277 Ja '92. Les Berkley (long)

Ensemble Organun

5042. The Chantilly Codex. Cunelier: Se Galaas et le puissant Artus. **Guido:** Dieux gart; Or voit tout. **Baude Cordier:** Tout par compas; Belle, bonne, sage. **Goscalch:** En nul estat. **J. de Senleches:** La harpe de mellodie. **Solage:** Fumeux fume par fumee. **F. Andrieu:** Armes, amour. **Anon:** Sans joie avoir; Toute clerte; Adieu vous di.
Marcel Peres (c). Ensemble Organum.
HARMONIA MUNDI 901252 DDD 54:00

★*Awards: Gramophone* Critics' Choice (Mary Berry), 1987.

"The performances under Marcel Peres are lovely....The sound is appropriate and each piece is tracked."

Fanfare 11:274-5 N/D '87. J. F. Weber (700w)

"Anyone interested in medieval music has to hear this recording, if for no other reason than curiosity's sake, and also to enjoy the surprisingly lucid, comprehending performances by the liquid-voiced Ensemble Organum."

Ovation 9:43-4 Je '88. David Patrick Stearns (350w)

"France's Ensemble Organum consists of countertenor, tenor, baritone, and bass, plus a viol and the instrument known in France as the *clavicytherium.* They perform these selections with unostentatious expertise and conviction—making the music austere but elegant, antique but viable—and are the beneficiaries of sonic engineering that is above reproach....all the texts, in Old French only."

High Fidelity 39:73 Je '89. Paul Moor (300w)

Gramophone 65:809 N '87 Mary Berry (275w)

The New York Times Jl 10 '88, p. H23. K. Robert Schwarz (250w)

Hi-Fi News & Record Review 33:103 F '88. Stephen Pettitt (350w)

Ensemble P.A.N.

5043 Project Ars Nova: Ars Magis Subtiliter. Symonis: Puisque je suis fumeux. **Suzay:** Pictagoras, Jabol et Orpheus. **Molins:** De ce que foul pense (two versions). **Goscalch:** En nul estate. **Solage:** Fumeux Fume par fumee. **Cordier:** Tout par compas; Belle, bonne, sage. **Grimace:** A l'arme, a l'arme. **Vaillant:** Par maintes foys. **Andrieu:** Armes, Amours/O flour. **Machaut:** Quant Theseus/Ne quier veoir. **Anon.:** Medee tu en amer veritable; Ha, fortune; A mon pouir.
Ensemble P.A.N. 1987.
NEW ALBION 021 DDD 61:23

★*Awards:* Editors' Choice, *Digital Audio's CD Review*, 6:32 Je '90; Cream of the Crop IV, *Digital Audio's CD Review*, 6:41 Je '90.

"The Ensemble P.A.N. is superb. Their vocalists are not afraid of attempting lively tempi even when executing the more difficult rhythmic passages featuring cross rhythms, subtle syncopations, or rapid melodic ornamental gestures. This is a disc I will use for illustrations in my classes as well as for listening enjoyment....most of the performances on this wonderful disc are excellent."

Musick 11:20-3 Spr '90. J. Evan Kreider (1850w)

"P.A.N. has put this charming disc together entirely from the Chantilly, compiled circa 1390. Of the fifteen numbers, I can find prior recordings of only five, making this a welcome addition to a specialized discography....It's one of the liveliest, prettist recordings of this repertoire available....On the downside, this isn't the clearest recording."

Fanfare 13:403-4 S/O '89. Kyle Gann (630w)

"The P.A.N. group here is highly competent and tasteful, but just a bit prissy and restrained-...Still, this is valuable repertoire....And the sound is quite respectable. Full texts with English translations and good notes are included."

American Record Guide 52:166-67 N/D '89. John W. Barker (330w)

"While some of this material was included on David Munrow's fine 1973 recording, *The Art of Courtly Love*, it receives fresh, pliant performances here which make the highly-wrought intricacies of the music almost natural sounding and which certainly betray no hint of the music's great difficulty."

Continuo 14:25 F '90. Scott Paterson (100w)

"The recording, made at Wellesley Chapel by WGBH-FM (Boston), is a clear and balanced job, although Kyle Gann (13:1, p. 403) found it less transparent than he would have liked-....Despite the overlapping, this is a valuable complement to the Ensemble Organum program...Highly recommended."

Fanfare 13:359 Mr/Ap '90. J. F. Weber (475w)

Gramophone 68:812 O '90. David Fallows (420w)

Digital Audio's CD Review 6:80 N '89. David Vernier (220w)

Fretwork

5044. Armada: Music from the Courts of Philip II and Elizabeth I. Byrd: Rejoice unto the Lord; Come to me, Grief, for ever; In angel's weed; The Carman's Whistle. **A. de Cabezon:** Differencias sobre el canto "La Dama le demanda"; Differencias sobre la Gallarda Milanesa. **H. de Cabezon:** Susana un jur; Dulce Memoria. **Lopez:** Fantasia. **M. de Fuenllana:** Morenica dame; Fantasia de Redobles. **E. Bevin:** Browning a 3. **D. Ortiz:** Recerecada segunda "sobra cant llano"; Recercada tercera. **R. Parsons:** Pour down, you pow'rs divine, "Pandolpho". **R. White:** Fantasia a 5. **E. Daza:** Quinte hizo. **Picforth:** In Nomine a 5.
Michael Chance (alto); Paul Nicholson (hpscd); Christopher Wilson (vihuela/lute). Fretwork.
VIRGIN 90722 DDD 66:30

✔**HC** ★*Awards:* Critics' Choice 1988, *Gramophone* D '88 (Julie Anne Sadie).

"Altogether these pieces form a delightful array in which variety offers novelty besides the charms of individual pieces; and the works of less famous composers present as much opportunity for sensitive performance as those of known masters....the sound is good, and one cannot fail to be entranced by this parcel of 16th-century goodies."

Hi-Fi News & Record Review 34:107 F '89. Helena Stoward (350w)

"Fretwork alternates...between the courts of Philip II and Elizabeth I....The engineering...is beautifully balanced....no texts are printed."

Fanfare 12:378-79 My/Je '89. J. F. Weber (170w)

"Fretwork...clearly prefers reticence, gravity and noble phrasing but still turns in some amazing virtuoso performances."

Continuo 13:25 Je '89. Colin Tilney (50w)

"This is a very attractive release that will please both specialists and those relatively uninitiated in the glories of renaissance music."

American Record Guide 52:126-27 Jl/Ag '89. Alan Heatherington (280w)

"I would like to be unqualified in my praise of this quadricentenary tribute to the days of the Armada...If, however, you ignore the whole business about the Armada, you are unlikely to find a better performance of this music...Sonically, there is almost nothing to fault."

Stereophile 12:177+ S '89. Les Berkley (450w)

Gothic Voices

5045. The Marriage of Heaven and Hell. Anonymous: Je ne chant pas/Talens m'est pris. Trois sereurs/Trois sereurs/Trois sereurs. Plus bele que flors/Quant revient/L'autrier jouer. Par un martinet/He, sire/He bergier! De la virge Katerine/Quant froidure/Agmina milicie. Ave parens/Ad gratie. Super te Jerusalem/Sed fulsit virginitas. A vous douce debonnaire. Mout souvent/Mout ai este en doulour. Quant voi l'aloete/Dieux? je ne m'en partire ja. En non Dieu/Quant voi la rose. Je m'en vois/Tels a mout. Festa januaria. **Blondel de Nesle:** En tous tans que vente bise. **Colin Muset:** Trop volontiers chanteroie. **Bernart de Ventadorn:** Can vei la lauzeta mover. **Gautier de Dargies:** Autre que je ne seuill fas.
Christopher Page (c). Gothic Voices.
HYPERION 66423 DDD 46:00

★*Awards:* The Gramophone Awards, Nominations, Early Music, *Gramophone*, N '91.

"This recording is a magisterial presentation of this charming but little-known area of music. The five voices (never more than four at a time) give graceful and lively performances with very sure intonation. They adopt a twangy sonority which seems to suit the music well."

Organists' Review 76:225 S '91. Marcus Huxley (long)

"The high quality of every disc of Gothic Voices should balance their rather skimpy running times....The recording was made at St. Cross, Winchester, the site of the previous disc, possibly a more pleasing venue to Page than his previous one at St. Jude's. Its warmth confers a lovely sound on the group."

Fanfare 14:468-9 Mr/Ap '91. J. F. Weber (325w)

Gramophone 68:1259 D '90. David Fallows (410w)

5046. Music for the Lion-Hearted King. Anon. (12th c.): Mundus vergens; Novus miles sequitur; Sol sub nube latuit; Hac in anni ianua; Anglia, planctus itera; Etras auri reditur; Vetus abit littera; In occasu sideris; Purgator criminum; Pange melos lacrimosum; Ver pacis apperit; Latex silice. **Gace Brule:** A la doucour de la bele seson. **Blondel de Nesle:** L'amours dont sui espris; Ma joie me semont. **Gui IV, "Li chastelain de Couci":** Li nouviauz tanz.
Christopher Page (c). Gothic Voices.
HYPERION 66336 DDD 60:00

★*Awards:* Record of the Eighties, *Gramophone*, D '89 (David Fallows).

"Most of the material here, *conductus* (ie, processional) pieces in Latin, either were written directly for ceremonial use or make some reflection upon public personalities and events in the world of Richard I....Nary an instrument in sight or sound here, much less any vocal doublings....if you like 'naked' medieval music, Gothic Voices can't be topped."
American Record Guide 53:162-63 N/D '90. John W. Barker (285w)

"The four singers (Philpot, Covey-Crump, Ainsley, Nixon) have been involved consistently on most of the Gothic Voices discs, and here Page is at pains to obtain well-tuned chords, made easier by the rhythmic approach. He is a most remarkable interpreter for this period, and each disc piles on new success-....Highly recommended."
Fanfare 13:376 Ja/F '90. J. F. Weber (500w)

"As music, the performances work perfectly. This marriage of performance and sound comes highly recommended."
Stereophile 13:189+ My '90. Les Berkley (220w)

Gramophone 67:737 O '89. David Fallows (380w)

5047. The Service of Venus and Mars. P. de Vitry: Gratissima virginis/Vos qui admiramini/Gaude gloriosa/Contratenor. **P. des Molins:** De ce que fol pense. **Pycard:** Gloria. **L. Power:** Sanctus. **L. Lebertoul:** Las, que me demanderoye. **J. Pyamour:** Quam pulchra es. **Dunstable:** Speicosa facta es. **Soursby:** Sanctus. **R. Loqueville:** Je vous pri que j'aye un basier. **Anon:** Singularis laudis digna; De ce fol pense (after des Molins); Lullay, lullay; There is no rose of swych virtu; Le gay playsir; Le grant pleyser; The Agincourt Carol.
Christopher Page (c). Andrew Lawrence-King (medieval harp). Gothic Voices.
HYPERION 66238 50:00

★★*Awards:* *Gramophone* Critics' Choice (David Fallows), 1987; Early Music (Medieval & Renaissance) Record Award 1988, *Gramophone* O '88.

"The familiar pieces are so well done as to inspire confidence in the renditions of the rare items....The singing throughout must be called flawless....it's a treasure."
Fanfare 11:275-6 N/D '87. J. F. Weber (350w)

"Quite simply, this is another superlatively beautiful recording from Gothic Voices....The vocal performances are, every one of them, exquisitely turned."
Hi-Fi News & Record Review 33:107 F '88. Stephen Pettitt (245w)

The New York Times Jl 10 '88, p. H23. K. Robert Schwarz (250w)

Gramophone 65:810 N '87 (310w) (rev. of LP); 66:549 O '88 (200w) (rev. of CD). David Fallows

5048. A Song for Francesca. Andreas de Florentia: Astio non mori mai; Per la ver'onesta. **Johannes de Florentia:** Quando la stella. **Landini:** Ochi dolenti mie; Per seguir la speranca. **Anonymous Trecento Italian:** Quando i oselli canta; Constantia; Amor mi fa cantar a la Francesca; Non na el so amante. **Dufay:** Quel fronte signorille in paradiso. **Richard de Loqueville:** Puisque je sjy amoureux; Pour mesdisans ne pour leur faulx parler; Qui ne veroit que vos deulx yeulx. **Hugu de Lantins:** Plaindre me'estuet. **Jean Haucourt:** Je demande ma bienvenue. **Etienne Grossin:** Va t'ent souspir. **Anonymous (Italian MS Canonici misc 213):** O regina seculi/Reparatrix Maria; Confort d'amours.
Christopher Page (c). Andrew Lawrence-King (medieval harp). Gothic Voices.
HYPERION 66286 DDD 50:00

★★*Awards:* Critics' Choice 1988, *Gramophone* D '88 (David Fallows). Early Music (Medieval & Renaissance) Record Award 1989, *Gramophone*, D '89.

"Page's singers and Hyperion's engineers-...need no more praise for the consistent high quality of their work....texts and translations are printed....I trust collectors who have experienced this ensemble have developed the habit of routinely adding all their new issues to their shelves without delay. This latest one will not disappoint them."
Fanfare 12:362-63 Mr/Ap '89. J. F. Weber (350w)

"It is rich fare, perhaps stretched to represent too diverse a pair of literatures, but fascinating and splendidly presented. The robust and stylish singing is up to the best standards of this group's previous work, and fanciers of early harp literature will want to note Lawrence-King's solos here. The sound is natural and unobtrusive. Full texts and English translations are given in the booklet along with admirably thorough notes by Page."
American Record Guide 52:122 My/Je '89. John W. Barker (410w)

Gramophone 66:1050 D '88. David Fallows (460w)

Hilliard Ensemble

5049. Sumer Is Icumen In. St. Godric: Sainte Marie viergene; Crist and Sainte Marie; Sainte Nicolas. **Anon.**"Sumer is icumen in; Fuweles in the frith; Edi beo thu; Worldes blisse; Gabriel fram hevenking; Stond wel moder under roode; Ut tuo propitiatus; Alleluya-Nativitatas; Kyrie - Rex virginum; Sanctus -Maria mater; Agnus Dei -Factushomo; Perspice Christicola; Mater ora filium; Valde mane diliculp; Ovet mundus letabundus; Gaude virgo mater Christi.
Hilliard Ensemble. May 1986.
HARMONIA MUNDI 901154 56:00

✔**HC** ★★*Awards:* *Gramophone* Critics' Choice 1986 (David Fallows). *Gramophone* Critics' Choice (Geoffrey Horn), 1987.

"Reviewed in *Fanfare* 9:6, p.272...Recommended in this format."
Fanfare 10:259 Mr/Ap '87 J.F. Weber (125w)

"All the music...is expertly performed on original instruments."

The New York Times F 26 '88, p. H27. Paul Turok (50w)

"The production is earnest and sincere...The CD was flawless, except for the poor documentation—a major shortcoming in unfamiliar works like this."

American Record Guide 51:117 Mr/Ap '88. Thomas W. Skladony (270w)

Gramophone 64:1318 Mr '87 Geoffrey Horn (90w)

Hillier, Paul

5050. Proensa. Guilhem IX Farai un vers de dreit nien. **Guiraut de Borneil:** Reis glorios, verais lums e clartatz. **Raimon der Miraval:** Aissi cum es genser pascors. **Marcabru:** L'autrier jost' una sebissa. **Bernart de Ventadorn:** Be m'an perdut lai enves Ventadorn; Can vei la lauzeta mover. **Peire Vidal:** Pos tornatz sui en Proensa. **Guiraut Riquier:** Be.m degra de chantar tener.
Paul Hillier (voc); Stephen Stubbs (lute/psaltery); Andrew Lawrence-King (harp/psaltery); Erin Headley (vielle).
ECM 837 360; ECM 1368 DDD 70:17

★*Awards:* Top Disks of the Year, *The New York Times* D 24, '89 (John Rockwell).

"Hillier's spare disc is a wonderful supplement to the more timbrally varied and vivacious recordings of Binkley and the Clemencic Consort (raucous is at times the word for the latter three-disc set, which remains one of my all-time favorites)."

Fanfare 13:408 S/O '89. Edward Strickland (160w)

"Hillier has an absolutely marvelous voice, and he has worked out a spare but moving technique of accompaniment that his colleagues perform perfectly....For me, the highlight of this performance was Bernart da Ventadorn's oft-recorded 'Can vei la lauzeta mover'...If there can be a definitive performance of a work 800 years old, this is it....This recording achieves something that digital had heretofore not accomplished, something *better* than any analog recording I have heard—it captures with uncanny accuracy the initial attack of a hammered dulcimer struck by wooden hammers....highly recommended."

Stereophile 12:215+ N '89. Les Berkley (825w)

"Proensa...was the home of the troubadours, 12th and 13th Century poet-musicians....About 300 troubadour poems survive, with about 42 set to music, but this music 'is so deeply sunk in time that no one knows precisely how the songs were uttered.' This record is an attempt, and a very effective one to my knowledge, to recreate eight of those troubadour songs of known composers."

American Record Guide 53:127 Ja/F '90. William Purcell (240w)

Gramophone 67:219 Jl '89. David Fallows (350w)

Digital Audio's CD Review 6:80-2 D '89. Roland Graeme (530w)

Madrid Atrium Musicae

5051. La Folia.
Gregorio Paniagua (c). Madrid Atrium Musicae.
HARMONIA MUNDI 901050 AAD 44:30

✔**HC** ★★*Awards:* *Fanfare* Want List 1987 (Jurgen Gothe). Records to Die for: 1 of 5 Recommended Recordings, *Stereophile* Ja '91 (Thomas J. Norton).

"This whole performance is absolutely wild-....certainly the players have captured the meaning and spirit of the 'folia.'...But the recording is crystal clear, and the whole thing is great fun."

American Record Guide 48:79 Ja '85. Carl Bauman (200w)

"A folia is apparently some sort of mad dance, a perfect description of this recording....I've often used this as a CD reference for soundstaging, transients, and dynamics....The LP is better in the expected ways, but sounds decidedly squashed in the more explosive portions of the work."

Stereophile 14:162 Ja '91. Thomas J. Norton (b.n.)

"In all, it's an entertaining and thoughtful diversion for anyone interested in music and sound."

The Sensible Sound 7:53-4 Fall '85. John J. Puccio (200w)

"The loose collection of compositions and arrangements...was greeted with enthusiasm here (*Fanfare* VI:1, p. 437)."

Fanfare 7:307-8 Jl/Ag '84. J. F. Weber (290w)

Martin Best Medieval Ensemble

5052. The Dante Troubadors. (**Anon.:** Lamento di Tristan; Trotto; Salterello; Lauda Novella; Istampitta. **Giraut de Bornelh:** Leu chansoneta; Si-Us Quer conselh. **Bertran de Born:** Ges de disnar; Chasutz sul; Ai, Lemozi. **Daniel:** Lo ferm voler; Chanson do-lh mot. **Bernart de Ventadorn** Can vei la lauzeta. **Vidal:** Pois tornaz. **Raimbaut de Vaquerias:** Kalenda Maia. **Faidit:** Non Alegra. **Almeric de Belenoi:** Nuls om en ren. **Folquet de Marseille:** Ben an mort).
Martin Best Medieval Ensemble.
NIMBUS 5002 DDD 49:13

★*Awards:* *Fanfare* Want List 1984 (John Bauman).

"The music is chosen from among composers specifically mentioned by Dante, or who frequented the courts of his time....The performances are outstanding, with each of the four members of the Martin Best Ensemble playing several instruments in dazzling succession.

This issue, more than most, supports the contention that the 13th century, the high point of the Middle Ages, was also a high point in musical history."

American Record Guide 47:79-80 My '84. Carl Bauman (300w)

Originally reviewed in *Fanfare* 7:4, p. 309. The recording was "spectacular on LP at 45 rpm quad encoded"and the CD "rank[s] with the best."

Fanfare 11:366 S/O '87. J. F. Weber (140w)

Ovation 10:52 F '89. David Patrick Stearns (320w)

Sequentia

5053. English Songs of the Middle Ages. St. Godric: Sainte Marie viegene; Crist and Sainte Marie; Sainte Nicholas. **Anon., 12-14th Century:** The milde Lomb, isprad or rode; Edi be thu, heven-queene (vocal and instrumental versions); Ar ne duth ich sorghe non (vocal and instrumental versions); Jesu Cristes milde moder; Worldes blis ne last no throwe; Fuweles in the frith; Man mai longe lives weene; Byrd one brere; Dance.
Sequentia.
EMI 49192 DDD 60:00

★*Awards:* Critics' Choice 1988, *Gramophone* D '88 (Mary Berry).

"If only because of the newly available items, this is a record worth owning....The singing, playing, and engineering are all superb....the printed medieval English texts are translated into modern English, French, and German."

Fanfare 12:361-62 Mr/Ap '89. J. F. Weber (500w)

"Those accustomed to hearing this and similar repertory in the 'big band' arrangements that were popular in the 1960s and 1970s may find these performances quite stark....The voices, as well as the recording, are pleasant without drawing attention to themselves."

High Fidelity 39:79 Jl '89. Christopher Rothko (250w)

Gramophone 66:472 S '88. Mary Berry (315w)

Sinfonye

5054. Bella Domna. The Medieval Woman: Lover, Poet, Patroness and Saint. Martin Codax: Cantigas de Amigo. **Anon.:** Domna, pos vos ay chausida; Estampies Royals—No's. 3, 4, 6; Danse Royale. **De Fournival:** Onques n'amai tant que jou fui amee. **La Comtesse de Die:** A chantar m'er de so qu'ieu non volria. **Anon.:** Lasse, pour quoi refusai. Stevie Wishart (medieval fiddle). Sinfonye.
HYPERION 66283 DDD 60:00

★*Awards:* Critics' Choice 1988, *Gramophone* D '88 (David Fallows).

"For an insight into the social and poetic, as well as the musical, values of the Middle Ages, this release is invaluable."

American Record Guide 51:105-6 S/O '88. John W. Barker (375w)

"For the unfamiliar half of the program, this is an interesting opportunity to hear some new artists, for Martin Codax I prefer Newnham. The sound is marvelous...An adventurous addition to the medieval shelf (and a must for the feminist contingent)."

Fanfare 12:325-6 S/O '88. J. F. Weber (300w)

"Sinfonye, the blurb says, is 'a new group specializing in the monophonic repertoire of medieval Europe'. It does its job exceedingly well, if this, their first disc, is anything from which to judge."

Hi-Fi News & Record Review 34:107 F '89. Stephen Pettitt (245w)

Gramophone 66:62 Je '88. David Fallows (350w)

CD Review Digest
Classical

Choral Music

BACH FAMILY

6001. Cantatas. (The complete cantatas of **Johann Michael Bach, Georg Christoph Bach, Johann Christoph Bach, Heinrich Bach).**
Reinhard Goebel (c). Maria Zedelius; Ulla Groenewold; David Cordier. Rheinische Kantorei; Cologne Musica Antiqua.
DEUTSCHE GRAMMOPHON 419 253 DDD
58:24; 52:56 2 discs

★★★**Awards:** *Fanfare* Want List 1987 (George Chien); *Gramophone* Critics' Choice (Nicholas Anderson); *Gramophone* Critics' Choice (Stanley Sadie), 1987.

"This is a fascinating and enjoyable two-record set, professionally produced in every way....All the performances are of the highest quality."
Organists' Review 72:253-4 Jl '87. Simon Mold (430w)

"For those who are really serious about the music that made that of Johann Sebastian not only possible but even inevitable, the Archiv set is a. must."
Fanfare 10:54-55 Jl/Ag '87 George Chien (1015w)

"This public dip into a family archive reveals, as one would expect, a very uneven sprinkling of talent."
Hi-Fi News & Record Review 32:93 Mr '87 Jeremy Siepmann (210w)

"This release is full of surprises, all pleasant."
The New York Times F 14, '88, p.H21. Edward Schneider (150w)

Gramophone 64:1163-4 F '87 Nicholas Anderson (1395w)

BACH, CARL PHILIPP EMANUEL

6002. Die Letzen Leiden des Erlosers, Wq.233.
Sigiswald Kuijken (c). Barbara Schlick (sop); Greta De Reyghere (sop); Catherine Patriasz (contr); Christophe Pregardien (ten); Max Van Egmond (bass). Ghent Collegium Vocale; La Petite Bande. reissue.
EMI 47753 ADD 120:00 2 discs

✔HC ★**Awards:** International Record Critics Award (IRCA) Winner 1988, *High Fidelity* N '88 and *Musical America* N '88.

"This performance seems an excellent one. The singers are all good, especially the women, and the Petite Band turns in its usual expert performance. The sound too is full and sharp."
Fanfare 12:100-1 My/Je '89. William Youngren (925w)

Gramophone 66:454+ S '88. Nicholas Anderson (765w)

BACH, JOHANN SEBASTIAN

6003. Cantatas (complete): No. 1, Wie schon leuchtet der Morgenstern; No. 2, Ach Gott, vom Himmel sieh' darein; No. 3, Ach Gott, wie manches Herzeleid; No. 4, Christ lag in Tobdesbanden.
("Das Kantatenwerk: Complete Cantatas." Volume 1).
Nikolaus Harnoncourt; Gustav Leonhardt (c). various soloists and choruses. Vienna Concentus Musicus; Leonhardt Consort.
TELDEC 35027

✔HC ★**Awards:** Special Achievement Award 1990, *Gramophone* D '90 (applies to v. 1-45).

"Anyone exposed to Bach's full range (as now, thanks to these records [Volume 1 +], one can be) knows that the hearty, genial, lyrical Bach of the concert hall is not the essential Bach. The essential Bach was an avatar of a pre-Enlightened—and when push came to shove, a violently anti-Enlightened—temper. His music was a medium of truth, not beauty. And the truth he served was bitter. His works persuade us—no, *reveal* to us—that the world is filth and horror, that humans are helpless, that life is pain, that reason is a snare....If he pleased, it was only to cajole. When his sounds were agreeable, it was only to point out an escape from worldly woe in heavenly submission. Just as often he aimed to torture the ear: when the world was his subject, he wrote music that for sheer deliberate ugliness has perhaps been approached—by Mahler, possible at times—but never equaled....Such music cannot be prettified in performance without essential loss. For with Bach—the essential Bach—there is no 'music itself.' His concept of music derived from and inevitably contained The Word, and the word was Luther's....It is for their refusal to flinch in the face of Bach's contempt for the world and all its creatures that Mr. Leonardhardt and Mr. Harnoncourt deserve our admiration. Their achievement is unique and well-nigh unbearable. Unless one has experienced the full range of Bach cantatas in these sometimes all but unlistenable renditions, one simply does not know Bach. More than that, one does not know what music can do, or all that music can be. Such performances could never work in the concert hall, it goes without saying, and who has time for church? But that is why there are records."

The New York Times Ja 27 '91, p. 25+ H. Donal Henahan (2100w)

Gramophone 68:729 O '90. James Jolly (140w)

6004. Cantatas (complete): No. 51, Jauchzet Gott in allen Landen; No. 52, Falsche Welt, dir trau' ich nicht; No. 54, Wilderstehe doch der Sunde; No. 55, Ich armer Mensch; No. 56, Ich will den Kreuzstab gerne tragen.
("Das Kantatenwerk: Complete Cantatas." Volume 14).
Gustav Leonhardt (c). Marjanne Kweksilber (sop); Seppi Kronwitter (treb); Paul Esswood (c-tenor); Kurt Equiluz (ten); Michael Schopper (bass); Heinz Hennig (choir director). Hanover Boys' Choir; Leonhardt Consort. reissue.
TELDEC 8.35304 AAD 34:42; 44:45 2 discs

"The performances, especially those of Paul Esswood, Kurt Equiluz and the obbligato instrumentalists, are up to the series' high standard, although Michael Schopper and the boy soprano are now and then somewhat unsteady. The CD transfer is a match for the already excellent LP pressing."

Continuo 12:16-7 O '88. Scott Paterson (90w)

"Volume 14 has the only female voice in any of the 41 volumes released to date. The aptly named Marjanne Kweksilber conquers the treacherous coloratura of Cantata 51 with breathtaking ease and persuasive elegance....this is a remarkable performance, and one of the highlights of the entire Teldec series....Schopper's performance is good, but it has great competition."

Fanfare 11:103-4 Jl/Ag '88. George Chien (275w)

Gramophone 66:830-35 N '88. Nicholas Anderson (770w)

6005. Cantatas (complete): No. 76, Die Himmel erzahlen die Ehre Gottes; No. 77, Du solist Gott, deinen Herren, lieben; No. 78, Jesu, der du meine Seele; No. 79, Gott, der Herr, ist Sonn' und Schild.
("Das Kantatenwerk: Complete Cantatas." Volume 20).
Nikolaus Harnoncourt; Gustav Leonhardt (c). Various soloists. Tolz Boys' Choir; Hanover Boys' Choir; Ghent Collegium Vocale; Vienna Concentus Musicus; Leonhardt Consort. 1979.
TELDEC 35362 ADD 84:00 2 discs

✔HC ★★*Awards:* Records to Die for: 1 of 5 Recommended Recordings, *Stereophile* Ja '91 (Mortimer H. Frank).

"Composed to celebrate the Protestant Reformation, this cantata [No. 79] stands as one of the peaks of the Bach canon....Directing period instruments, Leonhardt produces a reading that is colorful, transparent, joyous, and musical without any of the affectations that afflict some of the other performances in this Teldec series-....Among Bach-cantata recordings, this is a model of its kind."

Stereophile 14:135 Ja '91. Mortimer H. Frank (b.n.)

Gramophone 67:517-18 S '89. Nicholas Anderson (635w)

6006. Cantatas (complete): No. 140, Wachef auf, ruft uns die Stimme; No. 147, Herz und Mund und Tat und Leben.
("Das Kantatenwerk: Complete Cantatas." Volume 35).
Nikolaus Harnoncourt (c). Allan Bergius; Stefan Rampf; Paul Esswood; Kurt Equiluz; Thomas Hampson. Tolz Boys' Choir; Vienna Concentus Musicus. reissue.
TELDEC 8.43203 ADD 60:13

"The recordings were taken from the complete cantata series....Since Harnoncourt leads exemplary performance of both cantatas, collectors who have not started collecting the series but are thinking about it might want to test the waters with this fine disc."

Fanfare 11:62-3 Mr/Ap '88. George Chien (190w)

"A good coupling."

Hi-Fi News & Record Review 31:111 My '86. Stephen Daw (105w)

Digital Audio 2:60+ Ap '86. David Vernier (325w)

6007. Cantatas (complete): No. 164, Ihr, die ihr euch von Christo nennet; No. 165, O heliges Geist—und Wasserbad; No. 166, Wo gehest du hin; No. 167, Ihr Menschen, ruhmet Gottes Liebe; No. 168, Tue Rechnung! Donnerwort; No. 169, Gott soll allein mein Herze haben.
("Das Kantatenwerk: Complete Cantatas." Volume 39).
Nikolaus Harnoncourt; Gustav Leonhardt (c). Christoph Wegmann; Panito Iconomou; Christian Immler; Kurt Equiluz; Max Van Egmond. Tolz Boys' Choir; Collegium Vocale; Leonhardt Consort; Vienna Concentus Musicus.
TELDEC 35658 DDD 104:00 2 discs

✔HC ★*Awards:* *Gramophone* Critics' Choice (Nicholas Anderson), 1987.

"Those who have been collecting this series will be delighted to continue. Newcomers are urged to jump in."

Fanfare 11:83-4 N/D '87. George Chien (315w)

"The lowpoints are virtually all of the arias involving boy sopranos, several of which...are really acutely painful in terms of intonation, and unsatisfactory in terms of interpretative artistry."

Hi-Fi News & Record Review 32:109 O '87. Jeremy Siepmann (195w)

Gramophone 65:457-8 S '87. Nicholas Anderson (1190w)

6008. Cantatas (complete): No. 180, Schmucke dich, o liebe Seele; No. 181, Leichtgesinnte Flattergeister; No. 182, Himmelskonig, sei willkommen; No. 183, Sie werden euch in der

Bann tun; No. 184, Erwunschtes Freudenlicht. ("Das Kantatenwerk: Complete Cantatas." Volume 42).
Nikolaus Harnoncourt; Gustav Leonhardt (c). Jan Patrick O'Farrell (treb); Alexander Raymann (treb); Helmut Wittek (treb); Paul Esswood (alto); Kurt Equiluz (ten); Max Van Egmond (bass); Robert Holl (bass); Thomas Hampson (bass). Hanover Boys' Choir; Ghent Collegium Vocale; Tolz Boys' Choir; Leonhardt Consort; Vienna Concentus Musicus.
TELDEC 35799 DDD 107:00 2 discs

✔HC ★*Awards:* Critics' Choice 1989, *Gramophone* D '89 (Nicholas Anderson).

"The performances...contain some real gems-...something should have been done to prevent the slightly disjointed effect that one receives from successive movements which come from afar then near, and vice-versa."
Hi-Fi News & Record Review 34:86 Je '89. Stephen Daw (280w)

Fanfare 14:140-4 S/O '90. George Chien (510w)

Gramophone 66:1316-19 F '89. Nicholas Anderson (560w)

6009. Cantatas: No. 10, Meine Seele erhebt den Herrn; No. 130, Herr Gott, dich loven alle wir; No. 17, Wer Dank opferet, der preiset mich. ("Complete Cantatas." Volume 17).
Helmuth Rilling (c). Adalbert Kraus (ten); Wolfgang Schone (bass); Arleen Auger (sop); Margit Neubauer (alto); Aldo Baldin (ten); Kathrin Graf (sop); Gabriele Schnaut (alto); Gabriele Schreckenbach (alto); Walter Heldwein (bass). Stuttgart Gachinger Kantorei; Stuttgart Bach-Collegium; Figuralchor der Gedachtniskirche Stuttgart. reissue.
HANSSLER/LAUDATE 98868 AAD 55:42

"The performances are typical of Rilling's work....the listener who favors modern instruments and mixed choruses will find even more to admire here....The AAD code should cast some doubt on the publication date, but the recordings are entirely acceptable."
Fanfare 12:102-3 My/Je '89. George Chien (120w)

"Excellent recordings...Our summation of the series in Sept/Oct 1988 applies to these."
American Record Guide 52:12 Jl/Ag '89. Donald R. Vroon (50w)

6010. Cantatas: No. 8, Liebster Gott, wann werd' ich sterben; No. 78, Jesu, der du meine Seele; No. 99, Was Gott tut, das ist wohlgetan.
Joshua Rifkin (c). Julianne Baird (sop); Allan Fast (alto); Frank Kelley (ten); Jan Opalach (bass). Bach Ensemble.
OISEAU-LYRE 421 728 DDD 58:00

✔HC ★*Awards:* Top Disks of the Year, *The New York Times* D 24, '89 (John Rockwell).

"There are no surprises in this latest recording of Bach's cantatas from Joshua Rifkin's Bach Ensemble. He hasn't abandoned his practice of assigning each part to one singer, nor has he presided over a performance that diminishes in any way the vitality from Bach's living testament. So listeners who find Rifkin's hypothesis convincing should be delighted with the present release; others, which include yours truly, will probably have mixed feelings, as with Rifkin's prior efforts....Nevertheless, it would be hard to imagine a better solo quartet than the one Rifkin has assembled for this album, and the instrumentalists of the Bach Ensemble are predictably superb, with Christopher Krueger deserving special for his work in the demanding flute part of BWV 8....L'Oiseau-Lyre's sound and packaging are excellent. Recommended, with the usual caveat."
Fanfare 13:93-4 Ja/F '90. George Chien (300w)

Gramophone 67:715 O '89. John Duarte (385w)

6011. Cantatas: No. 202, Weichet nur (Wedding Cantata); No. 209, Non sa che sia dolore.
Joshua Rifkin (c). Julianne Baird (sop). Bach Ensemble.
OISEAU-LYRE 421 424 DDD 42:01

✔HC ★*Awards:* Top Disks of the Year, *The New York Times* D 24, '89 (John Rockwell).

"A joy from start to finish. If Julianne Baird hasn't dislodged Emma Kirkby from her particular pedestal in my personal pantheon, she looks like finding a place not far below. Her singing is of ravishing purity; small-toned, perhaps, but impeccably stylish, and musical to its figurative fingertips."
Hi-Fi News & Record Review 34:101 Ap '89. Jeremy Siepmann (200w)

"The Bach Ensemble is superb here, with high marks going to flutist Christopher Krueger and especially to oboist Stephen Hammer. But the success of the performances depends on the work of the soprano soloist....Julianne Baird's-...sweet, natural voice is ideally suited for these tender, intimate pieces, and she sings them impeccably....highly recommended."
Fanfare 12:71-2 Jl/Ag '89. George Chien (350w)

Gramophone 66:1319-20 F '89. Nicholas Anderson (540w)

6012. Cantatas: No. 206, Schleicht, spielende Wellen; No. 207, Auf, schmetternde Tone der muntern Trompeten.
Frieder Bernius (c). Ruth $$ Ziesak (sop); Michael Chance (alto); Christophe Pregardien (ten); Peter Kooy (bass). Stuttgart Chamber Choir; Cologne Concerto.
SONY 46492 DDD 67:00

★*Awards:* Critics' Choice 1991, *Gramophone*, Ja '92 (Nicholas Anderson).

"These works are a gentle riot of color and dance rhythm....Their every last shade and tick is relished by four exceptional soloists...Comparing these renditions with some ancient, respectable (and once loved) predecessors on LP was like comparing gliding skiffs with coughing jalopies. Anyone interested in modern Bach style at its light and airy best ought to hear this disk....Out of 14 recordings released thus far, most can be gladly recommended...although in no case but the Bach cantatas is one tempted to haul out the heavy superlatives."

The New York Times Ag 25 '91, sec H p. 19+. Richard Taruskin (long)

"All are performed with early instruments...Though all four soloists are excellent, tenor Christoph Pregardien impresses the most, his pure but lustrous timbre thinning out only at the very top. Frieder Bernius extracts solid, musicianly singing from his choir."

Musical America 111:36-7 N/D '91. James M. Keller (long)

"Except for the ever-familiar 'Coffee' and 'Peasant' cantatas and the increasingly popular wedding cantata (BWV 202), Bach's secular cantatas don't attract a lot of attention, perhaps because their librettos tend nowadays to sound a little overblown....To the best of my knowledge, this is the first CD version of either cantata, and it's a good one. Recommended."

Fanfare 15:248-9 N/D '91. George Chien (med)

Gramophone 69:106 S '91. Nicholas Anderson (long)

6013. Cantata No. 208, "Was Mir Behagt, Ist Nur Die Muntre Jagd" ("Hunt Cantata").
Roy Goodman (c). Roy Goodman; Jennifer Smith; Emma Kirkby; Simon Davies; Michael George. The Parley of Instruments. January, 1986.
HYPERION 66169 43:35

✔**HC** ★*Awards:* *Gramophone* Critics' Choice 1986 (John Duarte).

"With four excellent soloists and some of England's finest period instrumentalists, Goodman leads a performance that is expert, bright, and fresh...Excellent sound from Hyperion."

Fanfare 10:53-54 Ja/F '87 George Chien (200w)

"The performance is thoroughly enjoyable-....Recommended."

American Record Guide 50:12-13 Ja/F '87 Ralph V. Lucano (270w)

Hi-Fi News & Record Review 31:101 N '86. Stephen Daw (75w)

Gramophone 64:912 D '86 John Duarte (160w)

6014. Christmas Oratorio, BWV.248.
John Eliot Gardiner (c). Anthony Rolfe-Johnson (ten); Ruth Holton; Katie Pringle; Nancy Argenta (sop); Anne-Sofie von Otter (mez); Hans-Peter Blochwitz (ten); Olaf Bar (bass). Monteverdi Choir; English Baroque Soloists.
DEUTSCHE GRAMMOPHON 423 232 DDD 140:00 2 discs

✔**HC** ★*Awards:* The Want List 1988, *Fanfare* N/D '88 (Elliott Kaback). Critics' Choice 1988, *Gramophone* D '88 (Robert Layton).

"It strikes me as being an outstanding performance; and it has the edge over Schreier, and all the other four CD versions, in being accommodated on only two discs. This feat should not distract attention from its musical and technical excellence."

Hi-Fi News & Record Review 33:97 Mr '88. Peter Branscombe (300w)

"The Gardiner *Christmas Oratorio* is a high-spirited, propulsive, often thrilling account-...they make a much bigger (though never bloated) sound than the other original-instrument accounts, with the trumpets especially vibrant and excellently captured by Archiv. That more expansive splendor in itself is enough to warrant purchase, as a complement to the more intimate and delicate versions previously recorded. Gardiner continues his preference for brisk, at times breakneck, tempos, averaging about ten per cent faster than the once-jarringly fast Harnoncourt. His chorus and musicians are so proficient, however, that the effect is tremendously exhilarating rather than exhausting-....Evangelist Anthony Rolfe-Johnson is a model of decorum and cohesion, one of the real pluses of this excellent set."

Fanfare 12:72+ Mr/Ap '89. Edward Strickland (625w)

"It is a pity...that Gardiner has failed by and large to capture the innermost mystery, the spirituality of Christmas as conveyed by Bach. What we are offered, especially in the choruses, is a secular, lightweight, and at times downright superficial view."

Continuo 12:17-8 D '88. Pierre Savaria (575w)

Gramophone 65:984 D '87. Nicholas Anderson (845w)

6015. Easter Oratorio, BWV.249; Cantata: No. 6, Bleib bei uns, denn es will Aabend werden.
Helmuth Rilling (c). Arleen Auger; Julia Hamari; Adalbert Kraus; Philippe Huttenlocher; Edith Wiens; Carolyn Watkinson; Walter Heldwin. Stuttgart Gachinger Kantorei; Stuttgart Bach-Collegium. reissue.
HANSSLER/LAUDATE 98862 AAD 60:11

"When I received this last batch of discs from Laudate, I was both delighted and distressed—delighted by the contents of the discs; distressed because there was no indication of the specific contents of any disc on its spine."

Fanfare 11:68-70 My/Je '88. George Chien (175w)

6016. Magnificat in D, BWV.243; Cantata No. 51, Jauchzet Gott in allen Landen.
John Eliot Gardiner (c). Nancy Argenta; Emma Kirkby; Patrizia Kwella; Charles Brett; Anthony Rolfe-Johnson; David Thomas. Monteverdi Choir; English Baroque Soloists.
PHILIPS 411 458 41:44

★★*Awards:* *Fanfare* Want List 1985 (George Chien); *Stereo Review* Best of the Month, N '85.

"Overall I found myself caught by the infectious joy of all the performers in these superb examples of Bach's most brilliant vein."

Hi-Fi News & Record Review 30:81 Jl '85. Peter Branscombe (140w)

"Bach's *Magnificat* has been exceptionally well served on compact discs. There are three versions, including Gardiner's, available at present, all performed with period instruments, and all excellent....Though I prefer Harnoncourt's *Magnificat*, the Kirkby/Gardiner Cantata 51 is a rare gem, while Gardiner's *Magnificat* is a very good one. And for something completely different—or almost completely different—you might try Rifkin."

Fanfare 9:110-1 S/O '85. George Chien (490w)

"This is a wonderful album. Chalk one up for the authentic-performance gang."

Stereo Review 50:93 N '85. Stoddard Lincoln (350w)

6017. Magnificat in D. BWV.243. HANDEL, GEORGE FRIDERIC. Utrecht Te Deum and Jubilate.

Nikolaus Harnoncourt (c). Hildegard Heichele; Helrun Gardow; Felicity Palmer; Marjana Lipovsek; Paul Esswood; Kurt Equiluz; Thomas Moser. Arnold Schoenberg Choir; Vienna Concentus Musicus.
TELDEC 142955 DDD 52:00

✔HC ★*Awards:* Perfect 10/10, *Digital Audio*, Mr '88.

"Highly recommended."

Fanfare 8:96-7 My/Je '85. George Chien (240w)

Ovation 6:30 Ja '86. Scott Cantrell (180w)

Gramophone 64:603 O '86 Nicholas Anderson (420w)

Digital Audio 1:60-1 Je '85. David Vernier (125w)

6018. Magnificat in D, BWV.243. VIVALDI, ANTONIO. Gloria in D, R.589.

Robert Shaw (c). Dawn Upshaw (sop); Penelope Jensen (sop); Marietta Simpson (mez); David Gordon (ten); William Stone (bar). Atlanta Symphony Chamber Chorus; Atlanta Symphony Chamber Orchestra.
TELARC 80194 DDD 56:00

✔HC ★*Awards:* The Want List 1989, *Fanfare* N/D '89 (George Chien).

"Listeners who prefer the sound of mixed voices and modern instruments and the weight of a full orchestral-vocal ensemble should be especially pleased with this release, but it should be welcomed by anyone with an interest in this music, and it's a clear winner over the Corboz recording for Erato Bonsai, the only other version I know that pairs these popular scores."

Fanfare 13:120-21 S/O '89. George Chien (300w)

"Robert Shaw continues to bask in sound, and Telarc and his chorus and chamber orchestra do him proud. There is no real interpretation here: it's not a very pious reading, nor is it operatic or controversial. It's just lovely....the recorded sound is superb. My favorite coupling of these works on CD remains Michel Corboz's (Erato ECD-55002), but this set is definitely in the running."

Stereophile 12:203 O '89. Robert Levine (180w)

"This is an entirely admirable production, made by a man who has dedicated his life to the splendor and subtlety of choral sound, to its endless variety of tone color, and to its modern resurgence as a medium of true artistic expression....Of the chorus, it is hardly possible to say too much....This is a release to be recommended heartily."

Musical America 109:51-2 N '89. Denis Stevens (340w)

"Shaw's sustained concept of phrasing is beautifully realized throughout the Bach work, reaching a high point with women's voices in 'Suscepit Israel.' Less fortunate is Vivaldi on this recording...Indeed, Baroque enthusiasts will find this performance to be plodding at times...One notable exception is the duet between soprano Dawn Upshaw and solo oboe in 'Domine Deus,' where both soloists perform with inspired, lyric beauty. Dawn Upshaw also shines in the *Magnificat*."

HighPerformanceReview 8(1):86 '91. George S. T. Chu (320w)

"The instruments are not period dentistry; the orchestra sounds warm and healthy. We do not hear a loud, tinny harpsichord above everything else....But every time we have listened to this we have been disappointed....Too much control, too careful, too unspontaneous."

American Record Guide 52:135-36 N/D '89. Donald R. Vroon (145w)

"His conducting is precise, the music well tailored and rehearsed, beautifully controlled, the chorus accurate and indefatigable, just that Shaw-ish combination of 'amateur' blending and professional exactitude that he originated in his Collegiate Chorale so many years ago-....And yet nothing is really penetrating or profound."

Audio 74:138+ N '90. Edward Tatnall Canby (550w)

Gramophone 67:346 Ag '89. Nicholas Anderson (460w)

6019. Mass in B minor, BWV.232.

John Eliot Gardiner (c). Monteverdi Choir; English Baroque Soloists.
DEUTSCHE GRAMMOPHON 415 514 2 discs

✔HC ★★★★★*Awards:* *Fanfare* Want List 1986 (Edward Strickland); *Fanfare* Want List 1986 (George Chien); *Gramophone* Critics' Choice 1986 (John Steane); *Fanfare* Want List 1987 (William Youngren); *Fanfare* Want L1987 (Michael Ullman).

"Whether you've been wanting to update your library to a modern-day (read 'authentic') performance of this great work, or you're about to take your first plunge into the Mass in B Minor, this one is highly recommended."

Ovation 7:36 D '86 Robert Levine (345w)

"If you like extremes of contrast, Gardiner is for you: the sustained, very slow tempo of the Agnus Dei, tellingly sung by Michael Chance;

the massive sound of the Sanctus or the '*Gratias agimus*.' This performance never risks too much."

Opus 2:33-4 Ag '86. Nicholas Kenyon (515w)

"The flute's *ritornello* in *Benedictus qui venit in nomine domini* is simply the finest lyrical playing of this music that one can ever hope to hear....At times one could be forgiven for thinking Gardiner is driving these vocalists, pushing them more than necessary and getting a bit of strain into their voices. His tempi likewise are on the fast side. I sometimes wonder if Bach heard any of his music played as quickly as it is today."

Musick 12:23-4 Summ '90. J. Evan Kreider (330w)

Opus 3:50 D '86 Jon Alan Conrad (95w)

Gramophone 63:1054 F '86. Nicholas Anderson (940w); 64: 522 O '86 John Steane (70w)

Hi-Fi News & Record Review 31:76 Ag '86. Hugh Canning (420w)

6020. Motets (6), BWV.225/30.
Christoph Eschenbach (c). Rostock Motet Choir; Capella Fidicinia Leipzig.
CAPRICCIO 10030 DDD 68:04

✔**HC** ★*Awards:* Perfect 10/10, *Digital Audio*, Mr '88.

"The artists...provide performances above reproach, superbly recorded."

High Fidelity 36:61-2 Ag '86. Paul Moor (250w)

"Eschenbach resorts to mannered tempo manipulations in an attempt to create grandeur, distorting the rhythmic flow in the name of word-painting and cadential delineation."

High Fidelity 37:62-63 Jl '87 K. Robert Schwarz (160w)

Hi-Fi News & Record Review 30:82-3 Jl '85. Peter Branscombe (100w)

Fanfare 8:84-91 Jl/Ag '85. George Chien (190w)

Digital Audio 1:54-5 Ag '85. David Vernier (145w)

6021. Saint John Passion, BWV.245.
John Eliot Gardiner (c). Anthony Rolfe-Johnson; Stephen Varcoe; Cornelius Hauptmann; Nancy Argenta. Monteverdi Choir; English Baroque Soloists.
DEUTSCHE GRAMMOPHON 419 324 DDD 51:57; 54:39 2 discs

✔**HC** ★★*Awards:* *Stereo Review* Best of the Month, Jl '87; *Opus* Record Award Nominee, 1987; *Opus* Christmas List 1987 (Paul L. Althouse). Perfect 10/10, *Digital Audio*, Mr '88.

"Right from the start...you know that you are in a magnificent performance....The arias in this performance enter the most eloquent plea ever made on records for the use of period instruments and Baroque vocal styles, and thanks to the careful engineering, every musical subtlety has been faithfully captured."

Stereo Review 52:81 Jl '87 Stoddard Lincoln (500w)

"Of all the English conductors in the 'authentic' camp, Gardiner proves much the finest choral conductor....A wonderful job all around."

Opus 4:52 D '87. Paul L. Althouse (100w)

"This *Saint John* is perhaps the best balanced on disc. It is also the fastest....In the field of original instruments, it easily surpasses the interesting but vocally flawed Schneidt (also on Archiv) and makes up in overall conception for what it yields to the Harnoncourt account in color."

Fanfare 10:83-84 My/Je '87 Edward Strickland (650w)

"The particular success of this recording stems less from its 'authenticity' or lack of the same than from Gardiner's insightful treatment of the drama."

American Record Guide 50:3-4 Fall '87. Paul L. Althouse (740w)

"The forces are driven to do their technical best, but something is lacking, and it may be heart."

Ovation 8:38 N '87. Robert Levine (440w)

"Technically the issue meets the very high standard we expect from Archiv....But it is the singing which lets the issue down."

Hi-Fi News & Record Review 32:91 Je '87 Hugh Canning (280w)

Gramophone 64:1164 F '87 Lionel Salter (510w)

Digital Audio & Compact Disc Review 107:58 Jl '87 David Vernier (325w)

6022. Saint John Passion, BWV.245.
Philippe Herreweghe (c). Howard Crook (ten); Peter Lika (bass); Barbara Schlick (sop); Catherine Patriasz (contr); William Kendall (ten); Peter Kooy (bass). Ghent Collegium Vocale; Chapelle Royale Orchestra.
HARMONIA MUNDI 901264/5 DDD 115:00 2 discs

✔**HC** ★*Awards:* Editors' Choice, *Digital Audio's CD Review*, Je '89.

"This strikes me as our best *St John Passion* to date....The recording seems to have been as attentively achieved as the performance."

Hi-Fi News & Record Review 33:77 Ag '88. Stephen Daw (240w)

"It is not just for those who like to hear Bach without a strong operatic accent, but for those who prefer Bach with no accent at all. Even more than John Eliot Gardiner's excellent Deutsche Grammophon recording with authentic instruments, Herreweghe's interpretation epitomizes the basic idea of rediscovering original performance practices....So sincere, so unmannered is this approach that in comparison Gardiner's recording occasionally seems over-interpreted, even if brilliantly so, with touches that tell you more about the conductor's intelligence and style than about the story Bach lays before us."

Stereo Review 53:145-46 D '88. David Patrick Stearns (400w)

"As a meditative, singerly version, one focussed on the religious aspects of the piece, it would be hard to surpass. My first choice, however, would be John Eliot Gardiner's recording (DG 419 324) which, though similar to Herreweghe's, suggests a concert performance, not a liturgical one."

American Record Guide 51:10-11 N/D '88. Paul L. Althouse (275w)

"This is a first-class 'St. John,' done in a contemporary but not fussy manner, reasonably 'authentic' but claiming no exactitude since none really is possible."

Audio 72:112 Ag '88. Edward Tatnall Canby (830w)

"I'm still waiting for a *St. John* to admire as unreservedly as I do Herreweghe's *St. Matthew* or Gardiner's B-minor Mass. This will do in the meantime....The best thing about this performance...is its pacing....And that, probably, is why the whole is greater than the parts."

Fanfare 12:91-3 S/O '88. Edward Strickland (950w)

Gramophone 65:1628 My '88. Nicholas Anderson (825w)

Digital Audio 5:76+ N '88. David C. Vernier (375w)

Musick 12:17-9 Summ '90. J. Evan Kreider (765w)

6023. Saint Matthew Passion, BWV.244.
John Eliot Gardiner (c). Anthony Rolfe-Johnson (ten); Andreas Schmidt (bar); Barbara Bonney (sop); Ann Monoyios (sop); Anne-Sofie von Otter (mez); Michael Chance (alto); Howard Crook (ten); Olaf Bar (bar); Cornelius Hauptmann (bass). London Oratory Junior Choir; Monteverdi Choir; English Baroque Soloists.
DEUTSCHE GRAMMOPHON 427 648 DDD
167:00 3 discs

✔HC ★★★★Awards: Baroque (Vocal) Record Award 1990, *Gramophone* D '90; Critic's Choice: 1990, *American Record Guide* Ja/F '91 (Stephen Chakwin); Critics Choice, *Hi Fi News & Record Review*, Ap '91 Supplement (William McVicker). Top Disks of the Year, *The New York Times* D 24, '89 (John Rockwell); Best of the Month, *Hi-Fi News & Record Review*, F '90. The Year's Best, *Hi Fi News & Record Review*, May '90 Supplement.

"A vividly dramatic reading in which even the chorales take on a life of their own. There's nothing sanctimonious about this performance, not least because of the uniformly excellent and youthful team of soloists."

Music and Musicians International 38:45 Je '90. Antony Bye (b.n.)

"This is a noble and exhilarating performance of one of the greatest of all musical compositions. DG has given it recorded sound to match."

American Record Guide 53:18 My/Je '90. Stephen D. Chakwin, Jr. (625w)

"All things considered...I felt I was experiencing something special here." *P100 S95/100*

Hi-Fi News & Record Review 35:94 F '90. William McVicker (670w)

"Gardiner's *St. Matthew* is absorbing, exciting, and recorded in excellent sound. I fear its impact will prove ephemeral, however, because something essential is missing....There are a few things here...to draw the listener back, but there are also too many lacunae over which the music flies emptily and inconsequentially."

Fanfare 13:120-21 Mr/Ap '90. Ralph V. Lucano (1095w)

P100 S100/95

Hi-Fi News & Record Review p.15 My '90 Supplement. William McVicker (670w)

Gramophone 67:716 O '89 (1600w); 68:725 O '90 (140w). Nicholas Anderson

6024. Saint Matthew Passion, BWV.244.
Philippe Herreweghe (c). Barbara Schlick (sop); Rene Jacobs (alto); Peter Kooy (bar); Ulric Cold (bass); Howard Crook (ten). La Chapelle Royale Orchestra; Ghent Collegium Vocale.
HARMONIA MUNDI 901155/7

★Awards: *Fanfare* Want List 1985 (Edward Strickland).

"Altogether a first-rate job."

Stereo Review 50:174 S '85. Stoddard Lincoln (100w)

"While the LPs retain an edge in general warmth of ambience, the CDs do seem more revelatory of detail on many occasions and, particularly in the choral dynamics, more immediate....The Herreweghe is, I believe, superior overall to the landmark Harnoncourt among period-instruments accounts, a beautifully paced and nuanced performance featuring fine solo and choral work alike. It provides a perfect compliment to Richter II, with which it now shares the laurels."

Fanfare 9:109-10 N/D '85. Edward Strickland (150w)

"The soloists are very good indeed, particularly Howard Crook....I personally find this version so far superior to that done recently by Rilling that I see no reason to give further attention to Rilling's all-too-traditional interpretation....The carefully intellectualized approach by Herreweghe is far more pleasing, and, to my taste, the best now available."

Musick 9:27-9 Jl '87. J. Evan Kreider (1450w)

Ovation 7:32 Ag '86. Scott Cantrell (370w)

Gramophone 63:154-5 Jl '85 (560w) (rev. of LP); 63:664 N '85 (125w) (rev. of CD). Trevor Harvey

6025. Saint Matthew Passion, BWV.244.
Georg Solti (c). Hans-Peter Blochwitz (ten); Olaf Bar (bar); Kiri Te Kanawa (sop); Anne-Sofie von Otter (mez); Anthony Rolfe-Johnson (ten); Tom Krause (bar). Glen Ellyn Children's Chorus; Chicago Sym-

phony Chorus; Chicago Symphony Orchestra. 1987.
LONDON/DECCA 421 177 DDD 179:00 3 discs

★★*Awards:* Critics' Choice 1988, *Gramophone* D '88 (Robin Golding). Top Choices—1989, *American Record Guide* Ja/F '90 (Kurt Moses).

"The recorded sound...is superlative....It's a full-blooded performance, and the sound backs up the interpretation. My recommendation: It would be wrong to do without the Herreweghe; the Solti makes a superb complement."

Stereophile 11:180-81 D '88. Robert Levine (490)

"Like the historically invaluable Weissbach performance (Acanta LPs, deleted) recorded in concert in Leipzig in 1935...Solti's view of this masterpiece provides the listener with a tantalizing glimpse of the *St. Matthew* as it must have sounded in performances in Berlin in 1888....In short, this is a performance in the best conservative Brahmsian manner."

American Record Guide 52:17 Mr/Ap '89. Teri Noel Towe (300w)

"This is the best Bach opera I've ever heard-....For Herreweghe (in both Passions) the 'big' Bach works remain primarily religious meditations; for Solti they are theatrical experiences-....I find this recording, consequently, rather depressing."

Fanfare 12:93 S/O '88. Edward Strickland (425w)

Digital Audio 5:48-9 Ja '89. Roland Graeme (425w)

BARBER, SAMUEL

6026. Prayers of Kierkegaard, for Soprano, Orchestra and Mixed Chorus, Opus 30; Die Natali: Chorale Preludes for Christmans, Opus 37. CRESTON, PAUL. Corinthians XIII, for Orchestra, Opus 82. TOCH, ERNST. Jephta, Rhapsodic Poem (Symphony No. 5).
Jorge Mester; Robert Whitney (c). Gloria Capone (sop). Southern Baptist Theological Seminary Chorus; Louisville Orchestra. reissues.
ALBANY 021 AAD 69:47

★*Awards:* The Want List 1990, *Fanfare* N/D '90 (Walter Simmons).

"This latest CD reissue of items from the Louisville backlist is of great merit: Not only does it return to the catalog first and only recordings of four works, but two of them are among the finest creations of their respective composers-....All these performances are thoroughly adequate to convey the quality of the music, while leaving plenty of room for improvement with regard to both execution and interpretation. The sound quality of the CD transfers is vastly superior to the original LP releases."

Fanfare 13:110-11 My/Je '90. Walter Simmons (900w)

"A sincere thanks to Albany records for reminding me of the genius of these works and providing so much pleasurable listening."

American Record Guide 53:149 Jl/Ag '90. Karl Miller (285w)

Gramophone 68:103-4 Je '90. Peter Dickinson (360w)

BEETHOVEN, LUDWIG VAN

Fantasia in C minor for Piano, Chorus and Orchestra, Opus 80. See No. 2012, 2022.

6027. Missa Solemnis in D, Opus 123.
John Eliot Gardiner (c). Charlotte Margiono (sop); Catherine Robbin (mez); William Kendall (ten); Alastair Miles (bass). Monteverdi Choir; English Baroque Soloists.
DEUTSCHE GRAMMOPHON 429 779 DDD 72:00

★*Awards:* The Gramophone Awards, Nominations, Choral, *Gramophone*, N '91. The Record of The Year 1991, *Gramophone*, D '91. Pick of the Month, North American Perspective (Christie Barter), *Gramophone* Mr '91.

"Overall Gardiner's recording lacks the authoritativeness of the second recordings by Klemperer, Karajan, Toscanini (still the principal recommendations). In understanding of period instruments, this Archiv entirely supersedes the Harmonia Mundi...The Monteverdi Choir sings marvellously, and the solo quartet is decently matched, with a particularly good soprano cast." *P85 S85*

Hi-Fi News & Record Review 36:88 Mr '91. Christopher Breunig (340w)

Gramophone 68:1707 Mr '91. John Steane (665w)

6028. Missa Solemnis in D, Opus 123; Fantasia in C minor for Piano, Chorus and Orchestra, Opus 80.
Arturo Toscanini (c). Zinka Milanov (sop); Bruna Castagna; Jussi Bjoerling (ten); Alexander Kipnis (bass); Ania Dorfmann (pno); John Finley Williamson (choir director). NBC Symphony Orchestra; Westminster Choir. 1940; 1939.
MUSIC & ARTS 259 AAD (m) 95:18 2 discs

✔**HC** ★*Awards:* *Fanfare* Want List 1987 (Mortimer H. Frank).

"Although it [Opus 123] is probably familiar to many collectors from previous 'unofficial' editions, none of those releases is sonically competitive with this one....it is, of course, for the *Missa Solemnis* that one should grab this set while it remains available."

Fanfare 11:147-8 S/O '87. Mortimer H. Frank (280w)

American Record Guide 50:95-100 N/D '87. Peter J. Rabinowitz (445w)

6029. Missa Solemnis in D, Opus 123. MOZART, WOLFGANG AMADEUS. Mass in C minor, K.427, "The Great".
Robert Shaw (c). Sylvia McNair (sop); Janice Taylor (mez); John Aler (ten); Tom Krause (bar) (*Missa Solemnis*); Edith Wiens (sop); Delores Ziegler (mez);

John Aler (ten); William Stone (bar) (*"Great" Mass*). Atlanta Symphony Orchestra Chorus; Atlanta Symphony Orchestra. 1987.
TELARC 80150 DDD 139:00 2 discs

★★★*Awards:* The Want List 1988, *Fanfare* N/D '88 (Elliott Kaback); Critics' Choice 1988, *Gramophone* D '88 (John Steane). Top Choices—1989, *American Record Guide* Ja/F '90 (Paul Althouse).

"This is surely the state-of-the-art in recording large choral-orchestral music. There is much to admire among the singers and players also-....The sense of the mass as faith in God achieved in the face of the terrible reality of the world is not sensed....some of Shaw's long-familiar choral techniques...sound somewhat mannered under the scrutiny of the vivid recording. These strictures do not diminish the power, beauty, and sheer professional skill of this interpretation."
Fanfare 12:99-102 S/O '88. Elliott Kaback (865w)

"Klemperer saw it as a grand edifice to be climbed slowly and respectfully; Bernstein took great relish in its wild shifts of mood and tempo; Karajan found it something awesome but understandable in his first, very successful, recording, and a piece to approach gingerly in his latest. Shaw and his group play and sing the notes as they are written. No revolution, no revelation....Shaw makes the work absolutely valid without posturing or pondering its meaning....I love this performance; I am everything but moved or thrilled by it....[The performance of the *Mass*] is conscientious without being inspired, much like the *Missa*....With regard to the recording, the word 'mellow' comes to mind."
Stereophile 11:163+ N '88. Robert Levine (800w)

"Although it was Shaw who prepared the chorus for Toscanini's historic 1953 recording of the *Missa solemnis*, I cannot say that he achieves comparably incandescent results on his own. Nor does the performance catch fire in the manner of the two recordings by Leonard Bernstein or even the latest of Herbert von Karajan's four versions....The Mozart Mass-...has distinctly better choral presence, and the performance is marvelous."
Stereo Review 53:91 Ag '88. David Hall (450w)

"Telarc's sound lacks brilliance, such that the chorus sounds distant and lumpy. So swayed was I by the sound that until I boosted the treble, I felt the singers uninvolved and dull....I mean no disrespect if I find Klemperer on Angel more probing and revelatory. Shaw's is the equal of any of the remaining eight versions on my shelves—superior to most....recommended as long as you remember to boost the treble!"
American Record Guide 52:20-1 Mr/Ap '89. Paul L. Althouse (240w)

Gramophone 66:835 N '88. John Steane (300w)

Digital Audio 5:48-9 Ja '89. Lawrence Johnson (150w)

BERLIOZ, HECTOR

6030. Requiem, Opus 5 (Grande Messe des Morts); Symphonie funebre et triomphale, Opus 15.
Colin Davis (c). Ronald Dowd (dir). John Alldis Choir; Wandsworth School Boys' Choir; London Symphony Chorus; London Symphony Orchestra. reissue.
PHILIPS 416 283 ADD 126:39 2 discs

✔HC ★★★*Awards:* *Awards:* Pick of the Crop Reissues, *The New York Times* S 16, '90 (Sedgwick Clark); The Want List 1988, *Fanfare* N/D '88 (Mortimer H. Frank). *American Record Guide* Overview: Berlioz, Mr/Ap '91.

"The *Funeral & Triumphal Symphony* really comes into its own on CD...Colin Davis' masterly pacing of this extraordinary alfresco work for inflated military-band...retains my admiration after 16 years."*Hi-Fi News & Record Review* 31:107 Ap '86. John Crabbe (280w)

"The compact disc issue is entirely welcome. The sound in both works is spacious, clear, and detailed....Which is to say not merely *recommended*, but that this is an old love renewed and an indispensible cornerstone of any serious collection."
Fanfare 9:100 Jl/Ag '86. Adrian Corleonis (400w)

"A modicum of hiss remains...but is far less prominent than the assorted noises produced from the surfaces of the original releases...[this is] surely the preferred format for Davis's magnificent readings."
Stereophile 11:153+ Mr '88. Mortimer H. Frank (165w)

High Fidelity 36:83 D '86 Bill Zakariasen (288w)

6031. Requiem, Opus 5 (Grande Messe des Morts); Symphonie Fantastique, Opus 14.
Charles Munch (c). Leopold Simoneau (ten). New England Conservatory Chorus; Boston Symphony Orchestra. April 1959.
RCA 6210 ADD 130:17 2 discs

★*Awards:* *American Record Guide* Overview: Berlioz, Mr/Ap '91 (Requiem).

"The music is superb, the performance excellent to outstanding, and the original recording and digital remastering...are very good....much of the hiss from the master tapes was deliberately not removed, to preserve as much as possible of the high-frequency content. The result is perfectly acceptable....This is the kind of music-making we will regard in 20 years' time the same way we now do the classic Furtwangler and Toscanini performances of the '20s and '30s."
Stereophile 11:155+ Mr '88. L. Hunter Kevil (525w)

"Made in the late '50s...[this recording offers] relatively clear, somewhat bodiless sound piqued with marginal shrillness in the treble and accompanied by low-level tape hiss-....Munch's chiseled, polished, and inexorably brisk manner carries the work with an overall momentum...which is undeniably thrilling, sometimes hair-raising, and spellbinding throughout...The superb youthful chorus sings with conviction while the BSO smartly lays on the lash. And, as often noted, Leopold Simoneau delivers the most sublime *'Sanctus'* on discs...Munch's own 1968 remake with Peter Schreier and the Bavarian Radio Chorus and Orchestra (DG 413 523-1, *Fanfare* 9:1) proves a thin echo."

Fanfare 11:105-6 N/D '87. Adrian Corleonis (300w)

American Record Guide 51:20-1 Mr/Ap '88. Stephen D. Chakwin, Jr. (600w)

Gramophone 65:1216 F '88. Lionel Salter (510w)

6032. Romeo et Juliette (symphonie dramatique), for Mezzo-Soprano, Tenor, Baritone, Orchestra and Chorus, Opus 17; Symphonie Funebre et Triomphale, Opus 15.
Charles Dutoit (c). Florence Quivar (contr); Alberto Cupido (ten); Tom Krause; Jeffrey Budin (bar). Tudor Vocal Ensemble; Montreal Symphony Orchestra Chorus; Montreal Symphony Orchestra.
LONDON/DECCA 417 302 130:41 2 discs

★*Awards:* *Gramophone* **Critics' Choice (Lionel Salter), 1987.**

"This is the first *Romeo and Juliet* on CD [Muti's is announced by EMI] and the second *Funeral & Triumphal Symphony*. The latter joins the Davis reissue (coupled with the Requiem) and thus faces strong competition....But the main work here is *Romeo and Juliet*....The choruses are splendid, and Dutoit coaxes some beautiful sounds from his orchestra in what amounts to a generally well rounded view of the work. But I feel that *R & J* ideally needs more conviction, more intensity and nervous drive than we get here."

Hi-Fi News & Record Review 31:109-11 D '86 John Crabbe (270w)

"Dutoit's *Romeo* comes off short of superlatives."

Fanfare 10:83-84 Mr/Ap '87 Adrian Corleonis (490w)

Ovation 8:40 Je '87 Paul Turok (315w)

Gramophone 64:915 D '86 Lionel Salter (615w)

BRAHMS, JOHANNES

6033. Choral Music: Gesang der Parzen, Chorus and Orchestra, Opus 89; Nanie, for Chorus and Orchestra, Opus 82; Schicksalslied, Opus 54; Begrabnisgesang, for Chorus and Orchestra, Opus 13; Alto Rhapsody, Opus 53.
Herbert Blomstedt (c). Jard Van Nes (mez). San Francisco Symphony Chorus; San Francisco Symphony Orchestra.
LONDON/DECCA 430 281 DDD 63:00

★★*Awards:* The Gramophone Awards, Nominations, Choral, *Gramophone*, N '91. Critics' Choice 1990, *Gramophone* D '90 (James Jolly); Critics' Choice 1990, *Gramophone* D '90 (Alan Sanders).

"Herbert Blomstedt's expansive and idiomatic conducting and the first-rate San Francisco Symphony Chorus combine for a very satisfying recording of Brahms's beautiful choral works. The singing of the *Nanie* in particular is eloquent and moving....Except for the *Alto Rhapsody*, this fine new recording is a solid choice for this repertoire."

Fanfare 14:160 Mr/Ap '91. James Camner (190w)

"All in all...an enjoyable disc and a worthy companion to similar CDs from Sinopoli (DG) and Haitink (Orfeo)."

American Record Guide 54:47 Mr/Ap '91. Paul L. Althouse (145w)

Gramophone 68:399 Ag '90. Alan Sanders (450w)

6034. Ein Deutsches Requiem, Opus 45.
John Eliot Gardiner (c). Charlotte Margiono (sop); Rodney Gilfry (bar). Monteverdi Choir; Orchestre Revolutionnaire et Romantique. Notes, texts and translations included.
PHILIPS 432 140 DDD 66:00

★★★★★*Awards:* Best Recordings of the Month, *Stereo Review* N '91; The Gramophone Awards, Nominations, Choral, *Gramophone*, N '91. Critics' Choice 1991, *Gramophone*, Ja '92 (James Jolly); Honorable Mention, Records of the Year, 1991, *Stereo Review*, F '92. Disc of the Month, *Digital Audio's CD Review*, S '91; Pick of the Month, North American Perspective (Christie Barter), *Gramophone* Ap '91. Editors' Choice—Best CDs of the Year, *Digital Audio's CD Review*, Je '92.

"I have yet to hear a Brahms *Requiem* with such clarity of text and intensity of expression; the very close marriage between text and music is here convincingly elucidated....I came away from this recording feeling that much had been revealed about the work, and its composer."

Musick 13(2):23-7 Fall-Sept '91. Gerald Van Wyck (long)

"Gardiner...bring[s] out the grandeur and depth of expression in Brahms' masterwork within a context of clearly moving contrapuntal lines and subtly drawn textures....Technically the performances are top-flight and the recorded sound is also very good, featuring an exceptionally wide dynamic range."

Continuo 15:24 O '91. Scott Paterson (med)

"Gardiner's...performing techniques are used in such a way as to change one's perception of the [Brahm's Requiem]...profoundly. It's as if a veil had been lifted, and the discoveries are thrilling....Much of the success of the performance...[relates to] the near-perfect intonation and diction of Gardiner's Monteverdi Choir....a recording that's likely to set a new standard."

Stereo Review 56:71-2 N '91. David Patrick Stearns (med)

Gardiner "avoids the warm bath of Victorian sanctimony and delivers a strong, bracing account with rhythmic spring and vitality...his Monteverdi Choir sounds wonderful. Both soloists are very fine, though it is baritone Rodney Gilfry who commands the more attention-...This release...is an important document for our understanding of Brahms."

American Record Guide 54:44-5 N/D '91. Paul L. Althouse (long)

"Essentially an extension of the EBS, John Eliot Gardiner's new 'Orchestre Revolutionaire et Romantique' will allow him exploration of the later repertoire with appropriate orchestral timbres....One's overall response is that Gardiner satisfies all the demands we have come to expect of the *Requiem*: it's spacious, there's nothing freakishly 'revolutionary', simply none of the sorts of violations that Norrington perpetrates, or the preposterous idiosyncracies that litter Harnoncourt's work." *P100/85 S95*

Hi-Fi News & Record Review 36:68 Je '91. Christopher Breunig (595w)

"Stick with Klemperer on Angel, still the last word in Brahms Requiems."

Fanfare 15:281-2 N/D '91. Ralph V. Lucano (med)

Digital Audio's CD Review 7:56 S '91. David Vernier (460w)

Gramophone 68:1881 Ap '91. Lionel Salter (395w)

6035. Ein Deutsches Requiem, Opus 45. BRUCKNER, ANTON: Te Deum.
Herbert von Karajan (c). Jose Van Dam, Janet Perry, Helga Muller-Molinari, Gosta Winbergh, Alexander Malta, Vienna Singverein Barbara Hendricks. Vienna Philharmonic Orchestra.
DEUTSCHE GRAMMOPHON 410 521 DDD 2 discs

★*Awards:* Best of the Month, *Stereo Review* My '86.

"This is a deeply moving performance of Brahms which brings out the profound beauty of Brahms' writing....Bruckner's dramatic Te Deum is also given an exhilarating performance with the full sonic range of a live performance. Together, the Brahms and Bruckner receive definitive interpretations on this album, and it is most highly recommended."

HighPerformanceReview 4:103 Wint '86/'87 George S.T. Chu (290w)

"I find his latest go at it [the Requiem] to be not only the most stirring since his 1947 version but the most impressive yet in terms of sonic impact....While his new recording [of the Te Deum] offers fine work on the part of the soloists, I don't find the same controlled tension he achieved a decade ago."

Stereo Review 51:84 My '86. David Hall (600w)

Gramophone 63:380+ S '85. Richard Osborne (715w) (rev. of LP)

Ovation 7:32-3 Ag '86. Scott Cantrell (385w)

6036. Ein Deutsches Requiem, Opus 45.
Otto Klemperer (c). Elisabeth Schwarzkopf (sop); Dietrich Fischer-Dieskau (bar). Philharmonia Chorus; Philharmonia Orchestra. 1962 reissue.
EMI 47238 ADD 69:16

✔HC ★★★*Awards:* *Opus* Christmas List, 1987 (Paul L. Althouse); *Fanfare* Want List 1987 (Elliott Kaback). Records to Die for: 1 of 5 Recommended Recordings, *Stereophile* Ja '91 (Larry Archibald).

"One of the great recordings."

Fanfare 10:101 My/Je '87 Vincent Alfano (250w)

"There have been many fine Brahms Requiems over the years, but none to surpass this version-...now it is on CD, where it belongs."

Opus 4:52 D '87. Paul L. Althouse (100w)

"This is a heavy work—majestic, powerful and intensely, quietly moving—and this performance, dating from 1962, captures its essence as no other has since."

Ovation 9:45 F '88. Robert Levine (210w)

"I have the French EMI; I'm sure it was available on English and other EMIs, as well as Angel—but the EMI is *much* better than the Angel version."

Stereophile 14:120 Ja '91. Larry Archibald (225w)

Gramophone 65:88 Je '87 Richard Osborne (140w)

Gesang der Parzen, Chorus and Orchestra. See No. 1063.

BRITTEN, BENJAMIN

6037. A Ceremony of Carols, Opus 28; Hymn to St. Cecilia; Missa Brevis in D; Rejoice in the Lamb; Te Deum in C; Jubilate Deo.
David Willcocks (c). King's College Choir, Cambridge. 1972; 1974.
EMI 47709 ADD 70:00

"The most popular piece recorded here is *A Ceremony of Carols*, and I have always felt that this was the definitive version...there is not a weak performance to be found here."

Ovation 9:43 N '88. Robert Levine (170w)

"The music is wonderful, and the performances...are virtually perfect."

High Fidelity 38:66 Ap '88. Terry Teachout (85w)

Digital Audio 4:58 D '87. David Vernier and Andrew Taylor (200w)

6038. Hymn to St. Cecilia, Opus 27; Five Flower Songs, Opus 47; Sacred and Profane, Opus 91; A Wealden Trio; The Sycamore Tree; A Shepherd's Carol.
Quink Vocal Ensemble.
ETCETERA 1017 AAD 45:11

✔HC ★*Awards:* Top Choices—1989, *American Record Guide* Ja/F '90 (Charles Parsons).

"When the five very accomplished vocalists of Quink first turned up on LP in this Britten selection, *Fanfare* 7:6, pp. 145-46, I greeted them with unalloyed approval....I find my enjoyment of their polished manner and considerable spirit undiminished."

Fanfare 12:142 Ja/F '89. John Wiser (185w)

"It's almost like hearing these works with new ears, so refreshing and beguiling is their singing. This is a simply stunning recording."

American Record Guide 52:41 Ja/F '89. Charles H. Parsons (85w)

"My particular favorites are the *Hymn to Saint Cecilia*, the *Mediaeval Carol* and the *Shepherd's Carol*, but every piece is superbly sung. A quite exceptional disc."

Organists' Review 75:44 Mr '89. Richard Popple (340w)

"I recommend this disc both for its unusual selection of music and the sophisticated performance. The close miking of the singers gives the listener a very immediate and intimate experience with the music of Britten."

HighPerformanceReview 6:73 Je '89. George S. T. Chu (250w)

6039. War Requiem, Opus 66; Sinfonia da Requiem, Opus 20; Ballad of Heroes, Opus 14.
Richard Hickox (c). Heather Harper (sop); Philip Langridge (ten); Martyn Hill (ten); John Shirley-Quirk (bar). Saint Paul's Cathedral Choir; London Symphony Chorus and Orchestra. St. Jude's Church NW11; texts and translation included. February 1991.
CHANDOS 8983/4 DDD 125:00 2 discs

✔HC ★★★*Awards:* Pick of the Month, North American Perspective (Christie Barter), *Gramophone* N '91. Critics' Choice 1991, *Gramophone*, Ja '92 (Alan Blyth; Richard Osborne).

"The Boys of Paul's outdo themselves...their execution, Hickox's controlled interpretation, and Chando's engineering skill are a close match to the original version [of the War Requiem]...This package offers full measure-...with two substantial fillers."

Fanfare 15:188-9 Ja/F '92. J. F. Weber (long)

"Hickox and his production team have, I think, largely triumphed [in *War Requiem*]. The immediacy and bloomed sound character, the disposition of choirs—robust choristors and organ (Roderick Elms) are ethereally diffused at the far depths of St. Jude's—excite the senses; the chamber orchestra is spread wide, close at the front...Heather Harper is at her warm human best in the coda to the Requiem...Philip Langridge is, for me, conscientious, accurate, but rather grey-sounding with a narrow range of colour...Shirley Quirk is simply magnificent-...*Sinfonia da Requiem* is sensationally balanced to match what now (surely?) must be regarded as its merely sensationalist nature...*Heroes* proves a rather likeable work."

P95/85/100/85/95/95 S100/95/75/100/95

Hi-Fi News & Record Review 36:96 D '91. Christopher Breunig (long)

"There is no doubt in my mind that this is Hickox's finest venture to date—even more assured than his Elgar recordings....Hickox's firm direction evidently gives all performers the confidence and inspiration to give memorable performances, for all do. To hear Heather Harper sing on disc the work whose first performance she gave is to hear Britten himself at work; to hear John Shirley-Quirk in such superb form is equally exciting. The dramatic and beautiful singing of Philip Langridge is just right for the part. The LS chorus is crisper than it sometimes appears to be and greatly enhanced by having the St. Paul's Choristers 'in the gallery'. The LSO seem not just in good form, but committed to the experience (as one does not always get the impression they are for this conductor)....A must for all musicians."

Organists' Review 76:54-5 Mr '92. Paul Hale (long)

Gramophone 69:136 N '91. Alan Blyth (long)

Digital Audio's CD Review 8:54 Mr '92. Octavio Roca (long)

BRUCKNER, ANTON

6040. Mass No. 2 in E minor for Chorus and Brass; Afferentur Regi; Ave Maria (1861); Ave Maria (1882); Ecce Sacerdos Magnus; Locus Iste; Aequali for Three Trombones, No.'s 1 and 2.
Simon Halsey (c). Anne-Marie Owens (mez). City of Birmingham Symphony Chorus; Birmingham Symphony Orchestra Wind Ensemble. Great Hall, Birmingham University. March 1990.
CONIFER 192 DDD 64:00

★*Awards:* Critics' Choice 1991, *Gramophone*, Ja '92 (Michael Kennedy).

"All [the seven pieces in addition to the Mass] are well done, particularly the magnificent *Ecce sacerdos magnus*...Halsey's would be my first recommendation for the *E minor Mass*. It is on a par with Best's recording and includes more generous couplings."

American Record Guide 54:55 S/O '91. Paul L. Althouse (med)

"The start of the *Mass* is inspired and its performance here it utterly magical....I enjoyed every minute of this programme; it comes up fully to Matthew Best's memorable Corydon Singers' performance."

Organists' Review 76:138+ Je '91. Paul Hale (265w)

"The recording here is notable for the precise blending of voices both within themselves and when set against the brass....Simon Halsey cannot be said to take Herreweghe's 'urgent' view of the work...To some extent the couplings choose themselves because of the brass accompaniments...Both are sung beautifully, but unfortunately the works, listed (chronologically) as tracks 9 and 10 are actually performed on tracks 10 and 9 respectively....but it need not detract from the overall pleasure given by this nobly performed, grandly recorded presentation." *P95 S95/85*

Hi-Fi News & Record Review 36:89+ Mr '91. Antony Hodgson (180w)

Gramophone 68:1394 Ja '91. Michael Kennedy (365w)

Te Deum. See No. 6035.

DURUFLE, MAURICE

6041. Requiem, Opus 9. FAURE, GABRIEL. Requiem, Opus 48.
Robert Shaw (c). Judith Blegen (sop); James Morris (bass). Atlanta Symphony Chorus and Orchestra.
TELARC 80135 DDD 74:00

> ★★★*Awards:* The Want List 1988, *Fanfare* N/D '88 (George Chien). Records to Die for: 1 of 5 Recommended Recordings, *Stereophile* Ja '91 (Lewis Lipnick). The Super Compact Disk List, *The Absolute Sound*, Ap '92 (Harry Pearson).

"These are fine performances, treated in a manner more American than French, and magnificently recorded."

Stereophile 10:154 O '87. Harold Lynn (280w)

"Unequivocally splendid in every respect."

High Fidelity 37:80 N '87. Bill Zakariasen (210w)

"Warmly expressive singing...distinguished playing, and superb recording."

Opus 4:53 D '87. John Canarina (140w)

"Robert Shaw's name is almost a guarantee of excellence. The Duruflework, derived from Faure, has never sounded better in a recording and on one long (75 minute!) CD, the combination of the two is ideal."

American Record Guide 51:35 Mr/Ap '88. William L. Purcell (105w)

"These are subtle and deeply felt performances and highly recommended."

HighPerformanceReview 5:79 S '88. George S. T. Chu (235w)

"These performances of two great requiem masses have yet, in my opinion, to be equaled on recording....Sonics are excellent, with natural depth and width, and no highlighting (as with all Telarc releases)."

Stereophile 14:157 Ja '91. Lewis Lipnick (b.n.)

"By no means as expansive and overtly spiritual as some of its recorded rivals...Shaw's Faure makes its points with directness and simplicity...The lesser-known Durufle work gets, if anything, even more committed treatment."

Ovation 9:39 Je '88. John Von Rhein (270w)

"Overall, Shaw has given us a very fine, understated performance. I continue to prefer Rutter's reconstruction of Faure's original version, but Shaw's performance is a viable option for anyone who wants to hear the traditional version....Of the three Durufle *Requiems* I've heard on compact discs, this one is a clear winner over Corboz/Erato, but it's not so easy to choose between it and Best/Hyperion."

Fanfare 11:200-1 S/O '87. George Chien (560w)

Gramophone 65:608 O '87 Nicholas Anderson (585w)

ELGAR, EDWARD

6042. The Apostles, Opus 49.
Richard Hickox (c). Alison Hargan (sop); Alfreda Hodgson (contr); David Rendall (ten); Bryn Terfel (bass); Stephen Roberts (bass); Robert Lloyd (bass). London Symphony Chorus and Orchestra. St. Jude's Church. March 1990.
CHANDOS 8875/6 DDD 127:00 2 discs

> ★*Awards:* Best of the Month, *Hi-Fi News & Record Review*, Ap '91.

"The orchestra plays with great refinement—and, where necessary, with tremendous *eclat*. He is well served by his team of soloists...The choir is in good form, although the male semichorus still suffers from that unblending earnestness which I have mentioned before. A fine version then, whose many qualities and glorious recorded sound will earn it friends and lovers."

Organists' Review 76:54 Mr '91. Paul Hale (545w)

"It is difficult to find fault with this set. What minor misgivings I do have are more to do with the work itself, which is not a patch on *Gerontius*." *P95/100 S95/100*

Hi-Fi News & Record Review 36:84 Ap '91. Andrew Achenbach (200w)

"If you like Elgar, you will love this one."

American Record Guide 54:56 My/Je '91. Charles Parsons (310w)

"I do admit that there is a good deal of beautiful music in *The Apostles*, even though it is sickly'd o'er with Victorian religiosity and inflated by British Empire Grandiosity. This new recording unfortunately emphasizes the religiosity and grandiosity at the expense of the beauty, in part because Hickox chooses such gruelingly slow tempos and in part because his soloists sound like such a stiff-necked, proper-British bunch."

Fanfare 14:207-8 Mr/Ap '91. David Johnson (950w)

Gramophone 68:1244 D '90. Michael Kennedy (535w)

6043. The Dream of Gerontius (oratorio), Opus 38; Sea Pictures, for Contralto and Orchestra, Opus 37.
John Barbirolli (c). Janet Baker (mez); Richard Lewis (ten); Kim Borg (bass). Halle Choir; Sheffield Philharmonic Chorus; Ambrosian Singers; London Symphony Orchestra; Halle Orchestra. 1965.
EMI 63185 ADD 122:00 2 discs

"This wonderful version, for many people still the definitive performance, comes up ever fresh and should win many more admirers."

Organists' Review 76:53 Mr '90. Paul Hale (105w)

Music and Musicians International 38:40-1 Ag '90. Lewis Foreman (420w)

Gramophone 67:1183-84 D '89. Alan Blyth (475w)

6044. The Dream of Gerontius (oratorio), Opus 38.

Simon Rattle (c). Janet Baker (sop); John Mitchinson (ten); John Shirley-Quirk (bar). City of Birmingham Symphony Chorus; City of Birmingham Symphony Orchestra. The Great Hall, Birmingham University. September 1986.
EMI 49549 DDD 95:00 2 discs

★*Awards: Hi-Fi News & Record Review* Record of the Month, F '88.

"No praise can be too high for Rattle's achievement. I have spoken of wonderment, awe, mystery. Rarely can Elgar's ever-resourceful orchestrations have sounded quite as beautiful or as lucid as they do here."

Hi-Fi News & Record Review 33:93 F '88. Edward Seckerson (735w)

"As in all his interpretations Rattle gets right to what he perceives as the heart of the work-...He extracts some wonderful playing from the CBSO...Dare I say that I am somewhat less happy with the soloists?...It would not be my only recording of this work, but Rattle's insights make it a must for a comparative version."

Organists' Review 74:251 Jl '88. Paul Hale (290w)

"In summary, with but a few reservations, this recording can be recommended as the 'modern' *Gerontius* to own."

Fanfare 12:148-50 S/O '88. Walter Simmons (750w)

Digital Audio 5:78+ D '88. Roland Graeme (425w)

Music and Musicians International 38:40-1 Ag '90. Lewis Foreman (420w)

Gramophone 65:1113 Ja '88. Alan Blyth (865w)

FASCH, JOHANN FRIEDRICH. Music of Fasch. See No. 1145.

FAURE, GABRIEL

6045. Requiem, Opus 48.

John Rutter (c). Caroline Ashton; Stephen Varcoe. Cambridge Singers; Members of the City of London Sinfonia.
COLLEGIUM 101 DDD 41:14

✔**HC** ★★★★*Awards: Gramophone* Record Award Winner 1985—Choral Award. *Fanfare* Want List 1986 (Aaron M. Shatzman; Adrian Corleonis; George Chien).

"Not only highly recommended, but basic and indispensable."

Fanfare 9:139 Ja/F '86. Adrian Corleonis (250w)

This is a recording "of great beauty and devotion."

Music Journal 26 Spring '86. Bert Wechsler (70w)

"There have been better-played performances, to be sure, but this is perhaps the most wholly satisfying one ever to appear on record."

High Fidelity 36:68-9 Ap '86. Terry Teachout (225w) (rev. of cassette)

"No other recording of liturgical music exudes the wrapped, voluptuous mysticism of French Roman Catholicism the way this one does."

Stereo Review 50:79 O '85. Stoddard Lincoln (275w)

Digital Audio 2:54-5 Ap'86. David Vernier (175w)

Ovation 7:34-5 My '86. Paul Turok (260w)

Requiem, Opus 48. See No. 6041.

FINZI, GERALD

6046. Choral Music: All This Night, Opus 33; Let Us Now Praise Famous Men, Opus 35; Lo, the Full, Final Sacrifice, Opus 26; Magnificat, Opus 36; Seven Partsongs, Opus 17; Though Did'st Delight My Eyes, Opus 32; Three Anthems, Opus 27; Three Short Elegies, Opus 5; White-Flowering Days, Opus 37.

Paul Spicer (c). Harry Bicket (orgn). Finzi Singers. Texts included.
CHANDOS 8936 DDD 79:00

★*Awards:* The Want List 1991, *Fanfare* N/D '91 (Robert McColley).

"This disc easily established itself on my 1991 Want List....This is a splendid record in every respect."

Fanfare 15:319 N/D '91. Robert McColley (med)

"In what is both a chronologically wide-ranging and exceptionally well-filled collection from Chandos, the excellent Finzi Singers under the direction of Paul Spicer give beautifully prepared renditions of some of the finest choral offerings by their adopted namesake....a lovely disc." *P95 S95*

Hi-Fi News & Record Review 36:99 N '91. Andrew Achenbach (med)

"Paul Spicer's choir sings with just the right style to straddle the stylistic differences between the secular works...This record is a must for lovers of English music, let alone for all Finzi followers."

Organists' Review 76:302 D '91. Paul Hale (med)

"The works here represent Finzi's best choral writing and are a fine introduction for those who know him only by his Clarinet Concerto-....The choral blend is usually lovely except that on several occasions the altos throw it off. The organ accompaniments of Harry Bicket are frankly uneven, with a tendency towards a sameness of registration that is often too full for the chamber-like sound of the chorus....The diction is perfectly acceptable but would have benefitted from a less resonant acoustic. As usual, it seems as if I am dwelling on the negatives. Don't let this deter you from listening to and enjoying this program. You are unlikely to hear these works together on one disc again by performers so committed to portraying this composer's works in the best light possible."

American Record Guide 55:56-7 Mr/Ap '92. David Bower (long)

Gramophone 69:110 S '91. John Steane (med)

6047. Intimations of Immortality, Opus 29; Grand Fantasia and Toccata in D minor, Opus 38.
Richard Hickox (c). Philip Langridge (ten); Philip Fowke (pno). Liverpool Philharmonic Choir; Royal Liverpool Philharmonic Orchestra.
EMI 49913 DDD 61:00

★*Awards:* The Year's Best, *Hi Fi News & Record Review*, May '90 Supplement.

"If you already know *Intimations of Immortality* through the 1975 Lyrita recording...be assured that, on the basis of vastly superior choral and orchestral execution, this new release represents a distinct and significant improvement. Need I say more?"

Fanfare 14:196-97 Ja/F '91. Walter Simmons (350w)

"*Intimations of Immortality* is a setting of lines from Wordsworth's ode and throughout its 45m duration Finzi's sure sense of form and a wide range of moods sustain the listener's interest....I found the many havens of utter tranquillity and all of the final stanza deeply moving, especially in a performance as good as this one...Philip Fowke plays his part brilliantly [in the Grand Fantasia and Toccata], but the recording cannot disguise his sometimes steely tone....A rewarding disc." *P95/100 S95/85*

Hi-Fi News & Record Review 35:104 Mr '90; p.21-22 My '90 Supplement. Andrew Achenbach (410w)

Gramophone 67:1504 F '90. Michael Kennedy (300w)

GABRIELI, ANDREA. Music of Gabrieli. See No. 6048.

GABRIELI, GIOVANNI

6048. Music of Gabrieli: "A Venetian Coronation 1595" (ceremonial music by Andrea and Giovanni Gabrieli sequenced to to take the form of a Coronation Mass).
Paul McCreesh (c). Gabrieli Consort and Players.
VIRGIN 91110 DDD 71:17

✔HC ★★*Awards:* The Want List 1990, *Fanfare* N/D '90 (George Chien); Early Music Record Award 1990, *Gramophone* D '90.

"The disc opens with the ringing of church bells, which would have signaled the election of the new doge to the populace. The service follows, with twenty-eight musical numbers—organ intonations, instrumental fanfares and canzonas, polyphonic mass movements, and chants—given in liturgical context...The performances are excellent throughout....In many respects, this is the most interesting Gabrieli disc to date. Don't miss it!"

Fanfare 14:229-30 N/D '90. George Chien (300w)

"All the music is ordered and executed according to the liturgical styles and conventions of Renaissance Venice. The recording was made in Brinkburn Priory, Northumberland, England. Singers and instrumentalists (along with four organs) were placed around the building in accordance with indications in the written music and the traditions of St. Mark's....I applaud Virgin Classics for the quality of both the planning and execution of this project, and highly recommend it."

American Record Guide 53:58 N/D '90. Catherine Moore (400w)

"McCreesh and his Gabrieli Consort and Players have attempted to re-create one of these Venetian blowouts which took place in 1595 for the coronation of a popular new doge....one of the main organists of the time, Giovanni Gabrieli, provided much of the large-scale music, and his uncle Andrea provided most of the rest. The stirring sound of the younger Gabrieli's brass canzonas made them landmarks of instrumental music....Altogether a most fascinating album to bend the ear of even recalcitrant early music listeners." *P90 S90*

Audio 75:92+ F '91. John Sunier (465w)

GESUALDO, DON CARLO

6049. Lecons de Tenebres for Holy Saturday; Motets: Ave, dulcissima Maria; Precibus et meritis beatae Mariae; Ave, regina coelorum; Maria, mater gratiae.
Peter Phillips (c). The Tallis Scholars. 1987.
ABBEY-GIMELL 015 DDD 52:00

✔HC ★*Awards:* Editors' Choice, *Digital Audio's CD Review*, Je '89; Perfect 10s, *Digital Audio's CD Review*, Mr '89.

"The Tallis Scholars perform all with self-effacing beauty and perfect tuning."

Organists' Review 74:253 Jl '88. Paul Hale (190w)

"It must be stated immediately that the Tallis Scholars are by far the most technically secure and ingratiating of any group that has recorded these pieces...Comparison with the Deller recordings...reveals the vocal progress that has been made over the past 20 years in this repertoire."

American Record Guide 51:45-6 S/O '88. Arved Ashby (490w)

"Possibly the best issue yet from Peter Phillips and the Tallis Scholars."

Hi-Fi News & Record Review 33:95 S '88. Stephen Pettitt (250w)

"Highly recommendable."
High Fidelity 38:81-2 N '88. Christopher Rothko (170w)

"I have already pulled out all stops in praising Gimell's release of the Tallis Scholars' superb recording of three works by Josquin des Pres-...This one measures up to it."
Musical America 108:55-6 N '88. Paul Moor (325w)

Gramophone 65:989 D '87. John Milsom (350w)

Fanfare 11:167-8 Jl/Ag '88. J. F. Weber (500w)

Digital Audio 5:46 S '88. David C. Vernier (285w)

6050. Madrigals: Ahi, disperata vita; Sospirava il mio cor; O malnati messaggi; Non t'amo, o voce ingrata; Luci serene e chiare; Sparge la morte al mio Signor nel viso; Arde il mio cor; Occhi del mio cor vita; Merce grido piangendo; Asciugate i begli ochi; Se la mia morte brami; Io parto; Ardita Zanzaretta; Ardo per te, mio bene. **Canzon francese; Io tacero; Corrente.**
William Christie (c). Les Arts Florissants Vocal and Instrumental Ensemble. July 1987.
HARMONIA MUNDI 901268 DDD 54:54

✔HC ★*Awards:* Critics' Choice 1988, *Gramophone* D '88 (Iain Fenlon).

"The singing is always expressive, the voices perfectly balanced and in tune....The sound is clean and close-up."
Fanfare 12:156 S/O '88. J. F. Weber (240w)

"Their rendering of Gesualdo's work is of stunning ensemble, with impressive warmth and sympathy for this challenging musical fare-....As a traversal of Gesualdo's astonishing art—yes, astonishing even to our jaded ears—this album by Les Arts Florissants is a stunner-....A final note: If you are already tired of the white, pure sound of the Tallis Scholars, you will discover that, indeed, there *are* vocal groups breathing irresistible life into Renaissance music. This Arts Florissants CD will be a revelation."
Audio 72:168 D '88. Christopher Greenleaf (725w)

"Their utter confidence in spinning-out lines typically rife with dissonances completely avoids any risk of their sounding incompetent-...or of the expressive, naturalistic word-setting seeming unwieldy....Sparkling recorded sound too makes this release irresistible."
Hi-Fi News & Record Review 34:114 Ap '89. Helena Stoward (175w)

"The performances...beautifully demonstrate the group's ability to put across this highly mannered and difficult music....full texts with English translations. A splendid package altogether."
Stereo Review 54:90 Ag '89. Stoddard Lincoln (175w)

"At its best, Les Arts Florissants displays a sensitivity that does full justice to the works-....Sometimes a recurrent 'white,' hooting, tone quality becomes unpleasant and disturbing to the ear. The lower voices fortunately avoid this affliction....Recorded sound is clear, but the perspective a bit close."
HighPerformanceReview 5:78-9 D '88. June C. Ottenberg (230w)

Digital Audio 5:46 S '88. David C. Vernier (225w)

Gramophone 66:654 O '88. Iain Fenlon (355w)

6051. Responsories for Tenebrae; Benedictus; Miserere.
Hilliard Ensemble. Douai Abbey, England.
ECM 1422/3; ECM 843 867 DDD 76:41; 47:03 2 discs

✔HC ★★*Awards:* Disc Of The Month, *Digital Audio's CD Review*, O '91 (David Vernier). Editors' Choice—Best CDs of the Year, *Digital Audio's CD Review*, Je '92. Best of the Month, *Hi-Fi News & Record Review*, Ag '91.

"Some of the most searingly expressive music of all time, performed immaculately in a perfect acoustic....As is becoming a habit with this company, the literature provided in the beautifully produced booklet is enigmatic in the extreme...Still, this is but one blemish in what must surely be regarded as a further triumph for this most enterprising of ensembles." *P100 S100*
Hi-Fi News & Record Review 36:71 Ag '91. Simon Cargill (280w)

"Hilliard's style is almost uniquely right; if this is not how the composer heard the music, it is at least faithful to [Gesualdo's]...intentions."
Stereophile 14:247+ O '91. Les Berkley (med)

"How do the Hilliard Ensemble and ECM fare vis-a-vis the music itself?...magnificently. There's a wonderfully limpid quality to the voices and a deeply resonant ambience that belies the supposed brittleness of digital CD recording. The main quibble relates to the rationale behind packaging liturgical music in this highly cosmeticized and decontextualized way-....Wonderful music, but we need a bit more of a hand than this affords, lest it just becomes an exotic lifestyle accessory."
The Wire 88:56 Je '91. Brian Morton (long)

"As the only complete set now available on CD...the Hilliard group does put an aural magnifying glass to the music. It neatly complements the Montserrat version's special strength, and hearing both in turn is rewarding. The sound has great presence."
Fanfare 14:162-3 Jl/Ag '91. J. F. Weber (540w)

"These singers are so caught up in this music that one is drawn in with them. The textures are kept lucid and clean, while the singers take advantage of all the harmonic clashes and tensions of Gesualdo's often mannered but powerfully expressive and highly personal art."

American Record Guide 54:66-7 N/D '91. Carl Bauman (long)

Gramophone 69:97-8 Mr '92. Iain Fenlon (long)

GRIEG, EDVARD

6052. Fire Salmer (Four Psalms), for Baritone and Mixed Chorus, Opus 74. MENDELSSOHN, FELIX. Psalms (3), for Baritone and Mixed Chorus, Opus 78.
Terje Kvam (c). Hagegard Hakan (bar). Oslo Cathedral Choir. Oslo.
NIMBUS 5171 DDD 45:00

★*Awards:* Critics' Choice 1989, *Gramophone* D '89 (Mary Berry).

"The Grieg psalms...are works of supreme beauty...The Oslo Cathedral Choir sings these masterworks of the Norwegian choral repertoire as to the manner born...The three Mendelssohn psalms...have been recorded several times...I last reviewed them in a powerful performance by the Stuttgart Chamber Chorus-...The Oslo Cathedral Choir is no less eloquent an advocate of these psalm settings...and perhaps a bit stronger in its semi-choir of soloists."
Fanfare 13:222-23 N/D '89. David Johnson (525w)

"These are fine works, well served by this recording, and deserve wider dissemination."
The Musical Times 130:752-53 D '89. Antony Bye (285w)

"While not a blockbuster either musically or sonically, this [is an] attractive release...The *a cappella* performances are all first-rate. Hagegard is a sensitive, moving soloist in the Grieg...the sonics are good: spacious but not over-reverberant. Texts and translations are included."
American Record Guide 52:57-8 S/O '89. Kurt Moses (200w)

Gramophone 67:215 Jl '89. Mary Berry (250w)

HANDEL, GEORGE FRIDERIC

6053. Athalia.
Christopher Hogwood (c). Joan Sutherland; Emma Kirkby; Aled Jones; James Bowman; Anthony Rolfe-Johnson; David Thomas. New College Choir, Oxford; Academy of Ancient Music.
OISEAU-LYRE 417 126 121:39 2 discs

★★*Awards:* *Gramophone* Choral Award, 1987. *Opera News* Best of the Year, 1987.

"Bravos to all concerned!"
American Record Guide 50:19-20 Fall '87. David W. Moore (640w)

"There is little I don't like about this set....My listening partner, herself a chorister, described herself as 'paralyzed' by the proficiency of the Choir of New College as they leaped out of the Allisons and into our (collective) heart. Choirmaster Edward Higginbottom may be the unsung star of this star-studded show."
Fanfare 10:120-1 Jl/Ag '87 Edward Strickland (650w)

"The piping voice of Emma Kirkby (Josabeth), a baroque instrument in itself, matches the Handel line and the timbre of the Academy of Ancient Music, but the cavernous sonic ambience of St. Jude's Church, London, tends to muddy the textures. Christopher Hogwood's leadership provides resourcefully judged animation."
Opera News 52:64 O '87. John W. Freeman (290w)

"Emma Kirkby sings the role purely, brightly, fully, clearly, with perfect intonation. And if, despite all that, I don't respond with much enthusiasm, set it down to prejudice against what strikes me as rather sexless and somehow 'English' singing....on the whole Hogwood's pacing and progress are eloquent."
Opus 3:54-5 O '87. Andrew Porter (1250w)

Ovation 8:34 Ap '87 David Patrick Stearns (270w)

Stereo Review 52:112+ Je '87 Stoddard Lincoln (280w)

Gramophone 64:736 N '86 Stanley Sadie (665w) (rev. of LP); 64:1169 F '87 John Borwick (210w)

Hi-Fi News & Record Review 31:119 D '86 Hugh Canning (263w)

6054. Brockes-Passion (St. John Passion).
Nicholas McGegan (c). Maria Zadori; Katalin Farkas; Drew Minter; Martin Klietmann. Capella Savaria.
HUNGAROTON 12734/6 3 discs

✔HC ★*Awards:* *Fanfare* Want List 1987 (David Johnson).

"What, I wondered, could state-of-the-art period style do to lift the old battle-axe's face?-...she has emerged gleaming, lithe, buoyant, athletic, and vivacious. A miracle! Never have I run across a more magnificent testimonial to the power of late-twentieth-century 'historically informed' performance practice to enliven, to renew...Nor did I ever expect the finest period band in the world to turn up in Hungary, but that's what the Capella Savaria sounds like here."
Opus 4:40-1 D '87. Richard Taruskin (1105w)

"The performance shows Handel to have been the Liszt of his day, unafraid of bold ideas, eager to use traditional forces in gripping new ways."
Opera News 11:43 Ja 31 '87 John W. Freeman (90w)

"My first reaction on receiving this album for review was, 'Why another *Brockes* Passion? Didn't the 1967 DG recording do the job?'-...What struck me at once, even before putting Side I of the new Hungaroton edition on the turntable, was that the timings for the two recordings are staggeringly contradictory....DG's conductor, August Wenzinger, takes every-

thing at what now sounds a snail's pace, although I was beatifically satisfied with his tempos until Nicholas McGegan taught me differently....As for the singers, they are not so famous as DG's roster but they are, with a few exceptions, even better."
Fanfare 10:117-19 Ja/F '87 David Johnson (1125w) (rev. of LP)

"A beautiful score, excitingly realized and finely presented."
Hi-Fi News & Record Review 32:107 F '87 Peter Branscombe (345w) (rev. of LP)

"The cover art and design are lovely, the program notes require a separate, 100 page booklet, and both the jewel box and booklet are enclosed in a matching slip case. Simply first rate. And the recording itself, happily, is nothing less."
American Record Guide 51:42 Mr/Ap '88. Amy Stearns (357w)

Gramophone 64:916 D '86 Nicholas Anderson (1050w)

6055. Cantatas for Various Voices and Instruments: Tu Fedel? Tu Costante?; Mi Palpita Il Cor; Alpestre Monte; Tra le Fiamme.
Christopher Hogwood (c). Christopher Hogwood (harpsichord) Emma Kirkby. Academy of Ancient Music.
OISEAU-LYRE 414 473 54:36

★★***Awards:*** *Gramophone* Critics' Choice 1986 (Stanley Sadie); *Gramophone* Critics' Choice 1986 (Nicholas Anderson).

"In these four delightful Italian cantatas, Kirkby is in glorious voice...this is inspired music-making of very high order."
Audio 71:153 Je '87 Bert Whyte (200w)

"I urge not only her many international admirers, but also those who may not have taken to the sound of her voice hitherto, to hear this 1985 recording. It strikes me as excellent."
Hi-Fi News & Record Review 31:119 My '86. Stephen Daw (175w)

"To hear Emma Kirkby backed up by Hogwood's authentic instruments is to know what the 1980s has to offer in Handel interpretation. It's not just her voice...or the sounds of appropriate instruments, but the refined insight of both the singer and Hogwood....The digital engineering is exquisite."
Fanfare 10:153-4 S/O '86 J.F. Weber (330w)

"Emma Kirkby sings stylishly and sensitively-...her pert piping can be wearying, but then this isn't a program to absorb all at one sitting."
Ovation 8:40-41 F '87 Scott Cantrell (190w)

Opus 3:53 D '86 James Parsons (85w)

Opera News 51 (4):81 O '86. John W. Freeman (50w)

6056. Chandos Anthems, No.'s 1-3: O Be Joyful; In the Lord Put I My Trust; Have Mercy upon Me.
(Volume 1).
Harry Christophers (c). Lynne Dawson (sop); Ian Partridge (ten); Michael George (bass). Sixteen Choir; Sixteen Orchestra. St. Jude's Church, London. November and December 1987.
CHANDOS 8600 DDD 61:14

"These are definitive performances, lovingly and warmly recorded by producer Martin Compton and engineer Antony Howell...The acoustical venue, St. Jude's Church in London...has never sounded more flattering to a composer's intentions, or to the performers'."
Audio 74:102+ F '90. Christopher Greenleaf (275w)

"These performances are so musical and *sensible* in approach that I defy anyone not be moved by their sheer beauty....The players, choirs and soloists are faultless."
Organists' Review 75:279 D '89. Paul Hale (b.n.)

Harry Christophers's "ideas seem to spring mainly from the words (as did Handel's), and his choir and orchestra execute them with unusual grace and lyricism while never neglecting the music's rhythmic vitality. Given an extra sheen by the resonance of the recording locale, the vocal soloists are quite attractive, the standout being tenor Ian Partridge."
Stereo Review 54:90 Ag '89. David Patrick Stearns (300w)

"Lynne Dawson performs superbly in any repertory and I feel that Ian Partridge's light tenor sound is well-suited to this sort of music....The brilliance of The Sixteen's sound is reduced by the spacious acoustic of St. Jude's church, London, and this occasionally jumbles the more rapid sections."
Hi-Fi News & Record Review 34:107 Ap '89. William McVicker (300w)

"Despite some reservations about Partridge...a good, satisfying beginning to what is promised as a complete series of the eleven anthems."
American Record Guide 52:47 Jl/Ag '89. Paul L. Althouse (230w)"Notes and texts are fine...I hope further volumes are swiftly forthcoming, but there's no need to wait. This is as good a place to start as any."

Fanfare 12:209 My/Je '89. J. F. Weber (425w)

"What it lacks in terms of sheer sparkle it makes up for in a clean, straightforward and reliable performance. I personally find that the playing, singing particularly from the soloists...has a mellifluous quality that at times perhaps detracts from the sheer rhythmic vitality. These points are, however, comparatively minor."
Music and Musicians International 37:58 Mr '89. Jeremy Walbank (340w)

Digital Audio's CD Review 5:56+ Ap '89. Nigel Reid (225w)

Gramophone 66:1323 F '89. Nicholas Anderson (360w)

6057. Chandos Anthems, No.'s 4-6: O Sing unto the Lord; I Will Magnify Thee; As Pants the Hart.
(Volume 2).
Harry Christophers (c). Lynne Dawson (sop); Ian Partridge (ten). Sixteen Choir; Sixteen Orchestra. October 1988.
CHANDOS 0504 DDD 59:00

"These are definitive performances, lovingly and warmly recorded by producer Martin Compton and engineer Antony Howell...The acoustical venue, St. Jude's Church in London...has never sounded more flattering to a composer's intentions, or to the performers'."
Audio 74:102+ F '90. Christopher Greenleaf (275w)

"Critics who sniff at the lovely white tones of Emma Kirkby will find Dawson's warmer vocal output very much to their liking. All elements of this ensemble come together nicely. Splendid engineering, tracks for each movement, more notes by Simon Heighes to match the quality of his work in the first disc, and printed texts leave nothing missing."
Fanfare 13:213 S/O '89. J. F. Weber (235w)

"Highly recommended."
American Record Guide 52:64 N/D '89. Paul L. Althouse (b.n.)

"Harry Christophers leads a stylish performance...They are not strongly emotive or emotional interpretations, but they are clearly Baroque in their conception and these recordings are an accurate and welcome addition to the catalog of Handel's works."
HighPerformanceReview 8(1):67 '91. George S. T. Chu (280w)

See Volume 1 for review excerpt.
Organists' Review 75:279 D '89. Paul Hale (b.n.)

Gramophone 67:349 Ag '89. Nicholas Anderson (315w)

6058. Chandos Anthems, No.'s 7-9.
(Volume 3).
Harry Christophers (c). Patrizia Kwella (sop); James Bowman (alto); Ian Partridge (ten); Michael George (bass). Sixteen Choir; Sixteen Orchestra.
CHANDOS 0505 DDD 75:00

"This started out as an admirable series, but the latest entry may be the most revealing and rewarding of the group....Be sure to give this a hearing."
Fanfare 13:185 My/Je '90. J. F. Weber (320w)

"These are fine performances; I would recommend them without reservations were it not for some balance problems between soloists and orchestra."
American Record Guide 53:52-3 Jl/Ag '90. Paul Laird (230w)

Gramophone 67:1504 F '90. Nicholas Anderson (460w)

6059. Coronation Anthems (4) for George II; Royal Fireworks Music.
Robert King (c). New College Choir, Oxford; King's Consort.
HYPERION 66350 DDD 57:00

✔HC ★*Awards:* The Want List 1990, *Fanfare* N/D '90 (George Chien).

"The sound is full and rich and the ensemble is superb....The balance and recording are of equal standard and the whole CD makes a very enjoyable concert. Recommended: well worth buying."
Organists' Review 76:50 Mr '90. Richard Popple (320w)

"This disc is worth hearing for no other reason than its sound, but King's performance is equally persuasive....a remarkable, exciting release....Highly recommended."
Fanfare 13:186-87 Mr/Ap '90. George Chien (350w)

"The first choral entry in Handel's anthem *Zakok the Priest* is one of the most thrilling moments in music, and Robert King makes it even more shattering than usual....*Musick for the Royal Fireworks* continues the atmosphere of grand celebration and the period instrument band plays the original wind version of the score...The spacious recording copes well with the huge forces and the wide lateral spread is exciting." *P95 S95*
Hi-Fi News & Record Review 35:87 Ap '90. Antony Hodgson (420w)

"What a bone-rattling good show these *Fireworks* are! This huge baroque wind band at A=415 pitch creates a unique sound....Using a much smaller ensemble in the *Coronation Anthems*...King still raises the roof."
American Record Guide 53:57 My/Je '90. Charles Parsons (120w)

Gramophone 67:1184-85 D '89. Stanley Sadie (560w)

6060. Dixit Dominus; Nisi Dominus; Salve Regina (anthem), for Soprano and Orchestra.
Simon Preston (c). Arleen Auger (sop); Lynne Dawson (sop); Diana Montague (mez); Leigh Nixon (ten); John Mark Ainsley (ten); Simon Birchall (bass). Westminster Abbey Choir; Westminster Abbey Orchestra.
DEUTSCHE GRAMMOPHON 423 594 DDD 56:00

★★*Awards:* Critics' Choice 1989, *Gramophone* D '89 (John Durate); Top Choices—1989, *American Record Guide* Ja/F '90 (Paul Althouse).

"Just a few months ago London issued their *Dixit*...Now from DG Archiv comes a *Dixit* with period instruments, better acoustics and soloists and full of irrepressible Handelian spirit....the soloists, led by an opulent Arleen Auger, are all you could ask for....this disc is an all-around winner."

American Record Guide 52:47 Jl/Ag '89. Paul L. Althouse (200w)

"Preston excels whether performing as solo organist or as conductor....This recording comes with a substantial 32-page insert and the packaging coupled with outstanding performances from everybody rates as [A*:1*]."

Hi-Fi News & Record Review 34:89 Mr '89. William McVicker (315w)

"I haven't heard all of the many recordings of *Dixit Dominus*, but even if Preston's were the only one, I'd suggest holding out for something better....I can't complain about Preston's orchestra, nor Archiv's sound. Notes, texts, and translations are included. Recommended only for the two short compositions."

Fanfare 12:210 My/Je '89. Ralph V. Lucano (500w)

Gramophone 66:1323-24 F '89. John Duarte (330w)

6061. Esther.

Christopher Hogwood (c). Patrizia Kwella; Anthony Rolfe-Johnson; Ian Partridge; Emma Kirkby. Westminster Cathedral Boys' Choir; Academy of Ancient Music.
OISEAU-LYRE 414 423

★*Awards:* *Gramophone* Critics' Choice 1986 (Lionel Salter).

"The performances are sensitive and generally light in tone...the whole production is on a fine level of expertise which should give joy to both devotees of original instruments and lovers of good musical performances."

American Record Guide 50:20-1 Fall '87. David W. Moore (480w)

"Despite its historical significance, *Esther* apparently never before has been recorded in its entirety—a fact that makes this issue especially welcome....Christopher Hogwood's forces are fully up to conveying *Esther*'s attractions." Review of Cassette.

High Fidelity 36:57-8 Ag '86. R. D. Darrell (225w)

"Everything the work has to offer, these performers render wholeheartedly....While there is certainly room for a rival approach—the later, augmented score, perhaps with modern instruments—this recording is not likely to be challenged for some time."

Opus 3:38 F '87 John W. Barker (825w)

Opera News 51 (4):81 O '86. John W. Freeman (175w)

The Opera Quarterly 4:96-99 Wint '86/87 John Schauer (760w)

Gramophone 63:820+ D '85. Lionel Salter (455w)

6062. Hercules.

John Eliot Gardiner (c). Jennifer Smith; Sarah Walker; Catherine Denley; Anthony Rolfe-Johnson. Monteverdi Choir; English Baroque Soloists. reissue 1983.
DEUTSCHE GRAMMOPHON 423 137 153:00 3 discs

★*Awards:* Best of the Year, *Opera News* D 24 '88.

"First-rate presentation underpins this readily recommendable issue."

Music and Musicians International 36:41 My '88. Robert Hartford (140w)

Gramophone 65:1114 Ja '88. Julie Anne Sadie (315w)

6063. Israel in Egypt; The Ways of Zion Do Mourn.

John Eliot Gardiner (c). Jean Knibbs; Marilyn Troth; Daryl Greene; Elisabeth Priday; Norma Burrowes; Christopher Royall; Ashley Stafford; Brian Gordon; Julain Clarkson; Charles Brett; Paul Elliott; William Kendall; Martyn Hill; Stephen Varcoe; Marilyn Sansom (cello); Michael Lewin (theorbo); Malcolm Hicks (organ); Alastair Ross (hpschd). Monteverdi Choir; Monteverdi Orchestra. January, 1980; May, 1979.
ERATO 88182 AAD 138:00 2 discs

★*Awards:* *Gramophone* Critics' Choice (John Duarte), 1987.

"Two superb Handel productions by John Eliot Gardiner have been joined to make two very full CDs. I reviewed both on LP in *Fanfare* 4:1 and 5:1...these analog recordings...have made splendid transfers, with no audible background noise."

Fanfare 11:213 S/O '87. J. F. Weber (350w)

"Though soloists from the Monteverdi Choir do their work well, interest centers on the phenomenal variety of forms, moods and styles developed by Handel for the veritable Red Sea of massed episodes, brilliantly executed by the choir."

Opera News 52:42-3 D 19 '87. John W. Freeman (225w)

"Everything about the recording is big—the choir, the orchestra, the acoustic—and to my tastes, it is too big....This sense of the grandiose is further enhanced by a recording space that is too large and too reverberant for Handel's part-writing to be heard clearly....*The Ways of Zion* fares somewhat better than the oratorio, but perhaps only because the somber nature of the piece tied Gardiner's hands a bit. The recording is still too reverberant, however, and the chorus too large."

Musical America 108:59 Mr '88. Christopher Rothko (340w)

Stereo Review Presents: Compact Disc Buyers' Guide p. 50 Spr '87 William Livingstone and Christie Barter (130w)

Gramophone 64:1585 My '87 John Duarte (195w)

6064. Israel in Egypt.

Andrew Parrott (c). Nancy Argenta (sop); Emily Van Evera (sop); Tim Wilson (alto); Anthony Rolfe-Johnson (ten); David Thomas (bass); Jeremy White (bass). Taverner Choir; Taverner Consort and Players. Au-

gust, September 1989.
EMI 54018 DDD 135:00 2 discs

★*Awards:* The Gramophone Awards, Nominations, Baroque—vocal, *Gramophone*, N '91.

"*Israel in Egypt* has seldom been recorded, and that makes this vibrant performance all the more welcome. Furthermore, Parrott's is the first to present the work complete, with Handel's 1737 funeral anthem for Queen Caroline altered and tacked on at the start, adding about 45 minutes of music to the score. And finally, it is performed on period instruments—again, a first on discs...This is a real pearl of a set; there'll be no need for another *Israel in Egypt* for quite some time."
Stereophile 14:237+ D '91. Robert Levine (long)

"There is little to analyze here—everything just feels right. By comparison, John Eliot Gardiner's exaggerated tempos, dynamics, and declamation (on Erato; OP) seem campy, and most other performances rather dull and staid."
Musical America 111:77-8 My '91. Christopher Rothko (420w)

"There are four CD recordings of *Israel in Egypt* to choose from, and after due consideration, I'm inclined to award first prize to Parrott....If you're not interested in 'The ways of Zion' (or, to be exact in this case, 'The sons of Israel'), consider buying Mackerras's recording first. If you want a three-part *Israel*, you won't do better than Parrott's."
Fanfare 14:232-3 Mr/Ap '91. Ralph V. Lucano (620w)

"All in all, although Mr. Dean [*Handel's dramatic Oratorios and Masques*] may not find *Israel in Egypt* to be Handel's finest oratorio, parts of it are marvellous indeed and this performance is simply excellent. I have enjoyed adding it to my collection and would encourage others to consider purchasing it."
Musick 13(2):28-9 Fall-Sept '91. J. Evan Kreider (long)

"This is the tenth recording of *Israel in Egypt* but only the second that is truly complete as Handel conceived it....It is, in all, a superlative job....The solo work easily matches the competition...What gives one pause is that Parrott's pacing is often a bit relaxed and sedate."
American Record Guide 54:74 Mr/Ap '91. John W. Barker (430w)

"Andrew Parrott draws a sound of great beauty and refinement from his stylish players and singers. Indeed this aspect of his approach is that which lingers at the end. For my money there is consequently some lack of excitement."
Organists' Review 76:54 Mr '91. Paul Hale (345w)

"Parrott's Taverner Choir is well up to the task...The colourful depictions of the various plagues are particularly effective."
Continuo 15:26 F '91. Scott Paterson (130w)

"Handel oratorios are great, you don't need me to tell you, but not when they are given plodding performances with no inner tension, energy, or drive....this set is a big disappointment."
HighPerformanceReview 8(2):72 Summer '91. Bert Wechsler (b.n.)

Gramophone 68:1545-6 F '91. Stanley Sadie (805w)

6065. Jeptha.
John Eliot Gardiner (c). Lynne Dawson (sop); Ruth Holton (sop); Anne-Sofie von Otter (mez); Michael Chance (alto); Nigel Robson (ten); Stephen Varcoe (bar); Alastair Ross (hpscd); Paul Nicholson (orgn). Monteverdi Choir; English Baroque Soloists. Stadthalle, Gottingen. June 13-16, 1988 live.
PHILIPS 422 351 DDD 158:00 3 discs

★★★*Awards:* The Want List 1989, *Fanfare* N/D '89 (James Camner); Choral Record Award 1989, *Gramophone*, D '89; Record of the Month, *Hi-Fi News & Record Review*, D '89. The Year's Best, *Hi Fi News & Record Review*, May '90 Supplement.

"Predictably, John Eliot Garnier's Handelian forces make the strongest case for the oratorio yet on record....An outstanding issue in every respect—only one of Zebul's arias is missing (hardly a great loss musically)—which I cannot recommend too highly." *P100 S95*
Hi-Fi News & Record Review 34:117 D '89; p.9-10 My '90 Supplement. Hugh Canning (590w)

"Tenor Nigel Robson, though his tone has little inherent sensuous charm or smoothness, negotiates his coloratura in workmanlike style and projects Jephtha's dilemma with a wide range of feeling, culminating in the softly spun 'Waft her, angels,' rich with poignant despair and sublime restraint....John Eliot Gardiner's tempos for the most part are crisp and objectively even, while the choral work has conspicuously clear textures and a happy resilience. As a result, the oratorio, despite a fundamental lack of event, moves along, holding one's interest with its generous musical variety."
Opera News 54:31 Ja 20 '90. John W. Freeman (305w)

"*Jephtha* is not really in a class with the greatest of the Handelian oratorios. In John Eliot Gardiner's hands, though, it comes closer to that level than anyone might expect....I was struck by how...Gardiner and his performers exalt this troubled work to remarkable heights-....From the sublime to the ridiculous. *Stereo Review*'s critic found this recording to be so bad as to disqualify the performance from recommendation. I don't know what he was listening to. (In the more liberal Sixties, I would have asked what he was on.) This is not audiophile treasure—live recordings seldom are—but it is certainly good enough for the purpose."
Stereophile 13:185+ My '90. Les Berkley (475w)

"The old Vanguard...despite the modern instruments and some excessively fast tempos makes a better case for *Jephtha* than does the new Philips. This is mainly owing to its superior casting...On the other hand, the singing of Gardiner's small chorus, with its preponderance of countertenors on the alto line, is impressive, as is Gardiner's pacing of the work in general....The libretto is printed in four languages."
Fanfare 13:225-27 N/D '89. David Johnson (1200w)

"With upwards of fifty other large dramatic works by Handel to choose from which have not been recorded on period instruments, why re-record [this work?]...In every other way-...[the recording] under review [is] exemplary."
Continuo 13:22 O '89. Scott Paterson (270w)

"Though the chorus sings splendidly, the recorded sound is so harsh and opaque that you can barely hear, much less enjoy, the music's inner details—and Gardiner's fast tempos sometimes seem to lack purpose." *P70 S60*
Stereo Review 54:145 S '89. David Patrick Stearns (175w)

Gramophone 67:73 Je '89. Stanley Sadie (770w)

6066. Joshua.
Rudolph Palmer (c). Julianne Baird (sop); D'Anna Fortunato (mez); John Aler (ten); John Ostendorf (bass). Palmer Singers; Brewer Chamber Orchestra.
NEWPORT CLASSIC 85515 DDD 121:00 2 discs

★★*Awards:* The Want List 1991, *Fanfare* N/D '91 (Ralph V. Lucano). Critics' Choice 1991, *Gramophone*, Ja '92 (Stanley Sadie).

"Put to torture, I might, by the time my toenails were torn out, confess to the Hyperion recording (King, The King's Consort) as the more musically enjoyable; after recovering, though, I might whisper, 'But then, if you want more dramatic thrust, more clarity..."
American Record Guide 54:74-5 N/D '91. John W. Barker (long)

The New York Times Jl 14 '91, p. 21 H. Gerald Gold (brief)

Digital Audio's CD Review 8:38 Ap '92. Octavio Roca (long)

6067. Messiah.
Ton Koopman (c). Marjanne Kweksilber; James Bowman; Paul Elliott; Gregory Reinhart. Sixteen Choir; Amsterdam Baroque Orchestra.
ERATO 88050 DDD 140:52 3 discs

★*Awards: Stereo Review* Best of the Month, My '85.

"Koopman gives the *Messiah* all the dignity and spaciousness the sacred text requires, but at the same time he dispels any heaviness with clarity of tone and with the inner vitality afforded by sharply etched articulation in the singing and playing."
Stereo Review 50:87 My '85. Stoddard Lincoln (500w)

"A lithe, thoughtful account of a masterpiece that thrives on different interpretations."
Hi-Fi News & Record Review 30:79 Jl '85. Peter Branscombe (190w)

Fanfare 8:186-8 Jl/Ag '85. John Bauman (295w)

Ovation 6:27-8 Ja '86. Scott Cantrell (360w)

Digital Audio 2:65-6 Ap '86. David Vernier (375w)

6068. Messiah.
Andrew Parrott (c). Emma Kirkby (sop); Emily Van Evera (sop); Margaret Cable (contr); James Bowman (alto); Joseph Cornwell (ten); David Thomas (bass). Taverner Choir; Taverner Players. April 1988.
EMI 49801 DDD 146:00 2 discs

★★*Awards:* Critic's Choice: 1990, *American Record Guide* Ja/F '91 (Allen Linkowski). Top Disks of the Year, *The New York Times* D 24, '89 (John Rockwell).

"Without any sacrifice of majesty, Mr. Parrott has directed an intimately scaled performance-...Whether this is the style of performance Handel heard is beside the point; it works."
The New York Times D 3 '89, p. 27 H. Barrymore L. Scherer (100w)

"In all, the experience is both moving and exciting. Warmly recommended as one man's highly perceptive vision of this visionary and timeless work."
Organists' Review 76:51 Mr '90. Paul Hale (835w)

"Although period instruments are used, the temptation to go for a 1784-style Handel Commemoration performance (which used 525 musicians) has been resisted; the model has been the *Messiah* which took place at the Foundling Hospital in the 1750s....the orchestra is bolder than the choir, and this has both positive and negative points...Of the soloists, Emma Kirkby and David Thomas are outstanding." *P100/95 S95*
Hi-Fi News & Record Review 35:87 Ap '90. William McVicker (490w)

"With a few minor exceptions (why must there always be some?), this is one of the finest period-instrument editions currently available. Those exceptions include soprano Emily van Evera...The recorded sound is top-flight, easily matching Pinnock's superb Archiv set for clarity and balance....In short, this is a very fine version that will satisfy. I'll still stick with Pinnock and Hogwood for period-instrument versions, Tobin for the fascinating insights he provides, Beecham for sheer musicianship and quality of performance despite his outrageously corrupt texts, and the old Davis (Philips Silver Line) and Shaw/Telarc for 'standard' versions."
Fanfare 13:196-97 Ja/F '90. John Bauman (350w)

"For most of the movements Parrott chooses tempos which for his reduced forces are fairly conventional....Balances are good, if a little orchestra-heavy; the sound is terrific...Trevor

Pinnock's version is similar to Parrott's in many respects, but more energetic and alive; I admire it more, I think, than Teri Noel Towe did in Nov/Dec 1989 and would award it my recommendation among period versions."
American Record Guide 53:56-7 Mr/Ap '90. Paul L. Althouse (700w)

"The performance itself is an agreeable one, I think, without being especially memorable."
Stereo Review 54:150 D '89. Richard Freed (350w)

Gramophone 67:951 N '89. Stanley Sadie (860w)

Digital Audio's CD Review 6:58-9 Ja '90. David Vernier (530w)

6069. Messiah.
Trevor Pinnock (c). Arleen Auger (sop); Anne-Sofie von Otter (mez); Michael Chance (alto); Howard Crook (ten); John Tomlinson (bass). English Concert Choir; English Concert.
DEUTSCHE GRAMMOPHON 423 630 DDD
150:00 2 discs

✔HC ★★*Awards:* Critics' Choice 1988, *Gramophone* D '88 (Edward Greenfield). The Want List 1989, *Fanfare* N/D '89 (Robert Levine).

"There are currently more than ten readings available on CD alone, and no two of them could be confused for one another....Many are valid and enjoyable. A couple are spectacular. This is one of them....The soloists are among the best on discs....The whole reading is softer-edged than most original-instrument readings, and it's enormously effective and beautiful-....The recording is flawless...my other favorite *Messiah*...uses modern instruments, larger forces, and opera singers. It's Andrew Davis's, with the Toronto Symphony (EMI CDS-7 49027-2)....No home should be without two *Messiahs*, and these may as well be the two."
Stereophile 12:189-90 D '89. Robert Levine (550w)

"This version, with minor reservations, is probably my favorite at present, though it won't satisfy those who are unalterably opposed to period-instrument performances....I'll not give up the delights of Tobin, Hogwood, Gardiner, Shaw, or the old Davis issues, but this is the one to buy if you are buying only one. At least this year!"
Fanfare 12:175-76 Mr/Ap '89. John Bauman (600w)

"What sounds a wonderfully spontaneous performance has clearly been meticulously prepared. The singers embellish with taste and discretion, the choral and orchestral contributions are beautifully sensitive yet at the same time firm and poised, and the recording (Abbey Road Studios) is fresh, warm and full of atmosphere."
Hi-Fi News & Record Review 34:98 F '89. Peter Branscombe (310w)

"While the Pinnock *Messiah* is one of the best available, it does not challenge the supremacy of the Hogwood recording of the 1754 Foundling Hospital version as the period instrument *Messiah* of choice. Those who wish modern instruments should seek out the recording on the Word label of the Donald Neuen/Eastman School of Music performance based on the Alfred Mann edition."
American Record Guide 52:64 N/D '89. Teri Noel Towe (575w)

"But while Gardiner's failing was a certain Anglican-Evensong primness, Pinnock's is a curious lack of overview....Still, this is a *Messiah* not without merit."
Ovation 9:40 Ja '89. Scott Cantrell (425w)

Gramophone 66:838-41 N '88. Edward Greenfield (1340w)

The New York Times D 18 '88, p. H33. Barrymore L. Scherer (140w)

6070. Ode for St. Cecilia's Day.
Trevor Pinnock (c). Felicity Lott; Anthony Rolfe-Johnson. English Concert.
DEUTSCHE GRAMMOPHON 419 220 50:25

★★*Awards:* *Opus* Christmas List, 1987 (James R. Oestreich). *Fanfare* Want List 1987 (J. F. Weber).

"Utterly 'heav'nly harmony."
Opus 4:59 D '87. James R. Oestreich (110w)

"Despite its proof that this is not a perfect world we live in, I'd find it hard to turn to another version than this when I feel like listening to this glorious ode."
Fanfare 10:122 Jl/Ag '87 J.F. Weber (225w)

"I have no wish for period instrument performances to be driven into a ghetto of hairshirted fundamentalism, but Pinnock appears to be losing sight of the *stylistic* gains the authentic revolution has afforded."
Hi-Fi News & Record Review 32:105+ F '87 Hugh Canning (390w)

Gramophone 64:1051-2 Ja '87 Nicholas Anderson (290w)

6071. Roman Vespers.
Micahel Korn (c). Judith Blegen; Benita Valente; Maureen Forrester; Jon Garrison; John Cheek. Philadelphia Concerto Soloists Chamber Orchestra; Philadelphia Singers.
RCA 7182 55:41; 57:36 2 discs

★*Awards:* *Stereo Review* Best of the Month, O '86.

"All in all, this splendid album sheds a new light on Handel as a young master sowing his musical oats in Italy. The recorded sound, too, is excellent."
Stereo Review 51:86 O '86. Stoddard Lincoln (500w)

"I have listened to this set numerous times since receiving it and my enthusiasm for it has steadily grown. I warmly recommend it."

American Record Guide 50:35 Ja/F '87 Ralph V. Lucano (525w)

Blegen sings "with consistent brilliance and panache, although the digital recording overemphasizes the edginess of her powerful voice—as it does the fortissimo high-register tone of the other soloists, the organ, and the orchestra's strings and oboes. Valente's singing is admirably contrasted to Blegen's."

High Fidelity 37:82 Ja '87 R.D. Darrell (725w) (rev. of cassette)

"This Philadelphia performance is outstanding in the instrumental part...enthusiastically rowdy in the choruses...And, most important, it is good to excellent in the ever-present pair of solo sopranos."

Audio 72:102 O '88. Edward Tatnall Canby (660w)

"Of the soloists, only the two sopranos seem totally up to their difficult tasks; the usually wonderful Maureen Forrester sounds cloudy, and tenor Jon Garrison and bass John Cheek are less than enchanting. Nevertheless, these are important works, well recorded and performed, and we aren't likely to hear a competing set for quite a while. In all, a good find, highly recommended."

Ovation 7:38 N '86 Robert Levine (525w)

"With so little recording activity in this country by American companies employing American talent, I would like to be more encouraging, but this release proves a disappointment."

Opus 3:37-38 D '86 John W. Barker (735w) (rev. of LP)

Opera News 51 (4):81 O '86. John W. Freeman (80w)

6072. Solomon.

John Eliot Gardiner (c). Nancy Argenta; Carolyn Watkinson; Anthony Rolfe-Johnson; Stephen Varcoe. Monteverdi Choir; English Baroque Soloists.
PHILIPS 412 612 DDD 128:19 2 discs

✔**HC** ★★*Awards:* Perfect 10/10, *Digital Audio*, Mr '88; Record of the Eighties, *Gramophone*, D '89 (Edward Greenfield).

"Gardiner brings to this work a musicality and a technical superiority that make his results more telling than even Somary's. The cast is excellent, both musically and dramatically....A superb accomplishment for all hands."

Opus 2:39-40 Ag '86. John W. Barker (1380w)

Gramophone 63:832+ D '85. Roger Fiske (490w)

"The recording of this work has been so very well managed that it will not only continue to impress on repeated hearings: it will promote them. The performance is also extremely beautiful."

Hi-Fi News & Record Review 31:107 Ja '86. Stephen Daw (105w)

Opus 3:50 D '86 Jon Alan Conrad (105w)

Opera News 50 (12):45 Mr '86. John W. Freeman (105w)

Digital Audio 2:26+ My '86. David Vernier (575w)

High Fidelity 36:70 Je '86. R. D. Darrell (500w) (rev. of cassette)

The Opera Quarterly 4:151-3 Summer '86. Karin Pendle (950w)

6073. Sorge il Di (Aci, Galatea e Polifema), H.72; Sonatas for Recorder: H.369, H.365, H.358.

Charles Medlam (c). Emma Kirkby; Carolyn Watkinson; David Thomas; Michel Piguet (rec); John Toll (hpscd); Charles Medlam (cello). London Baroque. 1986; 1985.
HARMONIA MUNDI 901253/4 DDD 106:00 2 discs

✔**HC** ★★★*Awards:* *Gramophone* Critics' Choice (Lionel Salter), 1987; Perfect 10/10, *Digital Audio*, Mr '88; Editors' Choice, *Digital Audio*, 1988. Second Place Opera Mumm Champagne Classical Music Award 1988—Presented by *Ovation*, *Ovation* N '88.

"The performance is a treat in almost every way....in the two female voices we hear a unity of vocal and instrumental style that is rare even in early music....Mix and ambience are mostly good."

The Opera Quarterly 6:124-6 Autumn '88. Rodney Shewan (1050w)

"In all, these performers have rendered us a great service in bringing us this major Handel score in so satisfying a debut recording."

American Record Guide 51:27-9 Ja/F '88. John W. Barker (885w)

"The performance recorded here by Harmonia Mundi is extremely fine....[David Thomas's] brilliant account of Polifemo's above-mentioned entrance aria—with brazen trumpets—is worth the price of the discs alone."

Hi-Fi News & Record Review 33:101 Mr '88. Hugh Canning (625w)

"There's a real feeling of ensemble between singers and players...the recitatives are as intelligently sung as the arias...the second disc is filled out by workmanlike performances of three of Handel's solo sonatas."

HighPerformanceReview 5:79 Ap '88. Rodney Shewan (290w)

"The performances are splendid....The sound is flawless throughout: I love being able to hear the obbligato instruments so clearly and naturally."

Ovation 9:40 Je '88. Robert Levine (540w)

"This splendid release is a revelation."

Continuo 12:19-20 O '88. Pierre Savaria (1035w)

"The strings—exclusively gut, certainly, and of course entirely without vibrato—sound a bit shiny in crescendos at first, but you soon get used to hearing all the instruments sound the way we assume they did in Lully's day. The woodwinds have a softness and mellowness of timbre that modern instruments cannot emulate. All four of the main singers stand out in their roles, as do several of the supporting cast."

High Fidelity 39:60-2 F '89. Paul Moor (875w)

"Emma Kirkby's gentle virtuosity and Carolyn Watkinson's smooth, male-alto-ish tone enliven the title roles, but a halo of recorded resonance singles out David Thomas' Polifemo, depriving his work of comparable clarity and point....Medlam leads the London Baroque with ebullient security."

Opera News 53:48-9 My '89. John W. Freeman (110w)

"Unfortunately, the present recording of *Aci* is a victim of Murphy's Law of Baroque Performance, which frequently insures that the most interesting music goes to the least qualified performer. David Thomas simply doesn't have the range for Polifemo....The sound is lovely."

Fanfare 11:133-4 Ja/F '88. Ralph V. Lucano (525w)

Gramophone 65:796 N '87 Lionel Salter (525w)

Digital Audio 4:86+ D '87. David C. Vernier (475w)

6074. Susanna.

Nicholas McGegan (c). Lorraine Hunt (sop); Jill Feldman (sop); Drew Minter (alto); Jeffrey Thomas (ten); William Parker (bar); David Thomas (bass). University of California at Berkeley Chamber Chorus; Philharmonia Baroque Orchestra. Hertz Hall, University of California, Berkeley. September 16-17, 1989. HARMONIA MUNDI 907030/2 DDD 178:00 3 discs

★★★★★*Awards:* Pick of the Month, North American Perspective (Christopher Pollard), *Gramophone* O '90. Critics' Choice 1990, *Gramophone* D '90 (Stanley Sadie). The Gramophone Awards, Nominations, Baroque—vocal, *Gramophone*, N '91; The Want List 1991, *Fanfare* N/D '91 (Nicholas Deutsch); Best Baroque Recording Vocal 1991, *Gramophone*, D '91.

"In short, this *Susanna*, recorded complete for the first time by Harmonia Mundi USA, is essential Handel listening."

Stereo Review 55:128 D '90. David Patrick Stearns (290w)

"Now that we have heard *Susanna*, its neglect is inexplicable; it is a graceful piece, expertly crafted and deeply affecting, which ought to take a prideful place on the performance stage among Handel's other oratorios....Nicholas McGegan['s]...conducting is joyful, flexible, and utterly appropriate. The Philharmonia Baroque Orchestra's performance is rich of tone and quite bracingly fresh....The vocal parts are well taken. Lorraine Hunt, in the title role, does not have a particularly distinguished voice, but she uses it with real artistry....The chorus is superb."

Musical America 111:76-7 Mr '91. Jamie James (380w)

"There is some exciting choral work...and the solo singing is most commendable on all counts. Regarding sonics, I especially admired the accurately reproduced choral layout and the clarity of the instrument group, but the recording satisfies on many different levels." See also Handel's *Amadigi* for review excerpt.

Stereophile 14:235+ D '91. Igor Kipnis (long)

"Hunt as Susanna and David Thomas as the second Elder are especially successful at bringing their characters to life, while McGegan leads his forces in a production that unsentimentally and even warmly reinforces the work's praise of constancy and faith.The only elements of the recording which are less than completely satisfactory are the U.C. Berkeley choir...and the extremely dry acoustic and somewhat distorted balance resulting from the work's having been recorded live in U.C. Berkeley's Hertz Hall."

Continuo 15:29 Ap '91. Scott Paterson (220w)

"The performance is a strong, if imperfect one. No one on the present musical scene conducts Handel with greater authority than Nicholas McGegan....Only one of the soloists is equal in distinction to the orchestra and the chorus, but fortunately she sings the role of the protagonist-....But despite a variable cast, the power and beauty of this neglected oratorio comes across magnificently in this splendid recording."

Fanfare 14:253-6 S/O '90. David Johnson (1110w)

"Overall, this *Susanna* approaches the drama on a personal scale, not as a grand oratorio event. The orchestra doesn't make its best impression in the overture, where one begins to fear a thin original-instrument string tone and meandering attack, but soon there is plenty of vigorous execution under Nicholas McGegan's leadership....The soloists are solid and communicative rather than virtuosic."

Opera News 55:35 F 16 '91. John W. Freeman (310w)

"The sound is a little unkind to the singers, who seem a little remote. They are all expert and apt for their parts....Above all, there is the guiding presence of McGegan, who shapes this performance with obvious love and understanding."

American Record Guide 54:53-4 Ja/F '91. John W. Barker (560w)

Gramophone 68:801-2 O '90. Stanley Sadie (1015w)

Digital Audio's CD Review 7:72 N '90 Sebastian Russ (420w); 7:48 S '90 Octavio Roca (600w)

Utrecht Te Deum and Jubilate. See No. 6017.

HANSON, HOWARD. Song of Democracy, for Chorus and Orchestra. See No. 1165.

HARRISON, LOU

6075. La Koro Sutro ("The Heart Sutra"), for 100-Voice Chorus, American Gamelan, Harp and Organ; Varied Trio, for Violin, Piano and Percussion; Suite for Violin and American Gamelan.
John Bergamo (c). Philip Brett (chorus director); David Abel (vln); Julie Steinberg (pno); William Winant (perc); Karen Gottlieb (harp); Agnes Sauerbeck (orgn). University of California at Berkeley Chorus; University of California at Berkeley Chamber Chorus; American Gamelan.
NEW ALBION 015 ADD 72:45

✔HC ★*Awards:* Editors' Choice, *Digital Audio's CD Review*, Je '89.

"Let's hope this excellent disc by one of our most gifted composers is broadly distributed. It should be heard by anyone with any interest in American or contemporary music."
Fanfare 11:174 Jl/Ag '88. Edward Strickland (440w)

"The wide range and unusual timbres of the American Gamelan are such that, given the superlative recording provided by New Albion, the result is a disc of demonstration quality. The performances all appear to be first rate-...Recommended."
American Record Guide 51:26-7 Jl/Ag '88. Carl Bauman (470w)

"When the pendulum of fashion swings back from the extreme of minimalism, it may well pause for considerable appreciation of the gentle and lovely music of Lou Harrison."
Ovation 9:15 Ag '88. Joseph Fennimore (430w)

"One could not ask for more proficient performances or better recording."
High Fidelity 38:64 Ag '88. Paul Moor (325w)

"For listeners not familiar with Harrison's music the older pieces recorded here...might seem noteworthy primarily for their exotic sound. Repeated hearings, however, will reveal them to be just as dynamic, and in places just as gorgeously lyrical, as anything in the conservative Western tradition."
Musical America 108:59-60 S '88. James Wierzbicki (330w)

"Once provided with the possibility of re-creating the distinctive sounds of the Southeast Asian gamelan, Mr. Harrison in no way tries to write music indigenous to these instruments. Instead, he utilizes a completely eclectic range of rhythmic and melodic sources....the music floats on the gamelan sounds just as it does in Indonesia; if they happen to be vigorously Western, one is still aware of the unusual background coloration."
The New York Times Ag 14 '88, p. H25. Paul Turok (125w)

Digital Audio 5:66 O '88. Linda Kohanov (340w)

Gramophone 68:1024 N '90. Peter Dickinson (385w)

HAYDN, FRANZ JOSEPH

6076. The Creation (Die Schopfung) (oratorio).
Herbert Von Karajan (c). Gundula Janowitz (sop); Fritz Wunderlich (ten); Werner Krenn (ten); Dietrich Fischer-Dieskau (bar); Walter Berry (bass); Christa Ludwig (alto). Vienna Singverein; Chicago Symphony Chorus and Orchestra.
DEUTSCHE GRAMMOPHON 435 077 ADD 109:00

★★*Awards:* Critics' Choice 1991, *Gramophone*, Ja '92 (James Jolly; Hilary Finch).

Gramophone 69:112+ D '91. Hilary Finch (med)

6077. Mass (No. 11) in D minor, ("Nelson Mass"), H.XXII/11; Te Deum in C.
Trevor Pinnock (c). Felicity Lott (sop); Carolyn Watkinson (contr); Maldwyn Davies (ten); David Wilson-Johnson (bass-bar). English Concert Choir; English Concert. 1986.
DEUTSCHE GRAMMOPHON 423 097 DDD 50:00

✔HC ★*Awards:* Period Performance Record Award 1988, *Gramophone* O '88.

"For anyone seeking an 'authentic' edition of Haydn's glorious 'Nelson' Mass, this one is clearly a preferred edition....Haydn's eight-minute setting of the *Te Deum* is projected with a joyful pomp that suits the score perfectly and is a welcome bonus."
Fanfare 11:176 Jl/Ag '88. Mortimer H. Frank (150w)

"Another sparkling performance from Stephen Pinnock."
Organists' Review 74:250 Jl '88. Paul Hale (145w)

"Haydn's so-called 'Nelson' Mass...is indeed a work of troubled emotions springing from troubled times. It is a mark of the success of Pinnock and his ensemble's period-instrument account that this unease is conveyed most vividly through musical means."
Music and Musicians International 36:47 Ap '88. Robert Hartford (250w)

"There has been no lack of worthy recordings of the 'Nelson' mass...What makes this issue at a stroke the most desirable of the lot is its inclusion of the superb *Te Deum* of 1798-1800."
Hi-Fi News & Record Review 33:99 Ap '88. Peter Branscombe (210w)

"Pinnock and his colleagues give us a fine reading of the mass, coupled with a superb performance of the *Te Deum*....Pearlman's account [of the Nelson Mass] is brisker, more incisive, more transparent, and more exciting than Pinnock's."
American Record Guide 52:56 Ja/F '89. Teri Noel Towe (600w)

Gramophone 65:1220 F '88 (280w); 66:550 O '88 (200w) Hilary Finch

Digital Audio 4:36 Ag '88. David C. Vernier (280w)

6078. Mass (No. 12) in B flat, "Harmoniemesse".
Diethard Hellmann (c). Barbara Martig-Tuller (sop); Ria Bollen (alto); Adalbert Kraus (ten); Kurt Widmer (bass). Southwest German Radio Orchestra; Mainz Bachchoir.
CALIG 490 AAD 49:11

"This is as satisfying a performance of Haydn's sublime last Mass as can be heard today....The sound is remarkably clean."
Fanfare 12:177 Ja/F '89. J. F. Weber (100w)

6079. The Seasons (oratorio).
Karl Bohm (c). Gundula Janowitz (sop); Peter Schreier (ten); Martti Talvela (bass). Vienna Singverein; Vienna Symphony Orchestra. 1967.
DEUTSCHE GRAMMOPHON 423 922 ADD 67:24, 64:54 2 discs

★***Awards:*** *American Record Guide* Overview: Haydn, Mr/Ap '92.

"Everything is animated by clarity, incisiveness, and a firmly controlled momentum. And where apt, the conductor suggests a touching delicacy....Highly recommended."
Fanfare 13:217 S/O '89. Mortimer H. Frank (120w)

"No other recording of *The Seasons* comes close to this one in enthusiasm and grandeur-....This is a joyous experience from start to finish."
High Fidelity 39:65+ Jl '89. David Hurwitz (200w)

6080. Stabat Mater in G minor.
Trevor Pinnock (c). Patricia Rozario (sop); Catherine Robbin (mez); Anthony Rolfe-Johnson (ten); Cornelius Hauptmann (bass). English Concert Choir and Orchestra.
DEUTSCHE GRAMMOPHON 429 733 DDD 69:00

★★★***Awards:*** Pick of the Month, North American Perspective (Christopher Pollard), *Gramophone* S '90. Critics' Choice 1990, *Gramophone* D '90 (Hilary Finch); Best of the Month, *Hi-Fi News & Record Review*, Ja '91.

"The timbres are fascinating—cors anglais adding a strange deep-purple effect. The soloists's work is very evenly shared and all of them approach the music in a calm, reserved manner with no pressing of tone. The chorus provides strong dynamic contrasts in its relatively few contributions, and the beautifully balanced small orchestra plays with notable sweetness of tone." *P100/95 S100/95*
Hi-Fi News & Record Review 36:97-8 Ja '91. Antony Hodgson (350w)

"The performance is clear and richly expressive. The forces are pared down, but there is no compromise in quality. The four soloists-...are perfectly matched to the arias."
American Record Guide 54:76-7 Mr/Ap '91. David Bond (170w)

"Dissatisfaction with the work does not prevent admiration for this performance and recording, which is a great improvement over a ghastly performance on two Musical Heritage LPs, so this disc is recommended to Haydn devotees."
Fanfare 14:238 Mr/Ap '91. James H. North (350w)

Gramophone 68:589 S '90. Hilary Finch (460w)

HINDEMITH, PAUL

6081. When Lilacs Last in the Dooryard Bloom'd: A Requiem for Those We Love, for Mezzo-Soprano, Baritone, Orchestra and Chorus.
Robert Shaw (c). Jan De Gaetani (sop); William Stone (bar). Atlanta Symphony Chorus and Orchestra. Symphony Hall, Atlanta. March 31 - April 1, 1986.
TELARC 80132 DDD 52:54

✔**HC** ★★★***Awards:*** *Opus* Record Award Nominee, 1987; *Fanfare* Want List 1987 (John Ditsky); *Gramophone* Critics' Choice (Lionel Salter), 1987.

This "is a deeply moving piece and in this recording it receives the fine performance it deserves."
HighPerformanceReview 4:89 S '87. John Mueter (220w)

"Jan De Gaetani's enunciation of the text is not always clear (fortunately, texts are provided), but her singing is unalloyed gold. William Stone is excellent, and the Atlanta forces under Shaw's sympathetic direction catch both the monumentality and the humanity of what is probably Hindemith's best American work."
Stereo Review 53:156+ Ja '88. Eric Salzman (475w)

"This recording, which is this year's Grammy winner for nonoperatic choral performance, forcefully reminds us of how great our debt is to Robert Shaw."
High Fidelity 38:68 Je '88. Paul Moor (350w)

"In sum, a model CD premiere that can only be most highly recommended."
Fanfare 10:128-9 Jl/Ag '87 John Ditsky (815w)

"This new version is probably about as good a performance as the work is going to get for the foreseeable future and probably about as good a performance as it needs."
American Record Guide 50:38-9 N/D '87. Stephen D. Chakwin, Jr. (465w)

One of 20 classical CDs reviewed and recommended as "outstanding for their musical interest and their performance as well as for their technical quality."
Stereo Review Presents: Compact Disc Buyer's Guide 1988 p.40. William Livingstone and Christie Barter (125w)

"Much of this piece's success depends on a baritone's command of fine degrees of dynamic and timbral modulation, and on his ability to color his simple melodic outlines with a feeling for the sonorous and poetic possibilities of Whitman's words. In both respects Fischer-Dieskau lets us down."

Opus 4:35 D '87. Jon Alan Conrad (910w)

"Ultimately, the choice is between a highly disciplined, scrupulously faithful, excellently recorded but rather worthy performance [Telarc] and a moving, but flawed account [Orfeo] of a masterly and moving work which deserves to be better known."

Hi-Fi News & Record Review 33:111 O '88. Hugh Canning (210w)

Audio 72:150 Ja '88. Edward Tatnall Canby (500w)

Gramophone 65:211 Jl '87 Lionel Salter (330w); 68:827 O '90. Michael Stewart (110w)

HOLST, GUSTAV

6082. The Cloud Messenger, Opus 30; The Hymn of Jesus, Opus 37.

Richard Hickox (c). Della Jones (mez). London Symphony Chorus and Orchestra.
CHANDOS 8901 DDD 66:00

✔HC ★★★★*Awards:* The Want List 1991, *Fanfare* N/D '91 (Peter J. Rabinowitz; Paul Snook); Critics' Choice 1991, *Gramophone*, Ja '92 (Michael Kennedy). Best of the Month, *Hi-Fi News & Record Review*, My '91.

"*The Hymn of Jesus* is a masterpiece of 20th century choral music....Richard Hickox proves once again that he's one of our finest choral conductors in an assured, thrilling rendering with the LSO and Chorus."

High Fidelity 3:97 My '91. Clive Manning (b.n.)

"*The Cloud Messenger*...[is] full of striking ideas, most certainly worthy of investigation, and a stronger performance than Hickox's it would be impossible to envisage. Enjoying beautifully refined orchestral playing (trombones and cor anglais simply outstanding in the Prelude) and uncommonly assured choral work once again, Hickox's account of *The Hymn of Jesus* strikes me as easily the best version of Holst's visionary masterpiece we have had. Thrilling recorded sound, with finely judged balances throughout and organ supremely well integrated into the overall fabric—sonically speaking, Chandos can be proud of this one!" *P95/100 S100*

Hi-Fi News & Record Review 36:81 My '91. Andrew Achenbach (350w)

"Richard Hickox obviously believes in the work [The Cloud Messenger], and leads an impassioned performance. Chandos's sonics are the best I've heard from them, with visceral thrills a-plenty in the big orchestral climaxes with organ....This is the fourth recording [of the Hymn of Jesus—the Chandos]...takes pride of place."

American Record Guide 54:66-7 Jl/Ag '91. Richard E. Tiedman (550w)

"*The Cloud Messenger*...[is] a blemished but compelling piece, a far more worthy purchase than yet another recording of *The Planets*. The disc is made more attractive still by the inclusion of the more familiar, but hardly overexposed, *Hymn of Jesus*..In sum, a major release."

Fanfare 14:178-9 Jl/Ag '91. Peter J. Rabinowitz (550w)

Gramophone 68:2052 My '91. Michael Kennedy (350w)

HONEGGER, ARTHUR

6083. Jeanne d'Arc au Bucher, for Soloists, Orchestra and Chorus.

Seiji Ozawa (c). Francoise Pollet (sop); Michele Command (sop); Nathalie Stutzmann (contr); John Aler (ten); Marthe Keller (nar); Georges Wilson (nar); Pierre-Marie Escourrou (nar); Paola Lenzi (nar). French Radio Chorus; French Radio Children's Chorus; French National Orchestra. Basilique Saint-Denis, Paris. June 1989 live.
DEUTSCHE GRAMMOPHON 429 412 DDD 69:00

★★*Awards:* The Gramophone Awards, Nominations, Choral, *Gramophone*, N '91; The Gramophone Awards, Nominations, Engineering, *Gramophone*, N '91. Critics' Choice 1991, *Gramophone*, Ja '92 (Lionel Salter). Pick of the Month, North American Perspective (Christie Barter), *Gramophone* Ap '91.

Gramophone 68:1885-6 Ap '91. Lionel Salter (480w)

JANACEK, LEOS

6084. Slavonic Mass (M'sa Glagolskaja).

Charles Mackerras (c). Elisabeth Soderstrom; Drahomira Drobkova; Frantisek Livora; Richard Novak. Prague Philharmonic Chorus; Czech Philharmonic Orchestra.
DENON/SUPRAPHON 7448 DDD 39:55

✔HC ★★★*Awards:* *Stereo Review* Best of the Month, Ap '87; *Gramophone* Record Award Winner 1986—Choral Award; *Opera News* Best of the Year, 1987.

"For ferociously ecstatic commitment, this performance stands alone. The brawny yet consistently transparent sound on CD is splendid."

High Fidelity 36:63 Ja '86. Bill Zakariasen (130w)

"Mackerras drives this music with a completely appropriate passionate energy, inspiring his forces to pour their hearts and souls into the performance."

High Fidelity 38:84-5 N '88. Paul Moor (265w)

"While it's not *quite* the performance we've been waiting for, it so far outclasses the modern competition that even on a CD with less than 40 minutes, it's an easy recommendation."

Fanfare 10:129-30 Ja/F '87 Peter J. Rabinowitz (530w)

"This recording is, perhaps, only for the devotee of Janacek who must have one of everything, or for those who need the lovely sounds of Elisabeth Soderstrom."

Stereophile 10:155 O '87. Harold Lynn (225w)

Ovation 8:41-2 O '87. Paul Turok (310w)

Hi-Fi News & Record Review 31:103 Mr '86. Edward Seckerson (175w)

Gramophone 64:550 O '86 John Warrack (200w)

Music Journal p. 25 Spr '87 Bert Wechsler (70w)

Stereo Review 52:85-86 Ap '87 David Hall (260w)

American Record Guide 50:25-26 Mr/Ap '87 Carl Bauman (470w)

KLAMI, UUNO

6085. Psalmus.

Ulf Soderblom (c). Satu Vihavainen (sop); Juha Kotilainen (bar). Savonlinna Opera Festival Choir; Helsinki Philharmonic Orchestra.
FINLANDIA 369 DDD 50:10

★*Awards:* The Want List 1989, *Fanfare* N/D '89 (Paul A. Snook).

"This rare bird is a Finnish oratorio....Sung in archaic Finnish, this beautiful work is based on a 23-verse poem by the hymn writer Juhana Cajanus...Both solo artists sing boldly, excitingly. The chorus too sings well...The orchestral spirit matches that of the vocal artists."

American Record Guide 52:72 N/D '89. Charles Parsons (150w)

"*Psalmus* may well be Klami's masterpiece, even outshining the *Kalevala* suite and putting his achievement in a whole new perspective. The performance is plainly authoritative and also very dedicated, and Finlandia's digital sonics are flatteringly lifelike...A major release."

Fanfare 13:229 S/O '89. Paul A. Snook (505w)

"*Psalmus* uses the chorus and orchestra in massive sonorities. There are moments of lyric beauty, and also moments lacking depth, reminiscent of 'movie music'....Ulf Soderblom leads the Helsinki Philharmonic and Savonlinna Opera Festival Choir in a bold and forthright performance, and soloists Satu Vihavainen and Juha Kotilainen contribute outstanding and colorful interpretations."

HighPerformanceReview 8(1):70 '91. George S. T. Chu (300w)

"The performers on this disc tackle the music with complete assurance and notable enthusiasm....This is marvellous writing, and one must hope that Finlandia continue recording Klami's work."

Music and Musicians International 38:53+ D '89. David Bray (570w)

"More cantata than oratorio, Klami's *Psalmus* sets to music a 23-stanza 17th-century poetic mediation on death....The soloists, chorus, and orchestra, under the direction of Ulf Soderblom, bring fervor and dedication to their performance of this important piece, which had escaped the notice of even the Finns until 1960. Technical standards and musicianship are very high, and so are the production values."

Musical America 110:76-7 Mr '90. Andrew Stiller (470w)

LISZT, FRANZ

6086. Christus.

Antal Dorati (c). Sandor Solyom-Nagy; Veronika Kincses; Klara Takacs; Janos B. Nagy; Laszlo Polgar; Andras Viragh (harmonium); Bertalan Hock (orgn). Hungarian Radio and Television Chorus; The Nyiregyhaza Children's Chorus; Hungarian State Orchestra.
HUNGAROTON 12831/3 DDD 182:00 3 discs

★★*Awards:* *Opus* Christmas List, 1987 (Kenneth Furie). *Opera News* Best of the Year, 1987.

"Many thanks should go to Antal Dorati for this fine, sensitive performance...This is a wonderful work, wonderfully well-performed with sound of excellent, live quality."

HighPerformanceReview 4:90-1 S '87. June C. Ottenberg (840w)

"It would be impossible to fault the Dorati performance, which is remarkable for its lucidity of detail and for its overall ambience."

Organists' Review 72:133-4 May '87. Robert Ashfield (215w)

"Hungaroton's first *Christus* (LPX 11506-08, conducted by Miklos Forrai) was more than adequate....I wish Hungaroton had remastered Forrai's *Christus* for compact disc and spared themselves the trouble of producing a new one."

American Record Guide 49:22-23 N/D '86 Ralph V. Lucano (865w) (rev. of LP)

Fanfare 10:135-6 Ja/F '87 Peter J. Rabinowitz (525w); 10:144-5 Mr/Ap '87 Peter J. Rabinowitz (135w)

Opera News 11:42-43 Ja 31 '87 John W. Freeman (575w)

Gramophone 64:1170 F '87 Stephen Johnson (395w) (rev. of LP)

Digital Audio & Compact Disc Review 107:91-92 Je '87 Roland Graeme (600w)

Opus 4:55 D '87. Kenneth Furie (85w)

6087. Faust Symphony.

Thomas Beecham (c). Alexander Young (ten). Royal Philharmonic Orchestra; Beecham Choral Society. 1958 reissue.
EMI 63371 ADD 69:58

✔**HC** ★*Awards:* Pick of the Crop Reissues, *The New York Times* S 16, '90 (Sedgwick Clark).

"The news is that this classic 1958 performance has been generously knocked down from full-price to mid-price format apart from which the productions are identical....Self-commending."

Fanfare 14:277 S/O '90. Adrian Corleonis (b.n.)

"The *Faust Symphony*...has seldom been out of print since it was made (1959). And like most Beecham recordings it will continue to sell because *there is no better performance*—nor is there likely to be—and the sound is spectacular. That said, I should admit that I don't like Liszt's long-winded symphony very much."
American Record Guide 53:28+ S/O '90. Donald R. Vroon (210w)

Gramophone 67:2070 My '90. John Steane (270w)

The New York Times S 16 '90, p. 48 H. Sedgwick Clark (210w)

6088. Via Crucis.
Reinbert De Leeuw (c). Reinbert De Leeuw (pno). Netherlands Chamber Choir.
PHILIPS 416 649 DDD 49:27

★*Awards:* *Stereo Review* Best of the Month, D '86; *Gramophone* Critics' Choice 1986 (Hilary Finch).

"The performance throughout is marked by the greatest sensitivity and tenderness, with the choral work enhanced by fine solo contributions."
Stereo Review 51:112 D '86 David Hall (425w)

"Philips' version is first-rate in every way except, perhaps, the choice of accompanying instrument....in a work of this nature it is the organ, not the piano, that automatically establishes a sacred context. Here we have, too clearly, a concert performance rather than a religious occasion."
Opus 3:39 D '86 Paul L. Althouse (345w)

"Rieman's quicker tempo, coupled with his larger choral tone (especially in the *Stabat Mater* passages, where he uses a chorus rather than soloists), his more rounded attacks, and his gentler treatment of the music's contrasts, may make the Schwann recording more immediately attractive, especially for those new to Liszt's late output. Still, de Leeuw's more uncompromising reading has a perverse fascination of its own, and it's the one I'd choose if forced to make a choice...Highly recommended for the adventurous."
Fanfare 10:162-3 N/D '86 Peter J. Rabinowitz (520w)

Hi-Fi News & Record Review 31:104 Jl '86 (310w) (rev. of LP); 31:83 Ag '86 (40w) (rev. of CD). Barbara Jahn

LLOYD WEBBER, ANDREW

6089. Requiem.
Lorin Maazel (c). Placido Domingo; Sarah Brightman; Paul Miles-Kingston; James Lancelot. Winchester Cathedral Choir; English Chamber Orchestra.
EMI 47146 DDD 45:52

★*Awards:* *Fanfare* Want List 1985 (John Ditsky).

"Surely this is one of the top demonstration CDs and really the only way to experience Lloyd Webber's work in the home."
High Fidelity 37:75 Ja '87 Bill Zakariasen (240w)

"The performance, bearing as it does the imprimatur of the composer, would seem definitive."
High Fidelity 35:79-80 Je '85. Bill Zakariasen (960w) (rev. of LP)

"Should there be any of you out there still pondering its purchase, let me urge the deed upon you."
Fanfare 8:206-7 Jl/Ag '85. John Ditsky (1075w)

"Placido Domingo tends to overshadow the other soloists, if only because he is such an exceptional performer....Sarah Brightman seems a bit challenged by her difficult part, but she carries it off quite well....Conductor Lorin Maazel draws an exciting and quite moving performance out of the combined forces."
Hi-Fi News & Record Review 30:86 Je '85. Edward Seckerson (90w)

Gramophone 63L158 Jl '85. John Borwick (125w)

Digital Audio 1:67+ Jl '85. David Vernier (710w)

Ovation 6:37 O '85. Thor Eckert, Jr. (605w)

Audio 70:135-6 N '86 Steve Birchall (810w)

LULLY, JEAN BAPTISTE

6090. Motets: Omnes gentes; Regina coeli; O Sapientia; Laudate pueri; Salve Regina; Exaudi Deus; Anima Christi; Ave coeli; Dixit Dominus; O Dulcissime; Domine salvum fac.
William Christie (c). Les Arts Florissants Vocal and Instrumental Ensemble.
HARMONIA MUNDI 901274 DDD 64:30

★★*Awards:* The Want List 1988, *Fanfare* N/D '88 (Michael Ullman). Top Choices—1989, *American Record Guide* Ja/F '90 (Stephen Chakwin).

"If there is a better group performing this type of vocal music, I haven't heard it....The recorded sound is excellent."
American Record Guide 52:63 Ja/F '89. Stephen D. Chakwin, Jr. (200w)

"William Christie has brought the same intelligent insight to this unexplored field as he did to the other French Baroque material he has brought out with his vocal and instrumental ensemble....the engineering is exquisite as usual."
Fanfare 11:193-4 Jl/Ag '88. J. F. Weber (400w)

"Best of all here is the performing style...For once, there is lilt and rhythm and dance, irresistible, behind the formal Latin texts of the church. Why not? Only in recent times has church music turned solemn."
Audio 72:168 N '88. Edward Tatnall Canby (525w)

"Few ensembles are more highly qualified to make the most of these pieces than Les Arts Florissants....The clear, flexible voices blend well and the continuo section, consisting of chamber organ, bass lute and viola da gamba, lends supple, discreet support."

Music Magazine 11:43 N/D '88. Scott Paterson (315w)

"The singing is very accomplished; only tenor Jean-Paul Fouchecourt shows an occasional technical weakness....The sound on the disc is clear and well balanced."

High Fidelity 38:62 D '88. Christopher Rothko (200w)

"Taken individually, then, each of these performances is a small gem, but added together they become too much of a good thing. The recording is good enough to carry the readings with conviction but it lacks that last degree of sparkle, and pales beside that produced for Lully's *Atys.*"

Hi-Fi News & Record Review 33:109 N '88. Doug Hammond (245w)

MENDELSSOHN, FELIX

6091. Motets and Psalms (Opus 23/3; 69/1; 78/1,3; 79/1-6).
Philippe Herreweghe (c). Chapelle Royale Vocal Ensemble; Collegium Vocale.
HARMONIA MUNDI 901142 DDD 51:33

★***Awards:*** Perfect 10/10, *Digital Audio*, Mr '88.

"Here we have powerful, sensitive, and expressive singing in a very resonant church acoustic."

American Record Guide 48:69 Ja '85. Matthew B. Tepper (175w)

"The performances are on a consistently high level...In short, a splendid release, especially recommended to those who have turned up their noses at this side of Mendelssohn's output. Recording quality, as revealed on the CD, is first-rate."

Opus 2:46 Je '86. Paul L. Althouse (460w)

"The CD...comprises an interesting collection of fairly unfamiliar sacred works....The performances are entirely worthy, coming from an ensemble which has shown skill in a varied repertoire."

Fanfare 8:247-8 Mr/Ap '85. J.F. Weber (550w)

Hi-Fi News & Record Review 30:93 My '85. Doug Hammond (125w)

Gramophone 62:1107 Mr '85. Roger Fiske (140w)

Digital Audio 2:58 Ag '86. Pierre Beauregard (375w)

Psalms (3), for Baritone and Mixed Chorus, Opus 78. See No. 6052.

MEYERBEER, GIACOMO

6092. Gli Amori de Teolinda, for Soprano, Clarinet, Chorus and Orchestra.
Gerd Albrecht (c). Julia Varady (sop); Jorg Fadle (clar). Berlin Radio Symphony Orchestra; Berlin RIAS Chamber Choir.
ORFEO 054 831 DDD 35:13

★***Awards:*** Perfect 10/10, *Digital Audio*, Mr '88.

"The soloists are ideally suited to their roles-....The orchestral support is excellent. Orfeo has provided one of the finest recordings of any vocal CD I have ever heard."

American Record Guide 48:69-70 Ja '85. Carl Bauman (200w)

"Varady is fine, the clarinetist and orchestra proficient and the recording excellent."

Fanfare 8:200 Ja/F '85. Harry Townsend (75w)

Digital Audio 1:58 Mr '85. Roland Graeme (425w)

Opera News 50 (2):48 Ag '85. John W. Freeman (80w)

Ovation 5:57 D '84. George Jellinek (140w)

MONTEVERDI, CLAUDIO

6093. Madrigals: Book 6: Lamento d'Arianna a 5; Zefiro torna a 2; Una Donna fra l'altre; A dio, Florinda bella; Lagrime d'amante al sepolchro, "Sestina"; Ohime il bel viso; Qui rise, o Tirsi; Misero Alceo; Batto, qui pianse Ergasto; Presso un fiume tranquillo.
Anthony Rooley (c). Consort of Musicke.
VIRGIN 91154 DDD 68:00

★***Awards:*** The Gramophone Awards, Nominations, Baroque—Vocal, *Gramophone*, N '91.

"These are the first two installments of a projected complete set of the Monteverdi madrigals on this label....the special quality of ensemble that marks Rooley's group is never more evident than in their Monteverdi....The engineering at Forde Abbey is superlative....based on their opening gambit, this ensemble bids fair to dominate the Monteverdi bin in the near future."

Fanfare 14:283-4 Mr/Ap '91. J. F. Weber (300w)

"These are fine, expressive performances, rhythmically taut, though sensitive and flexible."

Continuo 15:27-8 Ap '91. David Klausner (440w)

P95 S95

Hi-Fi News & Record Review 36:82 My '91. Helena Stoward (350w)

Gramophone 68:1246 D '90. Iain Fenlon (275w)

6094. Mass of Thanksgiving.
Andrew Parrott (c). Joseph Cornwell (ten); Richard Wistreich (bass). Taverner Choir; Taverner Consort and Players.
EMI 49876 DDD 88:00 2 discs

✔**HC** ★★***Awards:*** Critics' Choice 1989, *Gramophone* D '89 (Tess Knighton). Critics' Choice 1990, *Gramophone* D '90 (Iain Fenlon).

"I recommend this highly for the way it puts Venetian music in the context of its times. A trumpet fanfare and two cannon salutes for Andrew Parrott!"

Fanfare 13:234-35 Mr/Ap '90. J. F. Weber (655w)

Gramophone 67:952 N '89. Tess Knighton (635w)

6095. Selve morale e spirituale (selections): Gloria a 7; Chi vol che m'innamori; O ciechi ciechi; Adoramus a 6; Confitebor III all francese; Confitebor tibi Domine a 6; Laudate Dominum; E questa vita un lampo; Beatus vir I a 6.
William Christie (c). Les Arts Florissants Vocal and Instrumental Ensemble.
HARMONIA MUNDI 901250 DDD 60:42

★*Awards:* *Opus* Christmas List, 1987 (Matthew Gurewitsch).

"This is gorgeous music, flawlessly served."
American Record Guide 50:54-5 N/D '87. Robert Levine (350w)

"The entire ensemble acquits itself nicely, and Christie guides them with his usual panache-....This is a very interesting collection."
Fanfare 11:243-4 S/O '87. J. F. Weber (320w)

"In Les Arts Florissants, Monteverdi has the daring, subtle and accomplished interpreters he deserves."
Opus 4:56 D '87. Matthew Gurewitsch (70w)

Gramophone 65:211 Jl '87 Iain Fenlon (490w)

6096. Vespro della Beata Vergine; Magnificat II a 6 voci.
John Eliot Gardiner (c). Ann Monoyios (sop); Marinella Pennicchi (sop); Michael Chance (alto); Mark Tucker (ten); Nigel Robson (ten); Sandro Naglia (ten); Bryn Terfel (bass); Alastair Milnes (bass). Monteverdi Choir; London Oratory Junior Choir; His Majesties Sagbutts and Cornets; English Baroque Soloists. Basilica of San Marco, Venice. May 10, 11, 1989 live.
DEUTSCHE GRAMMOPHON 429 565 DDD 106:00 2 discs

✔HC ★★*Awards:* The Highs, 1990, *The New York Times* D 30 '90 (John Rockwell); Best of the Month, *Hi-Fi News & Record Review*, D '90.

"First of the two outstanding features of this release (and the two most radically different from Gardiner's 1974 Decca recording), is the extraordinary depth of St Mark's acoustic. Thanks to its unique architecture, its long reverberation time adds flowing warmth to the utter clarity and precision of the performance. If the musicians sometimes sound distanced, they are never blurred or faint, and the excellent recording quality brings the massive dimensions of the great basilica right into your own earphones! Given that it's live, full credit must go to the engineers. A close second comes Gardiner's superb direction." *P100 S100*
Hi-Fi News & Record Review 35:95 D '90. Helena Stoward (490w)

"The field is crowded, but Gardiner has made a case and he deserves to be heard, along with the grand Montserrat (no CD yet but still hoping), the Parrott, the Christophers, and the Savall, largely because each of these has something different to tell us about one of the most fascinating masterpieces in the field of early music."
Fanfare 14:218-19 My/Je '91. J. F. Weber (900w)

"Gardiner's performance is full of early instruments, modern voices, bizarre effects, and quirky tempos....Monteverdi, as can be discovered from his life, letters, and music, was on the whole a serious man. but in this recording, he appears to suffer from chronic catalepsy of a lamentable kind."
Musical America 111:79-80 Jl '91. Denis Stevens (550w)

"These two recordings [Gardiner and Pickett] are performed, in the main, by English, nay *London* musicians, and both were recorded in May 1989....Each is impeccably performed...In general, the Pickett is more spartan, perhaps more English in sound, while the Gardiner is more lavish and captures a more Mediterranean spirit. So choose your preference!"
Continuo 15:21-2 Ag '91. JoAnne Harrop (290w)

"Recording in St. Mark's presents certain problems, especially when the various musical forces involved are dispersed in different locations around the building...Overall, Gardiner does not deliver what he claims to want to in this performance. Through use of excessive energy, inexplicable effects and response to musical rather than textual stimuli, Gardiner has give us a *Vespers* which though exciting, is restless, frantic, and inconsistently approached. In short, there is too much Gardiner here, and not enough Monteverdi."
Musick 13(2):23-7 Fall-Sept '91. Gerald Van Wyck (long)

"The St. Mark's sound is resonant and lively, but does not quite capture, for me, the extraordinary velvety acoustic resulting from the concave shapes of the many cupolae."
Stereophile 14:207+ S '91. Denis Stevens (med)

Gramophone 68:1399 Ja '91. David Fallows (575w)

6097. Vespro della Beata Vergine.
Philip Pickett (c). Catherine Bott (sop); Tessa Bonner (sop); Christopher Robson (alto); Andrew King (ten); John Mark Ainsley (ten); Rufus Muller (ten); Michael George (bar); Simon Grant (bass). New London Consort. May 1989.
OISEAU-LYRE 425 823 DDD 92:00 2 discs

★★*Awards:* The Gramophone Awards, Nominations, Baroque—vocal, *Gramophone*, N '91; The Want List 1991, *Fanfare* N/D '91 (Robert Levine). Critics' Choice 1991, *Gramophone*, Ja '92 (David Fallows).

"Briefly, Philips Pickett has chosen to set the polyphonic music within the framework of the chant for the second vespers of the Feast of the Nativity of the Blessed Virgin, thus giving a degree of liturgical procedure without involving us in a complete reconstructed service. Suffice it to say that the atmosphere generated is so convincing that it is a shock to see a picture of the performers at ease in casual clothes-...This recording cannot fail to bring joy."

Organists' Review 76:135 Je '91. Gordon Reynolds (600w)

"In many respects...PolyGram's two labels have offered highly contrasting versions, Gardiner hewing close to the score but being spectacularly engineered, Pickett adopting most of the recent innovations but using simpler techniques. Take your pick, or hear both."

Fanfare 14:221-2 Jl/Ag '91. J. F. Weber (575w)

See Gardiner on Deutsche Grammophone 429 565 (above) for review excerpt.

Continuo 15:22 Ag '91. JoAnne Harrop (290w)

"The writers don't know the source material...I wish it were possible to say that they had made up for it by adopting a more sensible attitude [than Gardiner] toward tempos and declamation. This, alas, is not so."

Musical America 111:79-80 Jl '91. Denis Stevens (550w)

Stereophile 14:207+ S '91. Denis Stevens (med)

Gramophone 68:1709 Mr '91. David Fallows (630w)

MOZART, WOLFGANG AMADEUS

6098. Mass in C minor, K.427, "The Great".
John Eliot Gardiner (c). Sylvia McNair (sop); Diana Montague (mez); Anthony Rolfe-Johnson (ten); Cornelius Hauptmann (bass). Monteverdi Choir; English Baroque Soloists. November 1986.
PHILIPS 420 210 DDD 54:00

★*Awards:* Critics' Choice 1988, *Gramophone* D '88 (Stanley Sadie).

"This is an excellent recording: outstanding in all technical respects. Mozart lovers will want to have this alongside Raymond Leppard's earlier Angel recording featuring Cotrubas and Te Kanawa."

HighPerformanceReview 6:83 Mr '89. George S. T. Chu (250w)

"Text and translations are printed....The sound is gloriously clean. This great Mass has not been neglected on records, but it has never been done better."

Fanfare 12:224 Mr/Ap '89. J. F. Weber (180w)

"As he's been able to do with so many other works, Gardiner brings a fresh perspective to the Mass, and his recording has become my favored vehicle for hearing this music."

Fanfare 12:215-16 Ja/F '89. George Chien (300w)

"Gardiner's grandly conceived interpretation—with spacious tempos to match the spacious acoustic of the London recording venue—is highly theatrical, a sort of abstract opera-....What keeps this recording from being ideal is the engineering....Rarely has such a rewarding performance been so hard to listen to."

Stereo Review 54:129 Ja '89. David Patrick Stearns (250w)

Gramophone 65:1630+ My '88. Stanley Sadie (375w)

6099. Mass in C minor, K.427, "The Great".
Christopher Hogwood (c). Arleen Auger (sop); Lynne Dawson (sop); John Mark Ainsley (ten); David Thomas (bass). Winchester Cathedral Choir; Winchester College Quiristers; Academy of Ancient Music. November 1988.
OISEAU-LYRE 425 528 DDD 51:00

✔HC ★*Awards:* Critics' Choice 1990, *Gramophone* D '90 (Stanley Sadie).

"This magnificent work receives an appropriately memorable performance here....The other two recorded performances worth considering alongside this one are by Marriner (Philips 412 932-1) and Leppard (EMI EG 29 0277 1). I would rate Hogwood's as the best, with Marriner's a close second and Leppard's some little way behind."

Organists' Review 76:222-23 S '90. Robert Lawrenson (585w)

"Hogwood's tempos are similar to Gardiner's (both use period instruments), but the boys of Winchester add an element of celebration to the work, singing with more continental tone than is usually heard in England. The whole performance is wonderfully pointed, and the soloists are superb....Pressed to choose between two fine recordings, I'd say the Winchester boys tip the scales to Hogwood."

Fanfare 14:292 N/D '90. J. F. Weber (240w)

"Hogwood keeps the work buoyant, with boisterous rhythms and wide but uninflated dynamic range, and an altogether more apt handling [than Schreier]. With little to choose between the reasonable sonic qualities of both recordings, Hogwood and his authentic-instrument band must be considered the more persuasive advocates of this delightful work."

Stereophile 14:259 Ap '91. Barbara Jahn (160w)

"Whether this can be called a definitive version of this truncated masterpiece is naturally difficult to say, but that it is an important contribution to our appreciation of Mozart's intentions as far as they can be determined is unquestionable." *P95/100 S95*

Hi-Fi News & Record Review 35:92-3 Ag '90. Kenneth Dommett (295w)

Musical America 111:81 My '91. Paul Moor (145w)

Gramophone 68:261 Jl '90. Stanley Sadie (595w)

Mass in C minor, K.427, "The Great". See No. 6029.

6100. Requiem, K.626; Kyrie in D minor, K.368a.
John Eliot Gardiner (c). Barbara Bonney (sop); Anne-Sofie von Otter (alto); Hans-Peter Blochwitz (ten); Willard White (bass). Monteverdi Choir; English Baroque Soloists.
PHILIPS 420 197 DDD 54:00

✔HC ★*Awards:* *Gramophone* Critics' Choice (Stanley Sadie), 1987.

"This is a winner on all fronts. The drama is strongly projected by both the conductors and the soloists."
Organists' Review 74:170 Ap '88. Paul Hale (115w)

"This is a performance that's going to be hard to equal."
Stereo Review 53:106 Jl '88. Stoddard Lincoln (130w)

"Gardiner brings to the *Requiem* much of the intellectual and motoric energy that mark his better Baroque recordings....I find that I have reflexively reached for his disc when my thoughts have turned to this music."
Fanfare 11:207-8 Jl/Ag '88. George Chien (260w)

"This is not a gently meditative interpretation, but one harsh and fearful, conjuring up the stark realities of life and death in Mozart's time and the composer's painful mental and physical state during the work's composition. There is real commitment and drive throughout-...Perhaps all this would have seemed less threatening had the venue's resonant acoustic been kinder."
Stereophile 11:173 Je '88. Barbara Jahn (450w)

"By comparison, [with Guest] the performances of John Eliot Gardiner, Riccardo Muti, and Hans Gillesberger sound like make-work projects for the studios rather than a record of musical events worth preserving."
Musical America 109:62-3 Ja '89. Thomas Hathaway (170w)

Opera News 52:48 Ap 9 '88. John W. Freeman (45w)

Music and Musicians International 36:47-8 Ja '88. Robert Hartford (75w)

Gramophone 65:801 N '87 Stanley Sadie (440w)

6101. Requiem, K.626.
Christopher Hogwood (c). Emma Kirkby; Carolyn Watkinson; Anthony Rolfe-Johnson; David Thomas. Westminster Cathedral Choir; Academy of Ancient Music.
OISEAU-LYRE 411 712 43:13

★★*Awards:* *Gramophone* Critics' Choice 1984 (Lionel Salter); *Gramophone* Critics' Choice 1984 (Robin Golding).

"Christopher Hogwood chooses to use an edition by C.R.F. Maunder...the greatest difference that listeners who are familiar with the *Requiem* will note is the absence of the Sanctus, Benedictus and Agnus dei, and a recomposed Lacrimosa (following the eight bars that Mozart completed), including a frugal Amen that is based on a sixteen-bar opening found about twenty years ago and completed by the editor. This addition is very convincing, but quite different from Sussmayr's completion."
Musick 7:32-3 Ja '86. John R. Burgess (485w)

"Christopher Hogwood's concept of "authentic" Mozart singing leads to frustrating listening, especially when he has Emma Kirkby making thin, squeaking sounds that seem like a parody of a boy soprano."
Stereo Review 50:70 F '85. Stoddard Lincoln (100w)

Digital Audio 3:34 Ja '86. Roland Graeme (585w)

Opera News 11:42-43 F 14 '87 John W. Freeman (200w)

Hi-Fi News & Record Review 30:103 Mr '85. Andrew Keener (175w)

Gramophone 62:639 N '84. Lionel Salter (175w)

Ovation 6:38 Ap '85. Scott Cantrell (310w)

6102. Requiem, K.626.
Ton Koopman (c). Barbara Schlick (sop); Carolyn Watkinson (alto); Christophe Pregardien (ten); Harry Van Der Kamp (bass). Netherlands Bach Association Chorus; Amsterdam Baroque Orchestra. Vredenburg, Utrecht. October 1989 live.
ERATO 45472 DDD 47:00

★*Awards:* Best of the Month, *Hi-Fi News & Record Review*, S '90.

"This is a dynamic, committed interpretation of tremendous insight, superbly recorded."
P100 S100
Hi-Fi News & Record Review 35:89 S '90. Antony Hodgson (340w)

"Listen to Ton Koopman's recording. Here is an 'early-music' version that has character as well as dynamic and dramatic power-....Koopman's Mozart/Sussmayr Requiem is a consistent and overwhelming experience and, quite simply, one of the best recordings of this work ever made."
Stereo Review 56:134 F '91. Eric Salzman (105w)

"For those interested in period instruments, Koopman's version has much to recommend it. It features generally fast tempos made utterly convincing with clean articulation, forceful accents, wide dynamics, and richly colored, clearly defined textures....In the main, this is a stark, intense reading that is sometimes fierce, other times delicately celestial (especially in the pure tone of the sopranos in the chorus), and always musical....A commanding and warmly recommended release."
Stereophile 14:199+ Ag '91. Mortimer H. Frank (180w)

"The sound is incredibly light and airy...For a light and quick approach to the score with tempos less extreme than these, my favorite is Stefan Skold's on Proprius (*Fanfare* 3:5), but that isn't available on CD. Koopman is the next best of its type among those I've heard."
Fanfare 14:295-96 N/D '90. J. F. Weber (280w)

"Briefly put, a blood-and-thunder baroque thriller. This recording would serve—and I guess I mean this disparagingly—as one's first

Requiem, particularly for those who don't ordinarily like this kind of music. (A teenager, for example!)."

American Record Guide 53:89-90 N/D '90. Paul L. Althouse (175w)

Musical America 111:83-4 Mr '91. Denis Stevens (225w)

Gramophone 68:1246+ D '90. Stanley Sadie (420w)

6103. Requiem, K.626.

Neville Marriner (c). Sylvia McNair (sop); Carolyn Watkinson (contr); Francisco Araiza (ten); Robert Lloyd (bass). Academy of St. Martin-in-the-Fields Chorus; Academy of St. Martin-in-the-Fields.
PHILIPS 432 087 DDD 50:10

★***Awards:*** Critics' Choice 1991, *Gramophone*, Ja '92 (Stanley Sadie).

"Marriner's is a Mozart *Requiem* for the ages, the one I will now play as a matter of choice."

Fanfare 15:292-93 S/O '91. J. F. Weber (med)

"Marriner's is by far the best of the four [Cascavelle 1012, Denon 9152, Teldec 72479]-...because of the well-balanced quartet of singers...Marriner's careful pacing [and]...the sheer elegance of his choral forces."

American Record Guide 54:118 N/D '91. Paul Schlueter (long)

Gramophone 69:46 Ja '92. Stanley Sadie (long)

ORFF, CARL

6104. Carmina Burana.

Seiji Ozawa (c). Evelyn Mandac; Stanley Kolk; Sherrill Milnes. Boston Symphony Orchestra; New England Conservatory Chorus; New England Children's Chorus.
RCA 6533 63:11

★***Awards:*** *American Record Guide* Overview: Carmina Burana, S/O '88.

"This Boston Symphony Orchestra account...always was one of the finest recorded versions and is doubly so now that it has been digitally remastered for CD."

High Fidelity 38:55 Ja '88. David Hurwitz (130w)

Gramophone 66:842 N '88. Edward Seckerson (70w)

PARRY, CHARLES HUBERT (HASTINGS)

6105. Songs of Farewell. STANFORD, CHARLES VILLIERS. Three Motets, Opus 38; Three Motets, Opus 135—Eternal Father; Magnificat in B flat, Opus 164.

Richard Marlow (c). Trinity College Choir, Cambridge. 1987.
CONIFER 155 DDD 60:00

★★***Awards:*** *Gramophone* Critics' Choice (Gordon Reynolds), 1987; Editors' Choice, *Digital Audio*, 1988. Perfect 10s, *Digital Audio's CD Review*, Mr '89.

"The performances here are both polished and loving. The rather live-sounding acoustic framework evokes a large church most effectively. A *capella* singing is not for all listeners, but for those who love it this will be a cherished disc."

American Record Guide 52:75-6 My/Je '89. Carl Bauman (130w)

"The Trinity College Choir may not be as well known or as abundantly recorded as King's College, but it is a comparably strong small ensemble, led with commitment and understanding. Conifer's recording is good in detail and sharply atmospheric."

Fanfare 11:192 N/D '87. John D. Wiser (300w)

Gramophone 65:469 S '87 Gordon Reynolds (415w)

Digital Audio 4:42 My '88. David C. Vernier (175w)

PART, ARVO

6106. Arbos; An den Wassem zu Babel sassen wir und weinten; Pari Intervallo; De Profundis; Es sang vor langen Jahren; Summa; Stabat Mater.

Dennis Russell Davies (c). Susan Bickley. Hilliard Ensemble; Stuttgart State Orchestra Brass Ensemble. 1987.
ECM 831 959; ECM 1325 DDD 59:00

★★★***Awards:*** *Gramophone* Critics' Choice (John Milsom), 1987; The Want List 1988, *Fanfare* N/D '88 (Paul Rapoport). Records to Die for: 1 of 5 Recommended Recordings, *Stereophile* Ja '91 (Richard Lehnert).

"This is deeply moving music, recorded in fine sound."

The $ensible Sound 9:56 Fall '87. Karl W. Nehring (60w)

"Very strongly recommended."

Fanfare 11:185-8 Mr/Ap '88. John D. Wiser (420w)

"Part's medieval sensibilities in both theology and music are anything but affectations or throwbacks: the man is capable of a depth of musical profundity that is both harrowing and comforting. I simply cannot imagine a better performance of the work."

Stereophile 14:153 Ja '91. Richard Lehnert (b.n.)

"These are all original deeply-considered, and potent works that should be ingested in small doses and listened to with care."

American Record Guide 50:63 N/D '87. Arved Ashby (630w)

"If ECM's initial offering of music by Arvo Part...presented him as a sort of East-European minimalist, this release displays him as a medievalizer. Several of the items here hew so close to ancient models that even a sophisticated listener might be forgiven for mistaking their provenance—especially with the Hilliard Ensemble singing at its level, antique best in four of the seven works....Of the two volumes of his work so far recorded, neither is better than the other, and neither gives a completely adequate overview of his music; together,however, they provide an excellent survey of his work in a number of media over the past decade, and they belong in any collection that pretends to even sample the late twentieth century. ECM, meeting its usual standard, provides flawless production and sonority; the *Stabat mater* ends with what may well be the most delicate *ppp* ever committed to plastic."

Opus 4:32+ F '88. Andrew Stiller (1640w)

"Though much has been alleged of the so-called minimalist spirituality, Part's work makes that of Reich, Riley, Glass, etc., seem minimalist only in inspiration and profundity, and only superficially 'spiritual'....The description [of "Arbos"] reads like an exercise, and 'Arbos' sounds it....From here on, however, the delights are endless....The Lithuanian Chamber Orchestra plays beautifully under Saulus Sondeckis. Re the recording in general: 'It is enough when a single note is beautifully played.' No other of Part's statements so sums up his work as this."

Stereophile 10:157+ N '87. Richard Lehnert (1060w)

The New York Times Mr 26 '89, p. 25. Allan Kozinn (375w)

Digital Audio 4:41-2 Ag '88. Linda Kohanov (370w)

Gramophone 65:469 S '87 John Milsom (540w)

6107. Passio Domini Nostri Jesu Christi Secundum Joannem.

Paul Hillier (c). Michael George (bass); John Potter (ten); Lynne Dawson (sop); David James (ctr-ten); Rogers Covey-Crump (ten); Gordon Jones (bar); Elizabeth Layton (vln); Melinda Maxwell (oboe); Elisabeth Wilson (cello); Catherine Duckett (bsn); Christopher Bowers-Broadbent (orgn). Evangelist Chorus; Western Wind Chamber Choir. 1988.
ECM 837 109; ECM 1370 DDA/DDD 70:55 2 discs

✔**HC** ★★★★★ ***Awards:*** Hall of Fame, *Digital Audio's CD Review*, Ja '92; Perfect 10s, *Digital Audio's CD Review*, Mr '89; Editors' Choice, *Digital Audio's CD Review*, Je '89. The Want List 1989, *Fanfare* N/D '89 (Robert Levine; Edward Strickland); Critics' Choice 1989, *Gramophone* D '89 (John Milsom); Top Choices—1989, *American Record Guide* Ja/F '90 (Arved Ashby); Cream of the Crop IV, *Digital Audio's CD Review*, 6:42 Je '90; Records to Die for: 1 of 5 Recommended Recordings, *Stereophile* Ja '91 (Robert Levine).

"All of the instrumentalists and singers perform as though this music were in their blood: it well may be. It is now in mine....While there is none of the repetitiveness common to the minimalists, there is not so much melodic development here as is evident in some of Part's shorter compositions (*vide* RL, Vol.10 No.8); nevertheless, the work can be recommended even to those who have hitherto balked at anything labeled 'contemporary'....I expect that the sound is exactly what Arvo Part wanted."

Stereophile 12:161-63 F '89. Les Berkley (650)

"The text [is provided] in Latin, English, and German. The music (from 1982) is sung in Latin....Arvo Part's recent music is truly minimal—not process music of Reich, Glass, et. al., but what Wilfred Mellers calls 'the eternal silence at the heart of sound'....the Hilliard Ensemble and associated musicians really outdo themselves. The haunting tone and color, the unanimity of blend, the precision of intonation and control are unequaled in my experience. This kind of singing makes you believe there is no other."

Fanfare 12:234-36 Mr/Ap '89. Paul Rapoport (450w)

"Non-believers will find *Passio* musically overwhelming, believers perhaps experience it on another level, closer to the creative passion that has clearly inspired the composer."

Fanfare 12:234-37 Mr/Ap '89. Edward Strickland (1250w)

"Following the example ECM set with its two previous releases of Part's work, the sound here is absolutely sublime, but it is the music itself that is the most enduringly awe-inspiring."

High Fidelity 39:68 Ap '89. James Wierzbicki (375w)

"Part's vision, no matter how compelling, could hardly have been conveyed without a group of exceptionally sympathetic performers. As on the recent recording of *Arbos* (ECM 831 959), the music is realized by members of the Hilliard Ensemble, who bring to it the same pure, pungent, nonvibrato vocal style they have perfected in recordings of Dufay and Josquin."

Musical America 109:82-3 My '89. K. Robert Schwarz (825w)

"A lustrous performance...The *Passio* is 70 minutes long, one seamless musico-dramatic statement comprising numerous tiny scenes sparingly depicted....Part's tone-painting of the events leading up to and including the crucifixion is subtle, sober, unspeakable. The opening choral statement is a downward plunge of irreversible tragedy....Part's *Passion According to Saint John* is a masterpiece, and one of the few indispensable works of the 1980s."

Ovation 10:54 S '89. Kenneth LaFave (540w)

"This is a staggeringly beautiful and reverential work—stark, rich, sensitive, brutal, simple, and complicated. Its sound is both ancient and modern—timeless....ECM has given it a recording that is ample and intimate at once, with a bass resonance which touches the soul."

Stereophile 14:155+ Ja '91. Robert Levine (b.n.)

"The performance is a magnificent one, and with the Hilliards' concert experience with the piece and their extensive work with the composer, it undoubtedly represents the music as Part himself now hears it....ECM provides a beautifully clear recording made in the rich acoustic of St. Jude's-on-the-Hill, London, but earns a severe grimace for its failure to provide any sort of internal access to the entire work."

American Record Guide 52:76 My/Je '89. Arved Ashby (675w)

"The writing is exquisitely beautiful and unbearably sad, and nothing ever happens. It makes for a long, intense, blank seventy minutes."

Stereo Review 54:88 Ap '89. Eric Salzman (90w)

The New York Times Mr 26 '89, p. 25. Allan Kozinn (375w)

Digital Audio 5:54 F '89. David Vernier (375w)

Gramophone 66:1326 F '89. John Milsom (360w)

PARTCH, HARRY

6108. Revelation in the Courthouse Park.
Danlee Mitchell (c). Suzanne Costallos; Christopher Durham; Obba Babatunde. Orchestra of Partch Instruments and Marching Band.
TOMATO 269 655 DDD 51:00; 33:42 2 discs

★★*Awards:* The Want List 1991, *Fanfare* N/D '91 (Peter Burwasser). The Want List 1990, *Fanfare* N/D '90 (Adrian Corleonis).

"Music succeeds or fails, endures or perishes, by (threading Fate's thousand irrelevant haphazards) sheer communicative power, and in this—as this stunning new production of *Revelation in the Courthouse Park* overwhelmingly demonstrates—Partch's great theater works are among the central achievements of music in our time."

Fanfare 14:328-31 S/O '90. Adrian Corleonis (2350w)

"*Revelation in the Courthouse Park* (1960) superimposes a modern tale having musical-mystical-religious trappings upon *The Bacchae* of Euripides....like so much of 1960s, expression—it now seems dated and naive; that is our loss. This performance has all the earmarks of authenticity....The performance may be counted a success on all counts....These discs may be more meaningful to those who attend to the drama of the work rather than the music; still, this is a major addition to recorded Partch."

Fanfare 14:328 S/O '90. James H. North (650w)

PENA, PACO

6109. Misa Flamenca.
Laszlo Heltay (c). La Susi (voc); Rafael El Chaparro" Montilla (voc); Dieguito (voc); Antonio Suarez "Gaudiana" (voc); Paco Pena (gtr); Tito Losada (gtr); Jose Losada (gtr/perc); Diego Losada (gtr); Cesar Victoriano (perc). Academy of St. Martin-in-the-Fields Chorus.
NIMBUS 5288 DDD 40:55

★*Awards:* Critic's Choice: 1991, *American Record Guide*, Ja/F '92 (William Ellis).

"Paco Pena, in my mind, 'is' flamenco, and with this Mass, he's a damn fine composer as well....The chorus, with faultless intonation and spirit in hand, performs exquisitely."

American Record Guide 54:131-2 N/D '91. William Ellis (long)

"No one should be misled into thinking that this is a traditional mass. It is really a group of works in flamenco style roughly organized into the form of the mass....I must admit to being completely captivated by this disc. It is not for all listeners. You must like the flamenco style with its sometimes melismatic, often gritty and harsh singing style. The vocal and instrumental soloists...perform almost as though of one mind and with tremendous brio. Nimbus's recorded sound, as expected, borders on the spectacular. The various solo voices are nicely spread and have so much presence that one sometimes feels that the singers are actually in the listening room. The first time the castanets cut loose, I literally jumped."

Fanfare 14:246 Jl/Ag '91. John Bauman (425w)

"If the reader enjoys flamenco, he will marvel at this music. If he doesn't know flamenco from Fado, he will marvel at it nonetheless....this is so unusual an assemblage of talent in the execution of so unusual an event that one's gratitude goes out to everyone who helped to get it right."

Fanfare 14:246-8 Jl/Ag '91. Mike Silverton (575w)

Gramophone 70:89 Jl '92. John Duarte (med)

PENDERECKI, KRZYSZTOF

6110. Saint Luke's Passion.
Krysztof Penderecki (c). Sigune Von Osten (sop); Stephen Roberts (bar); Kurt Rydl (bass); Edward Lubaszenko (nar). Cracow Boys' Choir; Warsaw National Philharmonic Chorus; Polish Radio National Symphony Orchestra. Cathedral of Christ, Katowice, Poland.
ARGO 430 328 DDD 76:00

"Recorded in the vast acoustic of the Cathedral of Christ, Katowice in Poland, the dynamic range of this powerful recording is vast. Coupled by moments of intense stillness and loud, anguished outbursts, it puts your speakers through a baptism of fire."

High Fidelity 3:98 Mr '91. Clive Manning (100w)

"What with all forces hand-picked and personally trained by the creator and conductor of these powerful, profoundly moving works [the Passion and the Requiem], one must obviously regard both these recordings as definitive, and as milestones in contemporary music."

Audio 75:76-7 Ag '91. Paul Moor (450w)

"On one level the *St Luke Passion* is not an easy work to listen to. The preponderance of chordal clusters and tortuous vocal lines seem, initially, to be an all too consistently graphic response to the subject-matter. But set in the massively resonant acoustic of the Cathedral of Christ the King, Katowice, the slow, monumental nature of proceedings and the wonderful performances of baritone Stephen Roberts and Edward Lubaszenko (as the narrator) give the disc an air of profound pathos, rarely equalled in religious works of this century....Spectacular recording." *P95 S95/100*

Hi-Fi News & Record Review 36:83 My '91. Simon Cargill (350w)

"Stephen Ellis reviewed a Muza CD reissue of the 1966 Philips recording, part of a seven-disc Penderecki release, in *Fanfare* 13:5...Both performances are excellent....That 1966 recording was a splendid one; Argo's fine 1989 one holds but a slight edge in sumptuousness....The two performances are so similar, and the recordings both so fine, that a blind hearing of this new disc might be mistaken for a remastering of the older one."

Fanfare 14:245 My/Je '91. James H. North (350w)

Gramophone 68:1709-10 Mr '91. Michael Stewart (360w)

PERGOLESI, GIOVANNI BATTISTA

6111. Missa Beata Virgine; Missa Ave Maria.
James O'Donnell (c). Westminster Cathedral Choir. 1989.
HYPERION 66364 DDD 73:44

★*Awards:* The Want List 1990, *Fanfare* N/D '90 (J.F. Weber).

"The Westminster Cathedral Choir has a rather more relaxed treble sound than the one to which we have become accustomed in recent years; consequently the music is less intense.There is however, some beautiful sustained legato singing....The ambient acoustics of the Cathedral have once again been expertly captured by the Hyperion team. Highly recommended."

Organists' Review 76:223-24 S '90. John Knott (450w)

"All the qualities that we expect to find in Palestrina are present here in abundance. The boys and men are beautifully balanced, they manage exquisite diminuendos when called for, and climactic passages are never overblown. The cathedral is a marvelous site for these beautifully engineered performances....This is a valuable addition to the Renaissance shelf."

Fanfare 14:325-6 S/O '90. J. F. Weber (320w)

"I have no reservations in recommending this. The choir (men and boys) is among the finest. The sound in Westminster Cathedral is clear, with subtle reverberation."

American Record Guide 53:95 N/D '90. Catherine Moore (185w)

Digital Audio's CD Review 6:40 Ag '90. David Vernier (270w)

6112. Stabat Mater, for Soprano, Contralto, String Orchestra, Female Chorus and Organ.
Claudio Abbado (c). Margaret Marshall; Lucia Valentini Terrani; Leslie Pearson (orgn). London Symphony Orchestra.
DEUTSCHE GRAMMOPHON 415 103

✔HC ★*Awards:* *Gramophone* Critics' Choice 1985 (Gordon Reynolds).

"Claudio Abbado has found the music's ideal pulse, and the beautiful sense of flow quite effectively offsets the rather static quality of the text....In every respect, this splendid recording leaves the nearest runner-up pretty far behind."

Stereo Review 50:177-8 S '85. Richard Freed (200w)

Fanfare 8:241-2 Jl/Ag '85. J.F. Weber (350w)

Gramophone 62:1264 Ap '85. Gordon Reynolds (210w)

6113. Stabat Mater, for Soprano, Contralto, String Orchestra, Female Chorus and Organ; Salve Regina in C minor.
Christopher Hogwood (c). Emma Kirkby (sop); James Bowman (alto). Academy of Ancient Music.
OISEAU-LYRE 425 692 DDD 52:00

★*Awards:* Critics' Choice 1988, *Gramophone D '88 (Lionel Salter).*

"The balance between voices and instruments is near perfectly judged....What pleases most is the complete commitment of the performers to the music, their attention to detail and, above all, the sheer beauty of the sound. Magnificent."

High Fidelity 1:119 Mr '90. Andrew Stuart (b.n.)

"The music exudes the sense of longing evoked by the texts, and is a must for all baroque enthusiasts."

Organists' Review 76:146 Je '90. Simon Mold (130w)

"Besides the inimitable Kirkby, Bowman is having one of his good days. The result is a very individual rendition, worthy of the highest standards....This release will be impossible to ignore, even if the obscure Adda issue is a close match."

Fanfare 13:221-22 Jl/Ag '90. J. F. Weber (325w)

"Originally scored for (male) soprano, (male) alto, strings, and organ, the work [Stabat Mater] does not make great technical demands on the performers, yet it requires that they concoct a subtle mixture of expressiveness and restraint, so as to capture both the operatic and spiritual elements of the piece. Christopher Hogwood and soloists Emma Kirkby and James Bowman manage this tightrope walk with remarkable suppleness and fluency....The performance of the coupling, Pergolesi's *Salve Regina*, reveals the same virtues."

Musical America 110:84 S '90. Christopher Rothko (300w)

Gramophone 67:1509 F '90. Nicholas Anderson (450w)

6114. Stabat Mater, for Soprano, Contralto, String Orchestra, Female Chorus and Organ; Salve Regina in A minor; In Coelestibus Regnis.
Robert King (c). Gillian Fisher (sop); Michael Chance (ctr-ten). King's Consort. December, 1987.
HYPERION 66294 DDD 54:23

★***Awards:*** Critics' Choice 1988, *Gramophone* D '88 (Lionel Salter).

"The idea of employing two fine voices (rather than a choir with soloists) and a single instrument to each line is an inspired one. It removes from the music the over-inflated effect often heard in performance, and returns it to the intimate dimensions in which its expressive qualities and its lighter moments are heard far more readily. The singing and playing are exquisite throughout, and the other two pieces a most worthy accompaniment."
Organists' Review 75:46 Mr '89. Paul Hale (460w)

"An absolute winner...The recording also sounds fairly natural, although slightly indirect in focus...one of the best baroque performances to have come to me recently on CD."
Hi-Fi News & Record Review 34:90-1 Je '89. Stephen Daw (220w)

"I'll have to call it a draw between Adda [581 016, Stradavaria Ensemble] and this, but the two are so similar that only the fillers give any reason to own both."
Fanfare 12:228-29 Ja/F '89. J. F. Weber (425w)

Gramophone 66:842-46 N '88. Lionel Salter (270w)

POULENC, FRANCIS

Gloria in G; Motets (4) pour un Temps de Penitence. See No. 2121.

6115. Stabat Mater; Salve Regina; Litanies a la Vierge Noire.
Serge Baudo (c). Michele Lagrange (sop). Lyon National Choir; Lyon National Orchestra.
HARMONIA MUNDI 905149 42:51

✔**HC** ★***Awards:*** *Stereo Review* Best of the Month, Ag '85.

"These performances are superb. The recordings are on a similar plane, with the CD, especially, revealing an almost uncanny capacity for spatial projection."
American Record Guide 48:59 N/D '85. Carl Bauman (350w)

These are "performances that make the most persuasive case for all three works."
Stereo Review 50:58-9 Ag '85. Richard Freed (470w)

"The sound is vivid and wide in dynamic range with a hint of analog origin if quiet passages are turned up above normal level....A beautiful program."
Fanfare 9:229 N/D '85. J. F. Weber (100w)

Hi-Fi News & Record Review 31:106 Ja '86. Andrew Keener (105w)

Gramophone 63:163 Jl '85. Lionel Salter (300w)

PROKOFIEV, SERGEI

6116. Alexander Nevsky (cantata), for Mezzo-soprano, Orchestra and Chorus, Opus 78; Lieutenant Kije Suite, Opus 60.
Andre Previn (c). Christine Cairns (mez). Los Angeles Master Chorale; Los Angeles Philharmonic Orchestra. 1986.
TELARC 80143 DDD 61:00

★★***Awards:*** Third Place Production and Engineering Mumm Champagne Classical Music Award 1988—Presented by *Ovation*, *Ovation* N '88. Records to Die for: 1 of 5 Recommended Recordings, *Stereophile* Ja '91 (Peter W. Mitchell).

"This is one of those rare recordings in which everything seems to have come together to produce a completely satisfying musical experience."
High Fidelity 38:64 F '88. David Hurwitz (250w)

"I have listened repeatedly to Abbado's silken recordings of *Lt. Kije* and the *Alexander Nevsky* cantata: this new recording sounds as good as Abbado's, and it is even more spirited."
Fanfare 11:188-9 Ja/F '88. Michael Ullman (100w)

"Prokofiev's marvelously varied sonic palette, with pseudo-oriental combinations of bass drum, tam-tam, tuba, cymbals, bells, tambourines, and large chorus, will give your system a real workout. Telarc's recording is superbly clear and naturally balanced, has a huge dynamic range, and produces a soundstage both wide and deep."
Stereophile 14:161 Ja '91. Peter W. Mitchell (b.n.)

"Those who want the sound of the demonstration-class recording that Telarc gives Previn, need not feel they are getting anything less than first-rate performances."
American Record Guide 51:67-8 Mr/Ap '88. Gerald S. Fox (500w)

"Andre Previn's unhurried manner and the urbanity of the Los Angeles sound are both well-suited to this work....Christine Cairns sings it beautifully...I'd prefer the darker timbre of a contralto. Likewise the chorus is pleasing to hear, but it's too refined to convey the brusque excitation of a medieval Russian army marching off to war. These reservations aside, the disc is highly recommended."
HighPerformanceReview 5:86 S '88. John Mueter (200w)

"In both works, the Los Angeles Philharmonic plays impressively; the *Kije* is altogether lovely, with Previn light-handedly 'on top' of the score, but the Nevsky performance (although excellently sung and played by soloist, chorus and orchestra and superbly recorded) simply lacks the excitement generated by other recent recordings, not to mention the classic versions by Reiner or Ormandy."

Ovation 10:52-4 Ag '89. Paul Turok (210w)

"It is the first CD to be recorded via Colossus, the new all-digital surround-sound system developed by Lou Dorren and Brad Miller-....These performances of the two Prokofiev scores are well worth having, quite aside from the potential resurrection of four-channel."

Audio 72:152 Ja '88. Edward Tatnall Canby (425w)

Digital Audio 4:54 Je '88. Daniel Kumin (375w)

Gramophone 65:1231 F '88. Ivan March (385w)

6117. Alexander Nevsky (cantata), for Mezzo-soprano, Orchestra and Chorus, Opus 78; Lieutenant Kije Suite, Opus 60. GLINKA, MIKHAIL. Overture: Rusland and Ludmilla.

Fritz Reiner (c). Rosalind Elias (mez). Chicago Symphony Chorus; Chicago Symphony Orchestra. 1957, 1959 reissues.
RCA 0176 ADD 67:30

★***Awards:*** *American Record Guide* Overview: Prokofieff and Shostakovich, S/O '91 (Alexander Nevsky).

"Shostakovich wrote a lot more film music but it fell to Sergei Prokofiev to write what may be the two most popular 'classical' film scores ever written, and here they are together on this mid-price CD in high-powered, well-recorded performances. I know that some more recent recordings are even clearer, but the sound on this CD continues to pay tribute to RCA Victor's mastery of Orchestra Hall, with the orchestra having presence without imposing itself on you....The Glinka overture is done as well as one would expect it to be."

Fanfare 13:263 Ja/F '90. James Miller (240w)

American Record Guide 53:75 Ja/F '90. Donald R. Vroon (125w)

P95/100 S75/85

Hi-Fi News & Record Review 34:137 D '89. Christopher Breunig (100w)

Digital Audio's CD Review 6:51+ Ja '90. Lawrence Johnson (105w)

PURCELL, HENRY

6118. Ode for St. Cecilia's Day, 1683: Welcome to All the Pleasures, Z.339.. **Funeral Sentences:** Man that is born of a woman, Z.27; In the midst of life, Z.17; Thou know'st, Lord, Z.58. **Ode for Queen Mary's Birthday, 1694:** Come ye sons of art, away, Z.323. **Funeral Music for Queen Mary:** March and Canzona, Z.860. **Thou know'st, Lord, Z.58.**

Andrew Parrott (c). Emily Van Evera (sop); Tim Wilson (ctr-ten); John Mark Ainsley (ten); Charles Daniels (ten); David Thomas (bass). Taverner Choir; Taverner Consort and Players. August 1988.
EMI 49635 DDD 55:00

✔**HC** ★***Awards:*** Critics' Choice 1990, *Gramophone* D '90 (David Fallows).

"From the standpoint of current performance practice, Parrott's renditions are above reproach....while I admire Parrott's accomplishment very highly, I can't avoid going back to older versions, some in an earlier style, for Purcell performances of high enduring art....This is a superb representation of Purcell in current garb."

Fanfare 13:267-68 Ja/F '90. J. F. Weber (500w)

"The soloists of the Taverner Consort provide all that could be asked for in the way of clarity; Parrott's direction is incisive; the chorus adds breadth when required. But I am left with the overriding impression that the interpretation—for all its scholarly insight and impact—is crucially lacking in deep-felt realisation of the fear, uncertainty and hope that are interwoven in the text."

New Hi-Fi Sound 7:108 N '89. Keith Howard (205w)

"It is curious how very few decent performances there are of *Come ye sons of art away* on record. You need look no further....The Choir, Consort and Players are all on fine form in the other works, which receive memorable performances...My only quibble really is over the tone of the solo soprano, Emily Van Evera, whose reedy, rather over-forward tone does not seem to me to suit the Funeral Sentences, where a more ethereal, detached boy's voice is altogether preferable."

Organists' Review 75:280 D '89. Paul Hale (375w)

"The exquisite Funeral Sentences suffer from occasional slips of intonation; however, the natural recording balance throughout this disc allows the ear to register Purcell's colorful harmonies."

High Fidelity 1:119 F '90. Andrew Stuart (b.n.)

"Without becoming oppressive this recording offers a sustained look at the melancholia of Purcell's music....The Taverner Consort plays with its usual skill, and the choir distinguishes itself in the harrowing, profoundly disturbing Funeral Sentences. Tenor Charles Daniels and Bass David Thomas are particularly appealing soloists."

American Record Guide 53:92 My/Je '90. Philip Kennicott (175w)

Gramophone 67:1510 F '90. David Fallows (230w)

6119. Ode for the Queen's Birthday, "Arise My Muse;" Ode for St. Cecilia's Day, "Welcome to All the Pleasures;" Ode for the

Queen's Birthday, "Now Does the Glorious Day Appear.
Robert King (c). Gillian Fisher (sop); Tessa Bonner (sop); James Bowman (alto); Michael Chance (alto); Charles Daniels (high ten); John Mark Ainsley (ten); Michael George (bar); Charles Potts (bass). King's Consort. May 1988.
HYPERION 66314 DDD 60:00

★*Awards:* Critics' Choice 1989, *Gramophone* D '89 (Julie Anne Sadie).

"*Welcome to all the Pleasures*...is full of delights....The two later works are similarly entrancing, and all their qualities are enhanced by the singers....Instrumental support from the strings, oboes, recorders, natural trumpets, theorbo, organ and harpsichord is skillfully woven around the vocal lines and the whole captured in a luminously resonant acoustic."
Organists' Review 75:46-7 Mr '89. Paul Hale (450w)

"At last we have a performance of Purcell's celebratory Odes where the voices have the right ring of exquisite confidence, the accompanying instrumentalists know how to make the music bloom without going 'over the top', and the whole effect is involving because it does not sound too precious....My most serious quibbles here concern the recording and the editing."
Hi-Fi News & Record Review 34:100 F '89. Stephen Daw (210w)

"Texts are printed...For the sensible grouping and stylish performances, this can be recommended."
Fanfare 12:281 My/Je '89. J. F. Weber (460w)

Gramophone 66:1326 F '89. Julie Ann Sadie (280w)

RACHMANINOFF, SERGEI

6120. Vespers (All-Night Vigil), for unaccompanied Chorus, Opus 37.
Mstislav Rostropovich (c). Maureen Forrester; Gene Tucker. Washington Choral Arts Society. National Cathedral, Washington.
ERATO 75319 DDD 57:22

★*Awards:* Second Place Choral Mumm Champagne Classical Music Award 1988—Presented by *Ovation, Ovation* N '88.

"A must-have, this one."
Ovation 9:43 O '88. Christopher Greenleaf (415w)

"I'm not a specialist in Slavic enunciation, but I hear nothing from the two soloists or the choral singers to offend my ear....This will please many listeners, and I'll return to it often for the gorgeous sound ands committed conducting."
Fanfare 11:196-7 Ja/F '88. J. F. Weber (380w)

"Unfortunately, Erato has not seen fit to include the Russian text, only the titles of the fifteen movements, given in French and English."
Stereo Review 53:106-7 Ap '88. Stoddard Lincoln (150w)

Gramophone 66:1200 Ja '89. John Warrack (400w)

RAMIREZ, ARIEL

6121. Missa Criolla; Navidad en Verano; Navidad Nuestra.
Jose Luis Ocejo; Damian Sanchez (c). Jose Carreras (ten); Ariel Ramirez (pno/hpscd). Laredo Choral Salve; Bilbao Choral Society; Instrumental Ensemble. Santuario de la Bien Aparecida, Cantabria, Spain. July 1987.
PHILIPS 420 955 DDD 44:00

★★*Awards:* Records to Die for: 1 of 5 Recommended Recordings, *Stereophile* Ja '91 (Lewis Lipnick, Thomas J. Norton).

"This July 1987 performance, recorded in the Santuario de la Bien Aparecida, Cantabria, Spain, has got to stand as one of the outstanding artistic and sonic achievements of the past ten years....Sonically, this recording is a knockout, especially if you're a soundstage freak."
Stereophile 14:159 Ja '91. Lewis Lipnick (105w)

"The engineering captures everything faithfully-....texts are omitted....If you like Carreras, or if you want this approach to music, you won't be disappointed."
Fanfare 12:244-45 Mr/Ap '89. J. F. Weber (260w)

"A superb sense of openness, spaciousness, and three-dimensional soundstage here is flawed only by occasional overloading on Carreras's crescendos. The work is moving, and the performance could hardly be bettered."
Stereophile 14:162 Ja '91. Thomas J. Norton (b.n.)

Gramophone 66:846 N '88. A.M.L. (245w)

REICH, STEVE

6122. The Desert Music.
Steve Reich; others. October 1984.
ELEKTRA 79101 DDD

★*Awards:* *Gramophone* Critics' Choice 1986 (John Milsom). Critics' Choice 1988, *Gramophone* D '88 (John Milsom).

"The performance itself is superb, and it is recorded with brilliant but unexaggerated vividness."
Stereo Review 51:96+ Ja '86. Richard Freed (350w)

"For Reich, the desert symbolizes hallucination and insanity and man's struggle for survival. In the third movement, Williams poetry is prophetic: 'Man has survived hitherto because he was too ignorant to know how to realize his wishes. Now that he can realize them, he must either change them or perish." *Desert Music* is scored for an orchestra of ninety players and a chorus of twenty-seven....This is not intellectually demanding music (it creates textures and mosaics and changing sounds in space)....It is more diverse in detail than the music of Philip Glass, but it also seems to be less powerful-....This recording is an important one if your are a follower of [Reich's] music."

HighPerformanceReview 4(1):179 '86 George S.T. Chu (560w) (rev. of LP)

"Michael Tilson Thomas, conducting members of the Brooklyn Philharmonic and of Reich's ensemble, provides a performance of unremitting energy and astonishing precision. Those who are at all interested in Reich's music should add this recording to their collections."

High Fidelity 36:67-8 Ap '86. K. Robert Schwarz (300w) (rev. of LP)

"When I heard the American premiere of *Desert Music* at the Brooklyn Academy, a few days before this recording was made, it seemed at bit tedious toward the end. Not so here-....Whatever the reason, the sense of forward movement never flags. Thomas' connection with Reich goes back some years...Here, his precise balancing of Reich's orchestral and choral forces points up the drama that seethes within the composer's layered blend of chord masses and insistent rhythms."

Opus 2:47-9 Ap '86. Allan Kozinn (860w)

"The *Desert Music* is...[Reich's] most ambitious work of all, scored for twenty-seven singers and a orchestra of eighty-nine players-....Like so many of this composer's works, *Desert Music* has an air of jauntiness, a glistening, bouncy quality and a good deal of wonderful, ornamental detail. Unfortunately, there are also problems with the piece, for the grandiosity of its aims seems to be undermined too often by poor text setting...and by a ponderousness and occasional lack of compelling direction."

Ovation 7:41-42 O '86 Michael Kimmelman (375w)

Opus 3:54 D '86 Andrew Stiller (105w)

Gramophone 64:81-2 Je '86. John Milsom (700w)

RHEINBERGER, JOSEF

6123. Sacred Choral Music: Mass in E flat, Opus 109, "Cantus Missae"; Hymn from Psalm 84, Opus 35; Stabat Mater in G minor, Opus 138; Hymns (5), Opus 140; Abendlied, Opus 69, No. 3.

Frieder Bernius (c). Stuttgart Chamber Choir; Stuttgart Ensemble.
CARUS 83113 DDD 65:02

> ★*Awards:* The Want List 1990, *Fanfare* N/D '90 (Haig Mardirosian).

"Frieder Bernius and his Stuttgart chorus, who have done such magnificent work in their many recordings of Mendelssohn's choral music, seem to fit this music as the proverbial hand the proverbial glove. This is choral singing at its best."

Fanfare 13:277 Ja/F '90. David Johnson (525w)

"Every one of these works has been painstakingly prepared and performed and even the organ chosen for this recording has been carefully selected...A fine series which is admirable in every respect."

American Record Guide 53:96 My/Je '90. David G. Mulbury (250w)

ROSNER, ARNOLD. Magnificat, Opus 72. See No. 1310.

ROSSI, LUIGI

6124. Oratorio per la Settimana Santa (Oratorio for Holy Week); Oratorio, "Un Peccator Pentitio" (A Repentant Sinner).

William Christie (c). Les Arts Florissants Vocal and Instrumental Ensemble.
HARMONIA MUNDI 901297 DDD 48:25

> ★*Awards:* Critics' Choice 1989, *Gramophone* D '89 (Tess Knighton).

"The merits of Christie's ensemble are well-known by now. The excellent solo work, especially for Mary (Agnes Mellon? Jill Feldman?), is particularly commendable for its (in this music, essential) attention to clear diction. The plangent sounds of the period strings in the oratorio are particularly well-suited to its affective intentions."

American Record Guide 53:96-7 Mr/Ap '90. John W. Barker (590w)

"While this work was recorded for West German Radio a few years ago, the brief filler was done for Radio France more recently....Appealing to a somewhat more special interest than the average Christie release, this will nevertheless be greeted without delay as an important byway of the early Italian oratorio."

Fanfare 13:306 S/O '89. J. F. Weber (340w)

Gramophone 67:728 O '89. Tess Knighton (385w)

ROSSINI, GIOACCHINO

6125. Stabat Mater.

Semyon Bychkov (c). Carol Vaness (sop); Cecilia Bartoli (mez); Francisco Araiza (ten); Ferruccio Furlanetto (bass). Bavarian Radio Chorus; Bavarian Symphony Orchestra.
PHILIPS 426 312 DDD 65:00

> ✔HC

"Nothing Semyon Bychkov has done on records prepared me for this revelation of Rossini's much-loved, much-ridiculed, ever-popular masterpiece....I find no reason not to put this at the top of the heap, pending the arrival of Hickox."

Fanfare 14:269-70 Jl/Ag '91. J. F. Weber (350w)

"Semyon Bychkov firmly places Rossini's *Stabat Mater* into the ecclesiastical tradition. While his view might not be what some listeners are familiar with or accustomed to, they owe it to themselves to hear this admirable version of an ever-rewarding masterpiece."

American Record Guide 54:117 Jl/Ag '91. Lee Milazzo (300w)

Gramophone 68:1710 Mr '91. Richard Osborne (700w)

RUTTER, JOHN

6126. Anthems for Chorus and Orchestra: O clap your hands; All things bright and beautiful; The Lord is my shepherd; A gaelic blessing; For the beauty of the earth; Praise ye the Lord; God be in my head; Open thou mine eyes; A prayer of Saint Patrick; The Lord bless you and keep you. Gloria.

John Rutter (c). Cambridge Singers; City of London Sinfonia.
COLLEGIUM 100 DDD

★*Awards:* *Gramophone* Critics' Choice (Malcolm Macdonald), 1987.

Gramophone 65:90 Je '87 Malcolm MacDonald (210w)

"Here is a composer who mixes the sophisticated and the naive in an utterly disarming way....The performances are all first-rate; Rutter knows how to get what he wants from his singers and instrumentalists."

Fanfare 10:195-6 Mr/Ap '87 David Johnson (350w)

SCELSI, GIACINTO. Uaxuctum, for Chorus and Orchestra. See No. 1320.

SCHEIN, JOHANN HERMANN

6127. Secular Vocal Music.

Konrad Junghanel (c). Cantus Colln.
DEUTSCHE HARMONIA MUNDI 77088 ADD 74:13

★*Awards:* Critics' Choice 1990, *Gramophone* D '90 (Tess Knighton).

"Cantus Colln...bring out both the Italianate wealth of musical imagery and the more Germanic solidity of construction in these pieces."

Continuo 14:22 Je '90. Scott Paterson (135w)

"The twenty-two works in this collection, settings of Schein's own poetry scored for five voices and continuo, cover a wide range of complementary styles and subjects—from artful madrigalian pastorales to folklike drinking songs. Under the direction of lutanist Konrad Junghanel, Cantus Colln succeeds in capturing the general spirit and subtle nuances of each composition....All the solo voices of Cantus Colln are attractive in their own right."

Musick 13(2):30 Fall-Sept '91. Gregory S. Johnston (long)

"The sound is clear and bright...This will be an automatic choice for anyone who wants to be familiar with seventeenth-century Germany, for it takes a block of material and renders it to perfection."

Fanfare 13:278 My/Je '90. J. F. Weber (350w)

Gramophone 68:808 O '90. Tess Knighton (525w)

SCHOENBERG, ARNOLD

6128. Gurrelieder.

Riccardo Chailly (c). Susan Dunn (sop); Brigitte Fassbaender (mez); Siegfried Jerusalem (ten); Peter Haage (ten); Hermann Becht (bass); Hans Hotter (nar). Saint Hedwig's Cathedral Choir; Dusseldorf Municipal Choral Society; Berlin Radio Symphony Orchestra. 1985.
LONDON/DECCA 430 321 DDD 101:00 2 discs

✔HC ★★★★*Awards:* The Gramophone Awards, Nominations, Choral, *Gramophone*, N '91; The Want List 1991, *Fanfare* N/D '91 (James H. North). Top Twelve Albums of the Year, 1991, *Stereo Review*, F '92. Pick of the Month, North American Perspective (Christie Barter), *Gramophone* Mr '91.

"Mr. Chailly achieves a lyrical sweep that is simply irresistible...[He] also appears to have transmitted this level of insight to his three principal singers. Two of them set new standards of eloquence in the piece."

The New York Times My 19 '91, p. 25+ H. Jon Alan Conrad (med)

"Chailly has a first-rate cast...I am a great fan of live performance and of music in the theater, but this is a work of magnitude and imagination that comes across in a recording like the Chailly/London version as it never can in real life."

Stereo Review 56:86 Ag '91. Eric Salzman (260w)

"Shaped like a first-rate dramatic production."

Stereo Review 57:42 F '92. (brief)

"*Gurrelieder* is one of those neglected 20th Century masterpieces that really deserves to be heard. Conductor Riccardo Chailly gives a persuasive account...The soloists are strong."

High Fidelity 3:98 Mr '91. Clive Manning (100w)

"The performance as a whole does give a sort of *Gurre-Lieder* experience that includes an uncommonly pleasant-sounding Waldemar."

Musical America 111:85-6 Jl '91. Kenneth Furie (500w)

"I had not been impressed by much of Chailly's conducting, on or off records, to date. This new release, however, is beyond complaint...Even the RSO's oft-sour woodwinds are on good behavior; and the build-up in the final chorus, thrillingly recorded, is expertly done...Jerusalem is terrific as Waldemar, encompassing the ardor and despair and the killing tessitura with aplomb...London's recorded sound is splendid, a characteristically fine combination of presence and hall resonance."

American Record Guide 55:103 Ja/F '92. Stephen D. Chakwin, Jr. (long)

"The 1979 Boston Symphony live performance under Ozawa is the only CD prior to this issue and the main competition for it; but that Philips recording is unsatisfactory....The Berlin Radio Symphony is made to sound a peer of the BSO. In addition, Chailly has a far more strongly characterized view of the score....The real competition for these wonderful discs may lie ahead: a Denon recording led by Eliahu Inbal is due shortly, and Sony is recording current performances by Zubin Mehta and the New York Philharmonic."

Fanfare 15:341-42 S/O '91. James H. North (long)

"The current dearth of really excellent Wagner singers that is affecting opera houses around the world makes casting this most Wagnerian of choral works a real headache....some of the choral singing is magnificent, and the final hymn does not fail to thrill. But, ultimately, this set is too uneven to endure repeated listenings—unless it be for the composer's spectacularly weighty tuttis. It is a pity to be so negative. But the faults are those of the times rather than of the performers engaged." *P85/75 S95*

Hi-Fi News & Record Review 36:76 Ag '91. Simon Cargill (180w)

"I wondered at first why the London discs had not been released since their 1985 recording date, but then I heard the *recording*. The balances are totally unnatural, in favor of the voice, and the recording blares and distorts during the louder passages—which make up 60% of the work. The soloists appear to have been taped on another planet, and the chorus seems to be yelling at us. It's disquieting."

Stereophile 15:271-3 Ja '92. Robert Levine (long)

Gramophone 68:1710+ Mr '91. Michael Oliver (635w)

SCHUBERT, FRANZ

6129. Mass No. 2 in G, D.167; Mass No. 6 in E flat, D.950.

Robert Shaw (c). Dawn Upshaw (sop); Benita Valente (sop); Marietta Simpson (mez); David Gordon (ten); Jon Humphrey (ten); Glenn Siebert (ten); William Stone (bar); Myron Myers (bar). Atlanta Symphony Chamber Chorus; Atlanta Symphony Chamber Orchestra. December 1988; February 1989.
TELARC 80212 DDD 78:00

✔**HC** ★*Awards:* The Want List 1990, *Fanfare* N/D '90 (David Johnson).

"While conducting his Atlanta Symphony and Chamber Chorus for both works, Shaw works with two entirely different sets of soloists. I don't know if that is by design or necessity, but both sets of soloists fulfill their assignments wondrously well....It is not only the Best E flat Mass ever put on records, it stands with the best choral-orchestral performances of past or present, not excluding those of Shaw's mentor, Toscanini. Both works have been captured with perfect fidelity, balance, and richness of detail by Telarc's recording engineer, Jack Renner."

Fanfare 13:251 Jl/Ag '90. David Johnson (600w)

"This latest in the distinguished series of Telarc recordings with Robert Shaw and the Atlanta Symphony lives up to the others....The orchestra, chorus and Telarc's recorded sound all add immeasurably to this quiet, yet impressive disc."

HighPerformanceReview 8(1):78 '91. Bert Wechsler (180w)

"I was so completely blown away (as the current vernacular has it) by this record that I doubt if I can write a coherent and objective review—and I don't think I am going to try to."

American Record Guide 53:102 My/Je '90. David Mason Greene (525w)

"Shaw always produces refined and musical results and these are no exception....Many will enjoy this sound (something of the old Decca 'Ace of Clubs' monaural all-embracing cosiness about it), but I'm a little uneasy on the whole."

Organists' Review 76:223 S '90. Paul Hale (180w)

Gramophone 68:592+ S '90. Stephen Johnson (175w)

SMYTH, ETHEL

6130. Mass in D; The Boatswain's Mate: Suppose You Mean to Do a Given Thing; March of the Women.

Philip Brunelle (c). Eiddwen Harrhy (sop); Janis Hardy (contr); Dan Dressen (ten); James Bohn (bass). Plymouth Festival Chorus and Orchestra.
VIRGIN 91188 DDD 75:00

★*Awards:* Critics' Choice 1991, *Gramophone*, Ja '92 (John Steane).

"This is one of the year's most interesting and worthwhile releases. Give it a shot."

The Wire 90:62 Ag '91. Brian Morton (long)

"A worthwhile issue in which excellent choral singing, orchestral playing and conducting combine to make as fine a case for a Smyth revival as could be hoped."

American Record Guide 54:131 S/O '91. Vivian A. Liff (long)

"This disc is a revelatory tribute to a much-neglected composer of considerable importance."

Fanfare 15:487-88 N/D '91. James H. North (med)

"Convention is the keynote, I'm afraid, to so much on offer here....Add to that some stolid, thick-textured choral writing, and a gloomy, quasi-Brahmsian orchestral palette (nowhere near as harmonically searching as that German master's), and you end up with a rather dispiriting hour-long experience." *P95/85 S95/85*

Hi-Fi News & Record Review 36:77 S '91. Andrew Achenbach (brief)

Gramophone 69:68 Ag '91. John Steane (435w)

STANFORD, CHARLES VILLIERS. Three Motets, Opus 38; Three Motets, Opus 135—Eternal Father; Magnificat in B flat, Opus 164. See No. 6105.

STENHAMMAR, WILHELM

6131. The Song (symphonic cantata); Ithaka, Ballade for Baritone and Orchestra, Opus 21; Two Sentimental Romances for Violin and Orchestra, Opus 28.
Herbert Blomstedt; Kjell Ingebretsen; Stig Westerberg (c). Iva Sorenson (sop); Anne-Sofie von Otter (m-sop); Stefan Dahlberg (ten); Per-Arne Wahlgren (bar); Hakan Hagegard (bar); Arve Tellefsen (vln). Swedish Radio Chorus; Adolf Frederik Music School Children's Choir; Swedish Radio Symphony Orchestra.
CAPRICE 21358 DDD; ADD 57:51

★*Awards:* The Want List 1988, *Fanfare* N/D '88 (Henry Fogel).

"Violinist Tellefsen is a deft, projective soloist, sympathetically supported by conductor Westerberg....All in all, this is an attractive collection....Heartily endorsed."
Fanfare 11:254 Jl/Ag '88. John D. Wiser (300w)

"What a wonderful disc this is!"
American Record Guide 51:390 N/D '88. Carl Bauman (89w)

Musical America 110:85-7 Ja '90. Thomas L. Dixon (110w)

STRAVINSKY, IGOR

6132. Symphony of Psalms; Symphony in C; Symphony in Three Movements.
Igor Stravinsky (c). Elmer Iseler (choir director). Toronto Festival Singers; CBC Vancouver Orchestra; Columbia Symphony Orchestra. 1962, 1964 reissues.
CBS 42434 ADD 70:10

✔HC ★*Awards:* The Want List 1988, *Fanfare* N/D '88 (Mortimer H. Frank).

"No one else has ever captured the violence and hard-won exultation of the *Symphony in Three Movements* better than their creator-....The older LPs are more aggressively brilliant and synthetic than the mellower, more natural CDs."
Fanfare 11:261-2 Jl/Ag '88. Elliott Kaback (210w)

"The *Symphony in Three Movements*...and the Symphony in C are superlative interpretations, crisply articulated and tenderly lyrical by turns; the *Symphony of Psalms*, on the other hand, is rather disappointing...and the sound is less well focused here than in the two instrumental symphonies, where it is clear and sharply defined."
Hi-Fi News & Record Review 34:97 Je '89. Kenneth Dommett (150w)

See *Petrouchka* for review excerpt.
Musical America 109:59-60 Mr '89. Terry Teachout (85w)

See *Petrouchka* for review excerpt.
Stereophile 11:175-6 N '88. Mortimer H. Frank (320w)

Gramophone 66:1049 D '88. Michael Oliver (95w)

TAVENER, JOHN

6133. Ikon of Light (1984); Funeral Ikos; Carol, the Lamb.
Peter Phillips; John Taverner (c). Members of the Chilingirian Quartet. Tallis Scholars. 1984 reissue.
ABBEY-GIMELL 005 DDD 55:00

★*Awards:* Critics' Choice 1991, *Gramophone*, Ja '92 (Michael Stewart).

"Strongly recommended to all...this is another stunning success in the Tallis Scholars series."
American Record Guide 54:160 N/D '91. Arved Ashby (long)

"In this welcome re-issue from GIMELL, the magnificent Tallis Scholars again demonstrate some of their ability: they not only manage to sound more numerous than sixteen, they also respond faithfully to the profound spirituality of the music. They are undaunted even when asked by the composer not to sing in a 'westernised manner'."
Organists' Review 76:138 Je '91. Francis O'Gorman (285w)

"This issue received little notice on LP, no reviews that I know of in this country, and no listing in our variously titled catalogs published by William Schwann's successors....The performances are clearly of the highest order...John Taverner's is undoubtedly a major talent...Curious collectors will find much to enjoy on this stunning disc."
Fanfare 14:305-6 Jl/Ag '91. J. F. Weber (350w)

Gramophone 69:78 Je '91. Michael Stewart (400w)

TIPPETT, MICHAEL

6134. The Mask of Time.
Andrew Davis (c). Faye Robinson (sop); Sarah Walker (mez); Robert Tear (ten); John Cheek (bass). BBC Singers; BBC Chorus; BBC Symphony Orchestra. Royal Festival Hall, London. March 2, 1986.
EMI 47705 DDD 91:30 2 discs

★★*Awards: Opus* Contemporary Music Award Nominee, 1987; *Gramophone* Contemporary Award, 1987. Critics' Choice 1989, *Gramophone* D '89 (David Fanning).

"It's a compelling reading—far and away the most gripping conducting I've ever heard form Andrew Davis...The soloists—especially Tear,-...are all in tune with Tippet's musical syntax, and the recording has both space and—in the climaxes—almost visceral impact."

Fanfare 11:327-9 S/O '87. Peter J. Rabinowitz (790w)

"It is an astonishing achievement on the performers' and the engineers' part."

The Musical Times 129:26 Ja '88. Peter Dickinson (440w)

"This is altogether a welcome issue that should enable the listener to gain an intimate knowledge of a major work of our time."

Hi-Fi News & Record Review 32:98-99 Ag '87 Doug Hammond (300w)

"Whatever the unevenness of the score, this account of it deserves nothing but praise-....Among the four admirable soloists, Faye Robinson takes top honors....Tippett...seems to have attempted nothing less than a summation of his long life's entire experience, as well as his conclusions—less than optimistic—concerning human fate."

Musical America 109:83-4 Mr '89. Paul Moor (170w)

"Faye Robinson...manages pretty well even in the seventh movement, where the writing exposes her most mercilessly; elsewhere she is consistently impressive...Robert Tear's trenchant diction, vivid musical intelligence, and trustworthy technique compensate here, as so often, for a certain dryness of tone...How John Cheek, the bass, landed this no doubt prestigious assignment is hard to guess...The BBC Singers, the BBC Symphony Chorus, and the BBC Symphony Orchestra, led by Andrew Davis, give a committed, sharply defined reading that deserves to stand unrivaled for a while—as on disc it in all likelihood will have to."

Opus 4:54-5 Ap '88. Matthew Gurewitsch (1500w)

Gramophone 64:1586+ My '87 Michael Oliver (320w) (rev. of LP)

TOCH, ERNST. Jephta, Rhapsodic Poem (Symphony No. 5). See No. 6026.

VAUGHAN WILLIAMS, RALPH

6135. Vocal Music: Serenade to Music; Flos Campi; Five Mystical Songs; Fantasia on Christmas Carols.

Matthew Best (c). Elizabeth Connell (sop); Linda Kitchen (sop); Anne Dawson (sop); Amanda Roocroft (sop); Sarah Walker (mez); Jean Rigby (mez); Diana Montague (mez); Catherine Wyn-Rogers (contr); John Mark Ainsley (ten); Martyn Hill (ten); Arthur Davies (ten); Maldwyn Davies (ten); Thomas Allen (bar); Alan Opie (bar); Gwynne Howell (bass); John Connell (bass); Nobuko Imai (vla). Corydon Singers; English Chamber Orchestra. February, June 1990.
HYPERION 66420 DDD 68:00

> ✔**HC** ★★*Awards:* Pick of the Month, North American Perspective (Christopher Pollard), *Gramophone* S '90. Critics' Choice 1990, *Gramophone* D '90 (Edward Greenfield). The Gramophone Awards, Nominations, Choral, *Gramophone*, N '91.

"Already a Hyperion best-seller; and not without good reason, for this is indeed a lovely issue, and the performances are consistently refined and thoughtful. The real jewel in this anthology comes in the shape of the *Serenade to Music*, which here receives magical treatment from a rapt ECO under Matthew Best and his 16 dedicated soloists." *P95/100 S95*

Hi-Fi News & Record Review 35:101 D '90. Andrew Achenbach (420w)

"This is one of the loviest records it has been my pleasure to listen to recently."

Organists' Review 76:54 Mr '91. Paul Hale (235w)

"This is a marvelous anthology exquisitely performed. I urge you to investigate it."

American Record Guide 54:121 My/Je '91. David Mason Greene (265w)

"Surely this is the most attractive performance of *Serenade to Music* so far to appear on CD in modern sound....This [*Five Mystical Songs*] is a festival piece *par excellence*....It is for the serenade and *Flos Campi* that one should want this CD, indeed, crave it. Strongly recommended!"

Fanfare 15:379-80 S/O '91. John Wiser (med)

High Fidelity 2:117 N '90. Clive Manning (80w)

Gramophone 68:598 S '90. Edward Greenfield (510w)

VERDI, GIUSEPPE

6136. Requiem Mass, in Memory of Manzoni; Choruses: from *Aida, Don Carlos, Macbeth, Nabucco, Otello.*

Robert Shaw (c). Susan Dunn (sop); Diane Curry (mez); Jerry Hadley (ten); Paul Plishka (bass). Atlanta Symphony Chorus and Orchestra. Symphony Hall, Atlanta, GA. April 11-12, 14, 1987.
TELARC 80152 DDD 59:00; 53:30 2 discs

> ★★★★★*Awards:* First Place Choral Mumm Champagne Classical Music Award 1988—Presented by *Ovation, Ovation* N '88; The Want List 1988, *Fanfare* N/D '88 (Ralph V. Lucano, James Miller); Choral Record Award 1988, *Gramophone* O '88; Best of the Year, *Opera News* D 24 '88. Records to Die for: 1 of 5 Recommended Recordings, *Stereophile* Ja '91 (Gordon Emerson).

"The recording is absolutely superb....It is a meticulous, thoughtful, altogether splendid performance, with not a weak element in it."

Ovation 9:42 My '88. Joseph Duchac (265w)

"Robert Shaw's account of the *Requiem* strikes me as the best since Giulini's....the voice-lover in me must take note of Susan Dunn's first major recording....This is a Verdi soprano of stature. Watch her."

American Record Guide 51:94-5 Mr/Ap '88. Ralph V. Lucano (265w)

"Shaw's Atlanta chorus is one of the greatest, and it easily outsings the La Scala group-...Shaw...catches the natural flow of the piece-

...creating an atmosphere of reverence that does not preclude drama. Telarc has helped him immeasurably by providing a rich, warm, beautifully balanced recording."
Musical America 108:80+ S '88. David Hurwitz (245w)

"Shaw's utterly straightforward interpretation is clearly cast in the Toscanini mold....The choral work is thrilling."
High Fidelity 38:62 D '88. Terry Teachout (150w)

"The soloists and assembled forces are first-rate, and Shaw molds a re-creation of this operatic yet deeply spiritual masterpiece that is wonderful in ways both obvious and subtle. Old Giuseppe must be smiling somewhere."
Stereophile 14:135 Ja '91. Gordon Emerson (b.n.)

"Despite—or because of—the absence of superstar performers, this latest entry in the *Requiem* sweepstakes has a great deal going for it....The casting of the vocal team...proves effectually attractive, particularly the three young singers."
Stereophile 11:135-7 Jl '88. Bernard Soll (1120w)

"One or two of my colleagues have been most enthusiastic. I don't see it myself. Certainly there is no finer *sounding* version currently before us...And yes, the singing...is generally excellent....I sorely miss the drama, the blazing hand-on-heart conviction that the likes of Muti and Toscanini breathe back into this music."
Hi-Fi News & Record Review 33:91 Je '88. Edward Seckerson (625w)

"This is a very 'safe' recording to recommend because of its middle-of-the-road stance and technical proficiency."
Fanfare 11:226-7 Mr/Ap '88. James Miller (425w)

"Telarc's recording...is surprisingly muted...the result is disappointedly lacking in immediacy, with some blurring of orchestral texture....the interpretation could use a more Italianate passion, more of the dramatic quality of opera-....Orchestra and chorus perform nobly."
HighPerformanceReview 5:87 D '88. George S. T. Chu (210w)

Gramophone 65:1339 Mr '88 (800w); 66:546 O '88 (200w). Alan Blyth

6137. Requiem Mass, in Memory of Manzoni; Te Deum (No. 4 of Pezzi Sacri).
Arturo Toscanini (c). Zinka Milanov (sop); Bruna Castagna (mez); Jussi Bjoerling (ten); Nicola Moscona (bass). NBC Symphony Orchestra. Carnegie Hall. 1940.
MUSIC & ARTS 240 99:50 2 discs

✔HC ★*Awards:* *Fanfare* Want List 1987 (Mortimer H. Frank).

"The performance of the Requiem, despite occasional fluffs from soloists and orchestra...is stupendous in virtually every way....The anonymous engineer who transferred the original acetate transcription discs to CD has done a surprisingly good cleanup job: the sound is noisy in spots but generally clear and intelligible."
Musical America 108:64 Mr '88. Terry Teachout (270w)

High Fidelity 38:62-3 Ja '88. Thomas Hathaway (800w)

VIERNE, LOUIS

6138. Messe Sonennelle for Chorus and 2 Organs, Opus 16; Triptyque, Opus 58; Symphony III for Organ, Opus 28.
Jehan Revert (c). Pierre Cochereau (orgn). Notre Dame (Paris) Cathedral Choir. December 1975.
FY 064 AAD 70:43

★*Awards:* The Want List 1988, *Fanfare* N/D '88 (Haig Mardirosian).

"This superb recording provides the listener with a sampler of Vierne's creative efforts-....Anyone who enjoys the sound of the organs of France, or has fond memories of visiting this ancient cathedral, or simply opts to wallow in acoustic splendor, will find this recording just the thing."
American Record Guide 51:92 S/O '88. Donald E. Metz (390w)

"Here is music meant to steady and console in the face of an uncertain future, an assessment which likely would have gladdened the composer. The performance, while grand and ceremonial, invites the hearer to spiritual reconciliation....a high recommendation."
Fanfare 11:227-8 Mr/Ap '88. Haig Mardirosian (750w)

VIVALDI, ANTONIO. Gloria in D, R.589.
See No. 6018.

WALTON, WILLIAM

6139. Sacred Choral Music: Magnificat and Nunc dimittis; Cantico del sole; Antiphon; Set me as a seal upon thine heart; Missa brevis; Where does the uttered music go?; Jubilate Deo; A Litany; The Twelve. *Carols:* All this time; What cheer?; King Herod and the Cock; Make we joy now in this fest.
Richard Marlow (c). Richard Jackson (orgn); Graham Pearce (orgn). Trinity College Choir, Cambridge. June 1988.
CONIFER 164 DDD 64:00

★★★*Awards:* Critics' Choice 1989, *Gramophone* D '89 (Mary Berry; Edward Greenfield); Best of the Month, *Hi-Fi News & Record Review*, S '89. Critics Choice, *Hi Fi News & Record Review*, Ap '91 Supplement (William McVicker).

"This well-planned disc fills a notable gap in Walton recordings. Performances are excellent; despite the richly resonant acoustics of Trinity College chapel, every note and word is clear, a tribute to the skills of Conifer's engineers."
Music and Musicians International 38:55 D '89. Anthony Milner (390w)

"This is a virtually ideal recording. Gripping, technically secure performances of excellent music that has been ignored by the record companies, with superbly reverberant (but still clear) recorded sound, accompanied by full texts and informative notes."

Fanfare 13:345-46 Ja/F '90. Henry Fogel (150w)

"I cannot imagine a finer collection of Walton's choral works—but what a pity that the great *Coronation Te Deum* was not included....The Trinity Metzler may have its idiosyncracies but its rich yet bright tones seem to suit the music well, and its distinctly 'live' wind somehow matches the breathing of the choir and the liveliness of much of the music. My record of the month."

Organists' Review 75:209 S '89. Paul Hale (415w)

"There are some very long phrases which Marlow asks the choir to sing without a breath-...In every case the control of tone is exemplary, the sense of 'line' is truly musical, the legato phrases being seamless and the intonation spot on." *P100/95 S100*

Hi-Fi News & Record Review 34:94 S '89; p.29 My '90 Supplement. William McVicker (300w)

"The Trinity College Choir excels in this flinty, sturdy, vigorous music."

American Record Guide 52:136 N/D '89. Charles Parsons (125w)

Gramophone 66:1766 My '89. Edward Greenfield (530w)

6140. Songs: Christopher Columbus, for Contralto, Tenor, Orchestra and Chorus; Anon in Love, for Tenor and Orchestra; A Song for the Lord Mayor's Table (song cycle), for Soprano and Orchestra; Songs after Edith Sitwell (Daphne; Through Gilded Trellises; Long Steel Grass; Old Sir Faulk), for Soprano (newly orchestrated Christopher Palmer); The Twelve (An Anthem for the Feast of any Apostle: text by W.H. Auden), for Soprano, Mezzo, Countertenor, Tenor, Baritone and Orchestra.

Richard Hickox (c). Jill Gomez (sop); Linda Finnie (mez); Martyn Hill (ten); Arthur Davies (ten). Westminster Singers; City of London Sinfonia.
CHANDOS 7724 DDD 65:05

★***Awards:*** Critics' Choice 1990, *Gramophone* D '90 (Edward Greenfield).

"One of the most assured exponents of English Choral music, Richard Hickox, conducts the City of London Sinfonia, soloists and singers in an exuberant disc."

High Fidelity 1:119 O '90. Clive Manning (100w)

"This is one of the most all-around enjoyable recordings I ever encountered. Where to point first?—to the music: almost an anthology of Walton's best—witty, inventive, colorful; to the text: a veritable compendium of great English poetry; to the artists: beautiful voices used with magical musicianship."

American Record Guide 54:121-2 Ja/F '91. Charles H. Parsons (500w)

"Although this is only the fourth CD in Chandos's Walton series, they have already arrived at some Walton esoterica, all of it vocal and all of it, at the very least, interesting....For Walton and vocal specialists."

Fanfare 14:348-49 Ja/F '91. James Miller (130w)

Musical America 111:62-3 Jl '91. Terry Teachout (165w)

Gramophone 68:1252+ D '90. Edward Greenfield (530w)

WEBER, CARL MARIA VON

6141. Mass No. 1 in E flat ("Freischutz Mass"); Mass No. 2 in G, Opus 76 ("Jubilee Mass").

Horst Stein; Gerhard Wilhelm (c). Krisztina Laki; Marga Schiml; Josef Protschka; Jan-Hendrik Rootering; Elisabeth Speiser; Helen Watts; Kurt Equiluz; Siegmund Nimsgern. Bamberg Symphony Chorus; Bamberg Symphony Orchestra; Stuttgart Hymnus Boys' Choir; Werner Keltsch Instrumental Ensemble.
EMI 47679 DDD/ADD 63:48

★***Awards:*** Critics' Choice 1988, *Gramophone* D '88 (John Warrack).

Originally reviewed in the November/December 1986 issue of *Fanfare.* "I have already expressed my unbounded enthusiasm for the two works and my approval of the performers...In my review of the LP issues, I mentioned that the Mass No. 1 needed a boost in volume. Not so on this CD; in fact, I recommend that you turn the volume down a fraction for comfortable listening."

Fanfare 11:347-8 S/O '87. David Johnson (375w)

Gramophone 66:472 S '88. John Warrack (420w)

XENAKIS, IANNIS

6142. Oresteia.

Dominique Debart (c). Spiros Sakkas (bar); Sylvio Gualda (perc); Women's voices of Colmar. Strasbourg University Music Department Chorus; Anjou Vocal Ensemble; Ensemble de Basse-Normandie. Church of Sainte Aurelie, Strasbourg. October 4 and 6, 1987 live.
SALABERT 8906 ADD 49:00

★★***Awards:*** The Want List 1991, *Fanfare* N/D '91 (William Wians). The Critics' Choice 1990—Composition Award: No. 7 of 15 *Wire* 82/3 '91.

"Subsequent ages must reinterpret past works to make them meaningful to the present. We may see this in the history of Shakespeare performance or in the many transformations of such mythic figures as Don Juan or Faust. So it is that Xenakis renders a strange and ancient story in such a way that we may find truth in it. In doing so, he enables us to find a further truth about ourselves in the choices behind his transformation."

Fanfare 14:329-30 Jl/Ag '91. William Wians (450w)

"*Oresteia*...sets sections of Aeschylus's trilogy in a style full of brutal oppositions between rhythmic chanting reminiscent of the Orthodox liturgy and Xenakis's own swathes of glissandi-....in many ways one of Xenakis's most approachable works for the new listener; the live recording underlines the compelling immediacy of this composer's best works."

Wire 85:63 Mr '91. Richard Barrett (170w)

Gramophone 68:598-9 S '90. David J. Fanning (315w)

ZEMLINSKY, ALEXANDER VON. Psalm XIII for Chorus and Orchestra, Opus 24. See No. 1485.

Choral Music—Collections

Cambridge Singers

6143. Faire is the Heaven: Music of the English Church. Parsons: Ave Maria. **Tallis:** Loquebantur variis linguis; If ye love me. **Byrd:** Miserere mei; Haec dies; Ave verum corpus; Bow thine ear. **Farrant: If ye love me; Hide not thou thy face; Lord, for thy tender mercy's sake. Gibbons:** O clap your hands. Hosanna to the Son of David. **Purcell:** Lord, how long wilt thou be angry?; Thou knowest, Lord, the secrets of our hearts. **Stanford:** Beati quorum via. **Trad. (arr. Wood): This joyful Eastertide. Howells:** Sing lullaby; A spotless rose. **Walton:** What cheer? **Vaughan Williams:** O taste and see. **Britten:** A hymn to the Virgin. **Poston:** Jesus Christ the apple tree. **Harris:** Faire is the Heaven.
John Rutter (c). Cambridge Singers. The Lady Chapel of Ely Cathedral, England. 1982 reissue.
COLLEGIUM 107 AAD 69:48

✔HC ★*Awards:* Critics' Choice 1988, *Gramophone* D '88 (Mary Berry).

"A splendid issue indeed, and highly recommended."

Music and Musicians International 36:42 Je '88. Robert Matthew-Walker (225w)

"Rutter's expressed enthusiasm for the acoustics of the chapel is justified by the superb results on this analog tape, expertly transferred to as fine a sounding CD as anything of its kind. Notes, texts, and the few needed translations are supplied for each piece. Worth hearing."

Fanfare 11:303 Jl/Ag '88. J. F. Weber (250w)

"I must agree that the magical acoustic of the Lady Chapel in Ely Cathedral has been superbly captured here. I would even go so far as to say that it is perfect for these *a cappella* works...The poise of the Cambridge Singers brings a trance-like tranquility and timelessness to a marvellously varied programme."

Hi-Fi News & Record Review 33:87-8 Ag '88. Barbara Jahn (270w)

Digital Audio 5:58+ O '88. David C. Vernier (350w)

Gramophone 66:62+ Je '88. Mary Berry (345w)

6144. There Is Sweet Music: English Choral Songs, 1890-1950. **Stanford:** The Bluebird. **Delius:** Two Unaccompanied Partsongs: To Be Sung of a Summer Night on the Water I and II. **Elgar:** There Is Sweet Music; My Love Dwelt in a Northern Land. **Vaughan Williams:** Three Shakespeare Songs: Full Fadom Five; The Cloud-capp'd Towers; Over Hill, Over Dale. **Britten:** Five Flower Songs: to Daffodils; The Succession of the Four Sweet Months; Marsh Flowers; The Evening Primrose; Ballad of Green Broom. **Grainger:** Brigg Fair; Londonderry Air. **Chapman:** Three Ravens. **Holst:** My Sweetheart's Like Venus. **Bairstow:** The Oak and the Ash. **Stanford:** Quick! We Have but a Second.
John Rutter (c). Cambridge Singers.
COLLEGIUM 104 DDD 56:20

✔HC ★*Awards:* Records to Die for: 1 of 5 Recommended Recordings, *Stereophile* Ja '91 (Barbara Jahn).

"This collection is assembled with extraordinary sensitivity and intelligence....If Rutter's direction runs to cool objectivity, it lacks nothing for vigor and fine-tuned control. The recording catches a solid vocal blend without suppressing timbral values of sections and solos. Detailed annotation by the director and full texts add to the value of this attractive collection."

Fanfare 11:361 S/O '87. John D. Wiser (360w)

"I have rarely been so stunned by the opening track of a disc before....The succeeding performances live up to the same high standard....I am equally enthusiastic about the recording."

Hi-Fi News & Record Review 32:99 F '87 Barbara Jahn (465w)

"I would still consider one four-minute snippet of *a cappella* singing on this disc, in Stanford's 'The Blue Bird,' the most hauntingly beautiful performance/recording I have ever heard. The control of this small, mixed-voice choir over all musical parameters is quite unbelievable, and this tiny record label-...has captured the essence of their unique qualities to perfection."

Stereophile 14:149 Ja '91. Barbara Jahn (b.n.)

"Taken a bit at a time, this is a gorgeous recording."

Fanfare 10:256-7 Mr/Ap '87 Henry Fogel (225w)

Digital Audio & Compact Disc Review 3:66 F '87 David Vernier (375w)

Gramophone 64:1452 Ap '87 Geoffrey Horn (105w)

Hi-Fi News & Record Review Record of the Month, F '87

Hilliard Ensemble

6145. Sacred and Secular Music. Music of **Machaut, Dufay, Fayrfax, Tallis, Byrd, Penalosa, Flecha, Isaac, Goudimel, Janequin, Anon.**
Hilliard Ensemble. 1987; 1989.
HYPERION 66370 DDD 62:00

★***Awards:*** Critics' Choice 1991, *Gramophone*, Ja '92 (David Fallows).

"While specialists may be drawn to this or that specific item in such a spectrum, the program as a whole is fascinating from beginning to end, a compact survey of vocal styles, and something no lover of early music or admirer of this group (and who, having heard them, is not?) should miss."

American Record Guide 54:152 My/Je '91. John W. Barker (335w)

"The historical range is as remarkable as the vocal range and no one will be able to resist Janequin's *Le Chant des Oiseaux*, a severe test of vocal dexterity and a witty catalogue of bird song which, as Paul Hillier's note points out, predates Messiaen by some 400 years."

Organists' Review 76:141 Je '91. Gordon Reynolds (235w)

"No vocal ensemble yields place to the Hilliard in scholarship, musicianship, tonal balance, or purity of intonation (I can think of two that are their equal, both also English). The quality of the recording is seamless...Recommended, as miscellanies go."

Fanfare 14:351 My/Je '91. J. F. Weber (300w)

Gramophone 69:82 Je '91. David Fallows (350w)

Digital Audio's CD Review 7:72 My '91. David Vernier (125w)

Saint Paul's Cathedral Choir

6146. The English Anthem. Bairstow: Blessed City, Heavenly Salem; Let All Mortal Flesh Keep Silence. **Finzi:** God Is Gone Up. **Gardiner:** Evening Hymn "Te lucis ante terminum". **Hadley:** My Beloved Spake. **Ireland:** Greater Love Hath No Man. **Naylor:** Vox dicentis clama. **Stainer:** I Saw the Lord. **Stanford:** Three Motets, Opus 38: Beati quorum via. **S. S. Wesley:** Blessed Be the God and Father. **Wood:** Hail, Gladdening Light.
John Scott (c). Andrew Lucas (orgn). Saint Paul's Cathedral Choir. June 1989.
HYPERION 66374 DDD 69:00

★***Awards:*** The Want List 1991, *Fanfare* N/D '91 (Haig Mardirosian).

"This is perfect for those who are fond of traditional Anglican anthems....Hyperion has captured the famed acoustics of St. Paul's to perfection....There is no finer collection available."

American Record Guide 54:167 Mr/Ap '91. Carl Bauman (b.n.)

"What a feast this is!...Every performance has great moments and the whole programme I'm sure will find many admirers."

Organists' Review 76:224 S '90. Robert Lawrenson (280w)

"It won't correct wrongs, heal the sick, or bring back the dead, but to hear the confident opening lines of, say, Balfour Gardiner's *Te lucis ante terminum* is to become convinced that a night of peaceful sleep will rest the weary spirit. Bairstow's *Blessed city, heavenly Salem* will restore heart and courage. Ireland's enduring *Greater love* will serve to remind that someone else is always worse off. Stanford's *Beati* will suggest that the righteous will have their recompense. It really is that good, and that touching."

Fanfare 14:421-22 N/D '90. Haig Mardirosian (300w)

Gramophone 68:599 S '90. John Steane (375w)

6147. My Spirit Hath Rejoiced. Noble: Evening Service in B minor, Opus 6. **Howells:** Gloucester Service. **Murrill:** Magnificat and Nunc dimittis in E. **Harwood:** Magnificat and Nunc dimittis in A flat, Opus 6. **Drake:** Evening Service in F. **sumsion:** Magnificat and Nunc dimittis in G. **Dyson:** Evening Service in D.
John Scott (c). Christopher Dearnley (orgn). Saint Paul's Cathedral Choir. 1988.
HYPERION 66305 DDD 61:00

★***Awards:*** Critics' Choice 1989, *Gramophone* D '89 (John Steane).

"The performances of this lovely music are uniformly superb."

Fanfare 12:377 My/Je '89. John Ditsky (200w)

"The choir is superb, as usual: nothing tentative here, but solid, forceful singing in the English tradition. Organ accompaniments are again a real treat, and many will treasure the perfectly-captured ambience of St. Paul's."

American Record Guide 52:125 My/Je '89. Donald R. Vroon (315w)

"Scott's control of the music is first-class. There can be few recording engineers who relish working in the vast acoustic of St. Paul's Cathedral....Hyperion and Scott have succeeded in getting these things right. The results are not quite perfect, but then I suppose that realistically they couldn't be."

Hi-Fi News & Record Review 34:99 Mr '89. William McVicker (350w)

Digital Audio's CD Review 5:66 Ap '89. David Vernier (125w)

Gramophone 66:1201-2 Ja '89. John Steane (215w)

Westminster Abbey Choir

6148. Sacred Concert. Palestrina: Missa Papae Marcelli; Tu es petrus. **Allegri:** Misere mei. **Anerio:** Venite ad me omnes. **Nanino:** Haec Dies. **Giovannelli:** Jubilate Deo.
Simon Preston (c). Westminster Abbey Choir.
DEUTSCHE GRAMMOPHON 415 517 59:05

★***Awards:*** *Gramophone* Critics' Choice 1986 (Gordon Reynolds).

"I would use this new Archiv to show my friends what this music ought to sound like-....Highly recommended."
Fanfare 10:287 O '86 J.F. Weber (375w)

"All the music...is expertly performed on original instruments."
The New York Times F 28 '88, p. H27. Paul Turok (75w)

"If it's to the seat of the Anglican church that we must go now to hear popish ditties at their best, so be it. This is an absolutely exquisite men-and-boys rendition of Palestrina's masterpiece."
Opus 3:61 Ap '87 Richard Taruskin (810w) (rev. of LP)

American Record Guide 50:69-71 My/Je '87 John W. Barker (1225w)

Hi-Fi News & Record Review 31:85 Ag '86. Hugh Canning (290w)

Gramophone 63:1455 My '86. Gordon Reynolds (385w)

CD Review Digest
Classical

Opera

ADAMS, JOHN

7001. Nixon in China.

Edo De Waart (c). Sanford Sylvan (bar); James Maddalena (bar); Thomas Hammons (bar); Mari Opatz (mez); Stephanie Friedman (mez); Marion Dry (mez); John Duykers (ten); Carolann Page (sop); Trudy Ellen Craney (sop). Saint Luke's Chorus; Saint Luke's Orchestra.
ELEKTRA 79177 DDD 62:54; 49:06; 32:45 3 discs

★★★★★*Awards:* First Place (Tie) Opera Mumm Champagne Classical Music Award 1988—Presented by *Ovation*, *Ovation* N '88; The Want List 1988, *Fanfare* N/D '88 (John Ditsky, Kyle Gann, Mike Silverton). Best of the Year, *Opera News* D 24 '88.

"This is not just a landmark recording; it is an involving musical experience that comes to life in recorded form even more than it did on the stage."

Stereo Review 53:128 O '88. Eric Salzman (880w)

"I love *Nixon in China*....As far as I'm concerned, America has only produced two operas—Virgil Thompson's *The Mother of Us All* and *Four Saints in Three Acts*—that come closer than *Nixon in China* to what I dream that an American operatic theater could be-....Sonically, the recording is less than ideal, but the cast is so thoroughly superb that any strong competition in the foreseeable future seems unthinkable."

Fanfare 11:92-4 Jl/Ag '88. Kyle Gann (1100w)

"Brilliantly engineered, intelligently programmed, and attractively designed, *Nixon in China* is a delight for the eye as well as the ear."

Musical America 108:78-9 S '88. K. Robert Schwarz (1130w)

"My nomination for Yuppie Opera of 1988-....his score is never as relentlessly boring as say, Glass's *Einstein on the Beach*, or of any Reilly's self-indulgent onanisms. This performance is enthusiastic."

Music and Musicians International 36:28 Ag '88. Robert Hartford (490w)

"Goodman's libretto is a masterpiece, and it cries out for music that projects the rise and fall of human emotions; Adam's music more often than not traffics in emotional stereotypes....The performances of soloists, chorus and orchestra are uniformly energetic and impeccable."

High Fidelity 38:63-4 D '88. James Wierzbicki (800w)

"Though the opera itself is a media event, and the visual elements are sorely missed here, this is a brilliant execution of the score."

Opera News 52:42 Jl '88. John W. Freeman (400w)

"Once each musical module is set in motion it simply trundles forward robotically until a change of pulse or harmony or both, with the occasional big crescendo to point a moment of climax. The essence remains that of a series of confrontations and conversations, with the ballet sequence the only element of drama."

Opera 39:1143-4 S '88. Noel Goodwin (400w)

"The performance seems excellent. There is fine singing, fine instrumental playing....But too much of *Nixon* is tiresome."

American Record Guide 51:8 Jl/Ag '88. Thomas Putnam (575w)

Digital Audio 5:62-3 S '88. Sebastian Russ (700w)

The New York Times Ap 3 '88, p. H31. Will Crutchfield (1000w)

Gramophone 66:670 O '88. John Milsom (825w)

AUBER, DANIEL-FRANCOIS

7002. La Muette de Portici.

Thomas Fulton (c). John Aler (ten); June Anderson (sop); Alfredo Kraus (ten); Jean-Philippe Lafont (bar); Frederic Vassar (bar). Monte Carlo Philharmonic Orchestra.
EMI 49284 DDD 149:00 2 discs

★*Awards:* Best of the Year, *Opera News* D 24 '88.

"The performance, under the enthusiastic direction of Thomas Fulton, carries almost complete conviction....I recommend this issue enthusiastically and with great confidence."

Hi-Fi News & Record Review 33:101 N '88. Peter Branscombe (350w)

"In the killingly demanding role of Masaniello, Alfredo Kraus makes a fine showing....Aler, with his lighter, brighter tenor, makes a nice contrast with Kraus, and delivers some of his best singing to date....Thomas Fulton delivers plenty of adrenaline to Auber's already hyperactive tempos."

Fanfare 12:113-5 N/D '88. David Johnson (1475w)

"Thomas Fulton and the Monte Carlo orchestra make the most of Auber's occasionally exciting pages; soprano June Anderson emerges as a worthy heir to what we used to identify as the Suterland/Caballe repertoire, and tenor John Aler gives yet another proof of his excellence in the French repertoire....[there is a] somewhat compressed quality of the recorded sound."

The Opera Quarterly 6:138-40 Winter '88/'89. George Jellinek (630w)

"Energetically paced by Thomas Fulton, the performance presents Auber's piece fair and square. Though Alfredo Kraus occasionally shows signs of dryness as Masaniello, evincing strain during heroic utterances, this after all is no standard lyric role, and through a sense of involvement he makes its distress real."

Opera News 53:64 S '88. John W. Freeman (540w)

Gramophone 66:71-2 Je '88. Lionel Salter (600w)

BARBER, SAMUEL

7003. Vanessa.

Dimitri Mitropoulos (c). Eleanor Steber (sop); Rosalind Elias (mez); Regina Resnik (mez); Nicolai Gedda (ten); Giorgio Tozzi (bass); George Cehanovsky (bar); Robert Nagy (ten). Metropolitan Opera Chorus; Metropolitan Opera Orchestra. 1978 reissue.
RCA 7899 ADD (m) 104:00 2 discs

✔HC ★*Awards:* The Want List 1990, *Fanfare* N/D '90 (Walter Simmons).

"This venerable performance is superb, the eminent soloists all at the top of their form. The sound quality is extraordinarily vivid and clear, with wide, 1950s-style stereo separation, and the text is fully audible."

Fanfare 14:144-45 Ja/F '91. Walter Simmons (1175w)

"No composer could have hoped for a finer cast for his first opera....In this reissue the occasional harshness of the original cast recording has been smoothed out, and the engineers have managed to sort out the vocal and instrumental lines in ensembles so that they are easier to follow."

American Record Guide 53:23-4 N/D '90. Desmond Arthur (750w)

"Barber relies on brass in an attempt to whip up the passion which is lacking in this slight Mills & Boon story of youth and love. There's an attractive Intermezzo in Act II but not even Nicolai Gedda saves the day."

High Fidelity 1:110 Ag '90. Clive Manning (b.n.)

Gramophone 68:272 Jl '90. Peter Dickinson (490w)

The New York Times D 16 '90, p. 35+. Martin Bookspan (280w)

BARTOK, BELA

7004. Bluebeard's Castle, Opus 11.

Istvan Kertesz (c). Christa Ludwig (mez); Walter Berry (bass). London Symphony Orchestra. 1966.
LONDON/DECCA 414 167 ADD 60:00

✔HC ★*Awards:* Records to Die for: 1 of 5 Recommended Recordings, *Stereophile* Ja '91 (Robert Levine).

"This version of Bartok's curiously evocative opera remains the most compelling on record."

Hi-Fi News & Record Review 34:101-2 Ap '89. Kenneth Dommett (145w)

"The recording has such depth that it actually scares the listener—there are groans and sighs which come from somewhere evil, and the terrifying and majestic C-major pull-out-the-stops chord with organ at the opening of the fifth door will blow you away. The singing by the two leads is unparalleled; I doubt whether they've ever sounded better."

Stereophile 14:155 Ja '91. Robert Levine (b.n.)

"Kertesz's idiomatic conducting, and the interplay of Christa Ludwig's Judith with Walter Berry's Bluebeard...are the great glories of this classic account of Bartok's only opera. A slight edginess at the top gives away the age of the recording, but the performance more than makes up for it."

Music and Musicians International 37:39 D '88. Robert Hartford (60w)

"The recent CBS recording (MK 44523) with Samuel Ramey and Eva Marton, conducted by Adam Fischer, will probably be the first choice of many collectors—it's extremely well played, conducted, sung, and engineered....no libretto, only a miserably inadequate plot summary....Often, the orchestra as recorded is simply too loud: certainly the winds are unrealistically prominent, and the climaxes often take on a fierce, glaring quality. Kertesz gives a taut, highly colored account of the score, and he has an excellent orchestra at his disposal. I have reservations about the soloists."

The Opera Quarterly 7:203-5 Summ '90. Roland Graeme (460w)

Gramophone 66:1202 Ja '89. Michael Oliver (425w)

BEETHOVEN, LUDWIG VAN

7005. Fidelio, Opus 72.

Bernard Haitink (c). Jessye Norman (sop); Reiner Goldberg (ten); Ekkehard Wlaschiha (bar); Kurt Moll (bass); Pamela Coburn (sop); Hans-Peter Blochwitz (ten); Andreas Schmidt (bar); Wolfgang Millgramm (ten); Egbert Junghanns (bass). Dresden State Opera Chorus and Orchestra.
PHILIPS 426 308 DDD 133:00 2 discs

✔HC ★★*Awards:* Top Twelve Albums of the Year, 1991, *Stereo Review*, F '92. Best Recordings of the Month, *Stereo Review* Jl '91; Editor's Choice, *Opera Canada* Summer '91.

"The Philips digital recording is perfection itself, far less conservative and distant than their usual style....Jessye Norman is a truly magnificent Leonore....With a better Florestan, I might rank this recording with the Klemperer EMI discs; it certainly ranks a close second among modern recordings. My advice is to play Haitink for act I and then switch to Klemperer."
Fanfare 14:111-3 Jl/Ag '91. James H. North (520w)

"This, for me, is the first recording of Beethoven's great monument to humanism, to measure up to the heroic resilience and spiritual intensity of Otto Klemperer's 1962 performance for EMI."
Opera Canada 32(2):53 Summer '91. Neil Crory (355w)

"This is a *Fidelio* with a mind of its own. Bernard Haitink has definite ideas about the score and digs right in, giving neither an unduly brisk nor an unduly drawn-out reading."
Opera News 55:48 My '91. John W. Freeman (385w)

"Vigorous, tasteful, and thoughtful."
Stereo Review 57:42 F '92. (brief)

"This may be the best-conducted *Fidelio* on records. Haitink understands, as he also demonstrated in his Met performance some years back, that you don't get at the opera's greatness by whipping up phony excitement or by announcing its profundity. All you get that way is empty platitudes....and sloppy sentimentality, instead of the extraordinary, even terrifying, standard of behavior exemplified by Florestan and Leonore, who probably don't see anything remarkable in their choices—they do what they have to do....The performance has a lovely, unforced flow and a fine supporting cast....The principals...make this recording, attractive as it is in many ways, difficult to recommend as a first choice."
Musical America 111:65-6 Jl '91. Kenneth Furie (840w)

"There are several fine recordings of *Fidelio* available. This new one, while not seriously challenging them, contains some singing of high quality....The central problem is that Haitink's conducting fails to supply the weight essential to the score, and he skates over many musical points as if they weren't there." *P85 S85*
Hi-Fi News & Record Review 36:87-8 F '91. George Hall (480w)

"The new *Fidelio* on Philips, admirably recorded, gives a full account of the excellences of the score thanks to the vigorous, tasteful, thoughtful conducting of Bernard Haitink. One could not ask for finer choral singing than that offered by the Staatsopernchor Dresden or for more expressive playing than that of the Staatskapelle Dresden....the set is indeed very well cast. As Leonore, Jessye Norman contributes one of her most opulent-sounding and dramatically convincing performances to date."
Stereo Review 56:58+ Jl '91. Robert Ackart (500w)

Haitink's approach is "careful and precise but emotionally uninvolved and cold....Jessye Norman's big and lustrous voice seems ideal for Leonore and she delivers many beautiful and vocally thrilling phrases. But phrases they remain; it's not a totally convincing characterization....The Dresden orchestra plays well for Haitink and the sound is excellent-....[the] main attractions [in this set] are the sound and Jessye Norman's voice."
American Record Guide 54:42-3 S/O '91. Kurt Moses (med)

Gramophone 68:1404 Ja '91. Edward Greenfield (1205w)

7006. Fidelio, Opus 72.
Otto Klemperer (c). Christa Ludwig (mez); Jon Vickers (ten); Walter Berry (bass); Gottlob Frick (bass); Ingeborg Hallstein (sop); Gerhard Unger (ten); Franz Crass (bass); Kurt Wehofschitz (ten); Raymond Wolansky (bar). Philharmonia Chorus; Philharmonia Orchestra. 1962.
EMI 69324 ADD 128:00 2 discs

✔HC ★★★★*Awards:* The Want List 1990, *Fanfare* N/D '90 (Elliott Kaback; David Claris; James H. North); Critics Choice, *Hi Fi News & Record Review*, Ap '91 Supplement (George Hall).

"This remains the best recording of Beethoven's only opera."
High Fidelity 1:121 F '90. Ian Brunskill (b.n.)

"I wouldn't want to be without Klemperer's *Fidelio*, and at mid-price it's even more enticing. I'd need other, more theatrical performances as well: Bernstein (DG) and Karajan (Angel) are good CD choices at the moment."
American Record Guide 53:24+ Mr/Ap '90. Ralph V. Lucano (400w)

"This 1962 recording was based on a stage production of extraordinary insight and devotion-...This is the CD reissue I have awaited above all others. Absolutely essential."
Fanfare 13:114-15 My/Je '90. James H. North (900w)

Gramophone 67:1368-69 Ja '90. Alan Blyth (525w)

BELLINI, VINCENZO

7007. Norma.
Tullio Serafin (c). Maria Callas (sop); Christa Ludwig (mez); Franco Corelli (ten); Nicola Zaccaria (bass). La Scala Chorus and Orchestra, Milan. La Scala, Milan. 1960.
EMI 63000 ADD 63:20, 52:25, 45:42 3 discs

✔HC

"There are pluses and minuses and all Callas/Bellini fans will need this—although I'm sure they already own it. The digital remastering is wonderful...To be thoroughly honest, I'd have to say that it's less successful on many levels than either the '55 RAI, Rome or the '52 Covent Garden recording (both available on compact disc), but it's still integral."
Fanfare 13:144-45 N/D '89. Robert Levine (300w)

"EMI has done a service in re-mastering the 1960 recording as an alternative to the previous Callas version (1954), both under Serafin. What her voice lost in the interval between is compensated by the greater experience in interpretation—finding, for instance, the added warmth and feeling in the early scenes, the anger and deeper resignation of the last. The present reissue has the better singers around Callas...Sound quality is fine."
Opera 40:1508-09 D '89.Noel Goodwin (265w)

BERG, ALBAN

7008. Wozzeck.

Claudio Abbado; Christoph von Dohnanyi (c). Franz Grundheber (bar); Hildegard Behrens (sop); Heinz Zednik (ten); Aage Haugland (bass); Philip Langridge (ten); Walter Raffeiner (ten); Anna Gonda (mez); Alfred Sramek (bass); Alexander Maly (bar); Peter Jelosits (ten); Eberhard Waechter (bar); Anja Silja (sop); Alexander Malta (ten); Horst Laubenthal (ten); Hermann Winkler (ten); Gertrude Jahn (mez); Alfred Sramek (bass); Franz Waechter (bar); Walter Wendig (ten). Vienna Boys' Choir; Vienna State Opera Chorus; Vienna Philharmonic Orchestra. Vienna State Opera. June 1987 live.
DEUTSCHE GRAMMOPHON 423 587 DDD
89:00 2 discs

✔**HC** ★★★***Awards:*** *Hi-Fi News & Record Review* Record of the Month, Mr '89. Critics' Choice 1989, *Gramophone* D '89 (Michael Oliver); Disks of the Year, *The New York Times* D 24, '89 (John Rockwell).

"One would have thought his Mahler 9, recorded in Vienna a couple of months before this, had taken the listener as close to the abyss as it was possible to go. Yet here we plunge into it, albeit with ferocious clear-sightedness, and not even in the final interlude, with its climax merely another terse twist of the knife, does Abbado let us look on the human inferno from a distance....I doubt if Vienna audiences ever registered Abbado's meticulously balanced orchestral eruptions as having quite the impact the recording gives them....Haugland's Doctor and Walter Raffeiner's Drum Major seem intent on the notes....The real subtlety comes from Zednik...and Behrens."
Hi-Fi News & Record Review 34:85 Mr '89. David Nice (595w)

"Few performances of *Wozzeck* can ever have been so well sung as Abbado's. Even the problem roles—the Doctor, Andres—are taken by singers who are not just content to sketch cartoons....On balance then one must salute the new Abbado version—all round it is the best *Wozzeck* ever put on record. But those who can afford the luxury of two sets should not be without Silja."
Opera 40:376-77 Mr '89. Andrew Clements (300w)

"The Vienna Philharmonic plays beautifully, but it is so overmiked and the sonic perspective so skewed that a listener feels almost as if he is sitting on the harpist's lap....There are wonderful moments...but too often everything becomes just too overwhelming."
The New York Times Mr 5 '89, p. 29. Mark Swed (175w)

"This is a vibrant, vital, resonant performance of *Wozzeck* which is, unfortunately very hard to listen to. It was taped live at the Vienna State Opera, and the engineers have got the perspective skewed."
Ovation 10:51-2 Jl '89. Robert Levine (365w)

"This new Deutsche Grammophon recording is first-rate. Admirably recorded and authoritatively conducted by Claudio Abbado—who approaches much of it, quite rightly, as though it were chamber music—it is a performance by artists who have not only mastered Berg technically but have also imbued themselves with the spirit of his work."
Stereo Review 54:88 Jl '89. Robert Ackart (375w)

"*Wozzeck* has been blessed in its recordings-...But even in the company of Mitropoulos, Bohm, Boulez, and Dohnanyi, Abbado stands out: this is quite simply the most vivid account of the orchestral score ever recorded....Recommendations? The Donanyi (London 417 348) remains perhaps the best-balanced performance on record; and since it's more generously packaged (with Schoenberg's *Erwartung*), it probably remains the safest choice for those seeking a single performance. Still, balance and safety are curious grounds on which to decide on a *Wozzeck*—and those who opt for Abbado will be amply rewarded."
Fanfare 12:97-9 Jl/Ag '89. Peter J. Rabinowitz (650w)

"Ultimately this is a gripping performance, one that neither hammers away nor plays in too literal, objective a manner. It shows *Wozzeck* basically as a theater piece...In this it fulfills Berg's aim."
Opera News 54:30 Ag '89. John W. Freeman (470w)

"This is a vibrant, vital, resonant performance of *Wozzeck*, which is, unfortunately, very hard to listen to. It was taped live at the Vienna State Opera, and the engineers have got the perspective skewed....Abbado's control and conception of the score are to be admired...this is a fine opportunity lost."
Stereophile 12:175+ Ag '89. Robert Levine (275w)

"Behrens has...made something of a specialty of this role...There is some audience and stage noise and there are problems of balance between stage and pit...but there is also an electricity and excitement which only a 'live' performance can generate."

Opera Canada 15:58 Fall '89. Neil Crory (200w)

"I still prefer the more discretely scaled performances offered by Boulez (CBS 30852) and Dohnanyi....The 1955 Mitropoulos (once available on CBS) was the first and is still in many ways the finest...These three earlier recordings may not scald the ears and bruise the emotions as this new one does, but their expressive gamut is more believable and their emotions more tangibly human, and thus ultimately moving and dramatically convincing in ways that the Abbado is not."

American Record Guide 52:26-7 Jl/Ag '89. Arved Ashby (650w)

"Deutsche Grammophon, in collaboration with Austrian television, recorded it live, onstage—and if ever a recorded opera cried out for the obvious advantages of having singers keep their eyes on the score while singing, *Wozzeck* does. Even more seriously, the practical necessity of miking the singers from a distance, onstage, means that many passages of text, including important ones, simply get swallowed or covered up...In spite of a splendid cast and some really magnificent orchestral interludes, I can hardly recommend this recording over its two competitors."

Musical America 110:41-3 Mr '90. Paul Moor (440w)

Gramophone 66:1336 F '89. Michael Oliver (230w)

Digital Audio's CD Review 5:54 Ag '89. Octavio Roca (615w)

BERLIOZ, HECTOR

7009. Benvenuto Cellini.

Colin Davis (c). Nicolai Gedda (ten); Christiane Eda-Pierre (sop); Jules Bastin (bass); Robert Massard (bar); Roger Soyer (bass). Royal Opera House Chorus, Covent Garden; BBC Symphony Orchestra. 1973 reissue.

PHILIPS 416 955 ADD 160:33 3 discs

✔HC ★*Awards:* The Want List 1989, *Fanfare* N/D '89 (Paul Sargent Clark).

"The sole recording of Berlioz's first opera paints such a vivid and exhilarating picture of the idealistic yet comic adventure which he constructed around his renaissance hero, that one can hardly imagine it ever being bettered."

Hi-Fi News & Record Review 33:103 O '88. John Crabbe (225w)

"Difficult to bring off in the theatre, the score reveals all its riches on record, especially when it is as resoundingly sung as here....The recorded sound, which was a marvel enough on LP, has been beautifully re-mastered for the new medium."

Music and Musicians International 37:35-6 O '88. Robert Hartford (170w)

"Nicolai Gedda gives as good an all-round portrait of the swashbuckling sculptor and mastercraftsman as one could find then, or for that matter now....One couldn't imagine a more sympathetic Teresa (a role which can fail to come to convincing life) than Christiane Eda-Pierre....Jane Berbie's apprentice Ascanio is excellent."

Opera 39:1463 D '88. Ronald Crichton (450w)

"This 1972 recording enjoys the authoritative presence of the reigning Cellini of that hour, Nicolai Gedda, still in ringing voice....one has only awed praise for chorus and orchestra as they bring this virtuoso score—taxing even by today's standards—to radiant, riotous life-....The dry boxy sound familiar from the SDs is disappointing, though this may be partially alleviated by a boost in treble."

Fanfare 12:109-11 Mr/Ap '89. Adrian Corleonis (360w)

Gramophone 66:1202 Ja '89. Edward Greenfield (320w)

7010. Les Troyens.

Colin Davis (c). Berit Lindholm; Josephine Veasey; Jon Vickers; Roger Soyer. Royal Opera House Orchestra, Covent Garden. May 1970.

PHILIPS 416 432 ADD 239:56 4 discs

✔HC ★★★*Awards: Awards: Gramophone* Critics' Choice (Edward Greenfield), 1987; Critics Choice, *Hi Fi News & Record Review*, Ap '91 Supplement (John Crabbe); The Want List 1988, *Fanfare* N/D '88 (Mortimer H. Frank).

"The CD transfer fully preserves all the glories and subtleties of the original ten LP sides."

Hi-Fi News & Record Review 32:97 Ja '87 John Crabbe (165w)

"A modicum of hiss remains...but is far less prominent than the assorted noises produced from the surfaces of the original releases...[this is] surely the preferred format for Davis's magnificent readings."

Stereophile 11:153+ Mr '88. Mortimer H. Frank (165w)

Gramophone 64:924 D '86 Edward Greenfield (680w)

Fanfare 10:95-96 My/Je '87 Adrian Corleonis (265w)

BERNSTEIN, LEONARD

7011. Candide.

Leonard Bernstein (c). Jerry Hadley (ten); June Anderson (sop); Adolph Green (ten); Christa Ludwig (mez); Nicolai Gedda (ten); Della Jones (mez); Kurt Ollmann (bar); Neil Jenkins (ten); Richard Suart (bass); John Treleaven (ten); Lindsay Benson (bar); Clive Bayley (bar). London Symphony Chorus and Orchestra. Barbican Hall, London. December 1989.

DEUTSCHE GRAMMOPHON 429 734 DDD
112:00 2 discs

★★★★★*Awards:* Best of the Month, *Hi-Fi News & Record Review*, O '91. Special Achievement, Records of the Year, 1991, *Stereo Review*, F '92; Critics' Choice 1991, *Gramophone*, Ja '92 (Richard Osborne). Editor's Choice, *Opera Canada*, Spr '92 (Harvey Chusid); Critical Choice, *Musical America*, N/D '91 (Susan Reiter).

"What a honey of a performance [*Candide*]-...gets here...The all-star operatic cast is exceptionally well chosen....This new recording firmly establishes *Candide*, along with *West Side Story* and the *Chichester Psalms*, as one of Bernstein's three greatest achievements as a composer."

Stereo Review 56:99 N '91. Roy Hemming (med)

"Through its turbulent 33-year history, the work had never once been performed under the direction of its composer, and this DG release, which derives from the wonderfully spirited performance heard on that historic occasion, proved to be Bernstein's last major recording in which he conducts his own music. And what a splendid valedictory!...Both singers (Jerry Hadley, June Anderson, Adolph Green, Christa Ludwig, Nicolai Gedda, Della Jones, Kurt Ollmann) and players (London Symphony), are galvanized by the great Bernstein personality—the performance can also be enjoyed on DG video—into a reading of intoxicating humor, energy and joy, and of deep commitment to the spirit of the composer's intention that the work be as affecting and emotional as it is entertaining." *PS 90*

Opera Canada 33:57 Spr '92. Harvey Chusid (long)

"Here we have the full text restored and assigned to the proper characters, and the music sparkles with an effervescence we associate with the young Bernstein." *P100 S95*

Hi-Fi News & Record Review 36:111 O '91. Kenneth Dommett (med)

"*Candide* has undergone numerous metamorphoses since its inception in 1956...but in whatever guise, it continues to grow in stature with the passing years. This recording—Leonard Bernstein's last—is of the 'final revised version,' capturing the verve and bounce of the score (which the composer never had conducted before) as well as its underlying seriousness....except for cultists who prefer the abridged original Broadway recording (CBS MK-38732), it is the *Candide* to have."

Opera News 56:40-1 O '91. Patrick J. Smith (medw)

"Now dubbed the 'final revised version'-...What emerges is a more profound, expansive *Candide* that blends grandeur with whimsy—a *Candide* of far greater musical coherence than before....restoration and reordering of several haunting chorales and previously lost sections of important thematic development greatly deepen the work....The casting of Jerry Hadley as Candide is one of the recording's coups. His clear, pure tenor and subtle characterization anchor the performance....*Candide* may remain difficult to categorize, but the score, as presented here, clearly represents a pinnacle of American musical theater. Drawing on the worlds of opera and Broadway...Bernstein created a work that is both stirring and diverting—and one that resonates with his compassion for human frailties and abiding belief in human possibility."

Musical America 111:44-5 N/D '91. Susan Reiter (long)

"The recording is well balanced, rock-solid, and brilliant...This may not be the best of all possible *Candides*, but it is one of them."

Fanfare 15:175-7 Ja/F '92. James H. North (long)

"The 'Candide' collector will find plenty of novelties here, and not just in music previously recorded in specialized anthologies or not at all: even some material that has been unchanged through all previous versions has been modified...For its inclusiveness, the new 'Candide' should be welcomed by anyone interested in Bernstein or musical theater. The performance has its attractions, too, but the composer's leadership is not one of them. He had not conducted 'Candide' before, and his advoacy here led him to a heavy-handed approach...The cast acquits itself well within this monumental framework....Deutsche Grammophon has helped its cause with excellent presentation: its booklet includes a helpful and thoughtful essay by Andrew Porter and all the lyrics...where does that leave someone who simply wants to enjoy a recording of 'Candide'? In need of at least two recordings to cover all the possibilities: for a spirited realization of the effervescent side of the work, the recording of the original production on CBS; and for its able cast, full ration of music and incorporation of the composer's last thoughts, the new Deutsche Grammophon."

The New York Times Ag 18 '91, sec H p. 25+. Jon Alan Conrad (long)

Digital Audio's CD Review 8:64 Ja '92. Steve Korte (long)

7012. Candide (1985 Opera House version). John Mauceri (c). David Eisler; Erie Mills; John Lankston; Maris Clement; Joyce Castle; Jack Harold; James Billings; Scott Reeve. New York City Opera Chorus; New York City Opera Orchestra. 1985. NEW WORLD 340/1 91:45 2 discs

★★*Awards:* *Fanfare* Want List 1986 (John Ditsky); *Gramophone* Critics' Choice 1986 (Adrian Edwards).

"[For] those of us who have gone around for three decades telling the world that *Candide* just might be the finest piece of musical theater that America has ever produced....This is in so many ways the *Candide* we have dreamed of. But wait! Whatever was wrong with that 1956 production...the early-stereo original-cast recording that ensued from it is probably one of the most important LPs ever made....In Fact, let's enjoy the luxury of *two Candides* at once, and count our blessings."

Fanfare 10:111-2 S/O '86 John Ditsky (550w)

"As J.D. so aptly points out, this New World set doesn't exactly replace the classic CBS recording of the 1956 version. But the performance, rather grander in conception, is excellent....Given...the quantity of music and the quality of the recording...this is...the place to start if you don't already own the work—and the next place to go if you do....Highest recommendation."

Fanfare 10:112-3 S/O '86 Peter J. Rabinowitz (950w)

"The operatic voices, far from being intrusive, fit very well within the concept of the show-...Sonically, the DDD sound is spacious, with an impressive bottom, excellent stereo imaging, and great ambient feel."

Show Music 5:16 N '86 Didier C. Deutsch (280w)

"The new album...does contain absolutely all the music, as the composer originally orchestrated it with help from Hershy Kay. It is exuberantly performed....These forces combine to do Bernstein's scintillating and ambitious—if occasionally pretentious—conception proud."

High Fidelity 36:78-79 D '86 Paul Kresh (950w) (rev. of LP)

"*Candide* still has not found its ideal form. A totally new book by a first-class librettist (whoever that might be) seems needed—one that would learn from the errors and achievements of all these versions, and accommodate the best alternatives in the score. That's a presumptuous proposal after all *Candide* has already been through, but what Bernstein and his lyricists have wrought is surely worth salvaging."

Opus 3:23+ D '86 Jon Alan Conrad (5190w)

"John Mauceri's conducting is workmanlike but unsubtle, as is the playing of the string-poor pit orchestra. One inevitably wonders why Bernstein himself was not brought in to work the same conductorial magic that he did with last year's DG *West Side Story*...Even so, the New York City Opera has done more than adequate service to the musical side of *Candide* in this recording, and lovers of the show will undoubtedly want to have it, flaws and all."

Musical America 107:59-60 Mr '87 Terry Teachout (760w)

"*Candide*, the opera, is not quite the best of all possible operas, nor is this new record the best of all possible operatic recordings."

The Opera Quarterly 4:94-96 Wint '86/87 Christopher J. Thomas (1140w) (rev. of LP)

Opera News 51 (2):48 Ag '86. John W. Freeman (275w)

Stereo Review Presents: Compact Disc Buyers' Guide p. 58 Spr '87 Didier C. Deutsch (90w)

Hi-Fi News & Record Review 31:101 O '86. Kenneth Dommett (330w)

Gramophone 64:617-8 O '86 Adrian Edwards (490w)

BIZET, GEORGES

7013. Carmen.

Thomas Beecham (c). Victoria De los Angeles (sop); Nicolai Gedda (ten); Janine Micheau (sop); Ernst Blanc (bar); Denise Monteil (sop). Les Petits Chanteurs de Versailles; French National Radio Chorus; French National Radio Orchestra. 1960 reissue.
EMI 49240 ADD 161:00 3 discs

✔HC ★★*Awards:* Critics Choice, *Hi Fi News & Record Review*, Ap '91 Supplement (George Hall). The Want List 1988, *Fanfare* N/D '88 (James Miller).

"Welcome back to the catalogue, one of the greatest opera recordings of all time."

Music and Musicians International 36:30 Ag '88. Robert Hartford (240w)

"This *Carmen* is an accumulation of small delights that add up to something even larger than their sum; the pacing and accenting have a 'rightness' that make them seem inevitable."

Fanfare 12:147-8 N/D '88. James Miller (465w)

Musical America 110:53-5 S '90. Denis Stevens (180w)

Gramophone 66:72 Je '88. Alan Blyth (450w)

7014. Carmen.

George Solti (c). Tatiana Troyanos (sop); Kiri Te Kanawa (sop); Placido Domingo (ten); Jose Van Dam (bar). London Philharmonic Orchestra.
LONDON/DECCA 414 489 3 discs

★*Awards:* *American Record Guide* Overview: Opera Favorites, Ja/F '91.

"One of the most imposing, and effective, performances of this opera you're likely to hear."

The $ensible Sound 8:55 Fall '86 John J. Puccio (45w)

Gramophone 63:396 S '85. Alan Blyth (245w)

7015. Les Pecheurs de Perles.

Michel Plasson (c). Barbara Hendricks (sop); John Aler (ten); Gino Quilico (bar); Jean-Philippe Courtis (bass). Toulouse Capitole Chorus; Toulouse Capitole Orchestra.
EMI 49837 DDD 127:00 2 discs

"The new recording...allows us to savor its languorous Oriental atmosphere and draws us into its emotional crises conveyed by three gifted young singers. They are knowingly guided by Michel Plasson, who conducts the Capitole Toulouse Orchestra in a relaxed, deliberate fashion, lovingly exploring Bizet's delicate score."

The New York Times Ja 14 '90, p. 29+ H. George Jellinek (440w)

"Except for the Nadir/Zurga duet, Bizet's original should be adhered to in the future. It is superior opera and theater. This set supersedes Pretre's....Barbara Hendricks is gorgeous....This is spectacularly beautiful singing, with a genuine glow on top, extraordinary hushed tones, no hint of stridency, and persuasive phrasing....For the general collector, the opera lover who will want but one *Pearl Fishers* in his library, the new EMI is the choice."
Fanfare 13:129-30 My/Je '90. Henry Fogel (1150w)

"In all, Plasson presides over an engaging performance and those tempted to buy on account of the famous tune will rarely be bored by the rest of Bizet's score, particularly in this luminous recording."
Music and Musicians International 38:46 Jl '90. Robert Hartford (330w)

"'Better than Pretre' is the watchword for this new recording. The playing and choral singing are good, though the chorus is placed a little too far back in the sound spectrum for ideal clarity....So, better than Pretre, and thus first choice for a recording of Bizet's opera, but I still have a soft spot for the previous EMI version of the corrupt score with Gedda, Micheau and Blanc, which is conducted with infectious elan by the veteran Pierre Dervaux."
Opera 41:492-93 Ap '90. Rodney Milnes (540w)

"Plasson's affection for the score is clear and his identification with the idiom strong, but polished though the reading is, it lacks spontaneity. There are drawbacks, too, in the casting."
PS 80
Opera Canada 31:53 Summ 90. Harvey Chusid (190w)

Gramophone 67:1369 Ja '90. John Steane (770w)

BRITTEN, BENJAMIN

7016. Billy Budd; The Holy Sonnets of John Donne; Songs and Proverbs of William Blake.
Benjamin Britten (c). Peter Glossop (bar); Peter Pears (ten); Michael Langdon (bass); John Shirley-Quirk (bar); Bryan Drake (bar); David Kelly (bass); Gregory Dempsey (ten); David Bowman (bar); Owen Brannigan (bass); Robert Tear (ten); Robert Bowman (ten); Delme Bryn-Jones (bar); Eric Garrett (bar); Nigel Rogers (ten); Benjamin Luxon (bar); Geoffrey Coleby (bar); Dietrich Fischer-Dieskau (bar); Benjamin Britten (pno). Ambrosian Opera Chorus; London Symphony Orchestra. 1968, 1969 reissue.
LONDON/DECCA 417 428 ADD 205:00 3 discs

✔HC ★★★*Awards:* The Want List 1989, *Fanfare* N/D '89 (Elliott Kaback). Editors' Choice, *Digital Audio's CD Review*, 6:36 Je '90.

"The remastered sound...is excellent."
Musical America 109:75 S '89. Terry Teachout (100w)

"For those who have to own composer-approved recordings of major works, or just for those who want to own some of these pieces in CD at all, highly recommended."
Fanfare 13:158-59 N/D '89. John Ditsky (b.n.)

"Vocal and dramatic performances of even the least of the numerous characters are vividly projected."
Opera Canada 15:51 Winter '89. John Kraglund (450w)

"*Billy Budd* is a great work of conscience and morality which can be carefully analyzed and nicely appreciated on disc. Despite the use of men's voices exclusively, the opera never lacks color....The digital remastering has brought some of the orchestral niceties and subtleties to the fore...Everyone in the cast is close to ideal...[In the song cycles] I wish the balance between piano and singer were better, but otherwise, these are crucial parts of any serious Britten collection."
Stereophile 13:192+ F '90. Robert Levine (225w)

"The performances...carry a unique authority because of the participation of the composer and that of artists who sang in the operas' first performances or who worked closely with Britten for a number of years....[The packaging] is highly satisfactory."
The Opera Quarterly 7:201-04 Spr '90. Joe K. Law (360w)

"Peter Pears is quite superb as the Captain; so is Peter Glossop as Budd."
High Fidelity 1:107 Je '90. Ian Brunskill (b.n.)

"Britten the conductor shirks the murky depths and shining peaks of *Billy Budd* as if he were almost afraid of what his unconscious has brought forth."
Hi-Fi News & Record Review 34:95 Ag '89. David Nice (260w)

Gramophone 67:81-2 Je '89. Michael Kennedy (490w)

Digital Audio's CD Review 6:90+ O '89. Octavio Roca (235w)

7017. Paul Bunyan.
Philip Brunelle (c). Pop Wagner (bar); James Lawless (spkr); Dan Dressen (ten); Elisabeth Comeaux Nelson (sop). Plymouth Music Series Chorus; Plymouth Music Series Orchestra.
VIRGIN 90710 DDD 113:00 2 discs

★★★*Awards:* Operatic Record Award 1988, *Gramophone* O '88.

"Excellent sound accompanies this admirable production. No true Brittenite will want to be without it."
Fanfare 12:153-5 N/D '88. John Ditsky (900w)

"In short, this is not a trifle, but an important, charming, unique work, and I recommend it highly."

Ovation 9:36 N '88. Robert Levine (425w)

"*Bunyan* has all the freshness and high spirits of a brilliant young composer at the top of his form, and it is a pleasure to have it on disc at last. The performance...is crisply confident, and although some of the singers lay on the popular mannerisms a trifle too heavily, the manifold beauties of this charming operetta come through unscathed."

High Fidelity 38:60 D '88. Terry Teachout (332w)

"I find it a wonderfully vibrant work, not typical Britten by any means, but a highly enjoyable hybrid of the Broadway musical, cabaret, country and Western song, and the spiritual; Britten himself, in his many letters during the time of its composition, was unable to settle on a name that justly described the genre of the piece, but it seems to me that is does work if you can accept its ironies and humor and its largely atypical style....And the recording? one of the finest I have heard this year."

Stereophile 12:209 Ja '89. Barbara Jahn (340)

"The recording is almost all-round successful-....A little more serious feeling could have been given the performance....For all its variety, this is a pleasurable work."

American Record Guide 52:41-2 Ja/F '89. Charles H. Parsons (550w)

"The recording...makes a very strong case for the work. The cast (uniformly praiseworthy), conductor, and Virgin Classics all deserve thanks for making it available to a wider audience."

The Opera Quarterly 7:201-04 Spr '90. Joe K. Law (360w)

"As far as the presentation is concerned, it is certainly praise deserved. The music is delivered with great zest, enthusiasm and charm, and though there may sometimes be rough passages in the singing, this is not a piece that needs great vocal sophistication, having been written for a college production and in a style bordering on the Broadway musical. Moreover, the booklet includes not only the full libretto but also a brief note by Auden and a substantial essay by Donald Mitchell....But in this very American piece, written for Americans by newcomers, the bravado and the adoption of the audience's language produce something at times condescending and didactic."

The Musical Times 130:31-2 Ja '89. Paul Griffiths (485w)

"*Paul Bunyan* simply lacks theatricality, even more in its text than in its music; but because so many of the songs are pleasant, it lends itself well to the broadcast or recorded format-....the performance is charming."

Opera News 53:45 D 24 '88. John W. Freeman (105w)

"Given the piece's provenance, this first recording is ideally cast with young American singers. Rather too many reedy tenors and brittle sopranos there may be, but this pales beside the strong feeling of ensemble and a freshness of approach that matches the music itself....A hugely enjoyable issue, and instructive too."

Opera 39:1252-3 O '88. Rodney Milnes (390w)

"Unlike many colleagues...I am not sure about the quality of the piece....Paul Bunyan is spoken by James Lawless with due authoritative resonance...The rest of the cast and chorus make an equally fine job of speech and song, and the orchestra plays soundly."

Hi-Fi News & Record Review 33:105 O '88. Stephen Pettitt (315w)

"I find it puzzling at times and not sufficiently engaging to expend effort...Still, if anything is going to persuade listeners it will be this clean-cut, enthusiastic account from a team of young-voiced American singers, conducted in fine style...it is an important and valuable issue."

Music and Musicians International 36:30-1 Ag '88. Robert Hartford (270w)

Gramophone 66:550 O '88. Michael Kennedy (200w)

7018. Peter Grimes.

Benjamin Britten (c). Peter Pears; Claire Watson; James Pease; Lauris Elms; Geraint Evens; Ned Keene; Jean Watson; others. Royal Opera House Chorus, Covent Garden; Royal Opera House Orchestra, Covent Garden. reissue.

LONDON/DECCA 414 577 ADD 2:21:59 3 discs

✔**HC** ★★★*Awards: Fanfare* Want List 1986 (Elliott Kaback); *Gramophone* Critics' Choice 1986 (Hilary Finch); *Gramophone* Record Award Winner 1986—Remastered Compact Disc Award.

"This is a wonderful recording, well worth adding to any collection."

High Fidelity 36:72 D '86 Robert E. Benson (205w)

"The digital remastering is... totally successful, bringing both voices and instruments closer without distortion. The moodiness of the work is perfectly captured....Peter Pears's portrayal of the titular crazed loner is still thoroughly convincing, even after Vickers's perspectives and insights....This crucial release should be in every serious collection."

Stereophile 13:192+ F '90. Robert Levine (225w)

"In general, the original cast is stronger and better balanced than that of the Philips recording [with Jon Vickers]....It is an unforgettable performance, brilliantly recreated here."

American Record Guide 49:57-59 N/D '86 Desmond Arthur (1425w)

"Pears' approach to the role, by contrast [to Jon Vickers], is more soulful and sensitive."

Ovation 8:45 F '87 George Jellinek (195w)

"London's release of this 1959 classic performance on three superbly remastered CDs provides an excellent opportunity for the modern listener to get acquainted with Britten, Pears, and *Peter Grimes* in sound fully equal to the extremely popular Philips recording conducted by Colin Davis and starring *the* Peter Grimes of most our times, Jon Vickers....The high level of achievement, bottom to top, in the London recording...helps us to somehow maintain a proper perspective on what is a multi-layered and complex stage work rather than the virtual mono-drama it has become since Vickers' ascendancy....If the...recording has a certifiably weak link, it's Claire Watson's Ellen-....London's originally excellent sound, with its wonderful stage and 'atmosphere' sounds...has blossomed even further in the remastering process....This is a great recording."

Fanfare 10:121-2 S/O '86 Vincent Alfano (1050w)

"There can really be no question that CD is the best thing to happen since denture adhesive, and it's edifying, in a bleakly amusing sort of way, to discover in a 29-year-old master-to-CD transfer a display of studio aptitude since more observed in the breach."

Fanfare 10:30+ Ja/F '87 Mike Silverton (450w)

"No clear-cut choice between the two complete recordings is possible. Those who are interested in the opera should have both, as well as the excerpts...Though *Peter Grimes* has tremendous flaws, it is a substantial, often beautiful work."

The Opera Quarterly 4:153-9 Autumn '86. Dale Harris (2980w)

"The technological progress of nearly three decades shows in the high level of background noise, which at times...is very intrusive....No reservations on performance, though, which is definitive."

Hi-Fi News & Record Review 31:115 My '86. Sue Hudson (240w)

Gramophone 63:1323-4 Ap '86. Alan Blyth (385w); 64:554 O '86 John Borwick (250w)

7019. The Turn of the Screw.

Benjamin Britten (c). Peter Pears (ten); Joan Cross (sop); Arda Mandikian (sop); Jennifer Vyvyan (sop); David Hemmings (treb); Olive Dyer (sop). English Opera Group Orchestra. 1985.
LONDON/DECCA 425 672 ADD (m) 105:00 2 discs

> ★★***Awards:*** The Want List 1990, *Fanfare* N/D '90 (Robert Levine); Critics' Choice 1990, *Gramophone* D '90 (Michael Kennedy).

"One would never guess its age, so vivid and wonderfully balanced is the original mono-....With Pears a matchless Quint, and Jennifer Vyvyan outstanding in the central role of the Governess, this must remain a classic." *P100 S85*

Hi-Fi News & Record Review 35:103 Je '90. Andrew Achenbach (200w)

Gramophone 67:2042+ My '90. Michael Kennedy (320w)

Music and Musicians International 39:37 O '90. Antony Bye (225w)

CASKEN, JOHN

7020. Golem (chamber opera).

Richard Bernas (c). Adrian Clarke (bar); John Hall (bass-bar); Patricia Rozario (sop); Christopher Robson (alto); Paul Wilson (ten); Richard Morris (bar); Paul Harrhy (ten); Mary Thomas (sop). Music Projects London. Texts and translations included.
VIRGIN 91204 ADD 99:00 2 discs

> ★★★***Awards:*** The Gramophone Awards, Nominations, Contemporary, *Gramophone*, N '91. Best Contemporary Recording 1991, *Gramophone*, D '91. Critics' Choice 1991, Opera, *The Wire*, D/Ja '91/92 (Nick Kimberley).

"*Golem*'s one hell of an opera!...But the reader who fancies Bellini had best move on to the next review. Mellifluous *Golem* isn't....Warmly recommended. Does Virgin intend to bring us more of Casken's things? (Hint, hint!)."

Fanfare 15:293-4 N/D '91. Mike Silverton (long)

"There's plenty to applaud here, not least the committed performances of cast and orchestra-...under conductor Richard Bernas. But despite the acclaim and the awards, I don't think *Golem* has uncovered the secret formula for an opera that is not only musically but also dramatically contemporary."

The Wire 91:53-4 S '91. Nick Kimberley (long)

"In 1990...[*Golem*] won the Britten Award for Composition, the prize of which included the funding for this recording....Vocally, the cast is strong and sensitive, especially baritone Adrian Clarke...*Golem*'s only fault is also a strength: the work's intensity and emotional concentration makes for very tiring listening. Still, this recording whets the appetite for seeing the drama staged, which is high praise for any opera disc."

Musical America 111:42-3 N/D '91. Philip Kennicott (long)

"There are moments when the chamber orchestra and vocal line flicker into life, but for the most part the hour-and-forty-minute opera traverses the post-Webernian sands that have been mashed flat by legions of previous exercises in gray—just the politically correct shade of gray, however, for awards committees. The performance, which represents the opera well, is strongest in the singing of Adrian Clarke and John Hull as rabbi and Golem, respectively. Richard Bernas leads the eleven-person band."

Opera News 56:35 Mr 14 '92. Patrick J. Smith (med)

"The first Britten Award for Composition was presented in 1990...The winner: John Casten's *Golem*...I suppose I should submit to the superior ears that awarded the prize, but I simply cannot...Do we really sympathize with the characters? Do we really care about them? No....I expected more from the work."

American Record Guide 54:51-2 N/D '91. Charles H. Parsons (long)

Gramophone 69:49 D '91. (med)

CATALANI, ALFREDO

7021. La Wally.

Pinchas Steinberg (c). Eva Marton (sop); Francesco Ellero D'Artegna (bass); Alan Titus (bar); Francisco Araiza (ten); Julie Kaufmann (sop); Birgit Calm (mez); Michele Pertusi (bass). Bavarian Radio Chorus; Munich Radio Orchestra.
EURODISC 69073 DDD 118:00 2 discs

★*Awards:* Editor's Choice, *Opera Canada*, Spr '91.

"In its combination of darkly melodious writing (it has a kind of Bellinian melancholy), passionate vitality and flashes of Tyrolean color, *La Wally* lies outside the mainstream of Italian opera altogether. But considered on its own merits, it has real value, to which this new recording gives strong evidence." *PS 100*

Opera Canada 32:49 Spr 91. Harvey Chusid (185w)

"A worthy, if not ideal performance of a much underestimated work by a composer who, according to his life-long ally, the lawyer and critic Depanis, suffered the worst misfortune that can befall a creative artist: to be 'tolerated'."

Opera 41:1455-6 D '90. Julian Budden (680w)

"I came away from this recording more convinced than ever of Catalani's greatness and his absolute uniqueness among nineteenth-century Italian composers. Though I cannot wholeheartedly recommend it above the Decca/London, it is nonetheless a must-have for Catalani enthusiasts. The sound, though it requires a slight volume boost, is excellent. The 262-page booklet contains a quattrolingual libretto."

Fanfare 14:176-7 Mr/Ap '91. David Johnson (850w)

"Titus does a first-rate job, vocally and dramatically. Araiza's lyric gifts are wasted on Hagenbach's hard-driving music....Julie Kaufman sings prettily as Walter...If Wally doesn't win our hearts in 'Ebben?...'in the First Act, she has little chance of holding our sympathies later on. Marton fails the initial test miserably-...The orchestral sound is very good and the vocal pickup is clear, but there could have been more simulated stage action....The London reissue (May/June 1990) offers Tebaldi as an endearing Wally and Del Monaco as a properly stentorian Hagenbach."

American Record Guide 54:53-4 Mr/Ap '91. Desmond Arthur (400w)

"This recording will scarcely lead to a clamor for a theatrical production, especially not in Italy. Pinchas Steinberg comes off best, with firm command of his orchestra and mostly suitable tempos, but he can't sing for his cast."

Musical America 111:72 My '91. Walter Price (340w)

Gramophone 68:600 S '90. Michael Oliver (625w)

CAVALLI, PIER FRANCESCO

7022. Giasone.

Rene Jacobs (c). Michael Chance (ctr-ten); Harry Van der Kamp; Michael Schopper (bass); Catherine Dubosc (sop); Bernard Deletre (bass); Agnes Mellon (sop); Gloria Banditelli (mez); Dominique Visse (ctr-ten); Guy De Mey (ten); Gianpaolo Fagotto (ten); instrumentalists. Concerto Vocale. May 1988.
HARMONIA MUNDI 901282/4 DDD 234:00 3 discs

✔HC ★★*Awards:* Critics' Choice 1989, *Gramophone* D '89 (Iain Fenlon); Critics' Choice 1989, *Gramophone* D '89 (Julie Anne Sadie).

"Jacobs—himself a countertenor—has chosen tempos that amply suit the music; his cast...provides a richly rewarding performance."

Fanfare 13:497-98 S/O '89. Nick Rossi (320w)

Included is an "ample booklet of notes (with libretto and multilingual translations)....This is, I think, not only one of the best Early Music recordings of recent vintage to come my way: it is, I would propose, one of the best opera recordings in general to appear of late."

American Record Guide 52:36-7 My/Je '89. John W. Barker (750w)

"The performances are very strong throughout the long score....The sound is splendid, the literary backing exemplary, the libretto and trilingual translations all one could wish."

Fanfare 12:158-61 My/Je '89. David Johnson (1505w)

"Even with judicious cuts, it [the opera] clocks in just under four hours; but it's well-prepared, intelligently cast, and strongly—sometimes brilliantly—performed....The engineering is good and largely inconspicuous, and the handsome 260-page booklet with quadrilingual libretto is conscientiously and thoughtfully compiled."

HighPerformanceReview 6:73-4 Je '89. Rodney Shewan (540w)

"Most of the notes have been captured, but sadly little of the elan of the piece. The reason lies partly with the conductor, who for all his undeniable musicality and sensitivity to voices still tends to favor sluggish tempi even in moments of comic repartee. Mainly, however, it is the cast that lets Cavalli down....The package...comes with a good background article by Professor Bianconi...The English translation [of the libretto] bears witness to some editorial sloppiness and sports a handful of howlers, to be sure....All in all, then, this recording is similar to the work itself—both are very mixed bags."

The Opera Quarterly 6:137-39 Summ '89. Dennis W. Wakeling (1785w)

Gramophone 67:229-30 Jl '89. Tess Knighton (800w)

CHARPENTIER, GUSTAVE

7023. Louise.

Georges Pretre (c). Ileana Cotrubas (sop); Placido Domingo (ten); Gabriel Bacquier (bar); Jane Berbie (sop); Michel Senechal (ten); Lyliane Guitton (mez). Ambrosian Opera Chorus; New Philharmonia Orchestra. 1976 reissue.
SONY 46429 DDD 172:00 3 discs

✔**HC** ★*Awards:* Editor's Choice, *Opera Canada* Summer '91.

"This 15-year-old recording makes an excellent case for the opera. The exquisite Ileana Cotrubas is everything the title role requires: passionate, impetuous, tender, with a wholly idiomatic approach to both words and music-....Sound is consistently spacious and bright." *P95/85 S95*

Hi-Fi News & Record Review 36:87 My '91. George Hall (545w)

"Pretre's conducting, supple, natural, with an incessantly flowing line, brings out the lyric grace and evocative charm of this music without sacrificing its veristic strength. And the cast is a joy."

Opera Canada 32(2):54 Summer '91. Neil Crory (300w)

Gramophone 69:87 Je '91. Lionel Salter (275w)

CHARPENTIER, MARC-ANTOINE

7024. Le Malade Imaginaire.

William Christie (c). Monique Zanetti (sop); Noemi Rime (sop); Claire Brua (sop); Dominique Visse (alto); Howard Crook (ten); Jean-Francois Gardeil (bar). Les Arts Florissants Chorus and Orchestra. Theatre des Champs-Elysees, Paris; complementary CD included (41 min, ADD) containing Charpentier's "'O' Anthems for Advent", H.36-43; "In nativitatem Domini nostri Jesus Christi canticum", H.414; "Noels sur les instruments", H.534. April 1990.
HARMONIA MUNDI 901336 DDD 79:00

★*Awards:* The Want List 1991, *Fanfare* N/D '91 (David Johnson).

"A premiere recording [of *Le malade imaginaire*] by Marc Minkowski and Les Musiciens du Louvre for Erato had already appeared some months before. William Christie's forces are larger than Minkowski's, however, resulting in richer, denser textures, particularly in the string parts, but also in the choir. His cast of soloists is very strong. Dominique Visse stands out for his irresistibly funny Pinocchio, and Monique Zanetti for her control and her feeling for the language, while Howard Crook's singing is as polished as ever. Care and attention to detail are everywhere in evidence....Moreover, as a final enticement to buy this set, Harmonia Mundi includes as a bonus CD a reissue of Charpentier's *Antiennes O* which brings back the magic of the first 'Arts Flo' records of almost a decade ago. Nobody could, or should, resist such largesse."

Continuo 15:24-5 D '91. Pierre Savaria (long)

"A captivating reading....Along with those of Marc Minkowski, it sets new standards of brilliance and daring for the authentic-performance era."

Fanfare 14:182-4 Mr/Ap '91. David Johnson (1300w)

"A tiny note at the back of the main release's booklet reveals that some cuts have been made in the recording—repeats in dances, elimination of one instrumental piece—in order to trim it down to 78:56 to be accommodated on one CD. (The full-length recording (87:16) may be had on cassette....the world premiere recording was made in June of 1988 by Marc Minkowski and his Musiciens du Louvre for Radio France, and that recording was issued by Erato (45002, reviewed Sept/Oct)....On balance, the quality of singing is better with Minkowski...But Christie scores through greater subtlety and more dramatic sense."

American Record Guide 54:54-5 Mr/Ap '91. John W. Barker (620w)

Gramophone 68:1894+ Ap '91. Nicholas Anderson (740w)

COPLAND, AARON

7025. The Tender Land.

Philip Brunelle (c). Elisabeth Comeaux (sop); Janis Hardy (mez); Maria Jette (sop); LeRoy Lehr (bass); Dan Dressen (ten); James Bohn (bar); Vern Sutton (ten); Agnes Smuda (sop); Merle Fristad (bass); Sue Herber (mez). Plymouth Music Series Chorus; Plymouth Music Series Orchestra.
VIRGIN 91113 DDD 107:00 2 discs

★*Awards:* Critics' Choice 1990, *Gramophone* D '90 (Edward Seckerson).

"This 'music drama', delivered with total conviction by a youthful cast, is set in mid-America in 1931. It's a atypical tale of the search for freedom and security with love thrown in for confusion."

High Fidelity 1:109 Jl '90. Clive Manning (b.n.)

"The performances under Philip Brunelle's fluent direction are dedicated and musically effective, particularly Elisabeth Comeaux's warm and pure-voiced Laurie, Dan Dressen's lyrical Martin, Janice Hardy's well-characterized Ma Moss, and LeRoy Lehr's sympathetic Grandpa Moss. Altogether, a warmly recommended set."

Stereo Review 55:159+ N '90. Robert Ackart (425w)

"Brunelle's is a performance which does at least proclaim the rightness of Copland's theatrical instincts; the curtain to every act is as good as anything in Britten. I could come to love the piece very easily, and I hope this recording will serve as an encouragement to many a college production." *P95(100)/(85) S95/85*

Hi-Fi News & Record Review 35:83+ S '90. David Nice (190w)

"Brunelle's conducting is admirably straightforward and unaffected, and producer Steve Barnett has provided suitably clear sound, with voices well to the fore. This is not always to the advantage, as the casting...is tilted a bit too heavily in the direction of 'character' voices-....Copland's music occasionally calls for something a little more opulent than the rather homespun singing heard here....Brunelle's singers-...clearly *believe* in *The Tender Land*, and their radiant, devoted performance leaves no possible doubt as to the opera's high musical quality."

Musical America 110:95-6 N '90. Terry Teachout (985w)

"This is the first complete recording of Copland's only full-length opera....Some 20 years ago there was an abridged recording (64 minutes) on Columbia conducted by the composer—an almost perfect affair (but it *should* have been complete), with performances by Joy Clements, Claramae Turner, Richard Cassilly, Richard Fredericks, and the legendary Norman Treigle that make the current singers pale in comparison....But this complete recording is a welcome addition to any collection of American opera or Copland."

American Record Guide 54:42 Ja/F '91. Charles Parsons (210w)

"The Plymouth Music Series singers and instrumentalists display a provincialism which Copland clearly expected from most of the groups that would perform his opera. The positive side of this lack of sophistication is their freshness and honesty of approach, and a fanatical scrupulousness toward the printed score....Unhappily, the anxiety to make the premiere recording as perfect as possible has drained much of the vitality, the rude energy of the work-....Virgin's recording is serviceable."

Fanfare 14:203-4 N/D '90. Elliott Kaback (1225w)

"This recorded production, first seen at the Ordway Music Theater in St. Paul, Minnesota with a cast of American singers, returns to the 1955 orchestration. Performed by the soloists, chorus and orchestra of Minnesota's Plymouth Music Series, under the diligent music direction of Philip Brunelle, it reveals itself as a work of slight dramatic resource, but one not bereft of considerable emotional resonance."

Opera Canada 31(4):49 Winter '90. Harvey Chusid (215w)

"*The Tender Land* is a slender reed. Even the most fervent admirers of Copland are inclined to admit its frailty....Minnesota's Philip Brunelle, dauntless friend of American opera, leads a modest-scaled ensemble performance with the warmth and simplicity required."

Opera News 55:40 Ag '90. John W. Freeman (190w)

Gramophone 68:407 Ag '90. Edward Seckerson (1025w)

The New York Times D 16 '90, p. 35+. Martin Bookspan (280w)

Digital Audio's CD Review 7:70 O '90. Sebastian Russ (780w)

High Fidelity 1:110 Ag '90. Clive Manning (b.n.)

DEBUSSY, CLAUDE

7026. Pelleas et Melisande. Pelleas et Melisande (excerpt): "Mes longs cheveux descendent (Melisande's song from the tower, Act 3). **Songs:** Ariettes outbliees—No. 2, Il pleure dans mon coeur; No. 3, L'ombre des arbres; No. 5, Aquarelles I—Green. Fetes galantes, Sets 1 and 2; Trois chansons de Bilitis; Le promenoir des deux amants; Proses lyriques—No. 2, De greve; Ballades de Francois Villon—No. 3, Ballade des femmes de Paris.

Roger Desormier (c). Jacques Jansen (bar); Irene Joachim (sop); Henri Etcheverry (bar); Paul Cabanel (bass); Germaine Cernay (mez); Mary Garden (sop); Claude Debussy (pno); Maggie Teyte (sop); Alfred Cortot (pno). Yvonne Gouverne Chorus; Symphony Orchestra. Paris. April and May 1941, May 1904 reissue.

EMI 61038 ADD 196:00 3 discs

✔**HC** ★★***Awards:*** Best of the Year, *Opera News* D 24 '88. The Want List 1989, *Fanfare* N/D '89 (Don C. Seibert).

"The performance [of *Pelleas*] is at once intimate, deeply perceptive and often dramatic. Time and again one notes the singers' sensitive response to Maeterlinck's haunting text and the far-reaching role identification that distinguishes each vocal performance....As if the greatest recorded *Pelleas* isn't enough, we are additionally treated to the classic Maggie Teyte/Alfred Cortot Debussy chansons sequence...and four tracks...featuring Mary Garden with Debussy at the piano."

Hi-Fi News & Record Review 33:89 Ag '88. Robert Cowan (245w)

"Karajan's *Pelleas* is larger-scaled and lusher than Desormiere's, which seems to use a smaller orchestra and whose faster (but certainly not rushed) pacing is probably closer to tradition. Yes, I know there's an obvious difference in sound, too, but the intimate 1941 sonics have held up very well and are quite appropriate for the opera....It is not necessary to prefer the Garden/Debussy duo to later performers even while conceding that their renditions are so 'historic' as to disarm criticism....In keeping with this classy enterprise, EMI has provided French-English-German texts ad extensive annotations....I realize that this set is almost self-recommending but I'll add mine."

Fanfare 12:150-51 Ja/F '89. James Miller (760w)

"The classic *Pelleas et Melisande* under Roger Desormiere leaves an indelible image of the work's Frenchness and its very soul. For many *Pelleas*-lovers it must remain the definitive version, and its sound—scratchy on wartime 78s, somewhat improved on hard-to-find LP—emerges surprisingly fresh and clear in Keith Hardwick's digital remastering for CD."

Opera News 53:42 Mr 18 '89. John W. Freeman (265w)

Gramophone 66:330-1 Ag '88. Lionel Salter (385w)

7027. Pelleas et Melisande.

Charles Dutoit (c). Didier Henry (bar); Colette Alliot-Lugaz (sop); Gilles Cachemaille (bar); Pierre Thau (bass); Claudine Carlson (contr); Francoise Golfier (sop); Philip Ens (bass). Montreal Symphony Chorus and Orchestra.
LONDON/DECCA 430 502 DDD 151:00 2 discs

★★★★★*Awards:* The Gramophone Awards, Nominations, Engineering, *Gramophone*, N '91; The Gramophone Awards, Nominations, Opera, *Gramophone*, N '91; Editor's Choice, *Opera Canada* Fall '91. Honorable Mention, Records of the Year, 1991, *Stereo Review*, F '92. Critics' Choice 1991, Opera, *The Wire*, D/Ja '91/92 (Nick Kimberley). Pick of the Month, North American Perspective (Christie Barter), *Gramophone* Mr '91.

This "recording...captures the haunting character of this unique music-drama almost to perfection....The playing of the OSM is a miracle of finesse, eloquence and rhythmic definition. Within this tonal tapestry...[the cast] supply the important vocal thread, all contributing strongly illuminated performances, rich in voice and expression."

Opera Canada 32(2):57 Fall '91. Harvey Chusid (med)

"Even if all the *Pelleas* recordings ever made were currently available on CD, this new one would hold its own...I don't hesitate to recommend Dutoit as a sensible first choice."

American Record Guide 54:56-7 N/D '91. Ralph V. Lucano (long)

"London's new *Pelleas* offers a strong challenge to its predecessors and isn't like any of the current CD competition (its nearest LP equivalent was probably the Fournet [Epic], similarly full-blooded and even similarly cast) so I can easily imagine someone who owns the Karajan and/or the Desormiere versions (which remain my personal favorites) getting Dutoit for a 'second opinion.' I can even imagine someone preferring Dutoit's to anyone else's—it's that good."

Fanfare 15:197-98 S/O '91. James Miller (long)

"While Dutoit's set doesn't reach all the high points of the opera, it's a better-rounded realization than most others."

Stereo Review 56:92 S '91. David Patrick Stearns (med)

"The performance, conducted by Charles Dutoit and played by his Montreal Symphony-...is well paced, often sensitive and musically unfailingly well mannered. The singers, all native to the French tongue, are vocally capable and an intelligent team—apart from Pierre Thau...Yet...this recording will not hide from the seasoned *Pelleas* fancier the ensemble's lack of experience performing this opera-...Among stereo recordings of *Pelleas*, one still recommends Eurodisc 7794, made in Lyons, led by Serge Baudo."

Opera News 56:40 N '91. C. J. Luten (long)

"Karajan's acclaimed 1979 recording offers splendid vocalism by an international cast that includes Frederica von Stade and Richard Stilwell (Angel/EMI 49350). But they tend to overinterpret the score; unable to depart from their correct but inflexible acquired diction, musical liberties remain their only outlet for 'characterization.' Dutoit's team, though not operatic all-stars, are vocally up to the task of the opera in question, and go further by employing exquisite shading redolent of native inflection...Unlike Karajan, who interpreted *Pelleas* as a vast symphonic rhapsody with obbligato voices, Dutoit follows Debussy's score fastidiously and keeps his virtuosic orchestra under tight rein...In a score that stresses similarity over contrast, I welcome Karajan's exploiting the extremes. I suspect, however, that Debussy would not have, at least not in *Pelleas*."

Musical America 111:50-1 S/O '91. James M. Keller (long)

Gramophone 68:1715 Mr '91. Lionel Salter (770w)

DELIUS, FREDERICK

7028. A Village Romeo and Juliet.

Charles Mackerras (c). Arthur Davies (ten); Helen Field (sop); Thomas Hampson (bass); Barry Mora (bar); Stafford Dean (bass); Samuel Linay (treb); Pamela Mildenhall (sop). Arnold Schoenberg Choir; Austrian Radio Symphony Orchestra. Vienna.
ARGO 430 275 DDD 111:00 2 discs

★★★*Awards:* Best of the Month, *Hi-Fi News & Record Review*, D '90; The Want List 1991, *Fanfare* N/D '91 (Adrian Corleonis). Critics' Choice 1991, *Gramophone*, Ja '92 (Michael Kennedy).

"Spellbound from first note to last of this astonishing feather in the new Argo caps, I can only hope that Mackerras's incandescent plea for a masterpiece does as much for anyone else who has so far admired Delius only from a cool distance....He has pulled off another recording triumph of the most valuable kind." *P100 S100*

Hi-Fi News & Record Review 35:93 D '90. David Nice (505w)

"Conductor Charles Mackerras underlines both the romanticism and dark tones of the music. Arthur Davies and Helen Field are in excellent voice."

High Fidelity 2:109 D '90. Clive Manning (100w)

"Prime Delius which resplendently repays the close scrutiny of digital."

Fanfare 14:169-71 My/Je '91. Adrian Corleonis (600w)

"Charles Mackerras proves to be the right conductor for [Delius' *A Village Romeo and Juliet*'s] pale, luminescent kind of radiance and cool kind of warmth. His protagonists...[are in] attractive voice, with Thomas Hampson relaxed and winsome as the shadowy Dark Fiddler who ushers them to their Liebestod. Mood, the essential ingredient of this poetic score, is always right, unviolated by the probing of high-fidelity engineering or too detached an interpretive hand."

Opera News 56:36 F 15 '92. John W. Freeman (med)

Gramophone 68:1260 D '90. Michael Kennedy (595w)

DONIZETTI, GAETANO

7029. L'Assedio di Calais.

David Parry (c). Christian Du Plessis (bar); Della Jones (mez); Russell Smythe (bar); Eiddwen Harrhy (sop); John Treleaven (ten); Norman Bailey (bar); Nuccia Focile (sop). Geoffrey Mitchell Choir; Philharmonia Orchestra.
OPERA RARA 009 DDD 124:00 2 discs

★***Awards:*** Critics' Choice 1989, *Gramophone* D '89 (John Steane).

"The performance does the work full justice-....presentation is excellent, with scrupulously documented essays, well-produced illustrations and clearly printed text and translation. The recorded sound is clear and well-balanced though at a rather low volume-level. This is one of the best and most enterprising of recent operatic recordings."

The Musical Times 130:481 Ag '89. John Steane (620w)

"This is an excellent performance....The recording is a bit cramped but perfectly acceptable... As usual Opera Rara's accompanying notes are scrupulous and fascinating, and full text and translation are included...Highly recommended."

Fanfare 13:187-88 S/O '89. Robert Levine (535w)

"In the central trouser role of Aurelio, Della Jones reveals dramatic power and vocal security throughout the soprano and mezzo range, and Norman Bailey, no less, puts in a cameo appearance as an English spy behind French lines. Baritone Christian du Plessis turns in an affecting portrayal of Eustachio, the Mayor of Calais, who is Aurelio's father and one of the five burghers. Nuccia Focile brings an edgy soprano to the role of Eleanora, Aurelio's wife, and David Parry musters the well-versed chorus and orchestra."

Opera News 54:38-9 F 17 '90. John W. Freeman (250w)

"My initial feelings about the performance itself were inclined to be negative...but, overall, this is an opera of genuine merit, both for the inspired pages of its score and its irrefutable evidence that the composer had a serious dramatist lurking within him."

Opera 40:1017-18 Ag '89. Richard Fairman (900w)

Gramophone 67:230 Jl '89. John Steane (630w)

7030. Lucia di Lammermoor.

Herbert Von Karajan (c). Maria Callas (sop); Giuseppe Di Stefano (ten); Rolando Panerai (bar); Nicola Zaccaria (bass); Luisa Villa (mez); Giuseppe Zampieri (ten); Mario Carlin (ten). La Scala Chorus, Milan; Berlin RIAS Symphony Orchestra. Berlin State Opera. September 29, 1955 live.
EMI 63631 ADD 119:00 2 discs

✔**HC** ★★★***Awards:*** ; Critics' Choice 1991, *Gramophone*, Ja '92 (David Patmore). Editor's Choice, *Opera Canada* Summer '90 (for same performance on Hunt 502).

"One of Callas's finest and most 'pirated' concert performances...is now available at mid-price on her 'legitimate' label....This *Lucia* is the most passionate, alive recording of the opera you will hear (this from a reviewer who adores Sutherland), even finer than the Callas-Di Stefano-Serafin studio version....As for Angel's sound, well, state of the art it isn't, but it is definitely streets ahead of previous issues-....Whether on worn LPs or shiny new CDs, you must have this *Lucia*."

American Record Guide 54:51 My/Je '91. Michael Mark (350w)

"The powerful Callas/Karajan alchemy makes for a performance whose emotional canvas is of compelling splendor. Callas' singing here is of exceptional beauty and poignancy, and her passagework is dazzling in its freedom. Dramatically, this is a more fragile and vulnerable Lucia than we find in Callas' 1954 and 1959 recordings with Tulio Serafin."

Opera Canada 32(2):54 Summer '91. Neil Crory (240w)

"Nothing quite like this Mad Scene can be found in any other Callas *Lucia*...and on its own terms the whole performance is a remarkable document of midcentruy operatic ideals and achievement....By comparison with the Turnabout LP edition, the bass is fuller, the top is duller, the 'room sound' less vivid, and the voices occasionally shadowed by touches of buzzing distortion."

Musical America 111:49-51 Jl '91. David Hamilton (820w)

"EMI's is remastered, but, frankly, I can hear no difference between it and any of the others—the sound was always pretty good, some nasty distortion in the Mad Scene notwithstanding. EMI's is the only one with a complete Italian-English libretto."

Fanfare 14:152 Jl/Ag '91. Robert Levine (100w)

High Performance Review 8:86-7 Wtr '91/92. Bert Wechsler (long)

Gramophone 68:1554 F '91. Richard Osborne (995w)

DVORAK, ANTONIN

7031. Rusalka, Opus 114.

Vaclav Neumann (c). Gabriela Benackova-Capova; Wieslaw Ochman; Drahomira Drobkova; Vera Soukupova; Jirina Markova; Richard Novak; Rene Tucek; Jindrich Jindrak. Czech Philharmonic Orchestra; Prague Philharmonic Chorus. Libretto, no English translation.

DENON/SUPRAPHON 7201/3 DDD 157:19 3 discs

★*Awards: Opera News* Best of the Year, 1987.

"Almost everything about the performance and recording is excellent or better, beginning with Vaclav Neumann's conducting."

Fanfare 9:154-6 N/D '85. Roger Dettmer (1550w)

"A worthy and long-overdue successor to Supraphon's pioneering old, and now decidedly murky-sounding, Chalabala recording. In almost every respect it could hardly be better."

Hi-Fi News & Record Review 30:91 S '85. Edward Seckerson (130w)

"Like its predecessors, Supraphon's new recording is complete to the last note...There is also a precious musical spirit here, which vividly communicates how everyone involved must adore this opera."

Opus 2:39-40 Je '86. Peter G. Davis (1250w)

Gramophone 64:206 Jl '86. John Warrack (490w)

Digital Audio 2:44 My '86. R. Sebastian Russ (575w)

Opera News 51:58 My '87 John W. Freeman (515w)

ENESCU, GEORGES

7032. Oedipe.

Lawrence Foster (c). Jose Van Dam (bass-bar); Barbara Hendricks (sop); Brigitte Fassbaender (mez); Marjana Lipovsek (contr); Gabriel Bacquier (bar); Nicolai Gedda (ten); Jean-Philippe Courtis (bass); Cornelius Hauptmann (bass); Gino Quilico (bar); John Aler (ten); Marcel Vanaud (bar); Laurence Albert (bass); Jocelyne Taillon (mez). Les Petits Chanteurs de Monaco; Orfeon Donostiarra; Monte Carlo Philharmonic Orchestra.

EMI 54011 DDD 157:00 2 discs

★★★★★*Awards:* The Gramophone Awards, Nominations, Opera, *Gramophone*, N '91; The Want List 1991, *Fanfare* N/D '91 (Henry Fogel; Robert Levine). Critics' Choice 1990, *Gramophone* D '90 (Lionel Salter); The Highs, 1990, *The New York Times* D 30 '90 (John Rockwell).

"*Oedipe* is a magnificent work....this is a powerful recording with an excellent cast...I do not believe that *Oedipe* has any real potential in the theater, but it is a moving and monumental work that deserves to have a life."

Stereo Review 55:127-8 D '90. Eric Salzman (380w)

"Conductor Lawrence Foster, who has already distinguished himself in Enesco's neglected orchestra works...has now crowned his services on the composer's behalf by championing this complex and fascinating opera. The way in which he controls its challenging complexities suggests intimate knowledge of the score, and he is immensely aided by the luxurious cast that EMI-France has lavished on the undertaking. It would have served little purpose indeed to have entrusted *Oedipe* to an ensemble unworthy of it....There is not a false note in Van Dam's Oedipe; Arrogance, rage, suffering, and serenity are all conveyed with total conviction and, where vigor and eloquence do not intrude on tonal beauty, expressed with a smooth and pliant vocalism."

Musical America 111:69-70 Mr '91. George Jellinek (940w)

"Although the music is more elevated in tone than Enesco's best-known works (his *Romanian Rhapsodies*), and though it uses quartertones and a variety of polyphony known as heterophony, the opera is quite tonal and approachable. This is not to say it is easy music, because the subject is not a comic romp-....Enesco's chef d'oeuvre is treated with proper respect by a glittering cast that any opera house would envy....Recommended to those in search of new operatic experiences."

Opera News 55:30 Mr 2 '91. Patrick J. Smith (520w)

"Lawrence Foster, Enescu's most consistently faithful and intelligent interpreter, has a profound understanding of the score, and his ability to draw from chorus and orchestra singing and playing of more than ordinary excellence is the cornerstone of the success of the venture. He has the advantage of an illustrious cast headed by Van Dam, superlative in the exhausting title role." *P95 S95*

Hi-Fi News & Record Review 36:93 Mr '91. Kenneth Dommett (240w)

"Jose Van Dam, a great artist, here surpasses himself in the title role. He reaches into his soul and draws a complete portrait of the tormented Oedipus...This is award-winning singing/action. There isn't a weak link in the cast-...[which] sings in flawless French...The orchestra is large and the texture intricate, but Lawrence Foster balances the various strands masterfully...Don't miss this one."

Stereophile 14:206 S '91. Robert Levine (long)

"Jose Van Dam creates a moving Oedipe...Conductor Lawrence Foster leads the Monte Carlo Philharmonic in a focused and energized reading of Enesco's fascinating score, captured in superb recorded sound."

The Nats Journal 48:31 S/O '91. Carol Kimball (long)

"The recording does justice to this monumental work. Just as the characters are dominated by the powerful character of Oedipus, so the recording is dominated by Jose Van Dam. His performance is a tour de force, not only sung to perfection, but characterized with amazing nuance and subtlety."

American Record Guide 54:56-7 My/Je '91. Charles Parsons (700w)

"The new recording, which presents *Oedipe* for the first time in its original French language, increases my respect but not my enthusiasm for this opera....There is simply nothing to take away with one after giving up two-and-a-half hours to this work....The performance and recording are magnificent....The sound is EMI at its best, and the English translation of the libretto, by the album's producer, John Rushby-Smith, does full justice to Edmond Fleg's elevated French diction."

Fanfare 14:208-10 Mr/Ap '91. David Johnson (1200w)

"*Oedipe*...merits repeated listenings and concentrated study. While I am not totally convinced by Foster's conducting, this is the most distinguished cast to be assembled in quite a while."

HighPerformanceReview 8(1):67 '91. Bert Wechsler (210w)

Gramophone 68:1045 N '90. Lionel Salter (700w)

ERKEL, FERENC

7033. Hunyadi Laszlo.

Janos Kovacs (c). Andras Molnar; Istvan Gati; Sylvia Sass; Denes Gulyas. Hungarian People's Army Male Chorus; Hungarian State Opera Chorus; Hungarian State Opera Orchestra.
HUNGAROTON 12581/3 154:01 3 discs

> ★*Awards:* *Gramophone* Critics' Choice 1985 (John Warrack).

"All in all, I find this issue very recommendable. The work is historically important. It is a great pleasure to listen to...the production is generally a fine one, which is very unlikely to be superseded within the foreseeable future."

Fanfare 9:137-8 Ja/F '86. John Bauman (1100w)

"The spatial and general balance qualities of the recording leave little to be desired, and give a good impression of a theatrical experience."

Hi-Fi News & Record Review 31:109 Ap '86. Kenneth Dommett (250w)

Gramophone 63:543 O '85. John Warrack (1120w)

GAY, JOHN AND JOHN CHRISTOPHER PEPUSCH

7034. The Beggar's Opera (arr. Bonynge/Gamley).

Richard Bonynge (c). Kiri Te Kanawa (sop); James Morris (bass); Joan Sutherland (sop); Stafford Dean (bass); Alfred Marks (bar); Angela Lansbury (mez); Regina Resnik (mez); Anthony Rolfe-Johnson (ten); Graham Clark (ten); Ann Murray (mez); Anne Wilkens (mez); John Gibbs (bar); Warren Mitchell (spkr); Michael Hordern (spkr). London Voices; National Philharmonic Orchestra. 1981 reissue.
LONDON/DECCA 430 066 DDD 125:00 2 discs

"A sparkling recording which switches between jazz, operetta and Hollywood musicals....In a bright recording, this pot-pourri of musical styles is almost certainly fun but ultimately wearing, and would certainly be more at home broadcast on, say, Radio 2 rather than Radio 3."

High Fidelity 3:97 My '91. Clive Manning (140w)

"Instead of period pastiche, let alone anything approaching authenticity, Bonynge and Gamley opted for a lavish 20th-century palette—full symphony orchestra with double woodwind and lots of percussion—resulting in a sound-world reminiscent at times of Strauss, Puccini and Korngold, at others of a high-class musical. They carry it through with enormous verve and gusto, and the result is well captured in this sumptuous Decca recording, with its admirable freshness, sharp profile and silky sheen....for me, at least, the blend is over-rich, and palls before the end; and it tips over into vulgarity on more than one occasion." *P95/85 S95*

Hi-Fi News & Record Review 36:73 Jl '91. George Hall (525w)

Gramophone 68:2060 My '91. Andrew M. Lamb (310w)

GERSHWIN, GEORGE

7035. Porgy and Bess.

Simon Rattle (c). Willard White (bass); Cynthia Haymon (sop); Harolyn Blackwell (sop); Cynthia Clarey (sop); Damon Evans (bar); Marietta Simpson (mez); Gregg Baker (bar); Bruce Hubbard. Glyndebourne Festival Chorus; London Philharmonic Orchestra. 1986.
ANGEL(EMI) 49568 DDD 189:00 3 discs

> ★★★★*Awards:* International Record Critics Award (IRCA) 1990, *Musical America* N '90. Operatic Record Award 1989, *Gramophone*, D '89; Top Disks of the Year, *The New York Times* D 24, '89 (John Rockwell); Cream of the Crop IV, *Digital Audio's CD Review*, 6:41 Je '90. Hall of Fame, *Digital Audio's CD Review* Ja '92.

"Both musically and dramatically (and sonically as well), this is the most fully realized account of *Porgy* yet recorded—surely one of the major operatic releases of the decade."
Stereo Review Presents: Compact Disc Buyers' Guide 1990 p.67 Richard Freed (125w)

"Most of the credit for the success of this outstanding recording of *Porgy* belongs not to the singers, good as they are, but to conductor Simon Rattle. Rattle's pronounced affinities for jazz and popular music—vividly demonstrated in his 1987 recording titled *The Jazz Album* (Angel EMI CDC 47991)—make him the perfect conductor for *Porgy and Bess*."
Musical America 110:68-9 Ja '90. Terry Teachout (620w)

"This recording is a marvellous testament to a significant event in the opera world. Gershwin's first and only opera has come of age, and in the most unlikely of settings."
New Hi-Fi Sound 6:96 Ag '89. Jonathan Kettle (450w)

"Gershwin's score provides everyone, especially the conductor, with a multifaceted challenge. Alongside brash big-band orchestration are passages (mostly in the interludes) of outright French impressionism...Simon Rattle knows how to make an orchestra sound alive in both kinds of scoring...He also has a few idiosyncratic ideas...A more pervasive problem stems from the musicians' lack of swing."
Opera News 54:50 S '89. John W. Freeman (275w)

"It may be a little too much to say that this recording and these artists make us realize that Gershwin was a prophet of postmodernism, but postmodern ears certainly let us hear Gershwin differently....but the magnitude of Gershwin's achievement can only be appreciated in the full-scale work, played and sung as it was conceived. And that, to put is simply, is what we have here."
Stereo Review 54:148-49 O '89. Eric Salzman (545w)

"The collector must make his or her own choice [of available recordings], but I would help—or hint—by pointing to that DDD and TT, and by noting that this album's annotation, amply illustrated with color stills is a model of its kind."
Fanfare 13:211-12 N/D '89. John Ditsky (630w)

"Not everything Rattle does is well considered....On the other hand, there is much that is blessedly right....If none of these young singers erases the memory of past recorded performances...their combined effort seems to me, as a complete performance, to be on the whole more musicianly than that of the Houston forces under John DeMain in 1977, and more dramatically compelling than that of the Cleveland forces under Lorin Maazel in 1976. Both of those were honorable recordings. But this is, I think, a more persuasive demonstration than either that in *Porgy* Gershwin wrote a compassionate opera, and a great one."
The Opera Quarterly 7:153-56 Summ '90. M. Owen Lee (1435w)

"While the slightly under-recorded, very spacious sound lost a certain amount of impact on cassette, the sense of occasion and atmosphere, the scale of the opera and the drama of key scenes such as the murder of Robbins and the passionate encounter between Crown and Bess are captured much more effectively on CD."
New Hi-Fi Sound 6:116 S '89. Jonathan Kettle (140w)

"It lacks theatrical excitement, especially when compared to the Houston recording on RCA (2109)....They all sound too much like ladies and gentlemen....The recording itself is too 'white,' and the soft parts are too soft if your volume is set at a reasonable level. In spite of these flaws this recording offers excellent singing and is well worth having."
American Record Guide 52:61 N/D '89. Sanford D. Schwartz (350w)

"It is, by and large, a brassy production, brilliant and controlled in orchestral execution, perhaps a bit manic in its orchestral drive (note especially its opening and the Jasbo Brown sequence), but exceedingly well sung. Dramatically, I find it somewhat more naturalistic but also less touching than Maazel's rather more stage-oriented (including sound effects) production...Soundwise, I must confess to some disappointment at the edgy and untransparent effect of the loudest orchestral passages...For the moment then...my preference remains Maazel."
Stereophile 13:195+ S '90. Igor Kipnis (325w)

"Instantly the orchestra, in Rattle's snappy direction, makes an impact, at times anticipating the frenzy of *West Side Story*, and occasionally drowning a soloist's entry....A benefit of Rattle's tight grasp is that the recitative never sags and large choral ensembles are telling—how original the independent strands of the prayer in Act 2 Scene 4 sound."
The Musical Times 130:687-88 N '89. Peter Dickinson (550w)

"It is beautifully sung as a full-scale opera by its cast...the London Philharmonic brings an urgent excitment and sweep to Gershwin's music not often captured. Yet, I can't help giving a slight edge to RCA Victor's recording, because of its dramatic, theatrical interpretation by a cast headed by Donnie Ray Albert and Clamma Dale, the latter a fiery, sexy, unforgettable Bess."
Show Music 7:13 Spr '91. Max O. Preeo (395w)

Digital Audio's CD Review 6:62 N '89. Octavio Roca (640w)

GLASS, PHILIP

7036. Akhnaten.

Dennis Russell Davies (c). Paul Esswood; Milagro Vargas; Melinda Liebermenn; Tero Hannula. Stuttgart State Opera Chorus; Stuttgart State Opera Orchestra. 1987.
CBS 42457 DDD 129:00 2 discs

★★★*Awards:* Classical Hall of Fame, *Fanfare*, Jl/Ag '91. Critics' Choice 1988, *Gramophone* D '88 (John Milsom); Best of the Year, *Opera News* D 24 '88; The Want List 1988, *Fanfare* N/D '88 (Robert Levine).

"From the chants of the chorus to the high-flying solos of Paul Esswood (Akhnaten) and his fellow principals...the singing is glorious-...*Ahknaten* is Glass's most vibrant opera to date; the same adjective, in a word, describes this recorded performance."
High Fidelity 38:61-2 Jl '88. James Wierzbicki (875w)

"It is an intelligently and fully conceived work, richly orchestrated and emotionally stirring, and this Stuttgart Opera performance...is a great achievement, brilliantly recorded."
Stereo Review 53:98 Mr '88. Mark Peel (365w)

"I love sections of both *Einstein* and *Satyagraha*, but neither held my interest nearly so continuously as *Akhnaten*....what I found most appealing here was the greater lyricism and humanity of the conception....this is a Glass-work to investigate even if you don't like Glass."
Fanfare 11:130-2 My/Je '88. Edward Strickland (825w)

"Musically...Glass has nearly equalled the achievement of *Satyagraha*."
Musical America 108:65+ Jl '88. K. Robert Schwarz (720w)

"The musical treatment is characteristic of Glass's minimalist style...The vocal parts play a subservient role....The chorus seems as splendid as could be expected in a Glass score and the orchestra has a fine rhythmic sense."
Opera Canada 14:51 Spr '88.John Kraglund (375w)

"It is absurd to call Glass' music minimal, redundant or simplistic: firmly traditional, it does contain both development and harmonic movement....Paul Esswood stands out in the title role."
Opera News 52:42 Mr 26 '88.John W. Freeman (400w)

"Among those impatient with the anti-intellectualism of Glass' earlier music, *Akhnaten* is unlikely to change any minds. But those attracted to the style and uneasy about only certain aspects may find Akhnaten, if not always Glass' most interesting work, at least his best unified and most consistently enjoyable."
Fanfare 11:111-2 Mr/Ap '88. Kyle Gann (900w)

"A muted welcome, then, for the score, and only a little more enthusiasm for the performance."
Opera 39:377 Mr '88. Richard Fairman (450w)

"Truth is, *Akhnaten* is a useful sonic blockage that should see me through next door's alterations. Makes a change from music."
Music and Musicians International 36:48 F '88. (225w)

Ovation 9:22 Ag '88. Dick Adler (280w)

Audio 72:97-8 My '88. John Diliberto (575w)

Digital Audio 4:56+ Je '88. Sebastian Russ (625w)

Gramophone 65:1236+ F '88. John Milsom (550w); 69:198 O '91. Alan Sanders (brief)

7037. Satyagraha.

Christopher Keene (c). Douglas Perry; Claudia Cummings; Rhonda Liss; McFarland. New York City Opera Chorus; New York City Opera Orchestra.
CBS 39672 3 discs

★★*Awards:* *Fanfare* Want List 1986 ((Don C. Seibert); *Gramophone* Critics' Choice 1986 (John Milsom).

"The present set makes the best possible claim for a work that many of us will be glad to own."
Fanfare 9:139 My/Je '86. John Ditsky (250w)

"Appreciating minimalism is a very personal thing. I prefer the music of Glass, John Adams, and Arvo Part to that of Terry Riley or Steve Reich; and for those who share these tastes I highly recommend CBS's world-premiere recording of *Satyagraha*....It is easy to praise tenor Douglas Perry's contribution to the recording because his role as Gandhi consists of several extended solo passages that exhibit the beauty of his voice: sweet, clear, and pure in every register. However, all of his colleagues give excellent performances....When the sympathetic listener immerses himself in Glass's music, he can expect a very moving experience. For those who are unfamiliar with this world, CBS's *Satyagraha* is the ideal introduction to it."
The Opera Quarterly 4:181-4 Spring '86. Christopher J. Thomas (1470w)

"Overall, the recording does *Satyagraha* justice."
Opus 2:16-21 F '86. Allan Kozinn (5660w)

"The recording has a strident, harsh sound, all too apparent on LPs, that comes close to being painful on the CDs, especially in the upper strings, winds, and keyboards....This recording may finally convince skeptics of what devotees knew all along: Glass is a composer who, when inspired, can create a work of true genius, one of the finest operas ever written in America."
High Fidelity 36:69-70 Ap '86. K. Robert Schwarz (800w)

Gramophone 64:437 S '86. John Milsom (265w)

Stereo Review 50:120 D '85. Mark Peel (715w)

Audio 70:110+ Jl '86. John Diliberto (290w)

GLINKA, MIKHAIL

7038. A Life for the Tsar.
Emil Tchakarov (c). Alexandrina Pendachanska (sop); Stefania Toczyska (contr); Chris Merritt (ten); Boris Martinovich (bass); Mincho Popov (ten); Stoil Georgiev (bass); Konstantin Videv (bass). Sofia National Opera Chorus; Sofia Festival Orchestra. Notes, text and translation included.
SONY 46487 DDD 210:00 3 discs

★★*Awards:* Editor's Choice, *Opera Canada*, Wtr '91; Critics' Choice 1991, *Gramophone*, Ja '92 (John Warrack).

"The present performance is spirited and stirring throughout. Each solo artist is fully engaged by his or her assignment, the Sofia National Opera Chorus sings with notable sensitivity, fire, and belief, and the Sofia Festival Orchestra, under the capable and convinced leadership of Emil Tchakarov, plays in exemplary fashion. The sound is excellent."
Stereo Review 56:99-100 N '91. Robert Ackart (brief)

"The second recording of this opera to emanate from Bulgaria in less than a year, this set has many musical and ancillary strengths, and no glaring weaknesses....The soundstage is wide and deep, and despite some opacity in loud orchestral tuttis and a few other climaxes that sound a bit raw, Sony's sound is superior to both EMI's and Balkanton's...Christoff and Markevitch make it impossible to forget the EMI set, but the many virtues of Sony's new *Life for the Tsar* make it deserve a long life in the catalog. Heartily recommended."
Fanfare 15:323-4 N/D '91. Ben Pernick (long)

"Tchakarov, while unable to disguise the opera's rambling structure, paces the work skillfully, and provides real impetus to the dances of the Polish act, while the Sofia National Opera Chorus seizes every opportunity to give of its best with superb enthusiasm. Susanin is sung by bass Boris Martinovich with commitment and resonant tone."
Opera Canada 32:49 Wtr '91. Harvey Chusid (long)

"Sony's new and welcome set fills a gap, since it is currently the only easily accessible version of this pathbreaking opera....Sony's main asset [over the Angel/EMI import] is completeness-...Emil Tchakarov...falls short of the dynamism and animation displayed by Igor Markevitch on EMI....Orchestra and chorus perform dependably, though the choral sonority of these eminent Bulgarians was revealed more impressively on earlier recordings. Sony's exemplary packaging contains informative essays and a quadrilingual libretto. With the stated reservations, this worthy effort is strongly recommended."
Musical America 111:45-6 N/D '91. George Jellinek (long)

"Boris Martinovich...is not as spellbinding a Susanin as Christoff [on a 1959 EMI]. Who is? However, the Yugoslav bass gives a strong performance...the superb EMI and excellent Sony version of *A Life for the Tsar* are the only recordings one need consider—musts for all lovers of Russian opera."
American Record Guide 54:67-8 N/D '91. Michael Mark (long)

"Boris Martinovich has neither the authority nor the noble, orotund sound one has expected from an Ivan Susanin since the days of Chaliapin...the Sofia Opera forces under Emil Tchakarov seem somewhat beyond their depth in terms of style...The barely adequate recording is second-rate by today's best standards."
Opera News 56:38 Ja 4 '92. C. J. Luten (long)

Digital Audio's CD Review 8:63-4 Ja '92. Sebastian Russ (long)

Gramophone 69:122 S '91. John Warrack (long)

GLUCK, CHRISTOPH WILLIBALD

7039. Le Cinesi (opera-serenade in one act).
Lamberto Gardelli (c). Kaaren Erickson (sop); Alexandrina Milcheva-Nonova (contr); Marga Schiml (contr); Thomas Moser (ten). Munich Radio Orchestra.
ORFEO 178 891 DDD 66:00

★*Awards:* Critics' Choice 1990, *Gramophone* D '90 (Julie Anne Sadie).

"An opera that is worthy of multiple representation in the catalog....Lamberto Gardelli leads his traditional symphonic forces in a respectful performance in which Gluck's melodies are well served. Excellent sound....With the exception of an inferior tenor, Jacobs's cast [on EMI 47752] is equal to Gardelli's but his orchestra has an unpleasant edge in its timbre."
Fanfare 13:185 Ja/F '90. James Camner (270w)

"The most interesting music is the overture, nicely played here by Gardelli's small orchestra. The women have pleasant voices and sing their music competently; Moser employs his light tenor skillfully in his slightly ironic love song. Discounting the rather tedious recitatives, *Le Cinesi* offers about a half hour of charming music."
American Record Guide 53:54 Mr/Ap '90. Desmond Arthur (300w)

Gramophone 67:1369-70 Ja '90. Julie Ann Sadie (300w)

7040. Iphigenie en Tauride.
John Eliot Gardiner (c). Diana Montague; Nancy Argenta; Colette Alliot-Lugaz; John Aler. Monteverdi Choir; Lyon Opera Orchestra.
PHILIPS 416 148 DDD 3 discs

✔HC ★★★★Awards: *Gramophone* Critics' Choice 1986 (Stanley Sadie; Alan Blyth); *Opus* Record Award Nominee, 1987; *Opus* Christmas List, 1987 (Andrew Stiller). *Opera News* Best of the Year, 1987.

"By quite a margin, Gardiner's recording is the finest available."
Ovation 8:39 N '87. David Patrick Stearns (710w)

"John Gardiner's performance does justice of a kind to this late and most magnificent flowering of Gluck's genius."
Opus 3:54 O '87. Matthew Gurewitsch (225w)

"More than decent: an absolutely superb, almost flawless performance and production."
Opus 4:58 D '87. Andrew Siller (130w)

"Gardiner's wonderful direction of his Lyon forces (modern instruments) takes this set out of the specialist category and into the universal domain....On CD, this magnificent performance leaps into your front room. Don't resist it!"
Hi-Fi News & Record Review 31:107 O '86. Hugh Canning (455w)

"The work is beautiful to hear in recording, especially with Diana Montague in the title role of Iphigenie....A gem of a recording."
Opera Canada 28:51 Summ '87 Ruby Mercer (220w) (rev. of LP)

"John Eliot Gardiner, who has made a richly deserved reputation as a conductor of Monteverdi and Rameau, fails signally with this Gluck recording because Gluck requires much more than a well-trained little orchestra and well-trained little singers."
Fanfare 10:116-8 Mr/Ap '87 David Johnson (1575w)

"Not only does Diana Montague manage very well as Iphigenie, but the performance as a whole is paced with lively, dynamic accents by John Eliot Gardiner, who steers the work with a sure sense of its dramatic destination."
Opera News 51:50 Mr 14, '87 John W. Freeman (330w)

"These aren't 'authentic instruments,' but the playing draws upon that burgeoning expertise-....Inhabiting this fresh—and wonderfully bracing—instrumental frame is a less exotic cast of soloists....What I miss is the livelier interaction among the characters in earlier versions, the sense of dramatic continuity that they generate; despite the new recording's opera house origins, its feeling is of the studio, and something less than the drama's full impact accumulates."
The Opera Quarterly 5:128-131 Spr '87 David Hamilton (1260w)

"Montague is a mezzo-soprano. At critical points in the opera, she simply finds it impossible to fill out the contours of her music with the requisite majesty....Thomas Allen...also finds some of his music too high for comfort-....The most successful feature of the recording is the conducting of John Eliot Gardiner."
The Opera Quarterly 5:131-134 Spr '87 Dale Harris (1200w)

Continuo 11:10-11 Summ '87 Scott Paterson (350w) (rev. of LP)

7041. Iphigenie en Aulis.
John Eliot Gardiner (c). Lynne Dawson (sop); Anne-Sofie von Otter (mez); Jose Van Dam (bar); John Aler (ten). Monteverdi Choir; Lyon Opera Orchestra. 1987. ERATO 45003 DDD 67:00, 65:50 2 discs

★★★★★Awards: The Want List 1990, *Fanfare* N/D '90 (James Camner); Critics' Choice 1990, *Gramophone* D '90 (Alan Blyth; Stanley Sadie); The Highs, 1990, *The New York Times* D 30 '90 (John Rockwell). Record of the Month, *Hi-Fi News & Record Review*, Jl '90.

"Gardiner's recording of Gluck's first Iphigenia opera...is a considerable achievement, and makes compelling listening. From the marvellous overture onwards, the incisive, disciplined playing of the Lyons Opera Orchestra...is a joy....The cast could not be bettered....This is a first-rate performance and a valuable addition to the catalogue." *P100 S95*
Hi-Fi News & Record Review 35:79 Jl '90. George Hall (605w)

"John Eliot Gardiner's splendidly recorded performance of *Iphigenie en Aulide* is even better than his fine recordings of two other Gluck operas...Highly recommended."
Fanfare 13:153-54 Jl/Ag '90. James Camner (920w)

"This great work, a Grand Opera *avant la lettre*, is very different in kind from the sublime 'interior' drama that is Gluck's later *Iphigenie* opera; in the excellent Erato sound it comes across as one of the peaks of 18th-century lyric theatre...the peculiar character of this opera, at once startlingly innovative and deeply respectful of French tradition, has been caught with immense perspicacity of form, style, and content....Gardiner's splendid cast is headed by Van Dam in one of the greatest of all his many performances for the gramophone...In sum, then, the first complete *Iphigenie en Aulide* on records is an absolute winner."
Opera 41:1006-7 Ag '90. Max Loppert (980w)

"This is easily the best of John Eliot Gardiner's Gluck recordings to date....And with perhaps one exception, it is hard to imagine that the cast here could be improved upon."
American Record Guide 53:60-1 N/D '90. George W. Loomis (510w)

"Jose Van Dam delivers Agamemnon whole, with fastidious attention to vocal detail yet broad and free expressive utterance. Close by him is Anne Sophie von Otter: gradually stepping forward in defense of her threatened daughter, this Clytemnestre avoids being dismissed as a ranting zany. It might be argued

that Lynne Dawson's more delicate timbre in the title role is weak casting, but the whole point about Iphigenie is her vulnerable innocence."
Opera News 55:33 Mr 30 '91. John W. Freeman (275w)

"This is a marvelous reading of Gluck's not-altogether-satisfying opera....The sound is rich and clear, with enough transparency to hear many of Gluck's inner harmonies, and the voice-instrument balance is just right."
Stereophile 14:198 Mr '91. Robert Levine (260w)

"This new recording from Lyons is an important, exciting restoration....Gluck operas can be a headache to cast, but you'd never know it from the elegant, idiomatic performances here-....John Eliot Gardiner is the hero of this set, however."
Stereo Review 55:93 Jl '90. David Patrick Stearns (350w)

Gramophone 68:108 Je '90. Stanley Sadie (820w)

7042. Orfeo ed Euridice.
Hartmut Haenchen (c). Jochen Kowalski (ctr-ten); Dagmar Schellenberger-Ernst (sop); Christian Fliegner (trbl). Carl Philipp Emanuel Bach Chamber Orchestra. Berlin, Christ Church. October 1988.
CAPRICCIO 60008 DDD 51:47; 60:53 2 discs

★*Awards:* Top Disks of the Year, *The New York Times* D 24, '89 (John Rockwell).

"Hartmut Haenchen has an inherent feel for the music, and both orchestra and chorus perform beautifully. Jochen Kowalski is not just a countertenor 'solution,' but is a major singer with a fine voice, who turns in a passionate and moving performance far superior to that of the other countertenor Orfeo, Rene Jacobs on Accent....Clear digital sound."
Fanfare 13:185-87 Ja/F '90. James Camner (350w)

"Jochen Kowalski is a fascinating young Polish countertenor who has been taking Europe by storm....for the most part, his is a remarkably vivid and moving portrayal, and it stays with the listener. His Euridice is good, and so is the little boy who sings amore...although their Italian diction is appalling...The orchestra and chorus are wonderful, and are recorded splendidly."
Stereophile 13:173+ Ag '90. Robert Levine (165w)

"East German countertenor Jochen Kowalski (see LG 45:1) is vocally and dramatically stunning as Orfeo....Dagmar Schellenberger-Ernst commits to a dramatic Euridice...Her creamy middle voice matches Kowalski's beautifully-...Under the direction of Hartmut Haenchen, the C.P.E. Bach Orchestra supplies buoyant accompaniment with only an occasional stodgy deviation....Excellent sound."
The Nats Journal 46:43 My/Je '90. Carol Kimball (390w)

"The Berlin-Capriccio *Orfeo* is very unauthentic indeed, with modern instruments playing in meaty modern style, but playing with tremendous fire under Haenchen's intense and dramatic direction. Gluck can take it, and on its own terms it works....But the point of this issue is Kowalski's incandescent performance as Orpheus....what we have here is a singer of remarkable imagination tackling one of opera's greatest roles and proving himself to be entirely worthy of it."
Opera 41:1007-8 Ag '90. Rodney Milnes (480w)

"A cultivated, resourceful artist, Kowalski plays Orfeo with seriousness and depth. Still, the countertenor voice inherently lacks as wide a range of dynamics and coloration as the female contralto or mezzo-soprano we are used to hearing. Similarly, a boy soprano (Christian Fliegner), while 'correct' for the music of Amor, seems pallid and tentative for this assertive arbiter of love....Though presentably sung, the performance is most attractive for its lean, incisive instrumental playing under Hartmut Haenchen."
Opera News 54:30 Ja 20 '90. John W. Freeman (205w)

Gramophone 67:1370 Ja '90. Stanley Sadie (405w)

GOUNOD, CHARLES

7043. Faust.
Michel Plasson (c). Richard Leech (ten); Cheryl Studer (sop); Jose Van Dam (bass-bar); Thomas Hampson (bass); Martine Mahe (mez); Marc Barrard (bar). French Army Chorus; Toulouse Capitole Chorus and Orchestra. Notes, texts and translations in French, English and German included.
EMI 54228 DDD 204:00 3 discs

✔HC ★★*Awards:* Editor's Choice, *Opera Canada*, Spr '92 (Harvey Chusid); Pick of the Month, *Gramophone*, D '91 (Christie Barter).

"In the title role, Richard Leech, though not strain-free, does not suffer by comparison with his predecessors...In the case of the Marguerite, Cheryl Studer, I have never heard the role sung better: such a meld of vocal competence and dramatic awareness has not been heard on any previous *Faust* recording, whether it be with Steber, de los Angeles, Sutherland, or Freni. Jose van Dam was a mild disappointment: I expected him to be the best Mephistopheles in my experience but he turned out to be only a very good one....As Valentin, Thomas Hampson...adds to [the recordings]...luster. The Siebel and Marthe, respectively, Martine Mahe and Nadine Denize, are strong performers, too. Michel Plasson's conducting isn't startling but he certainly gives the singers a strong foundation. Perhaps he bears some responsibility for the way their voices blend in the ensembles, another strength of this performance....All told, an impressive job."

Fanfare 15:199-200 Mr/Ap '92. James Miller (long)

"Cheryl Studer creates a Marguerite of vulnerability and haunting tenderness. Her youthful, clear soprano has agility and warmth, and though it is a little lighter in timbre than Freni's in the excellent 1979 recording with Domingo, it meets all the demands of the role, from innocence and excitability to despair. Happily, Richard Leech reaches similar heights-....Jose Van Dam's Mephistopheles, slightly husky in sound, is suitably sinister without hamming up the part. Thomas Hampson's Valentin musters plenty of anger in his rejection of Marguerite, and Martine Mahe is an ardent Siebel."

Opera News 56:34 Mr 14 '92. Shirley Fleming (med)

"Altogether, the combination here of masterly musicmaking and sensitive awareness to underlying dramatic values have yielded one of this opera's finest recorded realizations."

Stereo Review 57:81 Ap '92. Robert Ackart (long)

"Michel Plasson's exemplary new reading, an unmannered balance between 'French taste' and high emotion, makes for a genuinely stimulating theatrical experience, one to reinforce the conviction of confirmed enthusiasts for the opera. Plasson benefits strongly from the resources of a cast of wide-ranging, attractive voices: Richard Leech, a Faust with all the requisite lyricism, clarity and muscle; Jose van Dam, a great aristocratic singer, lacking only some of Mephistopheles' brash arrogance; Thomas Hampson, whose Valentin shows that vocal display is not incompatible with Gounod's dramatic intention; and Cheryl Studer as Marguerite—the one contentious piece of casting." *PS 90*

Opera Canada 33:58 Spr '92. Harvey Chusid (long)

Gramophone 69:125 D '91. Alan Blyth (long)

HALEVY, JACQUES-FRANCOIS

7044. La Juive.

Antonio De Almeida (c). Jose Carreras (ten); Julia Varady (sop); June Anderson (sop); Ferruccio Furlanetto (bass); Dalmacio Gonzalez (ten); Rene Massis (bass-bar); Rene Schirrer (bar). Ambrosian Opera Chorus; Philharmonia Orchestra.
PHILIPS 420 190 DDD 183:00 3 discs

★★***Awards:*** The Want List 1990, *Fanfare* N/D '90 (David Johnson). Critics' Choice 1989, *Gramophone* D '89 (Edward Greenfield).

"The main credit for its success must go to the conductor, Antonio de Almeida, whose assured leadership maintains a clear and balanced view over the diversified elements of this oversized but—in the right hands—colorfully effective score. The Philharmonia Orchestra and the Ambrosian Opera Chorus perform in exemplary fashion."

The New York Times Ja 14 '90, p. 29+ H. George Jellinek (440w)

"Aside from Varady, who deserves special mention, the other members of the cast are never less than successful in their roles-....Above all, praise must go to De Alameida, who...joins together his singers and players with consummate elegance, precision, and drama. Philips's sound is very fine. All told, this release constitutes one of the major operatic events in recent years."

Musical America 110:75-6 N '90. David Hurwitz (475w)

"This [recording]...though not ideal, is satisfying...*La Juive*...[is] more than a curiosity in its own right, and deserves to be heard—one would hope in stage performances."

Opera News 54:30 Mr 3 '90. Patrick J. Smith (865w)

"Though the Philips set is welcome, and presented with decent accomplishment (at least when measured by current standards of Romantic-opera singing, not to mention French Grand Opera), it's by no means the revival the work has been waiting for—there are too many weaknesses. It is heavily pruned....On records one might have expected a sharper, sparkier account of the score than that given by the Philharmonia (competent, routine, not always tidy in ensemble) and Ambrosians (ditto) under Antonio de Almeida's knowledgeable but slack direction....The single unqualified triumph of the performance is the casting of Varady in the title role...Rachel emerges as one of the most finely drawn of 19th-century Romantic-opera heroines; and for her above all the set can be recommended."

Opera 41:381-82 Mr '90. Max Loppert (1200w)

"There is some evidence of technical haste-...But a better performance of this seminal work in the history of the form is not likely to be issued in the near (or distant!) future."

Fanfare 13:183-84 My/Je '90. Adrian Corleonis (1190w)

"The singers are a mixed lot....Varady is a splendid Rachel...This is the finest work I have heard from her on records, and the set is worth acquiring for her performance alone."

American Record Guide 53:69-70 S/O '90. Desmond Arthur (680w)

"Though the score is not complete...it maintains musical and dramatic integrity in a kinetic, committed reading under Antonio de Almeida." *PS 90*

Opera Canada 31:53 Summ 90. Harvey Chusid (220w)

Digital Audio's CD Review 6:42+ Jl '90. Sebastian Russ (1200w)

Gramophone 67:965 N '89. Edward Greenfield (1580w)

HANDEL, GEORGE FRIDERIC

7045. Flavio.

Rene Jacobs (c). Christina Hogman (sop); Lena Lootens (sop); Bernarda Fink (mez); Jeffrey Gall (ctr-ten); Derek Ragin (ctr-ten). Ensemble 415. 1989.
HARMONIA MUNDI 901312/3 DDD 79:23; 76:15 2 discs

★*Awards:* Critics' Choice 1990, *Gramophone* D '90 (Stanley Sadie).

"The recording offers a good cast and all the solid virtues of the New Authenticity....In general, a splendid realization of this little-known Handel opera....The packaging and sound are exemplary."

Fanfare 14:250-2 S/O '90. David Johnson (1665w)

"*Flavio* may not be everyone's first choice for a Handel opera, but, as recorded here, it is a finely representative and splendidly realized illustration of the genre. I would rank it with Newport Classic's recent debut recording of *Imeneo* as among the most satisfying and worthwhile contributions to the Handel opera discography in years."

American Record Guide 53:72-3 S/O '90. John W. Barker (475w)

"The work is packed with vintage Handel-...Ugone...is the only weak(-ish) link in an otherwise flawless cast....Rene Jacobs...here emerges as a Handel opera conductor second to none in his understanding of dramatic pacing and character projection."

Opera 41:1372-73 N '90. Hugh Canning (980w)

"This recording proves *Flavio* to be well worth a revival. Rene Jacobs has assembled a marvelously balanced cast, and Chiara Banchini's Ensemble 415...plays beautifully for him....The sound here is very good for a small-opera recording....Recommended, even if you are unfamiliar with Handelian opera."

Stereophile 14:198-99 Mr '91. Les Berkley (465w)

Gramophone 68:272+ Jl '90. Stanley Sadie (1015w)

"The role of Vitige is sung by a soprano, an odd choice but it was Handel's. A good-sized orchestra of period instruments is used, Ensemble 415 led by Rene Jacobs, and the sound is quite wonderful."

The New York Times Jl 1 '90, p. 22+ H. George Jellinek (285w)

Digital Audio's CD Review 7:72 N '90. Sebastian Russ (420w)

7046. Giulio Cesare.

Rene Jacobs (c). Jennifer Larmore (mez); Barbara Schlick (sop); Bernarda Fink (mez); Marianne Rorholm (mez); Derek Lee Ragin (alto); Furio $$ Zanazi (bass); others. Cologne Concerto. libretto with translation included.
HARMONIA MUNDI 901385/7 DDD 244:00 3 discs

✔HC

This recording presents "a well-performed, occasionally thrilling *Giulio Cesare* that will serve nicely as a central version, albeit one that should be supplemented by one or two of the more eccentric, colorful readings [Sills and Treigle/RCA; Popp, Ludwig, Berry, and Wunderlich/Melodram; Janet Baker/Nuova Era; Karl Richter/DG]...Jacobs, a countertenor-turned-conductor, really digs into the drama....The Concerto Koln plays deftly, with especially fine contributions from the horns and winds....Larmore has a firm, easily produced voice and a regal manner....This is an extraordinarily accomplished performance, one that could hold its own in any company and the highlight of the set....The sound is excellent, but there's one odd production flaw. Recitatives are not tracked separately but tacked on after the arias."

Fanfare 15:203-4 Mr/Ap '92. Ralph V. Lucano (long)

Digital Audio's CD Review 8:64 My '92. Octavio Roca (long)

Gramophone 69:153-5 Ap '92. Stanley Sadie (long)

7047. Orlando.

Christopher Hogwood (c). James Bowman (alto); Arleen Auger (sop); Catherine Robbin (mez); Emma Kirkby (sop); David Thomas (bass). Academy of Ancient Music.
OISEAU-LYRE 430 845 DDD 158:00 2 discs

★★*Awards:* Wire Winner: Magic Operas, *The Wire* Ag '91; Wire Winner: Best New Releases, *The Wire* Ag '91. Critics' Choice 1991, *Gramophone*, Ja '92 (Lindsay Kemp). Critics' Choice 1991, Opera, *The Wire*, D/Ja '91/92 (Nick Kimberley).

"*Orlando*...[includes] some of Handel's most gorgeous arias—and (to quote Hogwood's book) 'more varied accompaniments than appear in any other of his operas'....*Orlando*, given a superlative performance that establishes it as one of the 18th century's finest operas, is absolutely unmissable....go for Baroque!"

The Wire 90:45 Ag '91. Graham Lock (long)

"Hogwood and his forces (many of whom were also involved in Pinnock's *Belshazzar*) turn in another spirited, technically adept reading. It is especially good to hear bass David Thomas and soprano Emma Kirkby in action in Handel again."

Continuo 16:26-7 Ap '92. Scott Paterson (med)

Gramophone 69:85 Ag '91. Lindsay Kemp (525w)

7048. Il Pastor Fido.

Nicholas McGegan (c). Katalin Farkas (sop); Paul Esswood (ctr-ten); Marta Lukin (mez); Maria Flohr (mez); Gabor Kallay (ten); Jozsef Gregor (bass). Sava-

ria Vocal Ensemble; Capella Savaria.
HUNGAROTON 12912/3 DDD 75:20, 71:43 2 discs

★*Awards:* Critics' Choice 1989, *Gramophone* D '89 (Stanley Sadie).

"McGegan's recording is...the third and final version of the opera in its entirety, omitting only the prologue...McGegan's reading of the opera, on period instruments, evinces a profound knowledge and respect for what is known about early 18th Century operatic performance practice in England; but it is not dry or academic and for most of its two and a half hours sparkles and charms....If you don't like the white timbre of the countertenor voice and the 'pure' focussed sound of female sopranos and mezzos who correctly treat vibrato as an embellishment...you would be advised to listen to this in small doses or avoid it altogether-....Esswood...is still equal to the demands of a role like Mirtillo and apparently still finds the florid writing easy sailing....Excellent annotations and a complete text, with translations into English, French, and German."
American Record Guide 52:59-60 S/O '89. Teri Noel Towe (520w)

"The performance is quite good, at times excellent....the sound is clear and warm with good balance and perspective. Dynamic range, however, seems a bit constrained....Highly recommended for either those with a taste for Baroque opera or those who wish to acquire such a taste."
HighPerformanceReview 7:57-8 Fall '90. June C. Ottenberg (500w)

"This recording is welcome because it is a 'first' for this opera, and also because the performance is quite good, at times excellent. Capella Savaria uses period instruments (or replicas), and is thoroughly experienced with 18th century style....Highly recommended for either those with a taste for Baroque opera or those who wish to acquire a taste for it."
HighPerformanceReview 7:1:76-7 '90. June C. Ottenberg (450w)

"Though obviously not the composer's finest work even in the pastoral genre—for it's certainly no *Acis and Galatea*—it is nevertheless good to have it available in such a credible performance."
Fanfare 13:498 S/O '89. Nick Rossi (175w)

"McGegan seems to favor understated solo singing. Katalin Farkas, who seems ill at ease in the role of Amarilli, and Jozsef Gregor, a capital character bass, both have been heard to better advantage in other recordings....The voices, notably those of Farkas and Gregor, seem disadvantaged by remote miking."
Opera News 55:35 F 16 '91. John W. Freeman (310w)

HASSE, JOHANN ADOLF

7049. Cleofide.
William Christie (c). Emma Kirkby; Agnes Mellon; Derek Ragin; Dominique Visse. Capella Coloniensis. 1986.
CAPRICCIO 10193/6 DDD 231:00 4 discs

★*Awards:* The Want List 1988, *Fanfare* N/D '88 (Robert Levine).

"What makes this set outstanding are...the precision and expressive beauty of the orchestral playing, the enthusiasm and sense of style of William Christie, and the superior quality of recording and documentation."
Hi-Fi News & Record Review 33:96 My '88. Peter Branscombe (375w)

"Kirkby shows a wide range of emotional projection...along with the technical poise needed to make the rather elaborate music sound natural....The period-instrument playing tends to favor a modern style of execution-...The effect is salutary, with William Christie's light-handed, spirited leadership essential to sparking the enterprise with life."
Opera News 52:43 F 27 '88.John W. Freeman (450w)

"William Christie's direction is urgent, his singers, led by Emma Kirkby in the title role, uniformly excellent....It comes with interesting notes and English translation (separate from the facsimile text)."
Music and Musicians International 36:48-9 F '88. Robert Hartford (275w)

"The performances of the principals here are of a very high caliber....The orchestral playing is neat and crisp...The recorded sound is crystal clear but a bit close and slightly bright."
Musical America 108:70-1 Jl '88. Christopher Rothko (520w)

"Christie's cast...is exceptionally strong, near ideal for such a 'showcase' piece. The Cappella Coloniensis...plays with brilliance and vitality."
Fanfare 13:497 S/O '89. Nick Rossi (275w)

"William Christie's direction is a model of period detail come to life....Emma Kirkby is splendid in the title role."
Ovation 9:42-3 Ja '89. Octavio Roca (220w)

"The performance is a model for clear textures and unaffected flow....There are only six roles in this long opera, and Hasse saw to it that even the subsidiary characters have showy and effective arias, though not one of them is excessive in length....The singers are closely miked, creating a front-row audio perspective, but the internal balances are good, with a strong, overall impact."
The Opera Quarterly 6:151-3 Autumn '88. George Jellinek (1225w)

"The singers...are mostly competent and pleasant...but...Emma Kirkby is no Faustina Bordoni...and none of the others approach what the brilliant singers of 1731 must have sounded like. The digital sound is splendid."

Fanfare 11:122-3 Mr/Ap '88. David Johnson (1150w)

Gramophone 65:1239-40 F '88. Stanley Sadie (990w)

Digital Audio 4:51 My '88. Roland B. Graeme (750w)

The New York Times Je 19 '88, p. H27. John Rockwell (550w); S 27 '88, p. H27+. Will Crutchfield (300w)

HENZE, HANS WERNER

7050. Die Bassariden.

Gerd Albrecht (c). Karan Armstrong (sop); Kenneth Riegel (ten); Andreas Schmidt (bar); Michael $$ Burt (bass); Robert Tear (ten); William B. $$ Murray (bass); Celina Lindsley (sop); Ortrun Wenkel (contr). Berlin Radio Chamber Choir; South German Radio Chorus; Berlin Radio Symphony Orchestra. Notes, text and translations included.
KOCH-SCHWANN 314 006 DDD 120:00 2 discs

★★★*Awards:* The Want List 1991, *Fanfare* N/D '91 (James H. North). Critics' Choice 1991, *Gramophone*, Ja '92 (Michael Stewart). Critics' Choice 1991, Opera, *The Wire*, D/Ja '91/92 (Nick Kimberley).

"Under Gerd Albrecht, the Berlin Radio forces deliver a gripping performance of *The Bassarids*. Kenneth Riegel's Dionysus is a miracle of tireless brightness and security."

Opera News 56:41 N '91. John W. Freeman (long)

"This...opera...[is] superbly performed and recorded."

American Record Guide 54:81 N/D '91. Mark L. Lehman (long)

"In his book *Opera in the Twentieth Century*, Ethan Mordden makes a case for *The Bassarids* as the culmination of a half century of operatic writing. The libretto, by W. H. Auden and Chester Kallman, is a distillation of Euripides' *The Bacchae*; the opera is sung in English, even in this German production....It is a masterful score, complex yet accessible. The large orchestra is lit with percussion; music for Penthus is stern and forceful, that for Dionysus lilting and seductive....Kenneth Riegel is stunning as Dionysus; this is the finest I have heard from him....The recording is clear and brilliant, and so well balanced that the blazing orchestra never drowns a soloist; of course that is Henze's doing too....a magnificent release, which goes straight onto Want List 1991. For anyone interested in modern opera, *The Bassarids* is a climactic work."

Fanfare 15:351-2 N/D '91. James H. North (long)

Gramophone 69:187 O '91; 69:47-8 Ja '92. Michael Stewart (long)

HUMPERDINCK, ENGELBERT

7051. Hansel und Gretel.

Jeffrey Tate (c). Anne-Sofie von Otter (mez); Barbara Bonney (sop); Hanna Schwarz (mez); Andreas Schmidt (bar); Barbara Hendricks (sop); Eva Lind (sop); Marjana Lipovsek (contr). Tolz Boys' Choir; Bavarian Radio Symphony Orchestra.
EMI 54022 DDD 103:00 2 discs

✔HC ★★★★*Awards:* Critics' Choice 1990, *Gramophone* D '90 (Edward Greenfield); Best Recordings of the Month, *Stereo Review* F '91; The Highs, 1990, *The New York Times* D 30 '90 (John Rockwell). Honorable Mention, Records of the Year, 1991, *Stereo Review*, F '92. Editors' Choice, *Digital Audio and CD Review*, Je '92.

"The new EMI/Angel recording of Humperdinck's opera *Hansel und Gretel* is pure enchantment, a fairy tale for children of all ages endowed with wonderful, inventive music....No *Hansel und Gretel* could be more glitteringly cast, but the artists work together so that the totality of performance is paramount....I cannot imagine a more satisfying *Hansel* than this one and take pleasure in recommending it to anyone who love children, fantasy, and appealing music."

Stereo Review 56:120 F '91. Robert Ackart (360w)

"For me, the only serious stereo competition for this set is on CBS, led by the late John Pritchard (M2K 35898)....What puts the set over the top is Elisabeth Soderstrom's Witch, a riotous characterization of a querulous, mean-spirited old woman, barely able to hide her true colors as she tries to lure the children to their doom."

Musical America 111:79 My '91. Thor Eckert Jr. (390w)

"Aside from Lind, there's not a weak performance in the cast....Jeffrey Tate really has a handle on this pearl of a work, and he gets lush yet lyrical playing out of the Bavarians. The Boys' Choir is a nice touch. This is also the best sounding *Hansel* on discs, with real ambience and great clarity....Highest recommendation."

Stereophile 14:244 Je '91. Robert Levine (200w)

"EMI's classic version of this opera, conducted by Karajan, has held sway in this field for a long time, and only now has the company managed to come up with a worthwhile successor. It has achieved, in fact, another winner. Bonney and Von Otter prove an almost ideal pair of children, perhaps not as smooth-voiced as their Karajan predecessors but as appealing as any of the 'children' in more recent sets-....The whole thing is joyously achieved."

Opera 41:1374-75 N '90. Alan Blyth (450w)

"The domestic Schwann/*Opus* catalog now lists four CD versions of *Hansel und Gretel*, with one (London's, under Solti) presumably still to come—an embarrassment of riches.

Those who opt for EMI's newest contribution will find the orchestral part set forth with clarity and warmth by conductor Jeffrey Tate and EMI's engineers. Despite its prominence, the orchestra doesn't upstage the singers."

Opera News 55:34 Mr 16 '91. John W. Freeman (320w)

"Tate's reading...is full of insights and good ideas (and I do hope he can persuade EMI over *Konigskinder*), but the supreme achievements of Solti and Karajan already stand guard over Humperdinck's enchanted forest." *P95/85 S95/85*

Hi-Fi News & Record Review 35:94 D '90. David Nice (525w)

"It has particularly strong performances of the title roles....The sound strikes me as bottom-heavy and unkind to the winds, although that may be an accurate reflection of what conductor Jeffrey Tate wants. Pacing is moderate. Of the four currently available CD sets, my first choice would be Karajan's, but it's mono (1953), which may disqualify it for some people."

Fanfare 14:244 Mr/Ap '91. James Miller (250w)

"Unfortunately, this producer seems to have persuaded his conductor to direct the score as if it were background to a horror movie: loud, shrill, fierce, unbending, and relentless are some of the adjectives I wrote down while listening to this misguided performance....Texts and translations, and a jacket picture that must have been designed by an expert in 'psycho-terror'."

American Record Guide 54:78-9 Mr/Ap '91. Kurt Moses (365w)

Digital Audio's CD Review 7:56 S '91. Sebastian Russ (320w)

Gramophone 68:1050 N '90. Edward Greenfield (700w)

JANACEK, LEOS

7052. Jenufa.

Charles Mackerras; David Atherton (c). Elisabeth Soderstrom (sop); Lucia Popp; Eva Randova; Peter Dvorsky (ten); Wieslaw Ochman; Vaclav Zitek; Dalibor Jedlicka (bass); Ivana Mixova; Vera Soukupova; Jindra Pokorna; Jana Jonasova. Vienna State Opera Chorus; Vienna Philharmonic Orchestra; London Sinfonietta.
LONDON/DECCA 414 483 130:22 2 discs

✔HC ★*Awards:* Record of the Eighties, *Gramophone*, D '89 (Arnold Whittall).

"The CD makes magical what has previously been merely sparkling."

Hi-Fi News & Record Review 31:103 Mr '86. Kenneth Dommett (170w)

"Mackerras, a champion of Janacek's music since his student days in Prague during the late 1940s, has undertaken to return as closely as possible to the composer's original intentions-....One of the attractions of this recording is that it offers two different versions of the concluding scene of the opera and makes it possible for one to compare Janacek's original ending with that devised by [Karel] Kovarovic-....Noted for her dramatic flair, as well as for her singing ability, Elisabeth Soderstrom offers an intensely moving and thoroughly thought-out portrayal of Jenufa: evolving from the simple, naive young girl, to the earnest and passionate young woman, the tender and loving mother, and a forgiving and accepting mature woman."

Opera Canada 27:50 Fall '86 Neil Crory (920w)

"The outstanding vocal dramatic performance in this well-recorded set...is Elisabeth Soderstrom's as the young girl Jenufa. But Eva Randova's portrayal of Jenufa's stepmother...is almost its equal."

High Fidelity 37:83 Ja '87 Thomas Hathaway (260w) (rev. of LP)

Gramophone 63:832 D '85. John Warrack (265w)

7053. Osud (sung in English).

Charles Mackerras (c). Helen Field (sop); Philip Langridge (ten); Kathryn Harries (sop); Peter Bronder (ten); Stuart Kale (ten). Welsh National Opera Chorus and Orchestra.
EMI 49993 DDD 79:00

★★★*Awards:* Pick of the Month, North American Perspective (Christopher Pollard), *Gramophone* S '90; Best of the Month, *Hi-Fi News & Record Review*, O '90. Critics' Choice 1990, *Gramophone* D '90 (John Warrack); The Gramophone Awards, Nominations, Opera, *Gramophone*, N '91.

"Even the opening seconds declare the white heat of genius, merry-go-round trumpet and bright woodwind joining glittering string ostinati to conjure up the sun-loving crowds of Luhacovice Spa...The ways of *Osud*, though, are stranger thereafter...Transition to the recording studio brings a perfect re-creation of Langridge's thoughts on stage; though Mackerras, turning to the Welsh National Opera Chorus and Orchestra, realizes effects only half grasped at the Coliseum." *P100 S100/95*

Hi-Fi News & Record Review 35:97+ O '90. David Nice (500w)

"The opera is performed in a highly singable English translation by Rodney Blumer, which makes the characters seem a little too precious but is more intelligible than the original and only minimally robs the vocal lines of their Czech speech rhythms....The recording as a whole offers a performance of genuine theatrical validity (unlike so many other studio creations) that not only rehabilitates Janacek's *Osud* but makes it one of the most listenable opera recordings of the year."

Stereo Review 55:164+ N '90. David Patrick Stearns (420w)

"Certainly there is no bar to the enjoyment of this inventive, frequently ravishing score in the new EMI recording with the forces of the Welsh National Opera under the experienced and authoritative direction of Charles Mackerras."

Opera 41:1375-76 N '90. Barry Millington (6000w)

"Langridge's words are crystal clear, and he plays his part with such sensitivity and intelligence that I quickly stopped wishing he had a more ringing voice. His timbre is always pleasing. Field and Harries won't win any prizes for *bel canto*, but they're at least adequate. The large supporting cast is at or above their level. Mackerras conducts with patent expertise and involvement...and the recorded sound is solid, lucid, and well-balanced. An English libretto is included."

American Record Guide 54:59 Ja/F '91. Ralph V. Lucano (230w)

"Under the knowledgeable leadership of Charles Mackerras, the opera blazes to life and overcomes—on disc, anyway—the inanities of the plot....The players of this Welsh National Opera production, if nowhere outstanding, are effective, singing the English translation of *Opera* magazine editor Rodney Milnes Blumer."

Opera News 55:34 F 16 '91. Patrick J. Smith (315w)

"The honors are about even: Mackerras's reading has more power, but the Brno forces do capture Janacek's unique sound more truly than the Welsh. So another great Janacek opera is now readily available, in about as fine a version as we could hope for.....For anyone who wallowed in the earlier Mackerras series, this disc is a must."

Fanfare 14:247-8 Mr/Ap '91. James H. North (800w)

High Fidelity 1:107 S '90. Clive Manning (b.n.)

Gramophone 68:605-6 S '90. John Warrack (595w)

The New York Times O 7 '90, p. 34. Jamie James (120w)

LECLAIR, JEAN MARIE

7054. Scylla et Glaucus.

John Eliot Gardiner (c). Donna Brown (sop); Howard Crook (ten); Rachel Yakar (sop); Catherine Dubosc (sop); Francoise Golfier (sop); Agnes Mellon (sop). Monteverdi Choir; English Baroque Soloists. London. February 1986.
ERATO 75339 DDD 170:00 3 discs

★★*Awards:* The Want List 1988, *Fanfare* N/D '88 (David Johnson); Early Music (Baroque) Record Award 1988, *Gramophone* O '88.

"One secret of performing this opera, clearly, is to find the link between the violinistic and vocal style of Leclair's music, and this is exactly what happens with Rachel Yakar, who sings the plum role of the sorceress Circe....As Glaucus, tenor Howard Crook produces a light, pointed, pliant tone that nevertheless conveys subtle sensuousness and physicality."

Opera News 53:64 S '88. John W. Freeman (400w)

"Work and performance will give keen pleasure as well as enlightenment even (or perhaps especially) to those who still feel shy of Baroque opera."

Opera 39:752 Je '88. Ronald Crichton (440w)

"John Eliot Gardiner...turns in a masterful reading...ably abetted by a large cast and orchestra who cope superbly with Leclair's often difficult and finely-wrought music. An added bonus is the accompanying booklet, a model of its kind."

Continuo 12:24-5 Je '88. Scott Paterson (200w)

"This is the music that Gardiner loves and performs best. The sound is a delight, the indexing generous, the libretto well translated...No *dix-septiemiste*, indeed no Francophile, will want to pass this wonderful recording up."

Fanfare 11:185-8 Jl/Ag '88. David Johnson (1550w)

"Fine as some of the performers are, I have reservations about the casting....Gardiner conducts a vigorous performance, highly dramatic but never in danger of going out of control. The sound is spot-on."

Musical America 108:71 Jl '88. Christopher Rothko (475w)

Gramophone 65:1492-3 Ap '88 (1400w); 66:549 O '88 (200w). Nicholas Anderson

LEONCAVALLO, RUGGERO

7055. I Pagliacci.

Renato Cellini (c). Jussi Bjoerling (ten); Victoria De los Angeles (sop); Leonard Warren (bar); Robert Merrill (bar); Paul Franke (ten). Robert Shaw Chorale; Columbus Boychoir; RCA Victor Orchestra. 1954.
EMI 49503 ADD 69:25

★*Awards: American Record Guide* Overview: Opera Favorites, Ja/F '91.

"I must admit to an extreme partiality for this recording...Now, digitally remastered, it is even more enjoyable....Vocally, the recording is gorgeous....The recording is surprisingly lifelike, by which I mean extremely theatrical."

Opera 41:1379 N '90. Elizabeth Forbes (380w)

"If this isn't a self-recommending cast, what is-...The recording sounds fine as far as it goes, but it seems to lack a certain brightness....Recommended, of course."

Fanfare 13:263 N/D '89. James Miller (220w)

Gramophone 67:1199 D '89. Alan Blyth (175w)

LULLY, JEAN BAPTISTE

7056. Atys.

William Christie (c). Guy De Mey (ten); Guillemette Laurens (mez); Agnes Mellon (sop); Jean-Francois Gardeil (bass). Les Arts Florissants Vocal and Instrumental Ensemble. 1987.
HARMONIA MUNDI 901257/9 DDD 167:21 3 discs

✔HC ★★★★★*Awards:* *Opus* Record Award, 1987; *Opus* Repertoire Enhancement Award Nominee, 1987; *Opus* Christmas List, 1987 (Malloch, William); *Fanfare* Want List 1987 (David Johnson); *Gramophone* Critics' Choice (Nicholas Anderson) 1987; *Opera News* Best of the Year, 1987. Second Place Opera Mumm Champagne Classical Music Award 1988—Presented by *Ovation*, *Ovation* N '88; Record of the Eighties, *Gramophone*, D '89 (Julie Anne Sadie).

"An album as near perfect as was the live performance I have heard and seen in Florence."
Fanfare 13:495 S/O '89. Nick Rossi (90w)

"Very few opera recordings in my experience possess the immediacy that this one has....Altogether a triumph for all concerned." Review 52:85 Ag '87 Christie Barter (360w)

"This superlative recording makes the best—perhaps the first—case for Lully's being a great master rather than merely an interesting Historical Personage....In an age of outstanding Baroque specialists, Christie belongs at the very top of the list. The compact disc sound is glorious."
Fanfare 11:232-5 S/O '87. David Johnson (2750w)

"The dream music of Act III, Scene 4, with its heavenly Aeolian winds, is itself worth the purchase price."
Opus 4:57 D '87. William Malloch (90w);

One of 20 classical CDs reviewed and recommended as "outstanding for their musical interest and their performance as well as for their technical quality."
Stereo Review Presents: Compact Disc Buyer's Guide 1988 p.40. William Livingstone and Christie Barter (125w)

"I reviewed the production when it arrived last January at the Opera-Comique....[This recording] confirms in every particular the excellence of the musical execution, the finely detailed preparation and delivery of recitative, and above all, the dramatic excitement that informed the live experience....I cannot recommend this *Atys* too highly."
Opera 38:1413-4 D '87. Max Loppert (300w)

"Outstanding among the singers are Agnes Mellon, Guillemette Laurens and Guy de Mey."
Opera News 52:58 D 5 '87. John W. Freeman (260w)

"This splendid release is a revelation."
Continuo 12:19-20 O '88. Pierre Savaria (1035w)

"The strings—exclusively gut, certainly, and of course entirely without vibrato—sound a bit shiny in crescendos at first, but you soon get used to hearing all the instruments sound the way we assume they did in Lully's day. The woodwinds have a softness and mellowness of timbre that modern instruments cannot emulate. All four of the main singers stand out in their roles, as do several of the supporting cast."
High Fidelity 39:60-2 F '89. Paul Moor (875w)

Ovation 9:40 Je '88. Dick Adler (450w)

American Record Guide 50:43-4 N/D '87. R. D. Darrell (750w)

Gramophone 65:215-6 Jl '87 Nicholas Anderson (1470w)

MAGNARD, ALBERIC

7057. Guercoeur.

Michel Plasson (c). Jose Van Dam (bass-bar); Hildegard Behrens (sop); Nadine Denize (mez); Gary Lakes (ten); Anne Salvan (mez); Michele Lagrange (sop). Orfeon Donostiarra; Toulouse Capitole Orchestra.
EMI 49193 DDD 183:00 3 discs

★★★★*Awards:* International Record Critics Award (IRCA) Winner 1988, *High Fidelity* N '88 and *Musical America* N '88; The Want List 1988, *Fanfare* N/D '88 (Adrian Corleonis). Critics' Choice 1988, *Gramophone* D '88 (Richard Osborne; Lionel Salter).

"Jose Van Dam's earnest, suffering Guercoeur speaks for the disillusion of all principled men, while Nadine Denize effectively conveys the earthbound anguish of his only too human wife, Giselle....*Guercoeur* is kept moving by Michel Plasson, and while it may not be much fun, it comes across as a substantial work, provoking both thought and emotion."
Opera News 53:64-5 S '88. John W. Freeman (390w)

"If anything could persuade one to rate *Guercoeur* as Magnard wanted it to be rated, it would be the French EMI performance, which is evidently a labour of love for Plasson, his orchestra, and the San Sebastian choir...The performance of the title role...is magnificent."
Opera 39:1253-4 O '88. Max Loppert (375w)

"This splendidly committed performance...carries the listener through turgid symbolism to concentrate on the very real musical rewards."
Music and Musicians International 36:42 My '88. Robert Hartford (210w)

"This is an opera in which the chorus vies notably with the soloists for the listener's loyalty. The Orfeon Donostiarra sings its finest music, in the scenes in paradise, with the tonal radiance and delicacy that this highly perfumed music requires. In the bustling of the scenes populated by the throngs of the third tableau of act 2, however, the men of the chorus sound too callow and underpowered to project this music, bombastic and rhetorical, with the force-

fulness that might otherwise make the most of what little it has to offer. The lineup of soloists is an able one....The Toulouse orchestral forces at Michel Plasson's disposal cope very nicely with the complexities of Magnard's rich scoring....The stereo sound is entirely adequate, if not much more than that, lacking but the added depth of perspective that would have been desirable to capture more fully the work's opulence in the choral and orchestral writing."
The Opera Quarterly 6:127-29 Winter '88/'89. C.P. Gerald Parker (1110w)

"Conductor Michel Plasson deserves great credit for molding the huge work into a listenable whole, and he has full support from the chorus, orchestra, and soloists."
Stereo Review 53:160-1 Ja '88. Robert Ackart (640w)

"If something less than a great singing actor, van Dam nevertheless essays the title role with authority. Behrens' vibrato-laden voice shows some strain above the staff, though without compromising a ringing and appropriately aloof rendering of Truth. But unqualified praise must be reserved for chorus, orchestra, and Michel Plasson."
Fanfare 12:188-91 S/O '88. Adrian Corleonis (645w)

The New York Times My 8 '88, p. H23. John Rockwell (300w)

Gramophone 65:1493-4 Ap '88. Lionel Salter (665w)

MASCAGNI, PIETRO

7058. Cavalleria Rusticana.
Renato Cellini (c). Zinka Milanov (sop); Jussi Bjoerling (ten); Robert Merrill (bar); Carol Smith (contr). Robert Shaw Chorale; RCA Victor Orchestra. 1953 reissue.
RCA 6510 ADD 71:08

★*Awards:* *American Record Guide* Overview: Opera Favorites, Ja/F '91.

"In tone and temperament, Milanov hardly suggests a young Sicilian girl. But Mascagni's music is grandly curvaceous as often as it is smolderingly tempestuous, and the soprano makes Santuzza a tragic heroine, not a fishwife-....Robert Merrill makes an uncommonly youthful and plump-toned Alfio, and Bjoerling, often criticized for placidity, is a supremely passionate Turiddu."
The Opera Quarterly 7:162+ Spr '90. William Albright (160w)

"No side breaks, no interruptions—just a thrilling performance."
Fanfare 11:142 Mr/Ap '88. Robert Levine (105w)

7059. Iris.
Giuseppe Patane (c). Ilona Tokody (sop); Placido Domingo (ten); Juan Pons (bar); Bonaldo Giaiotti (bass-bar); Maria Gabriella Ferroni (sop); Conchita Antunano (sop); Sergio Tedesco (ten); Heindrich Weber (ten). Bavarian Radio Chorus; Munich Radio Orchestra.
CBS 45526 DDD 124:00 2 discs

★*Awards:* Critic's Choice: 1990, *American Record Guide* Ja/F '91 (Lee Milazzo).

"The late Giuseppe Patane...unfolds the luxuriant score with absolute conviction and draws playing of rare refinement and beauty from the Munich Radio Orchestra...He has a well-nigh perfect cast, too....the revelation of the set is Ilona Tokody's thrilling and touching account of the title role...On the debit side there are some pretty hair-raising comprimarios."
Opera 40:1266-67 O '89. Hugh Canning (1200w)

"If one ignores the fact that Tokody's voice has a dark, dramatic quality that is difficult to associate with a young girl, she is excellent in the title role. Domingo's Osaka has the customary ring in the lyrical arias and is equally effective in more melodramatic passages....Patane coaxes expressive singing from the choir and precisely balanced playing from the orchestra."
Opera Canada 31:67 Spr 90. John Kraglund (370w)

"The performance is, for the most part, an excellent one, principally due to Patane's ministrations. Though my experience with the opera is limited to but two staged productions and a handful of private recordings, never have I heard such delicacy and lightness in what is basically a 'heavy' score....Recommended."
Fanfare 13:224-25 Ja/F '90. Adrian Corleonis (825w)

"The cast is a distinguished one and, despite my impatience at the time with the plot, the stronger moments linger on." *P95/(85) S95*
Hi-Fi News & Record Review 35:99 F '90. David Nice (360w)

"The opera belongs to the soprano, and Tokody has mastered the Italian style remarkably well....The chorus is splendid, and Patane conducts grandly and powerfully....The sound, while perhaps too bright on top, is deep and spacious...Unquestionably a worthwhile acquisition."
American Record Guide 53:73-4 My/Je '90. Ralph V. Lucano (315w)

"I find *Iris* a disturbing opera to listen to, because of the continual discrepancy between the brutal action and the quite ravishing beauty of the music....For a made-from-scratch studio version of an obscure opera, the CBS set is a considerable achievement....The conductor does obtain beautiful (if literal) playing from the solidly professional Munich orchestra....The cast is perhaps not ideal, but when I sat down with pencil and paper to decide how it could be improved upon, I discovered with some dismay that all of my candidates were either retired or dead....The digital recording is generally good and untricky."

The Opera Quarterly 7:231-37 Spr '90. Roland Graeme (1515w)

"Familiar with the idiom of the verismo composers, Patane was an ideal advocate for this problem score, on which Mascagni lavished colorful instrumentation but more ingenuity than melody....Most of Iris' solo scenes move slowly, and it takes an artist of Tokody's skill to keep them alive."

Opera News 54:54 N '89. John W. Freeman (325w)

Gramophone 67:533-34 S '89. Michael Oliver (410w)

MASSENET, JULES

7060. Manon. CHAUSSON, ERNEST. Poeme de l'Amour et de la Mer, for Voice and Piano (or Orchestra), Opus 19.

Pierre Monteux; Jean-Pierre Jacquillat (c). Victoria De los Angeles (sop); Henri Legay (ten); Michel Dens (bar); Jean Borthayre (bass); Jean Vieuille (bar); Rene Herent (ten); Liliane Berton (sop); Raymonde Notti (sop); Marthe Serres (sop). Paris Opera-Comique Chorus and Orchestra; Lamoureux Concerts Orchestra. 1956, 1973 reissue.
EMI 63549 ADD (m) 189:00 3 discs

★★*Awards:* The Want List 1990, *Fanfare* N/D '90 (James Miller); Editor's Choice, *Opera Canada* Winter '90.

"Pierre Monteux presided over the best recording of Massenet's opera ever made....I haven't actually tried to compile such a list, but if I did, this would probably be one of my choices among the 'Dozen Greatest Opera Recordings Ever Made.' Is that a high enough recommendation? That recommendation would stand even if EMI hadn't fattened the package by including Chausson's lyrical *Poem of Love and the Sea.*"

Fanfare 14:271 N/D '90. James Miller (625w)

"Thirty-five years after its release, this stylistically authentic reading still remains the opera's finest recording....A bonus on the CD reissue is los Angeles' magical account of Chausson's *Poeme de l'amour et de la mer.*"

Opera Canada 31(4):50 Winter '90. Harvey Chusid (200w)

"The orchestra sounds terrible....Victoria de los Angeles is wonderful—much better than Ileana Cotrubas...The rest of the cast is very French and sounds perfectly idiomatic....Angel has filled with a truly delicious recording [of the *Poeme*] from 14 years later."

American Record Guide 53:78 N/D '90. Donald R. Vroon (240w)

Gramophone 68:407-8 Ag '90. Alan Blyth (530w)

MESSAGER, ANDRE

7061. Fortunio.

John Eliot Gardiner (c). Thierry Dran (ten); Colette Alliot-Lugaz (sop); Gilles Cachemaille (bar); Francis Dudziak (ten); Michel Trempont. Lyon Opera Chorus; Lyon Opera Orchestra.
ERATO 75390 DDD 102:00 2 discs

★★★★★*Awards:* Record of the Month, *Hi-Fi News & Record Review* O '88; Critics' Choice 1988, *Gramophone* D '88 (Andrew Lamb; John Steane); Best of the Year, *Opera News* D 24 '88. The Want List 1989, *Fanfare* N/D '89 (David Johnson).

"Unmitigated delight and I defy anyone with a heart to resist it! It may, of course, be the kind of minor masterpiece which only works under certain conditions of performance. If so they are matchlessly met here."

Hi-Fi News & Record Review 33:99 O '88. (420w)

"This elegant and sensitive work well repays repeated hearings and the performance under review is unlikely to be surpassed....Very highly recommended!"

American Record Guide 51:61-2 N/D '88. Vivian A. Liff (405w)

"The performance is faultless under the baton-...of John Eliot Gardiner and his Lyons Opera forces, and the individual interpretations are not only delightful in themselves but scotch once and for all that ridiculous *canard* about there being no French singers any more...One of the special joys of *Fortunio* is the way the charm and sweetness of the score make us forget we are listening to a highly immoral little piece. I mean, what about the poor wretched husband?"

Opera 39:1336+ N '88. Rodney Milnes (550w)

"Messager's music is melodic (though not memorably tuneful) and his orchestrations are witty, pictorial, or sentimental, as the dramatic situation requires...*Fortunio* is a charming light opera...alive with musical and verbal wit....This cast strikes me as near-ideal....this recording-...deserves a place in any opera collection."

American Record Guide 53:64 Ja/F '90. Desmond Arthur (325w)

"This is connoisseurs' music, yet with popular appeal, so that it functions equally brilliantly on more than one level. The cast could scarcely help enjoying itself with *Fortunio.* As Jacqueline...Alliot-Lugaz has the field to herself."

Opera News 53:65 S '88. John W. Freeman (415w)

"As Fortunio, Thierry Dran has not the ultimate lyric eloquence of a Thill...but he does no serious damage to Messager's subtly contoured music. Colette Alliot-Lugaz... is a charming and lovable Jacqueline...Gilles Cachemaille is suitably macho and handsome-voiced as Clavaroche, and the remainder of the cast fulfill their tasks with style."

Fanfare 12:223-5 N/D '88. David Johnson (1250w)

"Just occasionally, one yearns for a bit more 'give' to the pacing, but Mr. Gardiner keeps a strong hand on the tiller—and he gets fine work from both chorus and orchestra."

The New York Times F 19 '89, p. 29+. Scott Cantrell (475w)

Gramophone 66:332 Ag '88. Andrew Lamb (595w)

MESSIAEN, OLIVIER

7062. Saint Francois d'Assise (Scenes Franciscaines).

Seiji Ozawa (c). Christiane Eda-Pierre (sop); Jose Van Dam (bass); Kenneth Riegel (ten); Michel Senechal. Paris Opera Chorus; Paris Opera Orchestra. Paris Opera. December 1983 live.
CYBELIA 833/6 DDD 246:00 4 discs

★★★★*Awards:* The Want List 1988, *Fanfare* N/D '88 (Kyle Gann); Critics' Choice 1988, *Gramophone* D '88 (David Fanning); Best of the Year, *Opera News* D 24 '88. Editors' Choice, *Digital Audio's CD Review*, Je '89.

"This performance...is fantastically good in many respects, and disappointments are few, if obvious....Quibbles notwithstanding, this disc will likely make a number of Want Lists, and it is guaranteed to be near the top of mine."

Fanfare 12:202-4 S/O '88. Kyle Gann (1390w)

"Under Seiji Ozawa's inspired direction, and with a dedicated cast headed by Jose van Dam in the title role, the music weaves its magic for anyone the least bit attuned to the composer's glinting, many-layered compositional style. The recording itself vividly conveys the fervor of the live performances at which it was made-....the libretto provided is in English only, which makes following Messiaen's French text almost impossible."

Stereo Review 53:150-52 D '88. Christie Barter (200w)

"There is little to fault in this remarkable performance...the sound is uncommonly clear and well balanced for a live recording."

Opera News 52:47 Je '88. John W. Freeman (500w)

"Such a sprawling and sectional composition ideally needs the coordination between voices and orchestra that only a studio performance, with scores in hand, can provide....The singing appears impeccable, however...The sound quality also suffers from live recording conditions."

American Record Guide 51:44-5 Jl/Ag '88. Arved Ashby (1200w)

"Everything is vividly captured by a sharply focused recording, impressive in its balance of orchestra and voices, though not entirely natural in that respect, and redolent of the spontaneity, vividness, and extraordinary staying power of all concerned in this four-hour musical feast. But, sadly, those at Cybelia...rather than stay with the inevitable mistakes that a live performance of such a lengthy work brings, they have chosen to give us the distraction of numerous tape edits, with their inherent alterations of ambience and changes in vocal quality."

Stereophile 11:157 S '88. Barbara Jahn (480w)

"There is some audible background noise, and the singers tend to wander from channel to channel and in and out of focus, depending upon their stage positions. The prompter is also clearly audible throughout the four CDs-....The orchestral playing and the singing is, on the whole, good." *P85/95 S75/85*

Hi-Fi News & Record Review 34:109+ O '89. William McVicker (1015w)

Digital Audio 5:55-6 S '88. Octavio Roca (570w)

Gramophone 66:1057 D '88. Michael Oliver (870w)

The New York Times Ag 13 '89, p. H 29. Paul Turok (415w)

MEYERBEER, GIACOMO

7063. Les Huguenots.

Cyril Diederich (c). Ghyslaine Raphanel (sop); Francoise Pollot (sop); Danielle Borst (sop); Richard Leech (ten); Gilles Cachemaille (bar); Nikolai Ghiuselev (bass); Boris Martinovich (bass); Jean-Luc Maurette (ten); Marc Barrard (bar); Antoine Garcin (bar); Herv Martin (bar); Christian Boulay (bass). Montpellier Opera Chorus; Montpellier Philharmonic Orchestra. 1988.
ERATO 45027 DDD 233:00 4 discs

★*Awards:* Editor's Choice, *Opera Canada*, Spr '91.

"The orchestra plays vigorously under Cyril Diederich's leadership, which only occasionally relaxes its momentum; and for the most part the singers do very well....Recorded sound takes on an old-fashioned aura in loud passages, which tend to sound shallow and cramped, but these moments are exceptions to a readily listenable overall standard."

Opera News 55:46 S '90. John W. Freeman (435w)

"Although this recording, which stems from 1988 concert readings of the opera in Montpellier, France, does not dispense the Golden Age singing vaunted by the Metropolitan Opera in performances at the turn of the century, it is an impressive achievement." *PS 90*

Opera Canada 32:50 Spr 91. Harvey Chusid (265w)

"*Les Hugeuenots* contains some delightful moments even though it hangs a little loose, in places."

High Fidelity 1:107 S '90. Clive Manning (100w)

"Montpellier...were able to cast most of the *Huguenots* roles adequately with native French singers, and they found a more-than-adequate Raoul and Marcel close to home....The Montpellier choral and orchestral forces may not be of ideal strength but they are well-prepared and enthusiastic....The sound is generally good...A fine release."

American Record Guide 53:81-2 N/D '90. Desmond Arthur (635w)

"The only CD rival to this new MF (for Musifrance) release, which was produced in cooperation with Erato and Radio France, is the classic 1962 revival of *Les Huguenots*, pirated live from La Scala and featuring a currently unmatchable cast...Its chief drawbacks are two: the sound is only so-so, and the score has been shorn of almost an hour's worth of music. A lesser drawback is the fact that it is sung in Italian rather than in the original French....The new performance is not only sung in French but four of its seven 'stars' *are* French, as is the chorus and orchestra....much of the performance is really good, really exciting."

Fanfare 14:279-81 N/D '90. David Johnson (1560w)

"Cyril Diederich leads with a sure hand and an obvious fondness for this behemoth, and the show hangs together well as a result. Both orchestra and chorus...play and sing with verve. Most of the soloists, too, turn in noble performances...The sound varies, it was recorded over a period of two months...but is never less than good. The chances of another *Huguenots* coming along, particularly one so correctly French and so lovingly prepared, warts and all, are slim. If the La Scala performance [available on CD, Melodram 37026] is not enough for you, you'll be pleased enough with this one. Recommended, with reservations."

Stereophile 15:263+ Ja '92. Robert Levine (long)

Gramophone 68:606 S '90. John Steane (840w)

MONTEVERDI, CLAUDIO

7064. Il Ballo delle Ingrate; Sestina (Lagrime d'Amante).

William Christie (c). Arts Florissants Vocal and Instrumental Ensemble.
HARMONIA MUNDI 901108 56:29

"A superb presentation of two important large works among Monteverdi's secular compositions....There's no evidence of analog original in the clean sound.'

Fanfare 9:203-4 N/D '85. J. F. Weber (175w)

"The whole effect is completely enchanting: a triumph."

Hi-Fi News & Record Review 30:81 Ag '85. Stephen Daw (110w)

Gramophone 63:264 Ag '85. John Milsom (140w)

7065. Il Combattimento di Tancredi e Clorinda; Lettera Amorosa; Volgendo il Ciel.

Rene Clemencic (c). Clemencic Consort. 1975.
HARMONIA MUNDI 90986 ADD 43:24

"When this was reviewed in *Fanfare* 3:2, it came as an American pressing as HNH 4006, but it has been available for most of the intervening time as HMU 986. It was a remarkable job....It's good to have it on a modest-priced CD."

Fanfare 11:176-7 N/D '87. J. F. Weber (240w)

7066. L'Incoronazione di Poppea.

Richard Hickox (c). Arleen Auger (sop); Della Jones (mez); Linda Hirst (mez); James Bowman (alto); Gregory Reinhart (bass); Juliet Booth (sop); Catherine Pierard (mez); Sarah Leonard (sop); Adrian Thompson (ten); Mark Tucker (ten); Brian Bannatyne-Scott (bass); Janice Watson (sop); Samuel Linay (treb); Catherine Denley (contr). City of London Baroque Sinfonia. 1968.
VIRGIN 90775 DDD 195:00 3 discs

"For readers wondering which to buy [the Hickox or the Jacobs, Harmonia Mundi 901330/2], I suggest that both are well worth the investment. The singing ranges from good to outstanding, with only the few problems I have outlined above. The decision depends upon one's attitude towards the role of the continuo. If you want the singing to predominate and are a purist towards the score, get the Hickox version. If imaginative ritornello writing and kaleidoscopic continuo orchestration appeals, get the Jacobs disc."

Musick 13(1):19-25 Summer-Jl '91. John E. Sawyer (1875w)

"For this production Hickox uses the Clifford Bartlett edition....While the old Harnoncourt is a milestone in the revival of this opera, I would be willing to settle for Hickox alone if I wanted only one. Even collectors who have several versions can profitably add this to their shelf (no, to the player!) for its strengths."

Fanfare 14:285-86 N/D '90. J. F. Weber (680w)

"Richard Hickox's new recording of *Poppea* deserves a warm welcome for the meticulous excellence of the edition prepared by Clifford Bartlett of what is a notoriously problematic opera, and for the idiomatic restraint of its instrumental palette in contrast to some more titillating, but historically questionable versions....With few exceptions, the singing rarely falls below a reasonable standard, and some of it is much better than that....what it misses above all is any grippingly theatrical or Italianate charge."

Opera 41:881-82 Jl '90. Robert Henderson (415w)

"This is a very delicate and pure version of Monteverdi's late masterpiece, and it is particularly distinguished by the exquisite and moving performance of Arleen Auger in the title role....The rest of the cast is somewhat uneven, mostly excellent but sometimes defeated by the usual gender problems of these old operas...and the recorded sound is exceptionally attractive."

Stereo Review 55:92 Ag '90. Eric Salzman (200w)

"The biggest casting problem in *Poppea* is Nero....There are other casting miscalculations as well....I have further reservations about some of the singing (as opposed to the actual casting)....Virgin has recorded the opera in fine, vivid sound....I like Leppard's *Poppea*, and both of Harnoncourt's, but I'll gladly find a place for Hickox on my shelves."
American Record Guide 54:66-7 Ja/F '91. Ralph V. Lucano (330w)

"James Bowman's countertenor sound simply cannot provide the passion needed for Ottone. The character may have many facets, but wimpishness is not one of them....Laudable though the attempts at authenticity in early music performance are—and the British have led the way—the results are too often essentially bloodless, as is the case here."
Musical America 110:83-4 S '90. Walter Price (220w)

The New York Times Jl 1 '90, p. 22 H. George Jellinek (350w)

Gramophone 67:2049 My '90. Iain Fenlon (1260w)

Opera News 55:30-1 Mr 2 '91. John W. Freeman (215w)

MOZART, WOLFGANG AMADEUS

Abduction from the Seraglio. See Die Entfuhrung aus dem Serall, K.384.

7067. La Clemenza di Tito, K.621.
Colin Davis (c). Stuart Burrows; Janet Baker; Yvonne Minton; Frederica Von Stade; Lucia Popp; Robert Lloyd. Royal Opera House Chorus and Orchestra, Covent Garden. 1976 reissue.
PHILIPS 420 097 ADD 127:44 2 discs

★*Awards:* *American Record Guide* Overview: Mozart Operas, N/D '91.

"This remains one of the most vividly theatrical Mozart recordings of all."
Hi-Fi News & Record Review 32:121 N '87 Hugh Canning (400w)

"There is little doubt that Davis' direction, with its firm grasp of pace, its clarity, and strong affinity for the Mozartean style, has become, in the main, the preferred edition of the work, even if all the singers are not always ideal....the sound of this reissue, if a trifle bright and close, is otherwise exemplary, without a trace of tape-hiss."
Fanfare 11:169 Ja/F '88. Mortimer H. Frank (150w)

Music and Musicians International 36:51-2 N '87. Robert Hartford (90w)

Gramophone 65:481 S '87 Hilary Finch (295w)

7068. La Clemenza di Tito, K.621.
Istvan Kertesz (c). Werner Krenn (ten); Maria Casula (sop); Teresa Berganza (mez); Brigitte Fassbaender (mez); Lucia Popp (sop); Tugomir Franc (bass). Vienna State Opera Chorus and Orchestra. 1967 reissue.
LONDON/DECCA 430 105 ADD 121:00 2 discs

★*Awards:* Editor's Choice, *Opera Canada*, Wtr '91.

"Istvan Kertesz's 1967 recording of *La Clemenza di tito* was long the preferred version; the beauty of the singing, the orchestral playing, and the Decca/London recording all contributed to make this *opera seria* seem the near-equal of the great Mozart operas....The 1967 sound is more sumptuous than ever in this ADRM digital remastering...This issue includes the necessary amenities: an index to the thirty-eight tracks and a four-language synopsis and libretto; each act is complete on one disc."
Fanfare 15:278-79] S/O '91. James H. North (long)

"This, the first worthy recording of *La Clemenza*, is still eminently treasurable, and Decca have refurbished it proudly in this digital remastering. Gruff the sound may be in the overture, but the ear soon grows accustomed, and there is rich detail as well as a spaciousness one normally associates with a stage performance." *P95 S85*
Hi-Fi News & Record Review 36:73 Jl '91. Peter Branscombe (210w)

"The performance...is excellently cast and is presented, under the leadership of Istvan Kertesz with power, urgency and flair...Kertesz provides a taut and transparent account of the score, securing beautifully clean, spacious playing from the Vienna State Opera Orchestra."
Opera Canada 32:50 Wtr '91. Harvey Chusid (long)

"Apart from some cuts in recitative, this version [of *Clemenza*] is substantially complete, and in its new form the splendidly balanced sound emerges with even greater clarity and impact."
American Record Guide 54:106-7 N/D '91. Vivian A. Liff (long)

7069. Cosi fan Tutte, K.588.
Daniel Barenboim (c). Lella Cuberli (sop); Cecilia Bartoli (mez); Joan Rodgers (sop); Kurt Streit (ten); Ferruccio Furlanetto (bass); John Tomlinson (bass). Berlin RIAS Chamber Choir; Berlin Philharmonic Orchestra.
ERATO 45475 DDD 177:00 3 discs

★★★*Awards:* Pick of the Month, North American Perspective (Christopher Pollard), *Gramophone* O '90. Best Recordings of the Month, *Stereo Review* D '90; Editor's Choice, *Opera Canada* Winter '90.

"I don't think you'll ever hear a better-played *Cosi*. I wish the singers were as accomplished as the orchestra!...On the whole, Barenboim's *Cosi* compares favorably with Levine's (reviewed *Fanfare* 13:4). It's less rambunctious, more of a piece; but Levine is note-complete and has the better cast....at the very top of my list is Karajan (a real bargain on two mid-price

EMI discs), with Schwarzkopf, Merriman, Simoneau, and Panerai. If you don't know this performance, don't live another day without hearing it."

Fanfare 14:249-50 Ja/F '91. Ralph V. Lucano (1155w)

"What are the excellences of this set?...I have seldom if ever heard such uniformly intelligible diction or such 'natural' handling of sung language. Secondly, the performance...is uncommonly energetic—and it is my firm belief that energy and concentration are the keys to effective performance....There are, however, matters to which objections may be made-....Faced with the problem of which *Cosi* to take to Crusoe's island, I should probably choose Karajan (mono and all). But if I could take two, this would probably be next on my list."

American Record Guide 54:69-70 Ja/F '91. David Mason Greene (490w)

"The women, Lella Cuberli, Cecilia Bartoloi and Joan Rogers excel, while casting the baritone roles as basses tends to shade some of the music in darker tones. This performance presents the work in a bold light where many may prefer a softer illumination for Mozart's music."

High Fidelity 2:109 D '90. Clive Manning (b.n.)

"This is not an 'early music' recording, and it is not a Mozart chamber-orchestra recording. But it has a freshness and a delicacy that are remarkable....Its nonstar cast (Barenboim is, of course, the star) is made up of first-class singing actors....the level is uniformly high, and the recording itself is gorgeous."

Stereo Review 55:97-8 D '90. Eric Salzman (590w)

"After the high-intensity experience of the Riccardo Muti Salzburg *Cosi* last August, a joyous, fully characterized reading of the performance seemed faceless in comparison. On second hearing, however, that proved not the case at all. Barenboim brings an air of relaxed, fluid control to this glorious music, but that is not to say that it is without personality-....The opera is well-served by a world-class ensemble of singers."

Opera Canada 31(4):49 Winter '90. Harvey Chusid (185w)

"The oddest feature of Barenboim's interpretation is his tendency to read *andante* in a romantic rather than a classical way...The recitatives are lively and responsive, as they must be in this opera...Appoggiaturas make their appearance all too sparingly."

Opera News 55:48 N '90. John W. Freeman (270w)

Digital Audio's CD Review 7:63-4 Ap '91. Octavio Roca (450w)

"This new version must be declared a disappointment on several counts." *P85 S85*

Hi-Fi News & Record Review 35:99 N '90. Peter Branscombe (320w)

"The recorded competition is too strong for this new entry. My preferences are Bohm (Angel EMI CDMC 69330), Karajan (Angel EMI CDHC 69635), or—if up-to-date sound is a major criterion—Levine."

Musical America 111:82-3 Mr '91. George Jellinek (455w)

Gramophone 68:815-6 O '90. Alan Blyth (1330w)

7070. Cosi fan Tutte.

Karl Bohm (c). Elisabeth Schwarzkopf (sop); Christa Ludwig (mez); Hanny Steffek (sop); Alfredo Kraus (ten); Giuseppe Taddei (bar); Walter Berry (bass). Philharmonia Chorus; Philharmonia Orchestra. 1963 reissue.
EMI 69330 ADD 165:00 3 discs

★***Awards:*** *American Record Guide* Overview: Mozart Operas, N/D '91.

Schwarzkopf's "partnership with Ludwig's adorable Dorabella remains the principal reason for acquiring the set."

Hi-Fi News & Record Review 34:90 Je '89. Hugh Canning (175w)

"I have no complaint about EMI's remastered sound...[No] English translation of the libretto-....I'm fond of Bohm's *Cosi*, and I've often derived pleasure from his glamorous cast, but I'd just as soon recommend the note-complete performances led by Solti (London) and Leinsdorf (RCA), both on CD."

Fanfare 12:241-42 My/Je '89. Ralph V. Lucano (750w)

"There's very little to choose from between the two casts [Bohm/Angel, Leinsdorf/RCA]. Price is a sexier Fiordiligi than Schwarzkopf, Ludwig and Troyanos are both great, Kraus is a bit more stylish than Shirley—the singing really is excellent all around....RCA includes and Italian/English libretto, while EMI stupidly offers Italian only, as is their custom on mid-price reissues."

Musical America 109:63 Mr '89. David Hurwitz (150w)

Gramophone 66:858-61 N '88. Alan Blyth (635w)

7071. Cosi fan Tutte, K.588.

Bernard Haitink (c). Carol Vaness (sop); Delores Ziegler (sop); Lillian Watson (sop); Dale Duesing (bar); John Aler (ten); Claudio Desderi (bass). Glyndebourne Festival Chorus; London Philharmonic Orchestra.
EMI 47727 DDD 186:25 3 discs

★★***Awards:*** *Opus* Christmas List, 1987 (Kenneth Furie); *Stereo Review* Best of Month, O '87.

"Fine Abbey Road recording confirms the virtues of the performance and makes this a very desirable *Cosi* indeed."

Hi-Fi News & Record Review 32:101 S '87 Kenneth Dommett (335w)

"A great opera in a shining performance that I am privileged to recommend."

Stereo Review 52:92 O '87. Robert Ackart (430w)

"These hard-working performers uncover perhaps more of *Cosi*'s radiant beauty and dramatic richness...than I've heard before in a single performance."

Opus 4:55 D '87. Kenneth Furie (80w)

"Haitink conveys energy tempered with deliberation."

Opera News 52:46 Je '88. John W. Freeman (425w)

"Some will find it carefully prepared and exquisite. I fear I find it so middle-of-the-road as to be forgettable...It's just slightly more fun than reading the score and slightly less than hearing any of the other performances [on CD]."

Ovation 9:22 Ag '88. Robert Levine (575w)

"One might say that this is a *Cosi* unsexed-...And this is where the Haitink performance falls short, somehow failing to convey all of the sensual emotion that is implicit in many of the opera's arias."

Fanfare 11:248-9 S/O '87. Mortimer H. Frank (435w)

"With Karajan's vintage *Cosi* lined up for CD release, and Davis's just transferred, it is a rash soul who goes for this latest version, outclassed at almost every turn by either of these others."

Music and Musicians International 36:51 N '87. Robert Hartford (115w)

"Though the production attracted attention by incorporating the alternative baritone aria, that aria is not performed here, even as an appendix. And the opera is not quite complete....it has real attractions too."

Opus 4:41+ Ap '88. Jon Alan Conrad (1500w)

Gramophone 65:216+ Jl '87 Hilary Finch (1120w)

7072. Cosi fan Tutte, K.588.

Herbert Von Karajan (c). Elisabeth Schwarzkopf (sop); Nan Merriman (mez); Lisa Otto (sop); Leopold Simoneau (ten); Rolando Panerai (bar); Sesto Bruscantini (bass). Philharmonia Chorus; Philharmonia Orchestra. 1955.
EMI 69635 ADD (m) 157:00 3 discs

✔**HC** ★★★*Awards:* The Want List 1989, *Fanfare* N/D '89 (Paul Sargent Clark); The Want List 1989, *Fanfare* N/D '89 (Ralph V. Lucano). *American Record Guide* Overview: The Operas of Mozart, N/D '91.

"It may not be for every taste, but it is one of Herbert von Karajan's great operatic recordings—a probing (if somewhat unorthodox) view of the work displaying an exceptional grasp of the music's prevailing sensuality. Although the action of some scenes may be underplayed, the overall sensuous ethos of the production conveys, more than any other I have encountered, the implicit eroticism underlying the music (and the drama), some portions having a sensual delicacy that is thrillingly unnerving....Not for every taste, perhaps, but a reading of exceptional elegance and one that in the next century will stand as cogent evidence of why Herbert von Karajan is considered one of the great conductors of this one."

Fanfare 12:195-96 Jl/Ag '89. Mortimer H. Frank (215w)

"There is no other production on record which condones such arbitrary butchery of the recitatives—ruining, to my ear, Mozart's subtle key transitions—though, of course, he makes no internal cuts in the musical numbers he does perform...If you want *Cosi* principally for the concerted numbers...this is the recording to have, despite aged sound."

Hi-Fi News & Record Review 34:90 Je '89. Hugh Canning (175w)

Gramophone 66:1057-58 D '88. Alan Blyth (385w)

7073. Cosi fan Tutte, K.588.

James Levine (c). Kiri Te Kanawa (sop); Ann Murray (mez); Marie McLaughlin (sop); Hans-Peter Blochwitz (ten); Thomas Hampson (bar); Ferruccio Furlanetto (bass). Vienna State Opera Chorus; Vienna Philharmonic Orchestra.
DEUTSCHE GRAMMOPHON 423 897 DDD 193:00 3 discs

★*Awards:* Best Recordings of the Month, *Stereo Review* Jl '90.

"I think I'd rate Levine's *Cosi* as the best since Solti's in 1973 or Davis's in '74, even if it lacks that elusive touch of elegance. These singers are just a little too extrovert. I prefer performances where the characters' sexuality smolders behind a courtly facade, and the conflict of propriety vs. passion adds tension to the drama."

Fanfare 13:239-41 Mr/Ap '90. Ralph V. Lucano (900w)

"This is the eighth *Cosi fan tutte* to appear on Compact Disc, and it certainly rates with the best. Conductor James Levine successfully combines muscular incisiveness with an abiding lightness of touch....while fully aware of the work's distinction as a great 'ensemble opera,' I would have welcomed more presence from some of the principals—that is, individual contributions on a more memorable level."

Musical America 110:78-9 My '90. George Jellinek (370w)

"Kiri Te Kanawa, as Fiordiligi, turns in what must be her finest operatic performance on disc....The joyous spirit of the performance remains the salient feature of the recording, and for that we are primarily and happily beholden to James Levine."

Stereo Review 55:75-6 Jl '90. Robert Ackart (400w)

"This new DG recording, if flawed, conveys—as all too few recordings have—the pathos and sensuality at the work's core. Much of the credit for this belongs to James Levine....Unfortunately, working against the conductor's style-consciousness and emotional grasp of the music is DG's choice of Vienna's Musikverein Grosser Saal for the recording, a hall that is fine for Bruckner, but whose dimensions and resonance run counter to the scale of this opera-....Obviously, no performance of this glorious work can be perfect...this new DG recording, its flaws notwithstanding, has a prevailing stylishness that will lead me to return to it often for the considerable pleasure it yields."

Stereophile 13:173+ Jl '90. Mortimer H. Frank (550w)

"Levine's way with *Cosi* is well worth hearing, but the somewhat lackluster cast will limit the appeal of this set."

American Record Guide 53:81 My/Je '90. Lee Milazzo (400w)

"Levine is still the natural Mozartian, letting the music breathe to produce a *Cosi* that is relaxed, loving, at ease with itself...Levine's recording was made in the studio and it sounds like it. The recorded balance is not convincing-...and the cast do not interact with much life. The most disappointing is Kiri Te Kanawa, whose Fiordiligi lacks not only spirit, but also the creamy tone that she has brought to the role on stage."

Opera 40:1381-82 N '89. Richard Fairman (415w)

"Sleek, homogenized performances of *Cosi Fan Tutte* have been the rule rather than the exception in the Schwann Catalog, and DG's new entry does not fly in its face. Yet there is always something special about James Levine's way with Mozart. Without bearing down too heavily on stresses or luxuriating in the sonic upholstery of the Vienna Philharmonic, his *Cosi* shows the buoyancy of a firm, light *sforzando* and the resilience of a hearty tone."

Opera News 54:36 Mr 17 '90. John W. Freeman (340w)

Gramophone 67:966 N '89. Alan Blyth (975w)

7074. Don Giovanni, K.527.

Carlo Maria Giulini (c). Eberhard Waechter (bar); Giuseppe Taddei (bar); Elisabeth Schwarzkopf (sop); Joan Sutherland (sop). Philharmonia Chorus; Philharmonia Orchestra. 1961 reissue.
EMI 47260 ADD 61:40; 64:50; 35:45 3 discs

✔**HC** ★★★*Awards:* The Want List 1988, *Fanfare* N/D '88 (Elliott Kaback, Ralph V. Lucano). Critics Choice, *Hi Fi News & Record Review*, Ap '91 Supplement (George Hall); Critics Choice, *Hi Fi News & Record Review*, Ap '91 Supplement (David Nice). *American Record Guide* Overview: The Operas of Mozart, N/D '91.

"Angel's *Don Giovanni* is surely one of the most celebrated complete opera recordings in history....The real hero was Carlo Maria Giulini....this is magnificent conducting (and playing, too). Angel's sound is splendid, clear and detailed, yet with lots of air and space."

American Record Guide 51:59-60 Mr/Ap '88. Lee Milazzo (435w)

"CD's enhanced dimensions only reaffirm the superlative combination of passion, vitality, and a thorough integration of dramatic elements that Giulini brought to this inspired production. Under his unerringly paced direction, the rich yet transparent orchestral execution supports an exceptional group of singers who form a model ensemble without submerging their individuality. There are no weaknesses in the singing, though admittedly, some of the stars shine brighter than others....The set is a masterpiece."

The Opera Quarterly 5:128-30 My '88. George Jellinek (385w)

"A treasure-house!"

Hi-Fi News & Record Review 33:111 Ja '88. David Nice (340w)

"I have never heard a *Don Giovanni* that is so excitingly conducted, that so reeks of the theater; it's a little heavy and a little humorless but it's also vibrant and powerful. If it had Siepi, it might be the greatest opera recording ever made....But it doesn't, and...the performance, wonderful as it is, has a big hole in the middle....when Wachter isn't present to mess things up, the performance takes off to heights unmatched by any other."

Fanfare 11:182-3 N/D '87. James Miller (500w)

Gramophone 65:996+ D '87. Hilary Finch (410w)

7075. Don Giovanni, K.527.

Bernard Haitink (c). Thomas Allen; Carol Vaness; Keith Lewis; Maria Ewing. Glyndebourne Festival Chorus; London Philharmonic Orchestra.
EMI 47036/7 DDD 171:36 3 discs

★★★★*Awards:* *Fanfare* Want List 1985 (James Miller); *Stereo Review* Best of the Month, O '84; *Gramophone* Critics' Choice 1984 (Alan Blyth); *Gramophone* Record Award Winner 1985—Operatic Award.

"In *Fanfare* VIII:2 I praised this performance highly...This is one performance that isn't likely to be topped very soon."

Fanfare 8:172 My/Je '85. James Miller (160w)

"This is a stunning performance on all counts."

Stereo Review 49:82 O '84. Christie Barter (550w)

Gramophone 62:793 D '84. Alan Blyth (210w)

Digital Audio 1:48-51 Mr '85. Roland Graeme (385w); 2:32-3 My '86. Rod McKuen (525w)

Ovation 6:71 F '85. Thor Eckert, Jr. (340w)

7076. Don Giovanni, K.527.

Nikolaus Harnoncourt (c). Thomas Hampson (bar); Edita Gruberova (sop); Roberta Alexander (sop); Barbara Bonney (sop); Hans-Peter Blochwitz (ten);

Laszlo Polgar (bass); Anton Scharinger (bar); Robert Holl (bass). Netherlands Opera Chorus; Royal Concertgebouw Orchestra.
TELDEC 44184 DDD 172:00 3 discs

★*Awards:* The Highs, 1990, *The New York Times* D 30 '90 (John Rockwell).

"This is a terrific *Don Giovanni*....Don has real swagger; he's a stud who has no morals and doesn't give diddly about what happens to him or anyone else....This is great, heady performing, filled with exquisite arrogance....This may not be the Nirvana of *Don Giovannis*—one may not exist—but if you love this opera, go out and buy this recording."
Stereophile 13:209+ N '90. Robert Levine (595w)

"My favorite has long been Angel's Giulini version...This new release is the first one I've heard that was a match for the Giulini. Overall, in fact, it seems to be an even finer performance and is now my first recommendation for this opera."
American Record Guide 53:86-7 N/D '90. Stephen D. Chakwin, Jr. (475w)

"Anybody who was brought up on the Viennese accounts of Krips or Bohm will probably find that Harnoncourt imposes himself on the score too forcefully; but there is no denying that his set carries with it much of the urgency of a live performance, so often found wanting when *Don Giovanni* is taken into the recording studio....the singers make a satisfactory team. Among the ladies, the Zerlina, Barbara Bonney, is superb....The recording is adequate, the booklet a generous addition to the set."
Opera 41:382+ Mr '90. Richard Fairman (800w)

"Mr. Hampson is the Don Giovanni, and not only does this fine young American singer deliver his most stirring performance to date, but he also singlehandedly revives the casting of the title part by a baritone....His fellow cast-members are impressive too....Best of all, Mr. Harnoncourt, conducting the Concertgebouw, brings a striking sympathy for all aspects of this multifaceted score, with wit and sensuality and grand Romantic drama at the end....Most highly recommended."
The New York Times Ap 1 '90, p. 33+ H. John Rockwell (250w)

"This is in many ways as fine a *Don Giovanni* as one could hope to hear with the only real drawback being the small-sounding Donna Anna. unless the listener prefers a Samuel Ramey (bass) to a Thomas Hampson (baritone), the disc is highly recommended."
HighPerformanceReview 8(2):70-1 Summer '91. Barbara Kierig (760w)

"The recording features a fine cast of youngish singers and a brilliantly accomplished orchestra. The dynamic of eighteenth-century music is realized with brilliant tempos, elegant and mostly flawless fioratura, and an overall energy that moves the opera along. Musically, that is. Rarely dramatically. The problem is a simple one. This is a brilliant concert reading, not a theatrical one."
Stereo Review 55:111+ Je '90. Eric Salzman (490w)

"Definitely one of my favourite's of the year."
High Fidelity 1:107 Je '90. Ian Brunskill (b.n.)

"Harnoncourt's *Don Giovanni* is stimulating and imaginative, and I've quickly developed a profound but guarded admiration for it....What checks my enthusiasm is nothing the conductor does but rather the tendency of the cast to undersing, as though they're rehearsing rather than actually performing. (I'll exempt Alexander, Polgar, and Scharinger from this charge)."
Fanfare 13:207-9 Jl/Ag '90. Ralph V. Lucano (1150w)

"This recording of *Don Giovanni* is full of moments in which conductor Nikolaus Harnoncourt's knowing way with the music makes the opera leap to life—a thousand and three, at least. It is also a showcase for some wonderful singing. Unfortunately, there are a few too many places where Teldec very nearly lets the enterprise down."
Musical America 110:77-8 N '90. Theodore W. Libbey, Jr. (510w)

"The cast suffers from across-the-board bloodlessness, imposed in large part by the aforementioned Viennese style (suppressed dynamics)....And the whole cast, along with Maestro Harnoncourt, needs a crash course in appoggiaturas. After two centuries, Don Giovanni is still eluding his would-be captors."
Opera News 55:37 D 22 '90. John W. Freeman (400w)

Gramophone 67:1683-84 Mr '90. Alan Blyth (945w)

7077. Don Giovanni, K.527.
Arnold Ostman (c). Hakan Hagegard (bar); Arleen Auger (sop); Della Jones (mez); Barbara Bonney (sop); Nico Van Der Meel (ten); Gilles Cachemaille (bar); Bryn Terfel (bass-bar); Kristinn Sigmundsson (bass). Drottningholm Theater Chorus and Orchestra.
OISEAU-LYRE 425 943 DDD 171:00 3 discs

★*Awards:* Critics Choice, *Hi Fi News & Record Review*, Ap '91 Supplement (Peter Branscombe).

"I have found this recorded performance enormously satisfying, and my immediate reaction would be to say that it must be the best there is....Well, there could hardly be a totally ideal account of the 'opera of all operas', yet this new version seems to me startlingly successful. There isn't a weak link in the cast, the whole team throw themselves into the enterprise heart and soul, and they are backed up by a recording that captures the feel of the theatre." *P100 S95*

Hi-Fi News & Record Review 36:99 Ja '91. Peter Branscombe (315w)

"Ostman has done a great service in his ground-breaking series of Mozart opera by presenting fully professional, intelligently realized performances which are at the same time strongly influenced by the use of period instruments and performing techniques, especially in terms of some rather quick tempos."

Continuo 15:23-5 Ag '91. Scott Paterson (140w)

"What exactly does an 'authentic' performance of the work offer us that a more conventional approach does not? For one thing, this is the most complete *Don Giovanni* on disc...What Ostman's account also provides that its current competitors cannot is the unique tonal and textural flavor of a period orchestra....Ostman's orchestra may be special, but then so is Harnoncourt's Royal Concertgebouw. That leaves us with the singing, where Ostman's cast, though fine and fairly restrained in its use of vibrato, is hardly so different from those fielded for other recordings."

Musical America 111:80-1 Jl '91. Christopher Rothko (630w)

"This is an intimate-scale, authentic-instrument performance of the original 1787 Prague version of *Don Giovanni* (K.527), given an spirited, fluent reading of well-pointed detail...The music proceeds at brilliant speed (though it wants for more breadth and elasticity at times), juxtaposing stark tragedy and high comedy with effective contrast."

Opera Canada 32(2):53 Summer '91. Neil Crory (355w)

"For those who have not been lucky enough to hear *Don Giovanni* at Drottningholm, the Ostman performance will be a minor revelation, a lithe and lucid account that strips away portentousness, is dramatically cogent and well sung. But for those who have experienced the opera in that priceless theatre—and the best *Giovanni* I have ever beheld was Jarvefelt's staging there five years ago—will be the same mixture of satisfaction and disappointment that attended the previous Da Ponte operas in this series; satisfaction that Ostman's period performances are gaining the wider audience they deserve, disappointment the Decca has felt it necessary to beef up the casting, to import some of its own roster rather than retain the light, young Scandinavian voices who had worked with Ostman in the theatre and to whom the style had become instinctive."

Opera 41:1454 D '90. Andrew Clements (480w)

"Ostman's pacing errs on the fast side, occasionally leaving the singers behind. Other potential drawbacks to his versions are the fact that international stars replace some of the ensemble soloists with whom the stage productions were prepared, and that the recordings were not made in the Court Theatre, whose acoustics are an important ingredient in the soft instrumental blend. The singing itself is more modern than the playing....Allowing for these discrepancies, Ostman and his troupe have put *Don Giovanni* back into the aesthetic of a small theater and intimate performing style. Swamped as we are by *Don Giovannis* of Wagnerian proportions, this is no small cause for rejoicing."

Opera News 55:32 Mr 30 '91. John W. Freeman (570w)

"Unlike this conductor's interesting *Cosi* and even finer *Figaro*—both domestic comedies and therefore more suitable for intimate treatment—his *Don Giovanni* sounds robbed of its true stature and transformed into a chamber work sung by technically proficient miniaturists. This is not to deny the loving, musicianly approach....With the exception of an Ottavio whose minimal vocal endowment makes Tito Schipa sound like a dramatic tenor, the cast is generally commendable."

American Record Guide 54:94-5 Mr/Ap '91. Vivian A. Liff (510w)

"This may be the first studio recording to give us the Prague version, and as such, I suppose it's valuable, more for the novelty of the period style than for the cuts, which any listener could have made at the touch of a button. There is, of course, no great merit in doing something differently; it must also be done well. Ostman's cast and orchestra attain excellence only intermittently, and one of the singers is a disaster....My previous *Don Giovanni* recommendations still stand: Giulini on Angel for general excellence, Krips on London for Siepi, and Harnoncourt on Teldec for an unorthodox but stimulating view."

Fanfare 14:230-31 My/Je '91. Ralph V. Lucano (1100w)

The New York Times F 3 '91, p. 24 H. John Rockwell (330w)

Digital Audio's CD Review 7:71 My '91. Sebastian Russ (215w)

Gramophone 68:1264+ D '90. Hilary Finch (815w)

7078. Die Entfuhrung aus dem Serail, K.384. Arias.

Thomas Beecham; Andre Jouve (c). Lois Marshall (sop); Ilse Hollweg (sop); Leopold Simoneau (ten); Gerhard Unger (ten); Gottlob Frick (bass); Hansgeorg Laubenthal (spkr). Beecham Choral Society; Royal Philharmonic Orchestra; Paris Champs-Elysees Theatre Orchestra. 1956 reissues.
EMI 63715 ADD (m) 146:00 2 discs

★*Awards: American Record Guide* Overview: Mozart Operas, N/D '91.

"Many of us who love this opera are sure this is the best recording and can't imagine a better

one coming along....This is a sparkling performance, perfectly judged in every detail."
American Record Guide 54:93 Mr/Ap '91. Donald R. Vroon (110w)

"This *Abduction* is now thirty-five years old. For many of us, it remains the finest ever recorded. The early stereo recording remains first-class, though clearly not quite the equal of the best digitalizations....A good synopsis is provided in three languages, but the libretto is German only. No texts are provided for the arias. All Beecham fans will buy this immediately, but lovers of Mozart should also consider it essential."
Fanfare 14:220 My/Je '91. John Bauman (645w)

Gramophone 68:1722+ Mr '91. Alan Blyth (455w)

7079. Die Entfuhrung aus dem Serail, K.384.
Nikolaus Harnoncourt (c). Yvonne Kenny (sop); Lillian Watson (sop); Peter Schreier (ten); Wilfried Gamlich (ten). Zurich Mozart Opera House Chorus and Orchestra. 1985 reissue.
TELDEC 35673 DDD 135:00 3 discs

✔HC ★*Awards:* The Want List 1988, *Fanfare* N/D '88 (Nick Rossi).

"Recently another magazine, concerned peripherally with classical music but committed to hosting annual international record awards, declared Nikolaus Harnoncourt's *Die Entfuhrung aus dem Serail* one of its prize-winners of the year....it is a matter of conscience to hand down a dissenting opinion, even if from another bench".
Opus 3:40-41 D '86 Matthew Gurewitsch (1635w)

Gramophone 63:677 N '85. Alan Blyth (770w) (rev. of LP)

7080. Die Entfuhrung aus dem Serail, K.384.
Josef Krips (c). Anneliese Rothenberger (sop); Lucia Popp (sop); Nicolai Gedda (ten); Gerhard Unger (ten); Gottlob Frick (bass); Leopold Rudolf (spkr). Vienna State Opera Chorus; Vienna Philharmonic Orchestra. Vienna. 1970.
EMI 63263 ADD (m) 114:00 2 discs

★*Awards:* The Want List 1990, *Fanfare* N/D '90 (David Claris).

"Krips's *Entfuhrung* loses some of the battles but bids fair to win the war, i.e., establish itself as the most desirable of the recordings of the opera. Its biggest drawback is the conductor himself....Urgently recommended, especially to anyone who hasn't heard this performance before."
Fanfare 13:241-42 Mr/Ap '90. Ralph V. Lucano (525w)

"The men are particularly strong...Balance favours singers rather than orchestra. Full German and English text...The true hero is Josef Krips, who directs a lively, straight-forward performance of lasting merit." *P95 S85/95*
Hi-Fi News & Record Review 34:125 D '89. Peter Branscombe (140w)

"Perhaps the best of this cast was still Frick, a spirited, wonderfully humorous Osmin disputing his then 60th birthday, and enchantingly bested by Popp's youthfully engaging Blonde. Rothenberger was a former Blonde who took on Constanze instead and reached new heights of eloquence as well as flexibility in a vehement 'Martern aller Arten', with Krips giving an object lesson of skill in phrasing to the singer's advantage, as he does throughout. Unger was among the best of his time as Pedrillo."
Opera 40:1508 D '89.Noel Goodwin (260w)

Gramophone 67:1199 D '89. Stanley Sadie (400w)

7081. Idomeneo, Re di Creta, K.366.
Colin Davis (c). George Shirley; Ryland Davies; Margherita Rinaldi; Pauline Tinsley. BBC Chorus; BBC Symphony Orchestra. 1969 reissue.
PHILIPS 420 130 ADD 166:00 3 discs

★*Awards:* *American Record Guide* Overview: Mozart Operas, N/D '91.

"Despite the minor cuts and a tenor Idamante (Ryland Davies) there has never been a more dramatic account of this great opera on record than Sir Colin Davis's...The sound is uncommonly life-like and 'present', too."
Hi-Fi News & Record Review 33:105 Mr '88. Hugh Canning (210w)

"Unfortunately, this transfer is the first of Philips' CDs that I have encountered that proves inferior to its LP predecessor."
Fanfare 11:159 Mr/Ap '88. Mortimer H. Frank (225w)

Gramophone 65:1240 F '88. Hilary Finch (585w)

7082. Idomeneo, Re di Creta, K.366.
John Eliot Gardiner (c). Anne-Sofie von Otter (mez); Anthony Rolfe-Johnson (ten); Sylvia McNair (sop); Hillevi Martinpelto (sop); Nigel Robson (ten); Glenn Winslade (ten); Cornelius Hauptmann (bass). Monteverdi Choir; English Baroque Soloists. Queen Elizabeth Hall, London. June 1990 live.
DEUTSCHE GRAMMOPHON 431 674 DDD 211:00 3 discs

✔HC ★★★★*Awards:* The Gramophone Awards, Nominations, Opera, *Gramophone*, N '91. Best Opera Recording 1991, *Gramophone*, D '91; Editor's Choice, *Opera Canada*, Wtr '91. Critics' Choice 1991, Opera, *The Wire*, D/Ja '91/92 (Nick Kimberley). Pick of the Month, North American Perspective (Christie Barter) *Gramophone* Je '91.

It is, in every way, a superlative release. The singing is consistently strong...Gardiner and his musicians are no less impressive; their experience in 18th Century opera, in Mozart's instrumental music and in authentic performance all used telling effect....an *Idomeneo* which is certain to stand a the definitive version for a long time to come."
The Wire 89:47-8 Jl'91. Graham Lock (575w)

"The singer who comes closest to free and uninhibited vocalism is Anthony Rolfe Johnson-

...his is a marvelously sung Idomeneo. He doesn't have half the voice of Pavarotti (the Idomeneo on London), but does have ten times the musicianship and technique...Anne Sophie von Otter is wonderful as Idamante...John Eliot Gardiner leads a taut performance that does, it must be noted, give more room than usual for his singers to maneuver...Despite the accomplishments of all, and the live venue of the recording, there is very little in this performance that sounds spontaneous....there is no doubt that this is now the *Idomeneo* to have."

Fanfare 15:276-8 Ja/F '92. James Camner (long)

"This magnificent recording, by-product of the QEH concert performances in June 1990, immediately becomes the clear all-round recommendation...Gardiner has easily the finest cast of any recording...And the playing of the EBS—delicate yet powerful, precise and superbly expressive—is irresistible...the recording is crisp, rounded and expertly balanced, and the booklet contains all one could hope for." *P100 S95*

Hi-Fi News & Record Review 36:101 D '91. Peter Branscombe (long)

"The present recording of the first of Mozart's seven great mature operas, is infused with rhythmic life and vibrant dramatic expression-...Of the singing, nothing falls below the level of imagination and compelling conviction...Finally, not the least of the recording's virtues is the spirited support of the Monteverdi Choir."

Opera Canada 32:49 Wtr '91. Harvey Chusid (long)

"There have been several good *Idomeneo* recordings over the years, but DG's new offering, a sleeper of the Mozart Year, goes to the head of the class...Credit a discerning choice of cast and sovereign leadership from John Eliot Gardiner."

Opera News 56:42 D 21 '91. John W. Freeman (long)

"Gardiner now offers us...the entire Munich version [of *Idomeneo*], including, as appendices, 12 1/2 minutes of ballet music and some alternate recitatives. He leads period instruments, of course, playing in a historically informed fashion, but I hear nothing revelatory in his performance. It's just another good *Idomeneo*, with strengths and weakness like every other recording, at its best when the splendid Monteverdi Choir digs into their more dramatic choruses and at its worst in some of the solo contributions....The best of the singers is Rolfe Johnson, clear and noble in utterance, proficient in the divisions of the original 'Fuor del mar'....I'll return to [Gardiner's]...performance for its Idomeneo and Elettra, as well as its many potent dramatic moments...I'll also remain faithful to many of my other recordings, starting with Pritchard's on EMI (not London). To hear Jurinac's Ilia and Simoneau's Idamante is to be transported to heights mere scholarship cannot reach."

American Record Guide 55:107-8 Mr/Ap '92. Ralph V. Lucano (long)

Continuo 15:27 O '91. Scott Paterson (med)

Gramophone 69:87-8 Je '91. Alan Blyth (1010w)

7083. Idomeneo, Re di Creta, K.366.
John Pritchard (c). Sena Jurinac (sop); Richard Lewis (ten); Leopold Simoneau (ten); Lucille Udovick (sop); James Milligan (bass-bar); William McAlpine (ten); Hervey Alan (bass). Glyndebourne Festival Chorus and Orchestra. 1957 reissue.
EMI 63685 ADD (m) 143:00 2 discs

★*Awards: American Record Guide* Overview: Mozart Operas, N/D '91.

"The monaural sound has held up very well. The stage-picture is narrow, but the voices register with great clarity, and the orchestra is amply solid. An Italian libretto is supplied, without translation...There have been other recordings of *Idomeneo* since 1956, and the two I mentioned above (Davis and Schmidt-Isserstedt) offer something beyond what Pritchard does: either more or different music. So does Harnoncourt on Teldec. But this EMI set will always be indispensable. It's a good, inexpensive introduction to the opera and, in its Ilia-Idamante pairing, a paradigm of incomparable Mozart singing."

Fanfare 14:231-33 My/Je '91. Ralph V. Lucano (1000w)

"Pritchard's conducting is...ideally flexible, always solicitous of his soloists, but perhaps in the final analysis slightly too lightweight to suit ideally this particular *opera seria*...If [Jurinac's Ilia]...here is a bit less inspired than under Busch, it still remains one of the most captivating and expressive on record...The mono sound is entirely satisfactory."

American Record Guide 54:110 N/D '91. Vivian A. Liff (long)

Gramophone 68:1557-8 F '91. Alan Blyth (395w)

The Magic Flute. See Die Zauberflote, K.620.

The Marriage of Figaro. See Le Nozze di Figaro, K.492.

7084. Le Nozze di Figaro, K.492.
Karl Bohm (c). Hermann Prey; Dietrich Fischer-Dieskau; Gundula Janowitz; Edith Mathis; Tatiana Troyanos. Berlin German Opera Chorus and Orchestra. reissue.
DEUTSCHE GRAMMOPHON 415 520 3 discs

✔**HC** ★*Awards: Fanfare* Want List 1986 (Elliott Kaback).

"With Fischer-Dieskau, Janowitz, Mathis and Prey leading a generally distinguished cast, and the conductor near his mercurial best, this is a performance to be reckoned with....this one will no doubt be surpassed technically; but the interpretation will continue to command respect."

Hi-Fi News & Record Review 31:117 Ap '86. Kenneth Dommett (130w)

"I've always liked the sound of this recording, and find little beyond the dynamic expansion on both ends to comment upon....Solti's diamond-and-sable London *Figaro* is currently the only competition on CD. Totally different, and quite enjoyable on its own terms, I cannot recommend it over Bohm's less electric but more comfortable performance."

Fanfare 10:179-80 N/D '86 Vincent Alfano (590w)

7085. Le Nozze di Figaro, K.492.

Erich Kleiber (c). Cesare Siepi (bass); Hilde Gueden (sop); Alfred Poell (bar); Lisa Della Casa (sop); Suzanne Danco (sop); Hilde Rossel-Majdan (contr); Fernando Corena (bass); Murray Dickie (ten); Hugo Meyer-Welfing (ten); Harald Proglhof (bass); Anny Felbermayer (sop). Vienna State Opera Chorus; Vienna Philharmonic Orchestra. 1954 reissue.
LONDON/DECCA 417 315 ADD 172:00 3 discs

★★★*Awards:* The Want List 1990, *Fanfare* N/D '90 (William Youngren). Critics Choice, *Hi Fi News & Record Review*, Ap '91 Supplement (Kenneth Dommett). *American Record Guide* Overview: The Operas of Mozart, N/D '91.

"If some recordings can be compared to fine wines then this is a vintage....I can think of no better way to spend a late summer's evening."

High Fidelity 1:110 Ag '90. Clive Manning (b.n.)

"Kleiber's [Figaro] is still unsurpassed in setting before us the tensions of the Almaviva household."

Opera 41:1138-39 S '90. Alan Blyth (210w)

"This still remains an impressive achievement, particularly for the extraordinary sparkle and charm of the overture and the remarkable sense of pacing throughout and for some distinguished singing from Cesare Siepi and Hilda Gueden, among others. On the debit side are rather wooden recitatives and engineering that, even by the standards of its time, is thin and harsh."

Fanfare 14:308 S/O '90. Mortimer H. Frank (190w)

"The merits of the EMI 2 CD *Figaro* under Giulini were discussed at length by HC in Dec....it's the incomparable expressive warmth of the VPO under Kleiber, his subtle pacing and attention to detail that gives the Decca the palm....My one disappointment is that the Decca booklet is so inferior to EMI's." *P100 S75*

Hi-Fi News & Record Review 35:104 F '90. Christopher Breunig (280w)

Gramophone 67:1525 F '90. Stanley Sadie (350w)

Music and Musicians International 39:37 O '90. Robert Hartford (185w)

7086. Le Nozze di Figaro, K.492.

Arnold Ostman (c). Petteri Salomaa (bass/bar); Barbara Bonney (sop); Hakan Hagegard (bar); Arleen Auger (sop); Alicia Nafe (mez); Della Jones (mez); Carlos Feller (bass); Edoardo Gimenez (ten); Francis Egerton (ten); Enzo Florimo (bass); Nancy Argenta (sop). Drottningholm Theater Chorus; Drottningholm Theater Court Orchestra.
OISEAU-LYRE 421 333 DDD 186:00 3 discs

★★★★*Awards:* Best of the Year, *Opera News* D 24 '88; The Want List 1989, *Fanfare* N/D '89 (Robert Levine); Critics' Choice 1989, *Gramophone* D '89 (Stanley Sadie); Top Choices—1989, *American Record Guide* Ja/F '90 (George Loomis).

"By his adroit choice of tempos, Ostman is able to inspire a performance which sounds spontaneous and proves to be musically exciting."

Fanfare 13:498-99 S/O '89. Nick Rossi (110w)

"The singers are all good and the women, in particular, are outstanding....the small orchestra is a delight and the recording quality could hardly be bettered. Interpretatively, there are questionable passages, but I am sure that they would not detract from enjoyment of this vital version and its reconstruction of the sound of Mozart's time. The informative booklet is already a part of my reference library."

Music and Musicians International 38:52-3 N '89. Robert Hartford (570w)

"In addition to generally brisk tempos and the welcome sounds of period instruments, we are introduced to some interesting rhythmic alterations, some of them jarring and a bit off-putting. But the performances pleases nonetheless."

Ovation 10:50 F '89. Robert Levine (270w)

"The Drottningholm production of *Le Nozze di Figaro* owes a great deal to the ambience of its chamber theater and to the stage direction of Goran Jarvefelt, both of which are absent from a sound-only recording....the CD versions of *Cosi Fan Tutte* and not *Le Nozze di Figaro* are making history on their own account, ranking with the Glyndebourne Festival albums of the late 1930's....Apart from its lively interplay, this performance is notable for its bracing juxtaposition of fleetness (in repartee and tempo) with relaxation (in natural characterizations)."

Opera News 53:64 D 10 '88. John W. Freeman (680w)

"This is the first *Figaro* that I have ever heard which attempts to reproduce the orchestral sound Mozart expected to hear from the pit-....This version will attract and enthral every serious student of Mozart."

Opera 40:198-99 F '89.William Mann (1340w)

"Ostman's *Figaro* is a must for the specialist, since it is the first on period instruments and, better still, includes all of the alternative music known to have been written for alternative stagings, in Prague and the 1789 Vienna revival, during Mozart's lifetime. Like the previous *Cosi* it presents a cast of singers not usually associated with Drottningholm's annual summer performances. On the whole, though, each has been carefully chosen to emulate the strong ensemble qualities which are such an appealing feature of the live performances....of the sets available on CD, this has undoubtedly the freshest cast and there are plenty of other compelling reasons for acquiring it, not least Peter Wadland's admirable production."

Hi-Fi News & Record Review 34:91 Mr '89. Hugh Canning (835w)

"This is an affectionate, highly musical, splendidly recorded *Figaro*. Hand on heart I could not recommend it as an only version, but as a vital adjunct to your favourite Karajan, Davis, Solti, Busch, etc., it should certainly be in your collection."

American Record Guide 52:60 Mr/Ap '89. Vivian A. Liff (550w)

"The new recording...is perhaps the most beautifully cast performance of *Figaro* that I have ever encountered....All are splendid Mozart singers....The sonority of the early instruments is quite distinctive from the very outset...you have only to hear their subtle interweaving in the introduction of the Countess's '*Porgi amor*' to realize that no modern orchestra can produce such ravishing sounds....The first recording of Mozart's comic masterpiece on period instruments, this is also one of the finest of the half-dozen or so available today on compact discs."

Stereo Review 54:119 My '89. Stoddard Lincoln (340w)

"This *Figaro*...an 'authentic' production...is superbly, if sometimes unconventionally, paced and molded....A four-language, eminently readable libretto is included...I cannot say this release will lead me to give up any of the several (traditional) Figaros that I cherish, particularly those led by Erich Kleiber and Colin Davis. But by making one hear this opera afresh, this set comprises a major release."

Fanfare 12:246-47 My/Je '89. Mortimer H. Frank (725w)

"If one takes 'authentic performance' to entail a thorough rethinking of the work in the light of what has been (and is being) learned about eighteenth-century practice, Ostman's operation must be regarded as relatively superficial-....he behaves much like any other present-day absolute-monarch conductor....In one respect Ostman overlooks a primary responsibility: balance....The major disappointment in Ostman's cast is the admired Arleen Auger, who (conceivably out of historical motives) affects a frail and whitish timbre."

The Opera Quarterly 6:107-11 Summ '89. David Hamilton (945w)

"My favorite recorded *Figaro* remains Sir Neville Marriner's (Philips 416 370),but this one should be in most collections as well....More than highly recommended."

Stereophile 12:201-3 Ap '89. Robert Levine (600w)

"To say it is undramatic is an understatement. It is downright chaste....Despite these drawbacks, many listeners...will be happy to settle for this beautiful concert."

Musical America 109:81 My '89. Paul Turok (450w)

Digital Audio's CD Review 6:77 S '89. Octavio Roca (525w)

Gramophone 66:1058 D '88. Stanley Sadie (1275w)

7087. Die Zauberflote, K.620 (complete).
Thomas Beecham (c). Erna Berger (sop); Wilhelm Strienz (bass); Helge Roswaenge (ten); Tiana Lemnitz (sop); Gerhard Husch (bar); Irma Beilke (sop); Heinrich Tessmer (ten). Berlin State Opera Chorus; Berlin Philharmonic Orchestra. 1937-1938.
EMI 61034 AAD (m) 61:12, 68:20 2 discs

★***Awards:*** Best of the Month, *Hi-Fi News & Record Review*, Ap '90. Critics Choice, *Hi Fi News & Record Review*, Ap '91 Supplement (Peter Branscombe).

"This is the third appearance on CD of this famous 50-year-old recording, and it is the best yet....Not much need be said about this performance except that you are not likely to encounter a cast of this overall quality in any opera house these days or on any new recording-....Highly recommended."

American Record Guide 53:82 My/Je '90. Kurt Moses (230w)

"This, the third CD edition of Beecham's long-familiar recording of *The Magic Flute*, is easily the best-sounding one available. It draws upon the excellent Keith Hardwick transfer used in a Seraphhaim LP set, but here equalized with slightly greater treble emphasis."

Fanfare 13:237 My/Je '90. Mortimer H. Frank (150w)

"Though one cannot help being aware from time to time of 78 hiss, even the incipient distortion in the loudest passages, the transfer has been triumphantly accomplished by Keith Hardwick...The performance, despite the total absence of dialogue, can still make strong claim to be the finest yet." *P100/85 S-historical*

Hi-Fi News & Record Review 35:89 Ap '90. Peter Branscombe (250w)

Gramophone 67:1706 Mr '90. John Steane (270w)

Musical America 110:53-5 S '90. Denis Stevens (180w)

7088. Die Zauberflote, K.620.
Nikolaus Harnoncourt (c). Barbara Bonney (sop); Edita Gruberova (sop); Edith Schmid (sop); Pamela Coburn (sop); Delores Ziegler; Marjana Lipovsek; Hans-Peter Blochwitz (ten); Peter Keller (ten); Anton Scharinger (bar); Thomas Hampson (bar); Matti

Salminen (bass). Zurich Opera House Chorus; Zurich Opera House Orchestra.
TELDEC 35766; TELDEC 42716 DDD 73:17, 70:26 2 discs

★*Awards:* Top Disks of the Year, *The New York Times* D 24, '89 (John Rockwell).

"Let me say at once that this is the finest and most revealing *Magic Flute* ever recorded-....The recording is splendid and wonderfully natural." *P100 S100*

Australian Hi-Fi 21(5):51:15 '90. John Aranetta (390w)

"The appeal of Harnoncourt's Mozart owes much to the conductor's uncanny ability to transfer the musical essence of a given score to the recording medium....the most salient feature of his new *Zauberflote* is the sound of the brass, revealing more than ever before the subtle contrasts of color and texture latent in the score...Mozart's orchestra emerges with as much individuality and life as the vocal lines, and the recording clearly captures the inner parts while maintaining acceptable balances throughout....Overall, the singing in this *Flute* is very distinguished."

The Opera Quarterly 7:220-22 Spr '90. E. Thomas Glasow (885w)

"It is beautifully recorded and boasts a cast of fresh young singers who will doubtless be doing the rounds of the record companies as members of an international Mozart ensemble-....Instrumental detail is Harnoncourt's great strength...So why, ultimately, do I prefer Karajan? Obviously not for the sound quality, which must needs be described as historic-....No, it is Harnoncourt's catastrophic decision to engage a narrator who tells the story between the musical numbers in a horribly patronising 'listen-with-motherish' tone with snatches of dialogue."

Hi-Fi News & Record Review 34:91-2 Mr '89. Hugh Canning (595w)

"Teldec's sound is deep and spacious, and the voices have lots of presence but don't sound too close....Teldec's booklet has a complete libretto with translation....I didn't particularly like this *Zauberflote*, if only because I don't want to be so aware of the conductor when I listen to a Mozart opera....I wouldn't be surprised if many listeners find him more refreshing than perverse."

Fanfare 12:244-46 My/Je '89. Ralph V. Lucano (1250w)

"His singers omit more appoggiaturas than they add—isn't this a universal complaint?—but the orchestra is something else. Woodwind articulation is simply phenomenal, while the strings do a good approximation of late-eighteenth-century bowing, attack and tone without resorting to actual period instruments....Because of the support they receive from this nimble footing, the cast can afford to sing softly without whispering...Viennese performing tradition, a handicap to Harnoncourt's recent *Don Giovanni* recording, is little hindrance to *Die Zauberflote*, since it fits the music and style of a singspiel so much better. there are a couple of examples of undercasting....On the other hand, Edita Gruberova, having gravitated toward more dramatic roles, is an enlightened choice for the Queen of the Night."

Opera News 55:32 F 2 '91. John W. Freeman (190w)

"It was found to be necessary to introduce an explanation of events by the expediency of introducing a *Zwischentext* Between-text) to replace much of the original spoken text....I feel it to be an error of judgement to introduce an explanation of the action rather than allow that very action to take place, so that we hear it evolve and emerge from the music as originally intended....a second and third hearing made me a little more tolerant of the approach. I am sure that this was because of the overall high musical standard and high recording standard with one or two minor lapses."

Music and Musicians International 37:58-60 Ap '89. Robert Hartford (1860w)

"It would be a recommendable set (heaven knows we need one) if it were not for the disastrous decision to scrap most of the spoken dialogue and introduce a female commentator who explains what is going on in the confidential, didactic tones of a primary schoolmistress. The spoken dialogue of *Zauberflote* is essential to Mozart music, I now realize, if I ever doubted it. The glutinous confidences of Gertraud Jesserer make this set an instant non-recommendation, though if the dialogue were restored I would doubtless hail it with three times three."

Opera 40:373 Mr '89. William Mann (440w)

Gramophone 67:234 Jl '89. Alan Blyth (330w)

Digital Audio's CD Review 7:56+ F '91. Sebastian Russ (225w)

7089. Die Zauberflote, K.620.

Neville Marriner (c). Kiri Te Kanawa (sop); Francisco Araiza (ten); Cheryl Studer (sop); Samuel Ramey (bass); Olaf Bar (bar); Eva Lind (sop); Jose Van Dam (bass-bar); Yvonne Kenny (sop); Iris Vermillion (mez); Anne Collins (contr); Aldo Baldin (ten); Edmund Barham (ten); Harry Peeters (bass); Christian Fliegner (treb); Markus Baur (treb); Christian Gunter (treb). Ambrosian Opera Chorus; Academy of St. Martin-in-the-Fields. 1989.
PHILIPS 426 276 DDD 142:00 2 discs

✔HC ★★*Awards:* Best of the Month, *Hi-Fi News & Record Review*, N '90. Editor's Choice, *Opera Canada*, Spr '91.

"Te Kanawa, predictably perhaps, is a superb Pamina...Araiza manages to reflect Tamino's heroism...without submerging him in the goody-goodyness which is always a threat to his credibility....for me the triumph of this triumphantly successful performance is Cheryl Studer's Queen of the Night...one of the finest versions of this opera so far committed to disc." *P100 S100*

Hi-Fi News & Record Review 35:99 N '90. Kenneth Dommett (455w)

"Neville Marriner's recording is notable for Francisco Araiza's superb Tamino and Jose Van Dam's calmly noble Speaker. Kiri Te Kanawa's Pamina, prettily vocalized, does not reach past sorrow to despair, and Cheryl Studer picks her way carefully through the Queen's music, missing its flash. Olaf Bar offers a mellow, gemutlich Papageno, intimate and soft in tone, with lieder-singer restraint. Samuel Ramey completes this international constellation with his orotund Sarastro, pronounced with bel canto fluidity."

Opera News 55:32 F 2 '91. John W. Freeman (190w)

"Marriner's readings, while consistently and sensitively alert to detail, sometimes proceed with more predictability than theatrical sparkle-...Best realized is the gentle radiance of *Die Zauberflote*, in which the supple playing of the Academy of St. Martin in the Fields propels a performance of exceptional warmth and sympathy. Kiri Te Kanawa's Pamina is perhaps the most ravishing on disc...Francisco Araiza makes a committed Tamino, though his tone lacks the endearing glow of a Tauber or Wunderlich; Samuel Ramey sings both Sarastro's arias to near-perfection; Olaf Bar, for all his considerable artistry, fails to capture Papageno's ebullience and charm; and Cheryl Studer fires off the Queen of the night's coloratura with authority but imprecise articulation." *PS 80*

Opera Canada 32:50 Spr 91. Harvey Chusid (140w)

"There are so many good *Zauberfloten* on compact disc—those conducted by Davis, Solti, Bohm, Sawallisch, and Levine lead the pack—that a new version was hardly needed....In any case, it is a pleasure to report that Philips's new entry is good enough for inclusion in the elite group cited above."

Musical America 111:80 My '91. George Jellinek (425w)

"The sound on this new *Flute* recording is exceptionally beautiful, the excellent playing heard in ideal balance with the voices. The problem is the almost complete lack of drama-....This issue, so promising on paper, is a grave disappointment."

Opera 41:1262 O '90. Rodney Milnes (420w)

"It has no glaring weaknesses. It may lack individual performances on a level with Wunderlich's Tamino or Seefried's Pamina, but every cast member is up to his or her assignment. Even the least satisfying of them Ramey, is about as good as anyone else you'll hear nowadays; the choral and orchestral work is fine; and there's enough dialog to suggest a real staging. It is, if I may resort to repellent modern jargon, a fine entry-level *Flute* at the very least, and often much better than that-....My favorite *Zauberflotes* remain Klemperer's and Bohm's. Between them, they leave nothing unsaid. I'm pleased with Marriner's also, and I wouldn't be surprised to find myself playing it more often then most of its rivals."

Fanfare 14:293-4 Mr/Ap '91. Ralph V. Lucano (1075w)

"At least the Papageno and Papagena, Olaf Bar and Eva Lind, have a bit of gruff humor and fun about what they do. On the other hand, how odd to cast a Pamina who, however great a singer, sounds much more mature than her mother, the Queen of the Night. The production lacks theatrical urgency. Somewhat surprisingly, it also lacks feeling for performance practice (the notes are all like columns holding up the temple) or anything at all that might give the music a particular point of view, or flavor, or dramatic edge."

Stereo Review 56:94 My '91. Eric Salzman (250w)

The New York Times F 3 '91, p. 24 H. John Rockwell (330w)

Gramophone 68:1050-1 N '90. Stanley Sadie (850w)

Digital Audio's CD Review 7:56+ F '91. Sebastian Russ (225w)

7090. Die Zauberflote, K.620 (complete).
Georg Solti (c). Pilar Lorengar (sop); Cristina Deutekom (sop); Stuart Burrows (ten); Hermann Prey (bar); Martti Talvela (bass). 1969.
LONDON/DECCA 414 568 155:43 3 discs

Vienna Philharmonic Orchestra; Vienna State Opera Chorus and Orchestra
★*Awards: American Record Guide* Overview: Mozart Operas, N/D '91.

"Solti's Mozart doesn't inhabit the same realm as Bohm's (his DG recording of the *Flute* remains, for the most part, unequaled), but what he achieves is, on its own correct, rhythmically unyielding terms, impressive in a grand and stately way....This is a *Flute* that thinks more than it smiles. I like it, but it could never be the only *Flute* on my shelves. Which brings us to the CD competition, Karajan's icy DG recording, and Davis' strongly cast but, in the end, disappointing version for Philips. I'd take Solti over either of them, but if RCA would move the entire Levine *Flute* onto CD I would, without hesitation, snap it up."

Fanfare 10:179 N/D '86 Vincent Alfano (450w)

Hi-Fi News & Record Review 31:93 S '86. Kenneth Dommett (90w)

MUSSORGSKY, MODEST

7091. Boris Gudounov.

Vladimir Fedoseyev (c). Alexander Vedernikov; Glafira Koroleva; Elena Shkolnikova; Nina Grigorieva. Spring Studio Children's Chorus; USSR Television and Radio Large Orchestra; USSR Television and Radio Large Chorus.
PHILIPS 412 281 3 discs

✔HC ★*Awards:* *Stereo Review* Best of the Month, O '85.

"The recording is uncommonly worthwhile because of the fine musical treatment of every scene....The recording has a fine balance between the orchestra and the voices, and there's a real sense f presence in the clarity and stereo imaging."

Stereo Review 50:74 O '85. Robert Ackart (400w)

"All in all, for the sake of having Mussorgsky's score complete and unadulterated and for the very high quality of the conducting by Vladimir Fedoseyev, the orchestral playing, the choral singing, and the performances of at least an important part of the principal cast, this set definitely supersedes all its predecessors, even if it cannot be said to represent the last word on the matter."

High Fidelity 35:59-61 My '85. Harry Halbreich (850w) (rev. of LP)

"In general, the recording is in wholly acceptable stereo, with above-average tonal quality for a Russian-originated recording. Vladimir Fedoseyev conducts a strong, convincing performance with some fine playing from the USSR TV and Radio Large Orchestra. Predictably, Yuri Mazurok makes the Jesuit Rangoni into a dominant role; and as the Polish princess Marina, Irina Arkhipova successfully belies her age with a deeply felt characterization-....Vladislav Piavko...presents a Grigory/Dmitri so unappealing in vocal talents as to seriously mar the enjoyment of every scene he is in. Overall...this is a fine set."

The Opera Quarterly 4:162-5 Spring '86. Christopher Hunt (1360w)

"If this is the best that could be assembled in Moscow, I can only note with grim satisfaction that what is sometimes referred to in opera circles as The Decline of the West has spread Eastward."

Fanfare 8:231-6 Jl/Ag '85. James Miller (3525w)

Gramophone 62:1117 Mr '85. Alan Blyth (155w)

Ovation 6:38 O '85. George Jellinek (590w)

Opus 2:43+ Ap '86. David Hamilton (815w)

Opera News 50 (2):48 Ag '85. John W. Freeman (275w)

7092. Khovanshchina.

Claudio Abbado (c). Aage Haugland (bass); Vladimir Atlantov (ten); Vladimir Popov (ten); Anatolij Kotscherga (bar); Paata Burchuladze (bass); Marjana Lipovsek (contr); Brigitte Poschner-Klebel (sop); Heinz Zednik (ten); Joanna Borowska (sop); Wilfried Gahmlich (ten). Vienna Boys' Choir; Slovak Philharmonic Chorus; Vienna State Opera Chorus and Orchestra. Vienna State Opera. September 1989 live.
DEUTSCHE GRAMMOPHON 429 758 DDD
171:00 3 discs

★★★*Awards:* Critics' Choice 1990, *Gramophone* D '90 (John Warrack). Record of the Month, *Hi-Fi News & Record Review*, Ap '91. Editor's Choice, *Opera Canada* Summer '91.

"Abbado's missionary zeal once again allows us to view anew an operatic masterpiece in a live recording. The impressive soloists include Aage Haugland and Marjana Lipovsek but the stars are the Vienna State Orchestra who, from the gorgeous Prelude to Act One, produce the most ravishing sound."

High Fidelity 3:105 F '91. Clive Manning (110w)

"Abbado's *Khovanshchina* comes on the heels of an estimable new recording of Shostakovich's edition, by Bulgarian forces-...The Rimsky orchestration is currently available on two CD imports...Abbado is the clear first choice, both musically and on the merit of its innovative edition."

Musical America 111:82-3 Jl '91. Jamie James (700w)

"This recording starts with the advantage of being compiled from live performances with a cast well rehearsed and working perfectly as a team. No single part of these forces is less than adequate, and under Abbado's inspired leadership we are vouchsafed as fine a reading of the score as could be wished....The well-balanced recording catches the full flavour of the theatre and does full justice to both the vocal and instrumental excellences of the performance."

American Record Guide 54:90 Jl/Ag '91. Vivian A. Liff (275w)

"The best *Khovanshchina* available, but those who already own the Sony Classical set, which rises well above its provincial origins, probably need not invest in this new one."

Stereo Review 56:80+ Jl '91. David Patrick Stearns (430w)

"Emma...is fairly served by Joanna Borowska, while the usually estimable Vladimir Atlantov sounds strangulated as Andrei. Paata Burchuladze wobbles as Dosifei...Vladimir Popov's haughty, steel-edged tone catches the volatility of Golitsin, and Aage Haugland's broad Ivan Khovansky fills the character's hulking outlines. Marjana Lipovsek offers a rich, impassioned yet smooth Marfa....In contrast with Russian-style conductors, who wade into Mussorgsky like a water buffalo into mud, Claudio Abbado works wonders with the score, clarifying its textures and highlighting details without sacrificing body weight, all the while keeping the pulse continuous."

Opera News 55:36 Ja 19 '91. John W. Freeman (275w)

"Marjana Lipovsek not only faces unflinchingly the grafted-on operatics of Marfa the Old Believer doubling, Kundry-like, as the discarded lover—that side of things is sensuously but firmly dealt with, lowest contralto register joined seamlessly to middle in Act 3 song—but she also manages to be calmly at one with Abbado's incandescent Vienna forces in the character's meditative moments. The final scene is an all-round consummation of those spiritual values....Casting seems appropriately to type throughout....but the Vienna venture remains an ensemble achievement, vividly thatrical (and, I stress, human) down to the vital contributions of Heinz Zednik's Scribe and Joanna Borowska's Emma. We shall not see a more important operatic release this year." *P100 S100*

Hi-Fi News & Record Review 36:81 Ap '91. David Nice (420w)

Gramophone 68:1051-2 N '90. John Warrack (920w)

NIELSEN, CARL

7093. Saul and David.

Neeme Jarvi (c). Aage Haugland (bass); Peter Lindroos (ten); Tina Kiberg (sop); Kurt Westi (ten); Anne Gjevang (contr); Christian Christiansen (bass); Jorgen Klint (bass). Danish Radio Choir; Danish Radio Symphony Orchestra.
CHANDOS 8911/2 DDD 124:00 2 discs

✔HC ★*Awards:* Pick of the Month, North American Perspective (Christie Barter), *Gramophone* Mr '91.

"Another triumph for the protean Mr. Jarvi!....a performance unlikely to be surpassed, at least for a long time to come." *P100 S95*

Hi-Fi News & Record Review 36:87 Ap '91. Kenneth Dommett (200w)

"The set is dominated by Aage Haugland whose dark, rich voice captures the torment of Saul perfectly."

High Fidelity 3:95 Ap '91. Clive Manning (b.n.)

"On balance...I would recommend the Chandos for listeners coming new to this powerful and beautiful opera. Later on, you will want to acquire the Unicorn-Kanchana as well, to round out the picture."

Fanfare 14:241-2 Jl/Ag '91. David Johnson (500w)

"If my marginal disappointment with some of the singing here makes me seem to damn with faint praise, I must stress that this remains a powerful performance, not totally eclipsing its recorded predecessors, but standing certainly as the one to get for those who seek either an introduction to this great score or a satisfying rendition to live with."

American Record Guide 54:99-100 Jl/Ag '91. John W. Barker (860w)

Gramophone 68:1727 Mr '91. Robert Layton (670w)

OFFENBACH, JACQUES

7094. La Belle Helene.

Michel Plasson (c). Jessye Norman; Colette Alliot-Lugaz; John Aler; Gabriel Bacquier. Toulouse Capitole Chorus; Toulouse Capitole Orchestra.
EMI 47156 108:30 2 discs

★★★*Awards:* *Fanfare* Want List 1986 (John Ditsky); *Opus* Christmas List, 1987 (Matthew Gurewitsch). *Gramophone* Critics' Choice 1986 (Andrew Lamb).

"Jessye Norman has a playful side that she gets to show too seldom. As Offenbach's purring queen, she seduces with creamy tone, lilting phrasing, and the mercurial temperament of the born *femme fatale*."

Opus 4:56 D '87. Matthew Gurewitsch (50w)

"I cannot but recommend it."

Fanfare 10:203 S/O '86 John Ditsky (175w)

"I gave the LP set high praise (March '86 p109) both for the idiomatic treatment and quality of sound. The CD is even better."

Hi-Fi News & Record Review 31:95 S '86. John Freestone (40w)

"Michel Plasson's conducting rightly emphasizes a buoyancy and zip not always apparent, for example, in the earlier *La Vie Parisienne* he did for EMI. Occasionally, his rapidity robs Offenbach's carefully plotted process of having the numbers build in speed, and fast tempos do *not* always seem funnier....Conversely, some of the frankly comic numbers are done with a precision that might seem dull in the theater....I have pangs of *nostalgie* for earlier *Belle Helenes*, especially the ancient set with Andre Dran as Paris, conducted by Rene Leibowitz....EMI's presentation is fine, with a warmly recorded sound and clean surfaces."

American Record Guide 49:28-29 S/O '86 Richard Traubner (1020w) (rev. of LP)

"Assigning Norman to this role is like using a howitzer to shoot a pigeon, but she aims her voice lightly and discreetly....In the tradition of opera-comique tenors, Aler sings rather thinly, but the guileless disposition and simple narcissism he conveys are right for Paris."

Opera News 51:68 N '86 John W. Freeman (205w)

Digital Audio & Compact Disc Review 3:90-2, Jl '87. Sebastian Russ (750w)

Gramophone 64:438 S '86. Geoffrey Horn (90w)

7095. Les Brigands.

John Eliot Gardiner (c). Ghylaine Raphanel (sop); Colette Alliot-Lugaz (sop); Tibere Raffalli (ten); Michel Trempont (bar); Francois Roux (bar). Lyon Opera Chorus; Lyon Opera Orchestra.
EMI 49830 DDD 105:00 2 discs

★*Awards:* Critics' Choice 1990, *Gramophone* D '90 (Andrew Lamb).

"This is a highly amusing and racily melodic burlesque of banditry....Comic waltzes, boleros and ensembles are zippily paced by John Eliot Gardiner. Colette Alliot-Lugaz is a feisty hero in the trouser role. Tibere Raffalli is a smug robber chief; Ghyslaine Raphanel, his spirited daughter."

The New York Times Ja 7 '90, p. 30 H. Richard Traubner (115w)

"This is a performance of ideal wit, elegance, and command of style....Gardiner's control is at once strict and marvellously true to the work-...The singing and, no less important, speaking are superb....Enough of overheated superlatives: 'go out and buy' is my bottom line."

Opera 41:493-94 Ap '90. Max Loppert (920w)

"With a generally excellent cast, he [Gardiner] gives an idiomatic and immensely entertaining account of one of Offenbach's less familiar works."

High Fidelity 1:113 Ap '90. Ian Brunskill (b.n.)

"Certainly it would be difficult to imagine a more persuasive account of this brilliant, sparkling score. Offenbach's rumbustious, diamantine, heartless style suits this conductor to perfection and the Lyon forces have never sounded in finer form. There is scarcely a single disappointment in the large cast...The full, warm, yet crystal clear sonics, excellent three-language libretto, sensible notes...make this set worthy of an award among the finest recordings of the year in its class."

American Record Guide 53:86 My/Je '90. Vivian A. Liff (350w)

"This is a nifty recording. The music is ideally suited to John Eliot Gardiner's racing baton, and the Lyon Opera Orchestra plays superbly for him. Although not star-studded, the cast of singers gives a spirited and idiomatic ensemble performance....Find sound...A welcome addition to any operetta library."

Fanfare 13:217 Jl/Ag '90. James Camner (200w)

Gramophone 67:1525 F '90. Andrew M. Lamb (485w)

7096. Les Contes d'Hoffmann (Tales of Hoffmann).

Richard Bonynge (c). Placido Domingo; Joan Sutherland; Gabriel Bacquier; Huguette Tourangeau; Jacques Charon; Hugues Cuenod; Andre Neury; Paul Plishka; Margarita Lilowa; Roland Jacques. Suisse Romande Orchestra; Suisse Romande Chorus; Lausanne Pro Arte Chorus; Du Brassus Chorus.
LONDON/DECCA 417 363 ADD 142:62 2 discs

✔HC

"I can't think of an opera recording any better than this; the sound could not be more pleasing, and the performance will probably never be matched."

The $ensible Sound 33:58 Spr '87 John J. Puccio (25w)

"However adept the great soprano is at tailoring her technique to the very different requirements of the three central roles...her vocal character seems to suit none of the women she portrays....Still, with Bacquier exemplary in the four villain's parts, and Cuenod extremely vivid if occasionally overdone in the four character tenor roles...and Bonynge (not usually a favourite of mine) giving one of his most committed and imaginative pieces of conducting on record, this will remain a strong CD contender. Decca's full-bodied sound captures the feel of a theatre performance, too."

Hi-Fi News & Record Review 32:109 Ja '87 Hugh Canning (330w)

Gramophone 64:747-8 N '86 Edward Greenfield (420w)

ORFF, CARL

7097. Die Kluge; Der Mond.

Wolfgang Sawallisch (c). *Die Kluge*; Marcel Cordes (bar); Gottlob Frick (bass); Elisabeth Schwarzkopf (sop); Rudolf Christ (ten); Georg Wieter (bass); Benno Kusche (bar); Paul Kuen (ten); Hermann Prey (bar); Gustav Neidlinger (bass-bar); *Der Mond*; Rudolf Christ (ten); Karl Schmitt-Walter (bar); Helmut Graml (bar); Paul Kuen (ten); Peter Lagger (bass); Albrecht Peter (bar); Hans Hotter (bass-bar); unnamed children's choir. Philharmonia Chorus; Philharmonia Orchestra. 1956; 1957.
EMI 63712 ADD 147:00 2 discs

★★*Awards:* Critic's Choice: 1991, *American Record Guide*, Ja/F '92 (David Greene); Critic's Choice: 1991, *American Record Guide*, Ja/F '92 (Stephen Chakwin).

"With star casts, a dedicated conductor, and a perfectionist producer, these have become classics, and the latest transfer is a remarkable replica of the early stereo sound ('early' in the best sense)....[no] librettos."

Fanfare 14:315 Mr/Ap '91. J. F. Weber (200w)

"In both instances [EMI and Eurodisc 69069] the CD sound is infinitely superior to the LP...Both pairs are very fine musically....I cannot in all honesty recommend one recording over the other. But I *can* say that you owe it to yourself to become acquainted with these works."

American Record Guide 54:102-3 Jl/Ag '91. David Mason Greene (550w)

Gramophone 68:1727-8 Mr '91. Michael Stewart (265w)

PAISIELLO, GOIVANNI

7098. Il Barbiere di Siviglia.

Adam Fischer (c). Krisztina Laki; Denes Guyas; Csaba Reti; Attila Fulop; Istvan Gati; Sandor Solyom-Nagy; Miklos Mersei; Gabor Vaghelyi; Jozsef Gregor; Aniko P. Szabo (hpscd). Hungarian State Orchestra.
HUNGAROTON 12525/6 DDD 121:30 3 discs

★*Awards:* Perfect 10/10, *Digital Audio*, Mr '88.

"The score sparkles, thanks to the transparency and rhythmic verve of the playing and the just, lively tempos. The singers all have attractive voices and work hard at projecting the drama-....Altogether, this recording is a wholly satisfactory replacement for the only earlier recorded performance."

The Opera Quarterly 4:154-6 Spring '86. Joe K. Law (930w)

"Adam Fischer conducts a lively and crisp performance and elicits a fine sense of ensemble from the singers and the orchestra."

Stereo Review 51:104 Jl '86. Robert Ackart (350w)

"As we listen to Paisiello's *Barber of Seville*, we are amazed at the originality and freshness of the musical language the buffa created for itself. This is no fledgling essay in a new genre, but a finished, stylistically settled work of art-....Adam Fischer, despite his youth an experienced and intelligent conductor, gives the score complete, the result of his studies of the manuscript (in Naples) and early editions. He takes absolute command, but the singers are not regimented....Krisztina Laki, with a clear, pleasant soprano, remains unerringly on pitch (as do all the singers) and floats some beautiful *pianos* heavenward....The orchestra is first-class and, though evidently well indoctrinated as to the singers' right of way, also asserts its own prerogatives....All in all, a fine performance, a fine recording....More such productions would propel Hungaroton into the Hall of Fame."

Opus 3:20-22 D '86 Paul Henry Lang (2880w)

"For those who don't know the Paisiello version of *Il barbiere di Siviglia*, there may be a pleasant surprise in store for them, especially if they listen to the version on Hungaroton.

Fanfare 10:38 Ja/F '87 Nick Rossi (300w)

Digital Audio 2:43-4 Je '86. R. Sebastian Russ (615w)

PEPUSCH, JOHN CHRISTOPHER. The Beggar's Opera (arr. Bonynge/Gamley). See No. 7034.

PERGOLESI, GIOVANNI BATTISTA

7099. La Serva Padronna.
Pal Nemeth (c). Katalin Farkas; Jozsef Gregor. Capella Savaria.
HUNGAROTON 12846 60:17

"In this early opera about the servant problem...a feeling of spontaneity and intimacy is essential...the Capella Savaria guarantees this, sine qua non, thanks to warm, lively playing under Pal Nemeth's alert, pliant leadership....Both [Farkas and Gregor] play their characters with evident enjoyment."

Opera News 28:48 Jl '87 John W. Freeman (125w)

"The recording is as lively and clear as the performance....This issue will give great and lasting pleasure."

Hi-Fi News & Record Review 32:102 S '87 Peter Branscombe (175w)

"Hungaroton gives us the first true digital *Serva*...Gregor and Farkas do a sweet job...Szabo does great things at the harpsichord, but Nemeth wants pulse and his band of authentic strings wanders from pitch far more often than is good for any of us." [Review of LP.]

Fanfare 10:154-5 Ja/F '87 Vincent Alfano (415w)

Fanfare 13:499 S/O '89. Nick Rossi (155w)

Gramophone 65:219 Jl '87 Stanley Sadie (350w)

Opus 3:44 Je '87 Matthew Gurewitsch (240w)

PROKOFIEV, SERGEI

7100. The Love for Three Oranges.
Kent Nagano (c). Gabriel Bacquier (bar); Jean-Luc Viala (ten); Helene Perraguin (mez); Vincent LeTexier (bass-bar); Georges Gautier (ten); Didier Henry (bar); Gregory Reinhart (bass); Michele Lagrange (sop); Consuelo Caroli (mez); Brigitte Fournier (sop); Catherine Dubosc (sop); Jules Bastin (bass); Beatrice Uria-Monzon (mez). Lyon Opera Chorus; Lyon Opera Orchestra.
VIRGIN 91084 DDD 102:00 2 discs

★★★★★*Awards:* Best of the Month, *Hi-Fi News & Record Review*, Ap '90; Record of the Year Award 1990, *Gramophone* O'90; Pick of the Month, North American Perspective (Christopher Pollard), *Gramophone* O '90. The Want List 1990, *Fanfare* N/D '90 (Peter J. Rabinowitz); Record of the Year Award 1990, *Gramophone* D '90; The Highs, 1990, *The New York Times* D 30 '90 (John Rockwell); Editor's Choice, *Opera Canada* Winter '90.

"Virgin's release...as nearly perfect a production as can be imagined—disarms criticism-....This sparkling recording, apparently issued in all formats except DAT, cannot be recommended too highly."

American Record Guide 53:88 Mr/Ap '90. Justin Herman (175w)

"The whole production is a triumph of wit and musical sense, and Virgin has done its part handsomely, with first-rate sound and documentation."

Stereo Review 55:98 Ap '90. Richard Freed (620w)

Nagano "conducts with an astonishing grasp of the mechanics of Prokofiev's score: he achieves an ideal balance of the music's grotesque humour...and its sinister undertones-....Virgin has caught the atmosphere in an extremely fine recording, revealing more real music in this usually noisy score than I would have ever thought possible." *P100 S95*

Hi-Fi News & Record Review 35:91 Ap '90. Hugh Canning (385w)

"The wit and energy of the piece are more than matched by the exuberance of this splendid performance."
High Fidelity 1:121 F '90. Ian Brunskill (b.n.)

"The orchestra plays as well for Nagano as it always did for Gardiner, the fleetness, wit and sparkle of the reading giving rise to dark thoughts about last year's rather lumpy effort nearer home. The sound is bright and clear. The singers are right inside their roles: I especially enjoyed Viala's agile Prince, Lagrange's spunky Fata Morgana and, of course, Bacquier's King and the fruity Cook of that great comedian Jules Bastin."
Opera 41:384+ Mr '90. Rodney Milnes (250w)

"The performance is energetic and delightful."
Opera News 54:30-1 Mr 3 '90. John W. Freeman (450w)

"Some people are mad about this piece of Dadaist fluff; I lose patience with it almost as soon as it begins....If you like this work, however, this recording will make you very happy. I wish repertory staples—and truly great operas—were so well served."
Stereophile 13:197 S '90. Robert Levine (250w)

"The sound is generally excellent, and the set comes with extensive notes and a French-German-English libretto (although, curiously, no plot summary). This is, I believe, the only version on CD; but even were the Dalgat and Leskovich recordings available, Nagano's would be the one to get."
Fanfare 13:249-51 My/Je '90. Peter J. Rabinowitz (490w)

"It is a joyous work, whose caustic wit, vivacity and gaiety are fully registered here by orchestra, soloists and chorus. Music director of the Opera de Lyon, Kent Nagano offers a view of the work which matches the score's infectious energy, and the cast...is uniformly excellent."
Opera Canada 31(4):50 Winter '90. Harvey Chusid (275w)

"If you are gaga about Dada, this is the opera for you. If not, enjoy Prokofiev's dazzling score and the enormous vitality with which Mr. Nagano and his cast serve it up."
The New York Times Ap 29 '90, p. 31 H. George Jellinek (220w)

Gramophone 67:1200 D '89 (680w); 68:724 O '90 (200w). Lionel Salter

7101. War and Peace, Opus 91.
Mstislav Rostropovich (c). Lajos Miller (bar); Galina Vishnevskaya (sop); Katherine Ciesinski (mez); Mariana Paunova (mez); Dimiter Petkov (bass/bar); Wieslaw Ochman (ten); Stefania Toczyska (mez); Nicolai Gedda (ten); Vladimir De Kanel (bass/bar); Mira Zakai (contr); Malcolm Smith (bass/bar); Kalin Topalov-Behar (bar); Nicola Ghiuselev (bass); Eduard Tumagian (bar). French Radio National Chorus; French National Orchestra. 1988.
ERATO 75480 DDD 247:00 4 discs

★★★***Awards:*** *Hi-Fi News & Record Review* Record of the Month, F '89; Editors' Choice, *Digital Audio's CD Review*, Je '89. *American Record Guide* Overview: Prokofieff/Shostakovich, S/O '91; Cream of the Crop IV, *Digital Audio's CD Review*, 6:42 Je '90.

"Under [Rostropovich's]...inspired leadership all the manifold glories of this score come alive in a way that makes even the excellent earlier recording seem a pale shadow....As for the singers, an ardently strong and vocally consistent cast is deployed, even in the very smallest roles."
The Opera Quarterly 7:227-30 Spr '90. Dennis W. Wakeling (1670w)

"There is no getting around the fact that the soprano's voice managed more freshly and easily in the earlier album, and steadiness of both tone and pitch is a recurrent problem; but she has a dramatic handle on the role and delivers it whole, with three-dimensional conviction-....Rostropovich's view of the score certainly does not lack breadth or power, but a want of underlying urgency in the more personal, lyrical episodes indicates less than immediate contact with the theatrical medium in which this opera was conceived, and which brings it to life."
Opera News 54:54 N '89. John W. Freeman (265w)

"This Paris-made *War and Peace*, originating in the studios of Radio-France in 1986, is the only version currently available....The solo voices are placed well forward and deal eloquently with the text....Sadly, the musical sound-quality is below the best expected today, with a lack of fullness and spaciousness in the big choral-orchestral climaxes....The booklet accompanying the discs has parallel English and French translations, with the original text (in Cyrillic script, reproduced from typewriting) on the following pages."
Opera 40:70 Ja '89. Arthur Jacobs (600w)

"I wish some of the singing conveyed the youthful vigour of the Coliseum performances-....The accompanying booklet contains the Russian text, as well as French, and English, translations, but laid out in a way to render them virtually useless to those intent on following the action. The recording is spacious, but at times not without congestion. Even with these reservations, I recommend this set wholeheartedly."
Music and Musicians International 37:61 Ja '89. Robert Hartford (350w)

"This new recording of War and Peace is the only one currently available in any format, as far as my researches indicate....The whole enterprise is directed with obvious love and dedication by Rostropovitch and the engineers have achieved an excellent recording, with exemplary integration of solo voice, chorus and orchestra. A magnificent achievement."

Music and Musicians International 37:53-4 F '89. Adrian Reynolds (575w)

"Galina Vishnevskaya created the role of Natasha in 1958, and the somewhat frayed, spreading tones of the opening scenes make one question the wisdom of her taking on the part of the debutante at this stage in her career. Yet as soon as Natasha's doubts begin...she absolutely commands the listener's involvement."

Hi-Fi News & Record Review 34:93 F '89. David Nice (665w)

"Most of the credit for the success of the performances has to go to Rostropovich...The orchestra plays well, and the sound, if a bit cushioned and lacking in presence, is more than satisfactory....while there are decent notes and a full libretto (excepting a few dropped lines) in French and English, there is, aggravatingly, no Russian text....A major contribution to the catalog."

Fanfare 12:241-42 Mr/Ap '89. Peter J. Rabinowitz (975w)

"Erato's sound is wonderfully wide and full-....Erato has blemished a praiseworthy achievement by failing to provide a Russian libretto. The text is given in English and French, and while that's better than nothing, the absence of even a Russian transliteration makes it hard to follow along. That cavil aside, I recommend this recording heartily."

American Record Guide 52:78 My/Je '89. Ralph V. Lucano (600w)

"When Vishnevskaya is singing lightly and lyrically, she is believable as the flighty and fascinating Natasha...But even where her singing is less graceful and more forced, it is always deeply impressive and true to Prokofiev's melodic genius. Most of the rest of the performers are well cast for character and style...The choral and orchestral performances are on an exceedingly large scale...full of strength and passion....The libretto is given in French and English only, and the two versions often do not agree with one another...Even so, I commend this *War and Peace* to you."

Stereo Review 54:93 Ag '89. Eric Salzman (725w)

"Erato made this recording during concert performances of *War and Peace*, and a few rough spots remain unplanned....The singers vary in quality but average out satisfactorily."

Musical America 109:63-4 S '89. Paul Moor (480w)

Gramophone 66:1206 Ja '89. Lionel Salter (1155w)

Digital Audio's CD Review 5:63-4 Ap '89. Octavio Roca (595w)

PUCCINI, GIACOMO

7102. La Boheme.

Thomas Beecham (c). Victoria De los Angeles (sop); Jussi Bjoerling (ten); Lucine Amara (sop); Robert Merrill (bar). Columbus Boychoir; RCA Victor Chorus; RCA Victor Symphony Orchestra. 1956.
EMI 47235 ADD 54:10; 54:00 2 discs

✔**HC** ★★★***Awards:*** Editors' Choice, *Digital Audio*, 1988. Record of the Eighties, *Gramophone*, D '89 (Michael Oliver). *American Record Guide* Overview: Getting to Know Your Opera, Ja/F '91.

"This famous set...remains the best of all possible *Bohemes* by a long shot."

High Fidelity 38:58 F '88. Terry Teachout (125w)

"The field is not devoid of competition...but no one who buys this fine Beecham *Boheme*...will have reason to regret it—it's strongly cast from top to bottom and the sound has aged well, mono or not."

Fanfare 11:264-5 S/O '87. James Miller (530w)

"Those who swear by the Beecham—and who can blame them?—need not hesitate...in the new medium, it comes up clean and fresh, and in certain well-known respects Beecham himself is unsurpassed."

Opera 38:1415 D '87. Alan Blyth (50w)

"It would practically be wrong not to own this set, for in many ways it serves as a reminder of what sort of singing we are currently missing."

Ovation 9:45-6 Ja '89. Robert Levine (155w)

Gramophone 65:101-2 Je '87 Michael Oliver (840w)

Musical America 110:53-5 S '90. Denis Stevens (180w)

Digital Audio 4:76 N '87. Sebastian Russ (450w)

7103. La Boheme.

Herbert Von Karajan (c). Mirella Freni; Elizabeth Harwood; Luciano Pavarotti; Rolando Panerai. Schoneberg Boys' Choir; Deutsche Oper Chorus, Berlin; Berlin Philharmonic Orchestra. 1973 reissue.
LONDON/DECCA 421 049 ADD 110:00 2 discs

★★***Awards:*** Records to Die for: 1 of 5 Recommended Recordings, *Stereophile* Ja '91 (Robert Deutsch). *American Record Guide* Overview: Getting to Know Your Opera, Ja/F '91.

"The tempi are a trifle eccentric, and the analytical tendency borders on fussiness, but von Karajan's approach to this opera *does* illuminate aspects of the score that remain unexplored on other recordings. The cast is generally first-rate....Then there's the sound: glorious '70s analog, featuring realistic vocal/instrumental timbres, a soundstage that's wide and deep, and powerful dynamics."

Stereophile 14:133 Ja '91. Robert Deutsch (b.n.)

"Glamorous, yes...but not a lot to do with an intimate little drama that once was *Boheme*....If you can stomach the conception you get Freni and Pavarotti in their prime."

Hi-Fi News & Record Review 32:135 D '87. Edward Seckerson (85w)

Digital Audio 4:76+ Je '88. Roland B. Graeme (800w)

Gramophone 65:814+ N '87 Michael Oliver (455w)

Opera 38:1415 D '87. Alan Blyth (50w)

7104. Madama Butterfly.
John Barbirolli (c). Renata Scotto (ten); Carlo Bergonzi (bar); Rolando Panerai (bar); Anna Di Stasio (mez); Piero De Palma (ten); Giuseppe Morresi (ten); Silvana Padoan (mez); Paolo Montarsolo (bass); Mario Rinaudo (bass). Rome Opera Chorus; Rome Opera Orchestra. 1967.
EMI 69654 ADD 142:00 2 discs

★*Awards:* *American Record Guide* Overview: Opera Favorites, Ja/F '91.

"Those who own Scotto's remake (CBS/with Placido Domingo, conducted by Lorin Maazel) already have an impressive souvenir of her Butterfly and might well resist owning another, but, good as that recording is, I think this one is superior on all fronts and if (what an unpleasant thought) I had to get by with one recording of *Madama Butterfly*, this EMI version is it."

Fanfare 13:287-88 S/O '89. James Miller (425w)

Gramophone 66:1778 My '89. Michael Oliver (560w)

7105. Madama Butterfly.
Giuseppe Sinopoli (c). Mirella Freni (sop); Jose Carreras (ten); Juan Pons (bar); Teresa Berganza (mez); Anthony Laciura (ten); Mark Curtis (ten); Marianne Rorholm (contr); Kurt Rydl (bass). Ambrosian Opera Chorus; Philharmonia Orchestra. April 1987.
DEUTSCHE GRAMMOPHON 423 567 DDD 154:00 3 discs

✔HC ★*Awards:* Top Disks of the Year, *The New York Times* D 24, '89 (John Rockwell).

"This is to my mind the crowning performance of her [Freni's] long and distinguished career in the recording studio. The reading is more detailed than it was for Karajan and, if possible, even more persuasively sung. This is a big, Italianate portrayal projected in an eloquent and telling manner that disarms criticism....Sinopoli obviously loves the score and...follows Butterfly's psychological development and downfall with a surefooted feeling for Puccini's masterly construction and his wonderful orchestration....I think this is my favourite among recent versions."

Opera 40:69 Ja '89. Alan Blyth (375w)

"Sinopoli confronts us with a deep and painful consciousness of the wrong inflicted by the unthinking westerner even before it properly begins....We shall be lucky if we see a *Butterfly* in the theatre as brutally theatrical as this."

Hi-Fi News & Record Review 34:92 Mr '89. David Nice (525w)

"The overall high quality of this all-digital recording almost makes it seem that another version of *Butterfly* was just what was most needed."

Opera Canada 15:51 Summ '89. John Kraglund (190w)

"Almost despite himself, Mr. Sinopoli produces a tremendously captivating and convincing performance. However over-blown the style or absurdly ponderous the tempos, Mr. Sinopoli's conducting does, nonetheless, demonstrate a real involvement with every note in the score and a great flair for aural theater....Mirella Freni and Jose Carreras have both recorded 'Butterfly' before, but not with this kind of dramatic conviction."

The New York Times Mr 5 '89, p. 29. Mark Swed (400w)

"This new recording of *Madama Butterfly* invites comparison with Herbert von Karajan's London set, which has been the standard of excellence for some time, particularly since both performances feature Mirella Freni as Cio-Cio-San....You won't go wrong with either of these well-played and well-recorded performances, and in both cases you will be enriched by the achievement of this rare artist."

Stereo Review 54:120+ Je '89. Robert Ackart (350w)

"Puccini's tempo and dynamic instructions, as always, are detailed and explicit. Sinopoli largely observes the latter; the former he follows or ignores in about equal measure. Most of his departures are on the side of enervating slowness...Vocally, DG's new set stands on firmer ground. Mirella Freni knows the title role inside and out, and with her tonal security, expressive color and personal charisma she makes it live....Several slightly noticeable splices attest to the fact that digital tape is trickier to edit than analog."

Opera News 53:44 Je '89. John W. Freeman (525w)

"This *Butterfly* is anything but a conventional reading. However, I was, and continue to be, deeply moved by it—and almost thoroughly convinced....[Freni] doesn't blow the listener away the way Callas did, but, still, this is a ravishing, probing portrayal....The rest of the cast is top-notch...The orchestra and chorus are in glorious form, performing what amounts to a sacred rite with proper solemnity. The recording could not be bettered."

Stereophile 12:172 Jl '89. Robert Levine (550w)

Gramophone 66:1060-62 D '88. Michael Oliver (1100w)

Digital Audio's CD Review 6:74 S '89. Sebastian Russ (600w)

"DG's sound is well balanced, but it cannot be called natural....The booklet has an insightful essay, plot summary and four-language libretto-....The Callas/Gedda/Karajan classic...the 1958 Tebaldi/Bergonzi/Serafin...[and] the Hungaroton entry, with Veronika Kincses and Peter Dvorsky, conducted by Giuseppe Patane-...All easily surpass this one, despite the admiration that one retains for Freni's freshness and vocal longevity."

Fanfare 12:276-78 My/Je '89. Henry Fogel (1100w)

7106. Manon Lescault.

Giuseppe Sinopoli (c). Mirella Freni; Placido Domingo; Renato Bruson; Kurt Rydl. Royal Opera House Chorus, Covent Garden; Philharmonia Orchestra.
DEUTSCHE GRAMMOPHON 413 893 2 discs

★★*Awards:* *Fanfare* Want List 1985 (James Miller); *Gramophone* Critics' Choice 1985 (Edward Greenfield).

"This is a Puccini interpretation of tremendous character and vitality, and I would—cautiously—put it in the same class as Victor de Sabata's *Tosca* (now on CD, Angel CDCB 47174)."

Opus 2:35-6 D '85. Peter G. Davis (1100w)

"Mirella Freni and Placido Domingo's new Deutsche Grammophon recording is certainly the finest all around of the modern versions of the opera....Giuseppe Sinopoli is, for me, the weakest link among the principals of this recording. He drives Puccini's score mercilessly-....Although this new recording is one's best bet for a *Manon Lescaut*, that does not mean that it alone represents the best."

The Opera Quarterly 3:103-4 Winter '85/86. William Huck (800w)

"It would be difficult to imagine a more convincing performance...The cast is a strong one, headed by two artists who have made the leading roles particularly their own."

Stereo Review 50:106 My '85. Robert Ackart (400w)

"In short, this version of *Manon Lescaut* is, in all musical, dramatic, and technical aspects, as close to definitive as one can rightfully expect in our time."

High Fidelity 35:66 Mr '85. Bill Zakariasen (750w) (rev. of cassette)

"Consider this a rave review."

Fanfare 8:185-6 My/Je '85. James Miller (700w)

Ovation 6:24 Jl '85. George Jellinek (325w) (rev. of LP)

Gramophone 62:1117 Mr '85. Edward Greenfield (140w)

7107. Suor Angelica.

Giuseppe Patane (c). Lucia Popp (sop); Marjana Lipovsek (mez); Maria Gabriella Ferroni (sop). Bavarian Radio Chorus; Munich Choir Boys; Munich Radio Orchestra. November 1987.
EURODISC 7806; EURODISC 258 208 DDD 56:23

★*Awards:* The Year's Best, *Hi Fi News & Record Review*, May '90 Supplement.

"What we have here is a beautifully sung *Angelica*—not only by Popp, who is close to perfection as she balances the title role's strength and sadness, but also by the supporting cast."

Ovation 10:54+ S '89. Dick Adler (335w)

"If you're...looking for a Suor Angelica, you really need look no further than this current one. It is an honest, well-sung performance with Lucia Popp as a lovely, touching Angelica-....The orchestra and chorus are superb, as is the sound....multilingual essay and libretto."

Fanfare 12:279 My/Je '89. Robert Levine (425w)

"He is the conductor, above all on record, I think, who captures the pulse of Puccinian ebb and flow, the while encouraging his Munich Radio band to revel in Puccini's overtly emotional, but richly orchestrated score...Patane extracts the maximum emotional pull from Angelica's painful encounter with her terrible aunt, The Princess, from the tragic outpouring of grief at the news of her baby's death, and the final apotheosis which protestant spirits have always found so unpalatable. Patane and Popp had me weeping buckets." *P95/100 S95*

Hi-Fi News & Record Review 34:127 D '89; p.26 My '90 Supplement. Hugh Canning (425w)

"Lucia Popp's soprano has a celestial purity that lends itself to the title role, though one would like a little more sense of inner conflict. Both here and in a recent disc of Slavic arias-...Popp's current mannerisms—squeezed vowels, sticky attacks and releases—militate against the natural loveliness of her voice, but they stand out less conspicuously than in her Mozart repertory."

Opera News 54:30 Ag '89. John W. Freeman (210w)

The New York Times Mr 12 '89, p. 29. George Jellinek (175w)

7108. Tosca.

Victor De Sabata (c). Maria Callas; Giuseppe Di Stefano; Tito Gobbi. Milan La Scala Orchestra.
EMI 47174 AAD 108:14 2 discs

★*Awards:* *American Record Guide* Overview: Opera Favorites, Ja/F '91.

"The laserlike top notes of Callas have been tamed by the laser of the CD player and, like the whole performance, have never sounded better—there isn't a trace of the distortion that inevitably creeps into her SDs, and the expected tape hiss is minimal, almost inaudible."

Fanfare 9:232-3 N/D '85. James Miller (240w)

"An essential recording for anyone who likes *Tosca*."

Musical America 107:61 My '87 Terry Teachout (215w)

Digital Audio 2:54 Mr '86. Rod McKuen (275w)

Ovation 7:34-6 Je '86. George Jellinek (140w)

7109. Turandot.
Zubin Mehta (c). Joan Sutherland (sop); Montserrat Caballe (sop); Luciano Pavarotti (ten); Nicolai Ghiarov (bass). Alldis Chorus; London Philharmonic Orchestra. 117:33.
LONDON/DECCA 414 274 AAD

✔**HC** ★★*Awards:* Critics Choice, *Hi Fi News & Record Review*, Ap '91 Supplement (George Hall). *American Record Guide* Overview: Opera Favorites, Ja/F '91.

"Twelve years on the market and still it startles-....This is top-flight Decca."
Hi-Fi News & Record Review 30:83+ Je '85. Edward Seckerson (175w)

"It's likely that someday this recording will have stronger competition in the CD format (i.e., the two recordings that feature Birgit Nilsson...would it be too much to hope for Maria Callas, too?): right now I'd rate it higher on most counts than CBS' Maazel version or DG's Karajan."
Fanfare 10:194-95 N/D '86 James Miller (365w)

Digital Audio 2:55+ O '85. Roland Graeme (725w)

High Fidelity 35:73 O '85. Robert E. Benson (65w)

Gramophone 62:1383 My '85. Edward Greenfield (265w)

PURCELL, HENRY

7110. Dido and Aeneas.
Raymond Leppard (c). Jessye Norman (sop); Thomas Allen (bar); Marie McLaughlin; Patricia Kern. English Chamber Orchestra.
PHILIPS 416 299 58:00

✔**HC** ★*Awards:* *Stereo Review* Best of the Month, S '86; *Gramophone* Critics' Choice 1986 (Edward Greenfield).

"If you're looking for a *Dido* with a bit of blood in its veins, this is the performance you should own."
Ovation 8:40 F '87 Robert Levine (265w)

This performance "will appeal particularly to admirers of Jessye Norman and to those who found the celebrated 1952 Mermaid Theatre/Kristen Flagstad version for EMI...to be nearly ideal."
High Fidelity 37:85-86 Ja '87 R.D. Darrell (185w)

"Whereas Flagstad creates a Dido of calm, stately, and ultimately resigned queenliness, Jessye Norman's Dido is finally stripped of regality to stand a woman denied, bereft, and desperate."
Stereo Review 51:99-100 S '86. Robert Ackart (750w)

"To my ears, a thin, girlish voice cannot begin to communicate the emotional range of the heroine of this compact little opera....I find Norman's new recording of the opera magnificent. It is not just that her unique voice fits the music so effortlessly but that she has an ability to inflect every phrase with the kind of import that produces a rich range of emotional responses."
Musical America 107:61 Jl '87 Thor Eckert, Jr. (650w)

"Devotees of Jessye Norman will probably form the principal audience for this recording of Purcell's superb chamber opera."
American Record Guide 50:64-5 N/D '87. George W. Loomis (530w)

"A lot of grand talent delivers a satisfying but in no way definitive performance of the opera-....Perhaps the presence of the two undeniably super-star leads has intimidated the conductor into a less assertive stance, but the too obvious reticence in the new recording was not present in 1977....Thomas Allen's Aeneas is among the best sung and most completely realized on records....The smoldering sexuality in the first aria, the rage and humiliation in the duet, and the enormously tragic final Lament are all typical Norman. Perhaps too typical. Can it be that this great personality has begun to fall back on a number of predictable effects? That this is one of the most exceptional voices I have heard, and one of the most striking stage presences I have seen, there can be no doubt. But it doesn't carry the day in this recording, and I would refer the listener to early Baker, late Troyanos, and D'Anna Fortunato on Joel Cohen's recording for nearly perfect assumptions of one of opera's great roles....I really cannot recommend against its purchase—it's very good. But the step into the truly memorable is not taken."
*Fanfare*10:195-8 N/D '86 Vincent Alfano (2200w)

"Leppard's first *Dido and Aeneas*, [on Erato] which appeared in America in 1978, is rhythmically livelier and relatively free of portentousness. Not so grand in aim, it achieves a better blend of drama and ritual, though the singing is far from memorable."
The Opera Quarterly 4:78-81 Wint '86/87 Dale Harris (940w) (rev. of LP)

"Given its surfeit of problems, this recording is difficult to recommend. Unfortunately, if you can't abide early instruments, there aren't many *Didos* to choose from, for domestically, at least, most modern-instrument accounts have fallen out of the catalog."
Opus 3:30-33 F '87 Allan Kozinn (2300w)

Hi-Fi News & Record Review 31:106-7 Jl '86. Arthur Jacobs (340w)

Opera News 51 (4):80 O '86. John W. Freeman (300w)

7111. The Fairy Queen.

William Christie (c). Nancy Argenta (sop); Lynne Dawson (sop); Isabelle Desrochers (sop); Willemijn Van Gent (sop); Veronique Gens (sop); Sandrine Piau (sop); Noemi Rime (sop); Charles Daniels (alto); Jean-Paul Fouchecourt (alto); Mark LeBrocq (alto); Christophe LePaludier (alto); Bernard Loonen (ten); Francois Piolino (ten); Thomas Randle (ten); Francois Bazola (bar); Jerome Correas (bass); George Banks-Martin (bass); Bernard Deletre (bass); Thomas Lander (bass); Richard Taylor (bass). Les Arts Florissants Vocal and Instrumental Ensemble.
HARMONIA MUNDI 901308/9 DDD 128:00 2 discs

✔HC ★★★★★*Awards:* Record of the Month, *Hi-Fi News & Record Review*, Mr '90; The Year's Best, *Hi Fi News & Record Review*, May '90 Supplement; Editors' Choice, *Digital Audio's CD Review*, 6:34 Je '90. The Want List 1990, *Fanfare* N/D '90 (Elliott Kaback; Michael Ullman); Critics' Choice 1990, *Gramophone* D '90 (Iain Fenlon); Records to Die for: 1 of 5 Recommended Recordings, *Stereophile* Ja '91 (Barbara Jahn).

"With an impressive line-up of soloists...supported with assurance and flair by chorus and period ensemble, not to mention the sympathetic acoustics, this is certainly a classic recording of an undisputed masterpiece." *P100 S100*

Hi-Fi News & Record Review 35:101 Mr '90. Helena Stoward (455w)

"A comparison with the recording by John Eliot Gardiner, hitherto the prime recommendation for this work, leaves no doubts. Gardiner may have the surer sense of rhythm, founded on precise articulation from his players; but it is Christie who has the better cast and has worked with them as a team to explore every corner of the score. The music has never sounded as full of joy, of magic and delight, as it does here."

Opera 41:492 Ap '90. Richard Fairman (635w)

P100 S100

Hi-Fi News & Record Review p.10 My '90 Supplement. Helena Stoward (455w)

"I didn't expect to hear [the Gardiner performance on Archiv]...made on original instruments and sung exquisitely, equaled, but this new *Fairy Queen* with William Christie conducting Les Arts Florissants does just that-....Some may prefer the sensuousness of the Christie; others may be bothered by the vagaries of pronunciation by some of his French singers. (A minor problem, in my opinion)."

Fanfare 13:266-67 Mr/Ap '90. Michael Ullman (750w)

"In all, Christie's recording represents a perspective on Purcell and one of his greatest works squarely in the light of the latest musicological thought but removed from the usual British baroque-revival mainstream. If one wants a more standardized approach, with more polished and appealing vocalism, in a sober and 'straight' interpretative style, Gardiner remains the choice."

American Record Guide 53:91-2 My/Je '90. John W. Barker (975w)

"This is, quite simply, a splendid recording...A handsome accompanying booklet provides a libretto in three languages. Excellent sound-....Highly recommended."

The Nats Journal 46:41 My/Je '90. Carol Kimball (405w)

"Christie's long associations with Les Arts Florissants and Harmonia Mundi show in the quality of both performance and recording achieved here."

Stereophile 14:149 Ja '91. Barbara Jahn (b.n.)

"A considerable theatrical atmosphere is conveyed in an approach that is straightforward and devoid of the kind of coyness that sometimes invades such presentations, and it is all captured in crisp and clear sonics."

The New York Times Jl 1 '90, p. 22 H. George Jellinek (170w)

"As we have come to expect from William Christie's recordings with Les Arts Florissant, the performance is indeed a very good one....It must be pointed out that Christie has refitted this work, which in its day would have been presented as a large-scale English theatrical event, to the overrefined setting of the French salon. I question his constant use of double-dotting and rhythmic alterations....Also, his mix of English and French singers presents some problems regarding diction....Altogether, though, this is a spirited and beautifully prepared production."

Stereo Review 55:124+ S '90. Stoddard Lincoln (580w)

"The spirit of the dance is never far away, Christie demanding a crisp but sprightly rhythmic lift from his exemplary players, who themselves create a fantastic battery of exotic sounds with theorbos, baroque guitar, gamba, harpsichords, organ, and authentic wind, brass, and string timbres....Some wonderful, dark-hued singing...Also, William Christie has been able to reinstate the instrumental sinfonias that had to be cut to make the live performance (still nearly four hours long) anything like a manageable length. All this has been captured by a recording typical of Harmonia Mundi's high standards in both its breadth and clarity."

Stereophile 13:197-98 S '90. Barbara Jahn (505w)

"A strength of this splendid recording is the attention paid to instrumental and vocal color in achieving a variety of special effects—sounds of nature, drunkenness, sleep, darkness, the four seasons."

Opera News 54:35 Ja 6 '90. John W. Freeman (b.n.)

"There is considerable musical scholarship here, but authenticity is never allowed to take the place of drama."

High Fidelity 1:121 Mr '90. Ian Brunskill (b.n.)

Digital Audio's CD Review 6:46 Je '90. Sebastian Russ (685w)

Gramophone 67:1374-75 Ja '90. Iain Fenlon (640w)

RAVEL, MAURICE

7112. L'Enfant et les Sortileges.
Lorin Maazel (c). Francoise Ogeas (sop); Jeanine Collard (contr); Jane Berbie (sop); Sylvaine Gilma (sop); Colette Herzog (sop); Heinz Rehfuss (bar); Camille Maurane (bar); Michel Senechal (ten). French Radio Children's Chorus; French Radio National Orchestra. 1961.
DEUTSCHE GRAMMOPHON 423 718 ADD 43:00

✔HC ★*Awards:* Remastered CDs Record Award 1989, *Gramophone*, D '89.

Gramophone 66:1492 Mr '89. Lionel Salter (245w)

ROSSINI, GIOACCHINO

7113. Il Barbiere di Siviglia.
Giuseppe Patane (c). Leo Nucci (bar); Cecilia Bartoli (mez); William Matteuzzi (ten); Enrico Fissore (bar); Paata Burchuladze (bass); Gloria Banditelli (contr); Michele Petrusi (bass). Bologna Teatro Comunale Chorus; Bologna Teatro Comunale Orchestra.
LONDON/DECCA 425 520 DDD 161:00 3 discs

"The overriding point of interest in this new *Barber* is the fact that conductor, orchestra, chorus and all the soloists save one are Italian...The advantages are obvious, especially in recitative that trips along with enormous zest. It's like hearing the work for the first time. But there are other reasons to recommend it. The sound is first-rate, clear, warm and full—it has *sun* in it....This reading is as relaxed, urbane and civilised as Rossini himself."
Opera 40:1506 D '89.Rodney Milnes (490w)

"There's a lot to be said for Patane's approach, particularly his supportive way with singers...If only the singers were a more accomplished crew....In general, then, this is a *Barbiere* with a provincial cast and a good conductor."
Opera News 54:34 Ja 6 '90. John W. Freeman (210w)

"It seems a shame to inaugurate the conspicuous arrival of Cecilia Bartoli on the operatic scene with so stiff-jointed a *Barber*." *P85/95 S75/95*
Hi-Fi News & Record Review 35:100 F '90. David Nice (390w)

"His Rosina is another promising newcomer, Cecilia Bartoli, who needs to polish her florid singing but who has a lovely voice and a bit of brio about her. William Matteuzzi provides a sweet but undersung Almaviva; the rest of the cast is poor, and the conducting, sad to say, is uneven and dull."
The New York Times F 25 '90, p. H 27. Will Crutchfield (210w)

"Overall, among the newer crop of *Barber* recordings, I prefer Neville Marriner's on Philips, which is somewhat crisper and frothier than Patane's and has superior lead performances."
Stereo Review 55:96 Ap '90. Robert Ackart (480w)

"This is a conventional *Barber*, big and extrovert, with lots of recitative and few embellishments or departures from the score other than some interpolated high notes....My favorite *Barbiere*, hands down, is Varviso's (London), currently out of print....I have no strong preference among the recordings now on the market....I don't think Patane is put in the shade by any of these efforts (Varviso excepted), so my recommendation is that you choose on the basis of the singers you like best."
Fanfare 13:269-70 My/Je '90. Ralph V. Lucano (675w)

"Termed a 'traditional recording' by its conductor, Giuseppe Patane, there is much to admire in his approach, marred though it is by some lack of consistency in style and spirit....I am not as captivated as some by the young...Cecilia Bertoli....to my mind, the performance lacks true Rossinian wit." *PS 80*
Opera Canada 31:54 Summ 90. Harvey Chusid (150w)

"There's less here than meets the eye, and for the most part, it's the late Giuseppe Patane's fault....Patane...never works the cast too hard, but as a result never manages to get any real life from them....The sound, by the way, is London's best—resonant, true, and rich."
Stereophile 13:215+ N '90. Robert Levine (300w)

Gramophone 67:537-38 S '89. Richard Osborne (805w)

7114. Le Comte Ory.
John Eliot Gardiner (c). John Aler (ten); Sumi Jo (sop); Diana Montague (mez); Gino Quilico (bar); Gilles Cachemaille (bar); Maryse Castets (sop); Raquel Pierotti (mez); Francis Dudziak (ten); Nicolas Rivenq (bar). Lyon Opera Chorus; Lyon Opera Orchestra.
PHILIPS 422 406 DDD 132:00 2 discs

★★★★*Awards:* Record of the Eighties, *Gramophone*, D '89 (Alan Blyth); Critics' Choice 1989, *Gramophone* D '89 (Richard Osborne); Editor's Choice, *Opera Canada*, Summ '90. The Want List 1990, *Fanfare* N/D '90 (Robert Levine).

"An excellent cast turn in an extremely stylish and enjoyable performance."
High Fidelity 1:121 F '90. Ian Brunskill (b.n.)

"The real reason to listen to *Le Comte Ory*...is that it is so much fun, especially when performed as well as here....In spite of its somber medieval setting, this is a comedy of the Enlightenment."
Opera News 54:30 Mr 31 '90. John W. Freeman (305w)

"On all counts, this is the neatest and best balanced recording of *Ory* to date, as well as the most complete. I recommend it to all Rossinians, even those who, like me, deplore it as a second-hand, second-rate work."
American Record Guide 53:97 My/Je '90. Desmond Arthur (420w)

"The first thing to observe about the new Philips recording is that it is complete, down to the last da capo....A major issue, which will certainly figure on my Five Best list come year's end."
Fanfare 13:270-72 My/Je '90. David Johnson (1075w)

"The superbly well-balanced cast includes a joyous performance by soprano Sumi Jo as Adele—sparkling in coloratura, affecting in legato, Diana Montague's fetching Isolier, and the verve and intelligence of tenor John Aler's accomplished account of the title role." *PS 100*
Opera Canada 31:54 Summ 90. Harvey Chusid (175w)

"Thanks to Gardiner's alert direction, and the fact that the recording came soon after stage performances, there is a tautness and crispness that pays off throughout but most notably in the ensembles. Vocally, there is much to enjoy and plenty to amaze."
Music and Musicians International 38:46 Jl '90. Robert Hartford (540w)

"This recording is better than good....The score is given complete, and the sound is Philips's best, which is to say, superb. Highly recommended."
Stereophile 14:263-4 Ja '91. Robert Levine (360w)

"As the rascally count, John Aler sings with a beautiful, easy, lyric tone....Sumi Jo...conveys the personality of her role with charm and playfulness....Indeed, the entire cast re-creates the youthful, often zany frolic of the characters with unusually engaging effect. And the Orchestra and Chorus of the Lyons Opera respond smoothly to John Eliot Gardiner's nicely paced direction."
Stereo Review 55:108 My '90. Robert Ackart (275w)

"Reservations may be noted about some of the singers, but certainly not about Diana Montague, who is firm-toned, confident, and charming in the role of the page Isolier....John Eliot Gardiner leads this well oiled orchestral ensemble with precision. He is in no way heavy-handed, yet there is a certain sparkle in the score that seems to elude him."
Musical America 110:82-3 Mr '90. George Jellinek (590w)

"Gardiner is superb here; what I think he misses is the essential Rossinian brio of the Count's raffish music—but that is a fairly common failing among modern conductors....I admire, too, Gardiner's insistence on voices which do justice to Rossini's virtuoso writing and comic spirit, rather than relying on the fashionable names—Baltsa, Raimondi and Co—whose laboured efforts have ruined at least two recent recordings...I am less happy, though, about the recording, which resembles a lot of DG's opera productions in favouring the voices at the expense of the players." *P95 S85*
Hi-Fi News & Record Review 34:127 D '89. Hugh Canning (735w)

"This is a very likeable performance....good, but in the context not quite good enough. Nevertheless, how marvellous to have the complete text of this supreme masterpiece of comic opera readily available."
Opera 40:1505 D '89. Rodney Milnes (370w)

Gramophone 67:744+ O '89. Richard Osborne (1185w)

7115. Ermione.

Claudio Scimone (c). Cecilia Gasdia (sop); Margarita Zimmerman (alto); Ernesto Palacio (ten); Chris Merritt (ten); William Matteuzzi (ten); Simone Alaimo; Mario Bolognesi; Elisabetta Tandura. Prague Philharmonic Chorus; Monte Carlo Philharmonic Orchestra. Monte Carlo. June 1986.
ERATO 75336 DDD 65:40, 56:55 2 discs

★★★*Awards:* The Want List 1988, *Fanfare* N/D '88 (Robert Levine, David Johnson, Ralph V. Lucano).

"At its exciting best, with ensembles culminating in reckless coloratura runs at energetic speed, *Ermione* is a new and wonderful operatic event."
Opera News 53:42-3 F 18 '89. John W. Freeman (515w)

"Merritt's kind of singing does not come along often and he will not possess it for long...Let's enjoy it while we can....The so-called minor roles are sung splendidly....Scimone has a first-rate chorus to work with...The accompanying book...is a model of its kind...A very important recording."
Fanfare 11:196-200 My/Je '88. David Johnson (2500w)

"Andromache is sung with character by Margherita Zimmerman. The tiresome Hermione of the title is dazzlingly taken by Cecilia Gasdia...The playing, under Scimone, is enthusiastic and, for the most part, accurate if splashy. The recording is excellent, and the opera itself a valuable addition to the CD repertory."
Music and Musicians International 36:48-9 Je '88. Robert Hartford (260w)

"If this premiere on compact disc fails to convince at every turn, it is not because *Ermione* is too lofty, or too puny, for modern audiences, but simply because it is so tall an order for the singers....If not the ultimate in revived Rossini, this is a welcome arrival to the recorded canon, and, until someone in this country mounts a fully staged production with majestic Sanquirico sets and a flawless cast, it will certainly do."

The Opera Quarterly 6:139-42 Summ '89. Rodney Shewan (1400w)

"It is a performance that serves the opera adequately without assuring it the masterpiece status claimed by its champions."

Ovation 9:38 O '88. George Jellinek (575w)

Gramophone 66:336 Ag '88. Richard Osborne (800w)

7116. La Gazza Ladra.

Gianluigi Gelmetti (c). Katia Ricciarelli (sop); William Matteuzzi (ten); Samuel Ramey (bass); Bernadette Manca di Nissa (contr); Luciana D'Intino (mez); Ferruccio Furlanetto (bar); Roberto Coviello (bass); Oslavio Di Credico (ten); Pierre Lefebre (ten); Francesco Musinu (bass); Marcello Lippi (bass). Prague Philharmonic Chorus; Turin Radio Symphony Orchestra. Teatro Rossini, Pesaro. Texts, translations and notes included. August 1989 live.
SONY 45850 DDD 194:00 3 discs

★★★*Awards:* The Want List 1991, *Fanfare* N/D '91 (David Johnson). Critics' Choice 1990, *Gramophone* D '90 (Richard Osborne); Editor's Choice, *Opera Canada* Winter '90.

"This live presentation from the 1989 Rossini Opera Festival in Pesaro is the work's first major digitally engineered recording. And if 'delirium' is not exactly the audience's pitch of emotion at the conclusion of the performance, the applause is strong and well-deserved for a vivacious, idiomatic account of a work shot through with musical genius."

Opera Canada 31(4):51 Winter '90. Harvey Chusid (250w)

"Gianluigi Gelmetti's leadership is inspired. The festival audience is almost Bayreuth-like in its decorum...Anyone inclined to shy away from this set because of ambivalence over the singers will be missing out on a real treat."

American Record Guide 54:98 My/Je '91. George W. Loomis (585w)

"The cast is a strong one....Gianluigi Gelmetti reveals himself as a first-rate Rossini conductor: the famous overture is thrilling, and throughout he paces the music to a nicety, relishing its spirit, wit and where appropriate grandeur and complexity. With minor reservations, warmly recommended." *P95/85 S95*

Hi-Fi News & Record Review 36:75-6 Ag '91. George Hall (330w)

"Katia Ricciarelli delivers an excellent performance as Ninetta and Samuel Ramey's voice commands the ear yet again."

High Fidelity 2:117 N '90. Clive Manning (110w)

"Gianluigi Gelmetti, along with Samuel Ramey, is the star of this recording....On the whole...a mixed offering, but with far more pluses than minuses—one of the greatest pluses being the decision to perform the opera in the Zedda critical edition, uncut save for small amounts of secco recitative....It's a recording one can live with for a lifetime, although I hope sometime down the road a more perfect one will come along."

Fanfare 14:342-6 Mr/Ap '91. David Johnson (3375w)

"The performance is by no means perfect, but any sensible Rossinian will want this valuable release...A full libretto in many languages, with essays and photos, is provided. This one matters; it may take a while to warm up to, but it's a splendid work well served."

Stereophile 15:196 F '92. Robert Levine (long)

Gramophone 68:816 O '90. Richard Osborne (910w)

Opera News 55:34 Ja 5 '91. John W. Freeman (250w)

7117. Semiramide.

Richard Bonynge (c). Joan Sutherland (sop); Marilyn Horne (mez); Joseph Rouleau (bass); John Serge (ten); Patricia Clark (sop); Spiro Malas (bass); Michael Langdon (bass); Leslie Fyson (ten). Ambrosian Opera Chorus; London Symphony Orchestra. 1966.
LONDON/DECCA 425 481 ADD 168:00 3 discs

"The partnership of Joan Sutherland and Marilyn Horne is one of the most brilliant on record...Nowhere is this more magnificently apparent than in this studio performance of *Semiramide*...Australian tenor John Serge's Idreno is rather pallid in tone, but Canadian bass Joseph Rouleau is a rich-voiced Assur, and Richard Bonynge conducts with (uncharacteristic) imaginative energy and structural insight." *PS 90*

Opera Canada 31:55 Summ 90. Harvey Chusid (125w)

"It matters little that supporting roles remain ciphers when the two principal ones are so splendidly portrayed. This is another essential CD library addition."

American Record Guide 53:156 Mr/Ap '90. Vivian A. Liff (b.n.)

Gramophone 67:1526 F '90. Richard Osborne (200w)

Digital Audio's CD Review 6:66+ Mr '90. Octavio Roca (145w)

7118. Il Viaggio a Reims.

Claudio Abbado (c). Cecilia Gasdia (sop); Katia Ricciarelli (sop); Lelia Cuberli (sop); Lucia Valentini-Terrani (mez); Edoardo Gimenez (ten); Francisco Araiza (ten); Enzo Dara (bass-bar); Leo Nucci (bar); Samuel Ramey (bass); Ruggero Raimondi. Prague Philharmonic Chorus; Chamber Orchestra of Europe. Auditorium Pedrotti, Pesaro. 1984.
DEUTSCHE GRAMMOPHON 415 498 2 discs

★★★★★*Awards:* *Stereo Review* Best of the Month, Je '86; *Fanfare* Want List 1986 (Elliott Kaback; David Johnson); *Gramophone* Record Award Winner 1986—Operatic Award; Best of the Month, *Stereo Review* Je '86; Record of the Eighties, *Gramophone*, D '89 (Alan Blyth). Critics Choice, *Hi Fi News & Record Review*, Ap '91 Supplement (Peter Branscombe).

This "is one of the best operatic recordings of recent years. The singing is excellent throughout, and some passages—notably Cecilia Gasdia's 'improvisations' in the sextet and the finale—will surely become vocal classics."

The Opera Quarterly 4:110-2 Wint '86/87 Roger Parker (1050w) (rev. of LP)

"Every member of the cast is musically strong-....Claudio Abbado conducts the opera crisply, delicately, wittily, and *con amore*."

Stereo Review 51:107 Je '86. Robert Ackart (525w)

"*Il Viaggio* was staged at the Rossini festival in Pesaro in 1984...The sound, on CD, is superb....This recording is a treasurable document of an event of immense importance to the musical world."

American Record Guide 49:77-9 My/Je '86. Desmond Arthur (1600w)

"In *Viaggio* itself, the nature of the game that is being played places an enormous burden on the performers: not only to sing the music, which is quite difficult enough, but to find what will make it personal and alive, and I'm afraid that our cast, abrim though it is with dedication and good intentions, and for all that these just may be the best singers who could have been assembled, isn't really up to the challenge....This is obviously a well-intentioned project that will be of interest to many opera lovers."

Opus 2:49-50 Je '86. Kenneth Furie (1090w)

Ovation 7:44 S '86. George Jellinek (550w)

Gramophone 64:549 O '86. Richard Osborne (400w)

Opera News 50 (16):49 My '86. John W. Freeman (435w)

7119. William Tell.

Riccardo Chailly (c). Sherrill Milnes; Luciano Pavarotti; Mirella Freni; Della Jones; Elizabeth Connell; Ferrucio Mazzoli; Nicolai Ghiaurov; John Tomlinson; Cesar Antonio Suarez; Piero De Palma; Richard Van Allan. Ambrosian Opera Chorus; National Philharmonic Orchestra.
LONDON/DECCA 417 154 234:44 4 discs

"Indeed, it would be difficult to find better representations of three of the finest singers of our time, all at the top of their form."

Hi-Fi News & Record Review 32:103 Mr '87 Arthur Jacobs (210w)

Gramophone 64:1178 F '87 Hilary Finch (375w)

SALIERI, ANTONIO

7120. Falstaff.

Tamas Pal (c). Maria Zempleni ,. Denes Gulyas, Eva Panczel, Istvan Gati, Tamas Csurja, Eva Vamossy Jozsef Gregor. Salieri Chamber Orchestra; Salieri Chamber Chorus.
HUNGAROTON 12789/91 155:22 3 discs

★*Awards:* *Opus* Record Award Nominee, 1987.

"This performance...is a thoroughly rewarding work on several levels....The performance is excellent and the compact disc sound is crystal clear, vibrant and warm."

HighPerformanceReview 4:88-89 Spr '87 June C. Ottenberg (600w)

"Jozsef Gregor is really not heavy enough to convey either the physical presence of Falstaff or to make his romantic aspirations obviously ridiculous...but Tamas Csurja (Baldof) turns his minor role to good account."

Hi-Fi News & Record Review 31:113 O '86. Kenneth Dommett (330w)

"In sum, this opera, fine almost throughout, demonstrates that Salieri was a major star in the galaxy, still little-known, that carried the buffa to its Classical apogee....For the excellence of the performance, the conductor, Tamas Pal, deserves the main accolade."

Opus 3:47-48 Ap '87 Paul Henry Lang (1845w) (rev. of LP)

"The newish Hungaroton recording of *Falstaff*-...is an excellent one, an outstanding performance with a well-balanced cast."

Fanfare 10:39 Ja/F '87 Nick Rossi (150w) (rev. of LP)

SCHOECK, OTHMAR

7121. Massimilla Doni.

Gerd Albrecht (c). Edith Mathis (sop); Hermann Winkler (ten); Josef Protschka (ten); Celina Lindsley (sop); Harald Stamm (bass); Roland Hermann (bar); Deon Van Der Walt (ten); Annette Kuttenbaum (mez). Cologne Radio Choir; Colonne Symphony Orchestra. January 1986 live.
KOCH-SCHWANN 314 025 DDD 128:00 2 discs

★*Awards:* Critics' Choice 1989, *Gramophone* D '89 (Robert Layton).

"Here is an intellectually stimulating plot, replete with beautiful, almost magical music, in an uncommonly well performed, knowing performance."

American Record Guide 53:83-4 Ja/F '90. Charles Parsons (475w)

"Schoeck's music is euphonious and searching, its basic romanticism tempered by twentieth-century turbulence and intellectuality....Like Strauss' *Capriccio*, it demands close attention to the text, and unfortunately the CDs come with a German-only libretto....As the aristocratic couple, Edith Mathis (Massimilla) and Josef Protschka (Emilio) scarcely could be bettered."

Opera News 54:30 F 3 '90. John W. Freeman (360w)

Originally reviewed in *Fanfare* 10:5. "Everyone involved in this performance seems to have given it their best shot and one takes leave of *Massimilla* with the conviction that something very close to the best possible case for it has been made. Would that such care had been lavished upon worthier works."

Fanfare 13:343-45 N/D '89. Adrian Corleonis (350w)

Gramophone 67:971 N '89. Robert Layton (450w)

SCHOENBERG, ARNOLD

7122. Moses und Aron.

Georg Solti (c). Franz Mazura; Philip Langridge; Aage Haugland. Members of the Glen Ellyn Children's Chorus; Chicago Symphony Chorus; Chicago Symphony Orchestra.
LONDON/DECCA 414 264 2 discs

✔HC ★★*Awards:* *Gramophone* Critics' Choice 1985 (Arnold Whittall; Max Harrison).

"If not the summit of Solti's musico-dramatic perception in this milestone recording, it ranks with the best here, to be savored, and cherished, and reverenced."

Fanfare 8:255-7 Jl/Ag '85. Roger Dettmer (1500w)

"Solti and his remarkable vocal and orchestral forces leave nothing to be desired in putting across its message, both dramatically and musically, and the London recording itself is a remarkably fine one."

Stereo Review 50:63 Ag '85. David Hall (425w)

Gramophone 62:914 Ja '85. Arnold Whittall (545w) (rev. of LP)

Opera News 50 (4):82 O '85. John W. Freeman (350w) (rev. of LP)

The Opera Quarterly 4:136-8 Summer '86. C.-P. Gerald Parker (1010w)

SCHREKER, FRANZ

7123. Der Ferne Klang.

Michael Halasz (c). Elena Grigorescu (sop); Thomas Harper (ten); Andreas Haller (bass-bar); Horst Fiehl (bar); Rudiger Bunse (bass); Paul Friess (bass); Werner Hahn (bar); Peter Nikolaus Kante (bass); Reinhard Leisenheimner (ten); William Pickersgill (bass-bar); Marisa Altmann-Althausen (mez). Hagen Opera Chorus; Hagen Philharmonic Orchestra.
MARCO POLO 8.223270 DDD 132:00 2 discs

★*Awards:* The Want List 1990, *Fanfare* N/D '90 (James H. North).

"The cast sings well, particularly tenor Thomas Harper in the role of Fritz...The chorus and orchestra are very well directed by Michael Halasz and they are extremely successful at projecting the very sumptuous sound that Schreker wrote into this work....The recording is big-sounding but clear even during this opera's most complex moments." *P95 S95*

Australian Hi-Fi 21(7):51:15 '90. Chris Green (610w)

"The Marco Polo performance...captures Schreker's nervy adventurousness most vividly. If Elena Grigorescu is a touch raw in the country-girl-to-courtesan role, her eager candour is a touching dramatic asset, and Thomas Harper makes an upstanding Fritz, with sterling support from (among others) Andreas Haller, Horst Fiehl and Werner Hahn."

Opera 41:1376-77 N '90. David Murray (585w)

"Gratitude is owed to Marco Polo for making the work accessible in a fine presentation in excellent sound. I have only two criticisms: A complete libretto is essential for getting the most out of such an unfamiliar work, and here we have only a scene-by scene synopsis....Second, the role of Grete (a lower middle-class German girl) is here played by an artist who, while she sings quite well, speaks with a heavy Slavic accent."

American Record Guide 53:100-01 My/Je '90. Kurt Moses (725w)

"We get no libretto here, but a German/English track-by-track synopsis of thirty-three tracks-...It sings better than it reads...Both protagonists have fine voices and sing effectively-...Marco Polo's recording gleams: quiet orchestral details are heard even in big vocal moments, and no singer is ever drowned by the orchestra...This is an extremely rewarding issue...this is a beautiful opera, well presented, and a joy to listen to."

Fanfare 13:68+ My/Je '90. James H. North (1160w)

Gramophone 68:408 Ag '90. Arnold Whittall (490w)

SCHUBERT, FRANZ

7124. Fierrabras, D.796.

Claudio Abbado (c). Josef Protschka (ten); Karita Mattila (sop); Robert Holl (bass); Thomas Hampson (bass); Robert Gambill (ten); Laszlo Polgar (bass); Cheryl Studer (sop); Brigitte Balleys (contr); Hartmut Welker (bar). Arnold Schoenberg Choir; Chamber Orchestra of Europe. Theater an der Wien, Vienna. May 1988 live.
DEUTSCHE GRAMMOPHON 427 341 DDD 144:00 2 discs

★★★★*Awards:* The Want List 1991, *Fanfare* N/D '91 (David Johnson; Susan Kagan). Critics' Choice 1990, *Gramophone* D '90 (John Warrack); Editor's Choice, *Opera Canada* Winter '90.

"This is the most alive and convincing recording of a Schubert opera yet, and if it serves as an example to future projects, it will remain hard to match."

Opera News 55:43 Je '91. John W. Freeman (375w)

"This magisterial recording of Schubert's last and grandest opera is the fulfillment of a lifelong passion for me....This is the fifth *Fierrabras* I have heard and it is so superior to the others that comparisons would be an im-

pertinence (save for the fact that the world has not yet found a replacement for Fritz Wunderlich). The live sound dazzles, and the audience's applause has been kept to it appropriate place at the ends of acts."
Fanfare 14:274-9 Jl/Ag '91. David Johnson (3420w)

"The score storms and roars like one of those dark, pseudo-medieval paintings of the period; there are rage arias, alarums and excursions, ignorant armies clashing by night. This is strong, exciting stuff, well suited to these performers and to the temperament of Maestro Abbado....The big trouble with the piece is that it has the quintessentially idiotic opera libretto-....Forget theater; as a recording, *Fierrabras* is lots of fun....The strong performance and recording are not ultrapolished, but the spirit and style are completely convincing."
Stereo Review 56:88+ My '91. Eric Salzman (375w)

"Each member of the cast is utterly convincing in this epic tale of friendship, love and loyalty against a background of a holy-war."
High Fidelity 2:117 N '90. Clive Manning (120w)

"The Vienna performance, led by Claudio Abbado, is captivating, sufficiently so as to render palatable the cliched conventions which permeate this story of chivalry, honor, love and war at the courts of Charlemagne."
Opera Canada 31(4):49-50 Winter '90. Harvey Chusid (225w)

"Abbado extracts a sensitive yet full-blooded performance from the Chamber Orchestra of Europe, which emphasizes some of the score's affinities with the composer's symphonic works of the same period. The cast is young and well-blended."
Musical America 111:86-7 Jl '91. Jamie James (355w)

"Of the singers the best are: Cheryl Studer, as Florinda the Moorish princess, who alone of the cast makes much of her melodrama in addition to her beautiful singing; Robert Gambill as Eginhard; Josef Protschka as Fierrabras (the noble Moorish prince), and Thomas Hampson, a suitably heroic Roland. I found Karita Mattila disappointingly wan and uninvolved-...Balance is uneasy at times, yet the sound quality is generally high." *P95 S95/85*
Hi-Fi News & Record Review 35:105 O '90. Peter Branscombe (635w)

Gramophone 68:819 O '90. John Warrack (810w)

"Conductor Abbado deserves praise for his part in the undertaking, and there's nothing tentative about the playing of his orchestra. The sound is excellent...I recommend *Fierrabras* wholeheartedly to lovers of Schubert, German romantic music, or operatic novelties. It just may be the most important opera recording of the year."
American Record Guide 54:121-22 S/O '91. Ralph V. Lucano (long)

SHOSTAKOVICH, DMITRI

7125. Lady Macbeth of Mtsensk.
Mstislav Rostropovich (c). Galina Vishnevskaya (sop); Nicolai Gedda (ten); Dimiter Petkov (bass); Werner Krenn (ten); Robert Tear (ten); Taru Valjakka (sop); Martyn Hill (ten); Leonard Mroz (bass); Aage Haugland (bass); Birgit Finnila (mez); Alexander Malta (bass); Leslie Fyson (ten); Steven Emmerson (bass); John Noble (bar); Colin Appleton (ten); Alan Byers (bar); James Lewington (ten); Oliver Broome (bass); Edgar Fleet (ten); David Beaven (bass); Lynda Richardson (mez). Ambrosian Opera Chorus; London Philharmonic Orchestra. 1979 reissue.
EMI 49955 ADD 155:00 2 discs

✔**HC** ★*Awards:* Critic's Choice: 1990, *American Record Guide* Ja/F '91 (Lee Milazzo).

"I cannot praise too highly the quality of the performances on this recording....Already devastatingly effective in its LP avator, this *Lady Macbeth of Mtsensk* becomes, on its CD reincarnation, one of the great recordings of all time."
Fanfare 13:269-70 Jl/Ag '90. Royal S. Brown (690w)

"This 1979 recording is the full, resurrected score and one of the best opera recordings that Rostropovich has given us. His wife, Galina Vishnevskaya, captures the rawness of *Lady Macbeth* and the LPO underline the composer's love for brass and percussion. A generously filled set."
High Fidelity 1:110 Ag '90. Clive Manning (b.n.)

"This is the classic recording of Shostakovich's harrowing tale of squalor, exploitation and betrayal."
High Fidelity 1:109 My '90. Ian Brunskill (b.n.)

"Just wait till this shocker hits CDV! Most of us will be content with Angel's reissue of its famous 1979 recording of the composer's original version. Indeed, I can't conceive of a more committed performance....Vishnevskaya has never done anything better on record."
American Record Guide 53:114 S/O '90. Lee Milazzo (300w)

"Vishnevskaya and Gedda are just a little too mature, the passion a bit overspent....the opera is too important, musically, historically, to be set aside for the sake of these imperfections. Until the ideal recording comes along it will serve."
Opera 41:1137-38 S '90. Andrew Clements (245w)

Digital Audio's CD Review 6:50+ Je '90. Octavio Roca (770w)

Gramophone 67:2053 My '90. Michael Oliver (475w)

SIBELIUS, JEAN

7126. Jungfrun i Tornet (The Maiden in the Tower (1896); Karelia Suite, Opus 11.
Neeme Jarvi (c). Mari Anne Haggander; Hakan Hagegard; Jorma Hynninen; Tone Kruse. Gothenburg Concert Hall Choir; Gothenburg Symphony Orchestra.
BIS 250 DDD 52:46

★*Awards:* *Fanfare* Want List 1984 (John Bauman).

"This issue is indispensable to all Sibelians."
American Record Guide 47:72 S'84. Carl Bauman (450w)

Digital Audio 2:54+ N '85. David C. Vernier (150w)

Hi-Fi News & Record Review 30:89 My '85. Edward Seckerson (80w)

High Fidelity 36:62 F '86. Bill Zakariasen (100w)

Gramophone 62:519-20 O '84 (755w); 62:1123 Mr '85 (210w). Robert Layton

Ovation 5:72 N '84. Thor Eckert, Jr. (700w)

Fanfare 8:260-2 N/D '84. Roger Dettmer (330w)

SMETANA, BEDRICH

7127. Libuse.
Zdenek Kosler (c). Gabriela Benackova-Capova; Eva Depoltova; Vera Soukupova; Vaclav Zitek. Prague Theater Orchestra; Prague Theater Chorus.
DENON/SUPRAPHON 7438/40 DDD 3 discs

★★*Awards:* *Opera News* Best of the Year, 1987; The Want List 1988, *Fanfare* N/D '88 (Justin R. Herman).

"In the main, the performance of this glorious paean to a people is done justice, especially by the orchestra and chorus...The soloists are a mixed bag, however."
High Fidelity 36:57 Mr '86. Bill Zakariasen (175w)

STRAUSS, JOHANN (II)

7128. Die Fledermaus.
Nikolaus Harnoncourt (c). Werner Hollweg (ten); Edita Gruberova (sop); Barbara Bonney (sop); Josef Protschka (ten); Marjana Lipovsek (contr). Netherlands Opera Chorus; Concertgebouw Orchestra.
TELDEC 35762 DDD 110:00 2 discs

★★*Awards:* The Want List 1988, *Fanfare* N/D '88 (Justin R. Herman). Best of the Year, *Opera News* D 24 '88.

"Not a quaint, stilted *Fledermaus* with its wings clipped but a fresh, pliant, natural one with all the accents, both musical and dramatic, put back to their proper emphasis and degree. The score is presented complete....With proportion restored, *Die Fledermaus* appears as a Viennese genre comedy rather than a tiresome paean to alcoholic escapism."
Opera News 53:42 Ja 7 '89. John W. Freeman (450w)

"A direct, sober, slightly contrived performance that I admire rather than warm to. Listen to the Czardas if you want to make up your mind—it seems to show the reading at its best and worst."
Opera 39:755-6 Je '88. Alan Blyth (450w)

"The question for the listener...is whether one wants a theatrical experience or an essay on Strauss' composition. This performance strikes me as the latter....The sound is superb."
Fanfare 11:255-6 Jl/Ag '88. Henry Fogel (650w)

"This release should be titled 'The music from *Die Fledermaus*'. It's clearly a documentation of a concert performance (though, it seems, without an audience), and even on those terms, it's flat champagne. Not that the cast is bad; it's the conductor whose rigid and often ponderous approach wet-blankets this affair."
American Record Guide 51:57-8 Jl/Ag '88. Kurt Moses (425w)

"The performance may lack the glossier talents of some of its rivals, but in general musical content and qualities of sound and balance, this new recording has decided and positive advantages."
Hi-Fi News & Record Review 33:85 Ag '88. Kenneth Dommett (490w)

Gramophone 65:1643 My '88. Andrew Lamb (415w)

Digital Audio 5:53-4 S '88. Octavio Roca (280w)

7129. Wiener Blut.
Otto Ackermann (c). Elisabeth Schwarzkopf; Nicolai Gedda; Erika Koth; Erich Kunz; Emmy Loose; Karl Donch; Alois Pernerstorfer. Philharmonia Chorus; Philharmonia Orchestra.
EMI 69529 (m) 70:00

★*Awards:* Best of the Year, *Opera News* D 24 '88.

"Conducting and singing...still sound close to perfection."
American Record Guide 52:124-25 Ja/F '89. Vivian A. Liff (85w)

STRAUSS, RICHARD

7130. Ariadne auf Naxos (2nd version, 1916).
Herbert Von Karajan (c). Elisabeth Schwarzkopf (sop); Rita Streich (sop); Irmgard Seefried (sop); Rudolf Schock (ten). Philharmonia Orchestra. 1955 reissue.
EMI 69296 (m) 128:00 2 discs

✔HC ★*Awards:* The Want List 1988, *Fanfare* N/D '88 (Ralph V. Lucano).

A "classic performance...the sound is warm and clear."
Opera Canada 14:50 Fall '88. Neil Croy (130w)

"CD's clarification of detail more than compensates for loss of a bit of the original LP's fullness. Karajan's conducting may not warm the music to the temperature of Karl Bohm's...but on the whole one will not find an equal in terms of style, elegance, grace or accuracy-....Apart from a weak Music Master, the cast is close to ideal."

Opera News 53:42 D 24 '88. C. J. Luten (140w)

"It's all too easy to eulogize a superior performance, ignoring the basic fact that, to many listeners, foreign-language opera and song without text is incomprehensible nonsense....Does EMI actually believe that a prospective purchaser would object to paying an extra dollar or two to better understand and enjoy a classic performance?"

Musical America 109:81-2 Ja '89. David Hurwitz (170w)

Hi-Fi News & Record Review 33:119 D '88. David Nice (315w)

Gramophone 65:1440 Ap '88. Michael Kennedy (375w)

7131. Ariadne auf Naxos (2nd version, 1916).
James Levine (c). Anna Tomowa-Sintow; Agnes Baltsa; Kathleen Battle; Gary Lakes; Hermann Prey. Vienna Philharmonic Orchestra. 1986.
DEUTSCHE GRAMMOPHON 419 225 DDD
124:54 2 discs

★★★★*Awards:* *Gramophone* Critics' Choice (Michael Kennedy), 1987; *Opera News* Best of the Year, 1987; First Place (Tie) Opera Mumm Champagne Classical Music Award 1988—Presented by *Ovation*, *Ovation* N '88. *Hi-Fi News & Record Review* Record of the Month, Ag '87.

"Sumptuous playing, and superb recording, for *Ariadne*'s welcome CD debut."

Music and Musicians International 36:43 O '87. Robert Hartford (70w)

One of 20 classical CDs reviewed and recommended as "outstanding for their musical interest and their performance as well as for their technical quality."

Stereo Review Presents: Compact Disc Buyer's Guide 1988 p.42. William Livingstone and Christie Barter (125w)

"The Vienna PO plays with velvety ease and stylistic poise throughout the new recording-...but it is the Zerbinetta of prologue and opera who steals the show. The American Kathleen Battle wanders among her highest notes as if she were gathering rosebuds (no pearls, real or artificial, here). The accuracy is impeccable, and she somehow makes exquisite music of a part that through lesser vocal cords can come out merely fussy or downright silly."

The Musical Times 128:699 D '87. Robert Anderson (270w)

"Perhaps no other ensemble in the world knows better or plays more lovingly this very special piece....Of her several recordings, this one shows Anna Tomowa-Sintow to best advantage....Kathleen Battle's Zerbinetta is staggering....Agnes Baltsa makes the Composer's youthful passion convincing....the recorded sound could hardly be improved upon."

Stereo Review 52:152+ D '87. Robert Ackart (480w)

"Tomowa-Sintow's Ariadne - surely the singer's most involved performance to date - challenges Schwarzkopf (Karajan) or Janowitz (Kempe) for tonal beauty, but far surpasses them in bringing a statue to life."

Hi-Fi News & Record Review 32:100 Ag '87

"Soprano Anna Tomowa-Sintow's account of the title role is a fine addition to recording annals....No one sings Zerbinetta's music quite like Kathleen Battle...[Levine's] approach is, at times, almost too reverential."

Opera Canada 28:50 Fall '87. Neil Crory (770w)

"This is a thoroughly enjoyable performance, although far from unflawed....Agnes Baltsa...is superb as the Composer....Hermann Prey's characterization of the Music Master is also excellently drawn and sung. Surprisingly, the 'cameo' introductions of the stars of Part Two don't make a good impression....These criticisms must be taken in the context of an extremely well-paced performance....that seems to allow the singers just enough time to breathe but never distorts the music's flow."

Ovation 10:52-3 Mr '89. Paul Turok (415w)

"Maybe it did deserve that Grammy."

High Fidelity 38:65 Ag '88. Paul Moor (725w)

"In this version, fine voices make beautiful sounds, but drama and characterization are largely left to the orchestra. If only the magnificent sound of the Vienna Philharmonic had been matched by a sense of excitement from the singers....So now for the glory of this set—the performance for which you should hasten forth to buy....Kathleen Battle ignores the possible technical obstacles and creates a character who projects the gentle, rueful irony which Hofmannsthal and Strauss intended. This is interpretive singing of the very highest order-....the sound of the CD is radiantly clear, with just enough stage presence."

Stereophile 11:173+ Ja '88. Harold Lynn (490w)

"*Ariadne*'s two 'acts'...are really two separate works...That said, the first 'work' fares rather better on this recording than the second, though neither can be recommended over performances previously (if, unfortunately, not currently) readily available."

Fanfare 11:215 Ja/F '88. Anthony D. Coggi (800w)

"James Levine's new set brings to seven the total of integral recordings...Despite the relative parity of casting credits and debits among [these]...one emerged from my comparative listening as distinctly preferable in theatrical, musical, and sonic terms...Kempe's Dresden set [1968, Angel]...If we are fortunate, it will have a revival on compact discs."

The Opera Quarterly 5:112-7 My '88. David Hamilton (2520w)

"Though the expressive terms of Levine's performance seem to me quite unacceptable, there is nothing technically mediocre about it. As always, Levine's empathy for his singers is exceptional...What is missing from Levine's performance is temperamental affinity for the opera's strengths...The opera is, on the whole, very well cast."

The Opera Quarterly 5:117-20 My '88. Dale Harris

"Recorded in the large hall of the Musikverein in Vienna, this *Ariadne auf Naxos*,,,comes across as self-important as the Major-domo played by Otto Schenk. Reproduction of instrumental timbres and balances is sharp, but the overall ambience tends toward resonance and generous bass in full-orchestra passages, making Strauss' chamber scoring sound more like a full symphony. And because the engineering places the listener so close to the pit, singers sometimes get overwhelmed...Counteracting this tendency is James Levine's adroit way of bringing out individual lines, both instrumental and vocal. Touches of brilliant casting help as well."

Opera News 52:72 O '87. John W. Freeman (340w)

Digital Audio 4:60-1 F '88. Brian J. Murphy (425w)

Gramophone 64:1595 My '87 Michael Kennedy (825w)

7132. Ariadne auf Naxos (2nd version, 1916).
Kurt Masur (c). Jessye Norman (sop); Julia Varady (sop); Edita Gruberova (sop); Paul Frey (ten); Dietrich Fischer-Dieskau (bar); Olaf Bar (bar); Gerd Wolf (bass); Martin Finke (ten); Eva Lind (sop); Marianne Rorholm (contr); Julie Kaufmann (sop); Rudolf Asmus. Leipzig Gewandhaus Orchestra. 1987.
PHILIPS 422 084 DDD 118:00 2 discs

★***Awards:*** Critics' Choice 1988, *Gramophone* D '88 (Michael Kennedy).

"Kurt Masur's new, admirably recorded version of the opera on Philips laudably captures its spirit and offers some fine interpretations, chief among them that of Masur himself-....Surely the title role has never been sung with greater amplitude of tone than it is here by Jessye Norman....Among the three recordings...on compact disc...a choice would not be easy."

Stereo Review 54:119 Mr '89. Robert Ackart (425w)

"This present recording now becomes the *Ariadne* of choice on CD."

Ovation 10:65-7 Ap '89. Robert Levine (330w)

"In addition to the generally high musical standards, the big attraction is the combination of Norman as Ariadne and Frey as Bacchus....Stylish support is provided by Masur and the orchestra."

Opera Canada 15:51 Summ '89. John Kraglund (225w)

"There is not quite so much sense of purpose and direction in Kurt Masur's leadership of the new *Ariadne*...his reading generates a gemutlich quality that suits the score extraordinarily well....Ariadne is not Jessye Norman's best role, but she brings it a mixture of warmth and deadpan nobility, plus that gleaming sound in the expansive moments....The choice catch of this cast is Julia Varady's purposeful, impulsive, high-strung Composer, focused with searing intensity, commanding a wide, mercurially shifting emotional range....Though the orchestra plays and sounds well, the recording somewhat undercuts the singers, especially Norman."

Opera News 53:42 Mr 4 '89. John W. Freeman (325w)

"This present recording now becomes the *Ariadne* of choice on CD. The only drawback I can find on this set is the rather uninspired leadership of Kurt Masur, who simply conducts without much charm...the playfulness and chamber-like feel are lacking. His soloists are, for the most part, superb....The recording is big and exciting and clear, although I found the voices a bit too closely miked."

Stereophile 12:220-21 Je '89. Robert Levine (275w)

"A most effective interpretation, although it falls just short of James Levine's recent version for Deutsche Grammophon."

The New York Times Mr 19 '89, p. 28. John Rockwell (200w)

"If you want a stereo *Ariadne*, you have two choices: Levine on DG...or this new set from Masur....Tallying up pluses and minuses for each cast, I'd reckon they come out even, but when I add the conductors, the balance tips slightly toward Levine. Toss a coin, buy both, or decide on the basis of whichever singers and roles are most important to you."

Fanfare 12:289-90 Mr/Ap '89. Ralph V. Lucano (705w)

"This will be know as the Norman *Ariadne*, which is a pity since Philips'...prima donna is this new set's least marketable asset....I can't readily accept the blowsy unsteadiness which has crept into the notes around the middle of the stave...she remains the visiting Diva descending on, rarely involved in, the performance. Which is a pity, since much else here is wondrously right."

Hi-Fi News & Record Review 33:119 D '88. Hugh Canning (560w)

Gramophone 66:862-68 N '88. Michael Kennedy (665w)

7133. Capriccio, Opus 83.
Wolfgang Sawallisch (c). Elisabeth Schwarzkopf; Eberhard Waechter; Nicolai Gedda; Dietrich Fischer-

Dieskau. Philharmonia Orchestra. 1957 reissue.
EMI 49014 ADD (m) 135:00 2 discs

★★*Awards:* *Gramophone* Critics' Choice (Alan Blyth), 1987; The Want List 1988, *Fanfare* N/D '88 (James Miller).

"To hear Schwarzkopf in a Strauss opera is to experience something quite unique...And just listen to what is going on around her!...Then there are the glories Sawallisch finds in the Philharmonia Orchestra...This is one of the great EMI opera sets and still sounds excellent in the mono transfers."
Hi-Fi News & Record Review 33:104 S '88. Hugh Canning (350w)

"The Sawallisch *Capriccio* is a recording for the ages, a meeting of some of the greatest singers of their time operating near the top of their form, and EMI has presented it in an appropriately classy way."
Fanfare 11:216 Ja/F '88. James Miller (620w)

"No version of the delectable *Capriccio* [is] guaranteed to give such unalloyed pleasure as this thirty-year-old product of Walter Legge's genius in the recording studio. His ensemble is well-nigh perfect."
Music and Musicians International 36:50-1 F '88. Robert Hartford (225w)

"I have already worn out one set of *Capriccio* LPs....This new CD set already sounds better than the records ever did, even when they were new—crisper, cleaner, richer."
Ovation 9:46 Ja '89. Dick Adler (180w)

"The CD transfer, though a trifle low-level in the opening scene, betters its vinyl predecessor in definition. As in the original...the orchestra continues to sue for parity with the voices."
Opera News 53:43 D 24 '88. C. J. Luten (140w)

Musical America 108:66-7 Jl '88. Thomas Hathaway (990w)

Digital Audio 4:66-7 Mr '88. Octavio Roca (480w)

Gramophone 65:818 N '87 Alan Blyth (525w)

7134. Daphne, Opus 82.
Karl Bohm (c). Hilde Gueden (sop); James King (ten); Vera Little (contr); Paul Schoeffler (bass); Fritz Wunderlich (ten); Hans Braun (bar); Kurt Equiluz (ten). Vienna State Opera Chorus; Vienna Symphony Orchestra. Theater an der Wien, Vienna. 1964 live.
DEUTSCHE GRAMMOPHON 423 579 ADD 95:00 2 discs

★*Awards:* Critics' Choice 1988, *Gramophone* D '88 (Michael Kennedy).

"I doubt whether this 'live' performance...can ever be superseded, not only because...the casting reflects a living tradition of native German Strauss singing which has all but vanished today."
Hi-Fi News & Record Review 34:117-8 Ja '89. Hugh Canning (385w)

"This is an historical document as well as a most enjoyable performance of an opera that rarely sees the light of day."
Music and Musicians International 37:63 Ja '89. Robert Hartford (245w)

"Deutsche Grammphon *does* provide a German-English libretto. So, although I think that Haitink, with some slightly slower tempos, actually milks a little more out of the score, Bohm has a better cast and better support and his, with virtually the same interior access points, would be my choice, despite his making three cuts, two of them in Apollo's music, one in Daphne's. They're not big ones."
Fanfare 12:294-300 Mr/Ap '89. James Miller (630w)

Gramophone 66:675-6 O '88. Michael Kennedy (320w)

7135. Elektra, Opus 58.
Seiji Ozawa (c). Hildegard Behrens (sop); Christa Ludwig (mez); Nadine Secunde (sop); Ragnar Ulfung (ten); Jorma Hynninen (bar); Brian Matthews (bass); Emily Rawlins (sop). Tanglewood Festival Chorus; Boston Symphony Orchestra. Boston Symphony Hall. November 1988 live.
PHILIPS 422 574 DDD 102:00 2 discs

★★*Awards:* Best Recordings of the Month, *Stereo Review* Ag '89. Top Choices—1989, *American Record Guide* Ja/F '90 (Kurt Moses).

"The *Elektra* orchestra requires about 115 musicians...Its full, visceral impact has been better captured by Philips in this new release than by the other two commercial recordings of the LP era...That is one reason why this is a highly commendable release. There are others, however....While the London set has Nilsson and Collier and is uncut, overall I would recommend this Philips as the best *Elektra* available today."
American Record Guide 52:123-24 N/D '89. Kurt Moses (825w)

"It is difficult to imagine a more fully realized performance of *Elektra*...no other recording of it [*Elektra*] surpasses the present one."
Stereo Review 54:71-2 Ag '89. Robert Ackart (725w)

"The double culmination of Wagnerian musical and sexual excess helps make the title role one of the most overwhelmingly difficult, even impossible roles in all the repertoire....The triumph of this recording is Hildegard Behrens' successful compromise between youthful pruri-ence and heavy Germanic wailing....The rest of the cast sings admirably and the orchestral fireworks are well managed by Seiji Ozawa."
Ovation 10:56-7 S '89. Philip Kennicott (425w)

"So much heat is generated in this performance that one is tempted to get the fire extinguisher....Ozawa might not have been everyone's first choice to conduct *Elektra*, but he comes through with flying colors, as does his orchestra....Orchestrally, this set has everything. The vocalists are to be reckoned with as well....The sound is spacious and spotless-...Highest recommendation—an experience not to be missed."

Stereophile 13:237+ Ja '90. Robert Levine (435w)

"I would absolutely recommend this *Elektra*, particularly for Christa Ludwig's performance."

HighPerformanceReview 7:1:89 '90. Barbara Kierig (235w)

"As 'live' recordings go, this set is a superior example of the genre from the engineering standpoint. The sound is full, clear, and well balanced....The real star of this performance is the Boston Symphony. The orchestral playing is on the highest level, actually more focused and dynamically varied than that of the Vienna Philharmonic, under Solti....most of the opera is beautifully *and* excitingly done....the cast, with certain inevitable reservations, is extremely strong....For most CD collectors, the choice will be between this set and London's-....I recommend acquisition of either...both, if affordable; their virtues are complementary."

The Opera Quarterly 7:240-43 Spr '90. Roland Graeme (1535w)

"At last!—competition for Nilsson and Solti some 20 years after their Decca *Elektra*, and from a generally thrilling recording which might well have claimed superiority, if it had not been for one major disappointment....the first thing to commend in it is the exceptionally high standard of playing that Seiji Ozawa gets from his Boston orchestra....For Hildegard Behrens's Elektra one can only have enormous admiration....the Klytemnestra of Christa Ludwig....is alone well worth the price of the discs....Why, then, the disappointment? Simply this: the score is cut as heavily as it ever has been in live performances."

Opera 40:498-99 Ap '89. Richard Fairman (1050w)

"There are, in broad terms, two ways to conduct *Elektra*—as a jumping-off point either for what Strauss might have become (like Schoenberg, Berg et al.), or for what he did become (i.e., *Der Rosenkavalier*). Seiji Ozawa adopts the latter course, and though it builds splendidly to its climax, the reading is memorable more for its lushness and tonal power than for any febrile or neurasthenic qualities....A strong, committed performance by a major set of artists. A drawback: Ozawa takes the standard cuts."

Opera News 54:31-2 Ag '89. Patrick J. Smith (500w)

"Ozawa's relative inexperience of the theatre disadvantages this issue...a pity because there is some distinguished singing and characterisation here....Philips have recorded the concerts in a natural and clean ambience and there are mercifully few of the 'horror' effects so beloved of John Culshaw."

Hi-Fi News & Record Review 34:85 Jl '89. Hugh Canning (665w)

"Ozawa's *Elektra*, then, is an uneven affair, its compelling middle tableaux set in a battered frame. Despite its flaws, it still packs considerable punch, and for that we must thank Ozawa, the Boston Symphony, and Strauss himself. It should not be anyone's only recording of the opera....Most essential for the *Elektra* library are Reiner's set of excerpts (RCA 5603) and Solti's complete recording (London 417 345)."

Fanfare 13:369-71 N/D '89. Ralph V. Lucano (1040w)

"What we are left with is an unexpectedly well conducted *Elektra* with no Elektra to speak of, a very fine Klytemnestra, and a remaining cast that at best fits all too squarely into the workaday category. Alas, poor Behrens—she once sang well, when firmly in her repertoire....this [is] the least recommendable *Elektra* currently available."

Musical America 110:85-6 Mr '90. Thor Eckert Jr. (1120w)

Gramophone 66:1638 Ap '89. Alan Blyth (875w)

Digital Audio's CD Review 6:73-4 O '89. Sebastian Russ (535w)

7136. Elektra, Opus 58.

Wolfgang Sawallisch (c). Eva Marton (sop); Marjana Lipovsek (contr); Cheryl Studer (sop); Hermann Winkler (ten); Bernd Weikl (bar); Carmen Anhorn (sop); Daphne Evangelatos (contr); Shirley Close (mez); Birgit Calm (mez); Julie Faulkner (sop); Caroline Maria Petrig (sop); Kurt Moll (bass); Victoria Wheeler (sop). Bavarian Radio Chorus; Bavarian Radio Symphony Orchestra.
EMI 54067 DDD 102:00 2 discs

★*Awards:* Editor's Choice, *Opera Canada*, Spr '91.

"An effective performance of *Elektra* is still about as overpowering an emotional experience as the opera stage has to offer, and virtually every aspect of this one achieves the desired impact. Under Wolfgang Sawallisch's command, the reading pulsates with the blood of tragedy....As the pathologically obsessed Mycenean princess, Eva Marton gives a blazing performance...Cheryl Studer is a richly feminine Chrysothemis, and while offering one of the best-*sung* Klytamnestras on record, Marjana Lipovsek's vivid histrionics conjure up a heady vision of the degenerate queen....All in all, a major addition to the catalogue." *PS 100*

Opera Canada 32:51 Spr 91. Harvey Chusid (220w)

"The orchestra—both its playing and its reproduction—sounds absolutely stupendous in this album....Aside from the handling of Klytamnestra's final shrieks, too close to make their ghastly effect, this is an outstandingly engineered recording and a vivid account of *Elektra*."

Opera News 56:36 Ag '91. John W. Freeman (275w)

"Three of the finest sopranos around storm their way through Strauss's passionate Elektra. Conductor Wolfgang Sawallisch drives them on, creating a glorious, passionate sound."

High Fidelity 3:98 Mr '91. Clive Manning (b.n.)

"This newest recording doesn't turn out to be completely satisfying. Its greatest assets are its Chrysothemis, its completeness, and its deep, detailed orchestral sound. Its most crippling drawback is its Elektra; and no matter how charitable my impulses, I'm hard put to find redeeming features in her....My *Elektra* recommendations from *Fanfare* 13:2 still stand. The best recording is Solti's (London), with Nilsson and Resnik."

Fanfare 14:396-7 Mr/Ap '91. Ralph V. Lucano (1000w)

"Eva Marton has both power and authority for the role and she's aided by Cheryl Studer, who is superb, as her sister Chrysothemis."

High Fidelity 3:105 F '91. Clive Manning (100w)

"This is the best-conducted and the best-recorded *Elektra* we have. Also, it's complete and uncut, unlike the Philips and DG versions. But, as you may have guessed already, it's not the best sung...Texts and translations are included in this well-produced set, which also has lots of access points."

American Record Guide 54:125-26 Mr/Ap '91. Kurt Moses (375w)

"Instead of milking the score's shock value, Wolfgang Sawallisch has pursued Strauss's generous indications of the undestroyed portion of the spirits of Elektra and her family, each of whom is created with a serving of the composer's most urgent as well as most beautiful music. The obvious difficulty is the scale of the resources required. To dramatize the situations of Elektra and her sister, mother, and brother, Strauss requires voices of tremendous size, range, and beauty, which he pushes to their limits in assorted ways. But what we almost inevitably hear are singers stretched *beyond* their limits."

Musical America 111:86 My '91. Kenneth Furie (530w)

Gramophone 68:1271 D '90. Alan Blyth (1265w)

7137. Elektra, Opus 58.

Georg Solti (c). Birgit Nilsson; Tom Krause; Regina Resnik; Gerhard Stolze; Marie Collier. 1967.
LONDON/DECCA 417 345 AAD 53:34; 54:16 2 discs

★*Awards:* The Want List 1988, *Fanfare* N/D '88 (Don C. Seibert).

"Nilsson for two decades was *the* Elektra in the world's major houses, and it is good to have her brilliant performance permanently preserved on Compact Disc....Regina Resnik is a superb Klytemnestra, both vocally and histrionically....Georg Solti's direction is dynamic, but rather insensitive....London's recording is remarkable....The only Compact Disc competition...is totally out-classed by this London set."

Musical America 107:62 Jl '87 Robert E. Benson (350w)

"Nilsson is awesome....Solti, brilliant and fervent, needs only a touch of ease in the recognition scene to fill all Strauss' requirements."

Opera News 53:43 D 24 '88. C. J. Luten (140w)

"'Neurasthenics beware': Solti's urgent 1967 recording spares none of this ever-startling opera's horrors, and the CD transfer renders Culshaw's 'Sonicstage' tricks and manners still more stomach-churningly vivid."

Hi-Fi News & Record Review 32:113 Ja '87 David Nice (215w)

Fanfare 10:189-90 Jl/Ag '87 Vincent Alfano (525w)

Gramophone 64:929-30 D '86 Alan Blyth (360w)

7138. Elektra, Opus 58 (excerpts); Salome: Dance; Final Scene.

Fritz Reiner (c). Inge Borkh (sop); Frances Yeend (sop); Paul Schoeffler (bar). Chicago Symphony Orchestra. reissue.
RCA 5603

★★★★*Awards:* *Opus* Christmas List, 1987 (Kenneth Furie); *Fanfare* Want List 1987 (Peter J. Rabinowitz). The Want List 1988, *Fanfare* N/D '88 (Don C. Seibert); Records to Die for: 1 of 5 Recommended Recordings, *Stereophile* Ja '91 (Richard Schneider).

"If RCA had recorded *Elektra* complete with these forces, it could have joined the Callas/Da Sabata *Tosca* as the 'other' most perfect opera recording ever made. As it is, these excerpts offer a compelling reminder of what dramatic singing, potent conducting, great orchestral playing, and natural stereo miking could produce during the 1950s....This CD is absolutely guaranteed to leave you limp and exhausted, but *not* from listening fatigue."

Stereophile 14:167 Ja '91. Richard Schneider (b.n.)

Opus 4:55 D '87. Kenneth Furie (90w)

7139. Die Frau ohne Schatten.

Wolfgang Sawallisch (c). Cheryl Studer (sop); Rene Kollo (ten); Ute Vinzing (sop); Alfred Muff (bass-bar); Hanna Schwarz (mez); Andreas Schmidt (bar); Julie Kaufmann (sop); Cyndia Sieden (sop). Tolz Boys' Choir; Bavarian Radio Chorus; Bavarian Radio Symphony Orchestra.
EMI 49074 DDD 191:00 3 discs

★★★★★*Awards:* Record of the Month, *Hi-Fi News & Record Review* N '88; Critics' Choice 1988, *Gramophone* D '88 (Michael Kennedy). The Want List 1989, *Fanfare* N/D '89 (Henry Fogel; Ralph V. Lucano); Top Disks of the Year, *The New York Times* D 24, '89 (John Rockwell); Top Choices—1989, *American Record Guide* Ja/F '90 (Kurt Moses).

"I urge you to hear this performance of a remarkable work. It is singularly beautiful, a vision of a world that never was, yet still might be, a world transfigured, a world that should be."

American Record Guide 52:92-3 Mr/Ap '89. Charles H. Parsons (775w)

"It is in its overall impact...that the new recording shines....In his leadership and interpretation, Sawallisch has proved himself a worthy successor to Karl Bohm, hitherto peerless in his handling of this score."

Stereo Review 54:170 F '89. Robert Ackart (405w)

"Mr. Sawallisch is, to this taste, not always an entirely persuasive conductor; his performances can sound perfunctory. But here he surpasses himself, and so do his orchestra and the EMI recording engineers. The cast is headed by Cheryl Studer's radiant Empress; why this fine American soprano has been so underrepresented at the Metropolitan Opera remains one of that house's casting anomalies."

The New York Times Mr 19 '89, p. 28. John Rockwell (375w)

"A masterpiece of epic stagecraft at last stands revealed in this performance....All that would count for less if the singers were unwilling to rise to their characters' respective crises....the playing is cultured but never tepid, and the supporting roles...are typical of the general polish. Like the opera, it's a generous labour of love, and generously flawed."

Hi-Fi News & Record Review 33:101 N '88. (830w)

"Sawallisch's new recording has one great advantage: it's absolutely complete....I wish the performance were better, but I'm sure there aren't a lot of singers lining up to record these difficult roles....The recorded sound is sumptuous....It's brought me vast pleasure in spite of my few strictures, and I'm sure it will do the same for all lovers of Strauss."

Fanfare 12:293-94 Mr/Ap '89. Ralph V. Lucano (1150w)

"Its only competition on compact discs is from the 'live' (1977) Karl Bohm performance recorded by Deutsche Grammophone...to which it is superior in all but two respects."

Ovation 10:67-8 Ap '89. Paul Turok (785w)

"The first uncut album of this large, noisy, difficult opera....Though Sawallisch is a more temperate conductor than Bohm, he understands the Strauss orchestral idiom equally well, and his cast for the most part is excellent. The one exception is Ute Vinzing....In general the teamwork of this group is awesome, with Sawallisch keeping things sorted out."

Opera News 53:48 My '89. John W. Freeman (375w)

"The leading singers in this new *Frau* range from the superlative to the disappointing....The real star of this recording is conductor Wolfgang Sawallisch, whose overall concept and judicious balancing of textures prove equally remarkable....In sum, although it has its flaws, this *Frau* offers many splendors."

High Fidelity 39:58-9 My '89. Robert E. Benson (875w)

"Wolfgang Sawallisch, I feel, is the true villain of the present undertaking. He is utterly scrupulous in his observance of dynamic markings as so is his cast, but there is more to Strauss than that. He appears to have no concept of the grandeur, intensity, and sweep of this work."

The Opera Quarterly 6:152-53 Spring '89. Robert Levine (875w)

"The CD is well balanced but rather lacking in feeling. It is a cold recording. The cast is variable....It is not an inspired reading."

Music and Musicians International 36:38-40 S '88. E. J. Benarroch (1415w)

"To make a long story short, it is a failure on practically every important level."

Stereophile 12:221+ Je '89. Robert Levine (650w)

Gramophone 66:481 S '88. Michael Kennedy (560w)

Digital Audio's CD Review 6:62 F '90. Octavio Roca (550w)

7140. Der Rosenkavalier, Opus 59.

Herbert Von Karajan (c). Elisabeth Schwarzkopf (sop); Otto Edelmann (bass); Christa Ludwig (mez); Teresa Stich-Randall (sop); Eberhard Waechter (bar); Ljuba Welitsch (sop). Loughton High School for Girls' Choir; Bancroft's School Chorus; Philharmonia Chorus; Philharmonia Orchestra. 1959 reissue.
EMI 49354 ADD 191:00 3 discs

✓HC ★***Awards:*** Remastered CDs Record Award 1988, *Gramophone* O '88.

"This justly celebrated performance needs little from me to commend it...Well worth ditching your LPs for."

Music and Musicians International 36:59 Ja '88. Robert Hartford (190w)

"A testimonial to digital art. Only the briefly available two-track tape came close to matching the clarity of sound now available."

Opera News 53:42 D 24 '88. C. J. Luten (140w)

"This is a generally strong performance."

Fanfare 11:209-10 Mr/Ap '88. James Miller (750w)

"If you followed EMI's libretto instead of the score, you would perhaps remain ignorant of this recording's principal flaw: two hefty cuts in Act I, three in Act II, and no fewer than seven in Act III....You will here some glorious singing here, though, and brilliant, virtuoso orchestral playing, and a performance of the final trio that at its climax attains a musical incandescence approaching levitation."

Musical America 109:81 Ja '89. Paul Moor (345w)

"For some [Schwarzkopf as Marschallin is] a likeable portrait of detailed character; for others (myself included) a mannered study of a woman whose musical personality is applied from outside, like make-up. Edelmann is endearingly dialect-ridden, Ludwig touchingly eloquent, Stich-Randall vocally virginal. Karajan's general pacing is good, and the acoustic quality of the reissue makes it deserving of new attention."

Opera 39:1387-8 N '88. Noel Goodwin (190w)

"For all the cleaning and defining which remasterings have achieved, that '57 sound can't give us the exaggerated edge of brass and wind with which Decca so splendidly gilded Solti's 1969 reading. Solti, besides, tolerates none of the numerous small cuts Karajan makes in the outer acts."

Hi-Fi News & Record Review 33:104-5 Ap '88. David Nice (375w)

Gramophone 65:1119 Ja '88. Hilary Finch (430w); 66:553 O '88. John Borwick (200w)

7141. Der Rosenkavalier: Suite; Die Frau ohne Schatten: Suite.
Antal Dorati (c). Detroit Symphony Orchestra.
LONDON/DECCA 411 893 45:33

★*Awards:* *Gramophone* Critics' Choice 1985 (Andrew Lamb).

"What we hear in this recording is sheer glory. As with the recent Bartok issue, the glory is enhanced no little by recorded sound that is itself of demonstration class."

Stereo Review 51:83 Ap '86. Richard Freed (400w)

Gramophone 63:354 S '85. Andrew Lamb (245w) (rev. of LP); 63:798 D '85. Geoffrey Horn (105w) (rev. of CD)

Fanfare 9:222 Ja/F '86. James Miller (350w)

Hi-Fi News & Record Review 30:107 N '85. Sue Hu(200w)

STRAVINSKY, IGOR. Le Rossignol; Mavra; The Rake's Progress; Oedipus Rex.
See No. 1425.

SZOKOLAY, SANDOR

7142. Blood Wedding (1964).
Andras Korodi (c). Erzsebet Hazy (sop); Erzsebet Komlossy (alto); Ferenc Szonyi (ten); Andras Farago (bar); Margit Szilvassy (sop); Stefania Moldovan (sop); Anita Szabo (contr); Endre Varhelyi (bass); Iren Szecsodi (sop); Sandor Palcso (ten); Zsuzsa Barlay (contr). Hungarian Radio and Television Children's Chorus; Hungarian State Opera Chorus and Orchestra. reissue.
HUNGAROTON 11262/3 ADD 53:56, 51:58 2 discs

★*Awards:* The Want List 1990, *Fanfare* N/D '90 (Henry Fogel).

"Thoughts of Bartok, Janacek, and Britten are not misplaced here: *Blood Wedding* belongs in such company. It is one of the most exciting operas of the last half century, although not the most subtle. This presentation is all one could ask, and it is enthusiastically recommended to everyone."

Fanfare 13:315-16 Mr/Ap '90. James H. North (790w)

"Eureka! This is it! Go for it! I don't know when I've been so excited about a new opera-....The performance is about all one could ask for, not one weak link in a cast of singing-actors (the true opera singer), committed to giving their all to a work they must believe in. I must single out especially Erzsebet Komlossy's Mother. This performance is beyond interpretation; this is life itself. I am in awe."

American Record Guide 53:119 My/Je '90. Charles Parsons (280w)

"Here is it: a major 20th century opera, quite unknown in this country. The excitement generated on the first hearing makes one hope that some company will snap up this musical feast and stage it as soon as possible....first-rate cast-....first-class recording....Highly recommended."

HighPerformanceReview 7:78-9 Winter '90-91. June C. Ottenberg (630w)

"From the opening bars of this opera the listener knows he is in the grips of some powerful storytelling....The performance and recording are about all one could ask for. The stereo separation is a bit artificial (that is, characters who are speaking to one another are not together; apparently this was done to clarify the vocal lines); I have no complaints."

Stereophile 13:227+ D '90. Robert Levine (270w)

Gramophone 68:1728+ Mr '91. Michael Oliver (630w)

TCHAIKOVSKY, PIOTR ILYICH

7143. Eugen Onegin, Opus 24.
James Levine (c). Thomas Allen (bar); Mirella Freni (sop); Neil Shicoff (ten); Anne-Sofie von Otter (mez); Paata Burchuladze (bass); Rosemarie Lang (mez); Ruthild Engert (mez); Michel Senechal (ten); Jurgen Hartfiel (bass); Gunter Emmerlich (bass). Leipzig Radio Chorus; Staatskapelle Dresden.
DEUTSCHE GRAMMOPHON 423 959 DDD 149:00 2 discs

★★★★★*Awards:* Critics Pick Some Favorites of the Year, *The New York Times* N 26, '89 (Barrymore L. Scherer); The Want List 1989, *Fanfare* N/D '89 (Don C. Seibert); Top Disks of the Year, *The New York Times* D 24, '89 (John Rockwell); Top Choices—1989, *American Record Guide* Ja/F '90 (Lawrence Hansen; George Loomis; Lee Milazzo).

"Perhaps there will be a recorded *Eugene Onegin* someday with a flawless Bolshoi cast under a top-notch conductor, to be universally recognized as the dream performance of this beautiful opera. None of the four Russian-origin productions that have emerged so far has fit that description...The choice is thus limited to two excellent West European entries: a 1974 account led by Sir Georg Solti (London 417 423-2) and this new set...My preference is for the DG, by a fairly comfortable margin."

Musical America 109:77 S '89. George Jellinek (330w)

"Levine's cast is as good as could be assembled today. Mirella Freni proves she is not just another pretty Mimi by offering a Tatyana of striking depth....All in all, this is a most distinguished production."

American Record Guide 52:109-10 S/O '89. Lee Milazzo (535w)

"The performance is driven with fully credible dramatic intensity; it could be more touching at some points, more subtly shaded at others, but it is hard to imagine it made more exciting or passionately charged. The foundation of that tension is the playing of the Dresden Staatskapelle and the singing of the Leipzig Chorus, both of whom give Levine tremendous support....Both Thomas Allen and Mirella Freni are capable of matching that passion most comprehensively."

Opera 40:374-76 Mr '89. Andrew Clements (750w)

"So integrated is the new recording that it is impossible to select a 'star,' but certainly James Levine merits highest commendation. His molding of the score is such that many nuances are heard afresh, and his exciting sense of orchestral coloration greatly enhances the performance throughout."

Stereo Review 54:92 Ap '89. Robert Ackart (430w)

"Freni is able to capture its [the role's] abandon and intensity as well as its vulnerable uncertainty....James Levine conducts with a satisfying blend of objectivity and dramatic concern, never falling to the lure of bathos."

Opera News 53:44 Je '89. John W. Freeman (420w)

"I've collected all the commercially issued *Onegins* I could get my hands on, and Levine's seems to me to be the most excitingly paced and beautifully shaped of any of them-....the singing...is quite uneven....The sound is rich and vibrant....My general recommendation is to buy this recording, whatever its imperfections."

Fanfare 13:340-42 S/O '89. Don C. Seibert (1250w)

"None of Levine's supporting ladies has quite the smiling charm of any of Solti's; Burchuladze's Gremin is another bland, big voice to set beside Ghaiurov. But the protagonists matter most, and in Freni and Allen you have an experienced, complex team unlikely to be surpassed."

Hi-Fi News & Record Review 34:93 My '89. David Nice (595w)

"It is the orchestra to which one's attention is continually drawn....this is a blandly sung 'Onegin,' one sung in Russian by a predominantly Western cast."

The New York Times Mr 5 '89, p. 29. Mark Swed (300w)

Gramophone 66:1497 Mr '89. John Warrack (840w)

TELEMANN, GEORG PHILIPP

7144. Der Geduldige Socrates.

Nicholas McGegan (c). Jozsef Gregor (bass); Eva Bartfai-Barta (sop); Julia Paszthy (sop); Guy De Mey (ten); Paul Esswood (counterten). Savaria Vocal Ensemble; Capella Savaria.
HUNGAROTON 12957/60 DDD 69:49; 61:33; 51:28; 60:47 4 discs

★*Awards:* Critics' Choice 1988, *Gramophone* D '88 (Nicholas Anderson).

"Every role requires virtuoso singing, and none of the cast is disappointing. McGegan...has the score well under control....The engineering is splendid....This is a long term contribution to the record catalog, and no use trying to improve on it in the foreseeable future."

Fanfare 11:219 Mr/Ap '88. J. F. Weber (575w)

"The performance is excellent, especially the male singers....The recorded sound favors the singers, but has the kind of wide dynamic range that requires one's volume control to be set carefully."

American Record Guide 51:69-70 My/Je '88. George W. Loomis (800w)

"The Capella Savaria performs on either authentic period instruments or accurate reproductions, and under McGegan's command presents a historically correct and undeniably pleasurable achievement. Jozsef Gregor gives an endearing portrayal as Socrates, although his thick Hungarian accent and Austrian-influenced pronunciation occasionally garble the German. Eva Bartfai-Barta and Julia Paszthy complement Gregor's sonorous bass voice with their bright, sometimes ear-piercing brilliance."

The Opera Quarterly 6:118-9 Autumn '88. Christopher J. Thomas (945w)

"The Capella Savaria seems to be the Baroque house band at Hungaroton, and they are very fine indeed....In this recording they have arranged to return not only to the lower pitch of the time, but also to use the pre-Bach untempered tuning."

Stereophile 11:183 Je '88. Harold Lynn (480w)

"The recording's strengths are its good humor and unflagging liveliness; also the stylish orchestra and various continuo groups, invigorated by McGegan's controlling hand, are fine. A major asset is bass Jozsef Gregor...The recording's weakness is the inconsistency of many of the singers."

HighPerformanceReview 5:91 S '88. Rodney Shewan (160w)

"Though there are lengthy recitatives, the cast packs them full of emotion and meaning."

Fanfare 13:497 S/O '89. Nick Rossi (225w)

"Students of baroque opera and the German singspiel will be interested in the recording as a document. Nicholas McGegan and his predominantly Hungarian forces give it their best effort, and for the most part the singing is cheerfully competent or better."

Opera News 54:30 Ja 20 '90. John W. Freeman (410w)

Digital Audio 5:56+ D '88. Sebastian Russ (550w)

Gramophone 65:1643-4 My '88. Nicholas Anderson (1500w)

The New York Times Je 19 '88, p. H27. John Rockwell (550w)

THOMSON, VIRGIL

7145. The Mother of Us All.

Raymond Leppard (c). Mignon Dunn (mez); James Atherton (ten); Philip Booth (bass); Linn Maxwell (sop); Helen Vanni (sop); Batyah Godfrey (mez); William Lewis (ten). Santa Fe Opera Orchestra. 1977 reissue.

NEW WORLD 288/9 AAD 61:01, 46:06 2 discs

> ★*Awards:* Critic's Choice: 1990, *American Record Guide* Ja/F '91 (Ralph Lucano).

"This is music that speaks to something in the American soul particularly, and we all share the capacity to respond to it in a way no foreigner could....The large cast is capable and apparently involved...The CD package lacks the copious annotations of the LP set, but a full libretto is included. The sound is quite good. Very heartily recommended."

American Record Guide 53:126 S/O '90. Ralph V. Lucano (785w)

"Virgil Thomson's and Gertrude Stein's glorious recreation of America past is hereby welcomed to compact discs, which are a tremendous improvement over the poorly pressed 1977 LPs....In short, the opera comes alive; Stein's poetry benefits as much as Thomson's music."

Fanfare 13:293-94 Jl/Ag '90. James H. North (420w)

"Limited though it is, the document is a worthy one. Not only is it the only recording ever made of the composer's 1947 collaboration with librettist Gertrude Stein, it is also a bright, energetic thing whose performances across the board—from the singing of the major roles to the stentorian thwackings of the bass drum—convey the sassy, and sometimes sentimental, whimsy of the opera as a whole. The recorded sound...is respectable—no more."

Musical America 111:82 Ja '91. James Wierzbicki (185w)

"This performance, recorded in 1977 in a theatrical ambience, benefits greatly from Leppard's sympathetic direction and a talented cast who wrestle skillfully with the dislocations of emphasis Thomson frequently imposes on the simplest lines. Whatever we may think of the artistic merits—I almost wrote pretensions—of such works we should be thankful to have at least one of the Thomson/Stein twins to tweak our ears and tease our intellects." *P95 S95/85*

Hi-Fi News & Record Review 35:107 O '90. Kenneth Dommett (360w)

Gramophone 68:276 Jl '90. Peter Dickinson (600w)

VERDI, GIUSEPPE

7146. Aida.

Herbert Von Karajan (c). Renata Tebaldi (sop); Giulietta Simionato (mez); Carlo Bergonzi (ten); Cornell MacNeil (bar); Arnold Van Mill (bass); Fernando Corena (bass); Piero De Palma (ten); Eugenia Ratti (sop). Vienna Singverein; Vienna Philharmonic Orchestra. 1959 reissue.

LONDON/DECCA 414 087 ADD 149:00 3 discs

> ★*Awards:* Records to Die for: 1 of 5 Recommended Recordings, *Stereophile* Ja '91 (Gary A. Galo).

"Renata Tebaldi is captured in one of her best roles, and Carlo Bergonzi *sings* Rhadames with a velvety tone and impeccable legato that eludes any of today's tenors....The recording is opulent and spacious, with realistic depth, flattering Karajan's approach to the score."

Stereophile 14:137 Ja '91. Gary A. Galo (b.n.)

"This is a difficult performance to get a handle on. On the one hand, it's an utterly masterful rendition of the music; on the other hand, it's an eccentric interpretation of the opera. When buffs discuss the great recordings of *Aida*, this is one of those that will be prominently mentioned....Other recordings have outstanding performances in some roles (Callas, Price, Vickers, Gobbi, to name a few) but this cast has no weak spots and the performance itself is so different, so individualistic, and so fascinating that, while it's too off-center to be number one, I'd suggest it as everyone's *second Aida*."

Fanfare 12:268-70 Jl/Ag '89. James Miller (1200w)

"This album was one of [Karajan's]...early examples of letting the orchestra take precedence over voices, who often sound placed in more distant perspective, almost like a secondary element in the texture. We also hear the conductor's fondness for tempos that are certainly unconventional and could even be called erratic, a preponderant slowness that can sometimes veer to the other extreme, with a range of dynamics also startling in its time. Those who can accept the conductor's approach will hear some memorable examples of Verdian vocal idiom."

Opera 40:754 Je '89. Noel Goodwin (175w)

Gramophone 66:1210-11 Ja '89. Alan Blyth (425w)

7147. Aida.

James Levine (c). Aprile Millo (sop); Dolora Zajick (mez); Placido Domingo (ten); James Morris (bass); Samuel Ramey (bass); Terry Cooke (bass); Charles Anthony (ten); Hei-Kyung Hong (sop). Metropolitan Opera Chorus and Orchestra.
SONY 45973 DDD 146:00 3 discs

★★★***Awards:*** Editor's Choice, *Opera Canada* Fall '91; The Want List 1991, *Fanfare* N/D '91 (James Miller). Pick of the Month, North American Perspective (Christie Barter), *Gramophone* My '91.

"Really, the performance is a parade of delights from beginning to end, conducted unhurriedly and imaginatively—even the chorus and orchestra sound like they mean it!...Balances are exemplary—I don't care how they did it. The overall sound seems a shade too bright, but that's my only complaint....in fact, although other *Aidas* may have occasionally reached greater heights, I believe that, all things considered, this is the greatest recording of the opera ever made."

Fanfare 15:380-82 S/O '91. James Miller (long)

"There's no want of excitement and grandeur in this performance, and I can't praise the Met chorus and orchestra highly enough. Sony's engineers have recorded it all in spacious, natural sound....By far, the most fascinating contribution comes from Millo....My favorite *Aida* remains Muti's on Angel, with Caballe, Cossotto, and—Domingo....If you've already bought the new Sony and happen to like Millo's Aida, make sure you also know the real thing: Tebaldi on London (with Bergonzi and Simionato)."

American Record Guide 54:139-40 S/O '91. Ralph V. Lucano (long)

The cast and orchestra "realize a performance of the world's most popular...opera which challenges the best in the catalogue. If there are no surprising revelations, the homogeneity, tragic force and no-holds-barred visceral excitement of this prodigious reading provide more than ample reason for commending the set."

Opera Canada 32(2):57-8 Fall '91. Harvey Chusid (brief)

"Much of Aprile Milo's singing here is of a high order...most of what she sings is correct and tasteful, but the sum does not yield a memorable Aida....Placido Domingo...sings with his customary taste and musicality, but frequently his voice sounds less than fresh, and in some passages his characterization lacks the necessary intensity...The Metropolitan Chorus sings admirably, and the orchestral playing is splendid, but more trenchant performances of the opera will be found in a number of earlier recordings."

Stereo Review 56:101 S '91. Robert Ackart (med)

"This first collaboration between Sony and the Met results in a no-nonsense *Aida* that is sinewy and propulsive. It's a strong performance, but don't look for subtlety or nuance."

Opera News 56:34 Jl '91. Patrick J. Smith (125w)

"This recording is a fair enough accomplishment....James Levine conducts with characteristic drive and discipline, although he is more successful in the surging ensemble than he is in the introspective, lyrical writing, particularly in the last two acts, where there is precious little poetic expression evident in his reading. The sonics are disappointing."

Musical America 111:54-5 S/O '91. Walter Price (med)

"In general the performance is pervaded by a depressing flaccidity and lack of sheer theatrical cut and thrust, for which Levine has to be held to account....A further drawback is the sound, with its lack of brilliance, clogged textures, and voices placed too far backward and consequently occasionally covered by the orchestra." *P95/85/75 S75*

Hi-Fi News & Record Review 36:70 Jl '91. George Hall (630w)

"In an arena which already holds 15 or so complete recordings of *Aida*, was another needed? Especially one with Domingo as Radames—his *fourth* recording of the role? The answer is decidedly "no"...That said, there's nothing wrong with this new Sony set, and one can actually find much to enjoy...The engineers have decided to record soft moments too softly and loud moments too loudly; the constant getting up and down to adjust volume may annoy some. Otherwise the recording is vivid and true...Should you buy it? Well, Millo is fascinating, and Levine has something to add to the opera, to be sure. But don't get rid of your other favorite recordings of *Aida*; listen before you buy. It's quite good; it just isn't crucial."

Stereophile 15:197 F '92. Robert Levine (long)

"This is an awful *Aida.* While there are quiet passages, they move as quickly as possible to the (very) loud ones. Temperance is in short supply everywhere. Voices yell at each other, without accord, as if the singers just arrived by plane, don't know or don't like each other much...The Aida is Levine's new phenom, Aprile Millo, coached to the ears but still not idiomatic or naturally musical...Presiding over this talent is Levine, caring for his orchestra, but did he listen to his singers?...As they say in German, I wonder me."

High Performance Review 8:86 Wtr '91/92. Bert Wechsler (long)

Digital Audio's CD Review 8:60+ O '91. Sebastian Russ (long)

Gramophone 68:2062 My '91. Alan Blyth (995w)

7148. Aida.

Riccardo Muti (c). Montserrat Caballe (sop); Placido Domingo (ten); Fiorenza Cossotto; Nicolai Ghiaurov; Piero Cappuccilli; Luigi Roni. Royal Opera House Chorus, Covent Garden; New Philharmonia Orchestra. February, 1975.
EMI 47271 146:07 3 discs

★*Awards: American Record Guide* Overview: Opera Favorites, Ja/F '91.

"This is one of those recordings where everything happens almost exactly as one hopes it will—the many exceptional components brought together for the event fall into place for as successful a final result as one has any right to hope for, and a phonograph classic is produced....Digital remastering adds some depth and detail to an already lifelike acoustic, and the wonder of CD guarantees that it will all sound just as good for our heirs."

Fanfare 10:224-6 Mr/Ap '87 Vincent Alfano (925w)

"If you want to prove how good your stereo system is—or, better yet, how good *Aida* can be—this release will please you immensely."

Ovation 8:46-47 F '87 Robert Levine (255w)

"Riccardo Muti's rendition, although having a much better cast than Abbado's, stultifies the listener with its artificiality and overly emphatic character, probably the fault only in part of the conductor. The recorded sound, perhaps the real and even full culprit, suffocates by means of its excessively close focus."

The Opera Quarterly 5:239-44 Sum/Aut '87. C.-P. Gerald Parker (330w)

Hi-Fi News & Record Review 32:105 Mr '87 Arthur Jacobs (180w)

Gramophone 64:1057-8 Ja '87 Alan Blyth (470w)

Stereo Review 52:107 D '87. Robert Ackart (100w)

7149. Aida.

Georg Solti (c). Leontyne Price (sop); Jon Vickers (ten); Rita Gorr (mez); Robert Merrill (bar); Giorgio Tozzi (bass). Rome Opera Chorus; Rome Opera Orchestra. reissue 1962.
LONDON/DECCA 417 416 ADD 152:51 3 discs

✔**HC** ★★*Awards:* Third Place Vocal Reissues Mumm Champagne Classical Music Award 1988—Presented by *Ovation, Ovation* N '88. *American Record Guide* Overview: Getting to Know Your Opera, Ja/F '91.

"Solti's performance, for all its dynamism, has a broad sweep and grandeur that the listener will not soon forget, yet without any vestige of the stagnant pomposity to which some maestros might fall prey in seeking to transmit such qualities."

The Opera Quarterly 5:238-44 Sum/Aut '87. C.-P. Gerald Parker (330w) (rev. of LP)

"Hearing it again after a lapse of many years I remain conscious of its faults but ask myself, as I have before, if not *this* one, which one?-...First and foremost, Solti has the benefit of Leontyne Price's Aida...When I hear a new Aida, she's always the one the newcomer is measured against....for now, his [Solti's] *Aida* is the choice one on compact disc."

Fanfare 11:225-6 Ja/F '88. James Miller (775w)

"If aural indulgence is your priority for Aida in this format, wait for Karajan on EMI; if it's the heroine, look no further than Solti."

Hi-Fi News & Record Review 32:107 S '87 David Nice (235w)

Gramophone 65:482 S '87 Alan Blyth (380w)

Stereo Review 52:107 D '87. Robert Ackart (70w)

7150. Un Ballo in Maschera.

Georg Solti (c). Luciano Pavarotti; Renato Bruson; Margaret Price; Christa Ludwig. London Opera Chorus; National Philharmonic Orchestra.
LONDON/DECCA 410 210 130:29 2 discs

★*Awards: Stereo Review* Best of the Month, Ap '86.

"A must for opera collectors....Solti shapes, unifies, and gives energy to this reading; it is he who brings out the best in each of his individual artists.

Stereo Review 51:69 Ap '86. Robert Ackart (650w)

"One's choice of a recording of *Un Ballo* depends, ultimately, upon one's preference for individual singers in key roles, but for a well-balanced performance in great sound, this one is recommended."

American Record Guide 49:45-6 My/Je '86. Desmond Arthur (825w)

"Margaret Price, whose voice is so well suited to the elegance of the Mozart repertory, is a restrained, graceful, and aristocratic-sounding Amelia, and yet her 'Morro, ma prima in grazia' is very moving....Solti's is the grandest, most lush approach, but occasional orchestral outbursts obscure the vocal lines."

The Opera Quarterly 5:223-6 Sum/Aut '87. Christopher J. Thomas (460w)

"In the end, Solti has once again failed to understand what a subtle score *Ballo* really is-...Pavarotti's second *Ballo* is also a win-a-few, lose-a-few proposition....Margaret Price strikes me as an ideal Amelia, possibly the best I've heard....An enchanting Oscar, Kathleen Battle-...sings the part irresistibly...I have only praise for the vibrant recorded sound."

Opus 2:53-4 Ag '86. Peter G. Davis (950w)

"This third try at the opera for London is not exactly definitive, but it has the flavor of a full-fledged operatic venture, a flavor that is rapidly being chased out of the studios and even the opera houses by directors and conductors (and in the case of recordings, producers) who believe that all that matters is note-to-note accuracy....Compact Disc buyers need search no further for a *Ballo*."

High Fidelity 37:66-67 Je '87 Thor Eckert, Jr. (800w)

"The cast is far from negligible, but the performance still misfires."

Fanfare 9:244-5 Mr/Ap '86. James Miller (900w)

The Opera Quarterly 4:96-105 Summer '86. David Hamilton (5215w)

Gramophone 63:405 S '85. Alan Blyth (700w)

Opera News 50 (14):45 Mr '86. John W. Freeman (405w)

Digital Audio 2:22-3 My '86. R. Sebastian Russ (900w)

Stereo Review 52:107 D '87. Robert Ackart (150w)

7151. Falstaff. Giuseppe Valdengo (bar); Frank Guarrera (bar); Herva Nelli (sop); Teresa Stich-Randall (sop); Antonio Madasi (ten); Cloe Elmo (contr); Nan Merriman (mez); Gabor Carelli (ten); John Carmen Rossi (ten); Norman Scott (bass). **Aida.** Herva Nelli (sop); Eva Gustavson (mez); Richard Tucker (ten); Giuseppe Valdengo (bar); Norman Scott (bass); Dennis Harbour (bass); Virginio Assandri (ten); Teresa Stich-Randall (sop). **Choral Works and Opera excerpts.** Quattro pezzi sacri: Te Deum. Requiem. *Nabucco:* Va, pensiero. *Luisa Miller:* Quando le sere al placido. Inno delle Nazioni.
Arturo Toscanini (c). NBC Symphony Orchestra; Robert Shaw Chorale; Westminster Choir.
RCA 0326 ADD (m) 373:00 7 discs

★★★★★*Awards:* Editor's Choice, *Opera Canada*, Fall '90. The Want List 1990, *Fanfare* N/D '90 (Robert Levine; Jon Tuska); Critics' Choice 1990, *Gramophone* D '90 (Alan Blyth); Critic's Choice: 1990, *American Record Guide* Ja/F '91 (Lee Milazzo).

"Because of some ineffective casting, the *Aida* has had less than its critical due....It is the conductor's noble conception of the opera, however, that gives the set its celebrity....Fine singing abounds in the Toscanini *Falstaff*, which remains one of the most glorious operatic performances ever recorded....The RCA package also includes an inspired account of the Verdi *Requiem* (oddly split between two discs), along with the *Te Deum* and a rousing performance of the *Inno delle nazione (Hymn of the Nations)." PS 100*

Opera Canada 31:58 Fall 90. Harvey Chusid (400w)

"The natural sound of most of the originals turns out, amazingly, to have been spacious, resonant, lustrous, and sweet—in short, everything a Toscanini recording has been perceived *not* to have been—and excellent for its period-....To hear these CDs, then, is to hear Toscanini's recordings as if for the first time, and to discover what audiences and musicians of his day found so impressive about his performances."

Musical America 110:42-6 Jl '90. Thomas Hathaway (1065w)

"Verdi's *Falstaff* [was] recorded from a broadcast made in 1950 when Toscanini was 83! He captures the work's comedy and colour with a brilliant ensemble of singers."

High Fidelity 1:109 Jl '90. Clive Manning (b.n.)

"There are revelations here, even after so many years. *Falstaff* was the work Toscanini conducted more than any other; *Aida* was second-....The minor works on these discs are also extraordinarily well served, with tenor Jan Peerce's contributions being particularly noteworthy."

Fanfare 13:299-300 Jl/Ag '90. Robert Levine (475w)

"Why invest in digitally remastered analog recordings from the early '50s when DDD recordings of these works abound? First, because tape noise notwithstanding, the sound is sumptuous. More importantly, because Toscanini's interpretations simply swing more; are more lyrical, in the sense of singer and song; are more organic from first note to last; and present a vigorous, unified conception of this as living, breathing music."

Musician 142:85-6 Ag '90. Chip Stern (490w)

American Record Guide 53:36-8 S/O '90. Kurt Moses (1010w)

7152. La Forza del Destino.
Riccardo Muti (c). Mirella Freni; Dolora Zajic; Francesca Garbi; Placido Domingo; Ernesto Gavazzi. Milan La Scala Chorus; Milan La Scala Orchestra.
EMI 47485 DDD 163:52 3 discs

★*Awards: Stereo Review* Best of the Month, My '87.

"Sumptuous sound and close attention to orchestral detail make Angel's new recording of Verdi's *La forza del destino* a conductor's showcase....The achievement of this performance is that you forget the opera's weaknesses and glory in its strengths."

Stereo Review 52:77-78 My '87 Robert Ackart (350w)

"Muti's performance...has the smell of theater in every measure....it is brisk, urgent, and restlessly on the move, an interpretation with not time to stop for philosophical introspection. Orchestral accents crack like whiplashes, tightly coiled rhythms spring with catlike grace, and the lean-limbed orchestral textures glow with crystalline clarity....I regret that Muti does not take more time over the lyrical pages."

Opus 4:47+ D '87. Peter G. Davis (795w)

"Readers may recall that I found Muti's *Don Pasquale* 'not much fun'...and indeed in *Forza* he is far from offering Serafin's flexibility. Still, his performance isn't dead like

Sinopoli's. This is due in part to his singers, who not only earn a better report card but also have some presence, something to say for themselves and to each other—and in part to the Scala forces, who outdo their opposite numbers in London, doubtless thanks to greater familiarity with the work in the theater and with the music's expressive intent."

The Opera Quarterly 5:227-32 Sum/Aut '87. David Hamilton (395w)

"But now, the big question: should you buy this *Forza*?....To be continued."

Fanfare 10:207-10 My/Je '87 James Miller (1950w)

Digital Audio 4:60-1 Ja '88. Sebastian Russ (325w)

Stereo Review 52:108 D '87. Robert Ackart (110w)

Hi-Fi News & Record Review 32:103 My '87 Benedict Sarnaker (300w)

Gramophone 64:1181 F '87 (1220w) (rev. of LP); 64:1595 My '87 (455w) (rev. of CD). Richard Osborne

7153. La Forza del Destino.

Giuseppe Sinopoli (c). Rosalind Plowright; Agnes Baltsa; Jose Carreras; Renato Bruson. Ambrosian Opera Chorus; Philharmonia Orchestra.
DEUTSCHE GRAMMOPHON 419 203 DDD
45:10; 65:30; 68:11 3 discs

★***Awards:*** *Gramophone* Operatic Award, 1987.

"A performance that treats Verdi's score with the utmost respect, illuminating it at every turn and, yes, realising the sombre aspects with such depth of feeling as to dispel any hints of depression. The overall impression is one of grandeur. Sinopoli's cast is virtually unsurpassable....Recording and presentation are fully up to the rest of the enterprise."

Music and Musicians International 36:57 N '87. Robert Hartford (165w)

"No, I haven't heard the Muti *Forza* yet, but I do know that Sinopoli here surpasses his own previous ventures in Verdi....With Levine's *Forza* now on CD (RCA) the competition is strong; but with unflawed casting, streamlined orchestral playing of the first order and a recording that pulls no punches, Sinopoli's stands secure."

Hi-Fi News & Record Review 32:99 Ag '87 David Nice (380w)

"Recommended."

Stereo Review 52:111 S '87. Robert Ackart (360w)

"I'll firmly straddle the fence right now and say that if I had to narrow them all down, the winner is...Levine *and* Sinopoli; either performance will, it seems to me, in terms of singing, acting, and conducting, give you a better idea of what *La forza del destino* is about than any of the competing ones, available or deleted-...If Giuseppe Sinopoli's men were as strong as his women, the choice of one recording would be much easier. Rosalind Plowright, without necessarily displacing Leontyne Price and Maria Callas from the top of my list, is a (literally) powerful Leonora."

Fanfare 11:333-6 S/O '87. James Miller (980w)

"With certain allowances made, this can be quite an enjoyable performance....It is hard to tell to what extent the sometimes misjudged instrumental balances, and proportion between voices and orchestra, are the conductor's or the engineers' doing"

Opera News 52:65 O '87. John W. Freeman (510w)

"At times Sinopoli's studied, every-note-in-place approach becomes so intent on making an Important Statement that the reality of the opera just flies out the window, leaving behind a great many provocative reflections on *Forza* rather than a performance....A general recommendation for *Forza* would still have to be RCA's 1977 edition, conducted by James Levine, with Leontyne Price, Domingo, and Sherrill Milnes, recently transferred to CD and technically much improved. The performance may be a trifle bland, but for musical consistency and overall vocal excellence, this set remains hard to beat."

Opus 4:47+ D '87. Peter G. Davis (795w)

"The newest recording of *La forza del destino*, led by Giuseppe Sinopoli, is a pretty chilling affair, for reasons that aren't revealed by a simple report card....this performance creates discomfort even when speed is not at issue; the absurd tempos are symptoms rather than causes."

The Opera Quarterly 5:227-32 Sum/Aut '87. David Hamilton (395w)

Stereo Review 52:108 D '87. Robert Ackart (90w)

Gramophone 64:1595 My '87 Richard Osborne (455w)

Stereo Review Presents: Compact Disc Buyer's Guide Summer 1988 p.52. William Livingstone (75w)

Digital Audio 4:60-1 Ja '88. Sebastian Russ (325w)

7154. Macbeth.

Karl Bohm (c). Christa Ludwig (mez); Sherrill Milnes (bar); Carlo Cossutta (ten); Karl Ridderbusch (bass). Vienna State Opera Chorus and Orchestra.
FOYER 2027 AAD 72:54, 57:41 2 discs

★***Awards:*** The Want List 1990, *Fanfare* N/D '90 (Marc Mandel).

"This is a spectacular *Macbeth*, unquestionably the best I've ever heard. As Lady Macbeth, Christa Ludwig offers an unrivaled combination of presence, intellect, and vocal security; she's nothing short of astonishing...Milnes, too, is in spectacular voice...Except for its last

few moments, I doubt you'll find a better *Macbeth* than this."
Fanfare 14:385-86 N/D '90. Marc Mandel (600w)

"I guarantee that if you are a Verdian and buy this you won't mind the sound *or* the heavier than usual cutting—it's *that* good."
American Record Guide 54:118-9 Ja/F '91. Michael Mark (260w)

7155. Rigoletto.
Tullio Serafin (c). Maria Callas; Adriana Lazzarini; Giuseppe Di Stefano; Tito Gobbi. Milan La Scala Chorus; Milan La Scala Orchestra. 1955 reissue.
EMI 47469 (m) 2 discs

★*Awards:* *American Record Guide* Overview: Opera Favorites, Ja/F '91.

"In so many ways this set will never be surpassed. Gobbi's distinctive, bitey, even hard-driven sound could be called a chore to listen to coming directly from Warren's massive smoothness, but once you accept the tone as valid, and really listen to the performance, you hear how vividly the deformed man is being re-created in all his bitter, malicious, and relentless vengeful glory. It is a performance that positively shatters the barrier between microphone and listener....[Callas] was not in pluperfect voice at these sessions, yet even that touch of stress she turns to her advantage. To hear once her E-flat at the end of 'Si, vendetta'—a piercing cry of anguish—is to be let down by anyone else in this moment."
The Opera Quarterly 5:197-203 Sum/Aut '87. Thor Eckert, Jr. (190w)

Callas "is, to my (and countless others') ears, the most interesting Gilda on disc, the one who best succeeds in making this imbecilic ninny into a memorable, sympathetic character. She touches the heart at every point....Her voice is in fine shape....Her soft singing is lovely...and she has plenty of strength when necessary-....The supporting players are adequate, and Serafin's conducting is authoritative and thoroughly idiomatic."
American Record Guide 50:64 My/Je '87 Ralph V. Lucano (375w)

"This time Callas becomes a young woman who grows up literally overnight, and the difference between her singing of *Caro Nome* and *Tutte le feste* is there to prove it, closely abetted by Serafin's incomparable feeling for pace and line."
Opera 38:1415-6 D '87. Noel Goodwin (135w)

"This is the recording which tells you more about the special character of Verdi's first undisputed masterpiece than any other....If you already have a *Rigoletto* on CD - there are already four others - sell it and get this one!"
Hi-Fi News & Record Review 32:101 Je '87 Hugh Canning (350w)

"The original sound of this release was a trifle flat, but the digital remastering has given it a new lease on life."
Ovation 8:45 D '87. Robert Levine (210w)

This is "a rather indifferent recording containing two of the most significant Verdi performances ever captured by the microphones-....There's not a player among the supporting cast who merits special mention....As far as Gobbi and Callas are concerned, it cannot be said too often that these performances are necessary to any collection of consequence."
Fanfare 10:228-30 Mr/Ap '87 Vincent Alfano (800w)

Ovation 8:39 My '87 Paul Turok (90w)

Digital Audio & Compact Disc Review 107:69 My '87 R. Sebastian Russ (575w)

Gramophone 64:1181 F '87 Alan Blyth (335w)

Stereo Review 52:110 D '87. Robert Ackart (110w)

7156. Rigoletto.
Giuseppe Sinopoli (c). Renato Bruson; Edita Gruberova; Neil Shicoff; Robert Lloyd. Santa Cecilia Academy Chorus, Rome; Santa Cecilia Academy Orchestra, Rome.
PHILIPS 412 592 DDD 128:02 2 discs

★*Awards:* *Stereo Review* Best of the Month, Mr '86.

"Enthusiastically recommended."
Stereo Review 51:76 Mr '86. Robert Ackart (600w)

"Heretofore, I have not really cared for Sinopoli's opera interpretations...but this way with this war-horse certainly works....the end result is exciting indeed, especially since the Saint Cecilia Academy forces seem to respond to his baton like the Berlin Philharmonic to Karajan's!"
Fanfare 9:248-9 Mr/Ap '86. Anthony D. Coggi (525w)

"In sum, then, this is an unusual, imperfect, but urgently arresting recording of *Rigoletto.*"
The Opera Quarterly 4:159-61 Spring '86. Dennis W. Wakeling (1120w)

"Neil Shicoff...is the only really decent thing on the Philips set....Sinopoli's is a hectic, even chaotic performance that has neither dramatic nor musical pulse."
The Opera Quarterly 5:198-203 Sum/Aut '87. Thor Eckert, Jr. (190w)

Stereo Review 52:110 D '87. Robert Ackart (115w)

Digital Audio 2:67+ Je '86. R. Sebastian Russ (560w)

High Fidelity 36:57-9 F '86. Gregory Sandow (1500w)

Gramophone 63:678+ N '85 (315w) (rev. of LP); 63:971 Ja '86 (195w) (rev. of CD). Richard Osborne

Opera News 50 (13):53 Mr '86. John W. Freeman (370w)

7157. La Traviata.
Franco Ghione (c). Maria Callas (sop); Alfredo Kraus (ten); Mario Sereni (bar); Laura Zannini (mez). San Carlos National Theater Chorus; San Carlos National Theater Orchestra. Lisbon. March 27, 1958 live.
EMI 49187 ADD (m) 123:00 2 discs

★***Awards:*** *Gramophone* Critics' Choice (Alan Blyth), 1987.

"I find it a riveting performance; Callas was, at times during it, in precarious voice, but she manages, as only she could, to turn that precariousness into a dramatic asset....the sound, while a great improvement over the black discs, is still thumpy...But who cares?"
Fanfare 11:228 Ja/F '88. Robert Levine (225w)

"In voice alone, Maria Callas is coarser than most of [her] rivals, but thanks to her art, she emerges as frail and aristocratic as any of them."
The Opera Quarterly 5:210-8 Sum/Aut '87. London Green (365w) (rev. of LP)

"If you don't own this, you should be ashamed of yourself."
Ovation 9:46 Ja '89. Robert Levine (155w)

Gramophone 65:818+ N '87 Alan Blyth (335w)

7158. La Traviata.
Carlo Maria Giulini (c). Maria Callas (sop); Giuseppe Di Stefano (ten); Ettore Bastianini (bar); Silvana Zanolli (sop); Luisa Mandelli (sop); Giuseppe Zampieri (ten); Arturo LaPorta (bass); Antonio Zerbini (bass); Silvio Maionica (bass); Franco Ricciardi (ten). La Scala Chorus and Orchestra, Milan. La Scala, Milan. May 28, 1955 live; reissue.
EMI 63628 ADD 124:00 2 discs

★***Awards:*** Critics' Choice 1991, *Gramophone*, Ja '92 (David Patmore).

"Callas' Milan performances of *La Traviata* in May 1955 had a spontaneity, intensity and reality that were astounding. Her singing unerringly portrays the spirit and fatality of Verdi's most touching heroine."
Opera Canada 32(2):54 Summer '91. John W. Freeman (brief)

"This is the *Traviata* to have."
American Record Guide 54:142 S/O '91. George W. Loomis (long)

"Rating Callas recordings is often like talking about wines: vintage is all-important. 1955 was a good year...highly recommended, even to somewhat non-Callas fans...There is strong commitment and enough beautiful singing for everyone...The conducting...is supreme."
High Performance Review 8:86-7 Wtr '91/92. Bert Wechsler (long)

"Though Callas is in good voice and never less than vivid, the whole doesn't add up nearly as well as the 1958 Covent Garden *Traviata*, with Cesare Valletti and Mario Zanasi—or, for that matter, as well as the Lisbon performance with Alfredo Kraus and Mario Sereni already available on EMI CDs (Angel/EMI CDS 49187/88), unfortunately plagued by an inordinately obtrusive prompter."
Musical America 111:49-51 Jl '91. David Hamilton (820w)

"Though this performance has shown up previously on Foyer, Price-Less, and Hunt CDs, I suppose EMI deserves a nod for legitimizing its release on a major label and ensuring its widespread distribution. On the other hand, I can't imagine how John Q. Record-Buying-Public will take to the sound, for which reason it may remain of interest primarily to collectors."
Fanfare 14:318-9 Jl/Ag '91. Marc Mandel (850w)

Gramophone 68:1558 F '91. John Steane (785w)

7159. Il Trovatore.
Renato Cellini (c). Zinka Milanov (sop); Leonard Warren (bar); Fedora Barbieri (mez); Jussi Bjoerling (ten). Robert Shaw Chorale; RCA Symphony Orchestra. 1954 reissue.
RCA 6643 ADD (m) 117:00 2 discs

★★***Awards:*** The Want List 1988, *Fanfare* N/D '88 (Henry Fogel). *American Record Guide* Overview: Opera Favorites, Ja/F '91.

"Though it uses the cuts made even in today's more score-faithful performances, RCA's 1952 recording of *Il Trovatore* is the yardstick against which all others are measured. And rightly so. Few if any versions made before or since have assembled four such musically potent and vocally resplendent singers."
The Opera Quarterly 7:149-51 Spr '90. William Albright (300w)

"While Milanov excels and Barbieri is quite glorious, the men are less satisfactory...The work is cut, and conducting is uninvolved...but there is still much to give pleasure, provided some allowance is made for the dryish mono sound."
Music and Musicians International 37:39 O '88. Robert Hartford (175w)

"The quartet of vocal stars...has achieved something of a legendary status. The performers, with one exception, do not really sustain their reputations."
The Opera Quarterly 5:203-9 Sum/Aut '87. Robert Baxter (350w) (rev. of LP)

"If I were recommending a recording of this opera...it would be a toss-up between Giulini (DG) and Mehta (RCA), both of them complete, conducted with more panache, and possessing casts that are, on the whole, at least as good as Cellini's."
Fanfare 12:287 S/O '88. James Miller (475w)

Gramophone 66:337-8 Ag '88. Hilary Finch (230w)

7160. Il Trovatore.

Carlo Maria Giulini (c). Giorgio Zancanaro; Rosalind Plowright; Brigitte Fassbaender; Placido Domingo; Evgeny Nesterenko. Santa Cecilia Academy Chorus, Rome; Santa Cecilia Academy Orchestra, Rome. DEUTSCHE GRAMMOPHON 413 355 DDD 3 discs

★*Awards:* *Gramophone* Critics' Choice 1984. Perfect 10/10, *Digital Audio*, Mr '88.

"Giulini's interpretation of *Il Trovatore* will probably stand as the exemplar for many years to come."

Stereo Review 50:83 Mr '85. Robert Ackart (550w)

"Not the most exciting *Trovatore* on records but a serious, intelligent performance that makes most others seem cheap and exhibitionistic by comparison. Like its only peer, the Mehta, it's uncut. It repays repeated listening, and my reaction to it has gradually changed from bemusement to admiration."

Fanfare 8:303-5 Mr/Ap '85. James Miller (1600w)

"Giulini is a subtle musician, and when he takes control of a performance, he rarely smothers it. Yet in this recording, for once, he has gone too far....Throughout the performance, the singers sound as though they are being held in check by an enormous metronome-....The orchestra plays with an awesome dynamic range...But none of this makes up for the recording's disappointing lack of dramatic intensity."

The Opera Quarterly 3:111-3 Winter '85/86. Gail Milgram Lavielle (850w) (rev. of LP)

"Giulini captures the dark, doom-laden qualities in Verdi's score and finds a wealth of exquisitely wrought details in his scrupulous reading. But the maestro gives his listeners too much time to savor those details, so slow and lugubrious, so lacking in vigorous rhythmic impulse are his tempos....Even at Giulini's ponderous tempo, Nesterenko cannot articulate the music. From her first entrance Rosalind Plowright sings commandingly....Domingo proves the all-purpose troubadour....Fassbaender compels attention with the vigor and clarity of her singing."

The Opera Quarterly 5:204-9 Sum/Aut '87. Robert Baxter (350w)

Stereo Review 52:110+ D '87. Robert Ackart (125w)

Digital Audio 1:61-2 My '85. Roland Graeme (890w))

Ovation 6:36 Je '85. George Jellinek (565w) (rev. of LP

Gramophone 62:651 N '84 (1120w) (rev. of LP); 62:1011 F '85 (125w) (rev. of CD). Alan Blyth

7161. Il Trovatore.

Zubin Mehta (c). Placido Domingo (ten); Leontyne Price (sop); Sherrill Milnes (bar); Fiorenza Cossotto (mez). Ambrosian Opera Chorus; New Philharmonia Orchestra. 1970.
RCA 6194 ADD 71:00; 66:05 2 discs

★*Awards:* *American Record Guide* Overview: Opera Favorites, Ja/F '91.

This "remains one of the finest versions of this opera....The *Trovatore* loses almost nothing in the remastering—though digital recording would have captured more of the bloom on Leontyne Price's high notes—and it gains immeasurably....warmly recommended to everyone."

Opera 39:120-1 Ja '88. Raymond Monelle (170w)

"For its third *Trovatore* RCA found a stellar cast, arguably the finest on record. This time RCA also located a high-energy conductor. And, for the first time, *Il trovatore* was recorded complete, without cuts. Mehta leads an animated performance more impressive for its detail than its overall musical structure. Placido Domingo ranks with Bjoerling and Pavarotti as the most elegant Manrico on record, although above G his voice has little ring....In some respects the recording marks an advance for Price."

The Opera Quarterly 5:204-9 Sum/Aut '87. Robert Baxter (350w)

"Ever since it came out, I've regarded this 1969 *Il trovatore* as the one other performances must be measured by, an attitude moderated two years ago with the appearance of Giulini's unorthodox but imposing DG set, a version that treats the music with unexpected (and effective) weight and gravity."

Fanfare 11:246-7 N/D '87. James Miller (900w)

"I hate to end a rave review on a negative note, but there is one serious problem with this reissue. The sound in virtually all loud passages suffers from distortion due to tape saturation....Shame on RCA's engineers in 1969, but top marks to everyone else!"

American Record Guide 51:93 Mr/Ap '88. Ralph V. Lucano (450w)

Gramophone 66:338-9 Ag '88. Hilary Finch (230w)

7162. I Vespri Siciliani.

James Levine (c). Martina Arroyo (sop); Placido Domingo (ten); Sherrill Milnes (bar); Ruggero Raimondi (bass). John Alldis Choir; New Philharmonia Orchestra. August 1973.
RCA 0370 ADD 66:21; 59:08; 61:30 3 discs

★*Awards:* The Want List 1990, *Fanfare* N/D '90 (John Wiser).

"The New Philharmonia Orchestra perform magnificently—maybe a little *too* magnificently, for the conductor and his recording engineers let the orchestra swamp the singers at many climaxes. The NPO keeps up with Levine's sometimes frantic tempi and maintains superb tone and rhythmic buoyancy throughout....The John Alldis Choir's vigorous, accurate singing tremendously enhances Levine's traversal of *Vespri's* challenging ensembles....Martina Arroyo wields a voice of Verdian weight that...can 'ride' over chorus and orchestra. However, she negotiates most of the *fioriture* effortfully and seems unable to use either voice or text to give essential energy and attack to this fearless character....It may be ungrateful to say it, but any number of Domingo portrayals sound just like this one: sincere but generalized, often overemotional when music and drama call for grace and restraint-....Last but not least is Sherrill Milnes, dominating the cast as Monforte, perhaps the baritone's most successfully realized role on records....In spite of less than perfect casting, the RCA performance makes a good case for *Vespri*."

The Opera Quarterly 5:218-21 Sum/Aut '87. Roger G. Pines (1060w) (rev. of LP)

"Levine's rather hard-driven account allows of no doubts in his headstrong enthusiasm. Playing and singing are first-rate....The remastered sound quality is most acceptable too."

Music and Musicians International 36:46 My '88. Robert Hartford (240w)

"The virtues are many...Arroyo is a disappointment but not a fatal one, and in relistening to this digital remastering I have revised my estimate of her contribution upward....RCA has redone its splendid recording even more splendidly and I find myself bowled over by the beauty and grandeur of this work."

Fanfare 11:270-1 Jl/Ag '88. David Johnson (650w)

Gramophone 66:483 S '88. Hilary Finch (465w)

VILLA-LOBOS, HEITOR

7163. Magdalena.

Evans Haile (c). Judy Kaye; George Rose; Faith Esham; Kevin Gray; Jerry Hadley. Connecticut Choral Artists; New England Orchestra.
CBS 44945 DDD 69:50

★***Awards:*** The Want List 1990, *Fanfare* N/D '90 (James Miller); Pick of the Month, North American Perspective (Christopher Pollard) *Gramophone* F '91.

"The music is pure Villa-Lobos all the way and would have done honor to a full-fledged opera....there's attractive singing-acting from everyone, including the chorus."

American Record Guide 53:119-20 Mr/Ap '90. Michael Mark (250w)

"Evans Haile, the moving spirit behind the concert revival that anteceded this recording, leads a well-organized, throbbingly energetic reading-....Not all the casting is quite ideal....Nevertheless, all sing well enough."

Opera News 54:31+ Mr 3 '90. John W. Freeman (325w)

"The trouble with *Magdalena* is that it should probably be staged by an opera company like the New York City Opera instead of being left to the mercy of your typical Broadway audience. I hope this will happen someday; in the meantime, here's that long-overdue recording."

Fanfare 13:330 Mr/Ap '90. James Miller (450w)

"Judy Kaye stands out in a well-chosen crossover cast of opera and Broadway names, and Evans Haile seems at home in this rain forest of steamy, tropical but often lovely orchestrations."

The New York Times Ja 21 '90, p. 26 H. Richard Traubner (130w)

WAGNER, RICHARD

7164. Gotterdammerung.

James Levine (c). Hildegard Behrens (sop); Reiner Goldberg (ten); Matti Salminen (bass); Ekkehard Wlaschiha (bar); Bernd Weikl (bar); Cheryl Studer (sop); Hanna Schwarz (mez); Hei-Kyung Hong (sop); Diane Kesling (mez); Meredith Parsons (contr); Helga Dernesch (mez); Tatiana Troyanos (mez); Andrea Gruber (sop). Metropolitan Opera Chorus and Orchestra.
DEUTSCHE GRAMMOPHON 429 385 DDD
270:00 4 discs

✔**HC** ★★***Awards:*** Editor's Choice, *Opera Canada*, Wtr '91. Critics' Choice 1991, Opera, *The Wire*, D/Ja '91/92 (Nick Kimberley).

"The new *Gotterdammerung* is an achievement to make [the] ensemble proud...Levine's mastery of Wagner's intricate world is fully documented here. His tempos are majestic, even too deliberate at times, but neither control nor cohesion is lacking. On the contrary, scenes follow one another in a giant arch of lustrous sound, with no orchestral detail glossed over...This recording is worthy to stand beside Solti's pioneering, gracefully aging, but still magnificent-sounding London set."

Stereo Review 57:100+ Ja '92. George Jellinek (long)

"This *Gotterdammerung*...conveys the musical values and emotional charge of this grandest of tragedies, the richest, most complex opera of Wagner's tetralogy...From a purely vocal viewpoint, this cast is not the equal of Solti's (Decca/London), but it does not shortchange emotional content nor blunt the dramatic edge."

Opera News 56:38 Ja 4 '92. C. J. Luten (long)

"In most of the crucial criteria, Levine's *Gotterdammerung* is superb and memorable-...The chorus is splendid, not only in the amazingly virile Act II sequences, but also in their reactions in the third act...for the most part, the soloists are equally impressive...DG's sound is too cavernous for my taste, but balances are clear as a bell and there's a nice distance between singers and orchestra."

Musical America 112:50-1 Ja/F '92. Robert Levine (long)

"It is with luminous presence and vitality that James Levine and the Metropolitan Opera Orchestra shape their reading of the score with a clearly formulated conception of the connected threads of the entire span of the work...But it is the absence of truly great Wagnerians in some of the principal roles which, in spite of strong teamwork, fails to raise the recording to truly classic stature."

Opera Canada 32:49-50 Wtr '91. Harvey Chusid (long)

"This performance...would be an almost perfect *Gotterdammerung* except for two things: the Brunhilde of Hildegard Behrens and the Siegfried of Reiner Goldberg...The other singers are all fine...But the real stars of the performance are Levine and his by now absolutely magnificent orchestra...I would...advise anyone who loves *Gotterdammerung* to get this performance—Behrens or no Behrens."

Fanfare 15:369-72 Ja/F '92. William Youngren (long)

"DG's sound tends to hedge the strings a little, but otherwise admirably reflects the careful balancing of the strands and the imposing bass lines of Levine's approach. It is the ideal recorded *Ring* to study with a score, missing just the last ounce of electricity that crackles in the Boulez recording (*still* unavailable on CD) but much more painstakingly detailed. In that respect, if in that respect only, no other cycle can quite match it." *P100/85/75 S95*

Hi-Fi News & Record Review 36:105+ N '91. David Nice (long)

"Levine does almost everything right here, and keeps on doing it until the final chord...The principals are simply awful...Goldberg squalls and bleats, and his vibrato needs a chokechain. I'd hoped this recording might mark the merciful end of a short, misguided career...Levine's *Gotterdammerung* demands praise as strongly as his *Rheingold* and *Walkure* deserved pans—it's that much better a story that much better told. With the Solti and Bohm recordings, and singing notwithstanding, definitely one of the top three to consider."

Stereophile 15:197+ F '92. Richard Lehnert (long)

Digital Audio's CD Review 8:62 My '92. Sebastian Russ (long)

7165. Lohengrin.

Rudolf Kempe (c). Jess Thomas (ten); Elisabeth Grummer (sop); Christa Ludwig (mez-sop); Dietrich Fischer-Dieskau (bar). Vienna State Opera Chorus; Vienna Philharmonic Orchestra. 1964 reissue.
EMI 49017 ADD 219:00 3 discs

✔HC ★*Awards:* Records to Die for: 1 of 5 Recommended Recordings, *Stereophile* Ja '91 (Richard Lehnert).

"I have praised this performance, Kempe's second *Lohengrin*...often in these pages—most recently, I think, in *Fanfare* 10:4. It is definitely the *Lohengrin* to have...The sound is excellent."

Fanfare 12:352 My/Je '89. William Youngren (100w)

"This 1962-63 *Lohengrin* is one of the finest operatic recordings ever made....EMI's studio recording—refreshingly hiss-free on the CD—is spacious, accurate, entirely believable, with a minimum of spot-miking. One of the timeless great ones."

Stereophile 14:153 Ja '91. Richard Lehnert (b.n.)

"Rudolf Kempe leads the forces of the Vienna State Opera with firmness and sensitivity, wanting only an extra touch of energy here and there....Jess Thomas, near the peak of his career, sings affectingly and musically in the title role, though the character's essential mystery eludes him."

Opera News 53:43 D 24 '88. C. J. Luten (140w)

"While the sound may not be as exceptional as the refurbished *Rosenkavalier* from EMI, nor as stunning as Decca's latest, it nevertheless has a burnished sheen that matched fully Kempe's unsurpassed conducting. The cast is a strong one...As to an out-and-out comparison with Solti, I would not be without either."

Music and Musicians International 36:51 F '88. Robert Hartford (170w)

Gramophone 65:1243-4 F '88. Arnold Whittall (250w)

Digital Audio 4:83 Je '88. Sebastian Russ (385w)

Opera Canada 14:50 Summ '88.Neil Croy (600w)

7166. Lohengrin.

Georg Solti (c). Placido Domingo (ten); Jessye Norman (sop); Eva Randova (mez); Siegmund Nimsgern (bar); Hans Sotin (bass); Dietrich Fischer-Dieskau (bar). Vienna State Opera Concert Choir; Vienna Philharmonic Orchestra. 1985-86.
LONDON/DECCA 421 053 DDD 223:00 4 discs

★★★*Awards:* *Gramophone* Critics' Choice (Arnold Whittall), 1987; *Stereo Review* Best Recordings of the Month Ap '88; Record of the Year, First Place, Mumm Champagne Classical Music Award 1988—Presented by *Ovation*, *Ovation* N '88.

"The performance is infused with the flowing lyricism that characterizes his [Solti's] more recent ones....The recording itself is well balanced, clear, and sonically opulent....every member of the cast is musically and dramatically convincing....Enthusiastically recommended."

Stereo Review 53:84 Ap '88. Robert Ackart (475w)

"The heroes of this set...are the chorus and orchestra, quite superbly recorded. Never on record have the grand ceremonial scenes sounded more imposing or been performed with such elan....Domingo's Lohengrin must be accounted another of his triumphs....I don't think that the Kempe version, which was recently reissued on LP by EMI, is quite eclipsed by this new one; as an interpretation, that is somewhat more idiomatic. But it is hard to resist the gorgeous sound on the new version, or indeed the persuasive qualities of its eponymous hero: indeed this recording is strong just where the EMI is weak."

Opera 38:1339 N '87. Alan Blyth (430w)

"It is a glorious performance, no mistake, and the set worth acquiring for Domingo (and Norman) no matter how good the rest."

Music and Musicians International 36:59 D '87. Robert Hartford (350w)

"After living for some time with the authoritative 1963 Kempe/VPO recording...it was hard to imagine a better performance. In many ways, that recording has not been bettered here—certainly not in the soloists....But in all other ways, including exciting, gripping drama from the podium, and orchestral sound of great fullness and beauty, I heartily recommend Solti's heroic *Lohengrin*."

Stereophile 11:171-3 Mr '88. Richard Lehnert (900w)

"This new arrival is splendidly recorded and, with Solti, Domingo and Norman, it has much going for it."

Ovation 9:40 Jl '88. George Jellinek (475w)

"The orchestral playing and the choral work are absolutely dazzling throughout, and Solti shapes and paces the work with (almost) unfailing sensitivity and effectiveness....But the singing of the soloists is something else again. It is (almost) all very beautiful...But there is throughout something just a little fussy, uninvolved, and self-contained about each singer's work....I kept having the nagging sense that I ought to be enjoying it more than I was....The sound is splendidly clear, full, and warm."

Fanfare 11:235-6 My/Je '88. William Youngren (535w)

"*Lohengrin*, sometimes called 'Slow 'n' Grim' by wags, is neither in this new recording."

Opera News 52(9):44 Ja '88. John W. Freeman (320w)

"Competitive recordings boast casts not merely 'this good,' but better, transmitted in sound that, perhaps not as clear in some respects, may be more illusion-producing in others. (The best of prior *Lohengrins*, Kempe's EMI Angel set...maintains a consistent level of dramatic involvement and idiomatic flavor, as well as making contact with a strain of ethereal spirituality in the opera that Solti's set more or less misses."

The Opera Quarterly 6:115-7 Autumn '88. David Hamilton (1365w)

"As conducted by Sir Georg Solti, *Lohengrin* is musically unintelligible. Worse, it is interminable, a protracted encounter with artistic confusion....Apart from the Vienna Philharmonic's stupendous brass section, the best thing about this performance is the Lohengrin of Placido Domingo...That the tenor doesn't fully succeed in his intentions has as much to do with his vocal as his imaginative limitations....Jessye Norman...cannot produce the kind of pure tone fundamental to any successful realization of Wagner's character."

The Opera Quarterly 6:113-5 Autumn '88. David Hamilton (1470w)

"The good news here is, in order of importance, the best sung recorded Lohengrin and Elsa ever, voluptuous sound, great playing by the VPO and superb singing by the chorus, and the fine leadership provided by Sir Georg Solti. The not-so-good news is the rest of the cast. For most opera-lovers, and surely for Wagnerites, there's enough good news here to warrant a buy recommendation."

American Record Guide 51:93-4 S/O '88. Kurt Moses (950w)

Opera Canada 14:50 Summ '88.Neil Croy (600w)

Gramophone 65:632 O '87 Arnold Whittall (1100w)

Hi-Fi News & Record Review 33:115+ Ja '88. David Nice (525w)

Digital Audio 4:83 Je '88. Sebastian Russ (385w)

7167. Die Meistersinger von Nurnberg.
Herbert Von Karajan (c). Elisabeth Schwarzkopf (sop); Otto Edelmann (bass); Hans Hopf (ten); Erich Kunz (bar); Friedrich Dalberg (bass); Gerhard Unger (ten); Ira Malaniuk (contr); Heinrich Pflanzl (bass); Erich Majkut (ten); Hans Berg (bass); Josef Janko (ten); Karl Mikorey (ten); Gerhard Stolze (ten); Heinz Tandler (bass); Heinz Borst (bass); Arnold Van Mill (bass); Werner Faulhaber (bass). Bayreuth Festival Chorus and Orchestra. Bayreuth Festival. 1951 reissue. EMI 63500 ADD (m) 267:00 4 discs

★*Awards:* Editor's Choice, *Opera Canada* Winter '90.

"Drawing the listener into the sweep of Wagner's music with almost reckless spontaneity, it is a reading far more vital and animated than the one Karajan would direct in Dresden for EMI nearly two decades later. Otto Edelmann offers a sympathetic, rich-voiced cobbler-poet; Elisabeth Schwarzkopf, who rarely returned to Eva (and never returned to Bayreuth) is incomparably radiant in the part; Hans Hopf, a rather stolid and monochromatic Walther, brings a genuinely heroic ring to his music."

Opera Canada 31(4):50-1 Winter '90. Harvey Chusid (140w)

"This evergreen performance of Wagner's timeless comedy is still unsurpassed, except in sound—and even that aspect has been cleaned and polished, though brightened, too, for the reissue."

American Record Guide 53:22+ S/O '90. Lee Milazzo (175w)

"This is an excellent *Meistersinger*, very satisfyingly shaped and paced, despite the weakness of two of its main links, Sachs and Walter. Eva, Beckmesser, David, and Magdalene are strong enough almost to make up for their failings. But if you already own the 1970 Karajan *Meistersinger*, I can't really recommend your buying this one unless you have a special interest in him or in Schwarzkopf....I should add that the mono sound on this CD version of the 1951 performance is excellent."

Fanfare 14:392-95 N/D '90. William Youngren (1825w)

Gramophone 68:621-2 S '90. Alan Blyth (660w)

7168. Parsifal.

James Levine (c). Peter Hofmann; Simon Estes; Matti Salminen; Hans Sotin. Bayreuth Festival Chorus; Bayreuth Festival Orchestra. The Festspielhaus, Bayreuth. July and August 1985 live.
PHILIPS 416 842 DDD 278:00 4 discs

★***Awards:*** The Record of the Month, *Music and Musicians International* F '88.

"The new Philips recording...may well stand as the definitive one for years to come."

Stereo Review 53:113 My '88. Robert Ackart (375w)

"For ecstatic revelation, topnotch singing, and orchestral sound as close as possible to what Wagner heard in head and hall, take Levine."

Stereophile 11:145+ My '88. Richard Lehnert (900w)

"Splendid general command of resources, fine orchestra...but a disappointing cast."

Fanfare 11:236-7 My/Je '88. William Youngren (675w)

"The cast of this *Parsifal* is not to be faulted-....My Record of the Year. Any year."

Music and Musicians International 36:47 F '88. Robert Hartford (500w)

"Levine's performance is enthralling precisely because he captures the ethos of suspended time that pervades this work....Regrettably this standard of excellence is not always matched by the singers....Notwithstanding the vocal deficiencies outlined above, the quality of Levine's interpretation puts his set among the front runners."

Opera 39:754-5 Je '88. Barry Millington (315w)

"Even in this age, one that is bereft of great Wagnerian singers, it should have been possible to assemble a stronger group of principals-....Levine's tempos are appropriate but on the slow side....It's unlikely that a better *Parsifal* will soon appear."

American Record Guide 51:72-4 My/Je '88. Kurt Moses (1075w)

"Some of the participants—James Levine, among them—seem virtually ideal. Others, including several of the principals, do not fare as well."

High Fidelity 38:65 Jl '88. Paul Moor (810w)

"This *Parsifal* has a reverential tone. So far, so good—but there is also a relaxed feeling that often threatens to impede the work's viscous lava flow....Much of what's best in this *Parsifal* emanates from Waltraud Meier's pointed, tensile Kundry....As a recording from stage performances, this one presents a reasonably accurate re-creation of how the Festspielhaus acoustics feel."

Opera News 52:42 Jl '88. John W. Freeman (460w)

"The orchestra is definitely the star of the recording, the fine playing and conducting being shown to advantage by the famous acoustics of the theater that Wagner took into consideration while composing the work. The singers are less well served...the sound being uneven as they move about on stage."

Music Magazine 11:48-9 N/D '88. Valerie Siren (540w)

"This whole undertaking cannot be dismissed; Levine's conducting is really quite wonderful. But my recommendation is that those seeking a fine *Parsifal* go for the reissue of the 1962 Knappertsbusch."

Ovation 9:47 O '88. Robert Levine (450w)

Hi-Fi News & Record Review 33:105 Ap '88. David Nice (485w)

Gramophone 65:1243 F '88. Arnold Whittall (830w)

7169. Das Rheingold.

James Levine (c). James Morris (bass-bar); Christa Ludwig (mez); Siegfried Jerusalem (ten); Heinz Zednik (ten); Ekkehard Wlaschiha (bar); Mari Anne Haggander (sop); Mark Baker (ten); Siegfried Lorenz (bar); Birgitta Svendsen (mez); Kurt Moll (bass); Jan-Hendrik Rootering (bass); Hei-Kyung Hong (sop); Diane Kesling (sop); Meredith Parsons (sop). Metropolitan Opera Orchestra. 1988.
DEUTSCHE GRAMMOPHON 427 607 DDD 157:00 3 discs

★***Awards:*** Best Recordings of the Month, *Stereo Review* O '90.

"James Levine's quite broad view of the score might not work so well with voices of less sustaining power, or with an orchestra of less clear, energetic articulation. But this is a gripping performance, both dramatically and musically. Too bad its libretto is printed in such small type."

Opera News 55:40 Ag '90. John W. Freeman (190w)

"Under Levine's unfailing sensitive, powerful leadership, the orchestral reading combines sensuous sound with energy and epic quality....In terms of dramatic propulsion and clear instrumental detail, the conducting and playing catch one's breath." *PS 100*

Opera Canada 31:57-8 Fall 90. Harvey Chusid (235w)

"Under Levine, the Met orchestra, at one time in low estate, has become one of the finest organizations of its kind, and *Das Rheingold*, a work full of colorful scene painting, is a wonderful showcase for the Lincoln Center band and its energetic conductor. Even more impressive is the casting. The recording offers some of the most lyrical Wagner singing I have ever heard, and after decades of Wagnerian hooting, it is much appreciated."
Stereo Review 55:87-8 O '90. Eric Salzman (430w)

"Earth, rather than fire or water, is Levine's element here. In other words, he may not have all the watery suppleness he needs for the Rhinemaidens, and he deliberately avoids Loge's tinder-box wit; but in all other respects this is a well-weighted, often searing drama in its own right rather than the opera-buffa juggling of types and ideas currently in production-fashion." *P95 S100*
Hi-Fi News & Record Review 35:95 S '90. David Nice (490w)

"The Culshaw/Solti *Rheingold* remains indispensable....I continue to admire the elegance and flow of Karajan's recording....The recent competition is, of course, from Haitink on Angel. When comparing his *Walkure* to Levine's, I didn't move far from the fence, and I'm not going to do so now....It's Jerusalem's remarkable performance that tips the balance toward Levine's *Rheingold*."
American Record Guide 53:129-30 S/O '90. Ralph V. Lucano (650w)

"What about the choice between this performance and Haitink's? Again I give Levine a very slight edge—and again it's because of his novel but convincing insight into the work at hand. But I certainly can't fault Haitink. Both are in superb sound, and one hears things never clearly heard before. On the other hand, I think it is safe to say that neither of these *Rings* will match such classic *Rings* of the past as Furtwangler's 1950 La Scala and 1953 Rome performances, or Clemens Krauss's 1953 Bayreuth performance, or even Solti's Vienna studio recording of 1958-66."
Fanfare 14:400-1 N/D '90. William Youngren (1375w)

"DGG's Met *Ring* is set against EMI's and it's swings and roundabouts all the way....but I think Haitink's EMI set just pips the post."
High Fidelity 1:110 Ag '90. Clive Manning (b.n.)

"If you're choosing between the two *Ring* recordings currently in production, Haitink's is, so far, the only choice."
Stereophile 13:201-2 S '90. Richard Lehnert (905w)

Levine "seems to conduct the work in segments, not organically as Bohm, Janowski or Haitink does. That said, Levine's magnificent orchestra is superior to Haitink's Bavarian Radio band (though not to Janowski's wonderful Dresden Staatskapell) and he is infinitely more theatrical....The casting, as in the two new *Walkuren*, is swings and roundabouts-....But for me, the set wins hands down in the casting of the most important roles in this opera, Loge and Alberich....DG's recording is characteristic: voices in the foreground, orchestra behind, quite wrong for Wagner...In sum then, I would not invest in this *Rheingold* as the first stage in a new *Ring*—on balance, Bohm's cycle retains my affections for its natural, theatrical pacing and mostly wonderful cast. Nor would I prefer it to Janowski."
Opera 41:1373-74 N '90. Hugh Canning (1120w)

Gramophone 68:276 Jl '90. Alan Blyth (770w)

Digital Audio's CD Review 7:50+ F '91. Sebastian Russ (255w)

7170. Der Ring des Nibelungen (Das Rheingold, Die Walkure, Siegfried, Gotterdammerung) (complete).
Georg Solti (c). Hans Hotter (bass/bar); Birgit Nilsson (sop); Gustav Neidlinger (bass); Wolfgang Windgassen (ten); Christa Ludwig (mez); George London (bass/bar); Kirsten Flagstad (sop). Vienna Philharmonic Orchestra. 1958-1965.
LONDON/DECCA 414 100 ADD 877:00 15 discs

✔HC ★★*Awards:* Records to Die for: 1 of 5 Recommended Recordings, *Stereophile* Ja '91 (Gary A. Galo); Records to Die for: 1 of 5 Recommended Recordings, *Stereophile* Ja '91 (Robert Levine).

"My number-one recommendation is still the London set....The first complete *Ring* on records, it was made in the early years of stereo-...and it remains a sonic marvel."
Stereo Review 52:156-7 D '87. William Livingstone (60w)

"Twenty-five years after its completion, Decca/London's *Ring* remains one of recorded music's greatest achievements....Overall, no stereo performance comes even close....A single CD excerpts disc (421 313-2) appears to be from analog copies of the originals and is *not* recommended."
Stereophile 14:137+ Ja '91. Gary A. Galo (b.n.)

"I'm going to beg the question and count this as *one-and-a-half* of the five all-time best recordings, only because it wouldn't be fair to count it as one and if I count it, correctly, as four, I would lose a turn and go directly to jail. This ground-breaking project remains epic in scope, execution, and quality."
Stereophile 14:157 Ja '91. Robert Levine (200w)

Gramophone 66:1498 Mr '89. Arnold Whittall (665w)

7171. Siegfried.
Georg Solti (c). Wolfgang Windgassen; Gerhard Stolze; Hans Hotter; Gustav Neidlinger. Vienna Phil-

harmonic Orchestra. reissue.
LONDON/DECCA 414 110 232:18 4 discs

"My number-one recommendation is still [this] London set....The first complete *Ring* on records, it was made available in the early years of stereo...and it remains a sonic marvel."
Stereo Review 52:156-7 D '87. William Livingstone (100w)

"Still the preferred choice if you want only one."
The New York Times F 7 '88, p. H30. John Rockwell (75w)

"Personally I would not want to be pressured into making a flat judgment about which *Ring* is 'the best'—there are now too many valid and stimulatingly different versions available to be dogmatic on the subject. But the attractions of London/Decca's pioneering achievement remain very real and considerable."
Ovation 6:42+ S '85. Peter G. Davis (440w)

Gramophone 62:794+ D '84. Alan Blyth (420w)

Stereo Review 51:100-1 Ja '86. William Livingstone (125w)

The Opera Quarterly 4:145-9 Summer '86. William Huck (360w)

Fanfare 9:283-9 N/D '85. William Youngren (315w)

American Record Guide 50:83+ Fall '87. John P. McKelvey (360w)

7172. Tristan und Isolde.
Wilhelm Furtwangler (c). Kirsten Flagstad (sop); Ludwig Suthaus (ten); Blanche Thebom (mez); Dietrich Fischer-Dieskau (bar); Josef Greindl (bar). Philharmonia Orchestra. 1957 reissue.
EMI 47321 ADD 67:02, 68:12, 64:21, 56:08 4 discs

✔HC ★★*Awards:* Critics Choice, *Hi Fi News & Record Review*, Ap '91 Supplement (Peter Branscombe); Critics Choice, *Hi Fi News & Record Review*, Ap '91 Supplement (George Hall).

"Here, in one of the greatest, most moving of all operatic masterpieces, you have the only contemporary of Toscanini to rank alongside him, the only Isolde of recent decades to transcend even her formidable younger colleague Birgit Nilsson, and, in the supporting role of Kurwenal, a most remarkable young singer on the threshold of one of the century's greatest singing careers—all that, plus one of the best symphony orchestras in the world....The refurbished sound emerges amazingly vibrant."
Musical America 108:67-8 Jl '88. Paul Moor (960w)

"Long available on LP from RCA, then Angel and Seraphim, the 1952 Tristan under Wilhelm Furtwangler remains a classic, and the CD reissue helps its cause."
Opera News 52:73 O '87. John W. Freeman (350w)

Stereo Review 52:112 D '87. Robert Ackart (140w)

7173. Die Walkure.
Wilhelm Furtwangler (c). Ludwig Suthaus (ten); Leonie Rysanek (sop); Martha Modl (sop); Ferdinand Frantz (bar); Margarete Klose (mez); Gottlob Frick (bass); Gerda Schreyer (sop); Erika Koth (sop); Judith Hellwig (sop); Dagmar Schmedes (sop); Dagmar Hermann (mez); Hertha Topper (mez); Johanna Blatter (mez); Ruth Siewert (mez). Vienna Philharmonic Orchestra. 1954 reissue.
EMI 63045 ADD 230:00 3 discs

✔HC ★*Awards:* Editors' Choice, *Digital Audio's CD Review*, 6:36 Je '90.

"Nobody on almost any other version of this opera can match Suthaus's wonderfully eloquent and heroically sung Siegmund...nor indeed Rysanek's Sieglinde...Choice must be for [this]...older set unless you must have modern stereo, but even here I much prefer the immediacy that was sought and achieved in the old days...I can promise anyone buying this historical reissue a revealing and stunning experience—and they can have it reasonably on only three, mid-price CDs."
Opera 40:750-51 Je '89. Alan Blyth (325w)

"This is a splendid performance, and should be in the collections even of those who already have Furtwangler's other versions....EMI has done its usual superb job in the transfer to CD. The brass and the bass lines in particular take on a life and presence they never had before."
Fanfare 13:335-36 Mr/Ap '90. William Youngren (1050w)

Gramophone 67:237 Jl '89. Alan Blyth (735w)

Digital Audio's CD Review 6:70-1 Mr '90. Sebastian Russ (630w)

WEBER, CARL MARIA VON

7174. Der Freischutz.
Joseph Keilberth (c). Elisabeth Grummer (sop); Rudolf Schock (ten); Lisa Otto (sop); Karl Christian Kohn (bass); Hermann Prey (bar); Gottlob Frick (bass); Ernst Wiemann (bass); Fritz Hoppe (spkr); Wilhelm Walter Dicks (bar); Maria Friederun (sop); Helga Hildebrand (sop); Herta Maria Schmidt (sop); Leonore Kirschstein (sop). Deutsche Oper Chorus; Berlin Philharmonic Orchestra. 1960 reissue.
EMI 69342 ADD 134:00 2 discs

"It is good to have this fine old recording back in circulation...This is the *Freischutz* to have." *P95 S95/85*
Hi-Fi News & Record Review 35:103 Je '90. Peter Branscombe (110w)

"There are several good recordings of *Der Freischutz*, but this is the one I'd choose first, for the sake of Grummer's truly definitive Agathe....The rest of the cast, if not extraordinary, are pretty good....Keilberth's conducting is unspectacularly satisfying."
American Record Guide 52:137 N/D '89. Ralph V. Lucano (305w)

Originally reviewed in *Fanfare* 12:6. "The fact remains that this is the best-sung *Der Freischutz*; you must decide for yourself between vocal and dramatic values. My own preference is still for the Erich Kleiber CDs...I dislike the two major CD releases, on DG and London."

Fanfare 13:411 N/D '89. James H. North (475w)

Gramophone 67:544 S '89. John Warrack (245w)

WEILL, KURT

7175. Der Zar Lasst Sich Photographieren (The Tsar Has His Photograph Taken).
Jan Latham-Keonig (c). Carla Pohl (sop); Marita Napier (sop); Barry McDaniel (bar); Thomas Lehrberger (ten); Ulla Tocha (mez); Heinz Kruse (ten); Hilke Helling (contr); Mario Brell (ten); Hans Franzen (bass). Cologne Radio Choir; Cologne Radio Orchestra. Cologne, Funkhaus. November 1984.
CAPRICCIO 60007; CAPRICCIO 10147 DDD 46:15

★*Awards:* Critics' Choice 1990, *Gramophone* D '90 (John Milsom).

"It's hard to imagine that such a fascinating little opera as this would have remained a mere footnote in Kurt Weill's output for so long-....Although a more stage-seasoned cast might have made a more convincing case for this opera, there's much to enjoy in this performance."

Stereo Review 55:116 Je '90. David Patrick Stearns (225w)"

"The artists on this disc perform very well and seem steeped in the style; the recording is quite convincing."

American Record Guide 53:106 Ja/F '90. Kurt Moses (335w)

"Barry McDaniel is an excellent Tsar...Carla Pohl as the real Angele is also vocally effective and the remaining cast members all provide sharply etched, neatly sung roles. The Cologne Radio Chorus offers solid support, and conductor Latham-Konig captures all the sizzle of Weill's energetic score in careful detail....Excellent sound."

The Nats Journal 46:41-2 My/Je '90. Carol Kimball (470w)

"Curiously, Latham-Konig has a much firmer grip on this work than heon *Aufstieg und Fall der Stadt Mahagonny* (Capriccio 10 160/61)-...A landmark issue, highly recommended."

Fanfare 13:348-50 Ja/F '90. Adrian Corleonis (465w)

In this 1984 recording, the characters play with appropriate manic dash. Only the Czar (Barry McDaniel) gets much chance for lyrical expansion: here the baritone's tendency toward a broad wobble is a minor liability...the ensemble is crisply coordinated."

Opera News 54:47 Ap 14 '90. John W. Freeman (250w)

"Overall, I'm not that taken with the score-...The cast is competent but not outstanding; I especially would have liked a suaver-sounding Tsar than Barry McDaniel."

Stereophile 13:202 S '90. Robert Deutsch (230w)

"The Capriccio recording...is poorly sung."

The New York Times Ag 19 '90, p. 36 H. John Rockwell (255w)

Gramophone 67:2054 My '90. John Milsom (485w)

WOLF, HUGO

7176. Der Corregidor.
Gerd Albrecht (c). Helen Donath (sop); Doris Soffel (contr); Ilse Hollweg (sop); Peter Maus (ten); Kurt Moll (bass); Dietrich Fischer-Dieskau (bar). Berlin Radio Symphony Orchestra; Berlin RIAS Chamber Choir.
SCHWANN 11641 DDD 130:03 2 discs

★★*Awards:* *Gramophone* Critics' Choice (Michael Oliver), 1987. Near-perfect 9/10, *Digital Audio*, Mr '88.

"This is it, at last—a loving, keenly versed, and (with one exception) note-complete presentation which supplants the no less dedicated 1944 Dresden recording (Acanta 40.21 408, *Fanfare* 9:4)."

Fanfare 11:256-7 N/D '87. Adrian Corleonis (450w)

"The performance...is exemplary....The libretto is in German only; shocking for a virtually unknown opera....fine sound."

American Record Guide 51:74-5 My/Je '88. Lee Milazzo (525w)

"A pity, then, that a theatre cut of some 200 bars in act four was made in a purely recorded account of the work. That apart, this must at last be the definitive version we have all been waiting for; I can not imagine it being surpassed."

Music and Musicians International 36:59 D '87. Robert Hartford (265w)

"Gerd Albrecht leads a vigorous and disciplined performance, although he hasn't always worked out the transitions between episodes smoothly. None of the singing, I'm sorry to say, is in the same league with that of the Dresden cast [1944 Urania LP]."

Opus 4:50-1 D '87. David Hamilton (2155w)

Digital Audio 4:74 D '87. Octavio Roca (390w)

WOLF-FERRARI, ERMANNO

7177. Il Segreto di Susanna.
John Pritchard (c). Renata Scotto (sop); Renato Bruson (bar). Philharmonia Orchestra. 1981.
CBS 36733 DDD 49:00

★*Awards:* Perfect 10s, *Digital Audio's CD Review*, Mr '89. Cream of the Crop IV, *Digital Audio's CD Review*, 6:43 Je '90.

"This 1981 recording finds baritone Renato Bruson at his most polished and dedicated-...Scotto is sassy and independent, giving languorousness a good name in her cigarette-enjoying stupor....The recording has a nice sitting-room intimacy which is just right."
Stereophile 11:161 S '88. Robert Levine (365w)

"This is one of those works that, at around 50 minutes, might have been made for CD. Renato Scotto and Renato Bruson make much of the slight piece, while Sir John Pritchard and the Philharmonia Orchestra underpin the fun."
Music and Musicians International 37:48-9 F '89. Robert Hartford (205w)

Digital Audio 5:48 Ja '89. Octavio Roca (215w)

Solo Vocal Music

ADAMS, JOHN

8001. Wound Dresser, for Baritone and Orchestra; Fearful Symmetries, for Orchestra.
Sanford Sylvan (bar). John Adams (c). Saint Luke's Orchestra.
ELEKTRA 79218 DDD 47:19

✔**HC** ★★★★*Awards:* Top Disks of the Year, *The New York Times* D 24, '89 (John Rockwell). The Want List 1990, *Fanfare* N/D '90 (Mike Silverton; Edward Strickland); Critics' Choice 1990, *Gramophone* D '90 (James Jolly). The Want List 1991, *Fanfare* N/D '91 (Leslie Gerber).

"I found *The Wound-Dresser* a wrenching experience, one that is likely to evoke the listener's own painful memories of the death of loved ones...It is most fully heard far from concert-hall distractions, or even listening-room distractions, in some physical correlative of the void Adams confronts in this outstanding composition. *Fearful Symmetries* is confrontational (the composer's word) in another sense—a trickster piece in the *Grand Pianola Music* vein. The more I hear it the more hilarious and ingenious I find it....this is certainly one of the best records of the year."
Fanfare 13:102 Mr/Ap '90. Edward Strickland (680w)

"With this latest collection, John Adams secures his position as America's leading minimalist....Taking as its text a poem of the same name by Walt Whitman, *The Wound Dresser* is an incomparably better work at conveying the emotions of war than that other recent, overly-touted composition, *Different Trains* by Steve Reich....*The Wound Dresser* is Adam's most powerful work to date, maybe the best thing he has yet written."
American Record Guide 53:14 Mr/Ap '90. William Ellis (360w)

"*The Wound-Dresser* is an exquisite and poignant evocation of the act of selfless love offered by those caring for the wounded. It avoids sentimentality (just) and, despite a few moments of obvious eclecticism, is a work of genuine vision and compassion....*Fearful Symmetries*, is an all too accurate exploration of some of the worst kinds of pop music." *P95 S95/75*
Hi-Fi News & Record Review 35:89 Ag '90. Simon Cargill (350w)

"'Fearful Symmetries'....amuses and intrigues the listener, but for musical importance it can hardly hold a candle to 'The Wound-Dresser,' the most affecting piece of music to come my way in long time."
Audio 74:134+ N '90. Paul Moor (665w)

"John Adams has noted an alternation between the solemn and the playful in his work...The contrast is nowhere more strikingly evident than in the two pieces recorded here: an earnest, careful, politically correct orchestral song that fails to touch the heart and a funky *perpetuum mobile* that leaves the listener physically exhausted and grinning like a maniac....The Orchestra of St. Luke's, under the composer's direction, presents polished, lively, informed, and enthusiastic readings of both works. The digital sound is admirably clear and entirely humane."
Musical America 110:72-3 S '90. Andrew Stiller (680w)

"The elements these works share is a continuous—generally even—rhythmic impulse, repeated patterns, slow harmonic change and special attention to orchestral color and dynamics. The liner notes by Sarah Cahill are very thorough and will be of help to the listener."
HighPerformanceReview 7:59 Winter '90-91. Allan Blank (260w)

Gramophone 68:88 Je '90. John Milsom (495w)

ARGENTO, DOMINICK

8002. From the Diary of Virginia Woolf. BENSON, WARREN. Songs for the End of the World.
Virginia Dupuy (mez); David Garvey (pno); Thomas Bacon (Fr horn); Rogene Russell (Eng horn); Douglas Howard (mrba); Barrett Sills (cello).
GASPARO 273 DDD 66:21

✔**HC** ★*Awards:* The Want List 1990, *Fanfare* N/D '90 (William Wians).

"Dupuy sings beautifully and intelligently-...these two works...share a quirky, sad lyricism, a spare musical frame, a feeling for sung words. More fundamentally, they show our common search for self-understanding and for our place in the world. They are beautiful explorations of deeply human concerns at once private and universal."

Fanfare 13:100-1 My/Je '90. William Wians (775w)

"Mezzo Virginia Dupuy handles both works with fine control and interpretive commitment-....In short, this is a highly complementary pairing of two contemporary American works."

The Nats Journal 46:42-3 My/Je '90. Carol Kimball (350w)

"Virginia Dupuy...does fine work on this disc of music by two American composers."

"Virginia Dupuy displays an absolutely even tone quality from bottom to top, a beautiful legato, and a naturalness and ease of performance that makes listening a pleasure. I found diction somewhat lacking in clarity. David Garvey is a fine accompanist, with flexibility and a sense of teamwork. The chamber ensemble in *Songs for the End of the World* also gives a first-rate performance.This disc is a must for anyone interested in present-day vocal music."

Pan Pipes; Sigma Alpha Iota 83:7 Spr '91. Jocelyn Mackey (1170w)

American Record Guide 53:151 Jl/Ag '90. Timothy D. Taylor (125w)

ARNE, THOMAS

8003. Songs: Frolick and free; The Morning; *Much Ado about Nothing:* Sigh no more, ladies; *The Desert Island:* What tho' his guilt; Cymon and Iphigenia; Thou soft flowing Avon; Jenny; *The Winter's Amusement:* The Lover's Recantation.
Emma Kirkby (sop); Richard Morton (ten); Roy Goodman (vln). Roy Goodman (c). Parley of Instruments.
HYPERION 66237 DDD 52:00

"An absolutely charming collection....all concerned acquit themselves beautifully....the whole package is calculated to put even the most curmudgeonly listener in a state of delighted good humour."

Hi-Fi News & Record Review 33:83 Je '88. Jeremy Siepmann (210w)

"Emma Kirkby sings her portion of the songs with the accuracy, clean coloratura and straight vibratoless tone for which she is known. Richard Morton's tenor is attractive and expressive, his diction excellent."

American Record Guide 51:11 S/O '88. Philip L. Miller (220w)

"I wish (vainly, of course) Emma Kirkby would risk a little vibrato so that her upper notes sounded less like a bos'n's whistle and more like a human voice, but her style is well known and, as always, she is supremely competent....The instrumental accompaniments...are delightfully played...Texts are provided."

Fanfare 12:83-4 S/O '88. Robert Levine (380w)

Gramophone 65:1627 My '88. Stanley Sadie (210w)

BARBER, SAMUEL

8004. Songs: Knoxville: Summer of 1915 (*Eleanor Steber, sop; Dumbarton Oaks Orch., William Strickland c*). Dover Beach, Opus 3 (*Dietrich Fischer-Dieskau, bar; Juilliard Quartet*). Hermit Songs, Opus 29 (*Leontyne Price, sop; Samuel Barber, pno*) Andromache's Farewell, Opus 39 (*Martina Arroyo, sop; New York Philharmonic Orchestra, Thomas Schippers, cond*).
reissues.
CBS 46727 ADD 51:00

✔HC ★*Awards:* Critics' Choice 1991, *Gramophone*, Ja '92 (David Gutman).

Gramophone 69:152 O '91. David Gutman (long)

8005. Songs: Three Songs, Opus 2; Three Songs, Opus 10; Four Songs, Opus 13; Two Songs, Opus 18; Nuvoletta, Opus 25; Hermit Songs, Opus 29; Despite and Still, Opus 41.
Roberta Alexander (sop); Tan Crone (pno).
ETCETERA 1055 DDD 61:00

★*Awards:* The Want List 1989, *Fanfare* N/D '89 (Walter Simmons).

"This disc can be recommended virtually without reservation."

Fanfare 12:84-6 Mr/Ap '89. Walter Simmons (1200w)

"The entire corpus is intelligently and lovingly sung here, and admirably recorded."

Hi-Fi News & Record Review 33:99+ O '88. Kenneth Dommett (335w)

"Barber wrote for generous voices, voices that could soar and fill out a lyrical line, rise above the staff without strain, spin out a phrase. At her best, Ms. Alexander answers these requirements very well indeed....Tan Crone's pianism—or perhaps the too-close recording of it—sounds prickly and wanting in legato."

The New York Times Ja 29 '89, p. H 27-28. Will Crutchfield (250w)

"Alexander's singing...is handsome and shapely, her diction adequate, her interpretations for the most part carefully worked out. What is missing is the intensity that comes from complete emotional involvement, a failing that causes her to be at her least distinctive when Barber is at his best. Pianist Crone, who is rather backwardly recorded, is perfectly competent, but Barber's piano parts require more vivid and pointed playing than Crone provides."

Musical America 109:50 Ja '89. Terry Teachout (430w)

Gramophone 66:459 S '88. Michael Oliver (400w)

BAX, ARNOLD

8006. Enchanted Summer; Walsinghame; Fatherland.

Anne Williams-King (sop); Lynore McWhirter (sop); Martyn Hill (ten). Vernon Handley (c). Brighton Festival Chorus; Royal Philharmonic Orchestra. 1988.
CHANDOS 8625 DDD 52:00

✔**HC** ★*Awards:* The Year's Best, *Hi Fi News & Record Review*, May '90 Supplement.

"This issue represents a considerable achievement for all involved. The spacious recording (All Saints, Tooting) copes beautifully with everything Bax can muster, and Chandos provide full texts." *P95/100 S95/100*

Hi-Fi News & Record Review 35:95 Ja '90; p.15+ My '90 Supplement. Andrew Achenbach (490w)

"Hadley turns in the kind of strong performances we have grown used to by now, and his soloists are fine; but I might draw attention to the presence here of the Brighton Festival Chorus directed by Laszlo Heltay, new to me but sweet and neat as Brighton rock. Recommended to all Baxites."

Fanfare 13:110-11 Ja/F '90. John Ditsky (220w)

"Soloists, chorus and orchestra are all excellent and one could not wish for a better advocate than Handley. I admit to a slightly favourable bias towards Bax's music but, even so, this is a CD well worth hearing."

Organists' Review 76:50 Mr '90. Richard Popple (425w)

Gramophone 67:716 O '89. Michael Oliver (455w)

Digital Audio's CD Review 6:54-5 F '90. David Vernier (225w)

BELLINI, VINCENZO

8007. Arias: *I Puritani:* Son salvo!..A una fonte afflitto...Corre a valle, corre a monte; A te, o cara. *La Sonnambula:* Vedi, o madre...Tutto e sciolto; Ah! perche non posso odiarti. **DONIZETTI, GAETANO. Arias:** *La Favorita:* Favorita del Re!..Spirto gentil; Una vergine, un angel di Dio. *La Fille du Regiment:* Ah! mes amis. *L'Elisir d'Amore:* Una furtiva lagrima. *Don Pasquale:* Povero Ernesto!..Cerchero lontana terra...E se fia ad altro oggetto; Come'e gentil. *Lucia di Lammermoor:* Tome degl'avi miei...Fra poco a e ricovero; Tu che a Dio spiegasti l'ali.
Raul Gimenez (ten). Michelangelo Veltri (c). Scottish Philharmonic Singers; Scottish Chamber Orchestra.
NIMBUS 5224 DDD 70:00

★*Awards:* Critics' Choice 1990, *Gramophone* D '90 (John Steane).

"The dozen numbers from Bellini and Donizetti that make up Raul Gimenez's showcase of *Operatic Arias*...certainly allow this young tenor from the Argentine to display his flexible, effortlessly-produced and always pleasing tenor to advantage."

Music and Musicians International 39:39-40 O '90. Robert Hartford (b.n.)

"Recording, conducting, and presentation maintain Nimbus's generally high standards. If this tenor's previous offerings pleased, no further recommendation is needed. Those who resisted then would do well to sample this—they will almost certainly be most pleasantly surprised."

American Record Guide 53:45-6 My/Je '90. Vivian A. Liff (330w)

"Gimenez is best, I think, when he's being mournful; second best when scornful. Still, when the sound is luscious, and Gimenez is feeling comfortable, it's really something to hear. Michelangelo Veltri's accompaniments are surprisingly flaccid and seem (like the chorus) to have been recorded in another room and at another time....uninteresting notes, texts, and translations. Recommended, but, somehow, it will leave you wanting a bit more in the energy department."

Fanfare 13:337 Jl/Ag '90. Robert Levine (300w)

"Phonographically speaking, his instrument sounds harmonious, wide-ranging, and eminently qualitative. Probably smallish in volume, it is employed with discreet, sensitive, communicative taste. One blemish of which I find myself becoming more and more conscious is the catarrhal nasality, most obvious on the 'ee' sound, that adulterates some of the bel in his canto....He is an intelligent interpreter with lyrical, yet impassioned portrayals that are both musically and dramatically rewarding....Despite qualifications, though, this is an album that should interest most voice devotees."

Stereophile 13:171+ Ag '90. Bernard Soll (485w)

Digital Audio's CD Review 7:80 O '90. Sebastian Russ (340w)

Gramophone 67:2042 My '90. John Steane (820w)

BENSON, WARREN. Songs for the End of the World. See No. 8002.

BERG, ALBAN

8008. Lulu: Suite, for Soprano and Orchestra; Der Wein (concert aria), for Soprano and Orchestra; Lyric Suite, for String Quartet (1926) or Orchestra (1929) (3 movts.).
Judith Blegen (sop); Jessye Norman (sop). Pierre Boulez (c). New York Philharmonic Orchestra. 1979, 1980 reissue.
SONY 45838 ADD 58:34

★*Awards:* The Want List 1991, *Fanfare* N/D '91 (William Youngren).

"With the NYPO at their peak and Judith Blegen and Jessye Norman making light of the composer's often angular vocal lines, it all adds up to a group of truly passionate performances. Doubters can try track 5." *P95 S95*

Hi-Fi News & Record Review 35:107 N '90. Simon Cargill (100w)

"In its LP form, this recording was a mainstay of my collection, so I'm happy to report that it has passed the remastering process with flying colors. The sound is, if anything, improved in definition and immediacy with more solid bass and less treble harshness and dryness than in the original."

American Record Guide 54:31 Ja/F '91. Stephen D. Chakwin, Jr. (120w)

Gramophone 68:1198 D '90. Arnold Whittall (310w)

Digital Audio's CD Review 7:45 Je '91. Octavio Roca (200w)

BERIO, LUCIANO

8009. Formazioni; Folk Songs (11), for Voice and 7 Instruments; Sinfonia, for 8 Voices and Orchestra.
Jard Van Nes (mez). Riccardo Chailly (c). Royal Concertgebouw Orchestra.
LONDON/DECCA 425 832 DDD 70:00

> ★★*Awards:* Critics' Choice 1990, *Gramophone* D '90 (John Milsom); The Highs, 1990, *The New York Times* D 30 '90 (John Rockwell). The Gramophone Awards, Nominations, Contemporary, *Gramophone*, N '91.

"This record unites on one disc three great pieces by Berio. If you're looking for a Berio sampler, you can't go wrong."

American Record Guide 54:35-6 Mr/Ap '91. William Ellis (400w)

"The London disc includes Berio's two best-loved works as well as a substantial new orchestral work, *Formazioni*, all played by a glorious orchestra and conducted by a devotee. *Folk Songs*...boasts luscious singing from Jard van Nes...*Formazioni*...is typical of the kind of many-layered and multi-colored instrumental music of which Berio is a master, and Chailly and the Concertgebouw, which commissioned it, make it sound tremendous. The *Sinfonia* performance, though, is a disappointment."

Musical America 111:69-70 My '91. Mark Swed (180w)

"Chailly takes it for granted that all the works here are masterpieces which need no special pleading. He plays them straight, and the results are taut and cogent in a way that seems to underplay the music's radicalism. This approach does have its disadvantages....Good but not stunning versions, then." *P95/85 S95*

Hi-Fi News & Record Review 35:83 S '90. Simon Cargill (350w)

"The London disc combines Berio's two most accessible and well-known works with *Formazioni* of 1987....sadly, neither receives one of its best performances here....And if you're tempted to get this disc for the sake of *Formazioni*, I'd say forget it."

Fanfare 15:160-62 S/O '91. Kyle Gann (long)

Gramophone 68:396+ Ag '90. John Milsom (555w)

High Fidelity 1:121 O '90. Andrew Stuart (110w)

BERLIOZ, HECTOR

8010. Les Nuits d'Ete (song cycle), Opus 7. MAHLER, GUSTAV. Des Knaben Wunderhorn: Wer hat dies Liedlein erdacht?; Verlor'ne Muh; Wo die schonen Trompeten blasen; Rheinlegendchen; Lob des hohen Verstandes. **Ruckert Lieder (5):** Blicke mir nicht in die Lieder; Ich atmet' einen linden Duft; Ich bin der Welt abhanden gekommen; Um Mitternacht; Liebst du um Schonheit.
Jan De Gaetani (mez). David Effron (c). Eastman Chamber Ensemble. May 1989.
BRIDGE 9017 DDD 65:00

> ★*Awards: American Record Guide* Overview: Berlioz, Mr/Ap '91 (Les Nuits d'Ete).

"If her voice is sometimes weary and frayed, what does it matter in relation to the peerless musicianship she evinces in every phrase? Her transcendent clarity of vision represents nothing less than the triumph of the human spirit, a courageous proclamation of life in the face of death."

The New York Times F 18 '90, p. 32 H. K. Robert Schwarz (105w)

"De Gaetani sounds as if she is singing in a reverie or hypnotic state, so intensely felt and strikingly nuanced are her performances....De Gaetani's voice was not large but her musical and interpretive intelligence were....Recommended."

American Record Guide 53:29 Mr/Ap '90. Michael Mark (250w)

"The valedictory nature of this album is inseparable from its content. Ranging from Schoenberg to Stephen Foster, or from Wolf to Wernick, Shifrin, Crumb, and Rochberg, DeGaetani filled, with tremendous authority, such a large and astonishingly adventurous place in our musical life that her passing is a literally incalculable loss....Bridge's presentation is exemplary. The sound is crisply immediate and startlingly detailed, though the eloquently expressive ensemble consistently threatens to overpower the voice."

Fanfare 13:356-57 My/Je '90. Adrian Corleonis (400w)

"Here and there DeGaetani's voice may seem a little smaller than some of us remember, but there is no mistaking its soundness, its purity, its genuineness. The special pathos in the last song on the disc, Mahler's *Ich bin der Welt abhanden gekommen*, derives simply and irresistibly from the total commitment of a great interpretive artist to the material she chose to sing....The sound quality is first-rate."

Stereo Review 55:109-10 Je '90. Richard Freed (330w)

"These were the remarkable Jan deGaetani's final recordings...At times the singer's tone whitens uncomfortably, and there's the occasional shortness of breath, but these are the exceptions rather than the rule, and few will complain. This is powerful stuff, and is recommended to anyone who loves this music."

Stereophile 13:171 Ag '90. Robert Levine (285w)

"I'm not crazy about the *Nuits d'ete*, which DeGaetani must once have sung beautifully but which seems to me to require more solidity of vocal line...But the Mahler songs are lovely."

Musical America 111:90-1 My '91. Kenneth Furie (385w)

8011. Les Nuits d'Ete (song cycle), Opus 7; La Mort de Cleopatre.
Kiri Te Kanawa; Jessye Norman. Daniel Barenboim (c). Paris Orchestra.
DEUTSCHE GRAMMOPHON 410 966

★***Awards:*** *American Record Guide* Overview: Berlioz, Mr/Ap '91 (Les Nuits d'Ete).

Gramophone 62:59 Je '84. Alan Blyth (225w)

BERNSTEIN, LEONARD

8012. Arias and Barcarolles (song cycle), for Mezzo-Soprano, Baritone and Piano Four Hands. Songs and Duets: *On the Town:* Some Other Time; Lonely Town; Carried Away; I Can Cook. *Peter Pan:* Dream with Me. *Wonderful Town:* A Little Bit in Love. *Songfest:* Storyette, H.M.; To What You Said.
Judy Kaye (sop); William Sharp (bar); Michael Barrett (pno); Steven Blier (pno); Sara Sant'Ambrogio (cello). 1989.
KOCH 7000 DDD 59:54

★★★★★***Awards:*** The Want List 1990, *Fanfare* N/D '90 (Ralph V. Lucano; Jon Tuska); Critics' Choice 1990, *Gramophone* D '90 (James Jolly; Edward Seckerson). Editors' Choice, *Digital Audio's CD Review*, Je '91.

"This is a beguiling recording—superbly performed...that comes closer to capturing the best of Mr. Bernstein's vocal music than perhaps any single disk ever has."

The New York Times Je 3 '90, p. 23 H. Mark Swed (375w)

"Judy Kaye and William Sharp sing with versatility, commitment, and sensitivity in performances which are simply first-rate. Duo-pianists Blier and Barrett furnish close-knit ensemble throughout the program....Outstanding recorded sound, texts for *Arias and Barcarolles*, and notes."

The Nats Journal 47:45 N/D '90. Carol Kimball (350w)

"This is a determined attempt to turn Broadway numbers into art songs, which is really not far removed from what nightclub artists like Julie Wilson and others do....Ms. Kaye clearly challenges singers like Edith Adams and Comden and Green, but I do miss the orchestras on the cast recordings. The 'Arias and Barcarolles'...were not written for show scores, and require another sensibility to be appreciated. Ms. Kaye and Mr. Sharp and the instrumentalists do them, and Mr. Bernstein, proud."

American Record Guide 53:168-71 S/O '90. Richard Traubner (270w)

"In this opinion, *Arias and Barcarolles* is a highly enjoyable, but possibly evanescent, pastiche and not the masterpiece of maturity most of us wished for....As these four artists constituted the team that introduced *Arias and Barcarolles* at the New York Festival in 1989, their performance should be—and certainly sounds—definitive."

Stereophile 14:251+ Ap '91. Bernard Soll (300w)

"It is unfortunate to report that this record is stillborn, which seems to be a minority opinion since everybody else has lauded it. Judy Kaye, of course, is a remarkable artist in many genres and I exclude her from these remarks....There is just under an hour of music on this CD, which is just as well."

HighPerformanceReview 7:61 Winter '90-91. Bert Wechsler (180w)

"His inability to tell the difference between a good text and a horrible one sinks *Arias and Barcarolles*...The music is minor Bernstein, lively and characteristic but not especially memorable....[the] performance...makes it sound suspiciously like a real piece of music."

Musical America 110:70 N '90. Terry Teachout (310w)

Digital Audio's CD Review 7:69-70 N '90. Octavio Roca (345w)

BLITZSTEIN, MARC

8013. Songs: Monday Morning Blues. Croon-Spoon. The New Suit ("Zipperfly"). In the Clear. I Wish It So. In Twos. Penny Candy. Emily (Ballad of the Bombardier). Displaced. o by the by. until and i heard. open your heart. jimmie's got a goil. What Will It Be for Me. Rose Song. Blues. Nickel Under the Foot. The Cradle Will Rock. Bird Upon the Tree. Stay in My Arms.
Karen Holvik (sop); William Sharp (bar); Steven Blier (pno).
KOCH 7050 DDD 67:30

★***Awards:*** Critic's Choice: 1991, *American Record Guide*, Ja/F '92 (David Greene).

"The performances are magnificent....Production values are outstanding: the recording is crystal-clear, so the lack of texts doesn't matter; to an American, every word is immediately intelligible. Every number is a highlight."

Fanfare 14:123-4 Jl/Ag '91. James H. North (750w)

"Holvik, Sharp, and Blier are simply stunning in a program which has equal impact...This recording is enthusiastically recommended."
The Nats Journal 48:39 N/D '91. Carol Kimball (long)

"Holvik has a fine voice and knows the style-...[William Sharp's] lyric baritone is beautifully controlled and prismatic in its range of color; his diction is faultless and natural...Steven Blier['s]...accompaniments are just right."
American Record Guide 54:36+ N/D '91. David Mason Greene (long)

"Mr. Sharp's light, airy vocal delivery, immaculate diction and vivid characterizations do much to bring these songs to life. Both he and Ms. Holvik find the perfect balance between Broadway and operatic styles...This is a flawless recording."
The New York Times S 22 '91, sec H p. 33. K. Robert Schwarz (med)

Gramophone 69:153 O '91. Peter Dickinson (long)

BOULEZ, PIERRE

8014. Le Visage Nuptial; Le Soleil des Eaux, for Soprano, Orchestra and Chorus; Figures, Doubles, Prismes, for Orchestra.
Phyllis Bryn-Julson (sop); Elisabeth Laurence (mez). Pierre Boulez (c). BBC Singers; BBC Symphony Orchestra.
ERATO 45494 DDD 62:00

> ★★ *Awards:* The Gramophone Awards, Nominations, Contemporary, *Gramophone*, N '91; The Want List 1991, *Fanfare* N/D '91 (Benjamin Pernick). Critics' Choice 1991, *Gramophone*, Ja '92 (Arnold Whittall).

"*Visage*, especially, reveals an ecstatic side of the composer that has all but disappeared, expressing an erotic passion whose lyricism borders on the Expressionistic."
The New York Times F 17 '91, p. 23 H. K. Robert Schwarz (b.n.)

"Sound quality is often close to ideal...these early works need to be listened to in the spirit of surrealist poems the composer sets. Image follows image: the effect is made more by juxtaposition than transition." *P95 S95*
Hi-Fi News & Record Review 36:89 Mr '91. Simon Cargill (225w)

"A release of major importance; highest recommendation."
Fanfare 14:159-60 Mr/Ap '91. Ben Pernick (550w)

"All the works on this disc are vividly performed, with Boulez's characteristic slight laxness of ensemble....Phyllis Bryn-Julson is too close to the microphone in this new issue. Erato's sound is otherwise very realistic, and this disc is strongly recommended to any and all students of 20th Century music."
American Record Guide 54:42 Mr/Ap '91. Arved Ashby (280w)

Option 38:87-7 My/Je '91. Steve Hahn (115w)

Gramophone 69:48 Ja '92. Arnold Whittall (long)

BRAHMS, JOHANNES. Ernste Gesange (4), Opus 121. See No. 8062.

BRITTEN, BENJAMIN

8015. Les Illuminations (Rimbaud) (song cycle for Soprano or Tenor and Strings), Opus 18; Serenade for Tenor, Horn and Strings, Opus 31; Nocturne, Opus 60.
Martyn Hill (ten); Frank Lloyd (horn); Duke Dobing (fl); Anthony Halstead (horn); Helen McQueen (Eng horn); Michael Pearce (clar); Rachel Masters (harp); Robert Jordan (bsn); Janos Keszei (timp). Richard Hickox (c). City of London Sinfonia.
VIRGIN 90792 DDD 77:00

> ★★*Awards:* Critics' Choice 1990, *Gramophone* D '90 (Christopher Headington). Best of the Month, *Hi-Fi News & Record Review*, Mr '90; The Year's Best, *Hi Fi News & Record Review*, May '90 Supplement.

"It's wonderfully well-recorded, with vibrant strings and a clear, clean, dynamic tenor voice. For the most part it is thoroughly, indeed passionately, compelling."
New Hi-Fi Sound 7:109 D '89. Jonathan Kettle (225w)

"With Martyn Hill's greater refinement not just in the *Nocturne*, but in *Les Illuminations* and the *Serenade* as well, and the City of London Sinfonia under Hickox at full stretch, the Virgin Classics CD wins my preference [over Chandos with Anthony Rolfe Johnson]."
Fanfare 13:110-11 Jl/Ag '90. John Wiser (350w)

"All three cycles are sensitively and stylishly performed. Martyn Hill sounds more ingratiating when he is not singing loudly (his tone is then inclined to roughen slightly and takes some getting used to), but his soft singing is often a delight and he is fortunate to have such a perceptive accompanist in Hickox."
P95(100) S95/100
Hi-Fi News & Record Review 35:102 Mr '90; p.18-19 My '90. Andrew Achenbach (445w)

"Tenor Hill is indeed a worthy successor to the original tenor Pears....Although not as incisive or menacing as Pears, Hill certainly has a more beautiful voice....This is a first-rate recording. You must get it!"
American Record Guide 53:35-6 Jl/Ag '90. Charles Parsons (155w)

Digital Audio's CD Review 8:56 Ja '92. Lawrence B. Johnson (long)

Gramophone 67:1183 D '89. Christopher Headington (580w)

8016. Les Illuminations (Rimbaud) (song cycle for Soprano or Tenor and Strings), Opus 18; Quatre Chansons Francaises for Soprano and Orchestra; Serenade (various poets) for Tenor, Horn and Strings, Opus 31.

Felicity Lott (sop); Anthony Rolfe-Johnson (ten); Michael Thompson (horn). Bryden Thomson (c). Scottish National Orchestra. Henry Wood Hall, Glasgow.
CHANDOS 8657 DDD 59:00

★★*Awards:* Critics' Choice 1989, *Gramophone* D '89 (Michael Kennedy). The Year's Best, *Hi Fi News & Record Review*, May '90 Supplement.

"*Les Illuminations*, to the poetry of Rimbaud, was originally dedicated to a soprano, but Pears co-opted them for tenor in his matchless performances. Felicity Lott sings them...in a way that only a fine soprano voice can achieve vocal effects....a superb performance."
HighPerformanceReview 7:63 Winter '90-91. Bert Wechsler (b.n.)

"Beautiful, stunningly accomplished performances are combined here with a subtly-balanced recording which conveys just the right degree of nearness to voices and orchestra. The result is an outstanding disc, one of the best ever made of Britten's music." *P100 S100*
Hi-Fi News & Record Review 34:95 Ag '89; p.18 My ' Supplement. Arthur Jacobs (350w)

"Lott's interpretation is well-nigh perfect, capturing the sensual overtones of Rimbaud's prose in excellent French. Vocally, the piece suits here to a 'T'....No less impressive is Anthony Rolfe Johnson's performance of the *Serenade for Tenor, Horn & Strings*....In short, for programming and performance, this is a Britten disc to have....Excellent sound."
The Nats Journal 46:38-9 N/D '89. Carol Kimball (640w)

"Two fine British singers, in their prime, feature on this welcome disc of Britten orchestral song cycles....Some directness of sound is lost in the boomy acoustic of Glasgow's Henry Wood Hall, but the strings of the Scottish National Orchestra sound resonant and sweet as a result."
Music and Musicians International 37:23 Je '89. Meurig Bowen (630w)

"This 'second generation' of Britten recordings (as opposed to recordings by the composer and his associates) bring to the ear new, if not always interesting, possibilities of interpretation. Chandos exceeds marvelously, especially with the work of tenor Johnson."
American Record Guide 52:48 N/D '89. Charles Parsons (160w)

"I wish tenor Anthony Rolfe Johnson would enunciate his English texts in the Serenade as cleanly and projectively as Lott does her French. His solid vocalism is more than adequate to the occasion but to those accustomed to leaner voices from Pears and Tear, he may seem positively beefy....Half of this Chandos CD I'll endorse heartily; the other half seems merely well intentioned."
Fanfare 13:143-44 Ja/F '90. John Wiser (180w)

Gramophone 67:69-70 Je '89. Michael Kennedy (300w)

8017. Les Illuminations (Rimbaud) (song cycle for Soprano or Tenor and Strings), Opus 18; Nocturne; Serenade for Tenor, Horn, and Strings, Opus 31.
Peter Pears (ten). Benjamin Britten (c). London Symphony Orchestra; English Chamber Orchestra.
LONDON/DECCA 417 153

✔HC ★★*Awards:* *Fanfare* Want List 1987 (Elliott Kaback). Record of the Eighties, *Gramophone*, D '89 (Christopher Headington).

CANTELOUBE, JOSEPH

8018. Songs of the Auvergne.
(Volume 1).
Kiri Te Kanawa (sop). Jeffrey Tate (c). English Chamber Orchestra.
LONDON/DECCA 410 004

"Reviewed in Lp form by JCO in Volume 2, Issue 4, pp.210-1. JCO commented that the orchestrations are overly lush for simple Auvergne folk songs, but Kiri Te Kanawa sings beautifully, and manages to convey the music's spirit."
High Performance Review 3 (1):91-2 Ag '84. (120w)

Gramophone 61:168 Jl '83. Edward Greenfield (210w)

Digital Audio 1:72-3 S '84. John Marks (200w)

8019. Songs of the Auvergne. VILLA-LOBOS, HEITOR. Bachianas Brasilieras No. 5.
(Volume 2).
Kiri Te Kanawa (sop); Lynn Harrell (cello). Jeffrey Tate (c). English Chamber Orchestra.
LONDON/DECCA 411 730 50:54

"The warmth, the 'satin-smoothness' of the voice are as beguiling as ever—irresistibly so in those songs of a more sensual, tantalising playfulness."
Hi-Fi News & Record Review 30:101 Mr '85. Edward Seckerson (165w)

"As a bonus, we get the celebrated *Bachianas Brasileiras No. 5*, including the *Dansa* in a performance that competes with the better ones."
Fanfare 8:159-60 Jl/Ag '85. James Miller (175w)

Gramophone 62:634 N '84. John Steane (385w) (rev. of LP); 62:902 Ja '85. Alan Blyth (85w) (rev. of CD)

Ovation 6:32 D '85. Philip L. Miller (290w)

Audio 69:136+ Je '85. Bert Whyte (250w)

CARCERES, BARTOMEU

8020. Villancicos and Ensaladas.
Montserrat Figueras (sop). Jordi Savall (c). La Capella Reial de Catalunya.
AUVIDIS-ASTREE 8723 DDD 67:50

★*Awards:* Critic's Choice: 1991, *American Record Guide*, Ja/F '92 (Paul Laird).

"Jordi Savall and soprano Montserrat Figueras continue to be definitive interpreters of Spanish Renaissance music. La Capella Reial de Catalunya...support the soloist Figueras, a soprano of great flexibility and clarity who sings this repertory with minute attention to nuance and shading...The sound is very live, particularly the realistic percussion."
American Record Guide 54:209 N/D '91. Paul Laird (long)

"This is unfamiliar music, and it's delightful to have it performed so well. The notes are informative, and texts are printed with translations, although the second and third verses of 'No la devemos dormir' are missing....The engineering matches the fine work of previous issues on this label."
Fanfare 14:134 Jl/Ag '91. J. F. Weber (350w)

"Most of the pieces come from the collection which originated at his court, *Villancicos de diversos autores* (Venice, 1556), usually known as the Uppsala Cancionero after the library where the unique copy survives....[The villancicos] are bright and lively pieces, a few of them quite well known, like 'Dadme albricias', which Savall presents with a no-l text from earlier in the century....The disc concludes with a 29-minute(!) ensalada of Carceres....Unfortunately, Carceres's pleasant style really can't sustain a piece of this length and the whole thing drags pretty quickly."
Continuo 16:24 Ap '92. David Klausner (long)

CARTER, ELLIOTT. A Mirror on Which to Dwell (6 poems of Elizabeth Bishop), for Soprano and Chamber Ensemble. See No. 2051.

CHAUSSON, ERNEST. Poeme de l'Amour et de la Mer, for Voice and Piano (or Orchestra), Opus 19. See No. 7060.

DOWLAND, JOHN

8021. Lute Songs: *Book 1:* Come away, come sweet loue; Come heauy sleepe; Wilt thou unkind thus reaue me of my hart?; If my complaints could passion moue; My thoughts are wingd with hopes; Awake sweet loue thou art returnd. *Book 2:* Sorrow sorrow stay, lend true repentant teares; Fine knacks for ladies; Flow my teares; Shall I sue, shall I seeke for grace?; I saw my Lady weepe. *Book 3:* When Phoebus first did Daphne loue; Say loue if euer thou didst finde; Fie on this faining, is loue without desire; Weepe you no more, sad fountaines. *Book 4:* A Pilgrimes Solace: Loue those beames that breede; Sweete stay a while, why will you?; To aske for all thy loue; Were euery thought an eye; Shall I striue with wordes to moue.
Nigel Rogers (ten); Paul O'Dette (lte).
VIRGIN 90726 DDD 61:00

> ✔**HC** ★*Awards:* Critics' Choice 1988, *Gramophone* D '88 (John Duarte).

"Nigel Rogers is the fortunate possessor of a fine and rare voice for music that demands unusual expressive qualities, and his flawless mastery of ornamentation is ideally suited to Dowland's songs....Lutist Paul O'Dette, through his sensitive playing of these time-honored tablatures, adds to the general ravishment."
Musical America 110:73 N '90. Denis Stevens (455w)

"*Gramophone* recently called Nigel Rogers 'the greatest living exponent of monody'; this is perhaps a bit too much, but it is more than justified to place him among the very finest-....this disc can very definitely be recommended for those seeking their first exposure to these songs....I am writing this copy immediately after reviewing the Dorian Recordings lute song disc (in the last issue); this rather prejudices me against the present recording. The sound here is very good; in most ordinary contexts, it would be highly praised, but there is no comparison with the Dorian."
Stereophile 12:189 D '89. Les Berkley (450w)

"Nigel Rogers...always had, and has still, is a high order of musical intelligence and a sensitivity to words. Every song here pays its way-...I'm sorry that Rogers omitted *In darkness let me dwell*...otherwise this selection displays both the composer's range and the singer's gifts."
Fanfare 12:134-35 Jl/Ag '89. Eric Van Tassel (400w)

"Nigel Rogers...sings with intelligence 20 of Dowland's songs selected from the different books....For those who do not have Dowland recordings...a good beginning."
American Record Guide 52:39 Jl/Ag '89. William Purcell (125w)

Gramophone 66:836 N '88. John Duarte (315w)

ELGAR, EDWARD. Sea Pictures, for Contralto and Orchestra, Opus 37. See No. 6043.

FELDMAN, MORTON

8022. Three Voices, for Solo Voice.
Jean LaBarbara (sop). 1988.
NEW ALBION 018 DDD 49:48

> ★★★★*Awards:* Critics' Choice 1990, *Gramophone* D '90 (John Milsom). Critics Pick Some Favorites of the Year, *The New York Times* N 26, '89 (K. Robert Schwarz); The Want List 1989, *Fanfare* N/D '89 (Kyle Gann). Cream of the Crop IV, *Digital Audio's CD Review*, 6:41 Je '90.

"*Three Voices* (1982) consists of Joan LaBarbara's neat, impassive voice live in counterpoint with two tapes of itself. The piece is kind of a requiem for Feldman's friends, Philip Guston and Frank O'Hara, and the singer-with-two-channel-tape medium was suggested by the look of onstage loudspeakers, which re-

minded Feldman of tombstones....The recording is wonderfully clear and close; it's noiseless enough to be played loud, yet present enough to play softly, as it should be....it grows on you within a few listenings...Top of my Want List, guaranteed."
Fanfare 12:146-47 Jl/Ag '89. Kyle Gann (700w)

"This music hypnotizes as do grains of sand in an hourglass: If the mind wanders, the sand is meaningless; concentrate, and it's fascinating-....This music, for its outward rejection of effusiveness, inwardly achieves an appeal to the emotions on a very elemental level....La Barbara's performance is extraordinary. Excellent intonation and rhythmic precision are required to create successfully the effects Feldman attempts to achieve. La Barbara does it without making us aware of the difficulties. Sonically, this disc is nothing special."
Stereophile 13:197+ Je '90. Robert Hesson (425w)

"*Three Voices for Joan La Barbara* (1982) is typical of Feldman's late work. Conceived within a vastly extended time frame, *Three Voices* consists of three superimposed vocal lines (in performances, one would be live, the other two on tape)....the emphasis is not on density but on the pristine clarity of the slowly shifting, intertwining voices. The effect is akin to that of some eerie celestial choir, and it is made all the more evocative because nearly the entire work is sung pianississimo (*ppp*) and in vocalise....Critic John Rockwell, disturbed that this performance clocks in at only 50 minutes (compared with Joan La Barbara's 90-minute California premiere of the work in 1983), feels that Feldman's intentions have been distorted-....Whatever the case, La Barbara's performance is a tour de force."
Musical America 109:59-60 S '89. K. Robert Schwarz (500w)

Gramophone 68:1244 D '90. John Milsom (530w)

Digital Audio's CD Review 6:78 O '89. John Diliberto (310w)

GLASS, PHILIP. Dances: No.'s 1, 3 and 5 for Voice and Instruments. See No. 4094.

HANDEL, GEORGE FRIDERIC

8023. Arias. *Serse:* Frondi tenere e belle...Ombra mai fu. *Acis and Galatea:* Love sounds the alarm; Would you gain the tender creature. *Esther:* Tune your harps to cheerful strains. *Athalia:* Gentle airs, melodious strains. *Judas Maccabaeus:* So shall the lute and harp awake. *Samson:* Total eclipse. *Messiah:* Comfort ye; Ev'ry valley. *Haman and Mordecai:* Praise the Lord with cheerful noise. *The Choice of Hercules:* There the brisk sparkling Nectar. *Joshua:* While Kedron's brook. *Rinaldo:* Lascia ch'io piange. *Semele:* Wher'er you walk; O Sleep, why dost thou leave me? *Ode for St. Cecilia's Day:* Sharp violins proclaim.
Robert White (ten). Ivor Bolton (c). City of London Baroque Sinfonia.
VIRGIN 90796 DDD 71:00

★*Awards:* Critic's Choice: 1990, *American Record Guide* Ja/F '91 (Ralph Lucano).

"White is backed up by period instruments, yet his program is curiously old-fashioned. He shamelessly appropriates arias written for soprano and castrato, presumably because he wants very much to sing them. And that is exactly what he communicates: affection for the music, and a vast delight in the words themselves....White is as communicative a Handel singer as you'll ever hear."
Fanfare 14:248-9 S/O '90. Ralph V. Lucano (250w)

"Considering the excellence of the performances in a generous length of over seventy minutes, the good clean digital sound, and the accompanying booklet with notes and texts, nothing remains but to write the obvious: recommended."
Fanfare 13:162 Jl/Ag '90. James Camner (300w)

"In top form in the Handel, the American tenor—who sounds very English—displays exemplary breath control enabling him to perform virtuosic runs, roulades, trills, and ornamentation while maintaining admirably even tonal emission. With meaningful, clear enunciation, he is also relatively free of those intrusive aspirates that so annoy many English critics. The voice, then, is estimably produced, applied, and recorded. However, it is the singer's masterly understanding of the composer's particular idiom that raises this disc to the apex of my preferred list of Handel vocal recordings."
Stereophile 14:201+ Mr '91. Bernard Soll (300w)

"A generous recital of this nature could have proved a wearing experience in lesser hands, but it is fortunately leavened by White's ability to color the voice and adapt his style to suit the many varied sentiments expressed....Handel purists will doubtless object to the appropriation of arias originally intended for other vocal ranges, but with singing of this excellence I am not prepared to carp. Bolton conducts the splendid 'period instrument' orchestra in lively, intelligent fashion, supporting the tenor sensitively."
American Record Guide 53:55 Mr/Ap '90. Vivian A. Liff (225w)

"White has a fine voice and impressive breath-control; diction and ornamentation are fine, and the programme has been well put together. All the same, it would be wise not to listen to it straight through." *P85/95 S85/95*
Hi-Fi News & Record Review 35:97 F '90. Peter Branscombe (170w)

Gramophone 67:1361 Ja '90. John Steane (430w)

8024. Love in Bath, for Soprano and Orchestra (arr. Beecham); The Gods Go a-Begging (arr. Beecham).
Ilse Hollweg (sop). Thomas Beecham (c). Royal Philharmonic Orchestra. 1951-58 reissues.
EMI 63374 ADD 75:15

★*Awards:* The Want List 1990, *Fanfare* N/D '90 (John Bauman).

"EMI has combined stereo recordings from 1956-8 with a single monaural one from 1951-...to give us the best of Beecham's Handel arrangements. There is charm, grace, wit, elegance—you name it—coupled with the polished leadership that marked all of the musical baronet's performances."
American Record Guide 53:65 N/D '90. Carl Bauman (155w)

"The performances on this CD, though not without momentary sloppiness, preserve the enthusiasm and skill of a master conductor put at the service of one of his favorite composers. If you think this sort of thing is for you, I couldn't recommend them highly enough."
Fanfare 14:253 S/O '90. James Miller (440w)

Salve Regina (anthem), for Soprano and Orchestra. See No. 6060.

HARVEY, JONATHAN. Song Offerings. See No. 1047.

LISZT, FRANZ

8025. Songs: S'il est un charmant gazon; Enfant, si j'etais roi; Comment, disaient-ils; Oh! quand je dors; Im Rhein, im schonen Strome; Morgens steh ich auf und frage; Vergiftet sind meine Lieder; Du bist wie eine Blume: Wie singt die Lerche schon; Kling leise, mein Lied; Schwebe, schwebe, blaues Auge; Ihr Glocken von Marling; Der Fischerknabe; Der Hirt; Der Alpenjager, Angiolin dal biondo crin; Three Petrarch Sonnets—Pace non trovo; Benedetto sia'l giorno; I vidi in terra angelici costumi.
John Aler (ten); Daniel Blumenthal (pno).
NEWPORT CLASSIC 60028 74:00

★*Awards:* Top Choices—1989, *American Record Guide* Ja/F '90 (Philip L. Miller).

"Aler's career is in high gear these days and rightly so. This recital displays not only his beautiful voice but an elegant sense of style and a splendid technique characterized by clean attacks, flawless intonation and a remarkable command of soft singing."
Ovation 10:58 Je '89. Joseph Duchac (250w)

"John Aler sings...with emotional conviction and a fine sense of style....Daniel Blumenthal's piano accompaniments are likewise on a highly satisfying level....there are no original-language texts."
Stereo Review 53:102 Jl '88. Robert Ackart (100w)

"Aler provides lots of healthy and attractive sound...but for the most part his sounds are unnuanced....Daniel Blumenthal's playing on this disc is superb technically and interpretively. It isn't his fault that he steals the show."
American Record Guide 51:35 Jl/Ag '88. Michael Mark (170w)

8026. Songs: Vergiftet sind meine Lieder, G.289; Uber allen Gipfeln ist Ruh, G.306; Ein Fichtenbaum steht einsam, G.309; Die drei Zigeuner, G.320; Es muss ein Wunderbares sein, G.314; Oh! quand je dors, G.282; Comment, disaient-ils, G.276; Si'il est un charmant gazon, G.284; Enfant, si j'etais roi, G.283.
STRAUSS, RICHARD. Songs.
Brigitte Fassbaender (mezzo-sop); Irwin Gage (pno).
DEUTSCHE GRAMMOPHON 419 238 DDD

★*Awards:* *Gramophone* Solo Vocal Award, 1987.

"Fassbaender's pulsating voice was in great form for these sessions...with her sometimes too prominent vibrato under control. Gage is superb throughout....One of the more remarkable recitals of the past few years."
Fanfare 10:214-5 Jl/Ag '87 Vincent Alfano (190w)

"Brigitte Fassbaender combines the better sides of Price and Behrens by proving how urgently Liszt needs *both* voice and understanding."
Opus 4:37-8 Ap '88. Jon Alan Conrad (330w)

"While Fassbaender offers some lovely moments, she does not communicate intense identification with her material the way that, say, Elly Ameling does in her recent recital of French songs for Philips."
Stereo Review 52:88-89 Ag '87 Robert Ackart (120w)

Gramophone 64:1446 Ap '87 Alan Blyth (420w)

Hi-Fi News & Record Review 32:95 Jl '87 Barbara Jahn (280w)

LOEWE, CARL

8027. Ballads: Die Heinzelmannchen; Die Uhr; Harald; Der Pilgrim vor St. Just; Odins Meeresritt; Meereleuchten; Im Strume; Heimlichkeit; Reiterlied; Die Verfallene Muhle; Herr Oluf; Tom der Reimer.
Kurt Moll (bass); Cord Garben (piano).
HARMONIA MUNDI 905171 52:50

★*Awards:* *Gramophone* Critics' Choice 1986 (Michael Oliver).

"Moll has enough trust in his range of vocal resources and in the material itself to take the enormous risk of presenting it without interposing those layers of interpretive attitude we've come to think of as part of the material itself. And the risk pays off."
Opus 2:43 Je '86. Kenneth Furie (375w)

"This magnificent album is strongly recommended to all lovers of German song."
Hi-Fi News & Record Review 31:104-5 Jl '86. John Freestone (190w) (rev. of LP)

Fanfare 10:183 S/O '86 John Bauman (125w)

LUTOSLAWSKI, WITOLD. Les Espaces du Sommeil, for Baritone and Orchestra. See No. 1209.

MAHLER, GUSTAV

8028. Das Lied von der Erde.
Janet Baker (alto); James King (ten). Bernard Haitink (c). Royal Concertgebouw Orchestra.
PHILIPS 432 279 ADD

✔HC

8029. Das Lied von der Erde.
Brigitte Fassbaender (mez); Francisco Araiza (ten). Carlo Maria Giulini (c). Berlin Philharmonic Orchestra.
DEUTSCHE GRAMMOPHON 413 459

★*Awards:* *Fanfare* Want List 1985 (Peter J. Rabinowitz).

"There have been great recorded realizations of *Das Lied von der Erde* in the past, and there will be great ones in the future. But, by any standard, this one by Giulini should retain a special place in the Mahler discography for many years to come."
Stereo Review 50:65 F '85. David Hall (575w)

"Giulini's luminous *Das Lied* (*Fanfare* VII:3) sounds even better on CD than it did on LP."
Fanfare 8:241 Mr/Ap '85. Peter J. Rabinowitz (100w)

"Certain performances of this music have bored me to tears, but so great are Giulini's powers of concentration and communication, his ability to sustain an extremely slow tempo convincingly and absorbingly, that I sat transfixed under his spell."
Opus 2:33 D '85. John Canarina (540w)

"Francisco Araiza...does considerably better than most tenors, but both he and Brigitte Fassbaender sing a number of clinkers, and with such firm conviction that one has the impression they've in fact learned them wrong—and neither conductor nor producer noticed them in time to correct them."
High Fidelity 35:69-70 My '85. Paul Moor (500w) (rev. of LP)

Audio 69:132 Je '85. Bert Whyte (160w)

Gramophone 62:513-4 O '84. Alan Blyth (700w)

8030. Das Lied von der Erde.
Kathleen Ferrier (alto); Julius Patzak (ten). Bruno Walter (c). Vienna Philharmonic Orchestra. May, 1952.
LONDON/DECCA 414 194 (m)

✔HC ★*Awards:* Critics Choice, *Hi Fi News & Record Review*, Ap '91 Supplement (Kenneth Dommett); Critics Choice, *Hi Fi News & Record Review*, Ap '91 Supplement (Antony Hodgson).

"More perhaps than any other, this compact disc of a mono recording made in 1952 is likely to level remaining walls of resistance to digitally encoded sound....[This is] *sine qua non* in any collection of Mahler."
Fanfare 8:242-3 Mr/Ap '85. Roger Dettmer (725w)

High Fidelity 36:70+ Ap '86. Paul Moor (100w)

Gramophone 62:905 Ja '85. Richard Osborne (385w)

Ovation 6:48 Ap '85. Paul Turok (360w)

8031. Das Lied von der Erde.
Alfreda Hodgson (alto); John Mitchinson (ten). Jascha Horenstein (c). BBC Northern Symphony Orchestra. Manchester. April 28, 1972 reissue.
DESCANT 001 71:43

★★★*Awards:* The Want List 1989, *Fanfare* N/D '89 (Benjamin Pernick); Top Choices—1989, *American Record Guide* Ja/F '90 (Gerald Fox). The Want List 1990, *Fanfare* N/D '90 (Henry Fogel).

"In short, the greatest *Das Lied* I have ever heard. Essential!"
Fanfare 13:104-6 S/O '89. Ben Pernick (485w)

This release is "magnificent in all important respects: performance, sonics, even album notes-....*Das Lied von der Erde* is simply the best-conducted version I know: expansive, dark, and weighty....no text."
American Record Guide 52:73+ S/O '89. Gerald S. Fox (380w)

"Horenstein's *Das Lied* is successful for the same reason other superior recordings are successful: because the conductor never loses sight of the piece's words and story. The sense of Horenstein's story is, of course, unique to him....Sound is true stereo, nicely proportioned, except for voices too large for the orchestral image. Timbres are exemplary for a radio check recording."
Stereophile 13:191+ Mr '90. Kevin Conklin (300w)

8032. Songs: *Des Knaben Wunderhorn:* No. 2, Verlorne Muh'; No. 7, Rheinlegendchen; No. 9, Wo die schonen Trompeten blasen; No. 10, Lob des hohen Verstands. *Lieder und Gesang:* No. 1, Fruhlingsmorgen; No. 2, Erinnerung; No. 4, Serenade aus Don Juan; No. 5, Phantasie aus Don Juan; No. 7, Ich ging mit Lust durch einen grunen Wald; No. 8, Aus! Aus! **WOLF, HUGO. Lieder:** Heiss mich nicht reden (Mignon I); Nur wer die Sehnsucht (Mignon II); So lasst mich scheinen (Mignon III); Kennst du das Land? (Mignon); Fruhling ubers Jahr; Frage nicht; Die Sprode; Der Schafer; Gesang Weylas.
Anne-Sofie von Otter (mez); Ralf Gothoni (pno).
DEUTSCHE GRAMMOPHON 423 666 DDD 59:00

★★★**Awards:** Critics' Choice 1989, *Gramophone* D '89 (Alan Blyth); Top Disks of the Year, *The New York Times* D 24, '89 (John Rockwell). The Want List 1990, *Fanfare* N/D '90 (David Mason Greene).

"Not perhaps the wittiest Mahler ever recorded-...but this young Swedish mezzo makes a deep impression with her recorded recital debut. Above all, she shows astonishing maturity—and courage—in her tackling of some of the most demanding Wolf songs. Rarely have I heard such impassioned, intelligent and beautiful singing of 'Kennst Du Das Land'...so superbly complemented by the playing of Ralf Gothoni, a great but sorely neglected singers' pianist...balance between voice and piano is naturally accomplished." *P95/100 S95*

Hi-Fi News & Record Review 34:133 D '89. Hugh Canning (350w)

"Every so often one encounters a record that makes one feel that it was worth living that long after all. This is, for me, such a record-....Gothoni emerges here as one of the best accompanists of the age. Luminous recording. Highly recommended!"

Fanfare 13:348-59 Mr/Ap '90. David Mason Greene (250w)

"Von Otter is an extroverted Lieder singer with a young, healthy voice....Greater subtlety and polish will certainly come with time, but even now, it's difficult to find fault with her....Ralf Gothoni is an accompanist both cooperative and expressive; DG's sound is excellent; texts and translations are included. I recommend this heartily."

American Record Guide 53:132-33 My/Je '90. Ralph V. Lucano (230w)

"Von Otter's debut recital, an imaginative selection of lieder by Wolf and Mahler, proves her to be a fully formed artist of the highest order...If you haven't heard Von Otter yet, this superlative recital is the place to start."

Musical America 110:89 Jl '90. Terry Teachout (270w)

"Von Otter's selections from Mahler's *Wunderhorn* songs are full of delightful characterization, *a la* Fassbaender....[the recording is] perfect in terms of balance and clarity...highly recommended."

Stereophile 13:225+ D '90. Barbara Jahn (140w)

Gramophone 67:74+ Je '89. Alan Blyth (420w)

The New York Times O 21 '90, p. 33-4. Thor Eckert Jr. (250w)

Songs. See No. 8010.

Songs from Ruckert (5). See No. 1215.

Songs of a Wayfarer. See No. 1218.

MOZART, WOLFGANG AMADEUS

8033. Arias: *Cosi Fan Tutte:* Temerari!...Come scoglio. *La Clemenza Di Tito:* Non piu di fiori. *Don Giovanni:* In Quali eccessi...Mi tradi quell'alma ingrata. *Die Entfuhrung Aus Dem Serail:* Marten aller Arten. *Idomeneo:* Oh smanie!-...D'Oreste e d'Aiace. *Le Nozze Di Figaro:* E Susanna non vien!...Dove sono i bei momenti; Porgi, amor. *Die Zauberflote:* O zittre nicht-...Zum Leiden bin ich auserkoren; Der Holle Rache; Ach, ich fuhl's.

Cheryl Studer (sop). Neville Marriner (c). Academy of St. Martin-in-the-Fields. 1990 reissue in part.
PHILIPS 426 721 DDD 55:00

★★**Awards:** The Want List 1991, *Fanfare* N/D '91 (Ralph V. Lucano). Honorable Mention, Records of the Year, 1991, *Stereo Review*, F '92.

"Marriner is certainly a capable conductor, and Philips's sound, though partial to the voice, is excellent....I'm willing to risk an enthusiastic endorsement of it now, and to declare it worthy of a place beside the handful of great Mozart-aria recitals on records."

Fanfare 15:277-78 S/O '91. Ralph V. Lucano (long)

"This program of unusually demanding music is sung expressively, accurately, and stylishly by Cheryl Studer...Her thoughtful performances are ably supported by Neville Marriner and his fine orchestra."

Stereo Review 56:73-4 O '91. Robert Ackart (brief)

"Studer's...bright, forward voice and intense delivery galvanize such dramatic arias as 'Come scoglio' and 'D'Oreste, d'Aiace'...and she proves herself equally capable of the softer characterizations required of the Countess (both arias) and of Pamina."

Opera News 56:39 Ja 4 '92. Shirley Fleming (long)

"This is an impressive record. Although devoted to a single composer, it nonetheless demonstrates Studer's much-heralded versatility, for each of the big seven operas is represented."

American Record Guide 54:99 N/D '91. George W. Loomis (long)

"In this selection of Mozart Arias, Ms. Studer continues to seduce the ear with her keen musical insight and ability to colour-in each note. Sir Neville Marriner and the Academy of St. Martins are the perfect partners in a recording that gives free rein to the voice with a warm, finely detailed sound."

High Fidelity 3:97 My '91. Clive Manning (100w)

"Cheryl Studer's remarkable range is amply demonstrated in this recital...Marriner's participation helps materially to ensure the success of this well planned recital." *P95 S95/85*

Hi-Fi News & Record Review 36:72-3 Ag '91. Kenneth Dommett (110w)

Gramophone 68:2060-1 My '91. John Steane (525w)

8034. Arias: *Die Zauberflote* (excerpts); *Cosi fan Tutte* (excerpts); *Idomeneo* (excerpts); *Zaide* (excerpts); *Lucio Silla* (excerpts); *Re Pastore* (excerpts); *Finta Giardinera* (excerpts); *Clemenzo de Tito* (excerpts).
Kiri Te Kanawa (sop). Colin Davis (c). London Symphony Orchestra.
PHILIPS 411 148 DDD 57:14

★*Awards:* Perfect 10/10, *Digital Audio*, Mr '88.

"The selection itself is outstanding...the CD is successful with rich, pleasing sound."
Fanfare 8:271 S/O '84. John Bauman (110w)

"Problem: you are depressed, on edge, unable to sleep, carrying the weight of the world on your shoulders. Solution: put this record on your turntable, play, and listen. Guarantee: the soothing, silken quality of Kiri Te Kanawa's voice will not only instantly calm you, but you will probably fall in love—with her, with the characters she sings, and most assuredly with the music. A voice like hers is truly a rare commodity....Indeed, Mozart's lyrical effusions seem written for her voice, and, thankfully, the repertoire chosen for this program emphasizes the lyrical—rather than the dramatic—Mozart-....One of the most difficult roles in Mozart's operatic lexicon is Pamina....Such is the artistry of Te Kanawa that one simply is unaware of the enormous difficulty of this aria."
The Opera Quarterly 1:144-5 Winter '83. Robert Chauls (560w) (rev. of LP)

Digital Audio 1:65-6 D '84. John Marks (350w)

Gramophone 61:1106 Mr '84. Edward Greenfield (140w)

Ovation 5:58+ Jl '84. Thor Eckert, Jr. (165w)

The NATS Journal 43:56 Mr/Ap '87 Barbara Kinsey Sable (200w)

MUSSORGSKY, MODEST

8035. Songs.
Boris Christoff (bass); Alexandre Labinsky (pno); Gerald Moore (pno). Georges Tzipine (c). French Radio National Orchestra. 1959, 1952 reissue.
EMI 63025 ADD 191:00 3 discs

✔**HC** ★★*Awards:* The Want List 1990, *Fanfare* N/D '90 (James H. North); The Want List 1990, *Fanfare* N/D '90 (Benjamin Pernick).

"The quality and rarity of repertoire, the magnificence of voice and artistry, and twenty-five years of unavailability combine to make this one of the most important reissues of the compact disc era. Want List 1990, item one."
Fanfare 13:250-51 Ja/F '90. James H. North (725w)

"In urging readers to purchase this set, which not only represents the crowning recorded achievement of Christoff's career but also one of EMI's finest offerings in the field of Russian song, I would raise only two very minor complaints."

American Record Guide 52:85 N/D '89. Vivian A. Liff (275w)

Gramophone 67:355-56 Ag '89. Alan Blyth (590w)

POULENC, FRANCIS

8036. Le Bal Masque (cantata), for Baritone, Oboe, Clarinet, Bassoon, Piano, Percussion, Violin, and Cello; Le Bestiaire, for Baritone, Flute, Clarinet, Bassoon and String Quartet; Sextuor for Piano and Woodwind Quintet; Trio for Oboe, Bassoon and Piano.
Thomas Allen (bar). Nash Ensemble.
CRD 3437

✔**HC** ★★*Awards:* *Gramophone* Critics' Choice 1986 (Lionel Salter); *Fanfare* Want List 1987 (Elliott Kaback).

"This is highly recommended to anyone interested in twentieth century music in all its diversity."
Hi-Fi News & Record Review 32:109 Ja '87 Barbara Jahn (255w)

"Recommended."
Fanfare 10:192 N/D '86 John D. Wiser (275w)

Gramophone 64:608-13 O '86 Lionel Salter (455w)

American Record Guide 50:48 My/Je '87 David W. Moore (125w)

Songs. See No. 8038.

PUCCINI, GIACOMO

8037. Songs: A te; Vexilla; Salve regina; Ad una morta; Mentia l'avviso; Storiella d'amore; Sole e amore; Avanti Urania!; Inno a Diana; E l'uccellino; Terra e mare (2 versions); Canto d'anime; Casa mia, casa mia; Morire?; Inno a roma.
(The Unknown Puccini).
Placido Domingo (ten); Julius Rudel (pno/orgn).
CBS 44981 DDD 45:00

★*Awards:* Critic's Choice: 1990, *American Record Guide* Ja/F '91 (Lee Milazzo).

"All but six of the songs on the disc have been recorded before...I can, however, safely recommend Domingo's performances as the ones to live with. He may miss some verbal felicities, but he's in strong, flowing voice. He's ably assisted by Justino Diaz in *Vexilla*, and Rudel is a fine accompanist."
Fanfare 13:266-67 Ja/F '90. Ralph V. Lucano (400w)

"Puccini's songs offer a fascinating insight into his more familiar, operatic, works."
High Fidelity 1:121 F '90. Ian Brunskill (b.n.)

"Not all the songs are jewels, of course, but each contains something of value. Domingo sings every one of them beautifully, demonstrating both care and commitment. Indeed, his-

tory may very well judge this one of Domingo's finest accomplishments."
American Record Guide 53:88-9 Mr/Ap '90. Lee Milazzo (350w)

"Julius Rudel's accompaniments are as thoroughly versed in the style as Domingo's singing."
Opera News 54:37 Mr 17 '90. John W. Freeman (140w)

"Some of Puccini's vignettes are very small indeed...and some, such as the religious selections, are more expansive. All, however, receive appropriate, honest performances by an artist in fine voice (ably assisted in *Vexilla* by bass-baritone Justino Diaz) with sensitive accompaniments by Julius Rudel. The recording itself is sonically well balanced throughout."
Stereo Review 55:134 Ja '90. Robert Ackart (180w)

"Under this title the American musicologist Michael Kaye published an assortment of Pucciniana (they hardly deserve a better description) mainly for solo voice...None, it must be said, add anything to his reputation....Placido Domingo dispatches them with easy fluency, if without particular attention to the composer's detailed markings."
Opera 41:753 Je '90. Julian Budden (753w)

"This is slightly more than a curiosity....much of this is salon stuff, early works, and a bit too easy-listening for my taste. But, that said, it's enjoyable enough....Throughout, with one exception noted above, the tenor is in fine voice."
Stereophile 13:201+ Ap '90. Robert Levine (225w)

Gramophone 67:1669-70 Mr '90. Michael Oliver (450w)

RAVEL, MAURICE

Sheherazade, for Mezzo-soprano and Orchestra. See No. 1300.

8038. Songs: Histoires naturelles. Cinq Melodies populaires greques. Don Quichotte a Dulcinee. **POULENC, FRANCIS. Songs:** Montparnasse. Hyde Park. Rosemonde. Dans le Jardin d'Anna. Aons plus vite. Bleuet. Le Bestiaire. Banalities. Quatre Poemes d'Apollinaire.
Jean-Francois Gardeil (bar); Billy Eidi (pno).
ADDA 581 210 DDD 63:23

> ★*Awards:* The Want List 1991, *Fanfare* N/D '91 (David Mason Greene).

"Gardeil and Eidi realize these songs more satisfyingly than any *team* in my experience....Recording is luminous. The accompanying booklet has an instructive rundown of the songs in French, English, and German, but the songtexts are given only in French. Recommended without qualification."
Fanfare 14:336-7 Mr/Ap '91. David Mason Greene (550w)

"Jean-Francois Gardeil and Billy Eidi, the booklet tells us, gave their first recital in Paris in March 1985, and their success was sensational. Hailed especially for their Ravel and their Poulenc, a new duo had been born. One can understand the enthusiasm of that first audience."
American Record Guide 54:106 Mr/Ap '91. Philip L. Miller (300w)

"An entire disc devoted to the *melodies* of Ravel and Poulenc is a welcome addition to the sparse CD offerings of the French vocal repertoire...One real gem is Ravel's *Histoires Naturelles*, a humorous, exotic and beguiling musical description of various animals...Baritone Jean-Francois Gardeil and pianist Billy Eidi do some fine work here...The Lebanese pianist, Billy Eidi, plays superbly throughout and is a true equal in the collaboration. The notes are informative but the booklet offers no translations."
High Performance Review 8:83 Wtr '91/92. John A. Mueter (long)

ROSSINI, GIOACCHINO

8039. Arias: *The Barber of Seville:* Cessa di piu resistere...E tu, infelice vittima. *Le Comte Ory:* Que les destins prosperes. *L'Italiana in Algeri:* Languir per una bella. *Elisabetta, Regina d'Inghilterra:* Che intesi, oh annunzio!...Deh! troncate i ceppi suoi. *Il Turco in Italia:* Tu seconda il mio disegno. *La Donna del Lago:* Oh fiamma soave.
(The Rossini Tenor).
Rockwell Blake (ten). John McCarthy (c). Ambrosian Singers; London Symphony Orchestra.
ARABESQUE 6582 DDD 47:00

> ★*Awards:* Third Place Vocal Solo Mumm Champagne Classical Music Award 1988—Presented by *Ovation*, *Ovation* N '88.

"Insofar as we know the Rossinian style of singing, Blake is certainly a masterly exponent of it, and the Ambrosian Opera Singers, London Symphony Orchestra, and conductor John McCarthy provide handsome support."
Stereo Review 53:114 S '88. Robert Ackart (125w)

"One of Blake's most endearing qualities is the apparently nonchalant bravura with which he attacks those extended florid passages, at the same time projecting verbal meaning by purely musical means. This places him in a class that would have been his and his alone—were it not for Gimenez. Yet Blake's omnipresent projection of spontaneity—extremely difficult to simulate in florid music—places him slightly ahead of the Argentinian in the virtuosity stakes....Enthusiastically recommended."
Stereophile 11:179+ O '88. Bernard Soll (450w)

"The American singer's timbre often is hard to take, with its weak low tones and blasting, penetrating top, but in such an episode as the rondo finale usually cut from *Il Barbiere di Siviglia*, done with chorus, the agility is simply breathtaking, and John McCarthy's conducting is exceptionally supportive."

Opera News 53:64-5 O '88. John W. Freeman (90w)

"In sum, the voice has a bright, edgy, shallow, relentless quality that is not shown to best advantage in sustained listening, so a solo recital is not a fair format for judgment."

Opera News 52:46-7 My '88. John W. Freeman (165w)

"There is little repose in this exciting, highly nervous temperament. Although he smudges some of the fioriture...he can be astounding when he is really with it."

Fanfare 11:194-5 My/Je '88. David Johnson (575w)

"This recital reveals distracting vocal mannerisms and technical flaws....But despite all these faults it is an interesting voice, and his high-energy singing is exciting. At least in small doses."

American Record Guide 51:52 Jl/Ag '88. Desmond Arthur (405w)

The New York Times Je 12 '88, p. 33+. Will Crutchfield (750w)

Gramophone 65:1494 Ap '88. Richard Osborne (530w)

8040. Arias: *Tancredi:* Pensa che sei mia figlia; Oh Dio! Crudel!...Ah! segnar invano io tento. *La Pietra del Paragone:* Oh, come il fosco impetuoso nembo...Quell'aime pupille. *Otello:* Che ascolto, ahime...Ah, come mai non senti. *The Barber of Seville:* Ecco ridente in cielo; Se il mio nome. *Il Signor Bruschino:* Deh! tu m'assisti, amore. *L'Occasion fa il Ladro:* D'ogni piu sacroimpegno. *L'Italiana in Algeri:* Languir per una bella; Concedi amor pietoso. *La Cenerentola:* Principe piu non sei...Si, ritrovaria io giuro.
Raul Gimenez (tenor); David Goodall (gtr). Michelangelo Veltri (c). Scottish Chamber Orchestra.
NIMBUS 5106 DDD 61:30

★***Awards:*** Best of the Year, *Opera News* D 24 '88.

"Raul Gimenez' disc of Rossini tenor arias is an almost unalloyed joy, showing that tightwire agility is not necessarily incompatible with agreeable tone."

Opera News 52:42-3 Ag '88. John W. Freeman (115w)

"His honeyed, lyrical eloquent voice caresses the sensibilities with the beauty of its unconstrained, unaffected purity....Vocally, his elegance, refinement, and technical accomplishments are of a standard seldom heard—even from legendary, Golden Age titans on creaky, noisy, ancient 78s....Enthusiastically recommended."

Stereophile 11:179+ O '88. Bernard Soll (450w)

"His voice is gorgeous. At times he sounds like a young Alfredo Kraus, with faultless legato and heroic Latinate timbre."

Ovation 9:40 My '88. Octavio Roca (300w)

"Although his generous selection is split evenly between comic and serious roles, I would judge that he is most valuable, and most at home in the ingenu roles of the comic operas."

Fanfare 11:194-5 My/Je '88. David Johnson (575w)

"Listening to this recital record, I find myself thrilling to Gimenez's manner and style in serious Rossini...but less certain of the voice in some of the more familiar buffo repertory."

Opera 39:378-9 Mr '88. Richard Osborne (650w)

"Gimenez tries for laid-back elegance which sometimes comes across as characterless. But his performance of Giocondo's recitative and aria from *La Pietra del Paragone* is a treasurable highlight of this disc...and there are many other fine moments throughout the program-....Nimbus provides excellent digital sound-...texts and translations [included]."

The Nats Journal 45:36-7 My/Je '89. Carol Kimball (770w)

"This is an auspicious record debut for a true *tenor de grazia*...The accompaniments are excellently played by the SCO, even though Veltri's conducting strikes me as routine...I find it impossible to rate the Nimbus single-miked recording."

Hi-Fi News & Record Review 33:93 Jl '88. Hugh Canning (315w)

"The repertoire here is unhackneyed, containing some of Rossini's happiest inspirations for the tenor voice and the disc is to be welcomed for this reason alone. Do not, however, expect another Fernando de Lucia, Hermann Jadlowker, Tito Schipa, nor even, in more recent times, Cesare Valletti."

American Record Guide 51:51-2 Jl/Ag '88. Vivian A. Liff (225w)

Gramophone 66:337 Ag '88. Richard Osborne (315w)

The New York Times Je 12 '88, p. H33+. Will Crutchfield (175w)

8041. Songs: La Pastorella; Belta Crudele; Il Trovatore; La Regata Veneziana; Mi Lagnero Tacendo; Il Risentimento; La Grande Coquette; Ariette a l'Ancienne; L'Orpheline du Tyrol; La Legende de Marguerite; Nizza; L'Ame Delaissee; Canzonette Spagnuola; En Medio a Mis Colores. Cantata: Giovanna d'Arco.
Cecilia Bartoli (mez); Charles Spencer (pno).
LONDON/DECCA 430 518 DDD 70:59

★★★***Awards:*** Best of the Month, *Hi-Fi News & Record Review*, Jl '91; The Want List 1991, *Fanfare* N/D '91 (Robert Levine). Honorable Mention, Records of the Year, 1991, *Stereo Review*, F '92.

"It is difficult to pick highlights when every number is a winner...It's hard to imagine some of these pieces being better done. Clear and responsive accompaniments from Charles Spencer, immaculate sound quality and balance." *P100 S100*

Hi-Fi News & Record Review, Jl '91. George Hall (550w)

"Not since Teresa Berganza came on the scene has a coloratura mezzo done such justice to this repertory....The miking is close...so that the voice is made to sound larger than it is in live performance. No matter. This recording is one of the finest of the year."

Musical America 111:50-1 S/O '91. Walter Price (med)

"Here is perhaps the most interesting all-Rossini song recital to come along since Sutherland devoted a side-and-a-half to Rossini's songs in the collection of Italian songs called *Serate musicali*, a three-LP London set still awaiting compact disc transfer....The voice has much to recommend it in the way of youthful strength and brilliance, but Bartoli has to learn to breathe quietly; her intakes of breath are audible and disruptive. And she needs to develop a more even production throughout her tessitura....But her temperament is fiery and exciting, she takes chances which are dazzling when they succeed, and at the age of twenty-five, or thereabouts, she bids fair to becoming one of the outstanding successors of Horne and Berganza in the coming decade....Bartoli's accompanist, Charles Spencer, makes the most of Rossini's piano parts, which are generally much more demanding and pianistic than those in the songs of Verdi, Bellini, or Donizetti."

Fanfare 15:326-28 S/O '91. David Johnson (long)

"This graceful recital album...has much to recommend it. Cecilia Bartoli's singing is fluid, finely phrased, stylish, and accurate. The well-engineered recording maintains a happy balance between voice and piano, and the accompaniments are sympathetically played."

Stereo Review 56:82+ Jl '91. Robert Ackart (150w)

"The range of mood and style is prodigious, from the quixotic to the tragic, muted sadness to cheerful sauciness, Tyrolean yodeling to a Spanish seductiveness that could have come straight out of *Carmen*. Capping the recital is the sixteen-minute cantata *Giovanna d'Arco* (Joan of Arc), probably the only reasonably well known work on the disc and certainly the one most likely to kill a singer in the shortest amount of time. Bartoli survives, negotiating this and the rest of her program's varied terrain with a nice perception of color and a strong sense of personality and dramatic projection."

Opera News 56:35 F 29 '92. Shirley Fleming (med)

SCELSI, GIACINTO. "Khoom", for Female Voice, Horn and Quartet (1962). See No. 3114.

SCHOENBERG, ARNOLD. Lied der Waltaube (arr. cpsr. for mezzo-soprano and chamber orchestra). See No. 1330.

SCHUBERT, FRANZ

Der Hirt auf dem Felsen, for Soprano, Clarinet and Piano, D.965. See No. 3124.

8042. Die Schone Mullerin, D.795.
Olaf Bar; Geoffrey Parsons (pno).
EMI 47947 65:13

★***Awards:*** Solo Vocal Record Award, *Gramophone* O '88.

"Once again, Bar's individuality, his light, evenly produced stream of tone, his flawless diction and instinctive, unexaggerated poetic sensibility combine to produce one of the most distinguished recorded performances of this favourite and much recorded cycle....I know of no more beautiful reading of this cycle, and the recording captures the freshness of voice and the complimentary musicianship of Parsons almost to perfection."

Hi-Fi News & Record Review 33:113 Ja '88. Hugh Canning (570w)

"Not for a long time has the art of a new singer excited me so much...To begin with, he has a creamy baritone of an extraordinarily beautiful timbre, seamless in its perfection from top to bottom and equally beautiful whether in intimate *mezza voce* or noble full voice. He has virtually flawless diction...More important, Baer's literary and dramatic intelligence matches his musicality."

High Fidelity 38:54-55 My '88. Paul Moor (300w)

"Although this is an outstanding account of Schubert's great song cycle, I must confess to a little disappointment after this singer's previous record, of Schumann's *Dichterliebe*."

Music and Musicians International 36:58 D '87. Robert Hartford (135w)

Gramophone 65:331 Ag '87 (595w); 66:550 O '88 (200w). Alan Blyth

8043. Die Schone Mullerin, D.795.
Peter Schreier (ten); Andras Schiff (pno).
LONDON/DECCA 430 414 DDD 63:00

✔**HC** ★★★***Awards:*** The Gramophone Awards, Nominations, Solo Vocal, *Gramophone*, N '91. Best Solo Vocal Recording 1991, *Gramophone*, D '91. Best of the Month, *Hi-Fi News & Record Review*, Jl '91.

"Schreier's...mastery of the quicksilvery, shadow-dappled emotional text is supreme-....what puts the present recording in a class of its own is the superb accompaniment of Andras Schiff."

Musical America 111:52-3 S/O '91. Jamie James (med)

"This is a treasurable experience: two magnificent musicians at the height of their powers...recorded with a telling combination of directness and warmth. Schiff's Bosendorfer has all the clarity one could wish for, yet never the stridency of certain other pianos." *P100 S100*

Hi-Fi News & Record Review 36:68 Jl '91. Peter Branscombe (235w)

"The Schreier-Schiff *Schone Mullerin* is far from run-of-the-mill performances (sorry)....I found this performance as instructive as it was unusual, and I know I'm going to return to it many times over; but I would hesitate to recommend it above less eccentric accounts, such as those of Underlich or Blochwitz (both on DG)."

Fanfare 15:346 S/O '91. Ralph V. Lucano (long)

Gramophone 68:2055-6 My '91. Alan Blyth (460w)

8044. Schwanengesang, D.957.
Dietrich Fischer-Dieskau; Alfred Brendel (pno).
PHILIPS 411 051

> ✔**HC** ★*Awards: Gramophone* Critics' Choice 1984 (John Warrack; Joan Chissell).

"There is quite a distance between the vocal image (very forward) and that of the piano, and I would have welcomed more air around the former. Nor is the vocal image as laterally stable as it might be, wandering occasionally from half-right (where it spends most of the time) to somewhere nearer the centre. The tonal quality of both singer and instrumentalist is, however, most impressively caught."

Hi-Fi News & Record Review 29:79 Je '84. Andrew Keener (140w)

Gramophone 61:1207 Ap '84. Alan Blyth (175w)

Ovation 5:74 N '84. Will Crutchfield (700w) (rev. of LP)

8045. Songs (complete): Der Jungling am Bache, D.30; Thekla, D.73; Schafers Klagelied, D.121 (1st version); Nahe de Geliebten, D.162 (2nd version); Meerestille, D.216; Amalia, D.195; Die Erwartung, D.159 (2nd version); Wandrers Nachtlied, D.224; Der Fischer, D.225 (2nd version); Erster Verlust, D.226; Wonne der Wehmut, D.260; An den Mond, D.296; Das Geheimnis, D.250; Lied, D.284; Der Fluchtling, D.402; An den Fruhling, D.587 (2nd version); Der Alpenjager, D.588 (2nd version); Der Pilgrim, D.794; Sehnsucht, D.636 (2nd version).
(Lieder, Volume 1).
Janet Baker (sop); Graham Johnson (pno).
HYPERION 33001 DDD 70:00

> ✔**HC** ★★★*Awards:* Critics' Choice 1988, *Gramophone* D '88 (Alan Blyth). Solo Vocal Record Award 1989, *Gramophone*, D '89; Top Choices—1989, *American Record Guide* Ja/F '90 (Paul Althouse).

"The intention is for Hyperion to record all Schubert's songs....with many different singers, each offering a programme appropriate to his or her voice and temperament....A finer beginning could hardly be imagined."

Hi-Fi News & Record Review 34:115-17 Ja '89. Peter Branscombe (380w)

"Dame Janet has been caught in singularly fine voice, and with just the right amount of expression there too."

Music and Musicians International 37:59-60 Ja '89. Robert Hartford (630w)

"This is the first volume of an undertaking which, if completed, will be one of the great achievements of the Age of Recordings....Certainly the quality of Volume I is a good augury-....each song has its own approach in Baker's searching interpretations....The poetic texts are printed in their correct stanzaic forms. The translations...are models of lucidity and accuracy."

Fanfare 12:304-6 My/Je '89. David Johnson (1000w)

"These volumes make an auspicious start to Hyperion's Schubert Edition. Janet Baker is-...in fine voice....Of special interest are the wonderful commentaries on each song by Johnson. His work is scholarly, but from a performer's, not a musicologist's, point of view. And, lest I forget, his pianism is first-rate."

American Record Guide 52:83-4 My/Je '89. Paul L. Althouse (160w)

"I would be remiss if I were to say that 30+ years of singing have taken no toll on this singer's voice, but the truth is that the problems are remarkably few....Perhaps now there are only six degrees of dynamic shading where previously there were ten—tsk, tsk. Graham Johnson's accompaniments are so much more than that—I wish there were a better word-....*Bravi!*"

Stereophile 12:173 Mr '89. Robert Levine (450w)

Gramophone 66:663 O '88. Alan Blyth (525w)

8046. Songs (complete): Fischerlied, D.351 (1st version); Fischerlied, D.562 (3rd version); Fischerweise, D.881 (2nd version); Widerschein, D.639 (2nd version); Fahrt zum Hades, D.526; Selige Welt, D.743; Am Bach im Fruhling, D.361; Am Flusse, D.766 (2nd version); Der Strom, D.565; Auf der Donau, D.553; Der Schiffer, D.536 (2nd version); Wie Ulfru fischt, D.525; Der Tauchner, D.111.
(Lieder, Volume 2).
Stephen Varcoe (bar); Graham Johnson (pno).
HYPERION 33002 DDD 59:00

> ✔**HC** ★*Awards:* Top Choices—1989, *American Record Guide* Ja/F '90 (Philip L. Miller).

"The second issue in this exciting series presents an excellent young baritone in a selection of Schubert's almost innumerable water songs-....The recording is lively and clean, apart from a couple of slightly edgy climaxes in 'Der Taucher', and the booklet with full texts, trans-

lations and notes enhances the value of the whole undertaking."
Hi-Fi News & Record Review 34:100 F '89. Peter Branscombe (350w)

"These volumes make an auspicious start to Hyperion's Schubert Edition....Stephen Varcoe's baritone is light-toned and musical—well cast for the simpler songs, but less rich and varied in texture than singers like Fischer-Dieskau, Prey, or particularly Hotter. Of special interest are the wonderful commentaries on each song by Johnson. His work is scholarly, but from a performer's, not a musicologist's, point of view. And, lest I forget, his pianism is first-rate."
American Record Guide 52:83-4 My/Je '89. Paul L. Althouse (160w)

"I have nothing negative to say about this undertaking....Throughout, as hinted at above, Graham Johnson doesn't miss a trick, and never intrudes....The sound is perfect...How can a lover of Schubert's songs do without this release?"
Stereophile 12:175 S '89. Robert Levine (460w)

"Varcoe encompasses the many and various moods with more conviction than I confess to having previously allowed him. Here he aspires to the very highest in the German art song, displaying a fine technique and appreciation of vocal expression."
Music and Musicians International 37:60 Ja '89. Robert Hartford (630w)

"Stephen Varcoe...proves to be a light, lyric baritone of seamless registers and caressing tone—a baritonino, to coin a word. This proves excellent in most of the repertoire on this disc but in a few of the stormier Mayrhofer songs (there are four of them) and in the big narrative ballad from Schiller, 'Der Taucher,' one feels the want of a larger sound and a darker color. On the whole Varcoe is good enough for one to hope to hear him often in this series."
Fanfare 12:240-41 Jl/Ag '89. David Johnson (850w)

Gramophone 66:1201 Ja '89. Alan Blyth (490w)

8047. Songs (complete): Der Liedler, D.209; Sangers Morgenlied, D.163; Sangers Morgenlied, D.165; Das war ich, D.174; Liebestandelei, D.206; Liebesrausch, D.179; Sehnsucht, D.180; Das gestorte Gluck, D.309; Auf der Riesenkoppe, D.611; Am See, D.124; Alte Liebe roster nie, D.477; Am Strome, D.539; Nachstuck, D.672; Liebeslauschen, D.698; An Herrn Josef von Spaun, Assessor in Linz, D.749, "Epistel".
(Volume 4).
Philip Langridge (ten); Graham Johnson (pno).
HYPERION 33004 DDD 69:00

★*Awards:* Critics' Choice 1989, *Gramophone* D '89 (Alan Blyth).

"The alert, responsive partnership of singer and pianist is a constant joy. Langridge's voice may be somewhat dry-toned, yet it is used with great artistry and insight...As for Graham Johnson, he plays throughout as a true Schubertian, and also provides the scholarly, and at times brilliantly funny, notes." *P95 S95*
Hi-Fi News & Record Review 34:107 N '89. Peter Branscombe (280w)

"Though I have been listening to this tenor for years on records, somehow his personality and the real beauty of his voice never fully reached me until I listened to this compact disc....More important still, he has studied these songs intensely and understands them thoroughly-....texts and excellent English translations."
Fanfare 13:295-96 Ja/F '90. David Johnson (1075w)

Langridge uses his voice "with charm and intelligence; he colors his words tellingly. This disc is a hot item."
Stereophile 14:261+ O '91. Robert Levine (brief)

"Most of the songs are relatively obscure...but most certainly are worth knowing and some are gems. Moreover, they are delivered with such style and conviction that you almost feel Schubert is speaking directly to you....The acoustic is just lively enough to suggest a fairly spacious room without veiling any of the apt details that make these readings so very special."
Audio 74:94+ Mr '90. Robert Long (400w)

Gramophone 67:524 S '89. Alan Blyth (458w)

8048. Songs (complete): Lied, D.483. Das Lied im Grunen, D.917. An die Natur, D.372. Wehmut, D.772. Die Mutter Erde, D.788. Die Erde, D.989. Ganymed, D.544. Taglich zu singen, D.533. Die Allmacht, D.852. Erinnerung, D.101. Klage der Ceres, D.323. Die Sternenwelten, D.307. Morgenlied, D.381. Dem Unendlichen, D.291.
(Volume 5).
Elizabeth Connell (sop); Graham Johnson (pno).
HYPERION 33005 DDD 62:00

★*Awards:* Critics' Choice 1990, *Gramophone* D '90 (Hilary Finch).

"Elizabeth Connell's assigned program deals with Spring, 'green,' and God expressed in nature....Connell is in sumptuous voice and offers fine, sensitive interpretations. There are a few smudged moments here and there, but the program offers many riches....This series is obviously a labor of love. Judging from the volumes released to date, it will become a distinguished reference in the Schubert discography."
The Nats Journal 47:46 S/O '90. Carol Kimball (280w)

"Connell...produces a bright, penetrating sound, sometimes pinched but always steady and even....Graham Johnson is not only a peerless accompanist, he also writes informative and absorbing notes....a must for all Schubertians."

American Record Guide 53:102 Jl/Ag '90. Ralph V. Lucano (305w)

"On the basis of this recital, Connell is ready for the big time, whether as a mezzo-soprano or dramatic soprano. Despite occasional problems at the bottom end of the range, this is a shining, indeed thrilling voice of the sort the French used to call 'Falcon'...The mastering of this laser disc strikes me as having been accomplished at too low a dynamic level. Increasing the volume a notch pretty well settles the problem, but a more generous approach to sound level would be desirable."

Fanfare 13:255-56 Jl/Ag '90. David Johnson (920w)

"Connell is impressive throughout the recital, aside from a few weakish low notes...This one's a gem."

Stereophile 14:261+ O '91. Robert Levine (brief)

Gramophone 67:1515 F '90. Alan Blyth (450w)

8049. Songs (complete): An den Mond, D.529; Romanze, D.114; Stimme de Liebe, D.418; Die Sommernacht, D.289; Die fruhen Graber, D.290; Die Mondnacht, D.238; An den Mond in einer Herbstnacht, D.614; Die Nonne, D.208; An Chloen, D.462; Hochzeit-Lied, D.463; In der Mitternacht, D.464; Trauer der Liebe, D.465; Die Perle, D.466; Abendlied der Furstin, D.495; Wiegenlied, D.498; Standchen, D.920 (with chorus); Bertas Lied in der Nacht, D.653; Erlkonig, D.328.
(Volume 8).
Sarah Walker (mez); Graham Johnson (pno).
HYPERION 33008 DDD 72:00

★★*Awards:* Best of the Month, *Hi-Fi News & Record Review*, O '90. Critics' Choice 1990, *Gramophone* D '90 (Alan Blyth). Critics Choice, *Hi Fi News & Record Review*, Ap '91 Supplement (Peter Branscombe).

"The emphasis here, in volume 8, is on songs of night. Sarah Walker's dusky mezzo may not be a flawless instrument, but it is a fine medium for these songs. Graham Johnson is again the superb pianist and his detailed notes on each song are an embarrassment of riches in this day when CDs seem to be accompanied by ever-more-meager material."

American Record Guide 54:90 Ja/F '91. Charles H. Parsons (240w)

"Volume 8 is as welcome as it was keenly awaited." *P95/100 S95*

Hi-Fi News & Record Review 35:103 O '90. Peter Branscombe (255w)

"Sarah Walker is another wise choice among the largely British singers who have peopled this series thus far. She can turn her handsome voice into a dignified, Erda-like contralto when required...or lighten it to a soprano in songs calling for a young-girl approach."

Fanfare 14:309-10 Ja/F '91. David Johnson (875w)

"Sarah Walker is an artist whose response to text and music invariably yields distinctive music-making. She is in superb voice throughout this excellent program....Graham Johnson provides his usual high measure of sensitivity in every accompaniment. Johnson's exceptional notes are a major contribution to each volume of the series....An outstanding disc in a superb series. Enthusiastically recommended."

The Nats Journal 47:49 Ja/F '91. Carol Kimball (300w)

This "disc...ranges from the almost unknown recitativo in tempo 'Die Sommernacht,' performed bhy singer and accompanist with exquisite taste, to the most famous of all Schubert lieder, 'Erlkonig,' which here receives an interpretation as subtle, thoughtfully phrased—and terrifying—as any on disc."

Musical America 111:51-2 S/O '91. Jamie James (med)

Audio 75:90 S '91. Robert Long (brief)

Gramophone 68:808+ O '90. Alan Blyth (525w)

8050. Songs (complete): An den Tod, D.518. Auf dem Wasser zu singen, D.774. Auflosung, D.807. Aus Heliopolis I, D.753. Aus Heliopolis II, D.754. Dithyrambe, D.801. Elysium, D.584. Der Geistertanz, D.116. Der Konig in Thule, D.367. Lied des Orpheus, D.474. Nachtstuck, D.672. Schwanengesang, D.744. Seligkeit, D.433. So lasst mich scheinen, D.727. Thekla. D.595. Der Tod und das Madchen, D.531. Verklarung, D.59. Vollendung, D.989. Das Zugenglocklein, D.871.
(Volume 11).
Brigitte Fassbaender (mez); Graham Johnson (pno).
HYPERION 33011 DDD 65:00

★★*Awards:* The Gramophone Awards, Nominations, Solo Vocal, *Gramophone*, N '91. Critics' Choice 1991, *The Wire*, D/Ja '91/92 (Brian Morton).

"These are exhilarating performances, full of life, ardent commitment and profound insight. The vocal quality is uneven, with harsh vibrato on many held high notes, but the immediacy of response of both artists to Schubert's challenging vocal line and harmonic daring, as well as to pacing and mood, is wonderfully rewarding." *P95/85 S95*

Hi-Fi News & Record Review 37:85 My '92. Peter Branscombe (long)

"A Fassbaender recital is always cause for rejoicing and often for controversy, for she is a performer who intuitively interprets, and that performance is totally committed, no holds barred....Particularly outstanding in the excellent program are 'Auflosung,' 'Dithyrambe,' and the two 'Heliopolis' settings.

Fassbaender's reading of the familiar 'Der Tod und das Madchen' is invested with chilling color. She also gives a persuasive performance of the eloquent 'Nachtstuck.'...Equally interesting is the inclusion of Schubert's first version of Mignon's 'So lasst mich scheinen,' and 'Der Geistertanz' with its black humor....Recorded quality is outstanding. This is vintage Fassbaender, in fine voice and at her interpretive best. Collectors of the series will want to add this one right away."

The Nats Journal 48:40 Ja/F '92. Carol Kimball (long)

"The motif here is 'Death and the Composer'-...But don't be put off by fears of morbidity-....Fassbaender is a variable and unpredictable artist—at times perfunctory and seemingly even bored, at others thrilling. Here we get both sides of the equation, but she is mostly on her best form and the natural beauty of her rich, chocolate-brown mezzo-soprano voice has never been more vividly captured on a recording....A final word about a new phenomenon that crops up in this volume: the repeat of a Lied (two Lieder in this case) that has already been programmed in an earlier volume-....The important thing is that all the songs be programmed at least once before the series ends. One can forgive some of them being programmed twice, but it will add a CD or two to an already long and, from the buyer's point of view, expensive project."

Fanfare 15:474-75 N/D '91. David Johnson (long)

8051. Songs: Der Hirt auf dem Felsen, D.965. Seligkeit, D.433. Gretchen am Spinnrad, D.118. Du liebst mich nicht, D.756. Heimliches Lieben, D.922. Im Fruhling, D.882. Die Vogel, D.691. Der Jungling an der Quelle, D.300. Der Musensohn, D.764. **SCHUMANN, ROBERT. Songs:** Myrthen, Opus 25: Widmung; Der Nussbaum. Auftrage, Opus 77, No. 5. Sehnsucht, Opus 51, No. 1. Frage, Opus 35, No. 9. ein schoner Stern, Opus 101, No. 4. Lieder Album fur die Jugend, Opus 79: Schmetterling; Kauzlein; Der Sandmann; Marienwurmchen; Er ists's; Schneeglockchen. Erstes Grun, Opus 35, No. 4. Die Sennin, Opus 90, No. 4. Sehnsucht nach der Waldgegend, Opus 35, No. 5. Jasminenstrauch, Opus 27, No. 4. Liederkreis, Opus 39: Waldesgesprach. Loreley, Opus 53, No. 2. Die Meerfee, Opus 125, No. 1.

Elly Ameling (sop); Jorg Demus (pno). 1965, 1968. DEUTSCHE HARMONIA MUNDI 77085 ADD (m) 69:00

★***Awards:*** Critics' Choice 1990, *Gramophone* D '90 (Nicholas Anderson).

"Quite a few of these songs are rarely done, and it's a joy to have them again in such expert performances. Most are nature pieces, and Ameling guides us through them confidently and likably. Her voice never sounded lovelier."

Fanfare 14:369-70 S/O '90. Ralph V. Lucano (325w)

Gramophone 67:2032+ My '90. Nicholas Anderson (385w)

8052. Songs: Auflosung, D.807; Hippolits Lied, D.890; Der Einsame, D.800; Wer sich der Einsamkeit ergibt, D.478; An die Turen will ich schleichen, D.479; Wer nie sein Brot mit Tranen ass, D.480; Gruppe aus dem Tartarus, D.583; Herbst, D.945; Nacht und Traume, D.827; Nachstuck, D.672; Im Abendrot, D.799; Der Wanderer, D.493; Uber Wildemann, D.884; Der Wanderer an den Mond, D.870.

Dietrich Fischer-Dieskau (bar); Alfred Brendel (pno). PHILIPS 411 421

✔HC ★***Awards:*** *Stereo Review* Best of the Month, N '84; *Gramophone* Critics' Choice 1984 (John Warrack).

"On the second of his Schubert releases from Philips...Fischer-Dieskau's voice is as beautiful as it was thirty years ago, with a remarkably youthful lightness and flexibility, and yet so much richer in the subtle ways only the experience of a lifetime can bring."

Stereo Review 49:82 N '84. Richard Freed (400w)

"Analytical to an almost alarming degree, the CD transfer reveals all the problems F-D has now with his ageing voice, though clearly he has lost none of his penetrating intellect."

Hi-Fi News & Record Review 29:93 S '84. Ivor Humphreys (120w)

Gramophone 62:63 Je '84. John Borwick (85w)

Ovation 5:74 N '84. Philip L. Miller (325w) (rev. of LP)

8053. Songs: Lieder der Mignon: Heiss mich nicht reden, D.877, No. 2; So lasst mich scheinen, D.877, No. 3; Nur wer der Sehnsucht kennt, K.877, No. 4; Kennst du das Land, D.321. Der Konig in Thule, D.367. Gretchen am Spinnrade, D.118. Gretchen im Zwinger, D.564. Szene aus "Faust", D.126b. Suleika I, D.720. Suleika II, D.717. Das Madchen, D.652. Die Junge Nonne, D.828. Ellens Gesange: Raste, Krieger, D.837; Jager, ruhe von der Jagd, D.383; Ave Maria, D.839.

Marjana Lipovsek (mez); Geoffrey Parsons (pno). ORFEO 159 871 DDD 67:24

★***Awards:*** Top Choices—1989, *American Record Guide* Ja/F '90 (Philip L. Miller).

"Recommended—these are performances that will wear well."

Fanfare 12:257 Ja/F '89. Ralph V. Lucano (220w)

"Her voice is a rich and true mezzo-soprano, her phrasing musicianly and her diction clear. She communicates....With Geoffrey Parsons at the piano she has given us one of the outstanding Lieder records of recent years."

American Record Guide 52:79-80 Mr/Ap '89. Philip L. Miller (525w)

Gramophone 66:846 N '88. Hilary Finch (355w)

8054. Songs: Schwanengesang, D.957; Herbst, D.945; Der Wanderer an den Mond, D.870; Am Fenster, D.878; Bei dir allein, D.866, No. 2.
Peter Schreier (ten); Andras Schiff (pno).
LONDON/DECCA 425 612 DDD 63:00

★★*Awards:* Record of the Month, *Hi-Fi News & Record Review*, Ag '90. Solo Vocal Record Award 1990, *Gramophone* D '90.

"This is an exciting recital, a happy marrying of the talents of Peter Schreier in his high maturity, and Andras Schiff's prodigious gifts-...Many of the songs gain greatly from being sung at the original tenor pitch, though it cannot be denied that Schreier is occasionally strained by low-lying passages, or that his tone whitens at the top of the range....Decca provides a recording of the utmost clarity and refinement: a true chamber acoustic." *P100/95 S100*

Hi-Fi News & Record Review 35:89 Ag '90. Peter Branscombe (320w)

"Schreier...hasn't much voice for the outbursts of the Heine songs....Moreover, the too close-up recording...exaggerates his sibilants, and puts an unpleasant edge on his tone. He's fascinating, nonetheless...making the most of every opportunity for drama. Even so, his pianist often upstages him....I get very little sense of collaboration here."

Fanfare 14:343-5 N/D '90. Ralph V. Lucano (275w)

Gramophone 68:98 Je '90 (535w); 68:729 O '90 (140w). Alan Blyth

8055. Songs: Der Jungling und der Tod; Nacht und Traume; Wehmut, D.772; Gehelmnis; Abensteern; Auflosung; Die Sterne, D.684; Das Madchen; Der Schmetterling; Die Rose; Das Zugenglockleln; Am Fenster; Marie; Dass sle hier gewesen; Die Junge Nonne; Der Blinde Knabe; Die Liebe hat Gelogen; Du Liebst mich Nicht; An den Mond, D.296.
Mitsuko Shirai (mez); Hartmut Holl (pno).
CAPRICCIO 10171 DDD 64:56

★*Awards:* Top Choices—1989, *American Record Guide* Ja/F '90 (Philip L. Miller).

"This is a beautiful disc, smoothly vocalized and penetratingly sung, and made even more effective by the colorful, sensitive pianism of Holl. In no way is this ordinary Schubert singing; Shirai has obviously spent time studying this repertoire....Song texts are unfortunately in German only....The voice-piano balance and perspective are natural and the sound quality is very good indeed."

Fanfare 12:237-38 Jl/Ag '89. Henry Fogel (350w)

"As with all outstanding recitals, the listener is left with memories to savor and a marvelous feeling of satisfaction that there are still artists who care about songs as a *genre* and perform it with the highest standards. The accompanying booklet is stingy—German texts only, and brief notes. Excellent sound."

The Nats Journal 46:39 S/O '89. Carol Kimball (595w)

"This is an interesting recording of Schubert songs, some of which rmake their way to a concert program....The recording reflects a thoughtful and sensitive approach on the part of the singer and accompanist who produce usually satisfying involving, (sometimes exciting) results."

HighPerformanceReview 7:1:87 '90. June C. Ottenberg (290w)

"Mitsuko Shirai and her husband/accompanist Hartmut Holl perform as a real team. Her voice is a rich and attractive mezzo-soprano capable of seemingly infinite expressiveness without overemphasis....Only one thing bothers me about the recording: there is a slight edge on the voice."

American Record Guide 52:84-5 My/Je '89. Philip L. Miller (460w)

"If in our worldly-wise age 'a musician's musician' were still a compliment...then I'd apply the term to Shirai and Holl....Recording is faithful and pleasing, though I could bear to be slightly further from the piano's bass strings. The leaflet contains no English translations except of its high-flown and rather fey article; the German texts are reproduced with a few inaccuracies. A valuable record on account of both its music and its performers."

Music and Musicians International 37:60-1 Ap '89. Leo Black (690w)

The New York Times O 21 '90, p. 33-4. Thor Eckert Jr. (250w)

Gramophone 67:728 O '89. Alan Blyth (315w)

8056. Winterreise, D.911.
Olaf Bar (bar); Geoffrey Parsons (pno).
EMI 49334 DDD 75:00

★★*Awards:* Critics' Choice 1989, *Gramophone* D '89 (Alan Blyth); Top Disks of the Year, *The New York Times* D 24, '89 (John Rockwell).

Gramophone 67:956 N '89. Alan Blyth (265w)

"Put out of mind other *Winterreises*...and Olaf Bar's heartfelt reflections on the subject cannot fail to refresh you....Moments of flashing insight may not come with every song here, but unforgettable phrases there certainly are...And any doubts previously entertained over Bar's ability to spin a forward-moving legato line are effectively dispelled by four of the songs here." *P95/85 S95*

Hi-Fi News & Record Review 35:109 Mr '90. David Nice (350w)

"All in all, this latest *Winterreise* takes its place among the best."

American Record Guide 53:104 Mr/Ap '90. Philip L. Miller (250w)

8057. Winterreise, D.911.
Brigitte Fassbaender (mez); Aribert Reimann (pno). EMI 49846 DDD 70:00

★★★★★*Awards:* The Gramophone Awards, Nominations, Solo Vocal, *Gramophone*, N '91; Critic's Choice: 1991, *American Record Guide*, Ja/F '92 (Stephen Chakwin). The Want List 1990, *Fanfare* N/D '90 (Ralph V. Lucano); Critics' Choice 1990, *Gramophone* D '90 (James Jolly; Hilary Finch).

"It is a noble [interpretation], seemingly effortless and uncontrived, projecting the directness and simplicity of the text with a power that is the greater for concealing the subtlety and thought behind it....Reimann is a partner here, and a superb one; I cannot imagine the songs or the singer being better served. The sonic focus, too, is exemplary."
Stereo Review 55:121 S '90. Richard Freed (400w)

"Of all the recordings of *Winterreise* I've reviewed for *Fanfare* over the past three years, this one wins top prize; and at the moment, I'm ready to place it beside my long-established favorites, Hotter and Fischer-Dieskau-....Reimann's accompaniments are crisp and forceful....For me, this is a very special, cherishable performance."
Fanfare 14:377-8 S/O '90. Ralph V. Lucano (655w)

"No matter how many recordings of these songs you have, no matter how well you think you know them, you are likely to find new insights and new beauties here. Don't expect flawless beauty—Fassbaender's mahogany-colored voice sounds worn at times and Reimann can be a clattery partner—but listen to the timeless truth of Schubert's music brought to life by two inspired artists."
American Record Guide 54:115 Mr/Ap '91. Stephen D. Chakwin, Jr. (130w)

"To get straight to the point, this is no material for a woman....The reasons lie not in principles but in the particular character of this work. 'Winterreise'—like Schubert's preceding song cycle, 'Die Schone Mullerin' and the cyclelike group of Heinne songs in his posthumous collection 'Schwanengesang'—is too close to the bone, too irreducibly confessional to permit any hint of artifice....Miss Fassbaender, to give her credit, makes them as real as she can."
The New York Times O 28 '90, p. 31+. Matthew Gurewitsch (2400w)

Gramophone 68:267 Jl '90. Hilary Finch (490w)

8058. Winterreise, D.911.
Dietrich Fischer-Dieskau; Alfred Brendel (pno). PHILIPS 411 463

✔HC ★★*Awards:* *Gramophone* Critics' Choice (Iain Fenlon); *Gramophone* Critics' Choice (Hilary Finch), 1987.

This issue "must be counted vocally the least of the six (the tone is too tired and frayed not to draw forth comment), but it's interpretively even more impressive that the volatile version he did with Barenboim in 1979 for DG....Recommended without hesitation."
Fanfare 10:190-2 My/Je '87 Vincent Alfano (425w)

"With acclaim at *The Gramophone's* award for Peter Schreier's 'Winter Journey' still resounding, Philips presents what must be the great German baritone's last trudge through Schubert's romantic snow-scape....This is Fischer-Dieskau's fifth recording of the complete cycle and Brendel's first....This is a great Schubertian partnership, preserved in the nick of time."
Hi-Fi News & Record Review 32:115 F '87 Hugh Canning (525w)

Gramophone 64:920 D '86 Alan Blyth (225w); Alfano, Vincent

Opus 3:49 Ap '87 Will Crutchfield (1005w)

SCHUMANN, ROBERT

8059. Dichterliebe, Opus 48; Liederkreis, Opus 39.
Olaf Bar (baritone); Geoffrey Parsons (pno). EMI 47397 67:03

★★★★*Awards:* *Fanfare* Want List 1986 (Elliott Kaback); *Gramophone* Critics' Choice 1986 (Hilary Finch; Alan Blyth); *Hi-Fi News & Record Review* Record of the Month, Ag '86.

"Remarkable recording of two of Schumann's most popular song cycles by a 29-year-old East German baritone....Bar's most prominent gift right now is one of the most beautiful baritone voices to be heard in the past half century-....Bar would be the better for wearing his heart on his sleeve a bit more every now and again....Perhaps the low emotional quota is due in part to Geoffrey Parson's uncharacteristically pedestrian accompaniment....EMI's sound, while clear enough, is so up-close that Bar's breathing is much too prominent....I certainly recommend this recording to all lovers of great singing, and especially to the nay-sayers fond of proclaiming that such a thing is dead."
Fanfare 10:226-7 S/O '86 Vincent Alfano (540w)

"Bar sings not one ugly note throughout, yet each verse is suffused with a vivid sense of verbal point and precisely defined mood."
Hi-Fi News & Record Review 31:75 Ag '86. Hugh Canning (400w)

"One magical feature of this recording is the attunement to pacing shared by these artists."
Hi-Fi News & Record Review 31:75 Ag '86. Christopher Breunig (1070w)

Bar "ventures into well-charted and highly competitive territory. He acquits himself well but these performances give rise to questions about the singer's vocal stature."

American Record Guide 50:56-57 My/Je '87 Kurt Moses (375w)

"Not for a long time has the art of a new singer excited me so much...To begin with, he has a creamy baritone of an extraordinarily beautiful timbre, seamless in its perfection from top to bottom and equally beautiful whether in intimate *mezza voce* or noble full voice. He has virtually flawless diction...More important, Baer's literary and dramatic intelligence matches his musicality."

High Fidelity 38:54-5 My '88. Paul Moor (300w)

"The only aspect of this recording that is less than outstanding is Geoffrey Parson's phlegmatic, monochrome piano part. Vocally, this ranks very high among current recordings."

Fanfare 10:226-7 S/O '86 Elliott Kaback (170w)

Gramophone 64:522 O '86 John Steane (245w)

Opus 3:30-31+ Je '87 Will Crutchfield (665w) (rev. of LP)

8060. Dichterliebe, Opus 48; Liederkreis (Eichendorff), Opus 39; Songs from Myrthen, Opus 25.
Dietrich Fischer-Dieskau; Christoph Eschenbach (pno). reissue.
DEUTSCHE GRAMMOPHON 415 190

✔HC

Hi-Fi News & Record Review 30:109 N '85. John Freestone (35w)

8061. Frauenliebe und -leben, for Solo Female Voice and Piano, Opus 42; Liederkreis, for Solo Voice and Piano, Opus 39.
Jessye Norman (sop); Irwin Gage (pno). 1977 reissue.
PHILIPS 420 784 ADD 54:00

"In terms of vocal allure, these marvelous performances are sui generis; there are none in the current catalog that even come close to what Norman gives us of beauty of tone and vocal security....while these renditions may not be the subtlest or the most profound interpretations ever recorded, they are not far from that...this is great Lieder singing and belongs in the library of everyone interested in this repertory."

American Record Guide 51:83 S/O '88. Kurt Moses (360w)

Gramophone 66:326 Ag '88. John Steane (210w)

8062. Liederkreis (Heine), Opus 24; Liederkreis (Eichendorff), Opus 39. BRAHMS, JOHANNES. Ernste Gesange (4), Opus 121.
Victor Braun (bar); Antonin Kubalek (pno).
DORIAN 90132 DDD 60:17

★*Awards:* Critic's Choice: 1991, *American Record Guide*, Ja/F '92 (David Greene).

"Braun masterfully portrays the character of each song through the music itself, subtly shaping and coloring every phrase....The rather reverberant recording is flattering to Braun's voice, but the piano sound often lacks impact....Warmly recommended."

HighPerformanceReview 8(3):83 '91. Andrew Colton (med)

"Each of the...performers is truly excellent, and there's no dead weight among the songs."

Audio 75:91+ N '91. Robert Long (brief)

"What I hear from this disc is a firm, clear baritone that is not afraid to be masculine....If the voice is not mellifluous or sensuous, the man sings with real legato, negotiates turns and such other ornaments with grace, and does not aspirate open vowels....Braun has a splendid accompanist in Kubalek...Crystalline recording. Trilingual texts and notes...For what it's worth, recommended enthusiastically."

American Record Guide 54:118 Mr/Ap '91. David Mason Greene (450w)

"Kubalek is an excellent accompanist, and the voice and piano are justly balanced. The recording was made in the acoustically legendary Troy Savings Bank Music Hall, which probably needs an audience in it for the optimal sound—the empty space surrounding the performers is readily perceptible here. Fine notes by Kurt Moses; texts and translations. Braun's accounts of the three cycles are not going to displace my favorites, but I admire his work, and I don't think anyone who purchases this disc will be sorry."

Fanfare 14:372-3 Mr/Ap '91. Ralph V. Lucano (300w)

The New York Times Ja 13 '91, p. 29+ H. Will Crutchfield (355w)

Songs. See No. 8051.

SHOSTAKOVICH, DMITRI. From Jewish Folk Poetry (song cycle), for Soprano, Contralto, Tenor and Piano, Opus 79. See No. 1361. **Seven Songs on Poems of Alexander Blok.** See No. 3136.

SIBELIUS, JEAN

8063. Songs: Arioso, Opus 3; Seven Songs, Opus 17; Souda, souda, sinisorosa; Six Songs, Opus 36; Five Songs, Opus 37; Les Trois Sœurs Aveugles; Six Songs, Opus 88.
Anne-Sofie von Otter (mez); Bengt Forsberg (pno).
BIS 457 DDD 57:00

★*Awards:* Critics' Choice 1990, *Gramophone* D '90 (Robert Layton).

"The performances by both artists are admirably judged and von Otter's treatment of the plaintive songs is especially attractive. A promising start to what one hopes will turn out to be a successful enterprise." *P95 S95*

Hi-Fi News & Record Review 35:105 O '90. Kenneth Dommett (290w)

"On the whole this disc is highly enjoyable. Good accompaniments, good sound and good liner notes; texts are included."
American Record Guide 53:110-11 My/Je '90. George W. Loomis (200w)

"This recital is quite a mixed bag: there are strophic and through-composed songs, love songs and lullabies, songs of ample melody, and others that merely develop a single phrase-....it is pleasing that von Otter goes some way toward rectifying his unjust neglect in this field....[the recording is] perfect in terms of balance and clarity...highly recommended."
Stereophile 13:225+ D '90. Barbara Jahn (140w)

Gramophone 68:103 Je '90. Robert Layton (655w)

STENHAMMAR, WILHELM. Ithaka, Ballade for Baritone and Orchestra, Opus 21. See No. 6131.

STRADELLA, ALESSANDRO. Arias: Lontanaza e gelosia; Si salvio chi puo. See No. 8068.

STRAUSS, RICHARD

Capriccio: Prelude; Intermezzo; Morgen mittag um elf!. See No. 1416

Drei Hymnen, Opus 71. See No. 1411.

8064. Four Last Songs. Songs: Cacillie; Morgen; Wiegenlied; Ruhe, meine Seele; Meinem kinde; Zueignung.
Jessye Norman (sop). Kurt Masur (c). Leipzig Gewandhaus Orchestra.
PHILIPS 411 052 DDD

★★★***Awards:*** *Stereo Review* Best of the Month, Mr '84; *Fanfare* Want List 1984 (Roger Dettmar); *Gramophone* Record Award Winner 1984—Solo Vocal Award.

"Not only is Jessye Norman a *virtuosa* vocally, as nearly perfect a technician as imaginable with that timbre of unique plangency and opulence, she's an interpreter of the frontmost rank in this century. Her singing of Strauss-...has no equivalent today, nor has it had for me in a performance-repertoire now stretching back nearly 50 years."
Fanfare 7:258-9 Jl/Ag '84. Roger Dettmer (230w)

"Surely no other soprano can encompass the wide range of these four songs with Norman's effortless command....This gifted soprano-...now seems to have reached the full realization of her amazing promise."
Stereo Review 49:59-60 Mr '84. George Jellinek (400w)

Gramophone 61:1002 F '84. Alan Blyth (245w)

High Fidelity 34:61+ Je '84. Paul Hume (150w)

Digital Audio 1:79-80 N '84. John Marks (475w)

Hi-Fi News & Record Review 29:86 Mr '84. Ivor Humphreys (160w)

8065. Four Last Songs. ***Capriccio:*** Morgen mittag um Elf. ***Arabella:*** Ich danke, Fraulein...Aber der Richtige; Mein Elemer; Sie wolheiraten; Das war sehr gut.
Elisabeth Schwarzkopf (sop); Anny Felbermayer (sop); Josef Metternich (bar). Otto Ackermann; Lovro von Matacic (c). Philharmonia Orchestra. 1954, 1955 reissues.
EMI 61001 68:00

"*Four Last Songs* have achieved remarkable popularity in the past decade, and there are currently at least ten CD versions available. For many listeners, however, the definitive recorded account remains this one.....Schwarzkopf was at her best in this recording, both vocally and interpretatively....It is unfortunate that no texts are provided."
High Fidelity 39:63 Mr '89. Robert E. Benson (235w)

"If Welitsch was indeed born to sing *Salome*, so it seems that Strauss wrote just about everything else to suit the glimmering beauty of Schwarzkopf's voice. He didn't, of course, but that popular misconception can only be reinforced by the high quality of this new compact disc."
Ovation 10:56 Ag '89. Dick Adler (135w)

"Powerful artisty, great music and sound. Not to be missed."
American Record Guide 51:58-9 Jl/Ag '88. Donald R. Vroon (180w)

"It's all too easy to eulogize a superior performance, ignoring the basic fact that, to many listeners, foreign-language opera and song without text is incomprehensible nonsense....Does EMI actually believe that a prospective purchaser would object to paying an extra dollar or two to better understand and enjoy a classic performance?"
Musical America 109:81-2 Ja '89. David Hurwitz (170w)

Gramophone 65:1488 Ap '88. Michael Kennedy (160w)

Four Last Songs. See No. 1414.

8066. Songs: Ruhe, meine Seele, Opus 27 No. 1; Waldseligkeit, Opus 49 No. 1; Freundliche Vision, Opus 48 No. 1; Morgen!, Opus 27 No. 4; Befreit, Opus 39 No. 4; Meinem Kinde, Opus 37 No. 3; Winterweihe, Opus 48 No. 4; Weigenlied, Opus 41 No.1; Die heiligen drei Konige aus Morgenland, Opus 56 No. 6. Metamorphosen for 23 Solo Strings.
Gundula Janowitz (sop). Richard Stamp (c). Academy of London.
VIRGIN 90794 DDD 60:00

★***Awards:*** Critics' Choice 1991, *Gramophone*, Ja '92 (Michael Kennedy).

"The first time I heard Janowitz, the exceptional warmth of her voice made me hers for life; very rarely does one find such a sunny radiance in the soprano register....Thirty-two years have passed since Janowitz's brilliant Vienna debut, but this recording shows that in this repertoire few sopranos can touch or even approach her even today. In addition to that exemplary warmth, she manifests unusual intelligence when it comes to texts and their enunciation."

Musical America 111:89 Jl '91. Paul Moor (400w)

"The soprano Gundula Janowitz brings a warmth and humanity to the nine songs in this recording that make them a deeply moving listening experience....The collaboration of the Academy of London under Richard Stamp's direction is faultless, and the sound from EMI's Abbey Road Studio 1 is richly textured, with inner lines beautifully delineated."

Stereo Review 56:97 Je '91. David Hall (155w)

"These could almost be Nine Last Songs as Gundula Janowitz now delivers them, their youthful poetry quite offset by a fragility in the voice which can be touching indeed—my eyes pricked at the quiet raptures of *Freundliche Vision* and *Wiegenlied*—but which never leaves you quite confident of what that voice can accomplish....Orchestral support, despite a distinguished contribution from Peter Manning in *Morgen* and telling clarinet work, is rather hazily recorded; *Metamorphosen* (All Saints Tooting notwithstanding) presents a much more immediate picture." *P95/85 S95/85 songs, P85/75 S95 Metamorphosen*

Hi-Fi News & Record Review 36:69 Jl '91. David Nice (250w)

"The voice here sounds splendidly equalized throughout its range with a luminous, easy top replacing the occasionally 'squeezed' tones that slightly marred its full effectiveness in her younger days. Almost all these songs have been oft recorded in the past, yet Janowitz manages to put an individual seal on many of them....The engineers have captured the massed strings superbly but I am not entirely happy with their work on the songs....However, the excellent notes, texts, and translations leave nothing to be desired; so this minor lapse on an otherwise superb disc should not put off prospective purchasers."

American Record Guide 54:126 Mr/Ap '91. Vivian A. Liff (275w)

"The Academy of London is as good as, if not better than any of its competitors, and the recording has a warmth and magical glow."

Australian Hi-Fi 22(5):92 '91. Cyrus Meher-Homji (brief)

"Janowitz may not challenge the rich vocalism of Jessye Norman—or even the confident ease of her own singing in the mid-seventies, when she spun out the *Four Last Songs* with Karajan. Nor is there much emotional specificity to her interpretations: all the songs seem to be inhabited by the same persona....it's hard not to be enraptured by the pure, almost disembodied beauty of these intimate and evocative readings, with their supple phrasing and their acute sensitivity to Strauss's aching harmonic turns."

Fanfare 14:301 Jl/Ag '91. Peter J. Rabinowitz (300w)

Gramophone 68:1549 F '91. Michael Kennedy (365w)

8067. Songs: Standchen; Mit deinen blauen Augen; Ich trage meine Minne; Kling!; Allerseelen; Die Nacht; Die Zeitlose; Einerlei; Lob des Leidens; Befreit; Ach Lieb, ich muss nun scheiden; Du meines Herzens Kronelein; Schlectes Wetter; Wir beide wollen springen; Wie sollten wir geheimk; Seitdem dein Aug; Stiller Gang; Heimliche Aufforderung; Malven; Traum durch die Dammerung.
Jessye Norman (sop); Geoffrey Parsons (pno).
PHILIPS 416 298 DDD

★*Awards:* *Opera News* Best of the Year, 1987.

"Norman is in great voice here. Everything is working just fine, and the sound is taking on some cello-like sounds in the lower range as the singer matures."

Fanfare 10:213-4 Mr/Ap '87 Vincent Alfano (475w)

Stereo Review 52:96+ Ap '87 Robert Ackart (150w)

Gramophone 64:992 Ja '87 John Steane (65w)

Hi-Fi News & Record Review 31:123 N '86. David Nice (315w) (rev. of LP)

Opera News 52:42 Mr 12 '88. John W. Freeman (80w)

Songs. See No. 8026.

STRAVINSKY, IGOR. Songs (complete). See No. 1425.

STROZZI, BARBARA

8068. Soprano Arias and Cantatas (7 selections from Opus 2, 3 and 7): Lamento; A pena il sol; L'amante bugiardo; Fin che tu spiri; Moralita amorosa; L'amante segreto; Tradimento. **STRADELLA, ALESSANDRO. Cantata, "L'Arianna"; Arias:** Lontanaza e gelosia; Si salvio chi puo.
Isabelle Poulenard (sop); Marianne Muller (vla da gamba); Elmer Buckley (hpscd).
ADDA 581 173 DDD 65:27

★*Awards:* The Want List 1990, *Fanfare* N/D '90 (Tom Moore).

"Poulenard's performances are absolutely stunning. What a range of expression! She captures the brilliance, the wit, the intensity of Barbara Strozzi with Kaleidoscopic shifts of mood-....She has a beautiful voice and superb technique....Praise also to her fine accompanists Muller and Buckley. What more can one ask? Superb!"

Fanfare 14:402-3 S/O '90. Tom Moore (200w)

"All three musicians are a pleasure to hear. Ms. Poulenard brings a most expressive voice to this music, and communicates its emotions well....All the accompaniments are imaginative and moving."

American Record Guide 53:123 N/D '90. Catherine Moore (385w)

TIPPETT, MICHAEL. Songs for Dov, for Tenor and Small Orchestra. See No. 1450.

VARESE, EDGAR. Offrandes, for Soprano and Chamber Orchestra (1921). See No. 1457.

VILLA-LOBOS, HEITOR. Bachianas Brasilieras No. 5. See No. 8019.

WAGNER, RICHARD

8069. Wesendonck Songs. Arias and Scenes: *Tannhauser:* Allmacht'ge Jungfrau. *Siegfried:* Ewig war ich. *Gotterdammerung:* Starke Scheite. *Tristan und Isolde:* Doch num von Tristan? Liebestod.

Kirsten Flagstad (sop); Gerald Moore (pno); various other artists. Abbey Road Studios. 1948 reissues.
EMI 63030 ADD (m) 75:00

"All in all...this is a fine disc to introduce Flagstad to what one hopes is a new audience out there, waiting to get to know her. The sound is good."

Fanfare 13:340-41 Ja/F '90. William Youngren (500w)

Gramophone 67:373 Ag '89. Alan Blyth (290w)

WEILL, KURT

8070. Songs: *Aufstieg und Fall der Stadt Mahagonny:* Alabama-Song; Denn Wie han sich bettet. *Berliner Requiem:* Zu Potsdam unter der Eichen. *Die Dreigroschenoper:* Die Ballade von der Sexuellen Horigkeit; Die Moritat von Mackie Messer; Salomon-Song; Je ne t'aime pas; Nannas Lied. *One Touch of Venus:* I'm a Stranger Here Myself; Speak Low; Westwind. *Der Silbersee:* Casars Tod; Finnimores Lied; Lied des Lotterieagenten. (Ute Lemper Sings Kurt Weill).

Ute Lemper (voc). John Mauceri (c). Berlin RIAS Chamber Ensemble. RIAS Studio 7, Berlin FRG. August 1988.
LONDON/DECCA 425 204 DDD 50:17

✔**HC** ★★*Awards:* Editors' Choice, *Digital Audio's CD Review*, Je '89. Critics' Choice 1989, *Gramophone* D '89 (Andrew Lamb). Cream of the Crop IV, *Digital Audio's CD Review*, 6:43 Je '90.

"Miss Lemper is nothing short of sensational in her recorded program of Weill's music-....Miss Lemper sings in German, in French, and in English, on this recording. She is equally facile in each of these languages."

Show Music 6:31 Summ 89. Max O. Preeo (440w)

"Lemper is awesome, with the necessary articulation, control and ironically jaded attitude to make Weill smile from beyond."

Jazziz 6:82 O/N '89. Wayne Lee (80w)

"Phenomenal the Lemper vocal equipment may not be, but governed by a shining intelligence and a strong sense of musical line it wears well through this selective appraisal of the German, French, and American Weill."

Hi-Fi News & Record Review 34:97 Mr '89. David Nice (385w)

"Her performance is indeed compelling. And she is certainly less eccentric and uneven than Teresa Stratas has been in her Weill recordings."

Stereo Review 54:98 Ap '89. Roy Hemming (275w)

"This is a very strong new entry. Recommended highly."

HighPerformanceReview 6:95 HPR Staff Je '89. (180w)

"Let's forget the niceties of competing versions: any good Weillian would want this CD. Texts are included, and overall production values are commendable."

Fanfare 12:282-83 Jl/Ag '89. John Ditsky (220w)

"On the evidence of this record, Lemper has a more attractive voice than did either Dietrich or Lenya, and she puts a lot of personality into her interpretations of the material...the sound quality...while having a rather close-up 'pop' perspective, is clear and unstrained."

Stereophile 12:189 Ag '89. Robert Deutsch (275w)

"This is, once again, a record about the way a singer can make up a lot of vocal styles and stick them willy-nilly, onto some powerful and cherishable music....John Mauceri's orchestral support is very fine, but most of the time there's not that much to support."

Kurt Weill Newsletter 7:25 Fall '89. Alan Rich (165w)

"Ute Lemper is no Lenya, nor does she rise to the level of Teresa Stratas or, most especially, Gisela May in this music. Lemper's problem lies in the fact that the style seems to be in place, but not the intelligence (or artistry) to apply it in the service of the music....London's production doesn't help Lemper at all."

Ovation 10:53-4 Mr '89. David Hurwitz (290w)

"Theatrically, she may have progressed astoundingly, but vocally, her Weill songs are not as ironic as Lenya's, nor as thoughtful as Teresa Stratas's. She has a yuppie approach that uses the bark rather than the incisors."

American Record Guide 52:107-9 Mr/Ap '89. Richard Traubner (105w)

8071. Songs.
(Berlin and American Theater Songs).
Lotte Lenya (voc). 1955, 1957 reissue.
CBS 42658 ADD 69:01

✔HC

"Highly recommended."
Fanfare 12:312 N/D '88. John Ditsky (240w)

"The remastered sound is startlingly clear and immediate....An indispensable disc."
American Record Guide 52:105-106 Ja/F '89. Ralph V. Lucano (335w)

"It comes in a double-CD jewel box...a fat little booklet with the lyrics for all the songs, in German, English, and French....a handy sampling of the work of Kurt Weill....One might question the wisdom of having had Miss Lenya sing such a 'masculine' song as 'September Song,' and she hasn't quite the 'zip' required for the showy 'Saga of Jenny,' but she is quite effective singing 'It Never Was You,' 'Foolish Heart,' 'Green-up Time,' and 'Trouble Man'....Ultimately, this release is a tribute not only to the work of Kurt Weill, but equally to the art of Lotte Lenya."
Show Music 6:39-40 Winter '88/89. Max O. Preeo (360w)

"Lenya's performances of Weill's songs are widely regarded as definitive, but her recording of Berlin and American theater songs merely makes one wonder what all the fuss is about."
Stereophile 12:161-65 Mr '89. Robert Deutsch (800w)

WISHART, TREVOR

8072. Vox (1980-88).
Electric Phoenix.
VIRGIN 91108 DDD 67:00

★*Awards:* Best of the Month, *Hi-Fi News & Record Review, Ap '90.*

"For those inclined to treat much recent electronic music as, at best, a cure for insommia, Wishart's *Vox* cycle may come as a pleasant surprise, for it has about it an imaginative precision of gesture, light years away from the exuberant sci-fi extravaganzas which characterize the work of lesser practitioners in the medium-....one cannot argue with the quality of the performances or recording." *P95 S100*
Hi-Fi News & Record Review 35:97+ Ap '90. Simon Cargill (315w)

"If a more polished 'experimental' vocal group exists, I've not heard it; Electric Phoenix's relationship to *Vox* is seamless and organic, a commendation which reads innocuously enough under conventional circumstances, but which, under these signally *un*conventional circumstances, speaks volumes—or better, phonemes-....the taped components integrate as elegantly with the voices as do the voices one with the other....A superbly crafted, recommended disc. The engineering is particularly fine—a gorgeously detailed soundstage and quite realistic vocal sounds."
Fanfare 14:405-6 N/D '90. Mike Silverton (370w)

"Trevor Wishart's (b 1946) *Vox* (1980-7) is one of those contemporary pieces that purports to mean something but doesn't really....Electric Phoenix is unbelievably excellent and virtuosic."
American Record Guide 54:125 Ja/F '91. Timothy D. Taylor (160w)

WOLF, HUGO

8073. Morike-Lieder: Auf einer Wanderung; Ein Stundlein wohl vor Tag; Erstes Liebeslied eines Madchens; Das verlassene Magdlein; Nixe Binsefuss; Gesang Weylas; Fussreise; Schlafendes Jesuskind; Lied vom Winde; Im Fruhling; Verborgenheit; Elfenlied; Zitronenfalter im April; Heimweh; Er ist's; Abschied.
Dinah Bryant (sop); Daniel Blumenthal (pno). Texts and translations included.
AUTOGRAPHE 148 003 DDD 47:30

★*Awards:* The Want List 1989, *Fanfare* N/D '89 (Adrian Corleonis).

"Not since the young Elly Ameling recorded twenty of these songs...with Dalton Baldwin nearly two decades ago...have these staples yielded such unalloyed pleasure....One complains, in fact, only of short measure...Enthusiastically recommended, anyway....a second Strauss recital is due for release as you read this...Meanwhile, get this album and stay tuned."
Fanfare 13:414-15 N/D '89. Adrian Corleonis (500w)

"The soprano...is at her best in the stark, disarming songs like 'Das verlassene Magdlein'-...Other songs find the vocal quality spreading slightly at climatic moments, and she lacks the kind of animated way with the texts that the quicker songs—taken in any event too slowly—demand."
American Record Guide 53:107-08 Ja/F '90. George W. Loomis (185w)

Gramophone 69:178 O '91. Alan Blyth (med)

Songs. See No. 8032.

Solo Vocal Music—Collections

Auger, Arleen

8074. Recital. Mozart. Die Verschweignung; Un moto di gioia; Das Veilchen; Als Luise die Briefe; Das Lied der Trennung; Abendempfindung. **Strauss:** Morgen; Hat gesagt; Gluckes genug; Gefunden. **Wolf:** Die vier Lieder der Mignon.
Arleen Auger (sop); Irwin Gage (pno).
CBS 42447 DDD 47:58

★★*Awards:* First Place Vocal Solo Mumm Champagne Classical Music Award 1988—Presented by *Ovation, Ovation* N '88. *Gramophone* Critics' Choice (Hilary Finch), 1987.

"An excellent, spotless acoustic catches the soprano voice and Gage's Bosendorfer to perfection."
Hi-Fi News & Record Review 33:102-3 F '88. Arthur Jacobs (310w)

"I have little to add (or to differ with) my late colleague's (V.A.) comments anent the performances on the 'warmly recommended' black-disc issue of this CD (*Fanfare* 10:6)."
Fanfare 11:260-1 N/D '87. Anthony D. Coggi (190w)

"The outstanding performances come at the end, in Wolf's four 'Mignon' songs....I wish I could feel quite as enthusiastic about the rest."
Opus 3:58 O '87. Jon Alan Conrad (650w)

Gramophone 65:474+ S '87 Hilary Finch (245w) (rev. of LP)

Baird, Julianne

8075. The English Lute Song. Anon.: This Merry Pleasant Spring; The French King's Masque; O Death, Rock Me Asleep; The Willow Song; I Must Complain; Nothing on Earth; Miserere, My Maker; Cupid Is Venus' Only Joy. **Johnson:** Woods, Rocks and Mountains; Where the Bee Sucks; Full Fathom Five; Come Away, Hecate; Alman; "Hit and Take It"; Come Hither You That Love; Have You Seen But a White Lily Grow; Alman; Care, Charming Sleep; O Let Us Howl. **Morley:** April Is My Mistress' Face. **Lanier:** No More Shall Meads Be Deck'd with Flow'rs. **Ferrabosco:** Come my Celia. **Wilson:** Dear, Do Not Your Fair Beauty Wrong; Turn, Turn Thy Beauteous Face Away; Take, O Take Those Lips Away. **Campion:** Fain Would I Wed. **Brewer:** O That Mine Eyes: **Webb:** As Life What Is So Sweet.
Julianne Baird (sop); Ron MacFarlane (lute). Music Hall, Troy Savings Bank, Troy, New York. October 6-7, 1987.
DORIAN 90109 DDD 65:00

✔**HC** ★★★*Awards:* The Want List 1989, *Fanfare* N/D '89 (John Wiser); The Want List 1989, *Fanfare* N/D '89 (William Zagorski). Cream of the Crop IV, *Digital Audio's CD Review*, 6:41 Je '90.

"Julianne Baird...gives the recital of her life-....The balance between singer, accompanist, and room sound are absolutely right—if there is a more believable recording of voice and solo instrument out there, I certainly haven't heard it."
Stereophile 12:214-15 N '89. Les Berkley (400w)

"Julianne Baird enjoys an enviable reputation as an authority on the history and performance of early music. Her voice is a straight, vibratoless soprano of extensive range, occasionally tending to hootiness. Her accomplished partner, the lutenist Ron MacFarlane, also plays three solos. The recording was made in the Music Hall of the Troy Savings Bank in Troy, New York, famous for its live acoustics. Obviously the hall was empty, which accounts for some diffuseness in the sound and a general clouding of the singer's diction."
American Record Guide 52:123-24 My/Je '89. Philip L. Miller (400w)

"It's one of the finest recordings, period, I have yet encountered, and it should lay to rest the notion that raspiness is an unfortunate by product of digital technology....A stunner-...highly recommended."
Fanfare 12:394 My/Je '89. William Zagorski (420w)

"*The English Lute Song* is only going to enhance Baird's considerable reputation as one of the finest interpreters of English Renaissance solo music."
Musick 11:23-5 Spr '90. J. Evan Kreider (555w)

"Baird has included some fiendishly difficult music which she brings off confidently."
Continuo 13:23-4 Je '89. Scott Paterson (70w)

"The recorded acoustics are a little annoying: sometimes there is a little too much echo in the voice, and sometimes the lute seems to get lost. But this is a minor complaint considering the disc's many outstanding points. Highly recommended."
HighPerformanceReview 6:91 Je '89. D. C. Culbertson (260w)

Gramophone 67:1858 Ap '90. David Fallows (225w)

Digital Audio's CD Review 5:89 My '89. Wayne Green (b.n.)

8076. Greensleeves: English Lute Songs. Morley: It was a lover and his lass. **Campion:** Author of light; Shall I come sweet love to thee? It fell on a summer's day; Never weather-beaten sail; If thou longst so much to learn. **A. Ferrabosco II:** So beauty on the waters stood. **Rosseter:** When Laura smiles. **Dowland:** In darkness let me dwell; Sorrow, sorrow stay; Come again sweet love; Away with these self-loving lads; Time stands still. **Cavendish:** Wand'ring in this place. **Lanier:** Mark how the blushful morn. **Anon. English:** Watkin's Ale; Bonny sweet boy; Packington's Pound; Kemp's Jig; Wilson's Wilde; Robinson's May. **Holborne:** Galliard; Cradle Pavan. Julianne Baird (sop); Ron MacFarlane (lute). Music Hall, Troy Savings Bank, Troy, New York. 1989. DORIAN 90126 DDD 68:00

★★★*Awards:* The Want List 1991, *Fanfare* N/D '91 (Michael Ullman). The Want List 1990, *Fanfare* N/D '90 (William Zagorski). The Want List 1991, *Fanfare* N/D '91 (Michael Ullman).

"This is, in my opinion, *the* lute song disc to buy if you are unfamiliar with the genre, and I think that those who know these works well will want this recording to compare with their personal favorites....Sound here is...excellent."
Stereophile 13:213 Je '90. Les Berkley (385w)

"The title *Greensleeves* here is misleading....Instead, what we have are richly crafted art songs of the most sophisticated variety....Recommended."
American Record Guide 53:149-50 Jl/Ag '90. George W. Loomis (260w)

"This beautifully recorded disc collects some familiar and some rare English lute songs...She has a pure sound, good diction, and a supple way of phrasing; her accompanist seems to me unemphatic, even for a lutenist."
Fanfare 13:371 Mr/Ap '90. Michael Ullman (150w)

Gramophone 67:1858 Ap '90. David Fallows (225w)

Digital Audio's CD Review 6:54+ Ap '90. Sebastian Russ (455w)

8077. Songs of Love and War: Italian Dramatic Songs of the Seventeenth and Eighteenth Centuries. Handel: Cantata "La Lucrezia." **Sances:** Cantata a voce sopra la Ciaccona. Cantata a voce sopra la Passacaglia. **Frescobaldi:** Toccata 8 (Book 2). **Caccini:** Amarilli (two versions). Caduca fiamma. Amor ch'attendi? **Monteverdi:** Lamento d'Arianna. **Hasse:** Cantata: "Pastorelle che piangete". Julianne Baird (sop); Colin Tilney (hpscd); Myron Lutzke (cello).
DORIAN 90104 DDD 64:00

✔**HC** ★*Awards:* The Want List 1990, *Fanfare* N/D '90 (Tom Moore).

"Julianne Baird has studied this repertoire from both a performer's and a musicologist's views, and her singing is informed by both perspectives....Although recorded before her successful lute-song recordings with Ronn McFarlane, this performance perhaps betters those superb efforts."
Stereophile 14:199+ F '91. Les Berkley (225w)

"This is singing of extraordinary beauty and expressive variety....in all Baird recordings I have heard an intelligence that misses not a thing. Yet nothing seems calculated."
American Record Guide 54:142-3 Ja/F '91. Michael Mark (120w)

"This program allows Baird to display not only her technical skill at division work, particularly in the English *Amarilli*, but also her gift for dramatic projection. While not as emotive as some, her *Arianna* is affecting because of her ability to portray the fullness of Ariadne's character."
Continuo 15:27-9 Je '91. Scott Paterson (110w)

"This is the latest in a series of fine recordings by Julianne Baird...Tilney and Lutzke are model accompanists, and the sound is first-rate-....Highly recommended."
Fanfare 13:329-30 Jl/Ag '90. Tom Moore (445w)

Gramophone 68:1402 Ja '91. John Duarte (315w)

Barstow, Josephine

8078. Opera Finales. (Josephine Barstow with various artists) R. Strauss: *Salome:* Es ist kein Laut zu vernehmen...Ah! Du wolltest mich nicht deinen Mund kussen lasses, Jokanaan! **Cherubini:** *Medee:* Eh quoi je suis Medee! **Janacek:** *The Makropulos Affair:* She's on the Whiskey! **Puccini (comp. Alfano):** *Turandot:* Principessa di morte! Josephine Barstow (sop). John Mauceri (c). Scottish Opera Chorus; Scottish Opera Orchestra. LONDON/DECCA 430 203 DDD 77:00

★*Awards:* Critics' Choice 1990, *Gramophone* D '90 (John Steane).

"This is an enthralling record, one of the most exciting to have come my way in a very long time. The programme is immensely valuable, offering as it does four substantial episodes, not bleeding chunks, on one exceptionally well-filled (76 minutes) CD.....Above all, Barstow's extraordinary powers are caught at their peak. If I wanted to demonstrate to the uninitiated how and why this artist is capable of inspiring such adoration to the point of idolatry, this Decca recital-record is the evidence to which I would turn first to support my argument."
Opera 41:1265-6 O '90. Max Loppert (540w)

"Josephine Barstow...is a rivetting, totally sincere singing actress who has always given 100% commitment in a wide-ranging repertoire...the disc is utterly fascinating and the Strauss, Janacek, and Puccini are very well done....The Scottish forces under Mauceri play splendidly....Definitely recommended."
American Record Guide 54:179 S/O '91. Vivian A. Liff (long)

"Barstow is an intelligent, thoughtful artist with a talent for verbal nuance, especially in roles, such as these, which benefit from psychological inflections....Altogether an impressive addition to the catalog."

Musical America 111:55 S/O '91. Walter Price (med)

"What her voice may lack in purity is more than made up by her understanding of the characters she portrays. In this clever programme of *Opera Finales*, Ms Barstow presents four tortured women including Turandot in the first recordings of the complete Puccini/Alfano ending."

High Fidelity 2:117 N '90. Clive Manning (110w)

Gramophone 68:615 S '90. John Steane (630w)

Opera News 55:41 Ap 13 '91. John W. Freeman (550w)

Battle, Kathleen

8079. Recital. Purcell: Come All Ye Songsters; Music for a While; Sweeter Than Roses. **Handel:** O Had I Jubal's Lyre. **Mendelssohn:** Bei der Wiege; Neue Liebe. **R. Strauss:** Schlagende Herzen; Ich wollt' ein Straus-slein binden; Sausle, liebe Myrte. **Mozart:** Ridente la calma; Das Veilchen; Un moto di gioia. **Faure:** Mandoline; Les roses d'Ispahan; En Prier; Notre amour. **Anon:** Honor, Honor; His Name So Sweet; Witness; He's Got the Whole World in His Hand).
Kathleen Battle; James Levine (pno). Salzburg Festival. August 25, 1984.
DEUTSCHE GRAMMOPHON 415 361 DDD 51:17

✔HC ★*Awards: Stereo Review* Best of the Month, Ap '87.

"This release is but further proof of what a phenomenal artist this superb American lyric soprano is."

American Record Guide 50:67 Fall '87. Michael Mark (190w)

"This recording...captures the gifted young recitalist at the top of her engaging form. Kathleen Battle's small soprano is beautifully focused and projected throughout the program, which is an attractive mixed bag of art songs-...Baroque chestnuts, and arrangements of spirituals....James Levine's piano playing is neat and orderly but rarely memorable."

High Fidelity 37:78+ N '87. Terry Teachout (175w)

One of 20 classical CDs reviewed and recommended as "outstanding for their musical interest and their performance as well as for their technical quality."

Stereo Review Presents: Compact Disc Buyer's Guide 1988 p.43. William Livingstone and Christie Barter (125w)

"This attractive and richly varied song recital was recorded live in the Kleines Festpielhaus during the Salzburg Festival of 1984....Levine proves himself to be a sympathetic, stylish and at times eloquent accompanist."

Hi-Fi News & Record Review 32:119 Ja '87 Peter Branscombe (240w)

"Why it has taken two and a half years for Deutsche Grammophon to get this into circulation, I wouldn't attempt to guess, but what a lovely release it is!"

Stereo Review 52:88 Ap '87 Richard Freed (350w)

"Miss Battle has one of the loveliest voices you could ever hope to hear, and she employs it purely, sweetly and truly. She sings pristine Purcell, followed by the most dazzling 'Jubal's Lyre' I've heard since the young Victoria de los Angeles knocked me out of my seat at an Edinburgh Festival recital almost forty years ago....Her spirituals evoke Dorothy Maynor; in this category, I have no higher praise."

Musical America 107:63 Jl '87 Paul Moor (350w)

"Battle is entirely suited to all of the material—she sings it to near-perfection and has yards of charm to reach across the platform to the listener....Pretty."

Fanfare 10:245-6 Mr/Ap '87 Vincent Alfano (400w)

"A big disappointment, this disc. It is beautifully produced, with the voice well in front, but the overall impression the recital leaves with the listener is one of detached purity—rather like listening to great songs through the aural equivalent of a microscope."

Ovation 8:43-4 O '87. Robert Levine (300w)

Gramophone 64:741 N '86 Hilary Finch (260w)

Opus 3:32 Je '87 Matthew Gurewitsch (435w)

Battle, Kathleen and Christopher Parkening

8080. The Pleasures of Their Company. Dowland: Songs. **Bach (arr. Gounod):** Ave Maria. **Villa-Lobos:** Aria from Bachianas Brasileiras No. 5; Three Brazilian Songs; Granados; La Maja de Goya. **De Falla:** Three Spanish Folk Songs. Six Spirituals.
Kathleen Battle (sop); Christopher Parkening (gtr). Wilshire United Methodist Church, Los Angeles, CA.
EMI 47196 44:09

✔HC ★*Awards: Fanfare* Want List 1986 (Vincent Alfano).

"Marked by delicacy and musicianship, this recording is a treasurable collaboration between two of America's most talented performing artists. The balance between voice and guitar is good, and the engineers have succeeded well in capturing the beauty of Ms. Battle's voice."

Stereo Review 51:146+ D '86 William Livingstone (290w)

"Highly recommended."

HighPerformanceReview 4:117 Wint '86/'87 Ann Viles (330w) (rev. of LP)

"Just the sort of thing to put one in a settled state of mind after a hard day at the salt mines-....One of the most startlingly immediate sound settings it's ever been my pleasure to hear....it can probably be said that Battle and Parkening have produced a classic."

Fanfare 10:281-2 S/O '86 Vincent Alfano (225w)

"The combination of Kathleen Battle's small, silvery voice and the light guitar of Christopher Parkening is a happy one. The balance is excellent."

Ovation 7:46 O '86 Philip L. Miller (165w)

"Guitar and voice combine as one melodious and harmonious instrument in the inspired, sensitive hands of these performers."

High Fidelity 37:58 Jl '87 Christopher Manion (160w)

"Although these are committed performances, I find many of them...over-indulgent. However, both artists show a commendable range of variety and approach that could never be considered dull."

Hi-Fi News & Record Review 33:107 F '88. Barbara Jahn (105w)

Stereo Review Presents: Compact Disc Buyers' Guide p. 52 Spr '87 William Livingstone and Christie Barter (80w)

Digital Audio 3:45-6 S '86. Brian J. Murphy (500w)

Battle, Kathleen and Jessye Norman

8081. Spirituals in Concert. In That Great Getting Up Morning; Sinner, Please Don't Let This Harvest Pass; Over My Head/Lil' David; Oh, What a Beautiful City; Lord, How Come Me Here; I Believe I'll Go Back Home/Lordy, Won't You Help Me; Ride On, King Jesus; Swing Low, Sweet Chariot/Ride Up in the Chariot; You Can Tell the World; Scandalize My Name; Great Day; Oh, Glory; Calvary/They Crucified My Lord; Talk about a Child; Gospel Train; My God Is So High; There Is a Balm in Gilead; He's Got the Whole World in His Hand.
Kathleen Battle (sop); Jessye Norman (sop); various others. James Levine (c). Carnegie Hall, New York. March 18, 1990 live.
DEUTSCHE GRAMMOPHON 429 790 DDD 68:00

> ★*Awards:* The Want List 1991, *Fanfare* N/D '91 (David Mason Greene).

"For sheer singing, this is one of the most exciting records to come my way in a long time-....This record gives us both singers in excelsis-....The recording is splendid....The one drawback is the trigger-happy audience which can't wait to get itself recorded and spoils one or two numbers with premature applause. Otherwise, highly recommended."

Fanfare 15:410-11 S/O '91. David Mason Greene (med)

"Both divas were in fine voice and obviously enjoying themselves, and so, judging by their audible interaction, was the audience...Good sound, texts, and only a minimum of distracting applause. Recommended."

American Record Guide 54:175 S/O '91. Kurt Moses (med)

"There's real magnificence here. If you like gorgeous singing and vaguely buttoned-down revival-meeting vibes, you can't go wrong with this disc. It's handsomely recorded, with real presence, too. Recommended."

Stereophile 15:279 Ja '92. Robert Levine (long)

"The arrangements...are performed with distinction by the pick-up orchestra and chorus under Levine's direction. While many listeners will find Kathleen Battle's patented brand of vocal sunshine too sugary...her devotees will doubtless find much to their liking. Jessye Norman's contribution is superbly crafted and deeply felt."

Musical America 111:56 S/O '91. Jamie James (med)

"Recorded live at Carnegie Hall, this disc should please virtually everyone. The selections are varied in mood and provide pleasant musical contrast....Kathleen Battle and Jessye Norman, in splendid form, give unstintingly of themselves....One gains from this record a sense of how the spiritual was an outlet for many different feelings and a source of enduring hope. The spiritual as an art form, however, is served with greater musical purity and with stronger emotional conviction in Miss Norman's solo album, 'Spirituals' on Philips."

Stereo Review 56:88 Ag '91. Robert Ackart (175w)

Gramophone 68:2060 My '91. Edward Greenfield (455w)

Digital Audio's CD Review 7:44-5 Je '91. Sebastian Russ (300w)

Berberian, Cathy

8082. MagnifiCathy: The Many Voices of Cathy Berberian (1928-1983). Monteverdi: La lettera amorosa. **Debussy:** Chansons de Bilitis. **Cage:** A Flower; The Wonderful Widow of Eighteen Springs. **Bussotti:** "O"—Atti Vocali. **Weill:** Surabaya-Johnny. **McCartney/Lennon:** A Ticket to Ride. **Gershwin:** Summertime. **Berberian: Stripsody.**
Cathy Berberian (sop); Bruno Canino (pno/hpscd). 1970.
WERGO 60054 ADD 44:20

> ★*Awards:* Critics' Choice 1989, *Gramophone* D '89 (John Milsom).

"Wergo's 'MagnifiCathy: the many voices of Cathy Berberian' is an outstanding example of Berberian's flexibility and range....the singer exhibits a voice of rich sonority as well as an impressive command of stylistic depth and dramatic inflection."

Ovation 10:59+ Jl '89. Karen Campbell (300w)

"In this material Berberian does indeed display a wide variety of voices without her performances ever sounding the least bit gimmicky-....it's a good introduction to Cathy Berberian for those listeners for whom a little Cage and Berio go a long way....I guess you could call this review a strong recommendation for a highly individualistic artist."
American Record Guide 52:122 Mr/Ap '89. Michael Mark (250w)

"The recordings, made over a long period of time as they were, are mostly excellent, but inconsistent....Texts are provided only in their original languages. This is an important, surprising, and surprisingly enjoyable recording, a tribute to an incredible musician, and a thought-provoking footnote to a turbulent era."
Fanfare 12:350 Mr/Ap '89. Kyle Gann (400w)

"Wergo's CD reissue...vividly lives up to its billing of documenting Berberian's 'many voices'."
Musical America 109:76-7 My '89. Paul Moor (425w)

Gramophone 67:226 Jl '89. John Milsom (350w)

Berganza, Teresa

8083. Spanish Songs. Granados: Six Songs. **Turina:** El Fantasma; Farruca; Peoma en forma de canciones. **Guridi:** Six Castilian Songs. **Toldra:** Six Songs.
Teresa Berganza (mez); Juan Antonio Alvarez-Parejo (pno). 1986.
CLAVES 8704 DDD 66:33

★*Awards:* International Record Critics Award (IRCA) Winner 1988, *High Fidelity* N '88 and *Musical America* N '88.

"This CD demonstrates that she can still sing well and retains a considerable amount of her charm."
Fanfare 11:246-7 Ja/F '88. James Miller (215w)

"The mezzo-soprano is in fine voice on this CD. Her characteristic covered tone, the beautiful line of her singing, the refinement and delicacy of her delivery are fully in evidence."
American Record Guide 51:115-6 Mr/Ap '88. Philip L. Miller (150w)

"The mezzo-soprano's voice and art seem to grow richer with each passing year, and this recital is an unalloyed pleasure."
Ovation 9:42 Je '88. Joseph Duchac (400w)

Carreras, Jose. Great Operatic Scenes. See No. 8103.

Chaliapin, Feodor

8084. Russian Opera Arias. Mussorgsky: *Boris Godunov:* Prologue; Coronation Scene; Boris's Monologue; Clock Scene; Farewell, prayer and death of Boris. **Glinka:** *A Life for the Tsar:* Susanin's aria. *Ruslan and Ludmilla: Farlaf's rondo.* **Dargomizsky:** *Rusaka:* Song of the Miller; Mad scene and death of the miller. **Rubinstein:** *The Demon:* Demon's aria. **Borodin:** *Prince Igor:* Khan Konchak's aria. **Rimsky-Korsakov:** *Sadko:* Song of the Viking Guest. **Rachmaninov:** *Aleko:* Aleko's aria.
Feodor Chaliapin (bass); various artists. 1908-1931.
EMI 61009 ADD 69:31

★★*Awards:* The Want List 1988, *Fanfare* N/D '88 (Howard Kornblum); Critics' Choice 1988, *Gramophone* D '88 (John Steane).

"It remains a source of amazement that a singer could characterize so powerfully, and that a character actor could sing so well."
Opera News 54:43 O '89. John W. Freeman (110w)

"A successful transfer of some classic Chaliapin recordings....A marvellous CD."
Hi-Fi News & Record Review 33:104-5 My '88. Robert Cowan (115w)

Gramophone 66:81 Je '88. John Steane (500w)

Corelli, Franco

8085. Opera Arias and Songs. Mascagni: Cavalleria Rusticana: Brindisi: Addio alla madre. **De Curtis:** Tu ca nun chiagne; Torna a Surriento. **Denza:** I'te vurria vasa. **Califano:** 'O surdato 'nnammurato. **Torelli:** Tu lo sai. **Puccini:** La Boheme: O soave fanciulla. Turandot: Non piangere Liu. Tosca: Recondita armonia. La Fanciulla Del West: Ch'ella mi creda. **Giordano:** Andrea Chenier: Vicino a te. Fedora: Amor ti vieta. **Verdi:** Un Ballo in Maschera: Teco io sto. **Lama:** Silenzio cantatore. **Tagliaferri:** Pusilleco. **Di capua:** O sole mio. **Tosti:** A vucchella.
Franco Corelli (ten); various others. 1962-1968 live.
STANDING ROOM ONLY 812 ADD (m) 76:40

★★*Awards:* The Want List 1991, *Fanfare* N/D '91 (Robert Levine); The Want List 1991, *Fanfare* N/D '91 (C.-P. Gerald Parker).

"The sound varies, because the sources do, but is always adequate....This disc captures Corelli's uniquely vibrant voice in its ringing prime, reminding us that we haven't heard its like since he retired....Yes, he played to the galleries, but that beats the bland all-purpose style of those who followed him."
Fanfare 14:335-36 My/Je '91. Henry Fogel (250w)

Crespin, Regine

8086. Vocal Recital. Berlioz: Les Nuits d'Ete. **Ravel:** Sheherazade. **Debussy:** Trois chansons de Bilitis. **Poulenc:** Banalities: Chansons d'Orkensise; Hotel. La Courte Paille: Le carafon; La reine de coeur. Chansons Villageoises: Les gars qui vont a la fete. Deux poemes de Louis Aragon.
Regine Crespin (sop); John Wustman (pno). Ernest Ansermet (c). Suisse Romande Orchestra. Texts and translations included. 1964, 1968.
LONDON/DECCA 417 813 ADD 68:00

★★*Awards:* Classical Hall of Fame, *Fanfare*, Mr/Ap '92 (Nicholas Deutsch). *American Record Guide* Overview: Berlioz, Mr/Ap '91 (Les Nuits d'Ete).

"This [is] an excellent anthology of Crespin's subtly expressive art. And the recorded sound is still not to be sneezed at."
Hi-Fi News & Record Review 34:97 Je '89. John Crabbe (140w)

"The hushed, luminous tone in 'Le spectre de la rose,' the naked emotional pain of 'Absence' (and the beautiful floated top notes), the deadened sound on 'Sur les lagunes,' the superb shaping of the line in 'Au cimetiere'—all these and more have made Crespin's recording of *Les Nuits d'ete* a true classic....The work of Ansermet and the orchestra has its rhythmic and ensemble shortcomings; none of it matters. This is a necessary recording. *Sheherazade* finds the conductor on more comfortable ground, and Crespin's performance is ravishing. The Debussy and Poulenc songs, well supported by pianist John Wustman, are an added attraction. Few artists have ever uttered the French language as beautifully as Crespin. Now for the bad news. On my equipment, at least, I find that the digitalizing of the Berlioz and Ravel has done appreciable damage to the characteristic sound of Crespin's voice, rendering it thinner and less recognizable in its individuality....I don't know what to recommend. If you still have a turntable, you might try to get hold of a copy of London CS 25821; if you have one already, I'd suggest holding on to it, at least until you've heard the CD transfer and decided for yourself. Sorry; this has left me upset."
Fanfare 15:472-3 Mr/Ap '92. Nicholas Deutsch (long)

Gramophone 66:835-36 N '88. Alan Blyth (265w)

De La Tomasa, Jose Maria La Burra and Maria Solea

8087. Cante Gitano—Gypsy Flamenco from Andalucia.
Jose De LaTomasa (voc); Maria LaBurra (voc); Maria Solea (voc); Paco Del Gastor (gtr); Juan Del Gastor (gtr).
NIMBUS 5168 DDD 75:12

★*Awards:* Top Choices—1989, *American Record Guide* Ja/F '90 (William Ellis).

"Against the singers' most fervent phrases, shouts of 'how beautiful' can be heard from the small cafe audience. The effect is like eavesdropping on a private conversation. The guitar playing is unadorned, without Pena's flash...The singing, especially by Jose de la Tomasa in 'Siguirilla' is direct and dusky, with melismas pushed to their breaking point....Singing, clapping, stamping, strumming—these Andalusian performers offer the rarest glimpse of a unique culture, a view not possible had the record been made in a cold studio. This recording will outlast most other flamenco records. Kudos to Nimbus for having the integrity to release it unfiltered, raw, and immediate."
American Record Guide 52:125 S/O '89. William Ellis (280w)

"An issue or two ago, I praised a recording of flamenco music led by Pepe Romero...it can be argued that this new Nimbus release contains even more impassioned performances...the difficult chore of setting down and translating lyrics has also been carried out for our better understanding of this culture of hot nights and violent love under the olive trees."
Fanfare 13:448 S/O '89. John Ditsky (225w)

Domingo, Placido

8088. Romanzas de Zarzuelas. J. Guerrero: *Los Gavilanes:* Mi aldea; Flor roja. *La Rosa del Azafran:* Cancion del Sembrador. *El Huesped del Sevillano:* Raquel. **Alonso:** *Coplas de Ronda:* Serenata. *La Parranda:* Canto a Murcia. **Sorozabal:** *La del Manojo de Rosas:* Madrilena bonita. *La Tabernera del Puerto:* No puede ser. **Moreno Torroba:** *Luisa Fernanda:* Los vareadores. *Maravilla:* Amor, vida de mi vida. **Breton:** *La Dolores:* Jota. **Soutullo/Vert:** *La del Soto del Parral:* Ya mis horas felices. **Serrano:** *La Cancion del Olvido:* Junto al puente de la pena. **Chapi:** *La Bruja:* Jota.
Placido Domingo (ten). Manuel Moreno-Buendia (c). National Zarzuela Theater Chorus; Madrid Rondalla Lirica; Madrid Symphony Orchestra.
EMI 49148 DDD 53:00

★*Awards:* Critics' Choice 1989, *Gramophone* D '89 (Andrew Lamb).

"The tenor is in fine, flexible voice throughout-....Idiomatic performances from orchestra and supporting choruses where required."
Opera 40:248 F '89. Noel Goodwin (300w)

"A much classier disc than you might at first think. I love it, and look forward to more (particularly if a female voice is included)."
Music and Musicians International 37:62 Ja '89. Robert Hartford (255w)

Gramophone 66:1212 Ja '89. Andrew M.Lamb (260w)

Gedda, Nicolai

8089. Russian Songs and Romances.
Nicolai Gedda (ten). Nicolai Nekrasov; Vladimir Popov (c). Leningrad Radio and Television Chorus; Russian Academic Orchestra; Russian Folk Orchestra. October 8, 1980 live.
MELODIYA 244 AAD 67:00

★*Awards:* The Want List 1990, *Fanfare* N/D '90 (James Miller).

"He is in almost flawless, luscious, gleaming voice throughout...You would have to return to the days of Fernando de Lucia in his prime to hear a tenor play with his voice and the music as Gedda does here. The effect is overwhelming, totally disarming all criticism....Since the recorded quality leaves little to be desired, the absence of texts and translations is the only minor blot on an enthralling recital which should be in the collection of everyone interested in truly great singing."

American Record Guide 53:151 Mr/Ap '90. Vivian A. Liff (250w)

"Anyone who admires this tenor's voice, thrills to great singing, or has a thing for Russian folk music is exhorted to obtain this disc immediately."

Fanfare 13:362-63 My/Je '90. David Claris (300w)

Hampson, Thomas

8090. Songs from "Des Knaben Wunderhorn." **Mendelssohn:** Jagdlied, Opus 84, No. 3. Altdeutsches Fruhlingslied, Opus 86, No. 6. **Mahler:** Scheiden und Meiden. Ablosung im Sommer. **Schumann:** Marienwurmchen, Opus 79, No. 13. **Brahms:** Der Uberlaufer, Opus 48, No. 2. Liebesklage eines Madchens, Opus 48, No. 3. **Mahler:** Nicht Wiedersehen! **Loewe:** Herr Oluf, Opus 2, No. 2. **Mahler:** Ich ging mit Lust. Um schlimme Kinder artig zu machen. Zu Strassburg auf der Schanz'. **R. Strauss:** Himmelsboten, Opus 32, No. 5. Junggesellenschwur, Opus 49, No. 6. **Zemlinsky:** Das bucklichte Mannlein. **Schoenberg:** Wie Georg von Frundsberg von sich selber sang, Opus 3, No. 1. **Weber:** Abendsegen, Opus 64, No. 5. **Brahms:** Wiegenlied, Opus 49, No. 4.
Thomas Hampson (bar); Geoffrey Parsons (pno).
TELDEC 44923 DDD 54:13

★★★★***Awards:*** Best Recordings of the Month, *Stereo Review* Je '90; International Record Critics Award (IRCA) Winner 1990, *Musical America* N '90. The Want List 1990, *Fanfare* N/D '90 (Marc Mandel); The Highs, 1990, *The New York Times* D 30 '90 (John Rockwell); Critic's Choice: 1990, *American Record Guide* Ja/F '91 (Ralph Lucano).

"Hampson here complements his operatic success with lieder singing of unusual subtlety and maturity....Superlative collaboration by Geoffrey Parsons."

American Record Guide 53:159 S/O '90. George W. Loomis (360w)

"A welcome change from the routine....Hampson sings each of the songs with skill and imagination. Only in Weber's *Abendsegen* does he miss the mark with his characterization-....Parsons provides splendid accompaniments, but his piano sounds woolly in the upper and middle range and is forwardly balanced to the point where it crowds Hampson just a bit."

Musical America 110:77-8 N '90. Theodore W. Libbey, Jr. (510w)

"Nine composers...are represented in the 18 songs on this record. Sweethearts, nightingales, betrayal and death are recurring subjects, but each song bears its composer's stylistic thumbprint. Mr. Hampson, whose voice combines clarity and strength, and Mr. Parsons are magicians in a magical world."

The New York Times Ja 7 '90, p. 30 H. Andrew L. Pincus (130w)

"Both the singer and the pianist are blessed with superb technical facility and uncommon musical intelligence, and their response, not only to the material itself but to each other in performing it, makes for a remarkably fulfilling experience....Teldec's engineers have provided an object lesson in how to record a singer and pianist in recital together."

Stereo Review 55:84 Je '90. Richard Freed (545w)

"I highly recommend this disc, as much for its intelligently chosen program as for the first-rate singing."

Fanfare 13:339-40 Jl/Ag '90. Marc Mandel (345w)

"The whole disc sounds not just vocally excellent but also carefully thought-out and rehearsed so that every song is dramatically convincing....This disc is most highly recommended for the artistry of both men and for the representation of so many composers' settings of these whimsical texts."

HighPerformanceReview 8(2):65-6 Summer '91. Barbara Kierig (540w)

"This would be a difficult recital to bring off in the throat and mind of a lesser baritone, but Thomas Hampson sails through it effortlessly...for the most part, this is very beautiful singing...Geoffrey Parsons understands this music and does more than accompany; he helps tell the stories, relate the sadness, express the jubilation. The sound is natural, with piano and voice well balanced. Highly recommended."

Stereophile 15:275 Ap '92. Robert Levine (long)

Gramophone 68:812 O '90. Hilary Finch (420w)

Hayes, Roland

8091. The Art of Roland Hayes. **Quilter:** It was a lover and his lass. **Purcell-Cochrane:** Passing by. **Handel:** Semele: Where'er you walk. **Downland:** Come again, sweet love doth now invite. **Schumann:** Der Nussbaum. **Arne:** Comus: Preach not me your musty rules. **Berlioz:** L'Absence. **Schubert:** Du bist die Ruh. **Haydn:** She never told her love. **Mendelssohn:** The May-bell and the flowers (with Afrika Hayes Lambe, soprano). **Beethoven: Wonne der Wehmut** ["Trocknet nicht"]. **Villa-Lobos:** Xango. **Afro-American Folksongs:** Weepin' Mary. Michieu banjo. Scandalize my name. Plenty good room. Ezekiel saw de wheel. I'm so glad trouble don't last alway. Lit'l David. Lay dis body down. There's a little wheel. I can tell the world (with Afrika Hayes Lambe). Swing low, sweet chariot (unaccompanied).
Roland Hayes (ten); Reginald Boardman (pno). reissues.
SMITHSONIAN 041 58:00

★★*Awards:* The Want List 1990, *Fanfare* N/D '90 (James Camner); The Want List 1990, *Fanfare* N/D '90 (David Mason Greene).

"Hayes, whose reputation hasn't survived as vividly as those of many of his peers, was a popular and gifted recitalist who had much in common with John McCormack....Although the original 78 recordings are variable in engineering quality, transfers have been accomplished creditably....Singing and song enthusiasts: investigate!"
Stereophile 13:181 Jl '90. Bernard Soll (375w)

"Whatever the voice was in the singer's heyday, what one hears on this record is remarkably consistent—a splendid example of the triumph of art over nature....Diction, phrasing, and musicianship are impeccable, and there is exquisite use, where appropriate, of mezza voce and head-tones....Recommended as a historical document and to listeners who value great artistry over sheer sound."
Fanfare 13:334-35 Jl/Ag '90. David Mason Greene (790w)

"Hayes's voice had a distinctive quality characterized by great sincerity. His art was most refined, his phrasing elegant, his diction crystal clear. He penetrated the secrets of the classical song repertoire as few artists have done. But at the same time he was deeply conscious of his own heritage of spirituals, many of which he sang in his own arrangements....Reginald Boardman, Hayes's longtime accompanist, assists sympathetically."
American Record Guide 53:152 Jl/Ag '90. Philip L. Miller (410w)

Digital Audio's CD Review 7:80 O '90. Sebastian Russ (300w)

Hirst, Linda

8092. Songs Cathy Sang. Berio: Folk Songs: Black is the colour; I wonder as I wander; Lossin yelav; Rossignolet du Bois; A la femminisca; La donna ideale; Ballo; Motettu de Tristura; Malurous qu'o uno fenno; Lo fiolaire; Azerbaijan Love Song; Sequenza III. **Cage:** Aria. **Pousseur:** Phonemes pour Cathy. **Berberian:** Stripsody.
Linda Hirst (mez). Diego Masson (c). London Sinfonietta.
VIRGIN 90704 DDD 58:00

★★*Awards:* Critics' Choice 1988, *Gramophone* D '88 (John Milsom). The Want List 1989, *Fanfare* N/D '89 (Benjamin Pernick).

"The stunning singer here is Linda Hirst...I don't think I have ever heard such intoxicatingly beautiful singing as in the first of Berio's Folk Songs, 'Black is the Color,' and such sensitive inflection in the remaining ten. The London Sinfonietta is also wonderful here-...I've run out of superlatives!"
Stereophile 11:159-162 Ag '88. Barbara Jahn (390w)

"With perception unusual in a vocal performer, she's begun the remarkable job of continuing the revolution in classical singing that Cathy Berberian started, and the fabulous beauty of this recording shows that she fully understands what she's doing....I find myself highly recommending most of the disc for pure listening beauty, and the whole thing as an audacious gesture of homage."
Fanfare 12:313 S/O '88. Kyle Gann (600w)

"Hirst has an admirable range and depth that give her an impressive command of the material on 'Songs Cathy Sang'....Throughout, Hirst is ably complemented by members of the London Sinfonietta."
Ovation 10:59+ Jl '89. Karen Campbell (300w)

"It's difficult to say on the basis of this record how well Linda Hurst would fare in less far-out stuff, but the Berio *Folk Songs* certainly reveal her to be an interesting vocal talent while the other selections demonstrate that she can shout and tickle the funny bone with the best of them. I commend this release to the truly adventurous."
American Record Guide 52:121-22 Ja/F '89. Michael Mark (310w)

"Hirst does all this music very well—until you start making odious but inevitable comparisons with her idol, who remains truly *sui generis*."
Musical America 109:76-7 My '89. Paul Moor (425w)

"Berberian was more 'abstract', the vocal sounds taking on the cast of some imaginary instrument....In terms of virtuosity, it's surely a dead heat."
Hi-Fi News & Record Review 33:75 Je '88. Christopher Breunig (325w)

Gramophone 66:192 Jl '88. John Milsom (420w)

Hvorostovsky, Dmitri

8093. Opera Recital. Tchaikovsky: *Eugene Onegin:* You have written to me...Had I wished to confine my life; Can it really be that same Tatyana?...No, there can be no doubt. *The Queen of Spades*: You are so downcast, my dear. *The Enchantress:* Business, official duties...But I cannot forget. *Iolantha:* Who can compare with my Mathilde? *Mazeppa:* O Maria! **Verdi:** *La Traviata:* Di Provenza il mar. *Macbeth:* Perfidi! All'anglo contra me v'unite...Pieta, rispetto, amore. *Luisa Miller:* Sacra la scelta. *Il Trovatore:* Tutto e deserto...Il balen. *Don Carlo:* Son io, mio Carlo...Per me giunto...O Carlo, ascolta.
Dmitri Hvorostovsky (bar). Valery Gergiev (c). Rotterdam Philharmonic Orchestra.
PHILIPS 426 740 DDD 57:00

★★*Awards:* The Highs, 1990, *The New York Times* D 30 '90 (John Rockwell); Critic's Choice: 1990, *American Record Guide* Ja/F '91 (Ralph Lucano).

"The voice itself, first of all, is phenomenal in its beauty and its amplitude. And, whether through instinct or cultivated taste, Hvorostovsky shows exceptional flexibility and sensitivity to his texts....From first track to last, in Tchaikovsky and Verdi alike, what confronts us is not just an exceptional voice but a noble artist....The Rotterdam Philharmonic is conducted very sympathetically by the Kirov Theater's superb Valery Gergiev, and the engineers have put voice and orchestra in the most effective perspective. There are also full texts and translations."

Stereo Review 55:109 O '90. Richard Freed (400w)

"While his arias show a refined sense of musical and linguistic style, with very few minor slips (on the order of 'quando' instead of 'quanto'), he is equally developed as a song interpreter, specifically in the Russian repertory-....Few baritones of any generation or nationality have shown such sensitivity of interpretation, such willingness and ability to sing a *diminuendo* or a *piano*: one has to go back to De Luca for a comparison."

Opera News 55:46 S '90. John W. Freeman (150w)

"The voice is big, handsome, and flexible, and Hvorostovsky is so completely in character in every one of the arias that one finds oneself not only eager to hear and see him in a stage production but eager to hear the little-known Tchaikovsky operas as well....first-rate sonics."

Stereo Review Presents: Compact Disc Buyers' Guide 1991 p.40 Richard Freed (100w)

"This recital program is sure-fire but demanding, and the artist meets his challenges impressively....In the Russian arias, the singing tone is not always firmly centered, allowing what is often characterized as a throbbing Slavic vibrato to intrude on tonal splendor-....nonetheless, the singing is characterful, the tone intelligently colored, and the dramatic presence undeniable."

Musical America 111:83-4 Ja '91. George Jellinek (330w)

"Hvorostovsky sings very beautifully. This is a full and rich baritone voice, glamourous in sheen, its chief glory being its middle register, which the singer proudly unfolds in one long cantilena after another...there is a lack of variety in this programme, right down to basics like dynamic levels and verbal point, that leaves the impression that the singer lacks personality."

Opera 41:1139 S '90. Richard Fairman (300w)

"When I heard Hvorostovsky in Tully Hall, I was slightly disappointed by the size of the voice and by the lack of fullness on top, yet I was certain he would sound wonderful on records....The Italian arias show up a few flaws-....Hvorostovsky's shortcomings grow less rather than more bothersome with each hearing, however: his singing is just too seductive."

American Record Guide 53:174-75 N/D '90. Ralph V. Lucano (420w)

"If the purpose of this disc is to call attention to an important new baritone voice on the international operatic scene, it succeeds. If, however, the purpose is to give us fully developed singing, it falls short....There is no question that the potential is here for a major international career....Valery Gergiev...brings far greater variety of color and intensity to the Verdi than does his singer. The sweep of the broad melody of the *Macbeth* aria is gorgeously molded."

Fanfare 14:419-20 N/D '90. Henry Fogel (525w)

"Although the paucity of charismatic baritones—especially those qualified to perform the Italian opera repertoire memorably—hasn't been chronicled as often as the lack of potential Pavarottis and Domingos, the need is just as great. Artistically speaking, it may be even greater. The 27-year-old Siberian singer, possessed of an undeniably handsome, luscious instrument, could help satisfy that need...Given additional time to reflect on the musical and theatrical demands of the characters he portrays—in conjunction, of course, with good coaching—he should be able to bring to bear an even more striking and individualized range of colors and nuances in both singing and interpretation....While the orchestra plays admirably...the singer is sometimes swamped. The fault appears to lie at the feet of the recording team, not the musicians."

Stereophile 14:253+ Je '91. Bernard Soll (430w)

"A beautiful and in many ways well-cultivated lyric baritone....the Tchaikovsky selections show the singer's promise best....The Verdi selections begin inauspiciously with Germont's 'Di Provenza il mar'; the lines are chopped up with careless 'h' sounds; the top notes are rough and uneasy, and there isn't much feeling for style or character. One can still tell it's a terrific voice, but here, off his home ground, he sounds like a singer with a long way yet to go."

The New York Times Jl 29 '90, p. 23-4 H. Will Crutchfield (1205w)

Gramophone 68:279 Jl '90. John Warrack (325w)

Jurinac, Sena

8094. Opera and Song Recital. Mozart: *Cosi fan Tutte:* Ah guarda, sorella; Come scoglio; Ei parte!..Per pieta. *Idomeneo:* Quando avran fine omai...Padre, germani, addio!; Si il padre perdei; Zeffiretti lusinghieri. **Smetana:** *The Bartered Bride:* O what sorrow...The dream of love. *The Kiss:* Cradle Song. **Tchaikovsky:** *Joan of Arc:* Farewell, forests. *Queen of Spades:* It will soon be midnight. **R. Strauss:** Four Last Songs.

Sena Jurinac (sop); Blanche Thebom (mez); various orchestras and conductors. 1950-51 reissue.
EMI 63199 ADD (m) 78:00

★★★★*Awards:* The Want List 1990, *Fanfare* N/D '90 (David Mason Greene); The Want List 1990, *Fanfare* N/D '90 (Ralph V. Lucano); Critics' Choice 1990, *Gramophone* D '90 (Alan Blyth). Best of the Month, *Hi-Fi News & Record Review*, D '89.

"She was at her peak in the early 1950s, whence these recordings derive....it is the Strauss which is the revelation, issued for the first time commercially...Applause greets each song, but I am prepared to live with this for the lyrical beauty of Jurinac's singing, her clear pointing of the words entirely devoid of Schwarzkopfian archness." *P95/100 S-historic*
Hi-Fi News & Record Review 34:129+ D '89. Hugh Canning (330w)

"When these recordings were made in 1950/51, Jurinac had the most beautiful soprano voice in the world....She had a warm, sensuous, feminine sound, distinctively smoky and absolutely even throughout her range. Her legato was faultless."
American Record Guide 53:149 My/Je '90. Ralph V. Lucano (300w)

"For me the best is left for the last. The Strauss songs...Jurinac is the voice and the singer that the old composer must have dreamed of and Busch conducts with passion and with complete understanding of the idiom-....By the end of the second hearing I was reduced to jelly. Though my more perfectly informed acquaintances generally snicker at my eccentric and inexplicable taste, I give this record my strongest possible recommendation."
Fanfare 13:352-53 My/Je '90. David Mason Greene (600w)

Gramophone 67:1386-87 Ja '90. Alan Blyth (455w)

Lehmann, Lotte

8095. Lotte Lehmann. Cimara: Canto di primavera. **Sadero:** Fa la nana, Bambin. **Gounod:** Vierge d'Athenes. **Paladilhe:** Psyche. **Duparc:** La Vie anterieure. **Hahn:** Infidelite.; L'Enamouree; D'une Prison. **Grechaninov:** My Native Land. **Worth:** Midsummer. **Sjoberg:** Visions. **Balogh:** Do Not Chide Me. **Trad.:** Drink to me only with thine eyes; Schiafe, mein susses kind. **Wolf:** Nun lass uns Frieden schliessen; Und willst du deinen Liebsten sterben sehen? Der Knabe und das immlein. **R. Strauss:** Die Zeitlose, Opus 10, No. 7. Wozu noch, Madchen, Opus 19, No. 1. Du meines Herzes Kronelein, Opus 21, No. 2. Brahms: Das Madchen spricht, Opus 107, No. 3; Mein Madel hat einen Rosenmund. **Schumann:** Waldesgesprach, Opus 39, No. 3. Du bist wie eine Blume, Opus 25, No. 24; Fruhlingsnacht, Opus 39, No. 12. **Schubert:** Im Abendrot, D.799; Der Jungling an der Quelle, D.300; An die Nachtigall, D.497; Nacht und Traume, D.827; An die Musik, D.547.

Lotte Lehmann (sop); Erno Balogh (pno); Paul Ulanowsky (pno). reissues.
RCA 7809 ADD (m) 73:43

✔HC ★*Awards:* Critics' Choice 1990, *Gramophone* D '90 (Alan Blyth).

"These recordings have been hard to come by for years, and four are first releases; so Lehmann's fans will need no coaxing. For the uninitiated, however, I'd sooner suggest, as starting points, the Centennial Album produced by the Lehmann Archives in Santa Barbara (reviewed in *Fanfare* 12:5) and EMI's two mid-priced CDs (the aria collection and *Die Walküre*, act I)."
Fanfare 13:430-31 N/D '89. Ralph V. Lucano (245w)

"Space precludes further rhapsodising over Lehmann's performances here so I will simply urge you to acquire this totally indispensable CD."
American Record Guide 53:130 Ja/F '90. Vivian A. Liff (b.n.)

"Lotte Lehmann's earlier recordings find the voice fresher, the breath longer and steadier than the later ones, but again it is for interpretation that one treasures these selections. Not the usual sort of lieder program, RCA's CD includes five first-time releases, all but one of them outside the German repertory."
Opera News 54:31 F 3 '90. John W. Freeman (100w)

Gramophone 67:1882 Ap '90. Alan Blyth (630w)

Musical America 109:69 N '89. Terry Teachout (b.n.)

Multiple or Unidentified Artists

8096. Great Singers, 1909-38. *MAFALA FAVERO* (ten); *TITO SCHIPA* (ten): **Mascagni:** *L'Amico Fritz:* Suzel, buon di. *AMELITA GALLI-CURCI* (sop): **Bellini:** *I Puritani:* Son vergin vezzosa. *CLAUDIA MUZIO* (sop): **Refice:** Ombre di nube. *ROSA PONSELLE* (sop): **Bellini:** *Norma:* Sedizione voci-...Casta diva. *LUISA TETRAZZINI* (sop): **Bellini:** *La Sonnambula:* Ah! no giunge. *EVA TURNER* (sop): **Puccini:** *Turandot:* In questa reggia. *ERNESTINE SCHUMANN-HEINK* (mez): **Donizetti:** *Lucrezia Borgia:* Brindisi. *CONCHITA SUPERVIA* (mez): **Bizet:** *Carmen:* Habanera. *MARIAN ANDERSON* (contr): **Saint-Saens:** *Samson et Dalila:* Mon coueur s'ouvre a ta voix. *ENRICO CARUSO* (ten): **Leoncavallo:** *Pagliacci:* No! Pagliaccio non son. *BENJAMIN GIGLIO* (ten): **Puccini:** *La Boheme:* Che gelida manina. *GIACOMO LAURI-VOLPI* (ten): **Bellini:** *I Puritani:* A te, o cara. *JOHN McCORMACK* (ten): **Mozart:** *Don Giovanni:* Il mio tesora. *RICHARD TAUBER* (ten): **Mozart:** *Die Zauberflote:* Dies Bildnis ist bezaubernd schon. *RICCARDO STRACCIARI* (bar): **Rossini:** *Il Barbiere di Siviglia:* Largo al factotum. *LAWRENCE TIBBETT* (bar): **Verdi:** *Un Ballo in Maschera:* Eri tu.

various conductors and orchestras. 1909-1938. NIMBUS 7801 ADD (m) 75:00

★*Awards:* Critics' Choice 1989, *Gramophone* D '89 (John Steane). The Want List 1990, *Fanfare* N/D '90 (Howard Kornblum).

"Richness, roundness, fullness of tone, resonance—now and again perhaps a shade too much—is what characterizes the recorded sound. The sound is pleasantly low level for CD, and the surface noise is greatly reduced; what remains is remarkably consistent for the duration of a particular piece."
American Record Guide 53:128-30 Ja/F '90. George W. Loomis (300w)

"Irresistible to the novice collector for their repertory and intriguing to the experienced devotee for their sound."
Opera News 54:30-1 F 3 '90. John W. Freeman (205w)

"In view of Nimbus' decision to effect as natural a transfer as possible, some very simple but radical steps were taken....The marriage of the old and the new audio is seamlessly done with exceptional taste. The results are musical, listenable, real."
Audio 74:100+ Ap '90. Christopher Greenleaf (120w)

"The ambient aspect has been dealt with here by placing the 'Expert' in an acoustically lively room as if it were itself the singer, and recording its output via an Ambisonic microphone....The 'natural' filtering combines with a surrounding acoustic to provide a fine sense of performing presence, and I only wish that the resulting vocal images had been properly centered....you will find wonders of vocal art." *P100 S-historic*
Hi-Fi News & Record Review 34:135 D '89. John Crabbe (75w)

"Voice lovers will have little problem in finding originals or finer transfers in virtually every case."
American Record Guide 53:128 Ja/F '90. Vivian A. Liff (100w)

Music and Musicians International 38:53 D '89. Robert Hartford (210w)

The New York Times D 31 '89, p. 27 H. Harold C. Schonberg (120w)

Gramophone 67:774 O '89. John Steane (220w)

HighPerformanceReview 7:66 Fall '90. Bert Wechsler (b.n.)

Newberry Consort

8097. Ay Amor: Spanish 17th Century Songs and Theatre Music. Hidalgo: Noble en Tinacria naciste; A todos miro; Credito es de mi decoro; En los floridos paramos; Ay, amor, ay ausencia; Ay, que si, ay, que no; De los cenos del diciembre; Como ha de saber Belilla; De las luces que en el mar; La noche tenebrosa; Trompicabals amor. **Falconiero:** Rinen y pelean entre Berzebillo con Stanasello y Caruf, y Pantul; Bayle de los dichos diabolos; Fantasia detta la Portia; L'Eroica a tre y Ciaccona. **Selma Y Salaverde:** Canzon 3; Canzon 1; Canzon 8. Mary Springfels (c). Newberry Consort. 1989. HARMONIA MUNDI 907022 DDD 68:35

★★*Awards:* The Want List 1991, *Fanfare* N/D '91 (Tom Moore). Disc of the Month, *Digital Audio's CD Review*, Je '91.

"The performances are all extremely virtuosic and stylish, as befits the music, though special mention should go to mezzo-soprano Judith Malafronte, who gives a 'Spanish' colour to her finely controlled and expressive voice in the manner of, but without slavishly imitating, the famous Montserrat Figueras."
Continuo 15:27-9 Je '91. Scott Paterson (110w)

"This disc is my first exposure to the singing of Judith Malafronte, and very fine it is too. She brings a warmth of tone, the plangent sound associated with Iberian singing since the Renaissance, and a wonderful clarity of diction. Praise all round is due to her instrumental colleagues—particularly beautiful is the accompaniment from Mary Springfels and David Douglass on two bass viols for 'La noche tenebrosa.' Warmly recommended."
Fanfare 14:355 Jl/Ag '91. Tom Moore (300w)

"The Newberry Consort, directed by Mary Springfels, has produced a collection of first-rate quality, and one hates to object to the slightly misleading packaging, but why not an accurate title for this disc? The eleven theatrical songs by Hidalgo are of prime interest."
American Record Guide 54:171 S/O '91. Paul Laird (med)

Digital Audio's CD Review 7:38 Je '91. Sebastian Russ (265w)

Norman, Jessye. Spirituals in Concert. See No. 8081.

Schipa, Tito

8098. Opera Arias. Gluck: *Orfeo ed Euridice:* Che faro senza Euridice? **A. Scarlatti:** *Sento nel cor. La donna ancora e fedele:* Son tutta duolo. *Pirro e Demetrio:* Rugiadose, odorose. **Bellini:** *La sonnambula:* Prendi l'anel ti dono. *L'elisir d'amore:* Una furtiva lagrima. *Lucia di Lammermoor:* Tu che a Dio spiegasti l'ali. *Don Pasquale:* Tornami a dir. **Verdi:** *Rigoletto:* Ella mi fu rapita...Parmi, veder le lagrime. *Falstaff:* Dal labbro il canto. **Ponchielli:** *La Gioconda:* Cielo e mar. **Massenet:** *Manon:* Io son sol-...Ah dispar, vision! *Werther:* Allor, sta proprio qua... O natura di grazia piena; Tradurre!... Ah! non mi ridestar. **Mascagni:** *Cavalleria rusticana:* O lola ch'ai di latti la cammisa (Siciliana). *L'amico Fritz:* Suzel, buon di! **Puccini:** *La Boheme:* Che gelida manina. *Tosca:* Recondita armonia; E lucevan le stelle.

Tito Schipa (ten); Toti Dal Monte (sop); Mafalda Favero (sop); various others. reissues.
EMI 63200 ADD (m) 74:00

★*Awards:* The Want List 1990, *Fanfare* N/D '90 (David Mason Greene).

"The sound is remarkably good, even in the 1913 recordings...very nice."
American Record Guide 53:154-55 Mr/Ap '90. Donald R. Vroon (b.n.)

"I am perfectly well aware of all the reservations the cognoscenti have about Schipa....But, all that said, how the man could sing! The control, the phrasing, the articulation, the interpretation were simply exquisite, and there has never been anything quite like it since....This record is essential to any serious vocal collection."
Fanfare 13:359-60 My/Je '90. David Mason Greene (540w)

Opera News 54:39 F 17 '90. John W. Freeman (b.n.)

Gramophone 67:1885 Ap '90. John Steane (560w)

Schreier, Peter

8099. Lieder and Song Recital. Brahms: Deutsche Volkslieder: No. 1, Sagt mire, o schonste Schaf'rin; No. 4, Guten Abend, mein tausiger Schatz; No. 15, Schwesterlein, Schwesterlein; No. 34, Wie komm'ich denn zur Tur herein? Wiegenlied, Opus 49, No. 4. **Prokofiev:** Three Children's Songs, Opus 68; The Ugly Duckling, Opus 18. **Schumann:** Dichterliebe, Opus 48; Der Nussbaum, Opus 25, No. 3.
Peter Schreier (ten); Wolfgang Sawallisch (pno). Munich. February 6, 1984 live.
PHILIPS 426 237 DDD 72:00

★*Awards:* Critics' Choice 1990, *Gramophone* D '90 (Hilary Finch).

"This live performance...has a fine natural balance and, while audience noise is sporadically intrusive, the gain in emotional spontaneity is more than adequate compensation."
High Fidelity 1:107 My '90. Andrew Stuart (b.n.)

"I've confessed, in the past, to having reservations about Schreier's singing....I am, however, enthusiastic about his artistry....Sawallisch is a responsive, understanding partner, and I can't complain about the recorded sound. Texts and translations are provided."
Fanfare 14:461 S/O '90. Ralph V. Lucano (260w)

The New York Times Ja 13 '91, p. 29+ H. Will Crutchfield (355w)

Gramophone 67:1861 Ap '90. Alan Blyth (630w)

Schwarzkopf, Elisabeth

8100. Elisabeth Schwarzkopf Sings Operetta. Works by **Heuberger, Zeller, Lehar, J. Strauss, Millocker, Suppe, Sieczynsky.**
Elisabeth Schwarzkopf (sop). Otto Ackermann (c). Philharmonia Chorus; Philharmonia Orchestra.
EMI 47284 43:43

★*Awards: Fanfare* Want List 1986 (James Miller).

"Yes, Schwarzkopf was occasionally given to heavy-handed coyness...but even her little mannerisms work here and she's in nearly prime voice...enthusiastically recommended."
Fanfare 9:250 Ja/F '86. James Miller (200w)

This reissue "can be highly recommended."
High Fidelity 36:56 Mr '86. Robert E. Benson (100w)

Gramophone 63:971 Ja '86. Andrew Lamb (140w)

8101. The Elisabeth Schwarzkopf Edition. (Elisabeth Schwarzkopf with various artists) **Disc 1: Wolf:** Elfenlied; Die Sprode; Die Bekehrte; Mignon I/II/III; Philine; Kennst du das Land; Ganymed; Morgenthau; Das Voglein; Die Spinnerin; Wiegenlied im Sommer; Wiegenlied im Winter; Mausfallen-Spruchlein; Wie glanzt der helle Mond; Wenn du zu den Blumen gehst; Die Zigeunerin; Im Fruhling; Auf einer Wanderung; Begegnung; Denk es, O Seele; Sonne der Schlummerlosen; An eine Aeolsharfe. **Disc 2: Schubert:** Die Vogel; Liebhaber in allen Gestalten; Heidenroslein; Die Forelle; Der Einsame; Der Jungling an der Quelle; An mein Klavier; Erlkonig; Suleika I/II; Hanflings Liebeswerbung; Meeres Stille; Gretchen an Spinnrade. **Schumann:** Der Nussbaum; Auftrage; Zwei venetianische Lieder; Die Kartenlegerin; Wie mit innigstem Behagen. **R. Strauss:** Hat gesagt, bleibt's nicht dabi; Schlechtes Wetter; Wiegenliedchen; Meinem Kinde; Drei Ophelia-Lieder; Die Nacht. **Disc 3:** Opera Arias. **Mozart:** *Le Nozze di Figaro:* Porgi amor. *Cosi Fan Tutte:* Per pieta. *Don Giovanni:* In quali eccessi...Mi tradi. **Verdi:** *Requiem:* Libera me. **Humperdinck:** *Hansel und Gretel:* Wo bin ich? **Lehar:** *Die Lustige Witwe:* Viljalied. **J. Strauss II:** *Die Fledermaus:* Csardas. **Puccini:** *Turandot:* Signore, ascolta. **R. Strauss:** *Ariadne auf Naxos:* Es gibt ein Reich. *Der Rosenkavalier:* Quinquin, er soll jetzt geh'n. *Capriccio:* Morgen mittag um elf. **Disc 4:** Encores. **Bach:** Bist du bei mir. **Gluck:** Einem Bach der fliesst. **Beethoven:** Wonne der Wehmut. **Loewe:** Kleiner Haushalt. **Wagner:** Traume. **Brahms:** Standchen; Da unten im Tale; Och Mod'r, ich well ein Ding han! In Stiller Nacht. **Mahler:** Um schlimme Kinder artig zu machen; Ich achmet' einen linden Duft; Des Antonius con Padua Fischpredigt. **Tchaikovsky:** Pimpinella. **Wolf-Ferrari:** Seven Italian Songs. **Martini:** Plaisir d'amour. **Hahn:** Si mes vers avaient des ailes. **Debussy:** Mandoline. **Quilter:** Drink to Me Only with Thine Eyes. **Arne:** When Daisies Pied; Where the Bee Sucks. **Gund (arr.):** Swiss Folk Songs. **Trad:** Maria auf dem Berge. **Weatherly (arr.):** Danny Boy. **J. Strauss II:**

Fruhlingsstimmen. **Disc 5:** Unpublished Recordings. **Bach:** Mein Herze Schwimmt im Blut, BWV.199. *Mass in B Minor:* Christe eleison; Laudamus te; Et in unum dominum. **Mozart:** Nehmt meinem Dank, K.383. **Gieseking:** Kinderlieder. **R. Strauss:** Vier letzte Lieder.
Elisabeth Schwarzkopf (sop); Gerald Moore (pno); Geoffrey Parsons (pno); various artists and orchestras. Also available separately (EMI 63653-57). reissues.
EMI 63790 ADD 79:08; 77:57; 79:15; 75:47; 78:39
5 discs

★★*Awards:* The Want List 1991, *Fanfare* N/D '91 (Charles Timbrell). Critic's Choice, 1991, *American Record Guide*, Ja/F '92 (Kurt Moses).

"It's an altogether astonishing collection: it not only gives evidence of this singer's versatility and staying power, but with few exceptions the performances are on a level that most singers only approach and few even attain occasionally, leading a reviewer to exhaust his store of superlatives much too quickly....In all, a historic release that should appeal to anyone who loves the art of singing."
American Record Guide 54:165-7 My/Je '91. Kurt Moses (215w)

"EMI has let us (and Schwarzkopf) down by failing to supply texts....The Schwarzkopf Edition is nonetheless an extravagant tribute, despite its shortcomings. A lifetime's work is documented here, and it cannot be appreciated in a few days' listening. Buy these discs, savor the best of what they offer."
Fanfare 14:334-6 Jl/Ag '91. Ralph V. Lucano (1450w)

Schwarzkopf, Elisabeth and Irmgard Seefried

8102. Soprano Duets. Monteverdi: Io son pur vezzosette pastorella; Ardo e scoprir; Baci soave e cari; Dialogo di ninfa e pastore (Bel pastor). **Carissimi:** Detesta la captiva sorte in amere; Lungi omai; Il mio core; A pie d'un verde alloro. **Dvorak:** 13 Moravian Duets, B60-62. **Humperdinck:** *Hansel und Gretel:* Suse, liebe Suse. **R. Strauss:** *Der Rosenkavalier:* Presentation of the Silver Rose.
Elisabeth Schwarzkopf (sop); Irmgard Seefried (sop); Gerald Moore (pno). Josef Krips; Herbert Von Karajan (c). Philharmonia Orchestra; Vienna Philharmonic Orchestra.
EMI 69793 ADD (m) 76:00

★*Awards:* Critics' Choice 1989, *Gramophone* D '89 (John Steane).

"The remastered sound is excellent. Once again, however, EMI is maltreating a 'Great Recording of the Century' by stinting on the packaging....I love this recording and warmly recommend it, but I can't countenance EMI's niggardliness, even with a mid-price issue."
Fanfare 12:296 Jl/Ag '89. Ralph V. Lucano (520w)

Gramophone 66:1487-88 Mr '89. John Steane (385w)

Scotto, Renata and Jose Carreras

8103. Great Operatic Scenes. Verdi: *La Traviata:* Brindisi, Un di felice, Che fai?...Amami lfredo, Invitato a qui seguirmi...Ogni suo aver, Signora...Parigi o cara; Prendi, quest'e l'immagine; *Lombardi:* Giselda! O ciel traveggo...O belle a questa misera. **Puccini:** *Madama Butterfly:* Dovunque al mondo-...Amore o grillo; Ancora un passo; Love duet.
Jose Carreras (ten); Renata Scotto (sop); various others. reissues.
LEGATO 150 AAD (m) 71:00

★*Awards:* The Want List 1990, *Fanfare* N/D '90 (C.P. Gerald Parker).

"This disc captures both singers in their primes-....For fans of both singers this disc can be very safely recommended."
Fanfare 14:421 N/D '90. Henry Fogel (175w)

"Even with Legato's often muddy, hissy sound, these two charismatic artists come to vivid life: beautiful singing, vocal acting with lots of stage savvy. When I get these qualities in my Verdi and Puccini, I'm a happy man-....Check this one out to catch two much-maligned artists at their best."
American Record Guide 53:151 S/O '90. Michael Mark (195w)

Seefried, Irmgard. Soprano Duets. See No. 8102.

Souzay, Gerard

8104. French Airs and Songs by Faure, Chausson.
Gerard Souzay (bar); Jacqueline Bonneau (pno). 1950-53 reissue.
LONDON/DECCA 425 975 ADD 67:29

★★*Awards:* The Gramophone Awards, Nominations, Historical—vocal, *Gramophone*, N '91. Best Historical Recording Vocal 1991, *Gramophone*, D '91.

"The command of nuance and dynamic control are masterly, with superbly articulated words invariably floated on an incomparable legato line of instrumental perfection....the piano and voice are ideally balanced in more-than-acceptable mono sound...Essential library material."
American Record Guide 54:186 S/O '91. Vivian A. Liff (med)

P95/100 S85/65
Hi-Fi News & Record Review 36:99 F '91. Christopher Breunig (120w)

Musical America 111:94 My '91. Terry Teachout (b.n.)

Gramophone 69:120 Jl '91. Alan Sanders (65w)

Studer, Cheryl

8105. Coloratura Arias. Bellini: *La Sonnambula:* Ah, non credea mirarti...Ah! non giunge. *Norma:* Casta diva. **Verdi:** *La Traviata:* E strano...Ah, fors e lui...Sempre libera. *Il Trovatore:* Timor di me?-

...D'amor sull'ali rosee. **Donizetti:** *Lucia Di Lammermoor:* Regnava nel silenzio...Quando rapito in estasi. *Lucrezia Borgia:* Tranquillo ei posa...Com'e bello! **Rossini:** *Il Barbiere Di Siviglia:* Una voce poco fa. *Semiramide:* Bel raggio lusinghier.
Cheryl Studer (sop). Gabriele Ferro (c). Munich Radio Orchestra.
EMI 49961 DDD 56:00

★★*Awards:* Pick of the Month, North American Perspective (Christopher Pollard), *Gramophone* S '90. Critics' Choice 1990, *Gramophone* D '90 (John Steane).

"Studer's voice has tremendous power with a wonderfully clear tone, but with an obvious brain at work behind the voice."
High Fidelity 1:119 O '90. Clive Manning (140w)

"Her vocalism encompasses with easy mobility and accuracy the hazards and hurdles of these eight coloratura arias, and she sings with a real feeling for character and dramatic moment-....every selection has something to recommend it,...and all are crisply accompanied by the Munich Radio Orchestra under Gabriele Ferro."
Stereo Review 56:104 Ja '91. Robert Ackart (175w)

"This is no dilettante tackling bravura arias for a lark. Studer is already phenomenally accomplished; and she can only improve with time, as her singing acquires more polish and personality and her verbal skills ripen. Eventually she'll have to face comparisons with Callas. That's the direction in which Studer is traveling, and she's packing a more dependable voice. We'll have to wait and see where she ends up. Angel's sound lends the timbre a touch of stridency I don't hear in the opera house, and it also takes away some of the lusciousness—which means that Studer may be even better than the recording suggests."
American Record Guide 54:151-2 Ja/F '91. Ralph V. Lucano (440w)

"Her vocal coloring is a touch monochromatic, but the singing is often quite beautiful, although she does not have a consistent trill. The Juliette aria and the rare Bizet are particularly haunting. A shocker, however, is the long *Vestale* scene, in which her vocal production is downright bad, effortful, and afflicted with a steady beat not apparent elsewhere. Retakes would have been in order, since the inclusion almost spoils what otherwise would have been a distinguished effort."
Musical America 111:88 My '91. Walter Price (160w)

"I'm not entirely convinced that Studer is a natural coloratura for starters, as say, Sutherland and Sills were. She sounds like a big lyric who can *sing* coloratura because of a superb technique. The difference is subtle but valid—all the little notes are there, but they're studied, I feel. This doesn't detract; it's merely an observation. In general, her singing is fabulous, and, heavens, she has a real trill....Complete texts and translations, and excellent sound. This could be historic—flaws and all."
Fanfare 14:359-60 Ja/F '91. Robert Levine (355w)
Gramophone 68:615 S '90. John Steane (455w)

Sutherland, Joan

8106. The Art of the Prima Donna. Arne: Artaxerxes (excerpts). **Handel:** Samson (excerpts). **Bellini:** Norma (excerpts); Puritani (excerpts); Sonnambula (excerpts). **Rossini:** Semiramide (excerpts). **Gounod:** Faust (excerpts); Romeo et Juliette (excerpts). **Verdi:** Otello (excerpts); Traviata (excerpts); Rigoletto (excerpts). **Mozart:** Entfuhrung (excerpts). **Thomas:** Hamlet (excerpts). **Delibes:** Lakme (excerpts). **Meyerbeer:** Huguenots (excerpts)).
Joan Sutherland (sop). Francesco Molinari-Pradelli (c). Rome Opera Chorus; Rome Opera Orchestra.
LONDON/DECCA 414 450 108:32 2 discs

★*Awards:* *Gramophone* Critics' Choice 1986 (Edward Greenfield).

"The standard of singing is amazingly high throughout this extremely testing recital....Altogether this is a series of gems and a superb demonstration of the art of *bel canto* by one of the truly great sopranos of this century."
Hi-Fi News & Record Review 31:121 Je '86. John Freestone (140w)

Sylvan, Sanford

8107. Beloved That Pilgrimage. Chanler: Eight Epitaphs. **Barber:** Hermit Songs. **Copland:** Twelve Poems of Emily Dickinson.
Sanford Sylvan (bar); David Breitman (pno).
ELEKTRA 79259 54:00

★★*Awards:* The Want List 1991, *Fanfare* N/D '91 (Marc Mandel). Critic's Choice: 1991, *American Record Guide*, Ja/F '92 (David Greene).

Sanford Sylvan's "voice itself is smooth, sweet, with enough body to fill out the bigger lines but no inclination to assert itself overtly-....David Breitman's clear delineation of the accompaniments is an asset."
The New York Times Jl 21 '91, p. 21 H. Will Crutchfield (long)

"The *Eight Epitaphs* of Theodore Chanler (1902-1961) are likely to be the most generally appealing songs on the disc...The Copland cycle is a highly original work that will grow on the listener with repeated hearings...Sylvan appears to be an intelligent and cultivated singer with a light voice that he uses with skill and imagination. The piano contribution of David Breitman is valuable, and the recording—aside from giving undue presence to the piano on occasion—is clear and resonant."
Stereo Review 57:104 Ja '92. George Jellinek (long)

"[Mr. Sylvan] is wholly sensitive to the texts and his diction is impeccable. Though I admire

Phyllis Curtin, Leontyne Price, and Robert Tear in their versions of the cycles, I like Sylvan even better. Breitman is highly competent."
American Record Guide 54:208 N/D '91. David Mason Greene (long)

"Sanford Sylvan [has] a small-voiced baritone with a tenorly timbre, precise, simple, and so self-effacing in his delivery that he is occasionally overwhelmed by the piano....His programming here stresses the accessible. Barber's *Hermit Songs* rarely fail to charm; Copland's *Emily Dickinson* settings demonstrate that he could write distinctly American songs without descending to kitsch."
Musical America 111:38-9 N/D '91. James M. Keller (long)

Gramophone 69:106 D '91. David Gutman (long)

Upshaw, Dawn

8108. American Elegies. J. Adams: Eros Piano. **Diamond:** Elegy in Memory of Maurice Ravel. **Feldman:** Madame Press Died Last Week at Ninety. **Ives:** The Unanswered Question. Songs (orch. Adams): At the River; Cradle Song; Down East; Serenity; Thoreau. **I. Marshall:** Fog Tropes.
Dawn Upshaw (sop); Paul Crossley (pno). John Adams (c). Saint Luke's Orchestra.
ELEKTRA 79249 DDD 50:00

★★***Awards:*** The Want List 1991, *Fanfare* N/D '91 (Edward Strickland). Critics' Choice 1991, *Gramophone*, Ja '92 (Peter Dickinson).

"This is an unusual and intriguing disc which weaves together American works on elegiac themes....For me, the transcendental Ives and the sonic *Fog Tropes* are the highlights of this unusual recording which I recommend to the listener seeking to expand horizons and to experience music which goes beyond the concert hall."
HighPerformanceReview 8(3):65 '91. George S. T. Chu (med)

"The Orchestra of St. Luke's has a lush sound that has been faithfully captured, the soloists are excellent, Adams's conducting usually rises to the occasion. It's worth having."
American Record Guide 54:177-8 N/D '91. Timothy D. Taylor (long)

The New York Times Jl 21 '91, p. 23 H. Gerald Gold (brief)

8109. Songs and Arias. Barber: Knoxville: Summer of 1915, for Soprano and Orchestra. **Harbison:** Mirabai Songs, for Soprano and Orchestra. **Menotti:** *The Old Maid and the Thief:* Act 1, Scene 6, "What a curse for a woman is a timid man". **Stravinsky:** *The Rake's Progress:* Act 1, Scene 3, "No word from Tom".
Dawn Upshaw (sop). David Zinman (c). Saint Luke's Orchestra. 1989.
ELEKTRA 79187 DDD 44:00

★★★★★***Awards:*** Top Disks of the Year, *The New York Times* D 24, '89 (John Rockwell); Top Choices—1989, *American Record Guide* Ja/F '90 (Karl Miller); Editors' Choice, *Digital Audio's CD Review*, 6:34 Je '90. The Want List 1991, *Fanfare* N/D '91 (Walter Simmons); The Want List 1990, *Fanfare* N/D '90 (William Wians); Best of the Month, *Hi-Fi News & Record Review*, D '90.

"These are not just 'performances' but total characterizations. The beauty lies not in the sound alone, enchanting as it is, but in the way Upshaw seems to give herself up completely to the sense and spirit of what she is singing. Everything here, whether humorous, wistful, nostalgic, or erotic, is incredibly touching."
Stereo Review 54:152 S '89. Richard Freed (475w)

"This is a magnificent disc....to put it simply, I am overwhelmed with Dawn Upshaw. Rarely have I ever heard such a superb voice....What I find even more amazing is the intelligence she brings to these performances....The Orchestra of St. Luke's plays beautifully....This is a very special release: don't miss it."
American Record Guide 52:32-3 N/D '89. Karl Miller (235w)

"This program is almost as striking for the imaginative choice of repertoire as for the beauty of the performances....Everything here, whether humorous, wistful, nostalgic, or erotic, is incredibly evocative and touching...The whole production is exceptional, with superb sound, printed texts for all four items, and an annotation by John Harbison."
Stereo Review Presents: Compact Disc Buyers' Guide 1990 p.68 Richard Freed (115w)

"It's been a long, long time since a soprano has come along who does all the right things: steers clear of vocal potholes, oozes intelligence, musicality, and common sense from every pore—and, to top it off, knows how to make pretty sounds....David Zinman, who conducts the Orchestra of St. Luke's in all four works, is an ideal accompanist....This whole album, in fact, is an absolute gem, a flawless setting for the deeply satisfying art of Dawn Upshaw."
Musical America 110:75 Ja '90. Terry Teachout (240w)

"The *Gramophone Awards* unpardonably passed this by, and so did we; WEA's swift reissue offers a chance to make amends. Upshaw has a silvery, open, light soprano voice, but intelligence and a love of words do more for it than you might have thought possible-....Acquire this disc while you can." P100 S100
Hi-Fi News & Record Review 35:103 D '90. David Nice (200w)

"This is an easy disc to review: a thoroughly delightful yet uncompromisingly artistic assemblage of twentieth-century American vocal music. Try it, you'll love it. There's virtually nothing to criticize—O.K., the timing is a little skimpy."

Fanfare 14:445 Mr/Ap '91. Walter Simmons (400w)

Gramophone 67:544+ S '89. Edward Seckerson (400w)

Digital Audio's CD Review 6:78 S '89. David Vernier (200w)

Voice of the Turtle

8110. From the Shores of the Golden Horn: Music of the Spanish Jews of Turkey.
Judith Wachs (dir). Voice of the Turtle. performed on traditional instruments of Turkey (mandolin, dembeks, naqqara, rebec, kamanja, shawm, 'ud).
TITANIC 173 DDD 63:32

★***Awards:*** Critic's Choice: 1990, *American Record Guide* Ja/F '91 (Paul Laird).

"The 19 songs collected here demonstrate a fascinating cultural blend: Some are indistinguishable from Arabic music; some cling to the Spanish heritage. Others are close to East European folk music. All are pervaded not only by a bittersweet poignancy but by an immense vitality in the face of adversity....Far from being esoteric, this powerfully expressive repertory will leave no one unmoved."

The New York Times F 18 '90, p. 32 H. K. Robert Schwarz (125w)

"The songs range from a sort of generic folksong style to ones with scales associated with Middle Eastern music. The performances are exemplary. The voices are delightful, and the moods of the songs are presented unfailingly....My frank response to the collection? *A mi me encanta!*"

American Record Guide 53:146-47 S/O '90. Paul Laird (330w)

"This New England ensemble has been devoting its attention in concert and on records to the heritage of the Sephardim (the Jews of southern Europe) for some years now. Their latest offering is the first in a new series, Paths of Exile...The performances are delightful-...This is clearly going to be a valuable series."

Fanfare 13:347 Jl/Ag '90. J. F. Weber (200w)

"These songs are performed in a charming and unaffected manner, with accompaniment on traditional folk instruments of the region. If the vocals are a touch amateurish, this only adds to the charm—these are not art songs intended to be sung by trained voices....Titanic's sound is very fine....honest and unaffected."

Stereophile 14:269 Ja '91. Les Berkley (225w)

CD Review Digest
Classical

Artist and Composer Index

Label Number Index

Label Number Index

Label Number Index

CD Review Digest
Classical

The Peri Press

Hemlock Ridge Rd., P.O. Box 348, Voorheesville, NY 12186-0348
(800) 677-4492, (518) 765-3163, Fax (518) 765-3163

Order by mail or toll-free number (U.S.). Check or credit card charge must accompany order.

Please include appropriate sales tax. Add $ 2.50 for shipping one volume plus $1.50 for each additional volume (U.S. and Canada); $5 surface, $15 air (all others). Subscriptions prepaid, inquire about airmail rates.

ORDER FORM

Qty	Title	Price
_____	Best Rated CDs—Classical (ISBN 1-879796-07-4)	19.95
_____	Best Rated CDs—Jazz, Popular etc. (ISBN 1-879796-06-6)	19.95
_____	CD Review Digest Annual—Classical, 1992 (ISBN 1-879796-08-1)	59.00
_____	CD Review Digest Annual—Jazz, Popular etc., 1992 (ISBN 1-879796-09-0)	59.00
_____	CDRD—Classical, subscription (4 quarterly issues, includes annual)	79.00
_____	CDRD—Jazz, Popular etc., subscription (4 quarterly issues, includes annual	79.00
_____	Please send ordering information for earlier CDRD annuals	

If other than current issue, please give starting date for subscription:______________________

Method of Payment: Check ___ Charge ___ Visa ___ Mastercard ___

Account Number ______________________ Expiration Date _____________

Signature ________________________________ Print Name ____________________________

Send to: ____

____

____

____

What reviewers are saying about CD Review Digest

"Make no mistake about it—these are **essential books for the serious CD collector**...A true CD-collectors' blessing." *Fanfare*

"An **outstanding** guice." *Cadence*

"This is the **most comprehensive** listing of CDs available. One may safely say...**a necessity for the Music Librarian**." *The Horn Call*

"An **amazing** reference work....If you collect CDs, you need this." *Factsheet Five*

"**Breaking new ground**...An **indispensable** reference source." *Show Music*

"**An invaluable survey** of CD materials **which will interest a wide audience**; from the personal collector to the music store owner, the music library, and any involved with music recordings on a professional level. An extensive and exhaustive collection: **weighty, but surprisingly easy to consult**." *The Midwest Book Review*

"Here is **help for the choosy compact disc shopper**....Over three-quarters of the citations are accompanied by sentence- to paragraph-length excerpts capturing the essence of reviewers' pans, raves, or ho-hums....This is **an indispensable guide for collectors of quality recordings**." *Magazines for Libraries, 6th edition*

"The CD Review Digest is **a great compilation of evaluations** - you have done a fine job. I immediately looked for some favorite works in the issue you sent and was pleased to read the different opinions. " *Joan Wittig, Lexington, MA*

"Highly recommended." *Library Journal*

See order form on reverse side of page.